DATE DUE

DEMCO 38-296

A Basic

Music

Library

A Basic

Library

Essential Scores and Sound Recordings

Third Edition

Compiled by the Music Library Association

Elizabeth Davis
Coordinating Editor

Pamela Bristah and Jane Gottlieb
Scores Editors

Kent Underwood and William E. Anderson
Sound Recordings Editors

American Library Association
Chicago and London
1997

Cover by Image House

Text design by Dianne Rooney in Caslon and Fenice

Printed on 50-pound Natural Smooth, a pH-neutral stock, and bound in Arrestox B cloth by Braun-Brumfield, Inc.

The paper used in this publication meets the minimum requirements of American National Standard for Information Sciences—Permanence of Paper for Printed Library Materials, ANSI Z39.48-1992.∞

Library of Congress Cataloging-in-Publication Data
A basic music library : essential scores and sound recordings / compiled by the Music Library Association : Elizabeth Davis, coordinating editor : Pamela Bristah and Jane Gottlieb, scores editors : Kent Underwood and William E. Anderson, sound recordings editors. — 3rd ed.
      p.   cm.
  Includes bibliographical references and index.
  ISBN 0-8389-3461-7
  1. Music—Bibliography. 2. Music libraries—Collection development. I. Davis, Elizabeth A., 1947– . II. Music Library Association.
ML113.B3 1997
016.78026—DC21   96-47351

01 00 99 98 97   5 4 3 2 1

CONTENTS

PREFACE

Purpose and Scope

A Basic Music Library, third edition (BML3), is a selection and buying guide to printed musical scores and sound recordings, intended for use by librarians and others who are responsible for collecting music materials. It will also serve a broad range of research and reference needs. The book is called a "basic" music library primarily for two reasons: its listings are both systematic and selective; and it represents the musical world in a way that is balanced and diverse, culturally and geographically.

BML3 is the first buying guide to include both printed and recorded music, with more than 3,000 scores and 7,000 recordings. The sound recordings listings, new to this edition, are worldwide in scope, including classical, traditional, and popular musics of the Americas, Europe, Africa, and Asia.

The decision to update *A Basic Music Library* in a third edition originated with the Music Library Association's Board of Directors, which charged MLA's Resource Sharing and Collection Development Committee to carry out this project.[1] Planning for the book,

as well as recruitment of editors and contributors, took place under the auspices of the committee and its chair, Daniel Zager, with committee member Elizabeth Davis serving as liaison to the project. The majority of editors and contributors are MLA members.

BML3 follows the committee's recommendation not to include books and periodicals on music (a departure from the previous two editions) because these are well covered in other current bibliographies, including *Books for College Libraries, Guide to Reference Books,* and *Magazines for Libraries.*[2]

Usage

A Basic Music Library can be used in a variety of ways. The book is expressly designed so that chapters and sections can be used independently and selec-

---

1. Committee members then included William Coscarelli, Robert Curtis, Elizabeth Davis, David Day, Cal Elliker,

Brenda Goldman, John Roberts, Brad Short, and Dan Zager, chair.

2. *Books for College Libraries: A Core Collection of 50,000 Titles,* 3rd ed. (Chicago: American Library Association, 1988); Robert Balay, Vee Friesner Carrington, and Murray S. Martin, *Guide to Reference Books,* 11th ed. (Chicago: American Library Association, 1996); *Magazines for Libraries* (New York: Bowker, 1992).

tively: to build a new collection, to assess existing holdings, to enhance targeted collection areas, and to serve in other ways. It will guide college libraries requiring scores and recordings of standard orchestral, solo, and chamber works in support of introductory music courses; junior high and high school libraries in need of instrumental methods to support the school's band program; public libraries that only collect recordings of contemporary popular genres; and many more institutional and individual users.

The concept of "basic" does not imply a need to own all the works cited in this book. Just as each library has different emphases and different needs, this book's recommendations should be implemented in relation to the mission, size, and overall resources of each institution. To make BML3 useful to the widest possible range of libraries, a three-tiered ranking system is built into the book, denoted in every individual citation with asterisks, as follows:

** (two asterisks) = The smallest, most selective "basic" collection (suited, for example, to small public libraries). On average (varying somewhat from section to section), about 10 percent of the citations have two asterisks.

* (one asterisk) = Midsize "basic" collection (suited, for example, to medium-size public libraries or small college libraries serving a general student body). With the addition of two-asterisk items, these comprise on average about 40 percent of the citations.

no asterisk = The most comprehensive "basic" collection (suited, for example, to larger metropolitan public libraries or to college and university libraries supporting undergraduate music studies). With the addition of one- and two-asterisk items, these comprise all citations.

The references here to "small," "medium-size," and "large" libraries are only illustrative examples and are not meant in any restrictive sense. In practice, BML3 is best used in conjunction with a library's own collection development policy, which would define which areas of music are in scope and at which collecting intensity levels. Thus, for example, an actual library might choose to collect blues recordings at 100 percent, Asian recordings at one and two asterisks only, and children's recordings not at all.

BML3 is also flexible in that for many cited works, more than one printed edition or recorded performance is given. Major works especially (i.e., those with one or two asterisks) are cited with multiple editions or performances whenever possible. A library can have the fullest possible "basic" collection by providing all of these choices, but it is equally possible to be selective.

Scores and Sound Recordings Compared

The content and arrangement of the book's two principal parts, "Scores" and "Sound Recordings," reflect some inherent differences between printed and recorded music. BML3 includes far more sound recordings than scores, simply because recordings are the primary documents for the numerous musical genres (such as jazz, rock, or most non-Western music) in which written notation plays little or no part in the creation or performance of the music. There are discrepancies as well in areas of Western classical music, mainly because some important compositions—especially of the medieval, Renaissance, baroque, and contemporary periods—have been recorded but are not available in score (at least not in practical editions suitable for this book). And because some smaller, very selective libraries are likely to want recorded music with little or no emphasis on scores, there are relatively few scores cited with two asterisks.

Scores and sound recordings are also organized differently within their chapters. Printed music is listed by format (scores and performing editions) and within those categories by performing medium (e.g., orchestra, chamber ensemble, solo instrument, voice). Recordings are categorized first by geography and culture (e.g., the Americas and Native American) and then by musical genre (polka). Recordings of Western classical music are subdivided by historical period (e.g., medieval). Vernacular genres with extensive histories are subdivided chronologically as well.

These differences reflect inherent, practical distinctions between print and recording: printed music is typically sought by players or students of a particular instrument (bassoon) or medium (choral), while recordings tend to be thought of in relation to a stylistic category (salsa) with less concern toward details of instrumentation. As a result, all the *recordings* of a composer are listed together (e.g., for Robert Schumann, under his name in the chapter on music of the romantic period). The composer's *scores* would be listed in several different places, according to the performing medium. The Scores index brings all of these titles together in a single list (e.g., under Schumann's name).

The format for individual entries is similar for both scores and recordings, and the information provides everything that should be needed to identify and order the item. The *Anglo-American Cataloguing Rules,* second edition (AACR2), 1988 revision, is the point of departure for bibliographic format, but for reasons of space and other considerations BML3 does not follow all AACR2 conventions, especially for sound recordings. BML3 does not constitute library cataloging and should not be taken as a cataloging authority.

CONTRIBUTORS

Scores

Richard AmRhein
University of Nevada, Las Vegas (Bassoon Music)

Bonna Boettcher
Bowling Green State University, Ohio (Music for Solo Piano; Piano, Four Hands; Two Pianos, Four Hands)

Anita Breckbill
University of Nebraska at Lincoln (Flute Music)

Pamela Bristah
Manhattan School of Music, New York City (Orchestral Music; Fake Books and Jazz Methods; Percussion Music; with Mark Palkovic, Harp Music)

Norbert Carnovale
University of Southern Mississippi, Hattiesburg (Trumpet and Cornet Music, with Wayne Shoaf)

James P. Cassaro
Cornell University, Ithaca, New York (Opera and Choral Works, in Full Score and Performing Editions)

Beth Christensen
Saint Olaf College, Northfield, Minnesota (Oboe and English Horn Music)

Brian Cockburn
Southwest Texas State University, San Marcos (Scores and Performing Editions for Wind Chamber Music; Chamber Music for Mixed Winds and Strings; Chamber Music for Unspecified Instruments)

Elizabeth Davis
Columbia University, New York City (Score Anthologies)

David Lasocki
Indiana University, Bloomington (Recorder Music)

Judy MacLeod
Southern Illinois University at Carbondale (Viola Music)

Jean Morrow
New England Conservatory of Music, Boston (Early Vocal Music and Early Anthologies)

Paul Orkiszewski
Rice University, Houston (Guitar Music)

Mark Palkovic
  University of Cincinnati (Harp Music, with Pamela Bristah)

Michael Rogan
  Longy School of Music, Boston (Classical Song for Solo Voice, Aria Anthologies, Sacred Song, Spirituals, Wedding Music, Christmas Anthologies, and Folk Song)

Elizabeth Sadewhite
  The Juilliard School, New York City (Scores and Performing Editions for String Chamber Music; Violoncello Music)

Wayne Shoaf
  Arnold Schoenberg Institute, University of California, Los Angeles (Music for Solo Trumpet and Cornet, Horn, Trombone, and Tuba)

Brad Short
  Washington University, St. Louis (Tuba Music, with Wayne Shoaf)

Charles Slater
  J. W. Pepper, Inc., Valley Forge, Pennsylvania (Musical Theater and Popular Song)

Carol Tatian
  Brown University, Providence (Violin Music)

Edie Tibbits
  East Carolina University, Greenville, North Carolina (Trombone Music, with Wayne Shoaf)

John Voigt
  Berklee College of Music, Boston (Double Bass Music)

Matthew Wise
  New York University (Clarinet Music; Saxophone Music)

Ross Wood
  Wellesley College, Massachusetts (Organ Music)

Recordings

William E. Anderson
  Cleveland Public Library (Colonial America and United States to about 1900; Blues; Jazz; Mainstream Popular and New Age; Rhythm and Blues and Soul; Rock; Gospel and Popular Christian Music; Jazz Motion Picture Soundtracks; Holidays, Special Occasions, Patriotic, and Miscellaneous; Folk and Traditional Musics of the United States and Canada; Traditional and Popular Musics of the Caribbean and Latin America; Traditional and Popular Musics of Europe; International Anthologies and Worldbeat Fusion; Traditional and Popular Musics of Sub-Saharan and Northern Africa, the Middle East, Asia, and Oceania)

Columbus Metropolitan Library, Children's Services Division, Columbus, Ohio (Children's Music)

Country Music Foundation (Linda Gross, Bob Pinson, Ronnie Pugh, John Rumble, Chris Skinker, Alan Stoker), Nashville (Country and Western)

Suzanne Flandreau
  Center for Black Music Research, Chicago (Traditional Music of Sub-Saharan Africa)

Mark McKnight
  University of North Texas, Denton (Traditional and Popular Musics of the Caribbean and Latin America)

Eunice Schroeder
  Lawrence University, Appleton, Wisconsin (Gregorian Chant)

Laurel Sercombe
  University of Washington, Seattle (Folk and Traditional Musics of the United States and Canada)

Wade Tolleson
  WRUW-FM, Cleveland (Gay and Lesbian Music)

Kent Underwood
  New York University (Western Classical; Musicals, Operettas, Motion Pictures, and Television Shows; Rap; Rock since 1980; Traditional Musics of Europe; Classical and Traditional Musics of Sub-Saharan and Northern Africa, the Middle East, Asia, and Oceania)

Scores

INTRODUCTION

estern art music—"classical" music—predominates in part 1, "Scores." The compilers and editors have included basic repertoire and methods for all instruments, including the less common solo instruments such as lower-pitched woodwinds, brass, and strings. The listings for certain instruments with classical and folk traditions, such as guitar, reflect their diverse history. Music for solo voice emphasizes art song and opera, with sacred song, musical theater, and some popular song as well. Jazz methods for specific instruments are listed with classical methods for those instruments. Jazz methods for groups of instruments (for example, B♭ or E♭ instruments) are given in a separate list.

Part 1, "Scores," includes printed music in all formats, including full scores, scores and parts for chamber music performance, music for solo instruments, and piano-vocal scores for stage and choral works.

Entries

Works by one composer are listed under the composer's name. Anthologies, works by more than one composer, are listed under title. Composers' names and uniform titles are given in AACR2 format, according to the *Anglo-American Cataloguing Rules,* 2nd edition.[1] For composers whose AACR2 form of name does not include dates, the editors added dates whenever they were verifiable.

A *uniform title* is the filing title for a work. It follows immediately after the composer heading and appears in brackets. A uniform title often differs from the publisher's title; it is commonly used for musical works because of the various names that different publishers may give one work. For example, different editions of a composer's first piano sonata may be titled *Piano sonata no. 1, Sonata no. 1 for piano, First piano sonata,* or *Première sonate pour piano.* The uniform title groups all editions of this work under the same title, in this case [Sonata, piano, no. 1], so the user will find all versions of the same work in one place.

For standard repertoire, many entries in "Scores" include more than one edition. These multiple editions

---

1. Michael Gorman and Paul W. Winkler, eds., *Anglo-American cataloguing rules,* 2nd ed., 1988 revision (Ottawa: Canadian Library Association; London: Library Association Publishing Ltd.; Chicago: American Library Association, 1988).

are listed under composer and title within the entry paragraph, separated by semicolons. The librarian can select among them or can acquire more than one edition of a work for a more comprehensive collection.

Selected works are marked with one or two asterisks. They assign two levels of priority to those items, according to levels of collecting (see the Preface for a full explanation of asterisk designations). In "Scores," the relatively few works marked with two asterisks are for public libraries that do not generally collect musical scores but wish to have on hand selected scores of often-heard works. Public libraries with a greater need for scores may prefer to acquire items marked with one asterisk.

Because BML3 is a buying guide, it emphasizes information useful for ordering, specifically publishers' numbers and prices, rather than place and date of publication. Each publisher's name is followed by the publisher's number, price, and, often, number of volumes; adding year of publication would have produced a confusing clutter of numbers, particularly for those entries with multiple editions. However, dates for revised versions of works, common to music of Stravinsky and certain other composers, are included when both original and revised versions of the work are currently available. Hymnals and certain instrumental methods are given publication dates, as they are commonly referred to and ordered by date of publication.

Availability and Prices

The majority of the scores listed were available as this book went to press. A very few were reported by their publishers as out-of-print or out-of-stock, but were re-tained here because of their importance, as they may again become available. These items are indicated by "OP" (out-of-print); because the status of a publication can change daily from out-of-stock to out-of-print, and back again, the designation OP serves for both. Additionally, a few scores were still in preparation, scheduled for publication later in 1996, and are designated as such.

Prices for scores were compiled from August 1995 through January 1996, and are current as of those months. All prices, of course, are subject to change, those for European publications particularly so because of currency fluctuations.

Prices for a small number of items could not be verified. Generally, these items were in transition from one publisher to another at press time, or are published by a European firm with no specific North American distributor. They are designated "price not available." However, any of the general or specialized music distributors listed under "Suppliers of Scores" (in the Appendixes) should be able to locate these works and import them as needed.

Index

The "All Scores" index lists all items in part 1, "Scores," each indexed to its entry number. Works by a single composer are indexed under the composer's name. Anthologies (collections of music by more than one composer) are indexed under title.

For those libraries particularly interested in the music of female or Black composers, a separate index is provided for each group; these works are included in the "All Scores" index as well.

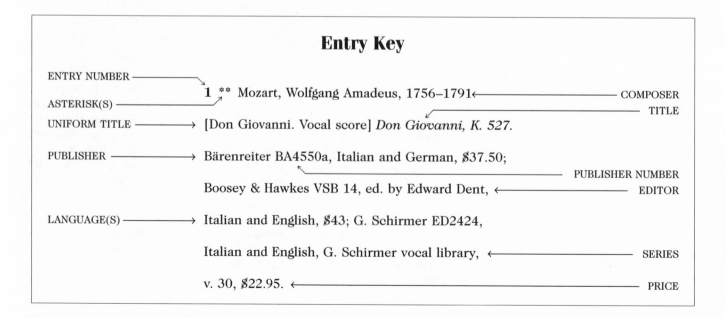

Entry Key

ENTRY NUMBER ⟶ **1** ** Mozart, Wolfgang Amadeus, 1756–1791 ⟵ COMPOSER

ASTERISK(S) ⟶

TITLE

UNIFORM TITLE ⟶ [Don Giovanni. Vocal score] *Don Giovanni, K. 527.*

PUBLISHER ⟶ Bärenreiter BA4550a, Italian and German, $37.50;

PUBLISHER NUMBER

Boosey & Hawkes VSB 14, ed. by Edward Dent, ⟵ EDITOR

LANGUAGE(S) ⟶ Italian and English, $43; G. Schirmer ED2424,

Italian and English, G. Schirmer vocal library, ⟵ SERIES

v. 30, $22.95. ⟵ PRICE

Acknowledgments

Part 1, "Scores," could not have been completed without the help of many people. Chief among these are the many contributors; this is truly their book. All gave generously of their time and expertise. I owe a great debt to Charles Slater, vice-president, distribution division, J. W. Pepper, Inc., who contributed nearly every one of approximately 5,000 prices for the score editions, a task that ended up taking a tremendous amount of work and time. Others who assisted with prices were Knut Dorn and Birgit Hausmann of Otto Harrassowitz, Inc.; Richie Henzler of Courtly Music Unlimited; and Toni Buffa of Lemur Music, Inc.

Christopher Lamb, principal percussionist of the New York Philharmonic, was kind enough to review my entries for the percussion section of BML3. My husband, David Wright, pianist and writer on music, advised me throughout this project on content and style. I would also like to thank the staff of the Frances Hall Ballard Library of the Manhattan School of Music for their invaluable support and assistance.

Pamela Bristah
Co-editor, Scores

Score Anthologies

Compiled by
Elizabeth Davis

nthologies of music provide a wide selection of musical works in one or a few volumes. They may be used in conjunction with classroom discussions and assignments involving listening and analysis, and they may also offer an inexpensive way to increase the number and variety of scores in a general collection.

This list includes 38 general anthologies, offering works representative of various periods of music history or collections of works specifically related to one particular stylistic period or genre. Most of these anthologies feature complete musical works, rather than excerpts.

Occasionally, sets of sound recordings are produced to accompany anthologies of printed music; the availability of such sets is indicated. A collection of anthologies of printed music, together with their recordings, can be a good start in building a score and sound recording collection.

Anthologies are arranged by title. Those items reported out-of-print or out-of-stock indefinitely are indicated by "OP" (out-of-print). Because the status of a publication can change daily, from out-of-stock to out-of-print and back again, the designation OP serves for both. Out-of-print anthologies have been retained

in this edition because of their importance, and in the hope they will again become available.

In 1995, the total cost of all the in-print anthologies listed below was $786.25. Available recordings in long-playing (LP), 33-1/3 rpm format cost a total of $133.95; cassettes $252.90; and compact discs $327.

A number of the anthologies are indexed in the following bibliographies, indicated by the presence of the editor's name at the end of an entry.

Heyer, Anna Harriett
Historical sets, collected editions, and monuments of music: a guide to their contents. 3rd ed. Chicago: American Library Association, 1980. 2 v. 0-8389-0288-X (set).

Hill, George R., and Norris L. Stephens
Collected editions, historical series & sets, & monuments of music: a bibliography. Fallen Leaf Reference Books in Music, v. 14. Berkeley: Fallen Leaf Press, 1997. 0-914913-22-0.

Hilton, Ruth B.
An index to early music in selected anthologies. Clifton, N.J.: European American Music Corp., 1978.

Murray, Sterling E.

Anthologies of music: an annotated index. 2nd ed. Warren, Mich.: Harmonie Park Press, 1992. 0-89990-061-5.

Perone, James E.

Musical anthologies for analytical study: a bibliography. Westport, Conn.: Greenwood Press, 1995. 0-313-29595-6.

Score Anthologies

1 * *Analytical anthology of music.* 2nd ed. by Ralph Turek. New York: McGraw-Hill, 1992. 0-07-065456-5, $38.

The objective of the work is to provide an "anthology of maximum practical value to students and instructors of musicianship and analysis courses at all levels" (Pref.). It contains a chronologically arranged selection of complete works or movements representing 47 known and several anonymous composers, with brief introductory remarks, related reading suggestions, and questions for discussion relating to the work's musical characteristics. An index of musical devices, a harmonic index, and a glossary complete the work. (Murray, Perone)

2 * *Anthology for musical analysis,* ed. by Charles Burkhart. 5th ed. Fort Worth: Harcourt Brace, 1994. 0-03-055318-0, $48.25.

Prev. eds.: 1986, 1979, 1972, 1964

Contains a collection of complete compositions and movements from the Middle Ages to the present, designed for theory and analysis classes. The 208 pieces by 68 composers are organized chronologically into five broad categories. Includes appendixes on jazz forms and chorale harmonizations. General index and index of chords, sequences, and modulations. (Hill/Stephens, Perone)

3 * *Anthology of classical music,* ed. by Philip G. Downs. The Norton introduction to music history. New York: W. W. Norton, 1992. 0-393-95209-6, $30.95.

Companion volume to the editor's *Classical music: the era of Haydn, Mozart, and Beethoven* (New York: W. W. Norton, 1992), this work contains 76 items with approximately half by these three masters and the remaining by lesser composers. The works are largely selections or excerpts of instrumental works in genres limited to 2–3 staves, rather than symphonic works. English translations are provided for foreign-language texts. (Hill/Stephens)

4 * *An anthology of early Renaissance music,* ed. by Noah Greenberg and Paul Maynard. New York: W. W. Norton, 1975. 0-393-02182-3, $20.

Contains 41 selections organized by the following genres: the Ordinary of the Mass, shorter liturgical pieces, secular vocal music, instrumental music, and music for special occasions. Includes an excellent introduction on performance practice; commentaries give historical as well as performance notes. Indexed by recommended performing media. (Heyer, Hill/Stephens, Murray)

5 * *Anthology of medieval music,* ed. by Richard H. Hoppin. The Norton introduction to music history. New York: W. W. Norton, 1978. 0-393-09080-9, $15.95.

Designed to accompany the editor's text *Medieval music* (New York: W. W. Norton, 1978) and relying on it for commentary. Provides a representative survey of medieval forms and styles in 71 complete or excerpted works. (Hill/Stephens, Murray)

6 *Anthology of music for analysis,* ed. by Albert Cohen and John D. White. New York: Appleton-Century-Crofts, 1965. OP

This anthology provides a body of music "for use in introductory, college level courses in form and style analysis" (Pref.). It includes excerpts, primarily of instrumental works by 18 composers from the eighteenth and nineteenth centuries. English translations included in the scores. (Murray, Perone)

7 *Anthology of musical structure and style,* ed. by Mary H. Wennerstrom. Englewood Cliffs, N.J.: Prentice-Hall, 1983. 0-13-038372-4. OP

Includes approximately 155 musical examples chosen because they represent important or typical examples of music literature and are useful for the study of harmony, counterpoint, and form. Many pieces relate to others in the anthology through some compositional process. Works are organized chronologically and 51 named composers are represented. A study guide, list of sources, composers' chart, and index conclude the work. (Hill/Stephens, Murray)

8 * *Anthology of romantic music,* ed. by Leon Plantinga. The Norton introduction to music history. New York: W. W. Norton, 1984. 0-393-01811-3, $28.95.

Designed to accompany the editor's text *Romantic music: a history of musical style in nineteenth-century Europe* (New York: W. W. Norton, 1984), this volume contains 24 complete works or excerpts by 16 composers. Emphasis is on standard repertory by major composers. (Hill/Stephens, Murray)

9 * *Anthology of twentieth-century music,* ed. by Robert P. Morgan. The Norton introduction to music history. New York: W. W. Norton, 1992. 0-393-95284-3, $31.95.

A collection of 29 complete works or excerpts, from Debussy's *Estampes* (1903) through Steve Reich's *Music for pieces of wood* (1973), designed to accompany the editor's separately published historical survey, *Twentieth-century music* (New York: W. W. Norton, 1990). Each work is accompanied by analytical comments. Indexed by form, genre, and analytical categories. (Hill/Stephens)

10 *Anthology of twentieth-century music.* 2nd ed. by Mary H. Wennerstrom. Englewood Cliffs, N.J.: Prentice-Hall, 1988. 0-13-038498-4, $45.

1st ed.: 1969

Presents 36 works, including complete pieces, individual movements, and long excerpts by 18 composers. Pieces are arranged alphabetically by composer and were selected based on their analytical interest and the availability of published analytical literature. Works are organized by composers, and each is accompanied by brief notes and analytical questions. (Hill/Stephens, Murray, Perone)

11 *Cantors: a collection of Gregorian chants,* ed. by Mary Berry. New York: Cambridge University Press, 1979. 0-521-22149-8. OP

Twenty-four chants are included with a brief introduction to the style and historical background of each. Compact but informative.

12 *Choral music,* ed. by Ray Robinson. New York: W. W. Norton, 1978. 0-393-02201-3, $42.95.

Contains 111 examples, mostly complete excerpts from larger works. Arrangement is chronological, with music dating from 1300 through 1974. (Hill/Stephens, Murray)

13 *Comparative anthology of musical forms,* ed. by David Ward-Steinman and Susan L. Ward-Steinman. Belmont, Calif.: Wadsworth, 1976. 0-534-00439-3 (v.1); 0-534-00459-8 (v.2). OP

Reprint: Lanham, Md.: University Press of America, 1986–87. OP

Contents: vol. 1. *Sectional forms, themes and variations, cantus firmus compositions.* vol. 2. *Ostinato compositions, contrapuntal textures,* *single-movement sonata forms, through-composed compositions.*

Contains complete movements and excerpts from more than 170 works organized around their common music structural or formal elements. Repertory includes Western classical, folk, and popular music, as well as non-Western music. Brief notes and suggested activities are included for instructional purposes. Indexed by composer, medium, style or period, non-Western, and folk, jazz, and popular music.

14 *The comprehensive study of music,* ed. by William Brandt, et al. 6 v. New York: Harper's College Press, 1976–80. 0-06-040922-3 (v.1); 0-06-161417-3 (v.2); 0-06-161422-X (v.3); 0-06-161420-3 (v.4); 0-06-161421-1 (v.5); 0-06-040921-5 (v.6). OP

Contents: vol. 1. *Plainchant through Gabrieli.* vol. 2. *Monteverdi through Mozart.* vol. 3. *Beethoven through Wagner.* vol. 4. *Debussy through Stockhausen.* vol. 5. *Piano reductions for harmonic study.* vol. 6. *Basic principles of music theory.*

Volumes 1–4 contain a chronological arrangement of standard repertory by prominent composers encompassing a wide variety of musical forms, types, and styles. The final two volumes are designed as pedagogical aids. (Hill/Stephens, Murray)

15 *The concerto, 1800–1900: a Norton music anthology,* ed. by Paul Henry Lang. New York: W. W. Norton, 1969. 0-393-09869-9. OP

Contains 11 complete works by nine composers, with an introductory essay. (Hill/Stephens, Murray)

16 * *The development of Western music: an anthology.* 2nd ed. by K Marie Stolba. Madison, Wisc.: Brown & Benchmark, 1994. 0-697-12549-1 (v.1), $29; 0-697-12550-5 (v.2), $29.

1st ed.: 1991

Contents: vol. 1. *Ancient through the classical era.* vol. 2. *Transition from classical to romantic, romantic, and modern.*

Designed to to be studied in conjunction with the editor's *Development of Western music: a history* (Madison, Wisc.: Brown & Benchmark, 1994). Selections are complete movements or complete compositions presented in the order in which they are discussed in the text. Contains 188 items, illustrating a wide range of the standard repertory. Indexes of composers and titles. (Hill/Stephens, Murray)

Accompanying recordings: vol. 1: 8 cassettes (0-697-12551-3), $57; 8 compact discs (0-697-12553-X),

$72; vol. 2: 5 cassettes (0-697-12552-1), $43; 8 compact discs (0-697-12554-8), $55.

17 *The European musical heritage, 800–1750,* ed. by Sarah Fuller. New York: McGraw-Hill, 1993. 0-07-554369-9, $39.50.

Prev. ed.: Knopf, 1987. 0-394-32951-1

A compendium of approximately 90 musical works arranged chronologically, beginning with chant and extending to the era of Bach and Handel. Pieces are further subarranged systematically by musical characteristics. Includes selective discography and index. (Hill/Stephens, Murray)

Accompanying recordings: LP recordings (0-07-555102-0), $56.

18 * *Historical anthology of music,* ed. by Archibald T. Davison and Willi Apel. Cambridge, Mass.: Harvard University Press, 1949–50. 0-674-39300-7 (v.1), $36; 0-674-39301-5 (v.2), $35.

Contents: vol. 1. *Oriental, medieval, and Renaissance music* (rev. ed., 1962). vol. 2. *Baroque, rococo, and pre-classical music.*

Long considered the standard anthology illustrating music history from antiquity to 1780. Includes commentary and translations of literary texts. (Heyer, Hill/Stephens, Hilton, Murray)

19 *Historical anthology of music by women,* ed. by James R. Briscoe. Bloomington, Ind.: Indiana University Press, 1987. 0-253-21296-0, $29.95.

Contains vocal and instrumental music from the Middle Ages to the present by 35 composers. An introductory essay on the composer, information on recordings, and suggestions for further reading precede each piece. Translations are provided for non-English texts. (Hill/Stephens, Murray)

Accompanying recordings: 3 cassettes (0-253-31268-X) (set), $29.95.

20 *Medieval music,* ed. by W. Thomas Marrocco and Nicholas Sandon. The Oxford anthology of music. New York: Oxford University Press, 1977. 0-19-323207-3. OP

The 106 complete compositions or movements included give examples of every important functional, technical, and stylistic aspect of Western art music from the sixth through the fifteenth centuries. The commentaries place each example in its context and note important technical features; they also include full translations of the text. (Hill/Stephens, Hilton, Murray)

21 *Music in America: an anthology from the landing of the pilgrims to the close of the Civil War, 1620–1865,* ed. by W. Thomas Marrocco and Harold Gleason. New York: W. W. Norton, 1964. 0-393-09296-8. OP

Historical and analytical notes tie the 131 complete works or movements to cultural and social changes. Includes a wide variety of scores, facsimiles of early printed music, and biographical notes on composers. Classified index and index of first lines. (Heyer, Hill/Stephens, Murray)

22 *Music in opera: a historical anthology,* ed. by Elaine Brody. Englewood Cliffs, N.J.: Prentice-Hall, 1970. 0-13-608109-6. OP

Contains 99 operatic scenes from works representing major composers and national schools from 1600 to 1967. Brief introductory remarks provide a historical framework and include translations. Accompaniments are presented in close (reduced) score, with details of instrumentation indicated in the music. Includes bibliography and index. (Heyer, Hill/Stephens, Murray)

23 *Music in the classic period: an anthology with commentary,* ed. by F. E. Kirby. New York: Schirmer Books, 1979. 0-02-870710-9, $34.

Contains 40 compositions from the late eighteenth and early nineteenth centuries. Most compositions are by Haydn, Mozart, and Beethoven, and are grouped accordingly. The remaining six works by six composers form an initial grouping labeled "background." Brief essays precede each work. (Hill/Stephens, Murray)

24 *Music in the romantic period: an anthology with commentary,* ed. by F. E. Kirby. New York: Schirmer Books, 1986. 0-02-871330-3, $34.

Comprises 58 separate items by 25 composers, including complete works, complete movements or parts of larger works, and fragments. The music is organized chronologically and further subarranged geographically. Emphasis is primarily on the German and Austrian repertory, secondarily on the French and Italian, and lastly on other national schools. Includes lists of editions and bibliography. (Hill/Stephens, Murray)

25 *Music of the Middle Ages: an anthology for performance and study,* ed. by David Fenwick Wilson. New York: Schirmer Books, 1990. 0-02-872952-8, $25.

Designed to accompany the editor's text *Music of the Middle Ages: style and structure* (New York:

Schirmer Books, 1990), but pieces have been chosen to avoid duplication with other anthologies. The 80 pieces include only complete compositions. Organization is roughly chronological, but primarily by musical characteristics (plainchant, free organum, early motet, etc.). English translations are provided, as are the complete texts for strophic songs. (Hill/Stephens, Murray)

26 *Music of the twentieth century: an anthology,* ed. by Bryan R. Simms. New York: Schirmer Books, 1986. 0-02-873020-8, $29.

Contains 29 works by 26 composers selected to provide "a representative sample of the major musical styles of this century" (Pref.). The pieces are organized by performing force (piano, solo voice, choral music, etc.) and subarranged chronologically by composer. Brief notes by the editor, a bibliography, and a discography accompany each piece. The editor refers to his separately published companion text, *Music of the twentieth century: style and structure* (New York: Schirmer Books, 1986), for fuller discussion. (Hill/Stephens, Murray)

27 *Music scores omnibus,* ed. by William J. Starr and George F. Devine. Englewood Cliffs, N.J.: Prentice-Hall, 1964. OP

Contents: vol. 1. *Earliest music through the works of Beethoven* (2nd ed., 1974; 0-13-608349-8). vol. 2. *Romantic and impressionistic music.*

Designed for the undergraduate student, this anthology includes many familiar titles in their entirety or excerpted in sufficient length to suggest their musical character. Arranged chronologically, the selections cover various media and illustrate forms, styles, or important compositional devices. (Heyer, Hill/Stephens, Hilton, Murray)

28 * *Norton anthology of Western music.* 2nd ed. by Claude V. Palisca. New York: W. W. Norton, 1988. 0-393-95642-3 (v.1), $27.95; 0-393-95644-X (v.2), $27.95.

1st ed.: 1980

Contents: vol. 1. *Medieval, Renaissance, baroque.* vol. 2. *Classic, romantic, modern.*

A historical anthology containing "a selection of music representing every important trend, genre, national school and historical development or innovation" (Pref.). Includes 163 selections in all genres; English translations provided. An index directs the user to discussions of the works included in Donald Jay Grout and Claude V. Palisca, *A history of Western music,* 4th ed. (New York: W. W.

Norton, 1988). Also includes indexes by composer, title, and forms and genres. (Hill/Stephens, Murray)

Accompanying recordings: vol. 1: 11 LP recordings, $45; 6 cassettes, $45; 7 compact discs, $70. vol. 2: 7 LP recordings, $32.95; 4 cassettes, $32.95; 5 compact discs, $50.

29 ** *The Norton scores: a study anthology,* 7th ed. by Kristine Forney. New York: W. W. Norton, 1995. 0-393-96688-7 (v.1), $32.95; 0-393-96687-9 (v.2), $32.95.

Prev. eds.: 1990, 1984, 1977, 1972, 1970, 1968

Contents: vol. 1. *Gregorian chant to Beethoven.* vol. 2. *Schubert to the present.*

Contains short pieces or excerpts from larger works arranged chronologically, from a Gregorian chant excerpt through contemporary computer music. Works included are judged to be masterworks from the standard repertory. A visual method of highlighting the scores enables users who cannot read music to follow an audio performance. Several appendixes with information related to reading scores complete each volume. (Hill/Stephens)

Accompanied by *The Norton recordings:* vol. 1: 4 cassettes (0-393-99187-3), $22.50; 4 compact discs (0-393-99186-5), $40. vol. 2: 4 cassettes (0-393-99207-1), $22.50; 4 compact discs (0-393-99208-X), $40.

30 *Schirmer scores: a repertory of Western music,* ed. by Joscelyn Godwin. New York: Schirmer Books, 1975. OP

Designed to serve teachers and students of introductory and appreciation courses, this anthology contains 73 works, each with a brief annotation and recording citation. Overall organization is by six categories, representing what the editor has designated as the "basic functions of music," then subarranged historically, from the medieval period through the twentieth century. A highlighting system provides visual guidance through a work's structure. Two charts provide a chronological index to the pieces. English translations and a glossary are provided. (Hill/Stephens, Hilton, Murray)

31 *Scores: an anthology of new music,* ed. by Roger Johnson. New York: Schirmer Books, 1981. 0-02-871190-4. OP

This book contains more than 160 compositions, most complete, chosen for their "musical interest, artistic quality, and accessibility to performance" (Pref.). All, according to the editor, are readily performable by a wide range of musicians and nonmusicians. They are listed in eight sections: seven by performing forces and one by purpose (exercises, rituals, and meditations). Several sections conclude the work: composer biographies, a listing of agents and distributors, a bibliography, and index. (Hill/Stephens)

32   *The solo song, 1580–1730,* ed. by Carol MacClintock. New York: W. W. Norton, 1973. 0-393-09982-2. OP

Provides examples from the late Renaissance and baroque eras organized by nationality (Italian, English, French, German) and subarranged chronologically. Texts, translations, and historical notes are provided. (Hill/Stephens, Murray)

33   *Study scores of historical styles,* ed. by Harry B. Lincoln and Stephen Bonta. Englewood Cliffs, N.J.: Prentice-Hall, 1986–87. 0-13-858911-9 (v.1), $42; 0-13-858853-8 (v.2). OP

Contents: vol. 1. *Medieval, Renaissance, baroque.* vol. 2. *Classic, romantic, 20th century.*

The aim of this anthology is to assemble musical works representing the best of the Western musical tradition, works that are readily available in recordings, and works representative of the tradition in which they were composed. Organization is chronological, with subarrangement by musical genre. A commentary containing the source and discography accompanies each work. (Hill/Stephens, Murray)

34   *The symphony, 1800–1900: a Norton music anthology,* ed. by Paul Henry Lang. New York: W. W. Norton, 1969. 0-393-09869-9. OP

Contains eight symphonies and one excerpt by nine composers, with an introductory essay. (Hill/Stephens, Murray)

35   *Twentieth century music scores,* ed. by Thomas DeLio and Stuart Saunders Smith. Englewood Cliffs, N.J.: Prentice-Hall, 1989. 0-13-934530-2. OP

Contains excerpts of movements and complete works by 50 composers. Pieces are arranged alphabetically by composer, and many are preceded by the composer's performance instructions. Also includes selected bibliography and discography. (Hill/Stephens, Murray)

Orchestral Music in Full and Study Score

Compiled by
Pamela Bristah

H ere are listed standard orchestral works in full or study score, divided into three sections: "Symphonies"; "Concertos" (including all works for solo instruments and orchestra, as well as concerti grossi and concertos for orchestra); and "Overtures, Program Music, and Other Orchestral Works."

Symphonies

36 Barber, Samuel, 1910–1981

[Symphonies, no. 1] *Symphony no. 1, in one movement.* G. Schirmer ED40720, $18.

37 ** Beethoven, Ludwig van, 1770–1827

[Symphonies, no. 1–4] *Symphonies no. 1, 2, 3, and 4.* Dover 0-486-26033-X, $10.95.

38 ** Beethoven, Ludwig van, 1770–1827

[Symphonies, no. 5–7] *Symphonies no. 5, 6, and 7.* Dover 0-486-26034-8, $10.95.

39 ** Beethoven, Ludwig van, 1770–1827

[Symphonies, no. 8–9] *Symphonies no. 8 and 9.* Dover 0-486-26035-6, $10.95.

—OR INDIVIDUALLY—

40 * Beethoven, Ludwig van, 1770–1827

[Symphonies, no. 1, op. 21, C major] *Symphony no. 1 in C major, op. 21.* Eulenburg 418, $8.75; Henle HN9801, $13.95; Kalmus K 00001, $6.50.

41 * Beethoven, Ludwig van, 1770–1827

[Symphonies, no. 2, op. 36, D major] *Symphony no. 2 in D major, op. 36.* Eulenburg 419, $10; Henle HN9802, $17.95; Kalmus K 00002, $7.50.

42 * Beethoven, Ludwig van, 1770–1827

[Symphonies, no. 3, op. 55, E♭ major] *Symphony no. 3 in E♭ major, op. 55, "Eroica."* Eulenburg 405, $12.75; Kalmus K 00003, $12.95.

43 * Beethoven, Ludwig van, 1770–1827

[Symphonies, no. 4, op. 60, B♭ major] *Symphony no. 4 in B♭ major, op. 60.* Eulenburg 414, $10.50; Kalmus K 00004, $6.50.

44 * Beethoven, Ludwig van, 1770–1827

[Symphonies, no. 5, op. 67, C minor] *Symphony no. 5 in C minor, op. 67.* Eulenburg 402, $11; Kalmus K 00005, $7.95; Norton Critical Scores 0-393-09893-X, ed. by Elliot Forbes, $10.95.

45 * Beethoven, Ludwig van, 1770–1827

[Symphonies, no. 6, op. 68, F major] *Symphony no. 6 in F major, op. 68, "Pastorale."* Eulenburg 407, $12.50; Kalmus K 00006, $7.50.

46 * Beethoven, Ludwig van, 1770–1827

[Symphonies, no. 7, op. 92, A major] *Symphony no. 7 in A major, op. 92.* Eulenburg 412, $12.75; Kalmus K 00007, $9.50.

47 * Beethoven, Ludwig van, 1770–1827

[Symphonies, no. 8, op. 93, F major] *Symphony no. 8 in F major, op. 93.* Eulenburg 416, $9.50; Kalmus K 00008, $6.50.

48 * Beethoven, Ludwig van, 1770–1827

[Symphonies, no. 9, op. 125, D minor] *Symphony no. 9 in D minor, op. 125.* Eulenburg 411, $16; Kalmus K 00057, $16.50.

———————

49 * Berlioz, Hector, 1803–1869

Symphonie fantastique. Bärenreiter TP331, $20.25; Dover 0-486-24657-4 (with Berlioz's *Harold in Italy*), $13.95; Eulenburg 422, $16.50; Norton Critical Scores 0-393-09926-1, ed. by Edward T. Cone, $10.95.

50 Bernstein, Leonard, 1918–1990

[Jeremiah] *Symphony no. 1, "Jeremiah."* Jalni/ Boosey & Hawkes FSB 597, $41.

51 Bizet, Georges, 1838–1875

[Symphony, no. 1, C major] *Symphony no. 1 in C major.* Eulenburg 556, $16.50; Kalmus K 00397, $9.50; Universal PH 391, $19.50.

52 Borodin, Aleksandr Porfir'evich, 1833–1887

[Symphonies, no. 2, B minor] *Symphony no. 2 in B minor.* Eulenburg 491, $15.

53 ** Brahms, Johannes, 1833–1897

[Symphonies] *Complete symphonies.* Dover 0-486-23053-8, $13.95; Kalmus K 00425-00426, 2 v., $12.95, $12.

—OR INDIVIDUALLY—

54 * Brahms, Johannes, 1833–1897

[Symphonies, no. 1, op. 68, C minor] *Symphony no. 1 in C minor, op. 68.* Eulenburg 425, $12.50; Kalmus K 00012, $5.95; Universal PH 130, $11.

55 * Brahms, Johannes, 1833–1897

[Symphonies, no. 2, op. 73, D major] *Symphony no. 2 in D major, op. 73.* Eulenburg 426, $11; Kalmus K 00014, $6.50; Universal PH 131, $11.

56 * Brahms, Johannes, 1833–1897

[Symphonies, no. 3, op. 90, F major] *Symphony no. 3 in F major, op. 90.* Eulenburg 427, $11; Kalmus K 00015, $5.50; Universal PH 132, $11.

57 * Brahms, Johannes, 1833–1897

[Symphonies, no. 4, op. 98, E minor] *Symphony no. 4 in E minor, op. 98.* Eulenburg 428, $12.75; Kalmus K 00016, $9.50; Universal PH 133, $11.

———————

58 Britten, Benjamin, 1913–1976

Simple symphony, for string orchestra, op. 4. Oxford University Press 0-19-361931-8, $21.95.

59 * Bruckner, Anton, 1824–1896

[Symphonies, no. 4, E♭ major] *Symphony no. 4 in E♭ major, "Romantic symphony,"* ed. by Robert Haas. Dover 0-486-26262-6 (with Bruckner's *Symphony no. 7*), $14.95.

60 * Bruckner, Anton, 1824–1896

[Symphonies, no. 5, B♭ major] *Symphony no. 5 in B♭ major (1878),* ed. by Robert Haas, Internationalen Bruckner Gesellschaft. Eulenburg 463, $21.50.

61 * Bruckner, Anton, 1824–1896

[Symphonies, no. 7, E major] *Symphony no. 7 in E major.* See 59

62 * Bruckner, Anton, 1824–1896

[Symphonies, no. 8, C minor] *Symphony no. 8 in C minor.* Eulenburg 466, 1887 version, ed. by Leopold Nowak, $25; Eulenburg 1526, 1890 version, ed. by Leopold Nowak, $25.

63 Bruckner, Anton, 1824–1896

[Symphonies, no. 9, D minor] *Symphony no. 9 in D minor.* Eulenburg 467, $17.50.

64 Carter, Elliott, 1908–

Symphony of three orchestras. Associated Music HL50238670, $42.50.

65 Copland, Aaron, 1900–1990

[Symphonies, no. 3] *Symphony no. 3.* Boosey & Hawkes HPS 629, $45.

66 Dvořák, Antonín, 1841–1904

[Symphonies, no. 7, op. 70, D minor] *Symphony no. 7 in D minor, op. 70 (B. 141).* Eulenburg 526, $17.50; Kalmus K 00050, $10.50.

67 Dvořák, Antonín, 1841–1904

[Symphonies, no. 8, op. 88, G major] *Symphony no. 8 in G major, op. 88 (B. 163).* Dover 0-486-24749-X (with Dvořák's *Symphony no. 9*), $12.95; Eulenburg 525, $15.

68 ** Dvořák, Antonín, 1841–1904

[Symphonies, no. 9, op. 95, E minor] *Symphony no. 9 in E minor, op. 95, "New world" (B. 178).* Eulenburg 433, $13.75; Kalmus K 00018, $7.50. *See also 67*

69 Elgar, Edward, 1857–1934

[Symphonies, no. 1, op. 55, A♭ major] *Symphony no. 1 in A♭ major, op. 55.* Eulenburg 8005, $36.

70 * Franck, César, 1822–1890

[Symphony, D minor] *Symphony in D minor.* Dover 0-486-24373-2, $9.95; Eulenburg 482, $13.75; Kalmus K 00019, $9.50.

71 Górecki, Henryk Mikolaj, 1933–

[Symphonies, no. 3, op. 36] *Symphony no. 3, op. 36, "Symphony of sorrowful songs."* Boosey & Hawkes PSB 21, $37.

72 Hanson, Howard, 1896–1981

[Symphonies, no. 2, op. 30] *Symphony no. 2, op. 30, "Romantic."* C. Fischer SC2, $18.

73 Harris, Roy, 1898–1979

[Symphonies, no. 3] *Symphony no. 3.* G. Schirmer ED38974, $25.

74 Haydn, Joseph, 1732–1809

[Symphonies, H. I, 6, D major] *Symphony no. 6 in D major, "Le matin."* Eulenburg 536, $6.75; Universal PH 706, ed. by H. C. Robbins Landon, $8.50.

75 Haydn, Joseph, 1732–1809

[Symphonies, H. I, 22, E♭ major] *Symphony no. 22 in E♭ major, "The philosopher."* Eulenburg 545, $6.75; Universal PH 722, ed. by H. C. Robbins Landon, $8.50.

76 Haydn, Joseph, 1732–1809

[Symphonies, H. I, 44, E minor] *Symphony no. 44 in E minor, "Trauer."* Eulenburg 544, $6.75; Universal PH 744, ed. by H. C. Robbins Landon, $8.50.

77 * Haydn, Joseph, 1732–1809

[Symphonies, H. I, 45, F♯ minor] *Symphony no. 45 in F♯ minor, "Farewell."* Eulenburg 486, $6.75; Universal PH 745, ed. by H. C. Robbins Landon, $8.50.

78 Haydn, Joseph, 1732–1809

[Symphonies, H. I, 49, F minor] *Symphony no. 49 in F minor, "La passione."* Eulenburg 535, $6.75; Universal PH 749, ed. by H. C. Robbins Landon, $8.50.

79 Haydn, Joseph, 1732–1809

[Symphonies, H. I, 82, C major] *Symphony no. 82 in C major, "The bear."* Eulenburg 488, $6.75; Universal PH 782, ed. by H. C. Robbins Landon, $8.50.

80 Haydn, Joseph, 1732–1809

[Symphonies, H. I, 83, G minor] *Symphony no. 83 in G minor, "The hen."* Eulenburg 530, $6.75; Universal PH 783, ed. by H. C. Robbins Landon, $8.50.

81 * Haydn, Joseph, 1732–1809

[Symphonies, H. I, 85, B♭ major] *Symphony no. 85 in B♭ major, "La reine."* Eulenburg 432, $6.75; Universal PH 785, ed. by H. C. Robbins Landon, $8.50.

82 Haydn, Joseph, 1732–1809

[Symphonies, H. I, 86, D major] *Symphony no. 86 in D major.* Eulenburg 484, $6.75; Universal PH 786, ed. by H. C. Robbins Landon, $8.50.

83 Haydn, Joseph, 1732–1809

[Symphonies, H. I, 87, A major] *Symphony no. 87 in A major.* Eulenburg 533, $6.75; Universal PH 787, ed. by H. C. Robbins Landon, $8.50.

84 * Haydn, Joseph, 1732–1809

[Symphonies, H. I, 88–92] *Paris symphonies, no. 88–92.* Dover 0-486-24445-8, $13.95.

—OR INDIVIDUALLY—

85 Haydn, Joseph, 1732–1809

[Symphonies, H. I, 88, G major] *Symphony no. 88 in G major.* Eulenburg 487, $6.75; Universal PH 788, ed. by H. C. Robbins Landon, $8.50.

86 * Haydn, Joseph, 1732–1809

[Symphonies, H. I, 92, G major] *Symphony no. 92 in G major, "Oxford."* Eulenburg 436, $6.75; Universal PH 792, ed. by H. C. Robbins Landon, $8.50.

87 ** Haydn, Joseph, 1732–1809

[Symphonies, H. I, 93–104] *Complete London symphonies, no. 93–104.* Dover 0-486-24982-4, 0-486-24983-2, 2 v., $15.95, $16.95.

—OR INDIVIDUALLY—

88 * Haydn, Joseph, 1732–1809

[Symphonies, H. I, 93, D major] *Symphony no. 93 in D major.* Eulenburg 468, $6.75; Universal PH 793, ed. by H. C. Robbins Landon, $8.50.

89 * Haydn, Joseph, 1732–1809

[Symphonies, H. I, 94, G major] *Symphony no. 94 in G major, "Surprise."* Eulenburg 435, $6.75; Universal PH 794, ed. by H. C. Robbins Landon, $8.50.

90 * Haydn, Joseph, 1732–1809

[Symphonies, H. I, 95, C minor] *Symphony no. 95 in C minor.* Eulenburg 480, $6.75; Universal PH 795, ed. by H. C. Robbins Landon, $8.50.

91 * Haydn, Joseph, 1732–1809

[Symphonies, H. I, 96, D major] *Symphony no. 96 in D major, "Miracle."* Eulenburg 481, $6.75; Universal PH 796, ed. by H. C. Robbins Landon, $8.50.

92 * Haydn, Joseph, 1732–1809

[Symphonies, H. I, 100, G major] *Symphony no. 100 in G major, "Military."* Eulenburg 434, $9; Universal PH 800, ed. by H. C. Robbins Landon, $8.50.

93 * Haydn, Joseph, 1732–1809

[Symphonies, H. I, 101, D major] *Symphony no. 101 in D major, "The clock."* Eulenburg 439, $10.50; Universal PH 801, ed. by H. C. Robbins Landon, $8.50.

94 * Haydn, Joseph, 1732–1809

[Symphonies, H. I, 103, E♭ major] *Symphony no. 103 in E♭ major, "Drum roll."* Eulenburg 469, $7.50; Universal PH 803, ed. by H. C. Robbins Landon, $8.50.

95 * Haydn, Joseph, 1732–1809

[Symphonies, H. I, 104, D major] *Symphony no. 104 in D major, "London."* Eulenburg 409, ed. by Harry Newstone, $7.75; Universal PH 804, ed. by H. C. Robbins Landon, $8.50.

---

96 Hindemith, Paul, 1895–1963

[Mathis der Maler (Symphony)] *Mathis der Maler: symphony.* Eulenburg 573, $11.75.

97 Ives, Charles, 1874–1954

[Holidays. Decoration Day] *Decoration Day: 2nd movement of a symphony, New England holidays.* Critical ed. by James B. Sinclair. Peer International 61623-856, $27.50.

98 Ives, Charles, 1874–1954

[Holidays. Fourth of July] *Fourth of July: 3rd movement of a symphony, New England holidays.* Critical ed. by Wayne D. Shirley. Associated Music AMP 8057, $20.

99 Ives, Charles, 1874–1954

[Holidays. Thanksgiving and Forefather's Day] *Thanksgiving and Forefather's Day: 4th movement of a symphony, New England holidays.* Critical ed., ed. by Jonathan Elkus. Peer International 61416-856, $27.50.

100 Ives, Charles, 1874–1954

[Holidays. Washington's Birthday] *Washington's Birthday: 1st movement of a symphony, New England holidays.* Critical ed. by James B. Sinclair. Associated Music AMP 8024, $15.

101 Ives, Charles, 1874–1954

[Symphonies, no. 2] *Symphony no. 2,* ed. by John Kirkpatrick and others. Peer International, $40.

102 Ives, Charles, 1874–1954

[Symphonies, no. 3] *Symphony no. 3: The camp meeting.* Critical ed., ed. by Kenneth Singleton. Associated Music AMP 8016, $20.

103 * Ives, Charles, 1874–1954

[Symphonies, no. 4] *Symphony no. 4.* Associated Music HL50237970, $85.

104 Janáček, Leoš, 1854–1928

Sinfonietta, for orchestra. Eulenburg 1369, $15.50.

105 ** Mahler, Gustav, 1860–1911

[Symphonies, no. 1–2] *Symphonies no. 1 and 2.* Dover 0-486-25473-9, $14.95.

106 ** Mahler, Gustav, 1860–1911

[Symphonies, no. 3–4] *Symphonies no. 3 and 4.* Dover 0-486-26166-2, $15.95.

107 ** Mahler, Gustav, 1860–1911

[Symphonies, no. 5–6] *Symphonies no. 5 and 6.* Dover 0-486-26888-8, $21.95.

—OR INDIVIDUALLY—

108 * Mahler, Gustav, 1860–1911

[Symphonies, no. 1, D major] *Symphony no. 1 in D major, "The titan."* Eulenburg 570, $20; Universal PH446, $21.

109 * Mahler, Gustav, 1860–1911

[Symphonies, no. 2, C minor] *Symphony no. 2 in C minor, "Resurrection."* Universal PH395, $32.

110 Mahler, Gustav, 1860–1911

[Symphonies, no. 3, D minor] *Symphony no. 3 in D minor.* Universal PH468, $32.

111 * Mahler, Gustav, 1860–1911

[Symphonies, no. 4, G major] *Symphony no. 4 in G major.* Eulenburg 575, $18.75; International Music 1201, $11.50; Universal PH214, $21.

112 * Mahler, Gustav, 1860–1911

[Symphonies, no. 5, C♯ minor] *Symphony no. 5 in C♯ minor.* Eulenburg 532, $24; Universal PH458, $28.

113 * Mahler, Gustav, 1860–1911

[Symphonies, no. 6, A minor] *Symphony no. 6 in A minor.* Eulenburg 586, $24.

———————

114 * Mahler, Gustav, 1860–1911

[Symphonies, no. 7, E minor] *Symphony no. 7 in E minor.* Dover 0-486-27339-3, $12.95; Eulenburg 492, $26; Universal PH473, $28.

115 * Mahler, Gustav, 1860–1911

[Symphonies, no. 8, E♭ major] *Symphony no. 8 in E♭ major, "Symphony of a thousand."* Dover 0-486-26022-4, $12.95; Universal PH490, $32.

116 * Mahler, Gustav, 1860–1911

[Symphonies, no. 9, D major] *Symphony no. 9 in D major.* Dover 0-486-27492-6, $9.95; Universal PH472, $28.

117 Mahler, Gustav, 1860–1911

[Symphonies, no. 10, F♯ minor] *Symphony no. 10,* completed by Deryck Cooke. Associated Music AMP7001, $65.

118 ** Mendelssohn-Bartholdy, Felix, 1809–1847

[Orchestral music. Selections] *Symphony no. 3 in A minor, op. 56, "Scotch"; Symphony no. 4, "Italian"; Midsummer night's dream excerpts; Hebrides overture; Calm sea and prosperous voyage overture.* Dover 0-486-23184-4, $16.95.

119 * Mendelssohn-Bartholdy, Felix, 1809–1847

[Symphonies, no. 3, op. 56, A minor] *Symphony no. 3 in A minor, op. 56, "Scotch."* Eulenburg 406, $13.50; Kalmus K 00117, $6.50.

120 * Mendelssohn-Bartholdy, Felix, 1809–1847

[Symphonies, no. 4, op. 90, A major] *Symphony no. 4 in A major, op. 90, "Italian."* Eulenburg 420, $10.50; Kalmus K 00486, $6.50.

121 Mendelssohn-Bartholdy, Felix, 1809–1847

[Symphonies, no. 5, op. 107, D minor] *Symphony no. 5 in D minor, op. 107, "Reformation."* Dover 0-486-27875-1, $10.95; Eulenburg 554, $10.50; Kalmus K 00321, $7.50.

122 Messiaen, Olivier, 1908–1992

Turangalîla-symphonie. 1990 revision. Durand 597-00559, $296.50.

123 * Mozart, Wolfgang Amadeus, 1756–1791

[Symphonies. Selections] *Symphonies no. 22–34.* Dover 0-486-26675-3, $13.95.

124 ** Mozart, Wolfgang Amadeus, 1756–1791

[Symphonies. Selections] *Later symphonies, no. 35–41.* Dover 0-486-23052-X, $11.95.

—OR INDIVIDUALLY—

125 Mozart, Wolfgang Amadeus, 1756–1791

[Symphonies, K. 183, G minor] *Symphony no. 25 in G minor, K. 183.* Bärenreiter TP76, $7.50; Eulenburg 547, $6.50.

126 * Mozart, Wolfgang Amadeus, 1756–1791

[Symphonies, K. 201, A major] *Symphony no. 29 in A major, K. 201.* Bärenreiter TP43, $7.50; Eulenburg 546, $6.50.

127 * Mozart, Wolfgang Amadeus, 1756–1791

[Symphonies, K. 297, D major] *Symphony no. 31 in D major, K. 297, "Paris."* Eulenburg 541, $10.

128 * Mozart, Wolfgang Amadeus, 1756–1791

[Symphonies, K. 319, B♭ major] *Symphony no. 33 in B♭ major, K. 319.* Bärenreiter TP178, $9; Eulenburg 543, $7.50.

129 * Mozart, Wolfgang Amadeus, 1756–1791

[Symphonies, K. 385, D major] *Symphony no. 35 in D major, K. 385, "Haffner."* Bärenreiter TP180, $10.25; Eulenburg 437, $9; Faber F0382, $13.75.

130 * Mozart, Wolfgang Amadeus, 1756–1791

[Symphonies, K. 425, C major] *Symphony no. 36 in C major, K. 425, "Linz."* Bärenreiter TP16, $9; Eulenburg 502, $7.75.

131 * Mozart, Wolfgang Amadeus, 1756–1791

[Symphonies, K. 504, D major] *Symphony no. 38 in D major, K. 504, "Prague."* Bärenreiter TP160, $11.25; Eulenburg 446, $10.

132 * Mozart, Wolfgang Amadeus, 1756–1791

[Symphonies, K. 543, E♭ major] *Symphony no. 39 in E♭ major, K. 543.* Bärenreiter TP39, $8.75; Eulenburg 415, $7.75.

133 * Mozart, Wolfgang Amadeus, 1756–1791

[Symphonies, K. 550, G minor] *Symphony no. 40 in G minor, K. 550.* Bärenreiter TP40, $8.25; Eulenburg 404, $7.75.

134 * Mozart, Wolfgang Amadeus, 1756–1791

[Symphonies, K. 551, C major] *Symphony no. 41 in C major, K. 551, "Jupiter."* Bärenreiter TP17, $9; Eulenburg 401, $10.

---

135 Nielsen, Carl, 1865–1931

[Symphonies, no. 3, op. 27] *Symphony no. 3, op. 27, "Sinfonia espansiva."* Kalmus A5726, $70.

136 Nielsen, Carl, 1865–1931

[Symphonies, no. 4, op. 29] *Symphony no. 4, op. 29, "Inextinguishable."* Kalmus A7720, $55.

137 Nielsen, Carl, 1865–1931

[Symphonies, no. 5, op. 50] *Symphony no. 5, op. 50.* Kalmus A5659, $50.

138 ** Prokofiev, Sergey, 1891–1953

[Orchestral music. Selections] *Symphony no. 1 in D major, op. 25, "Classical"; Lieutenant Kije suite; Peter and the wolf; Alexander Nevsky cantata.* Dover 0-486-20279-8, $18.95.

139 * Prokofiev, Sergey, 1891–1953

[Symphonies, no. 1, op. 25, D major] *Symphony no. 1 in D major, op. 25, "Classical."* Boosey & Hawkes HPS 33, $9.25; International Music 2275, $11. *See also* 138

140 Prokofiev, Sergey, 1891–1953

[Symphonies, no. 5, op. 100] *Symphony no. 5, op. 100.* Kalmus K 00263, $19.95.

141 * Rachmaninoff, Sergei, 1873–1943

[Symphonies, no. 2, op. 27, E minor] *Symphony no. 2 in E minor, op. 27.* Kalmus K 00141, $19.

142 Rachmaninoff, Sergei, 1873–1943

[Symphonies, no. 3, op. 44, A minor] *Symphony no. 3 in A minor, op. 44.* Belwin Mills SB899, $19.50.

143 Saint-Saëns, Camille, 1835–1921

[Symphonies, no. 3, op. 78, C minor] *Symphony for organ and orchestra in C minor, op. 78.* International Music 2122, $16.50.

144 Schoenberg, Arnold, 1874–1951

[Kammersymphonie] *Chamber symphony no. 1 in E major, op. 9.* Kalmus A6396, $30; Universal UE7147, $35.

145 ** Schubert, Franz, 1797–1828

[Symphonies. Selections] *Four symphonies: no. 4, D. 417, "Tragic"; no. 5, D. 485; no. 8, D. 759, "Unfinished"; no. 9, D. 944, "Great."* Dover 0-486-23681-1, $12.95.

—OR INDIVIDUALLY—

146 Schubert, Franz, 1797–1828

[Symphonies, D. 417, C minor] *Symphony no. 4 in C minor, D. 417, "Tragic."* Eulenburg 507, $11.75.

147 * Schubert, Franz, 1797–1828

[Symphonies, D. 485, B♭ major] *Symphony no. 5 in B♭ major, D. 485.* Eulenburg 508, $8.50.

148 * Schubert, Franz, 1797–1828

[Symphonies, D. 759, B minor] *Symphony no. 8 in B minor, D. 759, "Unfinished."* Eulenburg 403, $10.

149 * Schubert, Franz, 1797–1828

[Symphonies, D. 944, C major] *Symphony no. 9 in C major, D. 944, "Great."* Eulenburg 410, $18.75.

---

150 Schuman, William, 1910–1992

[Symphonies, no. 3] *Symphony no. 3.* G. Schirmer ED39886, $20.

151 ** Schumann, Robert, 1810–1856

[Symphonies] *Complete symphonies.* Dover 0-486-24013-4, $16.95.

—OR INDIVIDUALLY—

152 * Schumann, Robert, 1810–1856

[Symphonies, no. 1, op. 38, B♭ major] *Symphony no. 1 in B♭ major, op. 38, "Spring."* Eulenburg 417, $16.50.

153 * Schumann, Robert, 1810–1856

[Symphonies, no. 2, op. 61, C major] *Symphony no. 2 in C major, op. 61.* Eulenburg 421, $14.50.

154 * Schumann, Robert, 1810–1856

[Symphonies, no. 3, op. 97, E♭ major] *Symphony no. 3 in E♭ major, op. 97, "Rhenish."* Eulenburg 408, $12.75.

155 * Schumann, Robert, 1810–1856

[Symphonies, no. 4, op. 120, D minor] *Symphony no. 4 in D minor, op. 120.* Eulenburg 413, $11.75.

---

156 Scriabin, Aleksandr Nikolayevich, 1872–1915

[Poème èkstaza] *Symphony no. 4, op. 54, "Poem of ecstasy."* Dover 0-486-28461-1 (with Scriabin's *Symphony no. 5, "Prometheus unbound"*), $13.95; Eulenburg 497, $22.

157 * Scriabin, Aleksandr Nikolayevich, 1872–1915

[Prométhée] *Symphony no. 5, op. 60, "Prometheus, the poem of fire."* Eulenburg 8008, $22. *See also* 156

158 ** Shostakovich, Dmitrii Dmitrievich, 1906–1975

[Symphonies. Selections] *Symphonies no. 1 and 5.* Dover 0-486-28368-2, $13.95.

159 * Shostakovich, Dmitrii Dmitrievich, 1906–1975

[Symphonies, no. 1, op. 10, F major] *Symphony no. 1 in F major, op. 10.* Kalmus K 00157, $9.50.

160 * Shostakovich, Dmitrii Dmitrievich, 1906–1975

[Symphonies, no. 5, op. 47, D minor] *Symphony no. 5 in D minor, op. 47.* Eulenburg 579, $21.

161 Shostakovich, Dmitrii Dmitrievich, 1906–1975

[Symphonies, no. 7, op. 60, C major] *Symphony no. 7 in C major, op. 60, "Leningrad."* Kalmus K 01390, $15.50.

162 * Shostakovich, Dmitrii Dmitrievich, 1906–1975

[Symphonies, no. 9–10] *Symphonies no. 9 and 10.* Dover 0-486-28801-3, $16.95.

163 * Sibelius, Jean, 1865–1937

[Symphonies, no. 1–2] *Symphonies 1 and 2.* Dover 0-486-27886-7, $16.95.

—OR INDIVIDUALLY—

164 Sibelius, Jean, 1865–1937

[Symphonies, no. 1, op. 39, E minor] *Symphony no. 1 in E minor, op. 39.* Kalmus K 00322, $12.50.

165 * Sibelius, Jean, 1865–1937

[Symphonies, no. 2, op. 43, D major] *Symphony no. 2 in D major, op. 43.* Breitkopf & Härtel PB3323, $15.50.

---

166 Sibelius, Jean, 1865–1937

[Symphonies, no. 4, op. 63, A minor] *Symphony no. 4 in A minor, op. 63.* Breitkopf & Härtel PB3326, $14.10; Kalmus A6353, $40.

167 * Sibelius, Jean, 1865–1937

[Symphonies, no. 5, op. 82, E♭ major] *Symphony no. 5 in E♭ major, op. 82,* ed. by Paavo Berglund. W. Hansen 2103B, $26.95.

168 * Stravinsky, Igor, 1882–1971

[Symphonies d'instruments à vents] *Symphonies of wind instruments.* Rev. 1947 version. Boosey & Hawkes HPS 672, $13.

169 Stravinsky, Igor, 1882–1971

Symphony in three movements. Eulenburg 574, $18.50.

170 ** Tchaikovsky, Peter Ilich, 1840–1893

[Symphonies, no. 4–6] *Fourth, Fifth, and Sixth symphonies.* Dover 0-486-23861-4, $19.95.

—OR INDIVIDUALLY—

171 * Tchaikovsky, Peter Ilich, 1840–1893

[Symphonies, no. 4, op. 36, F minor] *Symphony no. 4 in F minor, op. 36.* Eulenburg 430, $14.50.

172 * Tchaikovsky, Peter Ilich, 1840–1893

[Symphonies, no. 5, op. 64, E minor] *Symphony no. 5 in E minor, op. 64.* Eulenburg 429, $16.50.

173 * Tchaikovsky, Peter Ilich, 1840–1893

[Symphonies, no. 6, op. 74, B minor] *Symphony no. 6 in B minor, op. 74, "Pathètique."* Eulenburg 479, $16.50.

---

174 * Vaughan Williams, Ralph, 1872–1958

[Symphonies, no. 1] *A sea symphony (Symphony no. 1).* E. C. Schirmer 3.0854.6, $49.

175 * Vaughan Williams, Ralph, 1872–1958

[Symphonies, no. 2, G major] *A London symphony (Symphony no. 2).* Rev. ed. E. C. Schirmer 3.0853.6, $32.95.

176 Vaughan Williams, Ralph, 1872–1958

[Symphonies, no. 5, D major] *Symphony no. 5 in D major.* Eulenburg 1506, $18.75.

177 Vaughan Williams, Ralph, 1872–1958

[Symphonies, no. 6, E minor] *Symphony no. 6 in E minor.* Eulenburg 1507, $24.

178 Zwilich, Ellen Taaffe, 1939–

[Symphonies, no. 1] *Symphony no. 1: three movements for orchestra.* Associated Music HL50481139, $30.

Concertos

Included here are solo concertos, works in concerto grosso form, concertos for orchestra, and other works for solo instrument(s) and orchestra.

179 ** Bach, Johann Sebastian, 1685–1750

[Brandenburgische Konzerte] *Brandenburg concertos no. 1–6, BWV 1046–1051.* Bärenreiter TP9, $39; or singly, Bärenreiter TP3-8, 6 v., $8, $7.25, $7.25, $7.25, $9, $6.75; Dover 0-486-23376-6 (with Bach's *Orchestral suites*), $10.95; Eulenburg 280, 257, 254, 281, 282, 255, 6 v., $6.50, $6.50, $6.50, $6.50, $7.75, $6.50.

180 * Bach, Johann Sebastian, 1685–1750

[Concertos, harpsichord, string orchestra] *Complete concerti for solo keyboard and orchestra.* Dover 0-486-24929-8, $10.95.

—OR INDIVIDUALLY—

181 * Bach, Johann Sebastian, 1685–1750

[Concertos, harpsichord, string orchestra, BWV 1052, D minor] *Concerto for harpsichord, D minor, BWV 1052.* Eulenburg 744, $9.

182 * Bach, Johann Sebastian, 1685–1750

[Concertos, harpsichord, string orchestra, BWV 1056, F minor] *Concerto for harpsichord, F minor, BWV 1056.* Eulenburg 745, $6.50.

———

183   Bach, Johann Sebastian, 1685–1750

[Concertos. Selections] *Complete concertos for two or more harpsichords.* Dover 0-486-24929-8, $10.95.

—OR INDIVIDUALLY—

184   Bach, Johann Sebastian, 1685–1750

[Concertos, harpsichords (2), string orchestra, BWV 1060, C minor] *Concerto for two harpsichords, BWV 1060, C minor.* Eulenburg 731, $7.50.

185   Bach, Johann Sebastian, 1685–1750

[Concertos, harpsichords (2), string orchestra, BWV 1061, C major] *Concerto for two harpsichords, BWV 1061, C major.* Eulenburg 730, $7.50.

———

186 * Bach, Johann Sebastian, 1685–1750

[Concertos. Selections] *Three violin concerti, BWV 1041, 1042, 1043.* Dover 0-486-25124-1, $5.95.

—OR INDIVIDUALLY—

187 * Bach, Johann Sebastian, 1685–1750

[Concertos, violin, string orchestra, BWV 1041–1042] *Violin concertos, BWV 1041 in A minor and BWV 1042 in E major.* Bärenreiter TP269, $13.50; Eulenburg 711–712, 2 v., $8.50, $6.75; Kalmus K 00908, $7.50.

188 * Bach, Johann Sebastian, 1685–1750

[Concertos, violins (2), string orchestra, BWV 1043, D minor] *Double concerto for 2 violins, strings, and continuo, BWV 1043, D minor.* Bärenreiter TP284, $7.50; Eulenburg 727, $6.50.

———

189   Barber, Samuel, 1910–1981

[Concertos, violin, orchestra, op. 14] *Violin concerto, op. 14.* G. Schirmer ED44057, $18.

190 * Bartók, Béla, 1881–1945

[Concertos, orchestra] *Concerto for orchestra.* 1993 rev. ed. by Peter Bartók. Boosey & Hawkes HPS 79, $16.50.

191   Bartók, Béla, 1881–1945

[Concertos, piano, orchestra, no. 2] *Piano concerto no. 2.* Boosey & Hawkes HPS 1006, $33.

192 * Bartók, Béla, 1881–1945

[Concertos, piano, orchestra, no. 3] *Piano concerto no. 3.* Boosey & Hawkes HPS 100, $35.

193   Bartók, Béla, 1881–1945

[Concertos, violin, orchestra, no. 2] *Violin concerto no. 2.* Boosey & Hawkes HPS 81, $38.

194 ** Beethoven, Ludwig van, 1770–1827

[Concertos, piano, orchestra] *Complete piano concertos.* Dover 0-486-24563-2, $14.95; Kalmus K 00302, $22.

—OR INDIVIDUALLY—

195 * Beethoven, Ludwig van, 1770–1827

[Concertos, piano, orchestra, no. 1, op. 15, C major] *Piano concerto no. 1 in C major, op. 15.* Bärenreiter TP274, $14.75; Eulenburg 724, $11.75.

196 * Beethoven, Ludwig van, 1770–1827

[Concertos, piano, orchestra, no. 2, op. 19, B♭ major] *Piano concerto no. 2 in B♭ major, op. 19.* Bärenreiter TP275, $11.25; Eulenburg 725, $10.

197 * Beethoven, Ludwig van, 1770–1827

[Concertos, piano, orchestra, no. 3, op. 37, C minor] *Piano concerto no. 3 in C minor, op. 37.* Bärenreiter TP276, $11.75; Eulenburg 704, $10.

198 * Beethoven, Ludwig van, 1770–1827

[Concertos, piano, orchestra, no. 4, op. 58, G major] *Piano concerto no. 4 in G major, op. 58.* Eulenburg 705, $10.50.

199 * Beethoven, Ludwig van, 1770–1827

[Concertos, piano, orchestra, no. 5, op. 73, E♭ major] *Piano concerto no. 5 in E♭ major, op. 73, "Emperor concerto."* Eulenburg 706, $15.

200 * Beethoven, Ludwig van, 1770–1827

[Concertos, violin, orchestra, op. 61, D major] *Violin concerto in D major, op. 61.* Bärenreiter TP277, $11.75; Eulenburg 701, $9.50; Kalmus K 00312, $6.95.

201 * Beethoven, Ludwig van, 1770–1827

[Concertos, violin, violoncello, piano, orchestra, op. 56, C major] *Triple concerto for piano, violin, and cello in C major, op. 56.* Bärenreiter TP285, $15; Eulenburg 729, $13.75; Kalmus K 01008, $7.95.

202 Beethoven, Ludwig van, 1770–1827

[Romances, violin, orchestra] *Two romances for violin and orchestra, op. 40 and op. 50.* Bärenreiter TP289, $8; Eulenburg 803, $6.50; Kalmus K 01004 (with Beethoven's *Septet, op. 20 and Sextet, op. 81b*), $6.

203 Berg, Alban, 1885–1935

[Concertos, violin, orchestra] *Concerto for violin.* Universal PH426, $29.

204 Berg, Alban, 1885–1935

Kammerkonzert for piano, strings, and winds. Univeral UE 12419, $39.

205 Berlioz, Hector, 1803–1869

[Harold en Italie] *Harold in Italy, for viola and orchestra, op. 16.* Dover 0-486-24657-4 (with Berlioz's *Symphonie fantastique*), $13.95; Eulenburg 423, $17.50.

206 Bloch, Ernest, 1880–1959

Schelomo: Hebrew rhapsody for cello and orchestra. Dover (with Bruch's *Kol nidrei*) 0-486-29039-5, $9.95, for sale in the United States only; G. Schirmer ED40760, $30.

207 Boccherini, Luigi, 1743–1805

[Concertos, violoncello, orchestra, G. 482, B♭ major; arr.] *Cello concerto in B♭ major.* Eulenburg 780, ed. by Richard Sturzenegger, $6.75; Eulenburg 780-01, ed. by Friedrich Wilhem Ludwig Grützmacher, $10.

208 ** Brahms, Johannes, 1833–1897

[Concertos] *Complete concertos, including the Piano concertos no. 1 and 2, Violin concerto, op. 77, and Concerto for violin and cello, op. 102.* Dover 0-486-24170-X, $14.95.

—OR INDIVIDUALLY—

209 * Brahms, Johannes, 1833–1897

[Concertos, piano, orchestra, no. 1, op. 15, D minor] *Piano concerto no. 1 in D minor, op. 15.* Eulenburg 713, $13.75; Kalmus K 00480, $9.50.

210 * Brahms, Johannes, 1833–1897

[Concertos, piano, orchestra, no. 2, op. 83, B♭ major] *Piano concerto no. 2 in B♭ major, op. 83.* Eulenburg 713, $13.75; Kalmus K 00481, $9.95.

211 * Brahms, Johannes, 1833–1897

[Concertos, violin, orchestra, op. 77, D major] *Violin concerto in D major, op. 77.* Eulenburg 716, $12.50; Kalmus K 00353, $7.50.

212 * Brahms, Johannes, 1833–1897

[Concertos, violin, violoncello, orchestra, op. 102, A minor] *Double concerto for violin and cello in A minor, op. 102.* Eulenburg 723, $13.50; Kalmus K 00319, $6.50.

213 * Bruch, Max, 1838–1920

[Concertos, violin, orchestra, no. 1, op. 26, G minor] *Violin concerto no. 1 in G minor, op. 26.* Eulenburg 714, $13.50.

214 Bruch, Max, 1838–1920

Kol nidrei, for cello and orchestra, op. 47. Kalmus A1360, $15. *See also 206*

215 Carter, Elliott, 1908–

[Concertos, piano, orchestra] *Piano concerto.* Associated Music AMP7011, $45.

216 Chausson, Ernest, 1855–1899

[Poème, violin, orchestra, op. 25] *Poème for violin and orchestra, op. 25.* Kalmus A3946, $15.

217 ** Chopin, Frédéric, 1810–1849

[Concertos, piano, orchestra] *The piano concertos.* Dover 0-486-25835-1, $8.95.

—OR INDIVIDUALLY—

218 * Chopin, Frédéric, 1810–1849

[Concertos, piano, orchestra, no. 1, op. 11, E minor] *Piano concerto no. 1 in E minor, op. 11.* Eulenburg 1215, $16.50.

219 * Chopin, Frédéric, 1810–1849

[Concertos, piano, orchestra, no. 2, op. 21, F minor] *Piano concerto no. 2 in F minor, op. 21.* Eulenburg 1216, $13.75; Kalmus K 00326, $12.50.

---

220 Copland, Aaron, 1900–1990

[Concertos, clarinet, string orchestra] *Concerto for clarinet and string orchestra.* Boosey & Hawkes HPS 831, $27.

221 * Copland, Aaron, 1900–1990

Quiet city, for trumpet, English horn, and orchestra. Boosey & Hawkes HPS 726, $7.25.

222 Corelli, Arcangelo, 1653–1713

[Concerti grossi, violins (2), violoncello, string orchestra, op. 6] *12 concerti grossi, op. 6.* Dover 0-486-25606-5, $12.95; Peters P618, $16.85.

223 Debussy, Claude, 1862–1918

Danse sacrée et danse profane, for harp and orchestra. Durand 597-00532, $24.

224 Dvořák, Antonín, 1841–1904

[Concertos, violin, orchestra, op. 53, A minor] *Violin concerto in A minor, op. 53 (B. 108).* Eulenburg 751, $12.50; Kalmus K 00026, $7.50.

225 * Dvořák, Antonín, 1841–1904

[Concertos, violoncello, orchestra, op. 104, B minor] *Cello concerto in B minor, op. 104 (B. 191).* Eulenburg 785, $12.50; Kalmus K 00298, $7.50.

226 Elgar, Edward, 1857–1934

[Concertos, violoncello, orchestra, op. 85, E minor] *Cello concerto in E minor, op. 85.* Eulenburg 1814, $19.95.

227 Falla, Manuel de, 1876–1946

[Noches en los jardines de España] *Nights in the gardens of Spain, for piano and orchestra.* Eschig ME 687, $63.50.

228 Fauré, Gabriel, 1845–1924

[Ballades, piano, orchestra, op. 19] *Ballade for piano and orchestra, op. 19.* Eulenburg 1384, $11.

229 Fauré, Gabriel, 1845–1924

[Elegy, violoncello, piano, op. 24; arr.] *Elégie for cello and orchestra, op. 24; orchestrated by the composer.* Eulenburg 1385, $8.50.

230 Franck, César, 1822–1890

[Variations symphoniques] *Symphonic variations for piano and orchestra.* Eulenburg 738, $9.50; Kalmus K 00381, $6.50.

231 * Gershwin, George, 1898–1937

[Concerto, piano, orchestra, F major] *Piano concerto in F major.* Warner Bros., $22.50.

232 * Gershwin, George, 1898–1937

Rhapsody in blue, for piano and orchestra. Warner Bros., $17.50.

233 * Grieg, Edvard, 1843–1907

[Concerto, piano, orchestra, op. 16, A minor] *Piano concerto in A minor, op. 16.* Dover 0-486-27931-6, $8.95; Eulenburg 726, $10.50; Kalmus K 00163, $7.95.

234 * Handel, George Frideric, 1685–1759

[Concerti grossi] *Concerti grossi, op. 3 and op. 6; Concerto grosso in C major, "Alexander's feast."* Dover 0-486-24187-4, $12.95.

—OR INDIVIDUALLY—

235 * Handel, George Frideric, 1685–1759

[Concerti grossi, op. 3] *Six concerti grossi, op. 3.* Bärenreiter TP65-70, 6 v., $6.50 each; Eulenburg 377-382, 6 v., $6.50 each.

236 * Handel, George Frideric, 1685–1759

[Concerti grossi, violins (2), violoncello, string orchestra, op. 6] *Twelve concerti grossi, op. 6.* Bärenreiter TP161-172, 12 v., $6.50 each; Eulenburg 263-274, 12 v., $6.50 each.

---

237 Handel, George Frideric, 1685–1759

[Concertos, organ, orchestra. Selections] *Twelve organ concerti, op. 4 and op. 7.* Dover 0-486-24462-8, $8.95.

238 Haydn, Joseph, 1732–1809

[Concertos, harpsichord, orchestra, H. XVIII, 11, D major] *Concerto in D major for piano and orchestra.* Eulenburg 791, $6.50.

239 Haydn, Joseph, 1732–1809

[Concertos, trumpet, orchestra, H. VIIe, 1, E♭ major] *Concerto in E♭ major for trumpet.* Bärenreiter TP351, $8; Eulenburg 798, $6.50; Kalmus K 00084, $5.50.

240 * Haydn, Joseph, 1732–1809

[Concertos, violin, orchestra, H. VIIa, 1, C major] *Concerto in C major for violin and orchestra.* Eulenburg 1202, $7.50.

241 Haydn, Joseph, 1732–1809

[Concertos, violoncello, orchestra, H. VIIb, 1, C major] *Concerto no. 1 in C major for cello and orchestra.* Bärenreiter TP291, $10.25.

242 * Haydn, Joseph, 1732–1809

[Concertos, violoncello, orchestra, H. VIIb, 2, D major] *Concerto no. 2 in D major for cello and orchestra.* Bärenreiter TP292, $8.25; Eulenburg 769, $6.75.

243 Hindemith, Paul, 1895–1963

The four temperaments, for piano and string orchestra. Schott ST06309, $20.

244 Hindemith, Paul, 1895–1963

Trauermusik, for viola and string orchestra. Schott ED3514, $10.

245 Khachaturian, Aram, 1903–1978

[Concertos, violin, orchestra, D minor] *Violin concerto in D minor.* Kalmus K 01480, $9.50.

246 * Lalo, Édouard, 1823–1892

Symphonie espagnole, for violin and orchestra, op. 21. Eulenburg 728, $13.75; Kalmus K 00267, $9.95.

247 * Liszt, Franz, 1811–1886

[Concertos, piano, orchestra] *The piano concerti.* Dover 0-486-25221-3, $8.95.

—OR INDIVIDUALLY—

248 * Liszt, Franz, 1811–1886

[Concertos, piano, orchestra, no. 1, E♭ major] *Concerto for piano in E♭ major, no. 1.* Editio Musica Budapest EMB 40118, $10.50; Eulenburg 710, $10.50.

249 * Liszt, Franz, 1811–1886

[Concertos, piano, orchestra, no. 2, A major] *Concerto for piano in A major, no. 2.* Eulenburg 720, $10.50; Kalmus K 09347, $5.95.

250 MacDowell, Edward, 1860–1908

[Concertos, piano, orchestra, no. 2, op. 23, D minor] *Piano concerto no. 2 in D minor, op. 23.* Kalmus A1668, $50.

251 * Mendelssohn-Bartholdy, Felix, 1809–1847

[Concertos, piano, orchestra, no. 1, op. 25, G minor] *Piano concerto no. 1 in G minor, op. 25.* Eulenburg 795, $11.75; Kalmus K 01187, $6.50.

252 Mendelssohn-Bartholdy, Felix, 1809–1847

[Concertos, piano, orchestra, no. 2, op. 40, D minor] *Piano concerto no. 2 in D minor, op. 40.* Eulenburg 1267, $11.75.

253 * Mendelssohn-Bartholdy, Felix, 1809–1847

[Concertos, violin, orchestra, op. 64, E minor] *Violin concerto in E minor, op. 64.* Eulenburg 702, $10.50; Kalmus K 00145, $5.50.

254 * Mozart, Wolfgang Amadeus, 1756–1791

[Concertos. Selections] *Concerti for wind instruments: bassoon K. 191, clarinet K. 622, flute K. 313 and K. 314, flute and harp K. 299, horn K. 412, K. 417, K. 447, and K. 495.* Dover 0-486-25228-0, $13.95.

—OR INDIVIDUALLY—

255 Mozart, Wolfgang Amadeus, 1756–1791

[Concertos, bassoon, orchestra, K. 191, B♭ major] *Bassoon concerto in B♭ major, K. 191.* Bärenreiter TP253, $8; Eulenburg 784, $6.50.

256 * Mozart, Wolfgang Amadeus, 1756–1791

[Concertos, clarinet, orchestra, K. 622, A major] *Clarinet concerto in A major, K. 622.* Bärenreiter TP254, $8.75; Eulenburg 778, $9; Kalmus K 00303, $5.

257 * Mozart, Wolfgang Amadeus, 1756–1791

[Concertos, flute, harp, orchestra, K. 299, C major] *Concerto for flute and harp in C major, K. 299.* Bärenreiter TP286, $9.75; Eulenburg 767, $9.

258 * Mozart, Wolfgang Amadeus, 1756–1791

[Concertos, flute, orchestra, K. 313, G major] *Flute concerto no. 1 in G major, K. 313.* Bärenreiter TP250, $8.25; Eulenburg 779, $7.50.

259 Mozart, Wolfgang Amadeus, 1756–1791

[Concertos, horn, orchestra] *Four horn concertos, K. 412, 417, 447, and 495.* Bärenreiter TP310, TP307, TP308, TP309, 4 v., $8, $8.75, $9.50, $9; Eulenburg 799, 792, 789, 797, 4 v., $6.50 each; Kalmus K 00091, $11.50.

260   Mozart, Wolfgang Amadeus, 1756–1791

[Concertos, oboe, orchestra, K. 314, C major] *Oboe concerto in C major, K. 314 (285d).* Bärenreiter TP252, $8.

261 * Mozart, Wolfgang Amadeus, 1756–1791

[Concertos, piano, orchestra, K. 271, E♭ major] *Piano concerto no. 9 in E♭ major, K. 271, "Jeunehomme."* Bärenreiter TP242, $12; Eulenburg 742, $9.50.

262 * Mozart, Wolfgang Amadeus, 1756–1791

[Concertos, piano, orchestra. Selections] *Piano concertos no. 11–16.* Dover 0-486-25468-2, $12.95.

263 * Mozart, Wolfgang Amadeus, 1756–1791

[Concertos, piano, orchestra. Selections] *Piano concertos no. 17–22.* Dover 0-486-23599-8, $14.95.

264 ** Mozart, Wolfgang Amadeus, 1756–1791

[Concertos, piano, orchestra. Selections] *Piano concertos no. 23–27.* Dover 0-486-23600-5, $12.95.

—OR INDIVIDUALLY—

265   Mozart, Wolfgang Amadeus, 1756–1791

[Concertos, piano, orchestra, K. 413, F major] *Piano concerto no. 11 in F major, K. 413.* Bärenreiter TP245, $11; Eulenburg 1208, $7.75.

266   Mozart, Wolfgang Amadeus, 1756–1791

[Concertos, piano, orchestra, K. 414, A major] *Piano concerto no. 12 in A major, K. 414.* Bärenreiter TP244, $10.50; Eulenburg 800, $9.50.

267   Mozart, Wolfgang Amadeus, 1756–1791

[Concertos, piano, orchestra, K. 415, C major] *Piano concerto no. 13 in C major, K. 415.* Bärenreiter TP246, $12; Eulenburg 1206, $9.50.

268 * Mozart, Wolfgang Amadeus, 1756–1791

[Concertos, piano, orchestra, K. 449, E♭ major] *Piano concerto no. 14 in E♭ major, K. 449.* Bärenreiter TP247, $11; Eulenburg 1204, $9.

269 * Mozart, Wolfgang Amadeus, 1756–1791

[Concertos, piano, orchestra, K. 450, B♭ major] *Piano concerto no. 15 in B♭ major, K. 450.* Bärenreiter TP248, $9.75; Eulenburg 743, $9.

270 * Mozart, Wolfgang Amadeus, 1756–1791

[Concertos, piano, orchestra, K. 451, D major] *Piano concerto no. 16 in D major, K. 451.* Bärenreiter TP249, $12.75; Eulenburg 1207, $11.75.

271 * Mozart, Wolfgang Amadeus, 1756–1791

[Concertos, piano, orchestra, K. 453, G major] *Piano concerto no. 17 in G major, K. 453.* Bärenreiter TP156, $11; Eulenburg 760, $9.50.

272 * Mozart, Wolfgang Amadeus, 1756–1791

[Concertos, piano, orchestra, K. 456, B♭ major] *Piano concerto no. 18 in B♭ major, K. 456.* Bärenreiter TP157, $12.50; Eulenburg 796, $9.50.

273 * Mozart, Wolfgang Amadeus, 1756–1791

[Concertos, piano, orchestra, K. 459, F major] *Piano concerto no. 19 in F major, K. 459.* Bärenreiter TP158, $12; Eulenburg 761, $10.

274 * Mozart, Wolfgang Amadeus, 1756–1791

[Concertos, piano, orchestra, K. 466, D minor] *Piano concerto no. 20 in D minor, K. 466.* Bärenreiter TP147, $11; Eulenburg 721, $9.50.

275 * Mozart, Wolfgang Amadeus, 1756–1791

[Concertos, piano, orchestra, K. 467, C major] *Piano concerto no. 21 in C major, K. 467.* Bärenreiter TP148, $11; Eulenburg 739, $8.50.

276 * Mozart, Wolfgang Amadeus, 1756–1791

[Concertos, piano, orchestra, K. 482, E♭ major] *Piano concerto no. 22 in E♭ major, K. 482.* Bärenreiter TP149, $6.60; Eulenburg 737, $9.50.

277 * Mozart, Wolfgang Amadeus, 1756–1791

[Concertos, piano, orchestra, K. 488, A major] *Piano concerto no. 23 in A major, K. 488.* Bärenreiter TP62, $10.50; Eulenburg 736, $9.50.

278 * Mozart, Wolfgang Amadeus, 1756–1791

[Concertos, piano, orchestra, K. 491, C minor] *Piano concerto no. 24 in C minor, K. 491.* Bärenreiter TP63, $10.50; Eulenburg 740, $9.50.

279 * Mozart, Wolfgang Amadeus, 1756–1791

[Concertos, piano, orchestra, K. 503, C major] *Piano concerto no. 25 in C major, K. 503.* Bärenreiter TP64, $10.50; Eulenburg 774, $9.50.

280 * Mozart, Wolfgang Amadeus, 1756–1791

[Concertos, piano, orchestra, K. 537, D major] *Piano concerto no. 26 in D major, K. 537, "Coronation concerto."* Bärenreiter TP90, OP; Eulenburg 719, $7.75.

281 * Mozart, Wolfgang Amadeus, 1756–1791

[Concertos, piano, orchestra, K. 595, B♭ major] *Piano concerto no. 27 in B♭ major, K. 595.* Bärenreiter TP91, $10.50; Eulenburg 775, $9.

282 * Mozart, Wolfgang Amadeus, 1756–1791

[Concertos, pianos (2), orchestra, K. 365, E♭ major] *Concerto for two pianos in E♭ major, K. 365.* Eulenburg 741, $9.

283 * Mozart, Wolfgang Amadeus, 1756–1791

[Concertos, violin, orchestra] *The five violin concerti and the Sinfonia concertante, K. 364.* Dover 0-486-25169-1, $11.95.

—OR INDIVIDUALLY—

284 Mozart, Wolfgang Amadeus, 1756–1791

[Concertos, violin, orchestra, K. 207, B♭ major] *Violin concerto no. 1 in B♭ major, K. 207.* Bärenreiter TP270, $8.25; Eulenburg 763, $7.50.

285 Mozart, Wolfgang Amadeus, 1756–1791

[Concertos, violin, orchestra, K. 211, D major] *Violin concerto no. 2 in D major, K. 211.* Bärenreiter TP271, $7.50; Eulenburg 764, $6.50.

286 * Mozart, Wolfgang Amadeus, 1756–1791

[Concertos, violin, orchestra, K. 216, G major] *Violin concerto no. 3 in G major, K. 216.* Bärenreiter TP272, $9; Eulenburg 747, $7.75.

287 * Mozart, Wolfgang Amadeus, 1756–1791

[Concertos, violin, orchestra, K. 218, D major] *Violin concerto no. 4 in D major, K. 218.* Bärenreiter TP273, $9; Eulenburg 748, $7.75.

288 * Mozart, Wolfgang Amadeus, 1756–1791

[Concertos, violin, orchestra, K. 219, A major] *Violin concerto no. 5 in A major, K. 219.* Bärenreiter TP20, $9.75; Eulenburg 717, $8.50.

289 Mozart, Wolfgang Amadeus, 1756–1791

[Rondos, piano, orchestra, K. 382, D major] *Rondo for piano and orchestra in D major, K. 382.* Eulenburg 783, $6.50.

290 Mozart, Wolfgang Amadeus, 1756–1791

[Rondos, violin, orchestra, K. 269, B♭ major] *Rondo concertante for violin and orchestra in B♭ major, K. 269 (K. 261a).* Kalmus A7764, $6.

291 Mozart, Wolfgang Amadeus, 1756–1791

[Rondos, violin, orchestra, K. 373, C major] *Rondo for violin and orchestra in C major, K. 373.* Kalmus A1777, $4.

292 Mozart, Wolfgang Amadeus, 1756–1791

[Sinfonia concertante, violin, viola, orchestra, K. 364, E♭ major] *Sinfonia concertante in E♭ major for violin, viola, and orchestra, K. 364.* Bärenreiter TP176, $11; Eulenburg 734, $9.50; Kalmus K 00316, $5.50.

293 * Paganini, Nicolò, 1782–1840

[Concertos, violin, orchestra, no. 1, op. 6, E♭ major; arr.] *Violin concerto no. 1, [transposed to] D major, op. 6.* Breitkopf & Härtel PB5260, $17.

294 Poulenc, Francis, 1899–1963

[Concertos, organ, string orchestra, G minor] *Concerto in G minor for organ, strings, and timpani.* Salabert SEAS 15404, $14.95.

295 Prokofiev, Sergey, 1891–1953

[Concertos, piano, orchestra, no. 1, op. 10, D♭ major] *Piano concerto no. 1 in D♭ major, op. 10.* Kalmus A2410, $50.

296 * Prokofiev, Sergey, 1891–1953

[Concertos, piano, orchestra, no. 3, op. 26, C major] *Piano concerto no. 3 in C major, op. 26.* Boosey & Hawkes HPS 52, $33; Kalmus K 00272, $14.95.

297 Prokofiev, Sergey, 1891–1953

[Concertos, violin, orchestra, no. 1, op. 19, D major] *Violin concerto no. 1 in D major, op. 19.* Boosey & Hawkes HPS 731, $28.

298 Prokofiev, Sergey, 1891–1953

[Concertos, violin, orchestra, no. 2, op. 63, G minor] *Violin concerto no. 2 in G minor, op. 63.* Boosey & Hawkes HPS 732, $27.

299 * Rachmaninoff, Sergei, 1873–1943

[Concertos, piano, orchestra, no. 2, op. 18, C minor] *Piano concerto no. 2 in C minor, op. 18.* Boosey & Hawkes HPS 17, $39; Kalmus K 00137, $9.50.

300 * Rachmaninoff, Sergei, 1873–1943

[Concertos, piano, orchestra, no. 3, op. 30, D minor] *Piano concerto no. 3 in D minor, op. 30.* Boosey & Hawkes HPS 18, $28.

301 * Rachmaninoff, Sergei, 1873–1943

[Rapsodie sur un thème de Paganini] *Rhapsody on a theme of Paganini, for piano and orchestra.* Kalmus K 00101, $13.

302 * Ravel, Maurice, 1875–1937

[Concertos, piano, 1 hand, orchestra, D major] *Concerto for piano, left hand, in D major.* Durand 597-00562, $48.75.

303 * Ravel, Maurice, 1875–1937

[Concertos, piano, orchestra, G major] *Piano concerto in G major.* Durand 597-00606, $48.25.

304 Ravel, Maurice, 1875–1937

[Tzigane; arr.] *Tzigane, for violin and orchestra.* Durand 597-00575, $29.25.

305 Rodrigo, Joaquín, 1901–

Concierto de Aranjuez, for guitar and orchestra. Eulenburg 1809, $24.

306 * Saint-Saëns, Camille, 1835–1921

[Carnaval des animaux] *Carnival of the animals, for 2 pianos and orchestra.* Durand 597-00605, $31.

307 Saint-Saëns, Camille, 1835–1921

[Concertos, piano, orchestra, no. 2, op. 22, G minor] *Piano concerto no. 2 in G minor, op. 22.* Dover (with Saint-Saëns's *Piano concerto no. 4 in C minor, op. 44*) 0-486-28723-8, $15.95; Durand 597-00593, $50.

308 Saint-Saëns, Camille, 1835–1921

[Concertos, piano, orchestra, no. 4, op. 44, C minor] *Piano concerto no. 4 in C minor, op. 44.* Kalmus K 01394, $12.50. *See also* 307

309 Saint-Saëns, Camille, 1835–1921

[Concertos, violoncello, orchestra, no. 1, op. 33, A minor] *Cello concerto no. 1 in A minor, op. 33.* Eulenburg 1285, $15.

310 Saint-Saëns, Camille, 1835–1921

[Introduction et rondo capriccioso] *Introduction and rondo capriccioso, op. 28, for violin and orchestra.* Durand 597-00594, $24; Kalmus K 00386, $8.

311 Schumann, Clara, 1819–1886

[Concerto, piano, orchestra, op. 7, A minor] *Piano concerto in A minor, op. 7.* Breitkopf & Härtel PB5183, $18.25.

312 * Schumann, Robert, 1810–1856

[Concerto, piano, orchestra, op. 54, A minor] *Piano concerto in A minor, op. 54.* Eulenburg 707, $12.50.

313 Schumann, Robert, 1810–1856

[Concertos, violoncello, orchestra, op. 129, A minor] *Cello concerto in A minor, op. 129.* Eulenburg 786, $10.50.

314 Shostakovich, Dmitrii Dmitrievich, 1906–1975

[Concertos, piano, orchestra, no. 1, op. 35] *Concerto no. 1 for piano, trumpet, and orchestra, op. 35.* Kalmus K 01462, $6.50.

315 * Sibelius, Jean, 1865–1957

[Concertos, violin, orchestra, op. 47, D minor] *Violin concerto in D minor, op. 47.* Eulenburg 770, $13.75; Kalmus K 00359, $9.50.

316 Strauss, Richard, 1864–1949

[Burlesque, piano, orchestra, D minor] *Burlesque in D minor for piano and orchestra.* Eulenburg 1253, $19.50.

317 Strauss, Richard, 1864–1949

[Concertos, oboe, orchestra] *Concerto for oboe and small orchestra.* Boosey & Hawkes HPS 645, $23.

318 Stravinsky, Igor, 1882–1971

[Concertos, violin, orchestra, D] *Violin concerto in D.* Eulenburg 1815, $10.50.

319 Stravinsky, Igor, 1882–1971

Ebony concerto, for clarinet with jazz ensemble. Boosey & Hawkes HPS 939, $13.

320 ** Tchaikovsky, Peter Ilich, 1840–1893

[Concertos, piano, orchestra, no. 1, op. 23, B♭ minor] *Piano concerto no. 1 in B♭ minor, op. 23.* Eulenburg 709, $15; Kalmus K 00590, $16.95.

321 * Tchaikovsky, Peter Ilich, 1840–1893

[Concertos, violin, orchestra, op. 35, D major] *Violin concerto in D major, op. 35.* Eulenburg 708, $12.50; Kalmus K 00595, $6.50.

322 Tchaikovsky, Peter Ilich, 1840–1893

[Variations sur un thème rococo] *Variations on a rococo theme, for cello and orchestra, op. 33.* Eulenburg 788, $8.50.

323 Vaughan Williams, Ralph, 1872–1958

The lark ascending: romance for violin and orchestra. Eulenburg 1388, $7.75.

324 Villa-Lobos, Heitor, 1887–1959

[Concertos, guitar, orchestra] *Concerto for guitar and orchestra.* Eschig ME 7993, $79.25.

325 ** Vivaldi, Antonio, 1678–1741

[Cimento dell'armonia e dell'inventione. N. 1–4] *The four seasons, op. 8, for violin and orchestra.* Dover 0-486-28638-X (with other violin concertos from Vivaldi's op. 8), $10.95; Eulenburg 1220-1223, 4 v. in 1, $14.50; Kalmus K 00305-00308, 4 v., $7.95, $5.50, $5.50, $5.50.

326 Vivaldi, Antonio, 1678–1741

[Estro armonico] *L'estro armonico, op. 3: 12 concertos for strings.* Eulenburg (concertos no. 1–2, 4, 6–12), $6.50 each; Peters (concertos no. 1–5, 7–10), $8.85 each; Ricordi (complete), 2 v., $37 each.

Overtures, Program Music, and Other Orchestral Works

327 * Bach, Johann Sebastian, 1685–1750

[Suites, orchestra, BWV 1066–1069] *Four suites (overtures) for orchestra, BWV 1066–1069.* Bärenreiter TP192-195, 4 v., $9 each; Dover 0-486-23376-6 (with Bach's *Brandenburg concertos*), $10.95; Eulenburg 856, 821, 818, 861, 4 v., $6.50 each; Kalmus K 00799, $6.

328 Barber, Samuel, 1910–1981

[Essays, orchestra, no. 1, op. 12] *First essay for orchestra, op. 12.* G. Schirmer OR42130, $7.50.

329 * Barber, Samuel, 1910–1981

[Quartets, strings, no. 1, op. 11, B major. Adagio; arr.] *Adagio for strings.* G. Schirmer, $4.

330 Bartók, Béla, 1881–1945

[Divertimento, string orchestra] *Divertimento for string orchestra.* Boosey & Hawkes HPS 28, $17.50.

331 * Bartók, Béla, 1881–1945

[Music, celesta, percussion, string orchestra] *Music for strings, percussion, and celesta.* Boosey & Hawkes HPS 609, $26.

332 Bartók, Béla, 1881–1945

[Roman népi táncok; arr.] *Roumanian folk dances for chamber orchestra,* rev. 1991 ed. by Peter Bartók. Universal UE6545/Boosey & Hawkes ORB55FS, $17.50.

333 Beethoven, Ludwig van, 1770–1827

Coriolan: overture, op. 62. Eulenburg 626, $6.50.

334 Beethoven, Ludwig van, 1770–1827

[Egmont. Overture] *Overture to Egmont, op. 84.* Eulenburg 604, $7.75; Kalmus K 00067, $4.50.

335 * Beethoven, Ludwig van, 1770–1827

[Fidelio (1806). Ouverture] *Leonore overture no. 3, op. 72a.* Eulenburg 601, $7.75; Kalmus K 00009, $5.50.

336 * Beethoven, Ludwig van, 1770–1827

[Fidelio (1814). Overture] *Overture to Fidelio, op. 72b.* Eulenburg 610, $6.50.

337 * Beethoven, Ludwig van, 1770–1827

[Overtures. Selections] *Six great overtures: Coriolan, Leonore overtures no. 1–3, Fidelio, Egmont.* Dover 0-486-24789-2, $13.95.

338 Berg, Alban, 1885–1935

[Orchesterstücke, op. 6] *Three pieces for orchestra, op. 6.* New version, 1929. Universal PH432, $26.

339 Berlioz, Hector, 1803–1869

[Béatrice et Bénédict. Overture] *Overture to Beatrice and Benedict.* Eulenburg 623, $8.50; Kalmus K 01223, $5.

340 Berlioz, Hector, 1803–1869

[Benvenuto Cellini. Overture] *Overture to Benvenuto Cellini.* Eulenburg 622, $8.50.

341 * Berlioz, Hector, 1803–1869

[Carnaval romain] *Roman carnival overture, op. 9.* Eulenburg 620, $8.50; Kalmus K 01221, $6.

342 * Berlioz, Hector, 1803–1869

[Overtures. Selections] *Roman carnival and other overtures.* Dover 0-486-28750-5, $12.95.

343 * Berlioz, Hector, 1803–1869

Roméo et Juliette: dramatic symphony, op. 17. Eulenburg 424, $30; Kalmus K 00502, $14.95.

344 * Bernstein, Leonard, 1918–1990

[Candide. Overture] *Overture to Candide.* Jalni/Boosey & Hawkes HPS 1207, $17.

345 Bernstein, Leonard, 1918–1990

[Divertimento, orchestra] *Divertimento for orchestra.* Jalni/Boosey & Hawkes HPS 986, $22.

346 Bernstein, Leonard, 1918–1990

[Symposium, after Plato] *Serenade after Plato's "Symposium."* Corrected ed. Jalni/Boosey & Hawkes HPS 1136, $31.

347 * Bernstein, Leonard, 1918–1990

[West side story. Selections] *Symphonic dances from "West side story."* New ed. Jalni/Boosey & Hawkes FSB 488, full score, $35; Jalni/Boosey & Hawkes HPS 1178, study score, in preparation.

348   Bizet, Georges, 1838–1875

[Arlésienne. Selections; arr.] *Suite no. 2 from "L'Arlésienne."* Eulenburg 829, $8.50.

349   Bizet, Georges, 1838–1875

[Arlésienne. Suite] *Suite no. 1 from "L'Arlésienne."* Eulenburg 828, $8.50; Kalmus K 00174, $4.95.

350 * Bizet, Georges, 1838–1875

[Carmen. Selections] *Carmen suite no. 1.* Kalmus K 00400, $8.50.

351   Bizet, Georges, 1838–1875

[Jeux d'enfants. Selections; arr.] *Jeux d'enfants, op. 22, for orchestra.* Eulenburg 898, $8.50; Kalmus K 00150, $5.50.

352   Borodin, Aleksandr Porfir'evich, 1833–1887

[Kniaz' Igor. Polovetskaia pliaska] *Polovetzian dances from "Prince Igor."* Eulenburg 886, $12.50; Kalmus K 00068, $6.50.

353 * Brahms, Johannes, 1833–1897

[Akademische Festouvertüre] *Academic festival overture, op. 80.* Eulenburg 656, $7.75; Kalmus K 00086, $5.50.

354 * Brahms, Johannes, 1833–1897

[Orchestral music. Selections] *Three orchestral works: Academic festival overture, Tragic overture, and Variations on a theme of Haydn.* Dover 0-486-24637-X, $8.95.

355 * Brahms, Johannes, 1833–1897

[Tragische Ouvertüre] *Tragic overture, op. 81.* Eulenburg 657, $7.75; Kalmus K 00304, $7.50.

356 * Brahms, Johannes, 1833–1897

[Variationen über ein Thema von Haydn] *Variations on a theme of Haydn, op. 56a.* Eulenburg 805, $8.50; Kalmus K 00140, $5.50; Norton Critical Scores 0-393-09206-2, ed. by Donald M. McCorkle (with Brahms's arrangement for two pianos, op. 56b), OP.

357   Britten, Benjamin, 1913–1976

[Peter Grimes. Selections] *Four sea interludes, op. 33a, from "Peter Grimes."* Boosey & Hawkes HPS 83, $32.

358   Britten, Benjamin, 1913–1976

Variations on a theme of Frank Bridge, for string orchestra, op. 10. Boosey & Hawkes HPS 64, $17.50.

359 ** Britten, Benjamin, 1913–1976

Young person's guide to the orchestra, op. 34. Boosey & Hawkes HPS 606, $16.50.

360   Carter, Elliott, 1908–

[Variations, orchestra] *Variations for orchestra.* 1967 corrected ed. Associated Music HL50237050, $60.

361   Chabrier, Emmanuel, 1841–1894

España. Eulenburg 893, $9.50.

362 * Copland, Aaron, 1900–1990

[Appalachian spring. Suite; arr.] *Appalachian spring suite, orchestral version.* Boosey & Hawkes HPS 82, $17.

363   Copland, Aaron, 1900–1990

[Billy the Kid. Suite] *Billy the Kid suite.* Boosey & Hawkes HPS 72, $37.

364 * Copland, Aaron, 1900–1990

Fanfare for the common man: included in *"Ceremonial music."* Boosey & Hawkes HPS 1125, $17.50.

365 * Copland, Aaron, 1900–1990

Lincoln portrait. Boosey & Hawkes HPS 61, $14.

366   Copland, Aaron, 1900–1990

[Rodeo. Selections] *Four dance episodes from "Rodeo."* Boosey & Hawkes HPS 684, $23.

367   Copland, Aaron, 1900–1990

El salon México. Boosey & Hawkes HPS 49, $23.

368   Debussy, Claude, 1862–1918

[Images, orchestra. Ibéria] *Ibéria, no. 2 from "Images pour orchestre."* Eulenburg 8010, $22; Kalmus K 09942, $12.50.

369   Debussy, Claude, 1862–1918

Jeux. Durand 597-00538, $48.25.

370 * Debussy, Claude, 1862–1918

La mer. Eulenburg 1321, $13.50; International Music 2126, $16.50; Kalmus K 00611, $16.95.

371 * Debussy, Claude, 1862–1918

[Nocturnes, orchestra] *Three nocturnes, for orchestra.* Eulenburg 1320, $13.75; International Music 1055, $13.25; Kalmus K 00103, $12.95; Peters 9156a, $30.40.

372   Debussy, Claude, 1862–1918

[Orchestral music. Selections] *Images, Jeux, and The martyrdom of St. Sebastian suite.* Dover 0-486-27101-3, $18.95.

373 * Debussy, Claude, 1862–1918

[Orchestral music. Selections] *Three great orchestral works: Prélude à l'après-midi d'un faune, Nocturnes, and La mer.* Dover 0-486-24441-5, $12.95.

374   Debussy, Claude, 1862–1918

[Petite suite; arr.] *Petite suite,* orchestrated by Henri Büsser. Durand 597-00544, $37; Kalmus K 01525, $9.50.

375 * Debussy, Claude, 1862–1918

Prélude à l'après-midi d'un faune. Eulenburg 1116, $6.50; Norton Critical Scores 0-393-09939-3, $9.95.

376   Dukas, Paul, 1865–1935

[Apprenti sorcier] *The sorcerer's apprentice.* International Music 1089, $9.50; Kalmus A1412, $35.

377   Dvořák, Antonín, 1841–1904

[Příroda, život a láska. Karneval] *Carnival overture, op. 92 (B. 169).* Eulenburg 690, $8.50; Kalmus K 00134, $5.50.

378   Dvořák, Antonín, 1841–1904

[Serenades, string orchestra, op. 22, E major] *Serenade for strings in E major, op. 22 (B. 52).* Eulenburg 896, $10.50.

379 * Dvořák, Antonín, 1841–1904

[Slovanské tance, op. 46; arr.] *Slavonic dances, op. 46 (B. 83), arranged for orchestra.* Dover 0-486-25394-5, $11.95; Eulenburg 1346-1347, 2 v., $15.50 each.

380   Dvořák, Antonín, 1841–1904

[Slovanské tance, op. 72; arr.] *Slavonic dances, op. 72 (B. 147), arranged for orchestra.* Eulenburg 1348-1349, 2 v., $15.50 each; Kalmus K 01473-01474, 2 v., $9.50 each.

381 * Elgar, Edward, 1857–1934

[Orchestral music. Selections] *Enigma variations and Pomp and circumstance marches no. 1–4.* Dover 0-486-27342-3, $13.95.

382   Elgar, Edward, 1857–1934

[Serenades, string orchestra, op. 20, E minor] *Serenade for strings in E minor, op. 20.* Kalmus K 01403, $7.50.

383 * Elgar, Edward, 1857–1934

[Variations on an original theme] *Enigma variations, op. 36.* Eulenburg 884, $15.

384   Enesco, Georges, 1881–1955

[Rhapsodies roumaines. No. 1] *Roumanian rhapsody no. 1.* Kalmus A2363, $40.

385   Enesco, Georges, 1881–1955

[Rhapsodies roumaines. No. 2] *Roumanian rhapsody no. 2.* Kalmus A2364, $15.

386   Falla, Manuel de, 1876–1946

El amor brujo: complete ballet. Chester JWC41, $45.

387   Fauré, Gabriel, 1845–1924

[Pavan, orchestra, op. 50, F♯ minor] *Pavane, op. 50.* Eulenburg 1383, $11.

388   Fauré, Gabriel, 1845–1924

[Pelléas et Mélisande. Suite] *Pelléas et Mélisande, op. 80.* Eulenburg 1386, $11.

389 ** Gershwin, George, 1898–1937

An American in Paris. Warner Bros., $17.50.

390   Glinka, Mikhail Ivanovich, 1804–1857

[Ruslan i Liudmila. Uvertiura] *Overture to "Russlan and Ludmilla."* Eulenburg 639, $8.50; Kalmus K 00291, $6.50.

391   Gould, Morton, 1913–1996

[Fall River legend. Suite] *Fall River legend: ballet suite.* G. Schirmer, $3.

392 * Grieg, Edvard, 1843–1907

[Fra Holbergs tid; arr.] *Holberg suite, for orchestra, op. 40.* Eulenburg 897, $6.50; Kalmus K 00168, $4.50.

393 * Grieg, Edvard, 1843–1907

[Peer Gynt. Suites no. 1–2] *Peer Gynt suites no. 1 and 2.* Eulenburg 1318, $8.50.

394   Griffes, Charles Tomlinson, 1884–1920

[Roman sketches. White peacock; arr.] *The white peacock, for orchestra.* G. Schirmer ED41170, $15.

395   Grofé, Ferde, 1892–1972

Grand canyon suite. CPP/Belwin, $20.

396 * Handel, George Frideric, 1685–1750

Music for the royal fireworks. Bärenreiter TP173, $8.75; Eulenburg 1307, $7.75.

397 * Handel, George Frideric, 1685–1750

[Orchestral music. Selections] *Water music and Music for the royal fireworks.* Dover 0-486-25070-9, $6.95.

398 * Handel, George Frideric, 1685–1750

Water music. Bärenreiter TP174, $10.25; Eulenburg 1308, $7.75.

399 Hindemith, Paul, 1895–1963

Symphonic metamorphosis of themes by Carl Maria von Weber. Eulenburg 1394, $11.75.

400 * Holst, Gustav, 1874–1934

The planets. Boosey & Hawkes HPS 22, $25.

401 Holst, Gustav, 1874–1934

St. Paul's suite, for string orchestra. Curwen OR42901, $7.50.

402 Honegger, Arthur, 1892–1955

Pacific 231. Eulenburg 1397, $7.50; Salabert SEMS6680, $12.95.

403 * Ives, Charles, 1874–1954

[Contemplations. Unanswered question] *The unanswered question.* Ives Critical Ed., ed. by Paul C. Echols and Noel Zahler. Peer International 61552-851, $20.

404 * Ives, Charles, 1874–1954

[Outdoor scenes. Central Park in the dark] *Central Park in the dark,* ed. by John Kirkpatrick and Jacques-Louis Monod. Boelke/Bomart BB22, $9.50.

405 * Ives, Charles, 1874–1954

Three places in New England, ed. by James B. Sinclair. Presser 456-40008, $20.

406 Janáček, Leoš, 1854–1928

Taras Bulba. Universal PH482, $44.

407 Kodály, Zoltán, 1882–1967

[Galánti táncok] *Dances of Galanta.* Universal PH275, $21.

408 * Kodály, Zoltán, 1882–1967

[Háry János. Suite] *Háry János suite.* Universal PH272, $26.

409 * Liszt, Franz, 1811–1886

Les préludes. Eulenburg 449, $10; Kalmus K 09331, $6.50.

410 Mendelssohn-Bartholdy, Felix, 1809–1847

[Hebriden] *Hebrides overture.* Eulenburg 637, $6.75.

411 Mendelssohn-Bartholdy, Felix, 1809–1847

[Meeresstille und glückliche Fahrt] *Calm sea and prosperous voyage: overture.* Eulenburg 653, $7.75.

412 ** Mendelssohn-Bartholdy, Felix, 1809–1847

[Orchestral music. Selections] *Major orchestral works: Midsummer night's dream, complete; Hebrides overture; Calm sea and prosperous voyage overture; Symphonies no. 3 and 4.* Dover 0-486-23184-4, $16.95.

413 * Mendelssohn-Bartholdy, Felix, 1809–1847

[Sommernachtstraum. Selections] *Five pieces from "A midsummer night's dream."* Eulenburg 804, $9.50.

414 * Milhaud, Darius, 1892–1974

La création du monde. Eschig ME2402, $62.25.

415 Mozart, Wolfgang Amadeus, 1756–1791

[Così fan tutte. Ouverture] *Overture to "Così fan tutte."* Eulenburg 662, $6.75.

416 * Mozart, Wolfgang Amadeus, 1756–1791

[Don Giovanni. Ouverture] *Overture to "Don Giovanni."* Eulenburg 608, $6.75.

417 * Mozart, Wolfgang Amadeus, 1756–1791

Eine kleine Nachtmusik, K. 525. Bärenreiter TP19, $7.50.

418 * Mozart, Wolfgang Amadeus, 1756–1791

[Nozze di Figaro. Ouverture] *Overture to "The marriage of Figaro."* Eulenburg 603, $6.75.

419 * Mussorgsky, Modest Petrovich, 1839–1881

[Kartinki s vystavki; arr.] *Pictures at an exhibition,* orchestrated by Maurice Ravel. Boosey & Hawkes HPS 32, $36.

420 * Mussorgsky, Modest Petrovich, 1839–1881

[Noch' na Lysoi gore] *Night on Bald Mountain,* completed and orchestrated by Nikolay Rimsky-Korsakov. Eulenburg 841, $10.

421 Pachelbel, Johann, 1653–1706

Canon in D major for string orchestra, or three violins with basso continuo. Schott CON 111, $15.

422 Piston, Walter, 1894–1976

The incredible flutist: ballet. Associated Music HL50488405, $25.

423 Prokofiev, Sergey, 1891–1953

[Liubov' k trem apel'sinam. Suite] *Love for three oranges: ballet suite, op. 33a.* Boosey & Hawkes HPS 967, $31.

424 ** Prokofiev, Sergey, 1891–1953

[Orchestral music. Selections] *Symphony no. 1 in D major, op. 25, "Classical"; Lieutenant Kije suite; Peter and the wolf; Alexander Nevsky cantata.* Dover 0-486-20279-8, $18.95.

425 * Prokofiev, Sergey, 1891–1953

[Romeo i Dzuhl'etta (Ballet). Suites no. 1–2] *Romeo and Juliet.* Kalmus K 00112 (Suite 1), $16.95; Kalmus K 00113 (Suite 2), $12.95.

426 Rachmaninoff, Sergei, 1873–1943

[Ostrov mertvykh] *Isle of the dead, op. 29.* Boosey & Hawkes HPS 886, $18.50.

427 Rachmaninoff, Sergei, 1873–1943

Symphonic dances, op. 45. Kalmus A7006, $80.

428 * Ravel, Maurice, 1875–1937

Boléro. Durand 597-00561, $41.

429 Ravel, Maurice, 1875–1937

[Daphnis et Chloé. Suite, no. 2] *Daphnis et Chloé: suite no. 2.* Durand 597-00564, $51.50; Kalmus A6754, $65.

430 * Ravel, Maurice, 1875–1937

[Ma mère l'oye] *Mother Goose suite: ballet.* Durand 597-00564, $26.75; Editio Musica Budapest EMB 40103, $7.50.

431 Ravel, Maurice, 1875–1937

[Miroirs. Alborada del gracioso; arr.] *Alborada del gracioso.* Durand 597-00820, $57.50.

432 * Ravel, Maurice, 1875–1937

[Orchestral music. Selections] *Four orchestral works: Rapsodie espagnole, Mother Goose suite, Valses nobles et sentimentales, Pavane for a dead princess.* Dover 0-486-25962-5, $11.95.

433 Ravel, Maurice, 1875–1937

[Pavane pour une infante défunte] *Pavane for a dead princess.* Eulenburg 1335, $7.50.

434 * Ravel, Maurice, 1875–1937

Rapsodie espagnole. Kalmus A3634, $45.

435 Ravel, Maurice, 1875–1937

Le tombeau de Couperin. Durand 597-00573, $44.

436 * Ravel, Maurice, 1875–1937

La valse. Durand 597-00576, $87.

437 Ravel, Maurice, 1875–1937

Valses nobles et sentimentales. Kalmus A6450, $25.

438 Respighi, Ottorino, 1879–1936

[Antiche arie e danze per liuto, no. 1–3] *Ancient airs and dances, suites no. 1–3.* Ricordi PR 1334, $25.

439 Respighi, Ottorino, 1879–1936

[Symphonic poems. Selections] *Three symphonic poems: Fontane di Roma, Pini di Roma, and Feste romane.* Ricordi PR 1282, $30.

440 * Rimsky-Korsakov, Nikolay, 1844–1908

Capriccio espagnol, op. 34. Eulenburg 842, $10.

441 * Rimsky-Korsakov, Nikolay, 1844–1908

[Shekherazada] *Scheherazade.* Dover 0-486-24734-1, $10.95; Eulenburg 493, $19.50.

442 Rimsky-Korsakov, Nikolay, 1844–1908

[Svetlyi prazdnik] *Russian Easter overture, op. 36.* Eulenburg 692, $12.50.

443 * Rossini, Gioacchino, 1792–1868

[Overtures. Selections] *William Tell and other overtures.* Dover 0-486-28149-3, $12.95.

444 * Ruggles, Carl, 1876–1971

Sun-treader. Presser 476-00187, $12.50.

445 Saint-Saëns, Camille, 1835–1921

Danse macabre. Kalmus K 00085, $7.95.

446 Satie, Erik, 1866–1925

[Gymnopédies; arr.] *Trois gymnopédies,* orchestrated by Claude Debussy. Eulenburg 1376, $8.50.

447 * Satie, Erik, 1866–1925

Parade: ballet. Salabert SEAS 16425, $24.95.

448 * Schoenberg, Arnold, 1874–1951

[Orchesterstücke, op. 16] *Five orchestral pieces, op. 16.* Eulenburg 1328, $13.50; Peters 3376a, $18.70.

449 Schoenberg, Arnold, 1874–1951

Pelleas und Melisande, op. 5. Universal UE14408, $35.

450   Schoenberg, Arnold, 1874–1951

Pierrot Lunaire. Corrected ed. Belmont Music BEL-1051, $25.

451 * Schoenberg, Arnold, 1874–1951

[Variations, orchestra, op. 31] *Variations for orchestra, op. 31.* Universal UE12196, $25.

452 * Schoenberg, Arnold, 1874–1951

[Verklärte Nacht; arr.] *Transfigured night, op. 4,* arranged for string orchestra by the composer. Associated Music HL50237870, $8.95.

453   Schuman, William, 1910–1992

New England triptych. Presser 446-41001, $8.50.

454 * Sibelius, Jean, 1865–1957

[Tone poems. Selections] *Tone poems: Finlandia, Valse triste, Swan of Tuonela, Lemminkainen's return, En saga, Pohjola's daughter, Night ride and sunrise, The oceanides.* Dover 0-486-26483-1, $16.95.

455 * Smetana, Bedřich, 1824–1884

[Má vlast. Vltava] *The Moldau, from "Má vlast."* Eulenburg 472, $10.50; Kalmus K 00148, $4.50.

456   Strauss, Johann, 1825–1899

[Fledermaus. Ouvertüre] *Overture to "Die Fledermaus."* Eulenburg 1103, $7.50.

457 * Strauss, Johann, 1825–1899

[Waltzes, orchestra. Selections] *The great waltzes.* Dover 0-486-26009-7, $13.95.

458   Strauss, Richard, 1864–1949

Eine Alpensinfonie, op. 64. Leuckart LEUFECL 7529, $21.

459 * Strauss, Richard, 1864–1949

Also sprach Zarathustra, op. 30. Eulenburg 444, $17.75; Kalmus K 00529, $12.50.

460 * Strauss, Richard, 1864–1949

Don Juan, op. 20. Eulenburg 440, $13.50; Kalmus K 00076, $14.95.

461 * Strauss, Richard, 1864–1949

Don Quixote, op. 35. Eulenburg 445, $16.50; Kalmus K 00132, $10.50.

462 * Strauss, Richard, 1864–1949

Ein Heldenleben, op. 40. Eulenburg 498, $18.75; International Music 1325, $13; Kalmus K 00258, $15.50.

463 * Strauss, Richard, 1864–1949

[Till Eulenspiegels lustige Streiche] *Till Eulenspiegel's merry pranks, op. 28.* Eulenburg 443, $13.50; Kalmus K 00040, $9.50.

464   Strauss, Richard, 1864–1949

[Tod und Verklärung] *Death and transfiguration, op. 24.* Eulenburg 442, $13.50; Kalmus K 00075, $12.95.

465 * Strauss, Richard, 1864–1949

[Tone poems. Selections] *Tone poems.* Dover 0-486-23754-0, Series I: *Don Juan, Tod und Verklärung, Don Quixote,* $13.95; Dover 0-486-23755-9, Series II: *Till Eulenspiegel, Also sprach Zarathustra, Ein Heldenleben,* $14.95.

466   Stravinsky, Igor, 1882–1971

Apollon musagète: ballet. Rev. 1947. Boosey & Hawkes HPS 611, $17.50.

467 * Stravinsky, Igor, 1882–1971

[Histoire du soldat. Polyglot] *L'histoire du soldat = The soldier's tale.* French, English, and German. Chester CH55726, $17.95.

468 * Stravinsky, Igor, 1882–1971

[Petruskha] *Petroushka: ballet.* Boosey & Hawkes HPS 639, rev. 1947 version, $29; Dover 0-486-25680-4, original 1912 version, $9.95; Norton Critical Scores 0-393-09770-6, original 1912 version, ed. by Charles Hamm, $11.95.

469 * Stravinsky, Igor, 1882–1971

[Pulcinella. Suite] *Pulcinella suite.* Rev. 1949. Boosey & Hawkes HPS 632, $23.

470 ** Stravinsky, Igor, 1882–1971

[Vesna sviaschennaia] *Le sacre du printemps = The rite of spring.* Boosey & Hawkes HPS 638, rev. 1947 and 1965, $23; Dover 0-486-25857-2, $9.95; Kalmus K 00078, $16.50.

471   Stravinsky, Igor, 1882–1971

[Zhar-ptitsa. Suite (1945)] *Firebird suite.* Schott ED4420, $25.

472   Tchaikovsky, Peter Ilich, 1840–1893

Capriccio italien, op. 45. Dover 0-486-25217-5 (with Tchaikovsky's *Romeo and Juliet fantasy-overture*), $9.95; Eulenburg 802, $11; Kalmus K 00579, $7.50.

473 * Tchaikovsky, Peter Ilich, 1840–1893

[1812 année] *1812 overture, op. 49.* Eulenburg 624, $9.50; Kalmus K 00580, $9.50.

474 Tchaikovsky, Peter Ilich, 1840–1893

Francesca da Rimini, op. 32. Eulenburg 840, $11; Kalmus K 00578, $14.95.

475 * Tchaikovsky, Peter Ilich, 1840–1893

[Lebedinoe ozero. Selections] *Swan lake: suite, op. 20a.* Eulenburg 1336, $11; Kalmus K 00262, $5.

476 Tchaikovsky, Peter Ilich, 1840–1893

Marche slave, op. 31. Eulenburg 851, $10; Kalmus K 00577, $6.50.

477 Tchaikovsky, Peter Ilich, 1840–1893

[Orchestral music. Selections] *1812 overture, Marche slave, and Francesca da Rimini.* Dover 0-486-29069-7, $14.95.

478 * Tchaikovsky, Peter Ilich, 1840–1893

[Romeo et Juliette (Fantasy-overture)] *Romeo and Juliet fantasy-overture.* Eulenburg 675, $8.50; Kalmus K 00575, $17.50. *See also* 472

479 Tchaikovsky, Peter Ilich, 1840–1893

[Serenade, string orchestra, op. 48, C major] *Serenade in C major for string orchestra, op. 48.* Eulenburg 857, $7.75; Kalmus K 00569, $5.50.

480 ** Tchaikovsky, Peter Ilich, 1840–1893

[Shchelkunchik. Suite] *Nutcracker suite, op. 71a.* Dover 0-486-25379-1, $6.95; Eulenburg 824, $12.50; Kalmus K 00042, $9.50.

481 Tchaikovsky, Peter Ilich, 1840–1893

[Spiashchaia krasavitsa. Selections] *Sleeping beauty suite, op. 66a.* Eulenburg 1329, $11.

482 Tower, Joan, 1938–

Silver ladders. Margun Music MM058SC, $25.

483 Varèse, Edgard, 1883–1965

Amériques. Colfranc, $25.

484 * Vaughan Williams, Ralph, 1872–1958

Fantasia on a theme by Thomas Tallis, for string orchestra. Boosey & Hawkes HPS 59, $17.50.

485 Vaughan Williams, Ralph, 1872–1958

Fantasia on "Greensleeves." Oxford University Press 0-19-360340-3, $17.95.

486 Wagner, Richard, 1813–1883

[Fliegende Holländer. Ouvertüre] *Overture to "The flying Dutchman."* Eulenburg 668, $8.50.

487 Wagner, Richard, 1813–1883

[Lohengrin. Vorspiel] *Preludes to acts I and III of "Lohengrin."* Eulenburg 652, $6.75.

488 * Wagner, Richard, 1813–1883

[Meistersinger von Nürnberg. Vorspiel] *Overture to act I of "Die Meistersinger von Nürnberg."* Eulenburg 665, $6.75.

489 * Wagner, Richard, 1813–1883

[Overtures. Selections] *Overtures and preludes.* Dover 0-486-29201-0, $17.95.

490 Wagner, Richard, 1813–1883

[Parsifal. Charfreitagszauber] *Parsifal: Good Friday music.* Eulenburg 812, $6.50.

491 Wagner, Richard, 1813–1883

[Parsifal. Vorspiel] *Prelude to "Parsifal."* Eulenburg 666, $6.50.

492 Wagner, Richard, 1813–1883

[Rienzi. Ouvertüre] *Overture to "Rienzi."* Eulenburg 667, $7.75.

493 * Wagner, Richard, 1813–1883

[Ring des Nibelungen. Götterdämmerung. Siegfried's Rheinfahrt] *Siegfried's Rhine journey.* Kalmus A4556, $35.

494 Wagner, Richard, 1813–1883

[Ring des Nibelungen. Götterdämmerung. Trauermusik] *Funeral music, from "Götterdämmerung."* Eulenburg 811, $6.50; Kalmus K 01455, $4.50.

495 * Wagner, Richard, 1813–1883

[Ring des Nibelungen. Siegfried. Waldweben] *Forest murmurs, from "Siegfried."* Eulenburg 809, $6.50; Kalmus K 00215, $2.50.

496 * Wagner, Richard, 1813–1883

[Ring des Nibelungen. Walküre. Walkürenritt] *Ride of the Valkyries.* Eulenburg 807, $8.50.

497 * Wagner, Richard, 1813–1883

Siegfried-Idyll. Eulenburg 810, $6.75; Kalmus K 00052, $4.50.

498 Wagner, Richard, 1813–1883

[Tannhäuser. Ouvertüre] *Prelude to act I of "Tannhäuser."* Eulenburg 669, $9.50.

499   Wagner, Richard, 1813–1883

[Tannhäuser. Venusberg] *Bacchanale (Venusberg music), from "Tannhäuser."* Eulenburg 814, $9.

500 ** Wagner, Richard, 1813–1883

[Tristan und Isolde. Einleitung] *Prelude and Liebestod, from "Tristan und Isolde."* Eulenburg 649, $7.75; Kalmus K 00048, $4.50; Norton Critical Scores 0-393-95405-6, $9.95.

501   Warlock, Peter, 1894–1930

Capriol suite, for string orchestra. G. Schirmer OR42899-1, $7.

502 * Weber, Carl Maria von, 1786–1826

[Aufforderung zum Tanze; arr.] *Invitation to the dance;* orchestrated by Hector Berlioz. Eulenburg 831, $7.75.

503   Weber, Carl Maria von, 1786–1826

[Euryanthe. Ouvertüre] *Overture to "Euryanthe."* Eulenburg 635, $6.75.

504 * Weber, Carl Maria von, 1786–1826

[Freischütz. Ouvertüre] *Overture to "Der Freischütz."* Eulenburg 602, $6.75; Kalmus K 00056, $5.50.

505 * Weber, Carl Maria von, 1786–1826

[Oberon. Ouvertüre] *Overture to "Oberon."* Eulenburg 607, $6.50.

506 * Weber, Carl Maria von, 1786–1826

[Overtures. Selections] *Great overtures: Der Freischütz, Euryanthe, Oberon, Preciosa, Jubilee.* Dover 0-486-25225-6, $8.95.

507   Webern, Anton, 1883–1945

[Passacaglia, orchestra, op. 1] *Passacaglia for orchestra, op. 1.* Universal PH428, $19.50.

508 * Webern, Anton, 1883–1945

[Stücke, orchestra, op. 6] *Six pieces, orchestra, op. 6.* Universal PH394, $12.50.

509   Webern, Anton, 1883–1945

[Stücke, orchestra, op. 10] *Five pieces, orchestra, op. 10.* Universal PH449, $11.

510 * Webern, Anton, 1883–1945

[Variations, orchestra, op. 30] *Variations for orchestra, op. 30.* Universal PH448, $13.50.

511   Wolf, Hugo, 1860–1903

[Italienische Serenade; arr.] *Italian serenade, for chamber orchestra.* Eulenburg 286, $6.50.

Chamber Music in Full and Study Score

Compiled by
Elizabeth Sadewhite (strings)
and Brian Cockburn
(winds and mixed winds and strings)

Chamber Music for Strings

Collections for Various Numbers of Strings

These collections may be acquired in place of individual editions. They include works for strings alone or strings with piano. For performance parts for these and other chamber works, see "Chamber Music for Strings," in chapter 9, "Chamber Music."

512 * Brahms, Johannes, 1833–1897

[Chamber music. Selections] *Complete chamber music for strings, and Clarinet quintet.* Dover 0-486-21914-3, $11.95.

513 * Brahms, Johannes, 1833–1897

[Chamber music. Selections] *Quintet and quartets for piano and strings.* Dover 0-486-24900-X, $14.95.

514 * Dvořák, Antonín, 1841–1904

[Chamber music. Selections] *Chamber works for piano and strings: includes Piano trios in F minor,*

op. 65, and E minor, op. 90, Piano quartets in D major, op. 23, and E♭ major, op. 87, and Piano quintet in A major.* Dover 0-486-25663-4, $15.95.

515 * Fauré, Gabriel, 1845–1924

[Chamber music. Selections] *Piano quartets no. 1 and 2, and Piano quintet no. 1.* Dover 0-486-28606-1, $14.95.

516 * Franck, César, 1822–1890

[Chamber music. Selections] *Great chamber works: includes Violin sonata in A major, Piano trio op. 1, no. 1, String quartet in D major, and Piano quintet in F minor.* Dover 0-486-26546-3, $13.95.

517 * Mendelssohn-Bartholdy, Felix, 1809–1847

[Chamber music. Selections] *Chamber works for piano and strings.* Dover 0-486-26117-4, $15.95.

518 * Mendelssohn-Bartholdy, Felix, 1809–1847

[Chamber music. Selections] *Complete chamber music for strings.* Dover 0-486-23679-X, $13.95.

519 * Mozart, Wolfgang Amadeus, 1756–1791

[Chamber music. Selections] *Complete piano trios and quartets, and Piano quintet.* Dover 0-486-26714-8, $13.95.

520 * Schubert, Franz, 1797–1828

[Chamber music. Selections] *Complete chamber music for piano and strings.* Dover 0-486-21527-X, $9.95.

521 * Schubert, Franz, 1797–1828

[Chamber music. Selections] *Complete chamber music for strings.* Dover 0-486-21463-X, $14.95.

522 * Schumann, Robert, 1810–1856

[Chamber music. Selections] *Chamber music of Robert Schumann: includes Three piano trios, Piano quartet, Piano quintet, and Three string quartets, op. 41.* Dover 0-486-24101-7, $12.95.

523 * *Seven string quartets: includes Grieg, Quartet in G minor, op. 27, and Quartet in F major (incomplete); Sibelius, Quartet in D minor, op. 56 (Voces intimae); Strauss, Quartet in A major, op. 2; Verdi, Quartet in E minor; Wolf, Quartet in D minor, and Italian serenade.* Dover 0-486-26891-8, $15.95.

String Trios (Violin, Viola, Violoncello)

524 * Beethoven, Ludwig van, 1770–1827

[Trios, strings] *Five string trios: op. 3; op. 8; op. 9, no. 1–3.* Eulenburg 41-45, 5 v., v.1, $7.50; v.2–5, $6.75 each.

525 Mozart, Wolfgang Amadeus, 1756–1791

[Divertimenti, string trio, K. 563, E♭ major] *Divertimento in E♭ major for string trio, K. 563.* Eulenburg 70, $6.50; International Music 1249, $6.

526 Schoenberg, Arnold, 1874–1951

[Trios, strings, op. 45] *String trio, op. 45.* Philharmonia PH 491, $13.50.

Piano Trios (Violin, Violoncello, Piano)

527 * Beethoven, Ludwig van, 1770–1827

[Trios, piano, strings. Selections] *Six great piano trios: op. 1, no. 1–3; op. 70, no. 1–2; op. 97.* Dover 0-486-25398-8, $11.95.

528 * Brahms, Johannes, 1833–1897

[Trios, piano, strings] *Three piano trios: op. 8, op. 87, op. 101.* Dover 0-486-25769-X (with Brahms's *Trio, piano, horn, violin, op. 40,* and *Trio, piano, clarinet, violoncello, op. 114*), $13.95; Eulenburg 246-248, 3 v., $7.75, $7.75, $6.50; Henle HN9245, in preparation; Kalmus K 00776, K 01239, 2 v., $6 each.

529 * Dvořák, Antonín, 1841–1904

[Trios, piano, strings, no. 4, op. 90, E minor] *Piano trio in E minor, op. 90, "Dumky."* Eulenburg 332, $7.50.

530 * Haydn, Joseph, 1732–1809

[Trios, piano, strings. Selections] *Great piano trios.* Dover 0-486-28728-9, $14.95.

531 * Mendelssohn-Bartholdy, Felix, 1809–1847

[Trios, piano, strings] *Piano trios: op. 49 in D minor; op. 66 in C minor.* Eulenburg 80-81, 2 v., $8.50, $9; Kalmus K 01193, $7.95.

532 * Mozart, Wolfgang Amadeus, 1756–1791

[Trios, piano, strings] *Piano trios: K. 254, K. 442, K. 496, K. 502, K. 542, K. 548, K. 564.* Kalmus K 00982-00983, 2 v. (with Mozart's *Trio in E♭ major for clarinet, viola, piano, K. 498*), $6 each.

533 Ravel, Maurice, 1875–1937

[Trio, piano, strings, A minor] *Piano trio in A minor.* Durand 597-00574, $28.25.

534 * Schubert, Franz, 1797–1828

[Trios, piano, strings] *Piano trios: op. 99, D. 898; op. 100, D. 929; Nocturne in E♭ major, op. 148, D. 897.* Eulenburg 84-85, 233, 3 v., $7.50, $7.75, $6.50; Henle HN9193, in preparation.

535 * Schumann, Robert, 1810–1856

[Trios, piano, strings] *Piano trios: op. 63, op. 80, op. 110.* Eulenburg 86-88, 3 v., $6.50, $6.75, $6.50.

536 Shostakovich, Dmitrii Dmitrievich, 1906–1975

[Trios, piano, strings, no. 2, op. 67, E minor] *Piano trio no. 2 in E minor, op. 67.* Philharmonia PH 181, $16.50.

537 Smetana, Bedřich, 1824–1884

[Trio, piano, strings, op. 15, G minor] *Piano trio in G minor, op. 15.* Eulenburg 335, $8.50.

538 * Tchaikovsky, Peter Ilich, 1840–1893

[Trios, piano, strings, op. 50, A minor] *Piano trio in A minor, op. 50.* Eulenburg 251, $11.75.

String Quartets
(Two Violins, Viola, Violoncello)

539 * Barber, Samuel, 1910–1981

[Quartets, strings, no. 1, op. 11, B minor] *String quartet, op. 11.* G. Schirmer HL50338950, $15.

540 * Bartók, Béla, 1881–1945

[Quartets, strings] *Six string quartets.* Boosey & Hawkes HPS 1028, $47; also available individually in 6 v., Boosey & Hawkes HPS 74-78, HPS 25, $14, $12.50, $11, $17.50, $12.50, $16.50.

541 * Beethoven, Ludwig van, 1770–1827

[Quartets, strings] *String quartets.* Dover 0-486-22361-2, $15.95; Kalmus K 00759-00762, 4 v., $7.50, $6, $7.95, $9.95.

—OR INDIVIDUALLY—

542 * Beethoven, Ludwig van, 1770–1827

[Quartets, strings, no. 1, op. 18, no. 1, F major] *String quartet no. 1 in F major, op. 18, no. 1.* Bärenreiter TP200 (first version), $7.25; Bärenreiter TP201 (final version), $6.75; Eulenburg 16, $6.75.

543 * Beethoven, Ludwig van, 1770–1827

[Quartets, strings, no. 2, op. 18, no. 2, G major] *String quartet no. 2 in G major, op. 18, no. 2.* Bärenreiter TP202, $5.75; Eulenburg 17, $6.75.

544 * Beethoven, Ludwig van, 1770–1827

[Quartets, strings, no. 3, op. 18, no. 3, D major] *String quartet no. 3 in D major, op. 18, no. 3.* Bärenreiter TP203, $6.75; Eulenburg 18, $6.75.

545 * Beethoven, Ludwig van, 1770–1827

[Quartets, strings, no. 4, op. 18, no. 4, C minor] *String quartet no. 4 in C minor, op. 18, no. 4.* Bärenreiter TP204, $6.75; Eulenburg 19, $6.75.

546 * Beethoven, Ludwig van, 1770–1827

[Quartets, strings, no. 5, op. 18, no. 5, A major] *String quartet no. 5 in A major, op. 18, no. 5.* Bärenreiter TP205, $6.75; Eulenburg 20, $6.75.

547 * Beethoven, Ludwig van, 1770–1827

[Quartets, strings, no. 6, op. 18, no. 6, B♭ major] *String quartet no. 6 in B♭ major, op. 18, no. 6.* Bärenreiter TP206, $6.75; Eulenburg 21, $6.75.

548 * Beethoven, Ludwig van, 1770–1827

[Quartets, strings, no. 7, op. 59, no. 1, F major] *String quartet no. 7 in F major, op. 59, no. 1.* Bärenreiter TP230, $6.50; Eulenburg 28, $7.75.

549 * Beethoven, Ludwig van, 1770–1827

[Quartets, strings, no. 8, op. 59, no. 2, E minor] *String quartet no. 8 in E minor, op. 59, no. 2.* Bärenreiter TP231, $6.50; Eulenburg 29, $6.75.

550 * Beethoven, Ludwig van, 1770–1827

[Quartets, strings, no. 9, op. 59, no. 3, C major] *String quartet no. 9 in C major, op. 59, no. 3.* Bärenreiter TP232, $5.75; Eulenburg 30, $6.75.

551 * Beethoven, Ludwig van, 1770–1827

[Quartets, strings, no. 10, op. 74, E♭ major] *String quartet no. 10 in E♭ major, op. 74.* Bärenreiter TP233, $8; Eulenburg 22, $6.75.

552 * Beethoven, Ludwig van, 1770–1827

[Quartets, strings, no. 11, op. 95, F minor] *String quartet no. 11 in F minor, op. 95.* Bärenreiter TP234, $6.50; Eulenburg 14, $6.75.

553 * Beethoven, Ludwig van, 1770–1827

[Quartets, strings, no. 12, op. 127, E♭ major] *String quartet no. 12 in E♭ major, op. 127.* Eulenburg 36, $7.50.

554 * Beethoven, Ludwig van, 1770–1827

[Quartets, strings, no. 13, op. 130, B♭ major] *String quartet no. 13 in B♭ major, op. 130.* Eulenburg 9, $6.75.

555 * Beethoven, Ludwig van, 1770–1827

[Quartets, strings, no. 14, op. 131, C♯ minor] *String quartet no. 14 in C♯ minor, op. 131.* Eulenburg 2, $6.75.

556 * Beethoven, Ludwig van, 1770–1827

[Quartets, strings, no. 15, op. 132, A minor] *String quartet no. 15 in A minor, op. 132.* Eulenburg 6, $6.75.

557 * Beethoven, Ludwig van, 1770–1827

[Quartets, strings, no. 16, op. 135, F major] *String quartet no. 16 in F major, op. 135.* Eulenburg 4, $6.75.

---

558 Berg, Alban, 1885–1935

[Lyrische Suite] *Lyric suite, for string quartet.* Philharmonia PH 173, $29.

559 Bloch, Ernest, 1880–1959

[Quartets, strings, no. 3] *String quartet no. 3.* G. Schirmer, $30.

560   Borodin, Aleksandr Porfir'evich, 1833–1887

[Quartets, strings, no. 2, D major] *String quartet no. 2 in D major.* Eulenburg 201, $7.75; International Music 1142, $8.50.

561 * Brahms, Johannes, 1833–1897

[Quartets, strings] *String quartets, op. 51, no. 1–2; op. 67.* Eulenburg 240-242, 3 v., $6.50 each; Kalmus K 00799, $9.

562   Carter, Elliott, 1908–

[Quartets, strings, no. 2] *String quartet no. 2 (1959).* 3rd corrected ed. Associated Music AMP-9609-62, $6.

563   Carter, Elliott, 1908–

[Quartets, strings, no. 3] *String quartet no. 3.* Associated Music HL50238300, $20.

564 * Debussy, Claude, 1862–1918

[Quartet, strings, op. 10, G minor] *String quartet in G minor, op. 10.* Eulenburg 210, $7.75; International Music 1098, $6.25; Kalmus K 00073, $5.50.

565 * Debussy, Claude, 1862–1918

[Quartet, strings, op. 10, G minor] *String quartets by Debussy and Ravel.* Dover 0-486-25231-0, $7.95.

566 * Dvořák, Antonín, 1841–1904

[Quartets, strings. Selections] *Five late string quartets, B. 92, B. 121, B. 179, B. 192, B. 193.* Dover 0-486-25135-7, $11.95.

567   Dvořák, Antonín, 1841–1904

[Quartets, strings, B. 75, D minor] *String quartet no. 9 in D minor, op. 34, B. 75.* Eulenburg 298, $7.50.

568   Dvořák, Antonín, 1841–1904

[Quartets, strings, B. 92, E♭ major] *String quartet no. 10 in E♭ major, op. 51, B. 92.* Eulenburg 299, $6.50.

569   Dvořák, Antonín, 1841–1904

[Quartets, strings, B. 121, C major] *String quartet no. 11 in C major, op. 61, B. 121.* Eulenburg 300, $8.50.

570 * Dvořák, Antonín, 1841–1904

[Quartets, strings, B. 179, F major] *String quartet no. 12 in F major, op. 96, B. 179, "American quartet."* Eulenburg 302, $6.75; International Music 1349, $6.50.

571   Dvořák, Antonín, 1841–1904

[Quartets, strings, B. 192, G major] *String quartet no. 13 in G major, op. 106, B. 192.* Eulenburg 304, $7.50.

572 * Dvořák, Antonín, 1841–1904

[Quartets, strings, B. 193, A♭ major] *String quartet no. 14 in A♭ major, op. 105, B. 193.* Eulenburg 303, $7.50.

573 * Fauré, Gabriel, 1845–1924

[Quartet, strings, op. 121, E minor] *String quartet in E minor, op. 121.* Durand 497-00208, $26.25; Peters P9895, $40.30.

574   Franck, César, 1822–1890

[Quartet, strings, D major] *String quartet in D major.* Eulenburg 323, $8.50; International Music 993, $7.75.

575   Ginastera, Alberto, 1916–1983

[Quartets, strings, no. 1, op. 20] *String quartet no. 1, op. 20.* Boosey & Hawkes HPS 1043, $16.50.

576 * Haydn, Joseph, 1732–1809

[Quartets, strings. Selections] *Eleven late string quartets, op. 74, no. 1–3; op. 76, no. 1–6; op. 77, no. 1–2.* Dover 0-486-23753-1, $12.95.

577 * Haydn, Joseph, 1732–1809

[Quartets, strings. Selections] *String quartets, op. 20 and op. 33, complete.* Dover 0-486-24852-6, $12.95.

578 * Haydn, Joseph, 1732–1809

[Quartets, strings. Selections] *String quartets op. 42, op. 50, and op. 54.* Dover 0-486-24262-5, $11.95.

579 * Haydn, Joseph, 1732–1809

[Quartets, strings. Selections] *Thirty celebrated string quartets, v. 3: op. 74, no. 1–3; op. 76, no. 1–6; op. 77, no. 1–2.* Kalmus K 00211-00213, 3 v., v.1-2, OP, v.3, $19.

580 * Haydn, Joseph, 1732–1809

[Quartets, strings. Selections] *Twelve string quartets, op. 55, op. 64, and op. 71.* Dover 0-486-23933-0, $11.95.

581   Hindemith, Paul, 1895–1963

[Quartets, strings, op. 22] *String quartet no. 3, op. 22.* Schott ED3435, $15.

582   Ives, Charles, 1874–1954

[Quartets, strings, no. 1] *String quartet no. 1.* Corrected ed. Peer International 61271-757, $6.

583 Ives, Charles, 1874–1954

[Quartets, strings, no. 2] *String quartet no. 2.* Peer International 61299-757, $6.

584 Janáček, Leoš, 1854–1928

[Quartets, strings, no. 2] *String quartet no. 2.* Philharmonia PH487, $19.50.

585 Lutosławski, Witold, 1913–

[Quartet, strings] *String quartet.* Chester, $39.95.

586 Mendelssohn-Bartholdy, Felix, 1809–1847

[Quartets, strings, no. 1, op. 12, E♭ major] *String quartet no. 1 in E♭ major, op. 12.* Eulenburg 47, $6.50.

587 * Mendelssohn-Bartholdy, Felix, 1809–1847

[Quartets, strings, no. 2, op. 13, A major] *String quartet no. 2 in A major, op. 13.* Eulenburg 68, $6.75.

588 * Mendelssohn-Bartholdy, Felix, 1809–1847

[Quartets, strings, no. 3, op. 44, no. 1, D major] *String quartet no. 3 in D major, op. 44, no. 1.* Eulenburg 48, $7.50.

589 * Mendelssohn-Bartholdy, Felix, 1809–1847

[Quartets, strings, no. 4, op. 44, no. 2, E minor] *String quartet no. 4 in E minor, op. 44, no. 2.* Eulenburg 7, $7.50.

590 * Mendelssohn-Bartholdy, Felix, 1809–1847

[Quartets, strings, no. 5, op. 44, no. 3, E♭ major] *String quartet no. 5 in E♭ major, op. 44, no. 3.* Eulenburg 49, $7.75.

591 Mendelssohn-Bartholdy, Felix, 1809–1847

[Quartets, strings, no. 6, op. 80, F minor] *String quartet no. 6 in F minor, op. 80.* Eulenburg 101, $6.75.

592 * Mozart, Wolfgang Amadeus, 1756–1791

[Kleine Nachtmusik] *Serenade in G major, K. 525, "Eine kleine Nachtmusik."* Bärenreiter TP19, $7.50; Eulenburg 217, $6.50; Kalmus K 00080, $8.

593 * Mozart, Wolfgang Amadeus, 1756–1791

[Quartets, strings] *Complete string quartets (23).* Dover 0-486-22372-8, $11.95.

594 * Mozart, Wolfgang Amadeus, 1756–1791

[Quartets, strings. Selections] *String quartets: K. 387, K. 421, K. 428, K. 458, K. 464; K. 465, K. 499, K. 575, K. 589, K. 590.* Bärenreiter TP140, $44.75; Kalmus K 00998-00999, 2 v., $6 each.

—OR INDIVIDUALLY—

595 * Mozart, Wolfgang Amadeus, 1756–1791

[Quartets, strings, K. 387, G major] *String quartet in G major, K. 387.* Bärenreiter TP141, $8; Eulenburg 1, $6.75; Universal PH327, $8.50.

596 * Mozart, Wolfgang Amadeus, 1756–1791

[Quartets, strings, K. 421, D minor] *String quartet in D minor, K. 421.* Bärenreiter TP142, $6.50; Eulenburg 32, $6.75; Universal PH328, $8.50.

597 * Mozart, Wolfgang Amadeus, 1756–1791

[Quartets, strings, K. 428, E♭ major] *String quartet in E♭ major, K. 428.* Bärenreiter TP144, $3.50; Eulenburg 33, $6.75; Universal PH329, $8.50.

598 * Mozart, Wolfgang Amadeus, 1756–1791

[Quartets, strings, K. 458, B♭ major] *String quartet in B♭ major, K. 458.* Bärenreiter TP143, $6.50; Eulenburg 34, $6.75; Universal PH330, $8.50.

599 * Mozart, Wolfgang Amadeus, 1756–1791

[Quartets, strings, K. 464, A major] *String quartet in A major, K. 464.* Bärenreiter TP145, $6.50; Eulenburg 35, $6.75; Universal PH331, $8.50.

600 * Mozart, Wolfgang Amadeus, 1756–1791

[Quartets, strings, K. 465, C major] *String quartet in C major, K. 465.* Bärenreiter TP146, $6.50; Eulenburg 8, $6.75; Universal PH332, $8.50.

601 * Mozart, Wolfgang Amadeus, 1756–1791

[Quartets, strings, K. 499, D major] *String quartet in D major, K. 499.* Bärenreiter TP86, $8; Eulenburg 24, $6.75; Universal PH333, $8.50.

602 * Mozart, Wolfgang Amadeus, 1756–1791

[Quartets, strings, K. 575, D major] *String quartet in D major, K. 575.* Bärenreiter TP87, $6.50; Eulenburg 25, $6.75; Universal PH334, $8.50.

603 * Mozart, Wolfgang Amadeus, 1756–1791

[Quartets, strings, K. 589, B♭ major] *String quartet in B♭ major, K. 589.* Bärenreiter TP88, $8; Eulenburg 26, $6.75; Universal PH335, $8.50.

604 * Mozart, Wolfgang Amadeus, 1756–1791

[Quartets, strings, K. 590, F major] *String quartet in F major, K. 590.* Bärenreiter TP89, $8; Eulenburg 27, $6.75; Universal PH336, $8.50.

605   Penderecki, Krysztof, 1933–

[Quartets, strings, no. 2] *String quartet no. 2.* Schott ED6302, $20.

606 * Prokofiev, Sergey, 1891–1953

[Quartets, strings, no. 1, op. 50] *String quartet no. 1, op. 50.* International Music 960, $6.50.

607   Prokofiev, Sergey, 1891–1953

[Quartets, strings, no. 2, op. 92] *String quartet no. 2, op. 92.* International Music 915, $7.

608 * Ravel, Maurice, 1875–1937

[Quartets, string, F major] *String quartet in F major.* International Music 539, $6.50. *See also* 565

609   Rochberg, George, 1918–

[Quartets, strings, no. 3] *String quartet no. 3.* Galaxy Music 1.2558, $15.75.

610   Schnittke, Alfred, 1934–

[Quartets, strings, no. 1] *String quartet no. 1 (1966).* Sikorski SIK 6715, $16.

611   Schoenberg, Arnold, 1874–1951

[Quartets, strings, no. 1, op. 7, D minor] *String quartet no. 1 in D minor, op. 7.* Kalmus K 00375, $8.95; Universal UE3665, $15.

612   Schoenberg, Arnold, 1874–1951

[Quartets, strings, no. 2, op. 10, F♯ minor] *String quartet no. 2 in F♯ minor, with soprano, op. 10.* Universal PH229, $15.

613   Schoenberg, Arnold, 1874–1951

[Quartets, strings, no. 3, op. 30] *String quartet no. 3, op. 30.* Universal PH228, $20.

614   Schoenberg, Arnold, 1874–1951

[Quartets, strings, no. 4, op. 37] *String quartet no. 4, op. 37.* G. Schirmer 21, $40.

615 * Schubert, Franz, 1797–1856

[Quartets, strings] *Complete string quartets (15).* Kalmus K 00788-00790, 3 v., $6 each.

616 * Schumann, Robert, 1810–1856

[Quartets, strings, op. 41] *Three string quartets, op. 41, no. 1–3.* Eulenburg 74-76, 3 v., $6.50 each.

617   Seeger, Ruth Crawford, 1901–1953

[Quartet, strings] *String quartet (1931).* Merion 144-40013, $10.

618 * Shostakovich, Dmitrii Dmitrievich, 1906–1975

[Quartets, strings, no. 1–5] *String quartets no. 1–5.* Dover 0-486-28140-X, $12.95.

619 * Shostakovich, Dmitrii Dmitrievich, 1906–1975

[Quartets, strings, no. 13–15] *String quartets no. 13–15.* Sikorski HL50159790, $40.

620   Smetana, Bedřich, 1824–1884

[Quartets, strings, no. 1, E minor] *String quartet no. 1 in E minor, "From my life."* Eulenburg 275, $6.75.

621   Stravinsky, Igor, 1882–1971

[Concertino, string quartet] *Concertino for string quartet.* W. Hansen WH2359, $16.95.

622   Stravinsky, Igor, 1882–1971

[Pieces, string quartet] *Three pieces for string quartet.* Boosey & Hawkes HPS 634, $16.50.

623   Tchaikovsky, Peter Ilich, 1840–1893

[Quartets, strings, no. 1, op. 11, D major] *String quartet in D major, op. 11.* Eulenburg 161, $6.50; Kalmus K 00598, $10.

624   Webern, Anton, 1883–1945

[Sätze, string quartet, op. 5] *Five movements for string quartet, op. 5.* Philharmonia PH358, $10.50.

625 * Wolf, Hugo, 1860–1903

[Italienische Serenade] *Italian serenade in G major for string quartet.* Eulenburg 286, $6.50.

Piano Quartets
(Violin, Viola, Violoncello, Piano)

626 * Brahms, Johannes, 1833–1897

[Quartets, piano, strings, no. 1, op. 25, G minor] *Piano quartet no. 1 in G minor, op. 25.* Eulenburg 243, $9.50; Kalmus K 00773, $6.

627 * Brahms, Johannes, 1833–1897

[Quartets, piano, strings, no. 2, op. 26, A major] *Piano quartet no. 2 in A major, op. 26.* Eulenburg 244, $10.50; Kalmus K 00774, $9.

628 * Brahms, Johannes, 1833–1897

[Quartets, piano, strings, no. 3, op. 60, C minor] *Piano quartet no. 3 in C minor, op. 60.* Eulenburg 245, $9; Kalmus K 00775, $6.

629   Copland, Aaron, 1900–1990

[Quartets, piano, strings] *Quartet for piano and strings.* Boosey & Hawkes HPS 671, $12.

630 * Dvořák, Antonín, 1841–1904

[Quartets, piano, strings, op. 87, E♭ major] *Quartet for piano and strings in E♭ major, op. 87.* Eulenburg 330, $8.50.

631 * Fauré, Gabriel, 1845–1924

[Quartets, piano, strings, no. 1, op. 15, C minor] *Quartet no. 1 in C minor for piano and strings, op. 15.* Eulenburg 1403, $10.50.

632 * Fauré, Gabriel, 1845–1924

[Quartets, piano, strings, no. 2, op. 45, G minor] *Quartet no. 2 in G minor for piano and strings, op. 45.* Eulenburg 1404, $10.50.

633 * Mozart, Wolfgang Amadeus, 1756–1791

[Quartets, piano, strings] *Two quartets for piano and strings: K. 478 in G minor, and K. 493 in E♭ major.* Eulenburg 158-159, 2 v., $7.50 each; Kalmus K 01244, $9.50.

634 * Schumann, Robert, 1810–1856

[Quartets, piano, strings, op. 47, E♭ major] *Quartet in E♭ major for piano and strings, op. 47.* Eulenburg 77, $10; Kalmus K 01106 (with Schumann's *Quintet for piano and strings, op. 44*), $6.50.

String Quintets (Two Violins, Two Violas, and Violoncello, Unless Otherwise Indicated)

635 * Beethoven, Ludwig van, 1770–1827

[Quintets, violins, violas, violoncello, op. 29, C major] *String quintet in C major, op. 29.* Eulenburg 31, $7.75.

636 Boccherini, Luigi, 1743–1805

[Quintets, violins, viola, violoncellos, G. 265–267] *String quintets no. 1–3, G. 265–267.* Eulenburg 209, $5.50. OP

637 * Brahms, Johannes, 1833–1897

[Quintets, violins, violas, violoncello, no. 1, op. 88, F major] *String quintet no. 1 in F major, op. 88.* Eulenburg 237, $6.75.

638 * Brahms, Johannes, 1833–1897

[Quintets, violins, violas, violoncello, no. 2, op. 111, G major] *String quintet no. 2 in G major, op. 111.* Eulenburg 238, $9.50.

639 Bruckner, Anton, 1824–1896

[Quintet, violins, violas, violoncello, F major] *String quintet in F major.* Eulenburg 310, $8.50.

640 Dvořák, Antonín, 1841–1904

[Quintets, violins, viola, violoncello, double bass, op. 77, G major] *String quintet in G major, op. 77* [originally numbered as op. 18]. Eulenburg 338, $8.50.

641 Dvořák, Antonín, 1841–1904

[Quintets, violins, violas, violoncello, op. 97, E♭ major] *String quintet no. 3 in E♭ major, op. 97.* Eulenburg 306, $10.50.

642 * Mozart, Wolfgang Amadeus, 1756–1791

[Quintets, violins, violas, violoncello] *Six string quintets, K. 174, K. 406, K. 515, K. 516, K. 593, K. 614.* Bärenreiter TP153, TP15, TP38, TP11 (OP), TP12, TP154, 6 v., $8, $8.75, $6.75, $6.75 (OP), $6.75, $8.75; Dover 0-486-23603-X (with Mozart's *Quintet in E♭ major for horn and strings, K. 407* and *Quintet in A major for clarinet and strings, K. 581*), $8.95; Kalmus K 00743-00744, 2 v., $6 each.

643 * Schubert, Franz, 1797–1828

[Quintets, violins, viola, violoncellos, D. 956, C major] *String quintet in C major, op. 163, D. 956.* Eulenburg 15, $7.75; Kalmus K 00791 (with Schubert's *Trout piano quintet, op. 114*), $6.

Piano Quintets (Piano, Two Violins, Viola, and Violoncello, Unless Otherwise Indicated)

644 * Brahms, Johannes, 1833–1897

[Quintets, piano, strings, op. 34, F minor] *Quintet in F minor for piano and strings, op. 34.* Eulenburg 212, $9; Kalmus K 00800, $6.

645 Dvořák, Antonín, 1841–1904

[Quintets, piano, strings, op. 81, A major] *Quintet in A major for piano and strings, op. 81.* Eulenburg 305, $10.

646 Franck, César, 1822–1890

[Quintet, piano, strings, F minor] *Quintet in F minor for piano and strings.* Eulenburg 329, $10.

647 * Schubert, Franz, 1797–1828

[Quintets, piano, violin, viola, violoncello, double bass, D. 667, A major] *Quintet in A major for piano and strings, op. 114, "Trout quintet," D. 667.* Eulenburg 118, $9.50; Kalmus K 00791 (with Schubert's *String quintet, op. 163*), $6.

648 * Schumann, Robert, 1810–1856

[Quintets, piano, strings, op. 44, E♭ major] *Quintet in E♭ major for piano and strings, op. 44.* Eulenburg 78, $9; Kalmus K 01106 (with Schumann's *Piano quartet, op. 47*), $6.50.

Sextets

649 * Brahms, Johannes, 1833–1897

[Sextets, violins, violas, violoncellos, no. 1–2] *Two sextets for strings: op. 18 in B♭ major, and op. 36 in G major.* Eulenburg 235-236, 2 v., $7.75, $8.50; Kalmus K 01149, $6.

650 Dvořák, Antonín, 1841–1904

[Sextet, violins, violas, violoncellos, op. 48, A major] *Sextet in A major for strings, op. 48.* Eulenburg 337, $8.50.

651 * Mendelssohn-Bartholdy, Felix, 1809–1847

[Sextet, piano, strings, op. 110, D major] *Sextet in D major for piano, violin, 2 violas, cello, and bass, op. 110.* Litolff/Peters L636, $31.25.

652 Schoenberg, Arnold, 1874–1951

Verklärte Nacht = Transfigured night, op. 4: sextet for violins, violas, and violoncellos. International Music 2156, $7; Kalmus K 00900, $6; Universal UE3662, $15.

Octets

653 * Mendelssohn-Bartholdy, Felix, 1809–1847

[Octet, violins (4), violas (2), violoncellos (2), op. 20, E♭ major] *Octet in E♭ major for strings, op. 20.* Eulenburg 59, $10.50; International Music 958, $10; Kalmus K 01182, $6.

Chamber Music for Winds

The following ensembles include works for wind ensemble, with or without piano or other keyboard instrument. For performance parts for these and other chamber works, see "Chamber Music for Winds," in chapter 9, "Chamber Music."

Collections for Various Numbers of Winds

These may be acquired in place of individual editions.

654 * Beethoven, Ludwig van, 1770–1827

[Chamber music. Selections] *Chamber music for winds, including Sextet, op. 71, Trio, op. 87, Octet, op. 103, and Rondino, K. 25.* Kalmus K 01007, $6.

655 * Mozart, Wolfgang Amadeus, 1756–1791

[Chamber music. Selections] *Divertimenti no. 11–17: K. 251, K. 252, K. 253, K. 270, K. 287, K. 289, K. 334.* Kalmus K 00960, $6.

Trios

656 * Beethoven, Ludwig van, 1770–1827

[Trios, oboes, English horn, op. 87, C major] *Trio in C major for 2 oboes and English horn, op. 87.* Eulenburg 104, $7.50.

657 Piston, Walter, 1894–1976

[Pieces, flute, clarinet, bassoon] *Three pieces for flute, clarinet, and bassoon.* Associated Music HL50234690, $18.50.

658 * Poulenc, Francis, 1899–1963

[Sonatas, horn, trombone, trumpet] *Sonata for horn, trumpet, and trombone.* Chester JWC 229, $8.95.

Quartets

659 Babbitt, Milton, 1916–

[Quartets, woodwinds] *Woodwind quartet in one movement.* Associated Music HL50237660, $8.

660 * Carter, Elliott, 1908–

[Etudes and a fantasy] *Eight etudes and a fantasy, for flute, oboe, clarinet and bassoon.* Associated Music HL50237430, $15.50.

Quintets

"Woodwind quintet" in the following entries indicates a work for flute, oboe, clarinet, horn, and bassoon.

661 * Beethoven, Ludwig van, 1770–1827

[Quintets, piano, oboe, clarinet, horn, bassoon, op. 16, E♭ major] *Quintet in E♭ major for piano, oboe, clarinet, horn, and bassoon, op. 16.* Eulenburg 200, $7.75; International Music 1199, $5.50.

662 * Carter, Elliott, 1908–

[Quintets, winds] *Woodwind quintet (1948).* Associated Music HL50237000, $15.

663 Davies, Peter Maxwell, 1934–

[Quintet, trumpets, horn, trombone, tuba] *Brass quintet (1981).* Chester CH55497, $45.

664   Etler, Alvin, 1913–1973

[Quintets, winds, no. 1] *Quintet no. 1 for woodwind instruments (1955)*. Associated Music HL50236750, $10.

665   Françaix, Jean, 1912–

[Quintets, winds] *Woodwind quintet.* Schott ED4103, $12.

666   Henze, Hans Werner, 1926–

[Quintet, winds] *Woodwind quintet.* Schott ED4414, $20.

667 * Hindemith, Paul, 1895–1963

Kleine Kammermusik, for woodwind quintet, op. 24, no. 2. Schott ED3437, $20.

668 * Mozart, Wolfgang Amadeus, 1756–1791

[Quintets, piano, oboe, clarinet, horn, bassoon, K. 452, E♭ major] *Quintet in E♭ major for piano and woodwind quartet, K. 452.* Eulenburg 160, $6.75; International Music 1181, $5.50.

669 * Nielsen, Carl, 1865–1931

[Quintets, winds, op. 43] *Woodwind quintet, op. 43.* W. Hansen 2283A, $22.95.

670 * Schoenberg, Arnold, 1874–1951

[Quintet, winds, op. 26] *Woodwind quintet, op. 26.* Universal PH230, $20.

671   Schuller, Gunther, 1925–

[Quintets, winds] *Woodwind quintet (1958).* Schott/Associated Music 6640, $20.

672   Stockhausen, Karlheinz, 1928–

Zeitmasse, for five woodwinds, no. 5. Universal UE12697, $49.

Sextets

673 * Beethoven, Ludwig van, 1770–1827

[Sextets, clarinets, bassoons, horns, op. 71, E♭ major] *Sextet for 2 clarinets, 2 bassoons, and 2 horns, E♭ major, op. 71.* Eulenburg 139, $11; International Music 1209, $9.

674 * Janáček, Leoš, 1854–1928

Mládí = Youth: suite for flute piccolo, oboe, clarinet, horn, bassoon, bass clarinet (1924). International Music 3111, $9.50; Peters P9864a, $31.95.

675 * Mozart, Wolfgang Amadeus, 1756–1791

[Divertimenti, K. 213, F major] *Divertimento in F major, for 2 oboes, 2 horns, and 2 bassoons, K. 213.* Eulenburg 394, $6.50.

676 * Mozart, Wolfgang Amadeus, 1756–1791

[Divertimenti, K. 240, B♭ major] *Divertimento in B♭ major, for 2 oboes, 2 horns, and 2 bassoons, K. 240.* Eulenburg 395, $6.50.

677 * Mozart, Wolfgang Amadeus, 1756–1791

[Divertimenti, K. 252, E♭ major] *Divertimento in E♭ major, for 2 oboes, 2 horns, and 2 bassoons, K. 252.* Eulenburg 396, $6.50.

678 * Mozart, Wolfgang Amadeus, 1756–1791

[Divertimenti, K. 253, F major] *Divertimento in F major for 2 oboes, 2 horns, and 2 bassoons, K. 253.* Eulenburg 351, $6.50.

679 * Mozart, Wolfgang Amadeus, 1756–1791

[Divertimenti, K. 270, B♭ major] *Divertimento in B♭ major for 2 oboes, 2 horns, and 2 bassoons, K. 270.* Eulenburg 352, $6.50.

680 * Poulenc, Francis, 1899–1963

[Sextet, piano, woodwinds, horn] *Sextet for piano, flute, oboe, clarinet, bassoon, and horn.* W. Hansen 3432, $29.95.

Septets

681 * Hindemith, Paul, 1895–1963

[Septet, woodwinds, trumpet, horn] *Septet for wind instruments (1948).* Schott ED3540, $20.

Octets

682 * Beethoven, Ludwig van, 1770–1827

[Octet, woodwinds, horns (2), op. 103, E♭ major] *Octet in E♭ major for 2 oboes, 2 clarinets, 2 bassoons, and 2 horns, op. 103.* Eulenburg 135, $6.50.

683 * Beethoven, Ludwig van, 1770–1827

[Rondino, woodwinds, horns (2), WoO 25, E♭ major] *Rondino in E♭ major for two oboes, two clarinets, two horns, and two bassoons, op. posth.* Eulenburg 252, $6.50; International Music 1173, $5.50.

684 * Mozart, Wolfgang Amadeus, 1756–1791

[Serenades, K. 375, E♭ major (1782)] *Serenade in E♭ major for 2 horns, 2 oboes, 2 clarinets, and 2 bassoons, K. 375.* Eulenburg 308, $6.75.

685 * Stravinsky, Igor, 1882–1971

[Octet, winds] *Octet for wind instruments.* Boosey & Hawkes HPS 630, $13.

Chamber Music for Mixed Winds and Strings

The following works include ensembles for mixed winds and strings, with or without piano or other keyboard instrument. For performance parts for these and other chamber works, see "Chamber Music for Mixed Winds and Strings," in chapter 9, "Chamber Music."

Trios

686 * Bartók, Béla, 1881–1945

Contrasts, for violin, clarinet and piano. Boosey & Hawkes HPS 723, $22.

687 * Beethoven, Ludwig van, 1770–1827

[Serenades, flute, violin, viola, op. 25, D major] *Serenade in D major for flute, violin, and viola, op. 25.* Eulenburg 103, $6.75.

688 * Beethoven, Ludwig van, 1770–1827

[Trios, piano, clarinet, violoncello, op. 11, B♭ major] *Trio for piano, clarinet (or violin) and violoncello, B♭ major, op. 11.* Eulenburg 223, $6.50.

689 * Brahms, Johannes, 1833–1897

[Trios, piano, clarinet, violoncello, op. 114, A minor] *Trio for piano, clarinet (or viola) and violoncello, A minor, op. 114.* Eulenburg 250, $6.50.

690 * Brahms, Johannes, 1833–1897

[Trios, piano, violin, horn, op. 40, E♭ major] *Trio for piano, violin, horn (or cello or viola), E♭ major, op. 40.* Eulenburg 249, $6.75.

691 * Debussy, Claude, 1862–1918

[Sonatas, flute, viola, harp] *Sonata for flute, viola, and harp.* Durand 597-00548, $20.

692 * Mozart, Wolfgang Amadeus, 1756–1791

[Trios, piano, clarinet, viola, K. 498, E♭ major] *Trio for piano, clarinet (or violin), and viola, E♭ major, K. 498.* Eulenburg 376, $6.50.

693 Reger, Max, 1873–1916

[Serenades, flute, violin, viola, op. 77a, D major] *Serenade in D major for flute, violin and viola, op.*
77a. Eulenburg 287, $6.50; International Music 3010, $5.50.

694 Reger, Max, 1873–1916

[Serenades, flute, violin, viola, op. 141a, G major] *Serenade in G major for flute, violin, and viola, op. 141a.* Eulenburg 313, $6.50.

Quartets

695 Britten, Benjamin, 1913–1976

[Phantasies, oboe, strings, op. 2] *Phantasy quartet for oboe, violin, viola and violoncello.* Boosey & Hawkes HPS 10, $15.50.

696 Carter, Elliott, 1908–

[Sonatas, harpsichord, flute, oboe, violoncello] *Sonata for flute, oboe, cello and harpsichord.* Associated Music AMP-9612-73, $15.

697 Crumb, George, 1929–

[Echoes of autumn] *Eleven echoes of autumn (1965), for violin, alto flute, clarinet, and piano.* Peters P66457, $33.85.

698 * Messiaen, Olivier, 1908–1992

Quatuor pour la fin du temps, for violin, B♭ clarinet, cello, and piano. Durand 597-00557, $24.

699 * Mozart, Wolfgang Amadeus, 1756–1791

[Quartets, flute, violin, viola, violoncello] *Four quartets for flute, violin, viola, and violoncello, K. 285, K. 285a, K. 285b, K. 298.* Bärenreiter TP150, $14.

700 Mozart, Wolfgang Amadeus, 1756–1791

[Quartets, flute, violin, viola, violoncello. Selections] *Two quartets for flute, violin, viola, and violoncello, K. 285, K. 298.* Eulenburg 192-193, 2 v., $6.50 each.

701 * Mozart, Wolfgang Amadeus, 1756–1791

[Quartets, oboe, violin, viola, violoncello, K. 370, F major] *Quartet in F major for oboe, violin, viola, and cello, K. 370 (368b).* Bärenreiter TP151, $7.50; Eulenburg 1294, $6.50.

Quintets

702 Babbitt, Milton, 1916–

Arie da capo, for flute, clarinet, violin, violoncello, piano. Peters P66584, $52.75.

703 Bliss, Arthur, Sir, 1891–1975

[Quintets, clarinet, violins, viola, violoncello] *Quintet for clarinet and strings.* Masters Music M2188, $12; Novello 235489, $16.95.

704 * Brahms, Johannes, 1833–1897

[Quintets, clarinet, violins, viola, violoncello, op. 115, B minor] *Quintet in B minor for clarinet and string quartet, op. 115.* Dover 0-486-21914-3 (with Brahms's *Complete chamber music for strings*), $11.95; Eulenburg 239, $6.75.

705 Diamond, David, 1915–

[Quintets, clarinet, violas, violoncellos] *Quintet for clarinet, 2 violas, and 2 cellos.* Peer International, $6.

706 * Mozart, Wolfgang Amadeus, 1756–1791

[Quintets, clarinet, violins, viola, violoncello, K. 581, A major] *Quintet in A major for clarinet, 2 violins, viola, cello, K. 581.* Bärenreiter TP14, $7.50; Eulenburg 71, $6.75.

707 * Mozart, Wolfgang Amadeus, 1756–1791

[Quintets, horn, violin, violas, violoncella, K. 407, E♭ major] *Quintet for horn (or cello), violin, two violas and cello in E♭ major, K. 407 (386c).* Bärenreiter TP13, $6.75; Eulenburg 347, $6.75.

708 Piston, Walter, 1894–1976

[Quintets, flute, strings] *Quintet for flute and string quartet (1942).* Associated Music AMP-96133, $18.

709 * Prokofiev, Sergey, 1891–1953

[Quintets, oboe, clarinet, violin, viola, double bass, op. 39, G minor] *Quintet in G minor for oboe, clarinet, violin, viola, and double bass, op. 39.* Boosey & Hawkes HPS 891, $13; International Music 992, $8.75; Masters Music M2161, $20.

Sextets

710 * Beethoven, Ludwig van, 1770–1827

[Sextets, horns (2), strings, op. 81b, E♭ major] *Sextet for 2 violins, viola, violoncello, and 2 horns, E♭ major, op. 81b.* Eulenburg 140, $6.50.

711 Copland, Aaron, 1900–1990

[Sextet, piano, clarinet, strings] *Sextet for string quartet, clarinet, and piano.* Boosey & Hawkes HPS 675, $19.50.

712 Falla, Manuel de, 1876–1946

[Concertos, harpsichord, instrumental ensemble] *Concerto for harpsichord or piano, flute, oboe, clarinet, violin, and cello.* Ediciones Manuel de Falla, $63.40.

713 Mozart, Wolfgang Amadeus, 1756–1791

[Divertimenti, K. 287, B♭ major] *Divertimento no. 15 in B♭ major for 2 violins, viola, bass, and 2 horns, K. 287.* Eulenburg 73, $6.75.

714 * Mozart, Wolfgang Amadeus, 1756–1791

Ein musikalischer Spass = The village musicians: a musical joke, K. 522, for two violins, viola, bass (or cello) and two horns. Eulenburg 217, $6.50.

715 Rochberg, George, 1918–

Serenata d'estate = Summer serenade, for flute, harp, guitar, violin, viola, and cello. Leeds, OP.

Septets

716 * Beethoven, Ludwig van, 1770–1827

[Septet, woodwinds, horn, strings, op. 20, E♭ major] *Septet for violin, viola, violoncello, double bass, clarinet, horn, and bassoon, E♭ major, op. 20.* Eulenburg 12, $7.75.

717 Boccherini, Luigi, 1743–1805

[Serenade, winds, violins (2), continuo, G. 501, D major] *Serenade in D major for 2 oboes, 2 horns, 2 violins, and continuo.* Eulenburg 373, $6.50.

718 Janáček, Leoš, 1854–1928

[Concertino, piano, winds, strings] *Concertino for piano, 2 violins, viola, clarinet, horn, and bassoon.* Kalmus A6385, $20.

719 * Ravel, Maurice, 1875–1937

[Introduction et allegro, harp, woodwinds, strings] *Introduction and allegro for harp with string quartet, flute, and clarinet.* Durand 597-00568, $22.25; International 2124, $11.50; Kalmus K 01513, $5.50.

720 * Schoenberg, Arnold, 1874–1951

[Suites, piano, clarinets (3), strings, op. 29] *Suite for E♭ clarinet, B♭ clarinet, bass clarinet, strings, piano, op. 29.* Universal PH603, $25.

721 Stravinsky, Igor, 1882–1971

[Septet, piano, winds, strings] *Septet for clarinet, horn, bassoon, piano, violin, viola, and violoncello.* Boosey & Hawkes HPS 682, $14.

Octets

722 Hindemith, Paul, 1895–1963

[Octets, woodwinds, horn, strings] *Octet for clarinet, bassoon, horn, violin, 2 violas, cello, and double bass.* Schott ED4595, $25.

723 Reich, Steve, 1936–

[Octet, pianos (2), woodwinds, strings] *Eight lines: octet.* Hendon/Boosey & Hawkes FSB 487, $55.

724 * Schubert, Franz, 1797–1828

[Octets, woodwinds, horn, strings, D. 803, F major] *Octet in F major for 2 violins, viola, violoncello, double bass, clarinet, horn, and bassoon, D. 803.* Bärenreiter TP302, $13; Eulenburg 60, $11.75.

725 * Varèse, Edgard, 1883–1965

Octandre, for flute, clarinet, oboe, bassoon, horn, trumpet, trombone, and double bass. Rev. ed. Colfranc HL50481068, $12.

Chamber Music for Unspecified Instruments

726 Bach, Johann Sebastian, 1685–1750

[Musikalisches Opfer] *Musical offering: canons, ricercars, and a trio sonata for flute, violin, and continuo; instruments not fully specified.* Bärenreiter TP198, $14.25; Eulenburg 1390, $7.50.

Vocal Music in Full and Study Score

Compiled by
James P. Cassaro (opera and choral)
and Michael Rogan (solo voice)

Operas

The following section lists operas in full or study score, for voices with orchestra. When ordering, one must distinguish between editions in orchestral score and those in vocal score, with the orchestral accompaniment reduced for piano. Specify "orchestral score" when placing orders.

Designation of the language of a work, usually found in the uniform title, is indicated after the title proper or after the publisher's name in order to accommodate different editions with different languages within a single entry. The language designations always refer to sung words (i.e., text set to the music), not to translations provided separately from the music.

727 * Beethoven, Ludwig van, 1770–1827
Fidelio. German. Dover 0-486-24740-6, $19.95.

728 Bellini, Vincenzo, 1801–1835
Norma. Italian. Dover 0-486-27970-7, $19.95.

729 Berg, Alban, 1885–1935
Wozzeck. German and English. Universal UE12100, $99.

730 Berlioz, Hector, 1803–1869
Les Troyens = The Trojans. French. Eulenburg 925, $77.

731 * Bizet, Georges, 1838–1875
Carmen. French. Dover 0-486-25820-3, $21.95; International Music 2000, $55.

732 Debussy, Claude, 1862–1918
Pelléas et Mélisande. French. International Music 2128, $55.

733 Donizetti, Gaetano, 1797–1848
Lucia di Lammermoor. Italian. Dover 0-486-27113-7, $19.95.

734 Gluck, Christoph Willibald Ritter von, 1714–1787
Orfeo ed Euridice. Italian and German. Dover 0-486-27324-5, $10.95.

735 Gounod, Charles, 1818–1893
Faust. French. Dover 0-486-28349-6, $24.95.

736   Handel, George Frideric, 1685–1759

Giulio Cesare. Italian. Dover 0-486-25056-3, $11.95.

737   Leoncavallo, Ruggiero, 1857–1919

I Pagliacci. Italian. Dover 0-486-27363-6, $15.95.

738   Mascagni, Pietro, 1863–1945

Cavalleria rusticana. Italian. Dover 0-486-27806-2, $11.95.

739   Monteverdi, Claudio, 1567–1643

L'Orfeo. Italian. Novello 260621, $24.95.

740   * Mozart, Wolfgang Amadeus, 1756–1791

Così fan tutte, K. 588. Dover 0-486-24528-4, Italian, $17.95, for sale in the United States only; Eulenburg 920, Italian and German, $31; Kalmus K 00421, Italian and German, $22.

741   * Mozart, Wolfgang Amadeus, 1756–1791

Don Giovanni, K. 527. Italian and German. Dover 0-486-23026-0, $19.95.

742   * Mozart, Wolfgang Amadeus, 1756–1791

Le nozze di Figaro = The marriage of Figaro, K. 492. Italian and German. Dover 0-486-23751-6, $17.95; Kalmus K 00419, $24.95.

743   * Mozart, Wolfgang Amadeus, 1756–1791

Die Zauberflöte = The magic flute. Dover 0-486-24783-X, German, $11.95; Eulenburg 912, Italian and German, $32; International Music 1499, German, $66; Kalmus K 00422, German, $22.

744   Mussorgsky, Modest Petrovich, 1839–1881

Boris Godunov. Orchestrated by Nikolay Rimsky-Korsakov. Russian. Dover 0-486-25321-X, $32.95.

745   * Puccini, Giacomo, 1858–1924

La bohème. Italian. Dover 0-486-25477-1, $16.95; International Music 1400, $55.

746   * Puccini, Giacomo, 1858–1924

Madama Butterfly. Italian. Dover 0-486-26345-2, $18.95; Ricordi 129166, $37.50.

747   * Puccini, Giacomo, 1858–1924

Tosca. Italian. Dover 0-486-26937-X, $19.95; Ricordi RR 1803, $37.50.

748   * Puccini, Giacomo, 1858–1924

Turandot. Italian. Ricordi RR 421, $37.50.

749   Purcell, Henry, 1659–1695

Dido and Aeneas. Dover 0-486-28746-7, English, $8.95; Norton 0-393-95528-1, ed. by Curtis Price, English, $9.95; Oxford University Press 0-19-337870-1, ed. by Ellen T. Harris, English and German, $75.

750   * Rossini, Gioacchino, 1792–1868

Il barbiere di Siviglia = The barber of Seville. Dover 0-486-26019-4, Italian and English, $16.95; International Music 1501, Italian, $45; Ricordi 1311809, critical ed., Italian and English, $85.

751   Schoenberg, Arnold, 1874–1951

Moses und Aron. German and English. Belmont E8004, $95.

752   Strauss, Richard, 1864–1949

Ariadne auf Naxos. German. Dover 0-486-27560-4, for sale in the United States only, $15.95.

753   Strauss, Richard, 1864–1949

Elektra. German. Boosey & Hawkes HPS 92, $150; Dover 0-486-26538-2, for sale in the United States only, $17.95.

754   * Strauss, Richard, 1864–1949 *Der Rosenkavalier.* German and English. Boosey & Hawkes HPS 90, $170; Dover 0-486-25498-4, for sale in the United States only, $16.95.

755   Strauss, Richard, 1864–1949

Salome. German. Boosey & Hawkes HPS 91, $130; Dover 0-486-24208-0, for sale in the United States only, $15.95.

756   * Verdi, Giuseppe, 1813–1901

Aïda. Italian. Dover 0-486-26172-7, $17.95; Ricordi 42602, $37.50.

757   Verdi, Giuseppe, 1813–1901

Un ballo in maschera = A masked ball. Italian. Dover 0-486-29141-3, $24.95; Ricordi 48180, $37.50.

758   * Verdi, Giuseppe, 1813–1901

Falstaff. Italian. Dover 0-486-24017-7, $17.95.

759   * Verdi, Giuseppe, 1813–1901

La forza del destino. Italian. Dover 0-486-26743-1, $24.95.

760   * Verdi, Giuseppe, 1813–1901

Otello. Italian. Dover 0-486-25040-7, $21.95; International Music 1150, $55.

761 * Verdi, Giuseppe, 1813–1901

Rigoletto. Italian and English. Dover 0-486-26965-5, $19.95; Ricordi RR 1980, $37.50.

762 * Verdi, Giuseppe, 1813–1901

La traviata. Dover 0-486-26321-5, Italian and English, $17.95; International Music 4004, Italian, $55; Ricordi RR2127, Italian and English, $37.50.

763 * Verdi, Giuseppe, 1813–1901

Il trovatore. Italian. Ricordi 109460, $46.

764 Wagner, Richard, 1813–1883

Der fliegende Holländer = The flying Dutchman. German and English. Dover 0-486-25629-4, $19.95; Eulenburg 902, $50.

765 Wagner, Richard, 1813–1883

Lohengrin. Dover 0-486-24335-4, German, $17.95; Eulenburg 904, German and English, $50.

766 * Wagner, Richard, 1813–1883

Die Meistersinger von Nürnberg = The mastersingers of Nuremberg. Dover 0-486-23276-X, German, $28.95; Eulenburg 906, German, English, and French, $75.

767 * Wagner, Richard, 1813–1883

Parsifal. Dover 0-486-25175-6, German, $19.95; Eulenburg 911, German, French, and Italian, $56.

768 * Wagner, Richard, 1813–1883

[Ring des Nibelungen. Götterdämmerung] *Götterdämmerung = The twilight of the Gods.* Dover 0-486-24250-1, German, $24.95; Eulenburg 910, German, English, and French, $89.

769 * Wagner, Richard, 1813–1883

[Ring des Nibelungen. Rheingold] *Das Rheingold.* Dover 0-486-24925-5, German, $14.95; Eulenburg 907, German, English, and French, $55.

770 * Wagner, Richard, 1813–1883

[Ring des Nibelungen. Siegfried] *Siegfried.* Dover 0-486-24456-3, German, $19.95; Eulenburg 909, German, English, and French, $69.

771 * Wagner, Richard, 1813–1883

[Ring des Nibelungen. Walküre] *Die Walküre.* Dover 0-486-23566-1, German, $24.95; Eulenburg 908, German, English, and French, $65.

772 Wagner, Richard, 1813–1883

Tannhäuser. German. Dover 0-486-24649-3, $21.95.

773 * Wagner, Richard, 1813–1883

[Tristan und Isolde] *Tristan and Isolde.* Dover 0-486-22915-7, German, $24.95; Eulenburg 905, German, English, and French, $75.

774 Weber, Carl Maria von, 1786–1826

Der Freischütz. German. Dover 0-486-23449-5, $11.95.

Choral Music

This section includes sacred and secular choral works in full or study score, for chorus and orchestra. When ordering, one must distinguish between editions in orchestral score and those in vocal score, with the orchestral accompaniment reduced for piano. Specify "orchestral score" when placing orders.

Designation of the language of a work, usually found in the uniform title, is indicated after the title proper or after the publisher's name in order to accommodate different editions with different languages within a single entry. The language designations always refer to sung words (i.e., text set to the music), not to translations provided separately from the music.

775 Adams, John, 1947–

Harmonium. English. Associated Music AMP 7924-7, $60.

776 * Bach, Johann Sebastian, 1685–1750

[Cantatas. Selections] *Eleven great cantatas: no. 4, 12, 21, 51, 56, 61, 78, 80, 82, 106, 140.* German. Dover 0-486-23268-9, $14.95.

777 * Bach, Johann Sebastian, 1685–1750

[Cantatas. Selections] *Six great secular cantatas: no. 201, 202, 205, 208, 211, 212.* German. Dover 0-486-23934-9, $13.95.

778 * Bach, Johann Sebastian, 1685–1750

Johannespassion = St. John Passion, BWV 245. Bärenreiter TP197, German, $28.50; Dover 0-486-27755-0, German, $9.95; Eulenburg 965, German and English, $15.

779 * Bach, Johann Sebastian, 1685–1750

[Magnificat, BWV 243, D major] *Magnificat in D major, BWV 243.* Latin. Bärenreiter TP2, $9; Dover (with Bach's *Six motets*) 0-486-28804-8, $13.95; Eulenburg 964, $9.

780 * Bach, Johann Sebastian, 1685–1750

[Masses, BWV 232, B minor] *Mass in B minor, BWV 232.* Latin. Bärenreiter TP1, $29.25; Dover 0-486-25992-7, $12.95.

781 * Bach, Johann Sebastian, 1685–1750

Matthäuspassion = St. Matthew Passion, BWV 244. Bärenreiter TP196, German, $28; Dover 0-486-26257-X, German, $13.95; Eulenburg 953, German and English, $23.

782 * Bach, Johann Sebastian, 1685–1750

Weihnachts Oratorium = Christmas oratorio, BWV 248. German. Bärenreiter TP85, $35.10; Dover 0-486-27230-2, $14.95; Eulenburg 962, $23.

783   Bartók, Béla, 1881–1945

[Kilenc csodaszarvas] *Cantata profana.* English and German. Universal PH359, $42.

784 * Beethoven, Ludwig van, 1770–1827

Missa solemnis in D major, op. 123. Latin. Dover 0-486-26894-2, $14.95; Eulenburg 951, $25; Universal PH74, $23.

785   Berlioz, Hector, 1803–1869

La damnation de Faust. French, English, and German. Eulenburg 994, $32.

786 * Berlioz, Hector, 1803–1869

[Grande Messe des morts] *Requiem, "Grande Messe des morts," op. 5.* Latin. Bärenreiter TP332, $29.25; Dover 0-486-29091-3 (with Berlioz's *Te Deum*), $17.95; Eulenburg 8003, $28.

787   Berlioz, Hector, 1803–1869

[Roméo et Juliette] *Romeo and Juliet.* French. Eulenburg 424, $30; Kalmus K00502, $7.50.

788   Berlioz, Hector, 1803–1869

Te Deum, op. 22. Latin. Eulenburg 1095, $20. *See also 786*

789   Brahms, Johannes, 1833–1897

[Choral music. Selections] *Alto rhapsody, Song of destiny = Schicksalslied, Nänie, and Song of the fates = Gesang der Parzen.* German. Dover 0-486-28528-6, $9.95.

790 * Brahms, Johannes, 1833–1897

Ein deutsches Requiem = A German requiem, op. 45. German. Dover 0-486-25486-0, $10.95; Eulenburg 969, $18.75.

791   Brahms, Johannes, 1833–1897

[Rhapsodies, alto, men's voices, orchestra, op. 53] *Alto rhapsody, op. 53.* German. Eulenburg 1054, $7.50.

792   Brahms, Johannes, 1833–1897

Schicksalslied = Song of destiny, op. 54. German, English, and French. Eulenburg 1601, $11.

793 * Britten, Benjamin, 1913–1976

War requiem. Latin alternating with English. Boosey & Hawkes HPS 742, $92.

794 * Bruckner, Anton, 1824–1896

[Masses, no. 2, E minor] *Mass no. 2 in E minor.* Latin. Universal PH204, $13.50.

795 * Bruckner, Anton, 1824–1896

Te Deum, op. 22. Latin. Eulenburg 960, $7.75.

796 * Fauré, Gabriel, 1845–1924

[Requiem, op. 48, D minor] *Requiem, op. 48.* Dover 0-486-27155-2, Latin, $9.95; Fitzsimmons IMG F8007, Latin and English, $50; Hinshaw Music HMB-147, with Fauré's original chamber instrumentation, newly ed. with English translation by John Rutter, Latin and English, $75; International Music 1451, Latin, $10.50.

797 ** Handel, George Frideric, 1685–1759

Messiah. Bärenreiter TP175, English and German, $34.25; Dover 0-486-26067-4, English, $11.95; Novello 900485, ed. by Watkins Shaw, English, $29.95.

798 * Haydn, Joseph, 1732–1809

[Masses, H. XXII, 11, D minor] *Mass no. 9 in D minor, Missa solemnis, "Nelson mass."* Latin. Bärenreiter TP98, $20; Dover 0-486-28108-6 (with Haydn's *Mass in time of war*), $12.95; Eulenburg 995, $24.

799 * Haydn, Joseph, 1732–1809

[Masses, H. XXII, 14, B♭ major] *Harmoniemesse.* Latin. Bärenreiter TP97, $30.

800 * Haydn, Joseph, 1732–1809

Die Schöpfung = The creation. Dover 0-486-26411-4, German and English, $12.95; Eulenburg 955, German, $28.

801   Ives, Charles, 1874–1954

Psalm 90. English. Presser 342-40021, $2.50.

802   Kodály, Zoltán, 1882–1967

Psalmus hungaricus, op. 13. Hungarian, English, and German. Universal PH233, $21.

803 * Mendelssohn-Bartholdy, Felix, 1809–1847

[Elias] *Elijah.* English and German. Dover 0-486-28504-9, $16.95.

804 * Monteverdi, Claudio, 1567–1643

Vespro della Beata Vergine (Vespers). Latin. Eulenburg 8024, ed. by Jerome Roche, $43; King's Music KM83, rev. 1990 ed. by Clifford Bartlett, $53; Novello 07.0211.00, ed. by Denis Stevens, $30; Universal PH470, ed. by Jürgen Jürgens, $50.

805 * Mozart, Wolfgang Amadeus, 1756–1791

[Masses, K. 427, C minor] *Mass in C minor, K. 427, "The great mass."* Latin. Eulenburg 983, $20.

806 * Mozart, Wolfgang Amadeus, 1756–1791

[Requiem, K. 626, D minor (Maunder)] *Requiem, K. 626,* ed. by Richard Maunder. Latin. Oxford University Press 0-19-337618-0, $110. [Excises Franz Xaver Süssmayr's contributions except for *Sanctus* and *Benedictus,* which appear in an appendix].

807 ** Mozart, Wolfgang Amadeus, 1756–1791

[Requiem, K. 626, D minor (Süssmayr)] *Requiem, K. 626,* completed by Franz Xaver Süssmayr. Latin. Bärenreiter TP152, $24; Dover 0-486-25311-2, $8.95; Eulenburg 954, $18.75.

808 * Orff, Carl, 1895–1982

Carmina burana: scenic cantata. Latin. Schott ED4425, $35.

809 *The play of Daniel: a medieval liturgical drama,* ed. for modern performance by Noah Greenberg. Sung portion in Latin; spoken narration in English, written by W. H. Auden. Oxford University Press 0-19-385195-4, $5.95.

810 * Poulenc, Francis, 1899–1963

Gloria in G major. Latin. Salabert SEAS16695, $19.95.

811 * Purcell, Henry, 1659–1695

[Ode for St. Cecilia's Day (1692)] *Ode for St. Cecilia's Day.* English and German. Schott ST10296, $25.

812 Reich, Steve, 1936–

Tehillim: parts I–IV. Rev. ed. Hebrew. Boosey & Hawkes HPS 1189, $65.

813 * Schoenberg, Arnold, 1874–1951

Gurre-Lieder. German. Universal UE6300, $45.

814 Schoenberg, Arnold, 1874–1951

A survivor from Warsaw, op. 46. Newly rev. ed. Sung portion in Hebrew; spoken narration in English. Universal UE478, $16.50.

815 * Schubert, Franz, 1797–1828

[Masses. Selections] *Masses no. 5, D. 678, and no. 6, D. 950.* Latin. Dover 0-486-28832-3, $17.95.

816 * Schubert, Franz, 1797–1828

[Masses, D. 678, A♭ major] *Mass in A♭ major, D. 678.* Latin. Eulenburg 974, $21.

817 * Schubert, Franz, 1797–1828

[Masses, D. 950, E♭ major] *Mass in E♭ major, D. 950.* Latin. Eulenburg 970, $21.

818 Schütz, Heinrich, 1585–1672

Historia von der Geburt Jesu Christi = Christmas oratorio. German. Bärenreiter TP132, $10.50; Eulenburg 980, $9.50.

819 * Stravinsky, Igor, 1882–1971

[Symphonie de Psaumes] *Symphony of Psalms.* Rev. 1947 version. Latin. Boosey & Hawkes HPS 637, $17.50.

820 Vaughan Williams, Ralph, 1872–1958

Serenade to music. English. Oxford University Press 0-19-339355-7, $21.95.

821 * Verdi, Giuseppe, 1813–1901

[Messa da Requiem] *Requiem.* Latin. Dover 0-486-23682-X, $10.95.

822 Verdi, Giuseppe, 1813–1901

[Pezzi sacri] *Quattro pezzi sacri = Four sacred pieces.* Latin. Eulenburg 1000, $9.50.

823 Webern, Anton, 1883–1945

[Cantatas, no. 2, op. 31] *Cantata no. 2, op. 31.* German and English. Universal PH466, $19.50.

Music for Solo Voice

This section includes works for solo voice(s) and orchestra or chamber ensemble in full score. When ordering, one must distinguish between editions in full score and those in vocal score, with the instrumental accompaniment reduced for piano. Specify "full score" when placing orders.

Designation of the language of a work, usually found in the uniform title, is indicated after the title proper or after the publisher's name in order to accommodate different editions with different languages within a single entry. The language designations always refer to sung words (i.e., text set to the music), not to translations provided separately from the music.

824 Berg, Alban, 1885–1935

[Orchester-Lieder, op. 4] *Altenberg Lieder, for voice and orchestra, op. 4.* German. Universal UE14325, $25.

825 Boulez, Pierre, 1925–

Le marteau sans maître, for alto voice, flute, marimba, vibraphone, percussion, guitar, and viola. French. Universal PH398, $29.

826 Crumb, George, 1929–

Ancient voices of children, for soprano, boy soprano, oboe, mandolin, harp, toy piano, electric piano, and percussion. English. Peters P66303, $43.

827 Mahler, Gustav, 1860–1911

Kindertotenlieder = Songs on the death of children, for voice and orchestra. German. Universal PH252, $11.

828 * Mahler, Gustav, 1860–1911

Das Lied von der Erde = The song of the earth: a symphony for tenor, contralto or baritone, and orchestra. German. Universal PH217, $22.

829 Mahler, Gustav, 1860–1911

Lieder eines fahrenden Gesellen = Songs of a wayfarer, for voice and orchestra. German. Universal PH251, $11.

830 * Strauss, Richard, 1864–1949

[Letzte Lieder] *Four last songs, for high voice and orchestra.* German and English. Boosey & Hawkes HPS 667, $17.50.

831 Stravinsky, Igor, 1882–1971

In memoriam Dylan Thomas, for tenor, string quartet, and four trombones. English. Boosey & Hawkes HPS 688, $14.

Music for Solo Woodwinds

Compiled by
**Anita Breckbill (flute), Beth Christensen (oboe and English horn),
Matthew Wise (clarinet and saxophone),
Richard AmRhein (bassoon), and David Lasocki (recorder)**

Flute Music

Solo Flute Music

832 * Bach, Carl Philipp Emanuel, 1714–1788

[Sonatas, flute, W. 132, A minor] *Sonata in A minor for flute.* Amadeus BP675, with facsimile, $15.30; Bärenreiter BA6820, $8; International Music 1857, $3.50.

833 * Bach, Johann Sebastian, 1685–1750

[Sonatas, flute, BWV 1013, A minor] *Partita in A minor for flute, BWV 1013.* Bärenreiter BA4401, $10.80; Henle HN457, $6.50; International Music 2380, ed. by Jean-Pierre Rampal, $3.50.

834 Berio, Luciano, 1925–

[Sequenza, no. 1] *Sequenza for flute.* Universal UE19957, $19.95.

835 Bozza, Eugène, 1905–

Image, for solo flute. Leduc AL19.908, $6.75.

836 * Debussy, Claude, 1862–1918

Syrinx, for solo flute. Jobert 524-000213, $4.25.

837 Fukushima, Kazuo, 1930–

Mei, for solo flute (1962). Zerboni S.5974Z., $12.

838 Hindemith, Paul, 1895–1963

[Stücke, flute] *Eight pieces for flute (1927).* Schott ED4760, $9.95.

839 Ibert, Jacques, 1890–1962

[Pieces, flute] *Pièce pour flûte seule.* Leduc AL19.306, $6.95.

840 * Telemann, Georg Philipp, 1681–1767

[Fantasias, flute] *Twelve fantasias for flute solo.* Amadeus BP370, with facsimile, $19.70; Bärenreiter BA2971, $10.50; International Music 3114, ed. by Jean-Pierre Rampal, $6.

841 * Varèse, Edgard, 1883–1965

Density 21.5, for flute. Colfranc, $4.95.

Flute and Keyboard Music

842 Bach, Carl Philipp Emanuel, 1714–1788

[Sonatas, flute, continuo. Selections] *6 sonatas for flute and continuo.* Zimmermann ZM1800, $16.50.

843 * Bach, Johann Sebastian, 1685–1750

[Sonatas. Selections] *Flute sonatas: vol. 1, The four authentic sonatas, BWV 1030, 1032, 1034, 1035; vol. 2, The three sonatas attributed to J. S. Bach, BWV 1020, 1031, 1033.* Bärenreiter BA4402, BA4418, 2 v., $20 each; Henle HN269, HN328, 2 v., $22.95, $18.95.

844 * Bach, Johann Sebastian, 1685–1750

[Sonatas, flute, continuo, BWV 1033–1035] *Sonatas no. 4–6 for flute and continuo.* International Music 1987, ed. by Jean-Pierre Rampal, $8; Peters P4461b, $11.10.

845 * Bach, Johann Sebastian, 1685–1750

[Sonatas, flute, harpsichord, BWV 1030–1032] *Sonatas no. 1–3 for flute or violin and piano.* International Music 1986, ed. by Jean-Pierre Rampal, $8.50; Peters P4461a, $11.10.

846 Blavet, Michel, 1700–1768

[Sonates melées de pièces] *Six sonatas for flute and continuo, op. 2.* Amadeus BP2474-2475, 2 v., $26.60 each; Bärenreiter BA6891, $19.

847 Copland, Aaron, 1900–1990

[Duet, flute, piano] *Duo for flute and piano.* Boosey & Hawkes WFB 19, $13.50.

848 *Flute music by French composers for flute and piano,* ed. by Louis Moyse. G. Schirmer ED2699, $9.95.

849 Handel, George Frideric, 1685–1759

[Sonatas, flute, continuo. Selections] *Eleven sonatas for flute and continuo.* Bärenreiter BA4225, $21; Henle HN483, in preparation.

850 Handel, George Frideric, 1685–1759

[Sonatas, flute, continuo. Selections] *Ten sonatas for flute and piano.* International Music 3031-3032, ed. by Jean-Pierre Rampal, 2 v., $8.50 each.

851 * Hindemith, Paul, 1895–1963

[Sonatas, flute, piano] *Sonata for flute and piano (1936).* Schott ED2522, $17.95.

852 Messiaen, Olivier, 1908–1992

Le merle noir, for flute and piano. Leduc AL21.053, $8.45.

853 Milhaud, Darius, 1892–1974

[Sonatinas, flute, piano, op. 76] *Sonatine for flute and piano, op. 76.* Durand 524-00501, $20.25.

854 Muczynski, Robert, 1929–

[Sonatas, flute, piano, op. 14] *Sonata for flute and piano, op. 14.* G. Schirmer ED3353, $15.95.

855 * Poulenc, Francis, 1899–1963

[Sonatas, flute, piano] *Sonata for flute and piano.* Chester Music CH1605, $15.95.

856 * Prokofiev, Sergey, 1891–1953

[Sonatas, flute, piano, op. 94, D major] *Sonata in D major, op. 94, for flute and piano.* International Music 1587, ed. by Jean-Pierre Rampal, $8.

857 * Reinecke, Carl, 1824–1910

[Sonatas, flute, piano, op. 167, E minor] *Undine sonata.* Boosey & Hawkes WFB 130, $13.50; International Music 1757, $6.50; G. Schirmer HL50336260, ed. by James Galway, $10.95.

858 Roussel, Albert, 1869–1937

Joueurs de flûte. Durand D&F10,702-D&F10,705, 4 v., $2.75, $7, $7, $2.75.

859 * Schubert, Franz, 1797–1828

[Introduction et variations sur un thème original] *Variations for flute and piano on "Trockne Blumen" from "Die schöne Müllerin," op. 160, D. 802.* Bärenreiter BA6819, $15; Henle HN474, $14.95; International Music 2179, ed. by Jean-Pierre Rampal, $6.50.

860 Vivaldi, Antonio, 1678–1741

Il pastor fido: six sonatas for flute (or recorder or oboe or violin) and continuo, op. 13. Bärenreiter HM135, $23.50.

Flute Concertos/Piano Reductions

The following section lists works for flute (or other solo instrument) and orchestra, with the orchestral score reduced for piano accompaniment. When ordering, specify "arranged for flute and piano; score and part."

861 Bach, Carl Philipp Emanuel, 1714–1788

[Concertos, harpsichord, string orchestra, H. 484.1, D minor; arr.] *Concerto in D minor for flute.*

International Music 3046, ed. by Jean-Pierre Rampal, $8; Kunzelmann GM838, $18.95.

862 * Bach, Johann Sebastian, 1685–1750

[Suites, orchestra, BWV 1067, B minor; arr.] *Suite no. 2 in B minor, BWV 1067, arranged for flute and piano.* International Music 2470, $5.50.

863 Griffes, Charles Tomlinson, 1884–1920

[Poem; arr.] *Poem for flute and orchestra,* ed. by James Galway. G. Schirmer ED3870, $8.95.

864 Hanson, Howard, 1896–1981

[Serenade, flute, harp, string orchestra, op. 35; arr.] *Serenade for flute and orchestra, op. 35.* C. Fischer W1923, $7.

865 Ibert, Jacques, 1890–1962

[Concertos, flute, orchestra; arr.] *Concerto for flute.* Leduc AL18.761, $18.30.

866 Kennan, Kent, 1913–

[Night soliloquy; arr.] *Night soliloquy, for flute and orchestra.* Eastman School of Music/C. Fischer 30215-6, $6.

867 Martin, Frank, 1890–1974

[Ballades, flute, string orchestra; arr.] *Ballade for flute, string orchestra, and piano.* Universal UE18034, $14.95.

868 * Mozart, Wolfgang Amadeus, 1756–1791

[Concertos, flute, orchestra, K. 313, G major; arr.] *Concerto for flute in G major, K. 313.* Amadeus BP2693, $14.95; Bärenreiter BA6817, $21; Breitkopf & Härtel EB2576, $14; International Music 1962, ed. by Jean-Pierre Rampal, $7.25.

869 * Mozart, Wolfgang Amadeus, 1756–1791

[Concertos, oboe, orchestra, K. 314, C major; arr.] *Concerto for flute [transposed to] D major, K. 314.* Amadeus BP2694, $10; Bärenreiter BA6818, $17.50; Breitkopf & Härtel EB2577, $13; International Music 2092, ed. by Jean-Pierre Rampal, $7.25.

870 * Nielsen, Carl, 1865–1931

[Concertos, flute, orchestra; arr.] *Concerto for flute.* Dan Fog Musikforlag, $30.

871 Telemann, Georg Philipp, 1681–1767

[Overtures, recorder, strings, continuo, TWV 55:a2, A minor; arr.] *Suite in A minor for recorder or flute, strings, and continuo.* Amadeus BP366, $19.70; International Music 2260, ed. by Jean-Pierre Rampal, $5.75; G. Schirmer HL50334860, $8.95.

872 Vivaldi, Antonio, 1678–1741

[Concertos, recorder, string orchestra, RV 443, C major; arr.] *Concerto in C major for piccolo (or flute or soprano recorder).* International Music 2782, ed. by Jean-Pierre Rampal, $6; Kunzelmann EES419, $18.30.

Flute Duets

873 Bach, Wilhelm Friedemann, 1710–1784

[Duets, flutes] *Six duets for two flutes.* Breitkopf & Härtel EB8517-8518, 2 v., $13.60 each; International Music 1812-1813, 2 v., $8.75 each.

874 * Hindemith, Paul, 1895–1963

Canonic sonatina, op. 31, no. 3, for 2 flutes. Schott ED2002, $9.95.

875 Kuhlau, Friedrich, 1786–1832

[Duets, flutes, op. 102] *Three duos brillants, op. 102, for two flutes.* C. Fischer CU189, $5; International Music 1359, $8.50.

876 Muczynski, Robert, 1929–

[Duets, flutes, op. 34] *Duos for two flutes, op. 34.* G. Schirmer ST47338, $11.95.

877 * Quantz, Johann Joachim, 1697–1773

[Duets, flutes, op. 2] *Six duets for two flutes, op. 2.* Amadeus BP2070-2071, 2 v., $14 each; Breitkopf & Härtel EB5581-5582, 2 v., $10 each; International Music 2293-2294, 2 v., $9.75 each.

878 * Telemann, Georg Philipp, 1681–1767

[Sonatas, flutes (2), op. 2] *Six sonatas for two flutes, op. 2.* Bärenreiter BA2979-2980, 2 v., $10.50 each; International Music 2744-2745, ed. by Jean-Pierre Rampal, 2 v., $6.75 each.

Flute Methods and Studies

879 * Andersen, Joachim, 1847–1909

[Grosse Etüden] *Twenty-four etudes, op. 15.* International Music 1664, $7; Novello 351257, corrected ed. by Trevor Wye, $14.95; Southern Music B419, $5.

880 Andersen, Joachim, 1847–1909

[Kleine Studien, flute, op. 63] *Twenty-four technical studies for flute, op. 63.* International Music 2038-2039, 2 v., $7.50 each.

881 Bozza, Eugène, 1905–

[Études sur des modes karnatiques] *Dix études sur des modes karnatiques pour flûte.* Leduc AL25.050, $14.95.

882   Cavally, Robert

Melodious and progressive studies for flute. Southern Music B413, B414, B426, B301, 4 v., $7, $8, $10, $12.

883   Filas, Thomas J.

Top register studies for flute: 90 melodious studies. C. Fischer O4739, $7.95.

884   Jeanjean, Paul, 1874–1928

Études modernes pour flûte. Leduc AL24.726, $30.

885   Karg-Elert, Sigfrid, 1877–1933

[Capricen, flute, op. 107] *Thirty studies for flute solo, op. 107.* International Music 1383, $5.75.

886   Moyse, Marcel, 1889–1984

Gammes et arpèges: 480 exercices. Leduc AL18.165, $20.95.

887   Moyse, Marcel, 1889–1984

Tone development through interpretation, for the flute and other wind instruments [some works with piano accompaniment]. McGinnis & Marx 5750, $15.

888 * Taffanel, Claude Paul, 1844–1908, and Philippe Gaubert, 1879–1941

[Méthode complète de flûte. Polyglot] *Méthode complète de flûte: in French, German, English, and Spanish.* New ed. Leduc AL16.588, 2 v. in 1, $66.95.

Oboe and English Horn Music

Solo Oboe Music

889   Arnold, Malcolm, 1921–

[Fantasies, oboe, op. 90] *Fantasy for oboe, op. 90.* Faber F323, $6.95.

890 * Britten, Benjamin, 1913–1976

[Metamorphoses after Ovid] *Six metamorphoses after Ovid, op. 49, for oboe solo.* Boosey & Hawkes WOB 35, $12.50.

891   Křenek, Ernst, 1900–1991

[Sonatinas, oboe] *Sonatina for oboe solo.* Rongwen, $5.50.

892   Persichetti, Vincent, 1915–1987

[Parable, no. 15] *Parable for oboe, Parable XV, op. 128.* Presser 164-00094, $2.95.

Oboe/English Horn and Keyboard Music

893   Carter, Elliott, 1908–

[Pastorale, English horn, piano] *Pastorale for English horn and piano.* Merion 144-40005, $14.50.

894   *Classical and romantic pieces for oboe and piano.* Arranged by Watson Forbes. Oxford University Press 0-19-356541-2, $15.95.

895   Dubois, Pierre Max, 1930–

[Sonatinas, English horn, piano] *Sonatine for English horn and piano.* Leduc AL23.507, $16.

896 * Handel, George Frideric, 1685–1759

[Sonatas, oboe, continuo] *The three authentic sonatas, oboe and continuo.* Bärenreiter HM242-244, 3 v., $18 each; Nova Music NM100, ed. by David Lasocki, 2nd ed., $15; Peters P3035, $18.70.

897   Hindemith, Paul, 1895–1963

[Sonatas, English horn, piano] *Sonata for English horn and piano.* Schott ED3672, $19.95.

898 * Hindemith, Paul, 1895–1963

[Sonatas, oboe, piano] *Sonata for oboe and piano (1938).* Schott ED3676, $17.95.

899   Milhaud, Darius, 1892–1974

[Sonatinas, oboe, piano, op. 337] *Sonatina for oboe and piano, op. 337.* Durand 524-01134, $37.25.

900 * Poulenc, Francis, 1899–1963

[Sonatas, oboe, piano] *Sonata for oboe and piano.* Chester, $15.95.

901 * Saint-Saëns, Camille, 1835–1921

[Sonatas, oboe, piano, op. 166] *Sonata for oboe and piano, op. 166.* Durand 524-01165, $25; Peters P9196, $33.85.

902 * Schumann, Robert, 1810–1856

[Romances, oboe, piano, op. 94] *Three romances for oboe (or violin or clarinet) and piano, op. 94.* Breitkopf & Härtel EB847, $10; Henle HN427, $10.95; Well-Tempered Press W7008, $4.50.

903 * Telemann, Georg Philipp, 1681–1767

[Sonatas, oboe, continuo, TWV 41:a3, A minor] *Sonata in A minor for oboe and keyboard.* Bärenreiter HM7, $14; Southern Music SS136, $4.50; Zimmermann ZM1892, arranged for oboe and guitar, $9.

904 Telemann, Georg Philipp, 1681–1767

[Sonatas, oboe, continuo, TWV 41:g10, G minor] *Sonata in G minor for oboe and keyboard.* Oxford University Press. OP

905 Vaughan Williams, Ralph, 1872–1958

[Studies in English folksong] *Six studies in English folksong, for English horn and piano.* Galaxy Music 1.5214, $8.95.

Oboe/English Horn Concertos/Piano Reductions

The following section lists works for oboe or English horn (or other solo instrument) and orchestra, with the orchestral score reduced for piano accompaniment. When ordering, specify "arranged for oboe (or English horn) and piano; score and part."

906 * Bach, Johann Sebastian, 1685–1750

[Concertos, harpsichord, string orchestra, BWV 1053, E major; arr.] *Concerto in D major for oboe d'amore, strings, and continuo* [reconstructed and transposed from Bach's *Concerto for harpsichord, BWV 1053*]. Kunzelmann GM921, $26.35.

907 * Bach, Johann Sebastian, 1685–1750

[Concertos, harpsichord, string orchestra, BWV 1055, A major; arr.] *Concerto in A major for oboe d'amore, strings, and continuo* [reconstructed from Bach's *Concerto for harpsichord, BWV 1055*]. Bärenreiter BA5145a, $16.

908 Cimarosa, Domenico, 1749–1801

[Concertos, oboe, chamber orchestra, C major; arr.] *Concerto in C major for oboe and chamber orchestra.* Billaudot, $14.25.

909 Françaix, Jean, 1912–

[L'horloge de flore; arr.] *L'horloge de flore, for oboe and orchestra.* Éditions Musicales Transatlantiques 524-01072, $22.

910 * Handel, George Frideric, 1685–1759

[Concertos, oboe, string orchestra, HWV 287, G minor; arr.] *Concerto no. 3 in G minor, for oboe.* Boosey & Hawkes WOB 15, $11.50; International Music 2738, $7.

911 * Haydn, Joseph, 1732–1809

[Concertos, oboe, orchestra, H. VIIg, C major; arr.] *Concerto in C major for oboe.* Breitkopf Härtel EB5349, $18.60; Oxford University Press, $24.95.

912 * Marcello, Alessandro, 1669–1747

[Concertos, oboe, string orchestra, D minor; arr.] *Concerto in D minor for oboe.* International Music 1289, $5.75; Musica Rara MR1891a, $9.50.

913 Milhaud, Darius, 1892–1974

[Concertos, oboe, orchestra, op. 365; arr.] *Oboe concerto, op. 365.* Heugel 524-01133, $15.

914 * Mozart, Wolfgang Amadeus, 1756–1791

[Concertos, oboe, orchestra, K. 314, C major; arr.] *Concerto for oboe in C major, K. 314.* Bärenreiter BA4856a, $16.50; Boosey & Hawkes WOB 7, $15.50.

915 Persichetti, Vincent, 1915–1987

[Concertos, English horn, string orchestra, op. 137A; arr.] *English horn concerto,* arranged for English horn and piano by the composer. Elkan-Vogel 164-00143, $8.

916 Piston, Walter, 1894–1976

[Fantasies, English horn, harp, string orchestra; arr.] *Fantasy for English horn, harp, and strings.* Associated Music. OP

917 Strauss, Richard, 1864–1949

[Concertos, oboe, orchestra; arr.] *Concerto for oboe and small orchestra.* Boosey & Hawkes WOB 13, $28.

918 Vaughan Williams, Ralph, 1872–1958

[Concertos, oboe, string orchestra; arr.] *Concerto for oboe and strings.* Oxford University Press 0-19-369231-7, $24.95.

Oboe/English Horn Methods and Studies

919 * Andraud, Albert J., b. 1884

Practical and progressive oboe method: reed making, melodious and technical studies. Southern Music B100, $25.

920 Bach, Johann Sebastian, 1685–1750

[Selections] *One hundred and five difficult passages from the works of J. S. Bach, for oboe, oboe d'amore, and oboe da caccia (cor anglais).* Selected and ed. by Evelyn Rothwell. Boosey & Hawkes WOB 39, $21.

921 * Barret, Apollon Marie Rose, 1804–1879

A complete method for the oboe. Boosey & Hawkes WOB 43, $30.

922   Ferling, Franz Wilhelm, 1796–1874

[Etudes, oboe, op. 31] *Forty-eight studies for the oboe, op. 31.* Universal UE17514, $11.95.

923   * Rothwell, Evelyn

Oboe technique. 3rd ed. Oxford University Press, $6.

924   Sellner, Joseph, 1787–1843

Méthode pour hautbois ou saxophone. New ed., rev. by Louis Bleuzet. Billaudot, 3 v., $16.50 each.

925   Voxman, Himie, 1912–

Selected studies for oboe: advanced etudes, scales and arpeggios in all major and minor keys. Rubank 04470710, $6.95.

926   Voxman, Himie, 1912– and Wm. (William) Gower

Rubank advanced method for oboe: an outline method designed to follow any of the various elementary or intermediate methods. Rubank 04470410, 04470420, 2 v., $6.95 each.

Clarinet Music

Solo Clarinet Music

927   * Osborne, Willson, 1906–1979

[Rhapsodies, clarinet] *Rhapsody for clarinet.* Peters P6006, $8.30.

928   * Stravinsky, Igor, 1882–1971

[Pieces, clarinet] *Three pieces for clarinet solo.* Chester 0-7119-2238-1, $7.95; International Music 2453, $6.25.

Clarinet and Keyboard Music

929   Berg, Alban, 1885–1935

[Stücke, clarinet, piano, op. 5] *Four pieces for clarinet and piano, op. 5.* Universal UE7485, $17.95.

930   * Brahms, Johannes, 1833–1897

[Sonatas, clarinet, piano, op. 120] *Sonatas for clarinet and piano, op. 120, no. 1–2.* Henle HN274, $22.95; Peters P3896, $21.30.

—OR INDIVIDUALLY—

931   * Brahms, Johannes, 1833–1897

[Sonatas, clarinet, piano, op. 120. No. 1] *Sonata for clarinet and piano in F minor, op. 120, no. 1.* Boosey & Hawkes WCB 89, $9.75; Breitkopf & Härtel EB6915, $11; International Music 418, $8.25; Wiener Urtext UT50015, $11.95.

932   * Brahms, Johannes, 1833–1897

[Sonatas, clarinet, piano, op. 120. No. 2] *Sonata for clarinet and piano in E♭ major, op. 120, no. 2.* Boosey & Hawkes WCB 90, $12.50; Breitkopf & Härtel EB6917, $11; International Music 419, $6.50; Wiener Urtext UT50016, $11.95.

933   * Debussy, Claude, 1862–1918

[Rhapsodies, clarinet, piano] *Première rhapsodie for clarinet and piano.* Durand 524-01336, $16.75; Chester CH55737, $11.95.

934   Finzi, Gerald, 1901–1956

[Bagatelles, clarinet, piano] *Five bagatelles for clarinet and piano.* Boosey & Hawkes WCB 21, $9.75.

935   * Goodman, Benny, 1909–1986

Benny Goodman, composer/artist: transcriptions for clarinet and piano. Hal Leonard HL00026703, $14.95.

936   * Hindemith, Paul, 1895–1963

[Sonatas, clarinet, piano] *Sonata for clarinet and piano.* Schott ED3641, $17.95.

937   * Poulenc, Francis, 1899–1963

[Sonatas, clarinet, piano] *Sonata for clarinet and piano.* Chester JWC1618, $19.95.

938   * Schumann, Robert, 1810–1856

[Fantasiestücke, clarinet, piano, op. 73] *Fantasy pieces for B♭ clarinet (or violin or cello) and piano, op. 73.* Henle HN416, $9.95; International Music 1789, $5.75; Peters P2366c, $13.15.

939   * Weber, Carl Maria von, 1786–1826

Grand duo concertante, for clarinet and piano, op. 48. International Music 1582, $8.50; Peters P3317, $22.25; Well-Tempered Press W7006, $7.50.

Clarinet Concertos/Piano Reductions

The following section lists works for clarinet and orchestra, with the orchestral score reduced for piano accompaniment. When ordering, specify "arranged for clarinet and piano; score and part."

940   * Copland, Aaron, 1900–1990

[Concertos, clarinet, string orchestra; arr.] *Concerto, clarinet and string orchestra with harp and piano.* Boosey & Hawkes WCB 8, $17.

941   * Mozart, Wolfgang Amadeus, 1756–1791

[Concertos, clarinet, orchestra, K. 622, A major; arr.] *Concerto in A major for clarinet, K. 622.* Bärenreiter

BA4733a, $20; Breitkopf & Härtel EB8523, $18; International Music 1878, $7.75.

942 * Weber, Carl Maria von, 1786–1826

[Concertinos, clarinet, orchestra, op. 26, E♭ major; arr.] *Concertino in E♭ major for clarinet, op. 26.* Breitkopf & Härtel EB1585, $11; International Music 1997, $5.50.

943 * Weber, Carl Maria von, 1786–1826

[Concertos, clarinet, orchestra, no. 1, op. 73, F minor; arr.] *Concerto no. 1 in F minor for clarinet, op. 73.* Breitkopf & Härtel EB1540, $15.50; International Music 1673, $7.25.

944 * Weber, Carl Maria von, 1786–1826

[Concertos, clarinet, orchestra, no. 2, op. 74, E♭ major; arr.] *Concerto no. 2 in E♭ major for clarinet, op. 74.* Breitkopf & Härtel 1541, $16; International Music 1674, $8.

Clarinet Duets

945 Persichetti, Vincent, 1915–1987

[Serenades, no. 13, op. 95] *Serenade no. 13 for two clarinets, op. 95.* Elkan-Vogel 164-00041, $2.

946 * Poulenc, Francis, 1899–1963

[Sonatas, clarinets (2)] *Sonata for two clarinets in B♭ and A.* Chester CH219, $11.95; Masters Music M2374, $5.50.

Clarinet Methods and Studies

947 * Baermann, Carl, 1811–1885

[Vollständige Clarinett-Schule, T. 1, op. 63] *Baermann complete method, op. 63.* Authentic ed. C. Fischer O32-O33, 2 v., $10.95 each.

948 Benham, Charles

Pro Art clarinet method. Pro Art, 2 v., $7 each.

949 Hendrickson, Clarence V.

Hendrickson method for clarinet. Belwin-Mills, 2 v., $7 each.

950 Jacobs, Frederick

Learn to play the clarinet! Alfred Music, 2 v., $5.95 each.

951 * Rose, Cyrille, 1830–1903

[Etudes, clarinet. Selections] *Forty studies for clarinet.* C. Fischer O437-O438, 2 v., $7.50; International Music 2162-2163, 2 v., $5 each.

952 * Rose, Cyrille, 1830–1903

[Etudes, clarinet. Selections] *Thirty-two etudes for clarinet.* C. Fischer O439, $7.50; International Music 2108, $6.25.

953 * Voxman, Himie, 1912–

Rubank advanced method for clarinet. Rubank, 2 v., $6.95 each.

Alto, Bass, and Contrabass Clarinet Methods and Studies

954 * Porter, Neal

Alto clarinet student: a method for individual instruction. Belwin-Mills, 3 v., $5.50 each.

955 * Porter, Neal

Bass clarinet student: a method for individual instruction. Belwin-Mills, 3 v., $5.50 each.

956 Rhoads, William E., 1918–

Eighteen selected studies for alto and bass clarinet. Southern Music B406, $9.

957 Rhoads, William E., 1918–

Thirty-five technical studies for alto and bass clarinet. Southern Music B110, $10.

958 Rhoads, William E., 1918–

Twenty-one foundation studies for alto and bass clarinet. Southern Music B217, $11.95.

959 * Voxman, Himie, 1912–

Introducing the alto or bass clarinet: a transfer method for intermediate instruction. Rubank, $5.

Bassoon Music

Solo Bassoon Music

960 Adler, Samuel, 1928–

[Canto, no. 12] *Canto XII: four concert etudes for bassoon solo.* Ludwig Music S-3D8, $11.50.

961 Arnold, Malcolm, 1921–

[Fantasies, bassoon, op. 86] *Fantasy for bassoon, op. 86.* Faber Music F500285, $6.95.

962 Jacob, Gordon, 1895–1984

[Partitas, bassoon] *Partita for solo bassoon.* Oxford University Press 0-19-357364-4, $5.

963 *Neue russische Musik für Fagott Solo.* Exempla nova, no. 141. Sikorski 1841, $27.95.

964 * Osborne, Willson, 1906–1979

[Rhapsody, bassoon] *Rhapsody for bassoon.* Peters P6005, $8.30.

965 * Perle, George, 1915–

[Inventions, bassoon] *Three inventions for solo bassoon.* Presser 114-40131, $3.50.

966 * Persichetti, Vincent, 1915–1987

[Parable, no. 4] *Parable for solo bassoon (Parable IV), op. 110.* Elkan-Vogel 164-00083, $3.50.

967 * Stockhausen, Karlheinz, 1928–

[In Freundschaft, bassoon] *In friendship, for bassoon, Werk Nr. 46 3/4, 1977.* 1st ed. Stockhausen-Verlag, $19.

Bassoon and Keyboard Music

968 Bozza, Eugène, 1905–

[Récit, sicilienne et rondo, bassoon, piano] *Récit, sicilienne et rondo, for bassoon and piano.* Leduc AL21.154, $8.45.

969 * Cascarino, Romeo, 1922–

[Sonata, bassoon, piano] *Sonata for bassoon and piano.* Southern Music ST-646, $5.

970 Dutilleux, Henri, 1916–

Sarabande et cortège, for bassoon and piano. Leduc AL20.097, $20.25

971 * Etler, Alvin, 1913–1973

[Sonatas, bassoon, piano] *Sonata for bassoon and piano (1952).* Associated Music HL50223680, $13.50.

972 * Galliard, John Ernest, 1687?–1749

[Sonatas, bassoon, continuo] *6 sonatas for bassoon and piano,* ed. by Arthur Weisberg; realization by Karl Heinz Füssl. International Music 2114, 2116, 2 v., $8 each.

973 * Hindemith, Paul, 1895–1963

[Sonatas, bassoon, piano] *Sonata for bassoon and piano.* Schott ED3686, $17.95.

974 * Pierné, Gabriel, 1863–1937

[Solo de concert] *Concertpiece, op. 35, for bassoon and piano.* International Music 1617, $6.

975 * Saint-Saëns, Camille, 1835–1921

[Sonatas, bassoon, piano, op. 168] *Sonata for bassoon and piano, op. 168.* Durand 524-01773, $31.

976 * Tansman, Alexandre, 1897–1986

[Sonatinas, bassoon, piano] *Sonatine for bassoon and piano.* Eschig ME6657, $28.50.

977 * Telemann, Georg Philipp, 1681–1767

[Sonatas, bassoon, continuo, TWV 41:f1, F minor] *Sonata in F minor for bassoon (or trombone or baritone) and piano.* International Music 1151, $5.

978 * Weber, Carl Maria von, 1786–1826

[Andante e rondo ongarese; arr.] *Andante and Hungarian rondo, for bassoon and piano.* International Music 1467, $5.50.

Bassoon Concertos/Piano Reductions

The following section lists works for bassoon and orchestra, with the orchestral score reduced for piano accompaniment. When ordering, specify "arranged for bassoon and piano; score and part."

979 Françaix, Jean, 1912–

[Concertos, bassoon, string ensemble; arr.] *Concerto for bassoon and 11 string instruments or piano (1979).* Schott FAG18, $19.95.

980 Hummel, Johann Nepomuk, 1778–1837

[Concertos, bassoon, orchestra, F major; arr.] *Grand concerto for bassoon and orchestra.* Musica Rara MR1505, $9.50.

981 Jolivet, André, 1905–1974

[Concertos, bassoon, string orchestra; arr.] *Concerto for bassoon, string orchestra, harp, and piano (1954).* Heugel 524-01703, $58.25.

982 * Mozart, Wolfgang Amadeus, 1756–1791

[Concertos, bassoon, orchestra, K. 191, B♭ major; arr.] *Concerto in B♭ major for bassoon, K. 191.* Bärenreiter BA4868a, $16.25.

983 Villa-Lobos, Heitor, 1887–1959

[Ciranda das sete notas; arr.] *Ciranda das sete notas, bassoon and string orchestra.* Peer-Southern 60186-368, $12.

984 * Vivaldi, Antonio, 1678–1741

[Concertos, bassoon, string orchestra. Selections; arr.] *Ten bassoon concerti.* G. Schirmer ED2889, ED2921, 2 v., $18.50, $18.

985 * Weber, Carl Maria von, 1786–1826

[Concertos, bassoon, orchestra, op. 75, F major; arr.] *Concerto in F major for bassoon, op. 75.* Universal UE18131, $14.95.

Bassoon Methods and Studies

986   Bitsch, Marcel, 1921–

[Etudes, bassoon] *Four etudes for bassoon.* Leduc AL20.602, $16.85.

987 * Milde, Ludwig

[Etüden, bassoon, op. 24] *Twenty-five studies in scales and chords, op. 24, for bassoon.* International Music 456, $6.

988 * Milde, Ludwig

[Etüden, bassoon, op. 26] *Concert studies, op. 26, for bassoon.* International Music 467, 497, 2 v., $8.25 each.

989   Orefici, Alberto

Twenty melodic studies for bassoon. International Music 2285, $8.50.

990 * Oubradous, Fernand

Enseignement complet du basson. Leduc AL19.634-19.635, AL19.709, 3 v., $33, $39.75, $33.

991   Spencer, William

The art of bassoon playing. Rev. ed. by Frederick A. Mueller. Summy-Birchard, $11.95.

992 * Stadio, Ciro

Passi difficili e a solo per fagotto = Difficult passages and solos for bassoon. Ricordi ER1221, $16.95.

993 * Weissenborn, Julius, 1837–1888

[Fagottstudien, op. 8] *Studies for bassoon.* International Music 1133-1134, 2 v., $6.75 each.

Saxophone Music

Solo Saxophone Music

994 * Bonneau, Paul, 1918–

[Caprices en forme de valse] *Deux caprices en forme de valse, for alto saxophone.* Leduc AL25.803, $23.95.

Saxophone and Keyboard Music

995 * Bozza, Eugène, 1905–

[Aria, saxophone, piano] *Aria for alto saxophone and piano.* Leduc AL19.714, $8.20.

996 * Creston, Paul, 1906–1985

[Sonatas, saxophone, piano, op. 19] *Sonata for Eb alto saxophone and piano, op. 19.* Shawnee Press, $20.

997   Heiden, Bernhard, 1910–

[Sonatas, saxophone, piano] *Sonata for Eb saxophone and piano.* Schott ST11195, $19.95.

998 * Hindemith, Paul, 1895–1963

[Sonatas, alto horn, piano] *Sonata for alto horn (mellophone in Eb) or French horn or alto sax and piano.* Schott ED4635, $19.95.

999   Jacobi, Wolfgang, 1894–

[Sonata, saxophone, piano] *Sonata for alto saxophone and piano.* Bourne 212100, $8.

1000   Lantier, Pierre, 1910–

Sicilienne for alto saxophone and piano. Leduc AL20.261, $11.85.

1001 * Milhaud, Darius, 1892–1974

[Scaramouche; arr.] *Scaramouche: suite for alto saxophone and piano.* Salabert SEAS15280A, $12.95.

1002 * Shorter, Wayne, 1933–

Wayne Shorter for tenor and soprano saxophones. Hal Leonard HL00660210, $16.95.

Saxophone Concertos/Piano Reductions

The following section lists works for saxophone and orchestra or chamber ensemble, with the full score reduced for piano accompaniment. When ordering, specify "arranged for saxophone and piano; score and part."

1003 * Creston, Paul, 1906–1985

[Concertos, saxophone, orchestra, op. 26; arr.] *Concerto for alto saxophone, op. 26.* G. Schirmer ED3546, $17.

1004 * Dubois, Pierre Max, 1930–

[Concertos, saxophone, string orchestra; arr.] *Concerto for alto saxophone and string orchestra.* Leduc AL22.834, $25.15.

1005 * Glazunov, Alexandr Konstantinovich, 1865–1936

[Concertos, saxophone, string orchestra, op. 109, Eb major; arr.] *Concerto in Eb major for alto saxophone, op. 109.* Leduc AL19.256, $18.95.

1006 * Ibert, Jacques, 1890–1962

[Concertino da camera; arr.] *Concertino da camera for alto saxophone and eleven instruments.* Leduc AL19.185, $23.90.

1007 * Villa-Lobos, Heitor, 1887–1959

[Fantasia, saxophone, chamber orchestra; arr.] *Fantasia for soprano or tenor saxophone and chamber orchestra.* Peer-Southern 60446-357, $12.

Saxophone Methods and Studies

1008 Jacobs, Frederick

Learn to play the saxophone! Alfred Music, 2 v., $6.50, $5.95.

1009 * Labanchi, Gaetano, 1829–1905

33 concert etudes. C. Fischer O2329-O2489, 2 v., $7, $8.95.

1010 * Mayeur, L. (Louis), 1837–1894

Grand collection of scales, arpeggio exercises and studies in interpretation for saxophone. C. Fischer. OP

1011 Pease, Donald J.

Pro Art saxophone method. Pro Art/Belwin, 2 v., $3.95, $5.50.

1012 * Voxman, Himie, 1912–

Rubank advanced method for saxophone. Rubank, 2 v., $6.95 each.

Recorder Music

The following music distributor specializes in recorder music:

> Courtly Music Unlimited, Inc.
> 84 Main Street
> Warrensburg, NY 12885
> (800) 274-2443 phone
> (518) 623-2869 fax
> courtlym@aol.com

Solo Recorder Music

1013 Eyck, Jacob van, 1589 or 1590–1657

Der Fluyten Lust-hof, chiefly for solo descant recorder, with several recorder duets. Amadeus Press BP 704-706, 3 v., $25 each.

1014 Linde, Hans Martin

Music for a bird, for treble recorder. Schott OFB0048, $9.95.

1015 Moser, Roland, 1943–

Alrune, for treble recorder. Hug GH 11464. OP

1016 Virgiliano, Aurelio, fl. 1600

[Dolcimelo. Libro 2. Selections] *Thirteen ricercate from "Il dolcimelo" for solo treble instrument,* ed. by Bernard Thomas. London Pro Musica LPM REP 1, $10.50.

Recorder and Keyboard Music

1017 Barsanti, Francesco, 1690–1772

[Sonatas, recorder, continuo, op. 1. Selections] *Two sonatas for recorder and continuo,* ed. by Gwilym Beechey. Musica da camera, no. 9. Oxford University Press, $9.75.

1018 Berkeley, Lennox, Sir, 1903–

[Sonatinas, recorder, piano] *Sonatina for treble recorder or flute and piano, op. 13.* Schott OFB1040, $12.95.

1019 Corelli, Arcangelo, 1653–1713

[Sonatas, violin, continuo, op. 5. No. 4; arr.] *Sonata in F major, op. 5, no. 4, for treble recorder and basso continuo,* ed. by John Madden. Musica Rara MR1899, $9.95.

1020 * Corelli, Arcangelo, 1653–1713

[Sonatas, violin, continuo, op. 5. No. 12; arr.] *La folia, op. 5, no. 12, for treble recorder and basso continuo,* ed. by Masahiro Arita. Zen-On Music R-145, $17.

1021 Dieupart, Charles, ca. 1670–ca. 1740

[Suittes de clavessin. No. 1; arr.] *Suite I for recorder and continuo in G major,* ed. by Hermann Moeck. Moeck EM 1002, $16.95.

1022 *The division recorder: a complete collection of English divisions on a ground bass for alto (treble) recorder and continuo (c. 1680–1708),* ed. by Peter Holman. Schattinger-International H1021, 2 v., v.1 $6.95, v.2 OP.

1023 * Handel, George Frideric, 1685–1759

[Sonatas, recorder, continuo] *The complete sonatas for treble recorder and continuo,* ed. by David Lasocki and Walter Bergmann. Faber Music F0566, $21.95.

1024 Hotteterre, Jacques, 1674–1763

[Pieces, op. 2. Suite, no. 1] *Suite in F major, op. 2, no. 1, for treble recorder and basso continuo,* ed. by David Lasocki. Nova Music NM162, $9.50.

1025 Paisible, James, 1656?–1721

[Sonatas, recorder, continuo. Selections] *Five sonatas for treble recorder and continuo,* ed. by Marianne Mezger. Dolce Edition DOL 250, $19.50.

1026 Rubbra, Edmund, 1901–1986

Meditazioni sopra "Coeurs désolés," op. 67, for recorder and harpsichord. Lengnick 3689, price not available.

1027 Sammartini, Giovanni Batista, 1700 (ca.)–1775

[Concertos, recorder, string orchestra, F major; arr.] *Concerto in F major for descant recorder, strings, and basso continuo, arranged for recorder and keyboard,* ed. by Winfried Michel. Amadeus BP 420, $10.

1028 Schickhard, Johann Christian, ca. 1680–1762

[Alphabet de la musique; arr.] *Twenty-four sonatas in all keys for recorder and continuo, op. 30,* ed. by Frans Brüggen and Walter Bergmann. Zen-On Music, 4 v., $25.50, $17.50, $17.50, $17.50.

1029 Telemann, Georg Philipp, 1681–1767

[Concertos, recorder, string orchestra, C major; arr.] *Concerto in C major for treble recorder, string orchestra, and harpsichord, arranged for recorder and keyboard,* ed. by Ilse Hechler. Moeck EM 1065, $25.

1030 * Telemann, Georg Philipp, 1681–1767

[Essercizii musici. Solo, no. 4] *Sonata in D minor from "Essercizii musici" for treble recorder and continuo,* ed. by Hugo Ruf. Schott OFB0104, $9.95.

1031 * Telemann, Georg Philipp, 1681–1767

[Essercizii musici. Solo, no. 10] *Sonata in C major from "Essercizii musici" for treble recorder and continuo,* ed. by Hugo Ruf. Schott OFB0103, $9.95.

1032 * Telemann, Georg Philipp, 1681–1767

[Getreue Music-meister. Sonatas, recorder, continuo] *4 sonatas from "Der getreue Musikmeister" for treble recorder and basso continuo,* ed. by Dietz Degen. Rev. ed. Bärenreiter HM6, $15.

1033 * Vivaldi, Antonio, 1678–1741

[Concertos, recorder, string orchestra, RV 441, C minor; arr.] *Concerto in C minor, P. 440, for treble recorder, strings, and basso continuo, arranged for recorder and keyboard,* ed. by David Lasocki. Musica Rara MR1204, $8.35.

1034 * Vivaldi, Antonio, 1678–1741

[Concertos, recorder, string orchestra, RV 444, C major; arr.] *Concerto in C major for piccolo or flute or soprano recorder and piano,* ed. by Yury Arbatsky. McGinnis & Marx, $8.

Music for Recorder Ensemble (Two or More Recorders)

1035 Bassano, Augustine, d. 1604

[Works] *Pavans and galliards in 5 parts,* ed. by Peter Holman. Parts. Royal wind music, v. 1. Nova Music NM201, $15.

1036 Bassano, Jerome, 1559–1635

[Fantasias, voices (5)] *Four fantasias in 5 parts,* ed. by Peter Holman. Parts. Royal wind music, v. 2. Nova Music NM202, $10.50.

1037 Hindemith, Paul, 1895–1963

[Plöner Musiktag. Abendkonzert. Trio] *Trio for recorders from "Plöner Musiktag."* Parts. Schott ST10094B, $7.95.

1038 Loeillet, John, 1680–1730

[Trio sonatas, op. 1. No. 1] *Sonata in F major, op. 1, no. 1 (Priestman IX) for treble recorder, oboe and basso continuo,* ed. by R. P. Block. Score and parts. Musica Rara MR1973, $10.70.

1039 Mancini, Henry, 1924–1994

[Pink Panther; arr.] *On the trail of the Pink Panther.* Arranged for recorder quartet by Paul Leenhouts. Parts. Moeck ED 2805, $29.95.

1040 * *The Schott recorder consort anthology,* ed. by Bernard Thomas. Parts. Schott ST12387-12392, 6 v., $19.95 each.

1041 Staeps, Hans Ulrich, 1909–

Reihe kleine Duette, for two treble recorders in F. Parts. Schott OFB0094, $7.95.

1042 * Telemann, Georg Philipp, 1681–1767

[Getreue Music-meister. Trio sonata, recorders, continuo, C major] *Trio sonata in C major from "Der getreue Musikmeister," for 2 treble recorders and basso continuo,* ed. by Dietz Degen. Rev. ed. Score and parts. Bärenreiter HM10, $9.

1043 Vaughan Williams, Ralph, 1872–1958

[Suites, pipes (4)] *Suite for 4 pipes or recorders.* Parts. Oxford University Press, OP.

Recorder Methods and Studies

1044   Brüggen, Frans, 1934–

Five etudes voor vingerveiligheid, altblokfluit = Five studies for finger control, treble recorder. Broekmans & Van Poppel 712, $9.

1045   Burakoff, Gerald, and William E. Hettrick

Sweet pipes recorder book: a method for adults and older beginners. Sweet Pipes, 2 v., v.1, soprano recorder, $5.25; v.2, alto recorder, $3.75.

1046 **   Donington, Margaret, and Robert Donington, 1907–

Scales, arpeggios, and exercises for the recorder. Oxford University Press, $6.50.

1047 *   Hauwe, Walter van

The modern recorder player. Schott ST12150, ST12270, ST12361, 3 v., $25, $29.95, $29.95.

1048 *   Linde, Hans Martin

Neuzeitliche Übungsstücke für die Altblockflöte = Modern exercises for treble recorder. Schott ED4797, $11.95.

1049   Staeps, Hans Ulrich, 1909–

Das tägliche Pensum: Übungen für fortschreitende Spieler der Altblockflöte in F. Universal UE12614, $9.95.

Music for Solo Brass

Compiled by
**Wayne Shoaf (horn, trumpet and cornet, trombone, and tuba),
Norbert Carnovale (trumpet and cornet),
Edie Tibbits (trombone), and Brad Short (tuba)**

The following company specializes in music for brass instruments. Its annual catalog can be used for bibliographic information as well as availability and prices:

Robert King Music Sales, Inc.
140 Main Street
North Easton, MA 02356-1499
(no telephone number available for orders)
(508) 238-2571 fax

Horn Music

Solo Horn Music

1050 Buyanovsky, Vitaly

[Pieces, horn] *Pieces for solo horn.* McCoy's Horn Library, $15.

Horn and Piano Music

1051 * Beethoven, Ludwig van, 1770–1827

[Sonatas, horn, piano, op. 17, F major] *Sonata in F major for horn and piano, op. 17.* Amadeus BP670,

$13; Breitkopf & Härtel EB7404, $15; C. Fischer W1631, $5; Henle HN498, $11.95; International Music 1205, $5.75; G. Schirmer ED3316, ed. by Barry Tuckwell, $7.50.

1052 Bozza, Eugène, 1905–

En forêt, for horn in F and piano. Leduc AL19.955, $18.25.

1053 Corelli, Arcangelo, 1653–1713

[Sonatas, violin, continuo, op. 5. No. 10; arr.] *Sonata in F major for horn and piano.* Editions Musicus 37, $3.50.

1054 * Dukas, Paul, 1865–1935

[Villanelle, horn, piano] *Villanelle, for horn and piano.* Masters Music M1686, $4.95.

1055 * Hindemith, Paul, 1895–1963

[Sonatas, horn, piano (1939)] *Sonata for horn and piano.* Schott ED3642, $17.95.

1056 Kogan, Lev, 1927–

Hassidic suite, for horn and piano. Israel Brass Woodwind Publications, $15.

1057 Musgrave, Thea, 1928–

[Music, horn, piano] *Music for horn and piano.* Chester JWC448, $24.95.

1058 Poulenc, Francis, 1899–1963

[Elegies, horn, piano] *Elégie in memory of Dennis Brain, for horn and piano.* Chester JWC1607, $11.95.

1059 Rheinberger, Joseph, 1839–1901

[Sonatas, horn, piano, op. 178, E♭ major] *Sonata for horn and piano in E♭ major, op. 178.* Schott COR 6, $11.95.

1060 * Schumann, Robert, 1810–1856

[Adagio und Allegro, horn, piano, op. 70, A♭ major] *Adagio and allegro in A♭ major for horn and piano, op. 70.* Breitkopf & Härtel EB842, $8.50; Billaudot 3356, $11.75; International Music 1542, $6; G. Schirmer ED3298, ed. by Barry Tuckwell, $9.95; Well-Tempered Press W7034, $5.50.

1061 *Solos for the horn player with piano accompaniment,* ed. by Mason Jones. G. Schirmer ED2462, $15.95.

1062 Strauss, Richard, 1864–1949

[Andantes, horn, piano, AV 86a, C major] *Andante for horn and piano in C major, op. posth. 86a.* Boosey & Hawkes BHB 13, $14.

1063 Wilder, Alec, 1907–1980

[Sonatas, horn, piano, no. 1] *Sonata no. 1 for horn and piano (1958).* Margun Music AW300, $10.

Horn Concertos/Piano Reductions

The following section lists works for horn and orchestra, with the orchestral score reduced for piano accompaniment. When ordering, specify "arranged for horn and piano; score and part."

1064 * Haydn, Joseph, 1732–1809

[Concertos, horn, orchestra, H. VIId, 3, D major; arr.] *Concerto no. 1 in D major for horn.* Boosey & Hawkes BHB 8, $25; Breitkopf & Härtel EB3031, $13.50; International Music 2736, $6.50.

1065 * Haydn, Joseph, 1732–1809

[Concertos, horn, orchestra, H. VIId, 4, D major; arr.] *Concerto no. 2 in D major for horn.* Boosey &

Hawkes BHB 9, $25; Breitkopf & Härtel EB3032, $15; Henle HN461, $9.95; International Music 2737, $6.50.

1066 * Hindemith, Paul, 1895–1963

[Concertos, horn, orchestra (1949); arr.] *Concerto for horn (1949).* Schott ED4024, $19.95.

1067 * Mozart, Wolfgang Amadeus, 1756–1791

[Concertos, horn, orchestra; arr.] *Four horn concertos and Concert rondo,* ed. by Barry Tuckwell. G. Schirmer LB1807, $13.95.

—OR INDIVIDUALLY—

1068 * Mozart, Wolfgang Amadeus, 1756–1791

[Concertos, horn, orchestra, K. 412, D major; arr.] *Concerto for horn, no. 1 in D major, K. 412.* Breitkopf & Härtel EB2561, $12.95; C. Fischer CU738, $5.50; International Music 1811, $6; Masters Music M1687, $5.50; Southern Music SS340, $7.50.

1069 * Mozart, Wolfgang Amadeus, 1756–1791

[Concertos, horn, orchestra, K. 417, E♭ major; arr.] *Concerto for horn, no. 2 in E♭ major, K. 417.* Breitkopf & Härtel EB2562, $12.95; International Music 1954, $7; Kalmus K 03705, $5.50; Southern Music SS341, $8.95.

1070 * Mozart, Wolfgang Amadeus, 1756–1791

[Concertos, horn, orchestra, K. 447, E♭ major; arr.] *Concerto for horn, no. 3 in E♭ major, K. 447.* Breitkopf & Härtel EB2563, $12.95; C. Fischer CU741, $6.95; International Music 1569, $6.50; Kalmus K 03709, $7.95; Southern Music SS342, $9.50.

1071 * Mozart, Wolfgang Amadeus, 1756–1791

[Concertos, horn, orchestra, K. 495, E♭ major; arr.] *Concerto for horn, no. 4 in E♭ major, K. 495.* Breitkopf & Härtel EB2564, $12.95; International Music 1991, $5; Southern Music SS343, $8.95.

1072 * Mozart, Wolfgang Amadeus, 1756–1791

[Rondos, horn, orchestra, K. 371, E♭ major; arr.] *Concert rondo for horn in E♭ major, K. 371.* Breitkopf & Härtel EB3033, $12; International Music 2739, $5.25; Kalmus K 04529, $5.50; Southern Music SS338, $4.50.

1073 * Saint-Saëns, Camille, 1835–1921

[Romances, horn, orchestra, op. 36; arr.] *Romance for horn and piano, op. 36.* Editions Musicus 879, $3.75; International Music 1521, $4; Masters Music M1989, $3.50.

1074 * Strauss, Richard, 1864–1949

[Concertos, horn, orchestra, no. 1, op. 11, E♭ major; arr.] *Concerto for horn, no. 1 in E♭ major, op. 11.* C. Fischer CU750, $8; International Music 1715, $5; Kalmus K 04130, $4; G. Schirmer LB1888, $6.95; Universal UE1039, $11.95.

1075 Strauss, Richard, 1864–1949

[Concertos, horn, orchestra, no. 2, E♭ major; arr.] *Concerto for horn, no. 2 in E♭ major.* Boosey & Hawkes BHB 1, $23.

Horn Duets

1076 Mozart, Wolfgang Amadeus, 1756–1791

[Duets, basset horns, K. 487; arr.] *12 pieces for 2 horns, K. 487.* Parts. Doblinger DM477, $9; International Music 2702, $5.50; McGinnis & Marx MM1076, $13; Medici Music Press FF01, $16.

Horn Methods and Studies

1077 * Gallay, Jacques François, 1795–1864

[Caprices, horn, op. 32] *Twelve grand caprices, op. 32.* Billaudot 534-00838, $13.50; International Music 2289, $7; Leduc AL20.545, $15.

1078 * Gallay, Jacques François, 1795–1864

[Préludes mesurés et non mesurés] *Forty preludes, op. 27.* International Music 2290, $6.50.

1079 * Kling, Henri, 1842–1918

[Etudes, horn] *Forty characteristic etudes for French horn.* International Music 1572, $8.50; Southern Music B131, $6.

1080 Kopprasch, G.

[Etudes, alto horn, op. 5] *Sixty selected studies.* C. Fischer O2790-O2791, 2 v., $7.50 each.

1081 Maxime-Alphonse

[Études nouvelles mélodiques et progressives, horn] *200 new studies for horn.* Leduc, 6 v., $14.50 each.

1082 Pottag, Max P., and Albert J. Andraud, b. 1884, editors

Selected melodious progressive and technical studies for French horn. Southern Music B134, B417, 2 v., $16.95 each.

1083 Reynolds, Verne, 1926–

[Etudes, horn] *Forty-eight etudes for French horn.* G. Schirmer ED2422, $11.95.

Trumpet and Cornet Music

Solo Trumpet Music

1084 Arnold, Malcolm, 1921–

[Fantasies, trumpet, op. 100] *Fantasy for B♭ trumpet, op. 100.* Faber Music F0322, $2.75.

Trumpet/Cornet and Piano Music

1085 Bernstein, Leonard, 1918–1990

Rondo for Lifey, for trumpet and piano. Boosey & Hawkes BAB 53, $6.75.

1086 *Carnaval: 11 solos for cornet and piano,* arranged by Donald Hunsberger. C. Fischer ATF114, $16.95.

1087 Clarke, Herbert L. (Herbert Lincoln), 1867–1945

[Cornet and piano music. Selections] *The music of Herbert L. Clarke: cornet solos with piano accompaniment.* Warner Bros. TF11-12, 2 v., $3.95 each. OP

1088 Clarke, Jeremiah, 1669?–1707

[Trumpet voluntary, harpsichord; arr.] *Trumpet voluntary,* attributed to Henry Purcell. International Music 2009, $3.25.

1089 * Enesco, Georges, 1881–1955

[Legenda] *Legend, for trumpet and piano.* International Music 916, $4.50; Masters Music M1676, $3.95.

1090 * Hindemith, Paul, 1895–1963

[Sonatas, trumpet, piano] *Sonata for trumpet in B♭ and piano.* Schott ED3643, $17.95.

1091 Honegger, Arthur, 1892–1955

[Intrada, trumpet, piano] *Intrada for trumpet in C and piano.* Salabert SEAS14920, $8.95.

1092 Ibert, Jacques, 1890–1962

[Impromptu, trumpet, piano] *Impromptu for trumpet and piano.* Leduc AL20.950, $12.20.

1093 Kennan, Kent, 1913–

[Sonatas, trumpet, piano] *Sonata for trumpet and piano.* Warner Bros. TS26, $10.

1094 Ropartz, Joseph Guy Marie, 1864–1955

[Andante et allegro, trumpet, piano] *Andante and allegro for trumpet in C and piano.* C. Fischer CU572, $5; International Music 1667, $4.

1095 Shapero, Harold, 1920–

[Sonatas, trumpet, piano] *Sonata for trumpet in C and piano.* Southern Music 360-22, $10.

1096 Stevens, Halsey, 1908–1989

[Sonatas, trumpet, piano] *Sonata for trumpet and piano.* Peters P6030, $15.70.

1097 Suderburg, Robert, 1936–

[Chamber music, no. 7] *Chamber music VII: ceremonies for trumpet and piano.* Presser 114-40402, $7.50.

Trumpet Concertos/Piano Reductions

The following section lists works for trumpet and orchestra, with the orchestral score reduced for piano accompaniment. When ordering, specify "arranged for trumpet and piano; score and part."

1098 * Arutiunian, Aleksandr Grigorévich, 1920–

[Concertos, trumpet, orchestra; arr.] *Concerto for trumpet.* International Music 2376, $6.50.

1099 Bloch, Ernest, 1880–1959

[Proclamation; arr.] *Proclamation, for trumpet and orchestra,* piano reduction by the composer. Broude Bros. 1040, $6.

1100 Chaynes, Charles, 1925–

[Concertos, trumpet, orchestra; arr.] *Concerto for C trumpet.* Leduc AL21.694, $18.

1101 Gregson, Edward, 1945–

[Concertos, trumpet, string orchestra; arr.] *Trumpet concerto,* arranged for trumpet and piano by the composer. Novello 12 0579, $17.95.

1102 * Haydn, Joseph, 1732–1809

[Concertos, trumpet, orchestra, H. VIIe, 1, E♭ major; arr.] *Concerto no. 1 in E♭ major for trumpet.* C. Fischer W1834, $7; Haydn-Mozart Presse HMP0223, ed. by H. C. Robbins Landon, $25; Henle HN456, $13.95; G. Schirmer LB1804, $4.95.

1103 * Hummel, Johann Nepomuk, 1778–1837

[Concertos, trumpet, orchestra, E♭ major; arr.] *Concerto in E♭ major for trumpet.* International Music 755, $7; Kalmus K 04550, $9.95; Robert King Music 801, $6.05; Musica Rara MR1176, $7.10; Universal UE25030C, $25.

1104 Mozart, Leopold, 1719–1787

[Concertos, trumpet, orchestra, D major; arr.] *Concerto in D major for trumpet.* Billaudot 1528, $13; C. Fischer W2455, $5; Kunzelmann GM809, $7.50.

1105 Purcell, Henry, 1659–1695

[Sonatas, trumpet, strings, continuo, Z. 850, D major; arr.] *Sonata transcribed for solo trumpet and organ.* Robert King Music, $4.50; Musica Rara MR1073, $5.

1106 Riisager, Knudåge, 1897–1974

[Concertinos, trumpet, string orchestra, op. 29; arr.] *Concertino for C or B♭ trumpet and strings, op. 29.* W. Hansen 3416, $21.95.

1107 Torelli, Giuseppe, 1658–1709

[Sinfonie, trumpet, string orchestra, D major; arr.] *Concerto in D major for trumpet.* International Music 1768, $5.75; Musica Rara MR1156, ed. by Edward Tarr, $5.75.

Trumpet/Cornet Methods and Studies

1108 * Arban, J.-B. (Jean-Baptiste), 1825–1889

[Méthode complète de cornet à pistons et de saxhorn. English] *Arban's complete conservatory method for trumpet.* C. Fischer O21, $25.95.

1109 Beeler, Walter, 1908–

Method book for trumpet: beginner to intermediate. Warner Bros. WB3-4, 2 v., $7.95 each.

1110 Charlier, Theo, 1868–1944

Thirty-six etudes transcendantes, trumpet. Leduc AL20.452, $51.25.

1111 Clarke, Herbert L. (Herbert Lincoln), 1876–1945

Characteristic studies for the cornet. C. Fischer O2281, $9.95.

1112 Clarke, Herbert L. (Herbert Lincoln), 1876–1945

Elementary studies for the cornet. C. Fischer O2581, $9.50.

1113 * Clarke, Herbert L. (Herbert Lincoln), 1876–1945

Technical studies for the cornet. C. Fischer O2280, $10.50.

1114   Colin, Charles, 1913–

Advanced lip flexibilities for trumpet. Charles Colin, $12.

1115   Concone, Giuseppe, 1801–1861

Advanced Concone studies for all brass instruments. Presser 464-00048, $6.95.

1116 * Gower, Wm. (William), and Himie Voxman, 1912–

Rubank advanced method for cornet or trumpet. Rubank 777-72, 1313-75, 2 v., $6.95 each.

1117   Sachse, Ernst

One hundred studies for trumpet, for transposition. International Music 1394, $10.

1118   Saint-Jacome, Louis Antoine, 1830–1898

Grand method for trumpet or cornet, complete. C. Fischer O457, $19.95.

1119   Schlossberg, Max, 1875–1936

Daily drills and technical studies for trumpet. M. Baron, $12.95.

1120   Stamp, James

Warm-ups and studies for trumpet. Editions BIM TP2, $16.

1121   Williams, Ernest S., 1881–1947

Modern method for trumpet or cornet. Charles Colin, $18.

Trombone Music

Solo Trombone Music

1122   Berio, Luciano, 1925–

[Sequenza, no. 5] *Sequenza V, for trombone solo.* Universal UE13725, $19.95.

1123 * Bernstein, Leonard, 1918–1990

[Brass music. Elegy for Mippy II] *Elegy for Mippy II, for unaccompanied trombone.* Boosey & Hawkes BTB 15, $5.75.

1124   Childs, Barney, 1926–

[Sonatas, trombone] *Sonata for solo trombone.* Tritone Press T 38, $15.

1125   Koetsier, Jan, 1911–

[Etudes, trombone, op. 122] *Three etudes for trombone, op. 122 (1990).* Donemus, $15.

1126   Xenakis, Iannis, 1922–

Keren, for trombone solo. Salabert EAS 18450, price not available.

Solo Bass Trombone Music

1127   Hamilton, Iain, 1922–

Spirits of the air, for solo bass trombone. Presser 114-40501, $7.

1128   Skolnik, Walter, 1934–

[Pieces, trombone] *Three pieces for solo bass trombone.* Tenuto 494-01773, $6.

Trombone and Piano Music

1129 * Bassett, Leslie, 1923–

[Sonatas, trombone, piano] *Sonata for trombone and piano.* Robert King Music 810, $5.85.

1130   Bigot, Eugène, 1885–1965

[Impromptu, trombone, piano] *Impromptu for trombone and piano.* Leduc AL17.141, $14.

1131   Hartley, Walter S. (Walter Sinclair), 1927–

[Sonatas, trombone, piano] *Sonata concertante for trombone and piano.* Fema Music, $7.50.

1132 * Hindemith, Paul, 1895–1963

[Sonatas, trombone, piano] *Sonata for trombone and piano (1941).* Schott ED3673, $17.95.

1133   Imbrie, Andrew, 1921–

[Sketches, trombone, piano] *Three sketches for trombone and piano.* Shawnee Press LA96, $10.

1134   Krenek, Ernst, 1900–1991

[Stücke, trombone, piano, op. 198] *Five pieces for trombone and piano.* Bärenreiter BA6107, $11.50.

1135   Nelhybel, Vaclav, 1919–1996

[Suites, trombone, piano] *Suite for trombone and piano.* General Music SU-21, $7.95.

1136 * Stevens, Halsey, 1908–1989

[Sonatas, trombone, piano] *Sonata for trombone and piano.* Southern Music, $6.50.

1137   White, Donald H., 1921–

[Sonatas, trombone, piano] *Sonata for trombone and piano.* Southern Music SS765, $10.95.

Bass Trombone and Piano Music

1138 Hartley, Walter S. (Walter Sinclair), 1927–

[Arioso, trombone, piano] *Arioso, bass trombone and piano.* Fema Music, $15.

Trombone Concertos/Piano Reductions

The following section lists works for trombone and orchestra, with the orchestral score reduced for piano accompaniment. When ordering, specify "arranged for trombone and piano; score and part."

1139 * Bloch, Ernest, 1880–1959

[Symphonies, trombone, orchestra; arr.] *Symphony for trombone and piano.* Broude Bros. 1002, $9.50.

1140 Chávez, Carlos, 1899–1978

[Concertos, trombone, orchestra; arr.] *Concerto for tenor trombone.* G. Schirmer B-1003, $10.75.

1141 Defaye, Jean Michel, 1932–

[Concerto, trombone, orchestra; arr.] *Concerto for trombone.* Leduc AL26.282, $31.

1142 * Martin, Frank, 1890–1974

[Ballades, trombone, orchestra; arr.] *Ballade for trombone (or tenor saxophone) and orchestra.* Universal UE11250, $19.95.

1143 Milhaud, Darius, 1892–1974

[Concertino d'hiver, trombone, orchestra; arr.] *Concertino d'hiver, op. 327, for trombone.* Associated Music HL50223790, $11.50.

1144 * Tomasi, Henri, 1901–1971

[Concertos, trombone, orchestra; arr.] *Concerto for trombone.* Leduc AL21.687, $23.20.

1145 Wagenseil, Georg Christoph, 1715–1777

[Concertos, trombone, orchestra, E♭ major; arr.] *Trombone concerto.* Universal UE25021C, $14.95.

1146 Zwilich, Ellen Taaffe, 1939–

[Concertos, trombone, orchestra; arr.] *Concerto for trombone.* Merion Music 144-40168, $38.50.

Trombone/Baritone Methods and Studies

1147 * Blume, O.

[Studies, trombone] *Thirty-six studies for trombone with F attachment.* C. Fischer O4948, $9.95; International Music 2472, 2473, 2183, 3 v., $6.25, $6.25, $5.75.

1148 * Bordner, Gerald

Practical studies for trombone and baritone. Belwin-Mills EL933, EL2165, 2 v., $5.50, $6.50.

1149 * Bordogni, Giulio Marco, 1788–1856

[Vocalises. Selections; arr.] *Melodious etudes for the trombone.* C. Fischer 01594-01596, 3 v., $9.95 each.

1150 * Gower, Wm. (William), and Himie Voxman, 1912–

Rubank advanced method for trombone or baritone. Rubank 96/179, $6.95.

1151 * Tyrrell, H. W.

Forty progressive studies for trombone in the bass clef. Boosey & Hawkes BTB 11, $10.50.

Bass Trombone Methods and Studies

1152 Fink, Reginald H.

Introducing the alto clef for trombone. Accura Music 002, $10.

1153 Marsteller, Robert L.

Advanced slide technique for trombone (B♭ tenor slide trombone and instruments with F and E attachments). Southern Music B-237, $16.95.

1154 Ostrander, Allen, 1909–

Method for bass trombone and F attachment for tenor trombone. C. Fischer O4517, $9.95.

Tuba Music

Solo Tuba Music

1155 * Hartley, Walter S. (Walter Sinclair), 1927–

[Suites, tuba] *Suite for unaccompanied tuba.* Elkan-Vogel 164-00061, $4.

1156 Kraft, William, 1923–

[Encounters, no. 2] *Encounters II, for solo tuba.* MCA Music 16441-030, $14.50.

1157 * Persichetti, Vincent, 1915–1987

[Serenades, no. 12, op. 88] *Serenade no. 12 for solo tuba.* Elkan-Vogel 164-00062, $3.

1158 Ziffrin, Marilyn J., 1926–

[Pieces, tuba] *Four pieces for tuba.* Music Graphics Press, $4.95.

Tuba and Tape

1159 Hiller, Lejaren Arthur, 1924–

Malta, for tuba and tape (1975). Presser 114-40223, $15.

1160 Lazarof, Henri, 1932–

[Cadence, no. 6] *Cadence VI, for tuba and tape (1973).* Bote & Bock, $10.50.

Tuba and Piano Music

1161 * Bernstein, Leonard, 1918–1990

[Brass music. Waltz for Mippy III] *Waltz for Mippy III, for tuba and piano.* Boosey & Hawkes BBB 17, $6.75.

1162 Beversdorf, Thomas, 1924–1981

[Sonatas, tuba, piano] *Sonata for tuba and piano.* Southern Music SS-773, $17.50.

1163 * Hartley, Walter S. (Walter Sinclair), 1927–

[Sonatas, tuba, piano] *Sonata for tuba and piano.* Presser 494-00111, $9.50.

1164 * Hindemith, Paul, 1895–1963

[Sonatas, tuba, piano] *Sonata for tuba and piano (1955).* Schott ED4636, $17.95.

1165 * Sibbing, Robert

[Sonatas, tuba, piano] *Sonata for tuba and piano.* Tenuto 494-00120, $12.

1166 * Wilder, Alec, 1907–1980

[Suites, tuba, piano, no. 1] *Suite no. 1 for tuba and piano, "Effie Suite."* Margun Music MM54, $11.

Tuba Concertos/Piano Reductions

The following section lists works for tuba and orchestra or wind ensemble, with the full score reduced for piano accompaniment. When ordering, specify "arranged for tuba and piano; score and part."

1167 Beversdorf, Thomas, 1924–1981

[Concertos, tuba, band; arr] *Concerto for tuba, winds, and percussion (1975).* Indiana Music Center, $60.

1168 Hartley, Walter S. (Walter Sinclair), 1927–

[Concertos, tuba, percussion; arr.] *Concerto for tuba and percussion orchestra.* J. Boonin EA259, $30.

1169 Ross, Walter, 1936–

[Concertos, tuba, band; arr.] *Tuba concert (1973).* Boosey & Hawkes BBB 7, $20.

1170 * Vaughan Williams, Ralph, 1872–1958

[Concertos, tuba, orchestra, F minor; arr.] *Concerto for tuba.* Corrected 1982 ed. Oxford University Press 71.002, $19.95.

Tuba Methods and Studies

1171 * Blazhevich, V. (Vladislav), 1881–1942

[Studies, tuba] *Seventy studies for B♭ tuba.* Robert King Music, 2 v., $4.55 each.

1172 Getchell, Robert W. (Robert Ward), 1916–

Practical studies for tuba. Belwin-Mills 774-775, 2 v., $5.50, $6.50.

1173 Gourse, Charles F.

Learn to play the tuba! (B♭ and E♭ sousaphone). Alfred Music, 2 v., $6.50, $5.95 (v.2 OP).

1174 * Gower, Wm. (William), and Himie Voxman, 1912–

Rubank advanced method for E♭ and B♭ bass. Rubank 142, 184, 2 v., $6.95 each.

1175 Tyrrell, H. W.

Advanced studies for B♭ bass. Boosey & Hawkes BBB 15, $10.

Percussion Music

Compiled by
Pamela Bristah

The following distributors specialize in percussion music:

Drums Unlimited, Inc.
4928 Saint Elmo Avenue
Bethesda, MD 20814
(301) 654-2719 phone
(301) 654-5517 fax

Steve Weiss Music
P.O. Box 20885
Philadelphia, PA 19141
(215) 329-1637 or (215) 324-3999 phone
(215) 329-3519 fax

Drum Set

1176 ** Beck, John, 1933–

A practical approach to the drum set. MCA Music, $5.95.

1177 *Contemporary drum solos by Buddy Rich, Louie Bellson, Lenny White, and others.* Hal Leonard HL2000000, $5.95.

1178 Magadini, Pete, 1942–

Drum ears: the drummer's digest to the rudiments of music. Hal Leonard, $5.95.

1179 Rothman, Joel

The compleat drum reader. J. R. Publications, $30.

Mallets

1180 * Bailey, Elden C.

Mental and manual calisthenics for the modern mallet player. Award Music, $15.

1181 Breuer, Harry, 1901–

[Selections] *Harry Breuer's mallet solo collection, for any keyboard [mallet] instrument and piano.* Alfred Music, $9.95.

1182 Creston, Paul, 1906–1985

[Concertinos, marimba, orchestra, op. 21; arr.] *Concertino for marimba and orchestra, op. 21; reduction for marimba and piano.* G. Schirmer ED3502, $18.

1183 DeLancey, Charles, 1959–

Malletree. M. Peters, $8.

1184 * Goldenberg, Morris, 1911–1969

Modern school for xylophone, marimba, and vibraphone. Hal Leonard, $12.95.

1185 Green, George Hamilton, 1893–1970

George Hamilton Green's instruction course for xylophone. Meredith Music, $20.

1186 Mann, Ed, 1955–

The essential mallet player. Monad/Hal Leonard, $9.95.

1187 Milhaud, Darius, 1892–1974

[Concertos, marimba, orchestra, op. 278; arr.] *Concerto for marimba (and vibraphone) and orchestra, op. 278; piano reduction by the composer.* Enoch, $100.

1188 *Modern Japanese marimba pieces,* ed. by Keiko Abe. Ongaku No Tomo Sha/Presser 544-00176, $25.50.

1189 Ptaszyńska, Marta, 1943–

Four preludes for vibraphone and piano. Marks Music, $5.

1190 Smadbeck, Paul, 1955–

Etudes, marimba, no. 1–3. Studio 4 Productions 2807-2809, 3 v., $3, $7, $4.50.

1191 * Stevens, Leigh Howard, 1953–

Method of movement for marimba, with 590 exercises. Marimba Productions, $20.

1192 Stout, Gordon, 1952–

[Etudes, marimba, no. 1–5] *Five etudes for marimba, book 1.* Music for Percussion, $6.

1193 Stout, Gordon, 1952–

[Etudes, marimba, no. 6–10] *Stout etudes for marimba, book 2.* Studio 4 Productions, $8.

1194 Stout, Gordon, 1952–

[Etudes, marimba, no. 11–14] *Stout etudes for marimba, book 3.* Studio 4 Productions, $5.

1195 * Van Geem, Jack, 1952–

Four-mallet democracy for marimba: studies and etudes for developing four-mallet independence. Belwin Mills EL03684, $6.95.

1196 Živković, Nebojša, 1962–

Macedonia, marimba and piano. Studio 4 Productions, $4.

Multiple Percussion

1197 Goldenberg, Morris, 1911–1969

Studies in solo percussion. Hal Leonard, $7.50.

1198 Jolivet, André, 1905–1974

[Concertos, percussion, orchestra; arr.] *Concerto for percussion and orchestra; reduction for percussion and piano.* Salabert EAS 16451, $39.40.

1199 Kraft, William, 1923–

English suite: multiple percussion solos in seven parts. Award Music, $15.

1200 Kraft, William, 1923–

French suite, for percussion solo. New Music West, $10.

1201 * Magadini, Pete, 1942–

Techniques for snare drum, timpani, and mallet percussion. Hal Leonard, $6.95.

1202 Milhaud, Darius, 1892–1974

[Concertos, percussion, orchestra; arr.] *Concerto for percussion and chamber orchestra; reduction for percussion and piano.* Universal UE 6453, $25.

1203 *Twentieth-century orchestra studies for percussion,* ed. by Alan Abel. G. Schirmer ED2740, $14.95.

Snare Drum

1204 Albright, Fred

Contemporary studies for the snare drum. Belwin HAB 1, $12.95.

1205 * Cirone, Anthony J., 1941–

Portraits in rhythm study guide: 50 studies for snare drum. Belwin EL03626, $10.

1206 * Delécluse, Jacques, 1933–

[Etudes, drum] *Twelve studies for snare drum.* Leduc AL23.410, $20.25.

1207 Delécluse, Jacques, 1933–

Initium II–IV: rhythm through percussion, percussion through rhythm [for snare drum]. Leduc AL25.340-25.342, 3 v. (v.2–4 of 4), $11.85, $14.45, $14.45.

1208 Delécluse, Jacques, 1933–
Method for snare drum. Leduc AL23.983, $19.80.

1209 *The drummer's heritage: a collection of popular airs and official U.S. Army music for fifes and drums combined with similiar pieces for field trumpets, cymbals, and drums,* ed. by Frederick Fennell. Eastman School of Music/C. Fischer ET4, $10.

1210 * Gardner, Carl E. (Carl Edward), b. 1885
The Gardner modern method for the drums, cymbals, and accessories: books 1 and 3. Rev. enl. ed. C. Fischer CF228, CF230, 2 v., $10.50 each.

1211 * Goldenberg, Morris, 1911–1969
Modern school for snare drum. Hal Leonard, $12.95.

1212 ** Goldenberg, Morris, 1911–1969
Snare drum for beginners. Hal Leonard, $7.95.

1213 * Lepak, Alexander, 1920–
Fifty contemporary snare drum etudes. Windsor Music, $8.

1214 Morello, Joe, 1929–
Master studies for snare drum. Modern Drummer Publications, $9.95.

1215 Peters, Mitchell, 1935–
Advanced snare drum studies. M. Peters, $11.

1216 * Peters, Mitchell, 1935–
Odd meter rudimental etudes for the snare drum. M. Peters, $9.

1217 Podemski, Benjamin
Podemski's standard snare drum method, including double drums and an introduction to tympani. Mills Music, $13.

1218 Sholle, Emil
The roll for snare drum: 83 exercises. Brook Publishing, $6.

1219 * Stone, George Lawrence, 1886–1967
Accents and rebounds for the snare drummer. G. B. Stone GS-2, $9.

1220 * Stone, George Lawrence, 1886–1967
Stick control for the snare drummer. G. B. Stone GS-1, $9.

1221 * Street, William G., 1896–1972
[Percussion music] *The complete works of William G. Street: 39 studies, solos, and duets for snare drum and timpani by an American master.* Eastman School of Music/C. Fischer ET34, $12.95.

1222 *Twelve progressive solos for snare drum,* ed. by Morris Goldenberg. Hal Leonard, $4.95.

1223 Živković, Nebojša, 1962–
[Etudes, snare drum] *Ten etudes for snare drum.* Studio 4 Productions, $6.

Timpani

1224 *Classic overtures for timpani, from Mozart to Wagner,* ed. by Morris Goldenberg. Hal Leonard HL00347780, $8.95.

1225 *Classic symphonies for timpani: Haydn, Mozart, Beethoven,* ed. by Morris Goldenberg. Hal Leonard HL00347781, $8.95.

1226 Delécluse, Jacques, 1933–
[Etudes, timpani (1968)] *Twenty studies for timpani.* Leduc AL23.933, $23.20.

1227 * Friese, Alfred, and Alexander Lepak
The Alfred Friese timpani method. Belwin Mills, $18.

1228 Goodman, Saul, percussionist
Modern method for timpani. Mills Music, $16.50.

1229 * Hinger, Fred D., 1920–
Technique for the virtuoso tympanist. Jerona Music, $17.95.

1230 * Hochrainer, Richard, 1922–1986
[Etudes, timpani] *Etudes for timpani.* Doblinger 05801, 05802, 05809, 3 v., $21.60, $21.60, $19.50.

1231 Kraft, William, 1923–
[Concertos, timpani, orchestra; arr.] *Concerto for timpani and orchestra, arranged for timpani and piano.* New Music West, $20.

1232 Leonard, Stanley, 1931–
Pedal technique for the timpani. Ludwig Music BK-63, $17.95.

1233 *Romantic symphonies for timpani,* ed. by Morris Goldenberg. Hal Leonard HL00347782, $10.95.

1234 *The timpani player's orchestral repertoire,* ed. by Fred D. Hinger. Jerona Music, 6 v., $24.95, $9.95, $13.95, $10.95, $13.95, $13.95.

1235 *Twentieth-century orchestra studies for timpani,* ed. by Alan Abel. G. Schirmer ED2741, $14.95.

Music for Solo Strings

Compiled by
**Carol Tatian (violin), Judy MacLeod (viola), Elizabeth Sadewhite (violoncello),
John Voigt (double bass), Mark Palkovic and Pamela Bristah (harp),
and Paul Orkiszewski (guitar)**

Violin Music

Solo Violin Music

1236 * Bach, Johann Sebastian, 1685–1750

[Sonaten und Partiten, violin, BWV 1001–1006] *Three sonatas and three partitas for violin, BWV 1001–1006.* Bärenreiter BA5116, $21.60; Henle HN356, $32.95; International Music 2525, ed. by Ivan Galamian, $15.50; Peters P4308, $21.15.

1237 Bartók, Béla, 1881–1945

[Sonatas, violin] *Sonata for unaccompanied violin,* ed. by Yehudi Menuhin. Boosey & Hawkes SAB 25, $23.

1238 * Paganini, Nicolò, 1782–1840

[Caprices, violin, op. 1] *Twenty-four caprices for unaccompanied violin, op. 1.* Henle HN450, $37.95; International Music 582, ed. by Carl Flesch, $8; Peters P1984, $10.10; G. Schirmer LB1663, $7.95.

1239 Rochberg, George, 1918–

[Caprice variations, violin] *Caprice variations, for unaccompanied violin.* Galaxy Music, $13.75.

1240 * Telemann, Georg Philipp, 1681–1767

[Fantasias, violin] *12 fantasies for violin.* Bärenreiter BA2972, $12.60; International Music 2887, $6; Peters P9365, $22.25.

1241 Tower, Joan, 1938–

Platinum spirals, for violin. Associated Music AMP7813-2, $3.

Violin and Keyboard Music

1242 Bach, Johann Sebastian, 1685–1750

[Sonatas. Selections] *Three sonatas for violin and piano or harpsichord, BWV 1020, BWV 1021, BWV 1023.* Henle HN458, $20.95.

1243 * Bach, Johann Sebastian, 1685–1750

[Sonatas, violin, harpsichord, BWV 1014–1019] *Six sonatas for violin and harpsichord, BWV 1014–1019.* Bärenreiter BA5118-5119, 2 v., $12.75, $12;

Henle HN223, $44.95; International Music 965-966, 2 v., $10.50 each; Kalmus K 03018-03019, 2 v., $9.95 each; Peters P232-233, 2 v., $18.70 each.

1244   Bartók, Béla, 1881–1945

[Rhapsodies, violin, piano, no. 1] *Rhapsody no. 1 for violin and piano.* Boosey & Hawkes SAB 1, $24.

1245   Bartók, Béla, 1881–1945

[Rhapsodies, violin, piano, no. 2] *Rhapsody no. 2 for violin and piano.* Boosey & Hawkes SAB 23, $18.50.

1246   Beach, H. H. A., Mrs., 1867–1944

[Sonata, violin, piano, op. 34, A minor] *Sonata in A minor for violin and piano, op. 34.* Da Capo Press 0-306-76250-1, $23.50.

1247 * Beethoven, Ludwig van, 1770–1827

[Sonatas, violin, piano] *Ten sonatas for violin and piano.* Henle HN7-8, 2 v., $31.95 each; International Music 2723, ed. by David Oistrakh, $26; Peters P9172a-b, ed. by David Oistrakh and Lev Oborin, 2 v., $38.05 each.

1248   Beethoven, Ludwig van, 1770–1827

[Violin and piano music. Selections] *Variations WoO 40, rondos, and German dances for violin and piano.* Henle HN291, $13.95.

1249   Biber, Heinrich Ignaz Franz, 1644–1704

[Sonatas, violin, continuo. Selections] *Eight violin sonatas.* Kalmus K 09193, $9.

1250 * Brahms, Johannes, 1833–1897

[Sonatas, violin, piano] *Three sonatas for violin and piano, op. 78, op. 100, op. 108.* Henle HN194, $32.95; International Music 1100, $14.75.

1251   Carter, Elliott, 1908–

[Duet, violin, piano] *Duo for violin and piano (1974).* Associated Music AMP7457, $40.

1252 * Corelli, Arcangelo, 1653–1713

[Sonatas, violin, continuo, op. 5] *12 sonatas for violin and basso continuo, op. 5.* International Music 908-909, 2 v., $14.50 each; Schott ED4380-4381, 2 v., $14.95, $15.95.

1253   Crumb, George, 1929–

[Nocturnes, violin, piano] *Four nocturnes for violin and piano: Night music II.* Peters P6740, $12.10.

1254 * Debussy, Claude, 1862–1918

[Sonatas, violin, piano, G minor] *Sonata in G minor for violin and piano.* Durand 514-00097, $28; Masters Music M2234, $7.95.

1255 * Dvořák, Antonín, 1841–1904

[Sonatas, violin, piano, op. 57, F major] *Sonata in F major for violin and piano, op. 57.* Critical ed. Masters Music M1287, $10.95.

1256 * Dvořák, Antonín, 1841–1904

[Sonatinas, violin, piano, op. 100, G major] *Sonatina in G major for violin and piano, op. 100.* Henle HN413, $12.95; International Music 2798, $5.75.

1257 * Fauré, Gabriel, 1845–1924

[Sonatas, violin, piano, no. 1, op. 13, A major] *Sonata in A major for violin and piano, op. 13.* International Music 1550, $9.50.

1258 * Franck, César, 1822–1890

[Sonatas, violin, piano, A major] *Sonata in A major for violin and piano.* Henle HN293, $19.95; International Music 322, ed. by Zino Francescatti and Robert Casadesus, $8.50; Peters P3742, $18.70.

1259   *Frauen Komponieren = Female composers: 13 pieces for violin and piano,* ed. by Barbara Heller and Eva Rieger. Schott, $39.95.

1260 * Handel, George Frideric, 1685–1759

[Sonatas, op. 1. Selections] *Seven sonatas for violin and continuo, op. 1, no. 3, 6, 10, 12–15.* Henle HN191, ed. by Stanley Sadie, $31.95; International Music 2261-2262 (omits no. 6), ed. by Zino Francescatti, 2 v., $8 each.

1261 * Ives, Charles, 1874–1954

[Sonatas, violin, piano, no. 4] *Sonata no. 4 for violin and piano, "Children's day at the camp meeting."* Associated Music AMP9638-21, $12.95.

1262 * Kreisler, Fritz, 1875–1962

[Violin and piano music. Selections] *Caprice viennois and other favorite pieces for violin and piano.* Dover 0-486-28489-1, $7.95.

1263 * Mozart, Wolfgang Amadeus, 1756–1791

[Sonatas, violin, piano. Selections] *Selected violin and piano sonatas.* Bärenreiter BA4774-4776, 3 v., $14.40, $15, $19.50; Henle HN77-79, 3 v., $24.95, $30.95, $28.95; International Music 862 (*19 selected sonatas*), ed. by Carl Flesch and Artur Schnabel, $30.

1264 * Prokofiev, Sergey, 1891–1953

[Sonatas, flute, piano, op. 94, D major; arr.] *Sonata for violin and piano in D major, no. 2, op. 94,* ed. by David Oistrakh. International Music 1588, $9.50.

1265 * Prokofiev, Sergey, 1891–1953

[Sonatas, violin, piano, op. 80, F minor] *Sonata no. 1 for violin and piano in F minor, op. 80.* International Music 1892, $9.

1266 * Ravel, Maurice, 1875–1937

[Sonatas, violin, piano (1927)] *Sonata for violin and piano.* Durand 514-00252, $36.25.

1267 Ravel, Maurice, 1875–1937

Tzigane, for violin and piano. Durand 514-00253, $42.25.

1268 Rorem, Ned, 1923–

Night music, for piano and violin. Boosey & Hawkes SAB 14, $11.95.

1269 * Schoenberg, Arnold, 1874–1951

[Phantasy, violin, piano, op. 47] *Phantasy for violin and piano, op. 47.* Peters P6060, $14.65.

1270 * Schubert, Franz, 1797–1828

[Sonatinas, violin, piano] *Three sonatinas, op. 137, no. 1–3, D. 384, D. 385, D. 408.* Bärenreiter BA5606, $12.75.

1271 * Schubert, Franz, 1797–1828

[Violin and piano music. Selections] *Three duos for violin and piano, D. 895, D. 934, D. 574.* Henle HN287, $33.95; International Music 935, 907, 601, 3 v., $8.50, $8.25, $7.75; Peters P156b, $37.60.

1272 Schumann, Clara, 1819–1896

[Romances, violin, piano, op. 22] *Three romances for violin and piano, op. 22.* Breitkopf & Härtel EB8383, $12.

1273 * Schumann, Robert, 1810–1856

[Fantasiestücke, clarinet, piano, op. 73] *Fantasy pieces, op. 73 for clarinet (or violin or cello) and piano.* Henle HN421, $9.95.

1274 Sessions, Roger, 1896–1985

[Duet, violin, piano] *Duo for violin and piano.* E. B. Marks Music, $7.50.

1275 Stravinsky, Igor, 1882–1971

[Duo concertante, violin, piano] *Duo concertante for violin and piano.* Boosey & Hawkes SAB 33, $24.

1276 Talma, Louise, 1906–

[Sonatas, violin, piano] *Sonata for violin and piano.* C. Fischer Facsimile Edition FE192, $10.

1277 Tartini, Giuseppe, 1692–1770

[Sonatas, violin, continuo, B. g 5, G minor] *Devil's trill sonata, for violin and piano.* C. Fischer F1193, ed. and cadenza by Leopold Auer, $6.50; Schott VLB34, cadenza by Fritz Kreisler, $9.95.

1278 * Vivaldi, Antonio, 1687–1741

[Sonatas, violin, continuo. Selections] *Twelve sonatas for violin and continuo, op. 2 (F. XIII, 29–40; RV 1, 8, 9, 14, 16, 20, 21, 23, 27, 31, 32, 36).* Schott ED4212-4213, 2 v., $14.95 each.

1279 Zwilich, Ellen Taaffe, 1939–

Sonata in three movements, for violin and piano. Elkan Vogel 144-40087, $10.

Violin Concertos/Piano Reductions

The following section lists works for violin and orchestra, with the orchestral score reduced for piano accompaniment. When ordering, specify "arranged for violin and piano; score and part."

1280 * Bach, Johann Sebastian, 1685–1750

[Concertos, violin, string orchestra, BWV 1041, A minor; arr.] *Concerto for violin in A minor, BWV 1041.* Bärenreiter BA5189a, $13.25; International Music 1598, ed. by Ivan Galamian, $6; Kalmus K 03020, $4.50; Peters P4996, ed. by David Oistrakh, $30.60.

1281 * Bach, Johann Sebastian, 1685–1750

[Concertos, violin, string orchestra, BWV 1042, E major; arr.] *Concerto for violin in E major, BWV 1042.* Bärenreiter BA5190a, $16.25; International Music 1893, ed. by Ivan Galamian, $6; Kalmus K 03021, $5.50; Peters P230, $10.10.

1282 Barber, Samuel, 1910–1981

[Concertos, violin, orchestra, op. 14; arr.] *Concerto for violin, op. 14.* G. Schirmer ED3491, $17.95.

1283 * Bartók, Béla, 1881–1945

[Concertos, violin, orchestra, no. 2; arr.] *Concerto for violin, no. 2.* Boosey & Hawkes SAB 27, $28.

1284 * Beethoven, Ludwig van, 1770–1827

[Concertos, violin, orchestra, op. 61, D major; arr.] *Concerto for violin in D major, op. 61.* Henle HN326, $20.95; International Music 430, ed. by Zino Francescatti, $8; Kalmus K 03140, $15; Peters P189, ed. by Carl Flesch, $18.70.

1285 * Beethoven, Ludwig van, 1770–1827

[Romances, violin, orchestra; arr.] *Two romances, op. 40 and op. 50.* Amadeus BP371A, $12.35; Henle HN324, $11.95; International Music 2720, ed. by Zino Francescatti, $6.

1286 Berg, Alban, 1885–1935

[Concertos, violin, orchestra; arr.] *Concerto for violin.* Universal UE10903, $39.

1287 * Brahms, Johannes, 1833–1897

[Concertos, violin, orchestra, op. 77, D major; arr.] *Concerto for violin in D major, op. 77.* International Music 1502, ed. by Zino Francescatti, $10.50; Peters P3893, $30.

1288 * Bruch, Max, 1828–1920

[Concertos, violin, orchestra, no. 1, op. 26, G minor; arr.] *Concerto for violin in G minor, op. 26.* International Music 865, ed. by Zino Francescatti, $8; Kalmus K 03272, $8.

1289 Chausson, Ernest, 1855–1899

[Poème, violin, orchestra, op. 25; arr.] *Poème, for violin and orchestra, op. 25.* International Music 1530, $6.

1290 Dvořák, Antonín, 1841–1904

[Concertos, violin, orchestra, op. 53, A minor; arr.] *Violin concerto in A minor, op. 53 (B. 108).* International Music 584, $12.50.

1291 * Haydn, Joseph, 1732–1809

[Concertos, violin, orchestra, H. VIIa, 1, C major; arr.] *Concerto no. 1 for violin in C major, Hob. VIIa:1.* Amadeus BP514, $14.25.

1292 Khachaturian, Aram, 1903–1978

[Concertos, violin, orchestra, D minor; arr.] *Violin concerto in D minor.* International Music 2246, $12.

1293 Lalo, Édouard, 1823–1892

[Symphonie espagnole; arr.] *Symphonie espagnole for violin and orchestra, op. 21.* International Music 1377, $9.

1294 * Mendelssohn-Bartholdy, Felix, 1809–1847

[Concertos, violin, orchestra, op. 64, E minor; arr.] *Concerto for violin in E minor, op. 64.* International Music 812, ed. by Zino Francescatti, $8; Kalmus K 03668, $12.50; Peters P1731a, ed. by Carl Flesch, $11.15.

1295 Mozart, Wolfgang Amadeus, 1756–1791

[Concertos, violin, orchestra, K. 207, B♭ major; arr.] *Concerto for violin, no. 1 in B♭ major, K. 207.* Bärenreiter BA4863a, $15.75; Peters P2193e, $15.60.

1296 Mozart, Wolfgang Amadeus, 1756–1791

[Concertos, violin, orchestra, K. 211, D major; arr.] *Concerto for violin, no. 2 in D major, K. 211.* Bärenreiter BA4864a, $14.75; International Music 2506, ed. by Zino Francescatti, $6.

1297 * Mozart, Wolfgang Amadeus, 1756–1791

[Concertos, violin, orchestra, K. 216, G major; arr.] *Concerto for violin, no. 3 in G major, K. 216.* Bärenreiter BA4865a, $15.75; International Music 2471, ed. by Zino Francescatti, $7; Peters P2193m, ed. by David Oistrakh, $27.75.

1298 * Mozart, Wolfgang Amadeus, 1756–1791

[Concertos, violin, orchestra, K. 218, D major; arr.] *Concerto for violin, no. 4 in D major, K. 218.* Bärenreiter BA4866a, $15.75; International Music 2042, ed. by Joseph Joachim, $6.50.

1299 * Mozart, Wolfgang Amadeus, 1756–1791

[Concertos, violin, orchestra, K. 219, A major; arr.] *Concerto for violin, no. 5 in A major, K. 219.* Bärenreiter BA4712a, $19.25; International Music 324, ed. by Ivan Galamian, $8; International Music 2043, ed. by Joseph Joachim, $7.75; Peters P2193a, $12.10.

1300 Mozart, Wolfgang Amadeus, 1756–1791

[Rondos, violin, orchestra, K. 373, C major; arr.] *Rondo for violin and orchestra in C major, K. 373.* International Music 565, $4.50; Schott ED6469, $8.95.

1301 * Paganini, Nicolò, 1782–1840

[Concertos, violin, orchestra, no. 1, op. 6, E♭ major; arr.] *Violin concerto no. 1, op. 6, [transposed to] D major.* International Music 3175, ed. by Zino Francescatti, $10; Well-Tempered Press W7035, ed. by Carl Flesch, $9.95.

1302 * Prokofiev, Sergey, 1891–1953

[Concertos, violin, orchestra, no. 1, op. 19, D major; arr.] *Concerto for violin, no. 1 in D major, op. 19.* Boosey & Hawkes SAB 29, $28; International Music 810, ed. by David Oistrakh, $9.

1303 Prokofiev, Sergey, 1891–1953

[Concertos, violin, orchestra, no. 2, op. 63, G minor; arr.] *Concerto for violin, no. 2 in G minor, op. 63.* International Music 503, ed. by Zino Francescatti, $10.50; Kalmus K 03804, $10.

1304 Saint-Saëns, Camille, 1835–1921

[Concertos, violin, orchestra, no. 3, op. 61, B minor; arr.] *Concerto for violin in B minor, no. 3, op. 61,* ed. by Zino Francescatti. International Music 1967, $9.

1305 * Saint-Saëns, Camille, 1835–1921

[Introduction et rondo capriccioso; arr.] *Introduction and rondo capriccioso for violin and orchestra, op. 28,* ed. by Zino Francescatti. International Music 1426, $6.

1306 * Sibelius, Jean, 1865–1957

[Concertos, violin, orchestra, op. 47, D minor; arr.] *Concerto for violin in D minor, op. 47.* International Music 529, ed. by Zino Francescatti, $8.50; Kalmus K 04690, $7.50.

1307 Stravinsky, Igor, 1882–1971

[Concertos, violin, orchestra, D; arr.] *Violin concerto in D.* Schott ED2190, $35.

1308 * Tchaikovsky, Peter Ilich, 1840–1893

[Concertos, violin, orchestra, op. 35, D major; arr.] *Concerto for violin in D major, op. 35.* International Music 1902, ed. by David Oistrakh and Leopold Auer, $9.50; Peters P3019a, ed. by Carl Flesch, $23.25.

1309 Vaughan Williams, Ralph, 1872–1958

[Lark ascending; arr.] *The lark ascending, for violin and orchestra.* Oxford University Press, $17.95.

1310 Vieuxtemps, Henri, 1820–1881

[Concertos, violin, orchestra, no. 5, op. 37, A minor; arr.] *Violin concerto in A minor, no. 5, op. 37.* International Music 2699, $8.50.

1311 * Vivaldi, Antonio, 1678–1741

[Cimento dell'armonia e dell'inventione. N. 1; arr.] *Concerto in E major, "Spring."* Ricordi, $9.95.

1312 * Vivaldi, Antonio, 1678–1741

[Cimento dell'armonia e dell'inventione. N. 2; arr.] *Concerto in G minor, "Summer."* Ricordi, $9.95.

1313 * Vivaldi, Antonio, 1678–1741

[Cimento dell'armonia e dell'inventione. N. 3; arr.] *Concerto in F major, "Autumn."* Ricordi, $9.95.

1314 * Vivaldi, Antonio, 1678–1741

[Cimento dell'armonia e dell'inventione. N. 4; arr.] *Concerto in F minor, "Winter."* Ricordi, $9.95.

1315 Wieniawski, Henri, 1835–1880

[Concertos, violin, orchestra, no. 2, op. 22, D minor; arr.] *Concerto for violin no. 2 in D minor,*

op. 22. International Music 1425, ed. by Ivan Galamian, $8; Kalmus K 03973, $6.50; Peters P3296, $16.85.

Violin Methods and Studies

1316 Applebaum, Samuel, 1904–

The Belwin string builder (violin): a string class method. Belwin-Mills, 3 v., with solo part, piano accompaniment, cassette tape, and compact disc for each volume. Solo part, $5.50 each; piano accompaniment, $7 each; cassette tape, $8.95 each; compact disc, $10.95 each.

1317 * Dont, Jacob, 1815–1888

[Etudes et caprices, violin, op. 35] *Etudes and caprices for violin, op. 35.* C. Fischer LB306, $7.95; International Music 2397, ed. by Ivan Galamian, $7; Schott ED6117, $11.95.

1318 * Galamian, Ivan, 1903–1981, and Frederick Neumann

Contemporary violin technique. Galaxy Music, 2 v., $22.95, $15.95.

1319 * Kreutzer, Rodolphe, 1766–1831

[Études ou caprices, violin] *Forty-two studies for violin.* C. Fischer LB120, $9; International Music 2073, ed. by Ivan Galamian, $9.25.

1320 Suzuki, Shinichi, 1898–

Suzuki violin school. Summy-Birchard, 10 v., with solo part, piano accompaniment, cassette tape, and compact disc for each volume. Violin part, $6.95 each; piano accompaniment, $6.95 each; cassette tape, $12.95 each; compact disc, $15.95 each.

1321 * Wohlfahrt, Franz, 1833–1884

[Etüden, violin, op. 45] *Sixty etudes for violin, op. 45.* C. Fischer LB122-123, 2 v., $6.50, $6.95.

Viola Music
Solo Viola Music

1322 * Bach, Johann Sebastian, 1685–1750

[Sonaten und Partiten, violin, BWV 1001–1006. Selections; arr.] *Sonatas and partitas for solo viola,* transcribed by Watson Forbes. Oxford University Press 0-19-355244-2, $11.95.

1323 * Bach, Johann Sebastian, 1685–1750

[Suites, violoncello, BWV 1007–1012; arr.] *Six cello suites,* arranged for viola and ed. by Leonard Davis. International Music 3064, $9.

1324 Berio, Luciano, 1925–

[Sequenza, no. 6] *Sequenza VI, for viola solo.* Universal UE13726, $19.95.

1325 Britten, Benjamin, 1913–1976

[Elegy, viola] *Elegy for viola.* Faber Music FO883, $6.95.

1326 * Hindemith, Paul, 1895–1963

[Sonatas, viola, op. 11, no. 5] *Sonata for viola solo, op. 11, no. 5.* Schott ED1968, $14.95.

1327 * Hindemith, Paul, 1895–1963

[Sonatas, viola, op. 25, no. 1] *Sonata for viola solo, op. 25, no. 1.* Schott ED1969, $17.95.

1328 * Reger, Max, 1873–1916

[Suites, viola, op. 131d] *Three suites for viola, op. 131d.* Amadeus BP2018, $14.25; Henle HN468, $10.95; International Music 3285, $9; Masters Music M1863, $4.95.

1329 Stravinsky, Igor, 1882–1971

[Elegy, viola] *Elégie for viola or violin, unaccompanied.* Boosey & Hawkes SVB 11, $11.

Viola and Keyboard Music

1330 Babbitt, Milton, 1916–

[Compositions, viola, piano] *Composition for viola and piano.* Peters P66408, $22.25.

1331 Bach, Carl Philipp Emanuel, 1714–1788

[Sonatas, viola da gamba, harpsichord, H. 510, G minor; arr.] *Sonata in G minor for viola and piano,* ed. by William Primrose. International Music 1731, $6.25.

1332 * Bach, Johann Sebastian, 1685–1750

[Sonatas, viola da gamba, harpsichord] *Three sonatas for viola da gamba (or viola) and harpsichord, BWV 1027–1029.* Bärenreiter BA5186, $22.50; Breitkopf & Härtel EB3359, $6; Well-Tempered Press W7060, $8.50.

1333 Beach, H. H. A., Mrs., 1867–1944

[Sonata, violin, piano, op. 34; arr.] *Sonata for viola and piano,* transcribed by Roger Hannay. Henmar/ Peters P66847, $37.25.

1334 Bloch, Ernest, 1880–1959

Meditation and processional, for viola and piano. G. Schirmer ST43208, $7.95.

1335 * Brahms, Johannes, 1833–1897

[Sonatas, clarinet, piano, op. 120; arr.] *Two sonatas for viola and piano, op. 120.* Henle HN231, $22.95; Kalmus K 04310, $9.50.

1336 * Brahms, Johannes, 1833–1897

[Sonatas, violin, piano, no. 1, op. 78, G major; arr.] *Sonata in D major, op. 78,* transcribed for viola and piano by Leonard Davis. International Music 488, $11.50.

1337 Carter, Elliott, 1908–

[Pastorale, English horn, piano] *Pastorale for viola (or clarinet or English horn) and piano.* Presser 144-40005, $14.50.

1338 * Cowell, Henry, 1897–1965

[Hymn and fuguing tune, no. 7] *Hymn and fuguing tune no. 7, for viola and piano.* Peer 237-17, $5.

1339 Enesco, Georges, 1881–1955

[Concertpiece, viola, piano] *Concertpiece for viola and piano.* International Music 1052, $5.50; Masters Music M1110, $5.

1340 * Hindemith, Paul, 1895–1963

[Sonatas, viola, piano, op. 11, no. 4, F] *Sonata in F for viola and piano, op. 11, no. 4.* Schott ED1976, $19.95.

1341 Ravel, Maurice, 1875–1937

[Pavane pour une infante défunte; arr.] *Pavane pour une infante défunte, arranged for viola and piano.* Masters Music M2124, $4.95.

1342 * Schubert, Franz, 1797–1828

[Sonatas, arpeggione, piano, D. 821, A minor; arr.] *Arpeggione sonata, arranged for viola and piano.* Henle HN612, $17.95; International Music 320, ed. by Milton Katims, $8; G. Schirmer LB1832, ed. by Paul Doktor, $13.95.

1343 * Schumann, Robert, 1810–1856

[Märchenbilder] *Fairy tales, for viola and piano, op. 113.* Breitkopf & Härtel EB8587, $12; International Music 2660, $7.75; Masters Music M1326, $9.95.

1344 * Shostakovich, Dmitrii Dmitrievich, 1906–1975

[Sonatas, viola, piano, op. 147] *Sonata for viola and piano, op. 147.* G. Schirmer VAAP ED3301, $13.95.

1345 *Solos for the viola player,* ed. by Paul Doktor. G. Schirmer ED2307, $14.95.

Viola Concertos/Piano Reductions

The following section lists works for viola and orchestra, with the orchestral score reduced for piano accompaniment. When ordering, specify "arranged for viola and piano; score and part."

1346 Bartók, Béla, 1881–1945

[Concertos, viola, orchestra; arr.] *Concerto for viola, op. posth.,* ed. by Tibor Serly. Boosey & Hawkes SVB 21, $35.

1347 * Berlioz, Hector, 1803–1869

[Harold en Italie; arr.] *Harold en Italie: symphony, op. 16, with viola solo;* transcription for viola and piano by Franz Liszt. Billaudot 514-01587, $43.

1348 * Bloch, Ernest, 1880–1959

[Suite hébraïque; arr.] *Suite hébraïque, for viola (or violin) and orchestra.* G. Schirmer ST42892, $7.50.

1349 Hindemith, Paul, 1895–1963

[Kammermusik, no. 5; arr.] *Kammermusik no. 5 (Viola concerto) for viola and large chamber orchestra, op. 36, no. 4.* Schott ED1977, $29.95.

1350 * Hindemith, Paul, 1895–1963

[Schwanendreher; arr.] *Der Schwanendreher: concerto on old folksongs, for viola.* Schott ED2517, $29.95.

1351 * Hindemith, Paul, 1895–1963

[Trauermusik; arr.] *Trauermusik, for viola (or cello or violin) and string orchestra.* Schott ED2515, $10.95.

1352 * Stamitz, Karl, 1745–1801

[Concertos, viola, orchestra, D major; arr.] *Concerto in D major for viola, op. 1.* International Music 542, $7.

1353 Vivaldi, Antonio, 1678–1741

[Estro armonico. N. 6; arr.] *Concerto in D minor for viola, op. 3, no. 6.* G. Schirmer ST46458, $11.95.

1354 * Walton, William, 1902–1983

[Concertos, viola, orchestra; arr.] *Concerto for viola.* Rev. ed. Oxford University Press, $29.95.

Viola Methods and Studies

1355 Applebaum, Samuel, 1904–

The Belwin string builder (viola): a string class method. Belwin, 3 v., with solo part, piano accompaniment, cassette tape, and compact disc for each volume. Solo part, $5.50 each; piano accompaniment, $7 each; cassette tape, $8.95 each; compact disc, $10.95 each.

1356 Kayser, Heinrich Ernst, 1815–1888

[Etudes, violin, op. 20; arr.] *Thirty-six elementary and progressive etudes for the viola, op. 20.* C. Fischer LB1065, $8.50; International Music 1872, $6.50; G. Schirmer LB1850, $6.95.

1357 Kreutzer, Rodolphe, 1736–1831

[Etudes ou caprices, violin; arr.] *Forty-two studies for viola.* Belwin Mills 4285, $7.95; International Music 976, $9.25; G. Schirmer LB1737, $8.95.

1358 * Ševčík, O. (Otakar), 1852–1934

[Schule der Violontechnik; arr.] *The celebrated Ševčík studies, arranged for viola with instructions for their application, from his "School of technique, op. 1."* Bosworth, $15.

1359 * Suzuki, Shinichi, 1898–

[Suzuki violin school; arr.] *Suzuki viola school.* Zen-on/Summy-Birchard, 6 v., with solo part, piano accompaniment, and cassette tape for each volume. Solo part, $6.95 each; piano accompaniment, $6.95 each; cassette tape, $12.95 each.

Violoncello Music

Solo Violoncello Music

1360 * Bach, Johann Sebastian, 1685–1750

[Suites, violoncello, BWV 1007–1012] *Six suites for unaccompanied violoncello, BWV 1007–1012.* Bärenreiter BA320, $24.30; Galaxy Music, $18.25; International Music 3125, ed. by Pierre Fournier, $8; International Music 805, with facsimile of manuscript, $10.50; Peters P238, $13.15; Presser 414-41059, $12.95.

1361 Bloch, Ernest, 1880–1959

[Suites, violoncello] *Three suites for unaccompanied violoncello.* Broude Bros., 3 v., $6.50 each.

1362 * Britten, Benjamin, 1913–1976

[Suites, violoncello] *Three cello suites.* Faber Music F0949, $17.95.

1363 * Gabrielli, Domenico, 1659–1690

[Ricercars] *Seven ricercari (1689).* Schott CB122, $9.95.

1364 * Hindemith, Paul, 1895–1963

[Sonatas, violoncello, op. 25, no. 3] *Sonata for unaccompanied violoncello, op. 25, no. 3.* Schott ED1979, $15.95.

1365 Jolas, Betsy, 1926–

Scion, for violoncello. Heugel H.32395, $9.50.

1366 * Kodály, Zoltán, 1882–1967

[Sonatas, violoncello, op. 8] *Sonata for unaccompanied violoncello, op. 8.* Universal UE6650, $17.95.

1367 * Ligeti, György, 1923–

[Sonatas, violoncello] *Sonata for violoncello.* Schott ED7698, $8.95.

1368 * Reger, Max, 1873–1916

[Suites, violoncello, op. 131c] *Three suites for violoncello, op. 131c.* Henle HN478, $13.95; International Music 826, rev. ed., $10.

1369 Stevens, Halsey, 1908–

[Sonatas, violoncello] *Sonata, violoncello.* Peters P6375, $12.10.

1370 Xenakis, Iannis, 1922–

Kottos. Salabert EAS 17296, $35.

Violoncello and Keyboard Music

1371 * Bach, Johann Sebastian, 1685–1750

[Sonatas, viola da gamba, harpsichord] *Three sonatas for cello and keyboard, based on BWV 1027–1029.* Bärenreiter BA6207, $20; Faber Music F50880, $20.95; International Music 882, $9.25; Peters P239, $23.25.

1372 Barber, Samuel, 1910–1981

[Sonatas, violoncello, piano, op. 6] *Sonata for violoncello and piano, op. 6.* G. Schirmer ED1552, $13.95.

1373 * Beethoven, Ludwig van, 1770–1827

[Sonatas, violoncello, piano] *Five sonatas for violoncello and piano: op. 5, no. 1–2; op. 69; op. 102, no. 1–2.* Henle HN252, $36.95; Peters P748, $33.30; G. Schirmer ED3119, ed. by Janos Starker, $19.50.

1374 * Boccherini, Luigi, 1743–1805

[Sonatas, violoncello, continuo, G. 4, A major] *Sonata no. 6 in A major.* International Music 653, $5.50; Schott CB24, $8.95.

1375 * Brahms, Johannes, 1833–1897

[Sonatas, violin, piano, no. 1, op. 78, G major; arr.] *Sonata in D major, op. 78,* transposed and arranged for cello and piano by the composer, ed. by Janos Starker. International Music 2499, $11.50.

1376 * Brahms, Johannes, 1833–1897

[Sonatas, violoncello, piano] *Two sonatas for violoncello and piano: op. 38 in E minor; op. 99 in F major.* Henle HN18-19, 2 v., $14.95 each; International Music 904, 901, ed. by Leonard Rose, 2 v., $7, $8.75; Wiener Urtext UT50039-50040, 2 v., $11.95 each.

1377 Britten, Benjamin, 1913–1976

[Sonatas, violoncello, piano, op. 65, C] *Sonata in C for cello and piano, op. 65.* Boosey & Hawkes SCB 42, $29.

1378 Carter, Elliott, 1908–

[Sonatas, violoncello, piano] *Sonata for violoncello and piano.* Associated Music AMP-6629, $18.

1379 Cassado, Gaspar, 1897–1966

Requiebros, for cello and piano. Schott ED1562, $14.95.

1380 * Chopin, Frédéric, 1810–1849

[Introduction et polonaise brillante] *Introduction and polonaise brillante.* International Music 1971, $5.75; Peters P1928 (with Chopin's *Sonata for violoncello and piano, op. 65, G minor*), $21.75.

1381 Couperin, François, 1668–1733

[Goûts réunis. Selections; arr.] *Pièces en concert.* Leduc AL16.920, $18.25.

1382 * Debussy, Claude, 1862–1918

[Sonatas, violoncello, piano] *Sonata for violoncello and piano.* Masters Music M1834, $6.50.

1383 Falla, Manuel de, 1876–1946

[Canciones populares españolas. Selections; arr.] *Suite populaire espagnole.* Eschig ME1718, $41.

1384 Fauré, Gabriel, 1845–1924

[Elegy, violoncello, piano, op. 24] *Elegy, op. 24, for cello and piano,* ed. by Leonard Rose. International Music 897, $5.

1385 * Fauré, Gabriel, 1845–1924

[Sonatas, violoncello, piano, no. 1, op. 109, D minor] *Sonata no. 1 in D minor for violoncello and piano, op. 109.* Durand 514-00499, $36.25; Masters Music M2238, $11.95.

1386 * Franck, César, 1822–1890

[Sonatas, violin, piano, A major; arr.] *Sonata in A major, arranged for cello and piano.* International Music 323, $8.50; Kunzelmann GM1184, $26.50.

1387 Ginastera, Alberto, 1916–1983

[Pampeana, no. 2] *Pampeana no. 2: rhapsody for violoncello and piano.* Boosey & Hawkes SCB 25, $12.

1388 Hindemith, Paul, 1895–1963

[Leichte Stücke] *Three easy pieces for violoncello and piano.* Schott ED2771, $9.95.

1389 * Kodály, Zoltán, 1882–1967

[Sonatas, violoncello, piano, op. 4] *Sonata, op. 4, violoncello and piano.* Universal UE7130, $19.95.

1390 Marcello, Benedetto, 1686–1739

[Sonatas, violoncello, continuo, op. 1] *Six sonatas for violoncello and continuo.* Masters Music M1541, $12.50; G. Schirmer LB1898, $10.95.

1391 Mendelssohn-Bartholdy, Felix, 1809–1847

[Lied ohne Worte, violoncello, piano] *Song without words in D major for cello and piano, op. 109.* International Music 1738, $3.75.

1392 * Mendelssohn-Bartholdy, Felix, 1809–1847

[Violoncello and piano music] *Compositions for cello and piano: Sonata, op. 45, B♭ major; Sonata, op. 58, D major; Lied ohne Worte, op. 109; Variations concertantes, op. 17.* Peters P1735, $23.25; Well-Tempered Press W7114, $20.

1393 * Prokofiev, Sergey, 1891–1953

[Sonatas, violoncello, piano, op. 119, C major] *Sonata in C major for violoncello and piano, op. 119,* ed. by Mstislav Rostropovich. International Music 1631, $10.

1394 Rachmaninoff, Sergei, 1873–1943

[Sonatas, violoncello, piano, op. 19, G minor] *Sonata in G minor for violoncello and piano, op. 19.* International Music 517, ed. by Leonard Rose, $12; Masters Music M1107, $8.50.

1395 Saint-Saëns, Camille, 1835–1921

[Allegro appassionato, violoncello, piano] *Allegro appassionato for violoncello and piano, op. 43.* International Music 1648, ed. by Leonard Rose, $5; Well-Tempered Press W7086, $3.95.

1396 * Schubert, Franz, 1797–1828

[Sonatas, arpeggione, piano, D. 821, A minor; arr.] *Sonata in A minor for violoncello and piano, D. 821, "Arpeggione sonata."* Bärenreiter BA6970, $15; International Music 552, ed. by Leonard Rose, $8.

1397 * Schumann, Robert, 1810–1856

[Adagio und allegro, horn, piano, op. 70, A♭ major] *Adagio and allegro, op. 70, for cello (or horn or viola) and piano.* International Music 1242, ed. by Leonard Rose, $6; Well-Tempered Press W7034, $5.50.

1398 * Schumann, Robert, 1810–1856

[Fantasiestücke, clarinet, piano, op. 73] *Fantasy pieces, op. 73, for cello (or violin or clarinet) and piano.* Henle HN422, $9.95; International Music 741, $5.75.

1399 Schumann, Robert, 1810–1856

[Stücke im Volkston] *Five pieces in folk style, for cello and piano, op. 102,* ed. by Leonard Rose. International Music 1520, $6.25.

1400 * Schumann, Robert, 1810–1856

[Violoncello and piano music] *Compositions for violoncello and piano: Adagio and allegro; Fantasy pieces, op. 73; Five pieces in folk style.* Peters P2373, $24.20.

1401 Shostakovich, Dmitrii Dmitrievich, 1906–1975

[Sonatas, violoncello, piano, op. 40] *Sonata for violoncello and piano, op. 40.* Belwin Mills 4445, $7.50; International Music 2087, ed. by Leonard Rose, $10.

1402 Strauss, Richard, 1869–1949

[Sonatas, violoncello, piano, op. 6, F major] *Sonata in F major for cello and piano, op. 6.* International Music 1794, $7.75; Masters Music M1637, $9.95; Universal UE1007, $12.95.

1403 * Stravinsky, Igor, 1882–1971

[Suite italienne, violoncello, piano] *Suite italienne for violoncello and piano.* Boosey & Hawkes SCB 15, $24.

1404 * Vivaldi, Antonio, 1678–1741

[Sonatas, violoncello, continuo. Selections] *Six sonatas for violoncello and continuo, op. 14, no. 1–6 (RV 40, 41, 43, 45–47).* International Music 1852, realized by Luigi Dallapiccola, $11; Peters P4938, $23.45; G. Schirmer LB1794, $11.95.

Violoncello Concertos/Piano Reductions

The following section lists works for violoncello and orchestra, with the orchestral score reduced for piano accompaniment. When ordering, specify "arranged for violoncello and piano; score and part."

1405 * Bloch, Ernest, 1880–1959

[Schelomo; arr.] *Schelomo: Hebraic rhapsody for violoncello and orchestra.* G. Schirmer ST28161, $18.95.

1406 * Boccherini, Luigi, 1743–1805

[Concertos, violoncello, orchestra, G. 482, B♭ major; arr.] *Cello concerto no. 1 in B♭ major.* Breitkopf & Härtel EB3596, $14; International Music 1720, ed. by Leonard Rose, $6.50.

1407 * Bruch, Max, 1838–1920

[Kol nidrei; arr.] *Kol Nidrei, op. 47, for cello and orchestra.* C. Fischer B2713, $4.75; International Music 1682, $6.

1408 Dohnányi, Ernő, 1877–1960

[Konzertstück, violoncello, orchestra, op. 12, D major; arr.] *Concertpiece in D major, op. 12, for cello and orchestra.* International Music 434, $12.

1409 * Dvořák, Antonín, 1841–1904

[Concertos, violoncello, orchestra, op. 104, B minor; arr.] *Concerto in B minor for cello, op. 104.* International Music 1080, ed. by Leonard Rose, $9.25; Masters Music M1562, $17.50; G. Schirmer ED3348, ed. by Janos Starker, $18; Schott ED4605, $12.95.

1410 * Elgar, Edward, 1857–1934

[Concertos, violoncello, orchestra, op. 85, E minor; arr.] *Violoncello concerto, op. 85.* Novello, $19.95.

1411 Goltermann, Georg, 1824–1898

[Concertos, violoncello, orchestra, no. 4, op. 65, G major; arr.] *Concerto no. 4 in G major for cello, op. 65,* ed. by Leonard Rose. International Music 1606, $7.

1412 * Haydn, Joseph, 1732–1809

[Concertos, violoncello, orchestra, H. VIIb, 1, C major; arr.] *Cello concerto no. 1 in C major.* Henle HN417, $14.95; International Music 2325, ed. by Mstislav Rostropovich, $8.

1413 * Haydn, Joseph, 1732–1809

[Concertos, violoncello, orchestra, H. VIIb, 2, D major; arr.] *Concerto for violoncello in D major, Hob. VIIb:2.* Henle HN418, $15.95.

1414 Kabalevsky, Dmitry Borisovich, 1904–1987

[Concertos, violoncello, orchestra, no. 1, op. 49; arr.] *Cello concerto no. 1, op. 49.* International Music 3113, $8.50; Well-Tempered Press W7029, $7.95.

1415 * Lalo, Édouard, 1823–1892

[Concertos, violoncello, orchestra, D minor; arr.] *Concerto in D minor for cello.* International Music 858, ed. by Leonard Rose, $10; Peters P3799, $22.25; G. Schirmer LB1870, $15.95.

1416 Milhaud, Darius, 1892–1974

[Concertos, violoncello, orchestra, no. 2; arr.] *Concerto no. 2 for violoncello.* Associated Music AMP 194555, $18.

1417 * Saint-Saëns, Camille, 1835–1921

[Carnaval des animaux. Cygne; arr.] *The swan, from "Carnival of the animals," for cello and orchestra.* C. Fischer B2789, $4; International Music 1630, ed. by Leonard Rose, $3.50.

1418 Saint-Saëns, Camille, 1835–1921

[Concertos, violoncello, orchestra, no. 1, op. 33, A minor; arr.] *Concerto for violoncello, no. 1 in A minor, op. 33.* Durand 514-00587, $27; International Music 1212, ed. by Leonard Rose, $7; Well-Tempered Press W7023, $7.50.

1419 * Schumann, Robert, 1810–1856

[Concertos, violoncello, orchestra, op. 129, A minor; arr.] *Concerto for violoncello in A minor, op. 129.* Breitkopf & Härtel EB1888, $15.60; International Music 1992, ed. by Leonard Rose, $8.75; Well-Tempered Press W7040, $8.95.

1420 * Shostakovich, Dmitrii Dmitrievich, 1906–1975

[Concertos, violoncello, orchestra, no. 1, op. 107, E♭; arr.] *Concerto for violoncello, no. 1, op. 107.* International Music 2191, ed. by Mstislav Rostropovich, $10; Well-Tempered Press W7024, $9.50.

1421 * Tchaikovsky, Peter Ilich, 1840–1893

[Variations sur un thème rococo; arr.] *Variations on a rococo theme, for cello and orchestra.* International Music 1263, ed. by Leonard Rose, $6; Well-Tempered Press W7039, $7.50.

1422 Walton, William, 1902–1983

[Concertos, violoncello, orchestra; arr.] *Concerto for violoncello.* Oxford University Press 0-19-368121-8, $39.95.

Violoncello Duets

1423 Stevens, Halsey, 1908–

[Duos, violoncellos] *Five duos for two cellos.* Peters P6028, $14.65.

Violoncello Methods and Studies

1424 Applebaum, Samuel, 1904–

The Belwin string builder (cello): a string class method. Belwin Mills, 3 v., with solo part, piano accompaniment, cassette tape, and compact disc for each volume. Solo part, $5.50 each; piano accompaniment, $7 each; cassette tape, $8.95 each; compact disc, $10.95 each.

1425 Cossmann, Bernhard, 1822–1910

Studies for developing agility, strength of fingers and purity of intonation, for cello. International Music 413, $6.50.

1426 Dotzauer, J. J. F. (Justus Johann Friedrich), 1783–1860

[Etudes, violoncello] *113 studies for cello.* International Music 1312, 1313, 967, 1287, 4 v., $7.75, $7.75, $8.25, $9.25.

1427 * Dotzauer, J. J. F. (Justus Johann Friedrich), 1783–1860

[Violoncellschule] *Violoncello method.* C. Fischer O364-O365, 2 v., $6.50 each.

1428 Duport, J. L. (Jean Louis), 1749–1819

[Exercices faisants suite à l'essai sur le doigté] *Twenty-one etudes for the violoncello.* International Music 2314, ed. by Pierre Fournier, $10.50; G. Schirmer LB637-638, 2 v., $9.50, $9.95.

1429 Grützmacher, Friedrich Wilhelm Ludwig, 1832–1903

[Tägliche Übungen] *Daily studies, op. 67, for cello.* International Music 2682, $7.25.

1430 Klengel, Julius, 1859–1933

[Technische Studien] *Technical studies for the violoncello.* International Music 1597, 2132, ed. by Leonard Rose, 2 v., $9 each; G. Schirmer LB1816, $7.95.

1431 * Lee, Sebastian, 1805–1887

[Melodic studies, violoncello, op. 31] *Forty melodic and progressive etudes for violoncello, op. 31.* International Music 2003-2004, ed. by Leonard Rose, 2 v., $5.50 each; G. Schirmer LB639-640, 2 v., $6.95, $7.95.

1432 * Popper, David, 1843–1913

[Hohe Schule des Violoncellspiels] *High school of cello playing: 40 etudes, op. 73, for cello.* International Music 811, $11; G. Schirmer LB1883, $10.95.

1433 Starker, Janos, 1924–

An organized method of string playing: violoncello exercises for the left hand. Peer International, $7.50.

1434 Suzuki, Shinichi, 1898–

Sato cello school. Rev. ed. Summy-Birchard, 3 v., with solo part, piano accompaniment, and cassette tape for each volume. Solo part, $6.95 each; piano accompaniment, $6.95 each; cassette tape, $12.95 each.

1435 Yampolsky, Mark

Violoncello technique. MCA U00247, $9.95.

Double Bass Music

Music for the double bass spans classic, jazz, and rock music, as reflected in this section. The following distributor specializes in music for double bass, as well as books, videos, and sound recordings featuring the double bass:

> Lemur Music, Inc.
> P.O. Box 1137
> San Juan Capistrano, CA 92693
> (800) 246-2277 phone
> (714) 493-8565 fax

Solo Double Bass Music

1436 * Coolman, Todd

The bass tradition: past, present, future: biographies, 36 transcribed solos, discographies. Jamey Aebersold, $9.45.

1437 Kreutzer, Rodolphe, 1766–1831

[Études ou caprices, violin. Selections; arr.] *Eighteen studies, transcribed for double bass.* International Music 1180, $7.75.

1438 * Pettiford, Oscar, 1922–1960

The music of Oscar Pettiford, v. 1: 80 bass solos. O. Pettiford (319 Nashua Road, Billerica, MA, 01821), $13.95.

Solo Electric Bass Music

1439 * Jamerson, James, 1936–1983

Standing in the shadows of Motown: the life and music of legendary bassist James Jamerson. Book and 2 compact discs. Hal Leonard, $32.95.

Double Bass and Keyboard Music

1440 Bach, Johann Sebastian, 1685–1750

[Sonatas, viola da gamba, harpsichord, BWV 1028, D major; arr.] *Sonata no. 2 in D major for string bass and piano.* International Music 2091, $5.50.

1441 * Bottesini, Giovanni, 1821–1889

[Double bass, piano music. Selections] *Yorke complete Bottesini, double bass, piano.* Yorke Edition YE0037, YE0045, YE0060, 3 v., $15 each.

1442 * Dragonetti, Domenico, 1783–1846

[Waltzes, double bass, piano] *Three waltzes for double bass and piano.* Yorke Edition YE0002, $4.95.

1443 * Eccles, Henry, fl. 1694–1735

[Sonatas, violin, continuo, book 1. No. 11; arr.] *Sonata in G minor, double bass, piano.* International Music 1712, $5.75.

1444 * Hindemith, Paul, 1895–1963

[Sonatas, double bass, piano (1949)] *Sonata for double bass and piano (1949).* Schott ED4043, $19.95.

1445 Koussevitsky, Serge, 1874–1951

Chanson triste, double bass, piano, op. 1. International Music 1155, $3.75.

1446 * Koussevitsky, Serge, 1874–1951

[Valse miniature, op. 1. No. 2] *Valse miniature, op. 1, no. 2, double bass, piano.* International Music 1154, $3.75.

1447 *Solos for the double bass player, with piano accompaniment,* ed. by Oscar G. Zimmermann. G. Schirmer ED2567, $14.95.

1448 * Vivaldi, Antonio, 1678–1741

[Sonatas, violoncello, continuo, RV 40, E minor; arr.] *Sonata no. 5 in E minor for string bass and piano.* International Music 1472, $6.

Double Bass Concertos/Piano Reductions

The following section lists works for double bass and orchestra, with the orchestral score reduced for piano accompaniment. When ordering, specify "arranged for double bass and piano; score and part."

1449 Bottesini, Giovanni, 1821–1889

[Concertos, double bass, orchestra, no. 2, B minor; arr.] *Concerto no. 2 in B minor for double bass.* International Music 2301, $11.50; Yorke Edition YE0072, $9.50.

1450 Dittersdorf, Karl Ditters von, 1739–1799

[Concertos, double bass, orchestra, K. 171, E♭ major; arr.] *Concerto in E♭ major for double bass.* Schott ED2449, $19.95.

1451 * Dittersdorf, Karl Ditters von, 1739–1799

[Concertos, double bass, orchestra, K. 172, E♭ major; arr.] *Concerto in E♭ major for double bass.* Schott ED2473, $19.95.

1452 * Dragonetti, Domenico, 1763–1846

[Concertos, double bass, orchestra, A major; arr.] *Concerto in A major for string bass.* International Music 2098, $7.

1453 Koussevitsky, Serge, 1874–1951

[Concertos, double bass, orchestra, op. 3, F♯ minor; arr.] *Concerto for string bass in F♯ minor, op. 3.* International Music 462, $8; Kalmus K 04459, $4.

Double Bass Duets

1454 *Album of 24 classical and modern duets for two string basses.* International Music 1725, $5.75.

1455 Telemann, Georg Philipp, 1681–1767

[Canons mélodieux; arr.] *6 canonic sonatas for two string basses.* International Music 3077, $8.

Double Bass Methods and Studies

1456 * Anderson, Gerald (Gerald E.), and Robert S. Frost

All for strings: comprehensive string method (double bass). Neil A. Kjos, 3 v., with separate solo part and piano accompaniment for each volume. Solo part, $4.95 each; piano accompaniment, $4.95 each.

1457 Nanny, Edouard, 1872–1942

Méthode complète pour la contrabass à quatre et cinq cordes = Complete method for the four- and five-stringed bass. Leduc AL15876-15877, 2 v., $45.50, $31.25.

1458 Rabbath, François, 1931–

[Nouvelle technique de la contrabasse] *A new technique for the double bass.* Leduc AL25.431, AL25.806, AL26.328, 3 v., $25.10, $27.10, $52.60.

1459 Reid, Rufus, 1944–

The evolving bassist. Myriad Limited, $18.50.

1460 Richmond, Mike

Modern walking bass technique. Ped Xing Music, $9.

1461 Simandl, Franz, 1840–1912

Gradus ad parnassum: 24 studies. International Music 1754, 1440, 2 v., $6.75, $7.25.

1462 * Simandl, Franz, 1840–1912

[Neueste Methode des Kontrabass-Spiels] *New method for the double bass.* Rev. ed. C. Fischer 0492, 03567, 2 v., $17.95, $14.95.

1463 Storch, Josef Emanuel, 1841–1877, and Josef Hrabe, 1816–1870

[Etudes, double bass. Selections] *57 studies for string bass.* International Music 1034-1035, 2 v., $6.50, $7.

1464 Streicher, Ludwig

[Mein Musizieren auf dem Kontrabass] *My way of playing the double bass: instruction and advice for the beginning and advanced double bassist.* Doblinger 03914-03917, 4 v., $18.90, $14.50, $11.25, $16.50.

1465 Sturm, Wilhelm, 1829–1898

[Studien, double bass, op. 20] *One hundred ten studies for string bass, op. 20.* International Music 2079-2080, 2 v., $7.75 each.

Electric Bass Methods

1466 * Dean, Dan

The Hal Leonard electric bass method, composite [contains books 1–3]. Hal Leonard HL00699283, $14.95.

1467 Filiberto, Roger

Mel Bay's electric bass method. Mel Bay MB93234-MB93235, 2 v., $5.95 each.

1468 Liebman, Jon, bass guitarist

Funk bass. Hal Leonard HL00699347, $14.95.

1469 * Rainey, Chuck

The complete electric bass player, books 1–5. Amsco AM 32705, AM 37268, AM 37284, AM 37276, AM 39405, $16.95, $10.95, $10.95, $10.95, $10.95.

Harp Music

The following distributors specialize in harp music:

International Music Service
133 West 69th Street
New York, NY 10023
(800) 959-5972 phone
(212) 874-3360 phone
(212) 580-9829 fax

Lyon and Healy
168 North Ogden
Chicago, IL 60607
Attn: Accessory Dept.
(800) 621-3881 phone
(312) 786-1881 phone
(312) 226-1502 fax

Vanderbilt Music Company
312-A South Swain Avenue
P.O. Box 456
Bloomington, IN 47402
(800) 533-7200 phone
(812) 333-5255 phone
(812) 333-5257 fax

For Claude Debussy's *Sonata for flute, viola, and harp,* see the study score and performing edition listings for "Chamber Music for Mixed Winds and Strings" in chapter 3 and chapter 9.

Solo Harp Music

1470 * *An anthology of music for the harp from the Elizabethan, baroque, classical, romantic, and modern periods,* ed. by Dewey Owens. Lyra Music, $10.

1471 Arnold, Malcolm, 1921–

[Fantasies, harp, op. 117] *Fantasy for harp, op. 117.* Faber Music F0539, $8.95.

1472 * Bach, Carl Philipp Emanuel, 1714–1788

[Solos, harp, H. 563, G major] *Sonata for harp in G major, Wotq. 139.* Breitkopf & Härtel EB6593, $10.

1473 Beethoven, Ludwig van, 1770–1827

[Variations über ein Schweizer Lied] *Variations on a Swiss air, for harp,* ed. by Nicanor Zabaleta. Schott ST38510, $7.95.

1474   Berio, Luciano, 1925–

[Sequenza, no. 2] *Sequenza II, harp.* Universal UE18101, $19.95.

1475 *   Britten, Benjamin, 1913–1976

[Suites, harp, op. 83] *Suite for harp, op. 83.* Faber Music, $13.50.

1476   Carter, Elliott, 1908–

[Trilogy. Bariolage] *Bariolage, harp solo from "Trilogy."* Hendon/Boosey & Hawkes SHB 20, $10.

1477   Castérède, Jacques, 1926–

[Preludes, harp] *Trois preludes, harp.* Leduc AL25.533, $20.

1478 *   Corri, Sophia, 1775–1847

[Sonatas, harp, op. 2. No. 3] *Sonata for harp in C minor, op. 2, no. 3,* ed. by Nicanor Zabaleta. Schott ST38511, $7.95. Often attributed to Jan Ladislaus Dussek (1760–1812).

1479 *   Debussy, Claude, 1862–1918

[Piano music. Selections; arr.] *Pour la harpe: piano pieces transcribed for harp: Claire de lune; Rêverie; Valse romantique.* Jobert, $19.75.

1480 *   Debussy, Claude, 1862–1918

[Preludes, piano, book 1. Fille aux cheveux de lin; arr.] *La fille aux cheveux de lin,* transcribed for harp by Marcel Grandjany. Durand 574-00085, $12.50.

1481   Del Tredici, David, 1937–

Acrostic paraphrase from "Final Alice," for harp. Boosey & Hawkes SHB 19, $17.50.

1482   Falla, Manuel de, 1876–1946

[Vida breve. Danza, no. 1; arr.] *Spanish dance no. 1 from the opera "La vida breve,"* transcribed for harp by Marcel Grandjany. Associated Music, $6.95.

1483 *   Fauré, Gabriel, 1845–1924

[Impromptus, harp, op. 86, D♭ major] *Impromptu for harp, op. 86.* Durand 574-00102, $18.

1484   Françaix, Jean, 1912–

[Suites, harp] *Suite for harp.* Schott ED6780, $12.95.

1485 *   Grandjany, Marcel, 1891–1975

[Chansons populaires françaises] *Deux chansons populaires françaises, harp: Le bon petit roi d'Yvetot; Et ron, ron, ron, petit patapon.* Durand 574-00113, 574-00116, 2 v., $12.75, $8.50.

1486 *   Handel, George Frideric, 1685–1759

[Suites, harpsichord, HWV 430, E major. Air con variazioni; arr.] *The harmonious blacksmith: air with variations,* transcribed for harp by Carlos Salzedo. Lyra Music, $5.

1487   Hindemith, Paul, 1895–1963

[Sonatas, harp] *Sonata for harp (1935).* Schott ED3644, $14.95.

1488   Milhaud, Darius, 1892–1974

[Sonatas, harp] *Sonata for harp.* Eschig ME8023, $16.

1489 *   Naderman, François Joseph, 1773 (ca.)–1835

[Sonates progressives] *Seven progressive sonatas for harp, op. 92.* Leduc AL20.037, $30.

1490   Persichetti, Vincent, 1915–1987

[Parable, no. 7] *Parable for solo harp.* Elkan-Vogel 574-00095, $5.75.

1491 *   Pierné, Gabriel, 1863–1937

Impromptu-caprice for harp, op. 9. Leduc AL10.381, $15.

1492 *   Renié, Henriette, 1875–1956

Feuillets d'album = Album leaves. New rev. ed. by Marcel Grandjany. E. B. Marks, $9.

1493   Rorem, Ned, 1923–

Sky music: ten pieces for harp. Boosey & Hawkes SHB 3, $17.

1494   Saint-Saëns, Camille, 1835–1921

[Fantaisies, harp, op. 95] *Fantaisie for harp, op. 95.* Durand 574-00195, $18.

1495 *   Salzedo, Carlos, 1885–1961

[Morceaux. Variations sur un thème dans le style ancien] *Variations sur un thème dans le style ancien, harp.* Leduc AL15.280, $20.

1496 *   *Solos for the harp player,* ed. by Lucile Lawrence. G. Schirmer, $12.95.

1497   *Spanish masters of the 16th and 17th century,* ed. by Nicanor Zabaleta. Schott AP360, $7.95.

1498   Tailleferre, Germaine, 1892–1983

[Sonatas, harp] *Sonata for harp.* Nouvelles Éditions Meridian NM1771, $8.

1499 Tcherepnin, Alexander, 1899–1977

[Caprices diatoniques] *Quatre caprices diatoniques, harp, op. posth.* Beliaeff Bel. Nr. 495, $20.

1500 Tournier, Marcel, 1879–1951

Vers la source dans le bois, for harp. Leduc, $16.

Harp and Keyboard Music

1501 * Debussy, Claude, 1862–1918

[Danse sacrée et danse profane; arr.] *Danses pour harpe chromatique ou harpe à pédales; transcription for harp and piano.* Durand 574-00082, $37.25.

1502 * Grandjany, Marcel, 1891–1975

Aria in classic style, harp and organ. Associated Music, $8.

Harp Concertos/Piano Reductions

1503 Dohnányi, Erno, 1877–1960

[Concertos, harp, orchestra, C major; arr.] *Concerto in C major for harp and orchestra, with piano reduction.* Lyra Music, $15.

1504 * Ginastera, Alberto, 1916–1983

[Concertos, harp, orchestra, op. 25; arr.] *Harp concerto, op. 25, with piano reduction.* Boosey & Hawkes SHB 14, harp and piano score, $31; Boosey & Hawkes SHB 7, harp part, $32.

1505 * Handel, George Frideric, 1685–1759

[Concertos, organ, orchestra, op. 4. No. 6; arr.] *Concerto in B♭ major, transcribed for harp solo or to be played with orchestral accompaniment;* with an original cadenza by Carlos Salzedo. G. Schirmer LB1960, $6.95.

1506 * Ravel, Maurice, 1875–1937

[Introduction et allegro; arr.] *Introduction and allegro for harp and chamber ensemble, with piano reduction.* Durand 574-00180, harp and piano score, $53.25; Durand 574-00179, harp part, $17.50.

1507 * Rodrigo, Joaquín, 1901–

[Concierto serenata; arr.] *Concierto serenata for harp and orchestra, with piano reduction,* ed. by Nicanor Zabaleta. Union Musical Ediciones UME19661, $27.

Harp Methods and Studies

1508 * Bochsa, Robert Nicolas Charles, 1789–1856, and Charles Oberthür, 1819–1885

Universal method for the harp. C. Fischer O531, $17.50.

1509 * Holý, Alfred, 1866–1948

[Studies, harp, op. 26] *Twenty-four easy studies for the harp, op. 26.* Lyra Music, $10.50.

1510 * Larivière, Edmond, 1811–1842

[Etudes, harp, op. 9] *Exercises and etudes for harp, op. 9.* Leduc AL20.032, $27.

1511 * Lawrence, Lucile, 1907– , and Carlos Salzedo, 1865–1961

Method for the harp: fundamental exercises [includes *Chanson dans la nuit* by Salzedo]. G. Schirmer, $13.95.

1512 * Zingel, Hans Joachim, 1904–1978

Neue Harfenlehre: Geschichte, Spielart, Musik = New harp instruction: history, method of playing, music. F. Hofmeister, 4 v., $32, $26, $37, $21.

Guitar Music

The following distributors specialize in guitar music. Their catalogs can be used for bibliographic information as well as for price and availability:

Editions Orphée
407 North Grant Avenue, Suite 400
Columbus, OH 43215-4304
(614) 224-4304 phone
(614) 224-1009 fax
http://www.orphee.com

Guitar Solo
514 Bryant Street
San Francisco, CA 94107
(415) 896-1144 phone
(415) 896-1155 fax

Solo Guitar Music

1513 * Albéniz, Isaac, 1860–1909

[Piano music. Selections; arr.] *Six pieces,* arranged by Julian Bream. Schott ST11428, $14.95.

1514 Albright, William, 1944–

Shadows: eight serenades for guitar. Mel Bay MB93973, $5.95.

1515 * *Andrés Segovia: die schönsten Stücke aus seinem Repertoire = Andrés Segovia: the finest pieces from his repertoire.* Schott GA520, $19.95.

1516 Babbitt, Milton, 1916–

[Compositions, guitar] *Composition for guitar.* Peters P67028, $20.45.

1517 * Bach, Johann Sebastian, 1685–1750

[Lute music; arr.] *The solo lute works of Johann Sebastian Bach,* arranged by Frank Koonce. Neil A. Kjos WG100, $24.95.

1518 ** *The baroque guitar,* ed. by Frederick Noad. Amsco AM 35890, $14.95.

1519 * Barrios Mangoré, Augustín, 1885–1944

[Preludes, guitar, op. 5. No. 1] *La catedral.* Belwin Mills SI 154, $6.50; G. Zanibon G.5311Z, $4.50.

1520 Berio, Luciano, 1925–

[Sequenza, no. 11] *Sequenza XI, for guitar solo (1988).* Universal UE19273, $19.95.

1521 Berkeley, Lennox, Sir, 1903–1989

[Theme and variations, guitar] *Theme and variations.* Chester JWC480, $7.95.

1522 * *The best of Bream,* ed. by Julian Bream. Faber Music FAB 0525, $7.50.

1523 * Britten, Benjamin, 1913–1976

Nocturnal after John Dowland, op. 70, ed. by Julian Bream. Faber Music ST47126, $12.95.

1524 Brouwer, Leo, 1939–

Elogia de la danza. Schott GA425, $9.95.

1525 * Castelnuovo-Tedesco, Mario, 1895–1968

[Sonatas, guitar, op. 77] *Sonata: omaggio a Boccherini,* ed. by Andrés Segovia. Schott GA149, $8.95.

1526 Chávez, Carlos, 1899–1978

Feuille d'album, for guitar solo. Carlanita Music CH101, $1.75.

1527 ** *The classical guitar,* ed. by Frederick Noad. Amsco AM 35908, $14.95.

1528 Davies, Peter Maxwell, 1934–

Hill runes. Boosey & Hawkes SRB 61, $9.75.

1529 * Dowland, John, 1563?–1626

[Lute music. Selections] *Solowerke, v. 1.* Universal UE16699, $11.95.

1530 Falla, Manuel de, 1876–1946

[Homenaje para Le tombeau de Debussy] *Homenaje: Le tombeau de Debussy.* Chester JWC 55675, $5.95.

1531 * Ginastera, Alberto, 1916–1983

[Sonatas, guitar, op. 47] *Sonata for guitar, op. 47.* Boosey & Hawkes SRB 3, $20.

1532 * Giuliani, Mauro, 1781–1829

[Guitar music. Selections] *Compositions for guitar.* Ricordi Americana BA 12407-12408, 2 v., $11.75, $7.25.

1533 * Granados, Enrique, 1867–1916

[Danzas españolas. No. 5; arr.] *Danza española no. 5: Andaluza.* Unión Musical Española UME15611, $6.25.

1534 Henze, Hans Werner, 1926–

[Royal winter music. No. 1] *Royal winter music: first sonata on Shakespearean characters,* ed. by Julian Bream. Schott GA467, $14.95.

1535 Kolb, Barbara, 1939–

[Lullabies, guitar] *Three lullabies for guitar solo.* Boosey & Hawkes SRB 59, $9.75.

1536 *Latin American solos for guitar,* ed. by Sophocles Papas and Carlos Barbosa-Lima. Columbia Music 494-01626, $6.25.

1537 * Llobet, Miguel, 1878–1938

[Canciones poulares catalanas] *Diez canciones populares catalanas.* Unión Musical Española UME20372, $4.

1538 * Milán, Luis, 16th cent.

[Maestro. Selections; arr.] *Six pavanas: facsimile and transcription,* ed. by Karl Scheit. Universal UE14458, $8.95.

1539 Montgomery, Wes, 1925–1969

Guitar transcriptions. Hal Leonard HL00675536, $15.95.

1540 * Moreno Torroba, Federico, 1891–1982

Nocturno, ed. by Andrés Segovia. Schott GA103, $5.95.

1541 Moreno Torroba, Federico, 1891–1982

[Sonatina, guitar] *Sonatina for guitar,* ed. by Andrés Segovia. Columbia CO.168, $4.50.

1542 Narváez, Luis de, 16th cent.

[Delphin de musica. Diferencias sobre Conde Clarós; arr.] *Veintidós variaciones sobre "Conde clarós,"* arranged by Graciano Tarrago. Unión Musical Española UME19692, $3.95.

1543   Piazzolla, Astor, 1921–1992

[Pieces, guitar] *Cinco piezas para guitarra.* Bérben E. 2343 B., $11.75.

1544 * Ponce, Manuel M. (Manuel María), 1882–1948

[Preludes, guitar] *Preludes.* Schott GA124-125, 2 v., $7.95, $6.95.

1545 * *The Renaissance guitar,* ed. by Frederick Noad. Amsco AM 35882, $14.95.

1546 * Rodrigo, Joaquín, 1901–

[Piezas españolas] *Tres piezas españolas.* Schott GA212, $8.95.

1547   Rorem, Ned, 1923–

[Suites, guitar] *Suite for guitar.* Boosey & Hawkes SRB 55, $12.50.

1548 * Sanz, Gaspar, 1640–1710

[Instrucción de música sobre la guitarra española. Selections] *Suite española.* Unión Musical Española UME21354, $9.95.

1549 * *Solos for jazz guitar: classic jazz solos as played by Django Reinhardt, Charlie Christian, Les Paul . . . [et al.].* C. Fischer ATJ306, $8.95.

1550 * Sor, Fernando, 1778–1839

[Fantaisie sur un air favori écossais] *Variations on a Scottish theme, "Ye banks and braes o bonnie Doon."* Tecla, $9.25.

1551 * Sor, Fernando, 1778–1839

[Fantaisies, guitar, no. 1, op. 7, C minor] *Fantasia no. 1, op. 7.* Oxford University Press 0-19-358860-9, $9.95.

1552 * Sor, Fernando, 1778–1839

[Introduction et variations sur l'air Malbroug] *Introduktion und Variationen über "Malborough s'en va-t-en guerre," op. 28.* Universal UE16702, $10.95.

1553 * Sor, Fernando, 1778–1839

[Introduction et variations sur un thème de Mozart] *Introduction and variations on a theme by Mozart from "The magic flute."* Schott GA612, $8.95.

1554 * Tárrega, Francisco, 1852–1909

[Guitar music. Selections] *Doce composiciones para guitarra.* Ricordi Americana BA 11248, $9.

1555   Tárrega, Francisco, 1852–1909

[Guitar music. Selections] *Transcriptions for guitar.* Universal UE16700, $19.95.

1556 * Tárrega, Francisco, 1852–1909

[Preludes, guitar] *Complete preludes.* Universal UE13408, $8.95.

1557   Tower, Joan, 1938–

Clocks, for guitar, ed. by Sharon Isbin. Associated Music HL50488702, $6.95.

1558 * Turina, Joaquín, 1882–1949

Fandanguillo, ed. by Andrés Segovia. Schott GA102, $5.95.

1559   Turina, Joaquín, 1882–1949

Hommage à Tárrega, ed. by Andrés Segovia. Schott GA136, $5.95.

1560 * Villa-Lobos, Heitor, 1887–1959

[Etudes, guitar] *Twelve etudes for guitar.* Eschig 564-01603, $38.

1561   Walton, William, 1902–1983

[Bagatelles, guitar] *Five bagatelles for guitar,* ed. by Julian Bream. Oxford University Press 0-19-359407-2, $17.95.

Guitar Concertos/Piano Reductions/Guitar and Keyboard Music

1562   Dodgson, Stephen, 1924–

Duo concertant, for guitar and harpsichord. Eschig, $35.

1563 * Rodrigo, Joaquín, 1901–

[Concierto de Aranjuez; arr.] *Concierto de Aranjuez for guitar and orchestra, with piano reduction.* Schott ED7242, $29.95.

1564 * Vivaldi, Antonio, 1678–1741

[Concertos, lute, violins (2), continuo, RV 93, D major; arr.] *Concerto in D major for guitar (or lute) and string orchestra, with piano reduction.* Columbia 494-00248, $3; Éditions Musicales Transatlantiques 564-00877, ed. by Narciso Yepes, $24.

Christmas and Wedding Music for Guitar

1565   *Carols for guitar: fifteen Christmas carols,* arranged by Hector Quine. Oxford University Press 0-19-358405-0, $8.95.

1566 ** *A guitar for Christmas,* arranged by Liona Boyd. Hal Leonard HL00699070, $9.95.

1567 ** *Wedding music for classical guitar,* ed. by Christopher Boydston. Mel Bay Music, $6.95.

Music for Guitar Ensemble (Two or More Guitars)

1568 Hindemith, Paul, 1895–1963

[Rondos, guitars (3)] *Rondo for 3 guitars (1925).* Schott GA412, $7.95.

1569 * Sor, Fernando, 1778–1839

[Duets, guitars, op. 34] *L'encouragement, op. 34, for 2 guitars.* Zimmermann ZM 1143, $7.00.

1570 *Spiel mit: 22 Gitarren-Duette = Play along: 22 guitar duets,* arranged and ed. by Heinz Teuchert. Ricordi 2281, $14.95.

Methods and Studies for Classical Guitar

1571 * Carcassi, Matteo, 1792 (ca.)–1853

[Méthode complète de guitare. English & Spanish] *Complete Carcassi guitar method: with 25 studies, in Spanish and English.* Mel Bay, $5.95.

1572 Giuliani, Mauro, 1781–1829

[Studi, guitar, op. 1a] *Studies for guitar, op. 1a.* Rev. ed. Schott GA30, $9.95.

1573 ** Noad, Frederick M.

Solo guitar playing. 2nd ed. G. Schirmer 0-02-871680-9, 0-02-871690-6, 2 v., $18, $16.95.

1574 Segovia, Andrés, 1893–1987

Diatonic major and minor scales. Columbia CO 127, $3.95.

1575 * Sor, Fernando, 1778–1839

[Guitar music. Selections] *Twenty studies for the guitar,* ed. by Andrés Segovia. E. B. Marks HL00006363, $6.95.

1576 Sor, Fernando, 1778–1839

[Méthode pour la guitare. English] *Method for the Spanish guitar.* Da Capo Press 0-306-80121-3, $7.95.

1577 Tárrega, Francisco, 1852–1909

[Guitar music. Selections] *Thirty-five etudes.* Zen-on Music 411239100x, $25.

Methods and Studies for Flamenco Guitar

1578 * Martín, Juan

El arte flamenco de la guitarra, English text. Presser 414-41132, 414-41133, 2 v., $20 each.

1579 * Serrano, Juan

Flamenco guitar: tecnicas basicas = Flamenco guitar: basic techniques. Mel Bay MB93632, $9.95.

Methods and Studies for Popular Guitar

1580 ** *Basic guitar,* from the editors of *Guitar player* and *Frets* magazines, rev. ed. by Helen Casabona. GPI Publications HL00183051, $14.95.

1581 * Traum, Happy

Traditional and contemporary guitar fingerpicking styles. Oak Publications OK62091, $7.95.

Methods and Studies for Jazz Guitar

1582 * Bell, Joe

Improvising jazz guitar. Amsco AM 37326, $12.95.

1583 ** De Mause, Alan

Beginning jazz guitar: everything you need to know to become an accomplished performer of jazz guitar, ed. by Jason Shulamn and Brenda Murphy. Amsco AM 32505, $9.95.

Chamber Music

Compiled by
Elizabeth Sadewhite (strings) and Brian Cockburn
(winds, mixed winds and strings, and unspecified instruments)

Chamber Music for Strings

String Duets
(Two Different String Instruments)

1584   Handel, George Frideric, 1685–1759

[Suites, harpsichord, HWV 432, G minor. Passacaille; arr.] *Passacaglia for violin and cello.* Parts. International Music 3363, $5.75.

1585 *   Paganini, Nicolò, 1782–1840

[Sonatas, violin, guitar, M.S. 3, A major] *Grosse Sonate, for guitar and violin accompaniment.* Parts. Zimmermann ZM1037, $9.50.

1586   Rossini, Gioacchino, 1792–1868

[Duets, violoncello, double bass, D major] *Duetto for cello and double bass.* Parts. Yorke Edition YE001, $10.50.

String Trios (Violin, Viola, Violoncello)

1587 *   Beethoven, Ludwig van, 1770–1827

[Trios, strings] *Five string trios: op. 3; op. 8, "Serenade"; op. 9, no. 1–3.* Parts. Henle HN192 (with Beethoven's *Duo for viola and cello, WoO 32, "Eyeglasses"*), $48.95; Kalmus K 03142, $10; Peters P194 (with Beethoven's *Serenade in D major for flute, violin and viola, op. 25*), $39.95.

1588   Dohnányi, Ernő, 1877–1960

[Serenade, string trio, op. 10, C major] *Serenade for violin, viola, and cello, op. 10.* Parts. International Music 541, $10.50.

1589   Fine, Irving, 1914–1962

[Fantasia, string trio] *Fantasia for string trio.* Parts. Boosey & Hawkes FIN 22, $17.50.

1590 *   Mozart, Wolfgang Amadeus, 1756–1791

[Divertimenti, string trio, K. 563, E♭ major] *Divertimento in E♭ major for string trio, K. 563.* Parts. Bärenreiter BA4844, $25.20; Breitkopf & Härtel KM744, $18.50; International Music 547, $8.50; Peters P1419, $10.75.

1591 * Schubert, Franz, 1797–1828

[Trios, strings] *String trios for violin, viola, and cello: D. 471 in B♭ major and D. 581 in B♭ major.* Parts. Bärenreiter BA5609, $19.80; Breitkopf & Härtel EB750, EB756, 2 v., $13.50, $11.50; International Music 827, 938, 2 v., $6.25, $6.75.

Piano Trios (Violin, Violoncello, and Piano, Unless Otherwise Indicated)

1592 Arensky, Anton Stepanovich, 1861–1906

[Trios, piano, strings, no. 1, op. 32, D minor] *Trio in D minor, op. 32, for violin, cello, and piano.* Score and parts. International Music 745, $15; Peters P4315, $22.25.

1593 * Bach, Johann Sebastian, 1685–1750

[Concertos, violins (2), string orchestra, BWV 1043, D minor; arr.] *Concerto for two violins, D minor, BWV 1043, with piano reduction.* Score and parts. Bärenreiter BA5188a, $14.25; Kalmus K 03022, $6.50; Peters P9032, ed. by David Oistrakh, $25.65.

1594 * Beethoven, Ludwig van, 1770–1827

[Trios, piano, strings] *13 piano trios (with Trio in B♭ major for clarinet or violin, cello and piano, op. 11, and Trio in G major for flute, bassoon and piano, K. 37).* Score and parts. Henle HN24, HN26, HN200, 3 v., $46.95, $48.95, $49.95; Peters P166a-I, P166a-II, P166b, 3 v., $40, $40, $55.

1595 * Beethoven, Ludwig van, 1770–1827

[Trios, piano, strings. Selections] *Six celebrated trios: op. 1, no. 1 and 3; op. 11; op. 70, no. 1; op. 97; op. 121a.* Score and parts. International Music 952, $29.75.

1596 Brahms, Johannes, 1833–1897

[Concertos, violin, violoncello, orchestra, op. 102, A minor; arr.] *Double concerto in A minor for violin and violoncello, op. 102; accompaniment arranged for piano.* Score and parts. International Music 548, $11.50.

1597 * Brahms, Johannes, 1833–1897

[Trios, piano, strings] *Three piano trios: op. 8, op. 87, and op. 101.* Score and parts. Henle HN245, $66.95; International Music 2670, 3062, 3061, 3 v., $13, $11, $11; Peters P3899a, P3899c, P3899d, 3 v., $15.40 each.

1598 Clarke, Rebecca, 1886–1979

[Trio, piano, strings] *Piano trio.* Score and parts. Da Capo Press 0-306-76053-3, $26.50.

1599 * Dvořák, Antonín, 1841–1904

[Trios, piano, strings, no. 4, op. 90, E minor] *Piano trio in E minor, op. 90, "Dumky trio."* Score and parts. Bärenreiter BA8301, $22; International Music 563, $14.50; Masters Music M1229, $16.50.

1600 * Haydn, Joseph, 1732–1809

[Trios, piano, strings] *31 piano trios.* Score and parts. Henle HN246, HN277, HN284, HN411, HN412, 5 v., $55.95, $64.95, $33.95, $61.95, $52.95; Peters P192a-192c, 3 v., $40, $50, $55.

1601 Ives, Charles, 1874–1954

[Trios, piano, strings] *Piano trio.* Score and parts. Peer International 61509-784, $30.

1602 * Mendelssohn-Bartholdy, Felix, 1809–1847

[Trios, piano, strings] *Two piano trios: op. 49 in D minor and op. 66 in C minor.* Score and parts. Henle HN250, $46.95; Peters P1740, $39.95.

1603 * Mozart, Wolfgang Amadeus, 1756–1791

[Trios, piano, strings] *Piano trios: K. 254, K. 442, K. 496, K. 502, K. 542, K. 548, K. 564, and Trio in E♭ major for clarinet, viola, piano, K. 498.* Score and parts. Bärenreiter BA4787 (omits K. 442), $38; Henle HN247, $55.95; International Music 951, $21; Peters P193a (omits K. 442), $68.90.

1604 * Ravel, Maurice, 1875–1937

[Trio, piano, strings, A minor] *Piano trio in A minor.* Score and parts. Masters Music M1808, $12.50.

1605 Schubert, Franz, 1797–1828

[Nocturne, piano trio, D. 897, E♭ major] *Nocturne in E♭ major, op. 148, D. 897.* Score and parts. International Music 775, $7.

1606 * Schubert, Franz, 1797–1828

[Trios, piano, strings] *Two piano trios: op. 99 in B♭ major, D. 898, and op. 100 in E♭ major, D. 929.* Score and parts. Henle HN193 (with Schubert's *Adagio, D. 897* and *Sonatensatz, D. 28*), $51.95; Peters P1673, $33.85.

1607 Schumann, Clara, 1819–1896

[Trio, piano, strings, op. 17, G minor] *Trio in G minor for piano, violin and violoncello, op. 17.* Score and parts. Amadeus BP2610, $24.05.

1608 * Schumann, Robert, 1810–1856

[Trios, piano, strings] *Three piano trios: op. 63, op. 80, and op. 110.* Score and parts. Peters P2377, $63.25.

1609 * Shostakovich, Dmitrii Dmitrievich, 1906–1975

[Trios, piano, strings, no. 2, op. 67, E minor] *Piano trio no. 2 in E minor, op. 67.* Score and parts. International Music 2086, $13.75; Kalmus K 09600, $14.95; Peters P4744, $38.05.

1610 Smetana, Bedřich, 1824–1884

[Trios, piano, strings, op. 15, G minor] *Piano trio in G minor, op. 15.* Score and parts. International Music 658, $14.25; Peters P4238, $31.25.

1611 * Tchaikovsky, Peter Ilich, 1840–1893

[Trios, piano, strings, op. 50, A minor] *Piano trio in A minor, op. 50.* Score and parts. International Music 943, $19.50; Kalmus K 09611, $16.95; Peters P3777, $46.60.

Trio Sonatas

Originating early in the seventeenth century, the trio sonata was a primary instrumental form of the baroque period. A trio sonata generally requires four performers: two solo players and two for the continuo part, one on harpsichord or other keyboard instrument, and one doubling the keyboard's bass line on cello, bassoon, or other low sustaining instrument. The examples listed here are but a few of hundreds, written by dozens of composers.

1612 * Bach, Johann Sebastian, 1685–1750

[Trio sonatas, violins, continuo, BWV 1037, C major] *Trio sonata in C major for 2 violins and continuo, BWV 1037, and Trio sonata in G minor for flute, violin and continuo, BWV 1038.* Score and parts. International Music 737, $7.

1613 Corelli, Arcangelo, 1653–1713

[Trio sonatas, violins, continuo, op. 2] *12 trio sonatas for 2 violins and continuo, op. 2.* Score and parts. International Music 1191-1193, 3 v., $10 each; Schott ED5430-5433, 4 v., $14.95 each.

1614 Handel, George Frideric, 1685–1759

[Trio sonatas, op. 2. No. 4] *Trio sonata op. 2, no. 4 in B♭ major for 2 violins and continuo.* Score and parts. International Music 752, $8.25; Schott ED4183, $10.95.

1615 Purcell, Henry, 1659–1695

[Trio sonatas, violins, continuo, Z. 807, G minor] *Sonata of IV parts, for 2 violins and basso continuo: Trio sonata VI in G minor (Chaconne in G minor), from "10 trio sonatas of IV parts (1697)."* Score and parts. Doblinger DM1136, in preparation.

1616 * Purcell, Henry, 1659–1695

[Trio sonatas, violins, continuo, Z. 810, F major] *Trio sonata in F major for 2 violins and continuo, "Golden sonata."* Score and parts. International Music 1553, $6.25; Schott ANT92, $11.95.

1617 Tartini, Giuseppe, 1692–1770

[Trio sonatas, violins, continuo, op. 3. No. 2] *Trio sonata in D major for 2 violins and continuo, op. 3, no. 2.* Score and parts. International Music 646, $5.50.

1618 * Telemann, Georg Philipp, 1681–1767

[Trio sonatas. Selections] *Six trio sonatas for 2 violins and continuo.* Score and parts. Schott ED4690-4691, 2 v., $14.95 each.

String Quartets (Two Violins, Viola, Violoncello)

1619 * Barber, Samuel, 1910–1981

[Quartets, strings, no. 1, op. 11, B minor] *String quartet no. 1 in B minor, op. 11.* Parts. G. Schirmer HL50341730, $15.

1620 * Bartók, Béla, 1881–1945

[Quartets, strings, no. 1] *String quartet no. 1, op. 7.* Parts. Boosey & Hawkes ENB 1937, $26; International Music 2690, $12; Masters Music M1164, $7.50.

1621 * Bartók, Béla, 1881–1945

[Quartets, strings, no. 4] *String quartet no. 4.* Parts. Boosey & Hawkes ENB 204, $29.

1622 * Beethoven, Ludwig van, 1770–1827

[Quartets, strings. Selections] *String quartets, vol. 1: op. 18, no. 1–6; op. 14, no. 1. vol. 2: op. 59, no. 1–3; op. 74; op. 95.* Parts. Henle HN139, HN268, 2 v., $54.95, $57.95.

1623 * Beethoven, Ludwig van, 1770–1827

[String quartet music] *Complete string quartets, including the Grosse Fuge.* Parts. Kalmus K 03143-03145, 3 v., $34.95, $25.50, $35; Peters P195a-P195c, 3 v., $35, $35, $50.

1624 * Borodin, Aleksandr Porfir'evich, 1833–1887

[Quartets, strings, no. 2, D major] *String quartet no. 2 in D major.* Parts. Breitkopf & Härtel EB5665, $22; International Music 510, $12; Well-Tempered Press W7003, $9.95.

1625 * Brahms, Johannes, 1833–1897

[Quartets, strings] *Complete string quartets: op. 51, no. 1–2; op. 67.* Parts. Breitkopf & Härtel EB6027-

6029, 3 v., $15 each; International Music 2870, $19.50; Peters P3903, $33.30.

1626 * Debussy, Claude, 1862–1918

[Quartet, strings, op. 10, G minor] *String quartet in G minor, op. 10.* Parts. Durand 514-00871, $46; International Music 1737, $12; Masters Music M1293, $13.50; Peters P9125, $40.

1627   Dvořák, Antonín, 1841–1904

[Quartets, strings, B. 75, D minor] *String quartet no. 9 in D minor, op. 34.* Parts. Bärenreiter BA8304, $18.

1628   Dvořák, Antonín, 1841–1904

[Quartets, strings, B. 92, E♭ major] *String quartet no. 10 in E♭ major, op. 51.* Parts. International Music 454, $12.50; Masters Music M1293, $12.50.

1629   Dvořák, Antonín, 1841–1904

[Quartets, strings, B. 121, C major] *String quartet no. 11 in C major, op. 61.* Parts. International Music 964, $13.75.

1630 * Dvořák, Antonín, 1841–1904

[Quartets, strings, B. 179, F major] *String quartet no. 12 in F major, op. 96, "American quartet."* Parts. Bärenreiter BA8302, $18; International Music 1084, $10.50; Kalmus K 03424, $7.50.

1631   Dvořák, Antonín, 1841–1904

[Quartets, strings, B. 192, G major] *String quartet no. 13 in G major, op. 106.* Parts. International Music 1085, $13.75; Masters Music M1250, $13.50.

1632   Dvořák, Antonín, 1841–1904

[Quartets, strings, B. 193, A♭ major] *String quartet no. 14 in A♭ major, op. 105.* Parts. International Music 463, $13.75.

1633 * Fauré, Gabriel, 1845–1924

[Quartets, strings, op. 121, E minor] *String quartet in E minor, op. 121.* Parts. Durand 514-00882, $66.75.

1634   Franck, César, 1822–1890

[Quartets, strings, D major] *String quartet in D major.* Parts. Masters Music M1157, $11; Peters P3746, $23.25.

1635   Ginastera, Alberto, 1916–1983

[Quartets, strings, no. 1, op. 20] *String quartet no. 1, op. 20.* Parts. Boosey & Hawkes ENB 128, $36.

1636 * Haydn, Joseph, 1732–1809

[Quartets, strings] *String quartets.* Parts. Henle HN205-209, HN212-213, v. 1–5 and 8–9, with more vols. forthcoming, $55.95, $49.95, $49.95, $51.95, $49.95, $49.95, $52.95; Peters P289a-289d, 4 v., $59.90, $59.90, $66.55, $66.55.

1637 * Haydn, Joseph, 1732–1809

[Quartets, strings. Selections] *30 celebrated string quartets: op. 3, no. 3 and 5; op. 9, no. 2; op. 17, no. 5; op. 20, no. 4–6; op. 33, no. 2–3; op. 33, no. 6; op. 50, no. 6; op. 54, no. 1–3; op. 64, no. 2–6; op. 74, no. 1–3; op. 76, no. 1–6; op. 77, no. 1–2.* Parts. International Music 1061-1062, 2 v., $25.75 each; Kalmus K 03543-03544, 2 v., $24.95 each.

1638   Ives, Charles, 1874–1954

[Quartets, strings, no. 1] *String quartet no. 1.* Corrected ed. Parts. Peer International, $20.

1639   Ives, Charles, 1874–1954

[Quartets, strings, no. 2] *String quartet no. 2.* Corrected ed. Parts. Peer International, $20.

1640 * Mendelssohn-Bartholdy, Felix, 1809–1847

[Quartets, strings. Selections] *String quartets: op. 12, op. 13, op. 44, op. 44a, op. 44b, op. 80, op. 81.* Parts. Henle HN270 (op. 12, op. 13), $33.95; HN443 (op. 44, no. 1–3), in preparation; Peters P1742 (complete), $53.20.

1641 * Mozart, Wolfgang Amadeus, 1756–1791

[Quartets, strings] *Quartets for 2 violins, viola, and cello, including Serenade, K. 525, "Eine kleine Nachtmusik"; Quartet for flute and strings, K. 298; Quartet for oboe and strings, K. 370; Adagio and fugue, K. 546.* Parts. Peters P16-17, 2 v., $43 each.

1642 * Mozart, Wolfgang Amadeus, 1756–1791

[Quartets, strings. Selections] *Ten celebrated string quartets: K. 397, K. 421, K. 428, K. 458, K. 464, K. 465, K. 499, K. 575, K. 589, K. 590.* Parts. Bärenreiter BA4750, $52.50.

1643   Prokofiev, Sergey, 1891–1953

[Quartets, strings, no. 1, op. 50] *String quartet no. 1, op. 50.* Parts. International Music 579, $12.

1644   Prokofiev, Sergey, 1891–1953

[Quartets, strings, no. 2, op. 92] *String quartet no. 2, op. 92.* Parts. International Music 877, $15.50.

1645 * Ravel, Maurice, 1875–1937

[Quartet, strings, F major] *String quartet in F major.* Parts. Durand 514-00931, $66.50; International Music 538, $12; Kalmus K 03840, $9.95.

1646 * Schubert, Franz, 1797–1828

[Quartets, strings] *String quartets.* Parts. Complete: Bärenreiter BA5625, BA5631, BA5636, 3 v., $29.75, $35.75, $50; selections: Kalmus K 03874-03875, 2 v., $25, $19; selections: Peters P168a-168b, 2 v., $33.85, $35.

1647 * Schubert, Franz, 1797–1828

[Quartets, strings. Selections] *Three celebrated string quartets: D. 804, D. 810, "Death and the maiden," D. 703.* Parts. International Music 2762, $19.75.

1648 * Schumann, Robert, 1810–1856

[Quartets, strings, op. 41] *Three string quartets, op. 41.* Parts. International Music 734, $18; Peters P2379, $29.90.

1649 Shostakovich, Dmitrii Dmitrievich, 1906–1975

[Quartets, strings, no. 1, op. 49] *String quartet no. 1, op. 49.* Parts. International Music 514, $13.50; Well-Tempered Press W7032, $10.

1650 * Shostakovich, Dmitrii Dmitrievich, 1906–1975

[Quartets, strings, no. 8, op. 110] *String quartet no. 8, op. 110.* Parts. Masters Music M1868, $9.95; Sikorski 2140, $40.

1651 Shostakovich, Dmitrii Dmitrievich, 1906–1975

[Quartets, strings, no. 15, op. 144] *String quartet no. 15, op. 144.* Parts. Sikorski 2204, $32.

1652 Smetana, Bedřich, 1824–1884

[Quartets, strings, no. 1, E minor] *String quartet no. 1 in E minor, "From my life."* Parts. International Music 511, $12; Peters P2635, $25.40; Well-Tempered Press W7031, $10.95.

1653 Stravinsky, Igor, 1882–1971

[Double canon, string quartet] *Double canon for string quartet.* Score; four scores required for performance. Boosey & Hawkes ENB 108, $11 each.

1654 Stravinsky, Igor, 1882–1971

[Pieces, string quartet] *Three pieces for string quartet.* Parts. Boosey & Hawkes ENB 202, $19.50; International Music 2547, $10.

1655 * Tchaikovsky, Peter Ilich, 1840–1893

[Quartets, strings, no. 1, op. 11, D major] *String quartet in D major, op. 11.* Parts. International Music 2611, $12; Peters P3172a, $16.35.

1656 Verdi, Giuseppe, 1813–1901

[Quartet, strings, E minor] *String quartet in E minor.* Parts. International Music 2613, $12; Peters P4255, $18.70.

1657 * Wolf, Hugo, 1860–1903

[Italienische Serenade] *Italian serenade, for string quartet.* Parts. International Music 515, $9.

Piano Quartets (Violin, Viola, Violoncello, and Piano, Unless Otherwise Indicated)

1658 Beethoven, Ludwig van, 1770–1827

[Concertos, violin, violoncello, piano, orchestra, op. 56, C major; arr.] *Triple concerto in C major for violin, violoncello and piano, op. 56, with orchestral reduction for 2nd piano.* Score and parts. International Music 2186, $27.50.

1659 * Brahms, Johannes, 1833–1897

[Quartets, piano, strings, no. 1, op. 25, G minor] *Piano quartet no. 1 in G minor, op. 25.* Score and parts. Breitkopf & Härtel EB6023, $15.50; Henle HN197, $38.95; International Music 2796, $16; Peters P3939a, $27.75.

1660 * Brahms, Johannes, 1833–1897

[Quartets, piano, strings, no. 2, op. 26, A major] *Piano quartet no. 2 in A major, op. 26.* Score and parts. Breitkopf & Härtel EB6024, $13; Henle HN275, $38.95; International Music 2861, $14.75; Peters P3939b, $27.75.

1661 * Brahms, Johannes, 1833–1897

[Quartets, piano, strings, no. 3, op. 60, C minor] *Piano quartet no. 3 in C minor, op. 60.* Score and parts. Breitkopf & Härtel EB6025, $13.50; Henle HN285, $35.95; International Music 2343, $18; Peters P3939c, $27.75.

1662 Copland, Aaron, 1900–1990

[Quartet, piano, strings] *Quartet for piano and strings.* Score and parts. Boosey & Hawkes ENB 30, $35.

1663 * Dvořák, Antonín, 1841–1904

[Quartets, piano, strings, op. 87, E♭ major] *Quartet in E♭ major, op. 87, for piano and strings.* Score and parts. International Music 954, $13.75; Masters Music M1314, $17.50.

1664 * Fauré, Gabriel, 1845–1924

[Quartets, piano, strings, no. 1, op. 15, C minor] *Quartet no. 1 in C minor for piano and strings.* Score and parts. International Music 1351, $21.

1665 * Fauré, Gabriel, 1845–1924

[Quartets, piano, strings, no. 2, op. 45, G minor] *Quartet no. 2 in G minor for piano and strings.* Score and parts. International Music 1095, $19.50.

1666 * Mozart, Wolfgang Amadeus, 1756–1791

[Quartets, piano, strings] *Two quartets for piano and strings: K. 478 in G minor; K. 493 in E♭ major.* Score and parts. Bärenreiter BA4728-4729, 2 v., $17 each; Henle HN196, $32.95; Peters P272, $21.15.

1667 * Schumann, Robert, 1810–1856

[Quartets, piano, strings, op. 47, E♭ major] *Quartet in E♭ major for piano and strings, op. 47.* Score and parts. International Music 750, $17.50; Peters P2380, $24.20.

String Quintets (Two Violins, Two Violas, and Violoncello, Unless Otherwise Indicated)

1668 * Beethoven, Ludwig van, 1770–1827

[Quintets, violins, violas, violoncello, op. 29, C major] *String quintet in C major, op. 29.* Parts. Henle HN267 (with Beethoven's *String quintets op. 4, op. 104, and op. 137*), $55.95; International Music 689, $13; Peters P1599 (with Beethoven's *String quintets op. 4, op. 104, and op. 137*), $32.50.

1669 Boccherini, Luigi, 1743–1805

[Quintets, guitar, violins, viola, violoncello, G. 448, D major] *Guitar quintet no. 1 in D major for 2 violins, viola, cello, and guitar, "Fandango-Quintett,"* ed. by Siegfried Behrend. Parts. Zimmermann ZM2544, $14.

1670 * Brahms, Johannes, 1833–1897

[Quintets, violins, violas, violoncello, no. 1, op. 88, F major] *String quintet no. 1 in F major, op. 88.* Parts. International Music 1514, $12; Peters P3905a, $20.25.

1671 * Brahms, Johannes, 1833–1897

[Quintets, violins, violas, violoncello, no. 2, op. 111, G major] *String quintet no. 2 in G major, op. 111.* Parts. International Music 1515, $12; Peters P3905b, $20.25; Well-Tempered Press W7005, $9.95.

1672 Bruckner, Anton, 1824–1896

[Quintet, violins, violas, violoncello, F major] *String quintet in F major.* Parts. International Music 568, $18; Peters P3842, $20.25.

1673 Dvořák, Antonín, 1841–1904

[Quintets, violins, viola, violoncello, double bass, op. 77, G major] *String quintet in G major, op. 77 (originally op. 18).* Parts. International Music 2537, $15.50.

1674 Dvořák, Antonín, 1841–1904

[Quintets, violins, violas, violoncello, op. 97, E♭ major] *String quintet no. 3 in E♭ major, op. 97.* Parts. International Music 622, $17; Masters Music M1209, $13.50.

1675 * Mozart, Wolfgang Amadeus, 1756–1791

[Quintets, violins, violas, violoncello] *Six string quintets: K. 174, K. 406, K. 515, K. 516, K. 593, K. 614.* Parts. Bärenreiter BA4771, $69; Peters P18-19, 2 v. (with Mozart's *String quintets K. Anh. 179 and K. 46; Quintet in A major for clarinet and strings, K. 581; Quintet in E♭ major for horn and strings, K. 407*), $35 each.

1676 * Schubert, Franz, 1797–1828

[Quintets, violins, viola, violoncellos, D. 956, C major] *String quintet in C major, op. 163, D. 956.* Parts. Barenreiter BA5612, $25.50; International Music 626, $13; Peters P775, $25.80.

Piano Quintets (Two Violins, Viola, Violoncello, and Piano, Unless Otherwise Indicated)

1677 * Brahms, Johannes, 1833–1897

[Quintets, piano, strings, op. 34, F minor] *Quintet in F minor for piano and strings, op. 34.* Score and parts. Breitkopf & Härtel EB6026, $16.25; Henle HN251, $44.95; International Music 2535, $17.50; Peters P3660, $30.

1678 * Dvořák, Antonín, 1841–1904

[Quintets, piano, strings, op. 81, A major] *Quintet in A major for piano and strings, op. 81.* Score and parts. International Music 2189, $18; Masters Music M1666, $19.50.

1679 Franck, César, 1822–1890

[Quintets, piano, strings, F minor] *Quintet in F minor for piano and strings.* Score and parts. International Music 2265, $19; Peters P3743, $25.40.

1680 * Schubert, Franz, 1797–1828

[Quintets, piano, violin, viola, violoncello, double bass, D. 667, A major] *Quintet in A major for piano and strings, op. 114, "Trout quintet," D. 667.* Score and parts. Bärenreiter BA5608, $35.25; Breitkopf & Härtel KM875, $27; Henle HN463, $43.95; International Music 558, $16.50; Peters P169, $21.75.

1681 * Schumann, Robert, 1810–1856

[Quintets, piano, strings, op. 44, E♭ major] *Quintet in E♭ major for piano and strings, op. 44.* Score and parts. International Music 2193, $20.50; Peters P2381, $31.25.

Sextets

1682 * Brahms, Johannes, 1833–1897

[Sextets, violins, violas, violoncellos, op. 18, B♭ major] *Sextet for strings in B♭ major, op. 18.* Parts. International Music 595, $15.50; Peters P3906a, $23.25.

1683 * Brahms, Johannes, 1833–1897

[Sextets, violins, violas, violoncellos, op. 36, G major] *Sextet for strings in G major, op. 36.* Parts. International Music 596, $16.50; Peters P3960b, $25.40.

1684 * Dvořák, Antonín, 1841–1904

[Sextet, violins, violas, violoncellos, op. 48, A major] *String sextet in A major, op. 48.* Parts. International Music 597, $15.50; Masters Music M1904, $17.50.

1685 Schoenberg, Arnold, 1874–1951

Verklärte Nacht = Transfigured night: sextet for violins, violas, and cellos, op. 4. Parts. International Music 598, $15.

Octets

1686 * Mendelssohn-Bartholdy, Felix, 1809–1847

[Octet, violins (4), violas (2), violoncellos (2), op. 20, E♭ major] *Octet in E♭ major for strings, op. 20.* Parts. International Music 743, $19; Peters P1782, $31.25.

Chamber Music for Winds

The following ensembles include works for two or more winds; trios through octets include works with or without piano or other keyboard accompaniment.

Duets (Two Different Wind Instruments)

1687 Bach, Jan, 1937–

[Two-bit contraptions] *Four 2-bit contraptions, for horn and flute.* Parts. Galaxy Music 7.0364, $14.95.

1688 * Beethoven, Ludwig van, 1770–1827

[Duets, clarinet, bassoon, WoO 27] *Three duets for clarinet and bassoon.* Parts. International Music 562, $7; Masters Music M1351, $8.50.

1689 Jacob, Gordon, 1895–1984

[Inventions, flute, oboe] *Three inventions for flute and oboe.* Parts. Stainer & Bell H351, $5.

Trios

1690 * Beethoven, Ludwig van, 1770–1827

[Trios, oboes, English horn, op. 87, C major] *Trio in C major for two oboes and English horn, op. 87.* Parts. Boosey & Hawkes ENB 163, $12.50; Breitkopf & Härtel KM1552, $15; Kalmus K 04831, $5.50; Peters P7167, $14.65.

1691 Jacob, Gordon, 1895–1984

[Pieces, oboes (2), English horn] *Two pieces for two oboes and cor anglais.* Score and parts. Stainer & Bell H220, $10.

1692 Milhaud, Darius, 1892–1974

[Pastorales, oboe, clarinet, bassoon, op. 147] *Pastorale for oboe, clarinet, and bassoon, op. 147.* Score and parts. Masters Music M1579, $6.50.

1693 Musgrave, Thea, 1928–

[Trio, piano, flute, oboe] *Trio for flute, oboe, and piano.* Score and parts. Chester JWC287, $7.95.

1694 Pinkham, Daniel, 1923–

[Trios, trumpet, horn, trombone] *Brass trio.* Score; three scores required for performance. Peters P66274, $22.25 each.

1695 * Piston, Walter, 1894–1976

[Pieces, flute, clarinet, bassoon] *Three pieces for flute, clarinet, and bassoon.* Parts. Associated Music HL50234690, $18.50.

1696 * Poulenc, Francis, 1899–1963

[Sonatas, horn, trombone, trumpet] *Sonata for horn, trumpet and trombone.* Parts. Chester CH55111, $17.95.

1697 * Poulenc, Francis, 1899–1963

[Trios, piano, oboe, bassoon] *Trio for piano, oboe, and bassoon.* Score and parts. Chester CH19245, $22.95.

1698 Rochberg, George, 1918–

[Trios, piano, clarinet, horn] *Trio for clarinet, horn and piano.* Score and parts. Presser 114-40270, $17.50.

1699 Still, William Grant, 1895–1978

Miniatures, for flute, oboe, and piano. Score and parts. Oxford University Press, $14.95.

1700 Villa-Lobos, Heitor, 1887–1959

[Trio, oboe, clarinet, bassoon] *Trio for oboe, clarinet, and bassoon.* Parts. Eschig 524-04899, $58.

Trio Sonatas

Originating early in the seventeenth century, the trio sonata was a primary instrumental form of the baroque period. A trio sonata generally requires four performers: two solo players and two for the continuo part, one on harpsichord or other keyboard instrument, and one doubling the keyboard's bass line on cello, bassoon, or other low sustaining instrument. The examples listed here are but a few of hundreds, written by dozens of composers.

1701 * Bach, Johann Christian, 1735–1782

[Trio sonatas, flutes, continuo, G major] *Trio in G major for 2 flutes and continuo.* Score and parts. Bärenreiter BA6894, $14.25.

1702 * Bach, Johann Sebastian, 1685–1750

[Trio sonatas, flutes, continuo, BWV 1039, G major] *Trio sonata in G major for 2 flutes and continuo, BWV 1039.* Score and parts. Bärenreiter BA4403, $10; Henle HN329, $17.95; Universal UE18026, $14.95.

1703 * Telemann, Georg Philipp, 1681–1787

[Essercizii musici. Trio, no. 12] *Trio sonata in E♭ major, oboe, obbligato harpsichord, and continuo.* Score and parts. Schott OBB 22, $11.95; Sikorski 392, $17.50.

1704 Telemann, Georg Philipp, 1681–1787

[Trio sonatas, recorder, viol, continuo, TWV 42:d7, D minor; arr.] *Trio sonata in D minor for flute, oboe, and continuo.* Score and parts. Amadeus BP 747, $25.

Quartets

1705 * Beethoven, Ludwig van, 1770–1827

[Equali, trombones (4), WoO 30] *Three equali for four-part trombone choir.* Score and parts. Chester CH55030, $17.95; Kalmus K 09420, $5.50; Robert King Music MFB26 (includes alternate parts for three horns and tuba), $5.85; Leduc AL26.164, $16.

1706 * Bernstein, Leonard, 1918–1990

Fanfare for Bima, for brass ensemble, for trumpet in B, horn in F, trombone, and tuba. Score and parts. Boosey & Hawkes ENB 263, $9.75.

1707 Carter, Elliott, 1908–

[Etudes and a fantasy] *8 etudes and a fantasy for woodwind quartet (1950).* Parts. Associated Music HL50235020, $30.

1708 * Hindemith, Paul, 1895–1963

[Plöner Musiktag. Morgenmusik] *Plöner Musiktag: Morgenmusik, for 2 trumpets and 2 trombones.* Score and parts. Schott ED1622, score, $12; Schott ED1622a-d, four parts, $3.95 each.

Quintets

"Woodwind quintet" in the following entries indicates a work for flute, oboe, clarinet, horn, and bassoon.

1709 * Arnold, Malcolm, 1921–

[Quintets, trumpets, horn, trombone, tuba, op. 73] *Quintet for two trumpets, horn, trombone and tuba, op. 73.* Parts. Paterson's Publications 0-85360-252-2, $15.95.

1710 * Barber, Samuel, 1910–1981

Summer music, for woodwind quintet. Score and parts. G. Schirmer HL50352030, $29.95.

1711 Beach, H. H. A., Mrs., 1867–1944

Pastorale, for woodwind quintet. Score and parts. Composers Press CP125, OP.

1712 * Beethoven, Ludwig van, 1770–1827

[Quintets, piano, oboe, clarinet, horn, bassoon, op. 16, E♭ major] *Quintet in E♭ major for piano, oboe, clarinet, horn, and bassoon, op. 16.* Score and parts. Breitkopf & Härtel KM854, $21; Henle HN222, $29.95; Musica Rara MR1040, $15.40; Peters P190, $25.40; Well-Tempered Press W7030, $10.

1713 Bozza, Eugène, 1905–

[Sonatinas, brasses] *Sonatine for 2 trumpets, horn, trombone, tuba.* Parts. Leduc AL20.934, $39.85.

1714 Chavez, Carlos, 1899–1978

[Soli, no. 2] *Soli no. 2, for wind quintet.* Parts. Mills Music, OP.

1715 * Danzi, Franz, 1763–1826

[Quintets, winds, op. 67. No. 2] *Woodwind quintet in E minor, op. 67, no. 2, for woodwind quintet.* Parts. International Music 3096, $14; Kneusslin 672, $17.50.

1716 Davies, Peter Maxwell, 1934–

[Quintets, trumpets, horn, trombone, tuba] *Brass quintet (1981).* Parts. Chester CH55497, $24.95.

1717 Etler, Alvin, 1913–1973

[Quintets, winds, no. 1] *Woodwind quintet no. 1 (1955).* Score; five scores required for performance. Associated Music AMP-96130, $10 each.

1718 Etler, Alvin, 1913–1973

Sonic sequence, for brass quintet. Score and parts. A. Broude A.B. 171-2, $20.

1719 Fine, Irving, 1914–1962

[Partita, wind quintet] *Partita for wind quintet.* Parts. Boosey & Hawkes ENB 12, $30.

1720 * Françaix, Jean, 1912–

[Quintets, winds] *Woodwind quintet.* Parts. Schott ED4121, $39.

1721 Henze, Hans Werner, 1926–

[Quintet, winds] *Woodwind quintet.* Parts. Schott ED4480, $39.

1722 * Hindemith, Paul, 1895–1963

Kleine Kammermusik, for woodwind quintet, op. 24, no. 2. Parts. Schott ED4389, $39.

1723 * Ibert, Jacques, 1890–1962

[Pièces brèves] *Trois pièces brèves for woodwind quintet.* Parts. Leduc AL17.772, $23.95.

1724 * Milhaud, Darius, 1892–1974

Cheminée du roi René = Chimney of King René, for woodwind quintet, op. 205. Parts. Southern SS-394, $15.95.

1725 * Mozart, Wolfgang Amadeus, 1756–1791

[Quintets, piano, oboe, clarinet, horn, bassoon, K. 452, E♭ major] *Quintet in E♭ major for piano, oboe, clarinet, horn, and bassoon, K. 452.* Score and parts. Bärenreiter BA4730, $18; Breitkopf & Härtel KM874, $20; International Music 942, parts, $12.50; International Music 1181, score, $5.50.

1726 * Nielsen, Carl, 1865–1931

[Quintets, winds, op. 43] *Woodwind quintet, op. 43.* Parts. Hansen 2285a, $32.95.

1727 Piston, Walter, 1894–1976

[Quintets, winds] *Quintet for wind instruments.* Parts. Associated Music HL50237300, $7.95.

1728 * Reicha, Anton, 1770–1836

[Quintets, winds, op. 91. No. 1] *Woodwind quintet, op. 91, no. 1, C major.* Parts. Kneusslin K20, $34.20.

1729 Reicha, Anton, 1770–1836

[Quintets, winds, op. 100. No. 4] *Woodwind quintet, op. 100, no. 4, E♭ major.* Parts. Kneusslin KKB15, $40.05.

1730 * Schuller, Gunther, 1925–

[Quintets, winds] *Woodwind quintet (1958).* Parts. Associated Music HL50225510, $20.

Sextets

1731 * Beethoven, Ludwig van, 1770–1827

[Sextets, clarinets, bassoons, horns, op. 71, E♭ major] *Sextet in E♭ major for 2 clarinets, 2 horns, and 2 bassoons, op. 71.* Parts. Breitkopf & Härtel KM1551, $18.80; International Music 946, $12.

1732 * Janáček, Leoš, 1854–1928

Mládí = Youth, suite for flute (piccolo), oboe, clarinet, horn, bassoon, bass clarinet (1924). Parts. International Music 3104, $14.50; Peters P9864, $42.15.

1733 * Mozart, Wolfgang Amadeus, 1756–1791

[Divertimenti, K. 213, F major] *Divertimento no. 8 in F major for 2 oboes, 2 horns, 2 bassoons, K. 213.* Parts. Breitkopf & Härtel KM2172, $19.

1734 * Mozart, Wolfgang Amadeus, 1756–1791

[Divertimenti, K. 240, B♭ major] *Divertimento no. 9 in B♭ major for 2 oboes, 2 horns, 2 bassoons, K. 240.* Parts. Breitkopf & Härtel KM2171, $19.

1735 * Mozart, Wolfgang Amadeus, 1756–1791

[Divertimenti, K. 252, E♭ major] *Divertimento no. 12 in E♭ major for 2 oboes, 2 horns, 2 bassoons, K. 252.* Parts. Breitkopf & Härtel KM2174, $19.

1736 * Mozart, Wolfgang Amadeus, 1756–1791

[Divertimenti, K. 253, F major] *Divertimento no. 13 in F major for 2 oboes, 2 horns, 2 bassoons, K. 253.* Parts. Breitkopf & Härtel KM2175, $19.

1737 * Mozart, Wolfgang Amadeus, 1756–1791

[Divertimenti, K. 270, B♭ major] *Divertimento no. 14 in B♭ major for 2 oboes, 2 horns, 2 bassoons, K. 270.* Parts. Breitkopf & Härtel KM2176, $19; Kalmus K 03733, $9.95.

1738 * Mozart, Wolfgang Amadeus, 1756–1791

[Divertimenti, K. 289, E♭ major] *Divertimento no. 16 in E♭ major for 2 oboes, 2 bassoons, and 2 horns, K. 289.* Parts. Breitkof & Härtel KM2177, $19.

1739 * Poulenc, Francis, 1899–1963

[Sextet, piano, woodwinds, horn] *Sextet, flute, oboe, clarinet, bassoon, horn, piano.* Score and parts. Petrucci, $19.95.

Septets

1740 Hindemith, Paul, 1895–1963

[Septet, woodwinds, trumpet, horn] *Septet for wind instruments.* Parts. Schott ED0919, $69.

Octets

1741 * Beethoven, Ludwig van, 1770–1827

[Octet, woodwinds, horns (2), op. 103, E♭ major] *Octet in E♭ major for 2 oboes, 2 clarinets, 2 horns and 2 bassoons, op. 103.* Parts. Breitkopf & Härtel KM1554, $28.50; Kalmus K 09461, $10.

1742 * Beethoven, Ludwig van, 1770–1827

[Rondino, woodwinds, horns (2), WoO 25, E♭ major] *Rondino in E♭ major, opus posth., for 2 oboes, 2 clarinets, 2 horns, and 2 bassoons.* Parts. International Music 1168, $8.50; Schott CON22-10, $18.

1743 Janáček, Leoš, 1854–1928

[Capriccio, piano, 1 hand, winds] *Capriccio for piano and winds (1926).* Score and parts. Supraphon H 610, $34.

1744 * Mozart, Wolfgang Amadeus, 1756–1791

[Serenades, K. 375, E♭ major (1782)] *Serenade no. 11 in E♭ major, K. 375, for 2 horns, 2 oboes, 2 clarinets and 2 bassoons.* Breitkopf & Härtel PB4394, score, $23, and Breitkopf & Härtel OB4394, parts, $33; Broude Bros. B.B. 37, parts, $20; Musica Rara MR1044, parts, $22.

1745 * Stravinsky, Igor, 1882–1971

[Octet, winds] *Octet for wind instruments.* Parts. Boosey & Hawkes ENB 44, $32.

Chamber Music for Mixed Winds and Strings

The following ensembles include works for mixed winds and strings; trios through octets include works with or without piano or other keyboard accompaniment.

Duets

1746 Hindemith, Paul, 1895–1963

[Plöner Musiktag. Abendkonzert. Duets, violin, clarinet] *Plöner Musiktag: two duets for violin and clarinet.* Parts. Schott ED1693, $7.95.

1747 Ibert, Jacques, 1890–1962

[Entr'acte, flute, guitar] *Entr'acte, for flute or violin and guitar.* Parts. Leduc AL21.346, $10.95.

1748 Jacob, Gordon, 1895–1984

Miniature suite, for clarinet in B♭ and viola. Parts. Musica Rara MR1138, $6.50.

1749 *The Rosewood book: 30 duets for guitar and flute (or any C instrument),* arranged and ed. by Peter Greenwood and Jean Rosenblum. Parts. C. Fischer O5004, $14.95.

1750 Villa-Lobos, Heitor, 1887–1959

Assobio a játo = The jet whistle, for flute and violoncello. Parts. Peer International, $10.

Trios

1751 * Bach, Johann Sebastian, 1685–1750

[Concertos, harpsichords (2), string orchestra, BWV 1060, C minor; arr.] *Concerto in C minor for oboe, violin, strings, and continuo, BWV 1060; arranged for oboe, violin, and piano.* Score and parts. Bärenreiter BA5147a, $17.25.

1752 * Bartók, Béla, 1881–1945

Contrasts, for violin, clarinet, and pianoforte. Score and parts. Boosey & Hawkes ENB 4, $25.

1753 * Beethoven, Ludwig van, 1770–1827

[Serenades, flute, violin, viola, op. 25, D major] *Serenade in D major for flute, violin, and viola, op. 25.* Score and parts. Henle HN300, $16.95; Kalmus K 03149, $7.50; Peters P194a, $19.20.

1754 * Beethoven, Ludwig van, 1770–1827

[Trios, piano, clarinet, violoncello, op. 11, B♭ major] *Trio in B♭ major for piano, clarinet (or violin), and* cello, op. 11. Score and parts. Breitkopf & Härtel KM1066, $15; Henle HN342 (with Beethoven's *Clarinet trio, op. 38*), $31.95; International Music 1028, $8.75; Peters P7126, $40.

1755 * Beethoven, Ludwig van, 1770–1827

[Trios, piano, clarinet, violoncello, op. 38, E♭ major] *Trio in E♭ major for piano, clarinet (or violin), and cello, op. 38.* Score and parts. International Music 2270, $10.50. *See also* 1754

1756 * Brahms, Johannes, 1833–1897

[Trios, piano, clarinet, violoncello, op. 114, A minor] *Trio in A minor for piano, clarinet, and cello, op. 114.* Score and parts. Breitkopf & Härtel EB6913, $15.50; Henle HN322, $22.95; Peters P3899e, $15.40.

1757 * Brahms, Johannes, 1833–1897

[Trios, piano, violin, horn, op. 40, E♭ major] *Trio in E♭ major for horn, violin and piano, op. 40.* Score and parts. Breitkopf & Härtel EB6913, $22; International Music 838, $11.50; Peters P3899b, $15.40.

1758 Debussy, Claude, 1862–1918

[Sonatas, flute, viola, harp] *Sonata for flute, viola, and harp.* Parts. Durand 554-00067, $53.25.

1759 * Holst, Gustav, 1874–1934

[Terzetto, flute, oboe, viola] *Terzetto (1925) for flute, oboe, and viola (or clarinet).* Parts. Masters Music M1172, $4.50.

1760 * Ives, Charles, 1874–1954

[Largo, piano, clarinet, violin] *Largo for violin, clarinet and piano.* Score and parts. Peer-Southern Music 60668-784, $7.

1761 Loeffler, Charles Martin, 1861–1935

[Rhapsodies, piano, oboe, viola] *Two rhapsodies for oboe, viola and piano.* Score and parts. Well-Tempered Press W1009, $12.50.

1762 * Mozart, Wolfgang Amadeus, 1756–1791

[Concertos, flute, harp, orchestra, K. 299, C major; arr.] *Concerto in C major for flute and harp, K. 299, with piano reduction.* Score and parts. Bärenreiter BA4598a, $20; Well-Tempered Press W7098, $10.95.

1763 * Mozart, Wolfgang Amadeus, 1756–1791

[Trios, piano, clarinet, viola, K. 498, E♭ major] *Trio in E♭ major for clarinet (or violin), viola, and piano, K. 498, "Kegelstatt-Trio."* Score and parts.

Bärenreiter BA5325, $14.75; Breitkopf & Härtel EB3737, $9.75; Henle HN344, $17.95; International Music 1144, $9.50.

1764 Reger, Max, 1873–1916

[Serenades, flute, violin, viola, op. 77a, D major] *Serenade in D major for flute, violin, and viola, op. 77a.* Parts. International Music 3005, $10; Masters Music M1932, $7.95.

Quartets

1765 Bach, Carl Philipp Emanuel, 1714–1788

[Quartets, keyboard instrument, flute, viola, violoncello, H. 539, G major] *Quartet in G major for flute, viola, cello, and cembalo, Wotq. 95.* Score and parts. G. Schirmer ED3376, $18.

1766 Bach, Johann Christian, 1735–1782

[Quartets, flute, strings, C major] *Quartet in C major for flute and string trio, or for string quartet.* Parts. Musica Rara MR1068, $8.35.

1767 Britten, Benjamin, 1913–1976

[Phantasies, oboe, strings, op. 2] *Phantasy quartet for oboe and strings, op. 2.* Parts. Boosey & Hawkes ENB 119, $31.

1768 * Danzi, Franz, 1763–1826

[Quartets, bassoon, violin, viola, violoncello, op. 40. No. 1] *Quartet, op. 40, no. 1, for bassoon, violin, viola, and cello.* Parts. Eulenburg GM771a, $21.60; Musica Rara MR1228, $17.90.

1769 * Devienne, François, 1759–1803

[Quartets, bassoon, violin, viola, violoncello, op. 73. No. 1] *Quartet in C major for flute or bassoon, violin, viola and violoncello, op. 73, no. 1.* Parts. Musica Rara MR2056, $12.75.

1770 Jacob, Gordon, 1895–1984

[Quartets, oboe, violin, viola, violoncello] *Quartet for oboe and strings.* Parts. Novello 16884, $49.25.

1771 * Messiaen, Olivier, 1908–1992

Quatuor pour la fin du temps, for violin, B♭ clarinet, cello, and piano. Score and parts. Durand 534-00150, $63.50.

1772 * Mozart, Wolfgang Amadeus, 1756–1791

[Quartets, flute, violin, viola, violoncello] *Four quartets for flute, violin, viola, and cello: K. 285, K. 285a, Anh. 171 (K. 285b), K. 298.* Parts. Bärenreiter BA4405, $18; International Music 2511, $12.

1773   Mozart, Wolfgang Amadeus, 1756–1791

[Quartets, flute, violin, viola, violoncello. Selections] *Three quartets for flute, violin, viola and cello: K. 285, Anh. 171 (K. 285b), K. 298.* Parts. Kalmus K 09687, $12.50; Peters P17a, $20.25; G. Schirmer ED3197, $18.

Quintets

1774   Bax, Arnold, 1883–1953

[Quintets, oboe, violins, viola, violoncello, no. 1] *Quintet for oboe and strings.* Score and parts. Chappell 39493, OP.

1775   Beach, H. H. A., Mrs., 1867–1944

Theme and variations, for flute and string quartet. Parts. G. Schirmer 29803, OP.

1776   Bliss, Arthur, Sir, 1891–1975

[Quintets, clarinet, violins, viola, violoncello] *Quintet for clarinet and strings.* 2nd ed. Parts. Novello 15899, $29.95.

1777   Bliss, Arthur, Sir, 1891–1975

[Quintets, oboe, violins, viola, violoncello] *Quintet for oboe and strings.* Parts. Masters Music M2188, $12; Oxford University Press 07.002-20, $34.95.

1778 *   Brahms, Johannes, 1833–1897

[Quintets, clarinet, violins, viola, violoncello, op. 115, B minor] *Quintet in B minor for clarinet and string quartet, op. 115.* Parts. Breitkopf & Härtel EB6048, $29; Kalmus K 09673, $10; Peters P3905c, $21.

1779   Diamond, David, 1915–

[Quintets, clarinet, violas, violoncellos] *Quintet for clarinet, 2 violas, and 2 cellos.* Parts. Peer International, $10.

1780   Jacob, Gordon, 1895–1984

[Quintets, clarinet, violins, viola, violoncello] *Quintet for clarinet and strings.* Score and parts. Novello 120232-01, $58.

1781 *   Mozart, Wolfgang Amadeus, 1756–1791

[Quintets, clarinet, violins, viola, violoncello, K. 581, A major] *Quintet in A major for clarinet, 2 violins, viola, and cello, K. 581.* Parts. Bärenreiter BA4711, $14.75; Breitkopf & Härtel KM84, $14; Peters P8286, $48.80; Well-Tempered Press W7096, $8.95.

1782 *   Mozart, Wolfgang Amadeus, 1756–1791

[Quintets, horn, violin, violas, violoncello, K. 407, E♭ major] *Quintet in E♭ major for horn, violin, 2 violas, cello, K. 407 (386c).* Parts. Bärenreiter BA4708, $14; International Music 437, $8.50; Peters P19d, $18.70.

1783   Musgrave, Thea, 1928–

[Serenade, flute, clarinet, viola, cello, harp] *Serenade for flute, clarinet, harp, viola and cello.* Score and parts. Chester JWC283, $29.95.

1784   Piston, Walter, 1894–1976

[Quintets, flute, violins, viola, violoncello] *Quintet for flute and string quartet.* Parts. Associated Music HL50488651, $20.

1785 *   Prokofiev, Sergey, 1891–1953

[Quintets, oboe, clarinet, violin, viola, double bass, op. 39, G minor] *Quintet in G minor for oboe, clarinet, violin, viola, double bass, op. 39.* Parts. Boosey & Hawkes ENB 201, $31; International Music 957, $17; Masters Music M2161, $20.

1786 *   Weber, Carl Maria von, 1786–1826

[Quintet, clarinet, violins, viola, violoncello, op. 34, B♭ major] *Quintet in B♭ major for clarinet and string quartet, op. 34.* Parts. Breitkopf & Härtel EB5830, $26; International Music 1387, $12; Kalmus K 09436, $10; Musica Rara MR1048, $15.

Sextets

1787   Bach, Johann Christoph Friedrich, 1732–1795

[Sextet, harpsichord, oboe, horns, violin, violoncello, C major] *Sextet in C major for oboe, violin, cello, 2 horns in C, and harpsichord.* Score and parts. Musica Rara MR1152, $13.

1788 *   Beethoven, Ludwig van, 1770–1827

[Sextets, horns (2), strings, op. 81b, E♭ major] *Sextet in E♭ major for two violins, viola, cello and 2 horns, op. 81b.* Parts. International Music 2153, $11; Litolff/Peters L192, $22.25.

1789 *   Copland, Aaron, 1900–1990

[Sextet, piano, clarinet, strings] *Sextet for clarinet, piano, and string quartet.* Score and parts. Boosey & Hawkes ENB 8, $52.

1790   Ives, Charles, 1874–1954

[All the way around and back] *Scherzo: All the way around and back, for small ensemble (clarinet or flute, violin, bugle or trumpet, middle bells or horn, piano 1 or right hand, and piano 2 or left hand).* Score and parts. Peer International 61068-794, $16.

1791 Mozart, Wolfgang Amadeus, 1756–1791

[Divertimenti, K. 287, B♭ major] *Divertimento no. 15 in B♭ major for 2 horns, 2 violins, viola, and bass (cello), K. 287.* Score and parts. Kalmus A1826, score $12, parts $38.

1792 * Mozart, Wolfgang Amadeus, 1756–1791

Ein musikalischer Spass = The village musicians: a musical joke, K. 522, for two violins, viola, bass (or cello) and two horns. Breitkopf & Härtel score PB4458, $17, and parts OB4458, $28; International Music 450, parts, $10.

Septets

1793 * Beethoven, Ludwig van, 1770–1827

[Septet, woodwinds, horn, strings, op. 20, E♭ major] *Septet in E♭ major for clarinet, bassoon, horn, violin, viola, violoncello, bass, op. 20.* Parts. Breitkopf & Härtel KM4, $26; Peters P2446, $22.25.

1794 * Janáček, Leoš, 1854–1928

[Concertino, piano, winds, strings] *Concertino for piano, 2 violins, viola, clarinet, horn, bassoon.* Score and parts. International Music 3105, $14.75; Supraphon H4342, $26.

1795 * Saint-Saëns, Camille, 1835–1921

[Septet, piano, trumpet, strings, op. 65, E♭ major] *Septet, op. 65, for two violins, viola, violoncello,* contrabass, trumpet, piano. Score and parts. International Music 1890, $15.50; Masters Music M1668, $15.95.

Octets

1796 * Schubert, Franz, 1797–1828

[Octets, woodwinds, horn, strings, D. 803, F major] *Octet in F major for string quartet, string bass, clarinet, horn and bassoon, op. 166, D. 803.* Parts. Bärenreiter BA5617, $42; International Music 975, $25; Kalmus K 09460, $18; Peters P1849, $31.25.

Chamber Music
for Unspecified Instruments

1797 Cage, John, 1912–1992

[Variations, no. 1] *Variations I, for any number of players and any sound-producing means.* Peters P6767a, $13.30.

1798 Crumb, George, 1929–

Vox balaenae, for three masked players. Peters P66466, $28.85.

1799 Stockhausen, Karlheinz, 1928–

Plus minus: 2 x 7 Seiten für Ausarbeitungen, Nr. 14. Universal UE13993, $29.

Fake Books/Jazz Methods

Compiled by
Pamela Bristah

Fake Books

1800 *The classical fake book: over 600 classical themes and melodies in their original keys.* Hal Leonard HL00240044, $21.95.

1801 * *The legal fake book: words, music, chord symbols, 700 songs.* Rev. ed. Warner Bros. VF066, $16.95.

1802 ** *The new real book: jazz classics, choice standards, pop-fusion classics: legal.* Sher Music, editions for Bb, C, and Eb instruments, 3 v. each key, $32 each volume.

1803 *The real little book: the most amazing, colossal, ultimate selection of the best songs ever assembled in a real legal fake book: over 1,200 songs.* Hal Leonard, editions for Bb, C, and Eb instruments, $39.95 each.

1804 * *The real little ultimate jazz fake book: over 625 songs,* compiled by Dr. Herb Wong. Hal Leonard, editions for Bb, C, and Eb instruments, $39.95 each.

Jazz Methods, Studies, and Transcriptions for All Instruments

1805 * Baker, David, 1931–
David Baker's jazz improvisation: a comprehensive method of study for all players. Rev. 2nd ed. Alfred Music 0-88284-370-2, $24.95.

1806 Corea, Chick, 1941–
The jazz solos of Chick Corea, for all instruments. Sher Music 0-9614701-8-6, $18.

1807 * Haerle, Dan
Scales for jazz improvisation: a practice method for all instruments. Studio P/R, $10.

1808 Mingus, Charles, 1922–1979
Charles Mingus, more than a fake book [transcriptions from recordings; lead sheets with chord symbols]. Jazz Workshop/Hal Leonard 0-7935-0900-9, $19.95.

1809 Monk, Thelonious, 1917–1982

A Thelonious Monk study album: includes parts for C, B♭, and E♭ instruments, ed. with transcriptions and biographical and analytical notes by Lionel Grigson. Novello 0-85360-156-9, $34.

1810 ** *A new approach to jazz improvisation: 61 play-a-long book and recording sets* [for all instruments, treble and bass clef, B♭ and E♭]. Jamey Aebersold Jazz (P.O. Box 1244C, New Albany, IN 47151-1244), $14.90 for book and compact disc, $13.95 for book and cassette.

   Selected volumes: vol. 1. *Jazz: how to play and improvise* (rev. 6th ed.). vol. 2. *Nothin' but blues.* vol. 3. *The II/V7/I progression.* vol. 5. *Time to play music.* vol. 6. *Charlie Parker, "All Bird."* vol. 7. *Miles Davis: eight classic jazz originals.* vol. 9. *Woody Shaw for all instruments.* vol. 11. *Herbie Hancock: eight classic jazz/rock originals.* vol. 12. *Duke Ellington: nine greatest hits.* vol. 21. *Gettin' it together.* vol. 24. *Major and minor in every key.* vol. 27. *John Coltrane: eight jazz originals.* vol. 33. *Wayne Shorter: jazz classics.* vol. 45. *Bill Evans.* vol. 54. *Maiden voyage.* vol. 56. *Thelonious Monk.*

1811 * Parker, Charlie, 1920–1955

Charlie Parker omnibook, transcribed exactly from his recorded solos by Jamey Aebersold and Ken Slone. Atlantic Music, editions for C, B♭, E♭, and bass-clef instruments, $14.95 each.

Music for Keyboard

Compiled by
**Bonna Boettcher (piano or harpsichord)
and Ross Wood (organ)**

Piano or Harpsichord Music

*Solo Piano or Harpsichord Music:
Composer Listing*

1812 Adams, John, 1947–

China gates. Associated Music AMP-7859-2, $6.

1813 Adams, John, 1947–

Phrygian gates. Associated Music AMP-7860-2, $16.

1814 * Albéniz, Isaac, 1860–1909

Iberia. Dover (with Albéniz's *España*), 0-486-25367-8, $10.95; International Music 2075-2078, 4 v., $8.75 each; Kalmus K 03004-03007, 4 v., $6.50 each.

1815 * Albéniz, Isaac, 1860–1909

[Piano music] *Piano solo: Chants d'espagne, Suite espanola, Iberia . . .* Salabert EAS 18908, $25.

1816 Albright, William, 1944–

[Chromatic dances] *Five chromatic dances.* Henmar/Peters P66797, $31.25.

1817 Albright, William, 1944–

[Sonatas, piano] *Grand sonata in rag.* Jobert JJ911, $25.25.

1818 Bach, Carl Philipp Emanuel, 1714–1788

[Keyboard music. Selections] *Sonatas and pieces.* Peters P4188, $14.65.

1819 Bach, Carl Philipp Emanuel, 1714–1788

[Keyboard music. Selections] *Twenty-three pièces characteristiques for keyboard,* ed. by Christopher Hogwood. Oxford University Press 0-19-372224-0, $32.50.

1820 * Bach, Carl Philipp Emanuel, 1714–1788

[Sonatas, keyboard instrument. Selections] *Great keyboard sonatas.* Dover 0-486-24853-4, 0-486-24854-2, 2 v., $8.95, $9.95.

1821 Bach, Carl Philipp Emanuel, 1714–1788

[Sonatas, keyboard instrument. Selections] *Piano sonatas.* Henle HN376-378, 3 v., $26.95, $24.95, $25.95.

1822 Bach, Carl Philipp Emanuel, 1714–1788

[Sonatas, keyboard instrument. Selections] *Six sonatas for harpsichord, "Württemberg sonatas."* Bärenreiter BA6498, $21.50; Kalmus K 03088-03089, 2 v., v.1, OP; v.2, no. 4–6, $4.50.

1823 Bach, Carl Philipp Emanuel, 1714–1788

[Sonatas, keyboard instrument, H. 24–29] *Six sonatas for harpsichord, "Prussian sonatas."* Bärenreiter BA6539, $20.70; Kalmus K 03090-03091, 2 v., $4.50 each; Performers' Facsimile Editions PF2, $15.

1824 * Bach, Johann Sebastian, 1685–1750

[Chromatische Fantasie und Fuge] *Chromatic fantasy and fugue in D minor for harpsichord, BWV 903.* Henle HN163, $7.95; Peters P9006, $5.45; Universal UE2540, ed. by Heinrich Schenker, $4; Well-Tempered Press W7050, $4.95.

1825 * Bach, Johann Sebastian, 1685–1750

[Englische Suiten] *Six English suites, for harpsichord, BWV 806–811.* Bärenreiter BA5165, $21; Henle HN100 (*Suites 1–6*), $23.95; Henle HN102 (*Suites 1–3*), $14.95; Henle HN103 (*Suites 4–6*), $14.95; Peters P4580a-b, 2 v., $14.65 each; Universal UE00326-327, 2 v., $9.95 each.

1826 * Bach, Johann Sebastian, 1685–1750

[Französische Suiten] *Six French suites, for harpsichord, BWV 812–817.* Bärenreiter BA5166, $19.15; Henle HN71, $15.95; Peters P4594, $13.15; Wiener Urtext UT50048, $14.95.

1827 * Bach, Johann Sebastian, 1685–1750

[Goldberg-Variationen] *Goldberg variations, for harpsichord, BWV 988.* Bärenreiter BA5162, $9.50; Henle HN159, $14.95; Peters P4462, $12.10.

1828 * Bach, Johann Sebastian, 1685–1750

[Inventions, harpsichord] *Two- and three-part inventions for harpsichord, BWV 772–801.* Bärenreiter BA5150, $14.25; Henle HN64, $13.95; Henle HN169 (*Two-part inventions*), $8.95; Henle HN360 (*Sinfonias, or Three-part inventions*), $8.95; Peters P4201, $10.10; Well-Tempered Press W7094, $7.95; Wiener Urtext UT50042A, practical ed., $11.95.

1829 * Bach, Johann Sebastian, 1685–1750

[Italienisches Konzert] *Italian concerto, for unaccompanied harpsichord, BWV 971.* Bärenreiter BA5161 (includes Bach's *French overtures, BWV 971 and BWV 831*), $13.25; Henle HN160, $7.95; Peters P4464 (includes Bach's *French overture,*

BWV 831), $10.10; G. Schirmer, ed. by Rosalyn Tureck, $14.95; Wiener Urtext UT50057, $8.95.

1830 * Bach, Johann Sebastian, 1685–1750

[Keyboard music. Selections] *Keyboard music: English suites, French suites, Partitas, Two- and Three-part inventions, Goldberg variations.* Dover 0-486-22350-4, $10.95.

1831 Bach, Johann Sebastian, 1685–1750

Der Kunst der Fuge = The art of fugue: keyboard study score. Henle HN9423, $10.95.

1832 * Bach, Johann Sebastian, 1685–1750

[Notenbuch der Anna Magdalena Bach (1725)] *Notebook for Anna Magdalena Bach.* Bärenreiter BA5115, $21.75; Henle HN349, $19.95; Masters Music M1034, ed. by Béla Bartók, $3; Peters P3829, $7.70.

1833 * Bach, Johann Sebastian, 1685–1750

[Partitas, harpsichord, BWV 825–830] *Six partitas for harpsichord, BWV 825–830.* Bärenreiter BA5152, $19.50; Henle HN28 (*Partitas 1–6*), $24.95; Henle HN30 (*Partitas 1–3*), $15.95; Henle HN31 (*Partitas 4–6*), $15.95; Peters P4463a-b, 2 v., $13.10 each; Universal UE00328-329, 2 v., $9.95 each.

1834 * Bach, Johann Sebastian, 1685–1750

[Toccatas, harpsichord, BWV 910–916] *Seven toccatas and fugues for harpsichord, BWV 910–916.* Henle HN126, $23.95; Peters P4665, $22.25.

1835 ** Bach, Johann Sebastian, 1685–1750

[Wohltemperierte Klavier] *The well-tempered clavier, books 1 and 2.* Bärenreiter BA5191-5192, 2 v., $20.25 each; Henle HN14, HN16, 2 v., $24.95 each; Peters P4691a-b, 2 v., $27.60 each; G. Schirmer ED3364-3365, 2 v., ed. by Anthony Newman, $14.95 each; Universal UE01547-01548, 2 v., $25 each; Wiener Urtext UT50050-50051, 2 v., $21.95 each.

1836 * Balakirev, Milii Alekseevich, 1837–1910

[Islamei] *Islamey, oriental fantasy for piano.* Peters P9167, $12.10.

1837 * Barber, Samuel, 1910–1981

Excursions, op. 20. G. Schirmer ED2138, $7.95.

1838 * Barber, Samuel, 1910–1981

[Piano music] *Complete piano music.* New ed. G. Schirmer ED3453, $12.95.

1839 Barber, Samuel, 1910–1981

[Sonatas, piano, op. 26] *Sonata for piano, op. 26.* G. Schirmer ED1971, $13.95.

1840   Bartók, Béla, 1881–1945

Allegro barbaro. Boosey & Hawkes PIB 39, $4.50; Masters Music M2222, $2.95.

1841   Bartók, Béla, 1881–1945

[Bagatelles, piano, op. 6] *14 bagatelles for piano, op. 6.* Editio Musica Budapest EMB934, $16; Kalmus K 03123, $5.

1842 * Bartók, Béla, 1881–1945

Mikrokosmos: progressive piano pieces. Boosey & Hawkes PAB 7-12, 6 v., $7 each.

1843 * Bartók, Béla, 1881–1945

[Piano music. Selections] *Piano music of Béla Bartók.* Dover 0-486-24108-4, 0-486-24109-2, 2 v., $9.95 each.

1844   Bartók, Béla, 1881–1945

[Rőgtőnzèsek magyar parasztdalokra] *Improvisations on Hungarian peasant songs, op. 20.* Boosey & Hawkes PAB 44, $9.75.

1845   Bartók, Béla, 1881–1945

[Sonatas, piano (1926)] *Sonata for piano.* Boosey & Hawkes PIB 41, $13.50.

1846 * Beach, H. H. A., Mrs., 1867–1944

[Piano music. Selections] *Piano music.* Da Capo Press 0-306-76088-6, $29.50.

1847   Beethoven, Ludwig van, 1770–1827

[Bagatelles, piano] *Bagatelles, op. 33, op. 119, op. 126.* Dover 0-486-25392-9 (includes other short works), $8.95; Henle HN158, $15.95; Peters P297c (includes other short works), $26.85; Wiener Urtext UT50054, $14.95.

1848 ** Beethoven, Ludwig van, 1770–1827

[Sonatas, piano] *32 sonatas for piano.* Associated Board of the Royal Schools of Music 490-00205–490-00207, 3 v., ed. by Harold Craxton and Donald Francis Tovey, $27.50 each; Dover 0-486-23134-8, 0-486-23135-6, 2 v., $11.95, $12.95; Henle HN32, HN34, 2 v., $42.95 each; Peters P8100a-b, 2 v., ed. by Claudio Arrau, $38.50 each; Universal UE8-9, 2 v., ed. by Heinrich Schenker, $14.95 each.

1849 * Beethoven, Ludwig van, 1770–1827

[Variations, piano] *Variations for piano.* Dover 0-486-25188-8, $11.95; Henle HN142, HN144, 2 v., $26.95 each; Peters P298aa-bb, 2 v., $22.90, $25.10; Wiener Urtext UT50024-25, 2 v., $22.95 each.

1850 * Berg, Alban, 1885–1935

[Sonatas, piano, op. 1] *Piano sonata, op. 1.* Universal UE08812, $14.95.

1851   Berio, Luciano, 1925–

[Piano music. Selections] *Six encores for piano: Brin, Leaf, Wasserklavier, Erdenklavier, Luftklavier, Feuerklavier.* Universal UE19918, $16.95.

1852   Blake, Eubie, 1883–1983

[Piano music. Selections] *Sincerely Eubie Blake: 9 original compositions for piano solo.* E. B. Marks 15780–61, OP.

1853   Boulez, Pierre, 1925–

[Sonatas, piano, no. 1] *Première sonate pour piano.* Amphion, $28.

1854   Boulez, Pierre, 1925–

[Sonatas, piano, no. 2] *Sonata no. 2 for piano.* Heugel, $36.

1855   Boulez, Pierre, 1925–

[Sonatas, piano, no. 3] *Third piano sonata: Formant 2, Trope.* Universal UE13292, $49. *Formant 3, Constellation-Miroir.* Universal UE13293b, $65.

1856 * Brahms, Johannes, 1833–1897

[Fantasien, piano, op. 116] *Fantasies, op. 116, no. 1–7.* Henle HN120, $10.95; Universal UE02267, $9.95; Wiener Urtext UT50072, $9.95.

1857 * Brahms, Johannes, 1833–1897

[Intermezzi, piano, op. 117] *Three intermezzi, op. 117.* Henle HN121, $8.50; Universal UE02294, $9.95; Wiener Urtext UT50023, $8.95.

1858 * Brahms, Johannes, 1833–1897

[Piano music] *Sonatas and variations, shorter works, and transcriptions for piano.* Dover 0-486-22651-4, 0-486-22650-6, 0-486-22652-2, 3 v., $8.95, $8.95, $10.95; International Music 459-461, 3 v., $19.50 each; Peters P8200a-e, 5 v., $30, $30, $27.50, $30, $35.

1859 * Brahms, Johannes, 1833–1897

[Piano music. Selections] *Sonatas, scherzo, and ballades.* Henle HN38, $29.95.

1860 * Brahms, Johannes, 1833–1897

[Rhapsodien, piano, op. 79] *Two rhapsodies, op. 79.* Henle HN119, $8.95; Universal UE02277, $7.95; Wiener Urtext UT50007, $8.95.

1861 * Brahms, Johannes, 1833–1897

[Stücke, piano] *Piano pieces, op. 76, op. 79, op. 116–119.* Henle HN36, $25.95.

1862 * Brahms, Johannes, 1833–1897

[Stücke, piano, op. 76] *Piano pieces, op. 76, no. 1–8.* Henle HN118, $9.95; Wiener Urtext UT50067, $14.95.

1863 * Brahms, Johannes, 1833–1897

[Stücke, piano, op. 118] *Piano pieces, op. 118, no. 1–6.* Henle HN122, $8.95; Universal UE02354, $8.95; Wiener Urtext UT50044, $8.95.

1864 * Brahms, Johannes, 1833–1897

[Stücke, piano, op. 119] *Piano pieces, op. 119, no. 1–4.* Henle HN123, $8.95; Universal UE02355, $8.95; Wiener Urtext UT50045, $8.95.

1865 * Brahms, Johannes, 1833–1897

[Variationen über ein Thema von Paganini] *Paganini variations, op. 35.* Henle HN394, $18.95.

1866 * Brahms, Johannes, 1833–1897

[Variationen und Fuge über ein Thema von Händel] *Handel variations, op. 24.* Henle HN272, $11.95.

1867 * Brahms, Johannes, 1833–1897

[Variations, piano] *Variations for piano.* Henle HN440, $33.95.

1868 * Brahms, Johannes, 1833–1897

[Waltzes, piano, 4 hands, op. 39; arr.] *Waltzes, op. 39,* arranged for solo piano by the composer. Henle HN42, $7.50; Universal UE01108, $17.95; Wiener Urtext UT50073, $7.95.

1869 * Brubeck, Dave, 1920–

The genius of Dave Brubeck. Belwin Mills TPF0130-0131, 2 v., $13.95 each.

1870 Cage, John, 1912–1992

4'33". Peters P6777, $4.05.

1871 * Cage, John, 1912–1992

[Sonatas and interludes, piano] *Sonatas and interludes, for prepared piano.* Peters P6755, $33.85.

1872 Carter, Elliott, 1908–

Night fantasies. Associated Music HL50236290, $25.

1873 Carter, Elliott, 1908–

[Sonatas, piano (1945–46)] *Sonata for piano.* Presser 450-00234, $12.50.

1874 Chaminade, Cécile, 1857–1944

[Piano music. Selections] *Selected pieces for piano solo.* Well-Tempered Press W7069-7070, 2 v., $7.95, $9.95.

1875 Chaminade, Cécile, 1857–1944

[Piano music. Selections] *Three piano works: Sonata in C minor, op. 21; Etude symphonique, op. 28; Six concert etudes, op. 35.* Da Capo Press 0-306-79551-5, $27.50.

1876 ** Chopin, Frédéric, 1810–1849

[Ballades, piano] *Ballades.* Dover 0-486-24164-5 (reprint of Polskie Wydawnictwo Muzyczne, with Chopin's *Impromptus and Sonatas*), $9.95; Henle HN295, $18.95; Peters P9902, ed. by Paul Badura-Skoda, $24.55; Polskie Wydawnictwo Muzyczne HL00008660, $8.

1877 * Chopin, Frédéric, 1810–1849

[Etudes, piano] *Etudes.* Dover 0-486-24052-5 (reprint of Polskie Wydawnictwo Muzyczne, with Chopin's *Preludes*), $8.95; Henle HN124, $22.95; Polskie Wydawnictwo Muzyczne HL00008664, $14; Wiener Urtext UT50030-50031, 2 v., $ 11.95, $14.95.

1878 * Chopin, Frédéric, 1810–1849

[Fantasia, piano, op. 49] *Fantasy in F minor, op. 49.* Dover 0-486-25950-1 (reprint of Polskie Wydawnictwo Muzyczne, with Chopin's *Barcarolle, Berceuse, and other shorter works*), $7.50; Henle HN321, $7.95; Polskie Wydawnictwo Muzyczne (with Chopin's *Berceuse and Barcarolle*) HL00008665, $14.95.

1879 * Chopin, Frédéric, 1810–1849

[Impromptus, piano] *Impromptus.* Henle HN235, $13.95; Polskie Wydawnictwo Muzyczne HL00008666, $7; Wiener Urtext UT50058, $11.95. *See also* 1876

1880 * Chopin, Frédéric, 1810–1849

[Mazurkas, piano] *Mazurkas.* Dover 0-486-25548-4 (reprint of Polskie Wydawnictwo Muzyczne), $8.95; Henle HN264, $32.95; Polskie Wydawnictwo Muzyczne HL00008667, $24.95.

1881 ** Chopin, Frédéric, 1810–1849

[Nocturnes, piano] *Nocturnes.* Dover 0-486-24564-0 (reprint of Polskie Wydawnictwo Muzyczne, with Chopin's *Polonaises*), $10.95; Henle HN185, $21.95; Polskie Wydawnictwo Muzyczne HL00008668, $12.

1882 * Chopin, Frédéric, 1810–1849

[Polonaises, piano] *Polonaises.* Henle HN217, $25.95; Polskie Wydawnictwo Muzyczne HL00008669, $14.95. *See also* 1881

1883 ** Chopin, Frédéric, 1810–1849

[Preludes, piano] *24 preludes, op. 28.* Henle HN73, $17.95; Polskie Wydawnictwo Muzyczne HL00008670, $9.95; Wiener Urtext UT50005, $14.95. *See also* 1877

1884 * Chopin, Frédéric, 1810–1849

[Scherzos, piano] *Scherzos.* Dover 0-486-24316-8 (reprint of Polskie Wydawnictwo Muzyczne, with Chopin's *Waltzes*), $9.95; Henle HN279, $19.95; Polskie Wydawnictwo Muzyczne HL00008672, $12; Wiener Urtext UT50061, $19.95.

1885 * Chopin, Frédéric, 1810–1849

[Sonatas, piano] *Two piano sonatas.* Henle HN289 (*Sonata op. 35*), $11.95; Henle HN290 (*Sonata op. 58*), $12.95; Polskie Wydawnictwo Muzyczne (with Chopin's *Waltzes*) HL00008674, $12. *See also* 1876

1886 ** Chopin, Frédéric, 1810–1849

[Waltzes, piano] *Waltzes.* Henle HN131, $21.95. *See also* 1884 and 1885

1887 * Clementi, Muzio, 1752–1832

[Sonatas, piano, op. 50. No. 3] *Piano sonata in G minor, op. 50, no. 3, "Didone abbandonata": scena tragica.* Henle HN86, $11.95.

1888 Clementi, Muzio, 1752–1832

[Sonatines progressives, piano, op. 36] *Sonatinas for piano, op. 36.* Kalmus K 03300, $4.50; Peters P3346, $7.70; G. Schirmer LB811, $4.95.

1889 Coleridge-Taylor, Samuel, 1875–1912

[Negro melodies] *Twenty-four Negro melodies, op. 59,* transcribed for the piano by Samuel Coleridge-Taylor. Da Capo Press 0-306-78023-1, $35.

1890 Copland, Aaron, 1900–1990

[Blues, piano] *Four piano blues.* Boosey & Hawkes PAB 75, $6.50.

1891 Copland, Aaron, 1900–1990

[Fantasy, piano] *Piano fantasy.* Boosey & Hawkes PIB 173, $21.

1892 * Copland, Aaron, 1900–1990

Piano variations. Boosey & Hawkes PIB 179, $8.50.

1893 * Copland, Aaron, 1900–1990

[Sonatas, piano] *Sonata for piano.* Boosey & Hawkes PIB 27, $16.50.

1894 * Couperin, François, 1668–1733

Pièces de clavecin = Pieces for harpsichord. Dover 0-486-25795-9, 0-486-25796-7, 2 v., $10.95 each; Heugel (Le pupitre, v. 21–24), 4 v., $82.85, $70.25, $60.40, $73.55; Performers' Facsimiles Editions PF41 (selections), $17.50.

1895 Cowell, Henry, 1897–1965

[Piano music. Selections] *Piano music.* Associated Music AMP 95611, AMP 7795, 2 v., $19.95, $14.95.

1896 Crumb, George, 1929–

[Makrokosmos, v. 1] *Makrokosmos, v. 1: for amplified piano.* Peters P66539a, $31.25.

1897 Crumb, George, 1929–

[Makrokosmos, v. 2] *Makrokosmos, v. 2: for amplified piano.* Peters P66539b, $31.25.

1898 Dallapiccola, Luigi, 1904–1975

Quaderno musicale di annalibera. Zerboni S.4959Z., $14.

1899 * Debussy, Claude, 1862–1918

[Arabesques, piano] *Arabesques, no. 1–2.* Durand 160-00041, $3.50; Henle HN380, $7.95; Peters P7259, $6.85.

1900 * Debussy, Claude, 1862–1918

Children's corner. Durand 460-00084, $5.95; Henle HN382, $9.95; Peters P9159c, $11.15.

1901 * Debussy, Claude, 1862–1918

Estampes. Durand 460-00056, $4; Henle HN387, $11.95; Peters P7267, $12.30.

1902 * Debussy, Claude, 1862–1918

[Etudes, piano] *12 etudes.* Durand 510-01310, 510-01311, 2 v., $21.50, $20.25; Henle HN390, $28.95; Masters Music M1845, M1878, 2 v., $4.95 each; Peters P7265a-b, 2 v., $22.25 each.

1903 * Debussy, Claude, 1862–1918

[Images, piano, 1st ser.] *Images, book I.* Durand 460-00012, $5.50; Henle HN388, $10.95; Peters P7266a, $10.40.

1904 * Debussy, Claude, 1862–1918

[Images, piano, 2nd ser.] *Images, book II.* Durand 510-01323, $21; Henle HN389, $10.95; Peters P7266b, $10.40.

1905 * Debussy, Claude, 1862–1918

L'isle joyeuse. Durand 160-00046, $5; Henle HN386, $8.95; Peters P7264, $7.15.

1906 * Debussy, Claude, 1862–1918

[Piano music. Selections] *Etudes, Children's corner, Images, book II, and other works for piano.* Dover 0-486-27145-5, $9.95.

1907 * Debussy, Claude, 1862–1918

[Piano music. Selections] *Piano music, 1888–1905* [includes all works in this section except Etudes, Children's corner, Preludes, and Images, book II; includes other short works as well]. Dover 0-486-22771-5, $7.95.

1908 * Debussy, Claude, 1862–1918

Pour le piano. Durand 460-00010, $6.95; Henle HN385, $9.95; Peters P7274, $10.40.

1909 * Debussy, Claude, 1862–1918

[Preludes, piano] *Preludes, books 1 and 2.* Dover 0-486-25970-6, $6.95; Durand 510-01346, 510-01347, 2 v., $14.75, $24.50; Henle HN383-384, 2 v., $21.95, $24.95; Peters P7255a-b, 2 v., $16.35 each; G. Schirmer ED1974, ed. by James Briscoe, $14.95.

1910 * Debussy, Claude, 1862–1918

Suite bergamasque. Durand 460-00011, $10; Henle HN381, $9.95; Peters P7261, $10.40.

1911 * Ellington, Duke, 1899–1974

Duke Ellington piano solos. Hal Leonard HL00294007, $16.95.

1912 Falla, Manuel de, 1876–1946

[Fantasía bética] *Fantasía baetica.* Chester CH02096, $15.95.

1913 Field, John, 1782–1837

[Nocturnes, piano] *Nocturnes.* Peters P491, $27.75; Salabert HL50489174, $12.50; Universal UE00061, $14.95.

1914 * Gershwin, George, 1898–1937

[Preludes, piano] *Three preludes for piano.* Warner Bros. NW50-11, $12.50.

1915 Gershwin, George, 1898–1937

[Rhapsody in blue; arr.] *Rhapsody in blue, arranged for solo piano.* Warner Bros. PS47, $15.

1916 Ginastera, Alberto, 1916–1983

Danzas argentinas, for piano. Durand 510-01361, $16.50.

1917 * Ginastera, Alberto, 1916–1983

[Sonatas, piano, no. 2, op. 53] *Sonata no. 2 for piano, op. 53.* Boosey & Hawkes PIB 437, $17.50.

1918 * Gottschalk, Louis Moreau, 1829–1869

[Piano music. Selections] *Piano music of Louis Moreau Gottschalk,* ed. by Richard Jackson. Dover 0-486-21683-7, $12.95.

1919 Grainger, Percy, 1882–1961

[Piano music. Selections] *Piano album.* G. Schirmer ED2436, $16.95.

1920 * Granados, Enrique, 1867–1916

[Goyescas (Piano work)] *Goyescas.* International Music 599, $10; Kalmus K 09223, $7.50.

1921 Granados, Enrique, 1867–1916

[Piano music] *Complete piano music.* Salabert HL50481365, $19.95.

1922 * Granados, Enrique, 1867–1916

[Piano music. Selections] *Goyescas, Spanish dances, and other works for solo piano.* Dover 0-486-25481-X, $8.95.

1923 Grieg, Edvard, 1843–1907

[Ballade i form av variasjoner over en norsk folkevise] *Ballade, op. 24.* Henle HN431, $11.95; Peters P1470, $11.15.

1924 * Grieg, Edvard, 1843–1907

[Fra Holbergs tid] *Holberg suite, op. 40.* Henle HN432, $9.95; Peters P2151, $9.60.

1925 * Grieg, Edvard, 1843–1907

[Lyriske stykker] *Complete lyric pieces for piano.* Dover 0-486-26176-X, $10.95.

1926 Grieg, Edvard, 1843–1907

[Piano music] *Works for piano.* Peters P3100a-c, 3 v., $40 each.

1927 Grieg, Edvard, 1843–1907

[Piano music. Selections] *Norwegian dances, op. 35, Ballade, op. 24, and other piano music.* Dover 0-486-26669-6, $11.95.

1928 * Grieg, Edvard, 1843–1907

[Piano music. Selections] *Peer Gynt suite, Holberg suite, and other works for piano solo.* Dover 0-486-27590-6, $14.95.

1929 * Griffes, Charles Tomlinson, 1884–1920

Roman sketches (includes *White peacock*). Masters Music M2113, $6.95; G. Schirmer ED2847, $7.95.

1930   Griffes, Charles Tomlinson, 1884–1920

[Sonatas, piano, A.85] *Sonata for piano.* G. Schirmer ST30184, $7.95.

1931 * Handel, George Frideric, 1685–1759

[Harpsichord music. Selections] *Selected harpsichord music.* Bärenreiter BA4221-4224, 4 v., $18.75 each; Dover 0-486-24338-9, $9.95; Henle HN336 (*Suites 1–8*), $26.95; Henle HN472 (*Suites 9–17*), in preparation; Peters P4981–4983, 3 v., $30, $30, $22.90.

1932   Haydn, Joseph, 1732–1809

[Piano music. Selections] *Piano pieces: variations, capriccios, and other short pieces.* Henle HN224, $18.95; Peters P4392, $20.35; Wiener Urtext UT50047, $17.95.

1933 * Haydn, Joseph, 1732–1809

[Sonatas, piano] *Sonatas for piano.* Associated Board of the Royal Schools of Music, 4 v. (selections), $14 each; Dover 0-486-24726-0, 0-486-24747-9, 2 v., $10.95, $11.95; Henle HN238, HN240, HN242, 3 v., $35.95, $35.95, $31.95; Peters 5 v., P713a-d, $17.40 each; P4443, $10.10; Wiener Urtext UT50026-29, 3 v. in 4: v. 1A, 1B, and 3, $24.95 each; v. 2, $29.95.

1934   Hensel, Fanny Mendelssohn, 1805–1847

Lieder ohne Worte = Songs without words, op. 8. Bote & Bock, $28.

1935 * Hensel, Fanny Mendelssohn, 1805–1847

[Piano music. Selections] *Selected piano works.* Henle HN392, $18.95.

1936   Hensel, Fanny Mendelssohn, 1805–1847

[Sonatas, piano] *Two piano sonatas.* Hildegard 09106, $38.50.

1937 * Hindemith, Paul, 1895–1963

Ludus tonalis. Schott ED3964, $25.

1938   Hindemith, Paul, 1895–1963

[Sonatas, piano] *Sonatas no. 1, 2, and 3.* Schott ED2518, ED2519, ED2521, 3 v., $17.95 each.

1939   Ives, Charles, 1874–1954

[Piano music. Selections] *Five piano pieces*, ed. by John Kirkpatrick. Presser 440-40007, $7.95.

1940 * Ives, Charles, 1874–1954

[Sonatas, piano, no. 2] *Sonata no. 2 for piano, "Concord, Mass., 1840–1860."* Associated Music AMP1581, $18.95.

1941   Ives, Charles, 1874–1954

Three-page sonata, ed. by John Kirkpatrick. Presser 150-40012, $8.50.

1942   Jacquet de La Guerre, Elisabeth-Claude, ca. 1664–1729

Pièces de clavecin. Heugel (Le pupitre, v. 66), H.32629, $66.95.

1943 ** Joplin, Scott, 1868–1917

[Rags, piano] *Complete piano rags.* Dover 0-486-25807-6, $8.95.

1944 * Kabalevsky, Dmitry Borisovich, 1904–1987

[Preludes, piano, op. 38] *Twenty-four preludes, op. 38.* International Music 856, $12; Kalmus K 03573, $7; Peters P4785, $27.25.

1945   Kabalevsky, Dmitry Borisovich, 1904–1987

[Sonatas, piano] *Sonatas for piano: no. 1, op. 6; no. 2, op. 45; no. 3, op. 46.* Boosey & Hawkes B&H9536, $19.95.

1946   Kabalevsky, Dmitry Borisovich, 1904–1987

[Sonatas, piano, no. 3, op. 46] *Piano sonata no. 3, op. 46.* International Music 1223, $5.75; Kalmus K 03572, $4.50.

1947   Kabalevsky, Dmitry Borisovich, 1904–1987

[Sonatinas, piano, no. 1, op. 13, no. 1, C major] *Sonatina no. 1 in C major, op. 13.* International Music 932, $3.50; Kalmus K 03561, $3.95; Peters P4708, $12.10.

1948 * Khachaturian, Aram, 1903–1978

[Toccata, piano] *Toccata.* International Music 933, $4.25; Kalmus K 03580, $3; Peters P4734, $11.15.

1949   Kuhnau, Johann, 1660–1722

[Biblische Historien] *Biblical sonatas.* Peters P4840a-f, 6 v., $11.15 each.

1950 * Liszt, Franz, 1811–1886

Années de pèlerinage, books I–III. Dover 0-486-25627-8, $11.95; Editio Musica Budapest 510-

01365, 510-00944, 510-00946, 3 v., $29.25, $29.25, $17.25; Henle HN173–175, 3 v., $22.95, $19.95, $18.95; Peters P3603, $31.95.

1951 * Liszt, Franz, 1811–1886

[Episoden auf Lenau's Faust. Tanz in der Dorfschenke; arr.] *Mephisto waltz no. 1.* Editio Musica Budapest 510-00353, $6.75; Peters P7203, $12.10.

1952 * Liszt, Franz, 1811–1886

[Etudes, piano] *Etudes, including the Transcendental etudes.* Dover 0-486-25815-7, 0-486-25816-5, 2 v., $11.95, $9.95; Editio Musica Budapest 510-01366–510-01367, 2 v., $31.50, $29.25; Peters P3600c-d, 2 v., $21.15, $24.20.

1953 Liszt, Franz, 1811–1886

[Piano music. Selections] *The final years: piano compositions of the late period.* G. Schirmer LB1845, $16.95.

1954 * Liszt, Franz, 1811–1886

[Rhapsodies hongroises] *Hungarian rhapsodies.* Dover 0-486-24744-9, $9.95; Editio Musica Budapest 510-01605, 510-01607, 2 v., $29.25 each; Peters P3600a-b, 2 v., $21.15 each.

1955 * Liszt, Franz, 1811–1886

[Sonata, piano, B minor] *Sonata in B minor.* Dover (with Liszt's *Consolations* and other works) 0-486-26182-4, $9.95; Editio Musica Budapest 510-02110, $8; Henle HN273, $12.95; Peters P3611, $8.45.

1956 * MacDowell, Edward, 1861–1908

[Piano music. Selections] *Piano works: Woodland sketches, complete sonatas and other pieces.* Dover 0-486-26293-6, $10.95.

1957 * MacDowell, Edward, 1861–1908

[Sonatas, piano] *Piano sonatas.* G. Schirmer ED3452, $8.95.

1958 * MacDowell, Edward, 1861–1908

[Woodland sketches] *Ten woodland sketches, op. 51.* International Music 1815, $5.50; Kalmus K 03649, $4.95; G. Schirmer LB1805, $4.95.

1959 * Mendelssohn-Bartholdy, Felix, 1809–1847

Lieder ohne Worte = Songs without words. Henle HN327, $34.95; Peters P1704a, $20.25; G. Schirmer LB58, $8.95.

1960 * Mendelssohn-Bartholdy, Felix, 1809–1847

[Piano music] *Complete works for piano.* Dover 0-486-23136-4, 0-486-23137-2, 2 v., $10.95 each.

1961 * Mendelssohn-Bartholdy, Felix, 1809–1847

[Piano music. Selections] *Selected piano works.* Henle HN281, $35.95.

1962 Mendelssohn-Bartholdy, Felix, 1809–1847

Rondo capriccioso, op. 14. Henle HN286, $7.50; Peter P1704f, $7.05.

1963 Mendelssohn-Bartholdy, Felix, 1809–1847

Variations sérieuses, op. 54. Kalmus K 03677, $5.95; Peters P1704g, $13.15.

1964 Messiaen, Olivier, 1908–1992

Catalogue d'oiseaux. Leduc AL22.937, AL22.940-AL22.941, AL22.943-AL22.944, AL22.946-AL22.947, 7 v., $38 each.

1965 Messiaen, Olivier, 1908–1992

[Études de rythme. Île de feu, 1] *Île de feu 1.* Durand 510-00423, $13.

1966 Messiaen, Olivier, 1908–1992

[Études de rythme. Île de feu, 2] *Île de feu 2.* Durand 510-00424, $20.50.

1967 Messiaen, Olivier, 1908–1992

[Études de rythme. Mode de valeurs et d'intensité] *Mode de valeurs et d'intensité.* Durand 510-00425, $12.75.

1968 Messiaen, Olivier, 1908–1992

[Études de rythme. Neumes rythmiques] *Neumes rythmiques.* Durand 510-00426, $19.75.

1969 Morton, Jelly Roll, d. 1941

[Piano music] *The collected piano music.* Smithsonian Institution/G. Schirmer ED3257, $35.

1970 Moszkowski, Moritz, 1854–1925

Fifteen virtuosic etudes, op. 72. International Music 2026, $8.50; Kalmus K 03685, $7.95; G. Schirmer LB1798, $8.95.

1971 * Mozart, Wolfgang Amadeus, 1756–1791

[Piano music. Selections] *Complete [shorter] piano pieces.* Henle HN22, $28.95; Peters P4240a, $31.90; Wiener Urtext UT50037, $14.95.

1972 * Mozart, Wolfgang Amadeus, 1756–1791

[Piano music. Selections] *Selected piano pieces.* Dover 0-486-26882-9, $10.95; Henle HN133, $16.95.

1973 * Mozart, Wolfgang Amadeus, 1756–1791

[Sonatas, piano] *Sonatas for piano.* Associated Board of the Royal Schools of Music 490-00273–490-00274, 2 v., $27.50 each; Bärenreiter BA4861-

4862, 2 v., $21 each; Dover 0-486-25417-8, $14.95; Henle HN1-2, 2 v., $25.95 each; Peters P1800a-b, 2 v., $26.85 each; Presser 410-41056, rev. ed. by Nathan Broder, $16.50; Wiener Urtext UT50035-36, 2 v., $22.95 each.

1974 * Mozart, Wolfgang Amadeus, 1756–1791

[Variations, piano] *Piano variations.* Henle HN116, $29.95; Wiener Urtext UT50008-09, 2 v., $14.95 each.

1975 Muczynski, Robert, 1929–

[Piano music. Selections] *Collected piano pieces.* G. Schirmer ED1972, $10.95.

1976 Muczynski, Robert, 1929–

[Preludes, piano, op. 6] *Six preludes, op. 6.* G. Schirmer ED2451, $6.95.

1977 * Mussorgsky, Modest Petrovich, 1839–1881

[Kartinki s vystavki] *Pictures at an exhibition, for piano.* Breitkopf & Härtel EB8112, with color reproductions of the Victor Hartmann paintings, $17; Dover 0-486-26515-3, $11.95; Henle HN477, $19.95; International Music 1250, with black-and-white reproductions of the Victor Hartmann paintings, $7.50; Peters P9585, $21.60; Wiener Urtext UT50076, ed. by Vladimir Ashkenazy, with selected color and black-and-white reproductions of the Victor Hartmann paintings, $28.95.

1978 Poulenc, Francis, 1899–1963

L'histoire de Babar, le petit elephant, pour recitant et piano. Hansen/Chester J.W.C. 9746, $15.95.

1979 Poulenc, Francis, 1899–1963

[Piano music. Selections] *Piano album.* Salabert SEAS18793, $19.95.

1980 * Prokofiev, Sergey, 1891–1953

[Mimoletnosti] *Visions fugitives, op. 22.* International Music 1629, $6; G. Schirmer LB1901, $7.95.

1981 * Prokofiev, Sergey, 1891–1953

[Piano music. Selections] *Shorter piano works: Sarcasms, Visions fugitives, sonatinas, and other works.* Dover 0-486-27166-8, $13.95.

1982 * Prokofiev, Sergey, 1891–1953

[Sarkazmy] *Sarcasms, op. 17.* Kalmus K 03797, $3.50; MCA/G. Schirmer HL00121202, $4.95.

1983 * Prokofiev, Sergey, 1891–1953

[Sonatas, piano] *Sonatas for piano.* Dover 0-486-25689-8, $11.95; International Music 2510, $27; MCA Music/G. Schirmer HL00123085, $15.95.

1984 * Rachmaninoff, Sergei, 1873–1943

[Etudes-tableaux, piano] *Etudes-tableaux, op. 33 and op. 39.* International Music 505, 983, 2 v., $7.50, $10.50; Kalmus K 03817, K 03821, 2 v., $4, $7.95; MCA Music/G. Schirmer HL00123087, $12.95. *See also* 1985

1985 * Rachmaninoff, Sergei, 1873–1943

[Preludes, piano] *Preludes, op. 3 no. 2, op. 23, and op. 32.* Dover 0-486-25696-0 (with Rachmaninoff's *Etudes-tableaux*), $10.95; International Music 879, 1143, 2 v., $7, $7.75; Kalmus K 03818-03819, 2 v., $5.50, $6.95; Peters P66900-66901, ed. by Ruth Laredo, 2 v., $20.25, $21.80.

1986 Rachmaninoff, Sergei, 1873–1943

[Sonatas, piano, no. 2, op. 36, B♭ minor] *Piano sonata no. 2 in B♭ minor, op. 36,* ed. by John Browning. International Music 3252, $14.

1987 Rameau, Jean Philippe, 1683–1764

Pièces de clavecin = Pieces for harpsichord. Bärenreiter BA3800, $37.50; Dover 0-486-27847-6, $9.95; Heugel (Le pupitre, v. 59), $95.35.

1988 Ran, Shulamit, 1947–

Hyperbolae, for piano. Israel Music Institute 510-03095, $9.

1989 * Ravel, Maurice, 1875–1937

Gaspard de la nuit. Durand 510-01380, $30.25; G. Schirmer, ed. by Gaby Casadesus, $12.95.

1990 * Ravel, Maurice, 1875–1937

Jeux d'eau. Kalmus K 03839, $3.50; G. Schirmer ED3508, ed. by Gaby Casadesus, $3.95.

1991 * Ravel, Maurice, 1875–1937

Miroirs. G. Schirmer ED3360, ed. by Gaby Casadesus, $5.95.

1992 * Ravel, Maurice, 1875–1937

Pavane pour une infante défunte. E. B. Marks/G. Schirmer, $3.95.

1993 * Ravel, Maurice, 1875–1937

[Piano music. Selections] *Piano masterpieces of Maurice Ravel.* Dover 0-486-25137-3 (includes all pieces listed except Tombeau and Valses nobles), $7.95.

1994 * Ravel, Maurice, 1875–1937

[Piano music. Selections] *Ravel album: Miroirs, Sonatine, Jeux d'eau.* Kalmus K 03826, $9.95.

1995 * Ravel, Maurice, 1875–1937

[Sonatina, piano] *Sonatine for piano.* Presser 460-00055, $4.50; G. Schirmer ED3509, ed. by Gaby Casadesus, $7.95.

1996 * Ravel, Maurice, 1875–1937

Le tombeau de Couperin. Durand 510-01397, $27; Masters Music M2257, $8.95.

1997 * Ravel, Maurice, 1875–1937

Valses nobles et sentimentales. Durand 510-01399, $26.50; Masters Music M1081, $5.50.

1998 Rzewski, Frederic, 1938–

The people united will never be defeated!: 36 variations on "El pueblo unido jamas sera vencido!" Zen-On Music 1410, $49.95.

1999 * Satie, Erik, 1866–1925

[Piano music] *Piano music.* Salabert SRL900X, SRL09871X, SMC194, 3 v., $11.95, $10.95, $10.95.

2000 * Satie, Erik, 1866–1925

[Piano music. Selections] *Gymnopédies, Gnossiennes and other works for piano.* Dover 0-486-25978-1, $9.95.

2001 * Satie, Erik, 1866–1925

[Sports et divertissements] *Twenty short pieces for piano: Sports et divertissements.* Dover 0-486-24365-6, $5.95.

2002 * Scarlatti, Domenico, 1685–1757

[Sonatas, harpsichord. Selections] *Sonatas for harpsichord.* Dover 0-486-24996-4, 0-486-25003-2, 0-486-27583-3, 0-486-27600-7, ed. by Alessandro Longo, 4 v., $8.95 each; Henle HN395, HN451, HN476, 3 v., $24.95, $25.95, $25.95; G. Schirmer ED3529, ED3530, ED3531 (*100 sonatas*), ed. by Eiji Hashimoto, 3 v., $15.95 each; G. Schirmer LB1774, LB1775 (*60 sonatas*), ed. by Ralph Kirkpatrick, 2 v., $9.95 each.

2003 * Schoenberg, Arnold, 1874–1951

Kleine Klavierstücke = Six little piano pieces, op. 19. Masters Music M1461, $3.50; Universal UE5069, $8.

2004 * Schoenberg, Arnold, 1874–1951

[Stücke, piano, op. 11] *Three piano pieces, op. 11.* Masters Music M1069, $3.95; Universal UE2991, $10.

2005 * Schoenberg, Arnold, 1874–1951

[Stücke, piano, op. 33] *Two piano pieces, op. 33a and op. 33b.* Universal/Belmont UE9773, UE15165, 2 v., $7, $6.

2006 * Schoenberg, Arnold, 1874–1951

[Suites, piano, op. 25] *Suite for piano, op. 25.* Universal UE7627, $10.

2007 * Schubert, Franz, 1797–1828

[Fantasien, piano, D. 760, C major] *Fantasy for piano, op. 15, D. 760, "Wanderer fantasy."* Associated Board of the Royal Schools of Music 490-00079, $8.50; Henle HN282, $9.95; Wiener Urtext UT50010, $9.95.

2008 ** Schubert, Franz, 1797–1828

[Piano music. Selections] *Impromptus and Moments musicaux.* Dover 0-486-22648-4, $10.95; Henle HN4, $17.95; Peters P3235, $16; Wiener Urtext UT50001, $17.95.

2009 * Schubert, Franz, 1797–1828

[Sonatas, piano] *Sonatas for piano.* Associated Board of the Royal Schools of Music 490-00070, 490-00074–490-00075, ed. by Howard Ferguson, 3 v., $33.75, $30.25, $33.75; Dover 0-486-22647-6, $13.95; Henle HN146, HN148, HN150, 3 v., $30.95, $40.95, $44.95; Universal UE257A-B, 2 v., $14.95 each.

2010 * Schumann, Clara, 1819–1896

[Piano music. Selections] *Selected piano works.* Bärenreiter BA6550, BA 6556, 2 v., $17 each; Da Capo Press 0-306-79554-X, $27.50; Henle HN393, $25.95.

2011 * Schumann, Robert, 1810–1856

[Album für die Jugend] *Album for the young, op. 68.* Henle HN45, $9.95; Peters P9500a, $13.10; Wiener Urtext UT50049, $10.95.

2012 * Schumann, Robert, 1810–1856

[Arabesque, piano, op. 18, C major] *Arabesque, op. 18.* Henle HN84, $6.50; Peters P9508 (with Schumann's *Blumenstück, op. 19*), $5.75; Wiener Urtext UT50059 (with Schumann's *Blumenstück, op. 19*), $9.95.

2013 * Schumann, Robert, 1810–1856

[Blumenstück] *Flower piece, op. 19.* Henle HN90, $7.95. *See also* 2012

2014 * Schumann, Robert, 1810–1856

Carnaval, op. 9. Henle HN187, $10.95; Peters P9503, $10.90.

2015 * Schumann, Robert, 1810–1856

[Davidsbündlertänze] *Davidsbündler dances, op. 6.* Henle HN244, $11.95; Peters P9502, $13.10.

2016 * Schumann, Robert, 1810–1856

[Etudes symphoniques] *Symphonic etudes, op. 13.* Henle HN248, $22.95; Peters P9515, $19.65.

2017 * Schumann, Robert, 1810–1856

[Fantasie, piano, op. 17, C major] *Fantasy in C major, op. 17.* Henle HN276, $11.95; Peters P9510, $13.10; Well-Tempered Press W7083, ed. by Clara Schumann, $6.50.

2018 * Schumann, Robert, 1810–1856

[Fantasiestücke, piano, op. 12] *Fantasy pieces, op. 12.* Henle HN91, $10.95; Peters P9512, $13.10; Wiener Urtext UT50038, $9.95.

2019 * Schumann, Robert, 1810–1856

[Faschingsschwank aus Wien] *Carnival jest of Vienna, op. 26.* Henle HN186, $10.95; Peters P9516, $10.90.

2020 * Schumann, Robert, 1810–1856

[Humoresque, piano, op. 20, B♭ major] *Humoresque, op. 20.* Henle HN441, $13.95; Peters P9514, $16.35.

2021 * Schumann, Robert, 1810–1856

[Kinderszenen, op. 15] *Scenes from childhood, op. 15.* Henle HN44, $7.50; Peters P9500b, $7.65; Wiener Urtext UT50006, $7.95.

2022 * Schumann, Robert, 1810–1856

Kreisleriana, op. 16. Henle HN253, $11.95; Peters P9504, $13.

2023 * Schumann, Robert, 1810–1856

Papillons, op. 2. Henle HN105, $7.50; Peters P9506, $7.65; Wiener Urtext UT50014, UT51021, 2 v., $7.95, $14.95.

2024 ** Schumann, Robert, 1810–1856

[Piano music] *Piano music.* Dover 0-486-21459-1, 0-486-21461-3, 0-486-23906-3, v. 1–2 ed. by Clara Schumann, v. 3 ed. by Clara Schumann and Johannes Brahms, 3 v., $12.95, $12.95, $10.95; Henle HN108, HN110, HN112, HN114, 4 v., $33.95, $40.95, $45.95, $48.95; Kalmus K 03923-03929, ed. by Clara Schumann, 7 v., $12.50 each.

2025 * Schumann, Robert, 1810–1856

[Sonatas, piano, no. 1, op. 11, F♯ minor] *Piano sonata no. 1 in F♯ minor, op. 11.* Henle HN337, $18.95; Peters P9509 (with Schumann's *Sonata no. 2 in G minor, op. 22*), $30.

2026 * Schumann, Robert, 1810–1856

[Sonatas, piano, no. 2, op. 22, G minor] *Piano sonata no. 2 in G minor, op. 22.* Henle HN331, $13.95. *See also* 2025

2027 * Schumann, Robert, 1810–1856

[Sonatas, piano, no. 3, op. 14, F minor] *Piano sonata no. 3 in F minor, op. 14.* Henle HN346, $24.95.

2028 * Schumann, Robert, 1810–1856

[Thème sur le nom Abegg varié] *Abegg variations, op. 1.* Henle HN87, $7.50; Peters P9501, $7.60.

2029 * Schumann, Robert, 1810–1856

[Toccata, piano, op. 7, C major] *Toccata, op. 7.* Henle HN201, $8.95; Peters P9518, $7.65.

2030 * Scriabin, Aleksandr Nikolayevich, 1872–1915

[Etudes, piano, op. 8] *Twelve etudes, op. 8.* International Music 1433, $6.75.

2031 * Scriabin, Aleksandr Nikolayevich, 1872–1915

[Etudes, piano, op. 42] *Eight etudes, op. 42.* International Music 537, $6.25; Peters P9077a (includes Scriabin's *Etudes op. 8 and op. 65*), $33.85.

2032 * Scriabin, Aleksandr Nikolayevich, 1872–1915

[Piano music. Selections] *Complete preludes and etudes for piano.* Dover 0-486-22919-X, $10.95.

2033 * Scriabin, Aleksandr Nikolayevich, 1872–1915

[Preludes, piano, op. 11] *Twenty-four preludes, op. 11.* Henle HN484, in preparation; International Music 1513, $6.75; Peters P9287b, $18.70.

2034 * Scriabin, Aleksandr Nikolayevich, 1872–1915

[Sonatas, piano] *Piano sonatas.* Dover 0-486-25850-5, $10.95; International Music 2799, $19.50; MCA Music/G. Schirmer, $14.95; Peters P9077e-f, 2 v., $33.85, $38.50.

2035   Seeger, Ruth Crawford, 1901–1953

[Preludes, piano, no. 1–5] *Preludes, no. 1–5.* Hildegard 09206, $29.50.

2036   Seeger, Ruth Crawford, 1901–1953

[Preludes, piano, no. 6–9] *Four preludes for piano.* Merion Music 440-40010, $5.95.

2037 * Shostakovich, Dmitrii Dmitrievich, 1906–1975

[Piano music. Selections] *Preludes, op. 34; Preludes and fugues, op. 87.* Dover 0-486-26861-6, $12.95.

2038 * Shostakovich, Dmitrii Dmitrievich, 1906–1975

[Preliudii i fugi, piano, op. 87] *24 preludes and fugues for piano, op. 87.* Kalmus K 03962-03964 (no. 1–12 only), 3 v., $4.50 each; MCA Music/G. Schirmer, $22.95; Peters P4716a-b, 2 v., $39.95, $30.

2039 Shostakovich, Dmitrii Dmitrievich, 1906–1975

[Preludes, piano, op. 34] *24 preludes, op. 34.* International Music 583, $7.25; Kalmus K 03967, $5.95; MCA Music/G. Schirmer, $9.95; Peters P4773, $20.25.

2040 Soler, Antonio, 1729–1783

[Sonatas, harpsichord. Selections] *Sonatas for harpsichord.* Faber F50886, $21.95; Henle HN475, v.1 $24.95.

2041 Still, William Grant, 1895–1978

[Traceries] *Seven traceries, for piano.* William Grant Still Music, $9.80.

2042 Still, William Grant, 1895–1978

[Visions] *Three visions, for piano.* William Grant Still Music, $8.

2043 Stockhausen, Karlheinz, 1928–

[Stücke, piano, I–IV, XI] *Klavierstücke, v. 1, no. 1–4; v. 2, no. 11.* Universal UE12251 (no. 1–4), UE12654 (no. 11), 2 v., $20, $25.

2044 * Stravinsky, Igor, 1882–1971

[Ballets. Selections; arr.] *Three early ballets: The firebird, Petrushka, The rite of spring, arranged for piano solo.* G. Schirmer LB1978, $17.95.

2045 Stravinsky, Igor, 1882–1971

[Piano music. Selections] *Short piano pieces.* Boosey & Hawkes PIB 46, $16.50.

2046 * Stravinsky, Igor, 1882–1971

[Serenade, piano, A] *Serenade in A for piano,* original ed. by Albert Spalding. Boosey & Hawkes PIB 334, $12.50; Masters Music M1763, $4.50.

2047 * Stravinsky, Igor, 1882–1971

[Sonatas, piano (1924)] *Sonata for piano (1924),* original ed. by Albert Spalding. Boosey & Hawkes PIB 341, $17.50; Masters Music M1075, $4.50.

2048 Szymanowska, Maria Agata Wolowska, 1789–1831

[Piano music. Selections] *Music for piano.* Hildegard 9005, $30.

2049 Szymanowski, Karol, 1882–1937

[Etiudy, piano, op. 33] *Etudes, op. 33.* Universal UE6998, $10.95.

2050 Szymanowski, Karol, 1882–1937

[Maski] *Masques, op. 34: three pieces for piano.* Masters Music M2412, $8.95; Universal UE5858, $14.95.

2051 * Tatum, Art, 1910–1956

Art Tatum: transcriptions of six important solo piano pieces as played by the legendary Art Tatum, selected and ed. by Jed Distler. Music for millions, v. 85. Amsco AM 30719, $11.95.

2052 Tchaikovsky, Peter Ilich, 1840–1893

[Vremena goda] *The seasons: 12 characteristic pieces for the piano, op. 37a.* Dover (with other piano works) 0-486-29128-6, $12.95; Peters P3781, $30; G. Schirmer LB909, $9.95.

2053 Villa-Lobos, Heitor, 1887–1959

Rudepoema. Eschig ME2169, $43.50.

2054 * Waller, Fats, 1904–1943

The genius of Fats Waller. Belwin-Mills TPF0120, $12.95.

2055 Weber, Carl Maria von, 1786–1826

[Aufforderung zum Tanze] *Invitation to the dance.* Henle HN415, $7.50.

2056 * Webern, Anton, 1883–1945

[Variations, piano, op. 27] *Variations for piano, op. 27.* Universal UE10881, $14.95

2057 Zaimont, Judith Lang, 1945–

[Calendar set] *Calendar collection: a set of 12 descriptive preludes.* Alfred Music 1872, $2.50, OP.

Solo Piano or Harpsichord Music: Anthologies

2058 *Alte Meister der Klaviermusik des 16.–18. Jahrhunderts = Old masters of piano music from the 16th–18th centuries.* Peters P4641a-d, 4 v., $33.85 each.

2059 *American contemporary masters: a collection of works for piano.* G. Schirmer ED3978, $29.95.

2060 *American keyboard music, 1866–1910,* ed. by Sylvia Glickman. Three centuries of American music, v. 4. G. K. Hall, $85.

2061 *American women composers: piano music, 1865–1959,* ed. by Sylvia Glickman. Hildegard 09004, $39.50.

2062 *Anthology of early English harpsichord music,* compiled and ed. by Anthony Newman. G. Schirmer ED3275, $13.95.

2063 * *An anthology of piano music,* ed. by Denes Agay. YMP, 4 v.

Contents: vol. 1. *The baroque period,* $12.95. vol. 2. *The classical period,* $17.95. vol. 3. *The romantic period,* $15.95. vol. 4. *The twentieth century,* $17.95.

2064 *The artistry of Bill Evans* [jazz piano versions of popular songs], ed. by David C. Olsen and Tom Roed; transcriptions by Pascal Wetzel. CPP/Belwin 0-89898-551-X, $13.95.

2065 *Best of jazz piano: 43 creative solos.* Warner Bros. PF0757, $22.95.

2066 *Black women composers: a century of piano music (1893–1990),* ed. by Helen Walker-Hill. Hildegard 09109, $43.50.

2067 *Classic piano rags,* ed. by Rudi Blesh. Dover 0-486-20469-3, $14.95.

2068 ** *The complete wedding music collection for piano.* CPP/Belwin, $16.95.

2069 *Contemporary styles for the jazz pianist,* ed. by John Mehegan. Sam Fox FX1008-1010, 3 v., $3 each.

2070 *Early keyboard music series: a series of anthologies,* ed. by Howard Ferguson. Oxford University Press, 4 v., $59.95 each.

Contents: vol. 1. *Early German keyboard music.* vol. 2. *Early Italian keyboard music.* vol. 3. *Early French keyboard music.* vol. 4. *Early English keyboard music.*

2071 *Early Spanish keyboard music: an anthology,* ed. by Barry Ife and Ry Truby. Oxford University Press, 3 v., $19.95 each.

Contents: vol. 1. *The sixteenth century.* vol. 2. *The seventeenth century.* vol. 3. *The eighteenth century.*

2072 *Eighteenth-century women composers for the keyboard,* ed. by Barbara Harbach. Vivace VIV 1801-1802, 2 v., $16.95 each.

2073 * *Fitzwilliam virginal book.* Dover 0-486-21068-5, 0-486-21069-3, 2 v., $12.50, $16.95.

2074 *Frauen Komponieren = Female composers: 22 piano pieces,* ed. by Eva Rieger and Käte Walter. Schott ED7197, $19.95.

2075 * *French piano music: an anthology,* ed. by Isidor Philipp. Dover 0-486-23381-2, $8.95.

2076 *Keyboard dances from the earlier sixteenth century,* transcribed into modern notation by Daniel Heartz. Corpus of early keyboard music, v. 8. American Institute of Musicology, OP.

2077 *Keyboard music of the fourteenth and fifteenth centuries,* ed. by Willi Apel. Corpus of early keyboard music, v. 1. American Institute of Musicology, OP.

2078 *Das neue Klavierbuch: leichte Klavierstücke zeitgenossischer Komponisten.* Schott ED6010, ED6011, ED7095, 3 v., $9.95, $9.95, $12.95.

2079 * *Nineteenth-century European piano music,* ed. by John Gillespie. Dover 0-486-23447-9, $15.95.

2080 * *Piano music for 1 hand,* ed. by Raymond Lewenthal. G. Schirmer ED2773, $13.95.

2081 *Ragtime rarities,* ed. by Trebor J. Tichenor. Dover 0-486-23157-7, $12.95.

2082 *Ragtime rediscoveries,* ed. by Trebor J. Tichenor. Dover 0-486-23776-1, $14.95.

2083 *Rare masterpieces of Russian piano music,* ed. by Dmitry Feofanov. Dover 0-486-24659-0, $8.95.

2084 * *Sonatas, classics to moderns,* ed. by Denis Agay. Music for millions, v. 67. Consolidated AM48737, $12.95.

2085 * *Style and interpretation: an anthology of 16th- through 19th-century keyboard music,* ed. by Howard Ferguson. Oxford University Press, v.1–4 of 6 (v.5–6 contain piano duets), $24.95 each.

Contents: vol. 1. *Early keyboard music (I): England and France.* vol. 2. *Early keyboard music (II): Germany and Italy.* vol. 3. *Classical piano music.* vol. 4. *Romantic piano music.*

2086 *Styles in twentieth-century piano music.* Universal UE12050, $25.

2087   *Themes and variations,* ed. by Denis Agay. Music for millions, v. 77. Consolidated MFM7, $12.95.

2088   *Thirty-six twentieth-century pieces for piano.* G. Schirmer ED2734, $11.95.

2089   *Le trésor des pianistes,* compiled and ed. by Aristide Farrenc and Louise Farrenc. Da Capo Press, 23 v., $55 each, $1,095 as set.

2090   *Various leaves: a collection of brief works for piano by contemporary American composers.* Fallen Leaf Press no. 52, $33.

2091   *Waltzes by 25 contemporary composers.* Peters P66735, $20.25.

Piano Methods and Studies

2092 * Brahms, Johannes, 1833–1897
[Übungen] *Fifty-one exercises for piano.* International Music 2030, $8; G. Schirmer LB1600, $6.95.

2093 * Clementi, Muzio, 1752–1832
Gradus ad Parnassum. Kalmus K 03303-3304, 2 v., $8.50 each; Peters P3013 (selections), $14.65; G. Schirmer LB167-168, 2 v., $14 each.

2094 * Czerny, Carl, 1791–1857
[Kunst der Fingerfertigkeit] *The art of finger dexterity: fifty studies for the piano, op. 740.* Kalmus K 03348, $10.50; Peters P2412, $32; G. Schirmer LB154, $12.95.

2095 * Czerny, Carl, 1791–1857
[Schule der Geläufigkeit] *School of velocity, op. 299.* Kalmus K 03345, $5.50; Peters P2411, $14.75; G. Schirmer LB161, $6.95.

2096   Czerny, Carl, 1791–1857
[Schule der linken Hand, op. 399] *School of the left hand, op. 399.* Peters P2842, $30.

2097 * Dobbins, Bill
The contemporary jazz pianist: a comprehensive approach to keyboard improvisation. GAMT Press, 4 v., $25 each.

2098   Dohnányi, Ernő, 1877–1960
Essential finger exercises. Editio Musica Budapest EMB2652, $11.

2099   Ganz, Rudolph, 1877–1972
Exercises for piano: contemporary and special. Summy-Birchard, $9.95.

2100   Gold, Arthur, 1917– , and Robert Fizdale, 1920–
Hanon revisited: contemporary piano exercises based on "The virtuoso pianist." G. Schirmer ED2697, $14.95.

2101 * Haerle, Dan
Jazz improvisation for keyboard players. Studio P/R, $7.50 each for basic, intermediate, and advanced editions; $17.50 for complete edition.

2102 * Hanon, Charles Lewis, 1820–1900
The virtuoso pianist in sixty exercises. Peters P4354, $14.50; G. Schirmer LB925, $5.95.

2103   Joseffy, Rafael, 1852–1915
School of advanced piano playing. G. Schirmer ED158, $15.95.

2104 * Pischna, Josef, 1826–1896
Technical studies. G. Schirmer LB792, $7.95.

2105   Suzuki, Shinichi, 1898–
Suzuki piano school. Summy-Birchard, 7 v., $6.95 each; 5 recordings (v.1–2, 3–4, 5, 6, 7): compact discs, $15.95 each; cassettes, $12.95 each.

Piano, Four Hands, and Two Pianos, Four Hands

Music for Piano, Four Hands

Piano duet literature, also referred to as *one piano, four-hand music,* consists of both original and transcribed works for two players at one keyboard.

2106   Barber, Samuel, 1910–1981
[Souvenirs, op. 28] *Souvenirs: ballet suite, op. 28.* G. Schirmer ED3565, $19.95.

2107 * Beethoven, Ludwig van, 1770–1827
[Piano music, 4 hands] *Music for piano, 4 hands.* Henle HN323, $22.95; International Music 628, $8.50; Kalmus K 03165, $7; Peters P285, $20.25; Universal UE13303, $14.95.

2108 * Bizet, Georges, 1838–1875
Jeux d'enfants = Children's games, op. 22. International Music 1116, $8.25; Kalmus K 03223, $6; G. Schirmer HL50481378, ed. by Noël Lee, $19.95.

2109 * Brahms, Johannes, 1833–1897

[Piano music, 4 hands] *Complete piano works for 4 hands.* Dover 0-486-23271-9, $11.95.

2110 * Brahms, Johannes, 1833–1897

[Ungarische Tänze] *Hungarian dances.* Henle HN68, $26.95; International Music 2581-2582, 2 v., $9, $11; Kalmus K 09527-09528, 2 v., $6.50 each; Peters P2100a-b, 2 v., $21.75 each.

2111 Brahms, Johannes, 1833–1897

[Variationen über ein Thema von Robert Schumann] *Variations on a theme by Robert Schumann, op. 23.* International Music 1959, $7.25; Peters P3659, $12.10.

2112 * Brahms, Johannes, 1833–1897

[Waltzes, piano, 4 hands, op. 39] *Waltzes for piano, 4 hands, op. 39.* Henle HN67, $10.95; International Music 947, $5.75; Kalmus K 03262, $5.50; Peters P3665, $7.70.

2113 * *Classical album for piano, 4 hands.* Kalmus K 09838, $6.50.

2114 Debussy, Claude, 1862–1918

[Épigraphes antiques] *Six épigraphes antiques.* Durand 510-01408, $24.50; Masters Music M1885, $5.95.

2115 * Debussy, Claude, 1862–1918

Petite suite: four original pieces. Durand 460-00062, $5.95; International Music 1830, $4.50; Masters Music M1010, $5.95; G. Schirmer LB1857, $4.95.

2116 * Debussy, Claude, 1862–1918

[Piano music, 4 hands and 2 pianos] *Works for piano four hands and two pianos.* Dover 0-486-26974-4, Series I: *Prélude à l'après-midi d'un faune, Petite suite,* $8.95; Dover 0-486-26975-2, Series II: *Danse sacrée et danse profane, La mer, En blanc et noir,* $8.95.

2117 * Dvořák, Antonín, 1841–1904

[Slovanské tance] *Complete Slavonic dances, for piano 4 hands.* Dover 0-486-27019-X, $8.95.

2118 * Dvořák, Antonín, 1841–1904

[Slovanské tance, op. 46] *Slavonic dances, op. 46.* International Music 2731, $19; Kalmus K 09523-09524, 2 v., $5.95, $6.50; G. Schirmer LB1028, $10.95; Schott ED4606-4607, 2 v., $7.95 each.

2119 * Dvořák, Antonín, 1841–1904

[Slovanské tance, op. 72] *Slavonic dances, op. 72.* Kalmus K 09525-09526, 2 v., $6.50 each; G. Schirmer LB1029, $10.95; Schott ED4408-4409, 2 v., $7.95 each.

2120 * Fauré, Gabriel, 1845–1924

[Dolly] *Dolly suite, op. 56.* International Music 1817, $8; Masters Music M1852, $8.95.

2121 *Forty-four original piano duets,* ed. by Walter Eckard. Presser 410-41166, $12.95.

2122 * *Four-hand piano music by nineteenth-century masters,* ed. by Morey Ritt. Dover 0-486-23860-1, $12.95.

2123 * Gershwin, George, 1898–1937

[I got rhythm variations; arr.] *I got rhythm: impromptu variations for piano duet.* Warner Bros. PS0149, $5.95.

2124 * Grieg, Edvard, 1843–1907

[Norwegische Tänze] *Norwegian dances, op. 35.* Peters P2056, $12.10; Schott ED4695, $7.95.

2125 * Hindemith, Paul, 1895–1963

Ragtime pieces, for piano, 4 hands. Schott ED7325, $14.95.

2126 * Hindemith, Paul, 1895–1963

[Sonatas, piano, 4 hands] *Sonata for piano, four hands.* Schott ED3716, $19.95.

2127 * Mendelssohn-Bartholdy, Felix, 1809–1847

[Piano music, 4 hands] *Works for piano, four-hands: Andante and variations, op. 83a; Allegro brillant, op. 92.* Henle HN325, $29.95; International Music 711, $10.50; G. Schirmer LB1732, $9.50.

2128 Milhaud, Darius, 1892–1974

Enfantines. Eschig 510-03225, $33.

2129 Milhaud, Darius, 1892–1974

Saudades do Brasil. Eschig 510-03207/03208, 2 v., $35 each.

2130 * Mozart, Wolfgang Amadeus, 1756–1791

[Piano music, 4 hands] *Music for piano, four hands.* Bärenreiter BA4786, $26.25; Dover (with Mozart's *Music for two pianos, four hands*) 0-486-26501-3, $9.95; Henle HN92, $34.95; International Music 569, $18; Kalmus K 03722, $9.95; Peters P12, $24.20; G. Schirmer LB1735, $13.95; Wiener Urtext UT13304, $14.95.

2131 Nancarrow, Conlon, 1912–

[Sonatinas, piano, 4 hands] *Sonatina for piano, four hands.* Peters P66990a, $20.95.

2132 Persichetti, Vincent, 1915–1987

[Concertos, piano, 4 hands, op. 56] *Concerto for piano, 4 hands, op. 56.* Presser 460-00052, $15.

2133 * Poulenc, Francis, 1899–1963

[Sonatas, piano, 4 hands] *Sonata for piano, 4 hands, or for 2 pianos.* Chester, $15.95.

2134 Rachmaninoff, Sergei, 1873–1943

[Pieces, piano, 4 hands, op. 11] *Six pieces for piano, 4 hands, op. 11.* Boosey & Hawkes PFB 58, $19.50; International Music 1343, $9.

2135 * Ravel, Maurice, 1875–1937

Ma mère l'oye = Mother Goose suite: pièces enfantines. Durand 510-01434, $24.50; Kalmus K 09949, $6.95.

2136 Satie, Erik, 1866–1925

[Morceaux en forme de poire] *Three pieces in the shape of a pear.* Masters Music M1013, $5.95; Salabert SRL09799, $13.95.

2137 * Schubert, Franz, 1797–1828

[Fantasies, piano, 4 hands, F minor, D. 940] *Fantasy in F minor, op. 103, D. 940.* Henle HN180, $11.95; Peters P155cc, $9.10.

2138 * Schubert, Franz, 1797–1828

[Piano music, 4 hands. Selections] *Music for piano, 4 hands.* [Contents vary slightly between the following editions; Henle is the most complete, followed by Peters.] Dover 0-486-23529-7, $12.95; Henle HN94, HN96, HN98, 3 v., $44.95, $46.95, $36.95; International Music 586, $13; Kalmus K 03889, K 03891-03893, v.1 and v.3–5 available of a 5-v. set, $12.95, $9.95, $8.50, $8.50; Peters P155a-d, 4 v., $29, $29, $29, $14.65.

2139 * Schumann, Robert, 1810–1854

[Piano music, 4 hands] *Music for piano, 4 hands: Bilder aus Osten, op. 66; 12 pieces, op. 85; Ballszenen, op. 109; Kinderball, op. 130.* International Music 2515, $16.50; Kalmus K 03921-03922, 2 v., $8.50, $6.50; Peters P2347, $33.85.

2140 * Stravinsky, Igor, 1882–1971

[Piano music, 4 hands. Selections] *Petrushka and The rite of spring, for piano 4 hands.* Dover 0-486-26342-8, $9.95.

2141 Stravinsky, Igor, 1882–1971

[Pièces faciles, piano, 4 hands (1915)] *Three easy pieces.* International Music 3075, $5.75.

2142 Stravinsky, Igor, 1882–1971

[Pièces faciles, piano, 4 hands (1917)] *Five easy pieces.* International Music 3074, $5.

2143 * *Style and interpretation: an anthology of 16th- through 20th-century keyboard music,* ed. by Howard Ferguson. Oxford University Press, v.5–6 of 6 (v.1–4 contain solo piano music), $24.95 each.

Contents: vol. 5. *Duets of the seventeenth and eighteenth centuries.* vol. 6. *Duets of the nineteenth and twentieth centuries.*

2144 Tchaikovsky, Peter Ilich, 1840–1893

[Piat desiat russkikh narodnykh pesen] *Fifty Russian folk songs.* International Music 2188, $8.75; Kalmus K 04076, $6.50; Peters P4493 (contains 36 of the 50 folk songs), $16.70.

2145 * Warlock, Peter, 1894–1930

[Capriol suite. Selections; arr.] *Capriol suite, for piano, 4 hands.* Curwen C99059, $6.95.

2146 Weber, Carl Maria von, 1786–1826

[Piano music, 4 hands] *Music for piano, 4 hands.* International Music 1541, $17; Peters P188a, $30.50.

Music for Two Pianos, Four Hands (Excluding Piano Concertos)

When ordering music for two pianos, four hands, one must distinguish between editions for which the publisher supplies two copies (indicated as "set" in the citations below) and those where each copy must be purchased separately. Because of the difficulty of determining to which category some editions belong, specify "one performance set" when placing orders.

2147 Arensky, Anton Stepanovich, 1861–1906

[Suites, pianos (2), no. 1, op. 15, F major] *Suite for 2 pianos, op. 15.* International Music 2416, $9.75, set; G. Schirmer LB1300, $8.95, set.

2148 * Bartók, Béla, 1881–1945

[Sonatas, pianos (2), percussion] *Sonata for 2 pianos and percussion.* Boosey & Hawkes PFB 96 (piano part), $29; Boosey & Hawkes, PFB 98 (percussion part), $28.

2149   Boulez, Pierre, 1925–

Structures no. 1 and 2, for 2 pianos. Universal UE12267, UE13833, 2 v., $39, $49.

2150 * Brahms, Johannes, 1833–1897

[Sonatas, pianos (2), op. 34b, F minor] *Sonata in F minor for 2 pianos, op. 34b.* International Music 836, $17.50, set; Peters P3662, $18.70.

2151 * Brahms, Johannes, 1833–1897

[Variationen über ein Thema von Haydn; arr.] *Variations on a theme by Haydn, op. 56b,* originally for orchestra; arranged by the composer. International Music 2556, $9.25, set; Kalmus K 03248, $5; Peters P3892, $12.10, set.

2152   Britten, Benjamin, 1913–1976

Introduction and rondo alla burlesca. Boosey & Hawkes PFB 122, $39, set.

2153   Chabrier, Emmanuel, 1841–1894

[Valses romantiques] *Trois valses romantiques.* International Music 2384, 671, 2385, 3 v., $6.50, $6, $7.25, sets; Masters Music M2363, $12.

2154 * Chopin, Frédéric, 1810–1849

[Rondos, pianos (2), op. 73, C major] *Rondo in C major for 2 pianos, op. 73.* Peters P1914, $9.10; G. Schirmer LB1508, $9.95.

2155   Copland, Aaron, 1900–1990

Danzón Cubano. Boosey & Hawkes PFB 105, $22, set.

2156   Crumb, George, 1929–

Music for a summer evening: Makrokosmos III for 2 amplified pianos and percussion. Peters P66590, $37.05.

2157 * Debussy, Claude, 1862–1918

En blanc et noir = In black and white. Durand 510-01446, $45.50, set. *See also* 2116

2158   Hindemith, Paul, 1895–1963

[Sonatas, pianos (2)] *Sonata for 2 pianos.* Schott ED4124, $29.

2159 * Lutosławski, Witold, 1913–

[Wariacje na temat Paganiniego] *Variations on a theme by Paganini, for 2 pianos.* Masters Music M2034, $7.95.

2160 * Messiaen, Olivier, 1908–1992

Visions de l'amen. Durand 510-01270, $71.

2161 * Milhaud, Darius, 1892–1974

[Scaramouche] *Scaramouche suite, op. 165b.* Salabert SEAS14914A, $24.95, set.

2162 * Mozart, Wolfgang Amadeus, 1756–1791

[Sonatas, pianos (2), K. 488, D major] *Sonata in D major, K. 488, and Fugue in C minor, K. 426.* Henle HN471 (with Mozart's *Adagio in C minor, K. 546*), $29.95; International Music 2044, $10.25, set; Kalmus K 09519, $5.50; Peters P1327 (with Mozart's *Adagio in C minor, K. 546*), $18.70, set; G. Schirmer LB1504, $6.95.

2163 * Poulenc, Francis, 1899–1963

[Sonatas, pianos (2)] *Sonata for 2 pianos.* Eschig 510-03231, $83, set.

2164 * Rachmaninoff, Sergei, 1873–1943

[Suites, pianos (2), no. 1, op. 5] *Suite no. 1 (Fantasy) for 2 pianos, op. 5.* International Music 522, $22.50, set.

2165 * Rachmaninoff, Sergei, 1873–1943

[Suites, pianos (2), no. 2, op. 17] *Suite no. 2 for 2 pianos, op. 17.* International Music 508, $14, set.

2166   Ravel, Maurice, 1875–1937

Sites auriculaires, for 2 pianos. Salabert SEAS17225, $17.95.

2167 * Saint-Saëns, Camille, 1835–1921

[Variations sur un thème de Beethoven] *Variations on a theme of Beethoven, op. 35.* Durand, $45.50, set; International Music 2558, $12, set; G. Schirmer LB1449, $11.95.

2168 * Schumann, Robert, 1810–1856

[Andante und Variationen, pianos (2), horn, violoncellos (2), B♭ major; arr.] *Andante and variations, op. 46, arranged for 2 pianos.* Peters P2362, $30.60, set; G. Schirmer LB1489, $9.95.

2169 * Stravinsky, Igor, 1882–1971

[Sonatas, pianos (2)] *Sonata for 2 pianos.* Boosey & Hawkes PFB 120, $23.

Piano Concertos/Piano Reductions

When ordering music for two pianos, four hands, one must distinguish between editions for which the publisher supplies two copies (indicated as "set" in the citations below) and those where each copy must be purchased separately. Because of the difficulty of determining to which category some editions belong, specify "one performance set" when placing orders. On the whole, piano concertos with orchestral accompaniment arranged for a second piano are much less likely to be published in a set of two copies than other works for two pianos, four hands.

2170 * Bach, Johann Sebastian, 1685–1750

[Concertos, harpsichord, string orchestra, BWV 1052, D minor; arr.] *Concerto for piano (harpsichord) in D minor, BWV 1052.* Kalmus K 03029, $7.50; Peters P9980, $30.80; G. Schirmer LB1527, $8.95.

2171 * Bach, Johann Sebastian, 1685–1750

[Concertos, harpsichord, string orchestra, BWV 1056, F minor; arr.] *Concerto for piano (harpsichord) in F minor, BWV 1056.* International Music 545, $5.25; Kalmus K 03030, $5.50; Peters P9983, $25.65.

2172 Barber, Samuel, 1910–1981

[Concertos, piano, orchestra, op. 38; arr.] *Piano concerto, op. 38.* G. Schirmer HL50296200, $17.95.

2173 Bartók, Béla, 1881–1945

[Concertos, piano, orchestra, no. 1; arr.] *Concerto for piano, no. 1.* Boosey & Hawkes PFB 3, $85.

2174 Bartók, Béla, 1881–1945

[Concertos, piano, orchestra, no. 2; arr.] *Concerto for piano, no. 2.* Boosey & Hawkes PFB 4, $85.

2175 * Bartók, Béla, 1881–1945

[Concertos, piano, orchestra, no. 3; arr.] *Concerto for piano, no. 3.* Rev. ed., 1994. Boosey & Hawkes PFB 5, $45.

2176 * Beethoven, Ludwig van, 1770–1827

[Concertos, piano, orchestra, no. 1, op. 15, C major; arr.] *Concerto for piano, no. 1 in C major, op. 15.* Henle HN433, $28.95; Peters P2894a, $12.40; G. Schirmer LB621, $7.95.

2177 * Beethoven, Ludwig van, 1770–1827

[Concertos, piano, orchestra, no. 2, op. 19, B♭ major; arr.] *Concerto for piano, no. 2 in B♭ major, op. 19.* Henle HN434, $23.95; Peters P2894b, $12.40; G. Schirmer LB622, $7.95.

2178 * Beethoven, Ludwig van, 1770–1827

[Concertos, piano, orchestra, no. 3, op. 37, C minor; arr.] *Concerto for piano, no. 3 in C minor, op. 37.* Henle HN435, $28.95; Peters P2894c, $12.40; G. Schirmer LB623, $7.95.

2179 * Beethoven, Ludwig van, 1770–1827

[Concertos, piano, orchestra, no. 4, op. 58, G major; arr.] *Concerto for piano, no. 4 in G major, op. 58.* Peters P2894d, $12.40; G. Schirmer LB624, $7.95.

2180 * Beethoven, Ludwig van, 1770–1827

[Concertos, piano, orchestra, no. 4–5; arr.] *Piano concertos no. 4 and 5, "Emperor."* Dover 0-486-28442-5, $10.95.

2181 * Beethoven, Ludwig van, 1770–1827

[Concertos, piano, orchestra, no. 5, op. 73, E♭ major; arr.] *Concerto for piano, no. 5 in E♭ major, op. 73, "Emperor."* Peters P2894e, $12.40; G. Schirmer LB625, $8.95.

2182 * Brahms, Johannes, 1833–1897

[Concertos, piano, orchestra, no. 1, op. 15, D minor; arr.] *Concerto for piano, no. 1 in D minor, op. 15.* International Music 2094, $13.75; Peters P3655, $13.65.

2183 * Brahms, Johannes, 1833–1897

[Concertos, piano, orchestra, no. 2, op. 83, B♭ major; arr.] *Concerto for piano, no. 2 in B♭ major, op. 83.* International Music 2095, $13.75; Peters P3895, $13.65.

2184 Britten, Benjamin, 1913–1976

[Concertos, piano, orchestra, no. 1, op. 13, D major; arr.] *Concerto for piano and orchestra, op. 13.* Boosey & Hawkes PFB 10, $21.

2185 Chaminade, Cécile, 1857–1944

[Konzertstück, piano and orchestra, C♯ minor, op. 46; arr.] *Konzertstück for piano and orchestra in C♯ minor, op. 46.* Enoch, $18.

2186 * Chopin, Frédéric, 1810–1849

[Concertos, piano, orchestra; arr.] *The piano concertos, arranged for two pianos.* Dover 0-486-27498-5, $10.95.

2187 * Chopin, Frédéric, 1810–1849

[Concertos, piano, orchestra, no. 1, op. 11, E minor; arr.] *Concerto for piano, no. 1 in E minor, op. 11.* Henle HN419, $26.95; Peters P2895a, $19.10; G. Schirmer LB1350, $10.95.

2188 * Chopin, Frédéric, 1810–1849

[Concertos, piano, orchestra, no. 2, op. 21, F minor; arr.] *Concerto for piano, no. 2 in F minor, op. 21.* Henle HN420, $26.95; Peters P2895b, $19.10; G. Schirmer LB1351, $11.50.

2189 Copland, Aaron, 1900–1990

[Concertos, piano, orchestra; arr.] *Concerto for piano and orchestra,* arranged by John Kirkpatrick. Boosey & Hawkes PFB 116, $25, set.

2190 Dohnányi, Ernő, 1877–1960

[Variationen uber ein Kinderlied; arr.] *Variations on a nursery tune, op. 25.* Simrock 490-00404, $70, set.

2191 Falla, Manuel de, 1876–1946

[Noches en los jardines de España; arr.] *Noches en los jardines de España = Nights in the gardens of Spain.* Eschig ME690, $88.50.

2192 Franck, César, 1822–1890

[Variations symphoniques; arr.] *Symphonic variations for piano.* International Music 2159, $8.75; Kalmus K 03442, $7.50; Peters P3741, $15.70.

2193 * Gershwin, George, 1898–1937

[Concerto, piano, orchestra, F major; arr.] *Concerto in F.* New World/Warner Bros., $17.50.

2194 * Gershwin, George, 1898–1937

[Rhapsody in blue; arr.] *Rhapsody in blue, for 2 pianos, 4 hands.* Warner Bros. PS161, $15.

2195 * Grieg, Edvard, 1843–1907

[Concerto, piano, orchestra, op. 16, A minor; arr.] *Concerto for piano in A minor, op. 16.* Peters P2164, $8.75; G. Schirmer LB1399, $7.95.

2196 Haydn, Joseph, 1732–1809

[Concertos, harpsichord, orchestra, H. XVIII, 11, D major; arr.] *Concerto for piano in D major, H. XVIII/11.* International Music 502, $6.50; Peters P4353a, $11.15; G. Schirmer LB1700, $7.95.

2197 * Liszt, Franz, 1811–1886

[Concertos, piano, orchestra, no. 1, E♭ major; arr.] *Concerto for piano, no. 1 in E♭ major.* Kalmus K 03613, $6.50; Peters P3606, $13.65; G. Schirmer LB1057, $7.95.

2198 * Liszt, Franz, 1811–1886

[Concertos, piano, orchestra, no. 2, A major; arr.] *Concerto for piano, no. 2 in A major.* Kalmus K 03614, $7.50; Peters P3607, $13.65; G. Schirmer LB1058, $8.95.

2199 Liszt, Franz, 1811–1886

[Fantasies, piano, orchestra; arr.] *Hungarian fantasy for piano and orchestra.* Kalmus K 09520, $7.50; Peters P3612, $16.70; G. Schirmer LB1056, $7.95.

2200 MacDowell, Edward, 1861–1908

[Concertos, piano, orchestra, no. 2, op. 23, D minor; arr.] *Concerto for piano, no. 2 in D minor, op. 23.* Well-Tempered Press W7131, $10.95, set.

2201 * Mendelssohn-Bartholdy, Felix, 1809–1847

[Concertos, piano, orchestra, no. 1, op. 25, G minor; arr.] *Concerto for piano, no. 1 in G minor, op. 25.* Kalmus K 03672, $6.95; Peters P2896a, $10.90; G. Schirmer LB61, $8.95.

2202 Mozart, Wolfgang Amadeus, 1756–1791

[Concertos, piano, orchestra. Selections; arr.] *Piano concertos no. 20, 21, and 22, with orchestra reduction for second piano.* Dover 0-486-28435-2, $12.95.

2203 * Mozart, Wolfgang Amadeus, 1756–1791

[Concertos, piano, orchestra, K. 271, E♭ major; arr.] *Concerto for piano, no. 9 in E♭ major, K. 271, "Jeunehomme."* Bärenreiter BA4790a, $26.70; Peters P8809, ed. by Christian Wolff, $22.90; G. Schirmer LB1704, $12.

2204 Mozart, Wolfgang Amadeus, 1756–1791

[Concertos, piano, orchestra, K. 413, F major; arr.] *Concerto for piano, no. 11 in F major, K. 413.* Bärenreiter BA4874a, $20.25; Peters P8811, ed. by Christian Wolff, $16.35; G. Schirmer LB1788, $9.95.

2205 Mozart, Wolfgang Amadeus, 1756–1791

[Concertos, piano, orchestra, K. 414, A major; arr.] *Concerto for piano, no. 12 in A major, K. 414.* Bärenreiter BA4876a, $21; International Music 922, $8.25; Peters P9028, ed. by Christian Wolff, $21.30; G. Schirmer LB1731, $11.95.

2206 Mozart, Wolfgang Amadeus, 1756–1791

[Concertos, piano, orchestra, K. 415, C major; arr.] *Concerto for piano, no. 13 in C major, K. 415.* Bärenreiter BA4878a, $21; Peters P8813, ed. by Christian Wolff, $17.35; G. Schirmer LB1789, $9.95.

2207 * Mozart, Wolfgang Amadeus, 1756–1791

[Concertos, piano, orchestra, K. 449, E♭ major; arr.] *Concerto for piano, no. 14 in E♭ major, K. 449.* Bärenreiter BA5381a, $21.75; International Music 1086, $6.75; Peters P8814, ed. by Christian Wolff, $19.65; G. Schirmer LB1756, $9.95.

2208 * Mozart, Wolfgang Amadeus, 1756–1791

[Concertos, piano, orchestra, K. 450, B♭ major; arr.] *Concerto for piano, no. 15 in B♭ major, K. 450.* Bärenreiter BA5382a, $22.25; International Music 570, $7.75; G. Schirmer LB1746, $10.95; Schott ED12434, $19.95.

2209 * Mozart, Wolfgang Amadeus, 1756–1791

[Concertos, piano, orchestra, K. 451, D major; arr.] *Concerto for piano, no. 16 in D major, K. 451.* Bärenreiter BA5383a, $22.25; Peters P8816, ed. by Christian Wolff, $20.75; G. Schirmer LB1854, $9.95.

2210 * Mozart, Wolfgang Amadeus, 1756–1791

[Concertos, piano, orchestra, K. 453, G major; arr.] *Concerto for piano, no. 17 in G major, K. 453.* Bärenreiter BA5384a, $22.25; International Music 920, $10; Peters P8817, ed. by Christian Wolff, $21.80; G. Schirmer LB1734, $12.95.

2211 * Mozart, Wolfgang Amadeus, 1756–1791

[Concertos, piano, orchestra, K. 456, B♭ major; arr.] *Concerto for piano, no. 18 in B♭ major, K. 456.* Bärenreiter BA5385a, $22.25; Peters P8818, ed. by Christian Wolff, $24; G. Schirmer LB1823, $10.95.

2212 * Mozart, Wolfgang Amadeus, 1756–1791

[Concertos, piano, orchestra, K. 459, F major; arr.] *Concerto for piano, no. 19 in F major, K. 459.* Bärenreiter BA5386a, $22.25; International Music 2867, $9.50; Peters P8819, ed. by Christian Wolff, $20.75; G. Schirmer LB1701, $8.95.

2213 * Mozart, Wolfgang Amadeus, 1756–1791

[Concertos, piano, orchestra, K. 466, D minor; arr.] *Concerto for piano, no. 20 in D minor, K. 466.* Bärenreiter BA4873a, $22.25; International Music 833, $10; Peters P8820, ed. by Christian Wolff, $20.75; G. Schirmer LB661, $7.95.

2214 * Mozart, Wolfgang Amadeus, 1756–1791

[Concertos, piano, orchestra, K. 467, C major; arr.] *Concerto for piano, no. 21 in C major, K. 467.* Bärenreiter BA5317a, $19.50; Peters P8821, ed. by Christian Wolff, $19.65; G. Schirmer LB662, $7.95.

2215 * Mozart, Wolfgang Amadeus, 1756–1791

[Concertos, piano, orchestra, K. 482, E♭ major; arr.] *Concerto for piano, no. 22 in E♭ major, K. 482.* Bärenreiter BA5387a, $22.25; Peters P8822, ed. by Christian Wolff, $24.55; G. Schirmer LB663, $8.95.

2216 * Mozart, Wolfgang Amadeus, 1756–1791

[Concertos, piano, orchestra, K. 488, A major; arr.] *Concerto for piano, no. 23 in A major, K. 488.* Bärenreiter BA4740a, $21.60; Peters P8823, ed. by Christian Wolff, $16.35; G. Schirmer LB1584, $8.95.

2217 * Mozart, Wolfgang Amadeus, 1756–1791

[Concertos, piano, orchestra, K. 491, C minor; arr.] *Concerto for piano, no. 24 in C minor, K. 491.* Bärenreiter BA4741a, $21.60; Peters P3309h, ed. by Christian Wolff, $12.40; G. Schirmer LB664, $11.95.

2218 * Mozart, Wolfgang Amadeus, 1756–1791

[Concertos, piano, orchestra, K. 503, C major; arr.] *Concerto for piano, no. 25 in C major, K. 503.* Bärenreiter BA4742a, $11.20; International Music 996, $14; Peters P8825, ed. by Christian Wolff, $19.65; G. Schirmer LB1786, $14.95.

2219 * Mozart, Wolfgang Amadeus, 1756–1791

[Concertos, piano, orchestra, K. 537, D major; arr.] *Concerto for piano, no. 26 in D major, K. 537, "Coronation."* Bärenreiter BA5318a, $22.25; Peters P8826, ed. by Christian Wolff, $24.55; G. Schirmer LB665, $6.95.

2220 * Mozart, Wolfgang Amadeus, 1756–1791

[Concertos, piano, orchestra, K. 595, B♭ major; arr.] *Concerto for piano, no. 27 in B♭ major, K. 595.* Bärenreiter BA4872a, $26.70; International Music 923, $10; Peters P8827, ed. by Christian Wolff, $20.75; G. Schirmer LB1721, $10.95.

2221 * Prokofiev, Sergey, 1891–1953

[Concertos, piano, orchestra, no. 3, op. 26, C major; arr.] *Concerto for piano, no. 3 in C major, op. 26.* Boosey & Hawkes PFB 13, $29; International Music 1413, $11; Kalmus K 03771, $12.

2222 * Rachmaninoff, Sergei, 1873–1943

[Concertos, piano, orchestra, no. 2, op. 18, C minor; arr.] *Concerto for piano, no. 2 in C minor, op. 18.* Boosey & Hawkes PFB 16, $40; International Music 1137, $8.75; Kalmus K 03815, $8.95; G. Schirmer LB1576, $8.95.

2223 * Rachmaninoff, Sergei, 1873–1943

[Concertos, piano, orchestra, no. 3, op. 30, D minor; arr.] *Concerto for piano, no. 3 in D minor, op. 30.* Boosey & Hawkes PFB 17, $29; International Music 1053, $9.50; Kalmus K 03816, $10; G. Schirmer LB1610, $8.95.

2224 * Rachmaninoff, Sergei, 1873–1943

[Rapsodie sur un thème de Paganini; arr.] *Rhapsody on a theme of Paganini, op. 43,* arranged for 2 pianos 4 hands by the composer. Belwin-Mills F2310, $14.95.

2225 * Ravel, Maurice, 1875–1937

[Concertos, piano, 1 hand, orchestra, D major; arr.] *Concerto in D major for piano, for the left hand, solo part.* Durand 510-01373, $32.75.

2226 * Ravel, Maurice, 1875–1937

[Concertos, piano, orchestra, G major; arr.] *Concerto for piano in G major.* Durand 510-01374, $39.75.

2227 Saint-Saëns, Camille, 1835–1921

[Concertos, piano, orchestra, no. 2, op. 22, G minor; arr.] *Concerto for piano, no. 2, op. 22 in G minor.* Durand 510-01762, $39.50, set; Kalmus K 03854, $7.50; G. Schirmer LB1405, $12.95.

2228 Saint-Saëns, Camille, 1835–1921

[Concertos, piano, orchestra, no. 4, op. 44, C minor; arr.] *Concerto for piano, no. 4, op. 44 in C minor.* G. Schirmer LB1486, $11.95.

2229 Schoenberg, Arnold, 1874–1951

[Concertos, piano, orchestra, op. 42; arr.] *Concerto for piano, op. 42.* G. Schirmer ST40728, $17.50.

2230 Schumann, Clara, 1819–1896

[Concertos, piano, orchestra, op. 7, A minor; arr.] *Piano concerto in A minor, op. 7.* Breitkopf EB 8568, $22; Hildegard 09205, $35.

2231 * Schumann, Robert, 1810–1856

[Concertos, piano, orchestra, op. 54, A minor; arr.] *Concerto for piano in A minor, op. 54.* Kalmus K 03897, $8; Peters P2898, $15.25; G. Schirmer LB1358, $10.95.

2232 Shostakovich, Dmitrii Dmitrievich, 1906–1975

[Concertos, piano, orchestra, no. 1, op. 35; arr.] *Concerto no. 1 for piano, string orchestra and trumpet.* Sikorski 2126, $28.

2233 Strauss, Richard, 1864–1949

[Burlesque, piano, orchestra, D minor; arr.] *Burleske in D minor.* Kalmus K 04010, $6.

2234 Stravinsky, Igor, 1882–1971

[Concertos, piano, instrumental ensemble; arr.] *Concerto for piano and instrumental ensemble.* Rev. 1920. Boosey & Hawkes PFB 20, $36.

2235 * Stravinsky, Igor, 1882–1971

[Concertos, pianos (2)] *Concerto for 2 unaccompanied pianos.* Schott ED2520, $35.

2236 Stravinsky, Igor, 1882–1971

[Movements, piano, orchestra; arr.] *Movements for piano and orchestra, arranged for two pianos.* Boosey & Hawkes PFB 132, $17.50.

2237 Tailleferre, Germaine, 1892–1983

[Ballades, piano, orchestra; arr.] *Ballade for piano and orchestra.* Chester CT02912 (authorized photocopy), $39.95.

2238 * Tchaikovsky, Peter Ilich, 1840–1893

[Concertos, piano, orchestra, no. 1, op. 23, B♭ minor; arr.] *Concerto for piano, no. 1 in B♭ minor, op. 23.* International Music 2190, $11.50; Kalmus K 04015, $7.95; Peters P3775, $23.25; G. Schirmer LB1045, $9.95.

2239 Tower, Joan, 1938–

[Concertos, piano, orchestra; arr.] *Concerto for piano and orchestra.* Associated Music HL50480241, $20.

2240 Weber, Carl Maria von, 1786–1826

[Konzertstück; arr.] *Konzertstück for piano and orchestra in F minor, op. 79.* International Music 2158, $8.50; Kalmus K 09509, $5.50; Peters P2899, $18.

2241 Zwilich, Ellen Taaffe, 1939–

[Concertos, piano, orchestra; arr.] *Concerto for piano and orchestra.* Presser 440-40015, $35, set.

Organ Music

2242 Alain, Jehan, 1911–1940

[Chorals, organ] *Deux chorals.* Masters Music M2119, $3.95.

2243 Alain, Jehan, 1911–1940

[Organ music] *L'oeuvre d'orgue.* Leduc AL20.091, AL20.102, AL20.184, 3 v., $36.50, $44.75, $37.75.

2244 * Alain, Jehan, 1911–1940

[Organ music. Selections] *Trois pièces.* Leduc AL19.744, $23.50.

2245 Albright, William, 1944–

[Organbook, no. 3] *Organbook III.* Henmar/Peters P66794, $37.25.

2246 Bach, Carl Philipp Emanuel, 1714–1788

[Organ music] *Complete organ works.* Peters P8009a-b, 2 v., $35.70, $37.05.

2247 * Bach, Johann Sebastian, 1685–1750

[Organ music] *Complete organ works.* Bärenreiter BA5171-5178, 8 v., $43.20, $37.50, $37, $23.50, $28.80, $37.50, $23.50, $33; Editio Musica Budapest Z. 12927-12936, Z. 13082, 11 v., $29 each; Novello, 18 v., $13.95 each (v.1–11) and $24.95 each (v.12–18); Peters P240a-248a, 9 v., $37.30 each; G. Schirmer ED841, ED851, ED867, ED870, ED885, ED2182, ED2707, ED2708, 8 v., $22.50 each.

2248 * Bach, Johann Sebastian, 1685–1750

[Organ music. Selections] *Complete preludes and fugues.* Dover 0-486-24816-X, $9.95.

2249 Bach, Johann Sebastian, 1685–1750

[Organ music. Selections] *Organ works: trio sonatas, Orgelbüchlein, Schübler chorales, Clavierübung part III, and other works.* Dover 0-486-22359-0, $12.50.

2250 ** Bach, Johann Sebastian, 1685–1750

[Organ music. Selections] *Toccatas, fantasias, passacaglia, and other works.* Dover 0-486-25403-8, $9.95.

2251 Bach, Johann Sebastian, 1685–1750

Orgelbüchlein. Concordia 97-5774, $20.

2252 Balbastre, Claude-Bénigne, 1727–1799

[Recueil de noëls] *Livre de noëls.* Kalmus K 03116-03117, 2 v., $4.95, $4.50; Schola Cantorum S. 5979, $22.

2253 Barber, Samuel, 1910–1981

Wondrous love: variations on a shape-note hymn. G. Schirmer ST44477, $4.95.

2254 Böhm, Georg, 1661–1733

[Organ music] *Collected organ works.* Breitkopf & Härtel EB8087, $43.50.

2255 * Brahms, Johannes, 1833–1897

[Organ music] *Organ works.* Breitkopf & Härtel EB8396, $18; Dover 0-486-26828-4 (with Mendelssohn's and Schumann's organ works), $11.95; Henle HN400, $22.95; Peters P6333a-c, 3 v., $18.70, $18.70, $15.70.

2256 * Bruhns, Nicolaus, 1665–1697

[Organ music] *Organ works.* Breitkopf & Härtel EB6670, $17; Doblinger D.17 887, D.17 956, 2 v., $30.25 each; Peters P4855, $22.25.

2257 * Buxtehude, Dietrich, 1637–1707

[Organ music] *Collected organ works.* Bärenreiter BA8221-8223, 3 v., $43.20 each; Breitkopf & Härtel EB6661-6664, 4 v., $30, $30, $27.50, $27.50; Hansen 3921-3922, 3927-3928, 4 v., $24.95 each.

2258 Buxtehude, Dietrich, 1637–1707

[Organ music. Selections] *Selected organ works.* Dover 0-486-25682-0, $12.95; Kalmus K 03277-03278, v.1–2 of 4, $9.50 each; Peters P4449, P4457, 2 v., $18.70 each.

2259 *Century of American organ music.* McAfee, 4 v., $10 each.

2260 * *Church organist's golden treasury.* Presser 433-40021, 433-41033, 433-41005, 3 v., $17.95, $22.50, $17.95.

2261 * Clérambault, Louis Nicolas, 1676–1749

Premier livre d'orgue. Kalmus K 03308, $5.95; Noetzel N 3633, $23; Schola Cantorum S. 5363, $22; Schott ED1874, $14.95.

2262 * Couperin, François, 1668–1733

[Pièces d'orgue] *Organ works.* Oiseau-Lyre OL1, $45; Schott ED1878, $14.95.

2263 Couperin, François, 1668–1733

[Pièces d'orgue. Messe à l'usage ordinaire des paroisses] *Mass for the parishes.* Dover (with Couperin's *Mass for the convents*) 0-486-28285-6, $8.95; Kalmus K 03314, $5.50; Schola Cantorum S. 5843, $25.

2264 Couperin, François, 1668–1733

[Pièces d'orgue. Messe pour les couvents] *Mass for the convents.* Kalmus K 03315, $5.50; Schola Cantorum S. 5943, $23. *See also 2263*

2265 * Daquin, Louis Claude, 1694–1772

Nouveau livre de noëls. Faber F0742, $17.95; Kalmus K 03368, $6.95; Schott ED1875, $14.95.

2266 Distler, Hugo, 1908–1942

[Wachet auf, ruft uns die Stimme] *Organ partita: Wachet auf, ruft uns die Stimme.* Bärenreiter BA6443, $31.75; Masters Music M1855, $3.95.

2267 Dupré, Marcel, 1886–1971

[Cortège et litanie; arr.] *Cortège et litanie.* Leduc AL16.850, $18.25.

2268 * Dupré, Marcel, 1886–1971

[Préludes et fugues, organ, op. 7] *Trois préludes et fugues, op. 7.* Leduc AL16.405, $51.25.

2269   Dupré, Marcel, 1886–1971

Variations sur un noël, op. 20. Leduc AL16.626, $29.

2270 * Dupré, Marcel, 1886–1971

[Vêpres de commun] *Fifteen pieces for organ founded on antiphons.* H. W. Gray, $7.95.

2271 * Duruflé, Maurice, 1902–1986

Prélude, adagio et choral varié sur le thème du "Veni Creator," op. 4. Durand 513-00199, $32.75.

2272 * Duruflé, Maurice, 1902–1986

Prélude et fugue sur le nom d'Alain, op. 7. Durand 513–00200, $26.75.

2273   Duruflé, Maurice, 1902–1986

[Suite, organ, op. 5] *Suite for organ, op. 5.* Durand 513-00201, $32.

2274   *Faber early organ series.* Faber F0771-0788, 18 v., $12.95 each.

2275 * Franck, César, 1822–1890

[Organ music] *Complete works for organ.* Durand 513-00243–513-00246, 4 v., $39.50, $38, $33.25, $32.75; Kalmus K 03443-03446, 4 v., $6.50 each; Wiener Urtext UT50140-50143, 4 v., $29.95 each.

2276 * Franck, César, 1822–1890

[Organ music. Selections] *Selected works for organ.* Bärenreiter BA6218, $22; Dover 0-486-25517-4, $10.95.

2277 * Frescobaldi, Girolamo, 1583–1643

[Keyboard music] *Organ and keyboard works.* Bärenreiter BA2201-2205, 5 v., $37.80, $41.40, $43.20, $43.20, $19.25.

2278   Froberger, Johann Jacob, 1616–1667

[Organ music] *Organ works.* Bärenreiter BA8063-8064, v.1–2 of 4 (v.3–4 in preparation), $55 each; Dover 0-486-28093-4, $13.95.

2279 * Grigny, Nicolas de, 1671–1703

Premier livre d'orgue. Heugel HE32.650 (Le pupitre, v. 68), $54.10; Kalmus K 04147, $8; Schola Cantorum S. 5212, $39.

2280   Guillou, Jean, 1930 April 18–

[Toccatas, organ] *Toccata for organ.* Leduc AL23.706, $18.

2281   Handel, George Frideric, 1685–1759

[Concertos, organ, orchestra] *Organ concertos.* Carus 40.538/01, 40.545/01, 3 v., v.1 in preparation; v.2, $69; v.3, $55; Dover 0-486-24462-8, $8.95.

2282 * Handel, George Frideric, 1685–1759

[Concertos, organ, orchestra, op. 4; arr.] *Six concertos for the harpsichord or organ, op. 4: Walsh's transcriptions.* A-R Editions 0-89579-159-5, $31.95; Bärenreiter BA1894-1895, 2 v., $14, $11.25.

2283 * Hindemith, Paul, 1895–1963

[Sonatas, organ, no. 1] *Organ sonata no. 1.* Schott ED2557, $17.95.

2284   Hindemith, Paul, 1895–1963

[Sonatas, organ, no. 2] *Organ sonata no. 2 (1937).* Schott ED2558, $17.95.

2285   Hindemith, Paul, 1895–1963

[Sonatas, organ, no. 3] *Organ sonata no. 3 on old folk songs.* Schott ED3736, $14.95.

2286   Howells, Herbert, 1892–1983

[Psalm preludes, organ, set 1] *Three psalm preludes.* Novello 59 0353 10, $11.95.

2287   Ives, Charles, 1874–1954

Variations on "America," and Adeste fidelis. Presser 153-00259, $6.50.

2288 * Karg-Elert, Sigfrid, 1877–1933

[Choral-Improvisationen, op. 65. Nun danket alle Gott] *Now thank we all our God.* G. Schirmer ST39511, $3.50.

2289   Langlais, Jean, 1907–

Hommage à Frescobaldi. Bornemann 513-00323, $36.50.

2290 * Langlais, Jean, 1907–

Organ book: 10 pieces. Elkan-Vogel 463-00006, $9.95.

2291   Langlais, Jean, 1907–

[Paraphrases grégoriennes] *Trois paraphrases grégoriennes.* Combre, 3 v., $18 each.

2292   Langlais, Jean, 1907–

[Pièces, organ (1943)] *Neuf pièces pour orgue.* Bornemann 513-00339, $51.

2293   Langlais, Jean, 1907–

Suite brève. Bornemann 513-00349, $25.25.

2294   Liszt, Franz, 1811–1886

[Organ music] *Organ works.* Peters P3628a-b, 2 v., $25.40, $21; Universal UE17883-17892, 10 v., $29 each.

2295 * Liszt, Franz, 1811–1886

[Organ music. Selections] *Organ works.* Dover 0-486-29083-2, in preparation; Kalmus K 03615-03616, 2 v., $5.50 each.

2296 Lübeck, Vincent, 1654?–1740

[Organ music] *Organ works.* Breitkopf & Härtel EB6673, $20.50; Kalmus K 09086, $6.95; Peters P4437, $18.70.

2297 Mendelssohn-Bartholdy, Felix, 1809–1847

[Organ music] *Complete organ works.* Novello 01 0215-01 0219, 5 v., $29.95, $19.95, $19.95, $23.95, $29.95.

2298 * Mendelssohn-Bartholdy, Felix, 1809–1847

[Organ music. Selections] *Selected organ works.* Henle HN426, $27.95; Kalmus K 03670, $12.95; Peters P1744, $26.85. *See also* 2255

2299 Messiaen, Olivier, 1908–1992

Apparition de l'église éternelle. Lemoine 22,673HL, $14.50; Masters Music M2148, $4.50.

2300 Messiaen, Olivier, 1908–1992

[Ascension, organ] *L'ascension.* Leduc AL18.826, $33.

2301 * Messiaen, Olivier, 1908–1992

Le banquet céleste. Leduc AL22.893, $12.50.

2302 Messiaen, Olivier, 1908–1992

Messe de la Pentecôte. Leduc AL20.906, $27.

2303 * Messiaen, Olivier, 1908–1992

Nativité du Seigneur. Leduc AL19.266, AL19.269, AL19.271, AL19.274, 4 v., $21, $18.25, $21, $21.

2304 * Messiaen, Olivier, 1908–1992

Verset pour la fête de la dédicace. Leduc AL23.042, $15.

2305 *Modern organ music.* Oxford University Press 0-19-375141-0, 0-19-375142-9, 0-19-375143-7, 3 v., v.1–2, $21.95 each; v.3 OP.

2306 Mozart, Wolfgang Amadeus, 1756–1791

[Adagio und Allegro, musical clock, K. 594, F minor] *Adagio and allegro, K. 594.* Oxford University Press 0-19-375583-1, $16.95.

2307 * Mozart, Wolfgang Amadeus, 1756–1791

[Organ music] *Organ works.* Universal UE17155-17157, UE17165-17166, 5 v., $19.95 each.

2308 * Mozart, Wolfgang Amadeus, 1756–1791

[Organ music. Selections] *Three pieces for organ.* Kalmus K 03707, $4.50.

2309 * Mozart, Wolfgang Amadeus, 1756–1791

[Sonatas, organ, orchestra] *Sämtliche Kirchensonaten = Complete church sonatas.* Bärenreiter BA4731, BA4732, BA4733, BA4735, 4 v., $21, $17.25, $13.50, $13.50.

2310 Mozart, Wolfgang Amadeus, 1756–1791

[Stück, mechanical organ, K. 608, F minor; arr.] *Fantasia in F minor.* G. Schirmer HL50292260, ed. by Anthony Newman, $6.

2311 Muffat, Georg, 1653–1704

Apparatus musico-organisticus. Doblinger D.16.276-16.279, 4 v., $12, $11.55, $10.05, $10.05.

2312 Mulet, Henri, 1878–1967

Esquisses byzantines. Leduc AL16.202, $36.50.

2313 Nivers, Guillaume Gabriel, 1632–1714

[Livre d'orgue, no. 3] *Troisième livre d'orgue.* Heugel, price not available.

2314 ** *The Oxford book of Christmas organ music,* compiled by Robin Gower. Oxford University Press 0-19-375124-0, $24.95.

2315 ** *The Oxford book of wedding music for manuals,* compiled by Malcolm Archer. Oxford University Press 0-19-375123-2, $12.95.

2316 * *The Oxford book of wedding music, with pedals,* compiled by Malcolm Archer. Oxford University Press 0-19-375119-4, $22.95.

2317 Pachelbel, Johann, 1653–1706

[Organ music] *Complete organ works.* Peters P8125a-d, ed. by Traugott Fedtke, 4 v., $37.05, $42.15, $37.05, $42.15.

2318 Pachelbel, Johann, 1653–1706

[Organ music. Selections] *Selected organ works.* Bärenreiter BA238-239, BA287, BA1016, BA5494, BA5498, BA6444-6446, 9 v., $28.50, $28.50, $34.50, $21.75, $20.25, $20.25, $17, $28, $27; Dover 0-486-27858-1, $10.95; Peters P9921a-b, ed. by A. M. Gurgel, 2 v., $49.50 each.

2319 * Peeters, Flor, 1903–1986

[Aria, organ] *Aria.* Heuwekemeijer 513-00436, $9.25.

2320 * Persichetti, Vincent, 1915–1987
Drop, drop, slow tears. Elkan-Vogel 163-00022, $3.25.

2321 Persichetti, Vincent, 1915–1987
[Parable, no. 6] *Parable for organ.* Elkan-Vogel 163-00034, $5.75.

2322 Persichetti, Vincent, 1915–1987
Shimah b'koli. Elkan-Vogel 163-00021, $3.75.

2323 * Persichetti, Vincent, 1915–1987
[Sonatas, organ, op. 86] *Sonata for organ.* Elkan-Vogel 463-0008, $6.50.

2324 Poulenc, Francis, 1899–1963
[Concertos, organ, string orchestra, G minor] *Concerto en sol mineur* [solo organ part]. Salabert EAS15404, $12.95.

2325 * Reger, Max, 1873–1916
Introduktion und Passacaglia. Breitkopf & Härtel EB2198, $5.

2326 Reger, Max, 1873–1916
[Organ music] *Complete organ works.* Breitkopf & Härtel EB8491-8497, 7 v., $31.50, $25.20, $32, $34, $31, $29, $31.

2327 Reger, Max, 1873–1916
[Organ music. Selections] *Fantasies, preludes, fugues, and other works for organ.* Dover 0-486-28846-3, $13.95.

2328 * Reger, Max, 1873–1916
[Phantasie und Fuge, organ, op. 46] *Fantasie and fugue on B-A-C-H, op. 46.* Kalmus K 09097, $3.50; Universal UE01222, $14.95.

2329 Reubke, Julius, 1834–1858
[Sonatas, organ, C minor] *94th Psalm.* Oxford University Press 0-19-375685-4, $16.30; Peters P4941, $12.10.

2330 Rorem, Ned, 1923–
Views from the oldest house. Boosey & Hawkes ONB 403, $17.50.

2331 Scheidemann, Heinrich, 1596 (ca.)–1663
[Organ music] *Organ works.* Bärenreiter BA5481, BA5480, BA5477, 3 v., $37, $34, $30.

2332 Scheidt, Samuel, 1587–1654
Tabulatura nova. Breitkopf & Härtel EB8565, new ed. by Harold Vogel, v. 1 only, $46.50; Deutscher Verlag für Musik DVfM 4756a-b, DVfM 4757, 3 v., $39, $34, $44.

2333 * Schumann, Robert, 1810–1856
[Pedal piano music] *Complete works for organ and pedal piano.* Henle HN367, $29.95. *See also* 2255

2334 Sowerby, Leo, 1895–1968
[Symphonies, organ, G major] *Symphony in G major.* Oxford University Press 0-19-375751-6, $7.50.

2335 Stanley, John, 1714–1786
[Voluntaries, organ] *Voluntaries.* Oxford University Press, $36.50.

2336 * Sweelinck, Jan Pieterszoon, 1562–1621
[Keyboard music. Selections] *Works for organ and keyboard.* Dover 0-486-24935-2, $12.95; Peters P4645a-b, 2 v., $20.25 each.

2337 Titelouze, Jean, 1563–1633
[Organ music] *Complete organ works.* Kalmus K 04139-04140, 2 v., $6.50 each; Schott ED1869, $14.95.

2338 Tunder, Franz, 1614–1667
[Organ music] *Complete organ works.* Breitkopf & Härtel EB6718, $30.

2339 * Vaughan Williams, Ralph, 1872–1958
[Preludes on Welsh hymn tunes] *Three preludes founded on Welsh hymn tunes.* Stainer & Bell MO 31, $6.95.

2340 Vierne, Louis, 1870–1937
Pièces de fantaisie: suites no. 1–4. Lemoine 21,916HL, 21,985HL, 22,099HL, 22,110HL, 4 v., $24.50, $32.25, $32.25, $32.25; Masters Music M2149, M2177, M2233, M2261, 4 v., $9.95 each.

2341 * Vierne, Louis, 1870–1937
[Pièces en style libre] *24 pièces en style libre.* Durand 513-00606/607, 2 v., $26.75, $27.75; Masters Music, M1705-1706, 2 v., $8.95 each.

2342 * Vierne, Louis, 1870–1937
[Symphonies, organ, no. 1, op. 14, D minor] *Symphony no. 1, op. 14.* Hamelle J. 6179 H., $62.75; Masters Music M2366, $11.95.

2343 Vierne, Louis, 1870–1937
[Symphonies, organ, no. 3, op. 28, F♯ minor] *Symphony no. 3, op. 28.* Durand 513-00617, $30; Masters Music M1767, $6.95.

2344 * Vierne, Louis, 1870–1937

[Symphonies, organ, no. 6, op. 59, B minor] *Symphony no. 6, op. 59.* Lemoine 22,406HL, $17.50; Masters Music M2121, $12.

2345 Walcha, Helmut, 1907–

Choralvorspiele. Peters P4850, P4871, P5999, P8413, 4 v., $30.60, $30.60, $30.60, $46.60.

2346 Walther, Johann Gottfried, 1684–1748

[Concertos, organ] *Concerto for organ.* Bärenreiter BA1290, $14.40.

2347 *Wedding music for organ.* Augsburg 11-9523—11-9526, 4 v., $10, $11, $8.50, $7.25.

2348 * Widor, Charles Marie, 1844–1937

[Symphonies, organ] *Complete organ symphonies.* Dover 0-486-26691-5, 0-486-26692-3, 2 v., $12.95 each.

2349 * Widor, Charles Marie, 1844–1937

[Symphonies, organ, no. 5, op. 42, no. 1, F minor] *Symphony no. 5 in F minor for organ, op. 42, no. 1.* A-R Editions 0-89579-276-1, Recent researches in the music of the nineteenth and early twentieth centuries, v. 15, $29.95; Kalmus K 04033, $5.50.

2350 Widor, Charles Marie, 1844–1937

[Symphonies, organ, no. 6, op. 42, no. 2, G minor] *Symphony no. 6 in G minor for organ, op. 42, no. 2.* A-R Editions 0-89579-284-2, Recent researches in the music of the nineteenth and early twentieth centuries, v. 16, $29.95; Kalmus K 04034, $6.95.

2351 Willan, Healey, 1880–1968

Introduction, passacaglia, and fugue. Oxford University Press 0-19-375909-8, $14.95.

2352 Zwilich, Ellen Taaffe, 1939–

[Praeludium, organ] *Praeludium for organ.* Mobart B 26965, $15.

Organ Methods

2353 Davis, Roger E.

The organist's manual. Norton, 1985. 0-393-95461-7, $40.

2354 * Gleason, Harold, 1892–1981

Method of organ playing. 8th ed., ed. by Catherine Crozier Gleason. Prentice-Hall, 1996. 0-13-207531-8, $49.50.

2355 Hurford, Peter, 1930–

Making music on the organ. Rev. ed. Oxford University Press, 1988. 0-19-816207-3, $29.95.

2356 * Ritchie, George, 1942–

Organ technique: modern and early. Prentice-Hall, 1992. 0-13-639873-1, $59.33.

2357 Soderlund, Sandra

Organ technique: an historical approach. 2nd ed. Hinshaw, 1986. 0-937276-00-6, $27.95.

Vocal Music in Performing Editions

Compiled by
**James P. Cassaro (opera and choral), Jean Morrow (early vocal music),
Charles Slater (musical theater and popular song), and
Michael Rogan (all remaining sections)**

Opera and Operetta

Operas in Vocal Score

The following section lists operas in vocal score, with the orchestral score reduced for piano accompaniment. When ordering, one must distinguish between editions in vocal score and those in full orchestral score. Specify "vocal score" when placing orders.

Designation of the language of a work, usually found in the uniform title, is instead indicated after the title proper or after the publisher's name in order to accommodate different editions with different languages within a single entry. The language designations always refer to sung words (i.e., text set to the music), not to translations provided separately from the music.

Certain operas published by G. Schirmer are available in both hardcover and paperbound editions. These are indicated; where no indication of binding is given, assume a paperbound edition.

2358 Adams, John, 1947–

[Nixon in China. Acts 2–3. Vocal score] *Nixon in China.* English. Boosey & Hawkes VSB 187, in preparation.

2359 Argento, Dominick, 1927–

[Postcard from Morocco. Vocal score] *Postcard from Morocco.* English. Boosey & Hawkes VSB 56, $60.

2360 Barber, Samuel, 1910–1981

[Antony and Cleopatra. Vocal score] *Antony and Cleopatra.* Rev. ed. English. G. Schirmer ED2669, $35.

2361 Barber, Samuel, 1910–1981

[Vanessa. Vocal score] *Vanessa.* Rev. ed. English. G. Schirmer ED2301, $45.

2362 Bartók, Béla, 1881–1945

[Kékszákallu herceg vára. Vocal score] *Bluebeard's castle, op. 48.* German and Hungarian. Boosey & Hawkes VSB 67, $100.

2363 * Beethoven, Ludwig van, 1770–1827

[Fidelio. Vocal score] *Fidelio, op. 72.* German and English. Boosey & Hawkes VSB 70, ed. by Edward Dent, $43; G. Schirmer ED620, $24.95 pbk., $45 hardcover.

2364 * Bellini, Vincenzo, 1801–1835

[Norma. Vocal score] *Norma.* Kalmus K 06089, Italian and English, $16.50; Ricordi RCP41684/05, Italian, $31; G. Schirmer ED2253, Italian, $20.95 pbk., $45 hardcover.

2365 Bellini, Vincenzo, 1801–1835

[Puritani. Vocal score] *I puritani.* Kalmus K 06774, Italian and English, $18.50; Ricordi RCP41685/01, Italian, $26.95.

2366 Bellini, Vincenzo, 1801–1835

[Sonnambula. Vocal score] *La sonnambula.* Italian and English. Ricordi RCP41686/05, $24.95; G. Schirmer ED509, $35.

2367 * Berg, Alban, 1885–1935

[Lulu. Vocal score] *Lulu.* German. Universal UT10745A-B, 2 v., $145 total.

2368 * Berg, Alban, 1885–1935

[Wozzeck. Vocal score] *Wozzeck.* German. Universal UE7382, $89.

2369 * Berlioz, Hector, 1803–1869

[Béatrice et Bénédict. Vocal score] *Béatrice et Bénédict.* French and German. Bärenreiter BA5443a, $70.

2370 * Berlioz, Hector, 1803–1869

[Troyens. Vocal score] *Les Troyens = The Trojans.* French. Kalmus K 06087, K 06106, 2 v., $15, $29.

2371 Bernstein, Leonard, 1918–1990

[Quiet place. Vocal score] *A quiet place* [this work incorporates Bernstein's *Trouble in Tahiti*]. English. Boosey & Hawkes VSB 154, $82.

2372 ** Bizet, Georges, 1838–1875

[Carmen. Vocal score] *Carmen.* Bärenreiter AE129a, French and German, $41; G. Schirmer ED421, French and English, $22.95.

2373 Blitzstein, Marc, 1905–1964

[Regina. Vocal score] *Regina: an opera based on "The little foxes"* by Lillian Hellman. English. Chappell HL00311578, $40.

2374 Boito, Arrigo, 1842–1918

[Mefistofele. Vocal score] *Mefistofele.* Italian and English. Ricordi RCP46855/05, $29.95.

2375 Britten, Benjamin, 1913–1976

[Albert Herring. Vocal score] *Albert Herring.* English. Boosey & Hawkes VSB 64, $87.

2376 * Britten, Benjamin, 1913–1976

[Billy Budd. Vocal score] *Billy Budd.* English. Boosey & Hawkes VSB 66, $130.

2377 Britten, Benjamin, 1913–1976

[Death in Venice. Vocal score] *Death in Venice.* English and German. Faber F0514, $66.

2378 * Britten, Benjamin, 1913–1976

[Midsummer night's dream. Vocal score] *Midsummer night's dream.* English and German. Boosey & Hawkes VSB 110, $120.

2379 * Britten, Benjamin, 1913–1976

[Peter Grimes. Vocal score] *Peter Grimes.* English. Boosey & Hawkes VSB 77, $110.

2380 Britten, Benjamin, 1913–1976

[Rape of Lucretia. Vocal score] *Rape of Lucretia.* English and German. Boosey & Hawkes VSB 79, $110.

2381 * Britten, Benjamin, 1913–1976

[Turn of the screw. Vocal score] *The turn of the screw.* English and German. Boosey & Hawkes VSB 91, $87.

2382 Caccini, Giulio, ca. 1545–1618

[Euridice. Vocal score] *Euridice.* Italian. Edizioni Musicali OTOS 2074, $72.

2383 Cavalli, Pier Francesco, 1602–1676

[Ormindo. Vocal score] *L'Ormindo,* ed. by Raymond Leppard. Italian, English, and German. Faber F0036, $50.

2384 Cilea, Francesco, 1866–1950

[Adriana Lecouvreur. Vocal score] *Adriana Lecouvreur.* E. Sonzogno M.1073S., Italian and German, $65.50; Well-Tempered Press W1147, Italian, $30.

2385 Cimarosa, Domenico, 1749–1801

[Matrimonio segreto. Vocal score] *Il matrimonio segreto.* Ricordi RCP131862/03, Italian and German, $59.95; Well-Tempered Press W1094, Italian, $30.

2386 Copland, Aaron, 1900–1990

[Tender land. Vocal score] *The tender land.* English. Boosey & Hawkes VSB 15, $55.

2387 Dallapiccola, Luigi, 1904–1975

[Prigioniero. Vocal score] *Il prigioniero = The prisoner.* Italian and English. Zerboni SZ-7685, $34.

2388 Davies, Peter Maxwell, 1934–

[Lighthouse. Vocal score] *The lighthouse.* English. Chester Music CH55350, $31.95.

2389 Davies, Peter Maxwell, 1934–

[Taverner. Vocal score] *Taverner.* English. Boosey & Hawkes VSB 130, $72.

2390 * Debussy, Claude, 1862–1918

[Pelléas et Mélisande. Vocal score] *Pelléas et Mélisande.* French and English. International Music 2127, $27.50; Kalmus K 06252, $19.

2391 Delibes, Léo, 1836–1891

[Lakmé. Vocal score] *Lakmé.* French and English. International Music 2800, $27.50.

2392 * Donizetti, Gaetano, 1797–1848

[Don Pasquale. Vocal score] *Don Pasquale.* Italian and English. Ricordi RCP132875/05, $27.95.

2393 * Donizetti, Gaetano, 1797–1848

[Élisir d'amore. Vocal score] *L'élisir d'amore = The elixir of love.* Ricordi RCP41688/05, Italian, $29.95; G. Schirmer ED2421, Italian and English, $21.95.

2394 * Donizetti, Gaetano, 1797–1848

[Fille du régiment. Vocal score] *The daughter of the regiment.* Kalmus K 06178, Italian and English, $14.50; Ricordi RCP46263/05, Italian, $18.95; G. Schirmer ED3003, French and English, $18.95 pbk., $45 hardcover.

2395 ** Donizetti, Gaetano, 1797–1848

[Lucia di Lammermoor. Vocal score] *Lucia di Lammermoor.* Ricordi RCP41689/05, Italian, $36; G. Schirmer ED361, Italian and English, $18.95 pbk., $45 hardcover.

2396 * Floyd, Carlisle, 1926–

[Susannah. Vocal score] *Susannah.* English. Boosey & Hawkes VSB 16, $38.

2397 ** Gershwin, George, 1898–1937

[Porgy and Bess. Vocal score] *Porgy and Bess.* English. New World VF1958, $85.

2398 Giordano, Umberto, 1867–1948

[Andrea Chénier. Vocal score] *Andrea Chénier.* International Music 1496, Italian and English, $22.50; Well-Tempered Press W1106, Italian, $30.

2399 Glass, Philip, 1937–

[Akhnaten. Vocal score] *Akhnaten.* English. Dunvagen, $30.

2400 * Gluck, Christoph Willibald, Ritter von, 1714–1787

[Orfeo ed Euridice. Vocal score] *Orfeo and Euridice* [1762 Vienna version in Italian; 1774 Paris version in French; customarily sung in Italian]. Bärenreiter BA2294a, 1762 Vienna version, Italian and German, $39; Bärenreiter BA2282a, 1774 Paris version, French and German, $51; G. Schirmer ED2323, French and English, $24.95 pbk., $45 hardcover; Well-Tempered Press W7126, Italian and English, $12.50.

2401 * Gounod, Charles, 1818–1893

[Faust. Vocal score] *Faust.* French and English. G. Schirmer ED2679, $24.95 pbk., $45 hardcover.

2402 Gounod, Charles, 1818–1893

[Roméo et Juliette. Vocal score] *Romeo and Juliet.* French and English. G. Schirmer ED454, $27.95; Well-Tempered Press W1145, $35.

2403 * Handel, George Frideric, 1685–1759

[Giulio Cesare. Vocal score] *Julius Caesar.* Bärenreiter BA4019a, $69; International Music 3150, Italian and English, $27.50; Well-Tempered Press W7210, Italian and German, $25.

2404 Haydn, Joseph, 1732–1809

[Mondo della luna. Vocal score] *Il mondo della luna.* Italian and English. Bärenreiter BA3816b, $74.25.

2405 * Humperdinck, Engelbert, 1854–1921

[Hänsel und Gretel. Vocal score] *Hansel and Gretel.* English translation. G. Schirmer ED1267, $16.95.

2406 Janáček, Leoš, 1854–1928

[Jenůfa. Vocal score] *Jenůfa.* Czech and German. Universal UE13982, $89.

2407 Janáček, Leoš, 1854–1928

[Kát'a Kabanová. Vocal score] *Kát'a Kabanová.* Czech and German. Universal UE7103, $89.

2408 ** Leoncavallo, Ruggiero, 1858–1919

[Pagliacci. Vocal score] *I pagliacci.* Italian and English. G. Schirmer ED2560, $20.95 pbk., $45 hardcover.

2409 ** Mascagni, Pietro, 1863–1945

[Cavalleria rusticana. Vocal score] *Cavalleria rusticana*. Italian and English. G. Schirmer ED2608, $16.95 pbk., $35 hardcover.

2410 * Massenet, Jules, 1842–1912

[Manon. Vocal score] *Manon*. French and English. G. Schirmer ED2627, $35.

2411 Massenet, Jules, 1842–1912

[Thaïs. Vocal score] *Thaïs*. Heugel HE 7644, French, $65; Kalmus K 06802, French and English, $22, OP.

2412 * Massenet, Jules, 1842–1912

[Werther. Vocal score] *Werther*. French and English. International Music 2500, $27.50; Kalmus K 06379, $26.

2413 ** Menotti, Gian Carlo, 1911–

[Amahl and the night visitors. Vocal score] *Amahl and the night visitors*. English. G. Schirmer ED2039, $20.

2414 Menotti, Gian Carlo, 1911–

[Consul. Vocal score] *The consul*. English. G. Schirmer ED1980, $35.

2415 * Menotti, Gian Carlo, 1911–

[Medium. Vocal score] *The medium*. English and French. G. Schirmer ED1911, $25.

2416 Meyerbeer, Giacomo, 1791–1864

[Huguenots. Vocal score] *Les huguenots*. English and Italian [no original-language French version currently available]. Kalmus K 06431, OP; Masters Music, in preparation.

2417 Monteverdi, Claudio, 1567–1643

[Incoronazione di Poppea. Vocal score] *L'incoronazione di Poppea = The coronation of Poppea*, ed. by Raymond Leppard. Italian, English, and German. Faber F0011, $61.95.

2418 Monteverdi, Claudio, 1567–1643

[Orfeo. Vocal score] *L'orfeo*. Italian. Carus CAR17275, $33; Zerboni SZ6634, ed. by Bruno Maderna, $57.

2419 Moore, Douglas, 1893–1969

[Ballad of Baby Doe. Vocal score] *The ballad of Baby Doe*. English. Chappell HL00312019, $40.

2420 * Mozart, Wolfgang Amadeus, 1756–1791

[Così fan tutte. Vocal score] *Così fan tutte, K. 588*. Bärenreiter BA4606a, Italian and German, $67.50;

Boosey & Hawkes VSB 68, Italian and English, $60; G. Schirmer ED2038, Italian and English, $22.95.

2421 ** Mozart, Wolfgang Amadeus, 1756–1791

[Don Giovanni. Vocal score] *Don Giovanni, K. 527*. Bärenreiter BA4550a, Italian and German, $45; Boosey & Hawkes VSB 14, ed. by Edward Dent, Italian and English, $43; G. Schirmer ED2424, Italian and English, $22.95.

2422 ** Mozart, Wolfgang Amadeus, 1756–1791

[Entführung aus dem Serail. Vocal score] *Die Entführung aus dem Serail = The abduction from the seraglio, K. 384*. Bärenreiter BA4591a, German and Italian, $33; International Music 1273, German and English, $25.

2423 Mozart, Wolfgang Amadeus, 1756–1791

[Idomeneo. Vocal score] *Idomeneo, K. 366*. Bärenreiter BA4562a, Italian and German, $99; International Music 1315, Italian and English, $27.50.

2424 ** Mozart, Wolfgang Amadeus, 1756–1791

[Nozze di Figaro. Vocal score] *Le nozze di Figaro = The marriage of Figaro, K. 492*. Bärenreiter BA4565a, Italian and German, $60; Boosey & Hawkes VSB 2, ed. by Edward Dent, Italian and English, $60; G. Schirmer ED2021, Italian and English, $22.95.

2425 ** Mozart, Wolfgang Amadeus, 1756–1791

[Zauberflöte. Vocal score] *Die Zauberflöte = The magic flute, K. 620*. Bärenreiter BA4553a, German, $27; Boosey & Hawkes VSB 8, ed. by Edward Dent, German and English, $40; G. Schirmer ED1728, German and English, $18.95 pbk., $35 hardcover.

2426 Musgrave, Thea, 1928–

[Christmas carol. Vocal score] *A Christmas carol*. English. Novello 268221, $74.95.

2427 Musgrave, Thea, 1928–

[Mary, Queen of Scots. Vocal score] *Mary, Queen of Scots*. English. Novello 260921, $95.

2428 * Mussorgsky, Modest Petrovich, 1839–1881

[Boris Godunov. Vocal score] *Boris Godunov*. Kalmus K 06353, Nikolay Rimsky-Korsakov version, ed. by Paul Lamm, German and English translations, $19; Oxford University Press 0-19-337701-2, original version, ed. by Paul Lamm, English translation, $89.

2429 Mussorgsky, Modest Petrovich, 1839–1881

[Khovanshchina. Vocal score] *Khovanshchina*, ed. by Paul Lamm. Russian and German. Kalmus K 08103, $78, OP.

2430 Nicolai, Otto, 1810–1849

[Lustigen Weiber von Windsor. Vocal score] *The merry wives of Windsor.* G. Schirmer ED2266, English, $22.95; Well-Tempered Press W7127, German and English, $20.

2431 * Offenbach, Jacques, 1819–1880

[Contes d'Hoffmann. Vocal score] *Les contes d'Hoffmann = The tales of Hoffmann.* French and English. Alkor-Edition AE 333c, critical ed., $70; G. Schirmer ED2639, $26.95.

2432 Pepusch, John Christopher, 1667–1752

[Beggar's opera. Vocal score] *The beggar's opera.* English. [This is generally listed in publishers' catalogs under librettist John Gay (1685–1732).] Boosey & Hawkes VSB 10, ed. by Frederic Austin, $46; Boosey & Hawkes VSB 65, ed. by Benjamin Britten, $77.

2433 Pergolesi, Giovanni Battista, 1710–1736

[Serva padrona. Vocal score] *La serva padrona = The maid as mistress.* Italian. Ricordi RCP45390/05, $12.95.

2434 Ponchielli, Amilcare, 1834–1886

[Gioconda. Vocal score] *La gioconda.* Kalmus K 06360, Italian and English, $19; Ricordi RCP44864/04, Italian, $44.

2435 * Poulenc, Francis, 1889–1963

[Dialogues des carmélites. Vocal score] *The dialogues of the Carmelites.* French and English. Ricordi RCP132874/05, $19.95.

2436 Prokofiev, Sergey, 1891–1953

[Liubov 'k trem apel'sinam. Vocal score] *The love for three oranges.* Russian and French. Kalmus K 05016, $38.

2437 ** Puccini, Giacomo, 1858–1924

[Bohème. Vocal score] *La bohème.* Italian and English. Ricordi RCP115494/05, $28.95; G. Schirmer ED2142, $24.95.

2438 Puccini, Giacomo, 1858–1924

[Fanciulla del West. Vocal score] *La fanciulla del West = The girl of the golden West.* Ricordi RCP113483/05, Italian and English, $35; Well-Tempered Press W1038, Italian, $25.

2439 ** Puccini, Giacomo, 1858–1924

[Madama Butterfly. Vocal score] *Madama Butterfly.* Italian and English. Ricordi RCP129166/05, $19.95; G. Schirmer ED2428, $24.95.

2440 * Puccini, Giacomo, 1858–1924

[Manon Lescaut. Vocal score] *Manon Lescaut.* Italian and English. International Music 3100, $32.50; Ricordi RCP97321/05, $30.95.

2441 ** Puccini, Giacomo, 1858–1924

[Tosca. Vocal score] *Tosca.* Italian and English. Ricordi RCP135431/05, rev. ed. by Roger Parker, $29.95; G. Schirmer ED2235, $22.95.

2442 * Puccini, Giacomo, 1858–1924

[Trittico. Gianni Schicchi. Vocal score] *Gianni Schicchi.* Ricordi RCP132848/05, Italian and English, $28.95; Well-Tempered Press W7213, Italian, $25.

2443 Puccini, Giacomo, 1858–1924

[Trittico. Suor Angelica. Vocal score] *Suor Angelica.* Ricordi RCP121612/05, Italian and English, $21.50; Well-Tempered Press W7211, Italian, $15.

2444 Puccini, Giacomo, 1858–1924

[Trittico. Tabarro. Vocal score] *Il tabarro = The cloak.* Ricordi RCP129782/05, Italian and English, $22; Well-Tempered Press W7212, Italian, $15.

2445 * Puccini, Giacomo, 1858–1924

[Turandot. Vocal score] *Turandot.* Italian and English. Ricordi RCP121329/05, $37.

2446 * Purcell, Henry, 1659–1695

[Dido and Aeneas. Vocal score] *Dido and Aeneas.* English. Boosey & Hawkes VSB 112, ed. by Benjamin Britten and Gustav Holst, $52; Novello 261421, $14.95; Oxford University Press 0-19-337865-5, rev. ed. by Ellen T. Harris, $26.95.

2447 ** Rossini, Gioacchino, 1792–1868

[Barbiere di Siviglia. Vocal score] *Il barbiere di Siviglia = The barber of Seville.* Italian and English. Ricordi RCP131809/07, critical ed., $55; G. Schirmer ED2495, $24.95.

2448 Rossini, Gioacchino, 1792–1868

[Cenerentola. Vocal score] *La cenerentola = Cinderella.* Kalmus K 06397, Italian and English, $29.95; Ricordi RCP45707/05, Italian, $29.95.

2449 Rossini, Gioacchino, 1792–1868

[Guillaume Tell. Vocal score] *William Tell.* French and Italian. Kalmus K 06393, $36.

2450 * Rossini, Gioacchino, 1792–1868

[Italiana in Algeri. Vocal score] *L'Italiana in Algeri.* Italian and English. Ricordi RCP132118/07, critical ed., $45; G. Schirmer ED2261, $29.95.

2451 * Saint-Saëns, Camille, 1835–1921

[Samson et Dalilah. Vocal score] *Samson and Delilah.* French and English. G. Schirmer ED2647, $21.95.

2452 Schoenberg, Arnold, 1874–1951

[Moses und Aron. Vocal score] *Moses und Aron.* German and English. Schott ED4935, $75.

2453 * Smetana, Bedřich, 1824–1884

[Prodaná nevěsta. Vocal score] *The bartered bride.* English translation. G. Schirmer ED2647, $26.95.

2454 * Strauss, Richard, 1864–1949

[Ariadne auf Naxos. Vocal score] *Ariadne auf Naxos.* German. Boosey & Hawkes VSB 9, $82; Well-Tempered Press W7250, $60.

2455 Strauss, Richard, 1864–1949

[Capriccio. Vocal score] *Capriccio.* German. Boosey & Hawkes VSB 85, $130.

2456 * Strauss, Richard, 1864–1949

[Elektra. Vocal score] *Elektra.* German and English. Boosey & Hawkes VSB 86, $57; Well-Tempered Press W1040, $40.

2457 * Strauss, Richard, 1864–1949

[Frau ohne Schatten. Vocal score] *Die Frau ohne Schatten.* German. Boosey & Hawkes VSB 89, $130.

2458 ** Strauss, Richard, 1864–1949

[Rosenkavalier. Vocal score] *Der Rosenkavalier.* Boosey & Hawkes VSB 5, German and English, $72; Dover 0-486-25501-8, German, $16.95.

2459 * Strauss, Richard, 1864–1949

[Salome. Vocal score] *Salome.* German and English. Kalmus K 06468, $22.

2460 Stravinsky, Igor, 1882–1971

[Rake's progress. Vocal score] *The rake's progress.* English. Boosey & Hawkes VSB 78, $100.

2461 * Tchaikovsky, Peter Ilich, 1840–1893

[Evgeniĭ Onegin. Vocal score] *Eugene Onegin.* Kalmus K 06456, Russian and English, $18.95; G. Schirmer ED650, English, $28.95.

2462 Tchaikovsky, Peter Ilich, 1840–1893

[Pikovaia dama. Vocal score] *Pique Dame = Queen of Spades.* Kalmus K 06757, Russian, $32; G. Schirmer ED1680, English, $32.50; Well-Tempered Press W7207, English, $30.

2463 Thomson, Virgil, 1896–1989

[Four saints in three acts. Vocal score] *Four saints in three acts.* English. G. Schirmer ED2799, $40.

2464 * Thomson, Virgil, 1896–1989

[Mother of us all. Vocal score] *The mother of us all.* English. G. Schirmer ED2809, $40.

2465 Tippett, Michael, 1905–

[Ice break. Vocal score] *The ice break.* English and German. Schott ST11253, $135.

2466 Tippett, Michael, 1905–

[Midsummer marriage. Vocal score] *The midsummer marriage.* English and German. Schott ST10778, $135.

2467 ** Verdi, Giuseppe, 1813–1901

[Aïda. Vocal score] *Aïda.* Italian and English. Ricordi RCP44628/05, $19.95; G. Schirmer ED2569, $24.95 pbk., $45 hardcover.

2468 * Verdi, Giuseppe, 1813–1901

[Ballo in maschera. Vocal score] *Un ballo in maschera = A masked ball.* Italian and English. International Music 2600, $27.50; G. Schirmer ED2233, $22.95 pbk., $45 hardcover.

2469 * Verdi, Giuseppe, 1813–1901

[Don Carlos. Vocal score] *Don Carlos.* Ricordi RCP48552/05, Italian, $24.95; G. Schirmer ED2712, Italian and English, $20.95.

2470 Verdi, Giuseppe, 1813–1901

[Ernani. Vocal score] *Ernani.* Italian. Ricordi RCP42308/05, $29.95.

2471 * Verdi, Giuseppe, 1813–1901

[Falstaff. Vocal score] *Falstaff.* Italian and English. Ricordi RCP96342/05, $28.95; G. Schirmer ED2538, $32.95 pbk., $45 hardcover.

2472 * Verdi, Giuseppe, 1813–1901

[Forza del destino. Vocal score] *La forza del destino.* Italian and English. International Music 3000, $32.50; G. Schirmer ED2790, $22.95 pbk., $45 hardcover.

2473 Verdi, Giuseppe, 1813–1901

[Luisa Miller. Vocal score] *Luisa Miller.* Italian. Ricordi RCP42310/05, $26.95.

2474 Verdi, Giuseppe, 1813–1901

[Macbeth. Vocal score] *Macbeth.* Italian and English. Ricordi RCP42311/05, $26.95; G. Schirmer ED2755, $26.95 pbk., $35 hardcover.

2475   Verdi, Giuseppe, 1813–1901

[Nabucco. Vocal score] *Nabucco*. Italian. Ricordi RCP42313/05, $29.95.

2476 ** Verdi, Giuseppe, 1813–1901

[Otello. Vocal score] *Otello*. Italian and English. Ricordi RCP52105/05, $24.95; G. Schirmer ED2936, $26.95 pbk., $45 hardcover.

2477 ** Verdi, Giuseppe, 1813–1901

[Rigoletto. Vocal score] *Rigoletto*. Italian and English. Ricordi RCP133058/07, critical ed. by Martin Chusid, $42; G. Schirmer ED2562, $19.95.

2478   Verdi, Giuseppe, 1813–1901

[Simon Boccanegra. Vocal score] *Simon Boccanegra*. Italian. Ricordi RCP47372/05, $24.95.

2479 ** Verdi, Giuseppe, 1813–1901

[Traviata. Vocal score] *La traviata*. Italian and English. Ricordi RCP133060/05, $31; G. Schirmer ED2420, $22.95.

2480 ** Verdi, Giuseppe, 1813–1901

[Trovatore. Vocal score] *Il trovatore*. Italian and English. Ricordi RCP109460/05, $24.95; G. Schirmer ED473, $22.95 pbk., $35 hardcover.

2481   Wagner, Richard, 1813–1883

[Fliegende Holländer. Vocal score] *Der fliegende Holländer = The flying Dutchman*. German and English. Breitkopf & Härtel EB4502, $42; G. Schirmer ED453, $22.95.

2482   Wagner, Richard, 1813–1883

[Lohengrin. Vocal score] *Lohengrin*. Breitkopf & Härtel EB4504, German, $44; G. Schirmer ED2564, German and English, $28.95.

2483 * Wagner, Richard, 1813–1883

[Meistersinger von Nürnberg. Vocal score] *Die Meistersinger von Nürnberg*. German and English. Breitkopf & Härtel EB4506, $51; G. Schirmer ED1697, $34.95.

2484 * Wagner, Richard, 1813–1883

[Parsifal. Vocal score] *Parsifal*. German and English. Breitkopf & Härtel EB4511, $44; G. Schirmer ED2850, $29.95 pbk., $45 hardcover.

2485 ** Wagner, Richard, 1813–1883

[Ring des Nibelungen. Götterdämmerung. Vocal score] *Götterdämmerung*. German and English. Breitkopf & Härtel EB4510, $49; G. Schirmer ED1562, $29.95 pbk., $45 hardcover.

2486 ** Wagner, Richard, 1813–1883

[Ring des Nibelungen. Rheingold. Vocal score] *Das Rheingold*. German and English. Breitkopf & Härtel EB4507, $42; G. Schirmer ED1563, $39.95 pbk., $45 hardcover.

2487 ** Wagner, Richard, 1813–1883

[Ring des Nibelungen. Siegfried. Vocal score] *Siegfried*. German and English. Breitkopf & Härtel EB4509, $44; G. Schirmer ED1564, $28.95 pbk., $45 hardcover.

2488 ** Wagner, Richard, 1813–1883

[Ring des Nibelungen. Walküre. Vocal score] *Die Walküre*. German and English. Breitkopf & Härtel EB4508, $44; G. Schirmer ED1565, $24.95 pbk., $35 hardcover.

2489 * Wagner, Richard, 1813–1883

[Tannhäuser. Vocal score] *Tannhäuser*. German and English. Breitkopf & Härtel EB4503, Paris version, $51; G. Schirmer ED414, $22.95 pbk., $45 hardcover.

2490 ** Wagner, Richard, 1813–1883

[Tristan und Isolde. Vocal score] *Tristan and Isolde*. Breitkopf & Härtel EB4505, German, $45; G. Schirmer ED619, German and English, $26.95 pbk., $35 hardcover.

2491   Ward, Robert, 1917–

[Crucible. Vocal score] *The crucible*. English. Galaxy Music, $39.95.

2492 * Weber, Carl Maria von, 1786–1826

[Freischütz. Vocal score] *Der Freischütz*. German and English. G. Schirmer ED573, $24.95 pbk., $45 hardcover.

2493   Weill, Kurt, 1900–1950

[Aufsteig und Fall der Stadt Mahagonny. Vocal score] *Aufsteig und Fall der Stadt Mahagonny = The rise and fall of the city of Mahagonny*. German. Universal UE9851, $89.

2494 * Weill, Kurt, 1900–1950

[Dreigroschenoper. Vocal score] *Die Dreigroschenoper = Threepenny opera*. German. Universal UE8851, $49.

2495   Weill, Kurt, 1900–1950

[Dreigroschenoper. Vocal score. Selections] *Kurt Weill's The threepenny opera*. English adaptation by Marc Blitzstein. Weill-Brecht-Harms/Warner Bros. SF0137, $11.95.

2496 Weisgall, Hugo, 1912–

[Tenor. Vocal score] *The tenor.* English. Merion Music 411-41001, $5.

2497 Wolf-Ferrari, Ermanno, 1876–1948

[Segreto di Susanna. Vocal score] *Il segreto di Susanna.* English, French, and German. Boosey & Hawkes VSB 139, $37.

Operettas in Vocal Score

2498 * Lehár, Franz, 1870–1948

[Lustige Witwe. Vocal score] *The merry widow.* English translation. Chappell HL00312259, $40; Dover 0-486-25414-4, $10.95.

2499 Offenbach, Jacques, 1819–1880

[Orphée aux enfers. Vocal score] *Orphée aux enfers = Orpheus in the underworld.* French. Heugel HE4425, $57.55.

2500 * Strauss, Johann, 1825–1899

[Fledermaus. Vocal score] *Die Fledermaus.* Boosey & Hawkes VSB 12, German and English, $47; G. Schirmer ED2027, English translation, $16.95 pbk., $45 hardcover.

2501 Strauss, Johann, 1825–1899

[Zigeunerbaron. Vocal score] *Der Zigeunerbaron = The gypsy baron.* German and English. Boosey & Hawkes VSB 198, $70.

2502 Sullivan, Arthur, Sir, 1842–1900

[Gondoliers. Vocal score] *The gondoliers.* English. G. Schirmer ED1673, $20.

2503 * Sullivan, Arthur, Sir, 1842–1900

[H.M.S. Pinafore. Vocal score] *H.M.S. Pinafore.* English. G. Schirmer ED1623, $13.95.

2504 Sullivan, Arthur, Sir, 1842–1900

[Iolanthe. Vocal score] *Iolanthe.* English. G. Schirmer ED1822, $14.95.

2505 ** Sullivan, Arthur, Sir, 1842–1900

[Mikado. Vocal score] *The Mikado.* English. G. Schirmer ED1624, $14.95.

2506 Sullivan, Arthur, Sir, 1842–1900

[Patience. Vocal score] *Patience.* English. G. Schirmer ED1982, $13.95.

2507 ** Sullivan, Arthur, Sir, 1842–1900

[Pirates of Penzance. Vocal score] *The pirates of Penzance.* English. G. Schirmer ED1655, $13.95.

2508 Sullivan, Arthur, Sir, 1842–1900

[Yeomen of the guard. Vocal score] *The yeomen of the guard.* English. G. Schirmer ED2118, $20.

Musical Theater
Musicals in Vocal Score and Vocal Selections

Musicals are published in vocal score and in vocal selections. Vocal scores provide a complete representation of the work, including all musical numbers, interludes, and reprises. Although more expensive, they are the preferred edition, particularly for musicals marked with asterisks. Vocal selections, while less costly, generally contain only the music to eight or nine songs, the "hits" of the show.

This list includes both vocal scores and vocal selections for a musical when both are available. When ordering, specify the desired version by adding "vocal score" or "vocal selections" after the work's title.

2509 Arlen, Harold, 1905–1986

The Wizard of Oz. CPP Belwin: vocal selections, $11.95.

2510 Bart, Lionel, 1930–

Oliver! Plymouth Music: vocal score, $40; vocal selections, $8.95.

2511 * Berlin, Irving, 1888–1989

Annie get your gun. Hal Leonard: vocal score, $40; vocal selections, $8.95.

2512 * Bernstein, Leonard, 1918–1990

Candide. Jalni/Boosey & Hawkes VSB 161: vocal score, Scottish Opera edition of the opera-house version (1989), $75.

2513 Bernstein, Leonard, 1918–1990

On the town. Warner Bros.: vocal selections, $9.95.

2514 ** Bernstein, Leonard, 1918–1990

West side story. G. Schirmer: vocal score, $40; vocal selections, $8.95.

2515 ** Bock, Jerry, 1928–

Fiddler on the roof. Times Square Music: vocal score, $75; Hal Leonard: vocal selections, $12.95.

2516 Casey, Warren

Grease. Hal Leonard: vocal score, $40; vocal selections, $12.95.

2517 Coleman, Cy, 1929–

City of angels. Warner Bros.: vocal score, $75; vocal selections, $16.95.

2518 * Coleman, Cy, 1929–

Sweet Charity. CPP Belwin: vocal score, $38.50; vocal selections, $11.95.

2519 * Coleman, Cy, 1929–

Wildcat. Hal Leonard: vocal score, $40; vocal selections, $8.95.

2520 Finn, William, 1952–

Falsettos. Warner Bros.: vocal selections, $24.95.

2521 Geld, Gary, 1935–

Shenandoah. Hal Leonard: vocal score, $40; vocal selections, $10.95.

2522 Gershwin, George, 1898–1937

Funny face. Warner Bros.: vocal score, $40; vocal selections, $8.95.

2523 Gershwin, George, 1898–1937

Girl crazy. Warner Bros.: vocal selections, $9.95.

2524 Gershwin, George, 1898–1937

Of thee I sing. New World Music: vocal score, $50; vocal selections, $9.95.

2525 Gershwin, George, 1898–1937

Oh, Kay! Warner Bros.: vocal selections, $9.95.

2526 Gesner, Clark

You're a good man, Charlie Brown. Plymouth Music: vocal score, $35; vocal selections, $8.95.

2527 ** Hamlisch, Marvin, 1944–

A chorus line. Hal Leonard: vocal score, $40; vocal selections, $9.95.

2528 Herbert, Victor, 1859–1924

Babes in Toyland. Warner Bros.: vocal score, $40; vocal selections, $9.95.

2529 * Herman, Jerry, 1933–

Hello, Dolly. Hal Leonard: vocal score, $40; vocal selections, $8.95.

2530 Herman, Jerry, 1933–

Mame. Hal Leonard: vocal score, $40; vocal selections, $8.95.

2531 * Kander, John, 1927–

Cabaret. Hal Leonard: vocal score, $40; vocal selections, $8.95.

2532 Kander, John, 1927–

Kiss of the spider woman. Fiddleback Music: vocal selections, $14.95.

2533 ** Kern, Jerome, 1885–1945

Showboat. Hal Leonard: vocal score, $40; vocal selections, $8.95.

2534 Lane, Burton, 1912–

Finian's rainbow. Hal Leonard: vocal score, $40; vocal selections, $8.95.

2535 * Leigh, Mitch, 1928–

Man of La Mancha. Hal Leonard: vocal score, $40; vocal selections, $9.95.

2536 * Lloyd Webber, Andrew, 1948–

Cats. Hal Leonard: vocal selections (complete songs), $17.95.

2537 Lloyd Webber, Andrew, 1948–

Jesus Christ superstar. Hal Leonard: vocal selections, $9.95.

2538 Lloyd Webber, Andrew, 1948–

Joseph and the amazing technicolor dreamcoat. Hal Leonard: vocal score, $17; vocal selections, $14.95.

2539 * Lloyd Webber, Andrew, 1948–

Phantom of the opera. Hal Leonard: vocal selections, $17.95.

2540 ** Loesser, Frank, 1910–1969

Guys and dolls. Hal Leonard: vocal score, $40; vocal selections, $10.95.

2541 Loesser, Frank, 1910–1969

How to succeed in business without really trying. Hal Leonard: vocal score, $40; vocal selections, $8.95.

2542 * Loesser, Frank, 1910–1969

The most happy fella. Hal Leonard: vocal score, $40; vocal selections, $8.95.

2543 * Loewe, Frederick, 1904–1988

Brigadoon. CPP Belwin: vocal score, $40; vocal selections, $12.95.

2544 * Loewe, Frederick, 1904–1988

Camelot. Hal Leonard: vocal score, $40; vocal selections, $8.95.

2545 Loewe, Frederick, 1904–1988

Gigi. Hal Leonard: vocal score, $40; vocal selections, $8.95.

2546 ** Loewe, Frederick, 1904–1988

My fair lady. Hal Leonard: vocal score, $40; vocal selections, $8.95.

2547 Loewe, Frederick, 1904–1988

Paint your wagon. Hal Leonard: vocal score, $40; vocal selections, $8.95.

2548 Menken, Alan

Beauty and the beast [Broadway version]. Hal Leonard: vocal selections, $19.95.

2549 Porter, Cole, 1891–1964

Anything goes. Warner Bros.: vocal selections, 1987 revival ed., $14.95.

2550 * Porter, Cole, 1891–1964

Can-can. Hal Leonard: vocal score, $40; vocal selections, $8.95.

2551 * Porter, Cole, 1891–1964

Kiss me, Kate. Hal Leonard: vocal score, $40; vocal selections, $8.95.

2552 Rodgers, Richard, 1902–1979

Allegro. Hal Leonard: vocal score, $40; vocal selections, $8.95.

2553 * Rodgers, Richard, 1902–1979

Babes in arms. Hal Leonard: vocal score, $40; vocal selections, $8.95.

2554 ** Rodgers, Richard, 1902–1979

Carousel. Hal Leonard: vocal score, $40; vocal selections, $8.95; vocal selections, 1994 revival ed., $16.95.

2555 Rodgers, Richard, 1902–1979

Do I hear a waltz? Hal Leonard: vocal score, $40; vocal selections, $8.95.

2556 Rodgers, Richard, 1902–1979

Flower drum song. Hal Leonard: vocal score, $40; vocal selections, $8.95.

2557 ** Rodgers, Richard, 1902–1979

The king and I. Hal Leonard: vocal score, $40; vocal selections, $8.95.

2558 ** Rodgers, Richard, 1902–1979

Oklahoma! Hal Leonard: vocal score, $40; vocal selections, $8.95.

2559 Rodgers, Richard, 1902–1979

On your toes. Hal Leonard: vocal score, $40; vocal selections, $8.95.

2560 Rodgers, Richard, 1902–1979

Pal Joey. Hal Leonard: vocal score, $40; vocal selections, $8.95.

2561 ** Rodgers, Richard, 1902–1979

The sound of music. Hal Leonard: vocal score, $40; vocal selections, $8.95.

2562 * Rodgers, Richard, 1902–1979

South Pacific. Hal Leonard: vocal score, $40; vocal selections, $8.95.

2563 Romberg, Sigmund, 1887–1951

The student prince. Warner Bros.: vocal score, $35; vocal selections, $9.95.

2564 Ross, Jerry, 1926–1955

Damn Yankees. CPP Belwin: vocal score, $38.50; vocal selections, $11.95.

2565 Ross, Jerry, 1926–1955

Pajama game. CPP Belwin: vocal score, $38.50; vocal selections, $12.95.

2566 ** Schmidt, Harvey, 1929–

The fantasticks. Hal Leonard: vocal score, $40; vocal selections, $8.95.

2567 Schmidt, Harvey, 1929–

I do! I do! Hal Leonard: vocal score, $40; vocal selections, $8.95.

2568 * Schönberg, Claude-Michel, 1944–

Les misérables. Hal Leonard: vocal selections, $17.95.

2569 * Schönberg, Claude-Michel, 1944–

Miss Saigon. Hal Leonard: vocal selections, $17.95.

2570 Schwartz, Stephen, 1948–

Godspell. Hal Leonard: vocal score, $40; vocal selections, $8.95.

2571 Schwartz, Stephen, 1948–

Pippin. CPP Belwin: vocal score, $40; vocal selections, $13.95.

2572   Sondheim, Stephen, 1930–
Anyone can whistle. Hal Leonard: vocal score, $40;
vocal selections, $8.95.

2573 ** Sondheim, Stephen, 1930–
Company. Hal Leonard: vocal score, $40; vocal
selections, $8.95.

2574 * Sondheim, Stephen, 1930–
Follies. Hal Leonard: vocal score, $40; vocal selec-
tions, $10.95.

2575 * Sondheim, Stephen, 1930–
A funny thing happened on the way to the forum.
Hal Leonard: vocal score, $40; vocal selections, $8.95.

2576   Sondheim, Stephen, 1930–
Into the woods. Warner Bros.: vocal score, $100;
vocal selections, $17.95.

2577 ** Sondheim, Stephen, 1930–
A little night music. Revelation: vocal score, $35;
vocal selections, $8.95.

2578   Sondheim, Stephen, 1930–
Merrily we roll along. Revelation: vocal score, $50;
vocal selections, $8.95.

2579   Sondheim, Stephen, 1930–
Pacific overtures. Revelation: vocal score, $35.

2580   Sondheim, Stephen, 1930–
Sunday in the park with George. Revelation: vocal
score, $50; vocal selections, $8.95.

2581 ** Sondheim, Stephen, 1930–
Sweeney Todd. Revelation: vocal score, $75; vocal
selections, $8.95.

2582 * Strouse, Charles, 1928–
Annie [Broadway version]. Hal Leonard: vocal
score, $40; vocal selections, $9.95.

2583   Strouse, Charles, 1928–
Bye bye Birdie. CPP Belwin: vocal score, $38.50;
vocal selections, $10.95.

2584 * Styne, Jule, 1905–1994
Bells are ringing. Hal Leonard: vocal score, $40;
vocal selections, $8.95.

2585   Styne, Jule, 1905–1994
Funny girl. Hal Leonard: vocal score, $40; vocal
selections, $8.95.

2586   Styne, Jule, 1905–1994
Gypsy. Hal Leonard: vocal score, $40; vocal selec-
tions, $9.95.

2587   Waller, Fats, 1904–1943
Ain't misbehavin'. Hal Leonard: vocal selections,
$12.95.

2588   Warren, Harry, 1893–1981
42nd Street. Warner Bros.: vocal selections, $14.95.

2589   Weill, Kurt, 1900–1950
Lady in the dark. Hal Leonard: vocal score, $40.

2590   Weill, Kurt, 1900–1950
Lost in the stars. Chappell: vocal score, $40.

2591 * Weill, Kurt, 1900–1950
Street scene. Chappell: vocal score, $40.

2592 * Willson, Meredith, 1902–1984
The music man. Hal Leonard: vocal score, $40;
vocal selections, $8.95.

2593   Wright, Robert, 1914–
Kismet. Hal Leonard: vocal score, $40; vocal selec-
tions, $8.95.

2594   Wright, Robert, 1914–
Song of Norway. Hal Leonard: vocal score, $40;
vocal selections, $8.95.

2595   Youmans, Vincent, 1898–1946
No, no, Nanette. Warner Bros.: vocal score, $75;
vocal selections, $9.95.

Songs from Musicals: Composer Collections

These song collections represent major composers
associated with the Broadway stage.

2596 * Arlen, Harold, 1905–1986
The Harold Arlen songbook. Hal Leonard, $19.95.

2597   Berlin, Irving, 1888–1989
Ballads. I. Berlin, $9.95.

2598 ** Berlin, Irving, 1888–1989
Broadway songs. I. Berlin, $12.95.

2599 * Berlin, Irving, 1888–1989
Movie songs. I. Berlin, $12.95.

2600   Berlin, Irving, 1888–1989
Novelty songs. I. Berlin, $12.95.

2601 Berlin, Irving, 1888–1989

Patriotic songs. I. Berlin, $8.95.

2602 Berlin, Irving, 1888–1989

Ragtime and early songs. I. Berlin, $10.95.

2603 ** Bernstein, Leonard, 1918–1990

Bernstein on Broadway. Jalni/Boosey & Hawkes VAB 236, $29.95.

2604 ** Gershwin, George, 1898–1937

Gershwin on Broadway. Warner Bros., $24.95.

2605 Gershwin, George, 1898–1937

Music by Gershwin. Warner Bros., $16.95.

2606 Gershwin, George, 1898–1937

Rediscovered Gershwin. Warner Bros., $22.95.

2607 ** Kern, Jerome, 1885–1945

Jerome Kern collection. Hal Leonard, $19.95.

2608 ** Lloyd Webber, Andrew, 1948–

Andrew Lloyd Webber anthology. Hal Leonard, $24.95.

2609 ** Loesser, Frank, 1910–1969

The best of Frank Loesser. Frank Music, $15.95.

2610 ** Porter, Cole, 1891–1964

Music and lyrics by Cole Porter. Chappell, 2 v., $16.95 each.

2611 ** Rodgers, Richard, 1902–1979

The Richard Rodgers collection. Williamson, $19.95.

2612 ** Rodgers, Richard, 1902–1979

Rodgers and Hart: a musical anthology. Hal Leonard, $19.95.

2613 ** Sondheim, Stephen, 1930–

All Sondheim. Valando/Revelation, 3 v., $14.95 each.

2614 * Weill, Kurt, 1900–1950

From Berlin to Broadway. Hal Leonard, $14.95.

Songs from Musicals: Anthologies

Listed here are major collections of songs from the Broadway stage.

2615 *Broadway musicals, show by show.* Hal Leonard, [7] v., $18.95 each.

Contents: vol. [1]. 1891–1916. vol. [2]. 1917–1929. vol. [3]. 1930–1939. vol. [4]. 1940–1949. vol. [5]. 1950–1959. vol. [6]. 1960–1971. vol. [7]. 1972–1988.

2616 *Comedy songs from Broadway musicals.* Hal Leonard, $9.95.

2617 ** *Singer's musical theatre anthology—baritone.* Hal Leonard, $17.95.

2618 ** *Singer's musical theatre anthology—duets.* Hal Leonard, $14.95.

2619 ** *Singer's musical theatre anthology—mezzo-soprano.* Hal Leonard, $17.95.

2620 ** *Singer's musical theatre anthology—soprano.* Hal Leonard, $17.95.

2621 ** *Singer's musical theatre anthology—tenor.* Hal Leonard, $17.95.

Solo Song

Classical Song: Composer Listing

In addition to art song, this section includes arias, cantatas, and other works for solo voice, accompanied by piano unless indicated otherwise.

Designation of the language of a work, usually found in the uniform title, is indicated after the title proper or after the publisher's name in order to accommodate different editions with different languages within a single entry. The language designations always refer to sung words (i.e., text set to the music), not to translations provided separately from the music.

2622 Argento, Dominick, 1927–

[Elizabethan songs] *Six Elizabethan songs, for high voice and piano.* English. Boosey & Hawkes VAB 64, $13.50.

2623 Argento, Dominick, 1927–

From the diary of Virginia Woolf, for medium voice and piano. English. Boosey & Hawkes VAB 77, $18.

2624 Argento, Dominick, 1927–

Letters from composers, for high voice and guitar. English. Boosey & Hawkes VAB 67, $19.

2625 Arne, Thomas Augustine, 1710–1778

[Songs. Selections] *Twelve songs for high voice and harpsichord or piano,* ed. by Michael Pilkington. English. Stainer & Bell 0-852-49461-0, 0-852-49462-9, 2 v., $12.50 each.

2626 * Bach, Johann Sebastian, 1685–1750

[Cantatas. Selections] *Arias from church cantatas, with obbligato instruments and piano or organ.* German, some with English. Kalmus K 06072, K 06818 soprano, 2 v., $22.95, $10.25; K 06819-06921 contralto, 3 v., $12.95, $24.95, $12.95; K 06825-06827 tenor, 3 v., $15, $9.95, $6.75; K 06828 bass, $9.

2627 * Bach, Johann Sebastian, 1685–1750

[Cantatas. Selections] *Arias from secular cantatas, for soprano with obbligato instruments and piano or organ.* German. Kalmus K 06817, $18.95.

2628 * Bach, Johann Sebastian, 1685–1750

[Cantatas. Vocal scores. Selections] *Arien album.* German. Peters P3335a soprano, P3335b alto, P3335c tenor, P3335d bass, $23.25, $18.70, $23.25, $18.70.

2629 Bach, Johann Sebastian, 1685–1750

[Ich habe genug. Vocal score] *Ich habe genug: cantata BWV 82, 1st version (1727), for bass and orchestra; accompaniment arranged for piano.* German and English. Breitkopf & Härtel EB7082, $8; Hänssler/Carus HE31.082/03, $4.50; Kalmus K 06017, $4.

2630 Bach, Johann Sebastian, 1685–1750

[Jauchzet Gott in allen Landen. Vocal score] *Jauchzet Gott in allen Landen: cantata BWV 51, for soprano and orchestra; accompaniment arranged for piano.* German, English, and French. Breitkopf & Härtel EB7051, $6.75; Hänssler/Carus HE 31.051/03, $6.50; Kalmus K 09402, $5.95.

2631 Bach, Johann Sebastian, 1685–1750

[Songs. Selections] *Geistliche Lieder und Arien aus "Schemellis Gesangbuch" und dem "Notenbuch der Anna Magdalena Bach,"* ed. by Ernst Naumann. German. Breitkopf & Härtel EB2817 high voice (original keys), EB4738 low voice, $13.50 each.

2632 Bach, Johann Sebastian, 1685–1750

[Vergnügte Ruh', beliebte Seelenlust. Vocal score] *Vergnügte Ruh', beliebte Seelenlust: cantata BWV 170, for alto and orchestra; accompaniment arranged for piano.* German and English. Breitkopf & Härtel EB7170, $7; Kalmus K 09326, $4.

2633 Bach, Johann Sebastian, 1685–1750

[Weichet nur, betrübte Schatten. Vocal score] *Weichet nur, betrübte Schatten (Wedding cantata), BWV 202, soprano and orchestra; accompaniment arranged for piano.* German. Breitkopf & Härtel EB7202, $8; Kalmus K 06638, $4.50; Peters P6281, $12.10.

2634 * Barber, Samuel, 1910–1981

[Songs] *Collected songs* [includes the cycle *Hermit songs*]. Chiefly English. G. Schirmer HL50328790 high voice, HL50328780 low voice, $19.95 each.

2635 * Barber, Samuel, 1910–1981

[Vocal music. Vocal scores. Selections] *Music for soprano and orchestra; reduction for soprano and piano* [includes *Knoxville: summer of 1915*]. English. G. Schirmer HL50331490, $8.95.

2636 * Beach, H. H. A., Mrs., 1867–1944

[Songs. Selections] *Twenty-three songs* [includes *Browning songs, op. 44*]. English. Da Capo Press 0-306-79717-8, $34.

2637 * Beethoven, Ludwig van, 1770–1827

[Songs] *Complete songs.* German, English, French, or Italian. Henle HN533-534, 2 v., $29.95, $28.95.

2638 * Beethoven, Ludwig van, 1770–1827

[Songs. Selections] *Songs for solo voice and piano.* German and English. Dover 0-486-25125-X, $9.95.

2639 * Beethoven, Ludwig van, 1770–1827

[Songs. Selections] *Thirty selected songs.* German. Peters P731 high voice, P732 medium and low voice, $27.25, $22.25.

2640 * Bellini, Vincenzo, 1801–1835

[Songs. Selections] *Fifteen composizioni da camera.* Italian. Ricordi HL50018410, $10.95.

2641 * Berg, Alban, 1885–1935

[Frühe Lieder] *Sieben Frühe Lieder = Seven early songs (1907).* German and English. Universal UE8853, $19.95.

2642 Berg, Alban, 1885–1935

[Lieder, op. 2] *Vier Lieder, op. 2.* German and English. Universal UE8813, $14.95.

2643 Berg, Alban, 1885–1935

[Songs. Selections] *Jugendlieder: 23 selected songs.* German. Universal UE18143-18144, 2 v., $29.95 each.

2644 * Berlioz, Hector, 1803–1869

Les nuits d'été = Summer nights, op. 7. Bärenreiter BA5784a, original keys, French, $21; International Music 1355 high voice, 1365 low voice, French and

English, $7 each; G. Schirmer ED2780 high voice, ED2779 low voice, French and English, $12.95 each.

2645 * Bernstein, Leonard, 1918–1990

[Songs. Selections] *Song album* [includes song cycles *I hate music, La bonne cuisine*]. Chiefly English. Boosey & Hawkes VAB 237, $20.

2646 Bizet, Georges, 1838–1875

[Songs. Selections] *Twenty mélodies.* French. Kalmus K06831 high voice, K06832 medium voice, $14.95 each.

2647 Bolcom, William, 1938–

Cabaret songs, for medium voice and piano. English. E. B. Marks HL00008273, $14.95.

2648 Boulanger, Lili, 1893–1918

[Songs. Selections] *Quatre chants.* French. G. Schirmer ED3217, $9.95.

2649 * Bowles, Paul, 1910–

Blue Mountain ballads. English words by Tennessee Williams. G. Schirmer ED3204, $7.95.

2650 * Brahms, Johannes, 1833–1897

[Songs] *Complete songs.* German and English. Dover 0-486-23820-2, 0-486-23821-0, 0-486-23822-9, 0-486-23823-7, 4 v., $11.95 each.

2651 Brahms, Johannes, 1833–1897

[Songs. Selections] *Fifty selected songs.* German and English. G. Schirmer LB1582 high voice, LB1581 low voice, $19.95 each.

2652 * Brahms, Johannes, 1833–1897

[Songs. Selections] *Lieder,* ed. by Max Friedlander. German. Peters, 4 v. for each voice: Peters P3201a, P3202a, P3691a, P3692a high voice, $31.95, $30.60, $31.95, $39.95; Peters P3201b, P3202b, P3691b, P3692b low voice, $31.95, $30.60, $39.95, $31.95.

2653 ** Brahms, Johannes, 1833–1897

[Songs. Selections] *Seventy songs,* ed. by Sergius Kagen. German and English. International Music 1270 high voice, 1271 low voice, $19 each.

2654 Britten, Benjamin, 1913–1976

A charm of lullabies, for mezzo-soprano and piano, op. 41. English. Boosey & Hawkes VAB 112, $22.

2655 * Britten, Benjamin, 1913–1976

Folk song arrangements. English. Boosey & Hawkes, 6 v.

Contents: vol. 1. *British Isles* VAB 8 high voice, VAB 8M medium voice, $15 each. vol. 2. *France* VAB 16H high voice, VAB 16 medium voice, $18 each. vol. 3. *British Isles* VAB 17 high voice, VAB 24 medium voice, $17 each. vol. 4. *Moore's Irish melodies* VAB 157, $20. vol. 5. *British Isles* VAB 99 medium voice, $15. vol. 6. *England* VAB 101, high voice and guitar, ed. by Julian Bream, $15.

2656 Britten, Benjamin, 1913–1976

[Illuminations. Vocal score] *Les illuminations de Rimbaud, op. 18, for tenor or soprano and string orchestra; reduction for voice and piano.* French. Boosey & Hawkes VAB 117, $22.

2657 Britten, Benjamin, 1913–1976

[Serenade, tenor, horn, string orchestra, op. 31. Vocal score] *Serenade for tenor, horn, strings, op. 31; reduction for tenor, horn, and piano.* English. Boosey & Hawkes VAB 123, $32.

2658 Britten, Benjamin, 1913–1976

Songs from the Chinese, op. 58, for high voice and guitar, ed. by Julian Bream. English. Boosey & Hawkes VAB 154, $20.

2659 Britten, Benjamin, 1913–1976

[Sonnets of Michaelangelo] *Seven sonnets of Michaelangelo, for tenor and piano.* Italian. Boosey & Hawkes VAB 5, $19.

2660 Carpenter, John Alden, 1876–1951

Gitanjali: song offerings. English. G. Schirmer ED909, high and medium voice, $16.95.

2661 Carter, Elliott, 1908–

[Poems of Robert Frost] *Three poems of Robert Frost.* English. Associated Music AMP-7454, $8.95.

2662 Chausson, Ernest, 1855–1899

[Songs. Selections] *Twenty songs,* ed. by Sergius Kagen. French and English. International Music 1130 high voice, 1131 low voice, $13 each.

2663 Copland, Aaron, 1900–1990

As it fell upon a day, for soprano, flute, and clarinet. English. Score and parts. Boosey & Hawkes VAB 30, $16.

2664 * Copland, Aaron, 1900–1990

Old American songs, sets 1 and 2. English. Boosey & Hawkes, set 1 VAB 25, set 2 VAB 26, $10.50 each.

2665 * Copland, Aaron, 1900–1990

[Poems of Emily Dickinson] *Twelve poems of Emily Dickinson, medium voice.* English. Boosey & Hawkes VAB 47, $14.50.

2666 * Copland, Aaron, 1900–1990

[Songs. Selections] *Song album, high voice.* English. Boosey & Hawkes VAB 61, $14.

2667 Corigliano, John, 1938–

The Cloisters: four poems by William Hoffman. English. G. Schirmer. Each song published separately: *Fort Tryon Park, September,* HL50290270; *Song to the witch of the Cloisters,* HL50290400; *Christmas at the Cloisters,* HL50290410; *The unicorn,* HL50290410; $3.95 each.

2668 Davies, Peter Maxwell, 1934–

The yellow cake review: comments in words and music on the threat of uranium mining in Orkney, for voice and piano. English. Boosey & Hawkes VAB 219, $18.

2669 Debussy, Claude, 1862–1918

[Songs. Selections] *Forty-three songs,* ed. by Sergius Kagen. French and English. International Music 1135 high voice, 1136 medium and low voice, $19 each.

2670 Debussy, Claude, 1862–1918

[Songs. Selections] *Songs, 1880–1904.* French and English. Dover 0-486-24131-9, $8.95.

2671 * Debussy, Claude, 1862–1918

[Songs. Selections] *Songs of Claude Debussy,* critical ed. by James R. Briscoe, based on primary sources, original keys only. French and English. G. Schirmer, HL00660164 high voice, HL00660283 medium voice, $18.95 each.

2672 Donaudy, Stefano, 1879–1925

[Arie di stille antico] *36 arie di stille antico.* Italian. Ricordi 117220, 117233, 118842, 3 v., $18.95 each.

2673 Donizetti, Gaetano, 1797–1848

[Songs. Selections] *Composizioni da camera.* Italian. Ricordi 130330-130331, 2 v., $17.95 each.

2674 * Dowland, John, 1563?–1626

[Songs, lute acc. Selections] *English lute songs, with the original lute tablature and guitar transcriptions.* English. Tecla, $11.75.

2675 Dowland, John, 1563?–1626

[Songs, lute acc. Selections; arr.] *Fifty songs, with accompaniment arranged for piano.* English.

Stainer & Bell/Galaxy, 2 v. for each voice: Stainer X5A and X6A high voice, Stainer X5B and X6B low voice, $15.95 each volume.

2676 Duke, John, 1899–1984

[Songs. Selections] *Songs of John Duke.* English. G. Schirmer HL50488485 high voice, HL50488486 low voice, $12.95 each.

2677 * Duparc, Henri, 1848–1933

[Songs. Selections] *Twelve songs.* French and English. Dover 0-486-28466-2 (original keys), $9.95; International Music 1112 high voice (*Eleven songs*), 1117 medium voice, 1113 low voice, $11 each.

2678 Dvořák, Antonín, 1841–1904

[Biblické písně] *Biblical songs: a cycle of ten songs, op. 99.* English. International Music, 2 v. for each voice: International 2237 and 2239 high voice, International 2238 and 2240 low voice, $5.50 each volume; G. Schirmer LB1834 high voice, LB1825 low voice, $7.95 each.

2679 Dvořák, Antonín, 1841–1904

[Cigánské melodie] *Gypsy songs: a cycle of seven songs, op. 55.* German and English. International Music 1995 high voice, 1996 low voice, $5.50 each.

2680 * Falla, Manuel de, 1876–1946

[Cancione populares españolas] *Seven Spanish folk songs.* Spanish, English, and French. Ediciones Manuel de Falla, 1 v. high voice, 1 v. medium voice, prices not available.

2681 * Fauré, Gabriel, 1845–1924

La bonne chanson: nine songs on poems by Verlaine. French and English. International Music 482 high voice, 1531 low voice, $7 each.

2682 * Fauré, Gabriel, 1845–1924

[Songs. Selections] *Fifty songs,* ed. by Laura Ward and Richard Walters. French. G. Schirmer HL007470741 high voice, HL004747070 medium/low voice, $19.95 each.

2683 Fauré, Gabriel, 1845–1924

[Songs. Selections] *Sixty songs for medium voice.* French. Dover 0-486-26534-X, $13.95.

2684 Fine, Irving, 1914–1962

Childhood fables for grownups. English. Boosey & Hawkes FIN 17, $9.50.

2685 * Foster, Stephen Collins, 1826–1864

[Songs. Selections] *Stephen Foster song book: original sheet music of 40 songs.* English. Dover 0-486-23048-1, $8.95.

2686 Gounod, Charles, 1818–1893

[Songs. Selections] *Fifteen mélodies.* French and English. Classical Vocal Reprints CVR 0567, $17.50.

2687 Granados, Enrique, 1867–1916

Canciones amatorias. Spanish. Unión Musical Española UME19807, $17.95.

2688 * Granados, Enrique, 1867–1916

[Tonadillas. Selections] *Eleven songs (Tonadillas).* Spanish and English. International Music 1262 (original keys), $9.

2689 Grieg, Edvard, 1843–1907

[Songs. Selections] *Thirty-six selected songs.* English and German. Kalmus K 06837 high voice, K 06836 low voice, $12.95, $9.75.

2690 * Handel, George Frideric, 1685–1759

[Vocal music. Vocal scores. Selections] *Forty-five arias from operas and oratorios,* ed. by Sergius Kagen. Original languages and English. International Music, 3 v. for each voice: International 1693, 1695, and 1697 high voice; International 1694, 1696, and 1698 low voice, $8 each volume.

2691 Harbison, John, 1938–

Mirabai songs, for soprano or mezzo-soprano and piano. English. Associated Music AMP-7977, $9.95.

2692 Haydn, Joseph, 1732–1809

Arianna a Naxos: cantata for solo voice with harpsichord or forte piano accompaniment (1789?). Italian. Haydn-Mozart Presse HMP 197, $19.95.

2693 * Haydn, Joseph, 1732–1809

[Songs. Selections] *Songs.* German and English. Henle HN535, $24.95.

2694 Hensel, Fanny Mendelssohn, 1805–1847

[Songs. Selections] *Selected songs.* German. Breitkopf & Härtel EB8596, $28. *See also* 2709

2695 Hensel, Fanny Mendelssohn, 1805–1847

[Songs. Selections] *Sixteen songs.* German and English. Alfred Music 4961 high voice, 4963 low voice, $9.95 each. *See also* 2709

2696 Hindemith, Paul, 1895–1963

[English songs] *Nine English songs for soprano or mezzo-soprano and piano.* English. Schott ED6839, $14.95.

2697 Hindemith, Paul, 1895–1963

Das Marienleben, op. 27. German. Schott ED2025 (original version, 1922–23), $25; Schott ED2026 (rev. version, 1948), $25.

2698 Honegger, Arthur, 1892–1955

[Psaumes] *Trois psaumes* [no. 34, 140, 138]. French. Salabert EAS13889, $6.95.

2699 Hundley, Richard, 1931–

[Songs. Selections] *Eight songs.* English. Boosey & Hawkes VAB 102, $13.50.

2700 Ives, Charles, 1874–1954

[Songs. Selections] *Forty earlier songs,* critical ed. by John Kirkpatrick. English. Peer International 61750-211, $27.50.

2701 * Ives, Charles, 1874–1954

[Songs. Selections] *One hundred fourteen songs.* Chiefly English. Peer International 60867-211, $29.95.

2702 Liszt, Franz, 1811–1896

[Songs. Selections] *Thirty songs for high voice.* German and English. Dover 0-486-23197-6, $9.95.

2703 * Mahler, Gustav, 1860–1911

[Kindertotenlieder. Vocal score] *Kindertotenlieder = Songs on the death of children, for voice and orchestra; accompaniment arranged for piano.* German and English. International Music 2144 high voice, 1040 medium voice, $6 each; Kahnt/Peters FK12 high voice, FK13 medium/low voice, $27.75 each.

2704 * Mahler, Gustav, 1860–1911

[Knaben Wunderhorn. Vocal score] *Wunderhorn songs.* German and English. G. Schirmer ED2767 high voice, ED2768 low voice, $15.95 each; Universal UE14786AE high voice, UE14786BE low voice, $25 each.

2705 * Mahler, Gustav, 1860–1911

[Lied von der Erde. Vocal score] *The song of the earth = Das Lied von der Erde: a symphony for tenor, contralto or baritone and orchestra; accompaniment arranged for piano.* German and English. Universal UE3391, $35.

2706 * Mahler, Gustav, 1860–1911

[Lieder eines fahrenden Gesellen. Vocal score] *Lieder eines fahrenden Gesellen = Songs of a wayfarer, for voice and orchestra; accompaniment arranged for piano.* German and English. Boosey & Hawkes VAB 137, original key, low voice, $30; International Music 2146 high voice, 1020 low voice, $6.50 each.

2707 * Mahler, Gustav, 1860–1911

[Song cycles. Vocal scores. Selections] *Three song cycles in vocal score: Songs of a wayfarer, Kindertotenlieder, Das Lied von der Erde.* German. Dover 0-486-26954-X, $10.95.

2708 * Mahler, Gustav, 1860–1911

[Songs. Selections] *Twenty-four songs.* German and English. International Music, 4 v. for each voice: International 1213-1216 high voice; International 1237 and 1232-1234 low voice, $6.50 each volume.

2709 Mendelssohn-Bartholdy, Felix, 1809–1847

[Songs. Selections] *Seventy-nine songs* [includes songs by Fanny Mendelssohn Hensel]. German. Kalmus K 09886 high voice, K 09887 medium voice, K 09888 low voice, $13, $15, $13.

2710 * Mozart, Wolfgang Amadeus, 1756–1791

[Arias. Vocal scores. Selections] *Mozart arias,* with recorded accompaniment on cassette by Robert L. Larsen, ed. by Robert L. Larsen and Richard Walters. Original languages and English. Hal Leonard, 4 v., HL00747019 soprano, HL00747020 mezzo-soprano, HL00747018 tenor, HL00747017 baritone/bass, $15.95 each.

2711 * Mozart, Wolfgang Amadeus, 1756–1791

[Arias. Vocal scores. Selections] *Twenty-one concert arias, for soprano.* Original languages and English. G. Schirmer LB1751-1752, 2 v., $11.95 each.

2712 * Mozart, Wolfgang Amadeus, 1756–1791

[Exsultate, jubilate. Vocal score] *Exsultate, jubilate: motet, K. 165, for soprano and orchestra; accompaniment arranged for piano.* Latin. Breitkopf & Härtel EB5232, $9; International Music 1174, $5.75; Kalmus K6332, $3.75; Oxford University Press 0-19-345593-5, ed. by Richard Maunder, $13.95.

2713 * Mozart, Wolfgang Amadeus, 1756–1791

[Songs. Selections] *Songs.* Bärenreiter BA5330, German, $20; Dover 0-486-27568-X, original languages and English, $9.95; Peters P299a high voice, P299b medium or low voice, original languages and German, $15.70 each.

2714 Musgrave, Thea, 1928–

A suite o' bairnsangs: poems by Maurice Lindsay. Scottish and English. Chester CH04063, $10.95.

2715 Mussorgsky, Modest Petrovich, 1839–1881

[Detskaia] *Nursery: seven songs.* Russian and English. International Music 1195, original key, medium-high voice, $6.50.

2716 Mussorgsky, Modest Petrovich, 1839–1881

[Pesni i pliaski smerti] *Songs and dances of death.* Russian and English. International Music 1795 high voice, 1129 medium voice, 1021 low voice, $8.50 each.

2717 Mussorgsky, Modest Petrovich, 1839–1881

[Songs] *Complete songs for voice and piano.* Russian, with transliteration. G. Schirmer LB2018, $59.95.

2718 * Niles, John Jacob, 1892–1980

[Songs. Selections] *The songs of John Jacob Niles.* Rev. and expanded ed. English. G. Schirmer ED3788 high voice, ED3841 low voice, $12.95 each.

2719 Pinkham, Daniel, 1928–

Letters from Saint Paul: six songs for high voice and organ or piano. English. E. C. Schirmer 142, $6.35.

2720 Poulenc, Francis, 1899–1963

Banalités: five songs on poems of Guillaume Apollinaire. French. Eschig 511-01729, $35.

2721 Poulenc, Francis, 1899–1963

Le bestiare, ou, Cortège d'Orphée. French. Eschig 511-01721, $17.75.

2722 * Poulenc, Francis, 1899–1963

[Songs. Selections] *Mélodies et chansons.* Chiefly French. Salabert EAS18889, $24.95.

2723 Poulenc, Francis, 1899–1963

Tel jour, telle nuit = As day, as night: nine songs on poems of Paul Eluard. French. Durand 511-00639, $26.75.

2724 Prokofiev, Sergey, 1891–1953

[Gadkii utënok] *Vilain petit canard = The ugly duckling, for mezzo-soprano and piano.* English, French, and German. Boosey & Hawkes VAB 144, $12.

2725 * Purcell, Henry, 1659–1695

[Songs. Selections] *Thirty songs,* ed. by Timothy Roberts. English. Oxford University Press, 2 v. for each voice: Oxford 0-19-345710-5 and 0-19-345713-X high voice (original keys), Oxford 0-19-345711-3 and 0-19-345714-8 medium voice, $18.95 each volume.

2726 Rachmaninoff, Sergei, 1873–1943

[Songs] *Songs with piano accompaniment in original keys.* Russian and English. Boosey & Hawkes VAB 178-179, 2 v., $34 each.

2727 Ravel, Maurice, 1875–1937

Chansons madécasses, for voice, flute, violoncello, and piano. French. Score and parts. Durand 511-00683, $44.50.

2728 Ravel, Maurice, 1875–1937

[Don Quichotte à Dulcinée. Vocal score] *Don Quichotte à Dulcinée, for voice and piano* [originally for tenor and orchestra]. French and English. Durand, 3 v., each available in high, medium, or baritone keys, $14–$18 each volume.

2729 Ravel, Maurice, 1875–1937

[Mélodies populaires grecques] *Five Greek folk songs.* French, Greek, and English. Masters Music M1812, $3.50.

2730 Ravel, Maurice, 1875–1937

[Shéhérazade (Song cycle). Vocal score] *Shéhérazade, for mezzo-soprano and orchestra; accompaniment arranged for piano.* French and English. International Music 1447, $8; Masters Music M1744, $5.50.

2731 * Ravel, Maurice, 1875–1937

[Songs. Selections] *Songs, 1896–1914.* French and English. Dover 0-486-26354-1, $9.95.

2732 Rorem, Ned, 1923–

Nantucket songs. English. Boosey & Hawkes VAB 98, $12.50.

2733 * Rorem, Ned, 1923–

Poems of love and the rain, for mezzo-soprano and piano. English. Boosey & Hawkes VAB 39, $15.

2734 * Rorem, Ned, 1923–

[Songs. Selections] *Song album.* Chiefly English. Boosey & Hawkes VAB 95, VAB 192, VAB 259, 3 v., $21, $22, $15.

2735 Rorem, Ned, 1923–

[Songs (1953). Vocal score] *Six songs for high voice and orchestra; accompaniment arranged for piano.* English. Peters P6373, $15.70.

2736 Rorem, Ned, 1923–

[Songs on American poetry] *Fourteen songs on American poetry.* English. Peters P66583, $23.25.

2737 Rossini, Gioacchino, 1792–1868

[Péchés de vieillesse. Album italiano. Regata veneziana] *La regata veneziana.* Italian. Masters Music M1317, $7.95; Ricordi ER 2558, high voice, $6.50.

2738 Rossini, Gioacchino, 1792–1868

[Soirées musicales. Part 1] *Serate musicali: parte 1, 8 Ariette.* Italian and French. Masters Music M2308, $12; Ricordi ER 2413, $9.95.

2739 * Satie, Erik, 1866–1925

[Songs. Selections] *Mélodies et chansons.* French. Salabert EAS 18683, $19.95.

2740 Scarlatti, Alessandro, 1660–1725

[Operas. Vocal scores. Selections] *Ten arias for high voice.* Italian and English. G. Schirmer LB1853, $7.95.

2741 Schoenberg, Arnold, 1874–1951

[Buch der hängenden Gärten] *Poems from The book of the hanging gardens, op. 15.* German and French. Masters Music M1740, $8.95.

2742 * Schoenberg, Arnold, 1874–1951

[Songs] *Collected songs.* German. Masters Music M1180-1181, 2 v., $5.50, $8.50.

2743 Schoenberg, Arnold, 1874–1951

[Songs. Selections] *The book of the hanging gardens, and other songs: op. 2, op. 3, op. 6, op. 8, op. 15, and others.* German. Dover 0-486-28562-6, $11.95, for sale in the United States only.

2744 * Schubert, Franz, 1797–1828

Die schöne Mullerin. German. Bärenreiter BA7000 high voice, BA7001 medium voice, $23.95, $16.95.

2745 * Schubert, Franz, 1797–1828

[Songs] *Lieder für Gesang und Klavier.* New ed., Urtext, ed. by Dietrich Fischer-Dieskau and Elmar Budde. German. Peters, 4 v. to date: Peters P8303a-8306a high voice; Peters P8303b-8306b medium voice, Peters P8303c-8306c low voice, $73.20 each volume.

2746 * Schubert, Franz, 1797–1828

[Songs] *Songs, complete in 7 volumes.* German. v. 1–3 in high, medium, and low voice: Peters P20a, P178a, P790a high voice, $34.60, $32.50, $48.80; Peters P20b, P178b, P790b medium voice, $34.60, $32.50, $48.80; Peters P20c, P178c, P790c low voice, $34.60, $32.50, $48.80; v.4–7 in original keys: P791-793, P2270, $48.80, $39.50, $22.25, $32.50.

2747 * Schubert, Franz, 1797–1828

[Songs. Selections] *Complete song cycles* [includes *Die schöne Mullerin, Die Winterreise,* and *Schwanengesang*]. German and English. Dover 0-486-22649-2, $9.95.

2748 * Schubert, Franz, 1797–1828

[Songs. Selections] *Fifty-nine favorite songs.* German and English. Dover 0-486-24849-6, $9.95.

2749 ** Schubert, Franz, 1797–1828

[Songs. Selections] *One hundred songs,* ed. by Sergius Kagen [v.1 of a 3-volume set of 200 Schubert songs; v.1 contains all song cycles and 42 selected songs]. German and English. International Music 2010 high voice, 2011 low voice, $28 each.

2750 * Schubert, Franz, 1797–1828

[Songs. Selections] *Schubert's songs to texts by Goethe.* German and English. Dover 0-486-23752-4, $13.95.

2751 Schubert, Franz, 1797–1828

[Songs. Selections; arr.] *Songs by Schubert,* with accompaniment arranged for guitar by John W. Duarte. German. Bérben, $11.

2752 Schubert, Franz, 1797–1828

Die Winterreise. German. Bärenreiter BA7002 high voice, BA7003 medium voice, $23.95, $18.95.

2753 Schumann, Clara, 1819–1896

[Songs] *Sämtliche Lieder = Complete songs.* German. Breitkopf & Härtel EB8558-8559, 2 v., $23.30, $22.50.

2754 ** Schumann, Robert, 1810–1856

[Songs. Selections] *Eighty-five songs* [includes the song cycles *Liederkreis, op. 39, Frauenliebe und Leben,* and *Dichterliebe*]. German and English. International Music 1487 high voice, 1402 low voice (*Ninety songs*), $20 each.

2755 * Schumann, Robert, 1810–1856

[Songs. Selections] *Lieder.* German. Peters, 3 v. for each voice: Peters P2383a-2385a high voice, $34.60, $34.60, $39.95; Peters P2383b-2385b medium voice, $34.60, $39.95, $39.95.

2756 * Schumann, Robert, 1810–1856

[Songs. Selections] *Selected songs,* ed. by Clara Schumann [includes the song cycles *Dichterliebe, Liederkreis, op. 24,* and *Liederkreis, op. 39*]. German and English. Dover 0-486-24202-1, original keys, $11.95.

2757 Strauss, Richard, 1864–1949

[Letzte Lieder. Vocal score] *Four last songs, high voice with piano reduction.* German and English. Boosey & Hawkes VAB 32, $12.

2758 Strauss, Richard, 1864–1949

[Songs. Selections] *Fifty-seven songs.* German and English. Dover 0-486-27828-X, original keys, $12.95.

2759 * Strauss, Richard, 1864–1949

[Songs. Selections] *Forty songs,* ed. by Laura Ward and Richard Walters. German. G. Schirmer HL00747062 high voice, HL00747063 medium/low voice, $18.95 each.

2760 Stravinsky, Igor, 1882–1971

Berceuses du chat = Cat's cradle, for medium voice and three clarinets. Russian and French. Score and parts. Masters Music M1175, $3.50.

2761 Stravinsky, Igor, 1882–1971

The owl and the pussy-cat, for voice and piano. English. Boosey & Hawkes SGB 5939, $9.

2762 Stravinsky, Igor, 1882–1971

[Songs from William Shakespeare] *Three songs from William Shakespeare, for mezzo-soprano, flute, clarinet, and viola.* English. Score and parts. Boosey & Hawkes VAB 128 score, $19, VAB128PT parts, $20.

2763 Stravinsky, Igor, 1882–1971

Two poems and three Japanese lyrics, for high voice and piano. Russian, French, English, and German. Boosey & Hawkes VAB 146, $22.

2764 Thomson, Virgil, 1896–1989

Le berceau de Gertrude Stein = The cradle of Gertrude Stein. French and English. Southern Music SMP 2370-12, $6.

2765   Thomson, Virgil, 1896–1989

[Songs from Willam Blake. Vocal score] *Five songs from William Blake, for baritone and orchestra; piano reduction.* English. Southern Music SMP 2255-29, $12.

2766   Tosti, F. Paolo (Francesco Paolo), 1846–1916

[Songs. Selections] *The songs of Francesco Paolo Tosti.* Italian. HLH Music Publications, VOC100 high voice, VOC102 low voice, $17.50 each.

2767   Turina, Joaquín, 1882–1949

Poema en forma de canciones, for soprano and piano. Spanish. Unión Musical Española UME15316, $14.95.

2768 *   Vaughan Williams, Ralph, 1872–1958

[Mystical songs. Vocal score] *Five mystical songs, for baritone solo, chorus and orchestra; reduction for voice and piano.* English. Well-Tempered Press W1071, $6.

2769   Vaughan Williams, Ralph, 1872–1958

On Wenlock Edge: a cycle of six songs for tenor and piano, with string quartet ad lib. English. Score. Boosey & Hawkes VAB 9, $26; Masters Music M2108, $15.

2770 *   Vaughan Williams, Ralph, 1872–1958

Songs of travel. English. Boosey & Hawkes VAB 78 high voice, VAB 78L low voice, $13.50 each.

2771   Villa-Lobos, Heitor, 1887–1959

[Bachianas Brasilieras, no. 5. Aria; arr.] *Bachianas Brasilieras no. 5: Aria (cantilena);* arranged by the composer for voice and guitar, ed. by Andrés Segovia. No text; sung on vowel. Associated Music HL50223640, $3.95.

2772   Vivaldi, Antonio, 1678–1741

[Arias. Vocal scores. Selections] *Four arias for high voice.* Italian and English. International Music 1203, $6.50.

2773 *   Wagner, Richard, 1813–1883

Wesendonk-Lieder. Dover 0-486-27070-X, German, $7.95; Peters P3445a high voice, P3445b low voice, German and English, $14.65 each.

2774   Webern, Anton, 1883–1945

[Lieder, clarinet, guitar acc., op. 18] *Three Lieder for voice, clarinet, and guitar, op. 18.* German. Score. Universal UE8684, $9.95.

2775   Webern, Anton, 1883–1945

[Lieder, op. 12] *Vier Lieder, op. 12.* German and English. Universal UE8257, $11.95.

2776   Webern, Anton, 1883–1945

[Lieder, op. 25] *Drei Lieder, op. 25.* German and English. Universal UE12418, $10.95.

2777   Weill, Kurt, 1900–1950

[Songs. Selections] *The unknown Kurt Weill: a collection of 14 songs.* German, English, and French. European American Music EA 493, $19.95.

2778   Wolf, Hugo, 1860–1903

[Mörike-Lieder] *The complete Mörike songs.* German. Dover 0-486-24380-X, $11.95.

2779   Wolf, Hugo, 1860–1903

[Songs. Selections] *Forty-five songs on poems of Goethe and Eichendorff.* German. Dover 0-486-28857-9, $12.95.

2780 *   Wolf, Hugo, 1860–1903

[Songs. Selections] *Sixty-five songs,* ed. by Sergius Kagen. German and English. International Music 1067 high voice, 1968 low voice, $20 each.

2781   Wolf, Hugo, 1860–1903

[Songs. Selections] *Spanish and Italian songbooks.* German. Dover 0-486-26156-5, $12.95.

Classical Song: Anthologies

These anthologies represent major national schools of song from the sixteenth century to the present.

2782   *All time favorite art songs from the modern repertoire.* Original languages and English. G. Schirmer HL50337000, $6.95.

2783   *American art songs of the turn of the century,* ed. by Paul Sperry. Dover 0-486-26749-0, $13.95.

2784 *   *Anthology of art songs by Black American composers,* compiled by Willis C. Patterson. E. B. Marks Music HL00008242, $16.95.

2785 *   *Anthology of French song: a collection of 39 songs,* ed. by Max Spicker. French and English. G. Schirmer HL50326040 high voice, HL50326050 low voice, $15.95 each.

2786 *   *Anthology of Italian song of the seventeenth and eighteenth centuries,* selected and ed. by Alessandro Parisotti. Italian and English. G. Schirmer HL50254010, HL50254020, 2 v., $9.95 each.

2787 *Anthology of songs.* Women composers series, no. 22. Chiefly French. Da Capo 0-306-76287-0, $32.

2788 * *Classical Spanish songs,* ed. by Fernando Obradors. Spanish and English. International Music 1748, $7.

2789 *A collection of art songs by women composers,* selected and ed. by Ruth Drucker and Helen Strine. Original languages. HERS Pub. Co. (available from Ruth Drucker, 1 Glencliffe Circle, Baltimore MD 21208), $12.95.

2790 *Contemporary American songs for high voice and piano,* ed. by John Belisle. American artsong anthology, v. 1. Galaxy Music, $12.95.

2791 *Contemporary art songs: 28 songs by American and British composers.* G. Schirmer HL50331880, $16.95.

2792 *Contemporary songs in English: 16 songs by American and English composers for recital, concert and studio use,* ed. by Bernard Taylor. C. Fischer 03819 medium-high voice, 03820 medium-low voice, $10.95 each.

2793 ** *Favorite French art songs.* With a companion cassette of recorded piano accompaniment (Gary Arvin, pianist) and French pronunciation lessons. Hal Leonard HL00312035 high voice, HL00312036 low voice, $14.95 each.

2794 ** *Favorite German art songs.* With a companion cassette of recorded piano accompaniment (Gary Arvin, pianist) and German pronunciation lessons. Hal Leonard HL00312033 high voice, HL00312034 low voice, $14.95 each.

2795 ** *Fifteen American art songs,* compiled by Gary Arvin. With a companion cassette of recorded piano accompaniment (Catherine Bringerud, pianist). G. Schirmer HL50482085 high voice, HL50482086 low voice, $14.95 each.

2796 * *Fifty art songs from the modern repertoire.* Original languages and English. G. Schirmer HL50327540, $19.95.

2797 *Fifty German songs* [including Schubert, Schumann, Franz, Brahms, Wolf, Mahler, and Strauss], ed. by Graham Bastable. German and English. International Music 3360 high voice, 3361 low voice, $22 each.

2798 *Fifty selected songs by Schubert, Schumann, Brahms, Wolf, and Strauss.* German and English. G. Schirmer HL50261420 high voice, HL50261430 low voice, $12.95 each.

2799 *First book of soprano solos; First book of mezzo-soprano/alto solos; First book of tenor solos; First book of baritone/bass solos:* 2 v. of each. Compiled by Joan Frey Boytim. Original languages and English. G. Schirmer HL50481173-50481176 (*First book . . . ,* vol. 1), HL50482064-50482067 (*First book . . . ,* vol. 2), $10.95 each. Piano accompaniment on cassette tape, Laura Ward, pianist. Hal Leonard HL00747080-00747083 (*First book . . . ,* vol. 1), HL00747084-00747087 (*First book . . . ,* vol. 2), $9.95 each cassette.

2800 * *Forty French songs,* ed. by Sergius Kagen. French and English. International Music, 2 v. for each voice: International 1121-1122 high voice; International 1123-1124 medium voice; International 1125-1126 low voice, $14.50 each volume.

2801 *Forty songs from Elizabethan and Jacobean songbooks,* ed. by Edmund Fellows. Stainer & Bell, 4 v. for each voice: Stainer 4003-4006 high voice; Stainer 3999-4002 low voice, $10.95 each volume (v.1–2 in high voice and v.1 in low voice OP).

2802 *Frauen Komponieren = Female composers: 25 songs for voice and piano,* ed. by Eva Rieger and Käte Walter. German. Schott ED7810, $29.95.

2803 *French art songs of the nineteenth century,* ed. by Philip Hale. French and English. Dover 0-486-23680-3, $9.95.

2804 *Great art songs of three centuries,* compiled by Bernard Taylor. Original languages and English. G. Schirmer HL50329610 high voice, HL50329620 low voice, $19.95 each.

2805 * *A heritage of twentieth-century British song.* Boosey and Hawkes VAB 91A-B, VAB 92A-B, 4 v., $15 each.

2806 * *Italian songs of the 17th and 18th centuries,* realized and ed. by Luigi Dallapiccola. Italian and English. International Music, 2 v. for each voice: International 2231 and 2234 high voice, International 2232 and 2235 medium voice, International 2233 and 2236 low voice, $8 each volume.

2807 *The library of vocal classics,* compiled by Amy Appleby and Peter Pickow. Original languages and English. Amsco AM 91735 medium voice, $17.95.

2808 *Lieder by women composers of the classic era*, v. 1, ed. by Barbara Garvey Jackson. German and English. ClarNan Editions CN7, $17.95.

2809 *Songs by 22 Americans*, ed. by Bernard Taylor. G. Schirmer HL50329400 high voice, HL50329410 low voice, $16.95 each.

2810 *Songs of an innocent age*, ed. by Paul Sperry. G. Schirmer HL50336790, $8.95.

2811 *Songs through the centuries: 41 vocal repertoire pieces from the 17th through the 20th centuries*, compiled and ed. by Bernard Taylor. Original languages and English. C. Fischer ATF110 high voice, ATF111 low voice, $14.95 each.

2812 *Twelve folk song arrangements for voice and guitar* by Benjamin Britten, Matyas Seiber, and Aaron Copland; ed. by Gregg Nestor. Boosey & Hawkes VAB 222, $25.

2813 *Twentieth-century art songs, for medium voice and piano: a collection of contemporary songs for recital and study.* English. G. Schirmer HL50331200, $18.95.

2814 ** *Twenty-six Italian songs and arias: an authoritative edition based on authentic sources.* With accompaniment on compact disc or cassette, ed. by John Glenn Paton. Italian and English. Alfred Music 3402 medium-high voice, 4861 CD, 4863 cassette; Alfred Music 3403 medium-low voice, 4862 CD, 4864 cassette; $8.95 each score, $10.95 each compact disc, $8.95 each cassette.

Opera Aria Anthologies

2815 *American arias for soprano: a diverse selection of arias from operas by American composers.* G. Schirmer HL50481197, $12.95.

2816 ** *G. Schirmer opera anthology: with historical notes and translations for study*, compiled and ed. by Robert L. Larsen. Original languages and English. G. Schirmer, 5 v., HL50481097 *Arias for soprano*, HL50481098 *Arias for mezzo-soprano*, HL50481099 *Arias for tenor*, HL50481100 *Arias for baritone*, HL50481101 *Arias for bass*, $16.95 each.

2817 *Italian tenor arias.* With a companion cassette of recorded accompaniment (Laura Ward, pianist). Italian and English. Hal Leonard HL00747045, $15.95.

2818 *Opera American style: arias for soprano*, compiled by Richard Walters. Hal Leonard HL00660180, $9.95.

2819 * *Operatic anthology: celebrated arias selected from operas by old and modern composers*, ed. by Kurt Adler. Original languages and English. G. Schirmer, 5 v., HL50325830 soprano, HL50325840 mezzo-soprano, HL50325850 tenor, HL50325860 baritone, HL50325870 bass, $19.95 each.

2820 * *The prima donna's album: 42 celebrated arias from famous operas* [for soprano], newly rev. and ed. by Kurt Adler. Original languages and English. G. Schirmer HL50325550, $17.95.

Anthologies of Sacred Songs and Arias from Oratorios

2821 * *Anthology of sacred song: celebrated arias selected from oratorios by old and modern composers*, ed. by Max Spicker. English. G. Schirmer, 4 v., HL50325780 soprano, HL50325790 alto, HL50325800 tenor, HL50325810 bass, $15.95 each.

2822 *Arias from oratorios by women composers of the eighteenth century*, ed. by Barbara Garvey Jackson [some with obbligato parts]. Italian. ClarNan Editions CN6, CN13-15, 4 v., $28, $30, $28, $30.

2823 *Contemporary American sacred songs.* G. Schirmer HL50502070, $5.95.

2824 *Fifty-two sacred songs you like to sing.* English. G. Schirmer HL50327490, $12.95.

2825 [World Charts presents] *The Jewish songbook* [includes *Hava Nagila* and *Kol-Nidre*]. Original languages only: Hebrew, English, or Yiddish. Hansen House D390, $8.95.

2826 *Lift up your voice, for medium voice and organ or piano: sacred songs from the seventeenth to the twentieth centuries*, compiled, ed. and adapted by M. B. Stearns. English. Coburn Press 491-00002, $10.

2827 ** *The oratorio anthology*, compiled and ed. by Richard Walters. Original languages and English. Hal Leonard, 4 v., HL00747058 soprano, HL00747059 alto/mezzo-soprano, HL00747060 tenor, HL00747061 baritone/bass, $18.95 each.

2828 ** *Sacred classics* [with cassette tape of both voice with piano and piano accompaniment without voice]. English. Hal Leonard HL00747013 high voice, HL00747014 low voice, $14.95 each.

2829 * *Sacred hour of song: a collection of sacred solos,* compiled, ed. and arranged by Mack Harrell. English. C. Fischer 02933 high voice, 02893 medium voice, $10.95 each.

2830 * *Sing unto the Lord: 20 sacred solos for medium voice and piano or organ,* compiled, ed. and arranged by Katherine Davis and Nancy Loring. English. C. Fischer 03534-03535, 2 v., $9.95 each.

2831 *Twelve sacred songs, including The Lord's prayer: with companion tape of recorded accompaniments.* English. G. Schirmer HL50482062 high voice, 50482063 low voice, $12.95 each.

Spirituals

2832 ** *The book of American Negro spirituals, and The second book of Negro spirituals,* ed. by James Weldon Johnson. Da Capo Press 0-306-80074-8, $14.95.

2833 *Spirituals for church and concert,* arranged by Phillip McIntyre. Fitzsimmons F0114 medium voice, $7.95.

2834 *Spirituals for solo singers: 11 spirituals for recitals, concerts and contests,* compiled and ed. by Jay Althouse. Alfred Music 11696 medium-high voice (book only) or 11697 (book and cassette), 11698 medium-low voice (book only) or 11699 (book and cassette), $7.95 book only, $16.90 book and cassette.

2835 * *Spirituals of Harry T. Burleigh.* CCP/Belwin EL3151 high voice, EL3150 low voice, $20 each.

2836 * *Thirty spirituals,* arranged by Hall Johnson. G. Schirmer HL50328310, $9.95.

Wedding Music

2837 * *Music for the Christian wedding* [vocal and instrumental selections, including Mendelssohn's *Wedding march* and Wagner's *Bridal chorus*]. Lillenas, 1968, $7.95.

2838 *The new complete book of wedding music: original sheet music editions in three categories: standard wedding songs, classical wedding songs, popular wedding songs.* Hansen House D304, piano/vocal, $12.95.

2839 *Wedding bouquet: 17 celebrated wedding songs,* collected and ed. by Bernard Taylor. Original languages and English. G. Schirmer HL50329280 high voice, HL50329290 low voice, $12.95 each.

2840 ** *Wedding classics* [with cassette tape of both voice with piano and piano accompaniment without voice]. Hal Leonard HL00747015 high voice, HL00747016 low voice, $16.95 each.

2841 * *A wedding garland: 32 songs of love and devotion from the classic and modern repertories,* compiled by Barry O'Neal. Original languages and English. G. Schirmer HL50333800, $9.95.

2842 *World's greatest book of wedding songs: the Royal Wedding special edition.* Hansen House D203, piano and vocal, $12.95.

Christmas Anthologies

2843 *American folk songs for Christmas.* Selected and ed. by Ruth Crawford Seeger. Oak Publications 0-685-65831-7, $12.95.

2844 ** *Classical carols: concert arrangements* by Richard Walters [with compact disc of both voice with piano and piano accompaniment without voice]. Hal Leonard HL00747024 high voice, HL00747025 low voice, $18.95 each.

2845 ** *The classical singer's Christmas album* [with cassette tape of both voice with piano and piano accompaniment without voice]. Hal Leonard HL00747022 high voice, HL00747021 low voice, $16.95 each.

2846 * *Favorite Christmas carols,* selected and arranged by Charles J. F. Cofone. Dover 0-486-20445-6, $14.95.

2847 *Sing solo Christmas.* Oxford University Press 0-19-345781-4 high voice, 0-19-345783-0 low voice, $14.95 each.

2848 *Songs of Christmas: 47 favourite songs,* arranged by Margery Hargest Jones. Boosey & Hawkes VAB 309, $19.95.

2849 *What child is this?: a Christmas songbook for medium voice and piano.* G. Schirmer HL50333580, $7.95.

Early Vocal Music

2850 *Chanter m'estuet: songs of the trouveres,* ed. by Samuel N. Rosenberg; music ed. by Hans Tischler. Indiana University Press 0-253-14942-8, $34.95.

2851 *English lute songs,* compiled by Michael Pilkington. Stainer & Bell 0-852496-16-8, 0-852496-17-6, 2 v., $16.95 each.

2852 *A medieval songbook: troubadour & trouvere,* ed. by Fletcher Collins Jr. University Press of Virginia, $14.95.

2853 *The monophonic songs in the Roman de Fauvel,* ed. by Samuel N. Rosenberg and Hans Tischler. University of Nebraska Press 0-8032-3898-3, $50.

2854 *Spanish Renaissance songs for voice and guitar, originally for voice and vihuela,* arranged and ed. by Daniel Benkő. Editio Musica Budapest Z.12235, $12.

2855 *Troubadours, trouveres, Minne- and Meistersinger,* compiled by Friedrich Gennrich. Anthology of music, v. 2. Arno Volk Verlag/Laaber, $23.

Folk Songs

2856 *American folk songs for children,* selected and ed. by Ruth Crawford Seeger. Zephyr/Doubleday 0-385-15788-6, $6.95.

2857 ** *American songbag,* selected and ed. by Carl Sandburg. Harvest Books/Harcourt Brace 0-15-605650-X, $16.95.

2858 * *Children sing around the world,* ed. by Jerry Silverman. Original languages and English. Mel Bay MB 94603, $7.95.

2859 *Collected reprints from "Sing Out!"* [the folk song magazine]. v.1–6 in 1 volume; v.7–12 in 1 volume, 1964–1973, ed. by *Sing Out!* magazine staff. Sing Out Corp. 0-9626704-0-5, 1-881322-00-9, $17.50 each.

2860 *Folk songs for schools and camps,* ed. by Jerry Silverman. Mel Bay MB 94558, $9.95.

2861 * *Folk songs of North America,* compiled by Alan Lomax. Dolphin Books/Doubleday 0-385-03772-4, OP.

2862 *Immigrant songbook,* ed. by Jerry Silverman. Original languages and English. Mel Bay MB 94630, $29.95.

2863 * *One hundred English folksongs,* ed. by Cecil J. Sharp. Dover 0-486-23192-5, $11.95.

2864 *Popular Irish songs,* ed. by Florence Leniston. Dover 0-486-26755-5, $9.95.

2865 *A Russian song book: Russian texts in Cyrillic and Latin-alphabet transliteration,* ed. by Rose N. Rubin and Michael Stillman. Russian and English. Dover 0-486-26118-2, $8.95.

2866 *Seventy Scottish songs,* ed. by Helen Hopekirk. Dover 0-486-27029-7, $10.95.

2867 *Songs of England: 106 favourite English songs,* ed. by Jerry Silverman. Mel Bay MB 94408, $12.95.

2868 *Songs of Ireland: 105 favourite Irish and Irish-American songs,* ed. by Jerry Silverman. Mel Bay MB 94395, $12.95.

2869 *Songs of Scotland: 86 favourite Scottish songs and ballads,* ed. by Jerry Silverman. Mel Bay MB 94391, $12.95.

Popular Song

The following are popular song collections, featuring either performers with an enduring influence on American popular music or songs that were significant or enormously popular at the time of their release.

2870 * Baez, Joan

The Joan Baez songbook. Amsco AM 10455, $19.95.

2871 ** Beatles

Complete Beatles. Hal Leonard HL00308170, $59.90.

2872 ** Beatles

Sgt. Pepper's Lonely Hearts Club Band. Hal Leonard HL00358168, $12.95.

2873 ** Beatles

Yellow submarine & The white album. Hal Leonard HL00356236, $17.95.

2874 * Cole, Nat King, 1917–1965

Nat King Cole: Unforgettable. CPP/Belwin TPF0150, $13.95.

2875 * Collins, Judy, 1939–

Judy Collins anthology . . . Trust your heart. Amsco AM 71200, $24.95.

2876 ** *The definitive jazz collection: 88 songs, piano, vocal, guitar.* Hal Leonard HL00359571, $24.95.

2877 Denver, John, 1942–

John Denver songbook. Cherry Lane, $14.95.

2878 * Doors (Musical group)

The Doors complete. CPP/Belwin, $18.95.

2879 Dylan, Bob, 1941–

The Bob Dylan collection. Amsco AM 80003, $15.95.

2880 ** Dylan, Bob, 1941–
The songs of Bob Dylan. Cherry Lane, $29.95.

2881 ** Ellington, Duke, 1899–1974
The great music of Duke Ellington. CPP/Belwin, $16.95.

2882 Garland, Judy, 1922–1969
The Judy Garland souvenir songbook. Hal Leonard HL00312157, $17.95.

2883 ** Grateful Dead (Musical group)
The Grateful Dead anthology. Warner Bros. VF0624, $22.95.

2884 ** Joel, Billy, 1949–
Billy Joel complete. Rev. ed. Hal Leonard HL00356297-298, 2 v., $27.95 each.

2885 John, Elton, 1947–
Elton John anthology. Rev. ed. Hal Leonard HL00357104, $18.95.

2886 * Joplin, Janis, 1943–1970
Janis. Hal Leonard HL00312220, $12.95.

2887 Led Zeppelin (Musical group)
Led Zeppelin. Warner Bros. GF0466, 2 v. in boxed set, $75.

2888 ** Lennon, John, 1940–1980
John Lennon: the solo years. Hal Leonard HL00307290, $17.95.

2889 * Mitchell, Joni, 1943–
Joni Mitchell anthology. Warner Bros. VF1052, $16.95.

2890 ** *Motown complete.* CPP/Belwin, 3 v., $18.95 each.

2891 * *New York Times great songs of the sixties,* ed. by Milt Okun. Cherry Lane, $19.95.

2892 *Peg o' my heart, and other favorite songs,* ed. by Stanley Appelbaum. Dover 0-486-25998-6, $12.95.

2893 * Peter, Paul and Mary (Musical group)
Peter, Paul & Mary deluxe anthology. Warner Bros. VF1483, $18.95.

2894 Pink Floyd (Musical quartet)
The wall. Amsco AM 64205, $19.95.

2895 ** Presley, Elvis, 1935–1977
Elvis Presley anthology. Hal Leonard HL00308198-199, 2 v., $24.95 each.

2896 * Prince, 1960–
Purple rain. Warner Bros. VF1179, $16.95.

2897 ** Rolling Stones
Rolling Stones singles collection. CPP/Belwin, $35.

2898 ** Simon and Garfunkel
Bridge over troubled water. Music Sales, $12.95.

2899 Simon and Garfunkel
Simon & Garfunkel: the concert in the park. Music Sales, $19.95.

2900 * Simon, Paul, 1941–
Graceland. Music Sales, $12.95.

2901 ** Sinatra, Frank, 1915–
Frank Sinatra songbook. Warner Bros. VF1495, $29.95.

2902 * Who (Musical group)
The Who anthology. Hal Leonard HL00358565, $19.95.

2903 * Williams, Hank, 1923–1953
Complete works: a 128-song legacy of his greatest hits. CPP/Belwin, $18.95.

Choral Music

Choral Music in Vocal Score

This section includes sacred and secular works, works originally for choir and keyboard, works originally for choir and orchestra in vocal score (with keyboard reduction), and works for unaccompanied voices. Cantatas for solo voice are listed in "Solo Song," above.

When ordering choral works in vocal score, one must distinguish between editions in vocal score and those in full orchestral score. Specify "vocal score" when placing orders.

Designation of the language of a work, usually found in the uniform title, is indicated after the title proper or after the publisher's name in order to accommodate different editions with different languages within a single entry. The language designations always refer to sung words (i.e., text set to the music), not to translations provided separately from the music.

2904 Bach, Johann Sebastian, 1685–1750

[Chorales. Selections] *Chorales, book I: chorales 1–91*, ed. by Charles N. Boyd and Albert Riemenschneider. German and English. G. Schirmer ED1628, $20.

2905 * Bach, Johann Sebastian, 1685–1750

[Christ lag in Todesbanden (Cantata). Vocal score] *Cantata no. 4, Christ lag in Todesbanden.* German and English. Bärenreiter BA10004a, $11; Breitkopf & Härtel EB7004, $6.25; Hänssler/Carus HE 314/03, $7.50; G. Schirmer HL50324490, $5.25.

2906 * Bach, Johann Sebastian, 1685–1750

[Feste Burg ist unser Gott (Cantata). Vocal score] *Cantata no. 80, Ein feste Burg ist unser Gott.* German and English. Bärenreiter BA10080a, $9.50; Breitkopf & Härtel EB7080, $4.75; Hänssler/Carus HE 31.080/03, $11.60.

2907 Bach, Johann Sebastian, 1685–1750

[Gottes Zeit ist die allerbeste Zeit. Vocal score] *Cantata no. 106, Gottes Zeit ist die allerbeste Zeit.* Bärenreiter BA10106a, German, $7; Breitkopf & Härtel EB7106, German and English, $8; Hänssler/Carus HE 31.106/03, German and English, $7.

2908 * Bach, Johann Sebastian, 1685–1750

[Jesu, meine Freude (Motet)] *Jesu, meine Freude, motet, BWV 227.* Bärenreiter BA5132, German, $7; Peters P6103, German and English, $5.65; G. Schirmer HL50500030, English, $5.95.

2909 * Bach, Johann Sebastian, 1685–1750

[Johannespassion. Vocal score] *Johannespassion = St. John Passion, BWV 245.* German and English. Bärenreiter BA5037a, $20.

2910 * Bach, Johann Sebastian, 1685–1750

[Magnificat, BWV 243, D major. Vocal score] *Magnificat in D major, BWV 243.* Latin. Bärenreiter BA5103a, $10.75; Peters P40, $7.15; G. Schirmer HL50324530, $5.95.

2911 ** Bach, Johann Sebastian, 1685–1750

[Masses, BWV 232, B minor. Vocal score] *Mass in B minor, BWV 232.* Latin. Bärenreiter BA5102a, $18.50; Kalmus K 06004, $10.50; Peters P37, $17.40; G. Schirmer HL50323910, $10.95.

2912 ** Bach, Johann Sebastian, 1685–1750

[Matthäuspassion. Vocal score] *Matthäuspassion = St. Matthew Passion, BWV 244.* German and En-glish. Bärenreiter BA5038a, $22.50; G. Schirmer ED2358, English translation by Robert Shaw, $12.95.

2913 * Bach, Johann Sebastian, 1685–1750

[Oster-Oratorium. Vocal score] *Oster-Oratorium = Easter oratorio, BWV 249.* German and English. Breitkopf & Härtel EB5750, $18.

2914 * Bach, Johann Sebastian, 1685–1750

[Wachet auf, ruft uns die Stimme (Cantata). Vocal score] *Cantata no. 140, Wachet auf, ruft uns die Stimme.* German and English. Bärenreiter BA10140a, $10.50; Breitkopf & Härtel EB7140, $7.50; G. Schirmer HL50324550, $4.95.

2915 * Bach, Johann Sebastian, 1685–1750

[Weihnachts Oratorium. Vocal score] *Weihnachts Oratorium = Christmas oratorio, BWV 248.* German and English. Bärenreiter BA5014a, $20; Breitkopf & Härtel EB13, $16.

2916 Bartók, Béla, 1881–1945

[Kilenc csodaszarvas. Vocal score] *Cantata profana.* Hungarian and English. Boosey & Hawkes LCB 239, $25.

2917 ** Beethoven, Ludwig van, 1770–1827

[Missa solemnis. Vocal score] *Missa solemnis in D major, op. 123.* Latin. Breitkopf & Härtel EB29, $15; Peters P45, $17.75; G. Schirmer ED602, $14.95.

2918 Berlioz, Hector, 1803–1869

[Damnation de Faust. Vocal score] *La damnation de Faust.* Bärenreiter BA5448a, French, $35; Kalmus K 06096, French and English, $30.

2919 * Berlioz, Hector, 1803–1869

[Enfance du Christ. Vocal score] *L'enfance du Christ = The childhood of Christ, op. 25.* Kalmus K 06091, French, German, and Italian, $10.95; G. Schirmer ED12, English, $7.95.

2920 * Berlioz, Hector, 1803–1869

[Grande messe des morts. Vocal score] *Requiem (Grande messe des morts), op. 5.* Latin. Bärenreiter BA5449a, $22; Kalmus K 06092, $7.50; G. Schirmer ED1, $7.95.

2921 Berlioz, Hector, 1803–1869

[Roméo et Juliette. Vocal score] *Romeo and Juliet.* Kalmus K 06090, French, German, and Italian, $19.

2922   Berlioz, Hector, 1803–1869

[Te Deum. Vocal score] *Te Deum, op. 22.* Latin. Bärenreiter BA5782a, $13; G. Schirmer ED2038, $18.95.

2923   Bernstein, Leonard, 1918–1990

[Chichester Psalms. Vocal score] *Chichester Psalms.* Hebrew. Boosey & Hawkes LCB214, $7.50.

2924   Bernstein, Leonard, 1918–1990

[Mass. Vocal score] *Mass: a theatre piece for singers, players and dancers.* Latin alternating with English. Boosey & Hawkes VSB 152, $87.

2925   Bloch, Ernest, 1880–1959

['Avodat ha-kodesh. Vocal score] *Avodat hakodesh = Sacred service.* Hebrew and English. Broude Bros. BB4077a, $15.

2926 **   Brahms, Johannes, 1833–1897

[Deutsches Requiem. Vocal score] *Ein deutsches Requiem = A German requiem, op. 45.* Kalmus K 06110, German, $6; Peters P3672, German, $10.10; G. Schirmer ED472, English, $6.25.

2927 *   Brahms, Johannes, 1833–1897

[Liebeslieder] *Liebeslieder waltzes, op. 52, for SATB voices and piano, 4 hands.* Lawson-Gould 834, German and English, $7.50; Peters P10514 (with Brahms's *Neue Liebeslieder, op. 65*), German, $20.90; Simrock 491-00230, German and English, $16.50.

2928 *   Brahms, Johannes, 1833–1897

[Neue Liebeslieder] *Neue Liebeslieder waltzes, op. 65, for SATB voices and piano, 4 hands.* Lawson-Gould 51136, German and English, $6.95; Simrock 491-00245, German and English, $14.75. *See also* 2927

2929   Brahms, Johannes, 1833–1897

[Rhapsodies, alto, men's voices, orchestra, op. 53. Vocal score] *Alto rhapsody, op. 53.* German. Peters P3916, $7.15.

2930   Brahms, Johannes, 1833–1897

[Schicksalslied. Vocal score] *Schicksalslied = Song of destiny, op. 54.* Kalmus K 06112, German and English, $3.50; Peters P3917, German, $7.15.

2931 *   Britten, Benjamin, 1913–1976

[Ceremony of carols. Vocal score] *A ceremony of carols, for voices and harp or piano, op. 28.* English. Boosey & Hawkes LCB 11, SSA version, $6.95; Boosey & Hawkes LCB 32, SATB version, $6.95.

2932   Britten, Benjamin, 1913–1976

[Rejoice in the Lamb. Vocal score] *Rejoice in the Lamb: festival cantata, op. 30.* English. Boosey & Hawkes LCB 147, SSAA version, $16.50.

2933 *   Britten, Benjamin, 1913–1976

[War requiem. Vocal score] *War requiem, op. 66.* Latin alternating with English. Boosey & Hawkes LCB 84VS, $72.

2934 *   Bruckner, Anton, 1824–1896

[Masses, no. 2, E minor. Vocal score] *Mass no. 2 in E minor.* Latin. Broude Bros. BB53, $5.50; Peters P8168, $7.15.

2935 *   Bruckner, Anton, 1824–1896

[Te Deum. Vocal score] *Te Deum, op. 22.* Latin. Kalmus K 06126, $5.95; G. Schirmer ED330, $4.95; Universal UE429, $15.

2936   Byrd, William, 1542 or 3–1623

[Masses, voices (3)] *Mass for three voices.* Latin. Eulenburg 998, $8.50.

2937 *   Byrd, William, 1542 or 3–1623

[Masses, voices (4)] *Mass for four voices.* Latin. Eulenburg 6456, $10; Stainer & Bell CS359, ed. by Philip Brett, $5.95.

2938 *   Byrd, William, 1542 or 3–1623

[Masses, voices (5)] *Mass for five voices.* Latin. Eulenburg 999, $9.50; Stainer & Bell CS373, ed. by Philip Brett, $6.

2939   Carissimi, Giacomo, 1605–1674

[Jephte] *Jephta.* Novello, Latin, $7.95; Ricordi 1313729, Latin and English, $19.95.

2940   Charpentier, Marc Antoine, 1634–1704

[Messe de minuit. Vocal score] *Messe de minuit pour Noël.* Latin. Concordia 97-5196, ed. by H. Wiley Hitchcock, $13.50.

2941   Cherubini, Luigi, 1760–1842

[Requiem, no. 1, C minor. Vocal score] *Requiem in C minor.* Latin and English. Kalmus K 06141, $7.95; G. Schirmer ED537, $8.95.

2942   Dufay, Guillaume, d. 1474

Missa "L'homme arme." Latin. Editio Musica Budapest Z.6437, $16.50.

2943 Duruflé, Maurice, 1902–1986

[Requiem. Vocal score] *Requiem.* Latin. Durand 512-00033, $34.25.

2944 * Elgar, Edward, 1857–1934

[Dream of Gerontius. Vocal score] *Dream of Gerontius.* English. Kalmus K 09406, $13.95; Novello 109233, $19.95.

2945 ** Fauré, Gabriel, 1845–1924

[Requiem, op. 48, D minor. Vocal score] *Requiem, op. 48.* Fitzsimmons F8001, Latin and English, $6.50; Hinshaw HMB-147, ed. by John Rutter, Latin and English, $6.50; Novello 110533, Latin, $7.95; G. Schirmer ED2243, Latin, $5.25.

2946 Guillaume, de Machaut, d. 1377

[Messe de Nostre Dame] *Notre Dame mass,* ed. by Daniel Leech-Wilkinson. Latin. Oxford University Press 0-19-337397-1, $17.95.

2947 Handel, George Frideric, 1685–1759

[Acis and Galatea. Vocal score] *Acis and Galatea.* Kalmus K 06208, English and French, $11; Peters P3633, English and German, $27.60.

2948 * Handel, George Frideric, 1685–1759

[Israel in Egypt. Vocal score] *Israel in Egypt.* English. Kalmus K 06205, $15; G. Schirmer ED479, $8.95.

2949 Handel, George Frideric, 1685–1759

[Judas Maccabaeus. Vocal score] *Judas Maccabaeus.* English. Kalmus K 06206, $19.95.

2950 ** Handel, George Frideric, 1685–1759

[Messiah. Vocal score] *Messiah.* English. Bärenreiter BA4012b, $22.50; Novello 07-0137, 1992 revision, ed. by Watkins Shaw, $6.95; G. Schirmer ED38, $6.95.

2951 Haydn, Joseph, 1732–1809

[Jahreszeiten. Vocal score] *Die Jahreszeiten = The seasons.* Breitkopf & Härtel EB116, German, English, and French, $18; Kalmus K 06237, German, English, and French, $16.95; Peters P67, German and English, $21.75.

2952 Haydn, Joseph, 1732–1809

[Masses, H. XXII, 9, C major. Vocal score] *Mass in C major (Mass in time of war, Missa in tempore belli, Paukenmesse).* Latin. Bärenreiter BA4652a, $25; Kalmus K 06245, $5.25; G. Schirmer ED2600, $6.25.

2953 * Haydn, Joseph, 1732–1809

[Masses, H. XXII, 11, D minor. Vocal score] *Mass in D minor (Missa solemnis, Nelson mass).* Latin. Bärenreiter BA4660a, $20; Peters P4351, $10.10; G. Schirmer ED409, $6.95; Schott ST10808, $14.95.

2954 * Haydn, Joseph, 1732–1809

[Schöpfung. Vocal score] *Die Schöpfung = The creation.* Breitkopf & Härtel EB118, German, English, and French, $15.50; Oxford University Press 0-19-335471-3, ed. by A. Peter Brown, German and English, $24.95; Peters P66, German and English, $15.70; G. Schirmer ED190, English, $8.95.

2955 Hildegard of Bingen, Saint, 1098–1179

[Symphonia armonie celestium revelationum. Selections] *Sequences and hymns.* Latin. Antico MCM1, $22.

2956 Honegger, Arthur, 1892–1955

[Jeanne d'Arc au bûcher. Vocal score] *Jeanne d'Arc au bûcher.* French, English, and German. Salabert HL50405490, $55.

2957 Honegger, Arthur, 1892–1955

[Roi David. Vocal score] *Le roi David = King David.* English. E. C. Schirmer, $29.95.

2958 Janáček, Leoš, 1854–1928

[Mša glagolskaja. Vocal score] *Glagolitic mass (Slavonic mass).* Universal UE9544, Slavonic and German, $39; Universal UE9544, Latin and English, $39.

2959 * Josquin, des Prez, d. 1521

[Missa Pange lingua] *Missa Pange lingua.* Latin. Kalmus K 06148 (reprint of Moeseler ed. without critical commentary), $4.95; Moeseler (Das Chorwerk, 1), $15.

2960 Kodály, Zoltán, 1882–1967

[Psalmus hungaricus. Vocal score] *Psalmus hungaricus, op. 13.* German and English. Universal UE84636, $11.95.

2961 * Mendelssohn-Bartholdy, Felix, 1809–1847

[Elias. Vocal score] *Elijah, op. 70.* Kalmus K 06300, German and English, $8.95; Novello 07-0201, ed. by Michael Pilkington, German and English, $11.95; G. Schirmer ED43, English, $8.95.

2962 * Monteverdi, Claudio, 1567–1643

[Madrigals. Selections] *Ten madrigals,* ed. by Denis Stevens. Italian. Oxford University Press 0-19-343676-0, $22.95.

2963 * Monteverdi, Claudio, 1567–1643

[Vespro della Beata Vergine. Vocal score] *Vespro della Beata Vergine (Vespers)*. Latin. Universal UE16648, $25.

2964 * Mozart, Wolfgang Amadeus, 1756–1791

[Masses, K. 317, C major. Vocal score] *Mass in C major, K. 317, "Coronation mass."* Latin. Bärenreiter BA4880a, $10.50; Breitkopf & Härtel EB8453, rev. ed. by Franz Beyer, $12.

2965 * Mozart, Wolfgang Amadeus, 1756–1791

[Masses, K. 427, C minor. Vocal score] *Mass in C minor, K. 427, "The great mass."* Latin. Bärenreiter BA4846a, $19; Peters P4856, ed. by H. C. Robbins Landon, $18.

2966 * Mozart, Wolfgang Amadeus, 1756–1791

[Requiem, K. 626, D minor (Maunder). Vocal score] *Requiem, K. 626,* ed. by Richard Maunder. Latin. Oxford University Press 0-19-337617-2, $9.95. [Excises Franz Xaver Süssmayr's contributions except for *Sanctus* and *Benedictus,* which appear in an appendix.]

2967 ** Mozart, Wolfgang Amadeus, 1756–1791

[Requiem, K. 626, D minor (Süssmayr). Vocal score] *Requiem, K. 626,* completed by Franz Xaver Süssmayr. Latin. Bärenreiter BA4538a, $10; Peters P76, $9.10; G. Schirmer ED1882, $4.95.

2968 * Orff, Carl, 1895–1982

[Carmina burana. Vocal score] *Carmina burana: scenic cantata.* Latin. Schott ED2877, $35.

2969 * Palestrina, Giovanni Pierluigi da, 1525?–1594

[Masses, book 2. Missa Papae Marcelli] *Missa Papae Marcelli.* Latin. Eulenburg 963, $6.50; Norton Critical Scores 0-393-09242-9, pbk., 0-393-02185-8, cloth, OP.

2970 Palestrina, Giovanni Pierluigi da, 1525?–1594

[Vocal music. Selections] *Masses and motets.* Latin. Dover 0-486-27631-7, $11.95.

2971 Pergolesi, Giovanni Battista, 1710–1736

[Stabat Mater. Vocal score] *Stabat Mater.* Latin. Kalmus K 06375, $4; Peters P774, $12.10; G. Schirmer ED498, $3.95.

2972 * Poulenc, Francis, 1899–1963

[Gloria. Vocal score] *Gloria in G major.* Latin. Salabert HL50418140, $19.95.

2973 Purcell, Henry, 1659–1695

[Come, ye sons of art. Vocal score] *Come, ye sons of art.* English. G. Schirmer ED2944, $5.95.

2974 Purcell, Henry, 1659–1695

[Ode for St. Cecilia's Day (1692). Vocal score.] *Ode for St. Cecilia's Day.* English. Novello, $12.95.

2975 Rossini, Gioacchino, 1792–1868

[Petite messe solennelle. Vocal score] *Petite messe solennelle (Missa solenne).* Latin. Kalmus K 06877, $14.50; Oxford University Press 0-19-345593-5, $24.95.

2976 Schoenberg, Arnold, 1874–1951

[Gurre-Lieder. Vocal score] *Gurre-Lieder.* German. Universal UE3696, $80.

2977 * Schubert, Franz, 1797–1828

[Masses, D. 678, A♭ major. Vocal score] *Mass in A♭ major, D. 678.* Latin. Kalmus K 06420, $8.95; Peters P1160, $29.

2978 * Schubert, Franz, 1797–1828

[Masses, D. 950, E♭ major. Vocal score] *Mass in E♭ major, D. 950.* Latin. Breitkopf & Härtel EB1626, $6.50; Kalmus K 06421, $6.50; Peters P1052, $18.70.

2979 * Schütz, Heinrich, 1585–1672

[Historia von der Geburt Jesu Christi. Vocal score] *Historia von der Geburt Jesu Christi = Christmas oratorio.* Bärenreiter BA1709, German, $3.90; Kalmus K 06435, German and English, $7.95; G. Schirmer ED1930, German and English, $6.95.

2980 Schütz, Heinrich, 1585–1672

Musikalische Exequien. German and English. G. Schirmer ED2270, $9.95.

2981 * Stravinsky, Igor, 1882–1971

[Mass. Vocal score] *Mass.* Latin. Boosey & Hawkes LCB 17, $9.

2982 Stravinsky, Igor, 1882–1971

[Noces. Vocal score] *Les noces = The wedding.* Chester JWC 9718, Russian and French, $37.95; Kalmus K 06452, English and German, $25.

2983 * Stravinsky, Igor, 1882–1971

[Symphonie de psaumes. Vocal score] *Symphony of psalms.* Latin. Boosey & Hawkes LCB 13, $6.50.

2984 Tallis, Thomas, 1505 (ca.)–1585

[Lamentations] *The lamentations of Jeremiah.* Latin. Oxford University Press 0-19-353415-0, AATTBB version, $12.95.

2985 Tallis, Thomas, 1505 (ca.)–1585

[Vocal music. Selections] *A Tallis anthology: 17 anthems and motets.* English or Latin. Oxford University Press 0-19-353410-X, $13.95.

2986 Thompson, Randall, 1899–1984

The peaceable kingdom: a sequence of sacred choruses for unaccompanied mixed voices. English. E. C. Schirmer 1730, $8.95.

2987 Tippett, Michael, 1905–

[Child of our time. Vocal score] *A child of our time: oratorio.* English. Schott ST10065, $35.

2988 * Vaughan Williams, Ralph, 1872–1958

[Mass, G minor. Vocal score] *Mass in G minor.* Latin. Curwen ED2044, $7.95.

2989 Vaughan Williams, Ralph, 1872–1958

[O clap your hands. Vocal score] *O clap your hands.* English. Stainer & Bell 222, $1.40.

2990 * Vaughan Williams, Ralph, 1872–1958

[This day. Vocal score] *Hodie = This day: a Christmas cantata.* Latin. Oxford University Press 0-19-339551-7, $18.95.

2991 ** Verdi, Giuseppe, 1813–1901

[Messa da Requiem. Vocal score] *Requiem in memory of Manzoni.* Novello 07-2403, Latin, $15.95; Peters P4251, Latin, $16.70; G. Schirmer ED180, Latin and English, $9.95.

2992 Verdi, Giuseppe, 1813–1901

[Pezzi sacri. Vocal score] *Quattro pezzi sacri = Four sacred pieces.* Latin. Kalmus K 06939, $4.50; Peters P4256a-d, 4 v., $2.05, $3.55, $2.65, $3.55.

2993 ** Vivaldi, Antonio, 1678–1741

[Gloria, RV 589, D major. Vocal score] *Gloria in D major.* Latin and English. Ricordi R131415, $9.95; G. Schirmer ED2922, $6.95.

2994 Walton, William, 1902–1983

[Belshazzar's feast. Vocal score] *Belshazzar's feast.* English and German. Oxford University Press 0-19-338461-2, $12.95.

Christmas Carols

2995 *Carols and songs for Christmastide: a collection of favorite carols, hymns, and songs of many countries and ages for unison singing or mixed voices, accompanied or unaccompanied,* compiled and arranged by John Verrall. Boston Music 11239, $2.50.

2996 *Carols for choirs,* ed. and arranged by Reginald Jacques and David Willcocks. Oxford University Press, 4 v., $11.95, $13.95, $13.95, $14.95.

2997 ** *Christmas carols and songs.* G. Schirmer ED3057, $7.95.

2998 ** *Christmas in song: a treasury of traditional songs, favorite hymns, and choice carols from all ages and from many lands, selected for your singing Christmas,* compiled and arranged for mixed voices (SATB) or unisonal singing by Theodore Preuss. Rubank, $2.50.

2999 *The New Oxford book of carols,* ed. by Hugh Keyte and Andrew Parrott. Oxford University Press 0-19-353323-5, $125.

3000 * *The Oxford book of carols,* collected and ed. by Ralph Vaughan Williams, Percy Dearmer, and Martin Shaw. Oxford University Press 0-19-353315-4, $24.95.

3001 ** *The shorter New Oxford book of carols,* ed. by Hugh Keyte and Andrew Parrott. Oxford University Press 0-19-353324-3, $16.95.

Early Music Anthologies

3002 *The art of the Netherlanders,* compiled by Rene Lenaerts. Anthology of music, v. 22. Arno Volk Verlag/Laaber, $38.

3003 *Canzone villanesche alla napolitana and villotte: Adrian Willaert and his circle,* ed. by Donna G. Cardamone. Recent researches in the music of the Renaissance, v. 30. A-R Editions 0-8957-9108-0, $31.95.

3004 *Canzoni villanesche and villanelle: Orlando di Lasso et al.,* ed. by Donna G. Cardamone. Recent researches in the music of the Renaissance, v. 82–83 (in 1 volume). A-R Editions 0-8957-9245-1, $63.90.

3005 *The combinative chanson: an anthology,* ed. by Maria Rika Maniates. Recent researches in the music of the Renaissance, v. 77. A-R Editions 0-8957-9236-2, $31.95.

3006 *Early Bodleian music: Dufay and his contemporaries,* transcribed by J. F. R. Stainer and C. Stainer. F. A. M. Knuf, OP; Gregg (reprint of Knuf), OP.

3007 *The English school, for 5 voices,* ed. by Anthony G. Petti. Chester book of motets, v. 9. Chester Music, $6.50.

3008 *The English school, for 6 voices,* ed. by Anthony G. Petti. Chester book of motets, v. 13. Chester Music, $7.95.

3009 *The Flemish and German schools, for 5 voices,* ed. by Anthony G. Petti. Chester book of motets, v. 15. Chester Music, $7.95.

3010 * *The flower of the Italian madrigal, for mixed voices,* ed. by Jerome Roche. Galaxy Music, 3 v., $12.95, $12.95, $24.95.

3011 *French chansons of the sixteenth century,* ed. by Jane A. Bernstein. Pennsylvania State University Press 0-271-00397-9, $30.

3012 *German part song from the 16th century to the present day.* Compiled by Helmuth Osthoff. Anthology of music, v. 10. Arno Volk Verlag/Laaber, $26.

3013 *Golden age of the madrigal: 12 Italian madrigals,* ed. by Alfred Einstein. AMS Press 0-404-12902-1 (reprint of G. Schirmer), $24.50; G. Schirmer ED1716, $6.

3014 * *Introduction to the Italian madrigal, for 4 voices,* newly rev. and ed. from the former *Penguin book of madrigals* by Jerome Roche. Galaxy Music, $10.95.

3015 *The Italian and Spanish schools, for 5 voices,* ed. by Anthony Petti. Chester book of motets, v. 10. Chester Music, $7.95.

3016 *The Italian and Spanish schools, for 6 voices,* ed. by Anthony G. Petti. Chester book of motets, v. 14. Chester Music, $7.95.

3017 *Italienische Madrigale, zu 4–5 Stimmen: Adrian Willaert und andere Meister,* ed. by Walter Wiora. Das Chorwerk, 5. Kallmeyer Verlag, $15.

3018 * *A medieval motet book: a collection of 13th-century motets in various vocal and instrumental combinations,* compiled and ed. by Hans Tischler. Associated Music, $5, OP.

3019 *Missae Caput: Guillaume Dufay, Johannes Ockeghem, Jacob Obrecht,* ed. by Alejandro Planchart. Collegium musicum, series 1, no. 5. Yale University Press, $24.95.

3020 * *The Oxford book of English madrigals,* ed. by Philip Ledger. Oxford University Press 0-19-343664-7, $17.95.

3021 * *The Oxford book of French chansons,* ed. by Franck Dobbins. Oxford University Press 0-19-343539-X, $26.95.

3022 * *The Oxford book of Italian madrigals,* ed. by Alec Harman. Oxford University Press 0-19-343647-7, $18.95.

3023 *The Oxford book of Tudor anthems: 34 anthems for mixed voices,* ed. by Christopher Morris. Oxford University Press 0-19-353325-1, $15.

3024 *Popular Italian madrigals of the sixteenth century, for mixed voices,* ed. by Alec Harman. Oxford University Press 0-19-343646-9, $14.95.

3025 *The sixteenth-century part song in Italy, France, England and Spain.* Anthology of music, v. 3. Arno Volk Verlag/Laaber, $26.

3026 *Thirty chansons for three and four voices from Attaingnant's collections,* ed. by Albert Seay. Collegium musicum, series 1, no. 2. Yale University Press, $24.95.

3027 *Thirty-five conductus for two and three voices,* ed. by Janet Knapp. Collegium musicum, series 1, no. 6. Yale University Press, $24.95.

3028 *The treasury of English church music.* Blandford Press, price not available.

National Anthems

3029 * *National anthems of the world,* ed. by W. L. Reed and M. J. Bristow. 8th rev. ed. Cappell/Sterling 0-304-34218-1, $90.

Hymnals and Synagogue Music

3030 *The English hymnal, 1933.* Oxford University Press 0-19-231111-5, $49.95.

3031 * *The hymnal 1982: according to the use of the Episcopal Church.* Church Hymnal Corp., 1985. 0-898-69121-4 pew ed., $11.95.

3032 *New hymnal for schools and colleges* [an ecumenical hymnal]. Yale University Press, 1992. $28.

3033 ** *The Presbyterian hymnal: hymns, psalms, and spiritual songs.* Westminster/John Knox Press, 1990. 0-664-10097-X pew ed., $15.95; 0-664-10110-0 ecumenical ed., $15.95.

3034 ** *Sha'arei Shirah = Gates of song: music for Shabbat,* ed. by Cantor Charles Davidson. Hebrew with transliteration or English. Transcontinental Music Publications 0-8074-0406-3, congregational ed., $14; Transcontinental 0-8074-0407-1, accompanist's ed., $87.

3035 ** *The United Methodist hymnal: book of United Methodist worship.* United Methodist Publishing House, 1989. 0-687-43132-8 pew ed., $15.95.

3036 *The worshiping church: a hymnal,* ed. by Donald Hustad. Hope Publishing Co., 1992. $10.95.

3037 *Yamim Nora'im = Days of awe* [music for solo voice, choir, and organ for the High Holy Days], ed. by Samuel Adler. Romanized Hebrew; some works also translated into English. Transcontinental Music Publications. vol. 1: *Rosh Hashannah = The new year,* 0-8074-04545-3, $40; vol. 2: *Yom Kippur = The day of atonement,* 0-8074-0455-1, $40; 5CD set, v.1–2, $90.

PART TWO

Sound Recordings

INTRODUCTION

For sound recordings, *A Basic Music Library,* 3rd edition (BML3), delineates the "basic" identity of a given musical genre by listing systematically the genre's definitive artists and their works. For Western classical music, the focus is on composers, whose works are included according to their importance to music history, their lasting popularity with classical-music audiences, or both. With respect to classical interpreters, there are many more superlative performances available on recordings (especially for standard repertory of the eighteenth to twentieth centuries) than can possibly be included in a book such as this, so we have selected interpreters according to the criterion "fully worthwhile artistically" rather than "best." For musical genres other than Western classical the composer and interpreter are most often one and the same, so we have selected and organized recordings in those chapters according to the principal performing artist or group. In the broad range of music recordings represented by BML3, the editors' and contributors' inevitably limited expertise has been aided by standard textbooks and historical surveys, and by the generous advice of the consultants acknowledged at the end of these introductory notes.

Citation Format

Example 1 (single title attached to name).

> **4388** * Johnson, James P., 1894–1955
> *Father of the stride piano.* Columbia: CL 1780. 1921–39. OP

Example 2 (first of multiple titles attached to name, with three different recorded interpretations).

> **3270** Bach, Johann Sebastian, 1685–1750
> **3270.1** ** *Brandenburgische Konzerte (Brandenburg concertos).*
> - (Musica Antiqua Köln/Reinhard Goebel). Archiv: 423 116-2. 2CD set. [With his *Concerto for flute, violin, harpsichord, and strings*].
> - (Orchestra of the Age of Enlightenment/Catherine Mackintosh). Virgin: CDCB 7 59152 2. 2CD set.
> - (English Concert/Trevor Pinnock). Archiv: 423 492-2. 2CD set.

Example 3 (anthology with title main entry).

> **6812** *Caribbean beat: soca, kaseko, merengue, cadence, zouk, ska, compas.* Intuition: INT 3112 2. [1993]. [Gazoline, Wilfrido Vargas, Laurel Aitken, and others].

Key to Citation Elements

Asterisks	One, two, or no asterisks after the citation number indicate one of the three levels of "basic" as described in the preface to BML.
Author	The composer or primary recording artist.
Title	For Western classical composers: The title given is that of the "basic" composition. Because of the need for a brief, clear, and consistent style, it is not possible for BML3 to adhere to all AACR2 conventions with respect to titles of recordings. Specific titles (e.g., operas) are given in their original language, followed by the English translation in parentheses, followed at times by additional identifying information in brackets. Generic titles (e.g., sonatas) are given in a modified AACR2 uniform-title format, indicating (in order) the form, instrumentation, opus or catalog number, and key.
	For Western classical anthologies and all other chapters: The title given is the album title. Bilingual, parallel titles are separated by an equals sign.
	For all personal name entries: A single title follows the name. Two or more titles attached to one name are indented and numbered as decimals to the main entry's whole number.
(Interpreters)	Optional, and shown in parentheses immediately following the title and translation of title. Always given for Western classical composers and sometimes with anthologies in various chapters. Multiple interpreters are separated within the parentheses by slash marks (e.g., soloist/orchestra/conductor). Where more than one recorded interpretation corresponds to a single composition, these are indented further and set off by bullets. Multiple interpretations are alphabetized by (in order of precedence) soloist's last name, conductor's last name, and ensemble name.

Publisher	The name of the record label, with multiple agencies separated by slash marks.
Publication Number	The alpha-numeric identification number of the recording, separated from the publisher/label by a colon. For most mail-order dealers this number is essential for ordering. BML3 makes every effort to transmit the numbers as completely and accurately as possible, but users of the book should be aware that inconsistencies abound in the way such numbers are cited in various catalogs and even by the record companies themselves.
	A second label name or number in parentheses indicates a previous release of the same recorded material. This may be valuable for the library that owns an earlier issue but it is not necessary or recommended for use in ordering.

Physical Format

No indication	One compact disc. Compact disc is the preferred and by far the most common format in BML3.
LP	One long-playing vinyl disc
AC	One cassette tape
2CD set	Two compact discs available only as a package
2 CDs	Two compact discs available separately

Recording Date: Not the publication, copyright, or release date, but the year in which the recording itself was produced. As used in the vernacular music chapters, where many citations are reissues of previously released material, the recording date is informative because it effectively identifies when the music was actually created. (The equivalent in Western classical music would be the dates of composition, but practical obstacles prevented BML3 from including these systematically.) The styles of citation for dates are:

1975	Recording date is firmly documented on the recording itself or by some other authoritative source.
1975–79	Recordings made originally between the two dates indicated.
1975, 1979	Recordings made on the dates indicated.
[1975]	Recording date is inferred from the release date.
[1975?]	Recording date is inferred from the release date, which is uncertain.
[197?]	Recording date is known only within the decade indicated.
[19-?]	Recording date is unknown.

[Free text note]	Optional and always in brackets. Notes contain additional information on performers, titles, or contents not previously given. The note "Item x covers material comparable to item y but in greater depth and with better packaging and notes" means that item y is a single-disc "highlights" album in relation to item x, which has at least two discs and is more expensive. Purchasing x would preclude the need for y.
OP	Out of print. The last possible element in a citation. Used in a small number of cases where the material is exceptionally important, in anticipation that there may be a reissue.
See and *See also* references	In italic, followed by a *citation* number (not page number). In the Western classical listings, *see* references are used whenever a single disc or package contains more than one "basic" composition. This way, the published recording itself is cited only once, and users of the book are prevented from inadvertently ordering the same item twice. In various other chapters, a limited number of *see* references guide the user to pertinent citations elsewhere in the book.

Prices

The current average price per compact disc is about $12, with individual labels ranging from $8 to more than $20 per disc. Because of the variability with respect to "list" prices and the actual retail costs (many mail-order dealers and other retailers give routine and substantial discounts to libraries, but others mark up), BML3 does not include prices for recordings.

Availability

All cited recordings (with the exception of the few out-of-print items noted above) are—to the best of the editors' knowledge—available as of this writing. They can readily be obtained from general dealers (*see* "Suppliers of Sound Recordings" in the Appendixes) or from specialty distributors for some of the smaller, hard-to-find record labels. Recordings of Latin American, African, Asian, and European music are limited to U.S.–produced or U.S.–distributed labels. Verifiable domestic sources for direct imports are given for exceptions. This policy results in relatively sparse listings for certain categories of music in certain countries (contemporary popular music of Asia, the Middle East, and much of Europe being the most notable), because the "basic" material is not readily available in the United States through mainstream commercial channels. Libraries finding these listings inadequate might benefit from developing ties to local merchants who cater to immigrant groups and who can obtain recordings directly from the country of origin.

Classical, Traditional, and Popular

In chapter headings for international recordings, the terms *classical, traditional,* and *popular* indicate in a general sense the range of musical styles within each country's listings. The ideal is to have as broad and balanced a representation as possible for the music of each country, but the meaning of these words in a given cultural context and in relation to particular recordings is complex and impossible to apply meaningfully and consistently without extensive annotations. For this reason, the book does not classify individual citations in this manner.

Indexing

The personal and corporate names in the index are almost without exception limited to the primary creators of the music, i.e., the composers for classical works and the principal recording artists for vernacular genres. For reasons of space, interpreters, editors, producers, and others who might also be included within a citation are not generally indexed. Subject terms in the index are given as a complement to the table of contents and provide an additional layer of access.

Acknowledgments

We gratefully acknowledge the advice and assistance of the following individuals, libraries, record companies, and distributors.

Michael Budd
    Columbus Metropolitan Library,
    Columbus, Ohio
    (rock)

Chuck Cody
    Columbus Metropolitan Library,
    Columbus, Ohio
    (rock)

Greg Denby
    Columbus Metropolitan Library,
    Columbus, Ohio
    (blues)

Constance S. Dickerson
    Cleveland, Ohio
    (children's)

Warren C. Dusenbury
    Sacramento, California
    (rhythm and blues)

Joe Fowler
    Columbus Metropolitan Library,
    Columbus, Ohio
    (jazz)

Jon Goldman
    Cleveland Heights, Ohio
    (jazz)

Greg Holtz
    WRUW-FM, Cleveland
    (North American and European
        traditional)

Dan Polletta
    WCPN-FM, Cleveland
    (jazz)

Gary Rozak
    WRUW-FM, Cleveland
    (North American and European
        traditional)

William L. Shurk
    Bowling Green State University
    Bowling Green, Ohio
    (mainstream popular)

Bert Stratton
Yiddishe Cup Klezmer Band
(North American and European
traditional)
Jennifer Tobin
Columbus Metropolitan Library,
Columbus, Ohio
(rock)
Used Kids Records
Columbus, Ohio
(rock)
Derek Van Pelt
Cleveland, Ohio
(rock)
Stuart Vandermark
Framingham, Massachusetts
(jazz)
Carl Woideck
Eugene, Oregon
(jazz)

Bowling Green State University Popular
 Music Library
Bowling Green, Ohio
Cleveland Public Library
Cleveland, Ohio
Columbus Metropolitan Library
Columbus, Ohio
New York University Library
Ohio State University Music Library
Columbus, Ohio
WRUW-FM, Case Western Reserve University
Cleveland

Arhoolie
Banjar
Blue Note
(Michael Cuscuna)
Canyon
Global Village
GRP
(Cara Bridgins)
MCA
(Andy McKaie)
Mosaic
(Charlie Laurie)
New World
Rhino
(Reggie Collins)
Rounder
(Leland Stein, Steve Burton)
Smithsonian Collection of Recordings
(Kathy Kim, Amy Pickworth)
Sony Music/Legacy
(Chris Barsa)
Stern's Music U.S.
(Ken Braun)
Verve
(Peter Pullman)
Warner Brothers
(Greg Geller)

Kent Underwood
William E. Anderson
Co-editors,
 Sound Recordings

Medieval Period

Compiled by

**Kent Underwood and
Eunice Schroeder**

Composers

3038 Adam, de La Halle, ca. 1235–ca. 1288

3038.1 *Le jeu de Robin et Marion* [musical play].

- (Schola Cantorum Basiliensis/Thomas Binkley). Focus: 913.
- (Ensemble Percival/Guy Robert). Arion: 68162.

3038.2 * *Songs. Selections. See 3105*

3039 * Alfonso X ("El Sabio"), King of Castile and León, 1221–1284. *Cantigas de Santa María. Selections.*

- (Montserrat Figueras/La Capella Reial de Catalunya/ Hespèrion XX/Jordi Savall). Astrée: E 8508.
- (Esther Lamandier). Astrée: E 7707.
- (Martin Best Medieval Ensemble). Nimbus: NI 5081.
- (Sequentia). [Series: Vox iberica, vol. 3]. Deutsche Harmonia Mundi: 05472-277173-2.

3040 Bernart, de Ventadorn, 12th cent.

Songs. Selections. (Martin Best). Hyperion: CDA66211. [Album title: *The testament of Tristan*].

3041 * Ciconia, Johannes, ca. 1335–1411. *Vocal music. Selections.*

- (Alla Francesca). Opus 111: OPS 30-101. [Album title: *Motets, virelais, ballate, madrigals*].
- (Ensemble Project Ars Nova). New Albion: NA 048. [Album title: *Hommage to Johannes Ciconia*].
- (Little Consort). Channel Classics: CCS 0290. [Album title: *Johannes Ciconia and his time*].

3042 Codax, Martin, fl. ca. 1230. *Cantigas de amigo* [song cycle].

- (Newberry Consort). *See 3108*
- (Sinfonye/Stevie Wishart). *See 3123*

3043 Guillaume, de Machaut, ca. 1300–1377

3043.1 ** *Messe de Nostre Dame.*

- (Ensemble Gilles Binchois). Harmonic: H/CD 8931. [With Gregorian chant Propers].
- (Hilliard Ensemble/Paul Hillier). Hyperion: CDA66358. [With his *Lai de la fonteinne* and *Ma fin est mon commencement*].

- (Taverner Consort/Andrew Parrott). EMI: CDC 7 47949 2. [With Gregorian chant Propers].

3043.2 * *Motets and songs. Selections.*

- (Gothic Voices/Christopher Page). Hyperion: CDA66087. [Album title: *The mirror of Narcissus*].
- (Ensemble Gilles Binchois/Dominique Vellard). Harmonic: H/CD 8825. [Album title: *Le vray remède d'amour*].

3044 Hildegard, Saint (Hildegard von Bingen), 1098–1179

3044.1 *Ordo virtutum* [sacred music-drama]. (Sequentia/Barbara Thornton). Deutsche Harmonia Mundi: 77051-2-RG. 2CD set.

3044.2 ** *Sequences and hymns. Selections.*

- (Gothic Voices/Christopher Page). Hyperion: CDA66039. [Album title: *A feather on the breath of God*].
- (Sequentia). Deutsche Harmonia Mundi: 05472-77320-2. [Album title: *Canticles of ecstasy*].
- (Sequentia). Deutsche Harmonia Mundi: 77020-2-RG. [Album title: *Symphoniae*].

3045 Jehannot, de Lescurel, 14th cent.
Songs. Selections. (Sequentia). *See* 3105

3046 * Landini, Francesco, ca. 1325–1397
Songs. Selections. See 3110–3115

3047 * Léonin, 12th cent. *Organum. Selections.*

- (Early Music Consort of London/David Munrow). *See* 3092
- (Ensemble Organum/Marcel Pérès). *See* 3091

3048 ** Pérotin, d. 1238?
Organum and conductus. Selections. (Hilliard Ensemble/Paul Hillier). ECM: 1385 (837 751-2).

3049 Petrus de Cruce, 13th cent.
Motets. Selections. (Sequentia). *See* 3105

3050 Riquier, Guiraut, ca. 1230–ca. 1300
Songs. Selections. (Martin Best Medieval Ensemble). Nimbus: NI 5261. [Album title: *The last of the troubadours*].

3051 Vitry, Philippe de, 1291–1361. *Motets. Selections.*

- (Orlando Consort). Amon Ra: CD-SAR 49. [Album title: *Philippe de Vitry and the Ars nova*].
- (Sequentia). Deutsche Harmonia Mundi: 77095-2-RC.

3052 Wolkenstein, Oswald von, 1377?–1445.
Songs. Selections. (Sequentia). Deutsche Harmonia Mundi: 05472-77302-2.

Anthologies and Recitals

Plainchant

3053 *Ambrosian liturgical chants.* (Schola Hungarica/Janka Szendrei/László Dobszay). Hungaroton: HCD 12889-2.

3054 *Chant cistercien.* (Ensemble Organum/Marcel Pérès). Harmonia Mundi: HMC 901392. [Cistercian chants].

3055 * *Chant gregorien.* (Deller Consort/Alfred Deller). Harmonia Mundi: HMA 190235/37. 3CD set. [Includes Requiem Mass and various other chants].

3056 *Chants de la Cathédrale de Benevento.* (Ensemble Organum/Marcel Pérès). Harmonia Mundi: HMC 901476. [Beneventan chants, including Easter Mass].

3057 *Chants de l'église de Rome des VIIe et VIIIe siècles: période byzantine.* (Ensemble Organum/Marcel Pérès). Harmonia Mundi: 901218. [Old Roman chants, principally for Easter].

3058 *Chants de l'église milanaise.* (Ensemble Organum/Marcel Pérès). Harmonia Mundi: HMC 901295. [Ambrosian chants].

3059 * *Deus, Deus meus: Gregorian chant.* (Schola Cantorum Gregoriana Essen/Godehard Joppich). Novalis: 150 009-2.

3060 *The feast of fools.* (New London Consort/Philip Pickett). L'Oiseau-Lyre: 433 194-2. [Mass and Office of the Circumcision with non-liturgical interpolations].

3061 *Gregorian chant.* (Choralschola der Wiener Hofburgkapelle/Hubert Dopf). Philips: 411 140-2. [*Mass of the Immaculate Conception of the Blessed Virgin Mary* with Propers].

3062 ** *Gregorian chant: Easter.* (Choir of St. Peter's Abbey, Solesmes/Jean Claire). Creative Joys: S.822.

3063 *Gregorian chant from Aquitaine.* (Schola Hungarica/Janka Szendrei/László Dobszay). Harmonia Mundi/Quintana: QUI 903031.

3064 * *Gregorian chant: Maundy Thursday.* (Choir of St. Peter's Abbey, Solesmes/Jean Claire). Creative Joys: S.831.

3065 ** *Gregorian chant: Vespers and Compline at the Abbey of Solesmes.* (Choir of St. Peter's Abbey, Solesmes/Jean Claire). Creative Joys: S.826.

3066 * *Gregorianische Gesänge: Advent, Weihnachten, Jahreskreis = Gregorian chants: Advent, Christmas, New Year.* (Mönchsschola der Erzabtei St. Ottilien/Johannes Berchmans Göschl). Calig: CAL 50858.

3067 * *Gregorianische Gesänge: die ältesten Marienproprien = Gregorian chants: the oldest Marian Propers.* (Mönchsschola der Erzabtei St. Ottilien/Johannes Berchmans Göschl). Calig: CAL 50884.

3068 *Old Roman liturgical chants.* (Schola Hungarica/Janka Szendrei/László Dobszay). Hungaroton: HCD 12741-2.

3069 *Sarum chant.* (Tallis Scholars/Peter Phillips). Gimell: CDGIM 017.

3070 *Les tons de la musique.* (Ensemble Gilles Binchois/Dominique Vellard). Harmonic: H/CD 8827. [Chants selected to illustrate the eight medieval modes].

England

3071 * *An English ladymass: medieval chant and polyphony in honor of the Virgin Mary.* (Anonymous IV). Harmonia Mundi: HMU 907080. [Anonymous compositions of the 13th–14th centuries].

3072 * *English songs of the Middle Ages.* (Sequentia). Deutsche Harmonia Mundi: 77019-2-RG. [Anonymous secular and spiritual songs in Latin and Middle English].

3073 *The lily and the lamb: chant and polyphony from medieval England.* (Anonymous 4). Harmonia Mundi: HMU 907125. [Anonymous compositions of the 13th–15th centuries].

3074 * *Medieval English music.* (Hilliard Ensemble/Paul Hillier). Harmonia Mundi: HMA 1901106. [Anonymous compositions of the 14th–15th centuries].

3075 *Music for the Lion-hearted King: music to commemorate the 800th anniversary of the coronation of King Richard I of England in Westminster Abbey, 3 September 1189.* (Gothic Voices/Christopher Page). Hyperion: CDA66336. [Music by Gace Brulé, Blondel de Nesle, Chastelain de Couci, and anonymous composers].

3076 *On Yoolis night: medieval carols and motets.* (Anonymous 4). Harmonia Mundi: HMU 907099. [Anonymous compositions].

3077 *The service of Venus and Mars: music for the Knights of the Garter, 1340–1440.* (Gothic Voices/Christopher Page). Hyperion: CDA66238. [Music by Richard Loqueville, Soursby, John Dunstable, John Pyamour, Franchois Lebertoul, Leonel Power, Pycard, Pierre des Molins, Philippe de Vitry, and anonymous composers].

3078 ** *Sumer is icumen in: chants médiévaux anglais.* (Hilliard Ensemble/Paul Hillier). Harmonia Mundi: HMC 901154. [Anonymous sacred and secular music in Latin and Middle English].

3079 *Worcester fragments: English sacred music of the late Middle Ages.* (Orlando Consort). Amon Ra: CD-SAR 59. [Anonymous compositions of the 13th–14th centuries].

France: Ars Antiqua, Ars Nova, and Ars Subtilior

3080 * *Ars magis subtiliter: secular music of the Chantilly Codex.* (Ensemble Project Ars Nova). New Albion: NA 021. [Music of the late 14th century by F. Andrieu, Jehan Vaillant, Baude Cordier, Guillaume de Machaut, Grimace, Solage, Goscalch, Pierre des Molins, Johannes Susay, Johannes Symonis, and anonymous composers].

3081 * *The art of courtly love.* (Early Music Consort of London/Munrow). Virgin: 7243 5 61284 2. 2CD set. [Music by Jehannot de Lescurel, Guillaume de Machaut, Pierre des Molins, F. Andrieu, Grimace, Franciscus, Borlet, Solage, Jehan Vaillant, Pykini, Anthonello da Caserta, Matteo da Perugia, Hasprois, Guillaume Dufay, Gilles Binchois, and anonymous composers]. OP

3082 *Campus stellae: Saint-Martial de Limoges-Santiago de Compostela, 12th century.* (Discantus/Brigitte Lesne). Opus 111: OPS 30-102. [Anonymous polyphony].

3083 *Le chant des cathédrales: organum, conduit, motets: École de Notre Dame de Paris, 1163–1245.* (Ensemble Gilles Binchois/Dominique Vellard). Harmonic: H/CD 8611. [Polyphony of the School of Notre Dame].

3084 *Codex Chantilly: airs de cour du XIVe siècle.* (Ensemble Organum/Marcel Pérès). Harmonia Mundi: HMC 901252. [Music of the late 14th century by F. Andrieu, Solage, Jacob de Senleches, Goscalch, Baude Cordier, Guido, Cuvelier, and anonymous composers].

3085 * *Danielis ludus (Play of Daniel)* [anonymous 12th-century liturgical drama].

- (Ensemble for Early Music/Frederick Renz). Fonè: 88 F 09-29 CD.
- (András Soós/Schola Hungarica/Janka Szendrei). Hungaroton: HCD 12457-2.
- (Clerkes of Oxenford/David Wulstan). Calliope: CAL 9848. [With White, Robert: *Lamentations of Jeremiah*].

3086 *Febus avant!: music at the court of Gaston Febus.* (Huelgas Ensemble/Paul van Nevel). Sony: SK 48195. [Late 14th-century music by Solage, Trebor, Cuvelier, and anonymous composers].

3087 * *Love's illusion: music from the Montpellier Codex, 13th century.* (Anonymous 4). Harmonia Mundi: HMU 907109. [Anonymous motets].

3088 * *The marriage of heaven and hell: motets and songs from 13th-century France.* (Gothic Voices/ Christopher Page). Hyperion: CDA66423. [Music by Blondel de Nesle, Colin Muset, Bernart de Ventadorn, and anonymous composers].

3089 *The medieval romantics: French songs and motets, 1340–1440.* (Gothic Voices/Christopher Page). Hyperion: CDA66463. [Music by Johannes de Lymburgia, Guillaume Dufay, Guillaume de Machaut, Jacob de Senleches, Paolo da Firenze, J. de Porta, Solage, Gilet Velut, and anonymous composers].

3090 *Messe de Tournai: XVIe siècle.* (Ensemble Organum/Marcel Pérès). Harmonia Mundi: HMC 901353. [Anonymous polyphonic Mass cycle of the earlier 14th century].

3091 *Messe du jour de Noël: (Léonin) École Notre-Dame.* (Ensemble Organum/Marcel Pérès). Harmonia Mundi: HMA 1901148. [Late 12th-century Christmas Mass with chant and polyphony, including music attributed to Léonin].

3092 ** *Music of the Gothic era.* (Early Music Consort of London/David Munrow). Archiv: 415 292-2. [Chronological survey of French polyphony of the 12th–14th centuries, with music by Léonin, Pérotin, Petrus de Cruce, Adam de La Halle, Philippe de Vitry, Guillaume de Machaut, and anonymous composers].

3093 *Notre-Dame Schule (School of Notre-Dame): Philippe le Chancelier.* (Sequentia). Deutsche Harmonia Mundi: 77035-3-RC. [Anonymous compositions of the later 12th century, to texts by Philip the Chancellor).

3094 *Le roman de Fauvel.* (René Zosso/Clemencic Consort/René Clemencic). Harmonia Mundi: HMA 190994. [Excerpts from the early 14th-century poetico-musical work with music by Philippe de Vitry and anonymous composers].

3095 * *The study of love: French songs and motets of the 14th century.* (Gothic Voices/Christopher Page). Hyperion: CDA66619. [Music of Guillaume de Machaut, Pycard, Solage, and anonymous composers].

3096 *12th century polyphony in Aquitaine (St. Martial de Limoges): excerpts from the Christmas Matins.* (Ensemble Organum/Marcel Pérès). Harmonia Mundi: HMC 901353. [Anonymous polyphony of the earlier 12th century].

France: Troubadours, Trobairitz, and Trouvères

3097 *Cansós de trobairitz.* (Hespèrion XX/Jordi Savall). EMI: CDM 7 63417 2. [Songs from the troubadour era with lyrics by women poets. Music by Gaucelm Faidit, Raimon de Miraval, Arnaut de Mareuil, Giraut de Borneil, Bernart de Ventadorn, Comtesse de Dia, and Cadenet].

3098 *Chansons de toile au temps du Roman de la Rose.* (Esther Lamandier). Aliénor: AL 1011. [Anonymous "spinning songs" of the 13th century].

3099 * *Dante and the troubadours.* (Sequentia). Deutsche Harmonia Mundi: 05472-77277-2. [Music by Aimeric de Peguilhan, Arnaut Daniel, Bertran de Born, Peire d'Alvernhe, Giraut de Borneil, and Folquet de Marseilla].

3100 *The Dante troubadours.* (Martin Best Medieval Ensemble). Nimbus: NI 5002. [Songs by Giraut de Borneil, Bertran de Born, Bernart de Ventadorn, Arnaut Daniel, Peire Vidal, Raimbaut de Vaqueiras, Gaucelm Faidit, Aimeric de Belenoi, Folquet de Marseilla, and anonymous composers].

3101 *Proensa.* (Paul Hillier). ECM: 1368 (837 360-2). [Troubadour songs by Guiraut Riquier, Peire Vidal, Bernart de Ventadorn, Marcabrun, Raimon de Miraval, Giraut de Borneil, and William IX, Duke of Aquitaine].

3102 *Songs of chivalry.* (Martin Best Medieval Ensemble). Nimbus: NI 5006. [Troubadour and trouvère songs by William X, Duke of Aquitaine, Huon d'Oisy, Thibaut de Navarre, Marcabrun, Blondel de Nesle, Moniot d'Arras, Bernart de Ventadorn, Jaufre Rudel, Comtesse de Dia, Raimbaut d'Aurenga, Peire Cardenal, and anonymous composers].

3103 *The sweet look and the loving manner: trobairitz love lyrics and chansons de femme.* (Sinfonye/Stevie Wishart). Hyperion: CDA66625. [Troubadour and trouvère songs with lyrics by or about women, by Bernart de Ventadorn, Comtesse de Dia, Audefroi le Bastart, and others].

3104 * *Troubadours & trouvères.* (Studio der Frühe Musik/Thomas Binkley). Teldec: 8.35519. 2CD set. [Music by Peire Vidal, Giraut de Borneil, Bernart de Ventadorn, Raimbaut de Vaqueiras, Comtesse de Dia, Jacques de Cambrai, Guiot de Dijon, Gillebert de Berneville, Gace Brulé, Etienne de Meaux, and anonymous composers].

3105 * *Trouvères: courtly love songs from northern France.* (Sequentia). Deutsche Harmonia Mundi: 77155-2-RC. 2CD set. [Music by Conon de Bethune, Gace Brulé, Blondel de Nesle, Adam de La Halle, Jehannot de Lescurel, Petrus de Cruce, and anonymous composers].

Germany

3106 * *Minnesänger und Spielleute.* (Studio der Frühe Musik/Thomas Binkley). Teldec: 8.44015. [Songs by Walther von der Vogelweide, Neidhart von Reuenthal, Reinmar von Brennenburg, Unverzagte, Frauenlob, Wizlav III, Prince of Rügen, and anonymous composers].

3107 *Minnesinger and Meistersinger: songs around Konrad von Würzberg.* (Andrea von Ramm). Christophorus: 74542. [Music by Lupold Hornburg, Goli, Frauenlob, Rudolf von Fenis-Neuenburg, Konrad von Würzburg, and Barthel Regenbogen].

3108 *Wanderers' voices: medieval cantigas and minnesang.* (Newberry Consort). Harmonia Mundi: HMU 907082. [German songs by Unverzagte, Neidhart von Reuenthal, Tannhäuser, and Oswald von Wolkenstein, plus the complete *Cantigas de amigo* by Martin Codax].

Italy

3109 * *Ars subtilis ytalica: polyphonie pseudo-française en Italie 1380–1410.* (Mala Punica). Arcana: 21. [Music by Bartolomeus de Bononia, Anthonello da Caserta, Matteo da Perugia, and Magister Zacharias].

3110 * *Decameron: ballate monodiques de l'Ars Nova florentine.* (Esther Lamandier). Astrée: E 7706. [14th-century monophonic songs by Lorenzo da Firenze, Gherardello da Firenze, and Francesco Landini].

3111 *Ecco la primavera.* (Early Music Consort of London/David Munrow). London: 436 219-2. [Music of the 14th century by Francesco Landini, Maestro Piero, Antonio Zacharia da Teramo, Giovanni da Cascia, Lorenzo da Firenze, Jacopo da Bologna, and anonymous composers].

3112 *Landini and his contemporaries.* (Ensemble Micrologus). Opus 111: OPS 30-112. [Music of the 14th century by Giovanni da Cascia, Francesco Landini, Lorenzo da Firenze, Donato da Cascia, Gherardello da Firenze, and anonymous composers].

3113 *Landini and his time.* (Ensemble Alta Musica Kyo). Channel: CCS 5793. [Music of the 14th century by Lorenzo da Firenze, Matteo da Perugia, Jacopo da Bologna, Francesco Landini, and anonymous composers].

3114 *Landini and the Italian Ars Nova.* (Alla Francesca). Opus 111: OPS 60-9026. [Music of the 14th century by Gherardello da Firenze, Jacopo Ripanda, Francesco Landini, Lorenzo da Firenze, and anonymous composers].

3115 *A Song for Francesca: music in Italy, 1330–1430.* (Gothic Voices/Christopher Page). Hyperion: CDA66286. [Music by Andrea da Firenze, Giovanni da Firenze, Francesco Landini, Guillaume Dufay, Richard Loqueville, Hugo de Lantins, Jean Haucourt, Estienne Grossin, and anonymous composers].

Spain

3116 * *Codex Las Huelgas: music from the royal convent of Las Huelgas de Burgos, 13th–14th century.* [Series: Vox iberica, vol. 2]. (Sequentia). Deutsche Harmonia Mundi: 15472-77238-2. [Anonymous polyphony].

3117 * *Codex Las Huelgas: 13th-century Spanish sacred vocal music.* (Discantus/Brigitte Lesne). Opus 111: OPS 30-68. [Anonymous polyphony].

3118 *Llibre vermell: pilgrim songs and dances.* (New London Consort/Philip Pickett). L'Oiseau-Lyre: 433 186-2. [Anonymous 14th-century compositions].

3119 *Pilgrimage to Santiago: a musical journey along the medieval pilgrim road to the shrine of St. James at Santiago de Compostela.* (New London Consort/Philip Pickett). L'Oiseau-Lyre: 433 148-2. [Anonymous 12th-century compositions].

3120 *Sons of thunder: music for St. James the Apostle from Codex Calixtinus.* [Series: Vox iberica, vol. 3]. (Sequentia). Deutsche Harmonia Mundi: 05472-77199-2. [Anonymous 12th-century compositions].

3121 *Visions and miracles: Gallician and Latin sacred songs from 13th-century Spain.* (Ensemble Alcatraz). Nonesuch: 79180-2. [Music by Alfonso el Sabio and anonymous composers].

Miscellaneous

3122 * *A l'estampida: medieval dance music.* (Dufay Collective). Continuum: CCD 1042. [Anonymous compositions of the 13th–14th centuries].

3123 * *Bella domna: the medieval woman: lover, poet, patroness, and saint.* (Sinfonye/Stevie Wishart). Hyperion: CDA66283. [Complete *Cantigas de amigo* by Martin Codax plus music by Comtesse de Dia and anonymous composers].

3124 *Beyond plainsong: tropes and polyphony in the medieval church.* (Pro Arte Singers/Thomas Binkley). Focus: 943. [Survey of organum and other types of improvised polyphonic chant elaboration of the 9th–15th centuries].

3125 * *Carmina burana* [early 13th-century collection of anonymous Latin songs].
- (Studio der Frühen Musik/Thomas Binkley). Teldec: 8.43775; 8.44012. 2CDs.
- (New London Consort/Philip Pickett). L'Oiseau-Lyre: 417 373-2; 421 062-2; 425 117-2. 4CDs in 3 vols.

3126 *Carmina burana. Grand mystère de la passion* [passion play with music from the 13th-century Carmina burana manuscript].
- (Indiana University Early Music Institute/Thomas Binkley). Musical Heritage Society: 533539T. 2CD set.
- (Ensemble Organum/Marcel Pérès). Harmonia Mundi: HMC 901323/24. 2CD set.

3127 *Codex Faenza.* (Ensemble Organum/Marcel Pérès). Harmonia Mundi: HMC 901354. [Anony-

mous late 14th-century instrumental transcriptions of songs, together with the vocal originals by Bartolino da Padova, Jacopo da Bologna, Francesco Landini, and Guillaume de Machaut].

3128 *A dance in the garden of mirth: medieval instrumental music.* (Dufay Collective). Chandos: CHAN 9320. [Anonymous compositions of the 13th–14th centuries].

3129 *Danse royale: French, Anglo-Norman, and Latin songs and dances from the 13th century.* (Ensemble Alcatraz). Nonesuch: 79240-2. [Anonymous compositions].

3130 *Domna.* (Esther Lamandier). Aliénor: AL 1019. [Secular and spiritual monodic songs from France, Germany, and Italy by Guillaume de Machaut, Peter von Aberg, Mönch von Salzburg, Peter von Sachsen, Folquet de Marseilla, Guiraut Riquier, Gherardello da Firenze, Masii da Firenze, and anonymous composers].

3131 *The island of St. Hylarion: music of Cyprus, 1413–1422.* (Ensemble Project Ars Nova). New Albion: NA 038. [Anonymous compositions].

3132 *Lancaster and Valois: French and English music, 1350–1420.* (Gothic Voices/Christopher Page). Hyperion: CDA66588. [Compositions by Guillaume de Machaut, Solage, Pycard, Sturgeon, Fonteyns, Cesaris, Baude Cordier, and anonymous composers].

3133 *Nova cantica: Latin songs of the high Middle Ages.* (Dominique Vellard/Emmanuel Bonnardot/Schola Cantorum Basiliensis). Deutsche Harmonia Mundi: 77196-2-RC. [Anonymous monodic songs of the 12th century].

3134 * *Popes and antipopes: music for the courts of Avignon and Rome.* (Orlando Consort). Metronome: MET 1008. [Music of the late 14th–early 15th centuries by Mayhuet de Joan, Egidius, Phillipus de Caserta, Bartolomeus de Bononia, Johannes Ciconia, Gilet Velut, Tapissier, Antonio de Civitate, Nicolaus Zacharie, Johannes Brassart, Guillaume Dufay, and anonymous composers].

3135 * *The spirits of England and France I: music of the later Middle Ages for court and church.* (Gothic Voices/Christopher Page). Hyperion: CDA66739. [Vocal and instrumental music of the 12th–14th centuries, by John Cooke, Matteo da Perugia, Guillaume de Machaut, Pykini, Pérotin?, and anonymous composers].

Renaissance Period

Compiled by
Kent Underwood

Composers

3136 Agricola, Alexander, 1446?–1506

    3136.1 *Sacred music. Selections.* (Chanticleer). *See* 3171.10

    3136.2 *Secular music. Selections.* (Ferrara Ensemble/Crawford Young). Deutsche Harmonia Mundi: 77038-2-RC.

3137 Arcadelt, Jacob, ca. 1505–1568

    Madrigals. Selections. (Consort of Musicke/Anthony Rooley). Deutsche Harmonia Mundi: 77162-2-RC.

3138 Banchieri, Adriano, d. 1634

    Barca di Venetia per Padova [madrigal comedy]. (Ensemble Clément Janequin). Harmonia Mundi: HMC 901281. [With Marenzio, Luca: *Madrigals*].

3139 Bertrand, Antoine de, d. ca. 1581

    Amours de Ronsard [chansons]. (Ensemble Clément Janequin). Harmonia Mundi: HMA 1901147. [With Morlaye, Guillaume: *Lute music.*]

3140 Binchois, Gilles, ca. 1400–1460. *Chansons. Selections.*

    • (Ensemble Gilles Binchois). *See* 3154.1

    • (Gothic Voices). *See* 3256

3141 Brumel, Antoine, ca. 1460–ca. 1515

    3141.1 *Missa Berzerette savoyenne.* (Chanticleer). Chanticleer: CR 8805. [With his selected motets].

    3141.2 * *Missa Et ecce terrae motus.*

    • (Huelgas Ensemble/Paul van Nevel). Sony: SK 46348. [With his *Dies irae*].

    • (Tallis Scholars/Peter Phillips). Gimell: CDGIM 026. [With his *Lamentations* and *Magnificat secundi toni*].

3142 * Bull, John, d. 1628. *Keyboard music. Selections.*

    • (Bob van Asperen) [harpsichord]. Teldec: 8.42874.

    • (Etienne Baillot) [organ]. K.617: K617 003.

    • (Pierre Hantaï) [harpsichord]. Astrée: E 8543.

3143 * Busnois, Antoine, d. 1492

Vocal music. Selections. (Pomerium/Alexander Blachly). Dorian: DOR-90184. [His *Missa O crux lignum triumphale* plus selected motets and chansons].

3144 Byrd, William, 1542 or 1543–1623

3144.1 *Cantiones sacrae, book 1* [motets]. (Choir of New College, Oxford/Edward Higginbottom). CRD: 3408.

3144.2 *Cantiones sacrae, book 2* [motets]. (Choir of New College, Oxford/Edward Higginbottom). CRD: 3439.

3144.3 *Consort songs. Selections.* (Consort of Musicke/Anthony Rooley). L'Oiseau Lyre: 443 187-2. [Album title: *Psalmes, sonets & songs*].

3144.4 *Gradualia, vol. 1.* (William Byrd Choir/Gavin Turner). Hyperion: CDA66451.

3144.5 * *The great service.* (Tallis Scholars/Peter Phillips). Gimell: CDGIM 011. [With his selected anthems].

3144.6 ** *Keyboard music. Selections.*
- (Ursula Duetschler). Claves: 50-9001.
- (Christopher Hogwood). L'Oiseau-Lyre: 430 484-2. 2CD set. [Album title: *My Ladye Nevells booke*].
- (Davitt Moroney). Harmonia Mundi: 901241/42. 2CD set. [Album title: *Pavans and galliards*].

3144.7 ** *Mass for 5 voices.* (Tallis Scholars/Peter Phillips). Gimell: 345. [With his *Mass for 4 voices* and *Mass for 3 voices*].

3144.8 * *Mass for 4 voices.* (Tallis Scholars/Peter Phillips). *See* 3144.7

3144.9 * *Mass for 3 voices.*
- (Choir of Christ Church Cathedral/Stephen Darlington). Nimbus: NI 5302. [With his Propers for the Mass].
- (Tallis Scholars/Peter Phillips). *See* 3144.7

3144.10 * *Viol consort music. Selections.* (Fretwork). *See* 3152.1

3145 Campion, Thomas, 1567–1620

Ayres. Selections. (Drew Minter/Paul O'Dette). Harmonia Mundi: HMU 907023.

3146 Cardoso, Manuel, 1566–1650

Requiem. (Tallis Scholars/Peter Phillips). Gimell: CDGIM 021. [With his *Magnificat* and selected motets].

3147 Carver, Robert, b. ca. 1490

Missa L'homme armé. [Series: Choral music, vol. 2]. (Cappella Nova/Alan Tavener). ASV Gaudeamus: GAU 126. [With his *Six-part Mass*].

3148 * Clemens non Papa, Jacobus, ca. 1510–ca. 1555

Missa Pastores quidnam vidistis. (Tallis Scholars/Peter Phillips). Gimell: CDGIM 013. [With his selected motets].

3149 Compère, Loyset, d. 1518

Vocal music. Selections. (Orlando Consort). Metronome: 1002-01.

3150 Cornago, Juan, 15th cent.

Missa de la mapa mundi. (His Majestie's Clerkes/Paul Hillier). Harmonia Mundi: HMU 907083. [With secular works from 15th-century Spain by Cornago and others].

3151 Cornysh, William, d. 1523

Vocal music. Selections. (Tallis Scholars/Peter Phillips). Gimell: 014.

3152 Dowland, John, 1563?–1626

3152.1 * *Lachrimae, or, seven teares.*
- (Fretwork). Virgin: 7 90795 2; 7 91117 2. 2 CDs. [With Byrd, William: *Viol consort music*].
- (Parley of Instruments/Peter Holman). Hyperion: CDA66637. [Complete pavans and dances].

3152.2 ** *Lute music. Selections.*
- (Jakob Lindberg). Bis: 722/24. 3CD set.
- (Paul O'Dette). Astrée: E 7715.
- (Paul O'Dette). [Series: Complete lute music, vol. 1]. Harmonia Mundi: HMU 907160. [Further volumes forthcoming].

3152.3 * *Songs or ayres.*
- (Emma Kirkby/Anthony Rooley) [selections]. Virgin: 7 59521 2 (7 90768 2).
- (Nigel Rogers/Paul O'Dette) [selections]. Virgin: 7 90726 2.
- (Consort of Musicke/Anthony Rooley). L'Oiseau-Lyre: 421 653-2; 425 889-2; 430 284-2; 436 188-2. 4 CDs.

3153 Du Caurroy, Eustache, 1549–1609

Fantasies [for instrumental ensemble—selections]. (Hespèrion XX/Jordi Savall). Astrée: E 7749.

3154 Dufay, Guillaume, d. 1474

3154.1 * *Chansons.*

- (Medieval Ensemble of London/Peter Davies and Timothy Davies). L'Oiseau-Lyre: D237D. 6LP set. OP

- (Ensemble Gilles Binchois). Harmonic: H/CD 8719. [With Binchois, Gilles: *Chansons*].

- (Early Music Consort/David Munrow). *See* 3081

3154.2 * *Missa Ecce ancilla Domini.* (Ensemble Gilles Binchois). Virgin: CDC 5 45050 2.

3154.3 ** *Missa L'homme armé.* (Hilliard Ensemble/Paul Hillier). EMI: CDC 7 47628 2. [With his selected motets].

3154.4 *Missa Se la face ay pale.*

- (Pro Arte Singers/Thomas Binkley). Focus: 934.

- (Early Music Consort of London/David Munrow). Seraphim: 60267. LP. OP

- (Chiaroscuro Ensemble/Nigel Rogers). Nuova Era: 6741. [With his selected chansons and works by Heinrich Isaac, Orlando di Lasso, and Ludwig Senfl].

3154.5 *Motets. Selections.*

- (Hilliard Ensemble). *See* 3154.3

- (Orlando Consort). *See* 3134

3155 ** Dunstable, John, ca. 1390–1453. *Motets. Selections.*

- (Hilliard Ensemble/Paul Hillier). EMI: CDC 7 49002 2. OP

- (Orlando Consort). Metronome: MET 1009.

3156 * Encina, Juan del, 1468–1529?

Vocal music. Selections. (Hespèrion XX/Jordi Savall). Astrée: E 8707.

3157 Fayrfax, Robert, 1464–1521

3157.1 *Missa Albanus.* (Sixteen/Harry Christophers). Hyperion: CDA66073.

3157.2 * *Missa O quam glorifica.* (Cardinall's Musick/Andrew Carwood/David Skinner). ASV Gaudeamus: GAU 142. [With his motet, *Ave Dei patris filia* and songs, *Sumwhat musyng* and *To complayne me, alas*].

3158 Francesco, da Milano, fl. 1502–1541

Lute music. Selections. (Paul O'Dette). Astrée: E 7705. *See also* 3222

3159 Frye, Walter, d. 1474 or 1475

Vocal music. Selections. (Hilliard Ensemble). ECM: 2476 (437 684-2).

3160 Gabrieli, Andrea, ca. 1533–1585

3160.1 *Organ music. Selections.* (Luigi Ferdinando Tagliavini/Liuwe Tamminga). Tactus: TC 510001. [Music for one and two organs. With Gabrieli, Giovanni: *Organ music*].

3160.2 *Sacred vocal music. Selections. See* 3261

3161 Gabrieli, Giovanni, 1557–1612

3161.1 ** *Canzonas and sonatas* [for instrumental ensembles—selections].

- (London Cornet and Sackbut Ensemble/Andrew Parrott). *See* 3161.3

- (Taverner Consort/Andrew Parrott). *See* 3161.3

- (London Brass/Philip Pickett). Teldec: 4509-90856-2. [With instrumental music by Biagio Marini, Lodovico da Viadana, Girolamo Frescobaldi, Andrea Gabrieli, and Tiburtio Massaino].

- (Hespèrion XX/Jordi Savall). EMI: CDM 7 63141 2. [With Guami, Gioseffo: *Canzonas*].

3161.2 *Organ music. Selections.* (Luigi Ferdinando Tagliavini). *See* 3160.1

3161.3 * *Vocal music. Selections.*

- (Gabrieli Consort/Paul McCreesh). *See* 3261

- (Currende/Concerto Palatino/Erik van Nevel). *See* 3205

- (Taverner Consort/Andrew Parrott). EMI: CDC 7 54265 2.

- (Taverner Choir/London Cornet and Sackbut Ensemble/Andrew Parrott). L'Oiseau-Lyre: 436 860-2. [Selections from *Symphoniae sacrae II, 1615*].

3162 Gesualdo, Carlo, principe di Venosa, ca. 1560–1613

3162.1 * *Madrigals. Selections.*

- (Les Arts Florissants/William Christie). Harmonia Mundi: HMC 901268.

- (Consort of Musicke/Anthony Rooley). L'Oiseau-Lyre: 410 128-2. [His *Book 5* complete].

3162.2 *Tenebrae responsories.*

- (Hilliard Ensemble/Paul Hillier). ECM: 843 867-2. 2CD set.

- (Tallis Scholars/Peter Phillips). Gimell: CDGIM 015.

3163 Gibbons, Orlando, 1583–1625

3163.1 *Consort music. Selections.*

- (Fretwork). Virgin: 7 59667 2 (7 90849 2).

- (Hespèrion XX/Jordi Savall). Astrée: E 7747.

3163.2 *Sacred music. Selections.* (Choir of New College, Oxford/Edward Higginbottom). CRD: 3451.

3164 * Gombert, Nicolas, 16th cent.

Missa in tempori paschali. (Huelgas Ensemble/Paul van Nevel). Sony: SK 48249. [With his *Magnificat secundi toni,* motets, and chansons].

3165 Guami, Gioseffo, ca. 1540–1611

Canzonas. Selections. (Hespèrion XX/Jordi Savall). *See* 3161.1

3166 Guerrero, Francisco, 1528?–1599

Motets. Selections. (Capella Reial de Catalunya/ Jordi Savall). Astrée: 8766. [Album title: *Sacrae cantiones*].

3167 Hassler, Hans Leo, 1564–1612

Missa I super Dixit Maria. (Chapelle Royale/ Philippe Herreweghe). Harmonia Mundi: HMC 901401. [With his selected motets and *Vater unser im Himmelreich.*

3168 Isaac, Heinrich, ca. 1450–1517

  3168.1 *Missa de apostolis.* (Tallis Scholars/Peter Phillips). Gimell: CDGIM 023. [With his selected motets].

  3168.2 * *Missa Paschale.* (Hilliard Ensemble/Kees Boeke Consort). EMI: CDM 7 63063 2. [Album title: *Sacred and secular works,* also including motets, instrumental, pieces, and vernacular songs].

3169 * Janequin, Clément, ca. 1495–ca. 1560. *Chansons. Selections.*

  • (Ensemble Clément Janequin). Harmonia Mundi: HMC 901099. [Album title: *Le chant des oyseaulx*].

  • (Ensemble Clément Janequin). Harmonia Mundi: HMC 901271. [Album title: *La chasse et autres chansons*].

  • (Ensemble Clément Janequin). Harmonia Mundi: HMC 901272. [Album title: *Les cris de Paris.* With Sermisy, Claudin de: *Chansons*].

3170 Johnson, Robert, ca. 1583–1633

Songs. Selections. (Emma Kirkby/David Thomas/ Anthony Rooley). Virgin: CDC 7 59321 2. [Album title: *Shakespeare's lutenist*].

3171 Josquin, des Prez, d. 1521

  3171.1 * *Chansons. Selections.*

  • (Ensemble Clément Janequin/Ensemble Les Elements). Harmonia Mundi: HMC 901279.

[Album title: *Adieu mes amours et autres chansons*].

  • (Hilliard Ensemble/Paul Hillier). *See* 3171.12

  • (King's Singers). *See* 3171.12

  • (Taverner Consort/Andrew Parrott). *See* 3171.2

  3171.2 * *Missa Ave maris stella.*

  • (A Sei Voci). Astrée: E 8507. [With his selected motets].

  • (Taverner Consort/Andrew Parrott). EMI: CDC 7 54659 2. [With his selected motets and chansons].

  3171.3 ** *Missa de Beata Virgine.*

  • (A Sei Voci). Astrée Auvidis: E 8560. [With his selected motets].

  • (Theatre of Voices/Paul Hillier). Harmonia Mundi: HMU 907136. [With Mouton, Jean: *Motets*].

  3171.4 *Missa di dadi.* (Medieval Ensemble of London/Peter and Timothy Davies). L'Oiseau-Lyre: 411 937-2. [With his *Missa Faisant regretz*].

  3171.5 *Missa Faisant regretz.* (Medieval Ensemble of London/Peter and Timothy Davies). *See* 3171.4

  3171.6 * *Missa Hercules Dux Ferrariae.* (Hilliard Ensemble/Paul Hillier). EMI: CDC 7 49960 2. [With his selected motets].

  3171.7 *Missa L'ami baudechon.* (Capella Alamire/Peter Urquhart). Dorian: DOR-80131. [With his *Magnificat, Credo sine nomine,* and *Credo De tous biens playne;* and Ockeghem, Johannes: *Credo sine nomine*].

  3171.8 * *Missa La sol fa re mi.* (Tallis Scholars/ Peter Phillips). *See* 3171.11

  3171.9 * *Missa L'homme armé* [two versions]. (Tallis Scholars/Peter Phillips). Gimell: CDGIM 019.

  3171.10 *Missa Mater Patris.* (Chanticleer). Chanticleer: CR 8808. [With Agricola, Alexander: *Magnificat* and motets].

  3171.11 * *Missa Pange lingua.*

  • (Ensemble Clément Janequin/Ensemble Organum). Harmonia Mundi: HMC 901239. [With plainchant Propers for the Mass].

  • (Tallis Scholars/Peter Phillips). Gimell: CDGIM 009. [With his *Missa La sol fa re mi*].

  3171.12 * *Motets. Selections.*

  • (A Sei Voci). *See* 3171.2 and 3171.3

- (Chapelle Royale/Philippe Herreweghe). Harmonia Mundi: HMC 901243.
- (Choir of New College, Oxford/Edward Higginbottom). Meridian: ECD 84093.
- (Hilliard Ensemble/Paul Hillier). EMI: CDC 7 49209 2. [With his selected chansons]. *See also* 3171.6
- (King's Singers). RCA: 09026-61814-2. [With his selected chansons].
- (Taverner Consort/Andrew Parrott). *See* 3171.2

3172 La Rue, Pierre de, d. 1518

3172.1 *Missa L'homme armé.* (Ensemble Clément Janequin). Harmonia Mundi: HMC 901296. [With his *Missa pro defunctis*].

3172.2 *Missa pro defunctis (Requiem).* (Ensemble Clément Janequin). *See* 3172.1

3173 Lasso, Orlando di, 1532–1594

3173.1 *Hieremiae prophetae lamentationes (Lamentations of Jeremiah).* (Chapelle Royale/ Philippe Herreweghe). Harmonia Mundi: HMC 901299.

3173.2 *Le lagrime di San Pietro (Tears of St. Peter)* [spiritual madrigal cycle]. (European Vocal Ensemble/Philippe Herreweghe). Harmonia Mundi: HMC 901483.

3173.3 *Missa Bell'Amfritit'altera.* (Sixteen/Harry Christophers). *See* 3251

3173.4 *Missa Osculetur me.* (Tallis Scholars/ Peter Phillips). Gimell: CDGIM 018. [With his selected motets].

3173.5 * *Motets. Selections.*

- (Collegium Vocale/Philippe Herreweghe). Astrée: E 7780. [From the collection *Moduli quinis vocibus (1571)*].
- (Hilliard Ensemble/Paul Hillier). Virgin: 5 61166 2. [With his selected chansons].
- (Currende Ensemble/Concerto Palatino/Erik van Nevel). Accent: ACC 8855 D. [From the collection *Patrocinium musices (1573–1574)*].
- (Tallis Scholars/Peter Phillips). *See* 3173.4

3173.6 * *Psalmi Davidis poenitentiales (Penitential psalms).* (Hilliard Ensemble/Kees Boeke Consort). Virgin: 5 61216 2. 2CD set.

3173.7 * *Secular music. Selections.*

- (Concerto Italiano/Rinaldo Alessandrini). Opus 111: OPS 30-94. [Album title: *Villanelle, moresche e altre canzoni*].

- (Ensemble Clément Janequin) Harmonia Mundi: HMC 901391. [Album title: *Chansons & moresche*].
- (Hilliard Ensemble/Paul Hillier). *See* 3173.5
- (King's Singers). EMI: CDC 7 49158 2. [Album title: *To all things a season*].

3174 Le Jeune, Claude, d. 1600

Meslanges [chansons and instrumental fantasias—selections]. (Ensemble Clément Janequin/Ensemble Les Elements). Harmonia Mundi: HMC 901182.

3175 Lobo, Duarte, 1565–1646

Requiem. (Tallis Scholars/Peter Phillips). Gimell: CDGIM 028. [With his *Missa Vox clamantis*].

3176 * Marenzio, Luca, 1553–1599. *Madrigals. Selections.*

- (Concerto Italiano/Rinaldo Alessandrini). Opus 111: OPS 30-117. [His First book of four-part madrigals, complete].
- (Ensemble Clément Janequin). *See* 3138
- (Concerto Vocale/René Jacobs). Harmonia Mundi: HMA 1901065.
- (Consort of Musicke/Anthony Rooley). Musica Oscura: 070992.

3177 * Milán, Luis, 16th cent.

El Maestro [vihuela music and songs with vihuela—selections]. (Montserrat Figueras/Hopkinson Smith). Astrée: E 7748; E 7777. 2 CDs.

3178 Monte, Philippe de, 1521–1603

Vocal music. Selections. (Hilliard Ensemble/Kees Boeke Consort). EMI: CDM 7 63428 2. [His *Missa La dolce vista*, plus selected motets, madrigals, and chansons].

3179 Morales, Cristóbal de, ca. 1500–1553

3179.1 *Missa Mille regretz.* (Chanticleer). Chanticleer: CR 8809. [With his selected motets].

3179.2 *Missa Quaeramus cum pastoribus.* (Westminster Cathedral Choir/James O'Donnell). Hyperion: CDA66635. [With his selected motets].

3179.3 * *Officium defunctorum (Requiem).* (Capella Reial de Catalunya/Hespèrion XX/Jordi Savall). Astrée: E 8765.

3180 * Morley, Thomas, 1557–1603?

Vocal and instrumental music. Selections. (Musicians of Swanne Alley/Red Byrd). Virgin: 7 59032 2 (7 91214 2). [Album title: *Joyne hands*].

3181 Mouton, Jean, d. 1522
Motets. Selections. See 3171.3

3182 * Mudarra, Alonso, ca. 1506–1580
Tres libros de musica en cifra para vihuela, 1546 [vihuela music—selections]. (Hopkinson Smith). Astrée: E 8740.

3183 Mundy, William, 1529–ca. 1591. *Sacred music. Selections.*
- (Sixteen/Harry Christophers). Hyperion: 66319. [Album title: *Cathedral music*].
- (Tallis Scholars/Peter Phillips). *See* 3267

3184 Narváez, Luis de, 16th cent. *Los seys libros del delphin de musica* [vihuela music—selections].
- (Lex Eisenhardt). Etcetera: KTC 1114.
- (Hopkinson Smith). Astrée: E 8706.

3185 Obrecht, Jacob, d. 1505
3185.1 * *Missa Maria zart.* (Tallis Scholars/Peter Phillips). Gimell: 032.
3185.2 *Motets. Selections.* (Clerkes Group/Edward Wickham). *See* 3186.2

3186 Ockeghem, Johannes, d. 1496?
3186.1 *Missa Ecce ancilla Domini.* (Clerkes Group/Edward Wickham). Proud Sound: PROU 133. [With his selected motets].
3186.2 ** *Missa Mi-mi.*
- (Hilliard Ensemble/Paul Hillier). EMI: CDC 7 49213 2. [With his *Requiem*].
- (Clerkes Group/Edward Wickham). ASV/Gaudeamus: GAU 139. [With motets by Ockeghem, Jacob Obrecht, Heinrich Isaac, and Antoine Busnois].
3186.3 * *Missa Prolationum.*
- (Hilliard Ensemble/Paul Hillier). EMI: CDC 7 49798 2. [With his selected motets].
- (Capella Nova/Richard Taruskin). ASV/Gaudeamus: GAU 103-R.
3186.4 *Missa Sine nomine.* (Schola Discantus/ Kevin Moll). Lyrichord: LEMS 8010. [With his *Missa Quinti toni*].
3186.5 *Missa Quinti toni.* (Schola Discantus/ Kevin Moll). *See* 3186.4
3186.6 * *Motets. Selections.*
- (Hilliard Ensemble/Paul Hillier). *See* 3186.3
- (Clerkes Group/Edward Wickham). *See* 3186.2
3186.7 * *Requiem.*
- (Hilliard Ensemble/Paul Hillier). *See* 3186.2

- (Ensemble Organum/Marcel Pérès). Harmonia Mundi: HMC 901441.
3186.8 *Secular music.* (Medieval Ensemble of London/Peter and Timothy Davies). L'Oiseau-Lyre: 436 194-2. 2CD set.

3187 Palestrina, Giovanni Pierluigi da, 1525?–1594
3187.1 * *Canticum canticorum Salomonis (Song of songs)* [motet cycle]. (Hilliard Ensemble/Paul Hillier). Virgin: 5 61168 2. 2CD set. [With his complete *Vergine* cycle of spiritual madrigals].
3187.2 *Magnificat primi toni.*
- (Chapelle Royale/Philippe Herreweghe). *See* 3187.16
- (Westminster Cathedral Choir/James O'Donnell). *See* 3187.3
3187.3 *Missa Aeterna Christi munera.* (Westminster Cathedral Choir/James O'Donnell). Hyperion: CDA66490. [With his *Magnificat primi toni* and selected motets].
3187.4 * *Missa Assumpta est Maria.*
- (Pro Cantione Antiqua/Mark Brown). *See* 3187.10
- (Chapelle Royale/Philippe Herreweghe). Ricercar: RIC 008029. [With his selected motets].
- (Tallis Scholars/Peter Phillips). Gimell: CDGIM 020. [With his *Missa Sicut lilium*].
3187.5 *Missa Ave Maria.* (Westminster Cathedral Choir/James O'Donnell). *See* 3187.8
3187.6 *Missa Benedicta es.* (Tallis Scholars/Peter Phillips). Gimell: CDGIM 001.
3187.7 * *Missa brevis.* (Tallis Scholars/Peter Phillips). Gimell: CDGIM 008. [With his *Missa Nasce la gioja mia*].
3187.8 *Missa de Beata Virgine.* (Westminster Cathedral Choir/James O'Donnell). Hyperion: CDA66364. [With his *Missa Ave Maria* and selected motets].
3187.9 * *Missa Hodie Christus natus es.* (Gabrieli Consort/Paul McCreesh). Archiv: 437 833-2. [With works by Josquin des Prez, Girolamo Frescobaldi, Tomás Luis de Victoria, Giovanni Francesco Anerio, and Domenico Mazzocchi].
3187.10 *Missa L'homme armé.* (Pro Cantione Antiqua/Mark Brown). Allegro: PCD 952. [With his *Missa Assumpta est Maria*].
3187.11 *Missa Nasce la gioja mia.* (Tallis Scholars/Peter Phillips). *See* 3187.7
3187.12 ** *Missa Nigra sum.* (Tallis Scholars/ Peter Phillips). Gimell: CDGIM 003. [With

motets by Jean Lhéritier, Andreas de Silva, and Tomás Luis de Victoria].

3187.13 *Missa O rex gloriae. See 3187.16*

3187.14 *Missa O sacrum convivium.* (Choir of Christ Church Cathedral, Oxford/Stephen Darlington). Nimbus: NI 5394.

3187.15 ** *Missa Papae Marcelli.* (Tallis Scholars/ Peter Phillips). *See 3267*

3187.16 * *Missa Viri Galilaei.*

- (Chapelle Royale/Philippe Herreweghe). Harmonia Mundi: HMC 901388. [With his *Magnificat primi toni*].
- (Westminster Cathedral Choir/James O'Donnell). Hyperion: CDA 66316. [With his *Missa O rex gloriae* and selected motets].

3187.17 * *Motets. Selections. See 3187.1, 3187.3, 3187.4, 3187.8, and 3187.16*

3187.18 *Le Vergine* [cycle of spiritual madrigals on Petrarch lyrics]. (Hilliard Ensemble). *See 3187.1*

3188 Peñalosa, Francisco de, ca. 1470–1528

Missa Ave Maria peregrina. (Westminster Cathedral Choir/James O'Donnell). Hyperion: CDA66629. [With his *Sacris solemniis* and *Missa Nunca fue pena mayor*].

3189 Power, Leonel, d. 1445

Sacred music. Selections. (Hilliard Ensemble/Paul Hillier). EMI: CDM 7 63064 2.

3190 Praetorius, Michael, 1571–1621

3190.1 *Christmas music.* (Westminster Cathedral Choir/Parley of Instruments/Peter Holman). Hyperion: CDA66200. [With selections from his *Terpsichore*].

3190.2 *Motets. Selections.* (Taverner Consort/ Andrew Parrott). *See 3347.11*

3190.3 * *Terpsichore* [instrumental dances—selections]. (Parley of Instruments/Peter Holman). *See 3190.1*

3191 Rore, Cipriano de, 1515 or 1516–1565

3191.1 *Madrigals. Selections.*

- (Hilliard Ensemble/Paul Hillier). Harmonia Mundi: HMA 1901107. [His complete *Vergine* cycle plus selected four-part madrigals].
- (Consort of Musicke/Anthony Rooley). Musica Oscura: 07099. [His *Book 5* complete].

3191.2 * *Missa Praeter rerum seriem.* (Tallis Scholars/Peter Phillips). Gimell: CDGIM 029. [With his selected motets].

3191.3 *Motets. Selections.* (Tallis Scholars/Peter Phillips). *See 3191.2*

3192 * Senfl, Ludwig, ca. 1486–1542 or 1543

Secular music. Selections. (Early Music Consort of London/David Munrow). *See 3260*

3193 Sermisy, Claudin de, ca. 1490–1562

3193.1 * *Chansons. Selections.* (Ensemble Clément Janequin). *See 3169*

3193.2 *Leçons de ténèbres.* (Ensemble Clément Janequin). Harmonia Mundi: HMA 1901131. [With his selected motets].

3194 Sheppard, John, ca. 1515–ca. 1560

3194.1 *Missa Cantate.* [Series: Church music, vol. 2]. (Sixteen/Harry Christophers). Hyperion: CDA66418. [With his hymns].

3194.2 * *Motets. Selections.*

- (Sixteen/Harry Christophers). [Series: Church music, vol. 1]. Hyperion: 66259.
- (Sixteen/Harry Christophers). [Series: Church music, vol. 3]. Hyperion: 66570.
- (Tallis Scholars/Peter Phillips). Gimell: CDGIM 016. [Album title: *Media vita*].

3194.3 * *Western wynde Mass.*

- (Sixteen/Harry Christophers). [Series: Church music, vol. 4]. Hyperion: 66603. [With his selected motets and English service music.]
- (Tallis Scholars/Peter Phillips). Gimell: CDGIM 027. [With Taverner, John: *Western wynde Mass* and Tye, Christopher: *Western wynde Mass*].

3195 * Susato, Tielman, fl. 1529–1561

Dance music. Selections. (New London Consort/ Philip Pickett). L'Oiseau-Lyre: 436 131-2.

3196 * Sweelinck, Jan Pieterszoon, 1562–1621. *Keyboard music. Selections.*

- (James David Christie) [organ]. Naxos: 8.550904.
- (Piet Kee) [organ]. *See 3275.3*
- (Gustav Leonhardt) [organ]. Deutsche Harmonia Mundi: 77148-2-RG.
- (Anneke Uittenbosch) [harpsichord and organ]. Globe: GLO 5030.

3197 Tallis, Thomas, ca. 1505–1585

3197.1 * *English anthems.* (Tallis Scholars/Peter Phillips). Gimell: CDGIM 007.

3197.2 ** *Lamentations of Jeremiah.*

- (Taverner Consort/Andrew Parrott). *See 3197.4*

- (Tallis Scholars/Peter Phillips). Gimell: CDGIM 025. [With his selected motets].

3197.3 *Mass Puer natus est.* (Clerkes of Oxenford/David Wulstan). Calliope: CAL 1623. [With his selected motets and White, Robert: *Motets*].

3197.4 * *Motets. Selections.*

- (Taverner Consort/Andrew Parrott). EMI: CDC 7 49555 2; 7 49563 2. 2CDs [Album title: *Latin church music,* including his *Lamentations of Jeremiah.*]

- (Tallis Scholars/Peter Phillips). Gimell: CDGIM 006. [Album title: *Spem in alium*]. *See also* 3197.2

- (Clerkes of Oxenford/David Wulstan). *See* 3197.3

3198   Taverner, John, ca. 1495–1545

3198.1 *Missa Corona spinea.* (Sixteen/Harry Christophers). Hyperion: CDA66360. [With his selected motets].

3198.2 * *Missa Gloria tibi Trinitas.*

- (Sixteen/Harry Christophers). Hyperion: CDA66134. [With his motet, *Audivi vocem*].

- (Tallis Scholars/Peter Phillips). Gimell: CDGIM 004. [With his *Leroy Kyrie* and motet, *Dum transisset Sabbatum*].

3198.3 *Missa Mater Christi sanctissima.* (Sixteen/Harry Christophers). Hyperion: CDA66639. [With his *Magnificat* and selected motets].

3198.4 *Missa O Michael.* (Sixteen/Harry Christophers). Hyperion: CDA66325. [With his *Leroy Kyrie* and motet, *Dum transisset Sabbatum*].

3198.5 *Missa Sancte Wilhelmi.* (Sixteen/Harry Christophers). Hyperion: CDA66427. [With his selected motets].

3198.6 *Motets. Selections.* (Sixteen/Harry Christophers). *See* 3198.1, 3198.2, 3198.3, 3198.4, 3198.5, and 3198.7

3198.7 * *Western wynde Mass.*

- (Sixteen/Harry Christophers). Hyperion: CDA66507. [With his selected motets].

- (Tallis Scholars). *See* 3194.3

3199   Tomkins, Thomas, 1572–1656

The great service. (Tallis Scholars/Peter Phillips). Gimell: CDGIM 024.

3200   Tye, Christopher, 1497?–1572

3200.1 * *Consort music. Selections.* (Hespèrion XX/Jordi Savall). Astrée: E 8708.

3200.2 *Western wynde Mass. See* 3194.3

3201   Vecchi, Orazio, 1550–1605

L'Amfiparnaso [madrigal comedy]. (Ensemble Clément Janequin). Harmonia Mundi: HMC 901461. [With his *Il convito musicale*].

3202   Victoria, Tomás Luis de, ca. 1548–1611

3202.1 *Missa Ascendens Christus in altum. See* 3202.3

3202.2 *Missa Ave maris stella. See* 3202.4

3202.3 * *Missa O magnum mysterium.* (Westminster Cathedral Choir/David Hill). Hyperion: CDA66190. [With his *Missa Ascendens Christus in altum* and selected motets].

3202.4 *Missa O quam gloriosum.* (Westminster Cathedral Choir/David Hill). Hyperion: CDA66114. [With his *Missa Ave maris stella* and selected motets].

3202.5 *Missa Vidi speciosam.* (Westminster Cathedral Choir/David Hill). Hyperion: CDA66129. [With his selected motets].

3202.6 * *Motets. Selections.*

- (Westminster Cathedral Choir/David Hill). *See* 3202.3, 3202.4, and 3202.5

- (Capella Reial de Catalunya/Jordi Savall). Astrée: 8767.

3202.7 * *Requiem.* (Tallis Scholars/Peter Phillips). Gimell: CDGIM 012. [With Lobo, Alonso: *Versa est in luctum*].

3202.8 *Tenebrae responsories.*

- (Westminster Cathedral Choir/David Hill). Hyperion: CDA66304.

- (Tallis Scholars/Peter Phillips). Gimell: CDGIM 022.

3203   Wert, Giaches de, 1535–1596

3203.1 *Madrigals. Selections.* (Consort of Musicke/Anthony Rooley). Virgin: 7 59161 2 (7 90763 20). [His *Book 7* complete].

3203.2 *Motets. Selections.* (Currende/Concerto Palatino/Erik van Nevel). Accent: ACC 9291 D. [Album title: *Musica religiosa,* also including excerpts from his *Missa Dominicalis*].

3204   White, Robert, d. 1574

3204.1 *Lamentations of Jeremiah.*

- (Tallis Scholars/Peter Phillips). Gimell: CDGIM 030. [With his selected motets].

- (Clerkes of Oxenford/David Wulstan). *See* 3085

3204.2 *Motets. Selections.*

- (Tallis Scholars/Peter Phillips). *See* 3204.1

- (Clerkes of Oxenford/David Wulstan). *See* 3197.3

3205 Willaert, Adrian, 1490?–1562

Motets. Selections. (Currende/Concerto Palatino/ Erik van Nevel). Accent: ACC 93101 S. [Album title: *Venetian music for double choir,* also including instrumental music by Willaert and motets and instrumental music by Giovanni Gabrieli].

Anthologies and Recitals

3206 *Al alva venid: música profana de los siglos XV y XVI.* (Ensemble La Romanesca/José Miguel Moreno). Glossa: GCD 920203. [Spanish secular music of the 15th–16th centuries by Luis de Narváez, Juan del Encina, Diego Ortiz, Alonso Mudarra, and others].

3207 ** *All at once well met: English madrigals.* (King's Singers). EMI: CDC 7 49265 2. [Music by John Farmer, Thomas Tomkins, Thomas Morley, Thomas Weelkes, John Wilbye, John Bennet, John Dowland, Giles Farnaby, Robert Jones, Francis Pilkington, John Mundy, George Kirbye, and William Byrd].

3208 *Ancient ayres and dances.* (Paul O'Dette). Hyperion: CDA66228. [Original solo lute versions of pieces arranged by Ottorino Respighi in his *Antiche arie e danze* suites. Music by Simone Molinaro, Vincenzo Galilei, Fabritio Caroso, Jean Baptiste Besard, Antoine Boësset, Bernardo Gianoncelli, Santino Garsi da Parma, Lodovico Roncalli, and anonymous composers].

3209 *Armada: music from the courts of Philip II and Elizabeth I.* (Michael Chance/Fretwork). Virgin: 7 90722 2. [English and Spanish vocal and instrumental music by William Byrd, Antonio de Cabezón, Miguel de Fuenllana, Elway Bevin, Diego Ortiz, Hernando de Cabezón, Robert Parsons, and Robert White].

3210 * *The art of the Netherlands.* (Early Music Consort of London/David Munrow). EMI: CMS 7 64215 2. 2CD set. [Sacred and secular vocal and instrumental music of the late 15th and early 16th centuries by Josquin des Prez, Heinrich Isaac, Hayne van Ghizeghem, Alexander Agricola, Antoine Brumel, Johannes Ghiselin, Jacques Barbireau, Paul Hofhaimer, Jacob Obrecht, Johannes Ockeghem, Antoine Busnois, Johannes Tinctoris, Francesco Spinacino, Pierre de La Rue, Loyset Compère, and Jean Mouton].

3211 *As I went to Walsingham: Elizabethan music.* (Musicians of Swanne Alley). Harmonia Mundi: HMC 905192. [Instrumental and vocal music by John Johnson, Richard Allison, William Byrd, Edward Collarde, Guillaume Tessier, Anthony Holborne, and anonymous composers].

3212 *Il ballarino: Italian dances ca. 1600.* (Broadside Band/Jeremy Barlow). Hyperion: CDA66244. [Music from the dance treatises of Fabritio Caroso and Cesare Negri, plus works by Giovanni Picchi, Antonio Valente, Giovanni Giacomo Gastoldi, and others].

3213 *The brightest heaven of invention: Flemish polyphony of the high Renaissance.* (New London Chamber Choir/James Wood). Amon Ra: CD-SAR 56). [15th-century sacred music by Johannes Regis, Jacob Obrecht, Josquin des Prez, Antoine Brumel, Guillaume Dufay, and Antoine Busnois].

3214 *Buxheimer Orgelbuch 1460–1470?: extraits.* (Ton Koopman). Astrée: E 7743. [Excerpts from an anonymous 15th-century collection of organ music].

3215 * *El cancionero de la Colombina: 1451–1506.* (Hespèrion XX/Jordi Savall). Astrée: E 8763. [Spanish secular music by Francisco de La Torre, Juan Urrede, Hurtado de Xerés, Juan Cornago, and others].

3216 * *El cancionero de palacio: 1474–1516.* (Hespèrion XX/Jordi Savall). Astrée: E 8762. [Spanish secular music by Francisco de La Torre, Francisco de Peñalosa, Juan de Anchieta, Juan Ponce, Juan del Encina, and others].

3217 * *The castle of fair welcome: courtly songs of the later 15th century.* (Gothic Voices/Christopher Page). Hyperion: CDA66194. [Music by Robert Morton, Johannes Regis, John Bedyngham, Gilles Binchois, Guillaume Dufay, Johannes Vincenet, Walter Frye, Charles the Bold, Enrique, and anonymous composers].

3218 ** *Chansons nouvelles et danceries.* (Ensemble Doulce Memoire). Astrée Auvidis: E 8545. [French chansons and dances of the early 16th century from collections of the publisher Pierre Attaingnant. Music by Claudin de Sermisy, Claude Gervaise, Pierre Sandrin, Jacotin, Pierre Certon, Pierre Cadéac, Antoine de Mornable, Jean Courtois, and anonymous composers].

3219 *Concerto delle donne: madrigali.* (Consort of Musicke/Anthony Rooley). Deutsche Harmonia Mundi: 77154-2-RC. [Virtuoso Italian madrigals featuring women's voice by Luca Marenzio, Luzzasco

Luzzaschi, Barbara Strozzi, Giacomo Carissimi, and Alessandro Scarlatti].

3220 * *Danses populaires françaises et anglaises du XVIe siècle.* (Broadside Band/Jeremy Barlow). Harmonia Mundi: HMC 901152. [16th-century popular dances from the collections of Thoinot Arbeau and John Playford].

3221 *La dolce vita: music in Renaissance Naples.* (King's Singers/Tragicomedia). EMI: CDC 7 54191 2. [Vocal and instrumental music, mostly 16th-century, by Pietro Antonio Giramo, Adrian Willaert, Gian Domenico da Nola, Giovanni de Macque, Alessandro Piccinini, Diego Ortiz, Francesco Lambardi, Alonso Mudarra, Lodovico Agostini, and anonymous composers].

3222 * *Dolcissima et amorosa: early Italian Renaissance lute music.* (Paul O'Dette). Harmonia Mundi: HMU 907043. [Music by Francesco da Milano, Pietro Paolo Borrono, Marco dall'Aquila, and Alberto da Ripa].

3223 *Draw on sweet night: English madrigals.* (Hilliard Ensemble/Paul Hillier). EMI: CDC 7 49197 2. [Works by Thomas Morley, Thomas Weelkes, John Wilbye, John Bennet, Orlando Gibbons, Thomas Tomkins, and John Ward].

3224 * *Elizabethan songs.* (Emma Kirkby/Anthony Rooley). L'Oiseau-Lyre: 425 892-2. [Solo songs with lute by Thomas Campion, John Dowland, John Danyel, Francis Pilkington, Thomas Morley, Robert Jones, and John Bartlett].

3225 *English and Italian madrigals.* (King's Singers). EMI: CDC 7 63052 2. [Music by Thomas Morley, Thomas Weelkes, John Wilbye, John Bennet, John Farmer, Sebastiano Festa, Fra Pietro da Hostia, Giaches de Wert, Gian Domenico da Nola, Adriano Banchieri, Orlando di Lasso, and others].

3226 *English lute duets.* (Jakob Lindberg/Paul O'Dette). Bis: 267. [Music by Alfonso Ferrabosco, John Dowland, John Danyel, John Johnson, Thomas Robinson, Jean Marchant, and anonymous composers].

3227 *The English lute song.* (Julianne Baird/Ronn McFarlane). Dorian: DOR-90109. [Music by Robert Johnson, Thomas Morley, Nicholas Lanier, Alfonso Ferrabosco, John Wilson, Thomas Campion, Thomas Brewer, William Webb, and anonymous composers].

3228 * *Faire, sweet, cruell.* (Christina Hogman/Jakob Lindberg). Bis: 257. [Solo songs with lute by Thomas Ford, Thomas Campion, John Danyel, John Dowland, Francis Pilkington, and anonymous composers].

3229 * *Fantasias, pavans & galliards.* (Gustav Leonhardt). Philips: 438 153-2. [English music for harpsichord and virginals by William Byrd, Robert Johnson, Peter Phillips, Thomas Morley, John Bull, William Randall, Giles Farnaby, and Orlando Gibbons].

3230 * *Fricassée parisiènne.* (Ensemble Clément Janequin). Harmonia Mundi: HMA 1901174. [16th-century French chansons by Clément Janequin, Claudin de Sermisy, Guillaume Morlaye, Thomas Crecquillon, Guillaume Costeley, Pierre Sandrin, Pierre Certon, Alberto da Ripa, Ninot le Petit, and others].

3231 *From a Spanish palace songbook: music from the time of Christopher Columbus.* (Margaret Philpot). Hyperion: CDA66454. [Music for voice and lutes by Juan del Encina, Francisco de La Torre, Francesco da Milano, Joan Ambrosio Dalza, Vincenzo Capirola, Juan de Anchieta, and others].

3232 *The garden of Zephirus: courtly songs of the early 15th century.* (Gothic Voices/Christopher Page). Hyperion: CDA66144. [Music by Guillaume Dufay, Francesco Landini, Bartolomeo Brolo, Francus de Insula, Matheus de Sancto Johanne, Gacian Reyneau, Briquet, Anthonello da Caserta, and anonymous composers].

3233 *Gentil madonna: a vision of the Italian Renaissance.* (London Pro Musica/Bernard Thomas). United: 88004. [16th-century secular vocal and instrumental music by Fillippo Azzaiolo, Diego Ortiz, Gian Domenico da Nola, Andrea Gabrieli, Sebastiano Festa, Francesco Patavino, Giovanni Pacoloni, Vincenzo Bell'Haver, Orlando di Lasso, and Adrian Willaert].

3234 *Greensleeves: a collection of English lute songs.* (Julianne Baird/Ronn McFarlane). Dorian: DOR-90126. [Songs and lute music by Thomas Morley, Thomas Campion, Alfonso Ferrabosco, Philip Rosseter, Anthony Holborne, John Dowland, Michael Cavendish, Nicholas Lanier, and anonymous composers].

3235 *In nomine: 16th-century English music for viols.* (Fretwork). Musical Heritage Society: 11231K; or Amon Ra: CD-SAR 29. [Music by Thomas Tallis, Christopher Tye, William Cornysh, John Taverner, William Byrd, John Bull, Alfonso Ferrabosco, and others].

3236 *In the streets and theatres of London: Elizabethan ballads and theatre music.* (Musicians of Swanne Alley). Virgin: 7 90789 2. [Music by Thomas Kete, Robert Johnson, John Johnson, Fillippo Azzaiolo, Clement Woodcocke, Thomas Campion, and anonymous composers].

3237 ** *The King's Singers madrigal history tour.* (King's Singers/Consort of Musicke). EMI: CDM 7 69837 2. [16th-century secular vocal music from Italy, England, France, Spain, and Germany by Giovanni Giacomo Gastoldi, Philippe Verdelot, Giaches de Wert, John Dowland, William Byrd, Thomas Tomkins, John Farmer, Orlando Gibbons, Thomas Morley, Jacob Arcadelt, Claude Le Jeune, Adrian Willaert, Alonso Mudarra, Juan del Encina, Mateo Flecha, Hans Leo Hassler, Ludwig Senfl, Paul Hofhaimer, and others].

3238 *The mannerist revolution.* (Pomerium/Alexander Blachly). Dorian: DOR-90154. [Motets and madrigals by Carlo Gesualdo, Giaches de Wert, Luca Marenzio, and Claudio Monteverdi].

3239 * *Music from the Eton Choirbook.* (Sixteen/Harry Christophers). [English sacred music of the late 15th century].

3239.1 [vol. 1] *The rose and the ostrich feather.* Collins: 13142. [Music by William Cornysh, John Browne, Edmund Turges, Richard Hygons, and Robert Fayrfax].

3239.2 [vol. 2] *The crown of thorns.* Collins: 13162. [Music by John Browne, Sheryngham, William Cornysh, and Richard Davy].

3239.3 [vol. 3] *The pillars of eternity.* Collins: 13422. [Music by Robert Wilkinson, Richard Davy, Walter Lambe, and William Cornysh].

3239.4 [vol. 4] *The flower of all virginity.* Collins: 13952. [Music by John Browne, Robert Fayrfax, John Nesbett, and Hugh Kellyk].

3239.5 [vol. 5] *The voices of angels.* Collins: 14622. [Music by Walter Lambe, William, monk of Stratford, John Plummer, and Richard Davy].

3240 *Music from the Spanish kingdoms.* (Circa 1500 Ensemble). CRD: 3447. [Music of the late 15th and early 16th centuries by Miguel de Fuenllana, Giovan Tomas di Maio, Diego Ortiz, Johannis Martini, Loyset Compère, Josquin des Prez, Juan Vasquez, Alonso Mudarra, Bartolomeo Tromboncino, Francesco da Milano, Marchetto Cara, Adrian Willaert, Alonso Hernandez, and Juan del Encina].

3241 * *Music of the Sistine Chapel.* (Taverner Choir and Consort/Andrew Parrott). EMI: CDC 7 47699 2.

[Sacred music by Giovanni Pierluigi da Palestrina, Gregorio Allegri, Cristóbal de Morales, and Josquin des Prez].

3242 *Musicque de joye.* (Hespèrion XX/Jordi Savall). Astrée: E 7724. [Instrumental ensemble music from the anthology of Jacques Moderne, ca. 1550. Works by Julio Segni, Gabriel Costa, Adrian Willaert, and others].

3243 * *Ein neues Lied wir heben an: Songs of the Reformation.* (Peter Schreier/Capella Fidicina Leipzig). Capriccio 11089. [16th-century Lutheran music by Johann Walter, Benedictus Ducis, Adam Puschman, Caspar Othmayr, Arnold de Bruck, and Ludwig Senfl].

3244 *O dolce vita mia: Italian music from the high Renaissance.* (London Early Music Group/James Tyler). Elektra Nonesuch: 79029-2. [Vocal and instrumental music by Giovanni Giacomo Gastoldi, Adrian Willaert, Claudio Merulo, Fillippo Azzaiolo, and others].

3245 *The Old Hall manuscript.* (Hilliard Ensemble/Paul Hillier). EMI: CDC 7 54111 2. [English sacred music of the early 15th century by Queldryk, Bittering, Damett, Pycard, Leonel Power, Pennard, Cooke, Forest, Oliver, Mayshuet, and others].

3246 *Il pastor fido: madrigals after texts by G. Guarini.* (Cantus Cölln/Konrad Junghänel). Deutsche Harmonia Mundi: 05472-77240-2. [Music by Heinrich Schütz, Marco da Gagliano, Sigismondo D'India, Giaches de Wert, Ruggiero Giovanelli, Luca Marenzio, Bernardo Pallavicino, Giovanni Giacomo Gastoldi, Steffano Bernardi, Claudio Monteverdi, and others].

3247 * *The pleasures of the royal courts.* (Early Music Consort of London/David Munrow). Elektra Nonesuch: 71326-2. [Music, primarily from the 15th and 16th centuries, by Adam de La Halle, Johannes Legrant, Guilaume Dufay, Heinrich Isaac, Ludwig Senfl, Marchetto Cara, Diego Ortiz, Antonio de Cabezón, Juan del Encina, and others].

3248 *Renaissance masterpieces.* (Oxford Camerata/Jeremy Summerly). Naxos: 8.550843. [Motets by Johannes Ockeghem, Josquin des Prez, Cristóbal de Morales, Jean Lhéritier, Philippe Rogier, Jacobus Clemens non Papa, Giovanni Pierluigi da Palestrina, Orlando di Lasso, Tomás Luis de Victoria, William Byrd, and Joaõ IV, king of Portugal].

3249 *Renaissance music from the courts of Mantua and Ferrara.* (Circa 1500 Ensemble). Chandos:

CHAN 0524. [Early 16th-century vocal and instrumental music by Marchetto Cara, Bartolomeo Tromboncino, Francesco Spinacino, Diomedes, Eustachio Romano, and others].

3250 * *Robin is to the greenwood gone: Elizabethan lute music.* (Paul O'Dette). Elektra Nonesuch: 79123-2. [Music by Daniel Bachelar, Francis Cutting, John Johnson, Anthony Holborne, Thomas Robinson, and others].

3251 *Sacred music from Venice and Rome.* (Sixteen/ Harry Christophers). Collins: 13602. [Includes *Missa Bell'Amfritit'altera* by Orlando di Lasso and music by Giovanni Gabrieli, Girolamo Frescobaldi, Pier Francecso Cavalli, and Antonio Caldara].

3252 *La Serenissima I: lute music in Venice, 1500– 1550.* (Jakob Lindberg). Bis: 399. [Music by Francesco da Milano, Vincenzo Capirola, Giovanni Maria da Crema, Francesco Spinacino, and Joan Ambrosio Dalza].

3253 *La Serenissima II: lute music in Venice, 1550– 1600.* (Jakob Lindberg). Bis: 599. [Music by Bernardino Balletti, Francesco da Milano, Giacomo Gorzanis, Giulio Cesare Barbetta, Lorenzini, Vincenzo Galilei, Simone Molinaro, Giovanni Battista della Gostena, and Giovanni Antonio Terzi].

3254 *Shakespeare songs and consort music.* (Deller Consort). Harmonia Mundi: HMA 190202. [Music by Thomas Morley, John Wilson, Thomas Weelkes, Robert Johnson, Francis Cutting, William Byrd, and anonymous composers].

3255 *Spanish and Mexican Renaissance vocal music.* (Hilliard Ensemble/Paul Hillier). EMI: CDS 7 54341 2. 2CD set. [Vocal music by Alonso de Mondéjar, Francisco de Peñalosa, Martín de Rivaflecha, Pedro de Escobar, Alonso de Alba, Juan del Encina, Luchas, Juan de Urrede, Francisco de Millán, Juan de Lienas, Cristóbal de Morales, Hernando de Franco, Alonso Lobo, Francisco Guerrero, Juan Gutiérrez de Padilla, and anonymous composers].

3256 * *The spirits of England and France III: Binchois and his contemporaries.* (Gothic Voices/ Christopher Page). Hyperion: CDA66783. [Music by Gilles Binchois, Cardot, Gilet Velut, Johannes Legrant, Johannes de Lymburgia, Leonel Power, John Dunstable, Pierre Fontaine, Guillaume de Machaut, Bittering, and anonymous composers].

3257 *Una stravaganza dei Medici: intermedi (1589) per La pellegrina.* (Taverner Consort/Andrew Parrott). EMI: CDC 7 47998 2. [Florentine stage work of 1589 with music primarily by Cristofano Malvezzi and Luca Marenzio].

3258 *Tabulatures de leut.* (Paul O'Dette). Astrée: E 7776. [16th-century French lute music by Adrian Le Roy, Guillaume Morlaye, Alberto da Ripa, and Jean-Paul Paladin].

3259 *Time stands still: lute songs on the theme of mutability and metamorphosis by John Dowland and his contemporaries.* (Emma Kirkby/Anthony Rooley). Hyperion: CDA66186. [English lute songs by William Lawes, Philip Rosseter, Alfonso Ferrabosco, John Danyel, George Handford, Thomas Ford, John Dowland, and anonymous composers].

3260 * *The triumphs of Maximilian.* (Early Music Consort of London/David Munrow). London: 436 998-2. [Music by Ludwig Senfl, Heinrich Isaac, Heinrich Finck, Hans Kotter, and others].

3261 ** *Venetian coronation, 1595.* (Gabrieli Consort/ Paul McCreesh). Virgin: 7 59006 2 (7 91110 2). [Vocal and instrumental works by Andrea and Giovanni Gabrieli, also with music by Cesare Bendinelli and others].

3262 *Venice preserved.* (Gentlemen of the Chapell/ His Majesties Sagbutts and Cornets/Peter Bassano). ASV/Gaudeamus: GAU 122. [Motets and instrumental music by Andrea Gabrieli, Giovanni Gabrieli, Augustine Bassano, Giovanni Bassano, Jerome Bassano, and Claudio Monteverdi].

3263 *Virtuoso lute music from Italy and England.* (Jakob Lindberg). Bis: 211. [Music by Lorenzini, Simone Molinaro, Giovanni Girolamo Kapsperger, Alessandro Piccinini, Bellerofonte Castaldi, Anthony Holborne, Peter Phillips, Francis Cutting, and others].

3264 *Virtuoso solo music for cornetto.* (Bruce Dickey/Tragicomedia). Accent: ACC 9173 D. [Italian music of the late 16th and early 17th centuries by Tarquinio Merula, Giovanni Battista Bovicelli, Giovanni Bassano, Girolamo Frescobaldi, Giovanni Battista Fontana, Francesco Rognoni Taeggio, Girolamo Dalla Casa, and Nicolaus à Kempis].

3265 * *Viva Rey Ferrando: Renaissance music from the Neapolitan court, 1442–1556.* (Hespèrion XX/ Jordi Savall). Virgin: 5 61222 2. [Vocal and instrumental music by Hayne van Ghizeghem, Juan Cornago, Gian Domenico da Nola, Diego Ortiz, Francisco de La Torre, Nicolas Gombert, Antonio de Cabezón, Antonio Valente, Adrian Willaert, and anonymous composers].

Baroque Period

Compiled by
Kent Underwood

Composers

3266 Albinoni, Tomaso, 1671–1750

3266.1 *Adagio* [arranged for organ and orchestra by Remo Giazotto]. *See* 3371

3266.2 * *Concertos. Selections.* (King's Consort/ Robert King). Hyperion: CDA66383. [With Vivaldi, Antonio: *Concertos*].

3267 Allegri, Gregorio, 1582–1652. *Miserere.*

- (Taverner Consort/Andrew Parrott). *See* 3241
- (Tallis Scholars/Peter Phillips). Gimell: CDGIM 339. [With Mundy, William: *Vox patris caelestis*; Palestrina, Giovanni Pierluigi da: *Missa Papae Marcelli*].

3268 Almeida, Francisco Antonio de, ca. 1720–1755

La Giuditta [oratorio]. (René Jacobs). Harmonia Mundi: 901411/12. 2CD set.

3269 Anglebert, Jean Henry d', 1628–1691

Harpsichord music. (Scott Ross). Musifrance: 2292-45007-2. 2CD set.

3270 Bach, Johann Sebastian, 1685–1750

ORCHESTRAL MUSIC

3270.1 ** *Brandenburgische Konzerte (Brandenburg concertos).*

- (Musica Antiqua Köln/Reinhard Goebel). Archiv: 423 116-2. 2CD set. [With his *Concerto for flute, violin, harpsichord, and strings*].
- (Orchestra of the Age of Enlightenment/Catherine Mackintosh). Virgin: CDCB 7 59152 2. 2CD set.
- (English Concert/Trevor Pinnock). Archiv: 423 492-2. 2CD set.

3270.2 *Concerto for flute, violin, harpsichord, and strings, BWV 1044 in A minor ("Triple concerto").*

- (Musica Antiqua Köln/Reinhard Goebel). *See* 3270.1
- (English Concert/Trevor Pinnock). *See* 3270.6

3270.3 * *Concertos (7) for harpsichord and strings, BWV 1052-1058.* (Trevor Pinnock/ English Concert). Archiv: 415 991-2; 415 992-2. 2 CDs.

3270.4 * *Concertos (3) for 2 harpsichords and strings, BWV 1060-1062.* (Trevor Pinnock/Kenneth Gilbert/English Concert). Archiv: 415 131-2.

3270.5 *Concertos (3) for 3 or 4 harpsichords and strings, BWV 1063-1065.*

- (Academy of Ancient Music/Christopher Hogwood). L'Oiseau-Lyre: 433 053-2.

- (English Concert/Trevor Pinnock). Archiv: 400 041-2.

3270.6 * *Concerto for oboe, violin, and strings, BWV 1060 in C minor.* (English Concert/Trevor Pinnock). Archiv: 413 731. [With his *Concerto for flute, violin, harpsichord, and strings* and *Concerto for oboe d'amore*].

3270.7 ** *Concertos (3) for 1 or 2 violins and strings, BWV 1041-1043.*

- (Sigiswald Kuijken/Petite Bande). Deutsche Harmonia Mundi: 77006-2-RG.

- (Gidon Kremer/Academy of St. Martin-in-the-Fields/Neville Marriner). Philips: 434 730-2.

3270.8 ** *Suites [overtures] (4) for orchestra, BWV 1066-1069.*

- (Musica Antiqua Köln/Reinhard Goebel). Archiv: 415 671-2. 2CD set.

- (Concentus Musicus Wien/Nikolaus Harnoncourt). Teldec: 92174-2. 2CD set.

CHAMBER AND SOLO MUSIC FOR STRINGS AND WINDS

3270.9 * *Lute music.* (Jakob Lindberg). Bis: 587/8. 2CD set.

3270.10 * *Musikalisches Opfer (Musical offering).* (Davitt Moroney and others). Harmonia Mundi: HMC 901260.

3270.11 ** *Sonatas and partitas (6) for violin unaccompanied, BWV 1001-1006.*

- (Gidon Kremer). Philips: 416 651-2. 2CD set.

- (Sigiswald Kuijken). Deutsche Harmonia Mundi: 77043-2-RG. 2CD set.

3270.12 * *Sonatas for flute and harpsichord (or continuo).* (Barthold Kuijken/Gustav Leonhardt). Deutsche Harmonia Mundi: 77026-2-RC. 2CD set.

3270.13 *Sonatas (3) for viola da gamba and obbligato harpsichord, BWV 1027-1029.* (Wieland Kuijken/Gustav Leonhardt). Deutsche Harmonia Mundi: 77044-2-RG.

3270.14 * *Sonatas (6) for violin and obbligato harpsichord, BWV 1014-1019.* (Sigiswald Kuijken/Gustave Leonhardt). Deutsche Harmonia Mundi: 77170-2-RG. 2CD set.

3270.15 ** *Suites (6) for violoncello unaccompanied, BWV 1007-1012.*

- (Anner Bylsma). Sony: S2K 48047. 2CD set.

- (Pablo Casals). EMI: 7 61028 2. 2CD set.

3270.16 *Trio sonatas.* (London Baroque). Harmonia Mundi: HMC 901173.

HARPSICHORD MUSIC

3270.17 * *Chromatische Fantasie und Fuge (Chromatic fantasy and fugue).*

- (Christophe Rousset). *See* 3270.23

- (Andreas Staier). *See* 3270.19

3270.18 * *Englische Suiten (English suites) (6), BWV 806-811.* (Colin Tilney). Music & Arts: 777. 2CD set.

3270.19 *Fantasias.* (Andreas Staier). Deutsche Harmonia Mundi: 77039-2-RC. [Includes his *Chromatic fantasy and fugue, Fantasia in C minor,* and other works].

3270.20 ** *Französische Suiten (French suites) (6), BWV 812-817.*

- (Glenn Gould). CBS: MK 42267.

- (Keith Jarrett). ECM: 78118-20001-2 (1513/1514). 2CD set.

3270.21 ** *Goldberg-Variationen (Goldberg variations).*

- (Glenn Gould) [piano]. CBS: MK 37779.

- (Pierre Hantaï) [harpsichord]. Opus 111: 30-84.

- (Gustave Leonhardt) [harpsichord]. Deutsche Harmonia Mundi: 77149-2-RG.

3270.22 ** *Inventions (Two-part and three-part inventions).* (Kenneth Gilbert). Archiv: 415 112-2.

3270.23 * *Italienisches Konzert (Italian concerto).* (Christophe Rousset). L'Oiseau-Lyre: 433 054-2. [With his *Chromatic fantasy and fugue* and *Partita in B minor*].

3270.24 * *Partitas (6), BWV 825-830.*

- (Gustav Leonhardt). Deutsche Harmonia Mundi: 77215-2-RG. 2CD set.

- (Christophe Rousset). L'Oiseau-Lyre: 440 217-2. 2CD set.

3270.25 *Toccatas. Selections.*

- (Kenneth Gilbert). Archiv: 437 555-2.

- (Charlotte Mattax). Koch: 3-7046-2.

3270.26 ** *Wohltemperierte Klavier (Well-tempered clavier).*

- (Kenneth Gilbert). Archiv: 413 439-2. 4CD set.
- (Keith Jarrett) [*Book 1* performed on piano; *Book 2* performed on harpsichord]. ECM: 7118-21362-2; 7118-21433-2. 4 CDs in 2 vols.
- (Gustav Leonhardt). Deutsche Harmonia Mundi: 77011-2-RG; 77012-2-RG. 4 CDs in 2 vols.

ORGAN MUSIC

3270.27 * *Chorales and chorale preludes. Selections.* (Helmut Rilling). Denon: C37-7809.

3270.28 *Complete organ music.*

- (Marie-Claire Alain). Erato: [vol. 1] 4509-96718-2; [vol. 2] 4509-96719-2; [vol. 3] 4509-96720-2; [vol. 4] 4509-96721-2; [vol. 5] 4509-96722-2; [vol. 6] 4509-96723-2; [vol. 7] 4509-96724-2; [vol. 8] 4509-96725-2; [vol. 9] 4509-96742-2; [vol. 10] 4509-96743-2; [vol. 11] 4509-96744-2; [vol. 12] 4509-96745-2; [vol. 13] 4509-96746-2; [vol. 14] 4509-96747-2. 14 CDs.
- (Lionel Rogg). Harmonia Mundi: 290772/83. 12CD set.

3270.29 ** *Toccatas and fugues; Preludes and fugues; Passacaglia and fugue. Selections.*

- (Marie-Claire Alain). Erato: 2292-45701-2; 2292-45702-2. 2 CDs.
- (Daniel Chorzempa). Philips: 420 860-2.
- (Herbert Tachezi). Teldec: 9031-74780-2.

3270.30 ** *Trio sonatas (6), BWV 525-530.*

- (John Butt). Harmonia Mundi: 907055.
- (Harald Vogel). Capriccio: 10 037; 10 040. 2 CDs. [With his *Canonic variations on Vom Himmel hoch*].

VOCAL MUSIC

3270.31 *Cantatas* [sacred, nos. 1–199 complete]. [Series: Das Kantatenwerk, vols. 1–45]. (Vocal Soloists/Concentus Musicus Vienna/Leonhardt Consort/Nikolaus Harnoncourt/Gustav Leonhardt). Teldec: [vol. 1] 2292-42497-2. 2CD set; [vol. 2] 2292-42498-2. 2CD set; [vol. 3] 2292-42499-2. 2CD set; [vol. 4] 2292-42500-2. 2CD set; [vol. 5] 2292-42501-2. 2CD set; [vol. 6] 2292-42502-2. 2CD set; [vol. 7] 2292-42503-2. 2CD set; [vol. 8] 2292-42504-2. 2CD set; [vol. 9] 2292-42505-2. 2CD set; [vol. 10] 2292-42506-2. 2CD set; [vol. 11] 2292-42556-2. 2CD set; [vol. 12] 2292-42559-2. 2CD set; [vol. 13] 2292-42560-2. 2CD set; [vol. 14] 2292-42422-2. 2CD set; [vol. 15] 2292-42423-2. 2CD set; [vol. 16] 2292-42565-2. 2CD set; [vol. 17] 2292-42571-2. 2CD set; [vol. 18] 2292-42572-2. 2CD set; [vol. 19] 2292-42573-2. 2CD set; [vol. 20] 2292-42576-2. 2CD set; [vol. 21] 2292-42577-2. 2CD set; [vol. 22] 2292-42578-2. 2CD set; [vol. 23] 2292-42582-2. 2CD set; [vol. 24] 2292-42583-2. 2CD set; [vol. 25] 2292-42584-2. 2CD set; [vol. 26] 2292-42602-2. 2CD set; [vol. 27] 2292-42603-2. 2CD set; [vol. 28] 2292-42606-2. 2CD set; [vol. 29] 2292-42608-2. 2CD set; [vol. 30] 2292-42609-2. 2CD set; [vol. 31] 2292-42615-2. 2CD set; [vol. 32] 2292-42617-2. 2CD set; [vol. 33] 2292-42618-2. 2CD set; [vol. 34] 2292-42618-2. 2CD set; [vol. 35] 2292-42630-2. 2CD set; [vol. 36] 2292-42631-2. 2CD set; [vol. 37] 2292-42632-2. 2CD set; [vol. 38] 2292-42633-2. 2CD set; [vol. 39] 2292-42634-2. 2CD set; [vol. 40] 2292-42635-2. 2CD set; [vol. 41] 2292-42428-2. 2CD set; [vol. 42] 2292-42738-2. 2CD set; [vol. 43] 2292-44179-2. 2CD set; [vol. 44] 2292-44193-2. 2CD set; [vol. 45] 2292-44194-2. 2CD set.

3270.32 ** *Cantata no. 4, "Christ lag in Todesbanden."* (Taverner Consort/Andrew Parrott). Virgin: CDC 5 45011 2. [With his *Oster-Oratorium*].

3270.33 ** *Cantata no. 51, "Jauchzet Gott in allen Landen."* (Emma Kirkby/English Baroque Soloists/John Eliot Gardiner). Philips: 411 458-2. [With his *Magnificat*].

3270.34 * *Cantatas nos. 61–62, "Nun komm der Heiden Heiland"* [two versions]. (Monteverdi Choir/English Baroque Soloists/John Eliot Gardiner). Archiv: 437 327-2. [With his *Cantata no. 36*].

3270.35 * *Cantata no. 78, "Jesu der du meine Seele."* (Chapelle Royale/Philipe Herreweghe). Harmonia Mundi: HMC 901270. [With his *Cantata no. 198*].

3270.36 * *Cantata no. 80, "Ein feste Burg ist unser Gott."* (Bach Ensemble/Joshua Rifkin). L'Oiseau-Lyre: 417 250-2. [With his *Cantata no. 147*].

3270.37 * *Cantata no. 82, "Ich habe genug."*

- (René Jacobs/Ensemble 415/Chiara Banchini). Harmonia Mundi: HMC 901273. [With his *Cantatas nos. 35 and 53*].
- (Emma Kirkby/Taverner Players/Andrew Parrott). Hyperion: CDA 66036. [With his *Cantata no. 202*].

3270.38 * *Cantata no. 106, "Gottes Zeit ist die allerbeste Zeit" (Actus tragicus).* (Monteverdi Choir/English Baroque Soloists/John Eliot Gardiner). Archiv: 429 782-2. [With his *Cantatas nos. 118 and 198*].

3270.39 ** *Cantata no. 140, "Wachet auf, ruft uns die Stimme."* (Monteverdi Choir/English Baroque Soloists/John Eliot Gardiner). Archiv: 431 809-2. [With his *Cantata no. 147*].

3270.40 * *Cantata no. 147, "Herz und Mund und Tat und Leben."* See 3270.36 or 3270.39

3270.41 * *Cantata no. 202, "Weichet nur, betrübte Schatten" ("Wedding cantata").* (Emma Kirkby/Taverner Consort/Andrew Parrott). See 3270.37

3270.42 *Cantata no. 205, "Der zufriedengestellte Aeolus."* (Mieke van der Sluis/René Jacobs/Orchestra of the Age of Enlightenment/Gustav Leonhardt). Philips: 431 161-2. [With his *Cantata no. 214*].

3270.43 * *Cantata no. 211, "Schweigt stille, plaudert nicht" ("Coffee cantata").* (Emma Kirkby/Academy of Ancient Music/Christopher Hogwood). L'Oiseau-Lyre: 417 621-2. [With his *Cantata no. 212*].

3270.44 *Cantata no. 212, "Mer han en neue Oberkeet" ("Peasant cantata").* (Emma Kirkby/Academy of Ancient Music/Christopher Hogwood). See 3270.43

3270.45 * *Johannespassion (St. John Passion).*
- (Monteverdi Choir/John Eliot Gardiner). Archiv: 419 324-2. 2CD set.
- (Chapelle Royale/Philippe Herreweghe). Harmonia Mundi: 901264/65. 2CD set.
- (Petite Bande/Sigiswald Kuijken). Deutsche Harmonia Mundi: 77041-2-RG. 2CD set.
- (Taverner Consort/Andrew Parrott). EMI: CDS 7 54083 2. 2CD set.

3270.46 * *Magnificat, BWV 243 in D major.*
- (Sixteen/Harry Christophers). Collins: 13202. [With Caldara, Antonio: *Stabat Mater* and Vivaldi, Antonio: *Gloria*].
- (Monteverdi Choir/John Eliot Gardiner). See 3270.33

3270.47 ** *Mass, BWV 232 in B minor.*
- (Monteverdi Choir/John Eliot Gardiner). Archiv: 415 514-2. 2CD set.
- (Chapelle Royale/Philippe Herreweghe). Virgin: 7 59634-2 (7 90757-2). 2CD set.

- (Taverner Consort/Andrew Parrott). Angel: CDS 7 47293 8. 2CD set.

3270.48 ** *Matthäuspassion (St. Matthew Passion).*
- (Monteverdi Choir/John Eliot Gardiner). Archiv: 427 648-2. 3CD set.
- (Chapelle Royale/Philippe Herreweghe). Harmonia Mundi: 901155/57. 3CD set.
- (Nicolai Gedda/Dietrich Fischer-Dieskau/Philharmonia Orchestra/Otto Klemperer). EMI: 7 63058 2. 3CD set.

3270.49 * *Motets.* (Sixteen/Harry Christophers). Hyperion: CDA66369. 2CD set.

3270.50 *Oster-Oratorium (Easter oratorio).* (Taverner Consort/Andrew Parrott). See 3270.32

3270.51 * *Weihnachts-Oratorium (Christmas oratorio).* (Monteverdi Choir/English Baroque Soloists/John Eliot Gardiner). Archiv: 423 232-2.

MISCELLANEOUS

3270.52 * *Kunst der Fuge (Art of fugue).*
- (Musica Antiqua Köln/Reinhard Goebel) [chamber ensemble]. Archiv: 431 704-2.
- (Davitt Moroney) [harpsichord]. Harmonia Mundi: 901169/70. 2 CDs.

3270.53 * *Notenbüchlein für Anna Magdalena Bach (Notebook for Anna Magdalena Bach).* (Tragicomedia/Stephen Stubbs). Teldec: 91183.

3270.54 * *Selections* [arranged for synthesizer]. (Wendy Carlos). CBS: MK 7194. 1973. [Album title: *Switched on Bach*].

3271   Bartolotti, Angelo Michele, ca. 1615–ca. 1681
Suites for guitar. Selections. (Lex Eisenhardt). Etcetera: KTC 1174.

3272   Biber, Heinrich Ignaz Franz, 1644–1704
3272.1 * *Sonatas for violin and continuo. Selections.* (Romanesca). Harmonia Mundi: HMU 907134/35. 2CD set.

3272.2 *String ensemble music. Selections.* (New London Consort/Philip Pickett). L'Oiseau-Lyre: 436 460-2. [With his *Requiem*].

3273   Blow, John, d. 1708
3273.1 *Organ music. Selections.* See 3333.4
3273.2 *Venus and Adonis* [opera]. (Charles Medlam). Harmonia Mundi: HMC 901276.

3274   Bononcini, Giovanni, 1670–1747
Muzio Scevola [opera—selections]. See 3306.36

3275 Buxtehude, Dietrich, 1637–1707

3275.1 * *Cantatas. Selections.*

- (James Bowman/King's Consort). *See* 3367

- (René Jacobs/Kuijken Consort). *See* 3369

- (Concerto Vocale/René Jacobs). Harmonia Mundi: HMC 901333. [Includes his *Membra Jesu nostri* and *Heut triumphierte Gottes Sohn*].

3275.2 * *Chamber music. Selections.*

- (Boston Museum Trio). Harmonia Mundi: HMA 1901089.

- (Musica Antiqua Köln/Reinhard Goebel). Archiv: 427 118-2. [With Pachelbel, Johann: *Chamber music*].

3275.3 * *Organ music. Selections.*

- (Piet Kee). Chandos: CHAN 0514. [With Sweelinck, Jan Pieterszoon: *Organ music*].

- (Piet Kee). Chandos: CHAN 0501. [With Bach, Johann Sebastian: *Organ music*].

- (Ton Koopman). Novalis: 150048.

3276 * Cabanilles, Juan, 1644–1712

Organ music. Selections. (John Butt). Harmonia Mundi: HMU 907047.

3277 Caccini, Francesca, 1587–after 1638

La liberazione di Ruggiero dall'Isola d'Alcina [opera]. (Ars Femina Ensemble). Nannerl: ARS-003.

3278 Caccini, Giulio, ca. 1545–1618

Le nuove musiche [for voice and continuo—selections]. (Monserrat Figueras/Schola Cantorum Basiliensis). Deutsche Harmonia Mundi: 77164-2-RG.

3279 Caldara, Antonio, 1670–1736

Stabat Mater. (Sixteen/Harry Christophers). *See* 3270.46

3280 Carissimi, Giacomo, 1605–1674

3280.1 * *Jephte* [oratorio].

- (John Eliot Gardiner). Erato: 2292-45466-2. [With his *Jonas* and *Judicum extremum*].

- (Cantus Cölln/Konrad Junghänel). Deutsche Harmonia Mundi: 05472-77322-2. [With Marazzoli, Marco: *Oratorios*].

3280.2 *Vocal chamber music. Selections.* (Concerto Vocale/René Jacobs). Harmonia Mundi: HMC 901262.

3281 * Castello, Dario, fl. 1621–1644

Sonatas. Selections. (Europa Galante). Opus 111: 30-62.

3282 Cavalli, Pier Francesco, 1602–1676

3282.1 *Calisto* [opera]. (Concerto Vocale/René Jacobs). Harmonia Mundi: 901282/84. 3CD set.

3282.2 * *Xerse* [opera]. (Concerto Vocale/René Jacobs). Harmonia Mundi: 901175/78. 4CD set.

3283 Cazzati, Maurizio, ca. 1620–1677

Sonatas. Selections. (Ensemble La Fenice). Adda: 581318. [With his *Requiem* and selected motets].

3284 Cesti, Antonio, 1623–1669

Orontea [opera]. (Concerto Vocale/René Jacobs). Harmonia Mundi: 901100/02. 3CD set.

3285 * Chambonnières, Jacques Champion de, ca. 1602–ca. 1672

Pièces de clavecin (Harpsichord pieces). Selections. (Skip Sempé). Deutsche Harmonia Mundi: 05472-77210-2.

3286 Charpentier, Marc Antoine, 1634–1704

3286.1 *Les arts florissants* [secular cantata]. (Les Arts Florissants/William Christie). Harmonia Mundi: HMC 1901083.

3286.2 * *Le malade imaginaire* [incidental music to Molière's play]. (Les Arts Florissants/William Christie). Harmonia Mundi: HMC 905124.

3286.3 *Medée* [opera]. (Les Arts Florissants/William Christie). Erato: 4509-96558-2. 3CD set.

3286.4 * *Messe de minuit (Midnight Mass).* (Boston Camerata/Joel Cohen). Elektra Nonesuch: 79265-2. [Album title: *A Baroque Christmas*. With works by Claudio Monteverdi, Henry Purcell, and Johann Hermann Schein].

3286.5 *Missa Assumpta es Maria.* (Les Arts Florissants/William Christie). *See* 3286.8

3286.6 * *"O" antiphons for Advent.* (Les Arts Florissants/William Christie). Harmonia Mundi: HMC 905124. [With his *Noël* and *In nativitaten D.N.J.C. canticum*].

3286.7 *Pastorale sur la naissance de N.S. Jésu-Christ* [sacred cantata]. (Les Arts Florissants/William Christie). Harmonia Mundi: HMC 901082. [With his *Magnificat for three voices*].

3286.8 *Te Deum.* (Les Arts Florissants/William Christie). Harmonia Mundi: HMC 901298. [With his *Missa Assumpta es Maria* and *Litanies of the Virgin*].

3287 Clarke, Jeremiah, 1669?–1707

Prince of Denmark's march. See 3371

3288   Clérambault, Louis Nicolas, 1676–1749
Medée [cantata]. *See* 3328

3289   Corelli, Arcangelo, 1653–1713

3289.1 ** *Concerti grossi op. 6.* (English Concert/ Trevor Pinnock). Archiv: 423 626-2. 2CD set.

3289.2 * *Sonatas for violin and continuo.* (Trio Sonnerie). Virgin: 7 45078 2 (7 90840 2). 2CD set; or Musical Heritage Society: MHS 522852H. 2CD set.

3289.3 * *Trio sonatas. Selections.*

   • (London Baroque). EMI: CDC 7 47965 2.

   • (English Concert/Trevor Pinnock). Archiv: 419 614-2.

3290   Couperin, François, 1668–1733

3290.1 *L'apothéose de Lully* [chamber suite].

   • (William Christie/Christophe Rousset) [two harpsichords]. Harmonia Mundi: 901269. [With his *Le Parnasse.*]

   • (English Baroque Soloists/John Eliot Gardiner) [chamber ensemble]. Musifrance: 245-011-2. [With his *Le Parnasse.*]

3290.2 *Concerts royaux (4)* [chamber suites]. (Trio Sonnerie). ASV: GAU 101.

3290.3 * *Leçons de ténèbres.* (Emma Kirkby/Judith Nelson). L'Oiseau-Lyre: 430 283-2. [With his motets].

3290.4 ** *Les nations* [chamber suites].

   • (Musica Antiqua Köln/Reinhard Goebel). Archiv: 427 164-2. 2CD set.

   • (Kuijken Ensemble). Accent: 9285/86. 2CD set.

   • (Hespèrion XX/Jordi Savall). Astrée: E 7700. 2CD set.

3290.5 *Organ Masses (2).* (Jean-Patrice Brosses). EMI: CDC 7 54224 2. [Includes plainchant alternations].

3290.6 *Le Parnasse (L'apothéose de Corelli)* [chamber suite]. *See* 3290.1

3290.7 * *Pièces de clavecin (Harpsichord pieces)* [Books 1–4].

   • (Kenneth Gilbert). Harmonia Mundi: [Book 1] 190351/53. 3CD set; [Book 2] 190354/56. 3CD set; [Book 3] 190357/58. 2CD set; [Book 4] 190359/60. 2CD set.

   • (Christophe Rousset). Harmonia Mundi: [Book 1] 901450/52. 3CD set; [Book 2] 901447/49. 3CD set; [Book 3] 901442/44. 3CD set; [Book 4] 901445/46. 2CD set.

   • (Skip Sempé). [Selected pieces]. Deutsche Harmonia Mundi: 77219-2-RC.

3291   Couperin, Louis, ca. 1626–1661

3291.1 *Organ music. Selections.* (Jan Willem Jansen). FNAC: 592291.

3291.2 * *Pièces de clavecin (Harpsichord pieces). Selections.*

   • (Bob van Asperen). EMI: CDC 7 54340 2.

   • (Gustav Leonhardt). Deutsche Harmonia Mundi: 77058-2-RG.

3292   D'India, Sigismondo, ca. 1580–1629. *Vocal music. Selections.*

   • (Consort of Musicke/Anthony Rooley). *See* 3370

   • (Emma Kirkby/Anthony Rooley). *See* 3382

   • (Emma Kirkby/Judith Nelson/Anthony Rooley). *See* 3365

3293   Dufaut, François, 17th cent. *Lute music. Selections.*

   • (Konrad Junghänel). *See* 3386

   • (Pascal Monteilhet). FNAC: 592267.

3294   Du Phly, Jacques, 1715–1789
Pièces de clavecin (Harpsichord pieces). Selections. (Mitzi Meyerson). ASV: GAU 108.

3295   Fischer, Johann Kaspar Ferdinand, ca. 1665–1746
Harpsichord music. Selections. (William Christie). Harmonia Mundi: HMC 90126.

3296   Forqueray, Antoine, 1671–1745
Bass viol music. Selections. (Jay Bernfeld/Skip Sempé). Deutsche Harmonia Mundi: 05472-77262-2. [With his *Harpsichord music (selections)*].

3297   Frescobaldi, Girolamo, 1583–1643

3297.1 *Arie musicale* [for voices and continuo]. (Concerto Italiano/Rinaldo Alessandrini). Opus 111: 30-105/106. 2CD set.

3297.2 * *Canzoni e partite* [for various chamber ensembles—selections]. (Ensemble Fitzwilliam). Astrée: 8514.

3297.3 *Fiori musicali* [for organ]. (Rinaldo Alessandrini). Astrée: 8714/15. 2CD set.

3297.4 * *Harpsichord music. Selections.*

   • (Bob van Asperen). Teldec: 8.43774.

   • (Gustav Leonhardt). Philips: 432 128-2.

3298 * Froberger, Johann Jacob, 1616–1667. *Keyboard music. Selections.*

   • (Gustave Leonhardt). Deutsche Harmonia Mundi: 7923-2-RC.

- (Christophe Rousset). Harmonia Mundi: HMC 901372.

3299 * Gaultier, Denis, d. 1672. *La rhétorique des dieux* [for lute—selections].
- (Konrad Junghänel). *See 3386*
- (Hopkinson Smith). Astrée: E 7778.

3300 * Gaultier, Ennemond, 1575–1651. *Pièces de luth (Lute pieces). Selections.*
- (Konrad Junghänel). *See 3386*
- (Hopkinson Smith). Astrée: E 8703.

3301 * Gay, John, 1685–1732
Beggar's opera. See 3332

3302 Geminiani, Francesco, 1687–1762
3302.1 *Concerti grossi. Selections.*
- (Petite Bande/Sigiswald Kuijken). Deutsche Harmonia Mundi: 77010-2-RG.
- (Tafelmusik/Jean Lamon). Sony: SK 48043.

3302.2 *Sonatas for violoncello and continuo.* (Anthony Pleeth). L'Oiseau-Lyre: 433 192-2.

3303 * Grandi, Alessandro, d. 1630. *Vocal music. Selections.*
- (Schola Cantorum Basiliensis/René Jacobs). Deutsche Harmonia Mundi: 05472-77281-2.
- (Gabrieli Consort/Paul McCreesh). *See 3395*

3304 Graun, Karl Heinrich, 1704–1759
Der Tod Jesu [oratorio]. (Pal Németh). Harmonia Mundi/Quintata: 903061.

3305 Guerau, Francisco, 17th cent.
Poema harmónico [for guitar—selections]. (Hopkinson Smith). Astrée: E 8722.

3306 Handel, George Frideric, 1685–1759
INSTRUMENTAL MUSIC
3306.1 *Ballet music. Selections.* (English Baroque Soloists/John Eliot Gardiner). Erato: 2292-88084-2. [Music from *Alcina, Terpsichore,* and *Il pastor fido*].

3306.2 * *Concerti grossi (6), op. 3.* (Brandenburg Consort/Roy Goodman). Hyperion: CDA66633.

3306.3 * *Concerti grossi (12), op. 6.* (English Concert/Trevor Pinnock). Archiv: 410 897-2; 410 898-2; 410 899-2. 3 CDs.

3306.4 * *Concerto for harp and orchestra, op. 4 no. 6.*

- (Ursula Holliger/English Concert/Trevor Pinnock). *See 3306.5*
- (Marisa Robles/Academy of St. Martin-in-the-Fields/Neville Marriner). *See 3402.1*

3306.5 *Concertos (6) for organ and orchestra, op. 4* [no. 4 for harp and orchestra]. (Simon Preston/English Concert/Trevor Pinnock). Archiv: 413 465-2. 2CD set.

3306.6 *Concertos (6) for organ and orchestra, op. 7.* (Simon Preston/English Concert/Trevor Pinnock). Archiv: 413 468-2. 2CD set.

3306.7 *Harpsichord music. Selections.* (Igor Kipnis). Elektra Nonesuch: 79037-2.

3306.8 * *Music for the royal fireworks.* (English Concert/Trevor Pinnock). Archiv: 415 129-2. [With his *Concerti a due cori, nos. 2–3*].

3306.9 *Sonatas for flute and continuo. Selections.* (Barthold Kuijken and others). Accent: ACC 9180.

3306.10 *Sonatas for oboe and continuo. Selections.* [Series: Handel chamber music, vol. 2]. (David Reichenberg/Ecole d'Orphée). CRD: 3374. [With his *Sonatas for violin and continuo*].

3306.11 * *Sonatas for recorder and continuo. Selections.*
- (Michala Petri/Keith Jarrett). RCA: 60441-2-RC.
- (Philip Pickett/Ecole d'Orphée). [Series: Handel chamber music, vol. 6]. CRD: 3378.

3306.12 *Sonatas for violin and continuo. Selections.* (Ecole d'Orphée). *See 3306.10*

3306.13 * *Trio sonatas op. 2.* (London Baroque). Harmonia Mundi: HMC 901379.

3306.14 * *Trio sonatas op. 5.* (London Baroque). Harmonia Mundi: HMC 901389.

3306.15 ** *Water music* [for orchestra].
- (Concentus Musicus Vienna/Nikolaus Harnoncourt). Teldec: 8.42368.
- (English Concert/Trevor Pinnock). Archiv: 410 525-2.

VOCAL MUSIC AND STAGE MUSIC

3306.16 * *Acis and Galatea* [oratorio]. (King's Consort/Robert King). Hyperion: CDA66361/2. 2CD set.

3306.17 *Agrippina* [opera]. (Susan Bradshaw/Lisa Saffer/Capella Savaria/Nicholas McGegan). Harmonia Mundi: 907063/65. 3CD set.

3306.18 * *Alessandro* [opera]. (Petite Bande/Sigiswald Kuijken). Deutsche Harmonia Mundi: GD-77110. 3CD set.

3306.19 * *Alexander's feast* [ode]. (Sixteen/Harry Christophers). Collins: 70162. 2CD set.

3306.20 *L'allegro, il penseroso ed il moderato* [oratorio]. (Banchetto Musicale/Martin Pearlman). Arabesque: Z6554. 2CD set.

3306.21 *Athalia* [oratorio]. (Joan Sutherland/ Academy of Ancient Music/Christopher Hogwood). L'Oiseau-Lyre: 423 406-2. 2CD set.

3306.22 *Belshazzar* [oratorio]. (English Concert/ Trevor Pinnock). Archiv: 431 793-2. 2CD set.

3306.23 *Brockes-Passion* [oratorio]. (Capella Savaria/Nicholas McGegan). Hungaroton: 12734/ 36. 3CD set.

3306.24 *Cantatas. Selections.*

- (Julianne Baird and others). Newport: NCD 60043.

- (Emma Kirkby/Academy of Ancient Music/ Christopher Hogwood). L'Oiseau-Lyre: 414 473-2.

3306.25 * *Chandos anthems.* (Sixteen/Harry Christophers). Chandos: CHAN 0504; CHAN 0505; CHAN 0509; CHAN 8600. 4 CDs.

3306.26 *Coronation anthems.* (Westminster Abbey Choir/Trevor Pinnock). Archiv: 410 030-2.

3306.27 * *Dixit Dominus.* (Westminster Abbey Choir/Simon Preston). Archiv: 423 594-2. [With his *Nisi Dominus* and *Salve Regina*].

3306.28 *Esther* [oratorio]. (Emma Kirkby/Drew Minter/Academy of Ancient Music/Christopher Hogwood). L'Oiseau-Lyre: 414 423-2. 2 CDs.

3306.29 ** *Giulio Cesare* [opera]. (Concerto Köln/René Jacobs). Harmonia Mundi: 901384/ 87. 4CD set.

3306.30 * *Hercules* [oratorio]. (John Tomlinson/ Sarah Walker/English Baroque Soloists/John Eliot Gardiner). Archiv: 423 137-2. 3CD set.

3306.31 * *Israel in Egypt* [oratorio].

- (Monteverdi Choir/English Baroque Soloists/ John Eliot Gardiner). Erato: 2292-45399-2. 2CD set.

- (Taverner Choir/Andrew Parrott). Angel: CDS 7 54018 2. 2CD set.

3306.32 *Jephthe* [oratorio]. (Monteverdi Choir/ English Baroque Soloists/John Eliot Gardiner). Philips: 422 352-2. 3CD set.

3306.33 * *Judas Maccabaeus* [oratorio]. (University of California Berkeley Chamber Choir/Philharmonia Baroque Orchestra/Nicholas McGegan). Harmonia Mundi: HMU 907077/78. 2CD set.

3306.34 * *Lucrezia* [cantata]. (Julianne Baird and others). *See 3390*

3306.35 ** *Messiah* [oratorio].

- (Academy of Ancient Music/Christopher Hogwood). L'Oiseau-Lyre: 430 488-2. 2CD set.

- (University of California Berkeley Chamber Choir/Philharmonia Baroque Orchestra/ Nicholas McGegan). Harmonia Mundi: HMU 907050/52. 3CD set. [Includes all music from all of Handel's performing versions].

- (English Concert/Trevor Pinnock). Archiv: 427 664-2. 2CD set.

3306.36 *Muzio Scevola* [opera]. (Julianne Baird/ John Ostendorf/Brewer Baroque Chamber Orchestra/Edward Brewer). Newport: NPD 85540. 2CD set. [Act 3 of Handel's opera, with excerpts from Giovanni Bononcini's *Muzio Scevola*].

3306.37 * *Orlando* [opera]. (Arleen Augér/Emma Kirkby/James Bowman Academy of Ancient Music/ Christopher Hogwood). L'Oiseau-Lyre: 430 845-2. 3CD set.

3306.38 *Ottone* [opera]. (Lisa Saffer/Patricia Spence/Freiburg Baroque Orchestra/Nicholas McGegan). Harmonia Mundi: HMU 907073/75. 3CD set.

3306.39 * *Partenope* [opera]. (Krisztina Laki/ Helga Müller-Molinari/René Jacobs/Petite Bande/ Sigiswald Kuijken). Deutsche Harmonia Mundi: 77109-2-RG. 3CD set.

3306.40 * *La Resurrezione* [oratorio].

- (Emma Kirkby/Carolyn Watkinson/Ian Partridge/Academy of Ancient Music/Christopher Hogwood). L'Oiseau-Lyre: 421 132-2. 2CD set.

- (Lisa Saffer/Judith Nelson/Jeffrey Thomas/ Philharmonia Baroque Orchestra/Nicholas McGegan). Harmonia Mundi: 907027/28.

3306.41 *Rodelinda* [opera]. (Barbara Schlick/ Claudia Schubert/David Cordier/La Stagione/ Michael Schneider). Deutsche Harmonia Mundi: 05472-77192-2. 3CD set.

3306.42 * *Semele* [oratorio]. (Monteverdi Choir/ English Baroque Soloists/John Eliot Gardiner). Erato: 2292-45982-2. 2CD set.

3306.43 * *Solomon* [oratorio]. (Monteverdi Choir/ English Baroque Soloists/John Eliot Gardiner). Philips: 412 612-2. 2CD set.

3306.44 *Susanna* [oratorio]. (University of California Berkeley Chamber Choir/Philharmonia Baroque Orchestra/Nicholas McGegan). Harmonia Mundi: HMU 907030.32. 3CD set.

3306.45 * *Teseo* [opera]. (Della Jones/Derek Lee Ragin/Musiciens du Louvre/Marc Minkowski). Erato: 2292-45806-2. 2CD set.

3307 Hasse, Johann Adolf, 1699–1783

3307.1 *Cantatas. Selections.* (Julianne Baird and others). CRD: 3488. [With his *Sonatas*].

3307.2 *Motets. Selections.* (Parlement de Musique/Martin Gester). Opus 111: 30-100.

3307.3 *Piramo e Tisbe* [opera]. (Barbara Schlick/Michel Lecocq/Capella Clementina/Helmut Müller-Brühl). Koch: 3-1088-2. 2CD set.

3308 Heinichen, Johann David, 1683–1729
Dresden concertos. (Musica Antiqua Köln/Reinhard Goebel). Archiv: 437 549-2. 2CD set.

3309 * Hidalgo, Juan, d. 1685
Vocal music. Selections. See 3360, 3362, or 3380

3310 Jacquet de La Guerre, Elisabeth-Claude, ca. 1664–1729

3310.1 *Cantatas. Selections.* (Sophie Boulin and others). Arion: 268012/13. 2CD set.

3310.2 *Harpsichord music. Selections.* (John Metz). Summit: CDC 136.

3311 Kapsperger, Giovanni Girolamo, ca. 1575–ca. 1650. *Lute and chitarrone music. Selections.*

- (Rolf Lislevand). Astrée: E 8515.
- (Paul O'Dette). Harmonia Mundi: HMU 907020.

3312 Lalande, Michel Richard de, 1657–1726

3312.1 *Petites motets.* (Les Arts Florissants/William Christie). Harmonia Mundi: HMC 901416.

3312.2 *Symphonies pour les soupers du roi* [for orchestra—selections]. (Simphonie du Marais/Hugo Reyne). Harmonia Mundi: HMC 901303.

3312.3 *Te Deum.* (Les Arts Florissants/William Christie). Harmonia Mundi: HMC 901351. [With his *Super flumina Babilonis* and *Confitebor tibi Domine*].

3313 Lawes, Henry, 1596–1662
Vocal music. Selections. (Consort of Musicke/Anthony Rooley). Hyperion: CDA66135.

3314 * Lawes, William, 1602–1645. *Chamber music for strings. Selections.*

- (Fretwork). Virgin: 7 59021 2 (7 91187 2).

- (Fretwork). Virgin: 7 59667 2.
- (London Baroque). Harmonia Mundi: HMC 901423.

3315 Leclair, Jean Marie, 1697–1764

3315.1 * *Concertos for violin and orchestra. Selections.* (Simon Standage/Collegium Musicum 90). Chandos: CHAN 0551; CHAN 0564. 2 CDs. [Further volumes forthcoming].

3315.2 *Sonatas for violin and continuo. Selections.*

- (Fabio Biondi/Rinaldo Alessandrini). Arcana: 39.
- (Trio Sonnerie). ASV Gaudeamus: GAU 106.

3316 * Legrenzi, Giovanni, 1626–1690
Sonatas. Selections. See 3389, 3393, or 3395

3317 Locatelli, Pietro Antonio, 1695–1764

3317.1 * *L'arte del violino* [12 concertos for violin and strings plus 24 caprices for violin solo]. (Elizabeth Wallfisch/Raglan Baroque Players/Nicholas Kraemer). Hyperion: 66721/23. 3CD set.

3317.2 *Concerti grossi. Selections.*

- (Europa Galante/Fabio Biondi). Opus 111: 30-104.
- (Concerto Köln). Teldec: 4509-94551-2.

3318 Locke, Matthew, 1621 or 1622–1677

3318.1 * *Chamber music for strings. Selections.*

- (Locke Consort). Globe: GLO 5027.
- (Hespèrion XX/Jordi Savall). Astrée: E 8519.

3318.2 *Choral music. Selections.* (Choir of New College, Oxford/Edward Higginbottom). Hyperion: CDA66373.

3318.3 *Organ music. Selections. See* 3333.4

3318.4 *The tempest* [incidental music]. (Academy of Ancient Music/Christopher Hogwood). L'Oiseau-Lyre: 433 191-2. [With his *Music for His Majesty's sackbuts and cornetts* and Purcell, Henry: *Abdelazer*].

3319 Lotti, Antonio, d. 1740
Crucifixus. See 3393

3320 Lully, Jean Baptiste, 1632–1687

3320.1 *Alceste* [opera]. (Colette Alliot-Lugaz/Howard Crook/Grand Ecurie et la Chambre du Roi/Jean-Claude Malgoire). Astrée: E 8527. 3CD set.

3320.2 * *Armide* [opera]. (Guillemette Laurens/Howard Crook/Chapelle Royale/Philippe Herreweghe). Harmonia Mundi: HMC 901456/57. 2CD set.

3320.3 *Atys* [opera]. (Les Arts Florissants/William Christie). Harmonia Mundi: HMC 901257/59. 3CD set.

3320.4 *Dies irae.* (Les Arts Florissants/Philippe Herreweghe). Harmonia Mundi: HMC 901167. [With his *Miserere*].

3320.5 *Petites motets.* (Les Arts Florissants/William Christie). Harmonia Mundi: HMC 901274.

3320.6 *Phaëton* [opera]. (Rachel Yakar/Howard Crook/Musiciens du Louvre/Marc Minkowski). Erato: 4509-91737-2. 2CD set.

3321 * Marais, Marin, 1656–1728. *Pieces for bass viol and continuo. Selections.*

- (Wieland Kuijken). Accent: ACC 78744 D [excerpts from his *Book 5*].
- (Jordi Savall). Astrée: E 7770 [excerpts from his *Book 2*]; E 8761 [excerpts from his *Book 3*]; E 7727 [excerpts from his *Book 4*].
- (Smithsonian Chamber Players). Deutsche Harmonia Mundi: 77146-2-RC [excerpts from his *Book 1*].

3322 Marazzoli, Marco, ca. 1605–1662

Oratorios. Selections. (Cantus Cölln/Konrad Junghänel). *See 3280.1*

3323 * Marcello, Alessandro, 1669–1747

Concerto for oboe and orchestra in D minor. (Academy of Ancient Music/Christopher Hogwood). L'Oiseau-Lyre: 421 655-2. [With Vivaldi, Antonio: *Concerto for recorder and string orchestra, RV 651 in C major; Trio sonata, op. 1 no. 12 ("La folia"); two cantatas*].

3324 Marcello, Benedetto, 1686–1739

3324.1 *L'estro poetico-armonico* [motets—selections]. (Capella Savaria/Pál Németh). Harmonia Mundi: HMA 1903048.

3324.2 *Sonatas for violoncello and continuo. Selections.* (Roel Dieltiens/Richte van der Meer/Konrad Junghänel). *See 3373*

3325 Marini, Biagio, 1597?–1665

Sonatas. Selections. See 3329.1 or 3391

3326 Mazzocchi, Domenico, 1592–1665

Vocal music. Selections. (René Jacobs). Harmonia Mundi: HMC 901357.

3327 Merula, Tarquinio, d. 1665

Vocal music. Selections. (Montserrat Figueras). Astrée: E 8503.

3328 Montéclair, Michel Pignolet de, 1667–1737

Cantatas. Selections. (Julianne Baird/American Baroque). Koch: 3-7096-2 H1. [*La bergère, La mort de Didon,* and *Pan et Sirinx.* With Clérambault, Louis Nicolas: *Medée.*]

3329 Monteverdi, Claudio, 1567–1643

SECULAR VOCAL MUSIC

3329.1 *Il combattimento di Tancredi e Clorinda* [dramatic cantata].

- (Les Arts Florissants/William Christie). Harmonia Mundi: HMC 901426. [With selected madrigals from his *Books 6–9*].
- (Nigel Rogers/Carolyn Watkinson/Musica Antiqua Köln/Reinhard Goebel). Archiv: 415 296-2. [With his *Lamento d'Arianna* plus instrumental works by Carlo Farina, Salomone Rossi, Giovanni Battista Fontana, Biagio Marini, and Giovanni Battista Buonamente].

3329.2 *Madrigals, book 2* [complete]. (Consort of Musicke/Anthony Rooley). Virgin: CDC 7 59282 2.

3329.3 *Madrigals, book 3* [complete]. (Consort of Musicke/Anthony Rooley). Virgin: CDC 7 59283 2.

3329.4 * *Madrigals, book 4* [complete]. (Concerto Italiano/Rinaldo Alessandrini). Opus 111: OPS 30-81.

3329.5 * *Madrigals, book 5* [complete]. (Consort of Musicke/Anthony Rooley). L'Oiseau-Lyre: 410 291-2.

3329.6 * *Madrigals, book 6* [complete]. (Concerto Italiano/Rinaldo Alessandrini). Arcana: A 66.

3329.7 ** *Madrigals, book 7* [selections].

- (Les Arts Florissants/William Christie). Harmonia Mundi: HMA 1901068. [With selections from *Book 8*].
- (Consort of Musicke/Anthony Rooley). L'Oiseau-Lyre: 421 480-2. [With selections from *Books 8–9*].

3329.8 * *Madrigals, book 8* [complete]. (Consort of Musicke/Anthony Rooley). Virgin: 7 59620 2 (7 91156 2); 7 59621 2 (7 91157 2). 2 CDs.

3329.9 *Madrigals, book 9* [selections].

- (Montserrat Figueras and others). *See 3329.15*
- (Emma Kirkby/Anthony Rooley). *See 3382*

SACRED VOCAL MUSIC

3329.10 *Masses.* (Chapelle Royale/Philippe Herreweghe). Harmonia Mundi: HMC 901355.

3329.11 * *Selva morale et spirituale* [motets—
selections].

- (Les Arts Florissants/William Christie). Harmonia Mundi: HMC 1250.

- (Taverner Consort/Andrew Parrott). EMI: CDC
7 47016 2.

3329.12 ** *Vespro della Beata Vergine (Vespers).*

- (Monteverdi Choir/John Eliot Gardiner). London: 429 656-2. 2CD set.

- (Taverner Consort/Andrew Parrott). EMI: 7
47078 2. 2CD set.

- (New London Consort/Philip Pickett). L'Oiseau-
Lyre: 425 823-2. 2CD set.

STAGE MUSIC

3329.13 *Ballo delle ingrate* [ballet].

- (Les Arts Florissants/William Christie). Harmonia Mundi: HMC 901108. [With his *Sestina
(from Madrigals, Book 6)*].

- (English Baroque Soloists/John Eliot Gardiner). Erato: 2292-45984-2. [With his *Tirsi e
Clori; De la bellezza; Vogendo il ciel; Orfeo
excerpts*].

3329.14 * *L'incoronazione di Poppea (The coronation of Poppea)* [opera].

- (Carmen Balthrop/Judith Nelson/Complesso
Barocco/Alan Curtis). Fonit Cetra: CDC 76.
3CD set.

- (Arleen Augér/Della Jones/City of London Baroque Sinfonia/Richard Hickox). Virgin: 7
45082 2 (7 90775 2). 3CD set.

- (Concerto Vocale/René Jacobs). Harmonia
Mundi: 901330/32. 3CD set.

3329.15 * *Lamento d'Arianna* [fragment of lost
opera].

- (Montserrat Figueras and others). Astrée:
8710. [With his selected secular and sacred
music for solo voice and continuo].

- (Carolyn Watkinson and others). *See* 3329.1

3329.16 ** *Orfeo* [opera].

- (Lajos Kozma/Cathy Berberian/Concentus
Musicus Vienna/Nikolaus Harnoncourt). Teldec: 2292-42494-2 (8.35020). 2CD set.

- (Nigel Rogers/Patrizia Kwella/London Baroque/
Charles Medlam). EMI: CMS 7 64947 2. 2CD
set.

- (Andrew King/Catherine Bott/New London
Consort/Philip Pickett). L'Oiseau-Lyre: 433
545-2. 2CD set.

3329.17 * *Il ritorno d'Ulisse in patria (The return
of Ulysses)* [opera]. (Concerto Vocale/René Jacobs). Harmonia Mundi: 901427/29. 2CD set.

3330 Mouret, Jean-Joseph, 1682–1738
Rondeau from Suite de symphonies no. 1. ["Masterpiece Theatre" theme]. *See* 3371

3331 Pachelbel, Johann, 1653–1706
3331.1 ** *Canon and gigue.*

- (Musica Antiqua Köln/Reinhard Goebel)
[original instrumentation]. *See* 3275.2

- (English Concert/Trevor Pinnock) [original in-
strumentation]. Archiv: 415 518-2. [With
works by Antonio Vivaldi, Tomaso Albinoni,
Henry Purcell, George Frideric Handel, Charles
Avison, and Joseph Haydn].

- (Various performers). RCA: 60712-2-RG.
["*Pachelbel's greatest hit*" in various instru-
mentations].

3331.2 *Organ music. Selections.* (John Butt).
Harmonia Mundi: HMU 907029.

3332 * Pepusch, John Christopher, 1667–1752
The beggar's opera. (Bob Hoskins/Broadside Band/
Jeremy Barlow). Hyperion: CDA66591/92. 2CD set;
or Musical Heritage Society: MHS 523361L. 2CD set.

3333 Purcell, Henry, 1659–1695

INSTRUMENTAL MUSIC

3333.1 * *Ayres for the theatre.* (Parley of Instru-
ments/Roy Goodman). Hyperion: CDA66001/3.
3CD set.

3333.2 * *Fantasias and In nomines for viol consort.*

- (Fretwork). Virgin: 7 45062 2.

- (Concentus Musicus Wien/Nikolaus Harnoncourt). Vanguard: 8091.

- (Hespèrion XX/Jordi Savall). Astrée: E 8536.

3333.3 *Harpsichord music.* (Kenneth Gilbert).
Harmonia Mundi: HMC 901496.

3333.4 *Organ music.* (John Butt). Harmonia
Mundi: HMU 907103. [With Blow, John: *Organ
music* and Locke, Matthew: *Organ music*].

3333.5 *Pavans and other works for violin consort.* (London Baroque). Harmonia Mundi: HMC
901327.

3333.6 * *Trio sonatas ("Sonatas of three parts"* (1683) and *"Sonatas of four parts"* (1697)). (London Baroque). Harmonia Mundi: HMC 901438; HMC 901439. 2 CDs.

VOCAL MUSIC

3333.7 * *Anthems, odes, and welcome songs, etc. Selections.*

- (King's Consort/Robert King). Hyperion: KING 2. [*"Essential Purcell"*].

- (English Concert/Trevor Pinnock). Archiv: 427 663-2. [*Come, ye sons of art, away; Welcome to all the pleasures; Of old, when heroes thought it base*].

- (Choir of Christ Church, Oxford/Simon Preston). Archiv: 427 124-2. [*My heart is inditing; O sing unto the Lord; They that go down to the sea in ships; Praise the Lord, O Jerusalem; Te Deum and Jubilate*].

3333.8 ** *Hail! bright Cecilia (Ode for St. Cecilia's Day, 1692).*

- (King's Consort/Robert King). [Series: Odes and welcome songs, vol. 2]. Hyperion: CDA66609.

- (Gabrieli Consort/Paul McCreesh). Archiv: 445 882-2. [With his *My beloved spake* and *O sing unto the Lord*].

3333.9 *Harmonia sacra* [sacred songs—selections]. (Gabrieli Consort/Paul McCreesh). Archiv: 445 829-2.

3333.10 * *Secular songs. Selections.*

- (Nancy Argenta and others). Virgin: 7 59324 2. [Album title: *O solitude: songs and airs*].

- (Barbara Bonney and others). Hyperion: 66710; 66720; 66730. 3 CDs.

- (Alfred Deller and others). Harmonia Mundi: HM 90249.

- (Drew Minter and others). Harmonia Mundi: HMU 907035.

STAGE MUSIC

3333.11 ** *Dido and Aeneas* [opera].

- (Lorrain Hunt/Lisa Saffer/Philharmonia Baroque Orchestra/Nicolas McGegan). Harmonia Mundi: HMU 907110.

- (Emma Kirkby/Judith Nelson/Taverner Players/Andrew Parrott). Chandos: CHAN 0521.

- (Lynn Dawson/Anne Sofie von Otter/English Concert/Trevor Pinnock). Archiv: 427 624-2.

3333.12 * *The fairy queen* [semi-opera]. (Jennifer Smith/Stephen Varcoe/English Baroque Soloists/John Eliot Gardiner). Archiv 419 221-2. 2CD set.

3333.13 *The history of Dioclesian, or The prophetess* [semi-opera]. (Lynn Dawson/Rogers Covey-Crump/English Baroque Soloists/John Eliot Gardiner). Erato: 2292-45327-2. 2CD set. [With his *Timon of Athens*].

3333.14 *King Arthur* [semi-opera]. (Nancy Argenta/Linda Perillo/English Concert/Trevor Pinnock). Archiv: 435 490-2.

———

3334   Rameau, Jean Philippe, 1683–1764

ORCHESTRAL MUSIC
(SUITES FROM OPERAS AND BALLETS)

3334.1 *Les Boréades suite.* (Orchestra of the 18th Century/Frans Brüggen). *See* 3334.2

3334.2 * *Dardanus suite.* (Orchestra of the 18th Century/Frans Brüggen). Philips: 420 240-2. [With suite from his *Boréades*].

3334.3 *Les fêtes d'Hebé suite.* (English Baroque Soloists/John Eliot Gardiner). Erato: 2292-95312-2.

3334.4 *Hippolyte et Aricie suite.* (Petite Bande/Sigiswald Kuijken). Deutsche Harmonia Mundi: 77009-2-RG.

3334.5 * *Les Indes galantes suite.* (Chapelle Royale/Philippe Herreweghe). Harmonia Mundi: HMC 1901130.

3334.6 *Les paladins suite.* (Orchestra of the Age of Enlightenment/Gustav Leonhardt). Philips: 432 968-2.

3334.7 *Les surprises de l'amour suite.* (Musiciens du Louvre/Marc Minkowski). Erato: 2292-45004-2.

CHAMBER AND SOLO INSTRUMENTAL MUSIC

3334.8 * *Pièces de clavecin (Harpsichord pieces).*

- (William Christie). Harmonia Mundi: HMA 1901120/21. 2CD set.

- (Christophe Rousset). L'Oiseau-Lyre: 425 886-2. 2CD set.

3334.9 ** *Pièces de clavecin en concert* [trios with harpsichord].

- (Christophe Rousset and others). Harmonia Mundi: HMC 901418.

- (Trio Sonnerie). Virgin: 7 59154 2 (7 90749 2).

VOCAL MUSIC

3334.10 *Cantatas. Selections.* (Barbara Schlick and others). Musikproduktion Dabringhaus und Grimm: MD+G L 3131. [*L'impatience* and *Orphée*.

With his *Pièces de clavecin en concert nos. 3 and 5*].

3334.11 * *Motets. Selections.*

- (Les Arts Florissants/William Christie). Erato: 2292-96967-2.

- (Chapelle Royale/Philippe Herreweghe). Harmonia Mundi: HM 901078.

STAGE MUSIC

3334.12 * *Les Boréades* [opera]. (Jennifer Smith/ Philip Langridge/English Baroque Soloists/John Eliot Gardiner). Musifrance: 2292-45572-2. 3CD set.

3334.13 * *Castor et Pollux* [opera]. (Howard Crook/Jérôme Corréas/Les Arts Florissants/William Christie). Harmonia Mundi: HMC 901435/ 37. 3CD set [complete opera]; HMC 9011501 [highlights].

3334.14 *Hippolyte et Aricie* [opera]. (Jean-Paul Fouchécourt/Véronique Gens/Musiciens du Louvre/ Marc Minkowski). Archiv: 445 853-2. 3CD set.

3334.15 * *Les Indes galantes* [opera-ballet]. (Les Arts Florissants/William Christie). Harmonia Mundi: HMC 901367/69. 3CD set.

3334.16 *Platée* [opera]. (Gilles Ragon/Jennifer Smith/Musiciens du Louvre/Marc Minkowski). Erato: 2292-45028-2. 2CD set.

3334.17 *Pygmalion* [ballet].

- (Les Arts Florissants/William Christie). Harmonia Mundi: HMC 901381.

- (Mieke van der Sluis/John Elwes/Petite Bande/ Gustav Leonhardt). Deutsche Harmonia Mundi: 77143-2-RG.

3334.18 *Zoroastre* [opera]. (Petite Bande/ Sigiswald Kuijken). Deutsche Harmonia Mundi: 77144-2-RG. 3CD set.

3335 Rebel, Jean-Féry, 1666–1747

Les élemens [ballet]. (Musiciens du Louvre/Marc Minkowski). Musifrance: 2292-45974-2. [With his *Les caractères de la danse* and *Le tombeau de M. de Lully*].

3336 Rosenmüller, Johann, 1619–1684

Trio sonatas. Selections. (Musica Antiqua Köln/ Reinhard Goebel). *See 3368*

3337 Rossi, Luigi, 1598–1653

3337.1 *Oratorios. Selections.* (Les Arts Florissants/William Christie). Harmonia Mundi: HMA 1901297.

3337.2 *Orfeo* [opera]. (Les Arts Florissants/ William Christie). Harmonia Mundi: HMC 901358/60. 3CD set.

3338 Rossi, Michelangelo, 17th cent. *Toccatas for harpsichord. Selections.*

- (Rinaldo Alessandrini). *See 3383*

- (Alan Curtis). *See 3363*

3339 * Rossi, Salamone, 1570?–ca. 1630

Song of songs. Selections. (Boston Camerata/Joel Cohen). Harmonia Mundi: HMA 1901021. [Album title: *Musique judeo-baroque*. With sonatas by Rossi, plus works by Louis Saladin and Carlo Grossi].

3340 * Royer, Pancrace, 1705–1755

Pièces de clavecin (Harpsichord pieces). Selections. (Christophe Rousset). L'Oiseau-Lyre: 436 127-2.

3341 Sainte-Colombe, sieur de, fl. 1713

Concerts for 2 bass viols. Selections. (Wieland Kuijken/Jordi Savall). Astrée: E 7729; E 8743. 2 CDs.

3342 Scarlatti, Alessandro, 1660–1725

3342.1 * *Arias. Selections.* (Judith Nelson and others). Harmonia Mundi: HMA 1905137. [With music by Alessandro Melani].

3342.2 *Cantatas. Selections.*

- (Cristina Miatello/Claudio Cavina/Rinaldo Alessandrini). Tactus: TC 661901.

- (Lynne Dawson/Purcell Quartet). Hyperion: CDA66254. [With his *Variations on La folia* for harpsichord].

3342.3 * *Passio secundum Joannem (St. John passion).* (Schola Cantorum Basiliensis/René Jacobs). Deutsche Harmonia Mundi: 77111-2-RG.

3342.4 *Il primo omocidio (Il Caino)* [oratorio]. (Gloria Banditelli/Concerto Italiano/Rinaldo Alessandrini). Opus 111: 30-75/76. 2CD set.

3342.5 *Stabat Mater.* (English Concert/Trevor Pinnock). *See 3357.10*

3343 Scarlatti, Domenico, 1685–1757

3343.1 ** *Sonatas for harpsichord. Selections.*

- (Vladimir Horowitz) [piano]. CBS: MK 42410.

- (Trevor Pinnock). Archiv: 419 632-2.

- (Scott Ross). Erato: 2292-45422-2. 3CD set.

- (Andreas Staier). Deutsche Harmonia Mundi: 05472-77224-2; 05472-77274-2. 2 CDs.

3343.2 * *Stabat Mater.* (Choir of Christ Church Oxford/Francis Grier). Hyperion: CDA66182. [With his *Salve Regina*].

3344 Scheidt, Samuel, 1587–1654

Consort music. Selections. (His Majesties Sagbutts and Cornetts). *See* 3378

3345 Schein, Johann Hermann, 1586–1630

3345.1 *Consort music. Selections.* (His Majesties Sagbutts and Cornetts). *See* 3378

3345.2 *Madrigals. Selections.* (Cantus Cölln/ Konrad Junghänel). Deutsche Harmonia Mundi: 77088-2-RC.

3346 Schmelzer, Johann Heinrich, ca. 1623–1680. *Music for strings and continuo. Selections.*

- (Musica Antiqua Köln/Reinhard Goebel). *See* 3387

- (Tafelmusik/Jean Lamon). Sony: SK 53963.

3347 Schütz, Heinrich, 1585–1672

3347.1 *Cantiones sacrae. Selections.* (Currende/ Erik van Nevel). Accent: ACC 9174 D; or Musical Heritage Society: MHS 513294A.

3347.2 *Geistliche Chormusik.* (Hannover Boys Choir/Heinz Hennig). Deutsche Harmonia Mundi: GD77171. 2CD set.

3347.3 *Madrigals.*

- (Cantus Cölln). Deutsche Harmonia Mundi: RD-77240.

- (Consort of Musicke/Anthony Rooley). Deutsche Harmonia Mundi: 77118-2-RG.

3347.4 *Motets. Selections.* (Cantus Cölln). Deutsche Harmonia Mundi: 77175-2-RC. [With his selected *Psalms* and *Concertos*].

3347.5 * *Musikalische Exequien.* (Monteverdi Choir/John Eliot Gardiner). Archiv: 423 405-2. [With his selected motets].

3347.6 *Psalmen Davids.* (Stuttgart Chamber Choir/Frieder Bernius). Sony: S2K 48042. 2CD set.

3347.7 *Schwanengesang.* (Capella Sagittariana/ Dieter Knothe). Berlin Classics: 1071-2. 2CD set.

3347.8 *Die sieben Worte Jesu Christi am Kreuz (Seven last words of Christ).* (Ensemble Clément Janequin). Harmonia Mundi: HMC 901255.

3347.9 * *Symphoniae sacrae op. 6.* (Barbara Borden/Rogers Covey-Crump/Concerto Palatino). Accent: ACC 9178/79. 2CD set.

3347.10 * *Symphoniae sacrae op. 10.* (Emma Kirkby/Purcell Quartet). Chandos: CHAN 0566/ 67. 2CD set.

3347.11 * *Weihnachtshistorie (Christmas oratorio).*

- (Stuttgart Chamber Choir/Frieder Bernius). Sony: 45943. [With his *Easter oratorio*].

- (Taverner Consort/Andrew Parrott). EMI: CDC 7 47633 2. [With Praetorius, Michael: *Motets*].

3348 Steffani, Agostino, 1654–1724

Duetti da camera [for voices and continuo— selections]. (Rossana Bertini/Claudio Cavina/ Arcadia). Glossa: 920902.

3349 Stradella, Alessandro, 1639–1682

3349.1 *Cantatas. Selections.* (La Stagione/ Michael Schneider). Deutsche Harmonia Mundi: 77180-2-RG. [Album title: *Weihnachtskantaten = Christmas cantatas*].

3349.2 * *San Giovanni Battista* [oratorio].

- (Catherine Bott/Musiciens du Louvre/Marc Minkowski). Erato: 2292-45739-2.

- (Ann Monoyios/Stagione/Michael Schneider). Deutsche Harmonia Mundi: RD-77034.

3350 * Strozzi, Barbara, 1619–ca. 1664. *Arias and cantatas. Selections.*

- (Julianne Baird and others). *See* 3379

- (Musica Secreta). Amon Ra: SAR 61.

- (Consort of Musicke/Anthony Rooley). *See* 3219

- (Glenda Simpson and others). Hyperion: CDA66303.

3351 Tartini, Giuseppe, 1692–1770

3351.1 * *Concertos. Selections.* (Ensemble 415/ Chiara Banchini). Harmonia Mundi: HMC 901548.

3351.2 *Sonatas for violin and continuo. Selections.*

- (Fabio Biondi and others). Opus 111: 59-9205.

- (Locatelli Trio). Hyperion: CDA66430.

3352 Telemann, Georg Philipp, 1681–1767

INSTRUMENTAL MUSIC

3352.1 * *Concertos, overtures, and suites for orchestra. Selections.*

- (Musica Antiqua Köln/Reinhard Goebel). Archiv: 419 633-2. [*Concertos for flute and strings in D major; For three oboes, three violins, and strings in B♭ major; For two chalumeaux and strings in D minor; For trumpet and strings in D major; For recorder, flute, and strings in C minor; For recorder, flute, and strings in E minor; For trumpet, violin, and strings in D major].*

- (Musica Antiqua Köln/Reinhard Goebel). Archiv: 413 788-2. [*Wassermusik (Hamburger Ebb' und Flut); Concertos for two recorders, two oboes, bassoon, and strings in B♭ major, F major, and A minor*].

- (New London Consort/Philip Pickett). L'Oiseau-Lyre: 433 043-2. [*Suite (overture) for recorder and strings in A minor; Concerto for recorder and strings in C major; Concerto for recorder, viola da gamba, and strings in A minor*].

- (English Concert/Trevor Pinnock). Archiv: 437 558-2. [*Overture-Suites for orchestra in C major, TWV 55:C6; D major, TWV 55:D19; and B♭ major, TWV 55:B10*].

- (English Concert/Trevor Pinnock). Archiv: 439 893-2. [*Concerto for three trumpets and orchestra in D major; Overture-Suite in G minor, TWV 55:g4; Overture in D major from Musique de table*].

3352.2 *Fantasias for solo flute.* (Barthold Kuijken). Accent: ACC 57803 D.

3352.3 * *Musique de table.* (Musica Antiqua Köln/Reinhard Goebel). Archiv: 427 619-2. 4CD set [complete]; 429 774-2 [selections].

3352.4 * *Paris quartets.* (Trio Sonnerie). Virgin: 7 45020 2; 7 59049 2. 2 CDs.

VOCAL MUSIC AND STAGE MUSIC

3352.5 *Cantatas. Selections.*

- (Julianne Baird/James Bowman). Meridian: 84159.

- (René Jacobs/Kuijken Consort/Parnassus Ensemble). *See* 3369

3352.6 *Ino* [dramatic cantata]. (Musica Antiqua Köln/Reinhard Goebel). Archiv: 429 772-2. [With his *Overture in D major, TWV 55 D:21*.]

3352.7 *Pimpinone* [comic intermezzo].

- (Julianne Baird/John Ostendorf/Baroque Orchestra of St. Luke's/Rudolph Palmer). Newport: 60117.

- (Stagione/Michael Schneider). Deutsche Harmonia Mundi: 05472-77284-2.

3352.8 *Der Tag des Gerichts* [oratorio]. (Monteverdi Choir/Concentus Musicus Wien/Nikolaus Harnoncourt). Teldec: 9031-77621-2. 2CD set.

3353 Torelli, Giuseppe, 1658–1709. *Concertos and sonatas for trumpet and strings. Selections.*

- (Musica Antiqua Köln/Reinhard Goebel). *See* 3364

- (Friedemann Immer/Concerto Köln). *See* 3392

3354 Uccellini, Marco, ca. 1603–1680

Sonatas and airs for violins and continuo. Selections. (Arcadian Academy). Harmonia Mundi: HMU 907066.

3355 Veracini, Francesco Maria, 1690–1768

Overtures. Selections. (Musica Antiqua Köln/Reinhard Goebel). Archiv: 439 937-2.

3356 Visée, Robert de, ca. 1650–ca. 1725

3356.1 *Pieces for guitar. Selections.* (Rafael Andia). Harmonia Mundi: HMC 901186.

3356.2 *Pieces for theorbo. Selections.* (Yasunori Imamura). Capriccio: 10404.

3357 Vivaldi, Antonio, 1678–1741

INSTRUMENTAL MUSIC

3357.1 * *Chamber concertos and trio sonatas for lute and strings.* (Jakob Lindberg and others). Bis: 290; or Musical Heritage Society: 512082Y.

3357.2 *Chamber concertos and trio sonatas. Selections.* (Marion Verbruggen and others). Harmonia Mundi: HMU 907046.

3357.3 *Il cimento dell'armonia e dell'inventione* [12 concertos for strings, of which *The four seasons* comprise the first four]. (Academy of Ancient Music/Christopher Hogwood). L'Oiseau-Lyre: 417 515-2. 2CD set.

3357.4 ** *Concertos for various instruments and orchestra. Selections.*

- (Europa Galante/Fabio Biondi). Opus 111: OPS 30-86. [RV 281 for violin; RV 286 for violin; RV 133 for strings; RV 407 for violoncello; RV 511 for two violins; RV 531 for two violoncellos; RV 541 for violin and organ].

- (King's Consort/Robert King). *See* 3266.2

- (Anner Bylsma/Tafelmusik/Jean Lamon). Sony: SK 48044. [RV 117, 134, 143, and 159 for strings; RV 413 and 418 for violoncello; RV 547 for violin and violoncello; RV 549 for four violins; RV 575 for two violins and two violoncellos].

- (English Concert/Trevor Pinnock). Archiv: 419 615-2. [RV 159 for strings; RV 271 ("L'amoroso") for violin; RV 436 for flute; RV

484 for bassoon; RV 540 for viola d'amore and lute; RV 545 for oboe and bassoon; RV 565 for two violins].

- (English Concert/Trevor Pinnock). Archiv: 431 710-2. [*RV 151 ("Alla rustica"); RV 439 for flute ("La notte"); RV 484 for bassoon; RV 532 for two mandolins; RV 549 for four violins; RV 558 for diverse instruments; RV 565 for two violins*].

3357.5 * *L'estro armonico op. 3* [12 concertos for strings]. (Academy of Ancient Music/Christopher Hogwood). L'Oiseau-Lyre: 414 554-2. 2CD set.

3357.6 ** *The four seasons.*

- (Fabio Biondi/Europa Galante). Opus 111: 56-9120.

- (Gidon Kremer/London Symphony/Claudio Abbado). Deutsche Grammophon: 413 726-2.

- (Nils Erik Sparf/Drottningholm Baroque Orchestra). Bis: 275.

  See also 3357.3

3357.7 *Sonatas for violin and continuo. Selections.* (Fabio Biondi). Arcana: 4-5. 2 CDs.

3357.8 *Sonatas for violoncello and continuo. Selections.*

- (Anner Bylsma and others). Deutsche Harmonia Mundi: 77909-2-RC. [*RV 40-41; 43; 45-47*].

- (Christophe Coin/Academy of Ancient Music/ Christopher Hogwood). L'Oiseau-Lyre: 433 052-2. [*Sonatas, RV 39, 42,* and *44,* plus *Concertos for violoncello and strings, RV 402, 406,* and *414*].

VOCAL MUSIC

3357.9 *Cantatas. Selections. See* 3323 and 3357.11

3357.10 * *Gloria, RV 589.*

- (Sixteen/Harry Christophers). *See* 3270.46

- (Taverner Consort/Andrew Parrott). Virgin: 7 59326 2. [With his *Magnificat*].

- (English Concert/Trevor Pinnock). Archiv: 423 386-2. [With Scarlatti, Alessandro: *Stabat Mater*].

3357.11 * *Magnificat, RV 610.*

- (Tafelmusik/Jean Lamon). Hyperion: CDA66247. [With his selected cantatas, motets, and concertos].

- (Taverner Consort/Andrew Parrott). *See* 3357.10

3357.12 *Stabat Mater, RV 621.* (James Bowman/ Academy of Ancient Music/Christopher Hogwood). L'Oiseau-Lyre: 414 329-2. [With his *Nisi Dominus* and selected concertos].

3358 * Weiss, Silvius Leopold, 1686-1750. *Lute music. Selections.*

- (Lutz Kirchhof). Sony: S2K 48391. 2CD set. Sony: SK 57964.

- (José Miguel Moreno). Glossa: 920102.

3359 Zelenka, Johann Dismas, 1679–1745

3359.1 * *Lamentations of Jeremiah.* (Schola Cantorum Basiliensis/René Jacobs). Deutsche Harmonia Mundi: 77112-2-RG.

3359.2 *Missa Dei Filii.* (Stuttgart Chamber Choir/ Frieder Bernius). Deutsche Harmonia Mundi: 7922-2-RC. [With his *Litaniae Laurentanae*].

3359.3 *Orchestral music. Selections.* (Camerata Bern/Alexander van Wijnkoop). Archiv: 423 703-2. 3CD set.

3359.4 *Trio sonatas. Selections.* (Paul Dombrecht and others). Accent: ACC 8848 D.

Anthologies and Recitals

3360 *¡Ay amor!: Spanish 17th century songs and theatre music.* (Newberry Consort). Harmonia Mundi: HMU 907022. [Vocal and instrumental music by Juan Hidalgo, Andrea Falconiero, and Bartolomé de Selma y Salaverde].

3361 *Baroque music for lute and guitar.* (Jakob Lindberg). Bis: 327. [Works by David Kellner, Robert de Visée, Johann Sebastian Bach, Lodovico Roncalli, and Silvius Leopold Weiss].

3362 * *El barroco español: tonos humanos und Instrumentalmusik um 1640–1700.* (Hespèrion XX/ Jordi Savall). EMI: CDM 7 63418 2. [Spanish vocal and instrumental music by Juan del Vado, Juan Cabanilles, Sebastián Durón, Antonio Martín y Coll, Juan Hidalgo, José Marín, and De Milanes].

3363 * *Il cimbalo cromatico napoletano.* (Alan Curtis). Nuova Era: 7177. [Harpsichord works by Giovanni de Macque, Luigi Rossi, Giovanni Maria Trabaci, Ascanio Mayone, Gioan Pietro del Buono, Giovanni Salvatore, Gregorio Strozzi, and Michelangelo Rossi].

3364 *Concerti.* (Musica Antiqua Köln/Reinhard Goebel). Archiv: 435 393-2. [Works by Giuseppe Torelli, Giovanni Mossi, Giuseppe Valentini, Pietro Antonio Locatelli, and Leonardo Leo].

3365 *Duetti da camera.* (Emma Kirkby/Judith Nelson/Anthony Rooley). L'Oiseau-Lyre: 436 861-2. [Italian 17th-century vocal duets by Angelo Notari, Sigismondo D'India, Giovanni Valentini, Girolamo

Frescobaldi, Alessandro Grandi, Nicolò Fontei, Giovanni Rovetta, and Galeazzo Sabbatini].

3366 * *English country dances: from Playford's Dancing master 1651–1703.* (Broadside Band/Jeremy Barlow). Saydisc: CD-SDL 393.

3367 *Eternal source of light.* (James Bowman/King's Consort/Robert King). Meridian: CDE 84126. [Handel, George Frideric: *Eternal source of light;* Buxtehude, Dietrich: *Jubilate Domino* and *Jesu, meine Freud und Lust;* Bach, Johann Christoph: *Ach, dass ich Wassers g'nug hätte;* Monn, Georg Mathias: *Maria, starke Sonnen* and *Lasst uns all' Mariam loben!;* Franck, Johann Wolfgang: *Jesu, ich in meinem Sinn*].

3368 * *German chamber music before Bach.* (Musica Antiqua Köln/Reinhard Goebel). Archiv: 437 089-2. [Works by Johann Adam Reincken, Dietrich Buxtehude, Johann Rosenmüller, Paul Westhoff, and Johann Pachelbel].

3369 *German church cantatas and arias.* (René Jacobs/Kuijken Consort/Parnassus Ensemble). Accent: ACC 77912 D. [Buxtehude, Dietrich: *Muss der Tod denn nun doch trennen* and *Jubilate Domino;* Bach, Johann Christoph: *Ach, dass ich Wassers g'nug hätte;* Telemann, Georg Philipp: *Ach Herr, strafe mich nicht* and *Ihr Völker, hört*].

3370 *Gerusaleme liberata: settings from Tasso.* (Consort of Musicke/Anthony Rooley). Musica Oscura: 070990. [Madrigals by Claudio Monteverdi, Giovanni Rovetta, Luca Marenzio, Sigismondo D'India, Piero Benedetti, Giaches de Wert, and Orazio Vecchi].

3371 ** *Greatest hits of the Baroque.* (Various performers). CBS: MLK 45738. [Works by Tomaso Albinoni, Johann Sebastian Bach, Jeremiah Clarke, George Frideric Handel, Alessandro Marcello, Jean-Joseph Mouret, Johann Pachelbel, Henry Purcell, and Antonio Vivaldi].

3372 * *Intermedios del barroco hispanico, 1580–1680.* (Hespèrion XX/Jordi Savall). Astrée: E 8729. [Spanish theater music by Mateo Romero, Sebastian Aguilera de Heredia, Juan Cabanilles, Manuel Machado, Francisco Correa de Araujo, Francisco Guerrero, Juan Blas de Castro, and José Marín].

3373 *Italian cello music.* (Roel Dieltiens/Richte van der Meer/Konrad Junghänel). Accent: ACC 9070 D. [Music by Domenico Gabrielli, Benedetto Marcello, Giovanni Bononcini, Alessandro Scarlatti, and Willem de Fesch].

3374 * *John Playford's popular tunes.* (Broadside Band/Jeremy Barlow). Amon Ra: CD-SAR 28.

3375 *Mas no puede ser: villancicos, cantatas, et al.* (Al Ayre Español/Eduardo Lopez Banzo). Deutsche Harmonia Mundi: 05472-77325-2. [Spanish baroque music by Antonio Literes, Cristóbal Galan, Jose de Torres, Francisco Valls, and Juan Francés de Iribarren].

3376 * *Masters of the baroque guitar.* (Barry Mason). Amon Ra: SAR-45. [Music by Santiago de Murcia, Gaspar Sanz, Robert de Visée, Francesco Corbetta, Domenico Pellegrini, and Carlo Calvi].

3377 * *Mexican Baroque: music from New Spain.* (Chanticleer). Teldec: 4509-96353-2. [Vocal music by Ignacio de Jerusalem and Manuel de Zumaya].

3378 *Music from 17th century Germany.* (His Majesties Sagbutts and Cornetts). Meridian: CDE 84096. [Music for cornett-and-sackbut ensemble, some with bass voice, by Samuel Scheidt, Johann Hermann Schein, Heinrich Schütz, Johannes Braun, and Matthias Weckmann].

3379 * *Musica dolce.* (Julianne Baird/Colin Tilney). Dorian: DOR-90123. [Vocal and harpsichord works by Claudio Monteverdi, Pier Francesco Cavalli, Giulio Caccini, Bernardo Storace, Luigi Rossi, Gregorio Strozzi, Barbara Strozzi, and Andrea Cima].

3380 * *Música en tiempos de Velásquez.* (Ensemble La Romanesca/Jose Miguel Moreno). Glossa: GCD 920201. [Spanish baroque music by Gaspar Sanz, Juan Hidalgo, Antonio Martín y Coll, José Marín, Bartolomé de Selma y Salaverde, Diego Huete de Fernández, Francisco Guerau, and Sebastián Durón].

3381 *Musiche veneziane per voce e strumenti.* (Teresa Berganza). Claves: 50-8206. [17th-century Venetian vocal and instrumental music by Barbara Strozzi, Simone Molinaro, Giovanni Felice Sances, Claudio Monteverdi, Carlo Milanuzzi, Nicolò Fontei, Guglielmo Miniscalchi, and Pietro Maria Lamoretti].

3382 * *Olympia's lament.* (Emma Kirkby/Anthony Rooley). Elektra/Nonesuch: 79125-2. [Works for soprano and continuo by Claudio Monteverdi and Sigismondo D'India].

3383 * *One hundred fifty years of Italian music, volume 1: harpsichord.* (Rinaldo Alessandrini). Opus 111: 30-118. [Works by Antonio Valente, Marco Facoli, Giovanni de Macque, Ascanio Mayone, Giovanni Maria Trabaci, Giovanni Picchi, Gioan Pietro del Buono, Girolamo Frescobaldi,

Francesco Lambardo, Tarquinio Merula, Michelangelo Rossi, Giovanni Salvatore, Bernardo Storace, Gregorio Strozzi, Alessandro Stradella, and Alessandro Scarlatti].

3384 *The organ in Santa Prisca: 17th and 18th century music of the Spanish and Portuguese.* (Donald Joyce). Titanic: Ti-187. [Works by Pablo Bruna, Sebastian Aguilera de Heredia, Francisco Correa de Araujo, Juan Cabanilles, and Antonio de Cabézon].

3385 *Le Parnasse français.* (Musica Antiqua Köln/ Reinhard Goebel). Archiv: 437 086-2. [French chamber music by Marin Marais, Jean-Féry Rebel, François Couperin, Jean Marie Leclair, Michel Blavet, and Michel Corrette].

3386 * *Pièces du luth, France 17. siècle.* (Konrad Junghänel). Deutsche Harmonia Mundi: 77037-2-RC. [17th-century French lute music by Ennemond Gaultier, Denis Gaultier, François Dufaut, Jacques Gallot, and Charles Mouton].

3387 *Scherzi musicali.* (Musica Antiqua Köln/ Reinhard Goebel). Archiv: 429 230-2. [String music by Heinrich Ignaz Franz Biber, Johann Heinrich Schmelzer, and Johann Walther].

3388 * *Se tu m'ami: arie antiche.* (Cecilia Bartoli/ György Fischer). London: 436 267-2. [Arias by Alessandro Scarlatti, Tommaso Giordani, Antonio Lotti, Giovanni Paisiello, Benedetto Marcello, Antonio Caldara, Giulio Caccini, Pier Francesco Cavalli, and Giacomo Carissimi].

3389 *Sonate concertate.* (Musicalische Compagney). Teldec: 8.44010. [17th-century Italian and German chamber music by Giovanni Battista Buonamente, Johann Heinrich Schmelzer, Heinrich Aloys Brückner, Marc Antonio Ferro, Giovanni Valentini, Johann Joseph Fux, and Giovanni Legrenzi].

3390 * *Songs of love and war.* (Julianne Baird). Dorian: DOR 90104. [Works by Giulio Caccini, Giovanni Felice Sances, Claudio Monteverdi, George Frideric Handel, Girolamo Frescobaldi, and Johann Adolf Hasse].

3391 *Three parts upon a ground.* (Three Parts upon a Ground). Harmonia Mundi: HMU 907091. [17th-century music for three violins and continuo by Henry Purcell, Giovanni Battista Buonamente, Giovanni Gabrieli, Biagio Marini, Marco Uccellini, Giovanni Battista Fontana, Louis Constantin, Johann Heinrich Schmelzer, Carolus Hacquart, Carl Rosier, and Johann Pachelbel].

3392 *Trompetenkonzerte des italienischen Barock.* (Friedemann Immer/Grant Nicholson/Concerto Köln). Musikproduktion Dabringhaus und Grimm: MD+G L 3271. [Italian baroque concertos for one and two trumpets by Giuseppe Torelli, Domenico Gabrielli, Arcangelo Corelli, Giovanni Bonaventura Viviani, Alessandro Stradella, and Francesco Manfredini].

3393 ** *Venetian church music.* (Taverner Consort/ Andrew Parrott). EMI: CDC 7 54117 2. [Vocal and instrumental works by Giovanni Gabrieli, Claudio Monteverdi, Alessandro Grandi, Dario Castello, Giovanni Legrenzi, Antonio Lotti, and Antonio Vivaldi].

3394 *Venetian Vespers.* (Gabrieli Consort/Paul McCreesh). Archiv: 437 554-2. 2CD set. [Vocal and instrumental music by Giovanni Antonio Rigatti, Alessandro Grandi, Claudio Monteverdi, Adriano Banchieri, Giacomo Finetti, Pier Francesco Cavalli, Biagio Marini, and Giovanni Battista Fasolo].

3395 *Venice preserv'd.* (Academy of Ancient Music/ Christopher Hogwood). L'Oiseau-Lyre: 425 891-2. [Vocal and instrumental music by Claudio Monteverdi, Giovanni Gabrieli, Andrea Gabrieli, Alessandro Grandi, Biagio Marini, Spiridion, Giovanni Paolo Cima, and Pier Francesco Cavalli].

Classical Period

Compiled by
Kent Underwood

Composers

3396 Arne, Thomas Augustine, 1710–1778

3396.1 *Concertos. Selections.* (Paul Nicholson/ Parley of Instruments/Peter Holman). Hyperion: CDA66509. [Album title: *Six favourite concertos for the organ, harpsichord or piano forte*].

3396.2 *Overtures. Selections.* (Academy of Ancient Music/Christopher Hogwood). L'Oiseau-Lyre: 436 859-2.

3396.3 *Trio sonatas. Selections.* (Le Nouveau Quatuor). Amon Ra: CD-SAR 42.

3396.4 * *Vocal music. Selections.* (Emma Kirkby/ Parley of Instruments/Roy Goodman). Hyperion: CDA66237. [Album title: *Dr Arne at Vauxhall Gardens*].

3397 Bach, Carl Philipp Emanuel, 1714–1788

ORCHESTRAL MUSIC

3397.1 *Concertos for flute and orchestra. Selections.* (James Galway/Württemburg Chamber Or-

chestra/Jörg Faerber). RCA: 60244-2-RC. [*H. 426 in F major; H. 438 in A major; H. 445 in G major*].

3397.2 * *Concertos for harpsichord and orchestra. Selections.*

- (Bob van Asperen/Melante 81 Orchestra). EMI: 7 49207 2. 2CD set. [*H. 471-476 ("Hamburg" concertos*)].

- (Ton Koopman/Amsterdam Baroque Orchestra). Philips: 416 615-2. [*H. 437 in A major. With his Quartets (3) for keyboard instrument, flute, viola, violoncello, H. 537-539*].

- (Gustav Leonhardt/Collegium Aureum). Deutsche Harmonia Mundi (Editio Classica): 77061-2-RG. [*H. 427 in D minor and H. 410 in F major (for two harpsichords). With his Concerto for oboe and orchestra, H. 468 in E♭ major*].

- (Andreas Staier/Freiburg Baroque Orchestra). Deutsche Harmonia Mundi: 77187-2-RC. [*H. 474 in C minor. With his Concerto for oboe and orchestra, H. 468 and Sinfonias, H. 659-661*].

3397.3 * *Concerto for harpsichord, piano, and orchestra, H. 479 in E major.* (Ton Koopman/

Tini Mathot/Amsterdam Baroque Orchestra). Erato: ECD 75396. [With his *Concerto for two harpsichords and orchestra in F major, H. 408*].

3397.4 * *Concerto for 2 harpsichords and orchestra, H. 408 in F major. See 3397.3 or 3399.1*

3397.5 *Concerto for oboe and orchestra, H. 468 in E♭ major. See 3397.2 or 3418.6*

3397.6 *Concertos for violoncello and orchestra. Selections.* (Anner Bylsma/Orchestra of the Age of Enlightenment/Gustav Leonhardt). Virgin: 7 59541 2 (7 90800 2) or Musical Heritage Society: 512931F. [*H. 432 in A minor; H. 436 in B♭ major; H. 439 in A major*].

3397.7 ** *Sinfonias (4) for full orchestra, H. 663-666.*

- (Amsterdam Baroque Orchestra/Ton Koopman). Erato: 2292-45361-2.

- (Orchestra of the Age of Enlightenment/Gustav Leonhardt). Musical Heritage Society: 512851Z or Virgin: 7 59543 2 (7 90806 2). [With his *Sinfonia for string orchestra, H. 661 in B minor*].

3397.8 * *Sinfonias (6) for string orchestra, H. 657-662 ("Hamburg symphonies").*

- (Academy of Ancient Music/Christopher Hogwood). L'Oiseau-Lyre: 417 124-2.

- (English Concert/Trevor Pinnock). Archiv: 415 300-2.

CHAMBER MUSIC AND SOLO INSTRUMENTAL MUSIC

3397.9 * *Keyboard music. Selections.*

- (Bob van Asperen). Teldec: 9031-77623-2. 2CD set. [Includes his complete *Prussian sonatas, H. 24-29*, complete *Wurttemberg sonatas, H. 30-35*, and *Concerto for harpsichord solo in C major, H. 190*].

- (Bernard Brauchli). Titanic: Ti-186. [Variations, sonatas, fantasias, and other works, performed on clavichord].

- (Gustav Leonhardt). *See 3436*

- (Andreas Staier). Deutsche Harmonia Mundi: 77025-2-RC. [Album title: *Sonatas and fantasien* [sic]. Performed on harpsichord and fortepiano].

3397.10 *Quartets (3) for keyboard instrument, flute, viola, violoncello, H. 537-539.*

- (Christopher Hogwood and others). L'Oiseau-Lyre: 433 189-2.

- (Ton Koopman and others). *See 3397.2*

3397.11 *Sonatas for bass viol and continuo.* (Paolo Pandolfo/Rinaldo Alessandrini). Tactus: 710201.

3397.12 *Sonatas for flute and harpsichord. Selections.* (Barthold Kuijken/Bob van Asperen). Sony: SK 253964. 2CD set.

3397.13 * *Trio sonatas for violins and continuo. Selections.* (London Baroque). Harmonia Mundi: HMC 901511.

VOCAL MUSIC

3397.14 *Die Auferstehung und Himmelfahrt Jesu* [oratorio]. (Philippe Herreweghe). Virgin: 7 59069 2 (7 91498 2).

3397.15 *Die Israeliten in der Wüste* [oratorio]. (William Christie). Harmonia Mundi: HMC 901321.

3397.16 *Die letzten Leiden des Erlösers* [oratorio]. (Sigiswald Kuijken). Deutsche Harmonia Mundi: 77042-2-RG. 2CD set.

3398 Bach, Johann Christian, 1735-1782

3398.1 *Amadis des Gaules* [opera]. (Ulrike Sonntag/James Wagner/Bach Collegium Stuttgart/Helmuth Rilling). Hänssler: 98.963. 2CD set.

3398.2 *Sinfonia concertante for violin, violoncello, and orchestra in A major.* (Pinchas Zukerman/Yo-Yo Ma/St. Paul Chamber Orchestra). *See 3401.1*

3398.3 *Sonatas (6) for piano, op. 17.* (Robert Woolley). Chandos: CHAN 0543.

3398.4 * *Symphonies. Selections.* (Academy of Ancient Music/Simon Standage). Chandos: CHAN 0540.

3399 Bach, Wilhelm Friedemann, 1710-1784

3399.1 * *Concertos for harpsichord and orchestra. Selections.*

- (Richard Egarr/London Baroque). Harmonia Mundi: HMC 901558. [*F. 44 in F major; F. 45 in A minor; F. 41 in D major*].

- (Andreas Staier/Musica Antiqua Köln/Reinhard Goebel). Archiv: 419 256-2. [*F. 46 in E♭ major; F. 10 in F major*. With Bach, Carl Philipp Emanuel: *Concerto for two harpsichords and orchestra, H. 408 in F major*].

3399.2 *Duets for flutes.* (Barthold Kuijken/Marc Hantai). Accent: ACC 9057 D.

3399.3 * *Keyboard music. Selections.* (Christophe Rousset). Harmonia Mundi: HMC 901305.

3400 Beethoven, Ludwig van, 1770–1827

ORCHESTRAL MUSIC

3400.1 ** *Concertos (5) for piano and orchestra.*
- (Vladimir Ashkenazy/Cleveland Orchestra). London: 421 718-2. 3CD set. [With his *Fantasia for piano, chorus, and orchestra*].
- (Alfred Brendel/Chicago Symphony/James Levine). Philips: 411 189-2. 3CD set.
- (Murray Perahia/Concertgebouw/Bernard Haitink). CBS: M3K 44575. 3CD set.

3400.2 ** *Concerto for violin and orchestra, op. 61 in D major.*
- (Jascha Heifetz/Boston Symphony/Charles Munch). RCA: RCD1-5402. [With Brahms, Johannes: *Concerto for violin and orchestra*].
- (Anne-Sophie Mutter/Berlin Philharmonic/Herbert von Karajan). Deutsche Grammophon: 423 064-2. [With his *Romances for violin and orchestra*].
- (Itzhak Perlman/Berlin Philharmonic/Daniel Barenboim). Angel: CDC 7 49567 2. [With his *Romances for violin and orchestra*].

3400.3 * *Concerto for violin, violoncello, piano, and orchestra, op. 56 in C major ("Triple concerto").*
- (Beaux Arts Trio/London Philharmonic/Bernard Haitink). Philips: 420 231-2. [With his *Trio for piano and strings no. 11*].
- (Anne-Sophie Mutter/Yo-Yo Ma/Mark Zeltser/Berlin Philharmonic/Herbert von Karajan). Deutsche Grammophon: 415 276-2. [With his *Egmont, Coriolan,* and *Fidelio* overtures].

3400.4 *Fantasia for piano, chorus, and orchestra, op. 80 in C minor ("Choral fantasia").* (Vladimir Ashkenazy/Cleveland Orchestra). *See* 3400.1

3400.5 ** *Overtures.*
- (Berlin Philharmonic/Herbert von Karajan). Deutsche Grammophon: 427 256-2. 2CD set. [Includes *Consecration of the house, Coriolan, Creatures of Prometheus, Egmont, Fidelio, King Stephen, Lenore nos. 1–3, Name-Day,* and *Ruins of Athens*].
- (NBC Symphony/Arturo Toscanini). RCA: 09026-60267-2. [Includes *Consecration of the house, Coriolan, Creatures of Prometheus, Egmont,* and *Lenore nos. 2 and 3*].
- *See also* 3400.3 and 3400.7

3400.6 *Romances (2) for violin and orchestra. See* 3400.2

3400.7 ** *Symphonies (9).*
- (Orchestre Revolutionnaire et Romantique/John Eliot Gardiner). Archiv: 439 900-2. 6CD set.
- (Cleveland Orchestra/George Szell). Sony: SB5K 48396. 5CD set. [With his *Egmont, Fidelio,* and *King Stephen* overtures].
- (NBC Symphony/Arturo Toscanini). RCA: 60324-2-RG. 5CD set. [With his *Leonore overture no. 3*].

CHAMBER MUSIC

3400.8 * *Quartets for strings (16).*
- (Alban Berg Quartet). EMI: CDS 7 47126 8; 7 47130 8; 7 47134 8. 10 CDs in 3 vols.
- (Guarneri Quartet). RCA: 60456-2-RG; 60457-2-RG; 60458-2-RG. 9 CDs in 3 vols.
- (Talich Quartet). Calliope: 9633/39. 7CD set.

3400.9 ** *Quartet for strings no. 11, op. 95 in F minor ("Serioso").* (Emerson Quartet). Deutsche Grammophon: 423 398-2. [With Schubert, Franz: *Quartet no. 14*].

3400.10 *Quintet for piano and winds, op. 16 in E♭ major. See* 3418.63

3400.11 *Septet for winds and strings, op. 20 in E♭ major.*
- (Hausmusik). EMI: CDC 7 54656 2. [With his *Quintet for strings, op. 29 in C major*].
- (Nash Ensemble). Virgin: 7 59597 2. [With his *Trio for piano, clarinet, and violoncello, op. 11*].

3400.12 * *Sonata for horn and piano, op. 17 in F major.*
- (Dennis Brain/Gerald Moore). Enterprise/Palladio: 4125. [With works by Paul Dukas, Wolfgang Amadeus Mozart, and Robert Schumann].
- (Lowell Greer/Stephen Lubin). Harmonia Mundi: HMU 907037. [With Brahms, Johannes: *Trio for horn, violin, and piano*].

3400.13 *Sonatas (10) for violin and piano [complete].*
- (David Oistrakh/Lev Oborin). Philips: 412 570-2. 4CD set.
- (Itzhak Perlman/Vladimir Ashkenazy). London: 421 453-2. 4CD set.

3400.14 * *Sonata for violin and piano no. 5, op. 24 in F major ("Spring").*
- (Gidon Kremer/Martha Argerich). Deutsche Grammophon: 419 787-2. [With his *Sonata for violin and piano no. 4*].

- (Pinchas Zukerman/Daniel Barenboim). EMI: 7 69021 2. [With his *Sonata for violin and piano no. 9*].

3400.15 ** *Sonata for violin and piano no. 9, op. 47 in A major ("Kreutzer")*.

- (Joseph Szigeti/Béla Bartók). Vanguard: 8008 (72025). [With Bartók, Béla: *Sonata for violin and piano no. 2* and *Rhapsody for violin and piano no. 1*; and Debussy, Claude: *Sonata for violin and piano*].

- (Pinchas Zukerman/Daniel Barenboim). *See* 3400.14

3400.16 * *Sonatas (5) for violoncello and piano*.

- (Anner Bylsma/Malcolm Bilson). Elektra Nonesuch: 79152-2; 79236-2. 2CDs.

- (Yo-Yo Ma/Emanuel Ax). CBS: M2K 42446. 2CD set. [With his *Variations on "Bei Männern, welche Liebe fühlen"* and *Variations on "Ein Mädchen oder Weibchen"* for violoncello and piano].

- (Mstislav Rostropovich/Sviatoslav Richter). Philips: 412 256-2. 2CD set. [With his *Variations on "Bei Männern, welche Liebe fühlen,"* *Variations on "Ein Mädchen oder Weibchen,"* and *Variations on "See, the conquering hero comes"* for violoncello and piano].

3400.17 *Trios for piano and strings*.

- (Daniel Barenboim/Pinchas Zukerman/Jacqueline Dupré). EMI: 7 63124 2. 3CD set.

- (Eugene Istomin/Isaac Stern/Leonard Rose). Sony: SM4K 46738. 4CD set.

3400.18 * *Trio for piano and strings no. 4, op. 70 no. 1 in D major ("Ghost")*.

- (Beaux Arts Trio). Philips: 412 891-2. [With his *Trio no. 6*].

- (Eugene Istomin/Isaac Stern/Leonard Rose). Sony: SBK 53514. [With his *Trio no. 6*].

3400.19 * *Trio for piano and strings no. 6, op. 97 in B♭ major ("Archduke")*.

- (Beaux Arts Trio). *See* 3400.18

- (Chung Trio). EMI: CDC 7 55187 2. [With his *Trio no. 7, op. 11 in B♭ major*].

- (Eugene Istomin/Isaac Stern/Leonard Rose). *See* 3400.17

- (Artur Rubinstein/Jascha Heifetz/Emanuel Feuermann). RCA: 09026-61760-2. [With Schubert, Franz: *Trio for piano and strings, D. 898 in B♭ major*].

3400.20 *Trio for piano, clarinet (or violin), and violoncello no. 7, op. 11 in B♭ major*.

- (Chung Trio). *See* 3400.19

- (Benny Goodman and others). *See* 3452.14

- (Nash Ensemble). *See* 3400.11

PIANO MUSIC

3400.21 * *Bagatelle, WoO 59 in A minor ("Für Elise")*. *See* 3400.22

3400.22 * *Bagatelles, op. 126*.

- (Alfred Brendel). Philips: 412 227-2. [With his *Variations, op. 35* and *Bagatelle "Für Elise"*].

- (Glenn Gould). *See* 3400.26

3400.23 ** *Sonatas (32)*.

- (Alfred Brendel). Vox Box: 5028; 5042; 5056; 5060. 8 CDs in 4 vols.

- (Richard Goode). Elektra Nonesuch: 9 79328 2. 10CD set.

- (Glenn Gould). Sony: SM3K 52638; Sony: SM3K 52642. 6 CDs in 2 vols. [*Sonatas 1–3, 5–10, 13–18, 23*, and *30–32* only].

- (Arthur Schnabel). Angel: CMS 7 63765 2. 8CD set.

3400.24 ** *Variationen über ein Walzer von Diabelli ("Diabelli variations")*.

- (Daniel Barenboim). Erato: 4509-94810-2.

- (Alfred Brendel). Philips: 426 232-2.

- (William Kinderman). Hyperion: CDA66763.

3400.25 * *Variations, op. 35 in E♭ major ("Eroica variations")*. *See* 3400.22 or 3400.26

3400.26 * *Variations, WoO 80 in C minor*. (Glenn Gould). Sony: SM2K 52646. 2CD set. [With his *Variations, op. 34; Variations, op. 35; Bagatelles, op. 34; Bagatelles, op. 126*].

VOCAL MUSIC AND STAGE MUSIC

3400.27 *Ah, perfido!* [concert scena for soprano and orchestra]. (Maria Callas/La Scala Orchestra/Tulio Serafin). *See* 3404.1

3400.28 *An die ferne Geliebte* [song cycle]. (Dietrich Fischer-Dieskau/Gerald Moore). Orfeo: C 140 501 A. [With his selected songs].

3400.29 * *Fidelio* [opera].

- (Christa Ludwig/Jon Vickers/Philharmonia Orchestra/Otto Klemperer). EMI: 7 69324 2 (7 55170 2). 2CD set.

- (Hildegard Behrens/Peter Hofmann/Chicago Symphony/Georg Solti). London: 410 227-2. 2CD set.

3400.30 ** *Missa solemnis, op. 123 in D major.*

- (Hilversum Choir/Concertgebouw Orchestra/ Leonard Bernstein). Deutsche Grammophon: 413 780-2. 2CD set.

- (Vienna Singverein/Berlin Philharmonic/Herbert von Karajan). Deutsche Grammophon: 423 913-2. 2CD set. [With Mozart, Wolfgang Amadeus: *Mass, K. 317 in C major*].

3401 Boccherini, Luigi, 1743–1805

3401.1 * *Concertos for violoncello and orchestra. Selections.*

- (Anner Bylsma/Tafelmusik/Jean Lamon). Sony: SK 53121. [*G. 476 in D major* and *G. 573 in C major*. With his *Symphonies, G. 519* and *G. 521*, and *Octet for woodwinds and strings, G. 470 in G major*].

- (Anner Bylsma/Tafelmusik/Jean Lamon). Deutsche Harmonia Mundi: 7867-2-RC. [*G. 480 in G major* and *G. 483 in D major*. With his *Symphonies, G. 497 and 506*].

- (Christophe Coin/Ensemble Baroque de Liège). Astrée: E 8517. [With his *G. 476 in D major; G. 480 in G major; G. 482 in B♭ major*. With his *Aria accademica no. 14*].

- (Pinchas Zukerman/Yo-Yo Ma/St. Paul Chamber Orchestra). CBS: MK 39964. [*G. 482 in B♭ major*. With Bach, Johann Christian: *Sinfonia concertante for violin, violoncello, and orchestra in A major* and *Symphony for double orchestra, op. 18, no. 1*].

3401.2 * *Quintets for guitar and strings, G. 445-450.* (Jakob Lindberg/Drottningholm Baroque Ensemble). Bis: 597/98. 2CD set.

3401.3 *Quintets for strings. Selections.*

- (Anner Bylsma/Boccherini Quartet). Channel Classics: 3692. [With his *Quartet for strings in A major, G. 213*, and *Trio for strings in C minor, G. 96*].

- (Ensemble 415). *See* 3401.5

- (Europa Galante). Opus 111: 30-82.

- (Smithsonian Chamber Players). Deutsche Harmonia Mundi: 77159.

3401.4 *Sonatas for violoncello and continuo. Selections.* (Anner Bylsma). Sony: SK 53362.

3401.5 *Stabat Mater.* (Agnes Mellon/Ensemble 415/Chiara Banchini). Harmonia Mundi: HMC 901378. [With his *Quintet for strings in C minor, G. 328*].

3401.6 * *Symphonies. Selections.*

- (Ensemble 415/Chiara Banchini). Harmonia Mundi: HMC 901291. [*G. 512 in F major; G. 490 in D major; G. 511 in A minor; G. 506 in D minor ("La casa del Diavolo")*].

- (Tafelmusik/Jean Lamon). *See* 3401.1

3401.7 *Trios for strings, G. 107-112.* (Europa Galante). Opus 111: OPS 41-9105.

3402 Boieldieu, François Adrien, 1775–1834

3402.1 *Concerto for harp and orchestra in C major.* (Marisa Robles/Academy of St. Martin-in-the-Fields/Iona Brown). London: 425 723-2. [With Handel, George Frideric: *Concerto for harp* and Dittersdorf, Karl Ditters von: *Concerto for harp*].

3402.2 *La dame blanche* [opera]. (Françoise Louvay/Germaine Baudoz/Michel Sénéchal/ Pierre Stoll). Accord: 220862. 2CD set.

3403 Boyce, William, 1711–1779

3403.1 *Anthems. Selections.* (Choir of New College, Oxford/Edward Higginbottom). CRD: 3483. [With his voluntaries for organ].

3403.2 * *Symphonies (8).*

- (Academy of Ancient Music/Christopher Hogwood). L'Oiseau-Lyre: 436 761-2.

- (English Concert/Trevor Pinnock). Archiv: 419 631-2.

3404 Cherubini, Luigi, 1760–1842

3404.1 * *Medea* [opera].

- (Sylvia Sass/Veriano Luchetti/Lamberto Gardelli). Hungaroton: 11904/05-2. 2CD set.

- (Maria Callas/Mirto Picchi/La Scala/Tulio Serafin). EMI: CDM 7 63627 2. 2CD set. [With Beethoven, Ludwig van: *Ah, perfido!*].

3404.2 *Requiem in C minor.* (Ambrosian Singers/ New Philharmonia Orchestra/Riccardo Muti). EMI: CDC 7 49678 2.

3405 Clementi, Muzio, 1752–1832

3405.1 * *Sonatas for piano. Selections.*

- (Vladimir Horowitz). RCA: 7753-2-RG. [*Op. 33 no. 3; Op. 34 no. 2; Op. 14 no. 3; Op. 26 no. 2*].

- (Jos van Immerseel). Accent: ACC 67911 D. [*Op. 24 no. 2; Op. 25 no. 5; Op. 37 no. 2; Op. 13 no. 6*].

3405.2 *Symphonies (6).* (Philharmonia Orchestra/Francesco D'Avalos). ASV: DCS 322. 3CD set [or separate CDs: ASV 802; 803; 804]. [Album title: *Complete orchestral works*, including his six symphonies, two overtures, and piano concerto].

3406 Danzi, Franz, 1763–1826

Quintets for woodwinds and horn. Selections. (Berlin Philharmonic Wind Quintet). Bis: 532. [With his *Quintet for piano and winds, op. 41*].

3407 Dussek, Johann Ladislaus, 1760–1812

Sonatas for piano. Selections. (Andreas Staier). Deutsche Harmonia Mundi: 05472-77286-2. [*Op. 35 nos. 1–3 and op. 31 no. 2*].

3408 Gluck, Christoph Willibald, Ritter von, 1714–1787

3408.1 *Don Juan* [ballet]. (English Baroque Soloists/John Eliot Gardiner). Erato: 2292-45980-2.

3408.2 * *Iphigénie en Aulide* [opera]. (José van Dam/Anne Sofie von Otter/Lynne Dawson/Opéra de Lyon/John Eliot Gardiner). Musifrance: 2292-45003-2. 2CD set.

3408.3 *Iphigénie en Tauride* [opera]. (Diana Montague/John Aler/Thomas Allen/Opéra de Lyon/John Eliot Gardiner). Philips: 416 148-2. 2CD set.Operas: Iphigénie en Tauride (Gluck)

3408.4 * *Orfeo ed Euridice* [opera] (*1762 Vienna version, in Italian*).

- (Nancy Argenta/Michael Chance/Tafelmusik/Frieder Bernius). Sony: SX2K 48040. 2CD set.

- (Marjanne Kweksilber/René Jacobs/Petite Bande/Sigiswald Kuijken). Accent: 48223/24 D. 2CD set.

3408.5 *Orphée et Eurydice* [opera] (*1774 Paris version, in French, revised by Hector Berlioz, 1866*). (Barbara Hendricks/Brigitte Fournier/Anne Sofie von Otter/Opéra de Lyon/John Eliot Gardiner). EMI: CDS 7 49834 2. 2CD set.

3409 Gossec, François Joseph, 1734–1829. *Requiem.*

- (Louis Devos). Erato: ECD 75359.

- (Jacques Houtmann). Koch Schwann: 313041. [With his *Symphony in F major*].

3410 Grétry, André Ernest Modeste, 1741–1813

3410.1 *Le caravane du Caire* [opera-ballet]. (Jules Bastin/Gilles Ragon/Philippe Huttenlocher/Ricercar Academy/Marc Minkowski). Ricercar: RIC 100084/85. 2CD set.

3410.2 *Le jugement de Midas* [opera]. (Mieke van der Sluis/John Elwes/Petite Bande/Gustav Leonhardt). Ricercar: RIC 063033.

3411 Haydn, Joseph, 1732–1809

ORCHESTRAL MUSIC

3411.1 * *Concerto for harpsichord (piano) and orchestra, H. XVIII, 11 in D major.*

- (Trevor Pinnock/English Concert). *See* 3331.1

- (Herbert Tachezi/Concentus Musicus Wien/Nikolaus Harnoncourt). *See* 3411.6

3411.2 * *Concerto for trumpet and orchestra, H. VIIe, 1 in E♭ major.*

- (Friedemann Immer/Academy of Ancient Music/Christopher Hogwood). L'Oiseau-Lyre: 417 610-2. [With his *Concerto for horn and orchestra, H. VIId, 3 in D major* and *Concerto for organ and orchestra, H. XVIII, 1 in C major*].

- (Wynton Marsalis/National Philharmonic Orchestra of London/Raymond Leppard). CBS: MK 37846. [With Hummel, Johann Nepomuk: *Concerto for trumpet and orchestra* and Mozart, Leopold: *Concerto for trumpet and orchestra*].

3411.3 *Concertos for violin and orchestra. Selections.* (Elizabeth Wallfisch/Orchestra of the Age of Enlightenment). *See* 3411.6

3411.4 * *Concertos (2) for violoncello and orchestra.*

- (Christophe Coin/Academy of Ancient Music/Christopher Hogwood). L'Oiseau-Lyre: 414 615-2.

- (Mischa Maisky/Chamber Orchestra of Europe). Deutsche Grammophon: 419 786-2.

3411.5 *Musica instrumentale sopra le sette ultime parole del nostro Redertore in croce (The seven last words of Christ on the cross).*

- (Arnold Schoenberg Choir/Concentus Musicus Wien/Nikolaus Harnoncourt) [oratorio version]. Teldec: 2292-46458-2.

- (Quatuor Mosaïques) [string quartet version]. Astrée: E 8742.

- (Concert des Nations/Jordi Savall) [orchestral version]. Astrée: E 8739.

3411.6 *Sinfonia concertante for oboe, bassoon, violin, violoncello, and orchestra, H. I, 105 in B♭ major.*

- (Concentus Musicus Wien/Nikolaus Harnoncourt). Teldec: 8.43674 (244 196-2). [With his *Concerto for harpsichord (piano) and orchestra, H. XVIII, 11* and *Overture Il mondo della luna*].

- (Orchestra of the Age of Enlightenment/ Elizabeth Wallfisch). Virgin: VC 7 59266 2. [With his *Concertos for violin and orchestra nos. 1 and 4*].

3411.7 *Symphonies (104)* [complete].

- (Hanover Band/Roy Goodman). [vol. 1] Hyperion: CDA66520; [vol. 2] Hyperion: CDA66521; [vol. 3] Hyperion: CDA66522; [vol. 4] Hyperion: CDA66523; [vol. 5] Hyperion: CDA66524; [vol. 6] Hyperion: CDA66525; [vol. 7] Hyperion: CDA66526; [vol. 8] Hyperion: CDA66527; [vol. 9] Hyperion: CDA66528; [vol. 10] Hyperion: CDA66529; [vol. 11] Hyperion: CDA66530; [vol. 12] Hyperion: CDA66531; [vol. 13] Hyperion: CDA66532; [vol. 14] Hyperion: CDA66533; [vol. 15] Hyperion: CDA66534; [vol. 16] Hyperion: CDA66535; [vol. 17] Hyperion: CDA66536. [Series includes individual discs listed below. Further volumes forthcoming].

- (Academy of Ancient Music/Christopher Hogwood). [vol. 1] L'Oiseau-Lyre: 436 428-2. 3CD set; [vol. 2] L'Oiseau-Lyre: 436 592-2. 3CD set; [vol. 3] L'Oiseau-Lyre: 433 661-2. 3CD set; [vol. 4] L'Oiseau-Lyre: 430 082-2. 3CD set; [vol. 5] L'Oiseau-Lyre: 433 012-2. 3CD set. [Further volumes forthcoming].

3411.8 * *Symphonies nos. 6–8 ("Le matin, Le midi, Le soir")*.

- (Hanover Band/Roy Goodman). Hyperion: CDA66523.

- (English Concert/Trevor Pinnock). Archiv: 423 098-2.

3411.9 * *Symphony no. 43 in E♭ major ("Mercury")*.

- (Hanover Band/Roy Goodman). Hyperion: CDA66530. [With his *Symphonies nos. 42 and 44*].

- (English Concert/Trevor Pinnock). Archiv: 429 400-2. [With his *Symphonies nos. 51 and 52*].

3411.10 * *Symphony no. 44 in E minor ("Trauer")*.

- (Hanover Band/Roy Goodman). *See* 3411.9

- (English Concert/Trevor Pinnock). Archiv: 429 756-2. [With his *Symphonies nos. 42 and 46*].

3411.11 * *Symphony no. 45 in F♯ minor ("Farewell")*.

- (Hanover Band/Roy Goodman). Hyperion: CDA66522. [With his *Symphonies nos. 46 and 47*].

- (English Concert/Trevor Pinnock). Archiv: 429 757-2. [With his *Symphonies nos. 47 and 50*].

3411.12 * *Symphony no. 48 in C major ("Maria Theresia")*.

- (Hanover Band/Roy Goodman). *See* 3411.13

- (English Concert/Trevor Pinnock). Archiv: 429 399-2. [With his *Symphonies nos. 41 and 65*].

3411.13 * *Symphony no. 49 in F minor ("La passione")*.

- (Hanover Band/Roy Goodman). Hyperion: CDA66531. [With his *Symphonies nos. 48 and 50*].

- (English Concert/Trevor Pinnock). Archiv: 427 662-2. [With his *Symphonies nos. 26 and 58*].

3411.14 * *Symphony no. 59 in A major ("Fire")*. (English Concert/Trevor Pinnock). Archiv: 427 661-2. [With his *Symphonies nos. 35, 38, and 39*].

3411.15 * *Symphony no. 82 in C major ("Bear")*. (Hanover Band/Roy Goodman). Hyperion: CDA66527. [With his *Symphonies nos. 83 and 84*].

3411.16 * *Symphony no. 83 in G minor ("Hen")*. (Hanover Band/Roy Goodman). *See* 3411.15

3411.17 * *Symphony no. 85 in B♭ major ("Reine")*. (Hanover Band/Roy Goodman). Hyperion: CDA66535. [With his *Symphonies nos. 86 and 87*].

3411.18 * *Symphony no. 86 in D major.* (Hanover Band/Roy Goodman). *See* 3411.17

3411.19 * *Symphony no. 87 in A major.* (Hanover Band/Roy Goodman). *See* 3411.17

3411.20 ** *Symphony no. 88 in G major.*

- (Vienna Philharmonic Orchestra/Leonard Bernstein). Deutsche Grammophon: 413 777-2. [With his *Symphony no. 92*].

- (Petite Bande/Sigiswald Kuijken). Virgin: VC 7 59070 2 (7 91499 2). [With his *Symphonies nos. 89 and 92*].

- (Columbia Symphony/Bruno Walter). Odyssey: MBK 44777. [With his *Symphony no. 100*].

3411.21 * *Symphony no. 92 in G major ("Oxford")*.

- (Vienna Philharmonic/Leonard Bernstein). *See* 3411.20

- (Hanover Band/Roy Goodman). Hyperion: CDA66521. [With his *Symphonies nos. 90 and 91*].

- (Petite Bande/Sigiswald Kuijken). *See* 3411.20

- (Cleveland Orchestra/George Szell). *See* 3411.25

3411.22 * *Symphony no. 93 in D major.*

- (Orchestra of the 18th Century/Frans Brüg-gen). Philips: 422 022-2. [With his *Symphony no. 90*].

- (Hanover Band/Roy Goodman). Hyperion: CDA66532. [With his *Symphonies nos. 94 and 95*].

3411.23 ** *Symphony no. 94 in G major ("Surprise").*

- (Hanover Band/Roy Goodman). *See* 3411.22

- (Concertgebouw Orchestra/Nikolaus Harnon-court). Teldec: 9031-73148-2. [With his *Symphony no. 95*].

- (Cleveland Orchestra/George Szell). *See* 3411.25

3411.24 * *Symphony no. 95 in C minor.*

- (Hanover Band/Roy Goodman). *See* 3411.22

- (Concertgebouw Orchestra/Nikolaus Harnon-court). *See* 3411.23

3411.25 * *Symphony no. 96 in D major ("Miracle").*

- (Petite Bande/Sigiswald Kuijken). Deutsche Harmonia Mundi: 05472-77294-2. [With his *Symphonies nos. 97 and 98*].

- (Cleveland Orchestra/George Szell). Sony: SBK 46332. [With his *Symphonies nos. 92 and 94*].

3411.26 * *Symphony no. 97 in C major.* (Petite Bande/Sigiswald Kuijken). *See* 3411.25

3411.27 * *Symphony no. 98 in B♭ major.* (Petite Bande/Sigiswald Kuijken). *See* 3411.25

3411.28 * *Symphony no. 99 in E♭ major.* (London Classical Players/Roger Norrington). *See* 3411.29

3411.29 ** *Symphony no. 100 in G major ("Military").*

- (Orchestra of the 18th Century/Frans Brüg-gen). Philips 434 096-2. [With his *Symphony no. 104*].

- (Orchestra of St. Luke's/Charles Mackerras). *See* 3411.32

- (London Classical Players/Roger Norrington). EMI: CDC 5 55192 2. [With his *Symphony no. 99*].

- (Columbia Symphony/Bruno Walter). *See* 3411.20

3411.30 ** *Symphony no. 101 in D major ("Clock").*

- (Orchestra of the 18th Century/Frans Brüg-gen). Philips: 422 240-2. [With his *Symphony no. 103*].

- (Hanover Band/Roy Goodman). Hyperion: CDA66528. [With his *Symphony no. 102* and *Overture to Windsor Castle*].

- (Orchestra of St. Luke's/Charles Mackerras). *See* 3411.33

- (London Classical Players/Roger Norrington). EMI: CDC 5 55111 2. [With his *Symphony no. 102*].

3411.31 * *Symphony no. 102 in B♭ major.* (London Classical Players/Roger Norrington). *See* 3411.30

3411.32 ** *Symphony no. 103 in E♭ major ("Drum roll").*

- (Orchestra of the 18th Century/Frans Brüg-gen). *See* 3411.30

- (Concertgebouw Orchestra/Nikolaus Harnon-court). Teldec: 8.43752 (243 526-2). [With his *Symphony no. 104*].

- (Orchestra of St. Luke's/Charles Mackerras). Telarc: 80282. [With his *Symphony no. 100*].

- (London Classical Players/Roger Norrington). EMI: CDC 5 55002 2. [With his *Symphony no. 104*].

3411.33 ** *Symphony no. 104 in D major ("London").*

- (Orchestra of the 18th Century/Frans Brüg-gen). *See* 3411.29

- (Concertgebouw Orchestra/Nikolaus Harnon-court). *See* 3411.32

- (Orchestra of St. Luke's/Charles Mackerras). Telarc: 80311. [With his *Symphony no. 101*].

- (London Classical Players/Roger Norrington). *See* 3411.32

CHAMBER MUSIC AND SOLO INSTRUMENTAL MUSIC

3411.34 *Musica instrumentale sopra le sette ul-time parole del nostro Redentore in croce (The seven last words of Christ on the cross)* [for string quartet]. *See* 3411.5

3411.35 *Quartets (6) for strings, op. 1.* (Tatrai Quartet). Hungaroton: HCD 31089/91. 3CD set. [With his *Quartets, opp. 2, 42, and 103*].

3411.36 * *Quartets (6) for strings, op. 20 (H. III, 31-36) ("Sun").*

- (Quatuor Mosaïques). Astrée: E 8785; E 8786. 2 CDs.

- (Tatrai Quartet). Hungaroton: 11332/33. 2CD set.

3411.37 *Quartets (6) for strings, op. 33 (H. III, 37-42).*

- (Salomon Quartet). Hyperion: 66681; 66682. 2 CDs. [With his *Quartets, op. 42*].

- (Tatrai Quartet). Hungaroton: 11887/88. 2CD set.

3411.38 *Quartets (6) for strings, op. 50 (H. III, 44-49) ("Prussian")*.

- (Salomon Quartet). Hyperion: CDA66821; CDA66822. 2 CDs.

- (Tatrai Quartet). Hungaroton: 11934/35. 2CD set.

3411.39 *Quartets (3) for strings, op. 54 (H. III, 57-59)*. (Tatrai Quartet). Hungaroton: 12506/07. 2CD set. [With his *Quartets (3), op. 55 (H. III, 60-62)*].

3411.40 *Quartets (6) for strings, op. 64 (H. III, 63-68)*. (Tatrai Quartet). Hungaroton: 11838/39. 2CD set.

3411.41 *Quartets (3) for strings, op. 71 (H. III, 69-71) ("Apponyi")*.

- (Salomon Quartet). Hyperion: CDA66065; 66098. 2 CDs. [With his *Op. 74, no. 1*].

- (Tatrai Quartet). Hungaroton: 12246/47. 2CD set. [With his *Quartets, op. 74*].

3411.42 *Quartets (3) for strings, op. 74 (H. III, 72-74)*.

- (Salomon Quartet). Hyperion: 66124. [*Op. 74, nos. 2–3; Op. 74, no. 1* on Hyperion: CDA66098*].

- (Tatrai Quartet). *See 3411.41*

3411.43 * *Quartets (6) for strings, op. 76 (H. III, 75-80)*. (Tatrai Quartet). Hungaroton: 12812/13.

3411.44 * *Quartets (3) for strings, op. 77 (H. III, 81-83)*.

- (Quatuor Mosaïques). Astrée: 8799.

- (Tatrai Quartet). Hungaroton: 11776.

3411.45 * *Sonatas and variations for piano. Selections*.

- (Glenn Gould). Sony: SM2K 52623. 2CD set.

- (Andreas Staier). Deutsche Harmonia Mundi: 77160-2-RC; 05472-77186-2; 05472-77285-2. 3 CDs.

3411.46 *Trios for flutes and violoncello ("London")*. (Barthold Kuijken/Marc Hantai/Wieland Kuijken). Accent: 9283/84. 2CD set. [With his *Quartets for flute and strings, op. 5*].

3411.47 * *Trios for piano, violin, and violoncello. Selections*.

- (Beaux Arts Trio). Philips: 422 831-2; 420 790-2. 2 CDs.

- (Robert Levin/Vera Beths/Anner Bylsma). Sony: SK 53120. [H. XV, 27 in C major; H. XV, 28 in E major; H. XV, 30 in E♭ major].

VOCAL MUSIC AND STAGE MUSIC

3411.48 *Arianna a Naxos* [cantata]. (Carolyn Watkinson/Glen Wilson). Virgin: 7 59033 2 (7 91215 2). [With his *English canzonettas*].

3411.49 * *Die Jahreszeiten (The seasons)* [oratorio].

- (John Eliot Gardiner). Archiv: 431 818-2. 2CD set.

- (Neville Marriner). Philips: 411 428-2. 2CD set.

3411.50 * *Mass no. 10, H. XXII, 9 in C major ("Missa in tempore belli")*. (James Levine). Deutsche Grammophon: 435 853-2. [With Mozart, Wolfgang Amadeus: *Mass, K. 317*].

3411.51 * *Mass no. 11, H. XXII, 11 in D minor ("Missa in angustiis" or "Nelson Mass")*. (Trevor Pinnock). Archiv: 423 097-2. [With his *Te Deum*].

3411.52 *Il mondo della luna* [opera]. (Edith Mathis/Barbara Hendricks/Lausanne Chamber Orchestra/Antal Dorati). Philips: 432 420-2. 3CD set.

3411.53 *Musica instrumentale sopra le sette ultime parole del nostro Redentore in croce (The seven last words of Christ on the cross)* [oratorio]. *See 3411.5*

3411.54 * *Die Schöpfung (The creation)* [oratorio].

- (Christopher Hogwood). L'Oiseau-Lyre: 430 397-2. 2CD set.

- (Neville Marriner). Philips 416 449-2. 2CD set.

3412 Haydn, Michael, 1737–1806. *Symphony, P. 16 in G major* [formerly attributed to Mozart as his *Symphony no. 37*].

- (Bournemouth Sinfonietta/Harold Farberman). MMG: 10026. [With his *Symphonies, P. 10 in C major* and *P. 43 in D major*].

- (Slovak Chamber Orchestra/Bohdan Warchal). CPO: 999 155-2. [With his *Symphonies P. 10 in C major* and *Divertimento, P. 8 in G major*].

3413 Hummel, Johann Nepomuk, 1778–1837

3413.1 *Chamber music. Selections*.

- (Consortium Classicum). Musikproduktion Dabringhaus und Grimm: MD+G 3440. [*Parthia for wind octet, op. 48; Serenade for winds and strings no. 2, op. 66 in E♭ major; Concertino, op. 73 in G major*].

- (Hausmusik). *See 3506.14*

3413.2 * *Concerto for trumpet and orchestra in Eb major.* (Wynton Marsalis/English Chamber Orchestra/Raymond Leppard). *See* 3411.2

3414   Jommelli, Nicolò, 1714–1774

Armida abbandonata [opera]. (Ewa Malas-Godlewska/Claire Brua/Gilles Ragon/Talens Lyriques/Christophe Rousset). FNAC: 592326. 3CD set.

3415   Martín y Soler, Vicente, 1754–1806

Una cosa rara [opera]. (Maria Angeles Peters/Montserrat Figueras/Ernesto Palacio/Concert des Nations/Jordi Savall). Astrée: E 8760. 3CD set.

3416   Méhul, Etienne Nicolas, 1763–1817

Symphonies 1–2. (Musiciens du Louvre/Marc Minkowski). Musifrance: 2292-45026-2.

3417   Mozart, Leopold, 1719–1787

3417.1 *Concerto for trumpet and orchestra.* (Wynton Marsalis/English Chamber Orchestra/Raymond Leppard). *See* 3411.2

3417.2 *Toy symphony (Cassation for orchestra in C major)* [formerly attributed to Joseph Haydn and also known as *"Berchtolsgadener Sinfonie"*]. (Hanover Band/Roy Goodman). Nimbus: NI 5126. [With Haydn, Joseph: *Symphonies nos. 94 and 95*].

3418   Mozart, Wolfgang Amadeus, 1756–1791

ORCHESTRAL MUSIC

3418.1 *Concerto for bassoon and orchestra, K. 191 in Bb major.*

- (Danny Bond/Academy of Ancient Music/Christopher Hogwood). *See* 3418.4
- (Dietmar Zeman/Vienna Philharmonic/Karl Böhm). *See* 3418.2

3418.2 ** *Concerto for clarinet and orchestra, K. 622 in A major.*

- (Eric Hoeprich/Orchestra of the 18th Century/Frans Brüggen). Philips: 420 242-2. [With his *Quintet for clarinet and strings*].
- (Robert Marcellus/Cleveland Orchestra/George Szell). *See* 3418.42
- (Alfred Prinz/Vienna Philharmonic/Karl Böhm). Deutsche Grammophon: 429 816-2. [With his *Concerto for bassoon and orchestra* and *Concerto for oboe and orchestra*].
- (Richard Stoltzman/English Chamber Orchestra). RCA: 60723-2-RC. [With his *Quintet for clarinet and strings*].

3418.3 * *Concerto for flute and orchestra, K. 313 in G major.*

- (Lisa Beznosiuk/Academy of Ancient Music/Christopher Hogwood). *See* 3418.4
- (James Galway/Chamber Orchestra of Europe). RCA: 7861-2-RC. [With his *Concerto for flute and orchestra, K. 314 in C major; Andante for flute and orchestra, K. 315 in C major; Concerto for flute, harp, and orchestra, K. 299*].

3418.4 * *Concerto for flute, harp, and orchestra, K. 299 in C major.*

- (Lisa Beznosiuk/Frances Kelley/Academy of Ancient Music/Christopher Hogwood). L'Oiseau-Lyre: 417 622-2. [With his *Concerto for bassoon and orchestra, K. 191; Concerto for flute and orchestra, K. 313; Andante for flute and orchestra, K. 315 in C major*].
- (James Galway/Marisa Robles/Chamber Orchestra of Europe). *See* 3418.3

3418.5 ** *Concertos (4) for horn and orchestra.*

- (Hermann Baumann/Concentus Musicus Wien/Nikolaus Harnoncourt). Teldec: 8.41272.
- (Dennis Brain/Berlin Philharmonic/Herbert von Karajan). EMI: CDH 7 61013 2.

3418.6 *Concerto for oboe (or flute) and orchestra, K. 314 in C major.*

- (Paul Goodwin/English Concert/Trevor Pinnock). Archiv: 431 821-2. [With Bach, Carl Philipp Emanuel: *Concerto for oboe and orchestra* and Lebrun, Ludwig August: *Concerto no. 1 for oboe and orchestra*].
- (Gerhard Turetschek/Vienna Philharmonic/Karl Böhm). *See* 3418.2

3418.7 *Concertos (27) for piano and orchestra* [complete, including no. 7 for three pianos and no. 10 for two pianos]. (Malcolm Bilson/English Baroque Soloists/John Eliot Gardiner). Archiv: 431 211-2. 9CD set. [Includes single discs listed below].

3418.8 * *Concerto for piano and orchestra no. 9, K. 271 in Eb major ("Jeunehomme").*

- (Malcolm Bilson/English Baroque Soloists/John Eliot Gardiner). Archiv: 410 905-2. [With his *Concerto no. 11*].
- (Alfred Brendel/Academy of St. Martin-in-the-Fields/Neville Marriner). Philips: 442 571-2. [With his *Concertos nos. 15, 22, 25, and 27*].
- (Murray Perahia/English Chamber Orchestra). *See* 3418.20

- (Mitsuko Uchida/English Chamber Orchestra/ Jeffrey Tate). Philips: 432 086-2. [With his *Concerto no. 8*].

3418.9 * *Concerto for 2 pianos and orchestra no. 10, K. 365 in E♭ major.*

- (Malcolm Bilson/Robert Levin/English Baroque Soloists/John Eliot Gardiner). Archiv: 427 317-2. [With his *Concertos nos. 6–7*].
- (Murray Perahia/Radu Lupu/English Chamber Orchestra). CBS: SK 44915. [With his *Concerto no. 7; Andante and variations for two pianos, K. 501 in G major;* and *Fantasia, K. 608 in F minor* (arranged for two pianos by Ferruccio Busoni)].

3418.10 * *Concerto for piano and orchestra no. 11, K. 413 in F major.*

- (Malcolm Bilson/English Baroque Soloists/ John Eliot Gardiner). *See* 3418.8
- (Alfred Brendel/Academy of St. Martin-in-the-Fields/Neville Marriner). *See* 3418.15
- (Murray Perahia/English Chamber Orchestra). CBS: MK 42243. [With his *Concertos nos. 12 and 14*].
- (Mitsuko Uchida/English Chamber Orchestra/ Jeffrey Tate). Philips: 422 458-2. [With his *Concerto no. 12*].

3418.11 * *Concerto for piano and orchestra no. 12, K. 414 in A major.*

- (Stephen Lubin/Mozartean Players). Arabesque: Z6552. [With his *Concerto no. 15*].
- (Murray Perahia/English Chamber Orchestra). *See* 3418.10
- (Mitsuko Uchida/English Chamber Orchestra/ Jeffrey Tate). *See* 3418.10

3418.12 * *Concerto for piano and orchestra no. 13, K. 415 in C major.*

- (Murray Perahia/English Chamber Orchestra). CBS: MK 39223. [With his *Concerto no. 6*].
- (Mitsuko Uchida/English Chamber Orchestra/ Jeffrey Tate). Philips: 422 359-2. [With his *Concerto no. 14*].

3418.13 * *Concerto for piano and orchestra no. 14, K. 449 in E♭ major.*

- (Murray Perahia/English Chamber Orchestra). *See* 3418.10
- (Mitsuko Uchida/English Chamber Orchestra/ Jeffrey Tate). *See* 3418.12

3418.14 * *Concerto for piano and orchestra no. 15, K. 450 in B♭ major.*

- (Alfred Brendel/Academy of St. Martin-in-the-Fields/Neville Marriner). *See* 3418.8
- (Stephen Lubin/Mozartean Players). *See* 3418.11
- (Murray Perahia/English Chamber Orchestra). CBS: MK 37824. [With his *Concerto no. 16*].
- (Mitsuko Uchida/English Chamber Orchestra/ Jeffrey Tate). Philips: 426 305-2. [With his *Concerto no. 16*].

3418.15 * *Concerto for piano and orchestra no. 16, K. 451 in D major.*

- (Alfred Brendel/Academy of St. Martin-in-the-Fields/Neville Marriner). Philips: 416 367-2. [With his *Concerto no. 11*].
- (Murray Perahia/English Chamber Orchestra). *See* 3418.14
- (Mitsuko Uchida/English Chamber Orchestra/ Jeffrey Tate). *See* 3418.14

3418.16 * *Concerto for piano and orchestra no. 17, K. 453 in G major.*

- (Richard Goode/Orpheus Chamber Orchestra). Elektra Nonesuch: 9 79024-2. [With his *Concerto no. 23*].
- (Murray Perahia/English Chamber Orchestra). CBS: MK 36686. [With his *Concerto no. 18*].
- (Mitsuko Uchida/English Chamber Orchestra/ Jeffrey Tate). Philips: 422 592-2. [With his *Quintet for piano and winds*].

3418.17 * *Concerto for piano and orchestra no. 18, K. 456 in B♭ major.*

- (Malcolm Bilson/English Baroque Soloists/ John Eliot Gardiner). *See* 3418.18
- (Murray Perahia/English Chamber Orchestra). *See* 3418.16
- (Mitsuko Uchida/English Chamber Orchestra/ Jeffrey Tate). Philips: 422 348-2. [With his *Concerto no. 19*].

3418.18 ** *Concerto for piano and orchestra no. 19, K. 459 in F major.*

- (Malcolm Bilson/English Baroque Soloists/ John Eliot Gardiner). Archiv: 415 111-2. [With his *Concerto no. 18*].
- (Murray Perahia/English Chamber Orchestra). CBS: MK 39064. [With his *Concerto no. 23*].
- (Mitsuko Uchida/English Chamber Orchestra/ Jeffrey Tate). *See* 3418.17

3418.19 ** *Concerto for piano and orchestra no. 20, K. 466 in D minor.*

- (Malcolm Bilson/English Baroque Soloists/ John Eliot Gardiner). Archiv: 419 609-2. [With his *Concerto no. 21*].

- (Alfred Brendel/Academy of St. Martin-in-the-Fields/Neville Marriner). Philips: 420 867-2. [With his *Concerto no. 24* and *Rondo for piano and orchestra in D major, K. 382*].

- (Stephen Lubin/Mozartean Players). Arabesque: Z6530. [With his *Concerto no. 23*].

- (Murray Perahia/English Chamber Orchestra). CBS: MK 42241. [With his *Concerto no. 27*].

- (Artur Rubinstein/RCA Victor Symphony/ Alfred Wallenstein). RCA: 7967-2-RG. [With his *Concerto no. 21*].

- (Mitsuko Uchida/English Chamber Orchestra/ Jeffrey Tate). Philips: 416 381-2. [With his *Concerto no. 21*].

3418.20 ** *Concerto for piano and orchestra no. 21, K. 467 in C major.*

- (Malcolm Bilson/English Baroque Soloists/ John Eliot Gardiner). *See 3418.19*

- (Murray Perahia/English Chamber Orchestra). CBS: MK 34562. [With his *Concerto no. 9*].

- (Artur Rubinstein/RCA Victor Symphony/ Alfred Wallenstein). *See 3418.19*

- (Mitsuko Uchida/English Chamber Orchestra/ Jeffrey Tate). *See 3418.19*

3418.21 ** *Concerto for piano and orchestra no. 22, K. 482 in E♭ major.*

- (Alfred Brendel/Academy of St. Martin-in-the-Fields/Neville Marriner). *See 3418.8*

- (Murray Perahia/English Chamber Orchestra). CBS: MK 42242. [With his *Concerto no. 24*].

- (Mitsuko Uchida/English Chamber Orchestra/ Jeffrey Tate). Philips: 420 187-2. [With his *Concerto no. 23*].

3418.22 ** *Concerto or piano and orchestra no. 23, K. 488 in A major.*

- (Richard Goode/Orpheus Chamber Orchestra). *See 3418.16*

- (Friedrich Gulda/Concertgebouw Orchestra/ Nikolaus Harnoncourt). *See 3418.25*

- (Stephen Lubin/Mozartean Players). *See 3418.19*

- (Murray Perahia/English Chamber Orchestra). *See 3418.18*

- (Artur Rubinstein/RCA Victor Symphony/ Alfred Wallenstein). RCA: 7968-2-RG. [With his *Concerto no. 24*].

- (Mitsuko Uchida/English Chamber Orchestra/ Jeffrey Tate). *See 3418.21*

3418.23 * *Concerto for piano and orchestra no. 24, K. 491 in C minor.*

- (Malcolm Bilson/English Baroque Soloists/ John Eliot Gardiner). Archiv: 427 652-2. [With his *Concerto no. 27*].

- (Alfred Brendel/Academy of St. Martin-in-the-Fields/Neville Marriner). *See 3418.19*

- (Murray Perahia/English Chamber Orchestra). *See 3418.21*

- (Artur Rubinstein/RCA Victor Symphony/ Alfred Wallenstein). *See 3418.22*

- (Melvyn Tan/London Classical Players/Roger Norrington). EMI: CDC 7 54295 2. [With his *Concerto no. 25*].

- (Mitsuko Uchida/English Chamber Orchestra/ Jeffrey Tate). Philips: 422 331-2. [With his *Concerto no. 25*].

3418.24 ** *Concerto for piano and orchestra no. 25, K. 503 in C major.*

- (Alfred Brendel/Academy of St. Martin-in-the-Fields/Neville Marriner). *See 3418.8*

- (Murray Perahia/English Chamber Orchestra). CBS: MK 37267. [With his *Concerto no. 5*].

- (Melvyn Tan/London Classical Players/Roger Norrington). *See 3418.23*

- (Mitsuko Uchida/English Chamber Orchestra/ Jeffrey Tate). *See 3418.23*

3418.25 ** *Concerto for piano and orchestra no. 26, K. 537 in D major ("Coronation").*

- (Alfred Brendel/Academy of St. Martin-in-the-Fields/Neville Marriner). Philips: 411 468-2. [With his *Concerto no. 8*].

- (Friedrich Gulda/Concertgebouw Orchestra/ Nikolaus Harnoncourt). Teldec: 8.42970. [With his *Concerto no. 23*].

- (Murray Perahia/English Chamber Orchestra). CBS: MK 39224. [With his *Rondos for piano and orchestra, K. 382 and K. 386*].

- (Mitsuko Uchida/English Chamber Orchestra/ Jeffrey Tate). Philips: 420 951-2. [With his *Concerto no. 27*].

3418.26 * *Concerto for piano no. 27, K. 595 in B♭ major.*

- (Malcolm Bilson/English Baroque Soloists/ John Eliot Gardiner). *See 3418.23*

- (Alfred Brendel/Academy of St. Martin-in-the-Fields/Neville Marriner). *See 3418.8*

- (Murray Perahia/English Chamber Orchestra). *See 3418.19*

- (Mitsuko Uchida/English Chamber Orchestra/ Jeffrey Tate). *See 3418.25*

3418.27 *Concerto for violin and orchestra no. 1, K. 207 in B♭ major.*

- (Monica Huggett/Orchestra of the Age of Enlightenment). Virgin: CDC 5 45010 2. [With his *Concertos for violin nos. 2 and 5*].
- (Pinchas Zukerman/St. Paul Chamber Orchestra). CBS: MDK 44653. [With his *Concertos for violin nos. 2 and 3*].

3418.28 *Concerto for violin and orchestra no. 2, K. 211 in D major. See 3418.27*

3418.29 * *Concerto for violin and orchestra no. 3, K. 216 in G major.*

- (Anne-Sophie Mutter/Berlin Philharmonic/ Herbert von Karajan). Deutsche Grammophon: 429 814-2. [With his *Concerto for violin no. 5*].
- (Pinchas Zukerman/St. Paul Chamber Orchestra). *See 3418.27*

3418.30 * *Concerto for violin and orchestra no. 4, K. 218 in D major.*

- (David Oistrakh/Berlin Philharmonic). EMI: CDM 7 64868 2. [With his *Concerto for violin no. 5; Rondos for violin and orchestra, K. 269 and 373; Adagio for violin and orchestra, K. 261*].
- (Pinchas Zukerman/St. Paul Chamber Orchestra). CBS: MDK 44654. [With his *Concerto for violin no. 5*].

3418.31 ** *Concerto for violin and orchestra no. 5, K. 219 in A major ("Turkish").*

- (Monica Huggett/Orchestra of the Age of Enlightenment). *See 3418.27*
- (Anne-Sophie Mutter/Berlin Philharmonic/ Herbert von Karajan). *See 3418.29*
- (David Oistrakh/Berlin Philharmonic). *See 3418.30*
- (Pinchas Zukerman/St. Paul Chamber Orchestra). *See 3418.30*

3418.32 ** *Eine kleine Nachtmusik (Serenade no. 13, K. 525 in G major).*

- (Concentus Musicus Wien/Nikolaus Harnoncourt). Teldec: 244 809-2. [With his *Divertimento, K. 251* and *Musikalischer Spass*].
- (Academy of Ancient Music/Christopher Hogwood). L'Oiseau-Lyre: 411 720-2. [With his *Notturno for four orchestras, K. 286* and *Serenata notturna*].
- (Boston Symphony/Erich Leinsdorf). *See 3418.50*
- (Talich Quartet). *See 3418.54*

3418.33 *Musikalischer Spass (Musical joke).*

- (Archibudelli). Sony: SK 46702. [With his *Quintet for horn and strings*].
- (Concentus Musicus Wien/Nikolaus Harnoncourt). *See 3418.32*

3418.34 ** *Overtures. Selections.* (Academy of St. Martin-in-the-Fields/Neville Marriner). EMI: CDC 7 47014 2. [Overtures to *Così fan tutte, La Clemenza di Tito, Don Giovanni, Die Entführung aus dem Serail, Idomeneo, Lucio Silla, Le Nozze di Figaro,* and *Der Schauspieldirektor*].

3418.35 *Serenade no. 5, K. 204 in D major.*

- (Concentus Musicus Wien/Nikolaus Harnoncourt). Teldec: 2292-72289-2. [With his *Symphony no. 27*].
- (Tafelmusik/Bruno Weil). *See 3418.38*

3418.36 *Serenade no. 6, K. 239 in D major (Serenata notturna).* (Academy of Ancient Music/Christopher Hogwood). *See 3418.32*

3418.37 * *Serenade no. 7, K. 250 in D major ("Haffner").*

- (Orchestra of the 18th Century/Frans Brüggen). Philips: 432 997-2.
- (Tafelmusik/Bruno Weil). *See 3418.38*

3418.38 * *Serenade no. 9, K. 320 in D major ("Posthorn").*

- (Dresden Staatskapelle/Nikolaus Harnoncourt). Teldec: 8.43063. [With his *Marches for orchestra, K. 335*].
- (Tafelmusik/Bruno Weil). Sony: S2K 47260. 2CD set. [With his *Serenades nos. 1, 3–5, and 7*].

3418.39 * *Serenade no. 10, K. 361 in B♭ major [for wind instruments] ("Gran partita").*

- (Vienna Mozart Winds/Nikolaus Harnoncourt). Teldec: 8.42981.
- (Octophorus). Accent: ACC 68642 D.

3418.40 * *Serenade no. 11, K. 375 in E♭ major [for wind instruments].*

- (Amadeus Winds). L'Oiseau-Lyre: 417 249-2. [With his *Serenade no. 12*].
- (Vienna Mozart Winds/Nikolaus Harnoncourt). Teldec: 8.43097. [With his *Serenade no. 12*].

3418.41 ** *Serenade no. 12, K. 388 in C minor [for wind instruments]. See 3418.40*

3418.42 ** *Sinfonia concertante for violin, viola, and orchestra, K. 364 in E♭ major.*

- (Rafael Druian/Abraham Skernick/Cleveland Orchestra/George Szell). CBS: MYK 37810. [With his *Concerto for clarinet*].
- (Itzhak Perlman/Pinchas Zukerman/Israel Philharmonic/Zubin Mehta). Deutsche Grammophon: 415 486-2. [With his *Concertone for two violins and orchestra*].

3418.43 *Symphonies (40)* [complete]. (Academy of Ancient Music/Christopher Hogwood). [vol. 1] L'Oiseau-Lyre: 417 140-2; [vol. 2] L'Oiseau-Lyre: 417 518-2; [vol. 3] L'Oiseau-Lyre: 417 592-2; [vol. 4] L'Oiseau-Lyre: 417 841-2; [vol. 5] L'Oiseau-Lyre: 421 104-2; [vol. 6] L'Oiseau-Lyre: 421 085-2; [vol. 7] L'Oiseau-Lyre: 421 135-2. 19 CDs in 7 vols.

3418.44 * *Symphony no. 25, K. 183 in G minor.*
- (Vienna Philharmonic/James Levine). Deutsche Grammophon: 419 234-2. [With his *Symphonies nos. 26 and 27*].
- (English Concert/Trevor Pinnock). Archiv: 431 679-2. [With his *Symphonies nos. 26 and 29*].

3418.45 * *Symphony no. 29, K. 201 in A major.*
- (English Baroque Soloists/John Eliot Gardiner). Philips: 412 736-2. [With his *Symphony no. 33*].
- (English Concert/Trevor Pinnock). *See* 3418.44

3418.46 ** *Symphony no. 35, K. 385 in D major* ("*Haffner*").
- (Berlin Philharmonic/Karl Böhm). Deutsche Grammophon: 429 521-2. [With his *Symphonies nos. 36 and 38*].
- (English Baroque Soloists/John Eliot Gardiner). Philips: 422 419-2. [With his *Symphonies nos. 32 and 36*].
- (Cleveland Orchestra/George Szell). Sony: SBK 46333. [With his *Symphonies nos. 40 and 41*].

3418.47 ** *Symphony no. 36, K. 425 in C major* ("*Linz*").
- (Vienna Philharmonic/Leonard Bernstein). Deutsche Grammophon: 415 962-2. [With his *Symphony no. 38*].
- (Berlin Philharmonic/Karl Böhm). *See* 3418.46
- (English Baroque Soloists/John Eliot Gardiner). *See* 3418.46
- (Boston Symphony/Erich Leinsdorf). *See* 3418.50

3418.48 *Symphony no. 37. See* 3412

3418.49 ** *Symphony no. 38, K. 504 in D major* ("*Prague*").
- (Vienna Philharmonic/Leonard Bernstein). *See* 3418.47
- (Berlin Philharmonic/Karl Böhm). *See* 3418.46
- (Orchestra of the 18th Century/Frans Brüggen). Philips: 426 231-2. [With his *Overture to Le Nozze di Figaro*].
- (English Baroque Soloists/John Eliot Gardiner). Philips: 426 283-2. [With his *Symphony no. 39*].

3418.50 ** *Symphony no. 39, K. 543 in E♭ major.*
- (English Baroque Soloists/John Eliot Gardiner). *See* 3418.49
- (Boston Symphony/Erich Leinsdorf). RCA: 09026-60907-2. [With his *Symphony no. 36* and *Eine kleine Nachtmusik*].
- (London Classical Players/Roger Norrington). Angel: CDC 7 54090 2. [With his *Symphony no. 41*].

3418.51 ** *Symphony no. 40, K. 550 in G minor.*
- (Vienna Philharmonic/Leonard Bernstein). Deutsche Grammophon: 431 040-2. [With his *Symphony no. 41*].
- (Vienna Philharmonic/Karl Böhm). Deutsche Grammophon: 413 547-2. [With his *Symphony no. 41*].
- (Orchestra of the 18th Century/Frans Brüggen). Philips: 434 149-2. [With his *Symphony no. 41*].
- (Cleveland Orchestra/George Szell). *See* 3418.46

3418.52 ** *Symphony no. 41, K. 551 in C major* ("*Jupiter*").
- (Vienna Philharmonic/Leonard Bernstein). *See* 3418.51
- (Vienna Philharmonic/Karl Böhm). *See* 3418.51
- (Orchestra of the 18th Century/Frans Brüggen). *See* 3418.51
- (London Classical Players/Roger Norrington). *See* 3418.50
- (Cleveland Orchestra/George Szell). *See* 3418.46

CHAMBER MUSIC AND SOLO INSTRUMENTAL MUSIC

3418.53 *Divertimento, K. 563 in E♭ major* [for string trio].
- (Archibudelli). Sony: SK 46497.
- (Gidon Kremer/Kim Kashkashian/Yo-Yo Ma). CBS: MK 39561.

3418.54 *Divertimentos (3) for string quartet, K. 136-138.* (Talich Quartet). Calliope: 9248. [With his *Eine kleine Nachtmusik*].

3418.55 *Duos (2) for violin and viola.* (Itzhak Perlman/Pinchas Zukerman). RCA: 60735-2-RC. [With Leclair, Jean Marie: *Sonata for two violins, op. 3 no. 4*].

3418.56 * *Quartets (4) for flute and strings.*

- (Les Adieux). *See 3418.57*

- (Kuijken Quartet). Accent: ACC 48225.

3418.57 * *Quartet for oboe and strings, K. 370 in F major.*

- (Les Adieux). Deutsche Harmonia Mundi: 77158-2-RC. [With his *Quartets for flute and strings*].

- (Heinz Holliger/Orlando Quartet). Philips: 412 618-2. [With his *Divertimento, K. 251*].

- (John Mack and others). *See 3437*

3418.58 * *Quartets (2) for piano and strings.*

- (Mozartean Players). Harmonia Mundi: HMU: 907018.

- (Artur Rubinstein/Guarneri Quartet). RCA: 60406-2-RG.

3418.59 ** *Quartets (6) for strings nos. 14–19 "dedicated to Haydn"* [K. 387 in G major; K. 421 in D minor; K. 428 in E major; K. 458 in B♭ major ("Hunting"); K. 464 in A major; K. 465 in C major ("Dissonance")].

- (Alban Berg Quartet). Teldec: 9031-72480-2. 4CD set. [With his *Quartets nos. 20–23*].

- (Emerson Quartet). Deutsche Grammophon: 431 797-2. 3CD set.

- (Quatuor Mosaïques). Astrée: 8746; 8747; 8748. 3 CDs.

3418.60 * *Quartets for strings nos. 20–23* [K. 499 in D major; K. 575 in D major; K. 589 in B♭ major; K. 590 in F major].

- (Alban Berg Quartet). *See 3418.59*

- (Melos Quartet). Deutsche Grammophon: 431 153-2.

3418.61 * *Quintet for clarinet and strings, K. 581 in A major.*

- (Erich Hoeprich and others). *See 3418.2*

- (Richard Stoltzman/Tokyo Quartet). *See 3418.2*

3418.62 *Quintet for horn and strings, K. 407 in E♭ major. See 3418.33*

3418.63 * *Quintet for piano and winds, K. 452 in E♭ major.*

- (Alfred Brendel and others) Philips: 420 182-2. [With Beethoven, Ludwig van: *Quintet for piano and winds*].

- (Jos van Immerseel and others). Accent: ACC 58538 D. [With Beethoven, Ludwig van: *Quintet for piano and winds*].

- (Murray Perahia and others). CBS: MK 42099. [With Beethoven, Ludwig van: *Quintet for piano and winds*].

- (Mitsuko Uchida and others). *See 3418.16*

3418.64 * *Quintet for strings no. 3, K. 515 in C major.*

- (Alban Berg Quartet). EMI: CDC 7 49085 2. [With his *Quintet for strings no. 4*].

- (Talich Quartet). Calliope: CAL 9231. [With his *Quintet for strings no. 4*].

3418.65 * *Quintet for strings no. 4, K. 516 in G minor. See 3418.64*

3418.66 * *Quintet for strings no. 5, K. 593 in D major.*

- (Hausmusik). EMI: 7 54858 2. [With his *Quintet for strings no. 6*].

- (Tatrai Quartet). White Label: 096. [With his *Quintet for strings no. 6*].

3418.67 * *Quintet for strings no. 6, K. 614 in E♭ major. See 3418.66*

3418.68 *Sonatas for violin and piano. Selections.* (Itzhak Perlman/Daniel Barenboim). Deutsche Grammophon: 415 102-2 [*Sonatas, K. 296, 305, and 306*]; Deutsche Grammophon: 410 896-2 [*Sonatas, K. 301-304*]; Deutsche Grammophon: 423 229-2 [*Sonatas, K. 378-380*].

3418.69 ** *Sonatas, variations, and other works for piano. Selections.*

- (Jos van Immerseel). Accent: ACC 58018 D. [*Variations on "Ah, vous dirai-je, Maman"; Fantasias, K. 397 and 475; Rondo, K. 511; and Sonata no. 14, K. 457*].

- (Mitsuko Uchida). Philips: 412 741-2 [*Sonatas nos. 7–9, K. 309-311*]; Philips: 412 616-2 [*Sonatas no. 10, K. 330 and 13, K. 333, plus Adagio in B minor, K. 540*]; Philips: 412 123-2 [*Sonatas nos. 11–12, K. 331-332, plus Fantasia in D minor, K. 397*]; Philips: 412 617-2 [*Sonatas no. 14, K. 457 and 17, K. 576, plus Fantasia in C minor, K. 475*]; Philips: 412 122-2 [*Sonata no. 15, K. 545, Allegro and andante, K. 533, and Rondo, K. 511*]; Philips: 420 185-2 [*Sonatas no. 6, K. 284 and 16, K. 570, plus Rondo, K. 485*].

3418.70   *Trios (6) for piano and strings.*
- (Beaux Arts Trio). Philips: 422 079-2. 3CD set.
- (London Fortepiano Trio). Hyperion: CDA66093; CDA66148; CDA66125. 3 CDs.

VOCAL MUSIC

3418.71   * *Ave verum corpus. See* 3418.75, 3418.76, *or* 3418.78

3418.72   *Concert arias.* (Kiri Te Kanawa, Edita Gruberova, Teresa Berganza, and others). London: 430 300-2. 5CD set.

3418.73   * *Exsultate jubilate.*
- (Cecilia Bartoli/Vienna Chamber Orchestra/ György Fischer). London: 443 452-2. [With his selected arias].
- (Emma Kirkby/Academy of Ancient Music/ Christopher Hogwood). L'Oiseau-Lyre: 411 832-2. [With his *Regina coeli, K. 108, Regina coeli, K. 127,* and *Ergo interest, K. 143.*]

3418.74   * *Mass, K. 317 in C major ("Coronation").*
- (Academy of Ancient Music/Christopher Hogwood). Argo: 436 585-2. [With his *Vesperae solennes de confessore, K. 339*].
- (Vienna Singverein/Berlin Philharmonic/ Herbert von Karajan). *See* 3400.30
- (RIAS Chamber Chorus/Berlin Symphony/ James Levine). *See* 3411.50

3418.75   ** *Mass, K. 427 in C minor ("Great").*
- (Monteverdi Choir/English Baroque Soloists/ John Eliot Gardiner). Philips: 420 210-2.
- (Academy of St. Martin-in-the-Fields/Neville Marriner). Philips: 438 999-2. [With his *Ave verum corpus*].

3418.76   ** *Requiem.*
- (Monteverdi Choir/English Baroque Soloists/ John Eliot Gardiner). Philips: 420 197-2. [In the version completed by Franz Xaver Süssmayr. With Mozart's *Kyrie, K. 341*].
- (Academy of Ancient Music/Christopher Hogwood). L'Oiseau-Lyre: 411 712-2. [In the version completed by Richard Maunder].
- (Schütz Choir/London Classical Players/Roger Norrington). EMI: CDC 7 54525 2. [In the version completed by Duncan Druce. With Mozart's *Masonic funeral music* and *Ave verum corpus*].

3418.77   *Songs.* (Julianne Baird/Colin Tilney). Dorian: DOR 90173.

3418.78   *Vesperae solennes de confessore, K. 339.*
- (Hilliard Ensemble/Choir of King's College Cambridge/Stephen Cleobury). EMI: CDC 7 49672 2. [With his *Vesperae, K. 321* and *Ave verum corpus*].
- (Academy of Ancient Music/Christopher Hogwood). *See* 3418.74

STAGE MUSIC

3418.79   *Bastien und Bastienne* [opera]. *See* 3424

3418.80   *La clemenza di Tito* [opera]. (Uwe Heilmann/Cecilia Bartoli/Della Jones/Academy of Ancient Music/Christopher Hogwood). L'Oiseau-Lyre: 444 131-2. 2CD set.

3418.81   * *Così fan tutte* [opera].
- (Elisabeth Schwarzkopf/Christa Ludwig/Alfredo Kraus/Philharmonia Orchestra/Karl Böhm). EMI: CMS 7 69330 2. 3CD set.
- (Kiri Te Kanawa/Ann Murray/Thomas Hampson/ Vienna Philharmonic/James Levine). Deutsche Grammophon: 423 897-2. 3CD set.
- (Rachel Yakar/Alicia Nafé/Gösta Winbergh/ Drottningholm Court Theatre/Arnold Östman). L'Oiseau-Lyre: 414 316-2. 3CD set.

3418.82   ** *Don Giovanni* [opera].
- (Thomas Allen/Carol Vaness/Maria Ewing/London Philharmonic/Bernard Haitink). EMI: CDS 7 47037 8. 3CD set.
- (Thomas Hampson/Edita Gruberova/Robert Holl/Concertgebouw/Nikolaus Harnoncourt). Teldec: 2292-44184-2. 3CD set.
- (Cesare Siepi/Hilde Gueden/Walter Berry/Vienna Philharmonic/Josef Krips). London: 411 626-2. 3CD set.
- (Andreas Schmidt/Alastair Miles/Amanda Halgrimson/London Classical Players/Roger Norrington). EMI: CDC 7 54859 2. 3CD set.

3418.83   * *Die Entführung aus dem Serail (The abduction from the seraglio)* [opera]. (Yvonne Kenney/Peter Schreier/Matti Salminen/Zurich Opera/Nikolaus Harnoncourt). Teldec: 8.35673. 3CD set.

3418.84   *Idomeneo* [opera].
- (Sylvia McNair/Anne Sofie von Otter/Anthony Rolfe Johnson/English Baroque Soloists/John Eliot Gardiner). Archiv: 431 674-2. 3CD set.
- (Rachel Yakar/Trudeliese Schmidt/Werner Hollweg/Zurich Opera/Nikolaus Harnoncourt). Teldec: 8.35547. 3CD set.

3418.85   ** *Le nozze di Figaro (The marriage of Figaro)* [opera].

- (Edith Mathis/Tatiana Troyanos/Hermann Prey/Deutsche Oper Berlin/Karl Böhm). Deutsche Grammophon: 415 520-2. 3CD set.
- (Hilde Gueden/Lisa Della Casa/Alfred Poell/Vienna Philharmonic/Erich Kleiber). London: 417 315-2. 3CD set.
- (Barbara Bonney/Arleen Augér/Håkan Hagegård/Drottningholm Court Theatre/Arnold Östman). L'Oiseau-Lyre: 421 333-2. 3CD set.

3418.86 ** *Die Zauberflöte (The magic flute)* [opera].

- (Hilde Gueden/Leopold Simoneau/Vienna Philharmonic/Karl Böhm). London: 414 362-2. 2CD set.
- (Lucia Popp/Siegfried Jerusalem/Bavarian Radio Orchestra/Bernard Haitink). EMI: CDS 7 47951 8. 3CD set.
- (Dawn Upshaw/Anthony Rolfe Johnson/London Classical Players/Roger Norrington). EMI: CDC 7 54287 2. 2CD set.
- (Uwe Heilmann/Michael Kraus/Vienna Philharmonic/Georg Solti). London: 433 210-2. 2CD set.

3419 Paisiello, Giovanni, 1740–1816

Il barbiere di Siviglia (The barber of Seville) [opera]. (Krisztina Laki/Dénes Gulyás/Hungarian State Orchestra/Adám Fischer). Hungaroton: 12525/26. 2CD set.

3420 Pergolesi, Giovanni Battista, 1710–1736

3420.1 * *La serva padrona* [opera].

- (Julianne Baird/John Ostendorf/Philomel Baroque Chamber Orchestra). Omega: 1016.
- (Katalin Farkas/József Gregor/Capella Savaria/Pál Németh). Hungaroton: 12846.

3420.2 *Stabat Mater.*

- (Gillian Fisher/Michael Chance/Robert King). Hyperion: CDA66294. [With his *Salve Regina* and *In coelestibus regnis*].
- (Emma Kirkby/James Bowman/Christopher Hogwood). L'Oiseau-Lyre: 425 692-2. [With his *Salve Regina*].

3421 Piccinni, Niccolò, 1728–1800

Iphigénie en Tauride (Iphigenia in Tauris) [opera]. (Silvia Baleani/René Massis/Aldo Bertolo/Teatro Petruzzelli di Bari/Donato Renzetti). Fonit Cetra: CDC 32. 2CD set.

3422 Quantz, Johann Joachim, 1697–1773. *See* 3434

3423 Reicha, Anton, 1770–1836

3423.1 *Quintets for strings. Selections.* (Anner Bylsma/Archibudelli). Sony: SK 53118.

3423.2 * *Quintets for winds. Selections.* (Academia Wind Quintet). Hyperion: CDA66268.

3424 Rousseau, Jean-Jacques, 1712–1778

Le devin du village (The village soothsayer) [opera]. (Eva Kirchner/Dongkyu Choi/Alpe Adria Ensemble/René Clemencic). Nuova Era: 7106/07. 2CD set. [With Mozart, Wolfgang Amadeus: *Bastien und Bastienne*].

3425 Saint-Georges, Joseph Boulogne, chevalier de, d. 1799

Concertos for violin and orchestra. Selections. (Jean Jacques Kantorow/Bernard Thomas Chamber Orchestra). Arion: ARN 68093.

3426 Salieri, Antonio, 1750–1825

Tarare (or, Axur, re d'Ormus) [opera]. (Andrea Martin/Curtis Rayam/Orchestra Filarmonica di Russe/René Clemencic). Nuova Era: 6852/54. 3CD set.

3427 Sammartini, Giovanni Battista, ca. 1700–1775

Orchestral music. Selections. (Ensemble 415/Chiara Banchini). Harmonia Mundi: HMA 1901245. [*Sinfonia in G major, Sinfonia in D major,* and *Quintet in G major* by Giovanni Battista Sammartini, plus *Concerto for recorder in F major, Concerto grosso in E minor,* and *Concerto grosso in G minor* by Giuseppe Sammartini].

3428 Sammartini, Giuseppe, 1695–1750

Concertos. Selections. See 3427

3429 * Soler, Antonio, 1729–1783. *Keyboard music. Selections.*

- (Virginia Black) [selected sonatas, performed on harpsichord]. CRD: 3452.
- (Bernard Brauchli) [selected sonatas, performed on clavichord]. Titanic: Ti-42.
- (Bernard Brauchli/Esteban Elizondo) [selected concertos for two keyboard instruments]. Titanic: Ti-152.
- (Maggie Cole) [selected sonatas, performed on harpsichord and fortepiano]. Virgin: 7 59624 2 (7 91172 2) or Musical Heritage Society: 513400M.
- (Gilbert Rowland) [selected sonatas, performed on harpsichord]. Nimbus: NI 5248.

3430 Stamitz, Johann, 1717–1757

Concertos. Selections. See 3431.1 and 3433

3431   Stamitz, Karl, 1745–1801

    3431.1   *Concertos. Selections.*

- (Barthold Kuijken/Tafelmusik/Jean Lamon). *See* 3433
- (Sabine Meyer/Academy of St. Martin-in-the-Fields/Iona Brown). EMI: CDC 7 54842 2. [*Concertos for clarinet and orchestra nos. 3, 10, and 11* by Karl Stamitz, plus *Concerto in B♭ major* by Johann Stamitz].

    3431.2   * *Symphonies. Selections.* (London Mozart Players/Matthias Bamert). Chandos: CHAN 9358.

3432   * Wassenaer, Unico Wilhelm, graaf van, 1692–1766

Concerti armonici [formerly attributed to Giovanni Battista Pergolesi]. (Brandenburg Consort/Roy Goodman). Hyperion: CDA66670.

Anthologies and Recitals

3433   *Flute concertos.* (Barthold Kuijken/Tafelmusik/Jean Lamon). Sony: SK 48045. [Concertos by Karl Stamitz, Franz Xavier Richter, Johann Stamitz, and Joseph Haydn, and the *Dance of the blessed spirits* from *Orfeo ed Euridice* by Christoph Willibald Gluck].

3434   *Music from the court of Frederick the Great.* (Collegium Musicum 90/Simon Standage). Chandos: CHAN 0541. [Chamber works by Carl Philipp Emanuel Bach, Franz Benda, Frederick the Great, Johann Gottlieb Graun, and Johann Joachim Quantz].

3435   * *Révolution française.* (Chorus and Orchestra of the Capitole de Toulouse/Michel Plasson). EMI: CDC 7 49470 2. [Music associated with the French Revolution by Claude Joseph Rouget de Lisle, Etienne Nicolas Méhul, Giovanni Paisiello, François Joseph Gossec, and Hector Berlioz].

Individual Artists

3436   * Leonhardt, Gustav. *Clavichord recital.* Philips: 422 349-2. [Music by Carl Philipp Emanuel Bach, Wilhelm Friedemann Bach, Johann Sebastian Bach, and Christian Ritter].

3437   Mack, John. *John Mack, oboe.* Crystal: CD323. [Mozart, Wolfgang Amadeus: *Quartet for oboe and strings;* Loeffler, Charles Martin: *Rhapsodies for oboe, viola, and piano;* Paladilhe, Emile: *Solo de concert;* Britten, Benjamin: *Metamorphoses after Ovid*].

Romantic Period

Compiled by
Kent Underwood

Composers

3438 * Albéniz, Isaac, 1860–1909

Piano music. Selections. (Alicia De Larrocha). London: 417 887-2. [Includes his *Iberia, Navarra,* and *Suite española*].

3439 Alkan, Charles Henri Valentin, 1813–1888

Piano music. Selections. (Marc-André Hamelin). Hyperion: CDA66794. [*Grande sonate "Les quatres âges"; Sonatine, op. 61; Barcarolle, op. 65 no. 6; Etude, op. 39 no. 12 "Le festin d'Esope"*].

3440 Arensky, Anton Stepanovich, 1861–1906

Trio for piano and strings no. 1, op. 32 in D minor. (Borodin Trio). Chandos: CHAN 8477. [With Glinka, Mikhail Ivanovich: *Trio pathétique*].

3441 Arriaga, Juan Crisóstomo, 1806–1826

Symphony in D major. (Concerts des Nations/Jordi Savall). Astrée: 8532. [With his *Overture, op. 1* and *Overture to Los esclavos felices*].

3442 Auber, Daniel François Esprit, 1782–1871

Fra Diavolo [opera]. (Mady Mesplé/Nicolai Gedda/Jules Bastin/Monte-Carlo Philharmonic/Marc Soustrot). EMI: CDS 7 54810 2. 2CD set.

3443 * Balakirev, Milii Alekseevich, 1837–1910

Islamey [for piano]. (Olli Mustonen). London: 436 255-2. [With Mussorgsky, Modest Petrovich: *Kartinki s vystavki* and Tchaikovsky, Peter Ilich: *Detskii albom*].

3444 Beach, H. H. A., Mrs., 1867–1944

3444.1 * *Symphony, op. 32 in E minor ("Gaelic").* (Detroit Symphony/Neeme Järvi). *See* 3543.14

3444.2 *Vocal and instrumental music. Selections.* (D'Anna Fortunato/Joseph Silverstein/Virginia Eskin). Northeastern: NR 9004-CD. [Album title: *Dark garden: songs, violin pieces, and piano music*].

3445 Bellini, Vincenzo, 1801–1835

3445.1 * *Norma* [opera].

- (Joan Sutherland/Marilyn Horne/John Alexander/London Symphony/Richard Bonynge). London: 425 488-2. 3CD set [complete opera]; London: 421 886-2 [highlights].

- (Maria Callas/Christa Ludwig/Franco Corelli/La Scala/Tullio Serafin). EMI: CMS 7 63000 2. 3CD set [complete opera]; EMI: CMS 7 63091 2 [highlights].

3445.2 *I Puritani* [opera]. (Maria Callas/Giuseppe Di Stefano/La Scala/Tullio Serafin). EMI: CDS 7 47308 8. 2CD set.

3445.3 *La Sonnambula* [opera].

- (Joan Sutherland/Luciano Pavarotti/Nicolai Ghiaurov/National Philharmonic/Richard Bonynge). London: 417 424-2. 2CD set.
- (Maria Callas/Nicola Monti/Nicola Zaccaria/La Scala/Antonio Votto). EMI: CDC 7 47378 2. 2CD set.

3446   Berlioz, Hector, 1803–1869

3446.1 *Béatrice et Bénédict (Beatrice and Benedict)* [opera]. (Susan Graham/Jean-Luc Viala/Lyon Opera/John Nelson). Musifrance: 2292-45773-2. 2CD set.

3446.2 * *La damnation de Faust (The damnation of Faust)* [dramatic cantata]. (Frederica von Stade/Kenneth Riegel/José van Dam/Chicago Symphony/Georg Solti). London: 414 680-2. 2CD set.

3446.3 *L'enfance du Christ (The childhood of Christ)* [oratorio]. (John Eliot Gardiner). Erato: 2292-45275-2. 2CD set.

3446.4 *Harold en Italie (Harold in Italy)* [for viola and orchestra]. (Pinchas Zukerman/Montreal Symphony/Charles Dutoit). London: 421 193-2. [With his *Rob Roy* and *Corsaire* overtures].

3446.5 * *Nuits d'été (Summer nights)* [song cycle].

- (Jessye Norman/London Symphony/Colin Davis). London: 412 493-2. [With Ravel, Maurice: *Shéhérazade*].
- (Anne Sofie von Otter). *See* 3446.8

3446.6 * *Overtures. Selections.*

- (Montreal Symphony/Charles Dutoit). *See* 3446.4
- (Berlin Philharmonic/James Levine). *See* 3446.7
- (London Classical Players/Roger Norrington). *See* 3531
- (Chicago Symphony/Georg Solti). *See* 3446.9

3446.7 * *Requiem.* (James Levine). Deutsche Grammophon: 429 724-2. 2CD set. [With his *Corsaire, Benvenuto Cellini,* and *Carnaval romain* overtures].

3446.8 * *Roméo et Juliette (Romeo and Juliet).* (Anne Sofie von Otter/Philip Langridge/Berlin Philharmonic/James Levine). Deutsche Grammophon: 427 665-2. [With his *Nuits d'été*].

3446.9 ** *Symphonie fantastique.*

- (Cleveland Orchestra/Christoph von Dohnanyi). London: 430 201-2. [With Weber, Carl Maria von: *Aufforderung zum Tanze*].
- (Orchestre Révolutionnaire et Romantique/John Eliot Gardiner). Philips: 434 402-2.
- (Boston Symphony/Charles Munch). RCA: 7735-2.
- (London Classical Players/Roger Norrington). EMI 7 49541 2.
- (Chicago Symphony/Georg Solti). London: 417 705-2. [With his *Francs-juges* overture].

3446.10 *Les Troyens* [opera]. (Berit Lindholm/John Vickers/Peter Glossop/Covent Garden/Colin Davis). Philips: 416 432-2. 4CD set.

3447   Berwald, Franz, 1796–1868

Symphonies (4). (Gothenburg Symphony/Neeme Järvi). Deutsche Grammophon: 415 502-2. 2CD set.

3448   Bizet, Georges, 1838–1875

3448.1 * *L'Arlésienne suites (2).*

- (Royal Philharmonic/Thomas Beecham). *See* 3448.5
- (Montreal Symphony/Charles Dutoit). London: 417 839-2. [With his *Carmen suites*].

3448.2 ** *Carmen* [opera].

- (Jessye Norman/Neil Shicoff/Simon Estes/French National Orchestra/Seiji Ozawa). Philips: 422 366-2. 2CD set.
- (Maria Callas/Nicolai Gedda/Robert Massard/Paris Opera/Georges Prêtre). EMI: 7 54368 2. 2CD set.
- (Tatiana Troyanos/Plácido Domingo/José van Dam/London Philharmonic/Georg Solti). London: 414 489-2. 2CD set.

3448.3 *Jeux d'enfants.*

- (Concertgebouw Orchestra/Bernard Haitink). *See* 3448.5
- (Katia and Marielle Labèque) [piano duet]. Philips: 420 159-2. [With Fauré, Gabriel: *Dolly;* and Ravel, Maurice: *Ma mère l'oye*].

3448.4 *Les pêcheurs de perles (The pearl fishers)* [opera]. (Barbara Hendricks/John Aler/Capitole de Toulouse Orchestra/Michel Plasson). EMI: CDS 7 49837 2. 2CD set.

3448.5 * *Symphony in C major.*

- (French National Radio Orchestra/Royal Philharmonic/Thomas Beecham). EMI: 7 47794 2. [With his *L'Arlésienne suites nos. 1–2*].

- (Concertgebouw Orchestra/Bernard Haitink). Philips: 416 437-2. [With his *Jeux d'enfants* and Debussy, Claude: *Danse sacrée et danse profane*].

3449 Boito, Arrigo, 1842–1918

Mefistofele [opera]. (Monterrat Caballé/Plácido Domingo/Norman Treigle/London Symphony/Julius Rudel). EMI: CDC 7 49522 2. 2CD set.

3450 Borodin, Aleksandr Porfirevich, 1833–1887

3450.1 *Kniaz Igor (Prince Igor)* [opera]. (Stefka Evstatieva/Kaludi Kaludov/Nicolai Ghiaurov/Sofia Festival/Emil Tchakarov). Sony: S3K 44878. 3CD set.

3450.2 * *Kniaz Igor. Polovestskaia pliaska (Polovtsian dances).* (London Symphony/Georg Solti). See 3533

3450.3 * *Quartet for strings no. 2 in D major.*
- (Emerson Quartet). See 3519.13
- (Talich Quartet). Calliope: 9202. [With Tchaikovsky, Peter Ilich: *Quartet for strings no. 1*].

3450.4 * *Symphony no. 2 in B minor.* (Royal Philharmonic/Vladimir Ashkenazy). London: 436 651-2. [With his *Symphony no. 1* and *V srednei Azii*].

3450.5 *V srednei Azii (In the steppes of Central Asia).* (Royal Philharmonic/Vladimir Ashkenazy). See 3450.4

3451 Bottesini, Giovanni, 1821–1889

Instrumental music. Selections. (Wolfgang Harrer and others). Koch Schwann Musica Mundi: 311112. [Album title: *Der Kontrabass = The doublebass.* Concerto for double bass and orchestra in B minor; Gran duo concertante for violin and double bass; and other works].

3452 Brahms, Johannes, 1833–1897

ORCHESTRAL MUSIC

3452.1 * *Akademische Festouvertüre (Academic festival overture).* See 3452.7 or 3452.8

3452.2 ** *Concerto for piano and orchestra no. 1, op. 15 in D minor.*
- (Alfred Brendel/Berlin Philharmonic/Claudio Abbado). Philips: 420 071-2.
- (Julius Katchen/London Symphony/Pierre Monteux). London: 440 612-2. 2CD set. [With his *Concerto for piano and orchestra no. 2; Variationen über ein Thema von Paganini; Variationen und Fuge über ein Thema von Händel*].

- (Artur Rubinstein/Chicago Symphony/Fritz Reiner). RCA: 61263-2.
- (Rudolf Serkin/Cleveland Orchestra/George Szell). CBS: MYK 37803.
- (Krystian Zimerman/Vienna Philharmonic/Leonard Bernstein). Deutsche Grammophon: 413 472-2.

3452.3 * *Concerto for piano and orchestra no. 2, op. 83 in B♭ major.*
- (Vladimir Ashkenazy/Vienna Philharmonic/Bernard Haitink). London: 410 199-2.
- (Julius Katchen). See 3452.2
- (Maurizio Pollini/Vienna Philharmonic/Claudio Abbado). Deutsche Grammophon: 419 471-2.
- (Sviatoslav Richter/Chicago Symphony/Erich Leinsdorf). RCA: 6518-2.

3452.4 ** *Concerto for violin and orchestra, op. 77 in D major.*
- (Jascha Heifetz/Boston Symphony/Charles Munch). See 3400.2
- (Gidon Kremer/Vienna Philharmonic/Leonard Bernstein). Deutsche Grammophon: 431 597-2. [With his *Concerto for violin, violoncello, and orchestra*].
- (Anne-Sophie Mutter/Berlin Philharmonic/Herbert von Karajan). Deutsche Grammophon: 400 064-2.
- (Itzhak Perlman/Chicago Symphony/Carlo Maria Giulini). EMI: 7 47166 2.
- (Isaac Stern/Philadelphia Orchestra/Eugene Ormandy). CBS: MK 42257. [With Dvořák, Antonín: *Concerto for violin and orchestra*].

3452.5 *Concerto for violin, violoncello, and orchestra, op. 102 in A minor ("Double concerto").*
- (Isaac Stern/Yo-Yo Ma/Chicago Symphony/Claudio Abbado). Sony: SK 45999. [With Berg, Alban: *Kammerkonzert*].
- (Gidon Kremer/Mischa Maisky/Vienna Philharmonic/Leonard Bernstein). See 3452.4
- (Anne-Sophie Mutter/António Meneses/Berlin Philharmonic/Herbert von Karajan). Deutsche Grammophon: 410 603-2. [With his *Tragische Ouvertüre*].

3452.6 * *Serenade no. 1, op. 11 in D major.* (St. Louis Symphony/Leonard Slatkin). RCA: 6247-2.

3452.7 *Serenade no. 2, op. 16 in A major.* (St. Louis Symphony/Leonard Slatkin). RCA: 7920-2. [With his *Akademische Festouvertüre* and *Variationen über ein Thema von Haydn*].

3452.8 ** *Symphonies (4).*

- (Vienna Philharmonic/Leonard Bernstein). Deutsche Grammophon: 415 570-2. 4CD set. [With his *Akademische Festouvertüre; Tragische Ouvertüre; Variationen über ein Thema von Haydn*].
- (London Classical Players/Roger Norrington). EMI: 7 54286 2 [*Symphony no. 1* and *Variationen über ein Thema von Haydn*]; EMI: 7 54875 2 [*Symphony no. 2* and *Tragische Ouvertüre*]. 2 CDs.
- (Chicago Symphony/Georg Solti). London: 421 074-2. 4CD set. [With his *Akademische Festouvertüre* and *Tragische Ouvertüre*].
- (Cleveland Orchestra/George Szell). Sony: SB3K 48398. 3CD set. [With his *Akademische Festouvertüre; Tragische Ouvertüre; Ungarische Tänze nos. 17–21; Variationen über ein Thema von Haydn*].

3452.9 * *Tragische Ouvertüre (Tragic overture).* See 3452.5 or 3452.8

3452.10 * *Ungarische Tänze (Hungarian dances)* [for orchestra—nos. 17–21]. Cleveland Orchestra/George Szell. See 3452.8

3452.11 * *Variationen über ein Thema von Haydn (Variations on a theme by Haydn).* See 3452.7 or 3452.8

CHAMBER MUSIC

3452.12 *Quartets (3) for piano and strings.*

- (Emanuel Ax/Isaac Stern/Jaime Laredo/Yo-Yo Ma). Sony: S2K 45846. 2CD set.
- (Borodin Trio/Rivka Golani). Chandos: 8809/10. 2CD set.

3452.13 *Quartets (3) for strings.*

- (Alban Berg Quartet). EMI: ZDCB 7 54829 2.
- (Bartók Quartet). Hungaroton: 11591/93. 3CD set. [With his *Quintets for strings* and *Sextets for strings*].

  See also 3508.11

3452.14 ** *Quintet for clarinet and strings, op. 115 in B minor.*

- (Benny Goodman/Berkshire String Quartet). Musicmasters: 62103Z/04X. 2CD set. [With his *Trio for clarinet, violoncello, and piano;* Beethoven, Ludwig van: *Trio for piano, clarinet, and violoncello, op. 11;* Weber, Carl Maria von: *Quintet for clarinet and strings*].
- (Bela Kovács/Bartók Quartet). Hungaroton: 11596-2. [With his *Quintet for piano and strings*].

3452.15 ** *Quintet for piano and strings, op. 34 in F minor.*

- (Maurizio Pollini/Quartetto Italiano). Deutsche Grammophon: 419 673-2.
- (Deszö Ránki/Bartók Quartet). See 3452.14

3452.16 *Quintets (2) for strings.* (Bartók Quartet/György Konrad). See 3452.13

3452.17 *Sextets (2) for strings.* (Bartók Quartet and others). See 3452.13

3452.18 *Sonatas (2) for clarinet (or viola) and piano.*

- (Richard Stoltzman [clarinet]/Richard Goode). RCA: 60036-2.
- (Pinchas Zukerman [viola]/Daniel Barenboim). Deutsche Grammophon: 437 248-2.

3452.19 *Sonatas (3) for violin and piano.*

- (Anne-Sophie Mutter/Alexis Weissenberg). EMI: 7 49299 2.
- (Itzhak Perlman/Vladimir Ashkenazy). EMI: 7 47403 2.

3452.20 *Sonatas (2) for violoncello and piano.*

- (Yo-Yo Ma/Emanuel Ax). Sony: SK 48191.
- (Mstislav Rostropovich/Rudolf Serkin). Deutsche Grammophon: 410 510-2.

3452.21 * *Trio for horn, violin, and piano, op. 40 in E♭ major.*

- (Lowell Greer/Stephanie Chase/Stephen Lubin). See 3400.12
- (William Purvis/Rolf Daniel Phillips/Richard Goode). Bridge: BCD 9012. [With Ligeti, György: *Trio for horn, violin, and piano*].
- (Barry Tuckwell/Itzhak Perlman/Vladimir Ashkenazy). See 3469.2

3452.22 *Trios (3) for piano and strings.*

- (Beaux Arts Trio). Philips: 416 838-2. 2CD set.
- (Borodin Trio). Chandos: 8834/35. 2CD set.

PIANO MUSIC

3452.23 *Ballades (4), op. 10.*

- (Glenn Gould). Sony: SM2K 52651. [With his *Rhapsodies, op. 79* and selections from *Opp. 116–119*].
- (Stephen Bishop Kovacevich). Philips: 411 103-4. [With his *Pieces, op. 76* and *Scherzo, op. 4*].
- (Dezsö Ránki). Quintana (Harmonia Mundi): 903082. [With his *Fantasies, op. 116, Intermezzos, op. 117,* and *Pieces, op. 118*].
- (Artur Rubinstein). See 3452.30

3452.24 * *Fantasies (7), op. 116.*
- (Richard Goode). *See 3452.26*
- (Evgeny Kissin). *See 3506.20*
- (Dezsö Ránki). *See 3452.23*

3452.25 * *Intermezzos (3), op. 117.*
- (Radu Lupu). *See 3452.29*
- (Ivo Pogorelich). Deutsche Grammophon: 437 460-2. [With his *Rhapsodies, op. 79* and selections from *Opp. 76 and 118*].
- (Dezsö Ránki). *See 3452.23*

3452.26 *Pieces (8), op. 76.*
- (Richard Goode). Elektra Nonesuch: 79154-2. [With his *Fantasies, op. 116* and *Pieces, op. 119*].
- (Stephen Bishop Kovacevich). *See 3452.23*

3452.27 * *Pieces (6), op. 118.*
- (Emanuel Ax). *See 3452.32*
- (Hélène Grimaud). *See 3452.30*
- (Radu Lupu). *See 3452.29*
- (Dezsö Ránki). *See 3452.23*

3452.28 * *Pieces (4), op. 119.*
- (Richard Goode). *See 3452.26*
- (Radu Lupu). *See 3452.29*

3452.29 *Rhapsodies (2), op. 79.*
- (Emanuel Ax). *See 3452.32*
- (Glenn Gould). *See 3452.23*
- (Radu Lupu). London: 417 599-2. [With his *Opp. 117, 118, and 119*].
- (Ivo Pogorelich). *See 3452.25*

3452.30 *Sonata no. 3, op. 5 in F minor.*
- (Hélène Grimaud). Denon: CO-79782. [With his *Pieces, op. 118*].
- (Artur Rubinstein). RCA: 5672-2. [With his *Ballades, op. 10*].

3452.31 *Variationen über ein Thema von Paganini (Variations on a theme of Paganini).* (Julius Katchen). *See 3452.2*

3452.32 *Variationen und Fuge über ein Thema von Händel (Variations and fugue on a theme of Handel).*
- (Emanuel Ax). Sony: SK 48046. [With his *Pieces, op. 118* and *Rhapsodies, op. 79*].
- (Julius Katchen). *See 3452.2*

VOCAL MUSIC

3452.33 *Alto rhapsody.* (Jessye Norman/Philadelphia Orchestra/Riccardo Muti). Philips: 426 253-2. [With his *Symphony no. 3*].

3452.34 ** *Deutsches Requiem (German Requiem)*
- (Monteverdi Choir/John Eliot Gardiner). Philips: 432 140-2.
- (Philharmonia Chorus and Orchestra/Otto Klemperer). EMI: 7 47238 2.

3452.35 * *Ernste Gesänge (Four serious songs), op. 121.* (Dietrich Fischer-Dieskau/Gerald Moore). Orfeo: 140201. [With his selected songs].

3452.36 *Liebeslieder waltzes.* (Barbara Bonney and others). EMI: CDC 7 55430 2.

3452.37 *Motets.* (Collegium Vocale/Philippe Herreweghe). Harmonia Mundi: 901122.

3452.38 *Songs. Selections.*
- (Elly Ameling/Rudolf Jansen). Hyperion: CDA66444.
- (Dietrich Fischer-Dieskau/Gerald Moore). *See 3452.35*
- (Jessye Norman/Daniel Barenboim). Deutsche Grammophon: 413 311-2.

3453 Bruch, Max, 1838–1920

3453.1 * *Concerto for violin and orchestra no. 1, op. 26 in G minor.*
- (Jascha Heifetz/New Symphony of London/Malcolm Sargent). RCA: 6214-2. [With his *Scottish fantasy* and Vieuxtemps, Henri: *Concerto for violin and orchestra no. 5*].
- (Itzhak Perlman/Concertgebouw/Bernard Haitink). *See 3492.3*

3453.2 *Kol nidre* [for violoncello and orchestra]. (Pablo Casals/London Symphony/Landon Ronald). *See 3464.3*

3453.3 *Schottische Fantasie (Scottish fantasy)* [for violin and orchestra]. *See 3453.1*

3454 Bruckner, Anton, 1824–1896

3454.1 *Motets.* (Stuttgart Chamber Choir/Frieder Bernius). Sony: SK 48037. [With his *Mass no. 2*].

3454.2 *Symphonies (9).* (Berlin Philharmonic/Bavarian Radio Symphony/Eugen Jochum). EMI: CZS 7 62935 2. 9CD set.

3454.3 ** *Symphony no. 4 in E♭ major ("Romantic").*
- (Vienna Philharmonic/Claudio Abbado) [1880 version]. Deutsche Grammophon: 431 719-2.
- (Frankfurt Radio Symphony/Elaihu Inbal) [1874 version]. Teldec: 8.42921.
- (Berlin Philharmonic/Herbert von Karajan) [1880 version]. Deutsche Grammophon: 415 277-2.

3454.4 * *Symphony no. 5 in B♭ major.* (Philharmonia Orchestra/Otto Klemperer). EMI: CDM 7 63612 2.

3454.5 * *Symphony no. 6 in A major.* (Bavarian Radio Symphony/Wolfgang Sawallisch). Orfeo: 241911.

3454.6 * *Symphony no. 7 in E major.*

- (Berlin Radio Symphony/Riccardo Chailly). London: 414 290-2.

- (Concertgebouw Orchestra/Bernard Haitink). Philips: 434 155-2.

3454.7 * *Symphony no. 8 in C minor.* (Vienna Philharmonic/Herbert von Karajan). Deutsche Grammophon: 427 611-2.

3454.8 * *Symphony no. 9 in D minor.* (Berlin Philharmonic/Herbert von Karajan). Deutsche Grammophon: 419 083-2.

3455   Chabrier, Emmanuel, 1841–1894

España. (New York Philharmonic/Leonard Bernstein). *See* 3532

3456   Chaminade, Cécile, 1857–1944

Piano music. Selections. (Enid Katahn). Gasparo: 247.

3457   Chausson, Ernest, 1855–1899. *Poème for violin and orchestra.*

- (Kyung-Wha Chung/Royal Philharmonic/Charles Dutoit). *See* 3504.6

- (Jascha Heifetz/RCA Symphony). *See* 3535

3458   Chopin, Frédéric, 1810–1849

3458.1 ** *Ballades (4).*

- (Vladimir Ashkenazy). London: 417 474-2. [With his *Scherzos*].

- (Murray Perahia). Sony: SK 64399. [With miscellaneous piano pieces].

- (Artur Rubinstein). RCA: RCD1-7156. [With his *Scherzos*].

3458.2   *Concerto for piano and orchestra no. 1, op. 11 in E minor.*

- (Martha Argerich/London Symphony/Claudio Abbado). Deutsche Grammophon: 415 061-2. [With Liszt, Franz: *Concerto no. 1*].

- (Murray Perahia/Israel Philharmonic/Zubin Mehta). Sony: SK 44922. [With his *Concerto no. 2*].

- (Artur Rubinstein/New Symphony Orchestra of London/Stanislaw Skrowaczewski). RCA: 5612-2. [With his *Concerto no. 2*].

- (Krystian Zimerman/Los Angeles Philharmonic/Carlo Maria Giulini). Deutsche Grammophon: 415 970-2. [With his *Concerto no. 2*].

3458.3 * *Concerto for piano and orchestra no. 2, op. 21 in F minor.*

- (Murray Perahia/Israel Philharmonic/Zubin Mehta). *See* 3458.2

- (Ivo Pogorelich/Chicago Symphony/Claudio Abbado). Deutsche Grammophon: 410 507-2.

- (Artur Rubinstein/Symphony of the Air/Alfred Wallenstein). *See* 3458.2

- (Krystian Zimerman/Los Angeles Philharmonic/Carlo Maria Giulini). *See* 3458.2

3458.4 ** *Etudes, opp. 10 and 25.*

- (Vladimir Ashkenazy). London: 414 127-2.

- (Maurizio Pollini). Deutsche Grammophon: 413 794-2.

3458.5 ** *Fantasy, op. 49 in F minor.*

- (Vladimir Ashkenazy). *See* 3458.13

- (Evgeny Kissin). RCA: 09026-60445-2. [With miscellaneous pieces for piano].

- (Murray Perahia). *See* 3458.6

3458.6 * *Impromptus (3), opp. 29, 36, and 51; and Fantasie-Impromptu, op. 66.*

- (Vladimir Ashkenazy). *See* 3458.11

- (Murray Perahia). Sony: MK 39708. [With his *Fantasy in F minor* and other pieces].

3458.7 * *Mazurkas.*

- (Vladimir Ashkenazy) [complete]. London: 417 584-2. 2CD set.

- (Emanuel Ax) [selections]. *See* 3458.12

3458.8 * *Nocturnes.*

- (Ivan Moravec). Elektra Nonesuch: 9 79233-2.

- (Artur Rubinstein). RCA: 5613-2.

3458.9 ** *Piano music* [miscellaneous pieces].

- (Vladimir Horowitz). RCA: 7752-2; 60376-2; 09026-60987-2. 3 CDs. [Album title: *Horowitz plays Chopin, vols. 1–3*].

- (Evgeny Kissin). *See* 3458.5 and 3458.14

- (Dinu Lipatti). *See* 3458.17

3458.10 * *Polonaises.*

- (Shura Cherkassky). Deutsche Grammophon: 429 516-2.

- (Artur Rubinstein). RCA: 5615-2.

3458.11 ** *Preludes.*

- (Martha Argerich). Deutsche Grammophon: 415 836-2.

- (Vladimir Ashkenazy). London: 417 476-2. [With his *Impromptus*].

- (Ivo Pogorelich). Deutsche Grammophon: 429 227-2.

- (Maurizio Pollini). Deutsche Grammophon: 413 796-2.

3458.12 * *Scherzos (4), opp. 20, 31, 39, and 54.*

- (Vladimir Ashkenazy). *See* 3458.1

- (Emanuel Ax). CBS: MK 44544. [With his *Mazurkas*].

- (Artur Rubinstein). *See* 3458.1

3458.13 * *Sonata for piano no. 2, op. 35 in B♭ minor.*

- (Vladimir Ashkenazy). London: 417 475-2. [With his *Sonata for piano no. 3* and *Fantasy in F minor*].

- (Van Cliburn). *See* 3458.14

- (Murray Perahia). CBS: MK 32780. [With his *Sonata for piano no. 3*].

3458.14 * *Sonata for piano no. 3, op. 58 in B minor.*

- (Vladimir Ashkenazy). *See* 3458.13

- (Van Cliburn). RCA: 09026-60417-2. [With his *Sonata for piano no. 2* and Liszt, Franz: *Piano pieces*].

- (Evgeny Kissin). RCA: 09026-62542-2. [With miscellaneous pieces for piano].

- (Murray Perahia). *See* 3458.13

3458.15 *Sonata for violoncello and piano, op. 65 in G minor.*

- (Jacqueline Du Pré/Daniel Barenboim). EMI: CDM 7 63184 2. [With Franck, César: *Sonata in A major; arranged for violoncello and piano*].

- (Mstislav Rostropovich/Martha Argerich). Deutsche Grammophon: 418 860-2. [With his *Polonaise brillante for violoncello and piano, op. 3* and Schumann, Robert: *Adagio and allegro, op. 70*].

3458.16 *Les sylphides* [ballet on piano pieces by Chopin, orchestrated by Alexander Glazunov].

- (Berlin Philharmonic/Herbert von Karajan). *See* 3495.2

- (Philadelphia Orchestra/Eugene Ormandy). Sony: SBK 46551. [With Delibes, Léo: *Coppélia suite* and *Sylvia suite;* Tchaikovsky, Peter Ilich: *Shchelkunchik*].

3458.17 * *Waltzes.*

- (Dinu Lipatti). EMI: CDH 7 69802 2. [With miscellaneous pieces for piano].

- (Artur Rubinstein). RCA: RCD1-5492.

3459 Cilèa, Francesco, 1860–1950

Adriana Lecouvreur [opera]. (Joan Sutherland/ Carlo Bergonzi/Leo Nucci/Welsh National Opera/ Richard Bonynge). London: 425 815-2. 2CD set.

3460 * Coleridge-Taylor, Samuel, 1875–1912

Scenes from The song of Hiawatha [cantata]. (Kenneth Alwyn). Argo: 430 356-2. 2CD set.

3461 Delibes, Léo, 1836–1891

3461.1 * *Coppélia* [suite from the ballet].

- (Berlin Philharmonic/Herbert von Karajan). *See* 3495.2

- (Philadelphia Orchestra/Eugene Ormandy). *See* 3458.16

3461.2 *Lakmé* [opera].

- (Joan Sutherland/Alain Vanzo/Gabriel Bacquier/ Monte Carlo Opera/Richard Bonynge). London: 425 485-2. 2CD set.

- (Mady Mesplé/Charles Burles/Roger Soyer/ Opéra-Comique Paris/Alain Lombard). EMI: 7 49430 2. 2CD set [complete opera]; EMI: 7 63447 2 [highlights].

3461.3 *Sylvia* [ballet suite]. (Philadelphia Orchestra/Eugene Ormandy). *See* 3458.16

3462 Donizetti, Gaetano, 1797–1848

3462.1 *Don Pasquale* [opera]. (Mirella Freni/Gösta Winbergh/Leo Nucci/Philharmonia Orchestra/ Riccardo Muti). EMI: CDS 7 47068 2. 2CD set.

3462.2 *L'elisir d'amore (Elixir of love)* [opera].

- (Joan Sutherland/Luciano Pavarotti/English Chamber Orchestra/Richard Bonynge). London: 414 461-2. 2CD set.

- (Kathleen Battle/Luciano Pavarotti/Metropolitan Opera/James Levine). Deutsche Grammophon: 429 744-2. 2CD set.

3462.3 *La fille du régiment (Daughter of the regiment)* [opera]. (Joan Sutherland/Luciano Pavarotti/Covent Garden/Richard Bonynge). London: 414 520-2. 2CD set.

3462.4 * *Lucia di Lammermoor* [opera]. (Joan Sutherland/Luciano Pavarotti/Covent Garden/ Richard Bonynge). London: 410 193-2. 3CD set [complete opera]; or London: 421 885-2 [highlights].

3463 Duparc, Henri, 1848–1933

Songs. Selections. See 3539

3464 Dvořák, Antonín, 1841–1904

3464.1 *Concerto for piano and orchestra, op. 33 in G minor.* (Rudolf Firkušný/Czech Philharmonic/Václav Neumann). RCA: 09026-60781-2. [With Janáček, Leoš: *Concertino* and *Capriccio*].

3464.2 *Concerto for violin and orchestra, op. 53 in A minor.*
- (Midori/New York Philharmonic/Zubin Mehta). CBS: MK 44923. [With his *Karneval* and *Romance for violin and orchestra*].
- (Isaac Stern/Philadelpha Orchestra/Eugene Ormandy). *See 3452.4*

3464.3 * *Concerto for violoncello and orchestra, op. 104 in B minor.*
- (Pablo Casals/Czech Philharmonic/George Szell). EMI: 7 63498 2. [With Elgar, Edward: *Concerto for violoncello and orchestra;* Bruch, Max: *Kol nidre*].
- (Yo-Yo Ma/Berlin Philharmonic/Lorin Maazel). CBS: MK 42206.
- (Mischa Maisky/Israel Philharmonic/Leonard Bernstein). Deutsche Grammophon: 427 347-2. [With Bloch, Ernest: *Schelomo*].
- (Mstislav Rostropovich/Berlin Philharmonic/Herbert von Karajan). Deutsche Grammophon: 413 819-2. [With Tchaikovsky, Peter Ilich: *Variations sur un thème rococo*].

3464.4 *Karneval (Carnival overture).* (Cleveland Orchestra/George Szell). *See 3464.2 or 3509.5*

3464.5 *Quartet for strings no. 9, op. 34 in D minor.* (American Quartet). Nonesuch: 79126-2. [With his *Quartet no. 10*].

3464.6 * *Quartet for strings no. 12, op. 96 in F major ("American").*
- (Alban Berg Quartet) EMI: CDC 7 54215 2. [With Smetana, Bedřich: *Quartet for strings no. 1*].
- (Emerson Quartet). Deutsche Grammophon: 429 723-2. [With Smetana, Bedřich: *Quartet for strings no. 1*].
- (Guarneri Quartet). Philips: 420 803-2. [With Smetana, Bedřich: *Quartet for strings no. 1*].
- (Juilliard Quartet). *See 3464.7*

3464.7 * *Quintet for piano and strings, op. 81 in A major.*
- (Rudolf Firkušný/Juilliard Quartet). Sony: SBK 48170. [With his *Quartet for strings no. 12*].
- (Menachem Pressler/Emerson Quartet). Deutsche Grammophon: 439 868-2. [With his *Quartet for piano and strings no. 2 in E♭ major, op. 87*].

3464.8 * *Serenade for string orchestra, op. 22 in E major.*
- (Berlin Philharmonic/Herbert von Karajan). *See 3519.15*
- (Academy of St. Martin-in-the-Fields/Neville Marriner). Philips: 400 020-2. [With his *Serenade for winds*].
- (Orpheus Chamber Orchestra). Deutsche Grammophon: 415 364-2. [With his *Serenade for winds*].

3464.9 *Serenade for winds, op. 44 in D minor.* *See 3464.8*

3464.10 *Slovanske tance (Slavonic dances). Selections.* (Cleveland Orchestra/George Szell). *See 3509.5*

3464.11 *Songs. Selections.* (Gabriela, Beňaćková-Cápová/Rudolf Firkušný). RCA: 09026-60823-2. [With songs by Leoš Janáček and Bohuslav Martinů].

3464.12 *Symphonic poems.* (Scottish National Orchestra/Neeme Järvi). Chandos: 8798/99. 2CD set; or Musical Heritage Society: 523031L. 2CD set.

3464.13 *Symphonies (9).* (Scottish National Orchestra/Neeme Järvi). Chandos: 9008/9013. 6CD set.

3464.14 * *Symphony no. 7, op. 70 in D minor.*
- (Cleveland Orchestra/Christoph von Dohnanyi). London: 421 082-2. 2CD set. [With his *Symphonies nos. 8–9*].
- (Czech Philharmonic/Václav Neumann). Supraphon: 11 0559-2. 2CD set. [With his *Symphonies nos. 8–9*].

3464.15 ** *Symphony no. 8, op. 88 in G major.*
- (Cleveland Orchestra/Christoph von Dohnanyi). *See 3464.14*
- (Czech Philharmonic/Václav Neumann). *See 3464.14*
- (Cleveland Orchestra/George Szell). CBS: MYK 38470.

3464.16 ** *Symphony no. 9, op. 95 in E minor ("From the new world").*
- (Cleveland Orchestra/Christoph von Dohnanyi). *See 3464.14*
- (Vienna Philharmonic/Herbert von Karajan). Deutsche Grammophon: 415 509-2. [With Smetana, Bedřich: *Vltava*].
- (Czech Philharmonic/Václav Neumann). *See 3464.14*

- (Cleveland Orchestra/George Szell). CBS: MYK 37763.

3464.17 * *Trio for piano and strings no. 4, op. 90 in E minor ("Dumky").*

- (Emanuel Ax/Young Uck Kim/Yo-Yo Ma). CBS: MY 44527. [With his *Trio for piano and strings no. 3 in F minor, op. 65*].

- (Borodin Trio). Chandos: 8445. [With Smetana, Bedřich: *Trio, op. 15*].

3465 Elgar, Edward, 1857–1934

3465.1 *Cockaigne overture.* (BBC Symphony/Andrew Davis). *See* 3465.8

3465.2 *Concerto for violoncello and orchestra, op. 85 in E minor.*

- (Pablo Casals/BBC Symphony/Adrian Boult). *See* 3464.3

- (Jacqueline Du Pré/London Symphony/John Barbirolli). EMI: CDC 7 47329 2. [With his *Sea pictures*].

3465.3 *The dream of Gerontius* [oratorio]. (London Symphony Chorus and Orchestra/Richard Hickox). Chandos: CHAN 8641/2. 2CD set.

3465.4 * *Falstaff* [symphonic study]. (Chicago Symphony/Georg Solti). *See* 3465.8

3465.5 *Introduction and allegro for string orchestra, op. 47.* (BBC Symphony/Andrew Davis). *See* 3465.8

3465.6 *Pomp and circumstance, op. 39.* (Royal Philharmonic/André Previn). *See* 3465.8

3465.7 *Serenade for string orchestra, op. 20 in E minor.* (BBC Symphony/Andrew Davis). *See* 3465.8

3465.8 ** *Variations on an original theme ("Enigma variations")* [for orchestra].

- (BBC Symphony/Andrew Davis). Teldec: 9031-73279-2. [With his *Introduction and allegro; Serenade for string orchestra;* and *Cockaigne overture*].

- (Royal Philharmonic/André Previn). Philips: 416 813-2. [With his *Pomp and circumstance*].

- (Chicago Symphony/Georg Solti). London: 425 155-2. [With his *Falstaff*].

3466 Farrenc, Jean-Louise Dumont, 1804–1875

Quintets (2) for piano and strings, opp. 30 and 31. (Linos Ensemble). CPO: 999 194-2.

3467 Fauré, Gabriel, 1845–1924

3467.1 *Ballade for piano and orchestra, op. 19.* (Louis Lortie/London Symphony/Raphael Frühbeck de Burgos). *See* 3617.4

3467.2 * *Barcarolles (13) for piano.*

- (Jean-Philippe Collard). EMI: 1113282.

- (Paul Crossley). CRD: 3422.

3467.3 *La bonne chanson.*

- (Barbara Hendricks/Michel Dalberto). EMI: CDC 7 49841 2. [With his selected songs].

- (Gérard Souzay/Dalton Baldwin). *See* 3539

3467.4 *Dolly* [suite].

- (Katia and Marielle Labèque) [original version for two pianos]. *See* 3448.3

- (Boston Symphony/Seiji Ozawa) [orchestration by the composer]. *See* 3467.7

3467.5 * *Nocturnes (13) for piano.*

- (Jean-Phillipe Collard). EMI: CMS 7 69149 2. 2CD set. [With his *Theme and variations; Ballade, op. 19;* and *Preludes, op. 103*].

- (Pascal Rogé). London: 425 606-2. 2CD set.

3467.6 *Pavane for orchestra, op. 50.* (Boston Symphony/Seiji Ozawa). *See* 3467.7

3467.7 * *Pelléas et Mélisande* [suite for orchestra]. (Boston Symphony/Seiji Ozawa). Deutsche Grammophon: 423 089-2. [With his *Pavane; Dolly suite;* and other works].

3467.8 *Quartet for strings, op. 121.* (Parrenin Quartet). [Series: Chamber music, vol. 2]. EMI: CMS 7 62548 2. 2CD set. [With his *Quartets for piano and strings* and *Quintets for piano and strings*].

3467.9 * *Quartets (2) for piano and strings, opp. 15 and 45.*

- (Jean-Phillipe Collard/Parrenin Quartet). *See* 3467.8

- (Nash Ensemble). CRD: 3403.

3467.10 * *Quintets (2) for piano and strings, opp. 89 and 115.* (Jean-Phillipe Collard/Parrenin Quartet). *See* 3467.8

3467.11 ** *Requiem.*

- (Monteverdi Choir/John Eliot Gardiner). Philips: 438 149-2. [With short choral works by Gabriel Fauré, Camille Saint-Saëns, Claude Debussy, and Maurice Ravel].

- (Ambrosian Singers/Michel Legrand). Teldec: 4509-90879-2. [With Duruflé, Maurice: *Requiem*].

- (Cambridge Singers/John Rutter). Collegium: 109. [With his *Ave verum corpus; Tantum ergo; Ave Maria; Maria, mater gratiae; Cantique de Jean Racine;* and *Messe basse*].

3467.12 *Sicilienne for violoncello and piano.* (Steven Isserlis/Pascal Devoyon). Hyperion: CDA66235. [With his *Sonata no. 2 for violoncello and piano* and other short works for violoncello and piano].

3467.13 *Songs. Selections.* (Barbara Hendricks/ Dalton Baldwin). *See 3467.3*

3467.14 *Violin and piano music.* (Augustin Dumay/Jean-Philippe Collard). [Series: Chamber music, vol. 1]. EMI: CMS 7 62545 2. 2CD set. [With his *Violoncello and piano music*].

3467.15 *Violoncello and piano music.* (Frédéric Lodéon/Jean-Philippe Collard). *See 3467.14*

3468 Field, John, 1782–1837

Nocturnes for piano. Selections. (John O'Conor). Telarc: 80199.

3469 Franck, César, 1822–1890

3469.1 *Organ music.*
- (Michael Murray). Telarc: 80234. 2CD set. [Album title: *Complete masterworks for organ*].
- (Anthony Newman). Newport: 60060/61. 2CD set. [Album title: *Complete organ music, vols. 1–2*].

3469.2 ** *Sonata for violin and piano in A major.*
- (Kyung-Wha Chung/Radu Lupu). London: 421 154-2. [With Debussy, Claude: *Sonata for violin and piano* and *Sonata for flute, viola, and harp*; Ravel, Maurice: *Introduction and allegro*].
- (Itzhak Perlman/Vladimir Ashkenazy). London: 414 128-2. [With Brahms, Johannes: *Trio for horn, violin, and piano*].

3469.3 * *Symphony in D minor.*
- (Concertgebouw Orchestra/Riccardo Chailly). London: 417 487-2. [With his *Variations symphoniques*].
- (Montreal Symphony/Charles Dutoit). London: 430 278-2. [With Indy, Vincent d': *Symphonie sur un chant montagnard français*].
- (New York Philharmonic/Kurt Masur). Teldec: 9031-74863-2. [With his *Eolides*].
- (Boston Symphony/Seiji Ozawa). Deutsche Grammophon: 437 827-2. [With Poulenc, Francis: *Concerto for organ and string orchestra*].

3469.4 *Variations symphoniques (Symphonic variations)* [for piano and orchestra]. (Jorge Bolet/Concertgebouw Orchestra/Riccardo Chailly). *See 3469.3*

3470 Giordano, Umberto, 1867–1948

Andrea Chénier [opera]. (Monserrat Caballé/ Luciano Pavarotti/National Philharmonic/Riccardo Chailly). London: 410 117-2. 2CD set.

3471 * Giuliani, Mauro, 1781–1829

Guitar music. Selections. (David Starobin). Bridge: 9029. *See also 3496.3*

3472 Glazunov, Aleksandr Konstantinovich, 1865–1936

3472.1 *Concerto for saxophone and orchestra, op. 109 in E♭ major.* (John Harle/Academy of St. Martin-in-the-Fields/Neville Marriner). *See 3667*

3472.2 * *Concerto for violin and orchestra, op. 82 in A minor.*
- (Itzhak Perlman/Israel Philharmonic/Zubin Mehta). *See 3636.2*
- (Oscar Shumsky/Scottish National Orchestra/ Neeme Järvi). *See 3472.4*

3472.3 *Quartet for saxophones, op. 109.* (Berlin Saxophone Quartet). *See 3662*

3472.4 *Vremena goda (The seasons)* [ballet].
- (Royal Philharmonic/Vladimir Ashkenazy). *See 3519.16*
- (Scottish National Orchestra/Neeme Järvi). Chandos: 8596. [With his *Concerto for violin and orchestra*].

3473 Glinka, Mikhail Ivanovich, 1804–1857

3473.1 *Capriccio brillante (Jota aragonesa)* [for orchestra]. (NBC Symphony/Arturo Toscanini). *See 3530*

3473.2 * *Ruslan i Liudmila (Russlan and Ludmilla) overture.* (London Symphony/Georg Solti). *See 3533*

3473.3 *Trio pathétique.* (Borodin Trio). *See 3440*

3474 Gottschalk, Louis Moreau, 1829–1869

3474.1 *Piano music. Selections.*
- (Eugene List). *See 3474.2*
- (Lambert Orkis). Smithsonian: ND 033.

3474.2 *Symphony no. 1 ("A night in the tropics").*
- (Syracuse Symphony/Christopher Keene). *See 3479*
- (Eugene List/Utah Symphony/Maurice Abravanel). Vanguard: 72026. [Album title: *The world of Louis Moreau Gottschalk*. With his *Grand tarantelle for piano and orchestra* and pieces for solo piano].

3475 Gounod, Charles, 1818–1893

3475.1 *Faust* [opera]. (Mirella Freni/Plácido Domingo/Nicolai Ghiaurov/Paris Opera/Georges Prêtre). EMI: CDS 7 47493 8. 2CD set [complete opera]; EMI: CDS 7 63090 2 [highlights].

3475.2 *Roméo et Juliette (Romeo and Juliet)* [opera]. (Catherine Malfitano/Alfredo Kraus/José van Dam/Capitole de Toulouse Orchestra/Michel Plasson). EMI: 1732058. 3CD set.

3476 Granados, Enrique, 1867–1916

3476.1 *Piano music. Selections.*

- (Alicia de Larrocha). RCA: 60408-2. [*Goyescas* and other works].

- (Alicia de Larrocha). EMI: CDM 7 64529 2. [*Danzas españolas* and other works].

3476.2 *Vocal music. Selections.* (Victoria de los Ángeles). *See* 3673

3477 Grieg, Edvard, 1843–1907

3477.1 ** *Concerto for piano and orchestra, op. 16 in A minor.*

- (Murray Perahia/Bavarian Radio Symphony/ Colin Davis). CBS: MK 44899. [With Schumann, Robert: *Concerto for piano and orchestra*].

- (Artur Rubinstein/Philadelphia Orchestra/Eugene Ormandy). RCA: 09026-60897-2. [With his *Ballade* and selected *Lyric pieces* for solo piano].

- (Krystian Zimerman/Berlin Philharmonic/ Herbert von Karajan). *See* 3508.1

3477.2 *Fra Holbergs tid (Holberg suite).* (Orpheus Chamber Orchestra). Deutsche Grammophon: 423 060-2. [With his *Elegiac melodies*; and Tchaikovsky, Peter Ilich: *Serenade for string orchestra*].

3477.3 * *Peer Gynt. Selections.*

- (Gothenburg Symphony/Neeme Järvi). Deutsche Grammophon: 427 807-2. [With *Lyric suite, op. 55* and *Three pieces from Sigurd Jorsalfar*].

- (Academy of St. Martin-in-the-Fields/Neville Marriner). EMI: 7 47003 2.

3477.4 * *Piano music. Selections.*

- (Emil Gilels). Deutsche Grammophon: 419 749-2.

- (Cyprien Katsaris). Teldec: 8.42925.

- (Artur Rubinstein). *See* 3477.1

3478 Halévy, Fromtental, 1799–1862

La juive [opera]. (Julia Varady/José Carreras/Ferruccio Furlanetto/Philharmonia Orchestra/Antonio de Almeida). Philips: 420 190-2. 3CD set.

3479 Heinrich, Anthony Philip, 1781–1861

The ornitholological combat of kings. (Syracuse Symphony/Christopher Keene). New World: 80208-2. [With Gottschalk, Louis Moreau: *Night in the tropics*].

3480 Hensel, Fanny Mendelssohn, 1805–1847

3480.1 *Das Jahr* [suite for piano]. (Lina Serbescu). CPO: 999 013-2.

3480.2 *Lieder. Selections.* (Donna Brown/François Tillard). Opus 111: 30–71. [With her *Trio for piano and strings*].

3480.3 *Piano music. Selections.* (Lina Serbescu). CPO: 999 015-2. [*Sonatas in E major, C minor, and G minor*, plus selected *Songs without words*]. *See also* 3480.1

3480.4 * *Trio for piano and strings, op. 11 in D major.*

- (Dartington Piano Trio). *See* 3507.4

- (Trio Brentano). *See* 3480.2

3481 * Humperdinck, Engelbert, 1854–1921

Hänsel und Gretel (Hansel and Gretel) [opera]. (Anne Sofie von Otter/Barbara Bonney/Bavarian Radio Symphony/Jeffrey Tate). Angel: 7 54022 2. 2CD set [complete opera]; Angel: 7 54327 2 [highlights].

3482 Indy, Vincent d', 1851–1931

Symphonie sur un chant montagnard français (Symphony on a French mountain air), for piano and orchestra. (Jean-Yves Thibaudet/Montreal Symphony/Charles Dutoit). *See* 3469.3

3483 Ippolitov-Ivanov, Mikhail Mikhailovich, 1859–1935

Kavkazskie eskizy (Caucasian sketches) [for orchestra]. (Sydney Symphony/Christopher Lyndon Gee). HK Marco Polo: 8.220369.

3484 Lalo, Edouard, 1823–1892

3484.1 *Concerto for violoncello and orchestra in D minor.* (Leonard Rose/Philadelphia Orchestra/ Eugene Ormandy). Sony: SBK 48278. [With Tchaikovsky, Peter Ilich: *Variations sur un thème rococo*; Bloch, Ernest: *Schelomo*; Fauré, Gabriel: *Élégie*].

3484.2 * *Symphonie espagnole* [for violin and orchestra].

- (Jascha Heifetz/RCA Symphony/William Steinberg). *See* 3535

- (Shlomo Mintz/Israel Philharmonic/Zubin Mehta). Deutsche Grammophon: 427 676-2. [With Vieuxtemps, Henri: *Concerto for violin and orchestra no. 5;* Saint-Saëns, Camille: *Introduction and rondo capriccioso*].

3485 * Lehár, Franz, 1870–1948

Die lustige Witwe (The merry widow) [operetta].

- (Elizabeth Harwood/Teresa Stratas/Werner Hollweg/Berlin Philharmonic/Herbert von Karajan). Deutsche Grammophon: 435 713-2. 2CD set [complete, in German].

- (Elisabeth Schwarzkopf/Hanny Steffek/Nicolai Gedda/Philharmonia Orchestra/Lovro von Matacic). EMI: CDS 7 47178 2. 2CD set [complete, in German].

- (Beverly Sills/New York City Opera/Julius Rudel). Angel: CDC 7 47585 2 [highlights, in English].

3486 ** Leoncavallo, Ruggiero, 1858–1919

Pagliacci [opera].

- (Luciano Pavarotti/Mirella Freni/Ingvar Wixell/National Philharmonic/Giuseppe Patané). *See* 3490

- (Plácido Domingo/Montserrat Caballé/Sherrill Milnes/London Symphony/Nello Santi). RCA: 60865-2.

3487 Liszt, Franz, 1811–1886

3487.1 *Années de pèlerinage (Pilgrimage years)* [three sets for piano].
- (Alfred Brendel) [Year 1]. Philips: 420 202-2.
- (Louis Lortie) [Year 2]. Chandos: CHAN 8900.
- (Zoltán Kocsis) [Year 3]. Philips: 420 174-2.

3487.2 * *Concerto for piano and orchestra no. 1 in E♭ major.*
- (Martha Argerich/London Symphony/Claudio Abbado). *See* 3458.2
- (Van Cliburn/Philadelphia Orchestra/Eugene Ormandy). RCA: 7834-2-RG. [With his *Concerto no. 2*].
- (Jean-Yves Thibaudet/Montreal Symphony/Charles Dutoit). London: 433 075-2. [With his *Concerto no. 2; Hungarian fantasy;* and *Totentanz*].
- (Krystian Zimerman/Boston Symphony/Seiji Ozawa). Deutsche Grammophon: 423 571-2. [With his *Concerto no. 2* and *Totentanz*].

3487.3 ** *Concerto for piano and orchestra no. 2 in A major. See* 3487.2

3487.4 *Episoden aus Lenau's Faust. Tanz in der Dorfschenke (Mephisto waltz no. 1)* [for orchestra]. *See* 3487.8

3487.5 * *Etudes d'execution transcendante (Transcendental etudes)* [for piano]. (Jorg Bolet). London: 414 601-2.

3487.6 *Faust-Symphonie* [for tenor, chorus, and orchestra].
- (Siegfried Jerusalem/Chicago Symphony/Georg Solti). London: 417 399-2.
- (Kenneth Riegel/Boston Symphony/Leonard Bernstein). Deutsche Grammophon: 431 470-2.

3487.7 ** *Piano music. Selections.*
- (Dag Achatz). Bis: 244. [Performed on Liszt's Chickering piano. *Hungarian rhapsody no. 2; Ballade no. 2; Jeux d'eau à la Villa d'Este; Nuages gris; La lugubre gondola; etc.*].
- (Claudio Arrau). London: 411 055-2. [*Dante sonata; Funérailles; etc.*].
- (Jorg Bolet). London: 425 689-2. [*Liebestraum no. 3; Au bord d'une source; Sonetto 104 del Petrarca; Jeux d'eau à la Villa d'Este; Gnomenreigen; etc.*].
- (Evgeny Kissin). *See* 3506.20
- (Andre Watts). EMI: CDC 7 47380 2. [*Au lac de Wallenstadt; Hungarian rhapsody no. 13; Jeux d'eau à la Villa d'Este; Il penseroso; Paganini etudes*].

See also 3487.1, 3487.5, 3487.10, and 3508.23

3487.8 *Les préludes* [symphonic poem].
- (New York Philharmonic/Leonard Bernstein). CBS: MYK 37772. [With his *Hungarian rhapsodies nos. 1 and 2* and *Mephisto waltz no. 1*].
- (Berlin Philharmonic/Herbert von Karajan). Deutsche Grammophon: 415 967-2. 2CD set. [With his *Mephisto waltz no. 1; Hungarian fantasy; Mazeppa; Tasso; Hungarian rhapsodies nos. 2 and 4*].

3487.9 *Rapsodies hongroises (Hungarian rhapsodies). Selections. See* 3487.8

3487.10 * *Sonata for piano in B minor.*
- (Emanuel Ax). Sony: SK 48484. [With his *Aida paraphrase, Rigoletto paraphrase,* and *Vallée d'Obermann*].
- (Alfred Brendel). Philips: 434 078-2. [With his *Funérailles, Nuages gris,* and other short works].

- (Vladimir Horowitz). RCA: 5935-2-RC. [With his *Ballade no. 2, Consolation no. 3, Funérailles,* and *Mephisto waltz no. 1*].
- (Maurizio Pollini). Deutsche Grammophon: 427 322-2. [With his late piano works].

3487.11 *Totentanz* [for piano and orchestra]. (Krystian Zimerman/Boston Symphony/Seiji Ozawa). *See* 3487.2

3488 Loeffler, Charles Martin, 1861-1935

Rhapsodies for oboe, viola, and piano. (John Mack/Abraham Skernick/Eunice Podis). *See* 3437

3489 MacDowell, Edward, 1860–1908

3489.1 *Concerto for piano and orchestra no. 1, op. 15 in A minor.* (Donna Amato/London Philharmonic/Paul Freeman). Olympia: OCD 353. [With his *Concerto for piano and orchestra no. 2, op. 23 in D minor*].

3489.2 *Piano music. Selections.* (Constance Keene). Protone: 2202/3. 2CD set. [*Sonatas 1–4; To a wild rose; etc.*]

3490 ** Mascagni, Pietro, 1863–1945

Cavalleria rusticana [opera].

- (Julia Varady/Luciano Pavarotti/National Philharmonic/Gianandrea Gavazzeni). London: 414 590-2. 2CD set. [With Leoncavallo, Ruggiero: *Pagliacci*].
- (Agnes Baltsa/Plácido Domingo/Philharmonia Orchestra/Giuseppe Sinopoli). Deutsche Grammophon: 429 568-2.

3491 Massenet, Jules, 1842–1912

3491.1 *Manon* [opera].

- (Victoria de Los Angeles/Henri Legay/Michel Dens/Paris Opéra-Comique/Pierre Monteux). EMI: 7 63549 2. 3CD set.
- (Beverly Sills/Nicolai Gedda/Gérard Souzay/New Philharmonia Orchestra/Julius Rudel). EMI: 7 69831 2. 3CD set.

3491.2 *Werther* [opera]. (Victoria de los Angeles/Nicolai Gedda/Jean-Christophe Benoit/Paris Orchestra/Georges Prêtre). EMI: CDM 7 63973 2. 2CD set.

3492 Mendelssohn-Bartholdy, Felix, 1809–1847

3492.1 *Concerto for piano and orchestra no. 1, op. 25 in G minor.*

- (Cyprien Katsaris/Leipzig Gewandhaus Orchestra/Kurt Masur). Teldec: 75860. [With his *Concerto for piano and orchestra no. 2*].

- (Murray Perahia/Academy of St. Martin-in-the-Fields/Neville Marriner). CBS: 42401. [With his *Concerto for piano and orchestra no. 2*; plus *Prelude and fugue, op. 35 no. 1; Variations serieuses,* and *Rondo capriccioso* for solo piano].

3492.2 *Concerto for piano and orchestra no. 2, op. 40 in D minor. See* 3492.1

3492.3 ** *Concerto for violin and orchestra in E minor, op. 64.*

- (Jascha Heifetz/Boston Symphony/Charles Munch). *See* 3519.3
- (Itzhak Perlman/Concertgebouw/Bernard Haitink). EMI: 7 47074 2. [With Bruch, Max: *Concerto for violin and orchestra*].
- (Pinchas Zukerman/St. Paul Chamber Orchestra). Philips: 412 212-2. [With his *Octet*].

3492.4 *Elias (Elijah)* [oratorio]. (Academy of St. Martin-in-the-Fields/Neville Marriner). Philips: 432 984-2. [Sung in English].

3492.5 * *Hebriden (Hebrides or "Fingal's cave" overture). See* 3492.16

3492.6 * *Lieder ohne Worte (Songs without words)* [for piano—selections]. (Andras Schiff). London: 421 119-2.

3492.7 *Lobgesang (Symphony no. 2).* (Berlin Philharmonic/Herbert von Karajan). Deutsche Grammophon: 431 471-2.

3492.8 * *Octet for strings, op. 20 in E♭ major.*

- (Cleveland and Meliora Quartets). Telarc: 80142. [With his *Quartet for strings no. 2*].
- (Pinchas Zukerman/St. Paul Chamber Orchestra). *See* 3492.3

3492.9 *Piano music. Selections.* (Murray Perahia). *See* 3492.1

3492.10 *Quartet for strings no. 2, op. 13 in A major. See* 3492.8

3492.11 ** *Sommernachtstraum (A midsummer night's dream)* [incidental music].

- (Chicago Symphony/James Levine). Deutsche Grammophon: 415 137-2. [With Schubert, Franz: *Rosamunde*].
- (Philharmonia Orchestra/Neville Marriner). Philips: 411 106-2.

See also 3492.17

3492.12 *Sonatas (2) for violoncello and piano.* (Lynn Harrell/Bruno Canino). London: 430 198-2. [With his *Variations concertantes, op. 17*].

3492.13 *Symphonies for string orchestra. Selections.* (Orpheus Chamber Orchestra). Deutsche Grammophon: 437 528-2. [*Nos. 8–10*].

3492.14 *Symphony no. 1, op. 11 in C minor.* (Leipzig Gewandhaus Orchestra/Kurt Masur). Teldec: 44933. [With his *Symphony no. 5*].

3492.15 *Symphony no. 2, op. 52 in B♭ major. See* 3492.7

3492.16 ** *Symphony no. 3, op. 56 in A minor* ("Scottish").

- (Berlin Philharmonic/Herbert von Karajan). Deutsche Grammophon: 419 477-2. [With his *Symphony no. 4* and *Hebriden*].
- (Chicago Symphony/Georg Solti). London: 414 665-2. [With his *Symphony no. 4*].
- (Cleveland Orchestra/George Szell). Sony: 46536. [With his *Symphony no. 4* and *Hebriden*].

3492.17 ** *Symphony no. 4, op. 90 in A major* ("Italian").

- (London Symphony/Claudio Abbado). Deutsche Grammophon: 415 974-2. [With his *Symphony no. 5*].
- (Orchestra of the 18th Century/Frans Brüggen). Philips: 432 123-2. [With Schubert, Franz: *Symphony no. 5*].
- (Berlin Philharmonic/Herbert von Karajan). *See* 3492.16
- (Orchestra of the Age of Enlightenment/Charles Mackerras). Virgin: 90725. [With his *Sommernachtstraum overture*].
- (Chicago Symphony/Georg Solti). *See* 3492.16
- (Cleveland Orchestra/George Szell). *See* 3492.16

3492.18 *Symphony no. 5, op. 107 in D major* ("Reformation").

- (London Symphony/Claudio Abbado). *See* 3492.17
- (Leipzig Gewandhaus Orchestra/Kurt Masur). *See* 3492.14

3492.19 * *Trios (2) for piano and strings.* (Trio Fontenay). Teldec: 44947.

3493   Meyerbeer, Giacomo, 1791–1864

3493.1 *Les Huguenots* [opera]. (Joan Sutherland/Huguette Tourangeau/Gabriel Bacquier/Philharmonia Orchestra/Richard Bonynge). London: 430 549-2. 4CD set.

3493.2 *Le prophète* [opera]. (Marilyn Horne/Renata Scotto/James McCracken/Royal Philharmonic/Henry Lewis). CBS: 34340. 3CD set.

3494   Mussorgsky, Modest Petrovich, 1839–1881

3494.1 * *Boris Godunov* [opera].

- (Anatoly Kotcherga/Berlin Philharmonic/Claudio Abbado) [1872 version]. Sony: 58977. 3CD set.
- (Boris Christoff/Concerts du Conservatoire Orchestra/André Cluytens) [Rimsky-Korsakov version]. EMI: 7 47993 2.
- (Yevgueni Nesterenki/Bolshoi Opera Moscow/Mark Ermler) [Rimsky-Korsakov version]. Chant du Monde: 278 853/55. 3CD set.
- (Alexander Vedernikov/USSR TV and Radio Large Symphony/Vladimir Fedoseyev) [1872 version]. Philips: 412 281-2. 3CD set.
- (Ruggiero Raimondi/National Symphony/Mstislav Rostropovich) [1872 version]. Erato: 45418. 3CD set.

3494.2 * *Kartinki s vystavki (Pictures at an exhibition)* [original version for piano].

- (Vladimir Ashkenazy). London: 414 386-2. [With the version orchestrated by Maurice Ravel].
- (Vladimir Horowitz). RCA: 60449-2-RG. [With Tchaikovsky, Peter Ilich: *Concerto for piano and orchestra no. 1*].
- (Olli Mustonen). *See* 3443

3494.3 ** *Kartinki s vystavki (Pictures at an exhibtion)* [orchestrated by Maurice Ravel].

- (Philharmonia Orchestra/Vladimir Ashkenazy). *See* 3494.2
- (Philadelphia Orchestra/Riccardo Muti). Philips: 431 170-2. [With his *Nochna Lysoi gore*].
- (Chicago Symphony/Georg Solti). London: 417 754-2. [With Bartók, Béla: *Concerto for orchestra*].

3494.4 *Khovanshchina* [opera]. (Aage Haugland/Vladimir Atlantov/Vladimir Popov/Vienna State Opera/Claudio Abbado). Deutsche Grammophon: 429 758-2. 3CD set.

3494.5 * *Nochna Lysoi gore (Night on Bare Mountain)* [for orchestra].

- (London Symphony/Claudio Abbado) [original version]. RCA: 3988-2. [With *Khovanshchina prelude* and other short orchestral works].
- (Philadelphia Orchestra/Riccardo Muti) [Rimsky-Korsakov version]. *See* 3494.3
- (London Symphony/Georg Solti) [Rimsky-Korsakov version]. *See* 3533

3494.6 *Pesni i pliaski smerti (Songs and dances of death)*. (Dmitri Hvorostovsky/Koriv Orchestra/Valery Gergiev). Philips: 438 872-2.

3495 Offenbach, Jacques, 1819–1880

3495.1 * *Les contes d'Hoffmann (Tales of Hoffmann)* [opera].

- (Edita Gruberova/Plácido Domingo/James Morris/French National Orchestra/Seiji Ozawa). Deutsche Grammophon: 427 682-2. 2CD set.
- (Eva Lind/Francisco Araiza/Samuel Ramey/Staatskapelle Dresden/Jeffrey Tate). Philips: 422 374-2. 2CD set.

3495.2 *Gaité parisiènne* [ballet arranged and orchestrated by Manuel Rosenthal].

- (Boston Pops Orchestra/Arthur Fiedler). RCA: 5478-2.
- (Berlin Philharmonic/Herbert von Karajan). Deutsche Grammophon: 423 215-2. [With Chopin, Frédéric: *Les sylphides;* Delibes, Léo: *Coppélia*].

3495.3 * *Orphée aux enfers (Orpheus in the underworld)* [operetta]. (Mady Mesplé/Miche Senechal/Capitole de Toulouse Orchestra/Michel Plasson). EMI: 7 49647 2. 2CD set.

3496 Paganini, Nicolò, 1782–1840

3496.1 * *Caprices (24) for violin, op. 1.*

- (Midori). CBS: MK 44944.
- (Itzhak Perlman). EMI: CDC 7 47171 2.

3496.2 *Concerto for violin and orchestra no. 1, op. 6 in E♭ major (D major).*

- (Itzhak Perlman/Royal Philharmonic/Lawrence Foster). EMI: CDC 7 47101 2. [With Sarasate, Pablo de: *Carmen fantaisie*].
- (Gil Shaham/New York Philharmonic/Giuseppe Sinopoli). Deutsche Grammophon: 429 786-2. [With Saint-Saëns, Camille: *Concerto for violin and orchestra no. 3*].

3496.3 *Violin and guitar music. Selections.* (Itzhak Perlman/John Williams). CBS: MK 34508. [*Centone di sonate, op. 64, no. 1; Sonata no. 6, op. 3 in E minor; Sonata concertata in A major; Cantabile.* With Giuliani, Mauro: *Sonata for violin and guitar*].

3497 Paine, John Knowles, 1839–1906

Symphony no. 2, op. 34 in A major. (New York Philharmonic/Zubin Mehta). New World: 350-2.

3498 Ponchielli, Amilcare, 1834–1886

3498.1 * *Danza delle ore (Dance of the hours)* [ballet from the opera, La Gioconda]. (Philadelphia Orchestra/Eugene Ormandy). Sony: SBK 48159. [With Bizet, Georges: *L'Arlésienne suites 1–2; Carmen suites 1–2*].

3498.2 *La Gioconda* [opera]. (Montserrat Caballé/Luciano Pavarotti/National Philharmonic/Bruno Bartoletti). London: 414 349-2. 3CD set.

3499 Puccini, Giacomo, 1858–1924

3499.1 ** *La Bohème* [opera].

- (Mirella Freni/Luciano Pavarotti/Berlin Philharmonic/Herbert von Karajan). London: 421 049-2. 2CD set.
- (Renata Tebaldi/Carlo Bergonzi/Accademia di Santa Cecilia, Rome/Tullio Serafin). London: 425 534-2. 2CD set.

3499.2 *La fanciulla del West (The girl of the golden West)* [opera]. (Renata Tebaldi/Mario Del Monaco/Cornell MacNeil/Accademia di Santa Cecilia, Rome/Franco Capuana). London: 421 595-2. 2CD set.

3499.3 * *Madama Butterfly* [opera].

- (Maria Callas/Nicolai Gedda/La Scala/Herbert von Karajan). EMI: CDS 7 47959 2. 2CD set.
- (Victoria de los Angeles/Jussi Björling/Rome Opera/Gabriele Santini). EMI: CMS 7 63634 2. 2CD set.

3499.4 *Manon Lescaut* [opera]. (Mirella Freni/Luciano Pavarotti/Metropolitan Opera/James Levine). London: 440 200-2. 2CD set.

3499.5 ** *Tosca* [opera].

- (Montserrat Caballé/José Carreras/Ingvar Wixell/Covent Garden/Colin Davis). Philips: 412 885-2. 2CD set.
- (Maria Callas/Giuseppe Di Stefano/Tito Gobbi/La Scala/Victor De Sabata). EMI: CDS 7 47175 8. 2CD set.

3499.6 *Trittico* [3 one-act operas: *Il tabarro; Suor Angelica; Gianni Schicchi*]. (Mirella Freni/Leo Nucci/Juan Pons/Maggio Musicale Florence/Bruno Bartoletti). London: 436 261-2. 3CD set.

3499.7 * *Turandot* [opera]. (Birgit Nilsson/Renata Scotto/Franco Corelli/Rome Opera/Francesco Molinari-Pradelli). EMI: CMS 7 69327 2. 2CD set.

3500 Regondi, Giulio, 1822–1872

Guitar music and concertina music. Selections. (David Starobin/Douglas Rogers). Bridge: 9039; 9055. 2 CDs. [Album title: *The great Regondi, vols. 1–2*].

3501   Reinecke, Carl, 1824–1910

Sonata for flute and piano, op. 167 in E minor ("Undine"). (Susan Milan/Ian Brown). Chandos: CHAN 8823. [With Schubert, Franz: *Introduction et variations sur un thème original*; Martinů, Bohuslav: *Sonata no. 1 for flute and piano*].

3502   Rimsky-Korsakov, Nikolay, 1844–1908

3502.1 * *Antar (Symphony no. 2).* (Bergen Philharmonic/Dimitrii Kitaenko). Chandos: 9178. [1897 version. With his *Symphony no. 1* and *Ispanskoe kaprichchio*].

3502.2 *Ispanskoe kaprichchio (Capriccio espagnol)* [for orchestra]. See 3502.1

3502.3 *Sadko* [opera]. (Vladimir Galusin/Kirov Orchestra/Valery Gergiev). Philips: 422 138-2. 3CD set.

3502.4 ** *Shekherazada (Scheherazade)* [symphonic poem].

- Philharmonia Orchestra/Vladimir Ashkenazy). London: 417 301-2. [With his *Tsar Saltan suite* and *Flight of the bumblebee*].

- (Israel Philharmonic/Zubin Mehta). CBS: MDK 45652. [With his *Russian Easter overture*].

- (Philadelphia Orchestra/Riccardo Muti). EMI: CDC 7 47023 2.

3502.5 * *Skazka o tsare Saltane. Nu, teper, moi shmel (The flight of the bumblebee).* See 3502.4

3502.6 * *Suites for orchestra. Selections* (Scottish National Orchestra/Neeme Järvi). Chandos: 8327. [*Snow maiden; Christmas eve; Mlada; Invisible city of Kitezh; Coq d'or; Tale of Tsar Saltan*].

3502.7 *Svetlyi prazdnik (Russian Easter overture).* See 3502.4

3503   Rossini, Gioacchino, 1792–1868

3503.1 * *Arias. Selections.*

- (Cecilia Bartoli/Teatro La Fenice Orchestra/Ion Marin). London: 436 075-2.

- (Marilyn Horne/Royal Philharmonic/Henry Lewis). London: 421 306-2.

3503.2 ** *Il barbiere di Siviglia (The barber of Seville)* [opera].

- (Frank Lopardo/Kathleen Battle/Plácido Domingo/Chamber Orchestra of Europe/ Claudio Abbado). Deutsche Grammophon: 435 763-2. 2CD set.

- (Leo Nucci/Cecilia Bartoli/Teatro Comunale Bologna/Giuseppe Patanè). London: 425 520-2. 3CD set.

3503.3 * *La Cenerentola (Cinderella)* [opera]. (Cecilia Bartoli/William Matteuzzi/Teatro Comunale Bologna/Riccardo Chailly). London: 436 902-2. 2CD set.

3503.4 *Guillaume Tell (William Tell)* [opera]. (Montserrat Caballé/Nicolai Gedda/Gabriel Bacquier/Royal Philharmonic/Lamberto Gardelli). EMI: CMS 7 69951 2. 4CD set.

3503.5 *L'Italiana in Algeri (The Italian girl in Algiers)* [opera]. (Kathleen Battle/Marilyn Horne/ Ernesto Palacio/I Solisti Veneti/Claudio Scimone). Erato: 2292-45404-2. 2CD set.

3503.6 *Otello* [opera]. (Nucci Condo/José Carreras/Samuel Ramey/Philharmonia Orchestra/ Jesús López-Cobos). Philips: 432 256-2. 2CD set.

3503.7 ** *Overtures. Selections.*

- (Chamber Orchestra of Europe/Claudio Abbado). Deutsche Grammophon: 431 653-2. [*Barbiere di Siviglia; Guillaume Tell; Cenerentola; L'Italiana in Algieri; La gazza ladra; La scala di seta; Semiramide*].

- (London Classical Players/Roger Norrington). EMI: CDC 7 54091 2. [*La scala di seta; Il signor Bruschino; L'Italiana in Algieri; Il barbiere di Siviglia; La gazza ladra; Semiramide; Giullaume Tell*].

- (NBC Symphony/Arturo Toscanini). RCA: 60289-2. [*L'Italiana in Algieri; Il signor Bruschino; Il barbiere di Siviglia; La Cenerentola; La gazza ladra; Le siège de Corinthe; Semiramide; Guillaume Tell*].

3503.8 *Petite Messe solenelle.* (Combattimento/ David Mason). Meridian: 84133.

3503.9 *Sonatas (6) for strings.* (I Musici). Philips: 434 734-2.

3504   Saint-Saëns, Camille, 1835–1921

3504.1 ** *Carnaval des animaux (Carnival of the animals).*

- (Pascal Rogé/Christina Ortiz/Montreal Symphony/Charles Dutoit). See 3504.8

- (Katia and Marielle Labèque/Israel Philharmonic/Zubin Mehta). See 3615.10

3504.2 *Concerto for piano and orchestra no. 2, op. 22 in G minor.* (Cecile Licad/London Philharmonic/Michael Tilson Thomas). See 3504.4

3504.3 *Concerto for violin and orchestra no. 3, op. 61 in B minor.*

- (Cho-Liang Lin/Philharmonia Orchestra/ Michael Tilson Thomas). See 3504.4

- (Gil Shaham/New York Philharmonic/Giuseppe Sinopoli). *See 3496.2*

3504.4 *Concerto for violoncello and orchestra no. 1, op. 33 in A minor.* (Yo-Yo Ma/French National Orchestra/Lorin Maazel). CBS: MDK 46506. [With his *Concerto for piano and orchestra no. 2* and *Concerto for violin and orchestra no. 3*].

3504.5 *Danse macabre.*

- (New York Philharmonic/Leonard Bernstein). *See 3532*

- (Philadelphia Orchestra/Eugene Ormandy). *See 3504.8*

3504.6 * *Introduction and rondo capriccioso* [for violin and orchestra].

- (Kyung-Wha Chung/Royal Philharmonic/Charles Dutoit). [With his *Havanaise for violin and orchestra*; Chausson, Ernest: *Poème for violin and orchestra*; Ravel, Maurice: *Tzigane*].

- (Jascha Heifetz/RCA Symphony/William Steinberg). *See 3535*

- (Jascha Heifetz/London Philharmonic/John Barbirolli). *See 3528*

- (Shlomo Mintz/Israel Philharmonic/Zubin Mehta). *See 3484.2*

3504.7 *Samson et Dalila (Samson and Delilah)* [opera]. (Agnes Baltsa/José Carreras/Jonathan Summers/Bavarian Radio Orchestra/Colin Davis). Philips: 426 243-2. 2CD set.

3504.8 * *Symphony no. 3, op. 78 in C minor ("Organ symphony")*.

- (Peter Hurford/Montreal Symphony/Charles Dutoit). London: 430 720-2. [With his *Carnival of the animals*].

- (Boston Symphony/Charles Munch). RCA: 09026-61500-2. [With Debussy, Claude: *La mer*; Ibert, Jacques: *Escales*].

- (Philadelphia Orchestra/Eugene Ormandy). CBS: MBK 38920. [With his *Bacchanale from Samson and Delilah*; *Danse macabre*; *Swan*; and *Marche militaire française*].

3505 Sarasate, Pablo de, 1844–1908

3505.1 *Carmen fantaisie* [for violin and orchestra]. (Itzhak Perlman/Royal Philharmonic/Lawrence Foster). *See 3496.2*

3505.2 * *Zigeunerweisen* [for violin and orchestra].

- (Jascha Heifetz/RCA Symphony/William Steinberg). *See 3535*

- (Jascha Heifetz/London Symphony/John Barbirolli). *See 3528*

- (Gil Shaham/London Symphony/Lawrence Foster). *See 3528.*

3506 Schubert, Franz, 1797–1828

ORCHESTRAL MUSIC

3506.1 *Rosamunde* [incidental music].

- (Chamber Orchestra of Europe/Claudio Abbado). *See 3506.2*

- (Chicago Symphony/James Levine). *See 3492.11*

3506.2 *Symphonies* [nos. 1–6, 8–9—no. 7 does not exist]. (Chamber Orchestra of Europe/Claudio Abbado). Deutsche Grammophon: 423 651-2. 5CD set. [Includes his *Rosamunde, Grand duo for two pianos in C major, D. 812 (arranged for orchestra by Joseph Joachim)* and individual symphonies listed below].

3506.3 * *Symphony no. 4, D. 417 in C minor ("Tragic")*.

- (Chamber Orchestra of Europe/Claudio Abbado). Deutsche Grammophon: 423 653-2. [With his *Symphony no. 3*].

- (London Classical Players/Roger Norrington). EMI: CDC 7 54210 2. [With his *Symphony no. 6*].

3506.4 ** *Symphony no. 5, D. 485 in B♭ major.*

- (Chamber Orchestra of Europe/Claudio Abbado). Deutsche Grammophon: 423 654-2. [With his *Symphony no. 6*].

- (Orchestra of the 18th Century/Frans Brüggen). *See 3492.17*

- (London Classical Players/Roger Norrington). EMI: CDC 7 49968 2. [With his *Symphony no. 8*].

3506.5 * *Symphony no. 6, D. 589 in C major.*

- (Chamber Orchestra of Europe/Claudio Abbado). *See 3506.4*

- (London Classical Players/Roger Norrington). *See 3506.3*

3506.6 ** *Symphony no. 8, D. 759 in B minor ("Unfinished")*.

- (Chamber Orchestra of Europe/Claudio Abbado). Deutsche Grammophon: 423 655-2. [With his *Grand duo for two pianos, D. 812 in C major (arranged for orchestra by Joseph Joachim)*].

- (Berlin Philharmonic/Herbert von Karajan). Deutsche Grammophon: 423 219-2. [With his *Symphony no. 9*].

- (London Classical Players/Roger Norrington). *See 3506.4*

- (Cleveland Orchestra/George Szell). Sony: SBK 48268. [With his *Symphony no. 9*].

- (NBC Symphony/Arturo Toscanini). RCA: 60290-2-RG. [With his *Symphony no. 9*].

3506.7 ** *Symphony no. 9, D. 944 in C major* ("Great").

- (Chamber Orchestra of Europe/Claudio Abbado). Deutsche Grammophon: 423 656-2. [With his *Rosamunde overture*].

- (Orchestra of the 18th Century/Frans Brüggen). Philips: 439 006-2.

- (Berlin Philharmonic/Herbert von Karajan). *See 3506.6*

- (Cleveland Orchestra/George Szell). *See 3506.6*

- (NBC Symphony/Arturo Toscanini). *See 3506.6*

CHAMBER MUSIC

3506.8 *Introduction et variations sur un thème original ("Trockne Blumen" variations)* [for flute and piano]. (Susan Milan/Ian Brown). *See 3501*

3506.9 * *Octet for winds and strings, D. 803 in F major.*

- (Academy of St. Martin-in-the-Fields Chamber Ensemble). Chandos: 8585.

- (Boston Symphony Chamber Players). Nonesuch: 9 79046-2.

- (Hausmusik). EMI: CDC 7 54118 2.

3506.10 *Quartet for strings no. 12, D. 703 in C minor ("Quartettsatz")*. (Juilliard Quartet). *See 3506.12*

3506.11 *Quartet for strings no. 13, D. 804 in A minor ("Rosamunde")*.

- (Alban Berg Quartet). *See 3506.12*

- (Tokyo Quartet). RCA: 7750-2-RC. [With his *Quartet no. 9*].

3506.12 * *Quartet for strings no. 14, D. 810 in D minor ("Death and the maiden")*.

- (Alban Berg Quartet). EMI: CDC 7 47333 2. [With his *Quartet no. 13*].

- (Emerson Quartet). *See 3400.9*

- (Juilliard Quartet). CBS: MBK 42602. [With his *Quartet no. 12*].

- (Talich Quartet). Calliope: 9234. [With his *Quartet no. 10*].

3506.13 *Quartet for strings no. 15, D. 887 in G major.* (Tokyo Quartet). RCA: 60199-2-RC.

3506.14 ** *Quintet for piano and strings in A major, D. 667 ("Trout quintet")*.

- (Alfred Brendel/Cleveland Quartet). Philips: 400 078-2.

- (Hausmusik). EMI: CDC 7 54264 2. [With Hummel, Johann Nepomuk: *Quintet for piano and strings in E♭ major*].

3506.15 * *Quintet for strings, D. 956 in C major.*

- (Alban Berg Quartet/Heinrich Schiff). EMI: CDC 7 47018 2.

- (Cleveland Quartet/Yo-Yo Ma). CBS: MK 39134.

3506.16 *Sonata for arpeggione and piano, D. 821 in A minor.*

- (Mischa Maisky/Martha Argerich). Philips: 412 230-2. [With Schumann, Robert: *Fantasiestücke, op. 73* and *Stücke im Volkston*].

- (Mstislav Rostropovich/Benjamin Britten). London: 417 833-2. [With Schumann, Robert: *Stücke im Volkston*; Debussy, Claude: *Sonata for violoncello and piano*].

3506.17 * *Trio for piano and strings no. 1, D. 898 in B♭ major.*

- (Beaux Arts Trio). Philips: 412 260-2. 2CD set. [With his *Trio no. 2, Notturno for piano, violin, and violoncello, D. 897* and other works].

- (Artur Rubinstein/Jascha Heifetz/Emanuel Feuermann). *See 3400.19*

3506.18 * *Trio for piano and strings no. 2, D. 929 in E♭ major.*

- (Beaux Arts Trio). *See 3506.17*

- (Borodin Trio). Chandos: 8324.

3506.19 *Violin and piano music.* (Isaac Stern/Daniel Barenboim). Sony: S2K 44504. 2CD set.

PIANO MUSIC

3506.20 ** *Fantasy, D. 760 in C major ("Wanderer fantasy")*.

- (Alfred Brendel). *See 3506.30*

- (Evgeny Kissin). Deutsche Grammophon: 435 028-2. [With Brahms, Johannes: *Fantasies, op. 116*; Liszt, Franz: *Hungarian rhapsody no. 12* and *Schubert song transcriptions*].

- (Murray Perahia). CBS: MK 42124. [With Schumann, Robert: *Fantasy, op. 17*].

- (André Watts). *See 3506.23*

3506.21 * *Impromptus, D. 899 and 935.*

- (Alfred Brendel). Philips: 422 237-2.

- (Murray Perahia). CBS: MK 37291.

  See also 3506.25

3506.22 *Moments musicaux, D. 780.*
- (Claudio Arrau). *See 3506.27*
- (Alfred Brendel). *See 3506.28*

3506.23 *Sonata, D. 664 in A major.*
- (Alfred Brendel). Philips: 410 605-2. [With his *Sonata, D. 537 in A minor*].
- (André Watts). EMI: CDC 7 54153 2. [With his *Fantasy, D. 760* and other works].

3506.24 *Sonata, D. 784 in A minor.*
- (Alfred Brendel). *See 3506.26*
- (Radu Lupu). *See 3506.29*

3506.25 *Sonata, D. 845 in A minor.*
- (Alfred Brendel). Philips: 422 075-2. [With his *Impromptus, D. 946*].
- (Richard Goode). Elektra Nonesuch: 79271-2. [With his *Sonata, D. 850 in D major*].
- (Radu Lupu). London: 417 640-2. [With his *Sonata, D. 894 in G major*].

3506.26 *Sonata, D. 850 in D major.*
- (Alfred Brendel). Philips: 422 063-2. [With his *Sonata, D. 784 in A minor*].
- (Richard Goode). *See 3506.25*

3506.27 *Sonata, D. 894 in G major.*
- (Claudio Arrau). Philips: 432 987-2. [With his *Moments musicaux, D. 780*].
- (Alfred Brendel). Philips: 422 340-2. [With his *Sonata, D. 840 in C major*].
- (Radu Lupu). *See 3506.25*

3506.28 * *Sonata, D. 958 in C minor.*
- (Alfred Brendel). Philips: 422 076-2. [With his *Moments musicaux, D. 780*].
- (Richard Goode). Elektra Nonesuch: 79064-2. [With his *Ländler, D. 790*].
- (Maurizio Pollini). Deutsche Grammophon: 419 229-2. 2CD set. [With his *Sonata, D. 959 in A major* and *Sonata, D. 960 in B♭ major*].

3506.29 * *Sonata, D. 959 in A major.*
- (Alfred Brendel). Philips: 422 229-2. [With his *German dances, D. 783* and other short works].
- (Richard Goode). Elektra Nonesuch: 78028-2.
- (Radu Lupu). London: 425 033-2. [With his *Sonata, D. 784 in A minor* and *Sonata, D. 157 in E major*].
- (Murray Perahia). *See 3508.24*
- (Maurizio Pollini). *See 3506.28*

3506.30 ** *Sonata, D. 960 in B♭ major.*
- (Alfred Brendel). Philips: 422 062-2. [With his *Fantasy, D. 760*].
- (Richard Goode). Elektra Nonesuch: 79124-2.
- (Maurizio Pollini). *See 3506.28*

VOCAL MUSIC

3506.31 *Fierrabras* [opera]. (Robert Holl/Karita Mattila/Thomas Hampson/Chamber Orchestra of Europe/Claudio Abbado). Deutsche Grammophon: 427 341-2. 2CD set.

3506.32 *Der Hirt auf dem Felsen (The shepherd on the rock).* (Elly Ameling/Hans Deinzer/Jörg Demus). *See 3506.36*

3506.33 *Mass no. 5, D. 678 in A♭ major.*
- (Wolfgang Sawallisch). EMI: CDM 7 69222 2. [With his *Mass no. 2*].
- (Bruno Weil). Sony: SK 53984. [With his *Deutsche Messe*].

3506.34 * *Die schöne Müllerin* [song cycle].
- (Dietrich Fischer-Dieskau/Gerald Moore). EMI: CDMC 7 63559 2. 3CD set. [With his *Winterreise, Schwanengesang,* and selected songs].
- (Peter Schreier/András Schiff). London: 430 414-2.

3506.35 * *Schwanengesang* [song cycle].
- (Brigitte Fassbaender/Aribert Reimann). Deutsche Grammophon: 429 766-2.
- (Dietrich Fischer-Dieskau/Gerald Moore). *See 3506.34*

3506.36 ** *Songs. Selections.*
- (Elly Ameling/Jörg Demus). Deutsche Harmonia Mundi: 77085-2-RG. [Includes his *Der Hirt auf dem Felsen* and selected songs, plus Schumann, Robert: *Songs*].
- (Jan DeGaetani/Gilbert Kalish). *See 3529.5*
- (Dietrich Fischer-Dieskau/Gerald Moore). EMI: CDM 7 69503 2 [Album title: *21 Lieder*]; or EMI: CMS 7 63566 2. 2CD set.
- (Elisabeth Schwarzkopf/Edwin Fischer). EMI: CDH 7 64026 2.

3506.37 * *Winterreise* [song cycle].
- (Olav Bär/Geoffrey Parsons). EMI: CDC 7 47947 2.
- (Dietrich Fischer-Dieskau/Gerald Moore). *See 3506.34*
- (Peter Schreier/András Schiff). London: 436 122-2.

3507 Schumann, Clara, 1819–1896

3507.1 *Concerto for piano and orchestra, op. 7 in A minor.* (Veronica Jochum/Bamberg Symphony/Joseph Silverstein). Tudor: 788. [With her *Romances for violin and piano* and *Trio for piano and strings*].

3507.2 *Piano music. Selections.* (Konstanze Eickhorst). CPO: 999 132-2.

3507.3 *Romances for violin and piano, op. 22.*

- (Fabio Biondi/Luigi Di Ilio). *See* 3508.13

- (Joseph Silverstein/Veronica Jochum). *See* 3507.1

3507.4 * *Trio for piano and strings, op. 17 in G minor.*

- (Dartington Piano Trio). Hyperion: CDA66331. [With Hensel, Fanny Mendelssohn: *Trio for piano and strings, op. 11*].

- (Veronica Jochum/Joseph Silverstein/Colin Carr). *See* 3507.1

3508 Schumann, Robert, 1810–1856

ORCHESTRAL MUSIC

3508.1 ** *Concerto for piano and orchestra, op. 54 in A minor.*

- (Martha Argerich/Chamber Orchestra of Europe/Nikolaus Harnoncourt). Teldec: 90696-2. [With his *Concerto for violin and orchestra*].

- (Daniel Barenboim/New Philharmonia/Dietrich Fischer-Dieskau). *See* 3508.3

- (Murray Perahia/Bavarian Radio Symphony/Colin Davis). *See* 3477.1

- (Maurizio Pollini/Berlin Philharmonic/Claudio Abbado). Deutsche Grammophon: 427 771-2. [With Schoenberg, Arnold: *Concerto for piano and orchestra*].

- (Krystian Zimerman/Berlin Philharmonic/Herbert von Karajan). Deutsche Grammophon: 410 021-2. [With Grieg, Edvard: *Concerto for piano and orchestra*].

3508.2 *Concerto for violin and orchestra in D minor.* (Gidon Kremer/Chamber Orchestra of Europe/Nikolaus Harnoncourt). *See* 3508.1

3508.3 * *Concerto for violoncello and orchestra, op. 129 in A minor.*

- (Jacqueline Du Pré/New Philharmonia Orchestra/Daniel Barenboim). EMI: 7 64626 2. [With his *Concerto for piano and orchestra*

and *Introduction and allegro appassionato for piano and orchestra*].

- (Yo-Yo Ma/Bavarian Radio Symphony/Colin Davis). CBS: MK 42663. [With his *Fantasiestücke for violoncello and piano, op. 73; Adagio and allegro for violoncello and piano, op. 70;* and *Stücke im Volkston, op. 102*].

- (Mstislav Rostropovich/French National Orchestra/Leonard Bernstein). *See* 3550.3

3508.4 *Konzertstück for 4 horns and orchestra, op. 86.* (Seattle Symphony/Gerard Schwarz). Delos: DE 3084. [With his *Symphony no. 1* and *Overture, scherzo, and finale for orchestra, op. 52*].

3508.5 * *Symphonies (4).* (Hanover Band/Roy Goodman). RCA: 09026-61931-2. 2CD set. [With his *Overture, scherzo, and finale, op. 52*].

3508.6 ** *Symphony no. 1, op. 38 in B♭ major ("Spring").* (Cleveland Orchestra/George Szell). CBS: MYK 38468. [With his *Symphony no. 4*].

3508.7 * *Symphony no. 2, op. 61 in C major.* (London Philharmonic/Kurt Masur). Teldec: 2292-46446-2. [With his *Symphony no. 3*].

3508.8 * *Symphony no. 3, op. 97 in E♭ major ("Rhenish").* (London Philharmonic/Kurt Masur). *See* 3508.7

3508.9 ** *Symphony no. 4, op. 120 in D minor.* (Cleveland Orchestra/George Szell). *See* 3508.6

CHAMBER MUSIC

3508.10 *Quartet for piano and strings, op. 47 in E♭ major.* (Emanuel Ax/Cleveland Quartet). RCA: 6498-2-RC. [With his *Quintet for piano and strings*].

3508.11 *Quartet for strings no. 3, op. 41 no. 3 in A major.* (Emerson Quartet). Deutsche Grammophon: 431 650-2. [With Brahms, Johannes: *Quartet for strings no. 1*].

3508.12 * *Quintet for piano and strings, op. 44 in E♭ major. See* 3508.10

3508.13 *Sonatas (2) for violin and piano.* (Fabio Biondi/Luigi Di Ilio). Opus 111: OPS 30-77. [With Schumann, Clara: *Romances for violin and piano*].

3508.14 *Stücke im Volkston (Pieces in folk style) for violoncello and piano, op. 102.*

- (Yo-Yo Ma/Emanuel Ax). *See* 3508.3

- (Mischa Maisky/Martha Argerich). *See* 3506.16

- (Mstislav Rostropovich/Benjamin Britten). *See* 3506.16

PIANO MUSIC

3508.15 * *Carnaval*

- (Claudio Arrau). Philips: 420 871-2. [With his *Kinderszenen* and *Waldszenen*].
- (Charles Rosen). *See* 3508.16
- (Artur Rubinstein). *See* 3508.18

3508.16 *Davidsbündlertänze.*

- (Vladimir Ashkenazy). *See* 3508.18
- (Murray Perahia). CBS: MK 32299. [With his *Fantasiestücke*].
- (Charles Rosen). Sony: SBK 68345. (With his *Carnaval* and *Papillons*].

3508.17 * *Etudes symphoniques.*

- (Murray Perahia). CBS: MK 34539. [With his *Papillons*].
- (Ivo Pogorelich). Deutsche Grammophon: 410 520-2. [With his *Toccata;* and Beethoven, Ludwig van: *Sonata for piano no. 32*].

3508.18 ** *Fantasiestücke.*

- (Martha Argerich). *See* 3508.19
- (Vladimir Ashkenazy). London: 425 109-2. [With his *Blumenstücke, op. 19* and *Davidsbündlertänze*].
- (Murray Perahia). *See* 3508.16
- (Artur Rubinstein). RCA: 5667-2-RC. [With his *Carnaval*].

3508.19 * *Fantasy, op. 17 in C major.*

- (Martha Argerich). EMI: CDM 7 63576 2. [With his *Fantasiestücke*].
- (Murray Perahia). *See* 3506.20
- (Artur Rubinstein). *See* 3508.21

3508.20 * *Kinderszenen.*

- (Martha Argerich). Deutsche Grammophon: 410 653-2. [With his *Kreisleriana*].
- (Claudio Arrau). *See* 3508.15
- (Vladimir Ashkenazy). *See* 3508.26
- (Vladimir Horowitz). *See* 3508.25

3508.21 ** *Kreisleriana.*

- (Martha Argerich). *See* 3508.20
- (Hélène Grimaud). Denon: 73336. [With Brahms, Johannes: *Sonata for piano no. 2 in F♯ minor*].
- (Vladimir Horowitz). *See* 3508.25
- (Artur Rubinstein). RCA: 09026-61264-2. [With his *Fantasy in C major*].

3508.22 * *Papillons.*

- (Murray Perahia). *See* 3508.17

- (Charles Rosen). *See* 3508.16

3508.23 *Sonata no. 1, op. 11 in F♯ minor.*

- (Vladimir Ashkenazy) *See* 3508.26
- (Hélène Grimaud). Denon: CO-1786. [With Chopin, Frédéric: *Ballade no. 1;* Liszt, Franz: *Dante sonata*].

3508.24 * *Sonata no. 2, op. 22 in G minor.* (Murray Perahia). CBS: MK 44569. [With Schubert, Franz: *Sonata in A major, D. 959*].

3508.25 * *Toccata, op. 7.*

- (Vladimir Horowitz). CBS: MK 42409. [With his *Kinderszenen; Kreisleriana; Arabesque, op. 18;* and *Blumenstück, op. 19*].
- (Ivo Pogorelich). *See* 3508.17

3508.26 *Waldszenen, op. 82.*

- (Claudio Arrau). *See* 3508.15
- (Vladimir Ashkenazy). London: 421 290-2. [With his *Kinderszenen* and *Sonata no. 1*].

VOCAL MUSIC

3508.27 *Dichterliebe, op. 48.* (Dietrich Fischer-Dieskau/Alfred Brendel). Philips: 416 352-2. [With his *Liederkreis*].

3508.28 * *Frauenliebe und Leben, op. 42.* (Jessye Norman/Irwin Gage). Philips: 420 784-2. [With his *Liederkreis*].

3508.29 *Liederkreis, op. 39.*

- (Dietrich Fischer-Dieskau/Alfred Brendel). *See* 3508.27
- (Jessye Norman/Irwin Gage). *See* 3508.28

3508.30 *Songs. Selections.* (Elly Ameling/Jörg Demus). *See* 3506.36

3509 Smetana, Bedřich, 1824–1884

3509.1 *Ma vlást* [cycle of symphonic poems]. (Czech Philharmonic/Vaclav Neumann). Supraphon: C37-7724/25. 2CD set. [With his *Richard III; Wallenstein's camp; Haakon Jarl; Solemn march*].

3509.2 * *Prodaná nevésta (The bartered bride)* [opera]. (Gabriela Beňačková/Peter Dovrský/ Czech Philharmonic/Zdeněk Košler). Supraphon: 10 3511/13-2. 3CD set [complete opera]; 11 0641-2 [highlights].

3509.3 * *Quartet for strings no. 1 in E minor ("From my life").*

- (Alban Berg Quartet). *See* 3464.6
- (Emerson Quartet). *See* 3464.6
- (Guarneri Quartet). *See* 3464.6

3509.4 *Trio for piano and strings, op. 15 in G minor.* (Borodin Trio). *See* 3464.17

3509.5 ** *Vltava (The Moldau)* [symphonic poem from the cycle, *Má vlast*].

- (Vienna Philharmonic/Herbert von Karajan). *See* 3464.16
- (Cleveland Orchestra/George Szell). CBS: MYK 36716. [With his *Dances from The bartered bride;* plus Dvořák, Antonín: *Carnival overture* and *Slavonic dances*].

3510 Smyth, Ethel, 1858–1944

Mass in D major. (Philip Brunelle). Virgin: 7 59022 2 (7 91188 2). [With her *Mrs. Water's aria* and *March of the women*].

3511 Sor, Fernando, 1778–1839

Guitar music. Selections. (Norbert Kraft). *See* 3536

3512 Spohr, Louis, 1784–1859

3512.1 *Double quartets nos. 3–4, opp. 87 and 136.* (Academy of St. Martin-in-the-Fields Chamber Ensemble). Hyperion: CDA66142.

3512.2 *Symphony no. 3, op. 78 in C minor.* (Berlin Radio Symphony/Gerd Albrecht). Schwann: 11620. [With his *Jessonda overture*].

3513 Spontini, Gaspare, 1774–1851

La vestale [opera]. (Rosalind Plowright/Francisco Araiza/Munich Radio Orchestra/Gustav Kuhn). Orfeo: C 256 922 H. 2CD set.

3514 Stenhammar, Wilhelm, 1871–1927

Symphony no. 2, op. 34 in G minor. (Gothenburg Symphony/Neeme Järvi). Bis: 251. [With his *Excelsior, op. 13*].

3515 Strauss, Johann, 1825–1899

3515.1 *Die Fledermaus* [operetta].

- (Edita Gruberova/Werner Hollweg/Josef Protschka/Concertgebouw Orchestra/Nikolaus Harnoncourt). Teldec: 8.35762.
- (Hilde Gueden/Anton Dermota/Alfred Poell/ Vienna Philharmonic/Clemens Krauss). London: 425 990-2. 2CD set.

3515.2 ** *Waltzes. Selections.*

- (Berlin Philharmonic/Herbert von Karajan). Deutsche Grammophon: 410 022-2.
- (Philadelphia Orchestra/Eugene Ormandy). RCA: 6799-2-RG.
- (Chicago Symphony/Fritz Reiner). RCA: 60177-2-RG. [With Strauss, Josef: *Waltzes*].

- (NBC Symphony/Arturo Toscanini). *See* 3530

3516 Suppé, Franz von, 1819–1895

3516.1 * *Dichter und Bauer (Poet and peasant) overture.* (NBC Symphony/Arturo Toscanini). *See* 3530. *See also* 3516.2

3516.2 *Overtures. Selections.* (Vienna Philharmonic/Zubin Mehta). CBS: MK 44932.

3517 Szymanowska, Maria Agata Wolowska, 1789–1831

Piano music. Selections. (Christine Harnisch). *See* 3534

3518 * Tárrega, Francisco, 1852–1909

Guitar music. Selections.

- (Julian Bream). RCA: 60429-2-RC. [With works by Joaquín Malats and Miguel Llobet].
- (Norbert Kraft). *See* 3536

3519 Tchaikovsky, Peter Ilich, 1840–1893

3519.1 *Capriccio italien* [for orchestra]. *See* 3519.8, 3519.14, or 3519.19

3519.2 * *Concerto for piano and orchestra no. 1, op. 23 in B♭ minor.*

- (Martha Argerich/Royal Philharmonic/Charles Dutoit). Deutsche Grammophon: 415 062-2. [With Prokofiev, Sergey: *Concerto for piano and orchestra no. 3*].
- (Van Cliburn/RCA Symphony/Kiril Kondrashin). RCA: 5912-2-RC. [With Rachmaninoff, Sergei: *Concerto no. 2*].
- (Vladimir Horowitz/NBC Symphony/Arturo Toscanini). *See* 3494.2
- (Ivo Pogorelich/London Symphony/Claudio Abbado). Deutsche Grammophon: 415 122-2.

3519.3 ** *Concerto for violin and orchestra, op. 35 in D major.*

- (Jascha Heifetz/Chicago Symphony/Fritz Reiner). RCA: 5933. [With Mendelssohn-Bartholdy, Felix: *Concerto for violin and orchestra*].
- (Nigel Kennedy/London Philharmonic/Okko Kamu). EMI: CDC 7 54127 2. [With Sibelius, Jean: *Concerto for violin and orchestra*].
- (Viktoria Mullova/Boston Symphony/Seiji Ozawa). Philips: 416 821-2. [With Sibelius, Jean: *Concerto for violin and orchestra*].
- (Itzhak Perlman/Philadelphia Orchestra/Eugene Ormandy). EMI: CDC 7 47106 2. [With his *Sérénade mélancolique for violin and orchestra*].

3519.4 *Detskii albom (Children's album)* [for piano]. (Olli Mustonen). *See 3443*

3519.5 ** *1812 année (1812 overture).*

- (Chicago Symphony/Claudio Abbado). Sony: SK 47179. [With his *Marche slave; Romeo et Juliette; Tempest*].

- (Israel Philharmonic/Leonard Bernstein). *See 3519.8*

3519.6 *Evgenii Onegin (Eugene Onegin)* [opera]. (Nuccia Focile/Dmitri Hvorostovsky/Neil Shicoff/ Paris Orchestra/Semyon Bychkov). Philips: 438 235-2. 2CD set.

3519.7 *Francesca da Rimini* [overture]. (Royal Philharmonic/Vladimir Ashkenazy). *See 3519.14*

3519.8 *Hamlet* [fantasy-overture]. (Israel Philharmonic/Leonard Bernstein). Deutsche Grammophon: 415 379. [With his *Marche slave; Capriccio italien; 1812 année*].

3519.9 * *Lebedinoe ozero (Swan Lake)* [ballet].

- (Philadelphia Orchestra/Riccardo Muti) [suite]. EMI: CDC 7 47075 2. [With his *Spiashchaia krasavitsa suite*].

- (Boston Symphony/Seiji Ozawa) [complete ballet]. Deutsche Grammophon: 415 367-2. 2CD set.

3519.10 *Manfred* [symphony]. *See 3519.19*

3519.11 *Marche slave* [for orchestra]. *See 3519.5 or 3519.8*

3519.12 *Pikovaia dama (Pique dame = The queen of spades)* [opera]. (Wieslaw Ochman/ Ivan Konsulov/Yuri Mazurok/Sofia Festival/Emil Tchakarov). Sony: S3K 45720. 3CD set.

3519.13 *Quartet for strings no. 1, op. 11 in D major.*

- (Emerson Quartet). Deutsche Grammophon: 427 618-2. [With Borodin, Aleksandr Porfirevich: *Quartet for strings no. 2*].

- (Talich Quartet). *See 3450.3*

3519.14 * *Romeo et Juliette (Romeo and Juliet)* [fantasy-overture].

- (Chicago Symphony/Claudio Abbado). *See 3519.5*

- (Royal Philharmonic/Vladimir Ashkenazy). London: 421 715-2. [With his *Capriccio italien; Francesca da Rimini; Élegie*].

3519.15 * *Serenade for string orchestra, op. 48 in C major.*

- (Berlin Philharmonic/Herbert von Karajan). Deutsche Grammophon: 400 038-2. [With Dvořák, Antonín: *Serenade for string orchestra*].

- (Orpheus Chamber Orchestra). *See 3477.2*

3519.16 ** *Shchelkunchik (Nutcracker)* [ballet].

- (Royal Philharmonic/Vladimir Ashkenazy) [complete ballet]. London: 433 000-2. 2CD set. [With Glazunov, Aleksandr Konstantinovich: *Vremena goda*].

- (Philadelphia Orchestra/Eugene Ormandy) [ballet suite]. *See 3458.16*

- (Boston Symphony/Seiji Ozawa) [complete ballet]. Deutsche Grammophon: 435 619-2. 2CD set. [With his *Spiashchaia krasavitsa suite*].

3519.17 *Spiashchaia krasavitsa (Sleeping beauty)* [ballet suite].

- (Philadelphia Orchestra/Riccardo Muti). *See 3519.9*

- (Boston Symphony/Seiji Ozawa). *See 3519.16*

3519.18 *Suite for orchestra no. 4, op. 61 in G major ("Mozartiana").* (Philharmonia Orchestra/Michael Tilson Thomas). CBS: MDK 46503. [With his *Suite no. 2*].

3519.19 *Symphonies (6)* [complete]. (Oslo Philharmonic/Mariss Jansons). Chandos: 8672/ 78. 6CD set. [With his *Manfred* and *Capriccio italien*].

3519.20 * *Symphony no. 2, op. 17 in C minor ("Little Russian").* (Chicago Symphony/Claudio Abbado). CBS: MK 39359. [With his *Tempest*].

3519.21 * *Symphony no. 4, op. 36 in F minor.*

- (Philharmonia Orchestra/Vladimir Ashkenazy). London: 425 586-2. 3CD set. [With his *Symphonies nos. 5 and 6*].

- (Oslo Philharmonic/Mariss Jansons). Chandos: 8361.

- (Chicago Symphony/Georg Solti). London: 430 745-2.

3519.22 * *Symphony no. 5, op. 64 in E minor.*

- (Philharmonia Orchestra/Vladimir Ashkenazy). *See 3519.21*

- (Oslo Philharmonic/Mariss Jansons). Chandos: 8351.

- (Cleveland Orchestra/George Szell). CBS: MYK 37767.

3519.23 ** *Symphony no. 6, op. 74 in B minor ("Pathétique").*

- (Philharmonia Orchestra/Vladimir Ashkenazy). *See 3519.21*

- (Oslo Philharmonic/Mariss Jansons). Chandos: 8446.

3519.24   *Tempest* [symphonic fantasy]. (Chicago Symphony/Claudio Abbado). *See* 3519.20

3519.25   *Trio for piano and strings, op. 50 in A minor.* (Vladimir Ashkenazy/Itzhak Perlman/Lynn Harrell). EMI: 7 47988 2.

3519.26   *Variations sur un thème rococo (Variations on a rococo theme)* [for violoncello and orchestra].

- (Leonard Rose/Philadelphia Orchestra/Eugene Ormandy). *See* 3484.1

- (Mstislav Rostropovich/Berlin Philharmonic/Herbert von Karajan). *See* 3464.3

3519.27   *Vremena goda (The seasons)* [for piano]. (Lydia Artymiw). Chandos: CHAN 8349.

3520   Tosti, Francesco Paolo, 1846–1916

Songs. Selections. (José Carreras/English Chamber Orchestra/Edoardo Müller). Philips: 426 372-2.

3521   Verdi, Giuseppe, 1813–1901

3521.1 ** *Aida* [opera].

- (Montserrat Caballé/Fiorenza Cossotto/Plácido Domingo/New Philharmonia Orchestra/Riccardo Muti). EMI: CDS 7 47271 2. 3CD set.

- (Zinka Milanov/Fedora Barbieri/Jussi Bjoerling/Rome Opera/Jonel Perlea). RCA: 6652-2-RC. 3CD set.

- (Maria Callas/Fedora Barbieri/Richard Tucker/La Scala/Tullio Serafin). EMI: CDS 7 49030 8. 3CD set.

- (Leontyne Price/Rita Gorr/Jon Vickers/Rome Opera/Georg Solti). London: 417 416-2. 3CD set.

3521.2   *Un ballo in maschera (A masked ball)* [opera].

- (Plácido Domingo/Katia Ricciarelli/Renato Bruson/La Scala/Claudio Abbado). Deutsche Grammophon: 415 685-2. 2CD set.

- (Margaret Price/Kathleen Battle/Luciano Pavarotti/National Philharmonic/Georg Solti). London: 410 210-2. 2CD set.

3521.3   *Don Carlos* [opera].

- (Montserrat Caballé/Shirley Verrett/Plácido Domingo/Covent Garden/Carlo Maria Giulini). EMI: CDS 7 47701 8. 3CD set.

- (Luciano Pavarotti/Samuel Ramey/Daniela Dessi/La Scala/Riccardo Muti). EMI: CDS 7 54867 2. 3CD set.

3521.4   *Ernani* [opera]. (Mirella Freni/Plácido Domingo/Renato Bruson/La Scala/Riccardo Muti). EMI: CDS 7 47083 8. 3CD set.

3521.5   *Falstaff* [opera].

- (Dietrich Fischer-Dieskau/Vienna Philharmonic/Leonard Bernstein). CBS: M2K 42535. 2CD set.

- (Leo Nucci/Los Angeles Philharmonic/Carlo Maria Giulini). Deutsche Grammophon: 410 504-2. 2CD set.

- (Giuseppe Valdegno/NBC Symphony/Arturo Toscanini). RCA: 60251-2-RG. 2CD set.

3521.6 * *La forza del destino* [opera].

- (Martina Arroyo/Carlo Bergonzi/Piero Cappuccilli/Royal Philharmonic/Lamberto Gardelli). EMI: CMS 7 64646 2. 3CD set.

- (Leontyne Price/Plácido Domingo/Sherrill Milnes/London Symphony/James Levine). RCA: RCD 3-1864. 3CD set.

- (Agnes Baltsa/Renato Bruson/José Carreras/Philharmonia Orchestra/Giuseppe Sinopoli). Deutsche Grammophon: 419 203-2. 3CD set.

3521.7   *Luisa Miller* [opera]. (Aprile Millo/Plácido Domingo/Vladimir Chernov/Metropolitan Opera/James Levine). Sony: S2K 48073. 2CD set.

3521.8   *Macbeth* [opera].

- (Sherrill Milnes/Fiorenza Cossotto/New Philharmonia Orchestra/Riccardo Muti). EMI: CMS 7 64339 2. 2CD set.

- (Renato Bruson/Maria Zampieri/Deutsche Oper Berlin/Giuseppe Sinopoli). Philips: 412 133-2. 3CD set.

3521.9   *Nabucco* [opera].

- (Elena Suliotis/Bruno Previdi/Tito Gobbi/Vienna State Opera/Lamberto Gardelli). London: 417 407-2. 2CD set.

- (Ghena Dimitrova/Plácido Domingo/Evgeny Neshterenko/Deutsche Oper Berlin/Giuseppe Sinopoli). Deutsche Grammophon: 410 512-2. 2CD set.

3521.10 * *Otello* [opera].

- (Mirela Freni/Jon Vickers/Peter Glossop/Berlin Philharmonic/Herbert von Karajan). EMI: CMS 7 96308 2. 2CD set.

- (Plácido Domingo/Renata Scotto/Sherrill Milnes/National Philharmonic/James Levine). RCA: RCD2-2951. 2CD set.

- (Herva Nelli/Ramón Vinay/Giuseppe Valdengo/NBC Symphony/Arturo Toscanini). RCA: 60302-2-RG. 2CD set.

3521.11   *Pezzi sacri* (Four sacred pieces).

- (Monteverdi Choir/John Eliot Gardiner). *See* 3521.13

- (Swedish Radio and Stockholm Chamber Choirs/Riccardo Muti). EMI: CDC 7 47066 2.

- (Atlanta Symphony Chorus/Robert Shaw). Telarc: 80254. [With Stravinsky, Igor: *Symphonie des psaumes*].

3521.12 *Quartet for strings.* (Juilliard Quartet). CBS: SK 48193. [With Sibelius, Jean: *Voces intimae*].

3521.13 * *Requiem.*

- (Monteverdi Choir/Orchestre Révolutionnaire et Romantique/John Eliot Gardiner). Philips: 442 142-2. 2CD set. [With his *Pezzi sacri*].

- (Philharmonia Chorus and Orchestra/Carlo Maria Giulini). EMI: CDS 7 47257 8. 2CD set. [With his *Pezzi sacri*].

- (La Scala Chorus and Orchestra/Riccardo Muti). EMI: CDS 7 49390 2. 2CD set.

- (Atlanta Symphony Chorus and Orchestra/Robert Shaw). Telarc: 80152. 2CD set. [With his selected operatic choruses].

- (Vienna State Opera Chorus/Vienna Philharmonic/Georg Solti). London: 411 944-2. 2CD set.

3521.14 ** *Rigoletto* [opera].

- (Sherrill Milnes/Joan Sutherland/Luciano Pavarotti/London Symphony/Richard Bonynge). London: 414 269-2. 2CD set.

- (Giorgio Zancanaro/Daniela Dessì/Vincanzo La Scola/La Scala/Riccardo Muti). EMI: CDS 7 49605 2. 2CD set.

- (Alexandru Agache/Leontina Vaduva/Richard Leech/Welsh National Opera/Carlo Rizzi). Teldec: 4509-90851-2. 2CD set.

- (Tito Gobbi/Maria Callas/Giuseppe di Stefano/La Scala/Tullio Serafin). EMI: CDS 7 47469 8. 2CD set.

3521.15 *Simon Boccanegra* [opera].

- (Mirela Freni/Piero Cappuccilli/La Scala/Claudio Abbado). Deutsche Grammophon: 415 692-2. 2CD set.

- (Kiri Te Kanawa/Leo Nucci/La Scala/Georg Solti). London: 425 628-2. 2CD set.

3521.16 ** *La traviata* [opera].

- (Joan Sutherland/Luciano Pavarotti/Matteo Manuguerra/National Philharmonic/Richard Bonynge). London: 410 154-2. 3CD set.

- (Maria Callas/Alfredo Kraus/Mario Sereni/San Carlos Opera Lisbon/Franco Ghione). EMI: CDS 7 49187 8. 2CD set.

- (Ileana Cotrubas/Plácido Domingo/Sherrill Milnes/Bavarian State Orchestra/Carlos Kieiber). Deutsche Grammophon: 415 132-2. 2CD set.

- (Edita Gruberova/Neil Shicoff/Giorgio Zancanaro/London Symphony/Carlo Rizzi). Teldec: 9031-76348-2. 2CD set.

3521.17 * *Il trovatore* [opera].

- (Joan Sutherland/Marilyn Horne/Luciano Pavarotti/National Philharmonic/Richard Bonynge). London: 417 137-2. 2CD set.

- (Rosalind Plowright/Brigitte Fassbaender/Plácido Domingo/Accademia Nazionale di Santa Cecilia/Carlo Maria Giulini). Deutsche Grammophon: 413 355-2. 3CD set.

- (Aprile Millo/Dolora Zajick/Plácido Domingo/Metropolitan Opera/James Levine). Sony: S2K 48070. 2CD set.

- (Leontyne Price/Fiorenza Cossotto/Plácido Domingo/New Philharmonia Orchestra/Zubin Mehta). RCA: 6194-2-RC. 2CD set.

3522 Vierne, Louis, 1870–1937

3522.1 *Pièces de fantaisie* [for organ]. (Wolfgang Rübsam). Bayer: 100 014/015. 2CD set.

3522.2 *Symphony for organ no. 1, op. 14.* (Michael Murray). Telarc: 80329. [With his *Symphony no. 3*].

3523 Vieuxtemps, Henri, 1820–1881

3523.1 *Concerto for violin and orchestra no. 4, op. 31 in D minor.* (Jascha Heifetz/London Philharmonic/John Barbirolli). *See* 3528

3523.2 *Concerto for violin and orchestra no. 5, op. 37 in A minor.*

- (Jascha Heifetz/New Symphony of London/Malcolm Sargent). *See* 3453.1

- (Shlomo Mintz/Israel Philharmonic/Zubin Mehta). *See* 3484.2

3524 Voříšek, Jan Hugo, 1791–1825

Symphony in D major. (Prague Chamber Orchestra/Ivan Parík). Supraphon: 10 3868-2. [With his *Variations de bravoure for piano and orchestra* and *Introduction et rondeau brillant for piano and orchestra*].

3525 Wagner, Richard, 1813–1883

3525.1 *Der fliegende Holländer (The flying Dutchman)* [opera].

- (Robert Hale/Hildegard Behrens/Vienna Philharmonic/Christoph von Dohnanyi). London: 436 418-2. 3CD set.

- (José van Dam/Junja Vajzovic/Berlin Philharmonic/Herbert von Karajan). EMI: CDC 7 47054 2. 3CD set.

3525.2 *Lohengrin* [opera].

- (Elisabeth Grümmer/Jess Thomas/Vienna Philharmonic/Rudolf Kempe). EMI: CDS 7 49017 8. 3CD set.

- (Cheryl Studer/Paul Frey/Bayreuth Festival/Peter Schneider). Philips: 434 602-2. 4CD set.

3525.3 * *Die Meistersinger von Nürnberg* [opera].

- (Helen Donath/René Kollo/Staatskapelle Dresden/Herbert von Karajan). EMI: CDS 7 49683 2. 4CD set.

- (Elisabeth Schwarzkopf/Hans Hopf/Bayreuth Festival/Herbert von Karajan). EMI: CHS 7 63500 2. 4CD set.

3525.4 ** *Orchestral music. Selections* [primarily excerpts from his operas].

- (Vienna Philharmonic/Herbert von Karajan). Deutsche Grammophon: 423 613-2. [*Tannhäuser overture; Siegfried-Idyll; Prelude and Liebestod from Tristan und Isolde*].

- (Metropolitan Opera Orchestra/James Levine). Deutsche Grammophon: 435 874-2. [Overtures and preludes from *Rienzi, Tannhäuser, Die Meistersinger, Lohengrin,* and *Der fliegende Holländer*].

- (Cleveland Orchestra/George Szell). CBS: MYK 38486. [*Prelude to Die Meistersinger; Prelude and Liebestod from Tristan und Isolde; Tannhäuser overture; Fliegende Holländer overture*].

- (Cleveland Orchestra/George Szell). CBS: SBK 48175. [Excerpts from the *Ring des Nibelungen*].

3525.5 * *Parsifal* [opera].

- (Waltraud Meier/Siegfried Jerusalem/Berlin Philharmonic/Daniel Barenboim). Teldec: 9031-74448-2. 4CD set.

- (Dunja Vejzovic/Peter Hofmann/Berlin Philharmonic/Herbert von Karajan). Deutsche Grammophon: 413 347-2. 4CD set.

- (Irene Dalis/Jess Thomas/Bayreuth Festival/Hans Knappertsbusch). Philips: 416 390-2. 4CD set.

3525.6 * *Der Ring des Nibelungen* [cycle of four operas: *Das Rheingold; Die Walküre; Siegfried; and Götterdämmerung*].

- (Daniel Barenboim). Erato: 4509-91185-2; 4509-91186-2; 4509-94193-2; 4509-94194-2. 14 CDs in 4 vols.

- (Karl Böhm). Philips: 420 325-2. 14CD set.

- (Wilhelm Fürtwängler). EMI: CDZM 67123. 13CD set.

- (Georg Solti). London: 414 1002. 15CD set.

3525.7 *Siegfried-Idyll* [for orchestra].

- (Vienna Philharmonic/Herbert von Karajan). *See 3525.4*

- (Orpheus Chamber Orchestra). *See 3537*

3525.8 *Tannhäuser* [opera].

- (René Kollo/Christa Ludwig/Vienna Philharmonic/Georg Solti). London: 414 581-2. 3CD set.

- (Wolfgang Windgassen/Anja Silja/Bayreuth Festival/Wolfgang Sawallisch). Philips: 420 122-2. 3CD set.

3525.9 ** *Tristan und Isolde* [opera].

- (Hildegard Behrens/Peter Hofmann/Bavarian Radio Symphony/Leonard Bernstein). Philips: 410 447-2. 5CD set.

- (Birgit Nilsson/Wolfgang Windgassen/Bayreuth Festival/Karl Böhm). Deutsche Grammophon: 419 889-2. 3CD set.

- (Kirsten Flagstad/Ludwig Suthaus/Philharmonia Orchestra/Wilhelm Fürtwängler). EMI: CDS 7 47322 8. 4CD set.

- (Margaret Price/René Kollo/Staatskapelle Dresden/Carlos Kleiber). Deutsche Grammophon: 413 315-2. 4CD set.

3525.10 *Wesendonk-Lieder.* (Jessye Norman/London Symphony/Colin Davis). Philips: 412 655-2. [With his *Prelude and Liebestod from Tristan und Isolde*].

3526 Weber, Carl Maria von, 1786–1826

3526.1 * *Aufforderung zum Tanze (Invitation to the dance)* [orchestrated by Hector Berlioz].

- (Cleveland Orchestra/Christoph von Dohnanyi). *See 3446.9*

- (NBC Symphony/Arturo Toscanini). *See 3530*

See also 3526.5

3526.2 *Concertos for clarinet and orchestra, op. 73 nos. 1–2 in F major and E♭ major.* (Anthony Pay/Orchestra of the Age of Enlightenment/Roy Goodman). Virgin: 59002 (7 90720-2).

3526.3 * *Der Freischütz* [opera].

- (Karita Mattila/Francisco Araiza/Staatskapelle Dresden/Colin Davis). Philips: 426 319-2. 2CD set.

- (Gundula Janowitz/Peter Schreier/Staatskapelle Dresden/Carlos Kleiber). Deutsche Grammophon: 415 433-2. 2CD set.

3526.4 *Overtures.* (Philharmonia Orchestra/Neeme Järvi). Chandos: 8766. [*Overtures to Euryanthe; Der Freischütz; Oberon; Der Beherrscher der Geister;* and *Turandot;* plus Hindemith, Paul: *Symphonic metamorphosis of themes by Carl Maria von Weber*].

3526.5 *Piano music. Selections.* Hamish Milne. CRD: 3485. [*Sonatas 1–2; Aufforderung zum Tanze;* and *Rondo brillante*].

3526.6 *Quintet for clarinet and strings in B♭ major, op. 34.* (Benny Goodman/Berkshire String Quartet). *See* 3452.14

3527 Widor, Charles Marie, 1844–1937

Symphony for organ no. 5, op. 42 no. 1 in F minor. (Daniel Chorzempa). Philips: 410 054-2. [With his *Symphony no. 10*].

3528 Wieniawski, Henri, 1835–1880. *Concerto for violin and orchestra no. 2, op. 22 in D minor.*

- (Jascha Heifetz/London Philharmonic/John Barbirolli). EMI: CDH 7 64251. [With Vieuxtemps, Henri: *Concerto no. 4;* Saint-Saëns, Camille: *Introduction and rondo capriccioso* and *Havanaise;* Sarasate, Pablo de: *Zigeunerweisen*].

- (Gil Shaham/London Symphony/Lawrence Foster). Deutsche Grammophon: 431 815-2. [With his *Concerto for violin and orchestra no. 1 in F♯ minor* and *Légend for violin and orchestra in G minor, op. 20,* plus Sarasate, Pablo de: *Zigeunerweisen*].

3529 Wolf, Hugo, 1860–1903

3529.1 *Goethe-Lieder.* (Arleen Auger/Irwin Gage). Hyperion: CDA66590. [With his *Mörike Lieder*].

3529.2 *Italienische Serenade (Italian serenade)* [for orchestra]. (Orpheus Chamber Orchestra). *See* 3537

3529.3 *Italienisches Liederbuch (Italian songbook).*

- (Barbara Bonney/Håkan Hagegård/Geoffrey Parsons). Teldec: 9031-72301-2.

- (Irmgard Seefried/Dietrich Fischer-Dieskau). Deutsche Grammophon: 435-752-2.

3529.4 *Mörike-Lieder.* (Brigitte Fassbaender/Jean-Yves Thibaudet). London: 440 208-2.

3529.5 *Spanisches Liederbuch (Spanish songbook). Selections.* (Jan DeGaetani/Gilbert Kalish). Elektra Nonesuch: 79263-2. [With Schubert, Franz: *Songs*].

Anthologies and Recitals

3530 ** *An der schönen, blauen Donau.* (NBC Symphony/Arturo Toscanini). RCA: 60309-2-RG. [Waldteufel, Emil: *Skater's waltz;* Strauss, Johann: *Tritsch-tratsch polka* and *Blue Danube waltz;* Suppé, Franz von: *Poet and peasant overture;* Ponchielli, Amilcare: *Dance of the hours;* Weber, Carl Maria von: *Invitation to the dance;* Glinka, Mikhail Ivanovich: *Jota aragonesa*].

3531 * *Early Romantic overtures.* (London Classical Players/Roger Norrington). EMI: 49889. [Weber, Carl Maria von: *Oberon;* Mendelssohn-Bartholdy, Felix: *Hebrides;* Berlioz, Hector: *Francs-juges;* Schumann, Robert: *Genoveva;* Wagner, Richard: *Fliegende Holländer*].

3532 ** *Favorite French spectaculars.* (New York Philharmonic/Leonard Bernstein). CBS: 37769. [Dukas, Paul: *Sorcerer's apprentice;* Saint-Saëns, Camille: *Danse macabre* and *Bacchanale from Samson and Delilah;* Chabrier, Emmanuel: *España;* Ravel, Maurice: *Pavane pour une infante défunte;* Offenbach, Jacques: *Overture to Orpheus in the Underworld*].

3533 ** *Weekend in Russia.* (London Symphony/Georg Solti). London: 417 689. [Glinka, Mikhail Ivanovich: *Russlan and Ludmilla overture;* Mussorgsky, Modest Petrovich: *Khovanshchina prelude* and *Night on Bare Mountain;* Borodin, Aleksandr Porfirevich: *Overture and Polovtsian dances from Prince Igor*].

Individual Artists

3534 Harnisch, Christine. *Concerto etudes and toccatas by 19th and 20th century women composers.* Aurophon: AU 31473. [Piano music by Maria Agata Wolowska Szymanowska, Grázyna Bacewicz, Wanda Landowska, Agathe Bäcker-Grøndahl, Maria Hofer, Clara Schumann, and Cécile Chaminade].

3535 * Heifetz, Jascha. *Showpieces.* RCA: 7709. [With RCA Symphony/William Steinberg/Izler Solomon. Lalo, Edouard: *Symphonie espagnole;* Saint-Saëns, Camille: *Havanaise* and *Introduction and rondo capriccioso;* Sarasate, Pablo de: *Zigeunerweisen;* Chausson, Ernest: *Poème*].

3536 Kraft, Norbert. *Sor, Aguado, Tárrega: 19th century guitar favorites.* Naxos: 8.553007. [Fernando Sor, Dionisio Aguado, Francisco Tárrega.

3537 * Orpheus Chamber Orchestra. *Siegfried-Idyll.* Deutsche Grammophon: 431 680-2. [Wagner, Richard: *Siegfried-Idyll;* Turina, Joaquín: *La oración del torero;* Wolf, Hugo: *Italienische Serenade;* Puccini, Giacomo: *Crisantemi;* Berlioz, Hector: *Rêverie et caprice;* Sibelius, Jean: *Valse triste;* Dvořák, Antonín: *Nocturno for strings.*].

3538 Paratore, Anthony, and Joseph Paratore. *Variations for four hands.* Koch Schwann Musica Mundi: 310 088. [Schumann, Robert: *Andante and variations in Bb major, op. 46;* Mendelssohn-Bartholdy, Felix: *Andante and variations in Bb major, op. 83a;* Beethoven, Ludwig van: *Variations in D major, WoO 74;* Saint-Saëns, Camille: *Variations on a theme by Beethoven, op. 35;* Lutoslawski, Witold: *Variations on a theme by Paganini*].

3539 Souzay, Gérard. *Mélodies françaises.* Denon: CO-2252-EX. [With Dalton Baldwin, piano. Fauré, Gabriel: *La bonne chanson;* Ravel, Maurice: *Don Quichotte à Dulcinée;* Duparc, Henri: *Songs*].

Modern Period to 1950

Compiled by
Kent Underwood

Composers

3540 Alain, Jehan, 1911–1940

Organ music. Selections. (Marie-Claire Alain). Erato: ECD 88194.

3541 Antheil, George, 1900–1959

3541.1 *Ballet mécanique.* (New Palais Royale Orchestra/Maurice Peress). MusicMasters: 01612-67094-2. [With his *Jazz symphony; Sonata no. 2 for violin, piano, and drum; Quartet for strings no. 1*].

3541.2 *Jazz symphony. See 3541.1*

3541.3 *Piano music. Selections.* (Steffen Schleiermacher). *See 3676*

3542 Auric, Georges, 1899–1983

3542.1 *Sonata for piano.* (Marie-Catherine Girod). *See 3750.3*

3542.2 *Trio for oboe, clarinet, and bassoon. See 3674*

3543 Barber, Samuel, 1910–1981

3543.1 ** *Adagio for strings. See 3543.7 or 3660*

3543.2 *Antony and Cleopatra* [opera]. (Esther Hinds/Jeffrey Wells/Spoleto Festival/Christian Badea). NW: 322/4. 2CD set.

3543.3 *Capricorn concerto, op. 21.* (Pacific Symphony/Keith Clark). Albany: TROY 064. [With his *Essay for orchestra no. 1*; Copland, Aaron: *Saga of the prairies*; Harris, Roy: *Symphony no. 6*].

3543.4 * *Concerto for piano and orchestra, op. 38.* (John Browning/St. Louis Symphony/Leonard Slatkin). RCA: 60732-2. [With his *Symphony no. 1* and *Souvenirs*].

3543.5 *Concerto for violin and orchestra.* (Elmar Oliveira/St. Louis Symphony/Leonard Slatkin). *See 3583*

3543.6 * *Dover beach* [for baritone and string quartet]. (Dietrich Fischer-Dieskau/Juilliard Quartet). *See 3543.9*

3543.7 *Essays (3) for orchestra.* (St. Louis Symphony/Leonard Slatkin). EMI: 7 49463 2. [With his *School for scandal overture; Adagio for strings; Medea's dance of vengeance*].

3543.8 *Hermit songs.* (Leontyne Price/Samuel Barber). *See* 3543.9

3543.9 * *Knoxville, summer of 1915.* (Eleanor Steber/Dumbarton Oaks Orchestra/William Strickland). Sony: MPK 46727. [With his *Dover beach; Hermit songs; Andromache's farewell*].

3543.10 * *Piano music.*

- (John Browning). MusicMasters: 01612-67122-2 or Musical Heritage Society: 513597L. [Includes his *Sonata, op. 26; Interlude no. 1; Nocturne, op. 33; Ballade, op. 46; Excursions, op. 20*].

- (Peter Lawson). [*Sonata* only]. *See* 3670

3543.11 * *Quartet for strings no. 1, op. 11 in B minor.*

- (Emerson Quartet). *See* 3590.7

- (Tokyo Quartet). *See* 3925.1

3543.12 *School for scandal overture. See* 3543.7

3543.13 * *Summer music* [for woodwind quintet].

- (Ensemble Wien-Berlin). *See* 4006

- (Marlboro Festival Ensemble). Sony: CMK 46250. [With Hindemith, Paul: *Octet;* Nielsen, Carl: *Quintet for woodwinds and horn*].

3543.14 * *Symphony no. 1.*

- (Detroit Symphony/Neeme Järvi). Chandos: CHAN 8958. [With Beach, H. H. A., Mrs.: *Symphony in E minor*].

- (St. Louis Symphony/Leonard Slatkin). *See* 3543.4

3543.15 *Vanessa* [opera]. (Eleanor Steber/Nicolai Gedda/Metropolitan Opera/Dmitri Mitropoulos). RCA: 7899-2-RG. 2CD set.

3544 * Barrios Mangoré, Agustín, 1885–1944

Guitar music. Selections. (John Williams). Sony: SK 64396. [Album title: *From the jungles of Paraguay*].

3545 Bartók, Béla, 1881–1945

3545.1 ** *Concerto for orchestra.*

- (Chicago Symphony/Pierre Boulez). Deutsche Grammophon: 437 826-2. [With his *Darab (Pieces) for orchestra, op. 12*].

- (Chicago Symphony/Fritz Reiner). RCA: 60175-2. [With his *Music for strings, percussion, and celesta*].

- (Chicago Symphony/Georg Solti). London: 400 052-2. [With his *Táncszvit (Dance suite)*]. *See also* 3494.3

- (Cleveland Orchestra/Christoph von Dohnanyi). London: 425 694-2. [With Lutoslawski, Witold: *Concerto for orchestra*].

3545.2 * *Concertos (3) for piano and orchestra.*

- (Vladimir Ashkenazy/London Philharmonic/Georg Solti). *See* 3545.15

- (Maurizio Pollini/Chicago Symphony/Claudio Abbado). Deutsche Grammophon: 415 371-2. [*Concertos 1–2 only*].

3545.3 *Concerto for violin and orchestra no. 1. See* 3545.4

3545.4 * *Concerto for violin and orchestra no. 2.*

- (Kyung-Wha Chung/London Philharmonic/Georg Solti). London: 425 015-2. [With his *Concerto no. 1*].

- (Midori/Berlin Philharmonic/Zubin Mehta). Sony: SK 45941.

3545.5 * *Contrasts* [for violin, clarinet, and piano].

- (Lucy Stoltzman/Richard Stoltzman/Richard Goode). RCA: 60170-2. [With Ives, Charles: *Largo for violin, clarinet, and piano;* Stravinsky, Igor: *Histoire du soldat suite*].

- (Joseph Szigeti/Benny Goodman/Béla Bartók). Sony: MPK 47676. [With works for piano solo, performed by Bartók].

3545.6 *Csodálatos mandarin (Miraculous mandarin) suite.* (Chicago Symphony/Georg Solti). *See* 3545.11

3545.7 *Divertimento for string orchestra.* (Orpheus Chamber Orchestra). Deutsche Grammophon: 415 668-2. [With his *Rumanian folk dances;* Janáček, Leoš: *Mládi*].

3545.8 *Fából faragott királyfi (Wooden prince)* [ballet]. *See* 3545.10

3545.9 * *Kécszakállú herceg vára (Bluebeard's castle)* [opera].

- (Tatiana Troyanos/Siegmund Nimsgern/BBC Symphony/Pierre Boulez). Sony: SMK 64110.

- (Sylvia Sass/Kolos Kováts/London Philharmonic/Georg Solti). London: 433 082-2.

3545.10 *Kilenc csodaszarvas (Cantata profana).* (Pierre Boulez). Deutsche Grammophon: 435 863-2. [With his *Fából faragott királyfi (Wooden prince)*].

3545.11 ** *Music for strings, percussion, and celesta.*

- (Berlin Philharmonic/Herbert von Karajan). EMI: CDM 7 69242 2. [With Hindemith, Paul: *Symphony Mathis der Maler*].

- (Chicago Symphony/Fritz Reiner). *See* 3545.1

- (Chicago Symphony/Georg Solti). London: 430 352-2. [With his *Divertimento* and *Csodálatos mandarin (Miraculous mandarin) suite*].

3545.12 * *Piano music.*

- (Béla Bartók). *See* 3545.5

- (Claude Helffer). Harmonia Mundi: 190194. [*Improvisations on Hungarian folk tunes; Out of doors suite; Sonata, op. 26; Suite, op. 14*].

- (Zoltán Kocsis). Denon: C37-7813. [*Allegro barbaro; Three rondos on folk tunes; Three Hungarian folk tunes; Suite, op. 14; Sonata, op. 26; Rumanian folk dances; Hungarian peasant songs*].

3545.13 * *Quartets for strings (6).* (Emerson Quartet). Deutsche Grammophon: 423 657-2.

3545.14 *Rhapsody for violin and piano no. 1.* (Joseph Szigeti/Béla Bartók). *See* 3400.15

3545.15 * *Sonata for two pianos and percussion.* (Vladimir Ashkenazy and others). London: 425 573-2. [With his *Concertos (3) for piano and orchestra*].

3545.16 *Sonata for violin* [unaccompanied]. (Nigel Kennedy). EMI: CDC 7 47621 2. [Ellington, Duke: *Black, brown, and beige (selections)*, arranged for violin and bass].

3545.17 * *Sonatas (2) for violin and piano.*

- (Gidon Kremer/Iury Smirnov). Hungaroton: HCD 11655-2.

- (Joseph Szigeti/Béla Bartók). [*Sonata no. 2* only]. *See* 3400.15

3545.18 *Táncszvit (Dance suite)* [for orchestra]. (Chicago Symphony/Georg Solti). *See* 3545.1

3546   Bax, Arnold, 1883–1953

Tintagel [symphonic poem]. (Ulster Orchestra/ Bryden Thomson). Chandos: CHAN 8312. [With his *Symphony no. 4*].

3547   Berg, Alban, 1885–1935

3547.1 ** *Concerto for violin and orchestra.*

- (Gidon Kremer/Bavarian Radio Symphony/ Colin Davis). Philips: 412 523-2. [With his *Pieces (3) for orchestra, op. 6*].

- (Anne-Sophie Mutter/Chicago Symphony/ James Levine). Deutsche Grammophon: 437 093-2. [With Rihm, Wolfgang: *Gesungene Zeit*].

3547.2 *Frühe Lieder (Early songs).* (Brigitte Balleys/Deutsches Symphonie-Orchester Berlin/ Vladimir Ashkenazy). *See* 3547.5

3547.3 * *Kammerkonzert (Chamber concerto)* [for violin, piano, and 13 winds].

- (Peter Serkin/London Symphony members/ Claudio Abbado). *See* 3452.5

- (Thomas Zehetmair/Oleg Maisenberg/Chamber Orchestra of Europe/Heinz Holliger). Teldec: 2292-46019-2. [With Schoenberg, Arnold: *Kammersymphonie no. 1*].

3547.4 *Lieder, op. 2.* (Brigitte Fassbaender/John Wustman). Acanta: 43579. [With lieder by Claus Ogermann and Gustav Mahler].

3547.5 * *Lieder, op. 4 ("Altenberglieder").* (Brigitte Balleys/Deutsches Symphonie-Orchester Berlin/Vladimir Ashkenazy). London: 436 567-2. [With his *Frühe Lieder; Pieces for orchestra, op. 6; Three pieces from Lyrische Suite, arranged for string orchestra*].

3547.6 * *Lulu* [opera; Act III completed by Friedrich Cerha]. (Teresa Stratas/Yvonne Minton/ Paris Opera/Pierre Boulez). Deutsche Grammophon: 415 489-2. 3CD set.

3547.7 *Lulu suite.* (Judith Blegan/New York Philharmonic/Pierre Boulez). Sony: SMK 45838. [With his *Wein; Three pieces from Lyrische Suite, arranged for string orchestra*].

3547.8 * *Lyrische Suite (Lyric suite) for string quartet.*

- (Alban Berg Quartet). EMI: 5 55190 2. [With his *Quartet for strings, op. 3*].

- (Arditti Quartet). Disques Montaigne: WM 789 001. [With his *Quartet for strings, op. 3*].

3547.9 *Pieces (4) for clarinet and piano, op. 5.* (Steven Kanoff/Catherine Collard). *See* 3669

3547.10 * *Pieces (3) for orchestra, op. 6.*

- (Deutsches Symphonie-Orchester Berlin/ Vladimir Ashkenazy). *See* 3547.5

- (Bavarian Radio Symphony/Colin Davis). *See* 3547.1

- (Chicago Symphony/James Levine). Deutsche Grammophon: 419 781-2. [With Schoenberg, Arnold: *Pieces (5) for orchestra, op. 16*; Webern, Anton: *Pieces (6) for orchestra, op. 6*].

3547.11 *Quartet for strings, op. 3. See* 3547.8

3547.12 * *Sonata for piano, op. 1.* (Maurizio Pollini). *See* 3563.7

3547.13 *Wein (Wine)* [for soprano and orchestra]. (Jessye Norman/New York Philharmonic/ Pierre Boulez). *See* 3547.7

3547.14 * *Wozzeck* [opera].

- (Franz Grundheber/Hildegard Behrens/Vienna Philharmonic/Claudio Abbado). Deutsche Grammophon: 423 587-2.

- (Dietrich Fischer-Dieskau/Evelyn Lear/Deutsche Oper Berlin/Karl Böhm). Deutsche Grammophon: 435 705-2. 3CD set.

3548 Bliss, Arthur, Sir, 1891–1975

A colour symphony. (Ulster Orchestra/Vernon Handley). Chandos: CHAN 8503. [With his *Checkmate suite*].

3549 Blitzstein, Marc, 1905–1964

3549.1 *Concerto for piano and orchestra.* (Michael Barrett/Brooklyn Philharmonic/Lukas Foss). *See 3878*

3549.2 *Regina* [opera]. (Katherine Ciesinski/Samuel Ramey/Scottish Opera/John Mauceri). London: 433 812-2.

3549.3 *Songs. Selections.* (Karen Holvik/William Sharp/Steven Blier). Koch: 3-7050-2. [Album title: *Zipperfly and other songs*].

3550 Bloch, Ernest, 1880–1959

3550.1 *Avodat ha-kodesh (Sacred service).* (Choir of the Metropolitan Synagogue/New York Philharmonic/Leonard Bernstein). Sony: SM2K 47533. 2CD set. [With Foss, Lukas: *Song of songs*; Ben-Haim, Paul: *Sweet psalmist of Israel*].

3550.2 * *Concerti grossi (2).* (Amadeus Chamber Orchestra/Agnieszka Duczmal). CPO: 999 096-2. [With his *Concertino for flute, viola, and string orchestra* and *Episodes (4) for chamber orchestra*].

3550.3 * *Schelomo* [for violoncello and orchestra].
- (Mischa Maisky/Israel Philharmonic/Leonard Bernstein). *See 3464.3*
- (Leonard Rose/Philadelphia Orchestra/Eugene Ormandy). *See 3484.1*
- (Mstislav Rostropovich/French National Orchestra/Leonard Bernstein). EMI: 7 49307 2. [With Schumann, Robert: *Concerto for violoncello and orchestra*].

3550.4 *Sinfonia breve.* (Minneapolis Symphony/Antal Dorati). *See 3574.1*

3551 Boulanger, Lili, 1893–1918

3551.1 *Du fond de l'abîme.* (Oralla Domínguez/Raymond Amade/Concerts Lamoureux Orchestra/Igor Markevitch). EMI: CDM 7 64281 2. [With her *Psalms 24 and 129; Vielle prière bouddhique; Pie Jesu;* and *Three pieces for violin and piano*].

3551.2 *Songs.* (Karin Ott/Jean Lemaire). Signum: SIG X39-00.

3552 Brian, Havergal, 1876–1972

Symphony no. 1 ("Gothic"). (Slovak Philharmonic/Ojdrej Lenard). Marco Polo: 8.223280/281. 2CD set.

3553 Britten, Benjamin, 1913–1976

3553.1 *Albert Herring* [opera]. (Sylvia Fisher/Peter Pears/Owen Brannigan/English Chamber Orchestra/Benjamin Britten). London: 421 850-2. 2CD set.

3553.2 * *Billy Budd* [opera]. (Peter Pears/Dietrich Fischer-Dieskau/London Symphony/Benjamin Britten). London: 417 428-2. 3CD set. [With his *Holy sonnets of John Donne* and *Songs and proverbs of William Blake*].

3553.3 *Canticles (5).* (Anthony Rolfe Johnson and others). Hyperion: CDA66498.

3553.4 * *Ceremony of carols.* (Choir of King's College, Cambridge/David Willcocks/Philip Ledger). EMI: 7 47709 2. [With his *Hymn to St. Cecilia; Rejoice in the lamb; Te Deum; Jubilate Deo; Missa brevis*].

3553.5 * *Death in Venice* [opera]. (Peter Pears/English Chamber Orchestra/Steuart Bedford). London: 425 669-2. 2CD set.

3553.6 *Lachrymae* [for viola and piano or viola and chamber orchestra]. (Kim Kashkashian/Stuttgart Chamber Orchestra/Dennis Russell Davies). *See 3586.16*

3553.7 *Metamorphoses (6) after Ovid* [for solo oboe]. *See 3437*

3553.8 *A midsummer night's dream* [opera]. (Elizabeth Harwood/Alfred Deller/Owen Brannigan/London Symphony/Benjamin Britten). London: 425 664-2. 2CD set.

3553.9 *Nocturnal* [for solo guitar]. *See 3999*

3553.10 * *Peter Grimes* [opera].
- (Claire Watson/Peter Pears/Covent Garden/Benjamin Britten). London: 414 577-2. 3CD set.
- (Felicity Lott/Anthony Rolfe-Johnson/Covent Garden/Bernard Haitink). EMI: 7 54832 2. 2CD set.

3553.11 *Phantasy quartet* [for oboe and strings]. (Derek Wickens/Gabrieli Quartet). Unicorn-Kanchana: UKCD 2060. [Album title: *Early chamber music.* With his *Temporal variations; Insect pieces;* and other works].

3553.12 * *Quartet for strings no. 2.*
- (Britten Quartet). Collins: 10252. [With his *Quartet no. 3*].
- (Tokyo Quartet). *See 3925.1*

3553.13 *The rape of Lucretia* [opera]. (Heather Harper/Janet Baker/Peter Pears/English Chamber Orchestra/Benjamin Britten). London: 425 666-2. 2CD set. [With his *Phaedra*].

3553.14 * *Sea interludes* [from Peter Grimes]. *See* 3553.17

3553.15 * *Serenade for tenor, horn, and strings.* (Peter Pears/Barry Tuckwell/London Symphony/Benjamin Britten). London: 417 153-2. [With his *Les illuminations* and *Nocturne*].

3553.16 *Simple symphony. See* 3553.21

3553.17 *Spring symphony.* (London Symphony/André Previn). EMI: CDC 7 47667 2. [With his *Sea interludes*].

3553.18 *Variations on a theme of Frank Bridge. See* 3553.21

3553.19 *Violoncello music.* Selections. (Mstislav Rostropovich/Benjamin Britten). London: 421 859-2. [*Suites for violoncello solo nos. 1–2; Sonata for violoncello and piano*].

3553.20 ** *War Requiem.*
- (Galina Vishnevskaya/Peter Pears/Dietrich Fischer-Dieskau/London Symphony/Benjamin Britten). London: 414 383-2. 2CD set.
- (Elisabeth Söderstrom/Thomas Allen/City of Birmingham Symphony/Simon Rattle). EMI: CDS 7 47034 8. 2CD set.

3553.21 * *Young person's guide to the orchestra.* (London Symphony/Benjamin Britten). London: 417 509-2. [With his *Simple symphony* and *Variations on a theme of Frank Bridge*].

3554 Busoni, Ferruccio, 1866–1924

3554.1 *Concerto for piano and orchestra, op. 39 in C major.* (Garrick Ohlsson/Cleveland Orchestra/Christoph von Dohnanyi). Telarc: CD-80207.

3554.2 * *Fantasia contrapputistica* [for piano]. (Christopher O'Riley). Centaur: 2036.

3554.3 *Sonatinas (6) for piano.* (Paul Jacobs). Nonesuch: H- 71359. LP. OP

3555 * Canteloube, Joseph, 1879–1957

Chants d'Auvergne. Selections. (Kiri Te Kanawa/English Chamber Orchestra/Jeffrey Tate). London: 410 004-2.

3556 Carpenter, John Alden, 1876–1951

Krazy Kat [for orchestra]. (Los Angeles Philharmonic/Calvin Simmons). New World: 80228-2. [With Gilbert, Henry: *Dance in Place Congo*; Weiss, Adolph: *American life*; Powell, John: *Rhapsodie nègre*].

3557 Chávez, Carlos, 1899–1978

3557.1 * *Symphonies* (6). (London Symphony/Eduardo Mata). Vox Box: CDX 5061. 2CD set.

3557.2 *Toccata* [for percussion ensemble]. *See* 3661

3558 Clarke, Rebecca, 1886–1979

Chamber music. Selections. (Patricia McCarty and others). Northeastern: NR 212. [Album title: *Music for viola*].

3559 Copland, Aaron, 1900–1990

3559.1 ** *Appalachian spring* [ballet].
- (New York Philharmonic/Leonard Bernstein). Sony: SMK 47543. [Version for orchestra. With his *Rodeo; Billy the Kid;* and *Fanfare for the common man*].
- (London Symphony/Aaron Copland). CBS: MK 42431. [Version for orchestra. With his *Lincoln portrait* and *Billy the Kid suite*].
- (Orpheus Chamber Orchestra). Deutsche Grammophon: 427 335-2. [Suite from the ballet. Version for 13 instruments. With his *Short symphony; Quiet city; Latin-American sketches*].
- (St. Paul Chamber Orchestra/Hugh Wolff). [Version for 13 instruments]. *See* 3559.8

3559.2 * *Billy the Kid* [ballet suite]. *See* 3559.1

3559.3 *Concerto for clarinet and orchestra.*
- (Stanley Drucker/New York Philharmonic/Leonard Bernstein). *See* 3559.15
- (Benny Goodman/Aaron Copland). *See* 3666

3559.4 *Concerto for piano and orchestra.* (Earl Wild/Symphony of the Air/Aaron Copland). Vanguard: OVC 4029.

3559.5 * *Connotations* [for orchestra]. *See* 3559.15

3559.6 *Fanfare for the common man. See* 3660 or 3559.1

3559.7 *Lincoln portrait.* (Henry Fonda/London Symphony/Aaron Copland). *See* 3559.1

3559.8 *Music for the theatre.*
- (New York Philharmonic/Leonard Bernstein). *See* 3559.15
- (St. Paul Chamber Orchestra/Hugh Wolff). Teldec: 2292-46314-2. [With his *Latin American sketches; Quiet city; Appalachian spring*].

3559.9 *Old American songs.*
- (Thomas Hampson/Dawn Upshaw/St. Paul Chamber Orchestra/Hugh Wolff). *See* 3559.11

- (Samuel Ramey/Warren Jones). Argo: 433 027-2. [With Ives, Charles: *Songs*].

3559.10 * *Piano music. Selections.*

- (Charles Fierro). Delos: 1013. [*Piano fantasy; Passacaglia; Night thoughts; Piano variations*].
- (Paul Jacobs). [His *Piano blues* only]. *See* 4011
- (Peter Lawson). [His *Piano sonata* only]. *See* 3670
- (David Lively). Etcetera: 1062. [*Piano fantasy; Piano variations; Piano sonata*].

3559.11 *Poems (8) of Emily Dickinson.* (Dawn Upshaw/St. Paul Chamber Orchestra/Hugh Wolff). Teldec: 77310. [With his *Old American songs*].

3559.12 *Quartet for piano and strings.*

- (Boston Symphony Chamber Players). *See* 3559.16
- (Romuald Tecco and others). *See* 3559.20

3559.13 * *Quiet city. See* 3559.1 or 3559.8 or 3559.18

3559.14 *Rodeo* [four dance episodes]. *See* 3559.1

3559.15 *El salón Mexico.* (New York Philharmonic/Leonard Bernstein). Deutsche Grammophon: 431 672-2. [With his *Concerto for clarinet and orchestra; Music for the theatre;* and *Connotations*].

3559.16 *Sextet for clarinet, piano, and string quartet.* (Boston Symphony Chamber Players). Elektra Nonesuch: 79168-2. [With his *Piano variations; Quartet for piano and strings*].

3559.17 * *Short symphony (Symphony no. 2).*

- (Orchestra of St. Luke's/Dennis Russell Davies). MusicMasters: 01612- 671-1-2. [With his *Dance panels* and *Poems of Emily Dickinson*].
- (Orpheus Chamber Orchestra). *See* 3559.1.

3559.18 *Symphony no. 3.* (New York Philharmonic/Leonard Bernstein). Deutsche Grammophon: 419 170-2. [With his *Quiet city*].

3559.19 *The tender land* [opera]. (Plymouth Music/Philip Brunelle). Virgin: 7 59207 2 (7 91113 2). 2CD set.

3559.20 *Vitebsk* [study on a Jewish theme for violin, violoncello, and piano]. (Romuald Tecco and others). MusicMasters: 7026-2-C. [With his *Quartet for piano and strings* and *Sonata for violin and piano*].

3560 Cowell, Henry, 1897–1965

3560.1 *Orchestral music. Selections.*

- (Manhattan Chamber Orchestra/Richard Auldon Clark). Koch: 3-7220-2.

- (Northwest Chamber Orchestra, Seattle/Alun Francis). CPO: 999 222-2.

3560.2 * *Piano music.*

- (Henry Cowell). Smithsonian/Folkways: 40801.
- (Steffen Schleiermacher). *See* 3676

3560.3 *Pulse* [for percussion ensemble]. *See* 4014

3560.4 *Quartet euphometric* [for strings]. (Emerson Quartet). *See* 4005

3560.5 ** *Set of five* [for violin, percussion, and piano]. *See* 3990

3561 Creston, Paul, 1906–1985

Orchestral music. Selections. (Seattle Symphony/ New York Chamber Symphony/Gerard Schwarz). Delos: DE 3127. [*Toccata; Choreographic suite; Symphony no. 5*].

3562 Dallapiccola, Luigi, 1904–1975

3562.1 *Liriche greche.* (Jane Manning/Alstralia Ensemble/Graham Hair). Entr'acte: ESCD 6504. [With his *Divertimento in quattro esercizi* and *Piccola musica notturna* for chamber ensembles].

3562.2 *Piano music. Selections.* (Ruggero Ruocco). *See* 3876.2

3562.3 * *Il prigioniero* [opera].

- (Phyllis Bryn-Julson/Jorma Hynninen/Swedish Radio Symphony/Esa-Pekka Salonen). Sony: SK 68323. [With his *Canti di prigionia*].
- (Helga Pilarczyk/Mario Basiola/Bavarian Radio Symphony/Hermann Scherchen). Stradivarius: 10034. [With his *Cinque canti* and *Preghiere* for baritone and instruments].

3563 Debussy, Claude, 1862–1918

3563.1 *Arabesques* [for piano]. (Zoltán Kocsis). *See* 3563.9

3563.2 * *Children's corner* [for piano].

- (Arturo Benedetti Michelangeli). *See* 3563.9
- (Alexis Weissenberg). *See* 3563.6

3563.3 * *Danse sacrée et danse profane* [for harp and strings]. (Vera Badings/Concertgebouw Orchestra/Bernard Haitink). *See* 3448.5

3563.4 *En blanc et noir* [for two pianos]. (Claude Helffer/Haakon Austbo). Harmonia Mundi: 90957. [With his *Épigraphes antiques; Petite suite;* and other works].

3563.5 *Épigraphes antiques. See* 3563.4

3563.6 ** *Estampes* [for piano].

- (Claudio Arrau). *See* 3563.17
- (Zoltán Kocsis). *See* 3563.24

- (Alexis Weissenberg). Deutsche Grammophon: 415 510-2. [With his *Suite bergamasque; Children's corner; L'isle joyeuse*].

3563.7 * *Etudes (12) for piano.*

- (Maurizio Pollini). Deutsche Grammophon: 423 678-2. [With Berg, Alban: *Sonata for piano*].

- (Mitsuko Uchida). Philips: 422 412-2.

3563.8 * *Images (3) for orchestra.*

- (Cleveland Orchestra/Pierre Boulez). *See* 3563.16

- (Montreal Symphony/Charles Dutoit). London: 425 502-2. [With his *Nocturnes*].

3563.9 * *Images [for piano], books 1–2.*

- (Claudio Arrau). *See* 3563.17

- (Zoltán Kocsis). Philips: 422 404-2. [With his *Arabesques; L'isle joyeuse;* and other works].

- (Arturo Benedetti Michelangeli). Deutsche Grammophon: 415 372-2. [With his *Children's corner*].

3563.10 *L'isle joyeuse [for piano]. See* 3563.6 or 3563.9

3563.11 * *Jeux [for orchestra].*

- (Cleveland Orchestra/Pierre Boulez). *See* 3563.13

- (Concertgebouw Orchestra/Bernard Haitink). *See* 3563.13

3563.12 ** *La mer [for orchestra].*

- (Cleveland Orchestra/Pierre Boulez). *See* 3563.13

- (Concertgebouw Orchestra/Bernard Haitink). Philips: 416 444-2. [With his *Prélude à l'après-midi d'un faune*].

- (Boston Symphony/Charles Munch). RCA: 09026-61500-2. [With his *Prélude à l'après-midi d'un faune* and *Nocturnes 1–2*].

3563.13 ** *Nocturnes (3) [for orchestra].*

- (Cleveland Orchestra/Pierre Boulez). Deutsche Grammophon: 439 896-2. [With his *Jeux* and *La mer*].

- (Montreal Symphony/Charles Dutoit). *See* 3563.8

- (Concertgebouw Orchestra/Bernard Haitink). Philips: 400 023-2. [With his *Jeux*].

3563.14 * *Pelleas et Mélisande [opera].*

- (Elizabeth Söderström/George Shirley/Covent Garden/Pierre Boulez). Sony: SM3K 47265. 3CD set.

- (Colette Alliot-Lugaz/Didier Henry/Montreal Symphony/Charles Dutoit). London: 403 502-2. 2CD set.

3563.15 * *Pour le piano.* (Zoltán Kocsis). *See* 3563.24

3563.16 ** *Prélude à l'après-midi d'un faune (Prelude to the afternoon of a faun) [for orchestra].*

- (Chicago Symphony/Pierre Boulez). Deutsche Grammophon: 435 766-2. [With his *Images* and *Printemps*].

- (Concertgebouw Orchestra/Bernard Haitink). *See* 3563.12

- (Boston Symphony/Charles Munch). *See* 3563.12

3563.17 * *Preludes for piano, books 1–2.*

- (Claudio Arrau). Philips: 420 393-2 / 420 394-2. 2 CDs. [With his *Estampes* and *Images*].

- (Krystian Zimerman). Deutsche Grammophon: 435 773-2. 2CD set.

3563.18 * *Quartet for strings, op. 10 in G minor.*

- (Alban Berg Quartet). EMI: CDC 7 47347 2. [With Ravel, Maurice: *Quartet for strings*].

- (Emerson Quartet). Deutsche Grammophon: 427 320-2. [With Ravel, Maurice: *Quartet for strings*].

3563.19 *Rhapsody for alto saxophone and orchestra.* (John Harle/Academy of St. Martin-in-the-Fields/Neville Marriner). *See* 3667

3563.20 *Sonata for flute, viola, and harp.*

- (Roger Bourdin/Colette Lequien/Annie Challan). *See* 3563.21

- (Osian Ellis/Melos Ensemble). *See* 3469.2

3563.21 * *Sonata for violin and piano.*

- (Borodin Trio members). *See* 3617.25

- (Kyung-Wha Chung/Radu Lupu). *See* 3469.2

- (Arthur Grimiaux/István Hadju). Philips: 422 839-2. [With his *Sonata for flute, viola, and harp; Sonata for violoncello and piano;* and *Syrinx*].

- (Joseph Szigeti/Béla Bartók). *See* 3400.15

3563.22 * *Sonata for violoncello and piano.*

- (Borodin Trio members). *See* 3617.25

- (Maurice Gendron/Jean Françaix). *See* 3563.21

- (Mstislav Rostropovich/Benjamin Britten). *See* 3506.16

3563.23 *Songs.* (Frederica von Stade/Dalton Baldwin). EMI: CDMC 7 64095 2. 3CD set.

3563.24 ** *Suite bergamasque [for piano].*

- (Zoltán Kocsis). Philips: 412 118-2. [With his *Pour le piano; Estampes;* and *Images oubliées*].
- (Alexis Weissenberg). *See* 3563.6

3563.25 *Syrinx* [for flute unaccompanied]. (Roger Bourdin). *See* 3563.21

3564 Delius, Frederick, 1862–1934

3564.1 * *Orchestral music. Selections.*
- (Royal Philharmonic/Thomas Beecham). EMI: CDS 7 47509 8. 2CD set. [Album title: *Beecham conducts Delius.* Includes *Over the hills and far away; Brigg Fair; Florida suite; Two pieces for small orchestra; Songs of sunset;* and other works].
- (Welsh National Opera Orchestra/Charles Mackerras). Argo: 433 704-2. [*Concerto for violin and orchestra; Dance rhapsodies; Aquarelles;* and other works].

3564.2 *A village Romeo and Juliet* [opera]. (Helen Field/Arthur Davies/ORF Symphony/ Charles Mackerras). Argo: 430 275-2. 2CD set.

3565 Dohnányi, Ernö, 1877–1960

Instrumental music. Selections. (István Lantos/ Budapest Symphony/György Lenel). White Label: HRC 121. [*Ruralia hungarica; Variations on a nursery song; Serenade for string trio*].

3566 Dukas, Paul, 1865–1935

3566.1 * *L'apprenti sorcier (The sorcerer's apprentice).*
- (New York Philharmonic/Leonard Bernstein). *See* 3532
- (Suisse Romande Orchestra/Ernest Ansermet). London: 433 714-2. [With his *La péri;* and Debussy, Claude: *La boite à joujoux*].

3566.2 *La péri. See* 3566.1

3566.3 *Villanelle for horn and piano.* (Dennis Brain/Gerald Moore). *See* 3400.12

3567 Dupré, Marcel, 1886–1971

Organ music. Selections. (Pierre Cochereau). FY: FYCD 020.

3568 Duruflé, Maurice, 1902–1986

3568.1 *Organ music. Selections.* (Philippe Lefebvre). FY: FYCD 100.

3568.2 *Requiem.* (Ambrosian Singers/Michel Legrand). *See* 3467.11

3569 Eisler, Hanns, 1898–1962

3569.1 * *Deutsche Sinfonie.* (Ernst Senff Chorus/ Gewandhaus Orchestra Leipzig/Lothar Zagrosek). London: 448 389-2.

3569.2 *Songs. Selections.* (Maria Tegzes/Geoffrey Burleson). Neuma: 450-83. [With his selected piano music].

3570 Enesco, Georges, 1881–1955

3570.1 *Chamber symphony, op. 33.* (Cluj-Napoca Philharmonic/Ion Baciu). Marco Polo: 8.223143. [With his *Symphony no. 3*].

3570.2 *Oedipe* [opera]. (José van Dam/Monte-Carlo Symphony/Lawrence Foster). EMI: CDS 7 54011 2. 2CD set.

3570.3 * *Rhapsodies roumaines (2)* [for orchestra]. (Royal Scottish Orchestra/Neeme Järvi). Chandos: CHAN 8947. [With Bartók, Béla: *Concerto for orchestra*].

3571 Falla, Manuel de, 1876–1946

3571.1 * *El amor brujo (Love the sorcerer)* [ballet for mezzo-soprano and orchestra]. (Teresa Berganza/Suisse Romand Orchestra/Ernest Ansermet). London: 433 908-2. 2CD set. [With his *Vida breve* (orchestral selections); *Sombrero de tres picos; Noches en los jardines de España; Retablo de maese Pedro; Psyché; Concerto*].

3571.2 *Canciones populares españolas.* (Victoria de los Angeles/Gerald Moore). *See* 3673

3571.3 * *Concerto for harpsichord and chamber ensemble.* (John Constable/London Sinfonietta/ Simon Rattle). *See* 3571.1

3571.4 *Noches en los jardines de España (Nights in the gardens of Spain)* [for piano and orchestra]. (Alicia de Larrocha/London Philharmonic/ Rafael Frühbeck de Burgos). *See* 3571.1

3571.5 *Psyché* [for soprano and instrumental ensemble]. (Jennifer Smith/London Sinfonietta/ Simon Rattle). *See* 3571.1

3571.6 *El retablo de maese Pedro (Master Peter's puppet show).* (London Sinfonietta/Simon Rattle). *See* 3571.1

3571.7 * *El sombrero de tres picos (The three-cornered hat)* [ballet]. (Teresa Berganza/Suisse Romande Orchestra/Ernest Ansermet). *See* 3571.1

3572 Françaix, Jean, 1912–

3572.1 *L'horloge de flore (The flower clock)* [for oboe and orchestra]. (John De Lancie/London Symphony/André Previn). *See* 3642.6

3572.2 *Petite quatuor (Little quartet)* [for saxophones]. (Berliner Saxophon-Quartett). *See* 3662

3572.3 * *Quintet for woodwinds and horn.*

- (Ensemble Wien-Berlin). *See* 4006
- (Pro Arte Wind Quintet). *See* 3674

3573 * Gerhard, Roberto, 1896–1970

Symphony no. 1. (Tenerife Symphony/Víctor Pablo Pérez). Auvidis Valois: V 4728. [With his *Symphony no. 3*].

3574 Gershwin, George, 1898–1937

3574.1 * *An American in Paris.*

- (New York Philharmonic/Leonard Bernstein) *See* 3574.5
- (Minneapolis Symphony/Antal Dorati). Mercury: 434 329-2. [With Copland, Aaron: *Dance episodes from Rodeo;* Schuller, Gunther: *Studies on themes of Paul Klee;* Bloch, Ernest: *Sinfonia breve*].
- (London Symphony/André Previn). *See* 3574.5

3574.2 *Concerto for piano and orchestra in F major.*

- (Oscar Levant/New York Philharmonic/Andre Kostelanetz). *See* 3574.5
- (André Previn/London Symphony). *See* 3574.5

3574.3 * *Piano music. Selections.*

- (William Bolcom). Elektra Nonesuch: 79151-2. [With his songs].
- (George Gershwin [from piano rolls]). Elektra Nonesuch: 79287-2.

3574.4 ** *Porgy and Bess. See* 6068.7

3574.5 ** *Rhapsody in blue* [for piano and orchestra].

- (Leonard Bernstein/Columbia Symphony). CBS: MYK 37242. [With his *American in Paris*].
- (Oscar Levant/Philadelphia Orchestra/Eugene Ormandy). CBS: MK 42514. [With his *Rhapsody no. 2; Concerto for piano and orchestra; "I got rhythm" variations for piano and orchestra;* and *Preludes for piano*].
- (André Previn/London Symphony). EMI: CDC 7 47161 2. [With his *American in Paris* and *Concerto for piano and orchestra*].

3574.6 *Rhapsody no. 2 for piano and orchestra.* (Oscar Levant/Morton Gould Orchestra). *See* 3574.5

3575 Ginastera, Alberto, 1916–1983

3575.1 * *Concerto for harp and orchestra.* (Nancy Allen/Mexico City Philharmonic/Enrique Bátiz). ASV: CD DCA 654. [With his *Estancia* and *Concerto for piano and orchestra*].

3575.2 *Estancia.* (Mexico City Philharmonic/ Enrique Bátiz). *See* 3575.1

3575.3 * *Pampanea no. 3.* (Simon Bolivar Symphony of Venezuela/Eduardo Mata). *See* 3620.6

3575.4 *Sonata for guitar.* (Joaquim Freire). Leman Classics: LC 42601. [With Ponce, Manuel M.: *Folias de España;* Villa Lobos, Heitor: *Preludes*].

3575.5 *Variaciones concertantes* [for orchestra]. (Israel Chamber Orchestra/London Symphony/ Gisèle Ben-Dor). Koch: 3-7149-2H1. [With his *Glosses on themes of Pablo Casals, opp. 46 and 48*].

3576 * Glanville-Hicks, Peggy, 1912–1990

Etruscan concerto [for piano and orchestra]. (Keith Jarrett/Brooklyn Philharmonic/Dennis Russell Davies). *See* 3781.5

3577 * Glière, Reinhold Moritsevich, 1875–1956

Krasnyi mak (The red poppy) [ballet suite]. (BBC Philharmonic/Edward Downes). Chandos: CHAN 9160. [With his *Symphony no. 1*].

3578 Grainger, Percy, 1882–1961

3578.1 * *Orchestral music. Selections.* (Bournemouth Sinfonietta/Kenneth Montgomery). Chandos: CHAN 6542. [Album title: *Famous folk-settings*].

3578.2 *Piano music. Selections.* [Series: *Dished up for piano, vol. 1*]. (Martin Jones). Nimbus: NI 5220.

3579 Griffes, Charles Tomlinson, 1884–1920

3579.1 * *Orchestral music. Selections.* (Seattle Symphony/Gerard Schwarz). Delos: CD 3099. [*Pleasure-dome of Kubla Khan; White peacock; Poem for flute and orchestra; Three tone pictures; Bacchanale.* With Taylor, Deems: *Through the looking glass*].

3579.2 *Sonata for piano in F major.* (Peter Lawson). *See* 3671

3580 Grofé, Ferde, 1892–1972

Grand Canyon suite. (New York Philharmonic/ Leonard Bernstein). CBS: MYK 37759. [With his *Mississippi suite*].

3581 Gruenberg, Louis, 1884–1964

Works. Selections. (Collage/Gunther Schuller). GM: 2015. [*The creation; White lilacs; Diversions; Jazz epigrams; Rhapsody*].

3582 Hába, Alois, 1893–1973

Chamber music. Selections. (Suk Quartet/Czech Nonet). Praga: PR 255 005. [*Quartets for strings nos. 7–8, 13–15; Nonets for woodwinds, horn, and strings nos. 1 and 4*].

3583 Hanson, Howard, 1896–1981

Symphony no. 2 ("Romantic"). (St. Louis Symphony/Leonard Slatkin). RCA: 60732-2. [With Barber, Samuel: *Concerto for violin and orchestra*].

3584 Harris, Roy, 1898–1979

3584.1 * *Symphony no. 3.* (New York Philharmonic/Leonard Bernstein). Deutsche Grammophon: 419 780-2. [With Schuman, William: *Symphony no. 3*].

3584.2 * *Symphony no. 6 ("Gettysburg").* (Pacific Symphony/Keith Clark). *See* 3543.3

3585 Hartmann, Karl Amadeus, 1906–1963

3585.1 *Gesangsszene.* (Siegmund Nimsgern/Bamberg Symphony/Karl Anton Rickenbacher). Koch: 3-1295-2. [With his *Sinfonia tragica* and *Adagio from Symphony no. 2*].

3585.2 *Symphony no. 3.* (Bamberg Symphony/Ingo Metzmacher). *See* 3590.8

3586 Hindemith, Paul, 1895–1963

3586.1 * *Chamber music. Selections.*

• (Malmö Brass Ensemble and others). Bis: 159. [*Morgenmusik; Sonata for trumpet and piano; Sonata for trombone and piano; Sonata for bass tuba and piano; Trio for three recorders from Plöner Musiktag; Sonata for alto saxophone and piano; Sonata for bassoon and piano*].

See also 3586.4, 3586.14, 3672

3586.2 *Concerto for violin and orchestra.* (David Oistrakh/London Symphony/Claudio Abbado). *See* 3586.8

3586.3 ** *Kammermusik 1–7.* (Concertgebouw Orchestra/Riccardo Chailly). London: 433 816-2. 2CD set. [With his *Kleine Kammermusik*].

3586.4 ** *Kleine Kammermusik* [for wind quintet].

• (Concertgebouw Orchestra members). *See* 3586.3

• (Netherlands Wind Quintet). CPO: 999229. [With his *Sonata for four horns; Sonata for horn and piano; Sonata for alto horn and piano*].

3586.5 *Konzertmusik for brass and string orchestra, op. 50.* (San Francisco Symphony/Herbert Blomstedt). *See* 3586.9

3586.6 *Ludus tonalis* [for piano]. (Sviatoslav Richter). Pyramid: 13497. [With his *Sonata no. 2*].

3586.7 *Das Marienleben* [song cycle]. (Gundula Janowitz/Irwin Gage). Jecklin: 574-2. [Revised version of 1948. With his songs].

3586.8 * *Mathis der Maler* [symphony].

• (Israel Philharmonic/Leonard Bernstein). Deutsche Grammophon: 429 404-2. [With his *Konzertmusik* and *Symphonic metamorphoses*].

• (London Symphony/Paul Hindemith). London: 433 081-2. [With his *Concerto for violin and orchestra* and *Symphonic metamorphoses* (Kletzki)].

• (Berlin Philharmonic/Herbert von Karajan). *See* 3545.11

3586.9 *Nobilissima visione* [ballet]. (San Francisco Symphony/Herbert Blomstedt). London: 433 809-2. [With his *Schwanendreher* and *Konzertmusik*].

3586.10 * *Octet for woodwinds, horn, and strings.* (Marlboro Festival Ensemble). *See* 3543.13

3586.11 *Der Schwanendreher* [for viola and orchestra]. (Geraldine Walther/San Francisco Symphony/Herbert Blomstedt). *See* 3586.9

3586.12 *Sonatas (3) for organ.* (Piet Kee). Chandos: CHAN 9097.

3586.13 *Sonatas (3) for piano.*

• (Glenn Gould). Sony: SMK 52670.

• (Sviatoslav Richter). [*Sonata no. 2* only]. *See* 3586.6

3586.14 *Sonatas (2) for viola unaccompanied.* (Kim Kashkashian/Robert Levin). ECM: 1330/32. 2CD set. [With his *Sonatas (3) for viola and piano*].

3586.15 * *Symphonic metamorphoses on themes by Carl Maria von Weber.*

• (Israel Philharmonic/Leonard Bernstein). *See* 3586.8

• (Suisse Romand Orchestra/Paul Kletzki). *See* 3586.8

3586.16 * *Trauermusik* [for viola and orchestra]. (Kim Kashkashian/Stuttgart Chamber Orchestra/

Dennis Russell Davies). ECM: 1506 (78118-20002-2). [With Britten, Benjamin: *Lachrymae*; Penderecki, Krzysztof: *Concerto for viola and chamber orchestra*].

3586.17 *When lilacs last in the dooryard bloom'd* [cantata]. (Atlanta Symphony Chorus and Orchestra/Robert Shaw). Telarc: 80132.

3587 Holst, Gustav, 1874–1934

3587.1 *Hammersmith* [for band]. (Dallas Wind Symphony). Reference: RR-39. [With his *Suite for band nos. 1–2* and *Moorside suite*].

3587.2 ** *The planets*.

- (Berlin Philharmonic/Herbert von Karajan). Deutsche Grammophon: 400 028-2.

- (London Symphony/Georg Solti). London: 414 567-2.

3588 Honegger, Arthur, 1892–1955

3588.1 *Concerto da camera for flute, English horn, and string orchestra*. (Timothy Hutchins/Pierre-Vincent Plante/Musici de Montreal/Yuli Turovsky). Chandos: CHAN 8632. [With his *Symphony no. 2* and *Prelude, arioso, and fughetta on the name of Bach*].

3588.2 *Jean d'Arc à bûcher* [oratorio]. (Serge Baudo). Supraphon: 11 0557-2. 2CD set.

3588.3 * *Pacific 231* [symphonic poem].

- (Czech Philharmonic/Serge Baudo). *See 3588.6*

- (Danish National Radio Symphony/Neeme Järvi). *See 3588.10*

3588.4 *Pastorale d'été* [for orchestra]. (Bournemouth Sinfonietta/Tamás Vásáry). *See 3588.9*

3588.5 *Le roi David* [oratorio]. (Charles Dutoit). Erato: 2292-45800-2. 2CD set.

3588.6 *Symphony no. 1*. (Czech Philharmonic/Serge Baudo). Supraphon: 11 1566-2. 2CD set. [With his *Symphonies 2–5*; *Pacific 231*; *Mouvement symphonique no. 3*; *Prélude pour la Tempête de Shakespeare*].

3588.7 *Symphony no. 2* [for string orchestra and trumpet].

- (Czech Philharmonic/Serge Baudo). *See 3588.6*

- (Musici de Montreal/Yuli Turovsky). *See 3588.1*

3588.8 * *Symphony no. 3* (*"Liturgique"*).

- (Czech Philharmonic/Serge Baudo). *See 3588.6*

- (Danish National Radio Symphony/Neeme Järvi). *See 3588.10*

3588.9 *Symphony no. 4 "Deliciae basilienses"*).

- (Czech Philharmonic/Serge Baudo). *See 3588.6*

- (Bournemouth Sinfonietta/Tamás Vásáry). Chandos: CHAN 8993. [With his *Pastorale d'été*; *Prelude, arioso, and fuguetta on the name of Bach*; *Concertino for piano and orchestra*].

3588.10 * *Symphony no. 5 ("De tre re")*.

- (Czech Philharmonic/Serge Baudo). *See 3588.6*

- (Danish National Radio Symphony/Neeme Järvi). Chandos: CHAN 9176. [With his *Pacific 231* and *Symphony no. 3*].

3589 Ibert, Jacques, 1890–1962

3589.1 *Concertino for saxophone and orchestra*. (John Harle/Academy of St. Martin-in-the-Fields/Neville Marriner). *See 3667*

3589.2 *Concerto for flute and orchestra*. (Timothy Hutchins/Montreal Symphony/Charles Dutoit). *See 3589.3*

3589.3 * *Escales (Ports of call)*.

- (Montreal Symphony/Charles Dutoit). London: 440 332-2. [With his *Concerto for flute and orchestra*; *Hommage à Mozart*; *Paris*; *Bacchanale*; *Bostoniana*; *Louisville concerto*].

- (Boston Symphony/Charles Munch). *See 3504.8*

3589.4 *Louisville concerto*. (Montreal Symphony/Charles Dutoit). *See 3589.3*

3589.5 *Trois pièces brèves* [for wind quintet]. *See 3674*

3590 Ives, Charles, 1874–1954

3590.1 * *Central Park in the dark*.

- (St. Louis Symphony/Leonard Slatkin). *See 3590.18*

- (Chicago Symphony/Michael Tilson Thomas). *See 3590.2*

3590.2 * *Holidays*. (Chicago Symphony/Michael Tilson Thomas). CBS: MK 42381. [With his *Central Park in the dark* and *Unanswered question* (2 versions)].

3590.3 *Instrumental music. Selections*. (Ensemble Modern/Ingo Metzmacher). EMI: 7 54552 2. [Album title: *Portrait of Charles Ives*. Includes 26 short works for chamber orchestra, instrumental ensemble, or voice and instruments].

3590.4 *Largo for violin, clarinet, and piano*. (Lucy Stoltzman/Richard Stoltzman/Richard Goode). *See 3545.5*

3590.5 * *Piano music. Selections*. (Herbert Henck/Deborah Richards) Wergo: 60112. [*Studies nos. 2, 9, 20–22*; *Waltz-rondo*; *Three-page sonata*; *Quarter-tone pieces*].

3590.6 * *Quarter-tone pieces (3)* [for two pianos]. (Herbert Henck/Deborah Richards). *See* 3590.5

3590.7 * *Quartets (2) for strings.* (Emerson Quartet). Deutsche Grammophon: 435 864-2. [With his *Scherzo "Holding your own" from Set of three short pieces*; Barber, Samuel: *Quartet for strings no. 1*].

3590.8 * *Robert Browning overture.* (Bamberg Symphony/Ingo Metzmacher). EMI: 7243 5 55254 2 0. [With Hartmann, Karl Amadeus: *Symphony no. 3*].

3590.9 * *Sonata for piano no. 1.*
- (Herbert Henck). Wergo: 60101-50.
- (Peter Lawson). *See* 3671

3590.10 * *Sonata for piano no. 2 ("Concord, Massachusetts, 1840–1860").*
- (Marc-André Hamelin). New World: 378-2. [With Wright, Maurice: *Sonata for piano*].
- (Gilbert Kalish). Elektra Nonesuch: 71337-2.

3590.11 *Sonatas (4) for violin and piano.* (Gregory Fulkerson/Robert Shannon). Bridge: 9024.

3590.12 *Songs. Selections.*
- (Jan DeGaetani/Gilbert Kalish). Elektra Nonesuch: 71325-2.
- (Henry Herford/Ensemble Modern/Ingo Metzmacher). *See* 3590.3
- (Samuel Ramey/Warren Jones). *See* 3559.9

3590.13 *Symphony no. 1.* (Chicago Symphony/ Michael Tilson Thomas). Sony: SK 44939. [With his *Symphony no. 4*].

3590.14 *Symphony no. 2.* (Concertgebouw Orchestra/Michael Tilson Thomas). Sony: SK 46440. [With his *Symphony no. 3*].

3590.15 ** *Symphony no. 3 ("The camp meeting").*
- (Orpheus Chamber Orchestra). *See* 3590.18
- (St. Louis Symphony/Leonard Slatkin). *See* 3590.18
- (Concertgebouw Orchestra/Michael Tilson Thomas). *See* 3590.14

3590.16 * *Symphony no. 4.*
- (Cleveland Orchestra/Christoph von Dohnanyi/ Jahja Ling). *See* 3650.1
- (Chicago Symphony/Michael Tilson Thomas). *See* 3590.13

3590.17 * *Three-page sonata* [for piano].
- (Herbert Henck). *See* 3590.5
- (Peter Lawson). *See* 3670

3590.18 ** *Three places in New England.*
- (Orpheus Chamber Orchestra). Deutsche Grammophon: 439 869-2. [With his *Unanswered question; Set of pieces for theatre or chamber orchestra; Symphony no. 3*].
- (St. Louis Symphony/Leonard Slatkin). RCA: 09026-61222-2. [With his *Central Park in the dark; Unanswered question; Symphony no. 3*].

3590.19 * *The unanswered question.*
- (Orpheus Chamber Orchestra). *See* 3590.18
- (St. Louis Symphony/Leonard Slatkin). *See* 3590.18
- (Chicago Symphony/Michael Tilson Thomas) [original and revised versions]. *See* 3590.2

3590.20 *Variations on "America"* [orchestrated by William Schuman]. (New York Philharmonic/ Kurt Masur). Teldec: 9031-74007-2. [With Brahms, Johannes: *Variationen über ein Thema von Haydn*; Reger, Max: *Variationen und Fuge über ein Thema von W. A. Mozart*].

3591 Janáček, Leoš, 1854–1928

3591.1 *Capriccio for piano (left hand) and chamber ensemble.* (Rudolf Firkušný/Czech Philharmonic/Václav Neumann). *See* 3464.1

3591.2 *Concertino for piano and chamber ensemble.* (Rudolf Firkušný/Czech Philharmonic/ Václav Neumann). *See* 3464.1

3591.3 * *Jenůfa* [opera]. (Elisabeth Söderström/ Vienna Philharmonic/Charles Mackerras). London: 414 483-2. 2CD set. [With his *Žárlivost overture*].

3591.4 *Kátá Kabanová* [opera]. (Elisabeth Söderström/Vienna Philharmonic/Charles Mackerras). London: 421 852-2. 2CD set.

3591.5 *Mládí (Youth)* [for woodwinds and horn].
- (London Sinfonietta/David Atherton). *See* 3591.16
- (Orpheus Chamber Orchestra). *See* 3545.7

3591.6 * *Mša Glagolskaja (Glagolitic Mass).*
- (Czechoslovak Radio Choir/Gewandhaus Orchestra/Kurt Masur). Philips: 432 983-2. [With his *Taras Bulba*].
- (City of Birmingham Symphony Chorus and Orchestra/Simon Rattle). *See* 3591.11

3591.7 *Piano music.*
- (Rudolf Firkušný). Deutsche Grammophon: 429 857-2. [Includes *Po zarostlém chodníčku (On an overgrown path); Sonata 1.X.1905; V mlhách (In the mists)*. Recorded 1972].

- (Rudolf Firkušný). RCA: 60147-2. [Same contents as above; recorded 1989].

3591.8 *Po zarostlém chodníčku (On an overgrown path)* [for piano]. See 3591.7

3591.9 ** *Příhody lišky Bystroušky (The cunning little vixen)* [opera].

- (Lucia Popp/Dalibor Jedlicka/Vienna Philharmonic/Charles Mackerras). London: 417 129-2. 2CD set. [In Czech].

- (Lillian Watson/Robert Tear/Covent Garden/Simon Rattle). EMI: CDS 7 54212 2. 2CD set. [In English. With his *Taras Bulba*].

3591.10 * *Quartets (2) for strings*. (Talich Quartet) Calliope: 9699.

3591.11 * *Sinfonietta*.

- (Berlin Philharmonic/Claudio Abbado). *See* 3591.17

- (Vienna Philharmonic/Charles Mackerras). London: 410 138-2. [With his *Taras Bulba*].

- (Philharmonia Orchestra/Simon Rattle). EMI: CDC 7 47504 2. [With his *Mša Glagolskaja*].

3591.12 *Sonata 1.X.1905* [for piano]. See 3591.7

3591.13 * *Taras Bulba* [for orchestra].

- (Vienna Philharmonic/Charles Mackerras). *See* 3591.11

- (Gewandhaus Orchestra/Kurt Masur). *See* 3591.6

- (Philharmonia Orchestra/Simon Rattle). *See* 3591.9

3591.14 *V mlhách (In the mists)* [for piano]. *See* 3591.7

3591.15 *Véc Makropulos (The Makropulos case)* [opera]. (Elisabeth Söderström/Peter Dvorský/Vienna Philharmonic/Charles Mackerras). London: 430 372-2. 2CD set.

3591.16 * *Z mrtvého domu (From the house of the dead)* [opera]. (Jiří Zahradníček/Vienna Philharmonic/Charles Mackerras). London: 430 375-2. 2CD set. [With his *Mládí* and *Říkadla*].

3591.17 *Zápisník zmizelého (Diary of one who vanished)* [song cycle]. (Philip Langridge/Berlin Philharmonic/Claudio Abbado). Deutsche Grammophon: 427 313-2. [With his *Sinfonietta*].

3592 Jolivet, André, 1905–1974

3592.1 * *Flute and piano music*. (Manuela Wiesler/Roland Pöntinen). Bis: 549. [*Incantations; Chant de Linos; Sonata; Ascèses*].

3592.2 *Sonata for piano no. 1*. (Marie-Catherine Girod). *See* 3750.3

3593 * Kabalevsky, Dmitry Borisovich, 1904–1987
Piano music. Selections. (Murray McLachlan). Olympia: 266. [*Preludes, op. 38; Sonatina, op. 13 no. 1 in C major; Sonata no. 3, op. 46*].

3594 Khachaturian, Aram Ilich, 1903–1978

3594.1 *Concerto for piano and orchestra*. (Alberto Portugheis/London Symphony/Loris Tjeknavorian). ASV: CD DCA 589. [With his *Sonatina* and *Toccata for piano* solo].

3594.2 *Concerto for violin and orchestra*. (Itzhak Perlman/Israel Philharmonic/Zubin Mehta). EMI: CDC 7 47087 2. [With Tchaikovsky, Peter Ilich: *Méditation*].

3594.3 * *Gaiane* [ballet suite].

- (Scottish National Orchestra/Neeme Järvi). Chandos: 8542. [With his *Concerto for piano and orchestra* and *Masquerade suite*].

- (Royal Philharmonic/Yuri Temirkanov). *See* 3594.4

3594.4 *Spartak (Spartacus)* [ballet suite]. (Royal Philharmonic/Yuri Temirkanov). EMI: CDC 7 47348 2. [With his *Gaiane suite*].

3594.5 *Toccata for piano*. (Alberto Portugheis). *See* 3594.1

3595 Kodály, Zoltán, 1882–1967

3595.1 *Duo for violin and violoncello, op. 7*. (Eleonora Turovsky/Yuli Turovsky). *See* 3595.6

3595.2 *Felszállot a páva (Peacock variations)* [for orchestra].

- (Hungarian State Orchestra/Antal Doráti). *See* 3595.5

- (Chicago Symphony/Neeme Järvi). *See* 3595.3

3595.3 *Galántai táncok (Dances of Galánta)* [for orchestra]. (Chicago Symphony/Neeme Järvi). Chandos: 8877. [With his *Háry János suite* and *Felszállot a páva*].

3595.4 * *Háry János suite* [for orchestra]. *See* 3595.3

3595.5 *Psalmus hungaricus*. (Budapest Chorus/Hungarian State Orchestra/Antal Doráti). Hungaroton: 11392-2. [With his *Felszállot a páva*].

3595.6 *Sonata for cello unaccompanied, op. 8*. (Yuli Turovsky). Chandos: 8427. [With his *Duo for violin and violoncello*].

3596 Koechlin, Charles, 1867–1950
The jungle book [for orchestra]. (Berlin Radio Symphony/David Zinman). RCA: 09026-61955-2.

3597 Korngold, Erich Wolfgang, 1897–1957

3597.1 *Sinfonietta.* (Northwest German Philharmonia/Werner Andreas Albert). CPO: 999 037-2. [With his *Schneemann* [excerpts] and *Schauspiel-Overtüre*].

3597.2 *Die tote Stadt* [opera]. (Carol Neblett/Rene Kollo/Munich Radio Orchestra/Erich Leinsdorf). RCA: GD-87767-2 (7767-2-RG). 2CD set.

3597.3 *Das Wunder der Heliane* [opera]. (Anna Tomowa-Sintow/Hartmut Welker/Berlin Radio Symphony/John Mauceri). London: 436 636-2. 3CD set.

3598 Kreisler, Fritz, 1875–1962. *Violin and piano music. Selections.*

- (Mischa Elman/Joseph Seiger). Vanguard: OVC 8028.
- (Itzhak Perlman/Samuel Sanders). EMI: CDC 7 47467 2.

3599 Krenek, Ernst, 1900–1991

3599.1 *Jonny spielt auf* [opera]. (Heinz Kruse/Alessandra Marc/Gewandhaus Orchestra Leipzig/Lothar Zagrosek). London: 436 631-2. 2CD set.

3599.2 *Lamentatio Jeremiae Prophetae.* (Netherlands Chamber Choir/Uwe Gronostay). Globe: 5085.

3599.3 *Quartet for strings no. 5.* (Sonare Quartet). Musikproduktion Dabringhaus und Grimm: MD+G L 3282.

3599.4 *Sonatas (7) for piano.* (Geoffrey Douglas Madge). Koch: 310047/48. 2CD set.

3600 Langlais, Jean, 1907–

Organ music. Selections. (Kevin Bowyer). Nimbus: NI: 5408.

3601 Lourié, Arthur, 1892–1966

3601.1 *Concerto da camera, for violin and string orchestra.* (Gidon Kremer/German Chamber Philharmonic). Deutsche Grammophon: 437 788-2. [With his *A little chamber music* and *Little Gidding*].

3601.2 *Poèmes (4) for piano.* (Sarah Rothenberg). *See 3675*

3602 Mahler, Alma, 1879–1964

Songs. (Isabel Lippitz/Barbara Heller). CPO: 999 018-2.

3603 Mahler, Gustav, 1860–1911

3603.1 * *Kindertotenlieder (Songs on the deaths of children)* [song cycle].

- (Janet Baker/Hallé Orchestra/John Barbirolli). *See 3603.3*
- (Thomas Hampson/Vienna Philharmonic/Leonard Bernstein). *See 3603.4*
- (Jessye Norman/Boston Symphony/Seiji Ozawa). *See 3603.12*

3603.2 *Des Knaben Wunderhorn (Youth's magic horn)* [song cycle].

- (Dietrich Fischer-Dieskau/Berlin Philharmonic/Daniel Barenboim). Sony: SK 44935. [With his *Lieder eines fahrenden Gesellen*].
- (Lucia Popp/London Philharmonic/Klaus Tennstedt). *See 3603.3*

3603.3 ** *Das Lied von der Erde (Song of the earth)* [song cycle].

- (Jessye Norman/Jon Vickers/London Symphony/Colin Davis). Philips: 411 474-2.
- (Murray Dickie/Dietrich Fischer-Dieskau/Philharmonia Orchestra/Paul Kletzki). EMI: CZS 7 62707 2. 2CD set. [With his *Lieder eines fahrenden Gesellen* (Janet Baker); *Kindertotenlieder* (Janet Baker); *Lieder nach Rückert* (Janet Baker); *Des Knaben Wunderhorn* (Lucia Popp)].
- (Mildred Miller/Ernst Häfliger/Columbia Symphony/Bruno Walter). Sony: MK 42034.

3603.4 *Lieder eines fahrenden Gesellen (Songs of a wayfarer)* [song cycle].

- (Janet Baker/Hallé Orchestra/John Barbirolli). *See 3603.3*
- (Dietrich Fischer-Dieskau/Berlin Philharmonic/Daniel Barenboim). *See 3603.2*
- (Thomas Hampson/Vienna Philharmonic/Leonard Bernstein). Deutsche Grammophon: 431 682-2. [With his *Kindertotenlieder*].

3603.5 *Lieder nach Rückert.*

- (Janet Baker/New Philharmonia Orchestra/John Barbirolli). *See 3603.3*
- (Hanna Schwarz/Chicago Symphony/Claudio Abbado). *See 3603.11*

3603.6 * *Symphony no. 1 in D major.*

- (Concertgebouw Orchestra/Leonard Bernstein). Deutsche Grammophon: 427 303-2.
- (Berlin Philharmonic/Bernard Haitink). Philips: 420 936-2.

- (Chicago Symphony/Georg Solti). London: 411 731-2.

- (Columbia Symphony/Bruno Walter). CBS: MYK 37235.

3603.7 * *Symphony no. 2 in C minor ("Resurrection").*

- (Vienna Philharmonic/Claudio Abbado). Deutsche Grammophon: 439 953-2. 2CD set.

- (New York Philharmonic/Leonard Bernstein). Deutsche Grammophon: 423 395-2. 2CD set.

- (London Symphony/Gilbert Kaplan). MCA: MCAD 11011. 2CD set.

- (Boston Symphony/Seiji Ozawa). Philips: 420 824-2. 2CD set.

3603.8 *Symphony no. 3 in D minor.*

- (Vienna Philharmonic/Claudio Abbado). Deutsche Grammophon: 410 715-2. 2CD set.

- (Chicago Symphony/James Levine). RCA: RCD2-1757. 2CD set.

3603.9 * *Symphony no. 4 in G major.*

- (Concertgebouw Orchestra/Bernard Haitink). Philips: 442 394-2.

- (Chicago Symphony/Georg Solti). London: 410 188-2.

- (Cleveland Orchestra/George Szell). Sony: SBK 46535.

3603.10 ** *Symphony no. 5 in C♯ minor.*

- (Berlin Philharmonic/Claudio Abbado). Deutsche Grammophon: 437 789-2.

- (Los Angeles Philharmonic/Zubin Mehta). London: 433 877-2.

- (Chicago Symphony/Georg Solti). London: 414 321-2.

3603.11 * *Symphony no. 6 in A minor.*

- (Chicago Symphony/Claudio Abbado). Deutsche Grammophon: 423 928-2. 2CD set. [With his *Lieder nach Rückert*].

- (Cleveland Orchestra/Christoph von Dohnanyi). Deutsche Grammophon: 436 240-2. [With Schoenberg, Arnold: *Pieces (5) for orchestra, op. 16*; Webern, Anton: *Im Sommerwind*].

- (Philharmonia Orchestra/Giuseppe Sinopoli). Deutsche Grammophon: 423 082-2. 2CD set. [With his *Adagio from Symphony no. 10*].

3603.12 *Symphony no. 7.*

- (Chicago Symphony/Claudio Abbado). Deutsche Grammophon: 413 773-2. 2CD set.

- (Boston Symphony/Seiji Ozawa). Philips: 426 249-2. 2CD set. [With his *Kindertotenlieder*].

3603.13 * *Symphony no. 8 in E♭ major ("Symphony of a thousand").*

- (Vienna Philharmonic/Leonard Bernstein). *See 3603.15*

- (Concertgebouw Orchestra/Bernard Haitink). *See 3603.15*

- (Chicago Symphony/Georg Solti). London: 414 493-2. 2CD set.

3603.14 * *Symphony no. 9.*

- (Concertgebouw Orchestra/Leonard Bernstein). Deutsche Grammophon: 419 208-2. 2CD set.

- (Berlin Philharmonic/Herbert von Karajan). Deutsche Grammophon: 410 726-2. 2CD set.

- (Vienna Philharmonic/Bruno Walter). EMI: CDH 7 63029 2.

3603.15 ** *Symphony no. 10. Adagio.*

- (Vienna Philharmonic/Leonard Bernstein). Deutsche Grammophon: 435 102-2. 2CD set. [With his *Symphony no. 8*].

- (Concertgebouw Orchestra/Bernard Haitink). Philips: 420 543-2. 2CD set. [With his *Symphony no. 8*].

- (Philharmonia Orchestra/Giuseppe Sinopoli). *See 3603.11*

3603.16 *Symphony no. 10* [completed by Deryck Cooke]. (Frankfurt Radio Symphony/Eliahu Inbal). Denon: CO-75129.

3604 Malipiero, Gian Francesco, 1882–1973
Orchestral music. Selections. (Veneto Philharmonic/Peter Maag). Marco Polo: 8.223397. [*Sette invenzioni; Quattro invenzioni; Il finto arlecchino; Vivaldiana*].

3605 Martin, Frank, 1890–1974

3605.1 *Ballade for flute, piano, and string orchestra.* (Philharmonia Virtuosi/Richard Kapp). *See 3605.3*

3605.2 *Ballade for trombone and piano.* (Christian Lindberg/Roland Pöntinen). *See 3672*

3605.3 *Concerto for winds (7), percussion, and string orchestra.*

- (Suisse Romande Orchestra/Armin Jordan). *See 3605.6*

- (Philharmonia Virtuosi/Richard Kapp). ESS.A.Y.: CD 1014. [With his *Petite symphonie concer-*

tante; Ballade for flute, piano, and string orchestra].

3605.4 *Mass.* (Christ Church Cathedral Choir/ Stephen Darlington). Nimbus: 5197. [With Poulenc, Francis: *Mass in G major; Salve Regina; Petites prières de Saint François d'Assise].*

3605.5 *Monologe aus Jedermann* [song cycle]. (Gilles Cachemaille/Suisse Romande Orchestra/ Armin Jordan). *See 3605.6*

3605.6 * *Petite symphonie concertante, for harp, harpsichord, piano, and 2 string orchestras.*

- (Suisse Romande Orchestra/Armin Jordan). Erato: 2292-45694-2. [With his *Monologe aus Jedermann* and *Concerto for winds, percussion, and string orchestra].*

- (Philharmonia Virtuosi/Richard Kapp). *See 3605.3*

3606 Martinů, Bohuslav, 1890–1959

3606.1 *Double concerto* [for piano, timpani, and 2 string orchestras]. (Prague Radio Symphony/ Charles Mackerras). Supraphon: 10 3393-2. [With his *Fresques de Piero della Francesca].*

3606.2 * *Fresques de Piero della Francesca* [for orchestra].

- (French National Orchestra/James Conlon). *See 3606.5*

- (Prague Radio Symphony/Charles Mackerras). *See 3606.1*

3606.3 *Madrigals* [for instrumental ensembles]. (Dartington Ensemble). Hyperion: CDA66133.

3606.4 *La revue de cuisine* [ballet]. (Dartington Ensemble). Hyperion: CDA66084. [With his *Nonet for woodwinds, horn, and strings; Trio for flute, violoncello, and piano].*

3606.5 *Sinfonietta La Jolla.* (French National Orchestra/James Conlon). Erato: 2292-45794-2. [With his *Toccata e due canzoni* and *Fresques de Piero della Francesca].*

3606.6 *Symphonies (6).* (Czech Philharmonic/ Václav Neumann). Supraphon: 11 0382-2. 3CD set.

3606.7 * *Symphony no. 6 ("Fantaisies symphoniques").* (Bamber Symphony/Neeme Järvi). Bis: 402. [With his *Symphony no. 5].*

3606.8 *Toccata e due canzoni* [for orchestra]. (French National Orchestra/James Conlon). *See 3606.5*

3607 McPhee, Colin, 1900–1964

Suite in 6 movements. (New Music Concerts/Robert Aitken). CBC: MVCD 1057. [Album title: *Ô Bali:*

Colin McPhee and his legacy. With his *Lagoe sesoeloelingan ardja* and *Kambing slem;* plus works by Jose Evanglista, Jon Siddall, and Andrew Timar].

3608 Milhaud, Darius, 1892–1974

3608.1 * *Le boeuf sur le toit.*

- (Lyon Opera Orchestra/Kent Nagano). Erato: 2292-45820-2. [With his *Création du monde* and *Concerto for harp and orchestra, op. 323].*

- (Czech Philharmonic/Vladimír Válek). *See 3628.2*

3608.2 * *La cheminée du roi René* [for wind quintet].

- (Athena Ensemble). Chandos: CHAN 6536. [With his *Suite d'après Corrette, op. 161b; Divertissement en trois parties, op. 299b; Pastoral, op. 147; Sketches, op. 227b].*

- (Pro Arte Wind Quintet). *See 3674*

3608.3 * *La création du monde.* (Lyon Opera Orchestra/Kent Nagano). *See 3608.1*

3608.4 *Quartets (18) for strings.* (Arcana Quartet/Aquitaine Quartet). Cybélia: 804/808. 5CD set (also available separately).

3608.5 * *Saudades do Brasil* [for piano]. (Martin Jones). DDC/AVM: AVZ: 3021. [With his *Suite, op. 8; Rag-caprices, op. 78; Sonata no. 1, op. 33].*

3608.6 *Scaramouche* [for 2 pianos]. (Katia and Marielle Labèque). *See 3614.6*

3608.7 ** *Sonatas. Selections.* (Aurèle Nicolet/ Heinz Holliger/Eduard Brunner/Oleg Maisenberg). Orfeo: 060831. [*Sonata for flute, oboe, clarinet, and piano; Sonatine for flute and piano; Sonatine for clarinet and piano; Sonatine for oboe and piano].*

3608.8 * *Suite provençale* [for orchestra].

- (Detroit Symphony/Neeme Järvi). *See 3624.4*

- (Capitol de Toulouse Orchestra/Michel Plasson). Deutsche Grammophon: 435 437-2. [With his *Symphonies nos. 1–2].*

3608.9 * *Symphonies (6) pour petite orchestre (Petites symphonies).* (Capella Cracoviensis/Karl Anton Rickenbacher). Koch Schwann: 3-1139-2. [With his *Opéras-minutes].*

3609 Mosolov, Aleksandr, 1900–1973

3609.1 *Piano music. Selections.* (Sarah Rothenberg). *See 3675*

3609.2 * *Zavod (The iron foundry)* [for orchestra]. (Concertgebouw Orchestra/Riccardo Chailly).

London: 436 640-2. [With Prokofiev, Sergey: *Symphony no. 3;* Varèse, Edgard: *Arcana*].

3610 Nielsen, Carl, 1865–1931

3610.1 *Concerto for clarinet and orchestra.* (Ollie Schill/Gothenburg Symphony/Myung-Wha Chung). *See 3610.5*

3610.2 *Concerto for flute and orchestra.* (James Galway/Danish Radio Symphony). RCA: 6359-2-RC. [With his *Quintet for woodwinds and horn* and other works with flute].

3610.3 *Quintet for woodwinds and horn.*

- (James Galway and others). *See 3610.2*
- (Marlboro Festival Ensemble). *See 3543.13*

3610.4 *Symphony no. 2 ("The four temperaments").*

- (San Francisco Symphony/Herbert Blomstedt). London: 430 280-2. [With his *Symphony no. 3*].
- (Swedish Radio Symphony/Esa-Pekka Salonen). CBS: MK 44934. [With his *Pan og Syrinx*].

3610.5 * *Symphony no. 3 ("Sinfonia espansiva").*

- (Royal Danish Orchestra/Leonard Bernstein). CBS: MK 44708. [With his *Symphony no. 5*].
- (San Francisco Symphony/Herbert Blomstedt). *See 3610.4*
- (Gothenburg Symphony/Myung-Wha Chung). Bis: 321. [With his *Maskarade overture* and *Concerto for clarinet and orchestra*].

3610.6 * *Symphony no. 4 ("The inextinguishable").*

- (San Francisco Symphony/Herbert Blomstedt). London: 421 524-2. [With his *Symphony no. 5*].
- (Gothenburg Symphony/Neeme Järvi). Bis: 600. [With his *Symphony no. 6*].
- (City of Birmingham Symphony/Simon Rattle). EMI: CDC 7 47503 2. [With his *Pan og Syrinx*].

3610.7 *Symphony no. 5.*

- (Royal Danish Orchestra/Leonard Bernstein). *See 3610.5*
- (San Francisco Symphony/Herbert Blomstedt). *See 3610.6*

3610.8 *Symphony no. 6 ("Sinfonia semplice").* (Gothenburg Symphony/Neeme Järvi). *See 3610.6*

3611 ** Orff, Carl, 1895–1982

Carmina burana.

- (Shinyukai Choir/Berlin Philharmonic/Seiji Ozawa). Philips: 422 363-2.
- (Atlanta Symphony Chorus and Orchestra/Robert Shaw). Telarc: 80056.

3612 Ornstein, Leo, 1892–

Piano music. Selections. (Steffen Schleiermacher). *See 3676*

3613 Piston, Walter, 1894–1976

3613.1 *Fantasy for English horn, harp, and string orchestra.* (Glen Danielson/Seattle Symphony/Gerard Schwarz). *See 3613.2*

3613.2 *The incredible flutist.*

- (Seattle Symphony/Gerard Schwarz). Delos: DE 3126. [With his *Fantasy for English horn, harp, and string orchestra; Suite for orchestra; Concerto for string quartet, winds, and percussion; Psalm and prayer of David*].
- (St. Louis Symphony/Leonard Slatkin). RCA: 60798-2. [With his *Symphony no. 6* and *New England sketches*].

3613.3 *Pieces (3) for flute, clarinet, and bassoon.* (Boehm Quintet). *See 3663*

3613.4 *Quintet for woodwinds and horn.* (Boehm Quintet). *See 3663*

3613.5 *Symphony no. 2.* (Boston Symphony/Michael Tilson Thomas). *See 3626.3*

3614 Poulenc, Francis, 1899–1963

3614.1 *Aubade for piano and orchestra.* (Gabriel Tacchino/Société des Concerts du Conservatoire/Georges Prêtre). EMI: 7 47369 2. [With his *Concerto for piano and orchestra* and *Concerto for two pianos and orchestra*].

3614.2 *Le bal masqué* [for baritone and chamber orchestra]. (Thomas Allen/Nash Ensemble/Lionel Friend). CRD: 3437. [With his *Trio for piano, oboe, and bassoon; Le bestiaire; Sextet for piano, woodwinds, and horn*].

3614.3 *Le bestiaire* [for voice and chamber ensemble]. (Thomas Allen/Nash Ensemble/Lionel Friend). *See 3614.2*

3614.4 *Les biches* [ballet]. (Czech Philharmonic/Vladimír Válek). *See 3628.2*

3614.5 * *Concerto for organ and string orchestra in G minor.*

- (Maurice Duruflé/R.T.F. Orchestra/Georges Prêtre). EMI: 7 47723 2. [With his *Gloria* and *Motets pour un temps de pénitence*].

- (Simon Preston/Boston Symphony/Seiji Ozawa). *See 3469.3*

3614.6 *Concerto for 2 pianos and orchestra in D minor.*

- (Katia and Marielle Labèque/Boston Symphony/Seiji Ozawa). Philips: 426 284-2. [With his *Sonata for piano, four hands; Capriccio for two pianos; L'embarquement pour Cythère for two pianos; Elégie for two pianos;* Milhaud, Darius: *Scaramouche*].
- (Gabriel Tacchino/Bernard Ringeissen/Société des Concerts du Conservatoire/Georges Prêtre). *See 3614.1*

3614.7 * *Dialogues des Carmélites* [opera]. (José van Dam/Catherine Dubosc/Lyon Opera/Kent Nagano). Virgin: 7 59227 2. 2 CD set.

3614.8 *L'embarquement pour Cythère* [for two pianos]. (Katia and Marielle Labèque). *See 3614.6*

3614.9 * *Gloria.*

- (R.T.F. Choir and Orchestra/Georges Prêtre). *See 3614.5*
- (Tanglewood Festival Chorus/Boston Symphony/Seiji Ozawa). Deutsche Grammophon: 427 304-2. [With his *Stabat Mater*].

3614.10 *Mass in G major.*

- (Christ Church Cathedral Choir/Stephen Darlington). *See 3605.4*
- (Robert Shaw Festival Singers/Robert Shaw). Telarc: 80236. [With his *Motets* and *Petits prières de Saint François d'Assise*].

3614.11 * *Piano music. Selections.* (Pascal Rogé). London: 417 438-2; 425 862-2. 2 CDs.

3614.12 * *Sextet for piano, woodwinds, and horn.*

- (Nash Ensemble). *See 3614.2*
- (Pascal Rogé and others). London: 421 581-2. [With his *Sonata for clarinet and piano; Sonata for flute and piano; Sonata for oboe and piano; Trio for piano, oboe, and bassoon*].

3614.13 * *Sonata for clarinet and piano.* (Michel Portal/Pascal Rogé). *See 3614.12*

3614.14 * *Sonata for flute and piano.* (Patrick Gallois/Pascal Rogé). *See 3614.12*

3614.15 * *Sonata for oboe and piano.* (Maurice Borugue/Pascal Rogé). *See 3614.12*

3614.16 *Sonata for piano, 4 hands.* (Katia and Marielle Labèque). *See 3614.6*

3614.17 *Songs. Selections.* (Pierre Bernac/Francis Poulenc). EMI: 7 54605 2.

3614.18 *Stabat Mater.* (Tanglewood Festival Chorus/Boston Symphony/Seiji Ozawa). *See 3614.9*

3614.19 *Trio for piano, oboe, and bassoon.*

- (Nash Ensemble). *See 3614.2*
- (Pascal Rogé and others). *See 3614.12*

3614.20 *La voix humaine* [opera]. (Julia Migenes/French National Orchestra/Georges Prêtre). Musifrance: 2292-45651-2.

3615 Prokofiev, Sergey, 1891–1953

3615.1 *Ala et Lolly (Scythian suite).*

- (Scottish National Orchestra/Neeme Järvi). *See 3615.2*
- (City of Birmingham Symphony/Simon Rattle). *See 3615.24*

3615.2 *Aleksandr Nevskii (Alexander Nevsky)* [cantata].

- (Elena Obraztsova/London Symphony Chorus and Orchestra/Claudio Abbado). Deutsche Grammophon: 419 603-2. [With his *Poruchik Kizhe (Lt. Kije) suite.*
- Linda Finnie/Scottish National Orchestra/ Neeme Järvi). Chandos: 8584. [With his *Ala et Lolly*].

3615.3 *Concertos (5) for piano and orchestra.* (Vladimir Ashkenazy/London Symphony/André Previn). London: 425 570-2. 2CD set.

3615.4 * *Concerto for piano and orchestra no. 2, op. 16 in G minor.* (Vladimir Feltsman/London Symphony/Michael Tilson Thomas). CBS: MK 44818. [With his *Concerto for piano and orchestra no. 1, op. 10 in Db major*].

3615.5 * *Concerto for piano and orchestra no. 3, op. 26 in C major.* (Martha Argerich/Royal Philharmonic/Charles Dutoit). *See 3519.2*

3615.6 * *Concertos (2) for violin and orchestra.*

- (Shlomo Mintz/Chicago Symphony/Claudio Abbado). Deutsche Grammophon: 410 524-2.
- (Isaac Stern/New York Philharmonic/Zubin Mehta). CBS: MK 42439.

3615.7 *Liubov k trem apelsinam (Love for three oranges)* [opera]. (Catherine Dubosc/Georges Gaultier/Gabriel Bacquier/Lyon Opera/Kent Nagano). Virgin: 7 59566 2 (7 91084 2). 2CD set.

3615.8 *Liubov k trem apelsinam (Love for three oranges)* [orchestral excerpts]. (Philadelphia Orchestra/Eugene Ormandy). *See 3615.22*

3615.9 *Mimoletnosti (Visions fugitives)* [for piano]. (Boris Berman). Chandos: 8881. [With his *Sarcasms; Tales of an old grandmother, op. 31; Sonata no. 7, op. 83*].

3615.10 ** *Petia i volk (Peter and the wolf)* [for narrator and orchestra].

- (Itzhak Perlman/Israel Philharmonic/Zubin Mehta). EMI: CDC 7 47067 2. [With Saint-Saëns, Camille, *Carnaval des animaux*].

- (Lina Prokofiev/Scottish National Orchestra/ Neeme Järvi). Chandos: 8511. [With his *Zolushka* [suite from the ballet].

- (Sting/Chamber Orchestra of Europe/Claudio Abbado). Deutsche Grammophon: 429 396-2. [With his *Symphony no. 1* and *Uvertiura na evreiskie temy*].

3615.11 * *Poruchik Kizhe (Lt. Kije)* [suite for orchestra].

- (Chicago Symphony/Claudio Abbado). *See* 3615.2

- (Philadelphia Orchestra/Eugene Ormandy). *See* 3615.22

- (Berlin Philharmonic/Seiji Ozawa). *See* 3615.24

3615.12 *Quartets (2) for strings.* (Emerson Quartet). Deutsche Grammophon: 431 772-2. [With his *Sonata for two violins, op. 56*].

3615.13 * *Romeo i Dzhuletta (Romeo and Juliet)* [ballet].

- (Royal Scottish National Orchestra/Neeme Järvi). Chandos: 8940. [Suites 1–3 from the ballet].

- (Philadelphia Orchestra/Riccardo Muti). EMI: CDC 7 47004 2. [Suites 1–2 from the ballet].

- (Boston Symphony/Seiji Ozawa). Deutsche Grammophon: 423 268-2. 2CD set. [Complete ballet].

3615.14 *Sarcasms* [for piano]. (Boris Berman). *See* 3615.9

3615.15 *Sonata for flute and piano, op. 94.* (Manuela Wiesler/Roland Pöntinen). *See* 4033

3615.16 *Sonatas (9) for piano.* (Frederic Chiu). Harmonia Mundi: HMU 907086.88. 3CD set.

3615.17 * *Sonata for piano no. 2, op. 14 in D minor.* (Sviatislav Richter). Praga: 250 015. [With his *Sonatas nos. 6–7*].

3615.18 * *Sonata for piano no. 6, op. 82.*

- (Ivo Pogorelich). *See* 3617.8

- (Sviatislav Richter). *See* 3615.17

3615.19 ** *Sonata for piano no. 7, op. 83.*

- (Boris Berman). *See* 3615.9

- (Yefim Bronfman). CBS: MK 44680. [With his *Sonata no. 8*].

- (Maurizio Pollini). *See* 3643.34

- (Sviatislav Richter). *See* 3615.17

3615.20 * *Sonatas (2) for violin and piano.* (Shlomo Mintz/Yefim Bronfman). Deutsche Grammophon: 423 575-2.

3615.21 *Symphonies (7).* (Royal Scottish National Orchestra/Neeme Järvi). Chandos: 8931/ 8934. 4CD set.

3615.22 ** *Symphony no. 1, op. 25 in D major ("Classical").*

- (Chamber Orchestra of Europe/Claudio Abbado). *See* 3615.10

- (Montreal Symphony/Charles Dutoit). London: 421 813-2. [With his *Symphony no. 5*].

- (Philadelphia Orchestra/Eugene Ormandy). CBS: MBK 39783. [With his *Poruchik Kizhe (Lt. Kije) suite* and *Liubov k trem apelsinam (Love for three oranges) suite*].

- (St. Louis Symphony/Leonard Slatkin). RCA: 09026-61350-2. [With his *Symphony no. 5*].

3615.23 * *Symphony no. 3, op. 44 in C minor.* (Concertgebouw Orchestra/Riccardo Chailly). *See* 3609.2

3615.24 * *Symphony no. 5, op. 100 in B♭ major.*

- (Montreal Symphony/Charles Dutoit). *See* 3615.22

- (Berlin Philharmonic/Seiji Ozawa). Deutsche Grammophon: 435 029-2. [With his *Poruchik Kizhe (Lt. Kije) suite*].

- (City of Birmingham Symphony/Simon Rattle). EMI: 7 54577 2. [With his *Ala et Lolly*].

- (St. Louis Symphony/Leonard Slatkin). *See* 3615.22

3615.25 *Uvertiura na evreiskie temy (Overture on Hebrew themes).* (Chamber Orchestra of Europe/Claudio Abbado). *See* 3615.10

3615.26 *Zolushka (Cinderella)* [ballet].

- (Cleveland Orchestra/Vladimir Ashkenazy). London: 410 162-2. 2CD set.

- (Scottish National Orchestra/Neeme Järvi). *See* 3615.10

3616 Rachmaninoff, Sergei, 1873–1943

3616.1 *Concertos (4) for piano and orchestra.* (Vladimir Ashkenazy/Concertgebouw Orchestra/ Bernard Haitink). London: 421 590-2. 2CD set.

3616.2 * *Concerto for piano and orchestra no. 2, op. 18 in C minor.*

- (Vladimir Ashkenazy/London Symphony/ André Previn). London: 417 702- 2. [With his *Rapsodie sur un thème de Paganini*].

- (Van Cliburn/RCA Symphony/Kiril Kondrashin). *See* 3519.2
- (Sergei Rachmaninoff/Philadelphia Orchestra/ Leopold Stokowski). RCA: 5997-2- RC. [With his *Concerto no. 3*].
- (Jean-Yves Thibaudet/Cleveland Orchestra/ Vladimir Ashkenazy). London: 440 653-2. [With his *Rapsodie sur un thème de Paganini*].

3616.3 * *Concerto for piano and orchestra no. 3, op. 30 in D minor.*

- (Vladimir Ashkenazy/Concertgebouw Orchestra/Bernard Haitink). London: 417 239-2.
- (Vladimir Horowitz/New York Philharmonic/ Eugene Ormandy). RCA: 09026-61564-2.
- (Sergei Rachmaninoff/Philadelphia Orchestra/ Eugene Ormandy). *See* 3616.2

3616.4 * *Etudes-tableaux for piano, opp. 33 and 39.*

- (John Browning) [selections]. *See* 3616.7
- (Hélène Grimaud). [Op. 33 complete]. *See* 3616.7
- (Ruth Laredo). [Opp. 33 and 39 complete]. Sony: SMK 48472.

3616.5 *Fantasie for orchestra, op. 7 ("The rock").* (London Symphony/André Previn). *See* 3616.12

3616.6 ** *Ostrov mertvykh (Isle of the dead).* (Concertgebouw Orchestra/Vladimir Ashkenazy). London: 430 733-2. [With his *Symphonic dances*].

3616.7 * *Piano music. Selections.*

- (John Browning). Delos: 3044. [*Sonata no. 2* plus selected *Preludes, Etudes-tableaux,* and other short pieces].
- (Hélène Grimaud). Denon: CO-1054. [*Sonata no. 2; Etudes-tableaux, op. 33;* selected *Preludes, op. 32*].
- *Rachmaninoff plays Rachmaninoff.* RCA: 7766.

3616.8 * *Preludes for piano, opp. 23 and 32.*

- (Vladimir Ashkenazy) [complete]. London: 414 417-2. 2CD set. [With his *Sonata no. 2*].
- (John Browning) [selections]. *See* 3616.7

3616.9 * *Rapsodie sur un thème de Paganini.*

- (Vladimir Ashkenazy/London Symphony/ André Previn). *See* 3616.2
- (Jean-Yves Thibaudet/Cleveland Orchestra/ Vladimir Ashkenazy). *See* 3616.2

3616.10 *Sonata for piano no. 2, op. 36 in B♭ minor.*

- (Vladimir Ashkenazy). *See* 3616.8
- (John Browning). *See* 3616.7
- (Hélène Grimaud). *See* 3616.7

3616.11 * *Symphonic dances.*

- (Concertgebouw Orchestra/Vladimir Ashkenazy). *See* 3616.6
- (Philadelphia Orchestra/Charles Dutoit). *See* 3616.13

3616.12 *Symphony no. 2, op. 27 in E minor.*

- (Concertgebouw Orchestra/Vladimir Ashkenazy). London: 400 081-2.
- (London Symphony/André Previn). RCA: 60791-2-RV. [With his *Fantasie for orchestra, op. 7*].
- (Baltimore Symphony/David Zinman). Telarc: 80312. [With his *Vocalise*].

3616.13 *Symphony no. 3, op. 44 in A minor.*

- (Philadelphia Orchestra/Charles Dutoit). London: 433 181-2. [With his *Symphonic dances*].
- (London Symphony/Neeme Järvi). Chandos: CHAN 8614.

3616.14 *Vocalise* [for soprano and orchestra]. (Sylvia McNair/Baltimore Symphony/David Zinman). *See* 3616.12

3616.15 *Vsenoshchnoe bdenie (Vespers).* (St. Petersburg Chamber Choir/Nikolai Korniev). Philips: 442 344-2.

3617 Ravel, Maurice, 1875–1937

3617.1 * *Alborada del gracioso.*

- (Montreal Symphony/Charles Dutoit). *See* 3617.13
- (Philadelphia Orchestra/Eugene Ormandy). *See* 3617.13

3617.2 ** *Bolero.*

- (Montreal Symphony/Charles Dutoit). *See* 3617.13
- (Boston Symphony/Charles Munch). *See* 3617.13
- (Philadelphia Orchestra/Eugene Ormandy). *See* 3617.13

3617.3 *Chansons madécasses.* (Jessye Norman/ Ensemble InterContemporain/Pierre Boulez). *See* 3617.22

3617.4 * *Concerto for piano, left hand and orchestra in D major.*

- (Michel Béroff/London Symphony/Claudio Abbado). *See* 3617.5

- (Leon Fleischer/Boston Symphony/Seiji Ozawa). Sony: SK 47188. [With Prokofiev, Sergey: *Concerto for piano and orchestra no. 4;* Britten, Benjamin: *Diversions*].

- (Louis Lortie/London Symphony/Raphael Frühbeck de Burgos). Chandos: CHAN 8773. [With his *Concerto for piano and orchestra in G major;* Fauré, Gabriel: *Ballade for piano and orchestra*].

3617.5 * *Concerto for piano and orchestra in G major.*

- Martha Argerich/London Symphony/Claudio Abbado). Deutsche Grammophon: 423 665-2. [With his *Concerto in D major; L'eventail de Jeanne; Menuet antique; Le tombeau de Couperin*].

- (Louis Lortie/London Symphony/Raphael Frühbeck de Burgos). *See* 3617.4

- (Arturo Benedetti Michelangeli/Philharmonia Orchestra/Ettore Gracis). EMI: CDC 7 49326 2. [With Rachmaninoff, Sergei: *Concerto for piano and orchestra no. 4*].

3617.6 * *Daphnis et Chloe* [ballet].

- (Montreal Symphony/Charles Dutoit). London: 400 055-2.

- (Boston Symphony/Bernard Haitink). Philips: 426 260-2.

- (Philadelphia Orchestra/Eugene Ormandy). [Suite no. 2 from the ballet]. *See* 3617.13

3617.7 *Don Quichotte à Dulcinée* [song cycle].

- (José van Dam/BBC Symphony/Pierre Boulez). *See* 3617.22

- (Gérard Souzay/Dalton Baldwin [piano]). *See* 3539

3617.8 * *Gaspard de la nuit* [for piano].

- (Ivo Pogorelich). Deutsche Grammophon: 413 363-2. [With Prokofiev, Sergey: *Sonata for piano no. 6*].

- (Jean-Yves Thibaudet). *See* 3617.15

3617.9 *Introduction and allegro for harp and ensemble.* (Osian Ellis/Melos Ensemble). *See* 3469.2

3617.10 *Ma mère l'oye (Mother Goose)* [version for two pianos]. (Katia and Marielle Labèque). *See* 3448.3

3617.11 *Ma mère l'oye (Mother Goose)* [version for orchestra].

- (Montreal Symphony/Charles Dutoit). *See* 3617.13

- (Boston Symphony/Charles Munch). *See* 3617.13

3617.12 * *Miroirs* [for piano]. (Jean-Yves Thibaudet). *See* 3617.15

3617.13 ** *Orchestral music. Selections.*

- (Montreal Symphony/Charles Dutoit). London: 410 254-2. [*Ma mère l'oye; Pavane pour une infante défunte; Le tombeau de Couperin; Valses nobles et sentimentales*].

- (Montreal Symphony/Charles Dutoit). London: 410 010-2. [*Alborada del gracioso; Bolero; Rapsodie espagnole; La valse*].

- (Boston Symphony/Charles Munch). RCA: 6522-2. [*Bolero; Ma mère l'oye; Pavane pour une infante défunte; Rapsodie espagnole; La valse*].

- (Philadelphia Orchestra/Eugene Ormandy). CBS: MBK 46274. [*Alborada del gracioso; Bolero; Daphnis et Chloe suite no. 2; Pavane pour une infante défunte; Rapsodie espagnole; La valse*].

3617.14 * *Pavane pour une infante défunte.*

- (New York Philharmonic/Leonard Bernstein). *See* 3532

- (Montreal Symphony/Charles Dutoit). *See* 3617.13

- (Boston Symphony/Charles Munch). *See* 3617.13

- (Philadelphia Orchestra/Eugene Ormandy). *See* 3617.13

3617.15 * *Piano music.* (Jean-Yves Thibaudet). London: 433 515-2. [*Jeux d'eau; Sonatina; Miroirs; Gaspard de la nuit; Valses nobles et sentimentales; Le tombeau de Couperin;* plus shorter works].

3617.16 * *Quartet for strings in F major.*

- (Alban Berg Quartet) *See* 3563.18

- (Emerson Quartet) *See* 3563.18

3617.17 * *Rapsodie espagnole* [for orchestra].

- (Montreal Symphony/Charles Dutoit). *See* 3617.13

- (Boston Symphony/Charles Munch). *See* 3617.13

- (Philadelphia Orchestra/Eugene Ormandy). *See* 3617.13

3617.18 *Shéhérazade.*

- (Heather Harper/BBC Symphony/Pierre Boulez). *See* 3617.22

- (Jessye Norman/London Symphony/Colin Davis). *See* 3446.5

3617.19 *Sonata for violin and piano (1927).* (Dmitry Sitkovetsky/Bella Davidovich). *See* 3617.26

3617.20 *Sonata for violin and violoncello.* (Eleonora Turovsky/Yuli Turovsky). Chandos: CHAN 8358. [Album title: *French music for violin and cello.* With Rivier, Jean: *Sonatine*; Honegger, Arthur: *Sonatine*; Martinů, Bohuslav: *Duo*]

3617.21 *Sonatina for piano.* (Jean-Yves Thibaudet). *See* 3617.15

3617.22 *Song cycles. Selections.* (Heather Harper and others). CBS: MK 39023. [*Shéhérazade; Poèmes de Stéphane Mallarmé; Chansons madécasses; Don Quichotte à Dulcinée; Mélodies populaires grecques*].

3617.23 * *Le tombeau de Couperin* [version for orchestra].
- (London Symphony/Claudio Abbado). *See* 3617.5
- (Montreal Symphony/Charles Dutoit). *See* 3617.13

3617.24 *Le tombeau de Couperin* [version for piano]. (Jean-Yves Thibaudet). *See* 3617.15

3617.25 *Trio for piano and strings.* (Borodin Trio). Chandos: CHAN 8458. [With Debussy, Claude: *Sonata for violin and piano; Sonata for violoncello and piano*].

3617.26 *Tzigane* [for violin and piano, or violin and orchestra].
- (Kyung-Wha Chung/Royal Philharmonic/Charles Dutoit). *See* 3504.6
- (Dmitry Sitkovetsky/Bella Davidovich). Orfeo: C 108 841 A. [With his *Sonata for violin and piano (1927); Sonata for violin and piano (posthumous); Berceuse sur le nom de Gabriel Fauré*].

3617.27 * *La valse* [for orchestra].
- (Montreal Symphony/Charles Dutoit). *See* 3617.13
- (Boston Symphony/Charles Munch). *See* 3617.13
- (Philadelphia Orchestra/Eugene Ormandy). *See* 3617.13

3617.28 *Valses nobles et sentimentales* [for orchestra]. (Montreal Symphony/Charles Dutoit). *See* 3617.13

3618 Reger, Max, 1873–1916

3618.1 *Organ music. Selections.*
- (Piet Kee). *See* 3586.12
- (Lionel Rogg). Bis: 242.

3618.2 *Serenades (2) for flute, violin, and viola, opp. 77a and 141a.* (Serenata of London). ASV: DCA 875. [With his *Suites for solo viola*].

3618.3 *Suites (3) for solo viola.* (George Robertson). *See* 3618.2

3618.4 *Variationen und Fuge über ein Thema von W. A. Mozart (Variations and fugue on a theme by W. A. Mozart).* (New York Philharmonic/Kurt Masur). *See* 3590.20

3619 Respighi, Ottorino, 1879–1936

3619.1 *Antiche arie e danze per liuto (Ancient airs and dances for lute)* [Suite no. 3, for orchestra]. (Academy of St. Martin-in-the-Fields/Neville Marriner). Philips: 420 485-2. [With his *Boutique fantasque* and *Uccelli*].

3619.2 *La boutique fantasque* [ballet after music by Rossini]. (Academy of St. Martin-in-the-Fields/Neville Marriner). *See* 3619.1

3619.3 *Feste romane (Roman festivals)* [for orchestra].
- (Montreal Symphony/Charles Dutoit). *See* 3619.5
- (Philadelphia Orchestra/Riccardo Muti). *See* 3619.5

3619.4 * *Fontane di Roma (Fountains of Rome)* [for orchestra].
- (Montreal Symphony/Charles Dutoit). *See* 3619.5
- (Philadelphia Orchestra/Riccardo Muti). *See* 3619.5

3619.5 * *Pini di Roma (Pines of Rome)* [for orchestra].
- (Montreal Symphony/Charles Dutoit). London: 410 145-2. [With his *Fontane di Roma* and *Feste romane*].
- (Philadelphia Orchestra/Riccardo Muti). EMI: 7 47316 2. [With his *Fontane di Roma* and *Feste romane*].

3619.6 *Gli uccelli (The birds)* [for orchestra]. (Academy of St. Martin-in-the-Fields/Neville Marriner). *See* 3619.1

3620 Revueltas, Silvestre, 1899–1940

3620.1 *Alcancías.* (New Philharmonia Orchestra/Eduardo Mata). *See* 3620.2

3620.2 * *Homenaje a Federico Garcia Lorca.*
- (Mexico City Philharmonic/Fernando Lozano). *See* 3620.7

- (New Philharmonia Orchestra/Eduardo Mata). Catalyst: 09026-62672-2. [With his *Sensemaya; Ocho X radio; Toccata; Alcancías; Planos; Noche de los Mayas*].

- (Ensemble 21/Arthur Weisberg). *See* 3847.7

3620.3 * *La noche de los Mayas (Night of the Mayas)*.

- (Mexico City Philharmonic/Fernando Lozano). *See* 3620.7

- (New Philharmonia Orchestra/Eduardo Mata). *See* 3620.2

3620.4 *Ocho X radio.* (New Philharmonia Orchestra/Eduardo Mata). *See* 3620.2

3620.5 *Planos.* (New Philharmonia Orchestra/Eduardo Mata). *See* 3620.2

3620.6 *Redes.*

- (Mexico City Philharmonic/Fernando Lozano). *See* 3620.7

- (Simon Bolivar Symphony of Venezuela/Eduardo Mata). Dorian: 90178. [With his *Sensemaya*; Orbón, Julián: *Concerto grosso for string quartet and orchestra*; Ginastera, Alberto: *Pampanea no. 3*].

3620.7 * *Sensemaya.*

- (Mexico City Philharmonic/Fernando Lozano). Forlane: UCD 16614. [With his *Homenaje a Federico Garcia Lorca; Noche de los Mayas; Redes*].

- (New Philharmonia Orchestra/Eduardo Mata). *See* 3620.2

- (Simon Bolivar Symphony of Venezuela/Eduardo Mata). *See* 3620.6

3620.8 *Toccata.* (New Philharmonia Orchestra/Eduardo Mata). *See* 3620.2

3621 Riegger, Wallingford, 1885–1961

Instrumental music. Selections. (Alfredo Antonini and others). CRI: 572. [*Romanza for string orchestra; Dance rhythms for orchestra; Music for orchestra; Concerto for piano and woodwind quintet; Music for brass choir; Movement for two trumpets, trombone, and piano; Nonet for brass; Symphony no. 3*].

3622 Rodrigo, Joaquín, 1901–

3622.1 * *Concierto de Aranjuez* [for guitar and orchestra].

- (Pepe Romero/Academy of St. Martin-in-the-Fields/Neville Marriner). Philips: 432 828-2. [With his *Fantasía para un gentilhombre* and *Concierto madrigal*].

- (John Williams/Philadelphia Orchestra/Eugene Ormandy). CBS: MYK 36717. [With his *Fantasía para un gentilhombre*].

3622.2 *Concierto madrigal* [for two guitars and orchestra]. (Pepe and Angel Romero/Academy of St. Martin-in-the-Fields/Neville Marriner). *See* 3622.1

3622.3 *Fantasía para un gentilhombre* [for guitar and orchestra].

- (Pepe Romero/Academy of St. Martin-in-the-Fields/Neville Marriner). *See* 3622.1

- (John Williams/Philadelphia Orchestra/Eugene Ormandy). *See* 3622.1

3623 Roslavets, Nikolai, 1881–1944

3623.1 *Chasi novoluniia (In the hour of the new moon).* (Saarbrucken Radio Symphony/Heinz Holliger). Wergo: WER 6207-2. [With his *Concerto for violin and orchestra no. 1*].

3623.2 *Piano music. Selections.* (Sarah Rothenberg). *See* 3675

3624 Roussel, Albert, 1869–1937

3624.1 *Bacchus et Ariane* [ballet]. (French National Orchestra/Georges Prêtre). EMI: CDC 7 47376 2. [With his *Festin de l'araignée*].

3624.2 *Le festin de l'araignée (The spider's feast)* [ballet]. (French National Orchestra/Georges Prêtre). *See* 3624.1

3624.3 *Sinfonietta, op. 52.* (Detroit Symphony/Neeme Järvi). *See* 3624.4

3624.4 *Symphony no. 4, op. 53.* (Detroit Symphony/Neeme Järvi). Chandos: CHAN 9072. [With his *Sinfonietta*; Milhaud, Darius: *Suite provençale*; Debussy, Claude: *La mer*].

3625 Rudhyar, Dane, 1895–1985

Instrumental music. Selections. (Kronos Quartet/Marcia Mikulak). CRI: 604. [*Advent; Crisis and overcoming; Transmutation*].

3626 Ruggles, Carl, 1876–1971

3626.1 *Angels* [for brass ensemble]. (Ensemble 21/Arthur Weisberg). *See* 3847.7

3626.2 *Evocations* [for piano]. (Michael Boriskin). New World: 80402-2. [With Shapero, Harold: *Sonatas for piano nos. 1 and 3*; Fine, Irving: *Music for piano*; Menotti, Gian Carlo: *Ricercar and toccata on a theme from The old maid and the thief*].

3626.3 * *Sun-treader.* (Boston Symphony/Michael Tilson Thomas). Deutsche Grammophon: 429

860-2. [With Piston, Walter: *Symphony no. 2*; Schuman, William: *Concerto for violin and orchestra*].

3627   Salzedo, Carlos, 1885–1961

Harp music. Selections. (Alice Giles). Koch Schwann: 312 232.

3628   Satie, Erik, 1866–1925

3628.1 * *Gymnopédies.*

- [Orchestral version]. (New London Orchestra/ Roland Corp). *See 3628.2*

- [Piano version]. (Yuji Takahashi). *See 3628.3*

3628.2   *Parade* [ballet].

- (New London Orchestra/Roland Corp). Hyperion: CDA66365. [With his *Gymnopédies; Mercure; Gnossiennes; Rêlache*].

- (Czech Philharmonic/Vladimír Válek). Supraphon: CO-1519. [With Poulenc, Francis: *Les biches*; Milhaud, Darius: *Le boeuf sur le toit*].

3628.3 ** *Piano music. Selections.*

- (Reinbert de Leeuw). Philips: 412 243-2. [*Gnossiennes; Petite ouverture à danser; Prélude de la porte héroïque du ciel; Danses gothiques*].

- (Yuji Takahashi). Denon: C37-7485. [*Gymnopédies; Gnossiennes; Prélude de la porte héroïque du ciel; Je te veux; Pièces froides; Nocturnes; Rag-time parade*].

- (Yuji Takahashi). Denon: C37-7486. [*Préludes flasques (pour un chien); Véritables préludes flasques (pour un chien); Descriptions automatiques; Embryons desséchés; Choses vues à droite et à gauche (sans lunettes); Valses distinguées du précieux dégoûte; Sports et divertissements; Avant-dernières pensées; Sonatine bureaucratique*].

3628.4   *Rêlache* [ballet]. (New London Orchestra/ Roland Corp). *See 3628.2*

3628.5   *Socrate* [for alto voice and piano]. (Hilke Helling/Deborah Richards). Wergo: 6186-2. [With Cage, John: *Cheap imitation*].

3628.6   *Vexations* [for piano]. (Alan Marks). London: 425 221-2.

3629   Schoenberg, Arnold, 1874–1951

3629.1   *Begleitmusik zu einer Lichtspielszene (Accompaniment to a cinematographic scene).*

- (BBC Symphony/Pierre Boulez). *See 3629.6*

- (London Symphony/Robert Craft). *See 3629.14*

3629.2   *Das Buch der hängende Gärten (Book of the hanging gardens)* [song cycle]. (Jan De-Gaetani/Gilbert Kalish). *See 3629.15*

3629.3   *Concerto for piano and orchestra op. 42.* (Maurizio Pollini/Berlin Philharmonic/Claudio Abbado). *See 3508.1*

3629.4 * *Erwartung* [monodrama]. (Jessye Norman/Metropolitan Opera Orchestra/James Levine). Philips: 423 231-2. [With his *Cabaret songs*].

3629.5   *Gurre-Lieder* [cantata]. (Jessye Norman/ Tatiana Troyanos/Boston Symphony/Seiji Ozawa). Philips: 412 511-2. 2CD set.

3629.6   *Jakobsleiter (Jacob's ladder)* [oratorio fragment]. (Pierre Boulez). Sony: SMK 48462. [With his *Kammersymphonie no. 1* and *Begleitmusik zu einer Lichtspielszene*].

3629.7 * *Kammersymphonie (Chamber symphony) no. 1, op. 9.*

- (Ensemble InterContemporain/Pierre Boulez). *See 3629.6*

- (Chamber Orchestra of Europe/Heinz Holliger). *See 3547.3*

- (Orpheus Chamber Orchestra). *See 3629.23*

3629.8   *Kammersymphonie (Chamber symphony) no. 2, op. 38.* (Orpheus Chamber Orchestra). *See 3629.23*

3629.9 * *Moses und Aron* [opera]. (Franz Mazura/ Philip Langridge/Chicago Symphony/Georg Solti). London: 414 264-2. 2CD set.

3629.10   *Ode to Napoleon Buonaparte.* (Ensemble InterContemporain/Pierre Boulez). *See 3629.18*

3629.11   *Pelleas und Melisande* [symphonic poem]. (Chicago Symphony/Pierre Boulez). Erato: 2292-45827-2. [With his *Variations for orchestra*].

3629.12   *Phantasy for violin and piano, op. 47.* (Schönberg Ensemble). *See 3629.23*

3629.13 * *Piano music.*

- (Glenn Gould). Sony: SM2K 52664. 2CD set. [With his *Concerto for piano and orchestra; Phantasy; Ode to Napoleon*].

- (Maurizio Pollini). Deutsche Grammophon: 423 249-2.

3629.14 ** *Pieces (5) for orchestra, op. 16.*

- (BBC Symphony/Pierre Boulez). *See 3629.18*

- (London Symphony/Robert Craft). Koch: 3-7263-2H1. [With his *Survivor from Warsaw; Begleitmusik zu einer Lichtspielszene; Herzgewächse; Serenade*].

- (Cleveland Orchestra/Christoph von Dohnanyi). *See* 3603.11
- (Berlin Philharmonic/James Levine). *See* 3547.10

3629.15 * *Pierrot lunaire* [for vocalist and chamber ensemble].

- (Jan DeGaetani/Contemporary Chamber Ensemble/Arthur Weisberg). Elektra Nonesuch: 79237-2. [With his *Buch der hängende Gärten*].
- (Lucy Shelton/Da Capo Chamber Players/ Oliver Knussen). Bridge: 9032. [Includes complete performances of the German original and the English translation by Andrew Porter. With his *Herzgewächse*].
- (Barbara Sukowa/Schönberg Ensemble/ Reinbert de Leeuw). Koch Schwann Musica Mundi: 310 117 H1. [With his *Suite for piano, clarinets, and strings, op. 29*].

3629.16 *Quartets (4) for strings.* (Arditti Quartet). Montaigne: 782024. 2CD set.

3629.17 *Quintet for woodwinds and horn, op. 26.* (London Sinfonietta). *See* 3629.19

3629.18 * *Serenade for bass* [voice] *and instrumental ensemble, op. 24.*

- (John Shirley-Quirk/Ensemble InterContemporain/Pierre Boulez). Sony: SMK 48463. [With his *Pieces (5) for orchestra, op. 16* and *Ode to Napoleon Buonaparte*].
- (Stephen Varcoe/20th Century Classics Ensemble/Robert Craft). *See* 3629.14

3629.19 *Suite for piano, clarinets (3), and strings, op. 29.*

- (Schönberg Ensemble/Reinbert de Leeuw). *See* 3629.15
- (London Sinfonietta). London: 433 083-2. [With his *Quintet for woodwinds and horn*].

3629.20 *Survivor from Warsaw.* (Simon Callow/ London Symphony/Robert Craft). *See* 3629.14

3629.21 *Trio for strings, op. 45.* (Schönberg Ensemble). *See* 3629.23

3629.22 * *Variations for orchestra, op. 31.*

- (Chicago Symphony/Pierre Boulez). *See* 3629.11
- (Berlin Philharmonic/Herbert von Karajan). *See* 3629.23

3629.23 * *Verklärte Nacht (Transfigured night)* [for string sextet or string orchestra].

- (Berlin Philharmonic/Herbert von Karajan). Deutsche Grammophon: 415 326- 2. [With his *Variations for orchestra*].

- (Orpheus Chamber Orchestra). Deutsche Grammophon: 429 233-2. [With his *Kammersymphonien, nos. 1–2*].
- (Schönberg Ensemble). Philips: 416 306-2. [With his *Trio* and *Phantasy*].

3630 Schreker, Franz, 1878–1934

Chamber symphony for 23 solo instruments. (Canadian Chamber Ensemble/Raffi Armenian). *See* 3656.4

3631 Schulhoff, Ervin, 1894–1942

3631.1 *Duo for violin and piano.* (Gidon Kremer/ James Tocco). *See* 3636.11

3631.2 *Jazz etudes* [for piano]. (James Tocco). *See* 3636.11

3631.3 *Sextet for strings.* (Gidon Kremer and others). *See* 3636.11

3632 Schwitters, Kurt, 1887–1948

Ursonate [for voice]. (Kurt Schwitters). Wergo: 6304.

3633 Scriabin, Aleksandr Nikolayevich, 1872–1915

3633.1 *Concerto for piano and orchestra, op. 20 in F♯ minor.* (Vladimir Ashkenazy/London Philharmonic/Lorin Maazel). *See* 3633.3

3633.2 ** *Piano music. Selections.*

- (Donna Amato). Altarus: 9020. [*Sonatas nos. 8–10; Preludes, opp. 67 and 74; Poèmes, opp. 69 and 71; Danses, op. 73*].
- (Vladimir Horowitz). RCA: 6215-2-RG. [*Sonatas nos. 3 and 5; Preludes from opp. 11, 15, 16, 27, 48, 59, and 67; Etudes from opp. 8 and 42*].

3633.3 * *Poema ekstaza ("Poem of ecstasy" = Symphony no. 4).*

- (Berlin Radio Symphony/Vladimir Ashkenazy). *See* 3633.6
- (London Philharmonic/Lorin Maazel). London: 417 252-2. [With his *Concerto for piano and orchestra; Promethée*].
- (New York Philharmonic/Giuseppe Sinopoli). *See* 3633.6

3633.4 *Promethée.* (London Philharmonic/Lorin Maazel). *See* 3633.3

3633.5 * *Sonatas (10) for piano.*

- (Robert Taub). Harmonia Mundi: 901741/42. 2CD set.

See also 3633.2

3633.6 *Symphony no. 3, op. 43 ("Divine poem").*

- (Berlin Radio Symphony/Vladimir Ashkenazy). London: 430 843-2. [With his *Reverie, op. 24* and *Poema ekstaza*].

- (New York Philharmonic/Giuseppe Sinopoli). Deutsche Grammophon: 427 324-2. [With his *Poema ekstaza*].

3634 Seeger, Ruth Crawford, 1901–1953

3634.1 * *Movements (2) for chamber orchestra.* (Boston Musica Viva/Richard Pittman). Delos: 1012. [With Musgrave, Thea: *Chamber concerto no. 2*; Mekeel, Joyce: *Planh*].

3634.2 * *Quartet for strings.* (Arditti Quartet). *See* 3992

3634.3 * *Solo and chamber music. Selections.*

- (Continuum/Cheryl Seltzer and Joel Sachs). Musical Heritage Society: 513493M. [*Suite for five wind instruments and piano; Sonata for violin and piano; Ricercari on poems of H. T. Tsiang; Study in mixed accents; Preludes for piano; Diaphonic suites nos. 1–2; Songs to poems by Carl Sandburg*].

- (Ida Kavafian and others). CRI: 658. [*Sonata for violin and piano; Study in mixed accents; Preludes for piano; Diaphonic suite no. 1 for solo oboe; Songs to poems by Carl Sandburg; Suite for wind quintet*].

3635 Sessions, Roger, 1896–1985

3635.1 *Chamber music. Selections.* (Group for Contemporary Music). Koch: 7113. [*Duo for violin and violoncello; Pieces (6) for violin; Duo for violin and piano; Sonata for violin*].

3635.2 *Concerto for orchestra.* (Boston Symphony/Seiji Ozawa). Hyperion: CDA66050. [With Panufnik, Andrzej: *Symphony no. 8*].

3635.3 * *Piano music.* (Barry David Salwen). Koch: 3-7106-2 H1. [*Sonatas nos. 1–3; From my diary; Pieces (5); Waltz*].

3635.4 *Quartet for strings no. 2.* (Juilliard Quartet). CRI: 587. [With Wolpe, Stefan: *Quartet for strings*; Babbitt, Milton: *Quartet for strings no. 4*].

3635.5 *Sonata for piano no. 2.* (Peter Lawson). *See* 3671

3635.6 *Symphony no. 2.* (San Francisco Symphony/Herbert Blomstedt). *See* 3779.1

3635.7 * *Symphony no. 4.* (Columbus Symphony/Christian Badea). New World: NW 345. [With his *Symphony no. 5* and *Rhapsody for orchestra*].

3635.8 *When lilacs last in the dooryard bloom'd* [cantata]. (Seiji Ozawa). New World: NW 296-2.

3636 Shostakovich, Dmitrii Dmitrievich, 1906–1975

3636.1 *Concerto for piano, trumpet, and orchestra no. 1, op. 35.* (Yevgeny Kissin/Moscow Virtuosi/Vladimir Spivakov). RCA: 7947-2-RC. [With his *Chamber symphony, op. 110a* and *Preludes for piano, op. 34*].

3636.2 *Concerto for violin and orchestra no. 1, op. 99* [revised from op. 77]. (Itzhak Perlman/Israel Philharmonic/Zubin Mehta). EMI: CDC 7 49814 2. [With Glazunov, Aleksandr Konstantinovich: *Concerto for violin and orchestra*].

3636.3 *Concerto for violoncello and orchestra no. 1, op. 107 in E♭.* (Yo-Yo Ma/Philadelphia Orchestra/Eugene Ormandy). *See* 3636.19

3636.4 * *Ledi Makbet Mtsenskogo uezda (Lady Macbeth of Mtsensk).* (Galina Vishnevskaya/Nicolai Gedda/London Philharmonic/Mstislav Rostropovich). EMI: CDS 7 49955 2. 2CD set.

3636.5 *Preludes and fugues for piano, op. 87.*

- (Keith Jarrett). ECM: 1469/1470 (437 189-2). 2CD set.

- (Tatiana Nikolayeva). Hyperion: CDA66441/43. 3CD set.

3636.6 *Preludes for piano, op. 34.* (Yevgeny Kissin). *See* 3636.1

3636.7 *Quartets (15) for strings.* (Brodsky Quartet). Teldec: 9031-71702-2. 6CD set.

3636.8 * *Quartet for strings no. 8, op. 110 in C minor.*

- (Borodin Quartet). Virgin: VC 7 91437-2 (261 610). [With his *Quartets nos. 7 and 9*].

- (Brodsky Quartet). Teldec: 244 919-2. (With his *Quartets nos. 7 and 9*].

3636.9 *Quartet for strings no. 8, op. 110 in C minor* [arranged by Shostakovich as his *Chamber symphony, op. 110a*]. *See* 3636.1 or 3636.24

3636.10 * *Quartet for strings no. 13, op. 138 in B♭ minor.* (Gidon Kremer and others). *See* 3636.11

3636.11 * *Quartet for strings no. 14, op. 142 in F♯ major.* (Gidon Kremer and others). [Series: Edition Lockenhaus, vols. 4–5]. ECM: 78118-21347-2 (833506-2). 2CD set. [With his *Quartet no. 13*; plus Schulhoff, Ervin: *Sextet for strings; Jazz etudes; Duo for violin and piano*].

3636.12 * *Quartet for strings no. 15, op. 144 in E♭ minor.* (Gidon Kremer and others). CBS: MK 44924. [With Gubaidulina, Sofia Asgatovna: *Rejoice!*].

3636.13 *Quintet for piano and strings, op. 57 in G minor.* (Borodin Trio and others). Chandos: CHAN 8342. [With his *Trio for piano and strings*].

3636.14 * *Sonata for viola and piano, op. 147.* (Kim Kashkashian/Robert Levin). ECM: 78118-21425-2. [With Bouchard, Linda: *Pourtinade*; Chihara, Paul: *Redwood*].

3636.15 * *Symphony no. 1, op. 10 in F minor.*

- (Royal Philharmonic/Vladimir Ashkenazy). London: 425 609-2. [With his *Symphony no. 6*].

- (Chicago Symphony/Leonard Bernstein). Deutsche Grammophon: 427 632-2. [With his *Symphony no. 7*].

- (London Philharmonic/Bernard Haitink). *See* 3636.23

3636.16 *Symphony no. 2, op. 14 in B major ("To October").* (London Philharmonic/Bernard Haitink). London: 421 131-2. [With his *Symphony no. 3* and *Zolotoi vek*].

3636.17 *Symphony no. 3, op. 20 in E♭ major ("First of May").* (London Philharmonic/Bernard Haitink). *See* 3636.16

3636.18 *Symphony no. 4, op. 43 in C minor.* (Royal Philharmonic/Vladimir Ashkenazy). London: 425 693-2.

3636.19 ** *Symphony no. 5, op. 47 in D minor.*

- (Royal Philharmonic/Vladimir Ashkenazy). London: 421 120-2. [With his *Fragmente (5) for orchestra, op. 42*].

- (Concertgebouw Orchestra/Bernard Haitink). London: 410 017-2.

- (Philadelphia Orchestra/Eugene Ormandy). CBS: MDK 44903. [With his *Concerto for violoncello and orchestra no. 1*].

3636.20 *Symphony no. 6, op. 54 in B minor.* (Royal Philharmonic/Vladimir Ashkenazy). *See* 3636.15

3636.21 *Symphony no. 7, op. 60 in C major ("Leningrad").* (Chicago Symphony/Leonard Bernstein). *See* 3636.15

3636.22 *Symphony no. 8, op. 65 in C minor.* (Scottish National Orchestra/Neeme Järvi). Chandos: CHAN 8757.

3636.23 *Symphony no. 9, op. 70 in E♭ major.* (London Philharmonic/Bernard Haitink). London: 414 677-2. [With his *Symphony no. 1*].

3636.24 *Symphony no. 10, op. 93 in E minor.* (Royal Philharmonic/Vladimir Ashkenazy). Lon-

don: 433 028-2. [With his *Chamber symphony, op. 110a*].

3636.25 *Symphony no. 11, op. 103 in G minor ("The year 1905").* (Helsinki Philharmonic/James De Preist). Delos: C/CD 3080.

3636.26 *Symphony no. 12, op. 112 ("The year 1917").* (Gothenburg Symphony/Neeme Järvi). Deutsche Grammophon: 431 688-2. [With his *Gamlet (Hamlet) suite* and *Zolotoi vek*].

3636.27 * *Symphony no. 13, op. 113 ("Babi Yar").* (Concertgebouw Orchestra/Bernard Haitink). London: 417 261-2.

3636.28 * *Symphony no. 14, op. 135.* (Concertgebouw Orchestra/Bernard Haitink). London: 417 514-2. [With his *Poems of Marina Tsvetaeva*].

3636.29 * *Symphony no. 15, op. 141 in A major.* (London Symphony/Mstislav Rostropovich). Teldec: 9031-74560-2.

3636.30 *Trio for piano and strings no. 2, op. 67 in E minor.* (Borodin Trio). *See* 3636.13

3636.31 *Zolotoi vek (The age of gold)* [ballet suite].

- (London Philharmonic/Bernard Haitink). *See* 3636.16

- (Gothenburg Symphony/Neeme Järvi). *See* 3636.26

3637 Sibelius, Jean, 1865–1957

3637.1 * *Concerto for violin and orchestra, op. 47 in D minor.*

- (Nigel Kennedy/London Philharmonic/Okko Kamu). *See* 3519.3

- (Gidon Kremer/London Symphony/Gennady Rozhdestvensky). RCA: 09026-60957-2. [With Schnittke, Alfred: *Concerto grosso no. 1*].

- (Viktoria Mullova/Boston Symphony/Seiji Ozawa). *See* 3519.3

3637.2 *En saga* [for orchestra]. (Philharmonia Orchestra/Vladimir Ashkenazy). *See* 3637.3

3637.3 * *Finlandia* [for orchestra].

- (Philharmonia Orchestra/Vladimir Ashkenazy). London: 417 762-2. [With his *Karelia; Tapiola; En saga*].

- (Berlin Philharmonic/Herbert von Karajan). Deutsche Grammophon: 413 755-2. [With his *Swan of Tuonela; Valse triste; Tapiola*].

3637.4 *Karelia* [suite for orchestra].

- (Philharmonia Orchestra/Vladimir Ashkenazy). *See* 3637.3

- (Berlin Philharmonic/Herbert von Karajan). See 3637.6

3637.5 *Lemminkäis-sarja (Four legends)* [for orchestra]. (Gothenburg Symphony/Neeme Järvi). Bis: 294.

3637.6 *Symphony no. 1, op. 39 in E minor.* (Berlin Philharmonic/Herbert von Karajan). EMI: CDM 7 69028 2. [With his *Karelia*].

3637.7 * *Symphony no. 2, op. 43 in D major.* (Berlin Philharmonic/Herbert von Karajan). EMI: CDM 7 69243 2.

3637.8 * *Symphony no. 3, op. 52 in C major.* (Gothenburg Symphony/Neeme Järvi). Bis: 228. [With his *Kunigas Kristian II suite*].

3637.9 ** *Symphony no. 4, op. 63 in A minor.*
- (Philharmonia Orchestra/Vladimir Ashkenazy). London: 430 749-2. [With his *Symphony no. 5*].
- (Berlin Philharmonic/Herbert von Karajan). Deutsche Grammophon: 415 108-2. [With his *Symphony no. 6*].

3637.10 ** *Symphony no. 5, op. 82 in E♭ major.*
- (Philharmonia Orchestra/Vladimir Ashkenazy). See 3637.9
- (Vienna Philharmonic/Leonard Bernstein). Deutsche Grammophon: 427 647-2. [With his *Symphony no. 7*].
- (Berlin Philharmonic/Herbert von Karajan). Deutsche Grammophon: 415 107-2. [With his *Symphony no. 7*].

3637.11 * *Symphony no. 6, op. 104 in D minor.* (Berlin Philharmonic/Herbert von Karajan). See 3637.9

3637.12 * *Symphony no. 7, op. 105 in C major.*
- (Vienna Philharmonic/Leonard Bernstein). See 3637.10
- (Berlin Philharmonic/Herbert von Karajan). See 3637.10

3637.13 * *Tapiola* [for orchestra].
- (Philharmonia Orchestra/Vladimir Ashkenazy). See 3637.3
- (Berlin Philharmonic/Herbert von Karajan). See 3637.3

3637.14 * *Tuonelan joutsen (Swan of Tuonela)* [from *Lemminkäis-sarja*] [for orchestra]. (Gothenburg Symphony/Neeme Järvi). See 3637.5

3637.15 * *Valse triste* [for orchestra].
- (Berlin Philharmonic/Herbert von Karajan). See 3637.3
- (Orpheus Chamber Orchestra). See 3537

3637.16 *Voces intimae* [for string quartet]. (Juilliard Quartet). See 3521.12

3638   Skalkottas, Nikos, 1904–1949

Epistrophi tou Odysseus (Return of Odysseus) [for orchestra]. (Danish Radio Symphony/Miltiades Caridis). Koch Schwann Musica Mundi: 311 110. [With Kalomiris, Manolis: *Symphony no. 1*].

3639 * Sorabji, Kaikhosru Shapurji, 1892–1988

Opus clavicembalisticum [for piano]. (John Ogden). Altarus: 9075. 4CD set.

3640   Sowerby, Leo, 1895–1968

Organ music. Selections. (Catharine Crozier). Delos: 3075. [*Fantasy for flute stops; Requiescat in pace; Symphony in G major*].

3641   Still, William Grant, 1895–1978

3641.1 *Miniatures for flute, oboe, and piano.* (Peter Christ and others). See 3664

3641.2 *Piano music. Selections.* (Denver Oldham). Koch: 3-7084-2 H1. [*Bells; Traceries; Blues from Lenox Avenue; Swanee River; Preludes; Summerland; Africa*].

3641.3 * *Symphony no. 1 ("Afro-American").* (Detroit Symphony/Neeme Järvi). Chandos: CHAN 9154. [With Ellington, Duke: *Suite from The river*].

3642   Strauss, Richard, 1864–1949

3642.1 *Alpensinfonie (Alpine symphony).* (Berlin Philharmonic/Herbert von Karajan). Deutsche Grammophon: 400 039-2.

3642.2 * *Also sprach Zarathustra (Thus spake Zarathustra)* [symphonic poem].
- (Berlin Philharmonic/Herbert von Karajan). Deutsche Grammophon: 410 959-2. [With his *Don Juan*].
- (Chicago Symphony/Georg Solti). London: 430 445-2. [With his *Don Juan* and *Till Eulenspiegels lustige Streiche*].

3642.3 *Ariadne auf Naxos* [opera]. (Jessye Norman/Julia Varady/Gewandhausorchestra Leipzig/Kurt Masur). Philips: 422 084-2. 2CD set.

3642.4 *Capriccio* [opera]. (Elisabeth Schwarzkopf/Christa Ludwig/Nicolai Gedda/Philharmonia Orchestra/Wolfgang Sawallisch). EMI: CDS 7 49014 8. 2CD set.

3642.5 *Concertos (2) for horn and orchestra.* (Barry Tuckwell/Royal Philharmonic/Vladimir Ashkenazy). London: 430 370-2.

3642.6 *Concerto for oboe and orchestra.*
- (John De Lancie/London Symphony/Max Wilcox). RCA: 7989-2-RG. [With Françaix, Jean: *Horloge de flore;* Ibert, Jacques: *Symphonie concertante*].
- (Heinz Holliger/New Philharmonia Orchestra/Edo de Waart). *See 3642.17*

**3642.7 ** ** *Don Juan* [symphonic poem].
- (Vienna Philharmonic/Christoph von Dohnanyi). London: 430 508-2. [With his *Metamorphosen* and *Tod und Verklärung*].
- (Berlin Philharmonic/Herbert von Karajan). *See 3642.2 or 3642.10*
- (Chicago Symphony/Georg Solti). *See 3642.2*
- (Cleveland Orchestra/George Szell). *See 3642.18*

3642.8 * *Don Quixote* [symphonic poem]. (Yo-Yo Ma/Boston Symphony/Seiji Ozawa). CBS: MDK 45804. [With his *Liebe der Danae*].

3642.9 * *Elektra* [opera]. (Birgit Nilsson/Regina Resnik/Vienna Philharmonic/Georg Solti). London: 417 345-2. 2CD set.

3642.10 * *Ein Heldenleben (A hero's life)* [symphonic poem].
- (Chicago Symphony/Daniel Barenboim). *See 3642.18*
- (Berlin Philharmonic/Herbert von Karajan). Deutsche Grammophon: 429 717-2. [With his *Don Juan*].

**3642.11 ** ** *Letzte Lieder (Four last songs).*
- (Jessye Norman/Gewandhaus Orchestra Leipzig/Kurt Masur). Philips: 412 653-2. [With his selected songs].
- (Kiri Te Kanawa/Vienna Philharmonic/Georg Solti). London: 430 511-2. [With his selected songs].

3642.12 * *Metamorphosen* [for 23 solo strings].
- (Vienna Philharmonic/Christoph von Dohnanyi). *See 3642.7*
- (Berlin Philharmonic/Herbert von Karajan). Deutsche Grammophon: 410 892-2. [With his *Tod und Verklärung*].

3642.13 * *Der Rosenkavalier* [opera].
- (Kiri Te Kanawa/Anne Sofie von Otter/Staatskapelle Dresden/Bernard Haitink). EMI: CDS 7 59259 2. 3CD set.
- (Elisabeth Schwarzkopf/Christa Ludwig/Philharmonia Orchestra/Herbert von Karajan). EMI: CDS 7 49354 2. 3CD set.

3642.14 * *Salome* [opera]. (Birgit Nilsson/Gerhard Stolze/Vienna Philharmonic/George Solti). London: 414 414-2. 2CD set.

3642.15 *Songs. Selections.*
- (Jessye Norman/Geoffrey Parsons). Philips: 416 298-2.

  See also 3642.11

3642.16 *Symphonia domestica* [symphonic poem]. (Chicago Symphony/Fritz Reiner). RCA: 60388-2-RG. [With his *Tod und Verklärung*].

3642.17 *Symphonie für Bläser (Symphony for winds).* (Netherlands Wind Ensemble/Edo de Waart). Philips: 438 733-2. [With his *Concerto for oboe and orchestra*].

**3642.18 ** ** *Till Eulenspiegels lustige Streiche (Till Eulenspiegel's merry pranks)* [symphonic poem].
- (Chicago Symphony/Daniel Barenboim). Erato: 2292-45621-2. [With his *Heldenleben*].
- (Chicago Symphony/Georg Solti). *See 3642.2*
- (Cleveland Orchestra/George Szell). CBS: MYK 36721. [With his *Don Juan* and *Tod und Verklärung*].

3642.19 * *Tod und Verklärung (Death and transfiguration)* [symphonic poem].
- (Vienna Philharmonic/Christoph von Dohnanyi). *See 3642.7*
- (Berlin Philharmonic/Herbert von Karajan). *See 3642.12*
- (Chicago Symphony/Fritz Reiner). *See 3642.16*
- (Cleveland Orchestra/George Szell). *See 3642.18*

3643 Stravinsky, Igor, 1882–1971

3643.1 *Abraham and Isaac* [cantata].
- (Stephen Varcoe/Orchestra of St. Luke's/Robert Craft). *See 3643.7*
- (David Wilson-Johnson/London Sinfonietta/Oliver Knussen). *See 3643.22*

3643.2 * *Agon* [ballet]. (Orchestra of St. Luke's/Robert Craft). [Series: Stravinsky the composer, vol. 4]. MusicMasters: 01612- 67113-2. [With his *Greeting prelude; Star-spangled banner; Concerto in E♭; Instrumental miniatures; Circus polka; Scherzo à la russe; Scènes de ballet; Balanchine-Stravinsky chorale; Vom Himmel hoch*].

3643.3 *Apollon musagète* [ballet].
- (Orchestra of St. Luke's/Robert Craft). *See 3643.49*

- (Montreal Sinfonietta/Charles Dutoit). *See* 3643.11

3643.4 *Le baiser de la fée (The fairy's kiss)* [ballet suite]. (London Sinfonietta/Riccardo Chailly). London: 417 114-2. [With his *Fanfare for a new theatre; Pieces for clarinet solo; Suites for chamber orchestra nos. 1–2; Octet*].

3643.5 *Berceuses du chat (Cat lullabies).*

- (Catherine Ciesinski/Robert Craft). *See* 3643.23

- (Denise Scharley and others). *See* 3643.45

3643.6 *Cantata.* (Gregg Smith Singers/Robert Craft). *See* 3643.7

3643.7 * *Capriccio for piano and orchestra.*

- (Paul Crossley/London Sinfonietta/Esa-Pekka Salonen). Sony: SK 45797. [With his *Symphonies d'instruments à vent; Concerto for piano and wind instruments; Movements for piano and orchestra*].

- (Mark Wait/Orchestra of St. Luke's/Robert Craft). MusicMasters: 01612-67158-2. [Series: Stravinsky the composer, vol. 8. With his *Cantata; Septet; Songs from William Shakespeare; In memoriam: Dylan Thomas; Abraham and Isaac*].

3643.8 *Chansons russes* [for soprano, flute, harp, and guitar]. (Jacqueline Brumaire/Pierre Boulez). *See* 3643.45

3643.9 * *Concertino for 12 instruments.* (Orchestra of St. Luke's/Robert Craft). *See* 3643.32

3643.10 * *Concertino for string quartet. See* 3643.42

3643.11 * *Concerto for orchestra in E♭ ("Dumbarton Oaks").*

- (Orchestra of St. Luke's/Robert Craft). *See* 3643.2

- (Montreal Sinfonietta/Charles Dutoit). London: 440 327-2. [With his *Concerto for string orchestra; Apollon musagète; Danses concertantes*].

- (Orpheus Chamber Orchestra). *See* 3643.37

3643.12 * *Concerto for piano and wind instruments.* (Paul Crossley/London Sinfonietta/Esa-Pekka Salonen). *See* 3643.7

3643.13 * *Concerto for 2 solo pianos.*

- (Alfons and Aloys Kontarsky). Wergo: 6228-2. [With his *Sonata for two pianos; Pièces faciles*].

- (Mark Wait/Tom Schultz). *See* 3643.44

3643.14 *Concerto for string orchestra in D.* (Montreal Sinfonietta/Charles Dutoit). *See* 3643.11

3643.15 * *Concerto for violin and orchestra.* (Anne-Sophie Mutter/Philharmonia Orchestra/Paul Sacher). Deutsche Grammophon: 423 696-2. [With Lutoslawski, Witold: *Partita for violin and orchestra* and *Chain no. 2*].

3643.16 *Danses concertantes.* (Montreal Sinfonietta/Charles Dutoit). *See* 3643.11

3643.17 *Divertimento for violin and piano.* (Cho-Liang Lin/André-Michel Schub). *See* 3643.43

3643.18 *Double canon* [for string quartet]. *See* 3643.42

3643.19 *Duo concertante* [for violin and piano].

- (American Chamber Players). *See* 3643.23

- (Cho-Liang Lin/André-Michel Schub). *See* 3643.43

3643.20 * *Ebony concerto* [for clarinet and band]. (Benny Goodman/Columbia Jazz Combo). *See* 3666

3643.21 *Elegy for viola solo.* (American Chamber Players). *See* 3643.23

3643.22 *The flood* [musical play]. (Peter Hall/David Wilson-Johnson/London Sinfonietta/Oliver Knussen). Deutsche Grammophon: 447 068-2. [With his *Abraham and Isaac; Variations; Requiem canticles.* Plus Wuorinen, Charles: *Reliquary for Igor Stravinsky*].

3643.23 * *L'histoire du soldat* [suite].

- (American Chamber Players) [version for violin, clarinet, and piano]. Koch: 3-7078-2H1. [With his *Duo concertante; Pieces for clarinet solo; Elegy for viola solo*].

- (Orchestra of St. Luke's/Robert Craft) [original instrumentation]. [Series: Stravinsky the composer, vol. 7]. MusicMasters: 01612-67152-2. [With his *Pribaoutki; Berceuses du chat; Mass; Canticum sacrum*].

- (Lucy Stoltzman/Richard Stoltzman/Richard Goode) [version for violin, clarinet, and piano]. *See* 3545.5

3643.24 *In memoriam: Dylan Thomas* [for tenor and instruments]. (Jon Humphries/Orchestra of St. Luke's/Robert Craft). *See* 3643.7

3643.25 *Jeu de cartes* [ballet]. (Philharmonia Orchestra/Esa-Pekka Salonen). *See* 3643.52

3643.26 * *Mass.*

- (English Bach Festival Chorus and Orchestra/Leonard Bernstein). *See* 3643.45

- (Gregg Smith Singers/Robert Craft). *See* 3643.23

- (Westminster Cathedral Choir/James O'Donnell). *See 3643.46*

3643.27 * *Movements for piano and orchestra.* (Paul Crossley/London Sinfonietta/Esa-Pekka Salonen). *See 3643.7*

3643.28 * *Octet for winds.*
- (London Sinfonietta/Riccardo Chailly). *See 3643.4*
- (Orchestra of St. Luke's/Robert Craft). *See 3643.32*
- (London Sinfonietta/Esa-Pekka Salonen). *See 3643.37*

3643.29 *Ode* [for orchestra]. (Orchestra of St. Luke's/Robert Craft). *See 3643.44*

3643.30 *Oedipus Rex* [opera].
- (Jon Humphrey/Wendy White/Orchestra of St. Luke's/Robert Craft). *See 3643.49*
- (Jessye Norman/Thomas Moser/Bavarian Radio Symphony/Colin Davis). Orfeo: C 071-831 A.

3643.31 * *Orpheus* [ballet]. (Philharmonia Orchestra/Esa-Pekka Salonen). *See 3643.33*

3643.32 *Perséphone* [melodrama]. (Gregg Smith Singers/Orchestra of St. Luke's/Robert Craft). [Series: Stravinsky the composer, vol. 3]. MusicMasters: 01612-67103-2. [With his *Zvezdoliki; Symphonies d'instruments à vent; Concertino for 12 instruments; Octet*].

3643.33 ** *Petrushka* [ballet].
- (Cleveland Orchestra/Pierre Boulez). Deutsche Grammophon: 435 769-2. [With his *Vesna sviashchennaia*].
- (London Philharmonic/Bernard Haitink). Philips: 420 491-2. [With his *Vesna sviashchennaia*].
- (Philharmonia Orchestra/Esa-Pekka Salonen). Sony: SK 53274. [With his *Orpheus*].

3643.34 *Piano music. Selections.*
- (Aleck Karis). Bridge: 9051. [*Movements (3) from Petrushka; Valse pour les enfants; Ragtime; Piano-rag music; Les cinq doigts; Serenade in A; Tango; Circus polka; Pièces faciles; Sonata for two pianos*].
- (Maurizio Pollini). Deutsche Grammophon: 419 202-2. [His *Movements (3) from Petrushka*; with Prokofiev, Sergey: *Sonata for piano no. 7*; Webern, Anton: *Variations, op. 27*; Boulez, Pierre: *Sonata for piano no. 2*].
- (Peter Serkin). New World: 344. [His *Serenade in A* and *Sonata*; with Lieberson, Peter:

Bagatelles; Wolpe, Stefan: *Pastorale; Form IV; Passacaglia*].

See also 3643.44

3643.35 *Pieces (3) for clarinet solo.*
- (American Chamber Players). *See 3643.23*
- (Steven Kanoff). *See 3669*

3643.36 *Pribaoutki* [for mezzo-soprano and instruments].
- (Catherine Ciesinski/Robert Craft). *See 3643.23*
- (Denise Scharley/Pierre Boulez). *See 3643.45*

3643.37 * *Pulcinella* [ballet with voices].
- (Orchestra of St. Luke's/Robert Craft). [Series: Stravinsky the composer, vol. 2]. MusicMasters: 01612-67086-2. [With his *Symphony in C; Russian peasant choruses; Russian sacred choruses; Svadebka*].
- (London Sinfonietta/Esa-Pekka Salonen) [complete ballet]. Sony: SK 45965. [With his *Ragtime; Renard; Octet*].
- (Orpheus Chamber Orchestra) [orchestral suite]. Deutsche Grammophon: 419 628-2. [With his *Concerto in E♭; Instrumental miniatures*].

3643.38 * *The rake's progress* [opera]. (Jane West/Jon Garrison/John Cheek/Orchestra of St. Luke's/Robert Craft). [Series: Stravinsky the composer, vol. 6]. MusicMasters: 01612-67131-2. 2CD set.

3643.39 *Renard* [burlesque].
- (Tom Baker/Orchestra of St. Luke's/Robert Craft). *See 3643.44*
- (John Aler/London Sinfonietta/Esa-Pekka Salonen). *See 3643.37*

3643.40 * *Requiem canticles.*
- (New York Choral Artists/Orchestra of St. Luke's/Robert Craft). *See 3643.49*
- (New London Chamber Choir/London Sinfonietta/Oliver Knussen). *See 3643.22*

3643.41 *Septet.* (Orchestra of St. Luke's/Robert Craft). *See 3643.7*

3643.42 *String quartet music.* (Alban Berg Quartet). EMI: CDC 7 54347 2. [*Trois pièces (1914); Concertino; Double canon*; with Haubenstock-Ramati, Roman: *Quartet for strings no. 2*; Einem, Gottfried von: *Quartet for strings no. 1*].

3643.43 *Suite italienne* [for violin and piano]. (Cho-Liang Lin/André-Michel Schub). CBS: MK 42101. [With his *Duo concertante* and *Divertimento*].

3643.44 *Suites (2) for chamber orchestra.*

- (London Sinfonietta/Riccardo Chailly). *See* 3643.4
- (Orchestra of St. Luke's/Robert Craft). [Series: Stravinsky the composer, vol. 5]. MusicMasters: 01612-67110-2. [With his *Etudes for piano, op. 7; Norwegian moods (4) for orchestra; Concerto for two solo pianos; Ode; Ragtime; Piano-rag music; Renard*].

3643.45 * *Svadebka (Les noces = The wedding).*

- (English Bach Festival Chorus/Leonard Bernstein). Deutsche Grammophon: 423 251-2. [With his *Mass*].
- (Paris Opera Chorus and Orchestra/Pierre Boulez). Adès: 13.236-2. [With his *Pribaoutki; Berceuses du chat; Chansons russes; Chansons paysanes*].
- (Gregg Smith Singers/Orchestra of St. Luke's/Robert Craft). *See* 3643.37
- (Dimitri Pokrovsky Singers). Elektra Nonesuch: 79335-2. [Includes traditional Russian village wedding songs].

3643.46 ** *Symphonie des psaumes (Symphony of psalms).*

- (New York Choral Artists/Orchestra of St. Luke's/Robert Craft). *See* 3643.49
- (Westminster Cathedral Choir/City of London Sinfonia/James O'Donnell). Hyperion: CDA66437. [With his *Motets (3); Mass; Canticum sacrum*].
- (Atlanta Symphony Chorus and Orchestra/Robert Shaw). *See* 3521.11

3643.47 * *Symphonies d'instruments à vent (Symphonies of wind instruments).*

- (Berlin Radio Symphony/Vladimir Ashkenazy). London: 436 416-2. [With his *Symphony in three movements; Symphony in C*].
- (Orchestra of St. Luke's/Robert Craft). *See* 3643.32
- (London Sinfonietta/Esa-Pekka Salonen). *See* 3643.7

3643.48 * *Symphony in C.*

- (Berlin Radio Symphony/Vladimir Ashkenazy). *See* 3643.47
- (Orchestra of St. Luke's/Robert Craft). *See* 3643.37

3643.49 * *Symphony in three movements.*

- (Berlin Radio Symphony/Vladimir Ashkenazy). *See* 3643.47

- (Orchestra of St. Luke's/Robert Craft). [Series: Stravinsky the composer, vol. 1]. MusicMasters: 01612-67078-2. 2CD set. [With his *Fanfare for a new theatre; Fanfare for three trumpets; Oedipus Rex; Apollon musagète; Requiem canticles; Symphonie des psaumes; Vesna sviashchennaia*].

3643.50 * *Variations: Aldous Huxley in memoriam* [for orchestra]. (London Sinfonietta/Oliver Knussen). *See* 3643.22

3643.51 ** *Vesna sviashchennaia (Le sacre du printemps = The rite of spring)* [ballet].

- (Cleveland Orchestra/Pierre Boulez). *See* 3643.33
- (Orchestra of St. Luke's/Robert Craft). *See* 3643.49
- (London Philharmonic/Bernard Haitink). *See* 3643.33

3643.52 ** *Zhar-ptitsa (The firebird)* [ballet].

- (Chicago Symphony/Pierre Boulez). Deutsche Grammophon: 437 850-2. [With his *Feu d'artifice* and *Etudes (4) for orchestra*].
- (Montreal Symphony/Charles Dutoit). London: 414 409-2. [With his *Scherzo fantastique* and *Feu d'artifice*].
- (Philharmonia Orchestra/Esa-Pekka Salonen). CBS: MK 44917. [With his *Jeu de cartes*].

3644 Szymanowski, Karol, 1882–1937

3644.1 *Piano music. Selections.* (Carol Rosenberger). Delos: D/CD 1002. [*Masques, op. 34; Etudes, opp. 4 and 33; Mazurkas, opp. 50 and 62*].

3644.2 *Quartets for strings (2).* (Varsovia Quartet). Olympia: OCD 328. [With Lutoslawski, Witold: *Quartet for strings*; Penderecki, Krzysztof: *Quartet for strings no. 2*].

3644.3 * *Stabat Mater.* (City of Birmingham Symphony Chorus and Orchestra/Simon Rattle). EMI: 5 55121 2. [With his *Litany to the Virgin Mary; Symphony no. 3*].

3644.4 *Symphony no. 3.* (City of Birmingham Symphony/Simon Rattle). *See* 3644.3

3645 Tailleferre, Germaine, 1892–1983

Chamber music. Selections. (Ilrike Siebler and others). Troubadisc: 01406. [*Image for eight instruments; Quartet for strings; Sonatas for violin and piano nos. 1–2; Sonata for clarinet; Arabesque for clarinet and piano; Forlane for flute and piano; Trio for piano and strings*].

3646 Thompson, Randall, 1899–1984

The peaceable kingdom [oratorio]. (Gregg Smith Singers). Orion: ORS 76228. LP. OP

3647 Thomson, Virgil, 1896–1989

3647.1 *Four saints in three acts* [opera]. (Betty Allen/Benjamin Matthews/Orchestra of Our Time/Joel Thome). Elektra Nonesuch: 79035-2. 2CD set.

3647.2 *The mother of us all* [opera]. (Mignon Dunn/James Atherton/Philip Booth/Santa Fe Opera/Raymond Leppard). New World: NW 288/89. 2CD set.

3647.3 *Piano music. Selections.* (Yvar Mikhashoff). New Albion: 034. [With his songs].

3647.4 *The plow that broke the plains.* (Los Angeles Chamber Orchestra/Neville Marriner). See 3660

3647.5 *Songs. Selections.* (Martha Herr and others). See 3647.3

3648 Tubin, Eduard, 1905–1982

Symphony no. 3. (Swedish Radio Symphony/Neeme Järvi). Bis: 342. [With his *Symphony no. 8*].

3649 Turina, Joaquín, 1882–1949

3649.1 *Guitar music. Selections.* (John Williams). See 3677

3649.2 *Oración del torero* [for chamber orchestra]. (Orpheus Chamber Orchestra). See 3537

3649.3 *Piano music.* (Alicia de Larocha). EMI: 7 64528 2. [*Sanlúcar de Barrameda; Danzas fantásticas; Zapateado; Sacromonte*].

3649.4 *Vocal music (selections).* (Victoria de los Angeles and others). See 3673

3650 Varèse, Edgard, 1883–1965

3650.1 *Amériques* [for orchestra].
- (New York Philharmonic/Pierre Boulez). See 3650.7
- (Cleveland Orchestra/Christoph von Dohnanyi). London: 443 172-2. [With Ives, Charles: *Symphony no. 4*].

3650.2 * *Arcana* [for orchestra].
- (New York Philharmonic/Pierre Boulez). See 3650.7
- (Concertgebouw Orchestra/Riccardo Chailly). See 3609.2

3650.3 * *Density 21.5* [for flute]. (Lawrence Beauregard). See 3650.7

3650.4 *Déserts* [for winds, piano, percussion, and electronic tape]. (Asko Ensemble/Cliff Crego). See 3650.6

3650.5 *Ecuatorial* [for baritone and chamber ensemble]. (Thomas Paul/Contemporary Chamber Ensemble/Arthur Weisberg). See 3650.9

3650.6 * *Intégrales* [for winds and percussion].
- (Ensemble InterContemporain/Pierre Boulez). See 3650.7
- (Asko Ensemble/Cliff Crego). Attaca Babel: 9263-2. [With his *Ionisation; Déserts; Poème electronique*].
- (Contemporary Chamber Ensemble/Arthur Weisberg). See 3650.9

3650.7 * *Ionisation* [for percussion ensemble].
- (Amadinda Percussion Group). See 3661
- (New York Philharmonic/Pierre Boulez). Sony: SK 45844. [With his *Amériques; Density 21.5; Offrandes; Arcana; Octandre; Intégrales*].
- (Asko Ensemble/Cliff Crego). See 3650.6

3650.8 *Octandre* [for woodwinds and brass].
- (Ensemble InterContemporain/Pierre Boulez). See 3650.7
- (Contemporary Chamber Ensemble/Arthur Weisberg). See 3650.9

3650.9 *Offrandes* [for soprano and chamber ensemble].
- (Jan DeGaetani/Contemporary Chamber Ensemble/Arthur Weisberg). Elektra Nonesuch: 71269-2. [With his *Intégrales; Octandre; Ecuatorial*].
- (Rachel Yakar/Ensemble InterContemporain/Pierre Boulez). See 3650.7 (Boulez)

3650.10 * *Poème electronique* [for electronic tape]. See 3650.6 or 3970

3651 Vaughan Williams, Ralph, 1872–1958

3651.1 *Concerto accademico* [for violin and orchestra]. (James Buswell/London Symphony/André Previn). See 3651.13

3651.2 *Concerto for tuba and orchestra in F minor.* (Patrick Harrild/London Symphony/Bryden Thomson). See 3651.17

3651.3 ** *Fantasia on a theme by Thomas Tallis* [for double string orchestra].
- (London Philharmonic/Bernard Haitink). See 3651.13
- (Academy of St. Martin-in-the-Fields/Neville Marriner). Argo: 414 595-2. [With his *Fanta-*

sia on Greensleeves; Lark ascending; Variants of Dives and Lazarus].

3651.4 *Fantasia on Greensleeves* [for orchestra]. (Academy of St. Martin-in-the-Fields/Neville Marriner). *See 3651.3*

3651.5 *Flos campi* [for viola, chorus, and orchestra]. (Nobuko Imai/Corydon Singers/Matthew Best). *See 3651.10*

3651.6 ** *The lark ascending* [for violin and orchestra]. (Iona Brown/Academy of St. Martin-in-the-Fields/Neville Marriner). *See 3651.3*

3651.7 *Mass.* (Christ Church Cathedral Choirs/Stephen Darlington). Nimbus: NI 5083. [With his *Shakespeare songs* and other choral works].

3651.8 *Mystical songs.* (Thomas Allen/English Chamber Orchestra/Matthew Best). *See 3651.10*

3651.9 *On Wenlock edge* [song cycle]. (Robert Tear/City of Birmingham Symphony/Simon Rattle). EMI: 7 64731 2. [With his *Songs of travel* and orchestral songs by Edward Elgar and George Butterworth].

3651.10 *Serenade to music* [oratorio]. (Corydon Singers/English Chamber Orchestra/Matthew Best). Hyperion: CDA66420. [With his *Mystical songs; Fantasia on Christmas carols; Flos campi*].

3651.11 *Songs of travel.* (Thomas Allen/City of Birmingham Symphony/Simon Rattle). *See 3651.9*

3651.12 *Symphony no. 1 ("A sea symphony").* (Felicity Lott/London Philharmonic Choir and Orchestra/Bernard Haitink). EMI: CDC 7 49911 2.

3651.13 * *Symphony no. 2 ("London symphony").*
- (London Philharmonic/Bernard Haitink). EMI: CDC 7 49394 2. [With his *Fantasia on a theme by Thomas Tallis*].
- (London Symphony/André Previn). RCA: 60581-2-RG. [With his *Concerto accademico* and *Wasps overture*].

3651.14 *Symphony no. 3 ("Pastoral symphony").*
- (New Philharmonia Orchestra/Adrian Boult). EMI: CDM 7 64018 2. [With his *Symphony no. 5*].
- (London Symphony/André Previn). RCA: 60583-2-RG. [With his *Symphony no. 4*].

3651.15 *Symphony no. 4 in F minor.* (London Symphony/André Previn). *See 3651.14*

3651.16 *Symphony no. 5 in D major.*
- (London Philharmonic/Adrian Boult). *See 3651.14*

- (Philharmonia Orchestra/Leonard Slatkin). RCA: 09026-60556-2. [With his *Symphony no. 6*].

3651.17 * *Symphony no. 6 in E minor.*
- (London Symphony/André Previn). RCA: 60588-2-RG. [With his *Symphony no. 9*].
- (Philharmonia Orchestra/Leonard Slatkin). *See 3651.16*
- (London Symphony/Bryden Thomson). Chandos: CHAN 8740. [With his *Concerto for tuba and orchestra*].

3651.18 *Symphony no. 7 ("Sinfonia antartica").* (Sheila Armstrong/London Philharmonic/Bernard Haitink). EMI: CDC 7 47516 2.

3651.19 *Symphony no. 8 in D minor.* (London Philharmonic/Adrian Boult). EMI: CDM 7 64021 2. [With his *Symphony no. 9*].

3651.20 *Symphony no. 9 in E minor.*
- (London Philharmonic/Adrian Boult). *See 3651.19*
- (London Symphony/André Previn). *See 3651.17*

3651.21 *Variants of Dives and Lazarus* [for orchestra]. (Academy of St. Martin-in-the-Fields/Neville Marriner). *See 3651.3*

3651.22 *Wasps overture.* (London Symphony/André Previn). *See 3651.13*

3652 Villa Lobos, Heitor, 1887–1959

3652.1 * *Bachianas brasileiras. Selections.*
- (Barbara Hendricks/Royal Philharmonic/Enrique Bátiz). EMI: CDC 7 47433 2. [*No. 1 for eight violoncellos; No. 5 for soprano and eight violoncellos; No. 7 for orchestra*].
- (Mady Mesplé/Michel Debost/Paul Capolongo and others). EMI: 7 47357 2. [*No. 2 for orchestra; No. 5 for soprano and eight violoncellos; No. 6 for flute and bassoon; No. 9 for string orchestra*].

3652.2 ** *Chôros. Selections.* (Various performers). Chant du Monde: LCD 278 835. [*No. 1 for guitar; No. 2 for flute and clarinet; No. 3 for male chorus and instruments; No. 4 for horns and trombone; No. 5 for piano; No. 7 for chamber ensemble; Chôros bis for violin and piano; Quintette en forme de chôros for woodwinds and horn*].

3652.3 *Fantasia for saxophone and orchestra.* (John Harle/Academy of St. Martin-in-the-Fields/Neville Marriner). *See 3667*

3652.4 * *Guitar music.* (Turibio Santos). Chant du Monde: LCD 278 869/70 2CD set. [*Etudes (12); Preludes (5); Suite populaire brésilienne; Distribution de fleurs, for guitar and flute; Chôros no. 1; Concerto for guitar and chamber orchestra; Sextuor mystique*]. *See also* 3575.4

3652.5 *Orchestral music. Selections.* (Czecho-Slovak Radio Symphony/Roberto Duarte). Marco Polo: 8.223357. [*Gênesis; Erosão; Amazonas; Dawn in a tropical forest*].

3652.6 *Piano music. Selections.* (Roberta Rust). Centaur: 2224. [*Ciclo brasileiro; Valsa; Rudepoema; Bachianas brasileiras no. 4; Suite floral; Chôros no. 5*].

3652.7 * *Quartets (17) for strings. Selections.* (Danubius Quartet). Marco Polo: 8.223389/92. 4 CDs [available separately].

3652.8 *Quintette en forme de chôros* [for woodwinds and horn]. *See* 3652.2

3652.9 * *Rudepoema* [for piano].

- (Volker Banfield). Wergo: 60110-50. [With Müller-Siemens, Detlev: *Under neonlight II*].
- (Roberta Rust). *See* 3652.6

3653 Walton, William, 1902–1983

3653.1 * *Belshazzar's feast* [oratorio]. (Benjamin Luxon/Brighton Festival Chorus/Royal Philharmonic/André Previn). RPO: 7013. [With his *Henry V suite*].

3653.2 *Concerto for viola and orchestra.* (Nigel Kennedy/Royal Philharmonic/André Previn). EMI: CDC 7 49628 2. [With his *Concerto for violin and orchestra*].

3653.3 *Concerto for violin and orchestra.* (Nigel Kennedy/Royal Philharmonic/André Previn). *See* 3653.2

3653.4 *Concerto for violoncello and orchestra.* (Lynn Harrell/City of Birmingham Symphony/Simon Rattle). EMI: 7 54572 2. [With his *Symphony no. 1*].

3653.5 *Façade* [for two speakers and chamber ensemble]. (Susanna Walton/Richard Baker/City of London Sinfonia/Richard Hickox). Chandos: CHAN 8869.

3653.6 *Symphony no. 1.* (City of Birmingham Symphony/Simon Rattle). *See* 3653.4

3654 Warlock, Peter, 1894–1930

Vocal and instrumental music. Selections. (James Griffett/Royal Philharmonic/Alan Barlow). ASV: QS 6143. [*Curlew; Capriol suite;* and other works].

3655 Webern, Anton, 1883–1945

3655.1 * *Pieces (6) for orchestra, op. 6.*

- (Berlin Philharmonic/Herbert von Karajan). *See* 3655.3 and 3655.4
- (Berlin Philharmonic/James Levine). *See* 3547.10

3655.2 ** *Variations for piano, op. 27.* (Maurizio Pollini). *See* 3643.34

3655.3 * *Works* [complete]. (Pierre Boulez and others). Sony: SM3K 45845. 3CD set.

3655.4 * *Works. Selections.*

- (Arditti Quartet). [Complete string trios and string quartets]. Montaigne: 789008.
- (Françoise Pollet/BBC Singers/Ensemble InterContemporain/Pierre Boulez). Deutsche Grammophon: 437 786-2. [*Pieces (5) for orchestra, op. 10; Quartet for violin, clarinet, saxophone, and piano, op. 22; Concerto, op. 24; Vocal music opp. 2, 8, 13, 14, 15, 18, 19; Quintet for piano and strings*].
- (Berlin Philharmonic/Herbert von Karajan). Deutsche Grammophon: 423 254-2. [*Passacaglia for orchestra, op. 1; Movements (5) for string orchestra, op. 5; Pieces (6) for orchestra, op. 6; Symphony, op. 21*].

3656 Weill, Kurt, 1900–1950

3656.1 * *Aufstieg und Fall der Stadt Mahagonny (Rise and fall of the city of Mahagonny)* [opera].

- (Lotte Lenya/North German Radio Orchestra/Wilhelm Brückner-Rüggeberg). CBS: M2K 77341. 2CD set.
- (Anja Silja/Cologne Radio Orchestra/Jan Latham-König). Capriccio: 10 160/61. 2CD set.

3656.2 *Concerto for violin and instrumental ensemble, op. 30.* (Naoko Tanaka/Orchestra of St. Luke's/Julius Rudel). MusicMasters: 7007- 2-C or Musical Heritage Society: MHS 512485Y. [With his *Kleine Dreigroschenmusik*].

3656.3 * *Dreigroschenoper (Threepenny opera).* (Ute Lemper/René Kollo/Berlin Radio Sinfonietta/John Mauceri). London: 430 075-2. 2CD set.

3656.4 * *Kleine Dreigroschenmusik (Little threepenny music).*

- (Canadian Chamber Ensemble/Raffi Armenian). CBC: SMCD5010. [With Schreker, Franz: *Chamber symphony*].
- (Orchestra of St. Luke's/Julius Rudel). *See* 3656.2

3656.5 *Lost in the stars.* See 6103.2

3656.6 *Mahagonny Songspiel* [cantata]. See 3656.7

3656.7 *Die sieben Todsünden (The seven deadly sins)* [cantata]. (Ute Lemper/RIAS Sinfonietta Berlin/John Mauceri). London: 430 168-2. [With his *Mahagonny Songspiel*].

3656.8 *Street scene.* See 6103.3

3656.9 *Symphony no. 1.* (Gewandhaus Orchestra/Edo de Waart). Philips: 434 171-2. [With his *Symphony no. 2*].

3657 Wolf-Ferrari, Ermanno, 1876–1948

Il segreto di Susanna (Susanna's secret) [opera]. (Renata Scotto/Renato Bruson/Royal Philharmonic/John Pritchard). CBS: MK 36733.

3658 Wolpe, Stefan, 1902–1972

3658.1 * *Piano music. Selections.*

- (Marc-André Hamelin) [*Battle piece*]. See 3709.2
- (Geoffrey Douglas Madge). CPO: 999 055-2. [*Passacaglia; Battle piece; Displaced spaces; Form IV;* and other works].
- (Peter Serkin) [*Pastorale; Form IV; Passacaglia*]. See 3643.34

3658.2 *Piece for trumpet and seven instruments.* (Parnassus/Anthony Korf). See 3658.5

3658.3 *Piece for two instrumental units.* (Parnassus/Anthony Korf). See 3658.5

3658.4 *Piece in three parts* [for piano and 13 instruments]. (Peter Serkin/Speculum Musicae/Oliver Knussen). See 3658.10

3658.5 *Piece in two parts for six players.* (Parnassus/Anthony Korf). Koch: 3-7141-2 H1. [With his *Quartet for piano, saxophone, trumpet, and percussion; Piece for two instrumental units; Piece for trumpet and seven instruments*].

3658.6 *Quartet for oboe, violoncello, percussion, and piano.* (Group for Contemporary Music). Koch: 3-7112-2 H1. [With his *Trio for flute, violoncello, and piano* and *Sonata for violin and piano*].

3658.7 *Quartet for piano, saxophone, trumpet, and percussion.* (Parnassus/Anthony Korf). See 3658.5

3658.8 *Quartet for strings.* (Juilliard Quartet). See 3635.4

3658.9 * *Quintet with voice.* (Jan Opalach/Speculum Musicae/William Purvis). See 3658.10

3658.10 *Suite im Hexachord* [for oboe and clarinet]. (Speculum Musicae). Bridge: 9043. [With his *Quintet with voice* and *Piece in three parts for piano and 13 instruments*].

3658.11 *Symphony.* (Orchestra of the 20th Century/Arthur Weisberg). CRI: 676. [With Sessions, Roger: *Concerto for violin and orchestra*].

3658.12 * *Trio for flute, violoncello, and piano.* (Group for Contemporary Music). See 3658.6

3659 Zemlinsky, Alexander, 1871–1942

3659.1 *Lyrische Symphonie (Lyric symphony)* [for voices and orchestra]. (Elisabeth Söderström/Berlin Radio Symphony/Bernhard Klee). Koch Schwann: 311 053.

3659.2 *Quartet for strings no. 2, op. 15.* (Schönberg Quartet). Koch Schwann: 310 118. [With his *Quartet no. 3*].

Anthologies and Recitals

3660 * *American miniatures.* (Various performers). Angel: CDM 7 64306 2. [Copland, Aaron: *Fanfare for the common man; Quiet city; Letter from home;* and *John Henry;* Thomson, Virgil: *Autumn* and *The plow that broke the plains;* Barber, Samuel: *Adagio for strings*].

Individual Artists

3661 * Amadinda Percussion Group. *Amadinda Percussion Group.* (Hungaroton: HCD 12991-2. [Varèse, Edgard: *Ionisation;* Chávez, Carlos: *Toccata;* Cage, John: *4'33"; Amores; Third construction;* Cage, John, and Lou Harrison: *Double music*].

3662 Berliner Saxophon-Quartett. *Saxophonquartette = Saxophone quartets.* Koch Schwann Musica Mundi: 310055. [Works by Aleksandr Konstantinovich Glazunov, Raymond Moulaert, Gustav Bumcke, and Jean Françaix].

3663 * Boehm Quintet. *American winds, vol. 1.* Premier: 1006. [Piston, Walter: *Quintet for woodwinds and horn* and *Pieces for flute, clarinet, and bassoon;* Fine, Irving: *Partita;* Siegmeister, Elie: *Ten minutes for four players;* Persichetti, Vincent: *Pastoral;* Carter, Elliott: *Quintet for woodwinds and horn*].

3664 Christ, Peter. *Oboist Peter Christ.* Crystal: CD 321. [Persichetti, Vincent: *Parable for solo oboe;* Still, William Grant: *Miniatures for flute, oboe, and piano;* plus works by Randall Thompson, Alberto Ginastera, William Schmidt].

3665 Gallois, Patrick. *Poulenc, Desbrière, Dutilleux, Roussel, Messiaen, Fauré.* Thesis: THC 82012. [Works for flute or flute and piano].

3666 * Goodman, Benny. *Benny Goodman collector's edition.* CBS: MK 42227. [Bernstein, Leonard: *Prelude, fugue, and riffs;* Copland, Aaron: *Concerto for clarinet and orchestra;* Stravinsky, Igor: *Ebony concerto;* Gould, Morton: *Derivations for clarinet;* Bartók, Béla: *Contrasts*].

3667 * Harle, John. *Saxophone concertos.* (Academy of St. Martin-in-the-Fields/Neville Marriner). EMI: CDC 7 54301 2. [Debussy, Claude: *Rhapsody;* Ibert, Jacques: *Concertino;* Villa Lobos, Heitor: *Fantasia;* Glazunov, Aleksandr Konstantinovich: *Concerto;* Bennett, Richard Rodney: *Concerto;* Heath, David: *Out in the cool*].

3668 * Hinderas, Natalie. *Piano music by African American composers.* CRI: 629. 2CD set. [Dett, R. Nathaniel: *In the bottoms;* Kerr, Thomas: *Easter Monday swagger;* Still, William Grant: *Visions;* Work, John Wesley III: *Scuppernong;* Walker, George: *Sonata no. 1;* Cunningham, Arthur: *Engrams;* Hakim, Talib Rasul: *Sound-gone;* Smith, Hale: *Evocation;* Wilson, Olly: *Piano piece*].

3669 Kanoff, Steven. *Clarinet music of the 19th & 20th century.* Doron: DRC 3014. [With Catherine Collard, piano. Schumann, Robert: *Fantasiestücke, op. 73;* Berg, Alban: *Pieces for clarinet and piano, op. 5;* Stravinsky, Igor: *Pieces for clarinet solo;* Poulenc, Francis: *Sonata for clarinet and piano;* Cage, John: *Sonata for clarinet;* Messiaen, Olivier: *L'abîme des oiseaux*].

3670 * Lawson, Peter. *American piano sonatas, vol. 1.* Virgin: CDC 7 59008 2 (7 91163 2). [Copland, Aaron: *Sonata;* Ives, Charles: *Three-page sonata;* Carter, Elliott: *Sonata;* Barber, Samuel: *Sonata*].

3671 * Lawson, Peter. *American piano sonatas, vol. 2.* Virgin: CDC 7 59316 2. [Griffes, Charles Tomlinson: *Sonata;* Sessions, Roger: *Sonata no. 2;* Ives, Charles: *Sonata no. 1*].

3672 * Lindberg, Christian. *The virtuoso trombone.* Bis: CD-258. [With Roland Pöntinen, piano. Martin, Frank: *Ballade for trombone and piano;* Hindemith, Paul: *Sonata for trombone and piano;* Berio, Luciano: *Sequenza no. 5;* plus works by Nikolay Rimsky-Korsakov, Stjepan Šulek, Vittorio Monti, Fritz Kreisler, and Arthur Pryor].

3673 Los Angeles, Victoria de. *Falla, Granados, Turina.* EMI: CDH 7 64028 2. [Songs, with Gerald Moore, piano and various orchestras].

3674 ** Pro Arte Wind Quintet. *French wind music.* Nimbus: NI 5327. [Ibert, Jacques: *Trois pièces brèves;* Françaix, Jean: *Quintet for woodwinds and horn;* Auric, Georges: *Trio for oboe, clarinet, and bassoon;* Honegger, Arthur: *La danse de la chèvre;* Milhaud, Darius: *La cheminée du roi René*].

3675 Rothenberg, Sarah. *Rediscovering the Russian avant-garde, 1912–1925.* GM: 2040. [Piano music by Aleksandr Mosolov, Nikolai Roslavets, and Arthur Lourié].

3676 * Schleiermacher, Steffen. *The bad boys!* Hat Hut: ART CD 6144. [Piano music by George Antheil, Henry Cowell, and Leo Ornstein].

3677 ** Williams, John, 1941– . *Spanish guitar favorites.* CBS: MK 44794. [Music by Enrique Granados, Isaac Albéniz, Manuel de Falla, Francisco Tárrega, Joaquín Turina, Joaquín Rodrigo, Miguel Llobet, and others].

Modern Period since 1950

Compiled by
Kent Underwood

Composers

3678 Abrahamsen, Hans, 1952–

Preludes for string quartet [String quartet no. 1].
(Kontra Quartet). Da Capo: CDDC 9006. [With his
String quartet no. 2; Ruders, Poul: *Quartets for
strings nos. 2–3*].

3679 Adams, John, 1947–

3679.1 ** *The chairman dances* [for orchestra].

- (City of Birmingham Symphony/Simon Rattle). *See* 3679.5

- (Baltimore Symphony/David Zinman). *See*
  3969

3679.2 * *China gates* [for piano]. (Christopher
O'Riley). *See* 4020

3679.3 *The death of Klinghoffer* [opera]. (Stephanie Friedman/Sanford Sylvan/James Maddalena/
Lyon Opera/Kent Nagano). Elektra Nonesuch:
79281-2. 2CD set.

3679.4 *Grand pianola music* [for voices and
instruments]. (Solisti di New York/Ransom Wilson). EMI: CDC 7 47331 2. [With Reich, Steve:
Octet ("Eight lines"); Vermont counterpoint].

3679.5 *Harmonielehre.* (City of Birmingham
Symphony/Simon Rattle). EMI: CDC 5 55051 2.
[With his *Chairman dances; Tromba lontana;
Short ride in a fast machine*].

3679.6 *Harmonium* [for chorus and orchestra].
(San Francisco Symphony Chorus and Orches-
tra/Edo de Waart). ECM: 1277 (78118-21277-2).

3679.7 * *Nixon in China* [opera]. (Sanford Sylvan/
Stephanie Friedman/James Maddalena/Orchestra
of St. Luke's/Edo de Waart). Elektra Nonesuch:
79177-2. 3CD set.

3679.8 * *Phrygian gates* [for piano].

- (Ursula Oppens). *See* 4018

- (Christopher O'Riley). *See* 4020

3679.9 *Shaker loops* [for orchestra].

- (San Francisco Symphony/Edo de Waart). *See*
  3886.15

- (London Chamber Orchestra/Christopher
  Warren-Green). *See* 4013

3680 Adler, Samuel, 1928–

Quartets for strings nos. 3, 6, and 7. (Meliora Quartet). CRI: CD 608.

3681 Albert, Stephen, 1941–

RiverRun [symphony]. (National Symphony/Mstislav Rostropovich). Delos: D/CD 1016. [With his *To wake the dead*].

3682 Albright, William, 1944–

Organbook no. 1. (David Craighead). Gothic: G 58627. [With his *Organbook no. 3*].

3683 Alvear, María de

En amor duro [for piano]. (Hildegard Kleeb). Hat Hut: ART CD 6112.

3684 Amirkhanian, Charles, 1945–

Vers les anges [electroacoustic music]. *See 3972*

3685 AMM Group

3685.1 * *AMMMusic—1966.* Matchless: 7 52725 00092 5. [Group compositions by Cornelius Cardew, Lou Gare, Eddit Prévost, Keith Rowe, and Lawrence Sheaff].

3685.2 *The Crypt, 12th June 1988: the complete session.* Matchless: MRCD05. 2CD set. [Group compositions by Cornelius Cardew, Lou Gare, Christopher Hobbs, Eddie Prévost, and Keith Rowe].

3686 Amram, David, 1930–

Orchestral music. Selections. (Manhattan Chamber Orchestra/Richard Auldon Clark). Newport: NPD 85546. [Album title: *An American original.* Contents: *American dance suite; Theme and variations on Red River Valley; Travels; Three songs for America*].

3687 Anderson, Laurie, 1947–

3687.1 ** *Big science.* Warner Bros.: 3674-2.

3687.2 *United States live.* Warner Bros: 9 25192-2. 4CD set.

3688 Andriessen, Louis, 1939–

3688.1 ** *De snelheid (Velocity).* (Icebreaker). *See 4010*

3688.2 *De staat (The republic).* (Schönberg Ensemble/Reinbert de Leeuw). Elektra Nonesuch: 79251-2.

3688.3 * *De tijd (Time).* (Schönberg Ensemble/Reinbert de Leeuw). Elektra Nonesuch: 79291-2.

3689 Argento, Dominick, 1927–

3689.1 * *From the diary of Virginia Woolf* [song cycle]. (Linn Maxwell/William Parker/William Hickaby). Centaur: CRC 2092.

3689.2 *Postcard from Morocco* [opera]. (Barbara Brandt/Yale Marshall/Barry Busse/Minnesota Opera/Philip Brunelle). CRI: CD 614.

3690 Arnold, Malcolm, 1921–

3690.1 *Chamber music* [selections]. [Series: Chamber music of Malcolm Arnold, vol. 3]. (Nash Ensemble). Hyperion: CDA66173. [*Quintet for woodwinds, horn, and strings, op. 7; Duo for flute and viola, op. 10; Divertimento for woodwinds, op. 37; Quartet for oboe and strings, op. 61; Sonata for flute, op. 121; Shanties for wind quintet, op. 4*].

3690.2 *Symphony no. 3, op. 63.* (London Symphony/Richard Hickox). Chandos: CHAN 9290. [With his *Symphony no. 4*].

3691 Ashley, Robert, 1930–

3691.1 * *Improvement* [opera]. (Robert Ashley and others). Elektra Nonesuch: 78289-2. 2CD set.

3691.2 *Yellow man with heart with wings* [for voices and electronics]. (Guillermo Grenier/Robert Ashley/"Blue" Gene Tyranny). Lovely Music: LCD 1003.

3692 Babbitt, Milton, 1916–

3692.1 *Correspondences* [for orchestra]. (Chicago Symphony/James Levine). *See 3721.19*

3692.2 *Elizabethan sextette* [for voices]. (Group for Contemporary Music). CRI: CD 521. [With his *Groupwise; Vision and prayer; Piano music*].

3692.3 *Groupwise* [for chamber ensemble]. (Group for Contemporary Music). *See 3692.2*

3692.4 *The head of the bed* [song cycle]. (Judith Bettina/Parnassus/Anthony Korf). New World: CD 346. [With his *Concerto for piano and orchestra*].

3692.5 * *Philomel* [for soprano and piano or electronic tape].
- (Bethany Beardslee). New World: 80466-2. [With his *Phonemena*].
- (Judith Bettina). *See 3970*

3692.6 * *Phonemena* [for soprano and piano or electronic tape].
- (Bethany Beardslee). *See 3692.5*
- (Judith Bettina). *See 3970*

3692.7 * *Piano music.* (Robert Taub). Harmonia Mundi: 905160.

3692.8 *Quartet for strings no. 4.* (Juilliard Quartet). *See* 3635.4

3693 Bacewicz, Grázyna, 1909–1969

3693.1 *Concerto for violin and orchestra no. 7.* (National Philharmonic Warsaw/Ajdrzej Markowski). Olympia: OCD 392. [With her *Sonata for violin and piano no. 4; Sonata for piano no. 2; Concerto for string orchestra*].

3693.2 *Quartets for strings* [selections]. (Wilanow Quartet). Olympia: OCD 387. [*Quartets nos. 3 and 5; plus her Quintet for piano and strings*].

3694 Bainbridge, Simon, 1952–

Orchestral music. Selections. (Simon Bainbridge and others). Continuum: CCD 1020. [*Fantasia for double orchestra; Concerto for viola and orchestra; Concertante in moto perpetuo*].

3695 Baird, Tadeusz, 1928–

Psychodrama [for orchestra]. (Polish Radio National Orchestra/Wojciech Michniewski). Olympia: OCD 326. [With his *Tomorrow*].

3696 * Barkin, Elaine, 1932–

Five collages [electroacoustic music]. Open Space: CD 3. [With Boretz, Benjamin, and others: *An experiment in reading: Samuel Beckett's Cascando*].

3697 Barraqué, Jean, 1928–1973

Concerto for clarinet, vibraphone, and instrumental ensemble. (Rémi Lerner/Ensemble 2e2m/Paul Méfano). Harmonia Mundi: HMC 905199. [With his *Le temps restitué*].

3698 Barron, Louis, 1920– , and Bebe Barron, 1927–

Forbidden planet [electronic film score]. *See* 6112

3699 * Behrman, David, 1937–

Leapday night [for trumpets and electronics]. (David Behrman and others). Lovely Music: CD 1042. [With his *Traveller's dream journal; Interspecies small talk*].

3700 Benjamin, George, 1960–

3700.1 * *Antara* [for orchestra]. (London Sinfonietta/George Benjamin). Nimbus: NI 5167. [With Boulez, Pierre: *Dérive* and *Mémoriale*; Harvey, Jonathan: *Song offerings*].

3700.2 *Orchestral music. Selections.* (London Sinfonietta/BBC Symphony/George Benjamin/ Mark Elder). Nimbus: NI 5075. [*At first light; A mind of winter; Ringed by the flat horizon*].

3701 Berberian, Cathy, 1925–1983

Stripsody [for voice]. (Cathy Berberian). *See* 3997

3702 Berger, Arthur, 1912–

Instrumental music. Selections. (Paul Jacobs and others). CRI: CD 622. [*Three pieces for two prepared pianos; Serenade concertante; String quartet; Two episodes for piano; Chamber music for 13 players*].

3703 Berio, Luciano, 1925–

3703.1 *Chemins no. 2* [for viola and chamber orchestra]. (Jean Sulem/Ensemble InterContemporain/Pierre Boulez). *See* 3703.10

3703.2 *Chemins no. 4* [for oboe and chamber orchestra]. (László Hadady/Ensemble InterContemporain/Pierre Boulez). *See* 3703.10

3703.3 * *Circles* [for mezzo-soprano, harp, and percussion]. (Cathy Berberian and others). Wergo: WER 6021-2. [With his *Sequenza nos. 1, 3, and 5*].

3703.4 * *Corale* [for violin and chamber ensemble].
- (Carlo Chiarappa/London Sinfonietta/Luciano Berio). *See* 3703.22
- (Carlo Chiarappa/Accademia Bizantina). *See* 3703.17
- (Maryvonne Le Dizès/Ensemble InterContemporain/Pierre Boulez). *See* 3703.10

3703.5 *Laborintus no. 2* [for solo voices and instrumental ensemble]. (Ensemble Musique Vivante/Luciano Berio). Harmonia Mundi: HMA 190764.

3703.6 *Opus number zoo* [for wind quintet]. (Ensemble Wien-Berlin). *See* 4006

3703.7 *Points on the curve to find* [for piano and chamber orchestra]. (Pierre-Laurent Aimard/ Ensemble InterContemporain/Pierre Boulez). *See* 3703.10

3703.8 *Quartet for strings.* (Arditti Quartet). *See* 3993

3703.9 *Requies* [for chamber orchestra]. (London Sinfonietta/Luciano Berio). *See* 3703.22

3703.10 *Ritorno degli snovidenia* [for violoncello and orchestra]. (Pierre Strauch/Ensemble InterContemporain/Pierre Boulez). Sony: SK 45862. [With his *Chemins no. 2; Chemins no. 4; Corale; Points on the curve to find*].

3703.11 ** *Sequenza no. 1* [for flute]. (Aurele Nicolet). *See* 3703.3

3703.12 *Sequenza no. 2* [for harp]. (Emily Lawrence). *See* 3980

3703.13 ** *Sequenza no. 3* [for voice]. (Cathy Berberian). *See* 3703.3

3703.14 *Sequenza no. 4* [for piano]. (Theo Bruins). Globe: GLO 6017. [With works by Paul Hindemith, Alban Berg, Arnold Schoenberg, Claude Debussy, and Francis Poulenc].

3703.15 *Sequenza no. 5* [for trombone].

• (Vinko Globokar). *See* 3703.3

• (Christian Lindberg). *See* 3672

3703.16 *Sequenza no. 7* [7a for oboe—7b for soprano saxophone]. (Claude Delangle). *See* 4002

3703.17 *Sequenza no. 8* [for violin]. (Carlo Chiarappa). Denon: CO-75448. [With his *Duets for two violins; Pieces for violin and piano; Corale*].

3703.18 *Sequenza no. 9* [9a for clarinet—9b for alto saxophone]. (Claude Delangle). *See* 4002

3703.19 *Sequenza no. 10* [for trumpet]. (Graham Ashton). *See* 3995

3703.20 *Sequenza no. 11* [for guitar]. (Eliot Fisk). MusicMasters: 01612-67150-2. [With transcriptions of works by Ludwig van Beethoven, Felix Mendelssohn-Bartholdy, Niccolò Paganini, and Domenico Scarlatti].

3703.21 * *Sinfonia* [for voices and orchestra]. (New Swingle Singers/French National Orchestra/Pierre Boulez). Erato: 2292-45228-2. [With his *Eindrücke*].

3703.22 *Voci* [for viola and chamber orchestra]. (Aldo Bennici/London Sinfonietta/Luciano Berio). RCA: 7898-2-RC. [With his *Requies* and *Corale*].

3704 * Bernstein, Leonard, 1918–1990

Selections. (Leonard Bernstein and others). Sony: SM3K 47162. 3CD set. [*Jeremiah symphony; Age of anxiety symphony; Kaddish symphony; Chichester psalms; Symposium, after Plato; Prelude, fugue, and riffs*].

3705 Birtwistle, Harrison, 1934–

3705.1 * *Punch and Judy* [opera]. (Phyllis Bryn-Julson/Jan DeGaetani/Philip Langridge/London Sinfonietta/David Atherton). Etcetera: 2014.

3705.2 *Ritual fragment* [for instrumental ensemble]. (London Sinfonietta/Oliver Knussen). NMC: D009. [With his *Melencolia I; Meridian*].

3705.3 * *Secret theatre* [for chamber ensemble]. (Ensemble InterContemporain/Pierre Boulez). *See* 3705.4

3705.4 * *Tragœdia* [for chamber ensemble]. (Ensemble InterContemporain/Pierre Boulez). Deutsche Grammophon: 439 910-2. [With his *Five distances; Three settings of Celan; Secret theatre*].

3705.5 *The triumph of time.* (Philharmonia Orchestra/Elgar Howarth). Collins: 13872. [With his *Gawain's journey*].

3705.6 *Verses for ensembles.* (Netherlands Wind Ensemble/Percussion Group The Hague/James Wood). Etcetera: KTC 1130. [With his *Refrains and choruses; For o, for o, the hobby-horse is forgot*].

3706 Blackwood, Easley, 1933–

Microtonal compositions. (Easley Blackwood/Jeffrey Kust). Cedille: CDR 90000 018.

3707 Blomdahl, Karl Birger, 1916–1968

Aniara [opera]. (Viveka Anderberg/Björn Haugan/Swedish Radio Symphony/Stig Westerberg). Caprice: 22016. 2CD set.

3708 Boesmans, Philippe, 1936–

Attitudes. (Ensemble Musique Nouvelle). Ricercar: 002040. [With his *Extases*].

3709 Bolcom, William, 1938–

3709.1 *Ghost rags (3)* [for piano]. (Paul Jacobs). *See* 4011

3709.2 * *New etudes* [for piano]. (Marc-André Hamelin). New World: NW 354-2. [With Wolpe, Stefan: *Battle piece*].

3709.3 *Quintet for brass.* (American Brass Quintet). New World: NW 377-2. [With Shapey, Ralph: *Quintet for brass*; Wright, Maurice: *Quintet for brass*; Druckman, Jacob: *Other voices*].

3709.4 *Symphony no. 4.* (Joan Morris/St. Louis Symphony/Leonard Slatkin). New World: 356-2. [With his *Session no. 1*].

3710 Borden, David, 1938–

The continuing story of counterpoint, parts 1–12. (David Borden and others). Cuneiform: Rune 16 CD; Rune 21 CD; Rune 28 CD. 3 CDs.

3711 Boucourechliev, André, 1925–

Archipels. (Claude Helffer and others). MFA/Radio France: 216001.

3712   Boulez, Pierre, 1925–

3712.1   *Cummings ist der Dichter.* (BBC Singers/ Ensemble InterContemporain/Pierre Boulez). *See* 3712.15

3712.2   *Dérive* [for instrumental ensemble].

- (London Sinfonietta/George Benjamin). *See* 3700.1

- (Ensemble InterContemporain/Pierre Boulez). *See* 3712.15

3712.3   *Dialogue de l'ombre double* [for clarinet and electronic tape]. (Alain Damiens). *See* 3712.15

3712.4   *Domaines* [for clarinet and chamber ensemble]. (Michel Portal/Musique Vivante/Diego Masson). Harmonia Mundi: HMA 1909930.

3712.5   * *Eclat-multiples* [for chamber ensemble]. (Ensemble InterContemporain/Pierre Boulez). *See* 3712.11

3712.6   *Figures, doubles, prismes* [for orchestra]. (BBC Symphony/Pierre Boulez). *See* 3712.17

3712.7   ** *Le marteau sans maître* [for mezzo-soprano and chamber ensemble].

- (Jeanne Deroubaix and others). Adès: 14.073-2. [With his *Sonatine for flute and piano*; Messiaen, Oliver: *Haikai*].

- (Elizabeth Laurence/Ensemble InterContemporain/Pierre Boulez). CBS: MK 42619. [With his *Notations for piano*; *Structures II for two pianos*].

3712.8   * *Mémoriale* [for flute and instrumental ensemble].

- (London Sinfonietta/George Benjamin). *See* 3700.1

- (Ensemble InterContemporain/Pierre Boulez). *See* 3712.15

3712.9   *Notations* [for orchestra].

- (Vienna Philharmonic/Claudio Abbado). *See* 3988

- (Paris Orchestra/Daniel Barenboim). *See* 3712.11

3712.10   * *Pli selon pli* [for soprano and orchestra]. (Phyllis Bryn-Julson/BBC Symphony/Pierre Boulez). Erato: 2292-45376-2.

3712.11   * *Rituel* [for orchestra].

- (Paris Orchestra/Daniel Barenboim). Erato: 2292-45493-2. [With his *Messagesequisse*; *Notations*].

- (BBC Symphony/Pierre Boulez). Sony: SMK 45839. [With his *Eclat-multiples*].

3712.12   *Sonata for piano no. 1.*

- (Pierre-Laurent Aimard). *See* 3712.15

- (Herbert Henck). Wergo: 60121-50. [With his *Sonatas nos. 2–3*].

3712.13   * *Sonata for piano no. 2.*

- (Herbert Henck). *See* 3712.12

- (Maurizio Pollini). *See* 3643.34

3712.14   *Sonata for piano no. 3.* (Herbert Henck). *See* 3712.12

3712.15   *Sonatina for flute and piano.* (Sophie Cherrier/Pierre-Laurent Aimard). Erato: 2292-45648-2. [With his *Sonata for piano no. 1*; *Dérive*; *Mémoriale*; *Dialogue de l'ombre double*; *Cummings ist der Dichter*].

3712.16   *Structures* [for two pianos]. (Alfons and Aloys Kontarsky). Wergo: 6011-2.

3712.17   *Le visage nuptial* [for voices and orchestra]. (BBC Singers/BBC Symphony/Pierre Boulez). Erato: 2292-45494-2. [With his *Soleil des eaux*; *Figures, doubles, prismes*].

3713   Branca, Glenn, 1948–

3713.1   *Symphony no. 3* ("*Gloria: music for the first 127 intervals of the harmonic series*"). (Glenn Branca). Atavistic: ALP08.

3713.2   * *Symphony no. 6* ("*Devil choirs at the gates of heaven*"). (Glenn Branca and others). Atavistic: ALP10.

3714   Brant, Henry, 1913–

3714.1   *Angels and devils* [for wind ensemble]. (Eastman Wind Ensemble/Donald Hunsberger). Centaur: CRC 2014. [With Hanson, Howard: *Dies natalis*; Benson, Warren: *Leaves are falling*].

3714.2   *Ghost nets* [for double bass and two instrumental groups]. (Lewis Paer/American Camerata for New Music/Henry Brant/John Elliott Stephens). AmCam: ACR-10303. [With Cyr, Gordon: *Quartet for strings no. 2*].

3714.3   * *Selections.* (Henry Brant/Boston Musica Viva/Richard Pittman). Newport: NPD 85588. [Album title: *Works of a lifetime*. Contents: *Hommage aux frères Marx*; *An era any time of year*; *All souls carnival*; *Pathways to security*; *Music for an imaginary ballet*].

3715   Brown, Earle, 1926–

3715.1   *Corroboree* [for three pianos]. (Peter Degenhardt and others). *See* 3729.3

3715.2   * *Folio* [for various instruments]. (Eberhard Blum and others). *See* 3982

3716 Bruzdowicz, Joanna, 1943–

Quartet for strings no. 1 ("La vita"). (Varsovia Quartet). Pavane: ADW 7218. [With her *Quartet for strings no. 2 ("Cantus aeternus"); Zarebski, Juliusz: Quintet for piano and strings*].

3717 Bryars, Gavin, 1943–

3717.1 *Jesus' blood never failed me yet* [for instruments and tape]. Point: 438 823-2.

3717.2 * *The sinking of the Titanic* [for instruments and electronics]. Point: 446 061-2.

3718 Bussotti, Sylvano, 1931–

3718.1 *O* [for mezzo-soprano, after the opera *La passion selon Sade*]. (Cathy Berberian). *See* 3997

3718.2 *Quartetto Grimsci* [for string quartet]. (Arditti Quartet). *See* 3993

3718.3 * *Rara requiem* [for voices and chamber orchestra]. (Saarbrücken Radio Symphony/ Gianpiero Taverna). Deutsche Grammophon: 437 739-2. [With his *Bergkristall; Lorenzaccio symphony*].

3719 Cage, John, 1912–1992

3719.1 * *Atlas eclipticalis* [for variable instrumental groupings, to be played with or without his *Winter music*].

- (Eberhard Blum and others) [Three flutes, with his *Winter music*]. *See* 3719.23

- (S.E.M. Ensemble/Petr Kotik) [orchestra]. *See* 3719.3

- (Chicago Symphony/James Levine) [orchestra]. *See* 3721.19

3719.2 *Cheap imitation* [for piano]. (Herbert Henck). *See* 3628.5

3719.3 *Concert for piano and orchestra.*

- (Joseph Kubera/S.E.M. Ensemble/Petr Kotik). Wergo: WER 6216-2. [With his *Atlas eclipticalis*].

- (David Tudor and others). *See* 3719.18

3719.4 ** *Constructions (3)* [for percussion ensemble].

- (Amadinda Percussion Group) [*Construction no. 3* only]. *See* 3661

- (New Music Consort) [*Constructions nos. 2–3* only]. *See* 4014

- (Quatuor Helios) [*Constructions 1–3*]. Wergo: WER 6203. [With his *She is asleep; Double music; Amores; Imaginary landscape no. 2*].

3719.5 *Double music* [co-written with Lou Harrison—for percussion ensemble].

- (Amadinda Percussion Group). *See* 3661

- (New Music Consort). *See* 4014

- (Quatuor Helios). *See* 3719.4

3719.6 *Etudes australes* [for piano]. (Stephen Drury). *See* 3721.9

3719.7 *Four* [for string quartet]. (Arditti Quartet). *See* 3719.20

3719.8 *4'33".* (Amadinda Percussion Group). *See* 3661

3719.9 *Four^3* [for instrumental ensemble]. (Martine Jost and others). [Series: The number pieces, vol. 1]. Mode: 44. [With his *One^5* and *Two^6*].

3719.10 *Freeman etudes, books 1–4* [for violin]. [Series: John Cage, vols. 7 and 9]. (Irvine Arditti). Mode: 32; 37. 2 CDs.

3719.11 * *Indeterminacy: new aspects of form in instrumental and electronic music.* Smithsonian/Folkways: CD/SF 40804/5. 2CD set. [Ninety stories written and read by John Cage with music by David Tudor and John Cage].

3719.12 *Music of changes* [for piano]. (Herbert Henck). Wergo: WER 60099-50.

3719.13 *Piano music. Selections* [including works for prepared piano and toy piano]. (Margaret Leng Tan). New Altion: NA070CD.

3719.14 *Roaratorio* [for live performers and taped sounds]. [Series: John Cage, vol. 6]. (John Cage and others). Mode: 28/29. 2CD set. [With his *Laughtears; Writing for the second time through Finnegans wake*].

3719.15 * *Ryoanji* [for flute and percussion]. (Dorothy Stone). *See* 4030

3719.16 *Ryoanji* [for flute, trombone, and percussion]. (Ives Ensemble). Hat Hut: ART CD 6159. [With his *Ten* and *Fourteen*].

3719.17 *Ryoanji* [for bass trombone and percussion]. (James Fulkerson and others). Etcetera: KTC 1137. [With his *Solo for sliding trombone from Concert for piano, combined with Fontana mix; Two^5 for trombone and piano*].

3719.18 *Selections.* (John Cage and others). Wergo: WER 6247-2. 3CD set. [Album title: *The 25-year retrospective concert of the music of John Cage (Town Hall, New York concert of 1959)*. Contents: *Short inventions (6); Construction no. 1; Imaginary landscape no. 1; The wonderful widow of eighteen springs; She is asleep; Sonatas and interludes (selections); Music for carillon no. 1; Williams mix; Concert for piano and orchestra*].

3719.19 ** *Sonatas and interludes* [for prepared piano]. (Yuji Takahashi). Denon: CM-7673.

3719.20 *String quartet music, vols. 1–2.* [Series: John Cage, vols. 3 and 5]. (Arditti Quartet). Mode: 17; 27. 2 CDs. [*Music for four; 30 pieces for string quartet; String quartet in four parts; Four*].

3719.21 *Vocal music. Selections.* (Joan La Barbara and others). New Albion: NA 035 CD. [Album title: *Singing through.* Contents: *A flower; Mirakus; Eight whiskus; The wonderful widow of eighteen springs; Nowth upon Nacht; Sonnekus; Forever and sunsmell; Songbooks. Selections; Music for two*].

3719.22 * *Williams mix* [for magnetic tape]. *See* 3719.18

3719.23 * *Winter music* [for 1–20 pianists]. (Nils Vigeland and three others). Hat Hut: ART CD 6141. [With his *Atlas eclipticalis,* with which it is heard simultaneously on track 2].

3720   Cardew, Cornelius, 1936–1981. *See* 3685

3721   Carter, Elliott, 1908–

3721.1 *Changes* [for guitar]. (David Starobin). *See* 3721.7

3721.2 ** *Concerto for harpsichord, piano, and orchestra* ("Double concerto"). (Paul Jacobs, Gilbert Kalish/Contemporary Chamber Ensemble/Arthur Weisberg). *See* 3721.14

3721.3 *Concerto for orchestra.* (London Sinfonietta/Oliver Knussen). *See* 3721.10

3721.4 * *Concerto for piano and orchestra.* (Ursula Oppens/Cincinnati Symphony/Michael Gielen). New World: NW 347-2. [With his *Variations for orchestra*].

3721.5 *Concerto for violin and orchestra.* (Ole Böhn/London Sinfonietta/Oliver Knussen). *See* 3721.10

3721.6 *Duo for violin and piano.* (Group for Contemporary Music). *See* 3721.7

3721.7 * *Enchanted preludes* [for flute and violoncello]. (Group for Contemporary Music). Bridge: BCD 9044. [With his *Gra; Duo for violin and piano; Scrivo in vento; Changes; Con leggerezza pensosa; Riconoscenza per Goffredo Petrassi; Sonata for violoncello and piano*].

3721.8 *Etudes (8) and a fantasy* [for wind quartet]. (Quintetto Arnold). *See* 4023

3721.9 *Night fantasies* [for piano].

- (Stephen Drury). Neuma: 450–76. [With Cage, John: *Etudes australes*].

- (Ursula Oppens). *See* 4018

- (Charles Rosen). Etcetera: KTC 1088. [With his *Sonata for piano*].

3721.10 *Occasions (3) for orchestra.* (London Sinfonietta/Oliver Knussen). Virgin: 7 59271 2. [With his *Concerto for violin and orchestra; Concerto for orchestra*].

3721.11 * *Quartets for strings (4).* (Arditti Quartet). Etcetera: KTC 1065/1066. 2CD set. [With his *Elegy for string quartet*].

3721.12 *Quintet for brass.* (Wallace Collection). *See* 4032

3721.13 *Quintet for woodwinds and horn.*

- (Boehm Quintet). *See* 3663

- (Quintetto Arnold). *See* 4023

3721.14 * *Sonata for flute, oboe, cello, and harpsichord.* (Harvey Sollberger and others). Elektra Nonesuch: 79183-2. [With his *Sonata for violoncello and piano; Concerto for harpsichord . . .*].

3721.15 * *Sonata for piano.*

- (Peter Lawson). *See* 3670

- (Charles Rosen). *See* 3721.9

3721.16 *Sonata for violoncello and piano.*

- (Group for Contemporary Music). *See* 3721.7

- (Joel Krosnick/Paul Jacobs). *See* 3721.14

3721.17 *Syringa* [for two voices and instrumental ensemble]. (Jan DeGaetani/Thomas Paul/Group for Contemporary Music). CRI: CD 610. [With his *Holiday overture; Pocahontas suite*].

3721.18 * *Triple duo* [for chamber ensemble]. (Fires of London/Peter Maxwell Davies). Wergo: 6278-2. [With his *In sleep, in thunder*].

3721.19 *Variations for orchestra.*

- (Cincinnati Symphony/Michael Gielen). *See* 3721.4

- (Chicago Symphony/James Levine). Deutsche Grammophon: 431 698-2. [With Schuller, Gunther: *Spectra*; Babbitt, Milton: *Correspondences*; Cage, John: *Atlas eclipticalis*].

3722   Celli, Joseph, 1944–

No world (trio) improvisations. O.O. Discs: 4. [With Jin Hi Kim, Alvin Curran, Malcolm Goldstein, Shelly Hirsch, Adam Plack, Mor Thiam].

3723   Chatham, Rhys, 1952–

Die Donnergötter. (Rhys Chatham and others). Dossier: DCD 9002. [With his *Waterloo no. 2; Guitar trio; Drastic classicism*].

3724 Chou, Lung, 1953–

Instrumental music. Selections. (Speculum Musicae and others). CRI: CD 679. [Album title: *Nature and spirit.* Contents: *Tian ling; Su; Wuji; Ding; Dhyana*].

3725 Chou, Wen-chung, 1923–

Instrumental music. Selections. (Group for Contemporary Music). CRI: CD 691. [*Pien; Yo ko; Cursive; The willows are new; Landscapes*].

3726 * Chowning, John M., 1934–

Computer music. Selections. Wergo: WER 2012-50. [*Turenas; Stria; Phoné; Sabelithe*].

3727 Collins, Nicholas

100 of the world's most beautiful melodies [for various performers and electronics]. (Nicholas Collins and others). Trace Elements: TE-1018-CD.

3728 Corigliano, John, 1938–

3728.1 *Pied piper fantasy* [for flute and orchestra]. (James Galway/Eastman Philharmonia/ David Effron). RCA: 6602-2-RC. [With his *Voyage*].

3728.2 * *Symphony no. 1.* (Chicago Symphony/ Daniel Barenboim). Erato: 2292-45601-2.

3729 Crumb, George, 1929–

3729.1 * *Ancient voices of children* [for solo voices and instruments]. (Jan DeGaetani/Contemporary Chamber Ensemble/Arthur Weisberg). Elektra Nonesuch: 79149-2. [With his *Music for a summer evening*].

3729.2 * *Black angels* [for amplified string quartet]. (Kronos Quartet). Elektra Nonesuch: 79242-2. [With works by Istvan Marta, Charles Ives, Dimitri Shostakovich, Thomas Tallis].

3729.3 *Celestial mechanics (Makrokosmos IV)* [for amplified piano 4 hands]. (Peter Degenhardt/Fuat Kent). Mode: 19. [With his *Zeitgeist*; Brown, Earle: *Corroboree*].

3729.4 *Piano music, vols. 1–2.* (Jeffrey Jacob). Centaur: CRC 2050; 2080. 2 CDs. [*Gnomic variations; Makrokosmos vols. 1–2; Little suite for Christmas A.D. 1979; Processional* (original and revised versions)].

3729.5 * *Songs, drones, and refrains of death* [for voice and chamber ensemble]. (Sanford Sylvan/ Speculum Musicae). Bridge: BCD 9028. [With his *Little suite for Christmas A.D. 1979; Apparition*].

3729.6 *Suite for violoncello.* (Matt Haimovitz). *See 3826.25*

3729.7 *Vox balaenae (Voice of the whale)* [for electric flute, electric violoncello, and electric piano]. (Zizi Mueller, Fred Sherry, James Gemmell). New World: NW 357-2. [With his *Idyll for the misbegotten; Madrigals*].

3730 Curran, Alvin S., 1938–

3730.1 *Canti e vedute del giardino magnetico (Songs and views of the magnetic garden)* [electroacoustic music]. (Alvin S. Curran). Catalyst: 09026- 61823-2.

3730.2 *Crystal psalms* [for seven choirs, instruments, and electronics]. (Performers from seven European radio stations). New Albion: NA067CD.

3731 Danielpour, Richard, 1956–

Instrumental music. Selections. (Christopher O'Riley and others). Koch: 3-7100-2H1. [*Urban dances for brass quintet; Psalms for piano; Enchanted garden for piano; Quintet for piano and strings*].

3732 Daugherty, Michael, 1954–

Instrumental music. Selections. (Michel Singher and others). Opus One: CD 138. [Album title: *New music from Oberlin.* Contents: *Celestial hoops no. 4; Mxyzptlk; Bounce no. 1; Blue like and orange; Snap!* With Miller, Edward J.: *Going home; Beyond the wheel; Seven sides of a crystal*].

3733 Davidovsky, Mario, 1934–

3733.1 *Scenes from Shir ha shirim* [cantata]. (Phyllis Bryn-Julson and others). CRI: SD 530. LP. [With his *Romancero*]. OP

3733.2 *Synchronisms no. 3* [for violoncello and electronic tape]. (Boston Musica Viva). *See 3998*

3733.3 * *Synchronisms no. 5* [for percussion and electronic tape]. *See 3984*

3733.4 * *Synchronisms no. 6* [for piano and electronic tape].
  - (Aequalis). *See 3991*
  - (Alan Feinberg). *See 4007*

3733.5 *Synchronisms no. 9* [for violin and electronic tape]. (Rolf Schulte). *See 3962*

3733.6 *Synchronisms no. 10* [for guitar and electronic tape]. (David Starobin). *See 3979*

3734 Davies, Peter Maxwell, 1934–

3734.1 ** *Ave maris stella* [for instrumental sextet]. (Fires of London/Peter Maxwell Davies). Unicorn-Kanchana: UKCD2038. [With his *Image, reflection, shadow; Runes from a holy island*].

3734.2 * *Image, reflection, shadow* [for instrumental sextet]. (Fires of London/Peter Maxwell Davies). *See* 3734.1

3734.3 *In nomine (7)* [for chamber ensemble]. (Aquarius Ensemble). Collins: 10952. [With his *Boyfriend suite; Devils suite*].

3734.4 *Miss Donnithorne's maggot* [chamber opera]. (Mary Thomas/Fires of London). Unicorn-Kanchana: DKPCD 9052. [With his *Songs for a mad king*].

3734.5 *Resurrection* [opera]. (Della Jones/Christopher Robson/BBC Philharmonic/Peter Maxwell Davies). Collins: 70342. 2CD set.

3734.6 *Runes from a holy island* [for instrumental sextet]. (Fires of London/Peter Maxwell Davies). *See* 3734.1 or 3734.12

3734.7 *Sinfonia* [for chamber orchestra]. (Scottish Chamber Orchestra/Peter Maxwell Davies). *See* 3734.8

3734.8 *Sinfonia concertante* [for wind quintet and string orchestra]. (Scottish Chamber Orchestra/Peter Maxwell Davies). Unicorn-Kanchana: UKCD2026. [With his *Sinfonia*].

3734.9 *Sonata for trumpet and piano.* (Graham Ashton/John Lenehan). *See* 3995

3734.10 * *Songs for a mad king.* (Julius Eastman/Fires of London/Peter Maxwell Davies). *See* 3734.4

3734.11 * *Symphony no. 1.* (BBC Philharmonic/Peter Maxwell Davies). Collins: 14352.

3734.12 * *Vesalii icones* [for chamber ensemble]. (Fires of London/Peter Maxwell Davies). Unicorn-Kanchana: UKCD2068. [With his *Bairns of Brugh; Runes from a holy island*].

3735 Davis, Anthony, 1951–

3735.1 *Wayang no. 5* [for piano and orchestra]. (Anthony Davis/Kansas City Symphony/William McGlaughlin). Gramavision: R2 79429. [Album title: *Ghost factory*. With his *Maps, for violin and orchestra*].

3735.2 * *X, the life and times of Malcolm X* [opera]. (Herbert Perry/Orchestra of St. Luke's/William Henry Curry). Gramavision: R2 79470. 2CD set.

3736 * Del Tredici, David, 1937–

An Alice symphony. (Phyllis Bryn-Julson/Tanglewood Orchestra/Oliver Knussen). CRI: CD 688.

3737 Dello Joio, Norman, 1913–

3737.1 *Ballet music. Selections.* [Series: Music for Martha Graham, vol. 3]. (Atlantic Sinfonietta/Edvard Tchivzhel). Koch: 3-7167-2H1. [*Seraphic dialogues; Exaltation of larks; Diversion of angels*].

3737.2 *Meditations on Ecclesiastes* [for orchestra].

- (Philharmonia Orchestra/David Amos). Harmonia Mundi: HMU 906012. [With works by Alan Hovhanness and Arnold Rosner].

- (Vienna Symphony/Dean Dixon). Bay Cities: BCD 1017. [With Moore, Douglas: *In memoriam*; Cowell, Henry: *Symphony no. 5*].

3738 Dempster, Stuart, 1936–

Standing waves (1976) [for trombone]. New Albion: NA013CD. [Album title: *In the great abbey of Clement VI*. With his *Didjeridervish; Standing waves (1978)*].

3739 Denisov, Edisson Vasilevich, 1929–

3739.1 *Chamber music. Selections.* (Alexandre Roudine and others). Le Chant du Monde: LCD 288 058. [*Variationen über ein Thema von Schubert; Pieces for violoncello and piano; Sonata for violoncello and piano; Reflexe; Quintet for piano and strings*]. *See also* 4033

3739.2 *Symphony.* (Paris Orchestra/Daniel Barenboim). Erato: 2292-45600-2.

3740 Diamond, David, 1915–

3740.1 * *Romeo and Juliet* [for orchestra]. (Seattle Symphony/Gerard Schwarz). Delos: DE 3103. [With his *Kaddish; Symphony no. 3*].

3740.2 *Symphony no. 2.* (Seattle Symphony/Gerard Schwarz). Delos: DE 3093. [With his *Concerto for small orchestra; Symphony no. 4*].

3741 Dick, Robert, 1950–

Instrumental music. Selections. (Robert Dick and others). O.O. Discs: 7. [Album title: *Venturi shadows*. Contents: *A black lake with a blue boat on it; Further down; Heart of light; Bassbamboo; Recombinant landscapes; Venturi shadows; Daytime; Times*].

3742 * Didkovsky, Nick

Selections. See 3958, 3971, 3981, 4003

3743 * Dockstader, Tod, 1932–

Electroacoustic music. Selections. Starkland: ST-201; 202. 2 CDs.

3744 * Dodge, Charles, 1942–

Electroacoustic music. Selections. New Albion: NA043CD. [Album title: *Any resemblance is purely coincidental*. Contents: *Any resemblance is purely coincidental; Speech songs; The waves; Viola elegy*].

3745 * Donatoni, Franco, 1927– . *Chamber music. Selections.*

- (Ensemble 2e2m/Paul Méfano). Adda: 581133. [*Ave; Toy; Nidi; Flag; Almari*].
- (Nieuw Ensemble). Etcetera: KTC 1053. [*Refrain; Etwas ruhiger im Ausdruck; De Pres; Fili; Spiri*].

See also 3993 and 4023

3746 Dresher, Paul, 1951–

Dark blue circumstance. (Paul Dresher and others). New Albion: NA053CD. [With his *Double ikat; Channels passing; Night songs*].

3747 Dreyblatt, Arnold, 1953–

Instrumental music. Selections. (Orchestra of Excited Strings/Arnold Dreyblatt). Tzadik: 004. [Album title: *Animal magnetism*].

3748 Druckman, Jacob, 1928–

3748.1 * *Aureole* [for orchestra]. (St. Louis Symphony/Leonard Slatkin). New World: NW 318-2. [With Colgrass, Michael: *Déjà vu; Light spirit*].

3748.2 *Chiaroscuro* [for orchestra]. (Juilliard Orchestra/Lukas Foss). New World: NW 381-2. [With Albert, Stephen: *Into eclipse;* Schwantner, Joseph: *Aftertones of infinity*].

3748.3 *Other voices* [for brass quintet]. (American Brass Quintet). *See 3709.3*

3748.4 *Prism* [for orchestra]. (New York Philharmonic/Zubin Mehta). New World: NW 335-2. [With Rochberg, George: *Concerto for oboe and orchestra*].

3749 Duckworth, William, 1943–

3749.1 * *Southern harmony* [for chorus]. (Gregg Smith Singers/Rooke Chapel Choir). Lovely Music: LCD 2033.

3749.2 * *Time curve preludes* [for piano]. (Neely Bruce). Lovely Music: LCD 2031.

3750 Dutilleux, Henri, 1916–

3750.1 * *Ainsi la nuit* [for string quartet]. (Arditti Quartet). Montaigne Auvidis: MO 782016. [With Dusapin, Pascal: *Time zones; Quartet for strings no. 3*].

3750.2 *Metaboles* [for orchestra]. (Paris Orchestra/Semyon Bychkov). *See 3750.4*

3750.3 *Sonata for piano.* (Marie-Catherine Girod). Solstice: SOCD 18. [With Auric, Georges: *Sonata for piano;* Jolivet, André: *Sonata for piano no. 1*].

3750.4 *Symphony no. 2 ("Le double").* (Paris Orchestra/Semyon Bychkov). Philips: 438 008-2. [With his *Timbres, espaces, mouvement; Metaboles*].

3750.5 *Timbres, espaces, mouvement* [for orchestra]. (Paris Orchestra/Semyon Bychkov). *See 3750.4*

3750.6 * *Tout un monde lointain* [for violoncello and orchestra]. (Mstislav Rostropovich/Paris Orchestra/Serge Baudo). EMI: CDC 7 49304 2. [With Lutoslawski, Witold: *Concerto for violoncello and orchestra*].

3751 Eaton, John, 1935–

3751.1 *Microtonal fantasy. See 3985*

3751.2 *Selections.* (Indiana University New Music Ensemble). Indiana University School of Music: IUSM-04. [Album title: *The music of John Eaton.* Contents: *The cry of Clytaemnestra. Selections; Sonority movement; Ars poetica; Fantasy romance; Ajax; Greek vision*].

3752 Enríquez, Manuel, 1926–

Selections. (Susana Enríquez and others). INBA-SACM: PCD 10152. [*Interminado sueño, for actress and orchestra; Diptico no. 3, for percussion and string orchestra; Manantial de soles, for soprano, actor, and orchestra; Recordando a Juan de Lienas, for string orchestra; A Juarez, for voices and orchestra*].

3753 Erb, Donald, 1927–

Instrumental music. Selections.

- (Stuart Dempster and others). New World: 80457-2. [*. . . and then toward the end . . . , for trombone and tape; Cenotaph (for E.V.), for symphonic band; Woody, for clarinet; Symphony for winds; Drawing down the moon, for piccolo and percussion*].
- (Gregory Fulkerson and others). Albany: TROY 092. [*The watchman's fantasy, for violin, piano, and synthesizer; Aura no. 2, for violoncello with audience participation; Red hot duets, for two contrabassoons; Quartet for strings no. 2*].

3754 Erickson, Robert, 1917–

Selections. (Edwin Harkins and others). CRI: CD 616. [*Kryl, for trumpet; Ricercar à 3, for double bass; Postcards, for soprano and lute; Dunbar's delight, for timpani; Quoq, for flute; Sierra, for baritone and instrumental ensemble*].

3755 Fast Forward

Percussion music. Selections. Lovely Music: LCD 2091. [Album title: *Panhandling*].

3756 Feldman, Morton, 1926–

3756.1 * *Crippled symmetry* [for flutes, piano, and mallet instruments]. (Eberhard Blum/Nils Vigeland/Jan Williams). Hat Hut: ART CD 60802. 2CD set. [With his *Why patterns?*].

3756.2 *For Philip Guston* [for flutes, piano, or celesta, and mallet instruments]. (Eberhard Blum/Nils Vigeland/Jan Williams). Hat Hut: ART CD 61041/44. 4CD set.

3756.3 * *For Samuel Beckett* [for chamber ensemble]. (San Francisco Contemporary Music Players/Stephen L. Mosko). Newport: NPD 85506.

3756.4 * *The king of Denmark* [for percussion].
  * (Michael Pugliese). *See* 4021
  * (Jan Williams). *See* 3983

3756.5 * *Piano and string quartet.* (Aki Takahashi/Kronos Quartet). Elektra Nonesuch: 79320-2.

3756.6 *Piano music. Selections.* (Marianne Schroeder). Hat Hut: ART CD 6035. [*Intermission no. 5; Piano piece; Vertical thoughts no. 4; Piano; Palais de Mari*].

3756.7 *Quartet for strings no. 1.* (Group for Contemporary Music). Koch: 3-7251-2H1.

3756.8 ** *Rothko Chapel* [for chorus and instruments]. (University of California Berkeley Chamber Chorus/Philip Brett). New Albion: NA039CD. [With his *Why patterns?*].

3756.9 *Routine investigations* [for chamber ensemble]. (Ensemble Recherche). Montaigne: MO 782018. [With his *For Frank O'Hara; Viola in my life, parts 1–3; I met Heine on the rue Fürstenberg*].

3756.10 *Structures, for string quartet.* (Arditti Quartet). *See* 3994

3756.11 *Three voices: for Joan La Barbara.* (Joan La Barbara). New Albion: NA018CD.

3756.12 * *The viola in my life, parts 1–3.* (Ensemble Recherche). *See* 3756.9

3756.13 * *Why patterns?* [for flute, piano, and glockenspiel].
  * (Eberhard Blum/Nils Vigeland/Jan Williams). *See* 3756.1
  * (California EAR Unit). *See* 3756.8

3757 Fennelly, Brian, 1937–

Fantasy variations [for orchestra]. (Louisville Orchestra/Lawrence Leighton Smith). Louisville: LCD003. [With Hanlon, Kevin: *Cumulus nimbus;* Schuller, Gunther: *Farbenspiel*].

3758 Ferneyhough, Brian, 1943–

3758.1 *Cassandra's dream song* [for flute]. (Pierre-Yves Artaud). *See* 3980

3758.2 *Chamber music. Selections.* (Nieuw Ensemble/Ed Spanjaard). Etcetera: KTC 1070. [*La chûte d'Icare, for clarinet and ensemble; Superscriptio, for piccolo; Intermedio alla ciaccona, for violin; Etudes transcendentales, for soprano and instruments; Mnemosyne, for bass flute and tape*].

3758.3 * *String quartet music. Selections.* (Arditti Quartet). Montaigne: 789002. [*Quartet for strings nos. 2–3; Adagissimo; Sonatas for string quartet*].

3759 Fine, Irving, 1914–1962

Selections. (Gerard Schwarz and others). Elektra Nonesuch: 9 79175-2. [*Notturno for strings and harp; Partita for wind quintet; Quartet for strings; The hour-glass, for chorus; Serious song, for orchestra*].

3760 Fine, Vivian, 1913–

Selections. (Reiko Honsho and others). CRI: CD 692. [*Concertante for piano and orchestra; Missa brevis, for four violoncellos and taped voice; Momenti, for piano; Quartet for brass; Sinfonia and fugato, for piano; Alcestis, for orchestra*].

3761 First, David

Resolver [for chamber ensemble]. (David First and others). O.O. Discs: 5.

3762 First Avenue

Hocus-opus. O.O. Discs: 13. [Group compositions by the First Avenue trio with guest artists Samm Bennett, Robert Dick, Steven Mackey, Pauline Oliveros, Ned Rothenberg, and Elliott Sharp].

3763 Foss, Lukas, 1922–

3763.1 * *Renaissance concerto* [for flute and orchestra]. (Carol Wincenc/Brooklyn Philharmonic/Lukas Foss). New World: NW 375-2. [With his *Salomon Rossi suite; Orpheus and Euridice*].

3763.2 *Thirteen ways of looking at a blackbird* [for mezzo-soprano and instruments]. (Lukas Foss and others). Koss: KC-1006. [With his *Early *song; Dedication; Composer's holiday; Paradigm; Curriculum vitae*].

3764   Galás, Diamánda, 1955–

3764.1 * *Plague mass (1984—end of the epidemic)* [for voice and instruments]. (Diamánda Galás). Mute: 9 61043-2.

3764.2   *Vena cava* [for voice and electronics]. (Diamánda Galás). Mute: 9 61459-2.

3765   García, Orlando Jacinto, 1954–

Selections. (Gregg Smith Singers and others). O.O. Discs: 6. [Album title: *La belleza del silencio = The beauty of silence.* Contents: *On the eve of the second year anniversary of Morton's death, for chorus; Improvisation with metallic materials, for MIDI breath controller and tape; Sitio sin nombre, for soprano; Metallic images, for percussion*].

3766   Garland, Peter, 1952–

Walk in beauty [for piano]. (Aki Takahashi). New Albion: NA052CD. [With his *Sones de flor, for piano, violin, and percussion; Jornada del muerto, for piano*].

3767 * Gideon, Miriam, 1906–

Selections. (Speculum Musicae and others). New World: 80393-2. [Album title: *A Miriam Gideon retrospective.* Contents: *Steeds of darkness; Suite for clarinet and piano; The shooting starres attend thee; Eclogue for flute and piano; Böhmische Krystall; Creature to creature;* and other works].

3768   Giteck, Janice, 1946–

Home (revisited) [for men's chorus, violoncello, gamelan, and synthesizer]. (Seattle Men's Chorus and others). New Albion: NA054CD. [With her *On Shanti, for soprano and instruments; Tapasya, for viola and percussion; Leningrad spring, for flutes, piano, and percussion*].

3769   Glass, Philip, 1937–

3769.1   *Akhnaten* [opera]. (Stuttgart State Opera/Dennis Russell Davies). CBS: M2K 42457. 2CD set.

3769.2 * *La belle et la bête* [opera]. (Janice Felty/Gregory Purnhagen/Philip Glass Ensemble/Michael Riesman). Elektra Nonesuch: 79347-2. 2CD set.

3769.3   *Company* [for string quartet]. (Kronos Quartet). *See* 3911.2

3769.4 ** *Einstein on the beach* [opera]. (Philip Glass Ensemble/Michael Riesman). Elektra Nonesuch: 79323-2. 3CD set.

3769.5   *Low symphony.* (Brooklyn Philharmonic/Dennis Russell Davies). Point: 438 150-2.

3769.6 * *Music in 12 parts.*
* (Philip Glass Ensemble/Michael Riesman) [parts 1–6 only]. Elektra Nonesuch: 79324-2.
* (Philip Glass Ensemble/Michael Riesman) [complete]. Virgin: 91311-2. 3CD set. OP

3769.7   *Two pages.* (Philip Glass and others). Elektra Nonesuch: 79326-2. [With his *Contrary motion; Music in fifths; Music in similar motion*].

3770   Globokar, Vinko, 1934–

Instrumental music. Selections. (Heinz Holliger and others). Koch Schwann: 3-1063-2. [*Discours no. 3, for five oboes; Toucher, for percussion; Discours no. 6, for string quartet; Voix instrumentalisée, for bass clarinet; Accord, for soprano and instruments*].

3771   Goehr, Alexander, 1932–

Selections. (Jeanine Thames/London Sinfonietta/Oliver Knussen). Unicorn-Kanchana: DKPCD 9102. [—*A musical offering (J.S.B. 1985)— for chamber ensemble; Behold the sun, for soprano and chamber ensemble; Lyric pieces, for chamber ensemble; Sinfonia, for orchestra*].

3772   Gordon, Michael, 1956–

3772.1   *Chamber music. Selections.* (Michael Gordon Philharmonic). CRI: CD 636. [Album title: *Big noise from Nicaragua.* Contents: *Thou shalt!, thou shalt not!; Low quartet; Four kings fight five; Acid rain*].

3772.2 * *Yo Shakespeare.* (Icebreaker). *See* 4010

3773   Gorécki, Henryk Mikolaj, 1933–

3773.1   *Already it is dusk* [String quartet no. 1, op. 62]. (Kronos Quartet). Elektra Nonesuch: 79319-2. [With his *Quasi una fantasia: String quartet no. 2, op. 64*].

3773.2 ** *Symphony no. 3.* (Dawn Upshaw/London Sinfonietta/David Zinman). Elektra Nonesuch: 79282-2.

3774   Gould, Glenn, 1932–1982

The solitude trilogy: three sound documentaries. CBC: PSCD 2003-2. 3CD set.

3775 * Gould, Morton, 1913–1996

Orchestral music. Selections. (Morton Gould and his orchestra). RCA: 09026-61651-2. [*Fall River legend; Interplay; Latin-American symphonette; Declaration*].

3776   Gruber, Heinz Karl, 1943–

Instrumental music. Selections. (Heinz Karl Gruber and others). Largo: 5124. [*Der rote Teppich wird ausgerollt, for chamber orchestra; Concerto for violin and orchestra no. 1 (". . . aus Schatten Duft gewebt . . ."); Episoden aus einer unterbrochenen Chronik; Pieces for solo violin; Bossa nova*].

3777   Guastavino, Carlos, 1912–

Songs. Selections. (Ulises Espaillat/Pablo Zinger). New Albion: NA058CD. [Album title: *Las puertas da la mañana*].

3778   Gubaidulina, Sofia Asgatovna, 1931–

3778.1 * *Offertorium* [for violin and orchestra]. (Gidon Kremer/Boston Symphony/Charles Dutoit). Deutsche Grammophon: 427 336-2. [With her *Hommage à T. S. Eliot, for soprano and chamber ensemble*].

3778.2 *Quartet for strings no. 2.* (Arditti Quartet). See 3812.3

3778.3 *Rejoice!* [for string quartet]. (Gidon Kremer and others). See 3636.12

3778.4 *Stimmen—vertsummen* [for orchestra]. (Royal Stockholm Philharmonic/Gennady Rozhdestvensky). Chandos: CHAN 9183. [With her *Stufen, for narrator and orchestra*].

3779   Harbison, John, 1938–

3779.1 *Concerto for oboe and orchestra.* (William Bennett/San Francisco Symphony/Herbert Blomstedt). London: 443 376-2. [With his *Symphony no. 2;* Sessions, Roger: *Symphony no. 2*].

3779.2 * *The flight into Egypt* [cantata]. (Cantata Singers/David Hoose). New World: 80395-2. [With his *The natural world; Concerto for double brass choir and orchestra*].

3779.3 *Quartets for strings nos. 1–2.* (Lydian Quartet). Harmonia Mundi: HMU 907057. [With his *November 19, 1828*].

3779.4 *Symphony no. 1.* (Boston Symphony/Seiji Ozawa). See 3944

3780 * Hardin, Louis ("Moondog"), 1916–

Selections. (Moondog and others). CBS: MK 44994. [Album title: *Moondog*].

3781   Harrison, Lou, 1917–

3781.1 *Concerto for piano and orchestra.* (Keith Jarrett/New Japan Philharmonic/Naoto Otomo). New World: NW366-2. [With his *Suite for violin, piano, and small orchestra*].

3781.2 * *Concerto in slendro* [for violin and ensemble]. (Daniel Kobialka and others). CRI: CD 613. [With his *Three pieces for gamelan with soloists; String quartet set; Suite for percussion*].

3781.3 *Double music* [for percussion—cowritten with John Cage].

- (Amadinda Percussion Ensemble). *See 3661*
- (New Music Consort). *See 4014*

3781.4 *Elegaic symphony.* (American Composers Orchestra/Dennis Russell Davies). *See 3788.2*

3781.5 *Pastorales (7)* [for orchestra]. (Brooklyn Philharmonic/Dennis Russell Davies). MusicMasters: 01612-67089-2. [With Glanville-Hicks, Peggy: *Etruscan concerto;* Riley, Terry: *June Buddhas*].

3781.6 * *Varied trio* [for violin, piano, and percussion]. (Abel-Steinberg-Winant Trio). *See 3990*

3782   Harvey, Jonathan, 1939–

3782.1 *Bhakti* [for chamber ensemble and electronic tape]. (Spectrum/Guy Protheroe). NMC: D001.

3782.2 * *From silence* [for soprano, instruments, and electronics]. (Karol Bennet and others). Bridge: BCD 9031. [With his *Nataraja; Ritual melodies*].

3782.3 ** *Mortuos plango, vivos voco* [electroacoustic music]. *See 3964*

3782.4 *Quartet for strings.* (Group for Contemporary Music). *See 3946.2*

3782.5 *Song offerings.* (Penelope Walmsley-Clark/London Sinfonietta/George Benjamin). *See 3700.1*

3783   Henze, Hans Werner, 1926–

3783.1 * *Die Bassariden (The bassarids)* [opera]. (Karen Armstrong/Michael Burt/Kenneth Riegel/Berlin Radio Symphony/Gerd Albrecht). Koch Schwann Musica Mundi: CD 314 006 K3. 2CD set.

3783.2 *Carillon, récitatif, masque* [for guitar, mandolin, and harp]. (David Starobin/Peter Press/Susan Jolles). *See 3978*

3783.3 * *El cimarrón* [cantata]. (Paul Yoder and others). Koch Schwann: 314 030. 2CD set.

3783.4 *Quartets for strings nos 1–5.* (Arditti Quartet). Wergo: WER 60114/15. 2CD set.

3783.5 *Royal winter music, no. 1* [suite for guitar]. (David Tanenbaum). Audiofon: 72029.

3783.6 *Symphonies nos. 1–6.* (Berlin Philharmonic/London Symphony/Hans Werner Henze). Deutsche Grammophon: 429 854-2. 2CD set.

3784 Hiller, Lejaren Arthur, 1924–

Selections. (Lejaren Hiller and others). Wergo: WER 60128-50. [Album title: *Computer music retrospective, 1957–1985.* Contents: *Expo '85, for multiple synthesizers; Quartet for strings no. 4 (Illiac suite); Computer music, for percussion and tape; Persiflage, for flute, oboe, and percussion; An avalanche, for voices, instruments, and electronics*].

3785 Hoddinott, Alun, 1929–

3785.1 *Orchestral music. Selections.* (BBC Welsh Symphony/Bryden Thomson). Chandos: CHAN 8762. [*Symphony no. 6; Lanterne des morts, for soprano and orchestra; A contemplation upon flowers; Scena*].

3785.2 *Sonatas for piano nos. 6–10.* (Martin Jones). Nimbus: NI 5370.

3786 Holliger, Heinz, 1939–

3786.1 * *Scardanelli-Zyklus 1985* [*for flute, chorus, and orchestra*]. (Aurèle Nicolet/London Voices/Ensemble Modern/Heinz Holliger). ECM: 78118-21472-2. 2CD set.

3786.2 * *Studie über Mehrklänge (Study in multiphonics)* [*for oboe*]. (Heinz Holliger). ECM: 78118-21340-2. [With his *Trema, for violoncello; Duo for violin and violoncello;* Bach, Johann Sebastian: *Suite no. 4 for violoncello*].

3787 Holmboe, Vagn, 1909–

3787.1 * *Symphonies nos. 1, 3, 10.* (Aarhus Symphony/Owain Arwel Hughes). Bis: 605.

3787.2 *Symphonies nos. 4–5.* (Aarhus Symphony/Owain Arwel Hughes). Bis: 572.

3787.3 *Symphonies nos. 6–7.* (Aarhus Symphony/Owain Arwel Hughes). Bis: 573.

3788 Hovhaness, Alan, 1911–

3788.1 *And God created great whales* [for orchestra and tape]. (Seattle Symphony/Gerard Schwarz). *See* 3788.2

3788.2 ** *Symphony no. 2, op. 132 ("Mysterious mountain").*

* (American Composers Orchestra/Dennis Russell Davies). MusicMasters: MMD 60204. [With his *Lousadzak, for piano and orchestra;* Harrison, Lou: *Elegaic symphony*].

* (Seattle Symphony/Gerard Schwarz). Delos: DE 3157. [With his *Prayer of St. Gregory; Prelude and quadruple fugue; And God created great whales; Alleluia and fugue; Celestial fantasy*].

3789 Hunt, Jerry, 1943–1994

Ground. (Jerry Hunt and others). O.O. Discs: 9.

3790 Husa, Karel, 1921–

3790.1 *Apotheosis of this earth* [for orchestra]. (Louisville Orchestra/Lawrence Leighton Smith). Louisville: LCD005. [With his *Monodrama;* Lutoslawski, Witold: *Fanfare for Louisville;* Creston, Paul: *Invocation and dance*].

3790.2 * *Music for Prague 1968.* (Slovak Radio Symphony/Barry Kolman). Marco Polo: 8.223640. [With his *Fresque; Reflections*].

3791 Hutchinson, Brenda

Eeeyah! [electroacoustic music]. *See* 3954

3792 Hykes, David, 1953–

3792.1 *Harmonic meetings.* (Harmonic Choir/David Hykes). Celestial Harmonies: 13013-2.

3792.2 * *Hearing solar winds.* (Harmonic Choir/David Hykes). Ocora: C 558607.

3793 Imbrie, Andrew, 1921–

3793.1 *Quartet for strings no. 4.* (Emerson String Quartet). *See* 4005

3793.2 *Selections.* (Parnassus/Anthony Korf). New World: 80441-2. [*Dream sequence, for chamber ensemble; Rothko songs, for soprano and piano; Three piece suite, for harp and piano; Campion songs, for vocal quartet; To a traveler, for clarinet, violin, and piano*].

3794 Johnson, Scott, 1952–

John Somebody [for guitar and tape]. (Scott Johnson). Elektra Nonesuch: 79133-2. [With his *No memory*].

3795 * Johnson, Tom, 1939–

Failing: a very difficult piece for string bass. (Robert Black). *See* 3956

3796 Johnston, Ben, 1926–

3796.1 * *Calamity Jane to her daughter* [cantata]. (Dora Ohrenstein and others). *See* 4017

3796.2 *Chamber music. Selections.* (Music Amici and others). New World: 80432-2. [*Septet; Chinese lyrics, for soprano and two violins; Gambit, for chamber ensemble; Fragments, for baritone and instruments; Trio, for clarinet, violin, and violoncello; Ponder nothing, for clarinet*].

3796.3 * *Quartet for strings no. 9.* (Stanford String Quartet). Laurel: LR-847CD. [With

Bolcom, William: *Quartet for strings no. 10*; Neikrug, Marc: "*Star's the mirror*"].

3797 Jolas, Betsy, 1926–

Instrumental music. Selections. (Claude Helffer and others). Adès: 14.087-2. [*Stances, for piano and orchestra; Points d'aube, for viola and 13 winds; J.D.E., for chamber ensemble; D'un opéra de voyage, for chamber ensemble*].

3798 Jordanova, Victoria

Requiem for Bosnia [for child's voice, broken piano, and harp]. (Olivia Dalrymple, Victoria Jordanova). CRI: CD 673. [With her *Preludes for harp; Once upon a time, for harp; Variations for harp*].

3799 Kagel, Mauricio, 1931–

3799.1 * *Chamber music. Selections.*

- (Arditti Quartet). [Series: Mauricio Kagel, vol. 1]. Montaigne: WMD 789004. [*Quartets for strings nos. 1–3; Pan, for piccolo and string quartet*].
- (Saschko Gawriloff and others). [Series: Mauricio Kagel, vol. 6]. Montaigne: MO 782043. [*Klangwolfe, for violin and piano; Unguis incarnatus est; An Tasten; Trio for violin, violoncello, and piano*].
- (Michael Riessler and others). [Series: Maurico Kagel, vol. 2]. Montaigne: 782003. [*Zwei Akte; Rrrrrrr—; Blue's blue*].

3799.2 *Exotica* [for non-European instruments]. (Ensemble Modern/Mauricio Kagel). Koch Schwann: 3-1391-2.

3800 Kancheli, Giia, 1935–

3800.1 * *Symphonies nos. 4–5.* (Georgian National Orchestra/Jansug Kakhizde). Elektra Nonesuch: 79290-2.

3800.2 *Vom Winde beweint (Mourned by the wind)* [for viola and orchestra]. (Kim Kashkashian/Beethovenhalle Orchestra Bonn/Dennis Russell Davies). ECM: 78118-21471-2. [With Schnittke, Alfred: *Concerto for viola and orchestra*].

3801 * Kernis, Aaron Jay, 1960–

Symphony in waves. (New York Chamber Symphony/Gerard Schwarz). Argo: 436 287-2. [With his *Quartet for strings*].

3802 Killmayer, Wilhelm, 1927–

3802.1 *Chamber music. Selections.* (Siegfried Mauser and others). CPO: 999 020-2. [*Quartet for strings; Trio for two violins and violoncello;*

Quartet for piano and strings; Brahms-Bildnis, for piano, violin, and violoncello; Vanitas vanitatum, for violin and piano].

3802.2 *Pieces for piano nos. 1–3.* (Siegfried Mauser). Wergo: WER 60141-50. [With Rihm, Wolfgang: *Pieces for piano nos. 1 and 7*].

3803 Kirchner, Leon, 1919–

Instrumental music. Selections. (Leon Kirchner and others). Elektra Nonesuch: 79188-2. [*Concerto for violin, violoncello, winds, and percussion; Trio for violin, violoncello, and piano; Pieces for piano; Music for 12*].

3804 Knussen, Oliver, 1952–

3804.1 * *Instrumental music* [selections]. (Oliver Knussen and others). Unicorn-Kanchana: UKCD2010. [*Symphony no. 3; Trumpets, for soprano and three clarinets; Ophelia dances, for chamber orchestra; Coursing, for chamber orchestra; Cantata, for chamber ensemble; Symphony no. 2, for soprano and chamber orchestra*].

3804.2 *Where the wild things are* [opera]. (Rosemary Hardy/Mary King/London Sinfonietta/Oliver Knussen). Unicorn-Kanchana: CKPCD9044.

3805 Kokkonen, Joonas, 1921–

—durch einen Spiegel— [for 12 strings and harpsichord]. (Lahti Symphony/Ulf Söderblom). Bis: CD528. [With his *Paesaggio, for chamber orchestra; Quintet for winds; Sinfonia da camera*].

3806 Kolb, Barbara, 1939– . *Selections.*

- (Igor Kipnis and others). CRI: CD 576. [*Toccata, for harpsichord; Appello, for piano; Looking for Claudio, for guitar and tape; Spring river flowers moon night, for two pianos, percussion, and tape*].
- (Nouvelle Ensemble Moderne and others). New World: 80422-2. [*Millefoglie, for computer-generated tape and chamber ensemble; Extremes, for flute and violoncello; Chromatic fantasy, for narrator and chamber ensemble; Solitaire, for piano, vibraphone, and tape*].

3807 Kosugi, Takehisa, 1938–

Violin improvisations. Lovely Music: LCD 2071.

3808 Kotík, Petr, 1942–

3808.1 *Integrated solos, no. 3* [for flute, tambourine, trumpet, trombone, and electronics]. (Petr Kotík and others). *See 4028*

3808.2 *Wilsie Bridge* [for chamber ensemble]. (S.E.M. Ensemble/Petr Kotík). Ear-Rational: ECD 1007. [With his *Solos and incidental harmonies; Explorations in the geometry of thinking*].

3809 Kraft, William, 1923–

3809.1 * *Concertos. Selections.* (Thomas Akins and others). Harmonia Mundi: HMU 907106. [*Concerto for timpani and orchestra; Concerto for piano and orchestra; Evening voluntaries, for orchestra; Veils and variations, for horn and orchestra*].

3809.2 *Percussion music. Selections.* (Barry Silverman and others). Crystal: CD124. [*Triangles; Theme and variations; Momentum; Soliloquy (Encounters no. 1); Quartet for percussion*].

3810 Kramer, Jonathan, 1942–

Instrumental music. Selections. (Harold Farberman and others). Leonarda: LE 332. [Album title: *KV: five compositions.* Contents: *Musica pro musica* (for orchestra); *Atlanta licks* (for chamber ensemble); *Music for piano nos. 3 and 5; Renascence* (for clarinet and tape).

3811 Kupferman, Meyer, 1926–

Jazz symphony. (Loretta Holkmann/Ron Fink/Lithuanian National Philharmonic/Juozas Domarkas). Soundspells: 104. [With his *Challenger*].

3812 Kurtág, György, 1926–

3812.1 * *Messages of the late Miss R. V. Troussova* [for soprano and chamber ensemble]. (Rosemary Hardy/Ensemble Modern/Peter Eötvös). Sony: SK 53290. [With his . . . *Quasi una fantasia . . . , for piano and chamber ensemble; Scenes from a novel, for soprano and three instruments*].

3812.2 *Quintet for woodwinds and horn.* (Quintetto Arnold). *See* 4023

3812.3 *String quartet music.* (Arditti Quartet). Montaigne: 789007. [*Quartet for strings, op. 1; Hommage à Mihály András Kurtág; Officium breve in memoriam Andreae Szervánszky.* With Lutosławski, Witold: *Quartet for strings;* Gubaidulina, Sofia Asgatovna: *Quartet for strings no. 2*].

3813 La Barbara, Joan, 1947–

3813.1 * *Poems (73)* [texts by Kenneth Goldsmith, for voice and electronics]. (Joan La Barbara). Lovely Music: LCD 3002.

3813.2 *Sound paintings* [for voice]. (Joan La Barbara). Lovely Music: LCD 3001. [*Urban tropics; ShadowSong; Time(d) trials and unscheduled events; Erin; Klee Alee; Berliner Träume*].

3814 Lachenmann, Helmut, 1935–

3814.1 *Chamber music. Selections.* (Ensemble Recherche). [Series: Helmut Lachenmann, vol. 2]. Montaigne: MO 782023. [*Trio for strings; TemA, for flute, voice, and violoncello; Trio fluido, for clarinet, viola, and percussion*].

3814.2 *Piano music. Selections.* (Roland Keller). Col Legno/Aurophon: AU 31813. [*Variationen über ein Thema von F. Schubert; Echo andante; Wiegenmusik; Guero; Ein Kinderspiel*].

3814.3 * *Reigen seliger Geister* [for string quartet]. (Arditti Quartet). [Series: Helmut Lachenmann, vol. 1]. Montaigne: MO 782019. [With his *Tanzsuite mit Deutschlandlied, for string quartet and orchestra*].

3815 Lam, Bun-Ching

EO-9066 [for vocal quartet and electronics]. *See* 3975

3816 Lang, David (David A.), 1957–

3816.1 * *The anvil chorus* [for percussion].

• (Evelyn Glennie). *See* 4008

• (Steve Schick). *See* 3957

3816.2 *Are you experienced?* [for narrator, electric tuba, and 13 instruments]. (Nouvel Ensemble Moderne and others). CRI: CD 625. [With his *Orpheus over and under, for two pianos; Spud, for chamber ensemble; Illumination rounds, for violin and piano*].

3817 Lansky, Paul, 1944–

3817.1 * *Fantasies on a poem by Thomas Campion* [electroacoustic music]. CRI: CD 883. [With his *Still time*].

3817.2 *Homebrew* [electroacoustic music]. Bridge: BCD 9035.

3818 Lanza, Alcides, 1929–

Trilogy [for actress/singer and electronics]. Shelan: eSp-9201-CD.

3819 Larsen, Libby, 1950–

Symphony ("Water music"). (Minnesota Orchestra/Neville Marriner). *See* 3870

3820 * Lebaron, Anne, 1953– . *Selections.*

• (New Music Consort/Theater Chamber Players). Mode: 30. [Album title: *Rana, ritual, and revelations.* Contents: *Lamentation/invocation; Rite of the black sun; Planxty bowerbird; Noh reflections; Concerto for active frogs*].

• (New Music Consort/Theater Chamber Players). Mode: 42. [Album title: *The musical realism of Anne Lebaron*. Contents: *Dog-gone cat act; The E. & O. line. Selections; Waltz for quintet; The sea and the honeycomb; I am an American . . . my government will reward you*].

3821   Leeuw, Ton de, 1926–

Selections. (Ed Spanjaard and others). Donemus: CV 23. [*Symphonies of winds; Haiku no. 2, for soprano and orchestra; Résonances for orchestra*].

3822 * Lentz, Daniel, 1942–

Choral music. Selections. (Daniel Lentz and others). New Albion: NA006CD. [*O-ke-wa; Missa umbrarum; Postludium; Lascaux*].

3823 * León, Tania, 1944–

Selections. (Tania León and others). CRI: CD 662. [*Indígena, for trumpet and chamber orchestra; Parajota delaté, for chamber ensemble; Rituál, for piano; A la par, for piano and percussion; Batéy, for voices and percussion*].

3824   Levin, Todd

Chamber music. Selections. (Todd Levin and others). Point: 434 872-2. [Album title: *Ride the planet*].

3825   Lieberson, Peter, 1946–

3825.1 *Bagatelles for piano.* (Peter Serkin). *See* 3643.34

3825.2 *Concerto for piano and orchestra.* (Peter Serkin/Boston Symphony/Seiji Ozawa). New World: 325-2.

3826   Ligeti, György, 1923–

3826.1 * *Artikulation* [electronic music]. Wergo: WER 60 161-50. [With his *Continuum, for harpsichord; Pieces for wind quintet; Etudes (2) for organ; Glissandi; Volumina, for organ*].

3826.2 ** *Atmospheres* [for orchestra].

• (Vienna Philharmonic/Claudio Abbado). *See* 3988

• (Southwest German Radio Orchestra/Ernest Bour). *See* 3826.12

3826.3 * *Aventures* [for voices and chamber ensemble]. (Bruno Maderna and others). *See* 3826.23

3826.4 *Bagatelles for wind quintet.* (Ensemble Wien-Berlin). *See* 4006

3826.5 * *Concerto for piano and orchestra.*

• (Pierre-Laurent Aimard/Ensemble InterContemporain/Pierre Boulez). Deutsche Grammophon: 439 808-2. [With his *Concerto for violoncello and orchestra; Concerto for violin and orchestra*].

• (Ueli Wiget/Ensemble Modern/Peter Eötvös). *See* 3826.7

3826.6 *Concerto for violin and orchestra.* (Saschko Gawriliff/Ensemble InterContemporain/Pierre Boulez). *See* 3826.5

3826.7 *Concerto for violoncello and orchestra.*

• (Siegfried Palm/Frankfurt Radio Orchestra/Michael Gielen). Wergo: WER 60163-50. [With his *Lontano; Double concerto; San Francisco polyphony*].

• (Miklos Perenyi/Ensemble Modern/Peter Eötvös). Sony: SK 58945. [With his *Concerto for piano and orchestra; Kammerkonzert*].

• (Jean-Guihen Queyras/Ensemble InterContemporain/Pierre Boulez). *See* 3826.5

3826.8 *Double concerto for flute, oboe, and orchestra.* (Gunilla von Bahr/Torielf Lännerholm/Swedish Radio Symphony/Elgar Howarth). Bis: CD-53. [With his *San Francisco polyphony; Quartet for strings no. 1; Continuum, for harpsichord; Musica ricercata, for piano*].

3826.9 *Glissandi* [electronic music]. *See* 3826.1

3826.10 *Le grand macabre* [opera]. (Dieter Weller/Penelope Walmsley-Clark/ORF Symphony/Elgar Howarth). Wergo: WER 6170/71-2. 2CD set.

3826.11 *Harpsichord music* [*Continuum; Hungarian rock; Passacaglia ungherese*].

• (Elisabeth Chojnacka). *See* 3826.26

• (Erika Haase). *See* 3826.18

3826.12 * *Kammerkonzert (Chamber concerto)* [for 13 instruments].

• (Ensemble "Die Reihe"/Friedrich Cerha). Wergo: WER 60162-50. [With his *Ramifications* (Bour and Janigro); *Lux aeterna* (Gottwald); *Atmospheres* (Bour)].

• (Ensemble Modern/Peter Eötvös). *See* 3826.7

3826.13 *Lontano* [for orchestra].

• (Vienna Philharmonic/Claudio Abbado). *See* 3988

• (Southwest German Radio Orchestra/Ernest Bour). *See* 3826.7

3826.14 * *Lux aeterna* [for chorus]. (Schola Cantorum Stuttgard/Clytus Gottwald). *See* 3826.12

3826.15 *Monument, Selbstporträt, Bewegung* [for 2 pianos].

• (Antonio Ballista/Bruno Canino). *See* 3826.26

- (Begonia Uriarte/Karl-Hermann Mrongovius). *See* 3826.18

3826.16 *Nouvelles aventures* [for voices and chamber ensemble]. (Bruno Maderna and others). *See* 3826.23

3826.17 * *Organ music.* (Karl-Erik Welin/Zsigmond Szathmáry). *See* 3826.1

3826.18 *Piano music.*

- (Erika Haase). Col Legno/Aurophon: AU-031 815 CD. [*Etudes, book 1; Invention; Capriccios nos. 1–2; Musica ricercata.* With his *Passacaglia ungherese; Hungarian rock; Continuum,* for harpsichord].

- (Begonia Uriarte/Karl-Hermann Mrongovius). Wergo: WER 60131-50. [*Musica ricercata; Capriccios; Invention.* With his *Monument, Selbstporträt, Bewegung,* for two pianos].

3826.19 *Pieces (10) for wind quintet.*

- (Quintetto Arnold). *See* 4023

- (Wind Quintet of the Southwest German Radio). *See* 3826.1

3826.20 *Poème symphonique* [for 100 metronomes]. Editions Michael Frauenlob Bauer: CD008.

3826.21 *Quartets (2) for strings.* (Arditti Quartet). Wergo: WER 60079-2.

3826.22 *Ramifications* [for 12 solo strings or string orchestra]. (Saarbrücken Radio Chamber Orchestra/Antonio Janigro [solo strings]/Southwest German Radio Orchestra/Ernest Bour [string orchestra]). *See* 3826.12

3826.23 * *Requiem.* (Bavarian Radio Chorus/ Frankfurt Radio Orchestra/Michael Gielen). Wergo: 60045-50. [With his *Aventures; Nouvelles aventures*].

3826.24 * *San Francisco polyphony* [for orchestra]. (Swedish Radio Symphony/Elgar Howarth). *See* 3826.8

3826.25 *Sonata for violoncello.* (Matt Haimovitz). Deutsche Grammophon: 431 813-2. [With Britten, Benjamin: *Suite no. 1;* Crumb, George: *Suite for violoncello;* Reger, Max: *Suite no. 1*].

3826.26 * *Trio for horn, violin, and piano.*

- (Hermann Baumann/Eckart Besch/Saschko Gawriloff). Wergo: WER 60100-50. [With his *Passacaglia ungherese; Hungarian rock;* and *Continuum* (Elisabeth Chojnacka); *Monument, Selbstporträt, Bewegung* (Antonio Ballista/Bruno Canino)].

- (William Purvis/Rolf Shulte/Alan Feinberg). *See* 3452.21

3827 Lindberg, Magnus, 1958–

3827.1 * *Instrumental music* [selections].

- (Ensemble InterContemporain/Peter Eötvös). Adda: 203 582. [*UR, for five instruments and electronics; Corrente* for instrumental ensemble; *Duo concertante,* for clarinet, violoncello, and instrumental ensemble; *Joy* for instrumental ensemble and electronics].

- (Matti Rantanen and others). Finlandia: 500342. [*Metalwork,* for accordion and percussion; *Ablauf,* for clarinet and percussion; *Twine,* for piano; *Kinetics,* for orchestra; *Jeux d'anches,* for accordion].

3827.2 * *Kraft* [for seven soloists and orchestra]. (Swedish Radio Symphony/Esa-Pekka Salonen). Finlandia: FACD 372. [With his *Action-situation-signification,* for five soloists and electronics].

3828 Lockwood, Annea, 1939–

Thousand year dreaming [for conch shell, winds, didjeridus, voice, and percussion]. (Art Baron and others). What Next?: WN0010.

3829 Loevendie, Theo, 1930–

Selections. (Nieuw Ensemble/Ed Spanjaard). Etcetera: KTC 1097. [*Venus and Adonis,* for five instruments; *Strides,* for piano; *Turkish folk poems,* for female voice and seven instruments; *Music,* for flute and piano; *Songs for mezzo soprano and eight instruments; Back Bay bicinium,* for seven instruments].

3830 Louie, Alexina, 1949–

Love songs for a small planet [for chorus, harp, and percussion]. (Vancouver Chamber Choir/Jon Washburn). CMC: 4893. [With Schafer, R. Murray: *Magic songs;* plus works by Imant Raminsh and Srul Irving Glick].

3831 Lucier, Alvin, 1931–

3831.1 *Crossings* [for instruments and oscillators]. (Thomas Ridenour and others). Lovely Music: LCD 1018.

3831.2 * *I am sitting in a room* [for electronically processed voice]. Lovely Music: LCD 1013.

3832 Luening, Otto, 1900–

Electronic music. Selections. See 3984

3833 Lutoslawski, Witold, 1913–1994

3833.1 * *Chain no. 2* [for violin and orchestra]. (Anne-Sophie Mutter/BBC Symphony/Witold Lutoslawski). *See* 3643.15

3833.2 *Chain no. 3* [for orchestra]. (BBC Symphony/Witold Lutoslawski). *See* 3833.4

3833.3 * *Concerto for orchestra.*

- (Chicago Symphony/Daniel Barenboim). Erato: 4509-91711-2. [With his *Symphony no. 3*].
- (Cleveland Orchestra/Christoph von Dohnanyi). *See* 3545.1

3833.4 *Concerto for piano and orchestra.* (Krystian Zimerman/BBC Symphony/Witold Lutoslawski). Deutsche Grammophon: 431 664-2. [With his *Chain no. 3*].

3833.5 *Concerto for violoncello and orchestra.* (Mstislav Rostropovich/Paris Orchestra/Witold Lutoslawski). *See* 3750.6

3833.6 *Les espaces du sommeil* [for baritone and orchestra].

- (Dietrich Fischer-Dieskau/Berlin Philharmonic/Witold Lutoslawski). *See* 3833.10
- (John Shirley-Quirk/Los Angeles Philharmonic/Esa-Pekka Salonen). *See* 3833.11 or 3847.23

3833.7 *Partita for violin and orchestra.* (Anne-Sophie Mutter/BBC Symphony/Witold Lutoslawski). *See* 3643.15

3833.8 ** *Quartet for strings.*

- (Arditti Quartet). *See* 3812.3
- (Varsovia Quartet). *See* 3644.2

3833.9 *Symphony no. 2.* (Polish Radio Symphony/Witold Lutoslawski). [Series: Matrix, vol. 3]. EMI: CDM 5 65076 2. [With his *Wariacje symfoniczne; Symphony no. 1; Muzyka za obna*].

3833.10 *Symphony no. 3.*

- (Chicago Symphony/Daniel Barenboim). *See* 3833.3
- (Berlin Philharmonic/Witold Lutoslawski). Philips: 416 387-2. [With his *Espaces du sommeil*].
- (Los Angeles Philharmonic/Esa-Pekka Salonen). *See* 3833.11 or 3847.23

3833.11 *Symphony no. 4.* (Los Angeles Philharmonic/Esa-Pekka Salonen). Sony: SK 66280. [With his *Symphony no. 3; Espaces du sommeil*].

3833.12 *Wariacje na temat Paganiniego (Variations on a theme of Paganini)* [for two pianos].

- (Martha Argerich/Nelson Freire). Philips: 411 034-2. [With Rachmaninoff, Sergei: *Suite for two pianos no. 2*; Ravel, Maurice: *La valse*].
- (Anthony and Joseph Paratore). *See* 3538

3834 Lutyens, Elisabeth, 1906–1983

Selections. (Jane Manning/Jane's Minstrels/Roger Montgomery). NMC: D011. [*Chamber concerto no. 1; The valley of Hatsu-Se, for soprano and chamber ensemble; Six tempi for ten instruments; Lament of Isis on the death of Osiris, for soprano; Triolet no. 1, for clarinet, mandolin, and violoncello; Requiescat (in memoriam Igor Stravinsky), for soprano and string trio; Triolet no. 2, for marimba, harp, and violoncello*].

3835 Machover, Tod, 1953–

3835.1 * *Selections.* (Carol Bennett and others). Bridge: BCD 9020. [*Flora, for computer-generated tape; Towards the center, for six instruments and live computer electronics; Famine, for four voices and computer-generated tape; Bug-mudra, for two guitars, percussion, and live computer electronics*].

3835.2 *Valis* [opera]. (Mary King/Thomas Bogdan/Tod Machover). Bridge: 9007.

3836 Mackey, Steven, 1956–

3836.1 *Never sing before breakfast* [for winds and electronics]. (Quintet of the Americas). *See* 4022

3836.2 * *Selections.* (Steven Mackey and others). Newport: NPD 85541. [*Indigenous instruments, for chamber ensemble; Moebius band, for chamber ensemble; Journey to Ixtlan, for chorus and orchestra*].

3837 MacMillan, James, 1959–

3837.1 *The confession of Isobel Gowdie* [for orchestra]. (BBC Scottish Symphony/Jerzy Maksymiuk). Koch Schwann: 3-1050-2. [With his *Tryst, for chamber orchestra*].

3837.2 * *Veni, veni, Emmanuel* [concerto for percussion and orchestra]. (Evelyn Glennie/Scottish Chamber Orchestra/Jukka-Pekka Saraste). Catalyst: 09026 61916-2. [With his *After the tryst, for violin and piano; ". . . as others see us . . .," for chamber orchestra; Dawn rituals, for chamber orchestra; Untold, for wind quintet*].

3838 Maconchy, Elizabeth, 1907–

Quartets (13) for strings. (Hanson Quartet/Bingham Quartet/Mistry Quartet). Unicorn-Kanchana: DKP(CD) 9080/9082. 3CD set.

3839 Maderna, Bruno, 1920–1973

3839.1 * *Hyperion* [dramatic cycle for vocal and instrumental soloists, chorus, and orchestra].

(Peter Eötvös and others). Montaigne: 782014. 2CD set.

3839.2 *Orchestral music. Selections.* (Bruno Maderna and others). Stradivarius: STR 10021. [*Concerto for violin and orchestra; Concerto for oboe and orchestra no. 2; Quadrivium*].

3839.3 *Quartet for strings.* (Arditti Quartet). *See* 3993

3840 * Marshall, Ingram, 1942–

Fog tropes [for brass sextet and tape]. (John Adams and others). New Albion: NA002CD. [With his *Gradual requiem, for instruments, voices, and electronics; Gambuh no. 1, for gambuh, synthesizer, and tape*].

3841 Martino, Donald, 1931–

3841.1 *Instrumental music. Selections.* (Michael Webster and others). CRI: CD 693. [*Set, for clarinet; Quodlibets, for flute; Trio for violin, clarinet, and piano; Fantasy-variations, for violin; Concerto for wind quintet; Strata, for bass clarinet*].

3841.2 * *Piano music. Selections.* (Eliza Garth). Centaur: CRC 2173. [*Fantasies and impromptus; Pianississimo; Suite in old form*].

3842 Martland, Steve, 1959–

3842.1 *Babi Yar* [for orchestra]. (Residentie Orkest Den Haag/Elgar Howarth). Catalyst: 09026-68397-2. [With his *Drill*].

3842.2 * *Danceworks* [for chamber ensemble]. (Steve Martland Band). Catalyst: 09026-62670-2. [With his *Principia, for chamber ensemble; Patrol, for string quartet*].

3842.3 *Drill* [for two pianos]. (Gerard Bouwhuis/Cees van Zeeland). *See* 3842.1

3843 Matthus, Siegfried, 1934–

Selections. (Theo Adam and others). Ars Vivendi: 2100238. [*Hyperion-Fragmente, for bass voice and orchestra; Der Wald, for percussion; Concerto for trumpet, kettledrums, and orchestra*].

3844 Mayuzumi, Toshiro, 1929–

Orchestral music. Selections. (Hong Kong Philharmonic/Yoshikazu Fukumura). HK Marco Polo: 8.220297. [*Samsara; Phonologie symphonique; Bacchanale*].

3845 McNabb, Michael, 1952–

Dreamsong [computer music]. Wergo: WER 2020-2. [With his *Love in the asylum; Mars suite*].

3846 Menotti, Gian Carlo, 1911–

3846.1 * *Amahl and the night visitors* [opera]. (Chet Allen/Rosemary Kuhlmann/Thomas Schippers). RCA: 6485-2-RG.

3846.2 *The telephone* [opera]. (Anne Victoria Banks/Gian Luca Ricci/Milan Chamber Orchestra/Paolo Vaglieri). Nuova Era: 7122. [With his *Ricercare and toccata on a theme from The old maid and the thief; Canti della lontananza*].

3847 Messiaen, Olivier, 1908–1992

3847.1 * *L'ascension* [for organ]. (Olivier Messiaen). *See* 3847.17

3847.2 *Catalogue des oiseaux, books 1–7* [for piano]. (Peter Hill). Unicorn-Kanchana: DKPCD9062; 9075; 9090. 3 CDs.

3847.3 *Chronochromie* [for orchestra]. (Cleveland Orchestra/Pierre Boulez). Deutsche Grammophon: 445 827-2. [With his *La ville d'en haut; Et expecto resurrectionem mortuorum*].

3847.4 *Couleurs de la cité céleste* [for piano, winds, brass, and percussion].
  * (Peter Donohoe/Netherlands Wind Ensemble/ Reinbert de Leeuw). *See* 3847.15
  * (Yvonne Loriod/Ensemble InterContemporain/ Pierre Boulez). *See* 3847.9

3847.5 * *Des canyons aux étoiles* [for piano, horn, percussion, and orchestra].
  * (Reinbert de Leeuw and others). [Series: Olivier Messiaen, vol. 2]. Montaigne: MO 782035. 2CD set.
  * (Esa-Pekka Salonen and others). CBS: M2K 44674. 2CD set. [With his *Oiseaux exotiques; Couleurs de la cité céleste*].

3847.6 *Eclairs sur l'au-delà* [for orchestra]. (Bastille Orchestra/Myung-Whun Chung). Deutsche Grammophon: 439 929-2.

3847.7 *Et expecto resurrectionem mortuorum* [for winds, brass, and percussion].
  * Cleveland Orchestra/Pierre Boulez). *See* 3847.3
  * (Netherlands Wind Ensemble/Reinbert de Leeuw). *See* 3847.15
  * (Ensemble 21/Arthur Weisberg). Summit: DCD 122. [With Revueltas, Silvestre: *Homenaje a Federico Garcia Lorca*; Ruggles, Carl: *Angels*].

3847.8 *Etudes de rythme (4) for piano.*
  * (Peter Hill). Unicorn-Kanchana: DKPCD9078. [With his *Preludes; Canteyodjaya*].
  * (Yuji Takahashi). *See* 3947.1

3847.9 *Haïkaï (7)* [for piano and chamber orchestra].

- (Peter Donohoe/Reinbert de Leeuw). *See* 3847.15
- (Yvonne Loriod/Ensemble InterContemporain/Pierre Boulez). Montaigne: MO 781111. [Album title: *Hommage à Olivier Messiaen.* With his *Couleurs de la cité céleste; Un vitrail-et-des oiseaux; Oiseaux exotiques*].

3847.10 *Harawi* [for soprano and piano]. (Dorothy Dorow/Carl-Axel Dominique). Bis: CD-86. [With his *Poèmes pour Mi*].

3847.11 * *Livre d'orgue.* (Olivier Messiaen). *See* 3847.17

3847.12 *La merle noir* [for flute and piano]. (Patrick Gallois/Elizabeth Sombart). *See* 3665

3847.13 *La nativité du Seigneur* [for organ]. (Olivier Messiaen). *See* 3847.17

3847.14 *O sacrum convivium* [motet]. (London Sinfonietta Chorus/Terry Edwards). *See* 3847.18

3847.15 ** *Oiseaux exotiques* [for piano, winds, and percussion].

- (Peter Donohoe/Netherlands Wind Ensemble/Reinbert de Leeuw). Chandos: CHAN 9301/2. 2CD set. [With his *Haïkaï; Couleurs de la cité céleste; Un vitrail-et-des oiseaux; La ville d'en haut; Et expecto resurrectionem mortuorum*].
- (Yvonne Loriod/Ensemble InterContemporain/Pierre Boulez). *See* 3847.9

3847.16 *Organ music* [complete].

- (Hans-Ola Ericsson). Bis: 409; 410; 441; 442; 464; 491/92. 7 CDs in 6 vols.
- (Gillian Weir). Collins: 70312. 7CD set.

3847.17 * *Organ music. Selections.* (Olivier Messiaen). EMI: CZS 7 67400 2. 4CD set. [Album title: *Messiaen par lui-même.* Contents: *Le banquet céleste; Diptyque; Apparition de l'église éternelle; L'ascension; La nativité du Seigneur; Les corps glorieux; Messe de Pentecôte; Livre d'orgue*].

3847.18 *Petites liturgies (3) de la présence divine* [for chorus and orchestra]. (London Sinfonietta Chorus/Terry Edwards). Virgin: 7 59051 2 (7 91472 2). [With his *Rechants; O sacrum convivium*].

3847.19 ** *Quatuor pour la fin du temps (Quartet for the end of time)* [for clarinet, violin, violoncello, and piano]. (Tashi). RCA: 7835-2-RG.

3847.20 *Rechants (5)* [for chorus]. (London Sinfonietta Chorus/Terry Edwards). *See* 3847.18

3847.21 *Saint-François d'Assise* [opera]. (José van Dam/Christiane Eda-Pierre/Paris Opera/Seiji Ozawa). Cybelia: CY 833/36. 4CD set.

3847.22 * *La transfiguration de Notre Seigneur Jésus-Christ* [oratorio].

- (Antal Dorati and others). London: 425 616-2. 2CD set.
- (Reinbert de Leeuw and others). [Series: Olivier Messiaen, vol. 4]. Montaigne: MO 782040. 2CD set.

3847.23 * *Turangalîla-symphonie* [for piano, ondes martenot, and orchestra].

- (Concertgebouw Orchestra/Riccardo Chailly). London: 431 626-2.
- (Bastille Orchestra/Myung-Whun Chung). Deutsche Grammophon: 431 781-2.
- (Los Angeles Philharmonic/Esa-Pekka Salonen). CBS: M2K 42271. 2CD set. [With Lutoslawski, Witold: *Espaces du sommeil; Symphony no. 3*].

3847.24 *Vingt regards sur l'enfant Jésus* [for piano].

- (Peter Hill). Unicorn-Kanchana: DKPCD9122/23. 2CD set.
- (Yvonne Loriod). Erato: 4509-91705-2. 2CD set.

3847.25 *Visions de l'amen* [for two pianos].

- (Martha Argerich/Alexander Rabinovitch). EMI: CDC 7 54050 2.
- (Peter Hill/Benjamin Frith). Unicorn-Kanchana: DKPCD9144.

3848 Monk, Meredith, 1942–

3848.1 *Book of days.* (Meredith Monk Ensemble). ECM: 78818-21399-2.

3848.2 *Do you be.* (Meredith Monk Ensemble). ECM: 78118-21336-2.

3848.3 ** *Dolmen music.* (Meredith Monk Ensemble). ECM: 78818-21197-2.

3848.4 * *Facing north.* (Meredith Monk/Robert Een). ECM: 78818-21482-2.

3848.5 *Our lady of late.* (Meredith Monk). Wergo: SM 1058-50.

3848.6 *Songs from the hill. Selections.* (Meredith Monk and others). Wergo: SM 1022-50. [With her *Tablet*].

3848.7 *Turtle dreams.* (Meredith Monk Ensemble). ECM: 78818-21240-2.

3849 Moondog. *See* 3780

3850 * Moran, John, 1966–

The Manson family [opera]. (John Moran and others). Point: 432 967-2.

3851 Moran, Robert, 1937–

Selections. (Robert Moran and others). Argo: 436 128-2. [*Arias, interludes, and inventions, from the opera Desert of roses, for soprano and chamber ensemble; Ten miles high over Albania, for eight harps; Open veins, for violin and chamber ensemble*].

3852 Mori, Ikue

Selections. Tzadik: 7201. [Album title: *Hex kitchen.* Works for drum machine, sampler, and various instruments or voices].

3853 Murail, Tristan, 1947– . *Instrumental music. Selections.*

- (Ensemble FA/Dominique My). Accord: 200842. [*Allégories, for chamber ensemble; Vues aériennes, for horn, violin, violoncello, and piano; Territoires de l'oubli, for piano*].

- (Alain Noël and others). Accord: 202122. [*Mémoire/érosion, for horn and chamber ensemble; Ethers, for flute and chamber ensemble; C'est un jardin secret, for viola; Les courants de l'espace, for ondes martenot and chamber ensemble*].

3854 Musgrave, Thea, 1928–

3854.1 *Chamber concerto no. 2.* (Boston Musica Viva/Richard Pittman). *See* 3634.1

3854.2 *Mary, Queen of Scots* [opera]. (Ashley Putnam/Virginia Opera Association/Peter Mark). Novello: NVLCD 108. 2CD set.

3855 Nancarrow, Conlon, 1912–

3855.1 *Instrumental music. Selections.*

- (Ensemble Modern/Ingo Metzmacher). RCA: 09026-61180-2. [Studies originally for player piano arranged for instrumental ensemble by Yvar Mikhashoff].

- (Continuum/Cheryl Seltzer/Joel Sachs). MusicMasters: 7068-2-C. [*Pieces nos. 1–2 for small orchestra; Toccata for violin and player piano; Trio for clarinet, bassoon, and piano; Quartet for strings no. 1;* and other short works].

3855.2 * *Studies for player piano, vols. 1–5.* Wergo: WER 6168/69-2; 60166/67-50; 60165-50. 5 CDs in 3 containers.

3856 Neill, Ben

I T S O F O M O: in the shadow of forward motion [for voice, mutantrumpet, percussion, and electronics]. (DavidWojnarowicz/Ben Neill/Don Yallech). New Tone: 6710 (129806710 2).

3857 Niblock, Phill, 1933– . *Instrumental music. Selections.*

- (Petr Kotik/Eberhard Blum/Susan Stenger). Experimental Intermedia: XI 101. [Album title: *Four full flutes*].

- (Susan Stenger/Eberhard Blum/Soldier String Quartet). Experimental Intermedia: XI 111. [*Five more string quartets, for string quartet and electronics; Early winter, for flute, bass flute, and electronics*].

3858 Nono, Luigi, 1924–1990

3858.1 * *Il canto sospeso* [for voices and orchestra]. (Berlin Radio Chorus/Berlin Philharmonic/Claudio Abbado). Sony: SK 53360. [With Mahler, Gustav: *Kindertotenlieder*].

3858.2 *Fragmente-Stille, an Diotima* [for string quartet]. (Arditti Quartet). [Series: Luigi Nono, vol. 1]. Montaigne: 789005.

3858.3 *Liebeslied* [for voices and orchestra]. (Vienna Philharmonic/Claudio Abbado). *See* 3988

3858.4 *La lontananza nostalgica utopica futura* [for violin and tape].

- (Irvine Arditti). [Series: Luigi Nono, vol. 2]. Montaigne: 782004.

- (Gidon Kremer). Deutsche Grammophon: 435 870-2. [With his *"Hay que caminar" soñando, for two violins*].

3858.5 *No hay caminos, hay que caminar—Andrei Tarkovskij, for seven instrumental groups.* (Southwest German Radio Orchestra/Michael Gielen). Auvidis/Astrée: E 8741. [With his *Variazioni canoniche, for orchestra; A Carlo Scarpa, architetto, ai suoi infiniti possibli, for orchestra*].

3859 Nordheim, Arne, 1931–

Tenebrae [for violoncello and orchestra]. (Truls Mørk/Oslo Philharmonic/Yoav Talmi). Aurora: ACD 4966. [With his *Magma, for orchestra*].

3860 Nørgård, Per, 1932–

3860.1 *Remembering child* [for viola and orchestra]. (Pinchas Zukerman/Danish National Radio Symphony/Jorma Panula). Da Capo/Marco Polo: DCCD 9002. [With his *Between, for violoncello and orchestra*].

3860.2 *Waves* [for percussion and tape]. (Michael Pugliese). *See* 4021

3861 Nunes, Emmanuel, 1941–

Musik der Frühe [for chamber ensemble]. (Ensemble InterContemporain/Peter Eötvös). Erato: ECD 75551. [With his *Esquisses, for string quartet*].

3862 Nyman, Michael, 1944–

3862.1 *The man who mistook his wife for a hat* [opera]. (Emile Belcourt/Sara Leonard/Frederick Westcott/Michael Nyman). CBS: MK 44669.

3862.2 *Quartets for strings nos. 1–3.* (Balanescu Quartet). Argo: 433 093-2.

3863 Ohana, Maurice, 1914–1992

Llanto por Ignacio Sánchez Mejías [cantata]. (Lionel Peintre/Ensemble Vocal et Instrumentale Musicatreize/Roland Hayrabedian). Calliope: CAL 9877. [With his *Syllabaire pour Phèdre*].

3864 Oliveros, Pauline, 1932–

3864.1 *Crone music* [for accordion]. (Pauline Oliveros). Lovely Music: LCD 1903.

3864.2 * *Deep listening* [for various instruments and voice]. (Pauline Oliveros/Stuart Dempster/Panaiotis). New Albion: NA022CD.

3864.3 *In memoriam Mr. Whitney* [for accordion and 12 voices]. (Pauline Oliveros/American Voices/Neeley Bruce). Mode: 40. [With her *St. George and the dragon, for accordion*].

3865 Ostertag, Bob, 1957–

All the rage [for string quartet and tape]. (Kronos Quartet). Elektra Nonesuch: 79332-2.

3866 Panufnik, Andrzej, 1914–1991

3866.1 *Sinfonia sacra.* (Concertgebouw Orchestra/Andrzej Panufnik). Elektra Nonesuch: 79228-2. [With his *Arbor cosmica, for string ensemble*].

3866.2 *Symphony no. 8 ("Sinfonia votiva").* (Boston Symphony/Seiji Ozawa). *See 3635.2*

3867 * Parkins, Zeena

Ursa's door [for chamber ensemble]. (Zeena Parkins and others). Victo: CD018. [With her *Flush, for chamber ensemble*].

3868 Pärt, Arvo, 1935–

3868.1 *Fratres* [for various instrumental combinations]. (I Fiamminghi/Rudolf Werthen). Telarc: 80387. [Versions for strings and percussion; violin, strings, and percussion; wind octet and percussion; eight violoncellos; string quartet; violoncello and piano. With his *Cantus in memory of Benjamin Britten; Festina lente*]. *See also 3868.3*

3868.2 * *Johannespassion (Passio Domini nostri Jesu Christi secundum Joannem)* [for voices and chamber ensemble]. (Paul Hillier and others). ECM: 78118-21370-2.

3868.3 ** *Tabula rasa* [for two violins, prepared piano, and string orchestra]. (Gidon Kremer and others). ECM: 78118-21275-2. [With his *Fratres, for violin and piano; Cantus in memory of Benjamin Britten, for orchestra; Fratres, for 12 violoncellos*].

3869 Partch, Harry, 1901–1974

3869.1 *And on the seventh day, petals fell in Petaluma* [for Partch ensemble]. (Gate 5 Ensemble/Harry Partch/John Garvey). CRI: 7000. [With his *Bewitched: final scene and epilogue; Castor and Pollux; The letter; Windsong*]. *See also 3869.5*

3869.2 *Barstow* [for voice and guitar]. (John Schneider). Bridge: 9041. [With his *Studies on ancient Greek scales;* plus music by John Cage, Lou Harrison, and La Monte Young].

3869.3 *The bewitched* [for Partch ensemble]. (University of Illinois Ensemble/Harry Partch/John Garvey). CRI: 7001. *See also 3869.5*

3869.4 * *Castor and Pollux* [for Partch ensemble]. (Harry Partch and others). *See 3869.1 or 3869.5*

3869.5 * *Cloud chamber music* [for Partch ensemble]. (Gate 5 Ensemble/Harry Partch). CRI: ACS 6001. AC. [With his *And on the seventh day, petals fell in Petaluma; Bewitched: final scene and epilogue; Castor and Pollux*].

3869.6 ** *Daphne of the dunes* [for Partch ensemble]. (Newband). *See 4016*

3869.7 *The letter* [for narrator and Partch ensemble]. (Harry Partch and others). *See 3869.1*

3869.8 *Lyrics of Li Po* [for voice and tenor violin]. (Stephen Kalm/Ted Mook). Tzadik: TZ 7012.

3869.9 *Revelation in the courthouse park* [for voices and Partch ensemble]. (Danlee Mitchell). Tomato: R2-73090 (2696552). 2CD set.

3869.10 *Studies on ancient Greek scales* [for guitar]. (John Schneider). *See 3869.2*

3869.11 *Windsong* [for Partch ensemble]. (Harry Partch and others). *See 3869.1*

3870 Paulus, Stephen, 1949–

Symphony in three movements ("Soliloquy"). (Minnesota Orchestra/Neville Marriner). Elektra Nonesuch: 79147-2. [With Larsen, Libby: *Symphony*].

3871 Payne, Maggi, 1945–

Crystal [electroacoustic music]. Lovely Music: LCD 2061.

3872 Penderecki, Krzysztof, 1933–

3872.1 *Chamber music. Selections.* (Silesian String Quartet and others). Wergo: WER 6258-2. [*Quartets for strings nos. 1–2; Trio for strings; Der unterbrochene Gedanke, for string quartet; Sonata for violin and piano; Miniatures (3), for violin and piano; Miniatures (3), for clarinet and piano; Cadenza, for viola; Per Slava, for violoncello; Prelude, for clarinet*].

3872.2 *Concerto for viola and chamber orchestra.* (Kim Kashkashian/Stuttgart Chamber Orchestra/Dennis Russell Davies). *See* 3586.16

3872.3 * *Ofiarom Hiroszimy (Threnody for the victims of Hiroshima)* [for orchestra]. (Polish National Radio Symphony/Krzysztof Penderecki). EMI: 7243 5 65077 2 3. [With his *Anaklasis, for strings and percussion; Fonogrammi, for flute and chamber orchestra; De natura sonoris nos. 1–2, for orchestra; Capriccio, for violin and orchestra; Canticum canticorum Salomonis, for voices and orchestra; The dream of Jacob, for orchestra*].

3872.4 * *Passio et mors Domini Nostri Jesu Christi secundum Lucam (St. Luke Passion).* (Krzysztof Penderecki and others). Argo: 430 328-2.

3873 Perle, George, 1915–

3873.1 * *Piano music. Selections.* (Michael Boriskin). New World: 342-2. [*Pantomime, interlude, and fugue; Fantasy-variations; Six new etudes; Suite in C; Short sonata*].

3873.2 ** *Quintets for winds nos. 1–4.* (Dorian Quintet). New World: 359-2.

3874 Persichetti, Vincent, 1915–1987

3874.1 * *Band music. Selections.* (Winds of the London Symphony/David Amos). Harmonia Mundi: HMU 907092. [Album title: *Divertimenti for winds.* Contents: *Divertimento, op. 42; Psalm, op. 53; Masquerade, op. 102; O cool is the valley, op. 118; Parable, op. 121*].

3874.2 *Sonatas for harpsichord. Selections.* (Elaine Comparone). Laurel: LR-838. [*Sonatas 2–5.* With selected sonatas by Domenico Scarlatti].

3874.3 *Symphony no. 5.* (Philadelphia Orchestra/Riccardo Muti). New World: NW 370-2. [With his *Concerto for piano and orchestra*].

3875 Peterson, Wayne, 1927–

Quartet for strings no. 1. (Group for Contemporary Music). *See* 3946.2

3876 Petrassi, Goffredo, 1904–

3876.1 *Chamber music* [selections].

• (Compania/Andrea Molino). Stradivarius: 33347. [*Sonata da camera for harpsichord and ten instruments; Beatitudines for baritone and five instruments; Grand septuor for clarinet and six instruments; Sestina d'autunno for six instruments*].

• (Gruppo Musica d'Oggi). Bongiovanni: GB 5534-2. [*Invenzioni for piano; Serenata for five instruments; Laudes creaturarum for reciter and six instruments; Duetto for violin and viola; Grand septuor for clarinet and six instruments*].

3876.2 *Piano music* [selections]. (Ruggero Ruocco). AS: 5006. [*Toccata; Invenzioni; Oh les beaux jours!; Petite pièce.* With Dallapiccola, Luigi: *Sonata canonica* and *Quaderno musicale di Annalibera*].

3877 Pettersson, Allan, 1911–1980

3877.1 * *Symphony no. 3.* (Saarbrücken Radio Orchestra/Alun Francis). CPO: 999 223. [With his *Symphony no. 4*].

3877.2 *Symphony no. 7.* (Noorköping Symphony/Leif Segerstam). Bis: 580. [With his *Symphony no. 11*].

3878 Picker, Tobias, 1954–

Keys to the city [for piano and orchestra]. (Tobias Picker/Brooklyn Philharmonic/Lukas Foss). CRI: CD 554. [With Blitzstein, Marc: *Concerto for piano and orchestra*].

3879 Polansky, Larry, 1954–

3879.1 * *Computer music. Selections.* Artifact: ART 1004. [Album title: *The theory of impossible melody.* Contents: *B'rey'sheet = In the beginning: cantillation study no. 1; Four voices canons nos. 3–6; Simple actions, rules of compossibility; Psaltery*].

3879.2 *Instrumental music. Selections.* (Alyssa Hess Reit and others). Artifact: ART 1011. [Album title: *Simple harmonic motion.* Contents: *Another you, for harp; Movement for Andrée Smith, for string quartet; Movement for Lou Harrison, for double bass quartet; Horn, for horn and computer*].

3880 Pousseur, Henri, 1929–

Phonèmes pour Cathy [for voice]. (Cathy Berberian). *See* 3996

3881 * Powell, Mel, 1923–

Duplicates [concerto for two pianos and orchestra]. (Alan Feinberg/Robert Taub/Los Angeles Philharmonic/David Alan Miller). Harmonia Mundi: HMU 907096. [With his *Setting, for two pianos; Modules, for chamber orchestra*].

3882 Radigue, Eliane, 1932–

Kyema [electroacoustic music]. Experimental Intermedia: XI 103.

3883 Ran, Shulamit, 1949–

Instrumental music. Selections. (Da Capo Chamber Players). Bridge: BCD 9052. [*Concerto da camera no. 2, for clarinet, string quartet, and piano; East winds, for flute; Inscriptions, for violin; Mirage, for chamber ensemble; For an actor, for clarinet; Private game, for clarinet and violoncello*].

3884 * Rands, Bernard, 1934–

Canti del sole [for soprano and instruments]. (Carol Plantamura/SONOR Ensemble/Bernard Rands). CRI: CD 591. [With his *Canti lunatici, for baritone and instruments; Obbligato, for trombone and string quartet*].

3885 Rautavaara, Einojuhani, 1928–

Cantus arcticus [for orchestra and tape]. (Leipzig Radio Symphony/Max Pommer). Ondine: ODE 747-2. [With his *Symphonies nos. 4–5*].

3886 Reich, Steve, 1936–

3886.1 *Clapping music.* (Steve Reich/Russ Hartenberger). *See* 3886.2

3886.2 * *Come out* [for electronic tape]. Elektra Nonesuch: 79169-2. [Album title: *Early works.* With his *Piano phase; Clapping music; It's gonna rain*].

3886.3 * *Different trains* [for string quartet and tape]. (Kronos Quartet). Elektra Nonesuch: 79176-2. [With his *Electric counterpoint*].

3886.4 * *Drumming.* (Steve Reich and Musicians). Elektra Nonesuch: 79170-2.

3886.5 *Four organs.* (Steve Reich and others). New Tone: RCD 5018. [With his *Phase patterns, for four organs*].

3886.6 *Four sections* [for orchestra]. (London Symphony/Michael Tilson Thomas). Elektra Nonesuch: 79220-2. [With his *Music for mallet instruments, voices, and organ*].

3886.7 *It's gonna rain* [for electronic tape]. *See* 3886.2

3886.8 ** *Music for 18 musicians.* (Steve Reich and Musicians). ECM: 78118-21129-2.

3886.9 *Music for mallet instruments, voices, and organ.* (Amadinda Percussion Group). Hungaroton: HCD 31358. [With his *Music for pieces of wood; Sextet*].

3886.10 *Music for pieces of wood.* (Amadinda Percussion Group). *See* 3886.9

3886.11 * *Octet ("Eight lines").*
- (London Chamber Orchestra/Christopher Warren-Green). *See* 4013
- (Solisti di New York/Ransom Wilson). *See* 3679.4

3886.12 * *Piano phase* [for two pianos]. (Nurit Tilles/Edmund Neimann). *See* 3886.2

3886.13 *Sextet* [for pianos and percussion].
- (Amadinda Percussion Group). *See* 3886.9
- (Steve Reich and Musicians). Elektra Nonesuch: 79138-2. [With his *Six marimbas*].

3886.14 ** *Tehillim* [for voices and instruments]. (Steve Reich and Musicians). ECM: 78118-21215-2.

3886.15 *Variations for orchestra.* (San Francisco Symphony/Edo de Waart). Philips: 412 214-2. [With Adams, John: *Shaker loops*].

3887 Reynolds, Roger, 1934–

3887.1 *Coconico—a shattered landscape* [for string quartet]. *See* 3992

3887.2 *Personae* [for violin, chamber ensemble, and electronics]. (Janos Negyesy/SONOR Ensemble/Rand Steiger). Neuma: 450-78. [With his *Vanity of words (Voicespace no. 5); Variation, for piano*].

3887.3 * *Transfigured wind no. 4* [for flute and electronic tape]. (Harvey Sollberger). *See* 3970

3887.4 *Voicespace. Selections* [for voice and electronics]. (Philip Larson). Lovely Music: LCD 1801. [*The palace (Voicespace no. 4); Eclipse (Voicespace no. 3); Still (Voicespace no. 1)*].

3887.5 * *Whispers out of time* [for solo strings and chamber ensemble]. (San Diego Symphony/Harvey Sollberger). New World: 80401-2. [With his *Transfigured wind no. 2, for flute and chamber ensemble*].

3888 Rihm, Wolfgang, 1952–

3888.1 *Depart* [for voices and orchestra]. (Vienna Philharmonic/Claudio Abbado). *See* 3988

3888.2 * *Fremde Szenen, nos. 1–3* [for violin, violoncello, and piano]. (Beethoven Trio Ravensburg). CPO: 999 119-2.

3888.3 *Gesungene Zeit (Time chant)* [for violin and orchestra]. (Anne-Sophie Mutter/Chicago Symphony/James Levine). *See 3547.1*

3888.4 *Music for 3 strings.* (Ensemble 13 Baden-Baden). CPO: 999 050-2.

3888.5 *Pieces for piano. Selections.* (Siegfried Mauser). *See 3802.2*

3888.6 * *String quartet music. Selections.* (Arditti Quartet). Montaigne: 782001. [*Im Innersten; Quartet for strings no. 8; Ohne Titel*].

3889 Riley, Terry, 1935–

3889.1 * *Cadenza on the night plain* [for string quartet]. (Kronos Quartet). Gramavision: R2 79444. [With his *Sunrise of the planetary dream collector; G song; Mythic birds waltz*].

3889.2 *The harp of New Albion* [for piano]. (Terry Riley). Celestial Harmonies: CEL 018/19-2. 2CD set.

3889.3 ** *In C* [for instrumental ensemble].

- (Terry Riley and others) [original 1968 recording]. CBS: MK 7178.
- (Terry Riley and others) [25th anniversary concert]. New Albion: NA071CD.

3889.4 *June Buddhas* [for orchestra]. (Brooklyn Philharmonic/Dennis Russell Davies). *See 3781.5*

3889.5 *Salome dances for peace* [for string quartet]. (Kronos Quartet). Elektra Nonesuch: 79217-2. 2CD set.

3889.6 *Songs for the ten voices of the two prophets* [for voice and synthesizer]. (Terry Riley). Kuckuck: 12047-2. 2CD set. [With his *Descending moonshine dervishes, for electronic organ*].

3890 Risset, Jean-Claude, 1938–

3890.1 * *Inharmonique* [for voice and tape]. INA. GRM: INA C 1003. [With his *Sud* (computer music); *Dialogues, for chamber ensemble and tape; Mutations* (computer music)].

3890.2 *Sud* [computer music]. Wergo: WER 2013-50. [With his *Songes; Passages; Computer suite from Little Boy*].

3891 Rochberg, George, 1918–

3891.1 *Concerto for oboe and orchestra.* (New York Philharmonic/Zubin Mehta). *See 3748.4*

3891.2 *Music for the magic theatre* [for chamber ensemble]. (New York Chamber Ensemble/Stephen Rogers Radcliffe). New World: 80462-2. [With his *Octet: a grand fantasia*].

3892 Rolnick, Neil B., 1947–

Electroacoustic music. Selections. (Neil B. Rolnick and others). Bridge: BCD 9030. [*Macedonian air drumming; Sanctus; Balkanization; ReBong*].

3893 Rorem, Ned, 1923–

3893.1 *Miss Julie* [opera]. (Theodora Fried/Philip Torre/Manhattan School of Music Opera/David Gilbert). Newport: NPD 85605-2. 2CD set.

3893.2 *Orchestral music. Selections.* (Atlanta Symphony/Robert Shaw/Louis Lane). New World: NW 353-2. [*String symphony; Sunday morning; Eagles*].

3893.3 * *Vocal music. Selections.* (Phyllis Bryn-Julson and others). CRI: CD 657. [*Nantucket songs; Some trees, and other songs; Women's voices*].

3894 Rosenboom, David, 1947–

Systems of judgment [computer music]. [CDCM computer music series, vol. 4]. Centaur: CRC 2077.

3895 Rouse, Christopher, 1949–

3895.1 * *Bonham* [for percussion]. (Baltimore Symphony/David Zinman). *See 3969*

3895.2 *Symphony no. 1.* (Baltimore Symphony/David Zinman). Elektra Nonesuch: 79230-2. [With his *Phantasmata, for orchestra*].

3896 Rouse, Mikel

3896.1 *Living inside design* [for voice, instruments, and electronics]. (Mikel Rouse). New Tone: NT 6724.

3896.2 *Soul menu* [for chamber ensemble]. (Mikel Rouse Broken Consort). New Tone: NT 6716.

3897 Ruders, Poul, 1949–

3897.1 *Chamber music. Selections.* (David Starobin and others). Bridge: BCD 9037. [*Psalmodies, for guitar and nine instruments; Vox in rama, for amplified violin, clarinet, and piano; Nightshade, for ten instruments*].

3897.2 *Quartets for strings nos. 2–3.* (Kontra Quartet). *See 3678*

3898 Russell, Arthur, d. 1992

Selections. (Arthur Russell and others). Point: 438 891-2. [Album title: *Another thought*].

3899 Rzewski, Frederic, 1938–

3899.1 *Coming together—Attica* [for narrator and instruments]. (Group 180). *See 3973*

**3899.2 ** *De profundis* [for speaking pianist]. (Frederic Rzewski). Hat Hut: ART CD 6134. [With his *Sonata for piano*].

3899.3 *North American ballads* [for piano]. (Paul Jacobs). *See* 4011

3899.4 * *The people united will never be defeated* [for piano]. (Frederic Rzewski). Hat Hut: ART CD 6066.

3900 Saariaho, Kaija, 1952–

3900.1 * *Du cristal* . . . [for orchestra]. (Los Angeles Philharmonic/Esa-Pekka Salonen). Ondine: ODE 804-2. [With her *À la fumée, for alto flute, violoncello, and orchestra; Nymphea, for string quartet and electronics*].

3900.2 * *Jardin secret no. 1* [computer music]. *See* 3964

3900.3 *Maa* [for chamber ensemble and electronics]. (Tapio Tuomela and others). Ondine: ODE 791-2.

3900.4 *Verblendungen* [for orchestra and tape]. (Avanti Chamber Orchestra/Jukka-Pekka Saraste). Finlandia: FACD 372. [With her *Lichtbogen, for chamber ensemble and electronics; Io, for chamber orchestra, tape, and live electronics; Stilleben, for tape*].

3901 Sallinen, Aulis, 1935–

3901.1 *Orchestral music. Selections.* (Tapiola Sinfonietta/Osmo Vänskä). Bis: CD 560. [*Variations for orchestra; Concerto for violin and orchestra; Some aspects of Peltoneimi Hintrik's funeral march (arranged for string orchestra from his Quartet for strings no. 3); Nocturnal dances of Don Juanquixote*].

3901.2 * *Quartet for strings no. 3 ("Some aspects of Peltoniemi Hintrik's funeral march").* (Kronos Quartet). *See* 3911.2

3902 Satoh, Somei, 1947–

Litania [for two pianos and electronics]. (Margaret Leng Tan and others). New Albion: NA008CD. [With his *Birds in warped time, for violin and piano; The heavenly spheres are illuminated by lights, for soprano, piano, and percussion; Incarnation no. 2 for piano and electronics*].

3903 Scelsi, Giacinto, 1905–1988

**3903.1 ** *Anahit* [for violin and chamber ensemble]. (Carmen Fournier/Polish Radio-Television Orchestra/Jurg Wyttenbach). Accord: 2000612. [With his *Pieces (4) for orchestra; Uzxuctum, for chorus and orchestra*].

3903.2 *Canti del Capricorno* [for voice and instruments]. (Michiko Hirayama and others). Wergo: WER 60127-50.

3903.3 *Orchestral music. Selections.* (Polish Radio-Television Orchestra/Jurg Wyttenbach). Accord: 201112. [*Hurqualia; Hymnos; Chukrum*]. *See also* 3903.1

3903.4 * *Quartets (5) for strings.* (Arditti Quartet). Salabert/Actuels: SCD8904/5. 2CD set. [With his *Trio for strings* and *Khoom, for soprano and six instruments*].

3903.5 *Suite for piano no. 8 ("Bot-ba").* (Marianne Schroeder). Hat Hut: ART CD 6092. [With his *Sonatas for piano nos. 2–3; Adieu*].

3904 Schaeffer, Pierre, 1910–1995

Works. INA-GRM: INA C 1006/1009. 4CD set. [His complete electroacoustic music. Some works co-written with Pierre Henry].

3905 Schafer, R. Murray, 1933–

3905.1 *Magic songs* [for chorus and orchestra]. (Vancouver Chamber Choir/CBC Vancouver Orchestra/Jon Washburn). *See* 3830

3905.2 *Quartets for strings nos. 1–5.* (Orford Quartet). Centrediscs: CMC CD 3990/4090. 2CD set.

3906 Schat, Peter, 1935–

Selections. (Gerard Bouwhuis and others). Donemus: CV 19. [*Anathema, for piano; Canto general, for voice, violin, and piano; Thema, for oboe and chamber ensemble; To you, for soprano, chamber ensemble, tape, and live electronics*].

3907 Schnittke, Alfred, 1934–

3907.1 *Concerto for viola and orchestra.* (Kim Kashkashian/Saarbrücken Radio Symphony/Dennis Russell Davies). *See* 3800.2

3907.2 * *Concerto grosso no. 1.*
- (Gidon Kremer/London Symphony/Gennady Rozhdestvensky). *See* 3637.1
- (Gidon Kremer/Chamber Orchestra of Europe/Heinrich Schiff). Deutsche Grammophon: 429 413-2. [With his *Quasi una sonata, for violin and chamber orchestra; Moz-Art à la Haydn, for strings*].

3907.3 *Concerto grosso no. 3.* (Concertgebouw Orchestra/Riccardo Chailly). London: 430 698-2. [With his *Concerto grosso no. 4 ("Symphony no. 5")*].

3907.4 ** *Quintet for piano and strings.*

- Fred Oldenburg/Mondriaan Quartet). Etcetera: KTC 1124. [With his *Quartet for strings no. 3*].

- (Roland Pöntinen/Tale Quartet). Bis: CD-547. [With his *Kanon in memoriam Igor Stravinsky; Quartet for piano and strings; Trio for strings*].

3908 Schuller, Gunther, 1925–

3908.1 *Farbenspiel* [for orchestra]. (Louisville Orchestra/Lawrence Leighton Smith). *See 3757*

3908.2 *Quartet for strings no. 2.* (Emerson String Quartet). *See 4005*

3908.3 *Spectra* [for orchestra]. (Chicago Symphony/James Levine). *See 3721.19*

3908.4 * *Studies on themes of Paul Klee* [for orchestra]. (Minneapolis Symphony/Antal Dorati). *See 3574.1*

3909 Schuman, William, 1910–1992

3909.1 *Concerto for violin and orchestra.* (Paul Zukofsky/Boston Symphony/Michael Tilson Thomas). *See 3626.3*

3909.2 *The mighty Casey* [opera]. (Juilliard Opera/Gerard Schwarz). Delos: DE 1030. [With his *A question of taste*].

3909.3 *New England triptych* [for orchestra]. (St. Louis Symphony/Leonard Slatkin). RCA: 09026-61282-2. [With his *American festival overture; Symphony no. 10;* Ives, Charles: *Variations on America*].

3909.4 * *Symphony no. 3.* (New York Philharmonic/Leonard Bernstein). *See 3584.1*

3909.5 * *Symphony no. 10* ("American muse"). (St. Louis Symphony/Leonard Slatkin). *See 3909.3*

3910 Schwantner, Joseph, 1943–

3910.1 * *Aftertones of infinity* [for orchestra]. (Juilliard Orchestra/Leonard Slatkin). *See 3748.2*

3910.2 *In aeternum* [for chamber ensemble]. (Boston Musica Viva). *See 3998*

3911 Sculthorpe, Peter, 1929–

3911.1 *Orchestral music. Selections.* (Sydney Symphony/Stuart Challender). ABC: 426481-2. [*Earth cry; Irkanda no. 4; Small town; Kakadu; Mangrove*].

3911.2 * *Quartet for strings no. 8.* (Kronos Quartet). Elektra Nonesuch: 79111-2. [With Sallinen, Aulis: *Quartet for strings no. 3;* Glass, Philip: *Company;* Nancarrow, Conlon: *Quartet for*

strings no. 1; Hendrix, Jimi: *Purple haze* (arr. Steve Rifkin)].

3912 Shapero, Harold, 1920–

Symphony for classical orchestra. (Los Angeles Philharmonic/André Previn). New World: NW 373-2. [With his *Nine-minute overture*].

3913 Shapey, Ralph, 1921–

3913.1 * *Concertante no. 1* [for trumpet and chamber ensemble]. (Ronald Anderson/University of Chicago Contemporary Chamber Players/Ralph Shapey). New World: NW 355-2. [With his *Kroslish sonata, for violoncello and piano;* Silverman, Faye-Ellen: *Restless winds; Speaking alone; Passing fancies*].

3913.2 *Movements for wind quintet.* (New York Woodwind Quintet). *See 4015*

3913.3 *Quintet for brass.* (American Brass Quintet). *See 3709.3*

3914 Shchedrin, Rodion Konstantinovich, 1932–

Carmen suite [for orchestra, after the opera by Georges Bizet]. (Virtuosi of Moscow/Vladimir Spivakov). Olympia: OCD 108. [With his *Freski Dionisiia (Frescoes of Dionysus), for orchestra*].

3915 Shea, David

Prisoner [for ensemble]. (David Shea and others). Sub Rosa: 73.

3916 Sheng, Bright, 1955–

H'un = Lacerations (for orchestra). (New York Chamber Symphony/Gerard Schwarz). New World: 80407-2. [With his *The stream flows, for violin; Chinese love songs, for soprano, viola, and piano; My song, for piano*].

3917 Shields, Alice, 1943–

Apocalypse. Selections [opera for live and recorded singers and electronics]. (Michael Willson/Jim Matus/Alice Shields). CRI: CD 647.

3918 Speach, Bernadette, 1948–

Selections. (Bowery Ensemble). Mode: 16. [Album title: *Without borders.* Contents: *Moto, for trombone, percussion, and piano; Pensées, for guitar; Trajet, for trombone and percussion; Sonata for piano; Shattered glass, for percussion; Telepathy, for reciter and chamber ensemble*].

3919 * Spiegel, Laurie, 1945–

Cavis muris [computer music]. *See 3987*

3920 Staley, Jim

Don Giovanni [for instrumental ensemble]. (Jim Staley and others). Einstein: 002.

3921 Starer, Robert, 1924–

Selections. (Abraham Kaplan and others). CRI: CD 612. [*Ariel (cantata); Concerto a tre, for clarinet, trumpet, trombone, and string orchestra; Anna Margarita's will, for soprano and chamber ensemble*].

3922 Stockhausen, Karlheinz, 1928–

3922.1 ** *Gesang der Jünglinge (Youth songs)* [electroacoustic music]. Stockhausen-Verlag: CD 3. [With his *Etude* (electroacoustic); *Studies nos. 1–2* (electroacoustic); *Kontake, for piano, percussion, and electronics*].

3922.2 *Gruppen (Groups)* [for three orchestras]. (West German Radio Orchestra/Karlheinz Stockhausen/Bruno Maderna/Pierre Boulez). Stockhausen-Verlag: CD 5. [With his *Carré, for four orchestras and choruses*].

3922.3 *Harlekin (Harlequin)* [for clarinet]. (Suzanne Stephens). Stockhausen-Verlag: CD 25. [With his *Kleine Harlekin, for clarinet*].

3922.4 *Kontakte (Contacts)* [for piano, percussion, and electronics]. (Bernard Wambach/Mircea Ardeleanu). *See* 3922.13

3922.5 *Kontra-punkte (Counterpoint)* [for chamber ensemble]. (Karlheinz Stockhausen and others). Stockhausen-Verlag: CD 4. [With his *Zeitmaße, for wind quintet; Stop, for orchestra; Adieu, for wind quintet*].

3922.6 * *Mantra* [for piano four hands and electronics].

- (Andreas Grau/Götz Schumacher). Wergo: WER 6267-2.
- (Alfons Kontarsky/Aloys Kontarsky). Stockhausen-Verlag: CD 16.
- (Ivar Mikashoff/Rosalind Bevan). New Albion: NA025CD.

3922.7 * *Michaels Reise (Michael's journey)* [soloist's version for trumpet, chamber ensemble, and electronics, from the opera *Donnerstag aus Licht*]. (Markus Stockhausen and others). ECM: 78118-21406-2.

3922.8 * *Piano music. Selections.*

- (Herbert Henck). Wergo: WER 60135/36050. 2CD set. [*Pieces 1–11*].
- (David Tudor). Hat Hut: ART CD 6142. [*Pieces nos. 1–8, 11*].

3922.9 *Spiral* [for solo performer with shortwave receiver]. (Eberhard Blum). Hat Hut: ART CD 6132.

3922.10 *Stimmung (Tuning)* [for six voices].

- (Collegium Vocale Köln) [Paris version]. Stockhausen-Verlag: CD 12. 2CD set.
- (Singcircle). Hyperion: CDA66115.

3922.11 *Tierkreis (Zodiac)* [for variable instrumentation]. (Susanne Stephens and others) [version for clarinet, flute, trumpet, and piano]. Acanta: 43201.

3922.12 *Zeitmaße (Time measurements)* [for wind quintet]. (Sebastian Bell and others). *See* 3922.5

3922.13 * *Zyklus* [for percussionist]. (Mircea Ardeleanu). Stockhausen-Verlag: CD 6; or Koch Schwann Musica Mundi: 310 020 H1. [With his *Refrain, for three instrumentalists: Kontakte, for piano, percussion, and electronics*].

3923 Stone, Carl, 1953–

Electroacoustic music. Selections. New Albion: NA049CD. [Album title: *Mom's*].

3924 Subotnick, Morton, 1933–

3924.1 *Key to songs* [for chamber ensemble and electronics]. (California Ear Unit). New Albion: NA012CD. [With his *Return: a triumph of reason* (electroacoustic music)].

3924.2 * *Silver apples of the moon* [electroacoustic music]. Wergo: WER 2035-2. [With his *Wild bull* (electroacoustic music)].

3925 Takemitsu, Tōru, 1930–1996

3925.1 *A way a lone* [for string quartet]. (Tokyo Quartet). RCA: 09026-61387-2. [With Barber, Samuel: *Quartet for strings no. 1*; Britten, Benjamin: *Quartet for strings no. 2*].

3925.2 * *Dorian horizon* [for orchestra]. (Yomiuri Nippon Symphony/Hiroshi Wakasugi). *See* 3925.4

3925.3 *Quatrain* [for clarinet, violin, violoncello, piano, and orchestra]. (Tashi/Boston Symphony/Seiji Ozawa). Deutsche Grammophon: 423 253-2. [With his *A flock descends into the pentagonal garden, for clarinet, violin, violoncello, piano, and orchestra; Stanza no. 1, for chamber ensemble; Sacrifice, for chamber ensemble; Ring, for chamber ensemble; Valeria, for chamber ensemble*].

3925.4 * *Requiem* [for string orchestra]. (Yomiuri Nippon Symphony/Hiroshi Wakasugi). Victor

(Japan): VDC-5507. [With his *Dorian horizon; Arc, for piano and orchestra*].

3925.5 * *RiverRun* [for piano and orchestra]. (Paul Crossley/London Sinfonietta/Oliver Knussen). Virgin: 7 59020 2 (7 91180 2). [With his *Water-ways, for chamber ensemble; Rain coming, for chamber orchestra; Rain spell, for chamber ensemble; Tree line, for chamber orchestra*].

3926   Tan, Dun, 1957–

Nine songs ["ritual opera"]. (Tan Dun and ensemble). CRI: CD 603.

3927   Tavener, John, 1944–

3927.1 *Choral music. Selections.* (Tallis Scholars/ Peter Phillips). Gimell: CDGIM 005. [*Ikon of light; Funeral ikos; The lamb*].

3927.2 * *The protecting veil* [for violoncello and orchestra]. (Stephen Isserlis/London Symphony/ Gennady Rozhdestvensky). Virgin: 7 59052 2. [With Britten, Benjamin: *Suite for violoncello no. 3*].

3928   Teitelbaum, Richard, 1939–

3928.1 *Concerto grosso* ["for human concertino and robotic ripieno"]. (Anthony Braxton/George Lewis/Richard Teitelbaum). Hat Hut: ART CD 6004.

3928.2 * *Golem* ["interactive opera"]. (Shelley Hirsch and others). Tzadik: 7105.

3929   * Tenney, James, 1934–

Critical band, for chamber ensemble. (Rêlache). *See* 4024

3930   Tippett, Michael, 1905–

3930.1 * *Byzantium* [for soprano and orchestra]. (Faye Robinson/Chicago Symphony/Georg Solti). London: 433 668-2. [With his *Symphony no. 4*].

3930.2 *Concerto for double string orchestra.* (Academy of St. Martin-in-the-Fields/Neville Marriner). London: 421 389-2. [With his *Fantasia concertante on a theme of Corelli; Little music, for string orchestra*].

3930.3 * *Fantasia concertante on a theme of Corelli* [for string orchestra]. (Academy of St. Martin-in-the-Fields/Neville Marriner). *See* 3930.2

3930.4 *King Priam* [opera]. (Heather Harper/ Norman Bailey/London Sinfonietta/David Atherton). London: 414 241-2. 2CD set.

3930.5 *Quartets for strings nos. 1–4.* (Britten Quartet). Collins: 70062. 2CD set.

3930.6 *Symphony no. 2.* (Bournemouth Symphony/Richard Hickox). Chandos CHAN 9299. [With his *New year suite*].

3930.7 *Symphony no. 4.* (Chicago Symphony/ Georg Solti). *See* 3930.1

3931   Torke, Michael, 1961–

Orchestral music. Selections. (Baltimore Symphony/David Zinman). Argo: 433 071-2. [Album title: *Color music*. Contents: *Green; Purple; Ecstatic orange; Ash; Bright blue music*].

3932   Tower, Joan, 1938–

Orchestral music. Selections. (St. Louis Symphony/ Leonard Slatkin). Elektra Nonesuch: 79245-2. [*Silver ladders, for orchestra; Island prelude, for oboe and string orchestra; Music, for violoncello and orchestra; Sequoia, for orchestra*].

3933   Tudor, David, 1926–

3933.1 * *Indeterminacy* [collaboration with John Cage]. *See* 3719.11

3933.2 *Neural synthesis nos. 6–9* [electroacoustic music]. Lovely Music: LCD 1602. 2CD set.

3934   Turnage, Mark-Anthony, 1960–

Greek [opera]. (Richard Bernas and others). Argo: 440 368-2.

3935   * Tyranny, "Blue" Gene, 1945–

Keyboard music. Selections. ("Blue" Gene Tyranny/ Timothy Buckley). Lovely Music: LCD 1064. [Album title: *Free delivery*].

3936   Ung, Chinary, 1942–

Spiral [for violoncello, piano, and percussion]. (Aequalis). *See* 3991

3937   Ussachevsky, Vladimir, 1911–1990

Electroacoustic music. Selections. See 3984

3938   Ustvolskaia, Galina Ivanovna, 1919–

3938.1 ** *Compositions nos. 1–3.* (Schönberg Ensemble/Reinbert de Leeuw). Philips: 442 532-2.

3938.2 *Instrumental music. Selections.*

- (Schönberg Ensemble/Reinbert de Leeuw). [Series: Galina Ustvolskaya, vol. 1]. Hat Hut: ART CD 6115. [*Trio for clarinet, violin, and piano; Sonata for piano no. 5; Duet for violin and piano*].

- (Marianne Schroeder and others). [Series: Galina Ustvolskaya, vol. 2]. Hat Hut: ART CD

6130. [*Preludes for piano; Grand duet for violoncello and piano; Composition no. 1*].

3939 Van de Vate, Nancy, 1930–

Orchestral music. Selections. (Polish Radio-Television Orchestra/Janusz Mirynski). Vienna Modern Masters: VMM 3008. [*Distant worlds; Dark nebulae; Journeys; Concertpiece for violoncello and small orchestra*].

3940 * Vierk, Lois V., 1951–

Red shift no. 4 [for chamber ensemble]. (Cloud Nine Consort). *See* 3957

3941 Viñao, Alejandro, 1951–

3941.1 * *Son entero* [for voices and computer]. (Singcircle). Wergo: WER 2019-50. [With his *Triple concerto, for flute, violoncello, piano, and computer*].

3941.2 * *Toccata del maga* [computer music]. *See* 3967

3942 Volans, Kevin, 1949–

3942.1 *Hunting, gathering* [Quartet for strings no. 3]. (Balanescu Quartet). Argo: 440 687-2. [With his *Songlines (Quartet for strings no. 2)*].

3942.2 * *White man sleeps* [Two versions: for two harpsichords, viola da gamba, and percussion; and for string quartet]. (Deborah James and others). United: CD 88034. [With his *Mbira, for two harpsichords and percussion; She who sleeps with a small blanket, for percussion*].

3943 Weir, Judith, 1954–

3943.1 *Instrumental music. Selections.* (Domus and others). Collins: 14532. [Album title: *Distance and enchantment: chamber works of Judith Weir*].

3943.2 * *Operas. Selections.* (Linda Hirst and others). Novello: NVLCD 109. [*The consolations of scholarship; Missa del Cid; King Harald's saga*].

3944 Wilson, Olly, 1937–

Sinfonia. (Boston Symphony/Seiji Ozawa). New World: 80331-2. [With Harbison, John: *Symphony no. 1*].

3945 Wolff, Christian, 1934–

3945.1 * *Chamber music. Selections.* (Eberhard Blum and others). *See* 3982–3983

3945.2 *Piano music. Selections.* (Sally Pinkas). Mode: 43. [Album title: *Bread and roses, piano works 1976–1983*].

3946 Wuorinen, Charles, 1938–

3946.1 * *Fortune* [for clarinet, violin, violoncello, and piano]. (Group for Contemporary Music). Koch: 3-7242-2H1. [With his *Cello variations no. 2; Album leaf, for violin and violoncello; Violin variations; Tashi, for clarinet, violin, violoncello, and piano*].

3946.2 *Quartet for strings no. 2.* (Group for Contemporary Music). Koch: 3-7121-2H1. [With Harvey, Jonathan: *Quartet for strings*; Peterson, Wayne: *Quartet for strings no. 1*].

3946.3 * *Spinoff* [for violin, double bass, and bongos]. (Speculum Musicae). Bridge: BCD 9008. [With his *Blue bamboula, for piano; Pieces (6) for violin and piano; The long and the short, for violin; Fantasia, for violin and piano*].

3946.4 *Trios. Selections.* (Group for Contemporary Music). Koch: 3-7123-2H1. [*Horn, violin, and piano; Bass trombone, tuba, and double bass; Piano and strings; Piano, trombone, and percussion*].

3947 Xenakis, Iannis, 1922–

3947.1 *Evryali* [for piano]. (Yuji Takahashi). Denon: CO-1052. [With his *Herma*; Messiaen, Olivier: *Etudes de rythme*].

3947.2 * *Jalons* [for chamber ensemble]. (Ensemble InterContemporain/Pierre Boulez). *See* 3947.6

3947.3 * *Metastasis* [for orchestra]. (O.R.T.F. Orchestra/Maurice Le Roux). Chant du Monde: LDC 278 368. [With his *Eonta, for brass and piano; Pithprakta, for orchestra*].

3947.4 * *Mycenae-alpha* [for electronic tape]. *See* 3970

3947.5 *Nomos alpha* [for violoncello]. (Pierre Strauch). *See* 3947.6

3947.6 *Phlegra* [for chamber orchestra]. (Ensemble InterContemporain/Pierre Boulez). Erato: 2292-45770-2. [With his *Jalons, for chamber ensemble; Keren, for trombone; Nomos alpha, for violoncello; Thallein, for chamber ensemble*].

3947.7 *Psappha* [for percussion]. (Michael Pugliese and others). *See* 4021

3947.8 *Tetras* [for string quartet]. *See* 3992

3948 Young, La Monte, 1935–

3948.1 * *Dreams of China. Second dream of the high-tension line stepdown transformer (90 XII 9 ca. 9:35-10:52 PM NYC. Melodic version)* [for eight trumpets with Harmon mutes]. (Theatre of

Eternal Music Brass Ensemble). Gramavision: R2 79467.

3948.2 *On remembering a naiad* [for string quartet]. (Arditti Quartet). *See* 3994

3948.3 * *The well-tuned piano (81 X 25: 6:17:50-11:18:59 PM NYC)* [for piano]. (La Monte Young). Gramavision: 18-8701-2. 5CD set.

3948.4 *Young's dorian blues in G (93 I 14 ca. 8:54-ca. 10:54:17 PM NYC)* [for guitar, bass guitar, synthesizer, and drums]. (La Monte Young/Forever Bad Blues Band). Gramavision: R2 79487. 2CD set. [Album title: *Just stompin: live at the Kitchen*].

3949 Yun, Isang, 1917–1995

3949.1 *Chamber music. Selections.* (Nomos Quartet and others). CPO: 999 075-2. [*Quartet for strings nos. 3–4; Concertino for string quartet and accordion; Tapis, for string quintet*].

3949.2 * *Symphony no. 3.* (Pomerian Philharmonic/Takao Ukigaya). CPO: 999 125-2. [With his *Symphony no. 1*].

3950 Zappa, Frank, 1940–1993

3950.1 * *Civilization phaze III* [opera-pantomime, for synclavier, taped voices, and ensemble]. (Ensemble Modern/Frank Zappa). Zappa: CDDZAP 56. 2CD set.

3950.2 * *Instrumental music. Selections.*

- (Ensemble InterContemporain/Pierre Boulez). EMI: CDC 7 47125 2. [Album title: *The perfect stranger*].

- (Ensemble Modern/Frank Zappa). Barking Pumpkin: R2 71600. [Album title: *The yellow shark*].

3951 Zimmermann, Bernd Alois, 1918–1970

3951.1 * *Intercommunicazione* [for violoncello and piano]. (Michael Bach/Bernard Wambach). CPO: 999 198-2. [With his *Enchiridion, for piano; Sonata, for violoncello solo; Kurze Studien (Short studies), for violoncello*].

3951.2 * *Die Soldaten (The soldiers)* [opera]. (Mark Munkittrick/Nancy Shade/Stuttgart State Theatre Orchestra/Berhard Kontarsky). Teldec: 9031-72775-2. 2CD set.

3952 Zorn, John, 1953–

3952.1 * *Absinthe* [for instrumental ensemble]. (Naked City). Disk Union/Avant: R-300194 (004).

3952.2 * *Cobra* [for variable ensemble].

- (Naked City). Hat Hut: ART CD 2034.

- (Norman Yamada and others). Knitting Factory Works: KFW 124.

3952.3 * *Forbidden fruit* [for voice, string quartet, and turntables]. (Ohta Hiromi/Kronos Quartet/Christian Marclay). *See* 3952.5

3952.4 * *Naked City.* (Naked City). Elektra Nonesuch: 79238-2.

3952.5 *Spillane* [for narrator and ensemble]. (John Zorn and others). Elektra Nonesuch: 79172-2. [With his *Two-lane highway; Forbidden fruit*].

3953 Zwilich, Ellen Taaffe, 1939–

3953.1 *Instrumental music. Selections.* (New York Philharmonic/Zubin Mehta). New World: NW 372-2. [*Concerto grosso, for orchestra; Symbolon, for orchestra; Concerto for trumpet and five players; Double quartet for strings*].

3953.2 * *Symphony no. 1.* (Indianapolis Symphony/John Nelson). New World: NW 336-2. [With her *Prologue and variations, for string orchestra; Celebration, for orchestra*].

Anthologies and Recitals

3954 * *The aerial #4: a journal in sound.* Nonsequitur Foundation: AER 1991/4. [Hutchinson, Brenda: *Eeeyah!;* works by Peter Van Riper, Erik Belgum, Leif Brush, Elodie Lauten, Elise Kermani, Anna Homler and Steve Moshier, Joseph Weber, Patsy Rahn, N. Sean Williams].

3955 * *The AIDS Quilt songbook.* (William Parker and others). Harmonia Mundi: HMU 907602. [Works by Donald Wheelock, Fred Hersch, John Musto, Ned Rorem, Chris DeBlasio, David Krakauer, Annea Lockwood, Donald St. Pierre, William Bolcom, Richard Thomas, John Harbison, Carl Byron, Lee Hoiby, Elizabeth Brown, Ricky Ian Gordon].

3956 * *Bang on a Can live, vol. 1.* CRI: CD 628. [Works by Tom Johnson, William Doerrfeld, Scott Lindroth, Michael Gordon, Julia Wolfe, Evan Ziporyn, Allison Cameron].

3957 * *Bang on a Can live, vol. 2.* CRI: CD 646. [Works by Shelley Hirsch and David Weinstein, Lois V. Vierk, Jeffrey Brooks, Elizabeth Brown, David Lang, Jeffrey Mumford, Phil Kline].

3958 * *Bang on a Can live, vol. 3.* CRI: CD 671. [Works by Nick Didkovsky, Bunita Marcus, Mary Wright, Orlando Jacinto García, Paul Reller, Linda Bouchard].

3959 *CDCM computer music series, vol. 3.* Centaur: CRC 2045. [Works by Salvatore Martirano, John Melby, Sever Tipei, Scott A. Wyatt, Herbert Brün, Carla Scaletti].

3960 *CDCM computer music series, vol. 5.* Centaur: CRC 2076. [Alternate title: *Inner voices: music from the Winham Laboratory at Princeton University.* Works by Paul Lansky, Brad Garton, Andrew Milburn, Martin Butler, Frances White, Alicyn Warren].

3961 *CDCM computer music series, vol. 7.* Centaur: CRC 2047. [Works by Neil B. Rolnick, Pauline Oliveros, Julie Kabat, Barton McLean, Joel Chadabe].

3962 *Computer music currents, vol. 2.* Wergo: WER 2022-50. [Davidovsky, Mario: *Synchronisms no. 9;* works by Gottfried Michael Koenig, Denis Lorrain, Emmanuel Ghent, Daniel Arfib, Loren Rush].

3963 *Computer music currents, vol. 4.* Wergo: WER 2024-50. [Works by David Evan Jones, Michel Decoust, Charles Dodge, Jean-Baptiste Barrier, Trevor Wishart, Roger Reynolds].

3964 ** *Computer music currents, vol. 5.* Wergo: WER 2025-2. [Harvey, Jonathan: *Mortuos plango, vivos voco;* Saariaho, Kaija: *Jardin secret no. 1;* works by Denis Smalley, Mesias Maiguaschca, Gareth Loy].

3965 *Computer music currents, vol. 6.* Wergo: WER 2026-2. [Works by Horacio Vaggione, Thomas Kessler, Denis Smalley, Amnon Wolman, Chris Chafe].

3966 *Computer music currents, vol. 7.* Wergo: WER 2027-2. [Works by Richard Karpen, Jean-Claude Risset, Lars-Gunnar Bodin, Tracy L. Petersen, Frances White, Joji Yuasa].

3967 * *Computer music currents, vol. 11.* Wergo: WER 2031-2. [Viñao, Alejandro: *Toccata del maga;* works by Stanislaw Krupowicz, Charles Dodge, Douglas Fulton, Paul Lansky].

3968 *A confederacy of dances, vol. 1: concert recordings from the Roulette series, New York.* Einstein: 001. [Music by Bill Frisell, Christian Marclay, Thoban Djan, Zeena Parkins, Billy Bang, Anthony Coleman, David Weinstein, Chris Cochrane, Ron Kuivila, John Zorn, Guy Klucevsek, Shelley Hirsch, Ikue Mori, David Shea, Jim Staley, Jeanne Lee, Wadada Leo Smith].

3969 * *Dance mix.* (Baltimore Symphony/David Zinman). Argo: 444 454-2. [Works by Leonard Bernstein, John Adams, Aaron Jay Kernis, David Schiff, Libby Larsen, John Harbison, Michael Torke, Robert Moran, Dominick Argento, Michael Daugherty, Christopher Rouse].

3970 ** *Electro acoustic music: classics.* Neuma: 450-74. [Varèse, Edgard: *Poème electronique;* Babbitt, Milton: *Phonemena; Philomel;* Reynolds, Roger: *Transfigured wind no. 4;* Xenakis, Iannis: *Mycenae-alpha*].

3971 *Flies in the face of logic.* Pogus: 21008-2. [Works for computer-controlled piano by Steve MacLean, C. W. Vrtacek, Nick Didkovsky].

3972 * *From A to Z.* Starkland: ST-203. [Electroacoustic works by Tod Dockstader, Paul Dresher, Joseph Kasinskas, Joseph Lukasik, Pamela Z., Charles Amirkhanian, Phillip Kent Bimstein].

3973 *Group 180.* Hungaroton: HCD 12545. [Rzewski, Frederic: *Coming together—Attica;* Reich, Steve: *Music for pieces of wood;* plus works by László Melis and Tibor Szemzo].

3974 * *Imaginary landscapes: new electronic music.* Elektra Nonesuch: 79235-2. [Works by Ron Kuivila, Shelley Hirsch and David Weinstein, Neil B. Rolnick, Mark Trayle, Gordon Monahan, Laetitia de Compeigne Sonami, Maryanne Amacher, Alvin Lucier, David Tudor, Nicholas Collins, Christian Marclay, "Blue" Gene Tyranny].

3975 *Jewel box.* [Series: Tellus, no. 26]. Harvestworks: 26. [Lam, Bun-Ching: *EO-9066;* works by Anne LeBaron, Laetitia de Compeigne Sonami, Sussan Deihim, Bun-Ching Lam, Catherine Jauniaux and Ikue Mori, Mary Ellen Childes, Michelle Kinney].

3976 *Journeys: orchestral works by American women.* (Carolann Martin and others). Leonarda: LE 327. [Van de Vate, Nancy: *Journeys;* Gardner, Kay: *Rainforest;* Larsen, Libby: *Overture—parachute dancing;* Richter, Marga: *Lament;* Mamlok, Ursula: *Elegy;* Brockman, Jane: *Perihelion no. 2*].

3977 *Mini-mall.* [Series: Tellus, vol. 27]. Harvestworks: 27. [Works by Charlie Ahearn, Ken Montgomery, Ben Neill, Jin Hi Kim, Brenda Hutchinson, Kato Hideki, Pauline Oliveros and Fanni Green, Takehisa Kosugi].

3978 * *New music with guitar: selected works from volumes 1, 2, & 3.* (David Starobin and others).

Bridge: BCD 9009. [Works by Elliott Carter, Stephen Sondheim, Milton Babbitt, Tōru Takemitsu, John Anthony Lennon, Barbara Kolb, Hans Werner Henze].

3979 *New music with guitar, vol. 5.* (David Starobin and others). Bridge: BCD 9042. [Davidovsky, Mario: *Synchronisms no. 10*; works by Roger Reynolds, Tom Flaherty, Milton Babbitt, Mel Powell, John Anthony Lennon].

3980 *New music series, vol. 2.* Neuma: 450-72. [Reynolds, Roger: *Autumn island, for marimba*; Scelsi, Giacinto: *Incantations, for piano*; Berio, Luciano: *Sequenza no. 2, for harp*; Barney, Nancy: *Strings of light, for guitar and harpsichord*; Ferneyhough, Brian: *Cassandra's dream song, for flute*; Cogan, Robert: *Utterances, for soprano*].

3981 *New York guitars.* CRI: CD698. [Works for electric guitar by Nick Didkovsky, David First, Brandon Ross, Judy Dunaway, Loren Mazzacane Connors, Ken Valitsky, Phil Kline].

3982 * *The New York School.* (Eberhard Blum/Frances-Marie Uitti/Nils Vigeland). Hat Hut: ART CD 6101. [Works by Earle Brown, Morton Feldman, John Cage, Christian Wolff].

3983 *The New York School #2.* (Eberhard Blum/Steffen Schleiermacher/Jan Williams). [Works by Earle Brown, Morton Feldman, John Cage, Christian Wolff].

3984 *Pioneers of electronic music.* CRI: CD 611. [Works by Alice Shields, Mario Davidovsky, Vladimir Ussachevsky, Bulent Arel, Pril Smiley, Otto Luening].

3985 *Tone over tone: microtonal keyboard works.* (Loretta Goldberg and others). Opus One: 135. [Works by John Cage, Sorrel Hays, George Boziwick, John Eaton, Mathew Rosenblum, Constance Cooper].

3986 *The virtuoso in the computer age, vol. 2.* [CDCM computer music series, vol. 11]. Centaur: CRC 2133. [Works by Larry Austin, Gareth Loy, Chris Chafe and Dexter Morrill, Neil B. Rolnick, Rodney Waschka, Jon Appleton, Larry Polansky].

3987 * *The virtuoso in the computer age, vol. 3.* [CDCM computer music series, vol. 13]. Centaur: CRC 2166. [Austin, Larry: *La Barbara: the name, the sounds, the music*; Spiegel, Laurie: *Cavis muris*; La Barbara, Joan: *L'albero dalle foglie azzure*; Pope, Stephen Travis: *Kombination no. 11*].

3988 * *Wien modern.* (Vienna Philharmonic/Claudio Abbado). Deutsche Grammophon: 429 260-2. [Rihm, Wolfgang: *Depart*; Ligeti, György: *Atmospheres; Lontano*; Nono, Luigi: *Liebeslied*; Boulez, Pierre: *Notations 1–4*].

3989 * *The Yellow River: piano concerto.* (Yin Cheng-Zong/Czecho-Slovak Radio Symphony/Adrian Leaper). Marco Polo: 8.223412. [Composed collaboratively by Yin Cheng-Zong, Chu Wan-Hua, Sheng Li-Hong, Liu Zhuang].

Individual Artists

3990 * Abel-Steinberg-Winant Trio. *Set of five.* New Albion: 036. [Cage, John: *Nocturne*; Cowell, Henry: *Set of five*; Hovhaness, Alan: *Invocations to Vahakn*; Satoh, Somei: *Toki no mon*; Harrison, Lou: *Varied trio*].

3991 * Aequalis. *Aequalis.* New World: 80412-2. [Works by Martin Brody, Miriam Gideon, Rand Steiger, Mario Davidovsky, Chinary Ung].

3992 * Arditti Quartet. *Arditti.* Gramavision: R2 79440. [Beethoven, Ludwig van: *Grosse Fuge*; Seeger, Ruth Crawford: *Quartet for strings*; Nancarrow, Conlon: *Quartet for strings no. 3*; Reynolds, Roger: *Coconico—a shattered landscape*; Xenakis, Iannis: *Tetras*].

3993 Arditti Quartet. *From Italy.* Montaigne: MO 782042. [Music for string quartet by Luciano Berio, Sylvano Bussotti, Niccolò Castiglioni, Franco Donatoni, Bruno Maderna, Alessandro Melchiorre, Giacinto Scelsi, Salvatore Sciarrino, Stefano Scodanibbio, Marco Stroppa].

3994 Arditti Quartet. *U.S.A.* Auvidis Montaigne: MO 782010. [Music for string quartet by Conlon Nancarrow, Elliott Carter, Charles Ives, Jay Alan Yim, Morton Feldman, Alvin Lucier, La Monte Young, John Cage].

3995 Ashton, Graham. *The contemporary trumpet.* Virgin: CDC 5 45003 2. [Works by Peter Maxwell Davies, André Jolivet, Michel Nyman, Hans Werner Henze, Luciano Berio, George Fenton].

3996 Berberian, Cathy. *Cathy Berberian.* Stradivarius: STR 10017. [Recorded live in concert, 1966–67. Works by Luciano Berio, Henri Pousseur, John Cage].

3997 * Berberian, Cathy. *Magnificathy.* Wergo: 60054-50. [Works by Claudio Monteverdi, Claude Debussy, Sylvano Bussotti, John Cage, Kurt Weill,

George Gershwin, Paul McCartney, and Cathy Berberian].

3998 Boston Musica Viva. *Boston Musica Viva plays.* Delos: D/CD 1011. [Works by Joseph Schwantner, Charles Ives, Luciano Berio, Mario Davidovsky, Donald Harris].

3999 Bream, Julian. *Nocturnal.* EMI: CDC 7 54901 2. [Martin, Frank: *Quatre pièces brèves*; Britten, Benjamin: *Nocturnal*; Brouwer, Leo: *Sonata for guitar*; Takemitsu, Tōru: *All in twilight*; Lutoslawski, Witold: *Melodie ludowe*].

4000 ** Bream, Julian. *20th century guitar.* [Series: Julian Bream edition, vols. 12–13]. RCA: 09026-61595/96-2. 2CD set. [Works by Lennox Berkeley, Albert Roussel, Reginald Smith Brindle, Frank Martin, Hans Werner Henze, Alan Rawsthorne, William Walton, Federico Mompou, Maurice Ohana, Federico Moreno Torroba, Roberto Gerhard, Heitor Villa Lobos].

4001 Cassatt Quartet. *Cassatt.* CRI: CD 671. [Works for string quartet by Tina Davidson, Julia Wolfe, Eleanor Hovda, Andrew Waggoner, Daniel S. Godfrey].

4002 Delangle, Claude. *The solitary saxophone.* Bis: CD-640. [Stockhausen, Karlheinz: *In Freundschaft*; Berio, Luciano: *Sequenza nos. 7b and 9b*; Scelsi, Giacinto: *Maknongan*; *Ixor*; and *Three pieces*; Jolas, Betsy: *Episode no. 4*; Takemitsu, Tōru: *Distance*].

4003 Doctor Nerve. *Beta 14 ok.* Cuneiform: Rune 26. [Compositions by Nick Didkovsky].

4004 Double Edge. *U.S. choice.* CRI: CD 637. [Works for two pianos by Meredith Monk, Duke Ellington and Billy Strayhorn, Mel Powell, David Borden, Paul Bowles, Morton Feldman, James Tenney, "Blue" Gene Tyranny].

4005 * Emerson String Quartet. *The Emerson String Quartet plays 50 years of American music, 1919–1969.* New World: 80453-2. [Cowell, Henry: *Quartet euphometric*; Shepherd, Arthur: *Tryptich*; Harris, Roy: *Quartet no. 2*; Schuller, Gunther: *Quartet no. 2*; Imbrie, Andrew: *Quartet no. 4*].

4006 * Ensemble Wien-Berlin. *20th century wind quintets.* Sony: SK 48052. [Françaix, Jean: *Quintet no. 1*; Barber, Samuel: *Summer music*; Berio, Luciano: *Opus number zoo*; Eder, Helmut: *Quintet no. 3*; Ligeti, György: *Bagatelles*].

4007 Feinberg, Alan. *The American innovator.* Argo: 436 925-2. [Piano music by Leo Ornstein, John Adams, Ruth Crawford Seeger, Henry Cowell, Mario Davidovsky, John Harbison, Charles Tomlinson Griffes, Milton Babbitt, Conlon Nancarrow, John Cage, Charles Ives, Ralph Shapey, and Thelonious Monk].

4008 Glennie, Evelyn. *Drumming.* Catalyst: 09026 68195-2. [Lang, David: *The anvil chorus*; with other works for solo percussionist by Evelyn Glennie, Roberto Sierra, Frederic Rzewski, and others].

4009 Goldstein, Malcolm. *Sounding the new violin.* What Next?: WN 0005. [Works for solo violin by John Cage, Malcolm Goldstein, Pauline Oliveros, Ornette Coleman, Philip Corner, James Tenney].

4010 * Icebreaker. *Terminal velocity.* Argo: 443 214-2. [Works by Michael Gordon, Louis Andriessen, Gavin Bryars, Damian Le Gassick, David Lang].

4011 * Jacobs, Paul. *Paul Jacobs plays blues, ballads & rags.* Elektra Nonesuch: 79006-2. [Bolcom, William: *Ghost rags*; Copland, Aaron: *Piano blues*; Rzewski, Frederic: *North American ballads*].

4012 Josel, Seth. *Long distance.* CRI: CD 697. [Works for guitars by Sidney Corbett, James Tenney, Martin Bresnick, Eric Lyon, Aaron Jay Kernis].

4013 * London Chamber Orchestra. *Minimalist.* Virgin: 5 61121 2. [Adams, John: *Shaker loops*; Glass, Philip: *Facades*; *Company*; Reich, Steve: *Octet ("Eight lines")*; Heath, Dave: *The frontier*].

4014 New Music Consort. *Pulse.* New World: 80405-2. [Cage, John, and Lou Harrison: *Double music*; Cage, John: *Constructions nos. 2–3*; Cowell, Henry: *Pulse*; Sollberger, Harvey: *The two and the one*].

4015 New York Woodwind Quintet. *New York Woodwind Quintet.* New World: 80413-2. [Roseman, Ronald: *Double quintet for woodwinds and brass*; Powell, Mel: *Quintet for winds*; Bresnick, Martin: *Just time*; Shapey, Ralph: *Movements*].

4016 ** Newband. *Microtonal works, vol. 2.* Mode: 33. [Partch, Harry: *Daphne of the dunes*; works by Dean Drummond, Thelonious Monk, James Pugliese, Mathew Rosenblum].

4017 * Ohrenstein, Dora. *Urban diva.* CRI: CD 654. [Works for soprano and instruments by Scott Johnson, Ben Johnston, Linda Bouchard, Anne LeBaron, Anthony Davis].

4018 Oppens, Ursula. *American piano music of our times.* Music & Arts: CD 604. [Carter, Elliott: *Night fantasies;* Adams, John: *Phrygian gates;* plus short works by Conlon Nancarrow, William Bolcom, Michael Sahl, Julius Hemphill, Lukas Foss, David Jaggard].

4019 Oppens, Ursula. *American piano music of our time* [sic], *vol. 2.* Music & Arts: CD 699. [Nancarrow, Conlon: *Canons for Ursula;* Rzewski, Frederic: *Mayn Yingele;* Wuorinen, Charles: *Blue bamboula;* Picker, Tobias: *Old and lost rivers;* Harbison, John: *Sonata no. 1;* Davis, Anthony: *Middle passage*].

4020 * O'Riley, Christopher. *Christopher O'Riley, piano.* Albany: TROY038-2. [Helps, Robert: *Homage à Fauré;* Adams, John: *China gates; Phrygian gates;* Brief, Todd: *Nightsong;* Sessions, Roger: *Sonata no. 1*].

4021 Pugliese, Michael. *Perkin' at Merkin.* Mode: 25. [Works for percussion by Iannis Xenakis, Morton Feldman, Nils Vigeland, John Cage, Per Nørgård, Henry Mancini].

4022 Quintet of the Americas. *Never sing before breakfast: a decade of new music.* Newport: NPD 85512. [Mackey, Steven: *Never sing before breakfast;* works for wind quintet by Jeffrey Wood, Roberto Sierra, Julia Wolfe, Stuart Balcomb, Jacob Druckman, Ursula Mamlok].

4023 * Quintetto Arnold. *Musica per quartetto e quintetto a fiati.* Stradivarius: STR 33304. [Carter, Elliott: *Etudes and a fantasy for wind quartet; Quintet for woodwinds and horn;* Donatoni, Franco: *Blow;* Kurtág, György: *Quintet for woodwinds and horn;* Ligeti, György: *Pieces (10) for wind quintet*].

4024 Rêlache. *On edge.* Mode: 22. [Tenney, James: *Critical band, for chamber ensemble;* plus works by Paul A. Epstein and Thomas Albert].

4025 Rêlache. *Outcome inevitable.* O.O. Discs: 17. [Ashley, Robert: *Outcome inevitable;* Vierk, Lois V.: *Timberline;* Hovda, Eleanor: *Borealis music;* Ho, Fred Wei-han: *Contradiction, please!*].

4026 * Rough Assemblage (Composers' collective). *Construction and demolition.* Avant/Disk Union: AVAN 017. [Works by Mark Degliantoni, Norman Yamada, Eric Qin].

4027 Schvartz, Haydee. *New piano music from Europe and the Americas.* Mode: 31. [Pärt, Arvo: *Variationen zur Gesundung von Arinuschka; Für Alina;* Cage, John: *Perpetual tango (five realizations);* Scelsi, Giacinto: *Quattro illustrazioni;* Kagel, Mauricio: *An Tasten;* Berio, Luciano: *Brin; Leaf;* plus works by Gerardo Gandini, Gabriel Valaverde, Robert Schumann].

4028 S.E.M. Ensemble. *Virtuosity with purpose.* Ear-Rational: ECD 1034. [Works by Petr Kotík, Ben Neill, Jon Gibson, David Behrman].

4029 Solomon, Nanette Kaplan. *Character sketches: solo piano works by 7 American women.* Leonarda: LE 334. [Works by Victoria Bond, Tania León, Jane Brockman, Ruth Schonthal, Gwyneth Walker, Marga Richter, Judith Lang Zaimont].

4030 Stone, Dorothy. *None but the lonely flute.* New World: 80456-2. [Babbitt, Milton: *None but the lonely flute;* Feldman, Morton: *Trio for flutes;* Mosko, Stephen: *For Morton Feldman; Indigenous music no. 2;* Alexander, Katherine: *And the whole air is tremulous;* Cage, John: *Ryoanji*].

4031 Svard, Lois. *With and without memory.* Lovely Music: LCD 3051. [Piano works by "Blue" Gene Tyranny, William Duckworth, Robert Ashley].

4032 Wallace Collection. *The Wallace Collection.* Collins: 12292. [Works for brass ensemble by Elliott Carter, Michael Tippett, and others].

4033 * Wiesler, Manuela. *The Russian flute.* Bis: 419. [With Roland Pöntinen, piano. Prokofiev, Sergey: *Sonata for flute and piano;* Denisov, Edisson Vasilevich: *Pieces for flute and piano;* Taktakishvili, Otar: *Sonata for flute and piano;* Amirov, Fikret: *Pieces for flute and piano*].

Music of Colonial North America and the United States to about 1900

Compiled by
William E. Anderson

This chapter covers vocal and instrumental music of the thirteen colonies and the United States before 1900, as well as American popular music around the turn of the century and extending (for some of the song and ragtime collections) up to World War I. Most of this music predates mechanical recording processes, so that recorded performances are interpretations or reconstructions based on sheet music, manuscripts, or descriptions by observers from the period. There are three main sections: "Religious Music" (the earliest chronologically), "Political Songs," and "Popular Vocal and Instrumental Music" (including songs, band music, and ragtime). Some anthologies may encompass more than one category.

Religious Music

Anthologies

4034 ** *America sings, vol. 1: the founding years (1620–1800).* (Gregg Smith Singers). Vox Box: CDX-5080 (SVBX-5350). 2CD set. 1975. [Selections from the *Ainsworth Psalter, Bay Psalm Book,*

James Lyon's *Urania,* and by William Selby, William Billings, Timothy Swan, Jeremiah Ingalls, Andrew Law, Justin Morgan, Daniel Read, Johann Friedrich Peter, John Antes, Johannes Herbst, and others. Also includes secular songs by Francis Hopkinson].

4035 *An American Christmas: carols, hymns and spirituals, 1770–1870.* (Boston Camerata/Joel Cohen). Erato: 4509-92874-2. 1993.

4036 *The American vocalist: spirituals and folk hymns, 1850–1870.* (Boston Camerata/Joel Cohen). Erato: 2292-45818-2. 1991.

4037 * *Early American vocal music: New England anthems and Southern folk hymns.* (Western Wind). Nonesuch: 71276-4. AC. [1972]. [Music by William Billings, Andrew Law, Daniel Read, Justin Morgan, and others].

4038 * *Make a joyful noise: mainstreams and backstreams of American psalmody, 1770–1840.* (Oregon State University Choir). New World: 80255-2. [1978]. [Music by William Billings, Supply Belcher, Timothy Swan, Daniel Read, and others].

4039 *Music of the Shakers.* (Glee Clubs of Smith and Amherst Colleges). Smithsonian/Folkways: 5378. AC. [1976].

4040 *New England harmony: a collection of early American choral music.* (Old Sturbridge Singers). Smithsonian/Folkways: 32377. AC. 1964. [Music by William Billings, Daniel Read, Justin Morgan, Supply Belcher, and others].

4041 * *Rivers of delight: American folk hymns from the Sacred Harp tradition.* (Word of Mouth Chorus). Nonesuch: 71360-2. 1978. [Music by Jeremiah Ingalls, Daniel Read, William Walker, and others].

4042 *Simple gifts: Shaker chants and spirituals.* (Boston Camerata/Schola Cantorum of Boston/Shaker Community of Sabbathday Lake, Maine). Erato: 4509-98491-2. 1994.

4043 *Vermont harmony 1.* (University of Vermont Choral Union). University Choral Union: UCVU-250. AC. 1990. [Music by Justin Morgan, Elisha West, Jeremiah Ingalls, Hezekiah Moors, and others].

4044 *Vermont harmony 3.* (University of Vermont Choral Union). Philo: PH 1073. LP. 1981. [Music by Elisha West, J. West, Ebenezer Child, and Eliakim Doolittle].

Individual Artist

4045 Billings, William, 1746–1800

  4045.1 * *The continental harmonist: hymns and fuging tunes.* (Gregg Smith Singers). Premier: PRCD 1008. [1991].

  4045.2 ** *A land of pure delight: anthems and fuging tunes.* (His Majestie's Clerkes/Paul Hillier). Harmonia Mundi: HMU 907048. 1991.

Political Songs

Revolutionary and Federal Periods

4046 *Ballads of the American Revolution, vol. 1: 1767–1775.* (Wallace House). Smithsonian/Folkways: 2151 (FP-48-1). AC. [1953].

4047 *Ballads of the American Revolution, vol. 2: 1776–1781.* (Wallace House). Smithsonian/Folkways: 2152. AC. [1959].

4048 *Ballads of the War of 1812.* (Wallace House). Smithsonian/Folkways: 5002 (FP-48-4). 2AC set. [1954].

4049 ** *The birth of liberty: music of the American Revolution.* (Sherrill Milnes and others). New World: 80276-2. [1976].

4050 * *Tippecanoe and Tyler too: a collection of American political marches, songs, and dirges.* (Chestnut Brass Company). Newport Classics: NPD 85548. 1992.

4051 *Winners and losers: campaign songs from the critical elections in American history, vols. 1 and 2.* (Peter Janovsky). Smithsonian/Folkways: 37260/37261. 2 ACs. [1978–80].

Civil War Period

4052 *The Civil War: its music and its sounds.* (Eastman Wind Ensemble/Frederick Fennell). Mercury: 432591-2. 2CD set. 1960, 1962.

4053 *The Civil War music collector's edition.* (Hutchinson Family Singers/Morning Sun Singers/Doug Green/James Bryan/Jerry Perkins/Princely Players). Time-Life Music: R103-12. 3CD set. [1991].

4054 *Honor to our soldiers: music of the Civil War.* (Classical Brass). MusicMasters: 67075-2. [1991].

4055 * *Music of the Civil War.* (Americus Brass Band). Summit: DCD 126. 1991.

4056 ** *Songs of the Civil War: first recordings from original editions.* New World: NW 202-2. [1976].

4057 *Union and liberty!* (D. C. Hall's New Concert and Quadrille Band). Dorian: DOR-90197. 1993.

Individual Artist

4058 Work, Henry Clay, 1832–1884

Who shall rule this American nation?: songs of the Civil War era. (Joan Morris/Clifford Jackson/William Bolcom). Nonesuch: H-71317. LP. 1975. OP

Popular Vocal and Instrumental Music

General Anthologies

4059 *American piano music of the 18th century.* (William Nabore). Doron: DRC 3001. 1992. [Music by Alexander Reinagle, John Christopher Moller, James Hewitt, and William Brown].

4060 ** *Come and trip it: instrumental dance music, 1780s–1920s.* (Federal Music Society/Dick Hyman/Gerard Schwarz). New World: 80293-2. [1978].

4061 *Grand concert! vocal and instrumental music heard in 19th-century America.* (D. C. Hall's New Concert and Quadrille Band). Dorian: DIS-80108. 1991.

4062 ** *Homespun America: music for brass band, social orchestra & choral groups from the mid-19th century.* (Eastman Wind Ensemble/Eastman Chorale/Donald Hunsberger/Robert DeCormier). Vox Box: CDX-5088 (SVBX-5309). 2CD set. 1976. [Music by the Manchester Cornet Band, the Hutchinson Family, Stephen Foster, and others].

4063 * *Music of the Federal Era.* (Federal Music Society). New World: 80299-2. [1978]. [Music by Samuel Holyoke, Benjamin Carr, Oliver Shaw, Raynor Taylor, and others].

4064 * *19th-century American ballroom music: waltzes, marches, polkas & other dances.* (Smithsonian Social Orchestra and Quadrille Band/James Weaver). Nonesuch: H-71313. LP. 1974. OP

4065 *Over the hills and far away: being a collection of music from 18th-century Annapolis.* (David and Ginger Hildebrand). Albany: H103. [1990].

4066 * *Piano music in America, vol. 1: 19th-century popular concert and parlor music.* (Neely Bruce). Vox Box: SVBX 5302. 3LP set. [1972]. [Music by Louis Moreau Gottschalk, Henry Weber, George Bristow, Anthony Philip Heinrich, Carl Reinecke, and others]. OP

Songs

4067 ** *After the ball: a treasury of turn-of-the-century popular songs: highlights from Vaudeville.* (Joan Morris/William Bolcom). Nonesuch: 79148-2 (71304). 1974, 1976. [Music by Charles K. Harris, Joseph E. Howard, Harry Von Tilzer, Bob Cole, J. Rosamond Johnson, Paul Dresser, Ernest R. Ball, Kerry Mills, and others].

4068 * *Angels' visits and other vocal gems of Victorian America.* (Kathleen Battle/Rose Taylor/Raymond Murcell/Harmoneion Singers). New World: 80220-2. [1977].

4069 *Coney Island baby: the Society for the Preservation and Encouragement of Barber Shop Quartet Singing in America: 1990 top twenty barber shop quartets.* Pro Arte: CDD 559. [1990].

4070 * *The early minstrel show.* (Robert Winans and others). New World: NW 338. LP. 1980. [Music by Dan Emmett, Stephen Foster, Billy Whitlock, A. F. Winnemore, and others].

4071 * *The great sentimental age: songs by Foster, Ives, Hawthorne, Hanby, and others.* (Gregg Smith Singers/New York Vocal Arts Ensemble). Vox Box: CDX-5016. 2CD set. [1990].

4072 * *The hand that holds the bread: progress and protest in the Gilded Age (songs from the Civil War to the Columbian Exposition).* (Cincinnati's University Singers). New World: NW 267. LP. [1976]. [Music by Jesse Hutchinson, George F. Root, Henry Clay Work, Septimus Winner, Charles K. Harris, and others]. OP

4073 *Let's do it: Bolcom and Morris at Aspen.* (Joan Morris/William Bolcom). Omega: OCD 3004. 1989. [Music by Harry Von Tilzer, Cole Porter, Jerome Kern, Paul Dresser, Richard Rodgers, Hank Williams, and others].

4074 *Listen to the mockingbird.* (New York Vocal Arts Ensemble). Arabesque: Z6555. 1985. [Music by Will S. Hays, the Hutchinson Family, Henry Clay Work, Scott Joplin, Septimus Winner, Stephen Foster, Henry R. Bishop, and Joseph E. Howard].

4075 *"There's a good time coming" and other songs of the Hutchinson Family.* (Lucy Shelton and others). Smithsonian: 1020. LP. 1978. OP

4076 * *Where home is: life in nineteenth-century Cincinnati, crossroads of the East and West.* (John Aler/Clifford Jackson/Harmoneion Singers). New World: 80251-2. [1977].

Individual Artist

4077 Foster, Stephen Collins, 1826–1864

4077.1 * *American dreamer.* (Thomas Hampson/Jay Ungar/Molly Mason/David Alpher). Angel: CDC 54621. 1992.

4077.2 ** *Songs of Stephen Foster.* (Jan DeGaetani and others). Nonesuch: 79158-2 (71268). 1972.

4077.3 *Stephen Foster's social orchestra: a collection of popular melodies published in 1854: arranged as solos, duets, trios & quartets by Stephen Foster.* (Columbia Social Orchestra/Gunther Schuller). Columbia: M 32577. LP. [1974]. OP

Band Music

4078 * *Carnaval.* (Wynton Marsalis/Eastman Wind Ensemble/Donald Hunsberger). CBS: MK 42137. 1987. [Compositions by Jean-Baptiste Arban, Herbert L. Clarke, Jules Levy, Hermann Bellstedt, and others].

4079 *Cornet favorites; highlights from cousins.* (Gerard Schwarz/William Bolcom/Ronald Barron/ Kenneth Cooper). Nonesuch: 79157-2. 1973, 1976.

4080 *The golden age of brass, vols. 1–2.* (David Hickman/Mark H. Lawrence/American Serenade Band/Henry Charles Smith). Summit: DCD 114/ DCD 121. 1990, 1991. [Music by Arthur Pryor, Herbert L. Clarke, Alessandro Liberati, and others].

4081 ** *The golden age of the American march.* (Goldman Band). New World: 80266-2. [1976].

4082 *Listen to the mockingbird: American brass band music from the nineteenth century performed on original instruments.* (Chestnut Brass Company). Newport Classics: NPD 85516. 1990.

4083 * *The music of Francis Johnson and his contemporaries: early 19th-century Black composers.* (Chestnut Brass Company). MusicMasters: 7029-2-C. 1988.

4084 *Silks and rags: a turn-of-the-century band concert.* (Great American Main Street Band). Angel/ EMI: CDC 54131. 1990. [Music by Scott Joplin, Tom Turpin, Eubie Blake, Herbert L. Clarke, and others].

4085 * *The Sousa and Pryor bands: original recordings, 1901–1926.* New World: NW 282. LP. 1901–26. OP

4086 *Under the big top: 100 years of circus music.* (Great American Main Street Band/Sam Pilafian/ Mark Gould). Angel: CDC 54728. 1992. [Music by Henry Fillmore, Karl L. King, and others].

4087 ** *The Yankee brass band: music from mid-nineteenth century America.* (American Brass Quintet Brass Band). New World: NW 312-2. [1981].

Individual Artist

4088 Sousa, John Philip, 1854–1932

    4088.1 ** *A grand Sousa concert.* (Nonpareil Wind Band/Timothy Foley). Angel/EMI: CDC 54130. 1990.

    4088.2 *Great marches and incidental music.* (Wallace Collection/John Wallace). Nimbus: NI 5129. 1988.

    4088.3 * *The Original all-American Sousa!* (New Sousa Band/Keith Brion/Sousa Band/John Philip Sousa). Delos: DE 3102. 1917–29, 1990. [Compilation of original Sousa recordings together with modern performances].

Ragtime

4089 * *The greatest ragtime of the century.* Biograph: BCD-103. [1987]. [From piano rolls recorded 1915–31 by the composers: Eubie Blake, Jimmy Blythe, James P. Johnson, Scott Joplin, Jelly Roll Morton, and Fats Waller].

4090 ** *Heliotrope bouquet: piano rags 1900–1970.* (William Bolcom). Nonesuch: 71257-4. AC. [1970]. [Music by Scott Joplin, Tom Turpin, Louis Chauvin, Joseph F. Lamb, James Scott, Luckey Roberts, and Bolcom].

4091 *I'll dance till de sun breaks through: ragtime, cakewalks & stomps.* Saydisc: CD-SDL-336. 1898–1923. [Original performances by James Europe, Victor Minstrels, Sousa's Band, Arthur Collins, Conway's Orchestra, Six Brown Brothers, and others].

4092 * *Maple leaf rag: ragtime in rural America.* New World: NW 235. LP. 1927–64. [Performances by Bunk Johnson, Cow Cow Davenport, Blind Blake, Rev. Gary Davis, Gid Tanner, Bill Boyd, Merle Travis, and others]. OP

4093 *Max Morath plays the best of Scott Joplin and other rag classics.* Vanguard: VCD-39/40. [1972]. [Music by Joplin, James Scott, Arthur Marshall, Joseph Lamb, Tom Turpin, and others].

4094 ** *Ragtime: pianos, banjos, saxophones, cakewalks, brass bands, jass . . .* RCA (France): PM 45687. 2LP set. 1900–1930. [Performances by Jim Europe, Sousa's Band, Victor Military Band, Original Dixieland Jazz Band, Earl Fuller, and others].

4095 Blake, Eubie, 1883–1983

    4095.1 * *The 86 years of Eubie Blake.* Columbia: C2S 847. 2LP set. 1969. OP

    4095.2 *Memories of you.* Biograph: BCD-112. [1990]. [From piano rolls recorded by the composer (1917–21) and electrical recordings (1973)].

4096   Joplin, Scott, 1868–1917

4096.1   *The complete piano rags of Scott Joplin.* (William Albright). MusicMasters: 7061-2-C. 2CD set. 1989.

4096.2 * *Elite syncopations.* Biograph: BCD-102. [1987]. [Items 4096.2, 4096.3, and 4096.4 are recorded from piano rolls, some cut by Joplin himself in 1916].

4096.3   *The entertainer.* Biograph: BCD-101. [1987].

4096.4   *King of the ragtime writers.* Biograph: BCD-110. [1989].

4096.5 ** *Piano rags.* (Joshua Rifkin). Nonesuch: 79159-2. 1969–72.

4096.6 * *Piano works, 1899–1904.* (Dick Hyman). RCA: 7993-2-RG. 1975.

4096.7 ** *The red back book; Elite syncopations.* (New England Conservatory Ragtime Ensemble/ Southland Stingers/Gunther Schuller). Angel: CDC 47193 (36060). 1973–74.

4097   Lamb, Joseph F., 1887–1960.

A study in classic ragtime. (Joseph F. Lamb). Smithsonian/Folkways: 3562. AC. 1959.

4098 *   Matthews, Artie, 1888–1958, and James Scott, 1885–1938

Pastimes and piano rags. (William Bolcom). Nonesuch: 71299-4. AC. [1974].

Blues

Compiled by
William E. Anderson

T his chapter covers blues from its beginnings to the present in three sections: "General Anthologies," "Pre–World War II," and "Post–World War II." The chronological sections are further subdivided into anthologies and individual artists or groups. Consult the index for listings under regional and genre terms such as *blues revival, Chicago blues, Louisiana blues, Memphis blues, Mississippi Delta blues, piano blues, Texas and West Coast blues,* etc.

General Anthologies

**4099 ** *The blues: a Smithsonian collection of classic blues singers.* Smithsonian: 2550 (RD 101). 4CD set. 1923–85. [Blind Lemon Jefferson, Papa Charlie Jackson, Ma Rainey, Robert Johnson, Bessie Smith, Sippie Wallace, Barbecue Bob, Texas Alexander, Furry Lewis, Blind Willie Johnson, Gus Cannon, Tommy Johnson, Henry Thomas, Leroy Carr, Frank Stokes, Mississippi John Hurt, Lonnie Johnson, Charley Patton, Roosevelt Sykes, Memphis Minnie, Sleepy John Estes, Blind Boy Fuller, Memphis Jug Band, Mississippi Sheiks, Walter

Davis, Son House, Skip James, Bumble Bee Slim, Blind Willie McTell, Bill Broonzy, Kokomo Arnold, Big Joe Williams, Little Brother Montgomery, Peetie Wheatstraw, Sonny Boy Williamson, Jimmy Rushing, Joe Turner, Bukka White, Tampa Red, Big Maceo, Washboard Sam, T-Bone Walker, Tommy McClennan, Louis Jordan, Eddie "Cleanhead" Vinson, Charles Brown, Wynonie Harris, John Lee Hooker, Lightnin' Hopkins, Jimmy Witherspoon, Muddy Waters, Howlin' Wolf, Lowell Fulson, Jimmy Yancey, Big Mama Thornton, Junior Parker, Junior Wells, Elmore James, Memphis Slim, Bobby Bland, Buddy Guy, Lightnin' Slim, Otis Rush, Jimmy Reed, Ray Charles, Latimore, and others].

**4100 ** *Blues masters, vol. 1: urban blues.* Rhino: 71121. 1940–66. [Guitar Slim, Pee Wee Crayton, Otis Rush, Lowell Fulson, Bobby Bland, T-Bone Walker, Junior Parker, Little Johnny Taylor, Albert King, Erskine Hawkins, Jimmy Witherspoon, Johnny Otis, Charles Brown, Eddie "Cleanhead" Vinson, Dinah Washington, Joe Turner, and others].

**4101 ** *Blues masters, vol. 3: Texas blues.* Rhino: 71123. 1927–87. [Blind Lemon Jefferson, Charles

Brown, T-Bone Walker, Percy Mayfield, Gatemouth Brown, Freddie King, Lightnin' Hopkins, Big Mama Thornton, Stevie Ray Vaughan, Albert Collins, Johnny Copeland, and others].

4102 * *Blues masters, vol. 6: blues originals*. Rhino: 71127. 1928–65. [Sonny Boy Williamson, Howlin' Wolf, Otis Rush, Elmore James, Muddy Waters, Ann Cole, Robert Johnson, Henry Thomas, Slim Harpo, and others].

4103 ** *Blues masters, vol. 8: Mississippi Delta blues*. Rhino: 71130. 1928–68. [Charley Patton, Robert Johnson, B. B. King, Willie Brown, Tommy Johnson, Son House, Muddy Waters, Howlin' Wolf, Elmore James, and others].

4104 * *Blues masters, vol. 10: blues roots*. Rhino: 71135. 1950–76. [Ed. by Samuel Charters. Music by Robert Pete Williams, Lightnin' Hopkins, Mandingo griots, Jali Nyama Suso, Furry Lewis, and others].

4105 ** *Blues masters, vol. 11: classic blues women*. Rhino: 71134. 1921–54. [Mamie Smith, Trixie Smith, Ma Rainey, Sippie Wallace, Ida Cox, Bessie Smith, Victoria Spivey, Alberta Hunter, Billie Pierce, and others].

4106 ** *Blues masters, vol. 12: Memphis blues*. Rhino: 71129. 1927–54. [Frank Stokes, Memphis Jug Band, Gus Cannon, Jim Jackson, Furry Lewis, Memphis Minnie, Sleepy John Estes, Jack Kelly, Joe Hill Louis, B. B. King, Willie Nix, Howlin' Wolf, James Cotton, Junior Parker, Rufus Thomas, Roscoe Gordon, Bobby Bland, and others].

4107 * *The roots of the blues*. New World: 80252-2. 1959. [Ed. by Alan Lomax. Music by Fred McDowell, Lonnie Young, Bessie Jones, and others].

4108 * *The story of the blues*. Columbia: 30008. 2LP set. 1928–68. [Available in the UK as a 2CD set: CBS 468992 2]. [Mississippi John Hurt, Blind Willie McTell, Charley Patton, Blind Lemon Jefferson, Peg Leg Howell, Leadbelly, Barbecue Bob, Memphis Jug Band, Bessie Smith, Leroy Carr, Peetie Wheatstraw, Bo Carter, Robert Johnson, Bukka White, Memphis Minnie, Blind Boy Fuller, Brownie McGhee, Bill Broonzy, Joe Turner, Otis Spann, Elmore James, Johnny Shines, and others]. OP

Pre–World War II

This section covers the recorded legacy of the blues from the earliest discs in the 1920s through the end of World War II. Musicians active during this period whose recording careers extend beyond 1945 are listed here.

Anthologies

4109 *Afro-American blues and game songs*. Library of Congress: AFS L4. LP/AC. 1933–41. [Vera Hall, Muddy Waters, Sonny Terry, and others].

4110 *Afro-American folk music from Tate and Panola Counties, Mississippi*. Library of Congress: L 67. LP/AC. 1942, 1969–71.

4111 * *Afro-American spirituals, work songs and ballads*. Library of Congress: AFS L3. LP/AC. 1933–39.

4112 *Alabama blues*. Yazoo: 1006. 1927–31. [Ed Bell, Barefoot Bill, Jaybird Coleman, and others].

4113 *Altamont: Black stringband music from the Library of Congress*. Rounder: CD 0238. 1942–49.

4114 *Better boot that thing: great women blues singers of the 1920's*. RCA Bluebird: 07863-66065-2. 1927–30. [Alberta Hunter, Victoria Spivey, Bessie Tucker, Ida May Mack].

4115 * *The blues*. ABC Music: 836-046-2 (BBC 683). 1923–33. [Ma Rainey, Bessie Smith, Ida Cox, Victoria Spivey, Eva Taylor, Ethel Waters, and others].

4116 *Blues from the western states*. Yazoo: 1032. 1929–49. [Ramblin' Thomas, Little Hat Jones, Oscar Woods, Texas Alexander, and others].

4117 *Blues in the Mississippi night*. Rykodisc: RCD-90155. 1946. [Alan Lomax interviews Big Bill Broonzy, Sonny Boy Williamson, and Memphis Slim].

4118 * *Canned heat blues: masters of Delta blues*. RCA Bluebird: 07863-61047-2. 1928. [Furry Lewis, Tommy Johnson, Ishman Bracey].

4119 ** *Chicago blues*. RCA (France): NL 89588. 2LP set. 1935–42. [Jazz Gillum, Sonny Boy Williamson, Big Bill Broonzy, Tampa Red, Washboard Sam, Joe McCoy, and others].

4120 * *Cuttin' the boogie: piano blues and boogie woogie*. New World: NW 259. LP. 1926–41. [Meade Lux Lewis, Pete Johnson, Albert Ammons, Jimmy Blythe, and others]. OP

4121 *Favorite country blues: guitar-piano duets*. Yazoo: 1015. 1929–37. [Roosevelt Sykes, Blind Blake, Walter Davis, Leroy Carr, Cripple Clarence

Lofton, Bumble Bee Slim, Charlie Spand, and others].

4122 *The Georgia blues.* Yazoo: 1012. 1927–33. [Peg Leg Howell, Barbecue Bob, Sylvester Weaver, Charlie Lincoln, Bumble Bee Slim, Blind Blake, and others].

4123 * *Good time blues: harmonicas, kazoos, washboards and cow-bells.* Columbia: CK 46780. 1930–41. [Memphis Jug Band, Roosevelt Graves, Charlie Burse, Bernice Edwards, Sonny Terry, Curley Weaver, Joe McCoy, Buddy Moss, and others].

4124 ** *Grinder man blues: masters of the blues piano.* RCA: 2098-2-R. 1935–45. [Big Maceo Merriweather, Little Brother Montgomery, Memphis Slim].

4125 * *Guitar wizards.* Yazoo: 1016. 1926–35. [Carl Martin, Blind Blake, Tampa Red, William Moore, and others].

4126 *Harmonica blues.* Yazoo: 1053. 1928–36. [Jaybird Coleman, DeFord Bailey, Jazz Gillum, and others].

4127 ** *Legends of the blues, vol. 1.* Columbia: CK 46215. 1925–65. [Bessie Smith, Blind Lemon Jefferson, Mississippi John Hurt, Blind Willie McTell, Lonnie Johnson, Charley Patton, Leroy Carr, Peetie Wheatstraw, Robert Johnson, Blind Boy Fuller, Bill Broonzy, Memphis Minnie, Bukka White, Big Joe Williams, Son House, and others].

4128 ** *Legends of the blues, vol. 2.* Columbia: CK 47467. 1929–41. [Roosevelt Sykes, Texas Alexander, Barbecue Bob, Tampa Red, Walter Roland, Bumble Bee Slim, Robert Wilkins, Victoria Spivey, Charlie Spand, Champion Jack Dupree, Brownie McGhee].

4129 * *Let's get loose: folk and popular blues styles from the beginning to the early 1940s.* New World: NW 290. LP. 1916–42. [Yank Rachell, Pillie Bolling, Hattie Hudson, Clara Smith, Leroy Carr, Walter Roland, Joe McCoy, Tommy McClennan, Sonny Boy Williamson, Five Breezes, and others]. OP

4130 *Lonesome road blues.* Yazoo: 1038. 1926–41. [Skip James, Big Joe Williams, Sam Collins, Robert Lockwood Jr., Robert Petway, and others].

4131 * *Masters of the Delta blues: the friends of Charley Patton.* Yazoo: 2002. 1928–34. [Son House, Willie Brown, Tommy Johnson, Bukka White, Louise Johnson, and others].

4132 *Mean mothers: independent women's blues, vol. 1.* Rosetta: RRCD-1300. 1926–49. [Martha Copeland, Ida Cox, Lil Green, and others].

4133 *Negro blues and hollers.* Library of Congress: AFS L59. LP/AC. 1941–42.

4134 *Negro work songs and calls.* Library of Congress: AFS L8. LP/AC. 1933–40.

4135 * *New Deal blues.* Mamlish: 3801. LP. 1933–39. [Joe McCoy, Bo Carter, Walter Davis, Memphis Minnie, Bill Broonzy, Bumble Bee Slim, Scrapper Blackwell, and others].

4136 *News and the blues: telling it like it is.* Columbia: CK 46217. 1927–47. [Bessie Smith, Victoria Spivey, Blind Willie McTell, Mississippi John Hurt, Charley Patton, Blind Boy Fuller, Bukka White, Memphis Minnie, and others].

4137 *The piano blues: Paramount, vol. 1.* Magpie: CD01. 1928–32. [Charlie Spand, Little Brother Montgomery, Will Ezell, and others].

4138 *The piano blues: Paramount, vol. 2.* Magpie: CD05. 1927–32. [Meade Lux Lewis, Henry Brown, Will Ezell, and others].

4139 * *The piano blues: Vocalion.* Magpie: CD03. 1928–30. [Cow Cow Davenport, Romeo Nelson, Montana Taylor, Pinetop Smith, Joe Dean, and others].

4140 *Raunchy business: hot nuts and lollypops.* Columbia: CK 46783. 1928–39. [Lil Johnson, Lonnie Johnson, Lucille Bogan, Bo Carter, Mississippi Sheiks, and others].

4141 * *The roots of Robert Johnson.* Yazoo: 1073. 1927–37. [Skip James, Kokomo Arnold, Leroy Carr, Son House, Lonnie Johnson, Charley Patton, Mississippi Sheiks, Scrapper Blackwell, and others].

4142 * *The roots of rock.* Yazoo: 1063. 1928–31. [Memphis Minnie, Charley Patton, Bukka White, Skip James, Bo Carter, Blind Blake, Blind Willie McTell, Henry Thomas, Tommy Johnson, Robert Wilkins, Gus Cannon, and others].

4143 * *Singin' the blues.* MCA: MCA2-4064. 2LP set. 1937–55. [Jimmy Rushing, Ella Johnson, Louis Armstrong, Dinah Washington, Joe Turner, Wynonie Harris, Helen Humes, Rosetta Tharpe, Walter Brown, Trixie Smith, Lonnie Johnson, and others]. OP

4144 *Sissy man blues.* Mojo: 304 (Jass 13). 1924–41. [Harlem Hamfats, Tampa Red, Ma Rainey, Bessie Jackson, Victoria Spivey, Sippie Wallace, Monette Moore, Peg Leg Howell, and others].

4145 *The slide guitar: bottles, knives and steel, vol. 2.* Columbia: CK 52725. 1927–36. [Tampa Red, Casey Bill Weldon, Sylvester Weaver, Curley Weaver, and others].

4146 * *Songsters and saints: vocal traditions on race records, vol. 1.* Matchbox: 2001/2002. 2LP set. 1927–31. [Peg Leg Howell, Pink Anderson, Charley Patton, Bo Chatmon, Washington Phillips, Roosevelt Graves, Rev. A. W. Nix, and others].

4147 * *Songsters and saints: vocal traditions on race records, vol. 2.* Matchbox: 2003/2004. 2LP set. 1925–30. [Papa Charlie Jackson, Gus Cannon, Jim Jackson, Frank Stokes, Henry Thomas, Luke Jordan, Blind Blake, Rev. J. M. Gates, Arizona Dranes, Blind Joe Taggart, Blind Willie Johnson, and others].

4148 *Sorry but I can't take you: women's railroad blues.* Rosetta: RRCD-1301. 1923–42. [Trixie Smith, Clara Smith, Bessie Smith, Bertha "Chippie" Hill, Sippie Wallace, Martha Copeland, Lucille Bogan, and others].

4149 *St. Louis blues: the Depression.* Yazoo: 1030. 1929–35. [Henry Townsend, Charlie Jordan, Hi Henry Brown, Peetie Wheatstraw, and others].

4150 *Ten years in Memphis.* Yazoo: 1002. 1927–37. [Gus Cannon, Robert Wilkins, Furry Lewis, Frank Stokes, and others].

4151 ** *Wild about my lovin': Beale Street blues 1928–30.* RCA: 2461-2-R. 1928–30. [Memphis Jug Band, Cannon's Jug Stompers, Jim Jackson, Frank Stokes].

Individual Artists or Groups

4152   Barbecue Bob, 1902–1931
Chocolate to the bone. Yazoo: 2005. 1927–30.

4153   Blake, Blind, ca. 1890–ca. 1933
Ragtime guitar's foremost fingerpicker. Yazoo: 1068. 1926–30.

4154 * Broonzy, Big Bill, 1893–1958
Good time tonight. Columbia: CK 46219. 1930–40.

4155   Cannon's Jug Stompers
Cannon's Jug Stompers. Yazoo: 1082. 1927–30.

4156   Carr, Leroy, 1905–1935
4156.1 ** *Leroy Carr, 1930–1935.* Magpie: CD 07. 1930–35.
4156.2 *Leroy Carr, vol. 2.* Magpie: CD 17. 1929–35.

4157   Carter, Bo, 1893–1964
Twist it babe. Yazoo: 1034. 1931–40.

4158   Crudup, Arthur "Big Boy," 1905–1974
That's all right mama. RCA Bluebird: 07863-61043-2. 1941–54.

4159   Davis, Gary, Reverend, 1896–1972, and Pink Anderson, 1900–1974
Gospel, blues and street songs. Original Blues Classics/Fantasy: OBCCD-524-2 (Riverside 148). 1950, 1956.

4160   Dorsey, Georgia Tom, 1899–1993
Come on mama do that dance. Yazoo: 1041. 1928–32.

4161   Dupree, Champion Jack, 1910–1992
4161.1 *Blues from the gutter.* Atlantic: 82434-2. 1958.
4161.2 *New Orleans barrelhouse boogie.* Columbia: CK 52834. 1940–41.

4162   Estes, Sleepy John, 1899–1977
I ain't gonna be worried no more. Yazoo: 2004. 1929–41.

4163   Fuller, Blind Boy, 1907–1941
East Coast Piedmont style. Columbia: CK 46777. 1935–39.

4164   Green, Lil, 1919–1954
Lil Green, 1940–1947. Rosetta: RRCD-1310 (Bluebird). 1940–47.

4165   House, Son, 1902–1988
4165.1 *Delta blues: the original Library of Congress sessions.* Biograph: BCD-118. 1941–42.
4165.2 *Father of the Delta blues.* Columbia: C2K 48867. 2CD set. 1965.

4166   Hunter, Alberta, 1895–1984
4166.1 *Amtrak blues.* Columbia: CK 36430. 1979.
4166.2 *Young Alberta Hunter.* Mojo: 310 (Jass 6). 1922–40.

4167 Hurt, Mississippi John, 1894–1966

4167.1 * *Avalon blues: the complete 1928 OKeh recordings.* Columbia: CK 64986. 1928.

4167.2 *Mississippi John Hurt today.* Vanguard: VMD 79220. 1964.

4168 James, Skip, 1902–1969

4168.1 *Complete early recordings.* Yazoo: 2009 (Paramount). 1931.

4168.2 *Skip James today.* Vanguard: VMD 79219. 1966.

4169 Jefferson, Blind Lemon, 1897–1929

4169.1 * *Blind Lemon Jefferson.* Milestone: MCD-47022-2. 1926–29.

4169.2 *King of the country blues.* Yazoo: 1069. 1926–29.

4170 * Johnson, Lonnie, 1889–1970

Steppin' on the blues. Columbia: CK 46221. 1925–32.

4171 ** Johnson, Robert, 1911–1938

The complete recordings. Columbia: C2K 64916 (46222). 2CD set. 1936–37.

4172 Leadbelly, 1885–1949

4172.1 ** *Huddie Ledbetter's best.* Capitol: 92075. 1944. OP

4172.2 *King of the 12-string guitar.* Columbia: CK 46776. 1935.

4172.3 * *The Library of Congress recordings, vols. 1–3.* Rounder: CD 1044/CD 1046. 1934–40.

4172.4 *The Library of Congress recordings, vols. 4–6.* Rounder: CD 1097/CD 1099. 1934–40.

4173 McTell, Blind Willie, ca. 1898–1959

4173.1 *The complete Victor recordings.* RCA Bluebird: 07863-66718-2. 1927–32.

4173.2 * *The definitive Blind Willie McTell.* Columbia/Legacy: C2K 53234. 2CD set. 1929–33.

4174 Memphis Jug Band

The Memphis Jug Band. Yazoo: 1067. 1927–34.

4175 * Memphis Minnie, 1896–1973

Hoodoo lady. Columbia: CK 46775. 1933–37.

4176 * Mississippi Sheiks

Stop and listen. Yazoo: 2006. 1930–34.

4177 * Patton, Charley, 1887–1934

Founder of the Delta blues. Yazoo: 1020. 1929–34.

4178 Rainey, Ma, 1886–1939

4178.1 * *Ma Rainey.* Milestone: MCD-47021-2. 1924–28.

4178.2 *Ma Rainey's black bottom.* Yazoo: 1071. 1924–28.

4179 Smith, Bessie, 1894–1937

4179.1 ** *The collection.* Columbia: CK 44441. 1923–33.

4179.2 * *The complete recordings, vol. 1.* Columbia: C2K 47091. 2CD set. 1923–24.

4179.3 *The complete recordings, vol. 2.* Columbia: C2K 47471. 2CD set. 1924–25.

4179.4 * *The complete recordings, vol. 3.* Columbia: C2K 47474. 2CD set. 1925–28.

4179.5 *The complete recordings, vol. 4.* Columbia: C2K 52838. 2CD set. 1928–31.

4179.6 *The complete recordings, vol. 5: the final chapters.* Columbia: C2K 57546. 2CD set. 1931–33.

4180 Stokes, Frank, 1883–1954

Creator of the Memphis blues. Yazoo: 1056. 1927–29.

4181 Sykes, Roosevelt, 1906–1983

The honeydripper. Story of Blues: 3542-2. 1929–41.

4182 Tampa Red, 1904?–1981

4182.1 * *The complete Bluebird recordings, vol. 1.* RCA Bluebird: 07863-66721-2. 2CD set. 1934–36. [Other volumes forthcoming].

4182.2 *The guitar wizard.* Columbia/Legacy: CK 53235. 1932–34.

4183 * Thomas, Henry, 1874–ca. 1959

Texas worried blues. Yazoo: 1080. 1927–29.

4184 Turner, Joe, 1911–1985

I've been to Kansas City, vol. 1. Decca Jazz: MCAD-42351. 1940–41.

4185 Wallace, Sippie, 1898–1986

Women be wise. Alligator: ALCD 4810 (Storyville). 1966.

4186 Washboard Sam, 1910–1966

Rockin' my blues away. RCA Bluebird: 07863-61042-2. 1941–47.

4187 Weldon, Casey Bill, 1909– , and Kokomo Arnold, 1901–1968

Bottleneck trendsetters of the 1930s. Yazoo: 1049. 1934–37.

4188   Wheatstraw, Peetie, 1902–1941

The devil's son-in-law. Story of Blues: 3541-2. 1930–41.

4189   White, Bukka, 1909–1977

The complete Bukka White. Columbia/Legacy: CK 52782. 1937–40.

4190   Wilkins, Robert, 1896–1987

The original rolling stone. Yazoo: 1077. 1928–35.

4191   Williams, Big Joe, 1903–1982

Shake your boogie. Arhoolie: CD 315. 1960, 1969.

4192 *   Williamson, Sonny Boy, ca. 1914–1948, and Big Joe Williams, 1903–1982

Throw a boogie woogie. RCA Bluebird: 9599-2-R. 1937–41.

Post–World War II

This section covers blues since 1945, including some older artists whose recording careers did not begin until after World War II.

Anthologies

4193 *   *The best of Duke-Peacock blues.* Duke-Peacock: MCAD-10667. 1949–62. [Gatemouth Brown, Big Mama Thornton, Johnny Ace, Larry Davis, Junior Parker, Otis Rush, Bobby Bland, and others].

4194   *The best of the Chicago blues.* Vanguard: VCD-1/2. 1965. [Junior Wells, J. B. Hutto, Otis Rush, James Cotton, Johnny Shines, Walter Horton].

4195 *   *Blue flames: a Sun blues collection.* Rhino: 70962 (Sun). 1951–55. [Jackie Brenston, Howlin' Wolf, Rufus Thomas, Little Milton, James Cotton, Little Junior Parker, Doctor Ross, B. B. King, Roscoe Gordon, and others].

4196 *   *The blues is alright, vol. 1.* Malaco: 7430. 1976–85. [Z. Z. Hill, Little Milton, Denise LaSalle, Bobby Bland, Latimore, Johnny Taylor, and others].

4197 **   *Blues masters, vol. 2: postwar Chicago blues.* Rhino: 71122. 1950–62. [Muddy Waters, Howlin' Wolf, Buddy Guy, Little Walter, Sonny Boy Williamson, Jimmy Reed, Otis Rush, Magic Sam, and others].

4198   *Blues masters, vol. 4: harmonica classics.* Rhino: 71124. 1952–81. [Little Walter, Walter Horton, Junior Wells, James Cotton, Paul Butterfield, Sonny Boy Williamson, and others].

4199 **   *Blues masters , vol. 7: blues revival.* Rhino: 71128. 1959–69. [Mississippi John Hurt, Son House, Fred McDowell, John Lee Hooker, John Mayall, Albert King, Paul Butterfield, Canned Heat, and others].

4200 **   *Blues masters, vol. 9: postmodern blues.* Rhino: 71132. 1968–86. [Albert Collins, Robert Cray, Stevie Ray Vaughan, Earl Hooker, B. B. King, Bobby Bland, Son Seals, Magic Slim, Koko Taylor, Johnny Winter, Fabulous Thunderbirds, and others].

4201 *   *Chess blues.* Chess: CHD4-9340. 4CD set. 1947–67. [Muddy Waters, Little Johnny Jones, Robert Nighthawk, Jimmy Rogers, Howlin' Wolf, Memphis Minnie, Little Walter, Eddie Boyd, John Brim, Lowell Fulson, Sonny Boy Williamson, Buddy Guy, Elmore James, Little Milton, and others].

4202   *The Cobra Records story: Chicago rock and blues.* Capricorn: 42012-2. 2CD set. 1956–58. [Otis Rush, Buddy Guy, Magic Sam, Ike Turner, Walter Horton, Sunnyland Slim, and others].

4203   *Deep blues* [original soundtrack]. Anxious/ Atlantic: 82450-2. 1992. [R. L. Burnside, Big John Jackson, Frank Frost, Jack Owens, and others]. OP

4204 *   *Drop down mama.* Chess: CHD-93002 (411). 1949–53. [Robert Nighthawk, Johnny Shines, Floyd Jones, Arthur "Big Boy" Spires, David "Honeyboy" Edwards, and others].

4205 *   *Great bluesmen—Newport.* Vanguard: VCD-77/78. 1959–65. [Robert Pete Williams, Sonny Terry, Brownie McGhee, Son House, John Lee Hooker, Sleepy John Estes, Mississippi John Hurt, Skip James, Fred McDowell, Lightnin' Hopkins, and others].

4206   *The Jewel/Paula Records story: the blues, rhythm & blues and soul recordings.* Capricorn: 42014-2. 2CD set. 1965–89. [Little Johnny Taylor, Lightnin' Hopkins, Ted Taylor, Toussaint McCall, Frank Frost, Carter Brothers, Little Joe Blue, Buster Benton, and others].

4207 **   *Legends of guitar: electric blues, vol. 1.* Rhino: 70716. 1948–74. [Muddy Waters, Otis Rush, B. B. King, T-Bone Walker, Bobby Bland, Howlin' Wolf, Albert King, Elmore James, Johnny Winter, Earl Hooker, and others].

4208 * *Legends of guitar: electric blues, vol. 2.* Rhino: 70564. 1948–89. [B. B. King, Electric Flag, John Mayall, John Lee Hooker, Magic Sam, Freddie King, Muddy Waters, Lowell Fulson, Albert Collins, Gatemouth Brown, Snooks Eaglin, and others].

4209 *Living Chicago blues, vol. 1.* Alligator: ALCD 7701. [1978]. [Jimmy Johnson, Eddie Shaw, Carey Bell, and others].

4210 *Living Chicago blues, vol. 2.* Alligator: ALCD 7702. [1978]. [Lonnie Brooks, Magic Slim, Pinetop Perkins, and others].

4211 *Living Chicago blues, vol. 3.* Alligator: ALCD 7703. [1980]. [A. C. Reed, Sons of Blues, and others].

4212 *Living Chicago blues, vol. 4.* Alligator: ALCD 7704. [1980]. [Luther Johnson, Queen Sylvia Embry, and others].

4213 ** *Mean old world: the blues from 1940 to 1994.* Smithsonian: RB0007 (RD 110). 4CD set. 1940–94. [Memphis Minnie, Louis Jordan, Arthur Crudup, Leadbelly, T-Bone Walker, Dinah Washington, Cecil Gant, Big Maceo, Doctor Clayton, Sonny Boy Williamson, Roy Brown, Amos Milburn, Charles Brown, John Lee Hooker, Tampa Red, Robert Nighthawk, Professor Longhair, Lowell Fulson, Johnny Otis, Memphis Slim, Percy Mayfield, Elmore James, Howlin' Wolf, Bill Broonzy, Jackie Brenston, Little Walter, Eddie Boyd, Big Mama Thornton, Big Maybelle, Muddy Waters, Guitar Slim, J. B. Lenoir, Gatemouth Brown, Ray Charles, Jimmy Rushing, Joe Turner, Otis Rush, Johnny "Guitar" Watson, Elizabeth Cotten, Jack Dupree, Jimmy Witherspoon, Sonny Terry, Brownie McGhee, Fred McDowell, Robert Pete Williams, Mance Lipscomb, Freddie King, Lightnin' Hopkins, Junior Parker, Jimmy Reed, Bobby Bland, Albert Collins, B. B. King, Slim Harpo, Jimmy McCracklin, Koko Taylor, Johnny Shines, Albert King, Magic Sam, Little Johnny Taylor, Little Milton, Jimmy Johnson, Z. Z. Hill, Denise LaSalle, Roosevelt "Booba" Barnes, Junior Kimbrough, Taj Mahal, Buddy Guy, Billy Branch, and others].

4214 * *The new bluebloods.* Alligator: ALCD 7707. [1987]. [Kinsey Report, Valerie Wellington, Sons of Blues, Gloria Hardman, Lil' Ed and the Blues Imperials, and others].

4215 *Soul shots, vol. 4: urban blues.* Rhino: 75758. 196071. [T-Bone Walker, Bobby Bland, B. B. King, Otis Rush, Buddy Guy, Junior Parker, Little Milton, Lowell Fulson, Albert Collins, Z. Z. Hill, and others].

4216 * *Sound of the swamp: the best of Excello Records, vol. 1.* Rhino: 70896. 1956–65. [Slim Harpo, Lazy Lester, Silas Hogan, Carol Fran, Lonesome Sundown, Lightnin' Slim, and others].

4217 *Stroll on: an Immediate blues collection.* Immediate/Sony Music Special Products: AK 47348. [196?]. [Yardbirds, Rod Stewart, Cyril Davies, Jeff Beck, John Mayall, Albert Lee, Savoy Brown, Eric Clapton, Jimmy Page, and others].

4218 *Superblues: all-time classic blues hits, vol. 1.* Stax: SCD-8551-2. 1957–81. [B. B. King, Z. Z. Hill, Albert King, Howlin' Wolf, Jimmy Reed, Koko Taylor, Bobby Bland, Little Johnny Taylor, Little Milton, and others].

4219 *The SwingTime Records story: r&b, blues, and gospel.* Capricorn: 42024-2. 2CD set. 1946–52. [Lowell Fulson, Floyd Dixon, Jimmy Witherspoon, Pete Johnson, Ray Charles, Lloyd Glenn, Jimmy McCracklin, Joe Turner, and others].

4220 *Texas blues: Bill Quinn's Gold Star recordings.* Arhoolie: CD 352. 1947–51. [Lil' Son Jackson, L. C. Williams, Thunder Smith, and others].

4221 * *Texas music, vol. 1: postwar blues combos.* Rhino: 71781. 1947–70. [T-Bone Walker, Charles Brown, Frankie Lee Sims, Albert Collins, Gatemouth Brown, Johnny Copeland, Pee Wee Crayton, Amos Milburn, Ivory Joe Hunter, Freddie King, Goree Carter, Lester Williams, Zuzu Bolin, and others].

4222 * *Willie Dixon: the Chess box.* Chess: CHD2-16500. 2CD set. 1951–68. [Little Walter, Eddie Boyd, Willie Mabon, Muddy Waters, Howlin' Wolf, Lowell Fulson, Willie Dixon, Bo Diddley, Sonny Boy Williamson, Koko Taylor, Little Milton, and others].

Individual Artists or Groups

4223 * Ace, Johnny, 1929–1954

Johnny Ace memorial album. MCA: MCAD-31183 (Duke). 1952–54.

4224 Adams, Johnny, 1932–

    4224.1 *I won't cry: original Ron recordings.* Rounder: CD 2083 (Ron). 1959–63.

    4224.2 *Walking on a tightrope.* Rounder: CD 2095. 1989.

4225 Bland, Bobby, 1930–

    4225.1 ** *The best of Bobby Bland.* MCA: MCAD-31219 (Duke). 1957–66.

    4225.2 *I pity the fool: the Duke recordings, vol. 1.* Duke/MCA: MCAD2-10665. 2CD set. 1952–60.

4225.3 * *Turn on your lovelight: the Duke recordings, vol. 2.* Duke/MCA: MCAD2-10957. 2CD set. 1960–64.

4225.4 *Two steps from the blues.* MCA: MCAD-27036 (Duke). 1958–61.

4226   Brooks, Lonnie, 1933–

Bayou lightning. Alligator: ALCD 4714. 1979.

4227   Brown, Clarence "Gatemouth," 1924–

4227.1 *Alright again!* Rounder: CD 2028. 1981.

4227.2 *The original Peacock recordings.* Rounder: CD 2039. 1952–59.

4228   Butterfield, Paul, 1942–1987

4228.1 * *East West.* Elektra: 7315-2. 1966.

4228.2 *Paul Butterfield Blues Band.* Elektra: 7294-2. 1965.

4229   Canned Heat

Best of Canned Heat. EMI: 48377 (Liberty). 1967–73.

4230   Clay, Otis, 1942–

I'll treat you right. Bullseye Blues: BBCD 9520. 1992.

4231   Collins, Albert, 1932–1993

4231.1 ** *Ice pickin'.* Alligator: ALCD 4713. 1978.

4231.2 *Truckin' with Albert Collins.* MCA: MCAD-10423 (TFC). 1962–63.

4232   Collins, Albert, 1932–1993, Robert Cray, 1953– , and Johnny Copeland, 1937–

Showdown! Alligator: ALCD 4743. 1985.

4233 * Copeland, Johnny, 1937–

Texas twister. Rounder: CD 11504. [1977–85].

4234   Cray, Robert, 1953–

4234.1 *False accusations.* Hightone: HCD-8005. 1985.

4234.2 ** *Strong persuader.* Hightone/Mercury: 830568-2. 1986.

4235   Eaglin, Snooks, 1936–

Country boy down in New Orleans. Arhoolie: CD 348. 1959–60.

4236   Fabulous Thunderbirds

The essential Fabulous Thunderbirds. Chrysalis: 21851. 1979–82.

4237   Fulson, Lowell, 1921–

4237.1 *Hung down head.* Chess: CHD-9325 (408). 1954–61.

4237.2 *Tramp/Soul.* Flair/Virgin: 86300 (Kent). 1964–66.

4238   Guitar Slim, 1926–1959

Suffering mind. Specialty: SPCD-7007-2. 1953–55.

4239   Guy, Buddy, 1936–

4239.1 *Damn right, I've got the blues.* Silvertone: 1462-2-J. 1991.

4239.2 * *The very best of Buddy Guy.* Rhino: 70280. 1958–81.

4240   Harpo, Slim, 1924–1970

The best of Slim Harpo. Rhino: 70169. 1957–70.

4241   Heartsman, Johnny, 1937–

The touch. Alligator: ALCD 4800. 1991.

4242 * Hill, Z. Z., 1935–1984

Greatest hits. Malaco: 7437. 1980–84.

4243   Hooker, Earl, 1930–1970

Two bugs and a roach. Arhoolie: CD 324. 1952–53, 1968–69.

4244   Hooker, John Lee, 1917–

4244.1 *Don't turn me from your door.* Atlantic: 82365-2 (SD 7228). 1953, 1961.

4244.2 *The healer.* Chameleon: 74808-2. 1989.

4244.3 ** *The legendary Modern recordings.* Flair/Virgin: 39658 (Ace 315). 1948–54.

4244.4 *The ultimate collection.* Rhino: 70572. 2CD set. 1948–90.

4245   Hopkins, Lightnin', 1912–1982

4245.1 *Complete Aladdin recordings.* EMI: 96843. 2CD set. 1946–48.

4245.2 * *Gold Star sessions, vols. 1–2.* Arhoolie: CD 330/CD 337. 2 CDs. 1947–50.

4245.3 *Mojo hand: the Lightnin' Hopkins anthology.* Rhino: 71226. 2CD set. 1946–74.

4245.4 *Texas blues.* Arhoolie: CD 302. 1961–69.

4246   Howlin' Wolf, 1910–1976

4246.1 * *Howlin' Wolf: the Chess box.* Chess: CHD3-9332. 3CD set. 1951–73.

4246.2 ** *Moanin' in the moonlight.* Chess: CHD-5908. 1951–61. [Item 4246.1 covers material comparable to item 4246.2 but in greater depth and with better packaging and notes].

4247   Jackson, John, 1924–

Don't let your deal go down. Arhoolie: CD 378. 1965–69.

4248 ** James, Elmore, 1918–1963
The sky is crying: the history of Elmore James. Rhino: 71190. 1951–61.

4249 Johnson, Jimmy, 1928–
Johnson's whacks. Delmark: DD-644. 1978.

4250 King, Albert, 1923–1992
4250.1 *The best of Albert King.* Stax: FCD-60-005. 1968–73.
4250.2 ** *King of the blues guitar.* Atlantic: 8213-2 (Stax). 1966–68.
4250.3 *Live wire/blues power.* Stax: SCD-4128-2 (STS-2003). 1968.
4250.4 *The ultimate collection.* Rhino: 71268. 2CD set. 1953–84.

4251 King, B. B., 1925–
4251.1 *B. B. King: the king of the blues.* MCA: MCAD4-10677. 4CD set. 1949–91.
4251.2 * *Back in the alley.* MCA: MCAD-27010 (BluesWay). 1964–67.
4251.3 *Best of B. B. King, vol. 1.* Flair/Virgin: 86230 (RPM, Kent). 1953–62.
4251.4 ** *Live at the Regal.* MCA: MCAD-31106 (ABC 509). 1964.
4251.5 * *Singin' the blues/The blues.* Flair/Virgin: 86296 (Crown). 1951–58.

4252 * King, Freddy, 1934–1976
Hide away: the best of Freddie King. Rhino: 71510 (El-Bee/Federal/Cotillion/Shelter). 1956–70.

4253 Kinsey Report
Edge of the city. Alligator: ALCD 4758. 1987.

4254 Lenoir, J. B., 1929–1967
Natural man. Chess: CHD-9323 (410). 1951–57. OP

4255 Lewis, Smiley, 1920–1966
I hear you knockin': the best of Smiley Lewis. EMI: 98824. 1950–60.

4256 * Lipscomb, Mance, 1895–1976
Texas songster. Arhoolie: CD 306. 1960–64.

4257 Little Milton, 1934–
Welcome to the club: the essential Chess recordings. Chess/MCA: CHD2-9350. 2CD set. 1961–70.

4258 Little Walter, 1930–1968
4258.1 ** *The best of Little Walter.* Chess: CHD-9192. 1952–55. [Item 4258.3 covers material comparable to item 4258.1 but in greater depth and with better packaging and notes].
4258.2 *The blues world of Little Walter.* Delmark: DD-648 (Parkway). 1950–51.
4258.3 * *The essential Little Walter.* MCA Chess: CHD2-9342 (Checker). 2CD set. 1952–63.

4259 Lockwood, Robert, Jr., 1915–
Steady rollin' man. Delmark: DD-630. 1973.

4260 Magic Sam, 1937–1969
4260.1 *West Side guitar.* Paula: PCD-02 (Cobra). 1957–66.
4260.2 *West Side soul.* Delmark: DD-615. 1967.

4261 * Martin, Bogan, and Armstrong
Martin, Bogan and Armstrong; That old gang of mine. Flying Fish: FF 70003. 1974–77.

4262 Mayall, John, 1933–
4262.1 * *Blues Breakers.* London: 800086-2. 1965.
4262.2 *London blues.* Deram: 844302-2. 2CD set. 1964–69.

4263 ** McDowell, Fred, 1904?–1972
Mississippi Delta blues. Arhoolie: CD 304. 1964–65.

4264 Muddy Waters, 1915–1983
4264.1 ** *The best of Muddy Waters.* Chess: CHD-31268. 1948–54. [Item 4264.4 covers material comparable to item 4264.1 but in greater depth and with better packaging and notes].
4264.2 *The complete plantation recordings: the historic 1941–42 Library of Congress field recordings.* Chess: CHD-9344. 1941–42.
4264.3 *Muddy "Mississippi" Waters live.* Blue Sky/CBS: ZK 35712. 1979.
4264.4 * *Muddy Waters: the Chess box.* Chess: CHD3-80002. 3CD set. 1947–72.

4265 Neal, Kenny, 1957–
Walking on fire. Alligator: ALCD 4795. 1991.

4266 Nighthawk, Robert, 1909–1967
Bricks in my pillow. Pearl: 11 (United). LP. 1952.

4267 * Parker, Junior, 1932–1971
Junior's blues: the Duke recordings, vol. 1. Duke/MCA: MCAD-10669. 1954–64.

4268 ** Reed, Jimmy, 1925–1976
Speak the lyrics to me, Mama Reed. Vee-Jay: NVD2-705. 1953–62.

4269 Rogers, Jimmy, 1924–

Chicago bound. Chess: CHD-93000 (407). 1950–56.

4270 Rush, Otis, 1934–

4270.1 * *Cobra recordings.* Paula: PCD-01 (Cobra). 1956–58.

4270.2 *Right place, wrong time.* Hightone: HCD 8007. 1971.

4271 * Seals, Son, 1942–

Midnight Son. Alligator: ALCD 4708. 1976.

4272 Shaw, Robert, 1908–1985

The ma grinder. Arhoolie: CD 377. 1963–77.

4273 Shines, Johnny, 1915–1992, and Robert Lockwood Jr., 1915–

Dust my broom. Paula: PCD-14 (JOB). 1951–55.

4274 Spann, Otis, 1930–1970

4274.1 ** *Otis Spann is the blues.* Candid: CCD-79001. 1960.

4274.2 *Walking the blues.* Candid: CCD-79025. 1960.

4275 Taj Mahal, 1940–

Giant step/Ole folks at home. Columbia: CKG 18. 1969.

4276 Taylor, Hound Dog, 1917–1975

Hound Dog Taylor and the Houserockers. Alligator: ALCD 4701. 1971.

4277 * Taylor, Koko, 1935–

I got what it takes. Alligator: ALCD 4706. 1975.

4278 Taylor, Little Johnny, 1943–

Greatest hits. Fantasy: FCD-4510-2 (Galaxy). 1963–68.

4279 Terry, Sonny, 1911–1986, and Brownie McGhee, 1915–1996

4279.1 ** *Brownie McGhee and Sonny Terry sing.* Smithsonian/Folkways: SF 40011 (FA2327). 1957.

4279.2 *Hometown blues.* Mainstream/Legacy: JK 53625 (Sittin' In). 1948–52.

4280 Thornton, Willie Mae "Big Mama," 1926–1984

4280.1 *Ball n' chain.* Arhoolie: CD 305. 1965–68.

4280.2 *Hound dog: the Peacock recordings.* Peacock/MCA: MCAD-10668. 1952–57.

4281 * Vaughan, Stevie Ray, 1954–1990

The sky is crying. Epic: EK 47390. 1991.

4282 Walker, Joe Louis, 1949–

The gift. Hightone: HCD 8012. 1988.

4283 Walker, T-Bone, 1910–1975

4283.1 * *The complete Capitol/Black & White recordings.* Capitol: 29379. 3CD set. 1940–49.

4283.2 *The complete Imperial recordings.* EMI: 96737. 2CD set. 1950–54.

4283.3 *Complete recordings of T-Bone Walker 1940–1954.* Mosaic: MD6-130 (Black & White/Imperial). 6CD set. 1940–54.

4283.4 ** *Low down blues.* Charly: CD 7 (Black & White). 1942–49.

4283.5 ** *T-Bone blues.* Atlantic: 8020-2. 1955–57.

4284 Walton, Mercy Dee, 1915–1962

4284.1 *One room country shack.* Specialty: SPCD-7036-2. 1952–53.

4284.2 *Troublesome mind.* Arhoolie: CD 369. 1961.

4285 Ward, Robert, 1938–

Fear no evil. Black Top: 1063. 1991.

4286 Watson, Johnny "Guitar," 1935–1996

3 hours past midnight. Flair/Virgin: 86233 (RPM). 1955–56.

4287 Webster, Katie, 1939–

Swamp boogie queen. Alligator: ALCD 4766. 1988.

4288 Wells, Junior, 1934–

4288.1 *Blues hit big town.* Delmark: 640 (States). LP/AC. 1953–54.

4288.2 *Hoodoo man blues.* Delmark: DD-612. 1965.

4289 Williams, Robert Pete, 1914–1980

I'm blue as a man can be. Arhoolie: CD 394. 1959–60.

4290 Williamson, Sonny Boy (Rice Miller), 1899–1965

4290.1 ** *Down and out blues.* Chess: CHD-31272 (Checker). 1955–58. [Item 4290.2 covers material comparable to item 4290.1 but in greater depth and with better packaging and notes].

4290.2 * *The essential Sonny Boy Williamson.* Chess: CHD2-9343 (Checker). 2CD set. 1955–64.

4290.3 * *King Biscuit time.* Arhoolie: CD 310 (Trumpet). 1951, 1965.

4291 Winter, Johnny, 1944–

Scorchin' blues. Columbia: CK 52466. 1968–79.

22

Jazz

Compiled by
William E. Anderson

T his chapter covers the recorded legacy of jazz from its beginnings to the present. In addition to "General Anthologies," there are two main sections, "Pre–World War II" and "Post–World War II," comprising the various historico-stylistic currents of jazz such as New Orleans, swing, bebop, cool, hard bop, free, fusion, third stream, etc. (Consult the index for listings under these and other categories.) The fourth and concluding section is devoted to jazz singers.

General Anthologies

4292 *Classic jazz piano.* RCA Bluebird: 6754-2-RB. 1927–57. [Jelly Roll Morton, James P. Johnson, Earl Hines, Fats Waller, Art Tatum, Duke Ellington, Count Basie, Bud Powell, Erroll Garner, Oscar Peterson, Bill Evans, and others].

4293 * *The Commodore story.* Commodore/GRP: CMD2-400. 2CD set. 1938–50. [Eddie Condon, Billie Holiday, Don Byas, Lester Young, Coleman Hawkins, Benny Carter, Lee Wiley, Jelly Roll Morton, Bunk Johnson, Bob Wilber, Wild Bill Davidson, Bobby Hackett, Jack Teagarden, Pee Wee Russell,

Bud Freeman, Chu Berry, Art Hodes, Joe Sullivan, Jess Stacy, Willie "The Lion" Smith, Ralph Sutton, and others].

4294 *50 years of jazz guitar.* Sony Music Special Products: A2 33566. 2CD set. 1921–71. [Lonnie Johnson, Eddie Lang, Teddy Bunn, Dick McDonough, Carl Kress, Charlie Christian, Slim Gaillard, Django Reinhardt, George Van Eps, Hank Garland, Kenny Burrell, Eddie Durham, Herb Ellis, George Benson, Charlie Byrd, John McLaughlin, and others].

4295 *Forty years of women in jazz.* Jass: J-CD 9/10. 2CD set. 1926–59. [Lovie Austin, Mary Lou Williams, Ina Rae Hutton, Lil Armstrong, Mary Osborne, International Sweethearts of Rhythm, Dorothy Donegan, Valaida Snow, Marian McPartland, Melba Liston, Vi Redd, Barbara Carroll, and others].

4296 ** *Jazz piano: a Smithsonian collection.* Smithsonian: 7002 [box set from Smithsonian]; or RD-039-1/RD-039-4 [4 individual CDs from other distributors]. 4CD set. 1924–78. [Jelly Roll Morton, James P. Johnson, Willie "The Lion" Smith, Fats Waller, Earl Hines, Teddy Wilson, Jimmy Yancey,

Meade Lux Lewis, Pete Johnson, Count Basie, Mary Lou Williams, Art Tatum, Duke Ellington, Jess Stacy, Nat King Cole, Thelonious Monk, Erroll Garner, Bud Powell, Lennie Tristano, Dave McKenna, Oscar Peterson, Jimmy Rowles, Horace Silver, Martial Solal, Herbie Nichols, Hank Jones, Tommy Flanagan, John Lewis, Randy Weston, Ray Bryant, Bill Evans, McCoy Tyner, Chick Corea, Keith Jarrett, Herbie Hancock, and others].

4297 * *The legends of guitar: jazz, vol. 1.* Rhino: 70717. 1927–86. [Eddie Lang, Eddie Durham, Freddie Green, George Barnes, Charlie Christian, Tiny Grimes, Tal Farlow, Howard Roberts, Wes Montgomery, Lenny Breau, Billy Bauer, Larry Coryell, John McLaughlin, Jim Hall, Derek Bailey, John Scofield, and others].

4298 * *The legends of guitar: jazz, vol. 2.* Rhino: 70722. 1934–82. [Carl Kress, Dick McDonough, Oscar Moore, Johnny Smith, Django Reinhardt, Herb Ellis, Kenny Burrell, Joe Pass, Jim Hall, Pat Metheny, Ralph Towner, Mary Osborne, and others].

4299 ** *The Smithsonian collection of classic jazz.* Rev. ed. Smithsonian: 2502 [box set from Smithsonian]; or RD-033-1/RD-033-5 [5 individual CDs from other distributors]. 5CD set. 1916–81. [Scott Joplin, Jelly Roll Morton, Bessie Smith, King Oliver, Sidney Bechet, James P. Johnson, Louis Armstrong, Earl Hines, Bix Beiderbecke, Jimmie Noone, Fletcher Henderson, Red Nichols, Bennie Moten, Fats Waller, Meade Lux Lewis, Benny Goodman, Coleman Hawkins, Billie Holiday, Ella Fitzgerald, Art Tatum, Jimmie Lunceford, Gene Krupa, Roy Eldridge, Benny Carter, Lionel Hampton, Django Reinhardt, Duke Ellington, Count Basie, Lester Young, Charlie Christian, Don Byas, Dizzy Gillespie, Charlie Parker, Erroll Garner, Bud Powell, Dexter Gordon, Tadd Dameron, Lennie Tristano, Red Norvo, Stan Getz, Sarah Vaughan, Thelonious Monk, Horace Silver, Miles Davis, Gil Evans, Charles Mingus, Modern Jazz Quartet, Sonny Rollins, Clifford Brown, Max Roach, Wes Montgomery, Bill Evans, Cecil Taylor, John Coltrane, Ornette Coleman, World Saxophone Quartet].

Pre–World War II

Beginning with the earliest jazz recording in 1917, this section covers the first three decades of jazz history up to the beginning of the bebop period. Artists who established themselves during these years but whose careers extended further are listed here.

Anthologies

4300 *An anthology of big band swing.* Decca Jazz: GRD2-629. 2CD set. 1930–55. [Duke Ellington, Luis Russell, Fletcher Henderson, Mills Blue Rhythm Band, Don Redman, Dorsey Brothers, Earl Hines, Jimmie Lunceford, Claude Hopkins, Tiny Bradshaw, Count Basie, Casa Loma Orchestra, Bob Crosby, Andy Kirk, Louis Armstrong, Spud Murphy, Benny Carter, Jay McShann, Lucky Millinder, Jack Teagarden, Roy Eldridge, Woody Herman, Charlie Barnet, Lionel Hampton, Tommy Dorsey, Benny Goodman, and others].

4301 ** *Barrelhouse boogie.* RCA Bluebird: 8334-2-RB. 1936–41. [Jimmy Yancey, Meade Lux Lewis, Pete Johnson, Albert Ammons].

4302 ** *Big band jazz: from the beginnings to the fifties.* Smithsonian: 2202 (SMI-CD-030). 4CD set. 1924–56. [Paul Whiteman, Fletcher Henderson, McKinney's Cotton Pickers, Luis Russell, Casa Loma Orchestra, Jesse Stone, Missourians, Bennie Moten, Earl Hines, Chick Webb, Jimmie Lunceford, Benny Goodman, Andy Kirk, Tommy Dorsey, Count Basie, Charlie Barnet, Artie Shaw, Glenn Miller, Harry James, Benny Carter, Erskine Hawkins, Duke Ellington, Lionel Hampton, Woody Herman, Billy Eckstine, Boyd Raeburn, Dizzy Gillespie, Claude Thornhill, Elliot Lawrence, Stan Kenton].

4303 *Chicago, vol. 2.* ABC Music: 836-181-2 (BBC 589). 1926–34. [Jelly Roll Morton, King Oliver, Frankie Trumbauer, Benny Goodman, Earl Hines, and others].

4304 *Chicago/New York Dixieland: at the jazz band ball.* RCA Bluebird: 6752-2-RB. 1929–39. [Eddie Condon, Muggsy Spanier, Bud Freeman, Jack Teagarden, and others].

4305 *The Chicagoans: the Austin High gang.* MCA: 1350 (Decca 9231). LP. 1928–30. [Frank Teschemacher, Eddie Condon, Wingy Manone, and others]. OP

4306 *The Chocolate Dandies 1928–1933.* DRG/Swing: CDSW-8448. 1928–33. [Coleman Hawkins, Benny Carter, Fats Waller, Teddy Wilson, and others].

4307 *The Duke's men: small groups, vols. 1–2.* Columbia: C2K 46995; C2K 48835. 4 CDs in 2 vols. 1934–40. [Rex Stewart, Barney Bigard, Johnny Hodges, Cootie Williams].

4308 * *Early Black swing: the birth of big band jazz.* RCA Bluebird: 9583-2-RB. 1927–34. [Fletcher Henderson, Bennie Moten, Jimmie Lunceford, Duke Ellington, Earl Hines, McKinney's Cotton Pickers, Charlie Johnson, Missourians, and others].

4309 *52nd Street swing: New York in the '30s.* Decca Jazz/GRP: GRD-646. 1934–41. [Roy Eldridge, Spirits of Rhythm, Stuff Smith, John Kirby, Joe Marsala, Pete Brown, Hot Lips Page, Sam Price, and others].

4310 *From spirituals to swing.* Vanguard: VCD2-47/48. 2CD set. 1938–39. [Benny Goodman, Count Basie, Lester Young, James P. Johnson, Sidney Bechet, Joe Turner, and others].

4311 *Giants of traditional jazz.* Savoy/Denon: SV-0277. (12038/12050). 1944–52. [Mutt Carey, Sidney Bechet, and others].

4312 * *The great Ellington units.* RCA Bluebird: 6751-2-RB. 1940–41. [Rex Stewart, Johnny Hodges, Barney Bigard].

4313 *Great trumpets: classic jazz to swing.* RCA Bluebird: 6753-2-RB. 1927–46. [Henry "Red" Allen, Louis Armstrong, Bix Beiderbecke, Bunny Berigan, Roy Eldridge, Hot Lips Page, and others].

4314 *Hot town.* ABC Music: 836-188-2. 1926–33. [Bennie Moten, Andy Kirk, Duke Ellington, Mart Britt, Slatz Randall, and others].

4315 * *Jammin' for the jackpot: big bands and territory bands of the 1930's.* New World: NW 217. LP. 1929–41. [Casa Loma Orchestra, Andy Kirk, Earl Hines, Chick Webb, Cab Calloway, Bennie Moten, and others]. OP

4316 *The jazz age: New York in the twenties.* RCA Bluebird: 3136-2-RB. 1927–30. [Red Nichols, Miff Mole, Benny Goodman, Jack Teagarden, Tommy Dorsey, Jimmy McPartland, Joe Venuti, Eddie Lang, and others].

4317 *Jazz in New York.* Commodore/Pair: CCD-7009. 1944. [Bobby Hackett, Miff Mole, Muggsy Spanier, and others].

4318 *Jazz in the thirties.* DRG/Swing: CDSW-8457/58. 2CD set. 1933–35. [Benny Goodman, Joe Venuti, Eddie Lang, Gene Krupa, Bud Freeman, and others].

4319 * *Jazz odyssey, vol. 1: the sound of New Orleans.* Columbia: C3L 30. 3LP set. 1917–47. [Original Dixieland Jazz Band, Louis Armstrong, Luis Russell, Bunk Johnson, Jelly Roll Morton, King Oliver, Jimmie Noone, New Orleans Rhythm Kings, Sam Morgan, and others]. OP

4320 * *Jazz odyssey, vol. 2: the sound of Chicago.* Columbia: C3L 32. 3LP set. 1923–40. [King Oliver, Louis Armstrong, Eddie Condon, Bud Freeman, Jimmy Yancey, Earl Hines, Roy Eldridge, and others]. OP

4321 * *Jazz odyssey, vol. 3: the sound of Harlem.* Columbia: C3L 33. 3LP set. 1920–42. [Eubie Blake, James P. Johnson, Fletcher Henderson, Fats Waller, Cab Calloway, Claude Hopkins, Chick Webb, Erskine Hawkins, Frankie Newton, Billie Holiday, Benny Carter, Jimmie Lunceford, and others]. OP

4322 * *Jive at five: style makers of jazz.* New World: NW 274. LP. 1927–46. [Count Basie, Benny Goodman, Coleman Hawkins, Louis Armstrong, Earl Hines, Johnny Hodges, Duke Ellington/Jimmy Blanton, and others]. OP

4323 *Kansas City: hot jazz.* ABC Music: 846-222-2 (BBC 691). 1926–30. [Bennie Moten, Walter Page, George E. Lee, Andy Kirk, and others].

4324 * *Little club jazz: small groups in the 30's.* New World: NW 250. LP. 1928–41. [Joe Venuti, Red Norvo, Teddy Wilson, Henry "Red" Allen, Coleman Hawkins, Stuff Smith, and others]. OP

4325 *New Orleans, vol. 1.* ABC Music: 836-180-2 (BBC 588). 1918–34. [Jelly Roll Morton, King Oliver, Johnny Dodds, Louis Armstrong, Henry "Red" Allen, Original Dixieland Jazz Band, and others].

4326 *New Orleans jazz.* Arhoolie: CD 346. 1959–85. [Kid Thomas Valentine, Billie and Dede Pierce, New Orleans Rag Time Orchestra, Captain John Handy, George Lewis, Kid Howard, Punch Miller.]

4327 *New York, vol. 3.* ABC Music: 836-182-2 (BBC 590). 1925–35. [Fletcher Henderson, Duke Ellington, Luis Russell, Casa Loma Orchestra, Cab Calloway, Jimmie Lunceford, and others].

4328 *The 1930s: big bands.* Columbia: CK 40651. 1930–39. [Casa Loma Orchestra, Fletcher Henderson, Chick Webb, Benny Goodman, Duke Ellington, Count Basie, Earl Hines, Jimmie Lunceford, Cab Calloway, and others].

4329 *The 1930s: the small combos.* Columbia: CK 40833. 1930–39. [Lester Young, Roy Eldridge, Cootie Williams, Teddy Wilson, and others].

4330 * *Piano in style.* MCA: 1332. LP. 1926–30. [Jelly Roll Morton, James P. Johnson, Pinetop Smith]. OP

4331 *Pioneers of the jazz guitar.* Yazoo: CD-1057. 1928–37. [Eddie Lang, Lonnie Johnson, Carl Kress, Dick McDonough, and others].

4332 *Reminiscing at Blue Note: Blue Note's early classic piano sessions.* Blue Note: 28893. 1939, 1943. [Earl Hines, Pete Johnson, James P. Johnson].

4333 *Ridin' in rhythm.* DRG/Swing: CDSW-8453/54. 2CD set. 1933–37. [Duke Ellington, Fletcher Henderson, Benny Carter, Coleman Hawkins, and others].

4334 * *Riverside history of classic jazz.* Riverside/ Fantasy: 3RBCD-005-2. 3CD set. ca. 1900–1954. [Scott Joplin, Jelly Roll Morton, King Oliver, Louis Armstrong, Sidney Bechet, New Orleans Rhythm Kings, Bix Beiderbecke, James P. Johnson, Duke Ellington, Fletcher Henderson, and others].

4335 ** *Steppin' on the gas: rags to jazz.* New World: NW 269. LP. 1913–27. [Jim Europe, Freddie Keppard, Kid Ory, Sam Morgan, Johnny Dunn, New Orleans Rhythm Kings, Clarence Williams, Perry Bradford, and others]. OP

4336 * *Sweet and low: big bands and territory bands of the 1920's.* New World: NW 256. LP. 1926–33. [Erskine Tate, Jabbo Smith, Walter Page's Blue Devils, Alphonso Trent, and others]. OP

4337 *Swing is here: small band swing.* RCA Bluebird: 2180-2-RB. 1935–39. [Gene Krupa, Frankie Newton, Mezz Mezzrow, Wingy Manone, and others].

4338 ** *Swing that music! the singers, the soloists, and the big bands.* Smithsonian: 2602 (RD 102). 4CD set. 1929–56. [Louis Armstrong, Mildred Bailey, Ella Fitzgerald, Cab Calloway, Earl Hines, Benny Goodman, Harry James, Jimmy Dorsey, Tommy Dorsey, Count Basie, Billie Holiday, Gene Krupa, Duke Ellington, Bob Crosby, Charlie Barnet, Billy Eckstine, Sarah Vaughan, Dizzy Gillespie, Boyd Raeburn, Woody Herman, Stan Kenton, Chris Connor, and others].

4339 *Three great swing saxophones.* RCA Bluebird: 9683-2-RB. 1929–46. [Coleman Hawkins, Benny Carter, Ben Webster].

4340 *The women: classic female jazz artists.* RCA Bluebird: 6755-2-RB. 1939–52. [Mary Lou Williams, International Sweethearts of Rhythm, Beryl Booker, Hazel Scott, Mildred Bailey, Barbara Carroll, and others].

Individual Artists or Groups

4341 Allen, Henry "Red," 1908–1967

4341.1 * *Henry "Red" Allen.* RCA: LPV-556. 1929–56. OP

4341.2 *Memorial album.* Prestige: 7755. LP. 1962. OP

4341.3 *1929–1933.* Classics: 540. 1929–33.

4341.4 *1933–1935.* Classics: 551. 1933–35.

4341.5 * *World on a string.* RCA Bluebird: 2497-2-RB (LPM-1509). 1957.

4342 Ammons, Albert, 1907–1949, and Meade Lux Lewis, 1905–1964

The first day. Blue Note: 98450. 1939.

4343 Armstrong, Louis, 1901–1971

4343.1 *All-time greatest hits.* MCA: MCAD-11032 (Decca/Kapp). 1964, 1970.

4343.2 *The complete Decca Studio recordings of Louis Armstrong and the All Stars.* Mosaic: MD6-146. 6CD set. 1950–58.

4343.3 *Heart full of rhythm.* Decca Jazz: GRD-620. 1936–38.

4343.4 * *The Hot Fives, vol. 1.* Columbia: CK 44049. 1925–26.

4343.5 ** *The Hot Fives and Hot Sevens, vol. 2.* Columbia: CK 44253. 1926–27.

4343.6 ** *The Hot Fives and Hot Sevens, vol. 3.* Columbia: CK 44422. 1927–28.

4343.7 * *Laughin' Louie.* RCA Bluebird: 9759-2-RB. 1932–33.

4343.8 * *Louis Armstrong: highlights from his Decca years.* Decca Jazz: GRD2-638. 2CD set. 1924–58.

4343.9 ** *Louis Armstrong: portrait of the artist as a young man.* Columbia: C4K 57176/Smithsonian: 1700 (RD 105). 4CD set. 1923–34.

4343.10 ** *Louis Armstrong and Earl Hines 1928.* Smithsonian: 2002. 2LP set. 1928. [Items 4343.10 and 4343.11 cover similar material, but item 4343.10 also includes Earl Hines's piano solos]. OP

4343.11 ** *Louis Armstrong and Earl Hines, vol. 4.* Columbia: CK 45142. 1928.

4343.12 *Louis Armstrong of New Orleans.* MCA: MCAD-42328. 1927–50.

4343.13 *Louis Armstrong plays W. C. Handy.* Columbia: CK 64925 (CL 591). 1954.

4343.14 *Louis in New York, vol. 5.* Columbia: CK 46148. 1929.

4343.15 *Pops: the 1940s small band sides.* RCA Bluebird: 6378-2-RB. 1946–47.

4343.16 *Rhythm saved the world.* Decca Jazz: GRD-602. 1935–36.

4343.17 *Satch plays Fats.* Columbia: CK 40378 (CL 708). 1955.

4343.18 *St. Louis blues, vol. 6.* Columbia: CK 46996. 1930.

4343.19 *Stardust.* Portrait/CBS: RK 44093. 1931–32.

4343.20 * *You're drivin' me crazy, vol. 7.* Columbia: CK 48828. 1930–31.

4344 Armstrong, Louis, 1901–1971, and Duke Ellington, 1899–1974

The complete sessions. Roulette: 93844. 1961.

4345 * Armstrong, Louis, 1901–1971, and Ella Fitzgerald, 1918–1996

Ella and Louis. Verve: 825373-2 (4003). 1956.

4346 * Armstrong, Louis, 1901–1971, and Sidney Bechet, 1897–1959

Louis Armstrong and Sidney Bechet in New York. Smithsonian: 2026. 2LP set. 1923–25. OP

4347 Barnet, Charlie, 1913–1991

4347.1 *Clap hands, here comes Charlie.* RCA Bluebird: 6273-2-RB. 1939–41.

4347.2 *Drop me off in Harlem.* Decca Jazz: GRD-612. 1942–46.

4348 Basie, Count, 1904–1984

4348.1 * *April in Paris.* Verve: 825575-2 (8012). 1955–56.

4348.2 * *The best of the Roulette years.* Roulette: 97969. 1957–62.

4348.3 *Brand new wagon.* RCA Bluebird: 2292-2-RB. 1947.

4348.4 *Chairman of the board.* Roulette: 52032. 1959. OP

4348.5 ** *The complete Atomic Basie.* Roulette: 28635 (52003). 1957.

4348.6 ** *The complete Decca recordings.* Decca Jazz: GRD3-611. 3CD set. 1937–39.

4348.7 *Count Basie in London.* Verve: 833805-2 (8199). 1956.

4348.8 *Count Basie jam: Montreux '77.* Fantasy: OJCCD-379-2 (Pablo 2308 209). 1977. [Roy Eldridge, Benny Carter, Zoot Sims, Vic Dickenson, Al Grey, and others].

4348.9 ** *The essential Count Basie, vol. 1.* Columbia: CK 40608. 1936–39.

4348.10 ** *The essential Count Basie, vol. 2.* Columbia: CK 40835. 1939–40.

4348.11 *The essential Count Basie, vol. 3.* Columbia: CK 44150. 1940–41.

4348.12 *For the first time.* Pablo: PACD-2310-712-2. 1974.

4348.13 *The golden years, vol. 1.* EPM: FDC-5502. 1937.

4348.14 *Kansas City suite.* Roulette: 94575 (52056). 1960.

4349 Bechet, Sidney, 1897–1959

4349.1 * *The best of Sidney Bechet.* Blue Note: 28891. 1939–53. [Item 4349.2 covers material comparable to item 4349.1 but in greater depth and with better packaging and notes].

4349.2 *The complete Blue Note recordings of Sidney Bechet.* Mosaic: MD4-110. 4CD set. 1939–53. OP

4349.3 ** *The legendary Sidney Bechet.* RCA Bluebird: 6590-2-RB. 1932–41. [Item 4349.4 covers material comparable to item 4349.3 but in greater depth and with better packaging and notes].

4349.4 *Sidney Bechet: the Victor sessions: master takes.* RCA Bluebird: 2402-2-RB. 3CD set. 1932–43.

4349.5 *Sidney Bechet, 1940.* Classics: 619 (HRS). 1940.

4350 Beiderbecke, Bix, 1903–1931

4350.1 ** *Bix Beiderbecke, vol. 1: singin' the blues.* Columbia: CK 45450. 1927–28.

4350.2 *Bix Beiderbecke, vol. 2: at the jazz band ball.* Columbia: CK 46175. 1927–28.

4350.3 *Bix Beiderbecke and the Chicago cornets.* Milestone: MCD-47019-2 (Gennett). 1924–25.

4350.4 *Bix lives!* RCA Bluebird: 6845-2-RB. 1927–30.

4351 Berigan, Bunny, 1908–1942

The pied piper. RCA Bluebird: 07863-66615-2. 1934–40.

4352 Berry, Chu, 1910–1941

Chu Berry/Lucky Thompson: giants of the tenor sax. Commodore/Pair: CCD-7004. 1938–44.

4353 Byas, Don, 1912–1972

4353.1 *Don Byas on Blue Star.* EmArcy: 833405-2. 1947–52. OP

4353.2 *Savoy jam party.* Savoy: SV-0268 (SJL-2213). 1944–46.

4354 Calloway, Cab, 1907–1994

4354.1 * *Are you hep to the jive?* Columbia: CK 57645. 1939–47.

4354.2 *Best of the big bands.* Columbia: CK 45336. 1932–42.

4354.3 * *Cab Calloway featuring Chu Berry.* Columbia: CK 48901. 1937–39.

4355 Carter, Benny, 1907–

4355.1 *All of me.* RCA Bluebird: 3000-2-RB. 1934–59.

4355.2 * *Cosmopolite: the Oscar Peterson Verve sessions.* Verve: 314 521673-2 (MGV8226). 1952, 1954.

4355.3 * *Further definitions.* MCA: MCAD-5651 (Impulse 12). 1961.

4355.4 *Jazz giant.* Fantasy: OJCCD-167-2 (Contemporary 7555). 1957.

4355.5 *Montreux '77.* Fantasy: OJCCD-374-2 (Pablo 2308-204). 1977.

4355.6 *Over the rainbow.* MusicMasters: 5015-2-C. 1988.

4355.7 * *Symphony in riffs.* ASV: CD AJA 5075. 1930–37.

4356 Carter, Benny, 1907– , and the American Jazz Orchestra

Central city sketches. MusicMasters: 5030-2-C. 1987.

4357 Christian, Charlie, 1916–1942

4357.1 ** *Genius of the electric guitar.* Columbia: CK 40846. 1939–41.

4357.2 * *Live sessions.* Vogue: 600135 (Everest 219). 1941.

4357.3 * *Swing to bop: live sessions at Minton's Playhouse New York, May 1941.* Natasha: NI-4020. 1941. [Items 4357.2 and 4357.3 cover similar material].

4358 Clayton, Buck, 1911–1991

4358.1 *The complete CBS Buck Clayton jam sessions.* Mosaic: MD6-144. 6CD set. 1953–56.

4358.2 *A swingin' dream.* Stash: ST-CD-16. 1989.

4359 Cole, Nat King, 1917–1965

4359.1 * *Best of the Nat King Cole Trio: instrumental classics.* Capitol Jazz: 98288 (11033). 1944–47.

4359.2 *Hit that jive, Jack: the earliest recordings.* Decca Jazz/GRP: GRD-662. 1936, 1940–41.

4360 Condon, Eddie, 1905–1973

4360.1 *Dixieland all-stars.* Decca Jazz: GRD-637. 1939–46.

4360.2 *Dixieland jam.* Columbia: CK 45145. 1957.

4361 Condon, Eddie, 1905–1973, and Bud Freeman, 1906–1991

Jammin' at Commodore. Commodore/Pair: CCD-7007. 1938.

4362 Crosby, Bob, 1913–1993

South Rampart Street parade. Decca Jazz: GRD-615. 1936–42.

4363 Dodds, Johnny, 1892–1940

4363.1 *Blue clarinet stomp.* RCA Bluebird: 2293-2-RB. 1926–30.

4363.2 *South Side Chicago jazz.* MCA: MCAD-42326. 1927–29. OP

4364 Dorsey, Jimmy, 1904–1957

Contrasts. Decca Jazz: GRD-626. 1936–43.

4365 * Dorsey, Tommy, 1905–1956

Yes indeed! RCA Bluebird: 9987-2-RB. 1939–45. [Sy Oliver arrangements].

4366 Dorsey Brothers

Best of the big bands. Columbia: CK 48908. 1928–33.

4367 Edison, Harry "Sweets," 1915–

Edison's lights. Fantasy: OJCCD-804-2 (Pablo 2310 780). 1976.

4368 Eldridge, Roy, 1911–1989

4368.1 * *After you've gone.* Decca Jazz: GRD-605. 1936, 1943–46.

4368.2 * *Little jazz.* Columbia: CK 45275. 1935–40.

4368.3 *Little jazz: the best of the Verve years.* Verve: 314 523338-2. 1951–60.

4368.4 *The nifty cat.* New World: NW-349-2 (MJR). 1970.

4369 Eldridge, Roy, 1911–1989, with Gene Krupa, 1909–1973, and Anita O'Day, 1919–

Uptown. Columbia: CK 45448. 1941–49.

4370 Ellington, Duke, 1899–1974

4370.1 *Afro-Eurasian eclipse.* Fantasy: OJCCD-645-2 (9498). 1971.

4370.2 * *. . . and his mother called him Bill.* RCA Bluebird: 6287-2-RB (LSP 3906). 1967.

4370.3 ** *Beyond category: the musical genius of Duke Ellington.* RCA: 755174-9000-2/Smithsonian: 1601 (RD 104) (Victor/Bluebird/RCA). 2CD set. 1927–67.

4370.4 * *Black, brown & beige.* RCA Bluebird: 6641-2-RB. 3CD set. 1944–46.

4370.5 ** *The Blanton-Webster band.* RCA Bluebird: 5659-2-RB. 3CD set. 1940–42.

4370.6 * *Braggin' in brass.* Portrait/CBS: R2K 44395. 2CD set. 1938.

4370.7 *The Brunswick era, vol. 1.* Decca Jazz: MCAD-42325. 1926–29. [Item 4370.10 covers material comparable to items 4370.7 and 4370.20 but in greater depth and with better packaging and notes].

4370.8 *Carnegie Hall concert 1943.* Prestige: 2PRCD-34004-2. 2CD set. 1943.

4370.9 ** *Early Ellington.* RCA Bluebird: 6852-2-RB. 1927–34.

4370.10 * *Early Ellington: the complete Brunswick and Vocalion recordings of Duke Ellington.* Decca Jazz: GRD-3-640. 3CD set. 1926–31.

4370.11 *Ellington at Newport.* Columbia: CK 40587 (CL 934). 1956.

4370.12 * *The Ellington era, vol. 1.* Columbia: C3L 27. 3LP set. 1927–40. OP

4370.13 * *The Ellington era, vol. 2.* Columbia: C3L 39. 3LP set. 1927–40. OP

4370.14 *The Ellington suites.* Fantasy: OJCCD-446-2 (Pablo 2310-762). 1959, 1971–72.

4370.15 * *The Far East suite: special mix.* RCA Bluebird: 07863-66551-2 (LPM 3782). 1966.

4370.16 *Fargo, North Dakota November 7, 1940.* Jazz Classics: 5009 (VJC 1019/20). 2CD set. 1940.

4370.17 *The great Paris concert.* Atlantic: 304-2. 2CD set. 1963.

4370.18 *Happy-go-lucky local.* Discovery/Warner Bros.: 70052 (Musicraft). 1946.

4370.19 *Jubilee stomp.* RCA Bluebird: 66038-2. 1928–34.

4370.20 *The jungle band.* [Series: The Brunswick era, vol. 2]. Decca Jazz: MCAD-42348. 1929–31. [Item 4370.10 covers material comparable to items 4370.7 and 4370.20 but in greater depth and with better packaging and notes].

4370.21 *Jungle nights in Harlem.* RCA Bluebird: 2499-2-RB. 1927–32.

4370.22 *Latin American suite.* Fantasy: OJCCD-469-2 (8419). 1968.

4370.23 *Money jungle.* Blue Note: 46398 (United Artists). 1962.

4370.24 *New Orleans suite.* Atlantic: 1580-2. 1970.

4370.25 * *1939.* Smithsonian: 2010. 2LP set. 1939. OP

4370.26 * *The OKeh Ellington.* Columbia: C2K 46177. 2CD set. 1927–30.

4370.27 *Piano reflections.* Capitol: 92863 (H477). 1953.

4370.28 *Reminiscing in tempo.* Columbia: CK 48654. 1928–60.

4370.29 *Second sacred concert.* Prestige: PRCD-24045-2 (Fantasy 8407/8). 1968.

4370.30 *Solos, duets and trios.* RCA Bluebird: 2178-2-RB. 1932–67.

4370.31 * *Such sweet thunder.* Columbia: COL 469140-2 (CL 1033). 1957.

4370.32 *Three suites.* Columbia: CK 46825. 1960.

4370.33 *Uptown.* Columbia: CK 40836. 1951–52.

4371 Ellington, Duke, 1899–1974, and Johnny Hodges, 1907–1970

4371.1 * *Back to back.* Verve: 823637-2 (8317). 1959.

4371.2 *Side by side.* Verve: 821578-2 (8345). 1958–59.

4372 Ellington, Duke, 1899–1974, and Ray Brown, 1926–

This one's for Blanton. Fantasy: OJCCD-810-2 (Pablo 2310-721). 1973.

4373 Garner, Erroll, 1921–1977

4373.1 * *Concert by the sea.* Columbia: CK 40589 (9821). 1955.

4373.2 *The original Misty.* Mercury: 834910-2. 1954–55.

4373.3 *Penthouse serenade.* Savoy/Denon: SV-0162. 1945, 1949.

4373.4 *Play piano play.* Spotlite: SPJ 119 (Dial). LP. 1947.

4374 Goodman, Benny, 1909–1986

4374.1 ** *After you've gone.* RCA Bluebird: 5631-2-RB. 1935–36.

4374.2 *All the cats join in, vol. 3.* Columbia: CK 44158. 1941–46.

4374.3 *Avalon: the small bands, vol. 2.* RCA Bluebird: 2273-2-RB. 1937–39.

4374.4 *Benny Goodman Sextet, featuring Charlie Christian.* Columbia: CK 45144. 1939–41.

4374.5 *The birth of swing.* RCA Bluebird: 61038-2. 3CD set. 1935–36.

4374.6 *Clarinet a la king, vol. 2.* Columbia: CK 40834. 1939–41.

4374.7 * *The Harry James years, vol. 1.* RCA Bluebird: 66155-2. 1937–38.

4374.8 * *Live at Carnegie Hall.* Columbia: G2K 40244 (OSL 160). 2CD set. 1938.

4374.9 *On the air.* Columbia: C2K 48836. 2CD set. 1937–38.

4374.10 *Roll 'em, vol. 1.* Columbia: CK 40588. 1937–39.

4374.11 ** *Sing sing sing.* RCA Bluebird: 5630-2-RB. 1935–38.

4374.12 *Undercurrent blues.* Capitol Jazz: 32086. 1947–49.

4375 Goodman, Benny, 1909–1986, and Jack Teagarden, 1905–1964

B.G. and Big Tea in New York. Decca Jazz: GRD-609. 1928–34.

4376 Grappelli, Stéphane, 1908–

4376.1 *Stephane Grappelli.* [Series: Verve jazz masters, vol. 11]. Verve: 314 516758-2. 1966–92.

4376.2 *Tivoli gardens.* Fantasy: OJCCD-441-2 (Pablo 2308-220). 1979.

4377 Gray, Glen, 1906–1963

Best of the big bands. Columbia: CK 45345. 1931–34. [With the Casa Loma Orchestra].

4378 Hackett, Bobby, 1915–1976, and Jack Teagarden, 1905–1964

Coast concert; Jazz ultimate. Dormouse International: DMI CDX 02 (Capitol 933/962). 1955, 1957. [Note: These two sessions are also available on a box set: Jack Teagarden, *The complete Capitol fifties Jack Teagarden sessions,* Mosaic: MD4-168, 4CD set, which also includes some less significant big band sessions.]

4379 Hampton, Lionel, 1909–

4379.1 * *Flying home.* Decca Jazz: MCAD-42349. 1942–45.

4379.2 * *Hot mallets.* RCA Bluebird: 6458-2-RB. 1937–39.

4379.3 *Jumpin' jive.* RCA Bluebird: 2433-2-RB. 1937–39.

4379.4 *Lionel Hampton with Oscar Peterson.* [Series: Verve jazz masters, vol. 26]. Verve: 314 521853-2. 1953–54.

4379.5 *Midnight sun.* Decca Jazz: GRD-625. 1946–47.

4379.6 *Tempo and swing.* RCA Bluebird: 66039-2. 1939–40.

4380 Hawkins, Coleman, 1904–1969

4380.1 *Bean and the boys.* Prestige: PRCD-24124-2. 1944–59.

4380.2 ** *Body and soul.* Victor Jazz: 09026-68515-2 (Bluebird 5717). 1939–56. [Items 4380.3 and 4380.2 include similar material].

4380.3 * *Coleman Hawkins: a retrospective.* RCA Bluebird: 07863-66617-2. 2CD set. 1929–63.

4380.4 * *The complete Coleman Hawkins on Keynote.* Mercury: 830960-2. 4CD set. 1944.

4380.5 *Giants of the tenor sax: Coleman Hawkins/Frank Wess.* Commodore/Pair: CCD-7003. 1940–43.

4380.6 *The high and mighty Hawk.* London: 820600-2 (Felsted). 1958.

4380.7 *Hollywood stampede.* Capitol: 92596 (11030). 1945–47.

4381 ** Hawkins, Coleman, 1904–1969, and Lester Young, 1909–1959

Classic tenors. Signature/CBS: AK 38446. 1943.

4382 * Hawkins, Erskine, 1914–1993

The original Tuxedo Junction. RCA Bluebird: 9682-2-RB. 1938–45.

4383 Henderson, Fletcher, 1897–1952

4383.1 ** *Developing an American orchestra.* Smithsonian: 2006. 2LP set. 1923–38. [Items 4383.1 and 4383.4 include similar material]. OP

4383.2 *First impressions.* MCA: 1310 (Decca 79227). LP. 1926–31. OP

4383.3 *Hocus pocus.* RCA Bluebird: 9904-2-RB (AXM2-5507). 1927–36.

4383.4 ** *A study in frustration.* Columbia: C3K 57596 (C4L19). 3CD set. 1923–38.

4383.5 *Swing.* ABC Music/DRG: 836-093-2 (BBC 682). 1929–37.

4383.6 * *Tidal wave.* Decca Jazz/GRP: GRD-643 (Decca 79228+). 1931–34.

4384 Herman, Woody, 1913–1987

4384.1 *Blues on parade.* Decca Jazz: GRD-606. 1937–42.

4384.2 *40th anniversary Carnegie Hall concert.* RCA Bluebird: 6878-2-RB. 1976.

4384.3 *Giant steps.* Fantasy: OJCCD-344-2 (9432). 1973.

4384.4 * *Keeper of the flame.* Capitol: 98453 (11034). 1948–50.

4384.5 ** *Thundering herds.* Columbia: CK 44108 (9291). 1945–47.

4385 Hines, Earl, 1903–1983

4385.1 ** *Earl Hines collection: piano solos 1928–1940.* Collector's Classics: COCD 11 (QRS/OKeh/Brunswick/Bluebird). 1928–40.

4385.2 *Earl Hines plays Duke Ellington.* New World: NW-361/362-2. 2CD set. 1971–75.

4385.3 *Harlem lament.* Portrait/CBS: RK 44119. 1933–38. OP

4385.4 * *Piano man.* RCA Bluebird: 6750-2-RB. 1939–42.

4385.5 * *Quintessential recording session.* Chiaroscuro: CR 101. LP. 1969. OP

4385.6 *South Side swing.* MCA: 1311. LP. 1934–35. OP

4385.7 *Tour de force.* Black Lion: BLCD-760140. 1972.

4386 Hodes, Art, 1904–1993

Pagin' Mr. Jelly. Candid: CCD-79037. 1988.

4387 Johnson, Bunk, 1889–1949

The king of the blues. American Music: AMCD-1. 1944.

4388 Johnson, James P., 1894–1955

4388.1 *Carolina shout.* Biograph: BCD-105. 1917–25. [Recorded from piano rolls].

4388.2 * *Father of the stride piano.* Columbia: CL 1780. 1921–39. OP

4388.3 ** *From ragtime to jazz: the complete piano solos.* Columbia/UK: 85387. 1921–39.

4388.4 *Snowy morning blues.* Decca Jazz: GRD-604. 1930, 1944.

4389 Jones, Jo, 1911–1985

The essential Jo Jones. Vanguard: VSD-101/02 (8503). 1955, 1958.

4390 Keppard, Freddie, 1890–1933

4390.1 *Complete heritage.* King Jazz/UK: KJCD-6111. 1923–27. [Items 4390.2 and 4390.1 cover similar material].

4390.2 *Legendary New Orleans cornet.* Smithsonian: 2020. LP. 1924–26. OP

4391 Kirby, John, 1908–1952

The biggest little band. Smithsonian: 2013. 2LP set. 1937–41. OP

4392 * Kirk, Andy, 1898–1992, and Mary Lou Williams, 1910–1981

Mary's idea. Decca Jazz: GRD-622 (MCA 1308). 1936–41.

4393 Leonard, Harlan, 1905–1983

Harlan Leonard and his Rockets: 1940. Classics: 670 (RCA LPV-531). 1940.

4394 Lewis, George, 1900–1968

4394.1 *Complete Blue Note recordings of George Lewis.* Mosaic: MD3-132. 3CD set. 1943–55. OP

4394.2 * *George Lewis with Kid Shots.* American Music: AMCD-2. 1944–45.

4395 Lunceford, Jimmie, 1902–1947

4395.1 * *For dancers only.* Decca Jazz: GRD-645 (Decca 5393+). 1935–37.

4395.2 *Lunceford special.* Columbia: CL 2715. LP. 1933, 1939–40. OP

4395.3 *Rhythm is our business.* ASV: AJA CD 5091. 1934–40.

4395.4 *Stomp it off.* Decca Jazz: GRD-608. 1934–35.

4396 * McKinney's Cotton Pickers

The band Don Redman built. RCA Bluebird: 2275-2-RB. 1928–30.

4397 * McShann, Jay, 1909–

Blues from Kansas City. Decca Jazz: GRD-614 (MCA 1338). 1941–43.

4398 Morton, Jelly Roll, 1890–1941

4398.1 *Anamule dance.* [Series: The Library of Congress recordings, vol. 2]. Rounder: CD 1092. 1938.

4398.2 ** *Jelly Roll Morton.* Milestone: MCD-47018-2 (Gennett). 1923–26.

4398.3 *The Jelly Roll Morton centennial: his complete Victor recordings.* RCA Bluebird: 2361-2-RB. 5CD set. 1926–30, 1939.

4398.4 *Kansas City stomps.* [Series: The Library of Congress recordings, vol. 1]. Rounder: CD 1091. 1938.

4398.5 *New York, Washington, and the rediscovery, vol. 3.* Smithsonian: RD-045. 1928–40.

4398.6 ** *The pearls.* RCA Bluebird: 6588-2-RB. 1926–34. [Item 4398.3 covers material comparable to item 4398.6 but in greater depth and with better packaging and notes].

4398.7   *The pearls.* [Series: The Library of Congress recordings, vol. 3]. Rounder: CD 1093. 1938.

4398.8   *Winin' boy blues.* [Series: The Library of Congress recordings, vol. 4]. Rounder: CD 1094. 1938.

4399   Moten, Bennie, 1894–1935

4399.1 * *Bennie Moten's Kansas City Orchestra: Basie beginnings.* RCA Bluebird: 9768-2-RB. 1929–32.

4399.2   *South.* RCA Bluebird: 3139-2-RB. 1926–29.

4400   New Orleans Rhythm Kings

The New Orleans Rhythm Kings and Jelly Roll Morton. Milestone: MCD-47020-2 (Gennett). 1922–23.

4401   Nicholas, Wooden Joe, 1883–1957

Wooden Joe Nicholas. American Music: AMCD-5. 1945–49.

4402   Nichols, Red, 1905–1965, and Miff Mole, 1898–1961

Great original performances. ABC Music: 836-185-2. 1925–30.

4403 * Noone, Jimmie, 1895–1944

Apex blues. Decca Jazz: GRD-633 (MCA 1313). 1928–30.

4404   Norvo, Red, 1908–

4404.1 * *Move!* Savoy/Denon: SV-0168 (Discovery). 1950–51.

4404.2   *Red Norvo featuring Mildred Bailey.* Portrait/CBS: RK 44118 (Epic 22010). 1933–38. OP

4404.3   *Red Norvo's fabulous jam session featuring Charlie Parker and Dizzy Gillespie.* Stash: STB-2514 (Comet). 1945.

4405   Oliver, Joe "King," 1885–1938

4405.1 ** *The complete Joseph "King" Oliver 1923/1931 heritage, vols. 1–2.* King Jazz/UK: KJ 112/KJ 113. 2 CDs. 1923.

4405.2 ** *King Oliver's Jazz Band.* Smithsonian: 2001 (OKeh). 2LP set. 1923. OP

4405.3 ** *Louis Armstrong and King Oliver.* Milestone: MCD-47017-2 (Gennett/Paramount). 1923–24.

[Item 4405.1 includes most of the material on items 4405.2 and 4405.3].

4406   Original Dixieland Jazz Band

75th anniversary. RCA Bluebird: 61098-2. 1917–21.

4407   Ory, Kid, 1886–1973

Kid Ory's Creole Jazz Band 1944–45. Good Time Jazz: GTJCD-12022-2. 1944–45.

4408   Quebec, Ike, 1918–1963

Blue and sentimental. Blue Note: 84098. 1961.

4409   Raeburn, Boyd, 1913–1966

Boyd meets Stravinsky. Savoy/Denon: SV-0185 (Jewell). 1946.

4410   Reinhardt, Django, 1910–1953

4410.1 ** *Djangologie U.S.A., vol. 1.* DRG/Swing: CDSW 8421/23. 2CD set. 1936–37.

4410.2 * *Djangologie U.S.A., vol. 2.* DRG/Swing: CDSW 8424/26. 2CD set. 1937–40.

4410.3   *Pêche à la mouche: the great Blue Star sessions.* Verve: 835418-2. 2CD set. 1947, 1953.

4411   Roberts, Luckey, 1887–1968, and Willie "The Lion" Smith, 1897–1973

Luckey and the Lion. Good Time Jazz: GTJCD-10035-2. 1958.

4412   Russell, Luis, 1902–1963

The Luis Russell collection, vol. 1. Gazell/Collectors Classics: COCD-7 (Columbia 32338). 1926–34.

4413 * Russell, Pee Wee, 1906–1969

Memorial album. Prestige: 7672 (Swingville 2008). 1960. OP

4414 * Russell, Pee Wee, 1906–1969, and Coleman Hawkins, 1904–1969

Jazz reunion. Candid: CCD-79020 (8020). 1961.

4415   Shaw, Artie, 1910–

4415.1 * *Begin the beguine.* RCA Bluebird: 6274-2-RB. 1938–41.

4415.2   *Blues in the night.* RCA Bluebird: 2432-2-RB. 1941–45.

4415.3   *The complete Gramercy Five sessions.* RCA Bluebird: 7637-2-RB (LPV-582). 1940, 1945.

4416   Smith, Jabbo, 1908–1991

Jabbo Smith's Rhythm Aces. Classics: 669 (MCA 1347). 1929–38.

4417   Smith, Stuff, 1909–1967

Stuff Smith/Dizzy Gillespie/Oscar Peterson. Verve: 314 521676-2. 2CD set. 1957–58.

4418 Smith, Willie "The Lion," 1897–1973

Piano solos. Commodore/Pair: CCD-7012. 1938–39.

4419 Spanier, Muggsy, 1906–1967

Muggsy Spanier 1939: the "ragtime band" sessions. RCA Bluebird: 07863-66550-2. 1939.

4420 Stacy, Jess, 1904–1995

Jess Stacy and friends. Commodore/Pair: CCD-7008 (15358). 1938–44.

4421 Tatum, Art, 1909–1956

  4421.1 * *Classic early solos.* Decca Jazz: GRD-607. 1934–36.

  4421.2 ** *The complete Capitol recordings, vols. 1–2.* Capitol Jazz: 92866/92867. 2 CDs. 1949.

  4421.3 *The complete Pablo solo masterpieces.* Pablo: 7PACD-4404-2 (Clef/Verve). 7CD set. 1953–56.

  4421.4 *God is in the house.* Onyx: 205. LP. 1940–41. OP

  4421.5 *I got rhythm, vol. 3.* Decca Jazz: GRD-630. 1934–44.

  4421.6 *Solos.* Decca Jazz: MCAD-42327. 1940.

4422 * Tatum, Art, 1909–1956, and Ben Webster, 1909–1973

The Tatum group masterpieces, vol. 8. Pablo: PACD-2405-431-2 (Verve MGV8220). 1956.

4423 Tatum, Art, 1909–1956, and Benny Carter, 1907–

The Tatum group masterpieces, vol. 1. Pablo: PACD-2405-424-2 (Clef 643). 1954.

4424 Tatum, Art, 1909–1956, and Buddy DeFranco, 1923–

The Tatum group masterpieces, vol. 7. Pablo: PACD-2405-430-2 (Verve MGV8229). 1956.

4425 Teagarden, Jack, 1905–1964

That's a serious thing. RCA Bluebird: 9986-2-RB. 1928–57.

4426 Thornhill, Claude, 1909–1965

Best of the big bands. Columbia: CK 46152. 1941–47.

4427 Venuti, Joe, 1903–1978

Violin jazz. Yazoo: CD-1062. 1927–34.

4428 * Venuti, Joe, 1903–1978, and Eddie Lang, 1902–1933

Stringing the blues. Sony Music Special Products: X2T-24 (C2L 24). 2AC set. 1927–32.

4429 Waller, Fats, 1904–1943

  4429.1 *Fats and his buddies.* RCA Bluebird: 61005-2. 1927–29.

  4429.2 *Fats Waller and his rhythm: the middle years, part 1.* RCA Bluebird: 66083-2. 3CD set. 1936–38.

  4429.3 ** *The Fats Waller piano solos: turn on the heat.* RCA Bluebird: 2482-2-RB (AXM2-5518). 2CD set. 1927–41.

  4429.4 ** *The joint is jumpin'.* RCA Bluebird: 6288-2-RB. 1929–41.

4430 Watters, Lu, 1911–1989

Yerba Buena Jazz Band, vol. 3: stomps, etc. & the blues. Good Time Jazz: GTJCD-12003-2. 1946.

4431 * Webb, Chick, 1909–1939

Spinnin' the Webb. Decca Jazz: GRD-635. 1929–39.

4432 Webster, Ben, 1909–1973

Soulville. Verve: 833551-2 (8274). 1957, 1959.

4433 Williams, Mary Lou, 1910–1981

  4433.1 *Free spirits.* Steeplechase: SCCD 31043. 1975.

  4433.2 *Solo piano and trios: the Asch and Disc recordings.* Smithsonian/Folkways: SF 40810. 1944–46.

4434 Wilson, Teddy, 1912–1986

  4434.1 *The complete Teddy Wilson.* Columbia (France): 467690-2 (Brunswick). 2CD set. 1934–41.

  4434.2 * *Piano solos.* Charly/UK: CDAFS 1016 (Columbia). 1934–37.

  4434.3 *Statements and improvisations.* Smithsonian: 2005. 2LP set. 1934–42. OP

4435 Young, Lester, 1909–1959

  4435.1 *Blue Lester/Immortal.* Savoy/Denon: SV-0112 (12068). 1944, 1949.

  4435.2 *The complete Aladdin sessions.* Blue Note: 32787 (Philo/Aladdin). 2CD set. 1942–48.

  4435.3 * *Complete Keynote sessions.* Mercury: 830920-2. 1943–44.

  4435.4 ** *The "Kansas City" sessions.* Commodore/GRP: CMD-402. 1938, 1944.

  4435.5 ** *The Lester Young story, vol. 1.* Columbia: CG 33502. 2LP set. 1936–37. OP

  4435.6 ** *The Lester Young story, vol. 4.* Columbia: JG 34843. 2LP set. 1939–40. OP

4435.7 *Pres and Teddy.* Verve: 831270-2 (8205). 1952, 1956.

Post–World War II

Anthologies

4436 * *Amarcord Nina Rota.* Hannibal: HNCD 9301. [1981]. [Hal Wilner, Jaki Byard, Carla Bley, Bill Frisell, Muhal Richard Abrams, David Amram, Steve Lacy, Sharon Freeman, and others].

4437 *The beat generation.* Rhino Word Beat: 70281. 3CD set. 1946–77. [Jack Kerouac, Langston Hughes, Babs Gonzales, Ken Nordine, Nelson Riddle, Tom Waits, William Burroughs, Lee Konitz, Gerry Mulligan, Dizzy Gillespie, Charles Mingus, Jean Shepherd, Kenneth Patchen, Lord Buckley, Lambert, Hendricks and Ross, Slim Gaillard, Charlie Ventura, David Amram, Charlie Parker, The Gordons, Oscar Brown Jr., Kenny Clarke, Elmer Bernstein, Allen Ginsberg, Steve Allen, and others].

4438 ** *Bebop.* New World: NW 271. LP. 1945–56. [Dizzy Gillespie, Charlie Parker, Thelonious Monk, Clifford Brown, Max Roach, Tadd Dameron, Fats Navarro, Horace Silver, and others]. OP

4439 *The bebop era.* Columbia: CK 40972. 1942–51. [Dizzy Gillespie, Woody Herman, Claude Thornhill, Charlie Parker, Metronome All-Stars, and others].

4440 ** *The bebop revolution.* RCA Bluebird: 2177-2-RB. 1946–49. [Dizzy Gillespie, Kenny Clarke, Fats Navarro, Sonny Stitt, Bud Powell, and others].

4441 * *Big band renaissance: the evolution of the jazz orchestra.* Smithsonian: RD 108. 5CD set. 1941–89. [Jay McShann, Boyd Raeburn, Duke Ellington, Benny Goodman, Charlie Barnet, Artie Shaw, Count Basie, Woody Herman, Stan Kenton, Sauter-Finegan, Ted Heath, Harry James, Maynard Ferguson, Buddy Rich, Herb Pomeroy, Johnny Richards, Dizzy Gillespie, Terry Gibbs, Gerry Mulligan, Quincy Jones, Gerald Wilson, Thad Jones, Mel Lewis, Duke Pearson, Clare Fischer, John Dankworth, Kenny Clarke, Francy Boland, Don Ellis, Toshiko Akiyoshi, Rob McConnell, Gil Evans, George Russell, Benny Carter, Manny Albam, Henry Mancini, Oliver Nelson, Muhal Richard Abrams, Sun Ra, Charlie Haden, and others].

4442 * *The birth of the cool, vol. 2.* Capitol: 98935. 1951–53. [Shorty Rogers, Gerry Mulligan, Miles Davis, and others].

4443 * *The birth of the Third Stream.* Columbia: CK 64929 (CL941/WL127). 1956–57. [Charles Mingus, George Russell, John Lewis, J. J. Johnson, Gunther Schuller, Jimmy Giuffre].

4444 *Conception.* Fantasy: OJCCD-1726-2 (Prestige 7013). 1949–51. [Miles Davis, Stan Getz, Lee Konitz].

4445 *Concord Jazz guitar collection, vols. 1–2.* Concord Jazz: CCD-4160. 1973–80. [Laurindo Almeida, George Barnes, Kenny Burrell, Charlie Byrd, Herb Ellis, Tal Farlow, Freddie Green, Barney Kessel, Joe Pass, Howard Roberts].

4446 *Conjure: music for the texts of Ishmael Reed.* American Clavé: 1006. 1983. [Kip Hanrahan, David Murray, Carla Bley, Olu Dara, Lester Bowie, Milton Cardona, Steve Swallow, Billy Hart, Taj Mahal, Allen Toussaint, and others].

4447 * *Introspection: neglected jazz figures of the 1950s and early 1960s.* New World: NW 275. LP. 1952–61. [Herbie Nichols, Curtis Counce, Jaki Byard, Serge Chaloff, Booker Little, Steve Lacy]. OP

4448 *Jam session: the Charlie Parker sides.* Verve: 833564-2. 1952. [Johnny Hodges, Benny Carter, Charlie Parker, Ben Webster, Oscar Peterson, and others].

4449 * *Jazz abstractions.* Atlantic: 1356. LP. 1960. [Gunther Schuller, Jim Hall, Ornette Coleman, Eric Dolphy, and others. Two selections from this album featuring Ornette Coleman solos are reissued on item 4532.2.]. OP

4450 *Jazz canto.* World Pacific: WP1244. 1955, 1958. LP. [John Carradine, Hoagy Carmichael, Ralph Pena, Ben Wright, Chico Hamilton, Bob Dorough, Roy Glenn, Gerry Mulligan, and others]. OP

4451 * *Jazz in revolution: the big bands in the 1940s.* New World: NW 284. LP. 1940–49. [Lionel Hampton, Billy Eckstine, Dizzy Gillespie, Claude Thornhill, Dexter Gordon, Fats Navarro, and others]. OP

4452 *Lost in the stars: the music of Kurt Weill.* A&M: 75021-5104-2. 1985. [Hal Wilner, John Zorn, Carla Bley, Phil Woods, Charlie Haden, Sharon Freeman, Henry Threadgill, and others].

4453 * *Mirage: avant-garde and third-stream jazz.* New World: NW 216. LP. 1946–61. [Duke Ellington, Woody Herman, Stan Kenton, Charles Mingus, Lennie Tristano, George Russell, John Lewis, and others]. OP

4454 ** *Nica's dream: small jazz groups of the 50s and early 60s.* New World: NW 242. LP. 1955–64. [Sonny Rollins, Charles Mingus, Modern Jazz Quartet, Art Blakey, Jazztet, and others]. OP

4455 * *Opus de bop.* Savoy/Denon: SV-0118 (12114). 1946–47. [Stan Getz, Fats Navarro, Tadd Dameron, Sonny Stitt, and others].

4456 * *The original mambo kings.* Verve: 314 513876-2 (VE2-2522). 1948–54. [Machito, Charlie Parker, Flip Phillips, Dizzy Gillespie, Chico O'Farrell].

4457 *That's the way I feel now: a tribute to Thelonious Monk.* A&M: CD 6600. [1984]. [Hal Wilner, Steve Lacy, Charlie Rouse, Sharon Freeman, Barry Harris, Randy Weston, Carla Bley, Johnny Griffin, Gil Evans, and others]. OP

4458 * *Weary blues.* Verve: 841660-2. 1958. [Langston Hughes, Charles Mingus, Leonard Feather, and others].

4459 * *West coast hot.* Novus: 3107-2-N (Flying Dutchman). 1969. [John Carter, Bobby Bradford, Horace Tapscott, Arthur Blythe]. OP

Individual Artists or Groups

4460 Abercrombie, John, 1944–

    4460.1 * *Gateway.* ECM: 78118-21061-2 (829192-2). 1975.

    4460.2 *Timeless.* ECM: 78118-21047-2. 1974.

4461 Abrams, Muhal Richard, 1930–

    4461.1 * *Blu blu blu.* Black Saint: 120117-2. 1990.

    4461.2 *Blues forever.* Black Saint: 120061-2. 1981.

    4461.3 *The hearinga suite.* Black Saint: 120103-2. 1989.

    4461.4 *Young at heart, wise in time.* Delmark: 423. 1968.

4462 Adams, George, 1940–1992, and Don Pullen, 1944–1995

Decisions. Timeless: SJP 205. 1984.

4463 Adams, Pepper, 1930–1986

The master. Muse: MCD-5213. 1980.

4464 Adderley, Cannonball, 1928–1975

    4464.1 *Best of Cannonball Adderley: the Capitol years.* Capitol: 95482. 1962–69.

    4464.2 * *Cannonball in Europe.* Landmark: LCD-1307-2 (Riverside 499). 1962.

    4464.3 ** *In San Francisco.* Fantasy: OJCCD-035-2 (Riverside 1157). 1959.

    4464.4 *Somethin' else.* Blue Note: 46338 (81595). 1958.

    4464.5 *Them dirty blues.* Landmark: LCD-1301-2 (Riverside 322). 1960.

4465 Adderley, Cannonball, 1928–1975, and John Coltrane, 1926–1967

Cannonball and Coltrane. EmArcy: 834588-2 (MG-20449). 1959.

4466 Air [Henry Threadgill, Fred Hopkins, Steve McCall]

    4466.1 ** *Air lore.* RCA Bluebird: 6578-2-RB (Novus 3014). 1979.

    4466.2 *Air mail.* Black Saint: 120049-2. 1980.

    4466.3 *Air time.* nessa: ncd-12. 1977.

4467 * Akiyoshi, Toshiko, 1929–

The Toshiko Akiyoshi/Lew Tabackin Big Band. Novus: 3106-2-N (RCA). 1974–76.

4468 Albany, Joe, 1924–1988, and Warne Marsh, 1927–1987

The right combination. Fantasy: OJCCD-1749-2 (Riverside 270). 1957.

4469 Alden, Howard, 1958– , and Dan Barrett, 1955–

The ABQ salutes Buck Clayton. Concord Jazz: CCD-4395. 1989.

4470 * Allen, Geri, 1957– , Charlie Haden, 1937– , and Paul Motian, 1931–

Segments. DIW: DIW-833. 1989.

4471 Almeida, Laurindo, 1917–1995, and Bud Shank, 1926–

Brazilliance, vol. 1. Pacific Jazz: 96339 (1412). 1953.

4472 American Jazz Quintet

From bad to badder. Black Saint: 120114-2. 1987. [Alvin Batiste, Harold Battiste, Ellis Marsalis, Richard Payne, Ed Blackwell].

4473 Ammons, Gene, 1925–1974

Boss tenor. Fantasy: OJCCD-297-2 (Prestige 7180). 1960.

4474 Ammons, Gene, 1925–1974, and Sonny Stitt, 1924–1982

Boss tenors. Verve: 837440-2 (MGV 8426). 1961.

4475 Anderson, Ray, 1952–

Right down your alley. Soul Note: 121087-2. 1984.

4476 Art Ensemble of Chicago [Roscoe Mitchell, Lester Bowie, Joseph Jarman, Malachi Favors, Don Moye]

4476.1 *Les stances à Sophie.* nessa: n-4. LP. 1970. OP

4476.2 *Full force.* ECM: 78118-21167-2 (1167). 1980.

4476.3 * *A Jackson in your house.* Affinity: AFF 752 (BYG/Actuel 529302). 1969.

4476.4 *Nice guys.* ECM: 78118-21126-2 (1126). 1978.

4476.5 * *People in sorrow.* nessa: n-3. LP. 1969. OP

4476.6 ** *Urban bushmen.* ECM: 78118-21211-2 (1211/12). 2CD set. 1980.

4477 Ayler, Albert, 1936–1970

4477.1 *Bells/Prophesy.* ESP DISK: 1010. 1964–65.

4477.2 *Live in Greenwich Village.* MCA: MCAD-39123 (Impulse 9155). 1966–67.

4477.3 *Spirits rejoice.* ESP DISK: 1020. 1965.

4477.4 * *Spiritual unity.* ESP DISK: 1002. 1964.

4477.5 *Vibrations.* Freedom: FCD-741000. 1964.

4477.6 *Witches and devils.* Freedom: FCD-741013. 1964.

4478 Bailey, Derek, 1930– , and Barre Phillips, 1934–

Figuring. Incus: CD 05. 1987–88.

4479 * Baker, Chet, 1929–1988

The best of Chet Baker plays. Pacific Jazz: 97161. 1953–57.

4480 Bang, Billy, 1947–

Rainbow gladiator. Soul Note: 121016-2. 1981.

4481 Barbieri, Gato, 1934–

Chapter one: Latin America. MCA: MCAD-39124 (Impulse 9248). 1973.

4482 Barron, Kenny, 1943–

Wanton spirit. Verve: 314 522364-2. 1994.

4483 Bellson, Louis, 1924–

Hot. MusicMasters: 5008-2-C. 1989.

4484 * Benson, George, 1943–

The George Benson collection. Warner Bros.: 3577-2. 1971–81.

4485 Berne, Tim, 1954–

Fractured fairy tales. JMT: 834431-2. 1989.

4486 Blake, Ran, 1935–

Breakthru. Improvising Artists: 123842-2. 1975.

4487 Blakey, Art, 1919–1990

4487.1 *Art Blakey's Jazz Messengers with Thelonious Monk.* Atlantic: 1278-2. 1957.

4487.2 ** *The best of Art Blakey and the Jazz Messengers.* Blue Note: 93205. 1958–64. [Item 4487.5 covers material comparable to item 4487.2 but in greater depth and with better packaging and notes].

4487.3 *The complete Blue Note recordings of Art Blakey's 1960 Jazz Messengers.* Mosaic: MD6-141. 6CD set. 1960–61.

4487.4 * *Free for all.* Blue Note: 84170. 1964.

4487.5 * *The history of Art Blakey and the Jazz Messengers.* Blue Note: 97190. 3CD set. 1947–81.

4487.6 *The jazz messenger.* Columbia: CK 47118 (CL 897). 1956.

4487.7 * *Moanin'.* Blue Note: 46516 (84003). 1958.

4487.8 *New York scene.* Concord Jazz: CCD-4256. 1984.

4487.9 *A night at Birdland, vols. 1–2.* Blue Note: 46519/46520 (81521/22). 2 CDs. 1954.

4487.10 *A night in Tunisia.* Blue Note: 84049. 1960.

4487.11 *Straight ahead.* Concord Jazz: CCD-4168. 1981.

4487.12 *Three blind mice, vols. 1–2.* Blue Note: 84451/84452. 2CD set. 1962.

4487.13 *Ugetsu.* Fantasy: OJCCD-090-2 (Riverside 9464). 1963.

4488 Blanchard, Terence, 1962– , and Donald Harrison, 1960–

New York second line. George Wein Collection/Concord Jazz: CCD-43002. 1983.

4489 Bley, Carla, 1938–

4489.1 * *Escalator over the hill.* ECM/Watt: 839310-2 (EOTH). 2CD set. 1968–71.

4489.2 *European tour.* ECM/Watt: 78118-23108-2 (Watt 8). 1977.

4489.3 * *Live!* ECM/Watt: 78118-23112-2 (Watt 12). 1981.

4489.4 *Social studies.* ECM/Watt: 78118-23111-2 (Watt 11). 1980.

4490 Bley, Paul, 1932–

4490.1 * *Footloose.* Savoy: SV-0140 (12182). 1962–63.

4490.2 *Open to love.* ECM: 78118-21023-2 (827751-2). 1972.

4491 Bley, Paul, 1932– , and John Gilmore, 1931–1995

Turning point. Improvising Artists: 123841-2. 1964.

4492 Bloom, Jane Ira, 1955–

Mighty lights. ENJA: 79662-2 (4044). 1982.

4493 Bluiett, Hamiet, 1940–

Resolution. Black Saint: 120014-2. 1977.

4494 Blythe, Arthur, 1940–

In concert (Metamorphosis/The grip). India Navigation: IN 1029-CD. 1977.

4495 Bolling, Claude, 1930–

Suite for flute and jazz piano. Columbia: MK 33233. 1975.

4496 Bowie, Lester, 1941–

ECM Works. ECM: 78118-20274-2 (837274-2). 1980–85.

4497 Brackeen, Charles, 1940–

Worshippers come nigh. Silkheart: SHCD-111. 1987.

4498 Brackeen, Joanne, 1938–

Special identity. Antilles: 422-848813-2 (1001). 1981.

4499 Bradford, Bobby, 1934– , and John Carter, 1929–1991

Comin' on. Hat Hut: ART CD 6016. 1988.

4500 Braff, Ruby, 1927– , and Scott Hamilton, 1954–

A sailboat in the moonlight. Concord Jazz: CCD-4296. 1985.

4501 Braxton, Anthony, 1945–

4501.1 *Anthony Braxton live.* RCA Bluebird: 6626-2-RB (Novus 5002). 1975–76.

4501.2 * *Creative orchestra music.* RCA Bluebird: 6579-2-RB (Novus 4080). 1976.

4501.3 *Three compositions of new jazz.* Delmark: DD-415. 1968.

4501.4 * *Willisau (quartet) 1991.* Hat Hut: ART CD 4-6100. 4CD set. 1991.

4502 Brecker, Michael, 1949–

Michael Brecker. MCA/Impulse!: MCAD-5980. 1987.

4503 Brecker Brothers (Michael, 1949– , and Randy, 1945–)

The Brecker Brothers collection, vol. 1. Novus: 3075-2-N. 1975–81.

4504 Breuker, Willem, 1944–

4504.1 *Bob's gallery.* BVHAAST: CD 8801. 1987.

4504.2 * *Live in Berlin.* BVHAAST: 008 (FMP SAJ06). LP. 1975.

4505 Brooks, John Benson, 1917–

Alabama concerto. Fantasy: OJCCD-1779-2 (Riverside 1123). 1958.

4506 Brooks, Tina, 1932–1974

True blue. Blue Note: 28975 (84041). 1960.

4507 Brötzman, Peter, 1941–

Machine gun. FMP (Free Music Production): CD 24. 1968.

4508 Brown, Clifford, 1930–1956

4508.1 *Brown and Roach Inc.* EmArcy: 814644-2 (MG-36008). 1954.

4508.2 *Brownie: the complete EmArcy recordings.* EmArcy: 838306-2. 10CD set. 1954–56.

4508.3 ** *Clifford Brown and Max Roach.* EmArcy: 814645-2 (MG-36036). 1954–55.

4508.4 * *Clifford Brown and Max Roach at Basin Street.* EmArcy: 814648-2 (MG-36070). 1956.

4508.5 *Clifford Brown memorial album.* Fantasy: OJCCD-017-2 (Prestige 7055). 1953. [Includes Tadd Dameron session].

4508.6 *Clifford Brown with strings.* EmArcy: 814642-2 (MG-36005). 1955.

4508.7 *A study in Brown.* EmArcy: 814646-2 (MG-36037). 1955.

4509 Brubeck, Dave, 1920–

4509.1 * *Jazz at Oberlin.* Fantasy: OJCCD-046-2 (Fantasy 3-245). 1953.

4509.2 * *Time out.* Columbia: CK 65122 (CL 1397). 1959.

4510 Bryant, Ray, 1931–

Alone with the blues. Fantasy: OJCCD-249-2 (New Jazz 8213). 1958.

4511 Burrell, Kenny, 1931–

Guitar forms. Verve: 825576-2 (68612). 1964–65. OP

4512 Burrell, Kenny, 1931– , and John Coltrane, 1926–1967

Kenny Burrell and John Coltrane. Fantasy: OJCCD-300-2 (New Jazz 8276). 1958.

4513 Burton, Gary, 1943–

    4513.1 * *Artist's choice.* RCA Bluebird: 6280-2-RB. 1963–68. OP

    4513.2 *Dreams so real.* ECM: 78118-21072-2 (833329-2). 1975.

4514 Burton, Gary, 1943– , and Carla Bley, 1938–

A genuine Tong funeral. RCA: LSP-3988. LP. 1968. OP

4515 Burton, Gary, 1943– , and Chick Corea, 1941–

Crystal silence. ECM: 78118-21024-2. 1972.

4516 * Byard, Jaki, 1922–

Empirical. Muse: MCD-6010 (Muse 5007). 1972.

4517 Byrd, Donald, 1932–

Free form. Blue Note: 84118. 1961.

4518 Byron, Don, 1959–

Tuskegee experiments. Elektra/Nonesuch: 79280-2. 1990–91.

4519 Carter, John, 1929–1991

    4519.1 * *Castles of Ghana.* Gramavision: 79423 (18-8603). 1985.

    4519.2 *Dance of the love ghosts.* Gramavision: 79424 (18-8704). 1986.

    4519.3 *Dauwhe.* Black Saint: 120057-2. 1982.

    4519.4 * *Fields.* Gramavision: 79425 (18-8809). 1988.

    4519.5 *Shadows on a wall.* Gramavision: 79422. 1989.

    [Items 4519.1–4519.5 comprise a suite entitled *Roots and folklore: episodes in the development of American folk music*].

4520 Carter, John, 1929–1991, and Bobby Bradford, 1934–

Seeking. Hat Hut: ART CD 6085 (Revelation 9). 1969.

4521 Chaloff, Serge, 1923–1957

    4521.1 *Blue Serge.* Capitol: M-11032 (742). LP. 1956. [Item 4521.2 covers all the material on item 4521.1 plus additional recording sessions and better packaging and notes]. OP

    4521.2 *The complete Serge Chaloff sessions.* Mosaic: MD4-147 (Dial/Savoy/Capitol, etc.). 4CD set. 1946–56.

4522 Charles, Ray, 1932–

Blues + jazz. Rhino/Atlantic: 71607. 2CD set. 1950–59.

4523 * Charles, Teddy, 1928–

The Teddy Charles Tentette. Atlantic: 90983-2 (1229). 1956.

4524 Charles, Teddy, 1928– , and Shorty Rogers, 1924–1994

Collaboration: West. Fantasy: OJCCD-122-2 (Prestige 7028). 1953.

4525 Cherry, Don, 1936–1995

    4525.1 * *The complete Blue Note recordings of Don Cherry.* Mosaic: MD2-145. 2CD set. 1965–66. [Original titles: *Complete communion, Symphony for improvisors,* and *Where is Brooklyn?*].

    4525.2 *Symphony for improvisors.* Blue Note: 28976 (84247). 1966. [Item 4525.1 covers all the material on item 4525.2 plus two additional sessions and better packaging and notes].

4526 Cherry, Don, 1936–1995, and Ed Blackwell, 1929–1992

Mu (the complete session). Affinity: CD AFF 774 (BYG Actuel 529301/529331). 1969.

4527 Circle

Paris concert. ECM: 78118-21018-2 (1018/19). 2CD set. 1971. [Chick Corea, Anthony Braxton, Dave Holland, Barry Altschul].

4528 * Clarinet Summit

In concert at the Public Theatre, vols. 1–2. India Navigation: IN 1062-CD. 1981. [Jimmy Hamilton, Alvin Batiste, John Carter, David Murray].

4529 Clark, Sonny, 1931–1963

    4529.1 *Cool struttin'.* Blue Note: 46513 (81588). 1958.

4529.2 *Leapin' and lopin'.* Blue Note: 84091. 1961.

4530 Cobham, Billy, 1944–

Best of Billy Cobham. Atlantic: 19238-2. [1973–76].

4531 Cohn, Al, 1925–1988, and Zoot Sims, 1925–1985

Body and soul. Muse: MCD-5356. 1973.

4532 Coleman, Ornette, 1930–

4532.1 *At the Golden Circle, vols. 1–2.* Blue Note: 84224/84225. 2CDs. 1965.

4532.2 * *Beauty is a rare thing: the complete Atlantic recordings.* Rhino/Atlantic: 71410. 6CD set. 1959–61. [Includes all material from items 4532.3, 4532.7, 4532.11, 4532.12, 4532.13, and 4532.16, two selections from 4449, plus additional material].

4532.3 ** *Change of the century.* Atlantic: 81341-2 (1327). 1959.

4532.4 *Crisis.* Impulse!: 9187. LP. 1969. OP

4532.5 * *Dancing in your head.* A&M: CD 0807 (SP-722). 1976. OP

4532.6 *Forms and sounds: the music of Ornette Coleman.* RCA Bluebird: 6561-2-RB (LSC-2982). 1968.

4532.7 * *Free jazz.* Atlantic: 1364–2. 1960.

4532.8 *In all languages.* Caravan of Dreams: 85008. 1987.

4532.9 *New York is now.* Blue Note: 84287. 1968.

4532.10 *Of human feelings.* Antilles: ANCD-2001. 1979.

4532.11 *Ornette!* Atlantic: 1378. LP. 1961. OP

4532.12 *Ornette on tenor.* Rhino/Atlantic: 71455 (1394). 1961.

4532.13 ** *The shape of jazz to come.* Atlantic: 1317-2. 1959.

4532.14 * *Skies of America.* Columbia: 31562. LP. 1972. OP

4532.15 *Something else!* Fantasy: OJCCD-163-2 (Contemporary 7551). 1958.

4532.16 *This is our music.* Atlantic: 1353. LP. 1960. OP

4532.17 *Tomorrow is the question!* Fantasy: OJCCD-342-2 (Contemporary 7569). 1959.

4533 Coleman, Steve, 1956–

Rhythm in mind. Novus: 63125-2. 1992.

4534 Coltrane, John, 1926–1967

4534.1 * *Africa/brass.* Impulse!/GRP: IMPD-2-168 (6 +). 2CD set. 1961.

4534.2 * *Blue train.* Blue Note: 46095 (81577). 1957.

4534.3 *Coltrane.* MCA: MCAD-5883 (Impulse 21). 1962.

4534.4 *Coltrane plays the blues.* Atlantic: 1382–2. 1960.

4534.5 *Crescent.* Impulse!/GRP: IMPD-200 (66). 1964.

4534.6 ** *Giant steps.* Atlantic: 1311-2. 1959.

4534.7 * *Impressions.* MCA: MCAD-5887 (Impulse 42). 1961–63.

4534.8 *Interstellar space.* Impulse!/GRP: GRD-110 (9277). 1967.

4534.9 * *John Coltrane and Johnny Hartman.* Impulse!/GRP: GRD-157 (40). 1963.

4534.10 *The last giant: the John Coltrane anthology.* Rhino: 71255. 2CD set. 1946–67.

4534.11 ** *Live at Birdland.* Impulse!/MCA: MCAD 33109 (50). 1963.

4534.12 *Live at the Village Vanguard.* Impulse!/MCA: MCAD-39136 (10). 1961.

4534.13 ** *A love supreme.* Impulse!/GRP: GRD-155 (77). 1964.

4534.14 *The major works of John Coltrane.* Impulse!/GRP: GRD2-113 (Impulse 95). 2CD set. 1965. [Includes *"Ascension"* and other works].

4534.15 *Meditations.* Impulse!/GRP: IMPD-199 (9110). 1965.

4534.16 * *My favorite things.* Atlantic: 1361-2. 1960.

4534.17 *Soultrane.* Fantasy: OJCCD-021-2 (Prestige 7142). 1958.

4534.18 *Traneing in.* Fantasy: OJCCD-189-2 (Prestige 7123). 1957.

4535 Company. *Company 6 and 7.* Incus: CD 07. 1977. [Leo Smith, Anthony Braxton, Steve Lacy, Evan Parker, Tristan Honsinger, Derek Bailey, Lol Coxhill, Han Bennink, and others].

4536 Corea, Chick, 1941–

4536.1 *A. R. C.* ECM: 78118-21009-2 (1009). 1971.

4536.2 *Akoustic Band: alive.* GRP: GRD-9627. 1991.

4536.3 *My Spanish heart.* Polydor: 825657-2 (PD2-9003). 1976.

4536.4 * *Now he sings, now he sobs.* Blue Note: 90055 (Solid State 18039). 1968.

4536.5 *Piano improvisations, vol. 2.* ECM: 78118-21020-2 (1020). 1971.

4536.6 * *Return to forever.* ECM: 78118-21022-2. 1971.

4536.7 *Trio music.* ECM: 78118-21232-2 (2-1232). 2CD set. 1981.

4537   Corea, Chick, 1941– , and Return to Forever

4537.1 *Hymn of the seventh galaxy.* Polydor: 825336-2 (5536). 1973.

4537.2 *Light as a feather.* Polydor: 827148-2 (5525). 1972.

4538   Coryell, Larry, 1943–

The essential Larry Coryell. Vanguard: VCD-75/76. 1968–72.

4539   Counce, Curtis, 1926–1963

You get more bounce with Curtis Counce. Fantasy: OJCCD-159-2 (Contemporary 7539). 1956–57.

4540   Cowell, Stanley, 1941–

Live at Maybeck Recital Hall, vol. 5. Concord Jazz: CCD-4431. 1990.

4541   Coxhill, Lol, 1932–

The Dunois solos. nato/Melodie: 53040.2. 1981.

4542   Crispell, Marilyn, 1947–

Gaia. Leo: CD LR 152. 1987.

4543   Criss, Sonny, 1927–1977

Sonny's dream. Fantasy: OJCCD-707-2 (Prestige 7576). 1968. [Horace Tapscott arrangements].

4544 * Crusaders

The golden years. GRP: GRD-3-5007. 3CD set. 1962–82.

4545   Dameron, Tadd, 1917–1965

4545.1 * *Fontainebleau.* Fantasy: OJCCD-055-2 (Prestige 7037). 1956.

4545.2 *The magic touch.* Fantasy: OJCCD-143-2 (Riverside 9419). 1962.

4546   Davern, Kenny, 1935–

One hour tonight. MusicMasters: 5003-2-C (60148). 1988.

4547   Davis, Anthony, 1951– , James Newton, 1953– , and Abdul Wadud, 1947–

I've known rivers. Gramavision: 79427. 1982.

4548   Davis, Eddie "Lockjaw," 1921–1986

Cookbook, vol. 1. Fantasy: OJCCD-652-2 (Prestige 7141). 1958.

4549   Davis, Miles, 1926–1991

4549.1 * *Bags' groove.* Fantasy: OJCCD-245-2 (Prestige 7109). 1954.

4549.2 ** *Birth of the cool.* Capitol: 92862 (T762). 1949–50.

4549.3 ** *Bitches brew.* Columbia: G2K 40577 (GP 26). 2CD set. 1969.

4549.4 * *The complete concert 1964 (My funny valentine + Four and more).* Columbia: C2K 48821 (9106/9253). 2CD set. 1964.

4549.5 * *Cookin'.* Fantasy: OJCCD-128-2 (Prestige 7094). 1956.

4549.6 *E. S. P.* Columbia: CK 46863 (9150). 1965.

4549.7 *Filles de Kilimanjaro.* Columbia: CK 46116 (9750). 1968.

4549.8 ** *In a silent way.* Columbia: CK 40580 (9875). 1969.

4549.9 ** *Kind of blue.* Columbia: CK 64935 (8163). 1959.

4549.10 ** *Miles ahead.* Columbia: CK 53225 (CL 1041). 1957. [Items 4546.10, 4546.18, and 4546.21 are all arranged by Gil Evans].

4549.11 * *Miles Davis and the Modern Jazz Giants.* Fantasy: OJCCD-347-2 (Prestige 7150). 1954.

4549.12 *Miles Davis: complete Prestige recordings.* Prestige: 8PRCD-012-2. 8CD set. 1951–56.

4549.13 ** *Miles smiles.* Columbia: CK 48849 (9401). 1966.

4549.14 *Milestones.* Columbia: CK 40837 (CL 1193). 1958.

4549.15 *Nefertiti.* Columbia: CK 46113 (9594). 1967.

4549.16 *On the corner.* Columbia: CK 53579 (31906). 1972.

4549.17 *Pangaea.* Columbia: C2K 46115. 2CD set. 1975.

4549.18 ** *Porgy and Bess.* Columbia: CK 65141 (CL 1274). 1958.

4549.19 *Relaxin'.* Fantasy: OJCCD-190-2 (Prestige 7129). 1956.

4549.20 * *Round about midnight.* Columbia: CK 40610 (CL 949). 1955–56.

4549.21 * *Sketches of Spain.* Columbia: CK 40578 (CL 1480). 1959–60.

4549.22 *Someday my prince will come.* Columbia: CK 40947 (8456). 1961.

4549.23 *Sorcerer.* Columbia: CK 52974 (CL 2732). 1967.

4549.24 *Steamin'.* Fantasy: OJCCD-391-2 (Prestige 7200). 1956.

4549.25 * *A tribute to Jack Johnson.* Columbia: CK 47036 (30455). 1970.

4549.26 *Tutu.* Warner Bros.: 25490-2. 1986.

4549.27 * *Walkin'.* Fantasy: OJCCD-213-2 (Prestige 7076). 1954.

4549.28 * *Workin'.* Fantasy: OJCCD-296-2 (Prestige 7166). 1956.

4550   DeJohnette, Jack, 1942–

4550.1 *Album album.* ECM: 78118-21280-2 (823467-2). 1984.

4550.2 * *Special edition.* ECM: 78118-21152-2 (827694-2). 1979.

4551   Dickerson, Walt, 1931– , and Richard Davis, 1930–

Divine Gemini. Steeplechase: SCCD 31089. 1977.

4552   DiMeola, Al, 1954–

Elegant gypsy. Columbia: CK 34461. 1976.

4553   DiMeola, Al, 1954– , John McLaughlin, 1942– , and Paco de Lucía, 1947–

Passion, grace and fire. Columbia: CK 38645. 1983.

4554   Dirty Dozen Brass Band

Live: Mardi Gras in Montreux. Rounder: CD 2052. 1985.

4555   Dolphy, Eric, 1928–1964

4555.1 *Conversations.* Metrotone: 72660-2 (FM 308). 1963.

4555.2 * *Eric Dolphy at the Five Spot, vol. 1.* Fantasy: OJCCD-133-2 (New Jazz 8260). 1961.

4555.3 *Eric Dolphy in Europe, vol. 1.* Fantasy: OJCCD-413-2 (Prestige 7304). 1961.

4555.4 * *Far cry.* Fantasy: OJCCD-400-2 (New Jazz 8270). 1960.

4555.5 *Last date.* Fontana: 822226-2 (Limelight 86013). 1964.

4555.6 ** *Out to lunch.* Blue Note: 46524 (84163). 1964.

4555.7 *Outward bound.* Fantasy: OJCCD-022-2 (New Jazz 8236). 1960.

4556   Donaldson, Lou, 1926–

Blueswalk. Blue Note: 46525 (81593). 1958.

4557   Dørge, Pierre, 1946–

4557.1 *Brikama.* Steeplechase: SCCD 31188. 1984.

4557.2 *Even the moon is dancing.* Steeplechase: SCCD 31208. 1985.

4558   Dorham, Kenny, 1924–1972

Whistle stop. Blue Note: 28978 (84063). 1961.

4559   Dyani, Johnny, 1945–1986

4559.1 *Song for Biko.* Steeplechase: SCCD 31109. 1978.

4559.2 *Witchdoctor's son.* Steeplechase: SCCD 31098. 1978.

4560 * Eckstine, Billy, 1914–1993

Mr. B and the band. Savoy/Denon: SV-0264 (National). 1945–47.

4561   Ehrlich, Marty, 1955–

The traveller's tale. ENJA: 79630 (6024). 1989.

4562   Ellis, Don, 1934–1978

4562.1 *Electric bath.* Columbia: CS 9585. LP. 1967. OP

4562.2 *How time passes.* Candid: CCD-79004 (8004). 1960.

4563   Ervin, Booker, 1930–1970

The freedom book. Fantasy: OJCCD-845-2 (Prestige 7295). 1963.

4564   Evans, Bill, 1929–1980

4564.1 *At the Montreux Jazz Festival.* Verve: 827844-2 (68762). 1968.

4564.2 *Bill Evans at Town Hall, vol. 1.* Verve: 831271-2 (68683). 1966.

4564.3 *Conversations with myself.* Verve: 821984-2 (68526). 1963.

4564.4 *Everybody digs Bill Evans.* Fantasy: OJCCD-068-2 (Riverside 1129). 1958.

4564.5 *Explorations.* Fantasy: OJCCD-037-2 (Riverside 9351). 1961.

4564.6 *Interplay.* Fantasy: OJCCD-308-2 (Riverside 9445). 1962.

4564.7 *Portrait in jazz.* Fantasy: OJCCD-088-2 (Riverside 1162). 1959.

4564.8 * *Sunday at the Village Vanguard.* Fantasy: OJCCD-140-2 (Riverside 9376). 1961.

4564.9 ** *Waltz for Debby.* Fantasy: OJCCD-210-2 (Riverside 9399). 1961.

4565 Evans, Bill, 1929–1980, and Eddie Gomez, 1944–

Intuition. Fantasy: OJCCD-470-2 (9475). 1974.

4566 Evans, Bill, 1929–1980, and Jim Hall, 1930–
Undercurrent. Blue Note: 90583 (UA 14003). 1962.

4567 Evans, Gil, 1912–1988

4567.1 *Gil Evans and ten.* Fantasy: OJCCD-346-2 (Prestige 7120). 1957.

4567.2 *Great jazz standards.* Pacific Jazz: 46856 (1270). 1959.

4567.3 ** *Individualism of Gil Evans.* Verve: 833804-2 (8555). 1964.

4567.4 *Live at the Public Theater, vol. 1.* Evidence: ECD-22089-2 (Blackhawk 525). 1980.

4567.5 *New bottle old wine.* Pacific Jazz: 46855 (1246). 1958.

4567.6 * *Out of the cool.* Impulse!/GRP: IMPD-186 (Impulse 4). 1960.

4567.7 *Priestess.* Antilles: 422-826770-2 (1010). 1977.

4567.8 *Svengali.* Atlantic: SD 1643. LP. 1973. OP

4567.9 *There comes a time.* RCA Bluebird: 5783-2-RB (APL1-1057). 1975.

4568 Farlow, Tal, 1921–

Tal Farlow. [Series: Verve jazz masters, vol. 41]. Verve: 314 527 365-2. 1954–58.

4569 Farmer, Art, 1928–

Something to live for. Contemporary: CCD-14029-2. 1987.

4570 Farmer, Art, 1928– , and Benny Golson, 1929–
Meet the Jazztet. Chess: CHD-91550 (Argo 664). 1960.

4571 Ferguson, Maynard, 1928–

4571.1 *M. F. horn.* Columbia: CGT 33660 (30466). AC. 1970.

4571.2 * *Message from Newport.* Roulette: 52012. LP. 1958. [This material is included on *The complete Roulette recordings of the Maynard Ferguson Orchestra* (Mosaic: MD10-156, 1958–62), a 10CD set that may exceed the "basic" scope of this book]. OP

4572 Flanagan, Tommy, 1930–

4572.1 * *Giant steps.* ENJA: 4022-2. 1982.

4572.2 *Jazz poet.* Timeless: CD SJP 301. 1989.

4572.3 *Thelonica.* ENJA: 4052-2. 1982.

4573 Freeman, Chico, 1949–
Chico. India Navigation: IN 1031-CD. 1977.

4574 Freeman, Russ, 1926– , and Richard Twardzik, 1931–1955
Trio. Pacific Jazz: 46861. 1954–56. OP

4575 * Frisell, Bill, 1951–
Look out for hope. ECM: 78118-21350-2 (833495-2). 1987.

4576 Ganelin Trio

4576.1 *Catalogue: live in East Germany.* Leo: CD LR 102. 1977–82.

4576.2 *Non troppo.* Hat Hut: ART CD 6059 (2027). 1980–82.

4577 Garbarek, Jan, 1947–
Witchi-tai-to. ECM: 78118-21041-2 (833330-2). 1973.

4578 Garrett, Kenny, 1961–
African exchange student. Atlantic: 82156-2. 1990.

4579 Getz, Stan, 1927–1991

4579.1 *Anniversary.* EmArcy: 838769-2. 1987.

4579.2 * *The artistry of Stan Getz, vol. 1.* Verve: 314 511468-2. 2CD set. 1952–67.

4579.3 *The complete recordings of the Stan Getz Quartet with Jimmy Raney.* Mosaic: MD3-131. 3CD set. 1951–53. OP

4579.4 *Focus.* Verve: 821982-2 (V6-8412). 1961.

4579.5 * *Jazz samba.* Verve: 810061-2 (MGV-8432). 1962.

4579.6 * *Pure Getz.* Concord Jazz: CCD-4188. 1982.

4579.7 *Quartets.* Fantasy: OJCCD-121-2 (Prestige 7002). 1949–50.

4579.8 ** *The Roost quartets.* Roulette Jazz: 96052. 1950–51. [Item 4579.3 covers all the material on items 4579.8 and 4579.9 but in greater depth and with better packaging and notes].

4579.9 * *Stan Getz at Storyville.* Roulette Jazz: 94507. 1951. [Item 4579.3 covers all the material on items 4579.8 and 4579.9 but in greater depth and with better packaging and notes].

4580 Getz, Stan, 1927–1991, and João Gilberto, 1931–

Getz/Gilberto. Verve: 810048-2 (V6-8545). 1963.

4581 Getz, Stan, 1927–1991, and J. J. Johnson, 1924–

Stan Getz and J. J. Johnson at the Opera House. Verve: 831272-2 (MGV-8265). 1957.

4582 Gibbs, Mike, 1937–

Big music. Venture/Caroline: CAROL-1604-2 (CDVE 27). 1988.

4583 Gibbs, Terry, 1924–

Dream band. Contemporary: CCD-7647-2. 1959.

4584 Gillespie, Dizzy, 1917–1993

4584.1 * *The complete RCA Victor recordings.* RCA Bluebird: 07863-66528-2. 2CD set. 1937–49.

4584.2 ** *Development of an American artist.* Smithsonian: 2004. 2LP set. 1940–46. OP

4584.3 *Dizzy Gillespie at Newport.* Verve: 314 513754-2 (MGV-8242). 1957.

4584.4 *Dizzy Gillespie's big 4.* Fantasy: OJCCD-443-2 (Pablo 2310 719). 1974.

4584.5 *Duets.* Verve: 835253-2 (MGV-8260). 1957.

4584.6 ** *Shaw 'nuff.* Discovery/Warner Bros.: 70053 (Musicraft). 1945–46.

4584.7 * *Sonny side up.* Verve: 825674-2 (MGV-8262). 1957.

4585 Giuffre, Jimmy, 1921–

4585.1 *The Jimmy Giuffre 3.* Atlantic: 90981-2 (1254). 1956.

4585.2 * *1961.* ECM: 78118-21438-2 (Verve 8397/8402). 2CD set. 1961.

4586 Globe Unity

Rumbling. FMP (Free Music Production): CD 40 (0220/0270). 1975.

4587 Gonzalez, Dennis, 1954–

Stefan. Silkheart: SHCD-101. 1986.

4588 Gordon, Dexter, 1923–1990

4588.1 *The chase: the complete Dial sessions, 1947.* Stash: STB-2513. 1947.

4588.2 *Dexter rides again.* Savoy/Denon: SV-0120 (12130). 1945–47.

4588.3 *Doin' alright.* Blue Note: 84077. 1960.

4588.4 * *Go!* Blue Note: 46094 (84112). 1962.

4588.5 *Homecoming.* Columbia: C2K 46824 (34650). 2CD set. 1976.

4588.6 *Nights at the Keystone, vols. 1–3.* Blue Note: 94848/94849/94850. 3 CDs. 1978–79.

4588.7 *Our man in Paris.* Blue Note: 46394 (84146). 1963.

4589 Gray, Wardell, 1921–1955

Memorial, vol. 1. Fantasy: OJCCD-050-2 (Prestige 7008). 1949–53.

4590 Green, Grant, 1931–1979

Idle moments. Blue Note: 84154. 1963.

4591 Grey, Al, 1925–

The new Al Grey Quintet. Chiaroscuro: 305. 1988.

4592 Griffin, Johnny, 1928–

4592.1 *Introducing Johnny Griffin.* Blue Note: 46536 (1533). 1956.

4592.2 *The man I love.* Black Lion: BLCD-760107. 1967.

4592.3 * *Return of the Griffin.* Fantasy: OJCCD-1888-2. (Galaxy 5117). 1978.

4593 Guaraldi, Vince, 1928–1976

Greatest hits. Fantasy: FCD-7706-2 (4505). 1962–66.

4594 Haden, Charlie, 1937–

4594.1 *The ballad of the fallen.* ECM: 78118-21248-2 (811546). 1982.

4594.2 * *Liberation Music Orchestra.* Impulse!/GRP: IMPD-188 (Impulse 9183). 1969.

4595 Haden, Charlie, 1937– , Egberto Gismonti, 1947– , and Jan Garbarek, 1947–

Folk songs. ECM: 78118-21170-2 (1170). 1979.

4596 Haig, Al, 1924–1982

Jazz will-o'-the-wisp. Fresh Sound: FSRCD-38 (Counterpoint 551). 1954.

4597 Hall, Jim, 1930–

Jazz guitar. Pacific Jazz: 46851 (1227). 1957.

4598 Hall, Jim, 1930– , and Ron Carter, 1937–

Alone together. Fantasy: OJCCD-467-2 (Milestone 9045). 1972.

4599   Hamilton, Chico, 1921–

4599.1 *Gong's east.* Discovery/Warner Bros.: 70831 (WB 1271). 1958.

4599.2 *Spectacular!* Pacific Jazz: PJ-1209 (39). LP. 1955. OP

4600   Hancock, Herbie, 1940–

4600.1 *Empyrean isles.* Blue Note: 84175. 1964.

4600.2 *Future shock.* Columbia: CK 38814. 1983.

4600.3 ** *Head hunters.* Columbia: CK 65123 (32731). 1973.

4600.4 * *Maiden voyage.* Blue Note: 46339 (84195). 1965.

4600.5 *Mwandishi Herbie Hancock: the complete Warner Bros. recordings.* Warner Archives: 45732-2 (1898/2617). 2CD set. 1969–72.

4600.6 *Quartet.* Columbia: CGK 38275. 1982.

4600.7 *Sound system.* Columbia: CK 39478. 1984.

4600.8 *Speak like a child.* Blue Note: 46136 (84279). 1968.

4601   Handy, John, 1933–

Live at the Monterey Jazz Festival. Koch Jazz: KOCCD-7820. (Columbia 9262). 1965.

4602   Harrell, Tom, 1946–

Sail away. Contemporary: CCD-14054-2. 1989.

4603   Harris, Craig, 1954–

Black bone. Soul Note: 121055-2. 1983.

4604   Hawes, Hampton, 1928–1977

The trio. Fantasy: OJCCD-316-2 (Contemporary 3505). 1955.

4605   Heath, Jimmy, 1926–

Picture of Heath. Xanadu: 118. LP. 1975.

4606   Hemphill, Julius, 1940–1995

4606.1 *Raw materials and residuals.* Black Saint: 120015-2. 1977.

4606.2 * *Reflections ('Coon bid'ness).* Freedom: 741012-2. 1972, 1975.

4607   Henderson, Joe, 1937–

4607.1 * *Best of Joe Henderson: the Blue Note Years.* Blue Note: 95627. 1963–85.

4607.2 *Mode for Joe.* Blue Note: 84227. 1966.

4607.3 * *The state of the tenor, vols. 1–2.* Blue Note: 28879 (46296/46426). 2CD set. 1985.

4608   Hill, Andrew, 1937–

4608.1 *Judgment.* Blue Note: 28981 (84159). 1964.

4608.2 * *Point of departure.* Blue Note: 84167. 1964.

4608.3 *Shades.* Soul Note: 121113-2. 1986.

4609   Holland, Dave, 1946–

4609.1 ** *Conference of the birds.* ECM: 78118-21027-2 (1027). 1972.

4609.2 *Jumpin' in.* ECM: 78118-21269-2 (817437-2). 1983.

4609.3 * *The razor's edge.* ECM: 78118-21353-2 (1353). 1987.

4609.4 *Triplicate.* ECM: 78118-21373-2 (837113-2). 1988.

4610   Hope, Elmo, 1923–1967

Elmo Hope Trio. Fantasy: OJCCD-477-2 (Contemporary 7620). 1959.

4611   Houn, Fred Wei-han (Fred Ho)

We refuse to be used and abused. Soul Note: 121167-2. 1987.

4612   Hubbard, Freddie, 1938–

Breaking point. Blue Note: 84172. 1964.

4613   Hutcherson, Bobby, 1941–

Components. Blue Note: 29027 (84213). 1965.

4614   Ibrahim, Abdullah (Dollar Brand), 1934–

4614.1 *African piano.* ECM: 78118-23302-2 (JAPO 60002). 1969.

4614.2 * *Water from an ancient well.* Tip Toe: TIP-888812-2 (Blackhawk). 1985.

4615   Jackson, Milt, 1923–

4615.1 * *Jackson's ville.* Savoy/Denon: SV-0175 (12080). 1956.

4615.2 *Milt Jackson.* Blue Note: 81509. 1948, 1952. [Includes Thelonious Monk session].

4615.3 *Milt Jackson Quartet.* Fantasy: OJCCD-001-2 (Prestige 7003). 1955.

4616   Jackson, Ronald Shannon, 1940–

Mandance. Antilles: 422 846397-2 (1008). 1982.

4617 * Jamal, Ahmad, 1930–

But not for me: live at the Pershing. Chess: CHD-9108 (Argo 628). 1958.

4618   Jang, Jon, and The Pan-Asian Arkestra

Self defense! Soul Note: 121203-2. 1991.

4619 Jarrett, Keith, 1945–

   4619.1 ** *Facing you.* ECM: 78118-21017-2 (827132-2). 1972.

   4619.2 *Foundations: the Keith Jarrett anthology.* Rhino/Atlantic: 71593. 2CD set. 1966–71.

   4619.3 * *Köln concert.* ECM: 78118-21064-2 (1064/65). 1975.

   4619.4 *Silence.* Impulse!/GRP: GRD-117 (Impulse 9331/9334). 1977.

   4619.5 *Standards, vol. 1.* ECM: 78118-21255-2 (811966-2). 1983.

4620 Jarrett, Keith, 1945– , and Jan Garbarek, 1947–

Belonging. ECM: 78118-21050-2 (829115-2). 1974.

4621 Jazz Composer's Orchestra

Communications. ECM: 841124-2 (JCOA 1001/02). 1968. [Michael Mantler, Cecil Taylor, Don Cherry, Roswell Rudd, Pharoah Sanders, Larry Coryell, Gato Barbieri].

4622 Jenkins, Leroy, 1932–

Mixed quintet. Black Saint: 120060-2. 1979.

4623 Johnson, J. J., 1924–

   4623.1 * *The eminent J. J. Johnson, vols. 1–2.* Blue Note: 81505/81506. 2 CDs. 1953–55.

   4623.2 *The great Kai and J. J.* MCA: MCAD-42012 (Impulse 1). 1961.

   4623.3 * *Jazz quintets.* Savoy/Denon: SV-0151 (12106). 1946–49.

   4623.4 *Trombone master.* Columbia: CK 44443. 1957–60.

4624 Johnson, Marc, 1953–

Bass desires. ECM: 78118-21299-2 (1299). 1985.

4625 Jones, Hank, 1918–

Live at Maybeck Recital Hall, vol. 16. Concord Jazz: CCD-4502. 1991.

4626 Jones, Quincy, 1933–

The best. A&M: 75021-3200-2. 1969–81.

4627 Jones, Thad, 1923–1986

The magnificent Thad Jones. Blue Note: 46814 (1527). 1956.

4628 Jones, Thad, 1923–1986, and Mel Lewis, 1929–1990

   4628.1 ** *The best of Thad Jones/Mel Lewis.* Capitol Jazz: [CD reissue forthcoming]. 1966–70. [Item 4628.2 covers material comparable to item 4628.1 but in greater depth and with better packaging and notes].

   4628.2 *The complete Solid State recordings of the Thad Jones/Mel Lewis Orchestra.* Mosaic: MD5-151. 5CD set. 1966–70.

4629 Jordan, Stanley, 1959–

Magic touch. Blue Note: 46092 (85101). 1984.

4630 Kelly, Wynton, 1931–1971

Kelly blue. Fantasy: OJCCD-033-2 (Riverside 1142). 1959.

4631 Kenton, Stan, 1912–1979

   4631.1 *The complete Capitol recordings of the Holman and Russo charts.* Mosaic: MD4-136. 4CD set. 1950–63.

   4631.2 *Cuban fire!* Capitol: 96260 (T 731). 1956.

   4631.3 * *New concepts of artistry in rhythm.* Capitol: 92865 (T 383). 1952.

   4631.4 *Retrospective.* Capitol: C24Z 97350. 4CD set. 1943–68.

4632 Kessel, Barney, 1923– , with Shelly Manne, 1920–1984, and Ray Brown, 1926–

The poll winners. Fantasy: OJCCD-156-2 (Contemporary 7535). 1957.

4633 Kirk, Rahsaan Roland, 1936–1977

   4633.1 *Does your house have lions: the Rahsaan Roland Kirk anthology.* Rhino/Atlantic: 71406. 2CD set. 1966–75.

   4633.2 * *Rip, rig & panic/Now please don't you cry, beautiful Edith.* EmArcy: 832164-2 (Limelight 86027). 1965, 1967.

4634 Klugh, Earl, 1954–

The best of Earl Klugh. Blue Note: 46625. 1976–84.

4635 Knepper, Jimmy, 1927–

I dream too much. Soul Note: 121092-2. 1984.

4636 Konitz, Lee, 1927–

Subconscious Lee. Fantasy: OJCCD-186-2 (Prestige 7004). 1949–50.

4637 Konitz, Lee, 1927– , and Gerry Mulligan, 1927–1996

Konitz meets Mulligan. Pacific Jazz: 46847 (PJ 20142). 1953.

4638 Kronos Quartet

Monk suite. Landmark: LCD-1505-2. 1984.

4639   Lacy, Steve, 1934–

4639.1   *The gleam.* Silkheart: SHCD 101. 1986.

4639.2   * *Morning joy (live at Sunset Paris).* Hat Hut: ART CD 6014. 1986.

4639.3   *Only Monk.* Soul Note: 121160-2. 1985.

4639.4   *The straight horn of Steve Lacy.* Candid: CCD-79007 (8007). 1960.

4640   Lacy, Steve, 1934– , and Don Cherry, 1936–1995

Evidence. Fantasy: OJCCD-1755-2 (New Jazz 8271). 1961.

4641   Lake, Oliver, 1944–

Compilation. Gramavision: 79458. 1982–88.

4642   Land, Harold, 1928–

The fox. Fantasy: OJCCD-343-2 (Hifijazz 612). 1959.

4643   Last Poets

This is madness. Metrotone: 72658-2 (Douglas). 1971.

4644   Lateef, Yusef, 1921–

Eastern sounds. Fantasy: OJCCD-612-2 (Prestige 7319). 1961.

4645   Laws, Hubert, 1939–

Afro-classic. CTI/CBS: ZK 44172 (6006). 1970.

4646   Lee, Jeanne, 1939– , and Ran Blake, 1935–

The legendary duets. RCA Bluebird: 6461-2-RB (LSP-2500). 1962.

4647   Legrand, Michel, 1932–

Legrand jazz. Philips: 830074-2 (Columbia CL 1250). 1957–58.

4648   Lewis, John, 1920– , and Bill Perkins, 1924–

2 degrees east, 3 degrees west. Pacific Jazz: 46859 (1217). 1956.

4649   Lewis, Ramsey, 1935–

4649.1   *Greatest hits of Ramsey Lewis.* Chess: CHD-6021. 1961–67.

4649.2   *Sun goddess.* Columbia: CK 33194. 1975.

4650   Little, Booker, 1938–1961

Out front. Candid: CCD-79027 (8027). 1961.

4651   * Lloyd, Charles, 1938–

Forest flower; Soundtrack. Rhino: 71746 (Atlantic 1473/1519). 1966, 1969.

4652   Loose Tubes

Open letter. Editions EG: CAROL-1501-2 (EGED 55). 1989.

4653   Lovano, Joe, 1952–

From the soul. Blue Note: 98636. 1991.

4654   Lowe, Frank, 1943–

Decision in paradise. Soul Note: 121082-2. 1984.

4655   Mahavishnu Orchestra

4655.1   *Birds of fire.* Columbia: CK 31996. 1972.

4655.2   * *Inner mounting flame.* Columbia: CK 31067. 1971.

4656   Mangelsdorff, Albert, 1928–

Three originals: The wide point/Trilogue/Albert live in Montreux. Verve: 314 519213-2 (MPS). 2CD set. 1975, 1976, 1980.

4657   Mangione, Chuck, 1940–

Feels so good. A&M: 75021-3219-2. 1977.

4658   Manne, Shelly, 1920–1984

4658.1   *At the Black Hawk, vol. 1.* Fantasy: OJCCD-656-2 (Contemporary 7577). 1959.

4658.2   *Shelly Manne and his men, vol. 1: the West Coast sound.* Fantasy: OJCCD-152-2 (Contemporary 3507). 1953, 1955.

4658.3   *"The Three" and "The Two."* Fantasy: OJCCD-172-2 (Contemporary 3584). 1954.

4659   Manne, Shelly, 1920–1984, and André Previn, 1929–

My fair lady. Fantasy: OJCCD-336-2 (Contemporary 7527). 1956.

4660   Mantler, Michael, 1943– , and Carla Bley, 1938–

13 for piano and two orchestras; 3/4 for piano and orchestra. Watt: 3. LP. 1975.

4661   Marsalis, Branford, 1960–

Renaissance. Columbia: CK 40711. 1987.

4662   Marsalis, Wynton, 1961–

4662.1   *Black codes (from the underground).* Columbia: CK 40009. 1985.

4662.2   *Citi movement (griot New York).* Columbia: M2K 53324. 2CD set. 1993.

4662.3   *The majesty of the blues.* Columbia: CK 45091. 1988.

4662.4 ** *Marsalis standard time.* Columbia: CK 40461. 1986.

4663 Martino, Pat, 1944–
East! Fantasy: OJCCD-248-2 (Prestige 7562). 1968.

4664 McCann, Les, 1935– , and Eddie Harris, 1936–
Swiss movement. Atlantic: 1537-2. 1969.

4665 McConnell, Rob, 1935–
Live in digital. Sea Breeze: CDSB 106. 1980.

4666 * McGregor, Chris, 1936–1990
Chris McGregor's Brotherhood of Breath. Repertoire: REP 4468-WP (Neon NE2). 1971.

4667 McKenna, Dave, 1930–
Dancing in the dark. Concord Jazz: CCD-4292. 1985.

4668 McKusick, Hal, 1924–
Now's the time. Decca Jazz: GRD-651. 1957–58.

4669 McLaughlin, John, 1942–
4669.1 *Extrapolation.* Verve: 841598-2 (Polydor 5510). 1969.
4669.2 *My goal's beyond.* Rykodisc: RCD-10051 (Douglas 9). 1970.

4670 McLean, Jackie, 1932–
4670.1 *Bluesnik.* Blue Note: 84067. 1961.
4670.2 * *Let freedom ring.* Blue Note: 46527 (84106). 1962.
4670.3 *Right now.* Blue Note: 84215. 1965.

4671 Metheny, Pat, 1954–
4671.1 *80/81.* ECM: 78118-21180-2 (843169-2). 1980.
4671.2 *Offramp.* ECM: 78118-21216-2 (1216). 1981.
4671.3 * *Pat Metheny Group.* ECM: 78118-21114-2 (825593-2). 1978.

4672 Metheny, Pat, 1954– , and Ornette Coleman, 1930–
Song X. Geffen: 24096-2. 1985.

4673 Mingus, Charles, 1922–1979
4673.1 *The black saint and the sinner lady.* Impulse!/MCA: IMPD-174 (Impulse 35). 1961.
4673.2 *Blues and roots.* Atlantic: 1305-2. 1959.
4673.3 ** *Charles Mingus presents Charles Mingus.* Candid: CCD-79005 (8005). 1960. [Item 4673.5 covers all the material on item 4673.3

plus additional recordings and better packaging and notes].
4673.4 *The clown.* Atlantic: 90142-2 (1260). 1957.
4673.5 *The complete Candid recordings of Charles Mingus.* Mosaic: MD3-111. 3CD set. 1960–61. OP
4673.6 *Cumbia and jazz fusion.* Rhino: 71785 (Atlantic 8801). 1976–77.
4673.7 *East coasting.* Bethlehem/Evidence: 3002 (6019). 1957.
4673.8 *Jazzical moods.* Fantasy: OJCCD-1857-2. (Period). 1954.
4673.9 *Let my children hear music.* Columbia: CK 48910 (31039). 1972.
4673.10 ** *Mingus ah um.* Columbia: CK 40648 (8171). 1959.
4673.11 *Mingus at Antibes.* Atlantic: 90532-2. 1960.
4673.12 * *Mingus dynasty.* Columbia: CK 52922 (8236). 1959.
4673.13 *Mingus revisited (pre-Bird).* EmArcy: 826496-2 (MG-20627). 1960.
4673.14 *New Tijuana moods.* RCA Bluebird: 5644-2-RB (LSC 2533). 1957.
4673.15 * *Pithecanthropus erectus.* Atlantic: 8809-2 (1237). 1956.
4673.16 *Thirteen pictures: the Charles Mingus anthology.* Rhino: 71402. 2CD set. 1952–77.

4674 Mitchell, Blue, 1930–1979
The thing to do. Blue Note: 84178. 1964.

4675 Mitchell, Roscoe, 1940–
4675.1 *Old/quartet.* nessa: n-5. LP. 1967. [*Old/quartet* has been reissued on *The Art Ensemble, 1967/68* (nessa: ncd-2500, 5CD set), a collectors' edition that may exceed the "basic" scope of this book]. OP
4675.2 *Snurdy McGurdy and her dancin' shoes.* Nessa: ncd-20. 1980.
4675.3 * *Sound.* Delmark: 408. 1966.

4676 Mobley, Hank, 1930–1986
4676.1 *No room for squares.* Blue Note: 84149. 1963.
4676.2 *Soul station.* Blue Note: 46528 (84031). 1960.

4677 Modern Jazz Quartet [John Lewis, Milt Jackson, Percy Heath, and Kenny Clarke or Connie Kay]

4677.1 * *The complete last concert.* Rhino: 81976 (Atlantic 909). 2CD set. 1974.

4677.2 *Concorde.* Fantasy: OJCCD-002-2 (Prestige 7005). 1955.

4677.3 ** *Django.* Fantasy: OJCCD-057-2 (Prestige 7057). 1953–54.

4677.4 *European concert.* Atlantic: CS2-603-4. AC. 1960.

4677.5 * *MJQ40.* Atlantic: 82330-2. 4CD set. 1952–88.

4677.6 *No sun in Venice.* Atlantic: 1284-2. 1957.

4677.7 *Third stream music.* Atlantic: 1345. LP. 1960. OP

4678 Moncur, Grachan, III, 1937–

Some other stuff. Blue Note: 32092 (84177). 1964.

4679 Monk, Thelonious, 1917–1982

4679.1 *At Town Hall.* Fantasy: OJCCD-135-2 (Riverside 1138). 1959.

4679.2 ** *The best of Thelonious Monk: the Blue Note years.* Blue Note: 95636. 1947–52. [Item 4679.5 covers material comparable to items 4679.2 and 4679.8 but in greater depth and with better packaging and notes].

4679.3 *Big band and quartet in concert.* Columbia: C2K 57636. 2CD set. 1963.

4679.4 ** *Brilliant corners.* Fantasy: OJCCD-026-2 (Riverside 226). 1956.

4679.5 * *The complete Blue Note recordings of Thelonious Monk.* Blue Note: 30363 (Mosaic MR4-101). 4CD set. 1947–52, 1957.

4679.6 *The complete Riverside recordings.* Riverside: 15RCD-022-2. 15CD set. 1955–61.

4679.7 *5 by Monk by 5.* Fantasy: OJCCD-362-2 (Riverside 1150). 1959.

4679.8 ** *Genius of modern music, vols. 1–2.* Blue Note: 81510/81511. 2 CDs. 1947–52. [Item 4679.5 covers material comparable to items 4679.2 and 4679.8 but in greater depth and with better packaging and notes].

4679.9 *The London collection, vol. 1.* Black Lion: BLCD-760101. 1970.

4679.10 *Misterioso.* Fantasy: OJCCD-206-2 (Riverside 1133). 1958.

4679.11 *Monk.* Fantasy: OJCCD-016-2 (Prestige 7053). 1953–54.

4679.12 * *Monk's dream.* Columbia: CK 40786 (8765). 1962.

4679.13 *Monk's music.* Fantasy: OJCCD-084-2 (Riverside 242). 1957.

4679.14 ** *Thelonious himself.* Fantasy: OJCCD-254-2 (Riverside 235). 1957.

4679.15 * *Thelonious Monk and John Coltrane.* Fantasy: OJCCD-039-2 (Jazzland 946). 1957.

4679.16 *Trio.* Fantasy: OJCCD-010-2 (Prestige 7027). 1952, 1954.

4679.17 *The unique Thelonious Monk.* Fantasy: OJCCD-064-2 (Riverside 209). 1956.

4680 Monterose, J. R., 1927–1993

Straight ahead. Xanadu: XCD 1233 (Jaro 5004). 1959.

4681 Montgomery, Wes, 1925–1968

4681.1 *Full house.* Fantasy: OJCCD-106-2 (Riverside 9434). 1962.

4681.2 ** *The incredible jazz guitar of Wes Montgomery.* Fantasy: OJCCD-036-2 (Riverside 9320). 1960.

4681.3 * *Smokin' at the Half Note.* Verve: 829578-2 (V6-8633). 1965.

4682 Montoliu, Tete, 1933–

Tete! Steeplechase: SCCD 31029. 1974.

4683 Moody, James, 1925–

4683.1 *Moody's mood for blues.* Fantasy: OJCCD-1837-2 (Prestige 7056/7072). 1954–55.

4683.2 *Return from Overbrook.* Chess: GRD-810. (Argo 603/637). 1956–58.

4684 Moody, James, 1925– , and Art Blakey, 1919–1990

New sounds. Blue Note: 84436. 1947–48.

4685 Moore, Brew, 1924–1973

The Brew Moore Quintet. Fantasy: OJC-100 (3-222). LP. 1955–56.

4686 Morgan, Frank, 1933–

Lament. Contemporary: CCD-14021-2. 1986.

4687 Morgan, Lee, 1938–1972

4687.1 * *Best of Lee Morgan.* Blue Note: 91138. 1957–65.

4687.2 *Candy.* Blue Note: 46508 (81590). 1957–58.

4687.3 *Leeway.* Blue Note: 32089 (84034). 1960.

4688 Moses, Bob, 1948–

When elephants dream of music. Gramavision: 79491 (8203). 1982.

4689 Motian, Paul, 1931–

It should have happened a long time ago. ECM: 78118-21283-2 (823641-2). 1984.

4690 Mulligan, Gerry, 1927–1996

4690.1 ** *The best of the Gerry Mulligan Quartet with Chet Baker.* Pacific Jazz: 95481. 1952–53.

4690.2 *Gerry Mulligan.* [Series: Compact jazz]. Mercury: 830697-2. 1955. OP

4690.3 * *Gerry Mulligan Concert Jazz Band.* Verve: 838933-2 (MGV 8396). 1960.

4690.4 *Gerry Mulligan Quartet featuring Chet Baker plus Chubby Jackson Big Band featuring Gerry Mulligan.* Fantasy: OJCCD-711-2 (3-220). 1950, 1952–53.

4691 Murray, David, 1955–

4691.1 *Deep river.* DIW: DIW-830. 1988.

4691.2 *Home.* Black Saint: 120055-2. 1981.

4691.3 ** *Ming.* Black Saint: 120045-2. 1980.

4691.4 *Morning song.* Black Saint: 120075-2. 1983.

4691.5 * *Murray's steps.* Black Saint: 120065-2. 1982.

4691.6 *3D family.* Hat Hut: ART CD 6020. 1978.

4692 Myers, Amina Claudine, 1943–

Amina Claudine Myers salutes Bessie Smith. Leo: 103. 1980.

4693 Navarro, Fats, 1923–1950

4693.1 * *Fats Navarro memorial.* Savoy/Denon: SV-0181 (12011). 1946–47.

4693.2 *Nostalgia.* Savoy/Denon: SV-0123 (12133). 1946–47.

4694 ** Navarro, Fats, 1923–1950, and Tadd Dameron, 1917–1965

The complete Blue Note and Capitol recordings of Fats Navarro and Tadd Dameron. Blue Note: 33373. 2CD set. 1947–49.

4695 * Nelson, Oliver, 1932–1975

Blues and the abstract truth. Impulse!/MCA: IMPD 154 (5). 1961.

4696 New York Art Quartet

New York Art Quartet. ESP DISK: 1004. 1964. [John Tchicai, Roswell Rudd, Lewis Worrell, Milford Graves].

4697 Newborn, Phineas, Jr., 1931–1989

A world of piano. Fantasy: OJCCD-175-2 (Contemporary 7600). 1961.

4698 * Newton, James, 1953–

African flower. Blue Note: 85109. 1985.

4699 * Nichols, Herbie, 1919–1963

The art of Herbie Nichols. Blue Note: 99176. 1955–56.

4700 Nordine, Ken

The best of word jazz, vol. 1. Rhino: 70773. 1957–60.

4701 * Old and New Dreams

Playing. ECM: 78118-21205-2 (829123-2). 1980. [Don Cherry, Dewey Redman, Charlie Haden, Ed Blackwell].

4702 * Oregon [Paul McCandless, Glen Moore, Ralph Towner, Collin Walcott]

Distant hills. Vanguard: VMD-79341. 1973.

4703 Parker, Charlie, 1920–1955

4703.1 *At the 1946 Jazz at the Philharmonic concert.* Verve: 314 513756-2. 1946.

4703.2 ** *Bird: Savoy master takes.* Savoy: ZDS-8801. 2CD set. 1945–48. [Item 4703.10 covers material comparable to item 4703.2 but in greater depth and with better packaging and notes]. OP

4703.3 *Bird: the complete Charlie Parker on Verve.* Verve: 837141-2. 10CD set. 1946–54.

4703.4 *Charlie Parker memorial, vol. 1.* Savoy/Denon: SV-0101 (12001). 1947–48.

4703.5 *Charlie Parker memorial, vol. 2.* Savoy/Denon: SV-0103 (12009). 1945–48.

4703.6 ** *The Charlie Parker story.* Savoy/Denon: SV-0105 (12079). 1945.

4703.7 *Charlie Parker with strings: the master takes.* Verve: 314 523984-2. 1947, 1949–52.

4703.8 *The complete birth of bebop.* Stash: ST-CD-535. 1940–45.

4703.9 * *The complete Dial sessions.* Jazz Classics: 5010 (Stash 567/70). 4CD set. 1946–47.

4703.10 * *Complete Savoy studio sessions.* Savoy: ZDS-5500. 3CD set. 1945–48. OP

4703.11 ** *Confirmation: best of the Verve years.* Verve: 314 527815-2. 2CD set. 1946–54.

4703.12 * *The genius of Charlie Parker.* Savoy/Denon: SV-0104 (12014). 1945–48.

4703.13 *The immortal Charlie Parker.* Savoy/Denon: SV-0102 (12001). 1944, 1947–48.

4703.14 * *Jazz at Massey Hall.* Fantasy: OJCCD-044-2 (Debut). 1953. [Charlie Parker, Dizzy

Gillespie, Bud Powell, Charles Mingus, Max Roach].

4703.15 ** *The legendary Dial masterpieces, vols. 1 and 2.* Jazz Classics: 5003 (Stash 23/25). 2CD set. 1946–47.

4703.16 *Now's the time.* Verve: 825671-2. 1952–53.

4703.17 *Swedish schnapps +.* Verve: 849393-2. 1949–51.

4704 Parker, Charlie, 1920–1955, and Dizzy Gillespie, 1917–1993

4704.1 *Bebop's heartbeat.* Savoy: ZDS-1177. 1945, 1947. OP

4704.2 *Bird and Diz.* Verve: 831133-2. 1950.

4705 Parker, Charlie, 1920–1955, and Jay McShann, 1909–

Early Bird. Stash: ST-CD-542. 1940–44.

4706 Parker, Evan, 1944–

Process and reality. FMP (Free Music Production): CD 37. 1991.

4707 Pass, Joe, 1929–1994

Virtuoso. Pablo: PACD-2310-708-2. 1973.

4708 Pastorius, Jaco, 1951–1987

4708.1 *Jaco Pastorius.* Epic: EK 33949. 1976.

4708.2 *Word of mouth.* Warner Bros.: 3535-2. 1981.

4709 Pepper, Art, 1925–1982

4709.1 * *Art Pepper meets the Rhythm Section.* Fantasy: OJCCD-338-2 (Contemporary 7532). 1957.

4709.2 *Landscape.* Fantasy: OJCCD-676-2 (Galaxy 5128). 1979.

4709.3 *Modern art.* Blue Note: 46848 (Intro 606). 1956–57.

4709.4 *Modern jazz classics.* Fantasy: OJCCD-341-2 (Contemporary 7568). 1959.

4710 Peterson, Oscar, 1925–

4710.1 * *At the Stratford Shakespearean Festival.* Verve: 314 513752-2 (8024). 1956.

4710.2 *The will to swing: Oscar Peterson at his very best.* Verve: 847203-2. 2CD set. 1947–73.

4711 Peterson, Oscar, 1925– , and Clark Terry, 1920–
Trio plus one. Mercury: 818840-2 (MG-60975). 1964.

4712 Peterson, Ralph, Jr., 1962–
Ralph Peterson presents the fo'tet. Blue Note: 95475. 1989.

4713 Pettiford, Oscar, 1922–1960
Deep passion (Oscar Pettiford Orchestra in hi-fi). Impulse!/GRP: GRD-143 (ABC 135/227). 1956–57.

4714 Pine, Courtney, 1964–
Destiny's song + The image of pursuance. Antilles: 422-842772-2. 1987.

4715 Ponty, Jean-Luc, 1942–
Imaginary voyage. Atlantic: 19136-2. 1976.

4716 Powell, Bud, 1924–1966

4716.1 ** *The amazing Bud Powell, vol. 1.* Blue Note: 81503. 1949–51.

4716.2 * *The amazing Bud Powell, vol. 2.* Blue Note: 81504. 1951–53.

4716.3 *The Bud Powell Trio plays.* Roulette Jazz: 93902 (Roost 2224). 1947–53.

4716.4 * *The genius of Bud Powell.* Verve: 827901-2. 1950–53.

4716.5 ** *Jazz giant.* Verve: 829937-2. 1949–50.

4717 Pukwana, Dudu, 1938–1990
In the townships. Earthworks: CAROL-2405-2 (Caroline 1504). 1973.

4718 Pullen, Don, 1944–1995
New beginnings. Blue Note: 91785. 1988.

4719 Raney, Jimmy, 1927–1995
"A." Fantasy: OJCCD-1706-2 (Prestige 7089). 1955.

4720 Redd, Freddie, 1928–
The connection. Blue Note: 89392 (84027). 1960.

4721 Revolutionary Ensemble
Vietnam. ESP DISK: 3007. 1972. [Leroy Jenkins, Sirone, Jerome Cooper].

4722 Rich, Buddy, 1917–1987

4722.1 *Buddy Rich.* [Series: Compact jazz]. Verve: 833295-2. 1955–61.

4722.2 *Swingin' new big band.* Pacific Jazz: 35232 (20113). 1966.

4723 * Rivers, Sam, 1923– , and Dave Holland, 1946–
Sam Rivers and Dave Holland, vols. 1–2. Improvising Artists (IAI): 123843-2/123848-2. 2 CDs. 1976.

4724 Roach, Max, 1924–

4724.1 *Drums unlimited.* Atlantic: 1467. LP. 1966. OP

4724.2 * *Percussion bitter suite.* Impulse!/GRP: GRD-122 (Impulse 8). 1961.

4724.3 *We insist: Freedom now suite.* Candid: CCD-79002 (8002). 1960.

4725 Roach, Max, 1924– , and Anthony Braxton, 1945–

Birth and rebirth. Black Saint: 120024-2. 1978.

4726 Rodney, Red, 1927–1994

Bird lives! Muse: MCD-5371. 1973.

4727 Rogers, Shorty, 1924–1994

Short stops. RCA Bluebird: 5917-2-RB. 1953–54.

4728 Rollins, Sonny, 1929–

4728.1 *Don't stop the carnival.* Milestone: MCD-55005-2. 1978.

4728.2 *East Broadway rundown.* Impulse!/GRP: IMPD-161 (9127). 1966.

4728.3 *Freedom suite.* Fantasy: OJCCD-067-2 (Riverside 258). 1958.

4728.4 *G man.* Milestone: MCD-9150-2. 1986–87.

4728.5 *Newk's time.* Blue Note: 84001. 1957.

4728.6 ** *A night at the Village Vanguard, vols. 1–2.* Blue Note: 46517/46518. 2 CDs. 1957.

4728.7 *On the outside.* RCA Bluebird: 2496-2-RB (LSP 2612). 1962.

4728.8 * *The quartets (The bridge).* RCA Bluebird: 5643-2-RB (LSP-2527). 1962, 1964.

4728.9 ** *Saxophone colossus.* Fantasy: OJCCD-291-2 (Prestige 7079). 1956.

4728.10 * *Sonny Rollins plus 4.* Fantasy: OJCCD-243-2 (Prestige 7038). 1956.

4728.11 *Tour de force.* Fantasy: OJCCD-095-2 (Prestige 7126). 1956.

4728.12 * *Way out west.* Fantasy: OJCCD-337-2 (Contemporary 7530). 1957.

4728.13 *Worktime.* Fantasy: OJCCD-007-2 (Prestige 7020). 1955.

4729 Roney, Wallace, 1960–

The standard bearer. Muse: MCD 5372. 1989.

4730 Rova Saxophone Quartet

Beat kennel. Black Saint: 120126-2. 1987.

4731 Rowles, Jimmy, 1918–1996

We could make such beautiful music together. EPM: FDC-5152 (Xanadu 157). 1977–78.

4732 Russell, George, 1923–

4732.1 * *Ezz-thetics.* Fantasy: OJCCD-070-2 (Riverside 375). 1961.

4732.2 *Jazz in the space age.* MCA: MCA2-4017 (Decca 9219). 2LP set. 1959–60. [The 2LP set also included *New York, N.Y.* (1959), which was last available on Decca Jazz: MCAD-31371]. OP

4732.3 *Jazz workshop.* RCA Bluebird: 6467-2-RB. 1956. OP

4732.4 *Live in an American time spiral.* Soul Note: 121049-2. 1982.

4733 Russell, Hal, 1926–1992, and the NRG Ensemble

The Finnish/Swiss tour. ECM: 314 511261-2 (1455). 1990.

4734 Sanborn, David, 1945–

The best of David Sanborn. Warner Bros.: 45768-2. 1978–88.

4735 Sanders, Pharoah, 1940–

4735.1 *Karma.* Impulse!/GRP: IMPD-153 (9181). 1969.

4735.2 *Tauhid.* Impulse!/GRP: GRD-129 (9138). 1966.

4736 Schlippenbach, Alexander von, 1938–

Elf Bagatellen. FMP (Free Music Production): CD 27. 1972–90.

4737 Schweizer, Irène, 1941–

Piano solo, vol. 1. Intakt: 020. 1990.

4738 * Scofield, John, 1951–

Time on my hands. Blue Note: 92894. 1989.

4739 Scott-Heron, Gil, 1949–

The revolution will not be televised. RCA Bluebird: 6994-2-RB (Flying Dutchman). 1970–72.

4740 Shakti

Shakti. Columbia: CK 46868. 1975. [John McLaughlin, Lakshminarayana Shankar, Zakir Hussain, and others].

4741 Sharrock, Sonny, 1940–1994

Ask the ages. Axiom: 422-848957-2. 1991.

4742 Shaw, Woody, 1944–1989

4742.1 *The complete CBS studio recordings of Woody Shaw.* Mosaic: MD3-142. 3CD set. 1977–81.

4742.2   *Solid.* Muse: MCD-5329. 1987.

4743 * Shearing, George, 1919–

George Shearing. [Series: Verve jazz masters, vol. 57]. Verve: 314 529 900-2 (MGM). 1949–54.

4744   Shepp, Archie, 1937–

4744.1 * *Fire music.* Impulse!/GRP: IMPD-158 (86). 1965.

4744.2   *New York City Contemporary Five in Europe.* Delmark: 409. LP. 1963.

4744.3   *On this night.* Impulse!/GRP: GRD-125 (97). 1965.

4745   Shepp, Archie, 1937– , and Horace Parlan, 1931–

4745.1 * *Goin' home.* Steeplechase: SCCD 31079. 1977.

4745.2   *Trouble in mind.* Steeplechase: SCCD 31139. 1980.

4746   Shorter, Wayne, 1933–

4746.1   *Adam's apple.* Blue Note: 46403 (84232). 1966.

4746.2   *Native dancer.* Columbia: CK 46159 (33418). 1974.

4746.3   *Night dreamer.* Blue Note: 84173. 1964.

4746.4 * *Speak no evil.* Blue Note: 46509 (84194). 1964.

4747   Silver, Horace, 1928–

4747.1 * *The best of Horace Silver, vol. 1.* Blue Note: 91143. 1954–64.

4747.2   *Blowin' the blues away.* Blue Note: 46526 (84017). 1959.

4747.3 ** *Horace Silver and the Jazz Messengers.* Blue Note: 46140 (81518). 1954–55.

4747.4   *The jody grind.* Blue Note: 84250. 1966.

4747.5 * *Song for my father.* Blue Note: 84185. 1963–64.

4748   Sims, Zoot, 1925–1985

If I'm lucky. Fantasy: OJCCD-683-2 (Pablo 2310-803). 1977.

4749   Smith, Jimmy, 1925–

4749.1 * *Jimmy Smith.* [Series: Compact jazz]. Verve: 831374-2. 1962–66.

4749.2   *Midnight special.* Blue Note: 84078. 1960.

4749.3   *The sermon.* Blue Note: 46097 (84011). 1957–58.

4750   Smith, Johnny, 1922–

Moonlight in Vermont. Roulette: 97747 (2211). 1952.

4751   Smith, Leo, 1941–

Spirit catcher. nessa: n-19. LP. 1979.

4752   Solal, Martial, 1927–

Bluesine. Soul Note: 121060-2. 1983.

4753   Spaulding, James, 1937–

Brilliant corners. Muse: MCD-5369. 1988.

4754   Spyro Gyra

Spyro Gyra collection. GRP: GRD-9642. 1979–90.

4755   Stadler, Heiner, 1942–

A tribute to Monk and Bird. Tomato: 2696302. 2CD set. 1978.

4756   Stitt, Sonny, 1924–1982

4756.1 * *Constellation.* Muse: MCD-5323 (Cobblestone 9021). 1972.

4756.2 * *Sonny Stitt/Bud Powell/J. J. Johnson (Bud's blues).* Fantasy: OJCCD-009-2 (Prestige 7024). 1949–50.

4756.3   *Stitt plays Bird.* Atlantic: 1418-2. [1964].

4757   Sun Ra, 1914–1993

4757.1   *Cosmic tones for mental therapy/Art forms of dimensions tomorrow.* Evidence: ECD 22036-2 (Saturn 408/404). 1961–63.

4757.2 * *Heliocentric worlds, vol. 1.* ESP DISK: 1014. 1965.

4757.3   *Heliocentric worlds, vol. 2.* ESP DISK: 1017. 1965.

4757.4 * *Jazz in silhouette.* Evidence: ECD 22012-2 (Saturn 205). 1958.

4757.5   *The magic city.* Evidence: ECD 22069-2 (Saturn 711). 1965.

4757.6   *Sun song.* Delmark: DD 411 (Transition 10). 1956.

4757.7   *Sunrise in different dimensions.* Hat Hut: ART CD 6099 (2R17). 1980.

4757.8 * *Super-sonic jazz.* Evidence: ECD 22015-2 (Saturn 216). 1956.

4758   Surman, John, 1944–

The amazing adventures of Simon Simon. ECM: 78118-21193-2 (829160-2). 1981.

4759   Sutton, Ralph, 1922–

At Cafe des Copains. Sackville: CD 2019. 1983–87.

4760 Tapscott, Horace, 1934–

The dark tree, vol. 1. Hat Hut: ART CD 6053. 1989.

4761 Taylor, Cecil, 1933–

4761.1 *Alms/Tiergarten (Spree).* FMP (Free Music Production): CD 8/9. 2CD set. 1988.

4761.2 *The complete Cecil Taylor/Buell Neidlinger Candid sessions.* Mosaic: MD4-127. 3CD set. 1960–61. OP

4761.3 *Conquistador.* Blue Note: 46535 (84260). 1966.

4761.4 *For Olim.* Soul Note: 121150-2. 1986.

4761.5 *Into the hot.* MCA: MCAD-39104 (Impulse 9). 1962. [This recording was released under Gil Evans' name, but is actually a Cecil Taylor session combined with a Johnny Carisi session]. OP

4761.6 *Jazz advance.* Blue Note: 84462 (Transition 19). 1956.

4761.7 *Looking ahead.* Fantasy: OJCCD-452-2 (Contemporary 7562). 1958.

4761.8 *Nefertiti, the beautiful one has come.* Freedom: 1905 (Debut). 2LP set. 1962. OP

4761.9 ** *Silent tongues.* Freedom: FCD-741005. 1974.

4761.10 * *Three phasis.* New World: NW 303-2. 1978.

4761.11 * *Unit structures.* Blue Note: 84237. 1966.

4761.12 *Winged serpent.* Soul Note: 121089-2. 1984.

4761.13 * *The world of Cecil Taylor.* Candid: CCD-79006 (8006). 1960. [Item 4761.2 covers all the material on item 4761.13 plus additional recordings and better packaging and notes].

4762 Tchicai, John, 1936–

Real Tchicai. Steeplechase: SCCD 31075. 1977.

4763 Terry, Clark, 1920– , and Bob Brookmeyer, 1929–

The power of positive swinging. Mainstream/CBS: JK 57115 (56054). 1965.

4764 Thompson, Charles, Sir, 1918–

Takin' off. Delmark: DD-450 (Apollo). 1945–47. [With Charlie Parker].

4765 Thompson, Lucky, 1924–

4765.1 *Lucky strikes.* Fantasy: OJCCD-194-2 (Prestige 7365). 1964.

4765.2 * *Tricotism.* Impulse!/GRP: GRD-135 (ABC 111). 1956.

4766 Threadgill, Henry, 1944–

4766.1 *Easily slip into another world.* Novus: 3025-2-N. 1987.

4766.2 ** *Just the facts and pass the bucket.* About Time: 1005. LP. 1983.

4766.3 *When was that?* About Time: 1004. LP. 1982.

4766.4 *You know the number.* Novus: 3013-2-N. 1986.

4767 Three Sounds

The best of the Three Sounds: featuring Gene Harris. Blue Note: 27323. 1958–62.

4768 Tjader, Cal, 1925–1982

Monterey concerts. Prestige: PRCD-24026-2. 1959.

4769 Tristano, Lennie, 1919–1978

4769.1 *The complete Lennie Tristano on Keynote.* Mercury: 830921-2. 1946–47.

4769.2 ** *Intuition.* Capitol Jazz: 52771. 1949, 1956. [With Warne Marsh].

4769.3 * *Lennie Tristano/The new Tristano.* Rhino/Atlantic: 71595 (1224/1357). 1955, 1961.

4770 Turre, Steve, 1948–

Viewpoints and vibrations. Stash: ST-CD-2 (ST 270). 1986–87.

4771 Turrentine, Stanley, 1934–

The best of Stanley Turrentine. Blue Note: 93201. 1960–84.

4772 29th Street Saxophone Quartet

The real deal. Antilles: 314 510941-2 (New Note 1006). 1987.

4773 Tyner, McCoy, 1938–

4773.1 * *Echoes of a friend.* Fantasy: OJCCD-650-2 (Milestone 9055). 1972.

4773.2 *Enlightenment.* Milestone: MCD-55001-2. 1973.

4773.3 *The real McCoy.* Blue Note: 46512 (84264). 1967.

4773.4 *Uptown/downtown.* Milestone: MCD-9167-2. 1988.

4774 * Ulmer, James "Blood," 1942–

Are you glad to be in America? DIW: DIW-400 (Artists House 13). 1980.

4775 V. S. O. P.

The quintet: V. S. O. P. live. Columbia: CGK 34976. 1976. [Herbie Hancock, Wayne Shorter, Freddie Hubbard, Ron Carter, Tony Williams].

4776 Vienna Art Orchestra

From no time to rag time. Hat Hut: ART CD 6073 (1999/2000). 1982.

4777 Walcott, Collin, 1945–1984, Don Cherry, 1936–1995, and Nana Vasconcelos, 1945–

Codona. ECM: 78118-21132-2 (1132). 1978.

4778 Waldron, Mal, 1926–

The quest. Fantasy: OJCCD-082-2 (New Jazz 8269). 1961.

4779 * Waldron, Mal, 1926– , and Steve Lacy, 1934–

Sempre amore. Soul Note: 121170-2. 1986.

4780 Wallace, Bennie, 1946–

Bennie Wallace plays Monk. ENJA: ENJ 3091 2. 1981.

4781 Wallington, George, 1924–1993

The George Wallington trios. Fantasy: OJCCD-1754-2 (Prestige). 1952–53.

4782 Walton, Cedar, 1934–

Eastern rebellion. Timeless: CDSJP-101. 1975.

4783 Washington, Grover, Jr., 1943–

4783.1 *Mister magic.* Motown: 37463-5175-2 (Kudu 20). 1975.

4783.2 *Winelight.* Elektra: 305-2. 1981.

4784 Watson, Bobby, 1953–

The inventor. Blue Note: 91915. 1989.

4785 Weather Report

4785.1 *Black market.* Columbia: CK 34099. 1976.

4785.2 ** *Heavy weather.* Columbia: CK 47481 (34418). 1977.

4785.3 * *I sing the body electric.* Columbia: CK 46107 (31352). 1971–72.

4785.4 *Mysterious traveler.* Columbia: CK 32494. 1974.

4786 Weber, Eberhard, 1940–

The colors of Chloe. ECM: 78118-21042-2 (1042). 1973.

4787 Westbrook, Mike, 1936–

On Duke's birthday. Hat Hut: ART CD 6021 (2012). 1984.

4788 Weston, Randy, 1926–

4788.1 * *African cookbook.* Atlantic: 1609. LP. 1964. OP

4788.2 *Blues to Africa.* Freedom: FCD-741014. 1974.

4788.3 *Carnival.* Freedom: FCD-741004. 1974.

4788.4 *Little Niles.* Blue Note: 598 (United Artists). 2LP set. 1958–59. OP

4788.5 *Uhuru Afrika/Highlife.* Blue Note: 94510 (Roulette 65001). 1960, 1964.

4789 Wheeler, Kenny, 1930–

Deer wan. ECM: 78118-21102-2 (1102). 1977.

4790 Wilkerson, Edward, Jr., 1955– , and 8 Bold Souls

Sideshow. Arabesque Jazz: AJ-0103. 1991.

4791 Williams, Tony, 1945–1997

4791.1 *Foreign intrigue.* Blue Note: 46289. 1985.

4791.2 *Spring.* Blue Note: 46135 (84216). 1965.

4792 * Williams, Tony, 1945–1997, and Lifetime

Emergency. Polydor: 849068-2 (25-3001). 1969.

4793 Wilson, Gerald, 1918–

Moment of truth. Pacific Jazz: 92928 (PJ61). 1962. OP

4794 Woods, Phil, 1931–

Integrity. Red: 123177-2. 1984.

4795 * Woods, Phil, 1931– , Tommy Flanagan, 1930– , and Red Mitchell, 1927–1992

Three for all. ENJA: 79614-2 (3081). 1981.

4796 World Saxophone Quartet [Julius Hemphill, Oliver Lake, David Murray, Hamiet Bluiett]

4796.1 ** *Revue.* Black Saint: 120056-2. 1980.

4796.2 * *Steppin' with the World Saxophone Quartet.* Black Saint: 120027-2. 1978.

4796.3 *World Saxophone Quartet plays Duke Ellington.* Nonesuch: 79137-2. 1986.

4796.4 *WSQ.* Black Saint: 120046-2. 1980.

4797 Yellowjackets

Politics. MCA: MCAD-6236. 1988.

4798 Young, Larry, 1940–1978

The art of Larry Young. Blue Note: 99177. 1964–69.

4799 Zawinul, Joe, 1932–

Zawinul. Atlantic: 1579-2. 1970.

4800 Zorn, John, 1953–

4800.1 *News for Lulu.* Hat Hut: ART CD 6005. 1987.

4800.2 *Spy vs. spy.* Elektra/Musician: 60844-2. 1989.

Jazz Singers

This section includes vocalists generally recognized as jazz singers. Popular singers who were influenced by jazz or who may have worked with jazz musicians (Fred Astaire, Connee Boswell, Rosemary Clooney, Nat King Cole, Bing Crosby, Lena Horne, Peggy Lee, Nina Simone, Frank Sinatra, Ethel Waters) are included in chapter 23, "Mainstream Popular and New Age." *See also 4338*

Anthologies

4801 *Legendary big band singers.* Decca Jazz/GRP: GRD-642. 1931–51. [Cab Calloway, Louis Armstrong, Sy Oliver, Pha Terrell, June Richmond, Jimmy Rushing, Helen Humes, Jack Teagarden, Helen O'Connell, Bob Eberly, Walter Brown, Rosetta Tharpe, Ella Fitzgerald, Kay Starr, Dinah Washington, Ella Johnson, Arthur Prysock].

4802 *1930s: the singers.* Columbia: CK 40847. 1930–39. [Red Allen, Louis Armstrong, Mildred Bailey, Connie Boswell, Jack Teagarden, and others].

4803 *1940s: the singers.* Columbia: CK 40652. 1940–49. [Billie Holiday, Anita O'Day, Cab Calloway, and others].

4804 * *When Malindy sings.* New World: NW 295. LP. 1938–61. [Billie Holiday, Ella Fitzgerald, Dinah Washington, Betty Carter, Sarah Vaughan, Joe Turner, Chris Connor, and others]. OP

Individual Artists

4805 Allison, Mose, 1927–

Greatest hits. Fantasy: OJCCD-6004-2. 1957–59.

4806 Anderson, Ernestine, 1928–

Never make your move too soon. Concord Jazz: CCD-4147. 1980.

4807 Armstrong, Louis, 1901–1974. *See 4343–4345*

4808 * Bailey, Mildred, 1907–1951

The rockin' chair lady. Decca Jazz/GRP: GRD-644. 1931–50.

4809 Carter, Betty, 1930–

4809.1 * *The audience with Betty Carter.* Verve: 835684-2 (BetCar 1003). 2CD set. 1979.

4809.2 *The Betty Carter album.* Verve: 835682-2 (BetCar 1002). [1975].

4809.3 *Finally.* Roulette: 95333 (5000). 1969.

4809.4 *I can't help it.* Impulse!/GRP: GRD-114 (Peacock 90/ABC 363). 1958–59.

4809.5 * *Inside Betty Carter.* Capitol Jazz: 89702 (UA 6379). 1964–65.

4809.6 *Look what I got.* Verve: 835661-2. 1988.

4810 Christy, June, 1925–1990

Something cool. Capitol: 96329 (T516). 1953–55.

4811 Connor, Chris, 1927–

Chris Connor sings the George Gershwin almanac of songs. Atlantic: 601-2. 2CD set. 1957.

4812 Fitzgerald, Ella, 1918–1996

4812.1 ** *The best of the song books.* Verve: 314 519804-2. 1956–64. [Item 4812.13 covers similar material].

4812.2 *Cole Porter songbook, vols. 1–2.* Verve: 821989-2/821990-2 (4001-2). 2 CDs. 1956.

4812.3 *Ella in London.* Pablo: PACD-2310-711-2. 1974.

4812.4 * *Ellington songbook.* Verve: 837035-2 (4008/9-2). 3CD set. 1956–57.

4812.5 * *First lady of song.* Verve: 314 517898-2. 3CD set. 1949–66.

4812.6 * *George and Ira Gershwin songbook.* Verve: 825024-2 (4029-5). 3CD set. 1959.

4812.7 * *Harold Arlen songbook, vols. 1–2.* Verve: 817527-2/817528-2 (64057/58). 2 CDs. 1960–61.

4812.8 *Jerome Kern songbook.* Verve: 825669-2 (64060). 1963.

4812.9 *Mack the knife: the complete Ella in Berlin concert.* Verve: 314 519564-2 (64041). 1960.

4812.10 ** *Pure Ella (Ella sings Gershwin).* Decca Jazz: GRD-636 (DL8378+). 1950, 1954.

4812.11 *Rodgers and Hart songbook, vols. 1–2.* Verve: 821579-2/821580-2 (4002-2). 2 CDs. 1956.

4812.12 * *75th birthday celebration: greatest hits.* Decca Jazz: GRD2-619. 2CD set. 1935–55.

4812.13 * *The songbooks.* Silver Collection. Verve: 823445-2. 1956–61. [Item 4812.1 covers similar material].

4813   Fitzgerald, Ella, 1918–1996, and Joe Pass, 1929–1994

Speak love. Pablo: PACD-2310-888-2. 1983.

4814   Frishberg, Dave, 1933–

Classics. Concord Jazz: CCD-4462. 1982–83.

4815   Hartman, Johnny, 1923–1983. *See* 4534.9

4816   Holiday, Billie, 1915–1959

4816.1 * *Billie's best.* Verve: 314 513943-2. 1952–59. [Item 4816.4 covers material comparable to item 4816.1 but in greater depth and with better packaging and notes].

4816.2 * *The complete Commodore recordings.* Commodore/GRP: CMD2-401. 2CD set. 1939, 1944.

4816.3   *Complete Decca recordings.* Decca Jazz: GRD-2-601. 2CD set. 1944–50.

4816.4   *First issue: the great American songbook.* Verve: 314 523003-2. 2CD set. 1952–59.

4816.5   *The quintessential Billie Holiday, vol. 1.* Columbia: CK 40646. 1933–35.

4816.6 * *The quintessential Billie Holiday, vol. 2.* Columbia: CK 40790. 1936.

4816.7 * *The quintessential Billie Holiday, vol. 3.* Columbia: CK 44048. 1936–37.

4816.8 ** *The quintessential Billie Holiday, vol. 4.* Columbia: CK 44252. 1937.

4816.9 ** *The quintessential Billie Holiday, vol. 5.* Columbia: CK 44423. 1937–38.

4816.10   *The quintessential Billie Holiday, vol. 6.* Columbia: CK 45449. 1938.

4816.11   *The quintessential Billie Holiday, vol. 7.* Columbia: CK 46180. 1938–39.

4816.12 * *The quintessential Billie Holiday, vol. 8.* Columbia: CK 47030. 1939–40.

4816.13 * *The quintessential Billie Holiday, vol. 9.* Columbia: CK 47031. 1940–42.

4816.14   *Solitude.* [Series: The Billie Holiday story, vol. 2]. Verve: 314 519 810-2. 1952.

4817   Horn, Shirley, 1934–

Close enough for love. Verve: 837933-2. 1988.

4818   Humes, Helen, 1913–1981

Songs I like to sing. Fantasy: OJCCD-171-2 (Contemporary 7582). 1960.

4819   Jarreau, Al, 1940–

Look to the rainbow: Al Jarreau live in Europe. Warner Bros.: 3052-2. 1977.

4820   Jefferson, Eddie, 1918–1979

Body and soul. Fantasy: OJCCD-396-2 (Prestige 7619). 1968.

4821   Jordan, Sheila, 1928–

4821.1 * *Lost and found.* Muse: MCD 5390. 1989.

4821.2   *Portrait of Sheila.* Blue Note: 89002. 1962.

4822   Lambert, Hendricks & Ross

4822.1   *Everybody's boppin'.* Columbia: CK 45020. 1959–61.

4822.2   *Sing a song of Basie.* Impulse!/GRP: GRD-112 (ABC 223). 1957.

4822.3 * *Twisted: the best of Lambert, Hendricks and Ross.* Rhino: 70328. 1957–61.

4823   Lea, Barbara

Lea in love. Fantasy: OJCCD-1742-2 (Prestige 7100). 1957.

4824   Lincoln, Abbey, 1930–

4824.1   *Abbey is blue.* Fantasy: OJCCD-069-2 (Riverside 1153). 1959.

4824.2   *You gotta pay the band.* Verve: 314 511110-2. 1991.

4825   McCorkle, Susannah, 1949–

No more blues. Concord Jazz: CCD-4370. 1988.

4826   McFerrin, Bobby, 1950–

The voice. Elektra/Musician: 60366-2. 1984.

4827   McRae, Carmen, 1922–1994

4827.1 ** *The great American songbook.* Atlantic: 904-2. [1972].

4827.2   *Here to stay.* Decca Jazz: GRD-610. 1955–59.

4828   Merrill, Helen, 1930–

Helen Merrill. [Series: Compact jazz]. Mercury: 832831-2. 1954–76.

4829   Merrill, Helen, 1930– , and Gil Evans, 1912–1988

Collaboration. EmArcy: 834205-2. 1987.

4830   Murphy, Mark, 1932–

Bop for Kerouac. Muse: MCD 5253. 1981.

4831 O'Day, Anita, 1919–

4831.1 *Anita O'Day.* [Series: Compact jazz]. Verve: 314 517954-2. 1952–62.

4831.2 * *Anita O'Day sings the winners.* Verve: 837939-2 (8283). 1958.

4832 Pleasure, King, 1922–1981, and Annie Ross, 1930–

King Pleasure sings/Annie Ross sings. Fantasy: OJCCD-217-2 (Prestige 7128). 1952–54.

4833 Rushing, Jimmy, 1902–1972

4833.1 * *The essential Jimmy Rushing.* Vanguard: VCD 65/66. 1954–57.

4833.2 *The you and me that used to be.* RCA Bluebird: 6460-2-RB. 1971.

4834 Sloane, Carol, 1937–

The real thing. Contemporary: CCD-14060-2. 1991.

4835 Sullivan, Maxine, 1911–1987

The great songs from the Cotton Club. Mobile Fidelity: MFCD 836 (Stash 244). 1984. OP

4836 Swingle Singers

Anyone for Mozart, Bach, Handel, Vivaldi? Philips: 826 948-2. 1964–65.

4837 Teagarden, Jack, 1905–1964. *See 4425*

4838 Tormé, Mel, 1925–

4838.1 *Mel Tormé swings Schubert Alley.* Verve: 821581-2 (6146). 1960.

4838.2 *Reunion.* Concord Jazz: CCD-4360. 1988.

4839 Vaughan, Sarah, 1924–1990

4839.1 *The complete Sarah Vaughan on Mercury, vol. 1: great jazz years.* Mercury: 826320-2. 6CD set. 1954–56.

4839.2 *Crazy and mixed up.* Pablo: PACD-2312-137-2. 1982.

4839.3 *The divine Sarah.* Columbia: C2K 44165. 2CD set. 1949–53.

4839.4 * *How long has this been going on?* Pablo: PACD-2310-821-2. 1978.

4839.5 *It's you or no one.* Discovery/Warner Bros.: 70055 (Musicraft). 1946–48.

4839.6 *Live in Japan.* Mainstream/Legacy: J2K 57123 (2401). 2CD set. 1973.

4839.7 * *No Count Sarah.* Polydor: 824057-2 (Mercury MG-20441). 1958.

4839.8 *The Rodgers and Hart songbook.* EmArcy: 824864-2. 1954–58.

4839.9 ** *Sarah Vaughan.* EmArcy: 814641-2 (MG-36004). 1954.

4839.10 *Sarah Vaughan at Mister Kelly's.* EmArcy: 832791-2 (MG-20326). 1957.

4839.11 *Sarah Vaughan sings George Gershwin, vol. 1.* EmArcy: 846895-2. 1957.

4839.12 *Swinging easy.* EmArcy: 314-514072-2 (MG-36109). 1954, 1957.

4839.13 *Tenderly.* Discovery/Warner Bros.: 70057 (Musicraft). 1946–48.

4840 Wiley, Lee, 1915–1975

4840.1 *As time goes by.* RCA Bluebird: 3138-2-RB. 1956–57.

4840.2 *Lee Wiley sings the songs of Rodgers & Hart and Harold Arlen.* Audiophile: ACD-10. 1940, 1943.

4841 Williams, Joe, 1918–

4841.1 * *Count Basie swings, Joe Williams sings.* Verve: 314 519852-2. 1955–56.

4841.2 *Every day: the best of the Verve years.* Verve: 314 519813-2. 2CD set. 1955–57, 1987–90.

4841.3 *Nothin' but the blues.* Delos: 13491-4001-2. 1983.

4841.4 *The overwhelming Joe Williams.* RCA Bluebird: 6464-2-RB. 1963–65.

4842 Wilson, Cassandra, 1955–

4842.1 *Blue light 'til dawn.* Blue Note: 81357. 1993.

4842.2 *Blue skies.* JMT: 834419-2. 1988.

Mainstream Popular and New Age

Compiled by
William E. Anderson

T his chapter comprises American mainstream commercial popular music in the twentieth century, excluding rock, country, jazz, and other categories with their own chapters. There are five sections: "General Anthologies," "Songwriter Anthologies," "Pre–World War II," "Post–World War II," and "New Age."

General Anthologies

4843 ** *American popular song: six decades of songwriters and singers.* Smithsonian: 1502 [direct from Smithsonian]; RD-031 [from other distributors]. 5CD set. 1911–80. [Sophie Tucker, Bessie Smith, Billy Murray, Al Jolson, Marion Harris, Fred Astaire, Ethel Waters, Gene Austin, Helen Morgan, Bing Crosby, Russ Columbo, Mildred Bailey, Louis Armstrong, Billie Holiday, Helen Forrest, Judy Garland, Connie Boswell, Lena Horne, Nat King Cole, Dinah Shore, Jo Stafford, Frank Sinatra, Billy Eckstine, Dick Haymes, Perry Como, Margaret Whiting, Mabel Mercer, Peggy Lee, Rosemary Clooney, Sarah Vaughan, Ella Fitzgerald, Carmen McRae, Joe Williams, Mel Tormé, Teddi King, Barbara Cook, Tony Bennett, Barbra Streisand, and others].

Songwriter Anthologies

Anthologies in this section focus on the major American popular songwriters of the twentieth century. Each collection features interpretations by a variety of singers.

4844   Arlen, Harold, 1905–1986

Harold Arlen. [Series: American songbook, vol. 5]. Smithsonian: RD 048-5. 1933–85. [Judy Garland, Jack Teagarden, Ethel Merman, Lena Horne, Nat King Cole, Margaret Whiting, Bing Crosby, Andrews Sisters, Frances Wayne, Pearl Bailey, Bobby Short, Joe Williams, Mabel Mercer, Fred Astaire, Ella Fitzgerald, Tony Bennett, Oscar Peterson, Maureen McGovern, Mel Tormé].

4845   Berlin, Irving, 1888–1989

4845.1 *Irving Berlin.* [Series: American songbook, vol. 1]. Smithsonian: RD 048-1. 1930–87. [Al Jolson, Connie Boswell, Ella Fitzgerald, Kate Smith, Bing Crosby, Judy Garland, Fred Astaire, Dinah Shore, Mary Martin, Teddi King, Ethel

Merman, Johnny Mathis, Mel Tormé, Eileen Farrell, Max Morath, Dorothy Loudon, Tony Bennett, Barbara Cook, and others].

4845.2 *Irving Berlin: a hundred years.* Columbia: CGK 40035. 1930–58. [Ben Selvin, Jan Garber, Connie Boswell, Victor Young, Eddie Cantor, Ethel Waters, Fred Astaire, Bunny Berigan, Billie Holiday, Mildred Bailey, Peggy Lee, Dinah Shore, Tony Bennett, Rosemary Clooney, Judy Holliday, Andre Kostelanetz, and others].

4846 Carmichael, Hoagy, 1899–1981

4846.1 ** *The classic Hoagy Carmichael.* Smithsonian: 2302 [direct from Smithsonian]; RD-038 [from other distributors]. 3CD set. 1927–84. [Bix Beiderbecke, Paul Whitemen, Louis Armstrong, Boswell Sisters, Hoagy Carmichael, Mills Brothers, Bing Crosby, Benny Goodman, Mildred Bailey, Ethel Waters, Shirley Ross, Kate Smith, Billie Holiday, Frank Sinatra, Betty Hutton, Jo Stafford, Ella Fitzgerald, Ray Charles, Sarah Vaughan, Margaret Whiting, and others].

4846.2 *Hoagy Carmichael.* [Series: American songbook, vol. 9]. Smithsonian: RD 048-9. 1932–64. [Frank Sinatra, Mildred Bailey, Bing Crosby, Ethel Waters, Mills Brothers, Billy Eckstine, Ray Eberle, Dick Haymes, Sarah Vaughan, Johnny Mercer, Marilyn Monroe, Teddi King, Four Aces, Barbara Lea, Carmen McRae, Tony Bennett, Rosemary Clooney, and others].

4847 Coleman, Cy, 1929–

Cy Coleman. [Series: American songbook, vol. 19]. Smithsonian: RD 048-19. 1958–90. [Mabel Mercer, Johnny Mathis, Liza Minnelli, Peggy Lee, Jack Jones, Barbra Streisand, Gwen Verdon, Morgana King, Shirley MacLaine, Rosemary Clooney, Tony Bennett, Sarah Vaughan, Lainie Kazan, Sylvia Syms, Jackie and Roy, Mel Tormé, and others].

4848 Ellington, Duke, 1899–1974

Duke Ellington. [Series: American songbook, vol. 10]. Smithsonian: RD 048-10. 1938–71. [Frank Sinatra, Rosemary Clooney, Billie Holiday, Billy Eckstine, Mildred Bailey, Carmen McRae, Tony Bennett, Peggy Lee, Dinah Shore, Jo Stafford, Joe Williams, Nat King Cole, Kitty Kallen, Lena Horne, Ella Fitzgerald, Mel Tormé, and others].

4849 Fields, Dorothy, 1905–1974

Dorothy Fields. [Series: American songbook, vol. 13]. Smithsonian: RD 048-13. 1932–87. [Louis Armstrong, Mills Brothers, Adelaide Hall, Frances Langford, Fred Astaire, Billie Holiday, Ethel Merman, Bing Crosby, Nat King Cole, Pearl Bailey, Shirley Booth, Mae Barnes, Joe Williams, Judy Garland, Margaret Whiting, Tony Bennett, Mabel Mercer, Maureen McGovern, Aretha Franklin, Peggy Lee, Sylvia Syms, Gwen Verdon].

4850 Gershwin, George, 1898–1937

4850.1 *George Gershwin.* [Series: American songbook, vol. 2]. Smithsonian: RD 048-2. 1920–88. [Al Jolson, Paul Whiteman, Gertrude Lawrence, Lee Wiley, Nat King Cole, Judy Garland, Mel Tormé, Mary Martin, Ella Fitzgerald, Fred Astaire, Chris Connor, Nancy Walker, Kaye Ballard, Sarah Vaughan, Mabel Mercer, Cab Calloway, Bobby Short, Lena Horne, Michael Feinstein, Maureen McGovern, and others].

4850.2 * *I got rhythm: the music of George Gershwin.* Smithsonian: RD 107. 4CD set. 1923–92. [Ethel Waters, Maxine Sullivan, Fred Astaire, Helen Forrest, Lena Horne, Jo Stafford, Bing Crosby, Judy Garland, Lee Wiley, Vaughn Monroe, Teddi King, Sarah Vaughan, Diahann Carroll, Dinah Shore, Tony Bennett, Nancy Walker, Joan Morris, Marti Webb, Linda Ronstadt, Cliff Edwards, Gertrude Lawrence, Abbie Mitchell, Lawrence Tibbett, Todd Duncan, Ella Logan, Al Jolson, Gene Kelly, John W. Bubbles, William Warfield, Leontyne Price, Paul Whiteman, Leonard Pennario, Juilliard String Quartet, Don Redman, Jimmie Noone, Billie Holiday, Count Basie, Lester Young, Benny Goodman, Artie Shaw, Eddie Condon, Chet Baker, Erroll Garner, Louis Armstrong, Ella Fitzgerald, Miles Davis, Gil Evans, Buddy DeFranco, Art Tatum, Bob Brookmeyer, Shelly Manne, Milt Jackson, Joe Pass, and others].

4851 Hammerstein, Oscar, 1895–1960

Oscar Hammerstein II. [Series: American songbook, vol. 7]. Smithsonian: RD 048-7. 1943–65. [Alfred Drake, Joan Roberts, John Raitt, Billie Holiday, Margaret Whiting, Dick Haymes, Judy Garland, Jo Stafford, Ezio Pinza, Mary Martin, Louis Armstrong, Perry Como, Teddi King, David Allyn, Judy Holliday, Mabel Mercer, Marilyn Horne, Barbara Cook, Mel Tormé, Julie Andrews, and others].

4852 Harburg, E. Y. (Edgar "Yip"), 1898–1981

E. Y. Harburg. [Series: American songbook, vol. 16]. Smithsonian: RD 048-16. 1932–90. [Bing Crosby, Judy Garland, Groucho Marx, Tommy Dorsey, Frank Sinatra, Deanna Durbin, Billie Holiday, Ella Logan, David Wayne, Barbara Cook, Sarah Vaughan, Dinah Washington, Rosemary Clooney,

Carmen McRae, Doris Day, Bobby Short, Lena Horne, Jeri Southern, Tony Bennett, Susannah McCorkle, Margaret Whiting, and others].

4853 Kern, Jerome, 1885–1945

Jerome Kern. [Series: American songbook, vol. 4]. Smithsonian: RD 048-4. 1932–64. [Frank Sinatra, Paul Robeson, Helen Morgan, Billie Holiday, Kate Smith, Margaret Whiting, Helen Forrest, Dick Haymes, Judy Garland, Lena Horne, Mabel Mercer, Bobby Short, Teddi King, Sarah Vaughan, David Allyn, Ella Fitzgerald, Eileen Farrell, Nat King Cole, and others].

4854 Lerner, Alan Jay, 1918–1986

Alan Jay Lerner. [Series: American songbook, vol. 8]. Smithsonian: RD 048-8. 1950–87. [Robert Goulet, Fred Astaire, Hi-Los, Julie Andrews, Vic Damone, Louis Jourdan, Gogi Grant, John Raitt, Andy Williams, Richard Burton, Felicia Sanders, Nat King Cole, Barbara Harris, Marilyn Maye, Alfred Drake, Jackie and Roy, Barbra Streisand, and others].

4855 Loesser, Frank, 1910–1969

Frank Loesser. [Series: American songbook, vol. 15]. Smithsonian: RD 048-15. 1938–67. [Billie Holiday, Marlene Dietrich, Dick Haymes, Betty Hutton, Bing Crosby, Andrews Sisters, Ray Bolger, Margaret Whiting, Kay Kyser, Doris Day, Sarah Vaughan, Dinah Shore, Mabel Mercer, Four Lads, Peggy Lee, Dinah Washington, Johnny Mathis, Robert Morse, and others].

4856 Mercer, Johnny, 1909–1976

Johnny Mercer. [Series: American songbook, vol. 11]. Smithsonian: RD 048-11. 1937–86. [Frances Langford, Louis Armstrong, Helen Ward, Mildred Bailey, Dinah Shore, Jo Stafford, Helen O'Connell, Bob Eberly, Bing Crosby, Mary Martin, Billie Holiday, Woody Herman, Mills Brothers, Judy Garland, Gordon MacRae, Margaret Whiting, Tony Bennett, Mel Tormé, Johnny Mathis, Andy Williams, and others].

4857 Porter, Cole, 1891–1964

4857.1 *Cole Porter.* [Series: American songbook, vol. 3]. Smithsonian: RD 048-3. 1932–71. [Ethel Merman, Fred Astaire, Ethel Waters, Artie Shaw, Mary Martin, Billie Holiday, Lee Wiley, Bing Crosby, Andrews Sisters, Judy Garland, Gene Kelly, Peggy Lee, Mabel Mercer, Lena Horne, Ella Fitzgerald, Jeri Southern, Eileen Farrell, Bobby Short, Marlene Dietrich, and others].

4857.2 * *From this moment on: the songs of Cole Porter.* Smithsonian: RD-047. 4CD set. 1928–86. [Cole Porter, Marion Harris, Fred Waring, Fred Astaire, Alberta Hunter, Mary Martin, Lee Wiley, Judy Garland, Ethel Merman, Bing Crosby, Peggy Lee, Billie Holiday, Mabel Mercer, Margaret Whiting, Frank Sinatra, Ella Fitzgerald, Bobby Short, Lena Horne, Maurice Chevalier, and others].

4857.3 *Red, hot and blue: a tribute to Cole Porter to benefit AIDS research and relief.* Chrysalis: 21799. [1990]. [Neneh Cherry, Neville Brothers, Sinead O'Connor, David Byrne, Tom Waits, Annie Lennox, U2, k.d. lang, Jungle Brothers, and others].

4858 Rodgers, Richard, 1902–1979

Rodgers/Hart. [Series: American songbook, vol. 6]. Smithsonian: RD 048-6. 1932–87. [Lee Wiley, Bing Crosby, Maurice Chevalier, Margaret Whiting, Dick Haymes, Judy Garland, Lena Horne, Mel Tormé, Mary Martin, Peggy Lee, Bobby Short, Doris Day, Ella Fitzgerald, Sarah Vaughan, Elaine Strich, Carmen McRae, Joe Williams, Billie Holiday, Tony Bennett, Maureen McGovern, Nat King Cole, and others].

4859 Schwartz, Arthur, 1900–1984

Arthur Schwartz. [Series: American songbook, vol. 23]. Smithsonian: RD 048-23. 1931–92. [Bing Crosby, Boswell Sisters, Ethel Waters, Mildred Bailey, Tony Martin, Margaret Whiting, Dinah Shore, Buddy Clark, Pearl Bailey, Mary Martin, Fred Astaire, Dick Haymes, Helen Merrill, Mel Tormé, Judy Holliday, Judy Garland, Barbara Cook, Weslia Whitfield, and others].

4860 Styne, Jule, 1905–1994

Jule Styne. [Series: American songbook, vol. 12]. Smithsonian: RD 048-12. 1942–86. [Helen Forrest, Dinah Shore, Kitty Kallen, Frank Sinatra, Glenn Miller, Tex Beneke, Jo Stafford, Doris Day, Carol Channing, Tony Bennett, Judy Holliday, Ethel Merman, Johnny Mathis, June Christy, Judy Garland, Lena Horne, Barbra Streisand, Maxine Sullivan, and others].

4861 Van Heusen, Jimmy, 1913–1990

James Van Heusen. [Series: American songbook, vol. 18]. Smithsonian: RD 048-18. 1938–91. [Paul Whiteman, Cab Calloway, Ray Eberle, Frank Sinatra, Bing Crosby, Chris Connor, Margaret Whiting, Dick Haymes, Dinah Shore, Doris Day, Hi-Los, June Christy, Lena Horne, Tony Bennett, Sarah

Vaughan, Jack Jones, Joe Williams, Peggy Lee, Julie Andrews, Mary Cleere Haran, and others].

4862 Waller, Fats, 1904–1943

Waller/Razaf. [Series: American songbook, vol. 21]. Smithsonian: RD 048-21. 1928–94. [Ted Lewis, Bing Crosby, Ethel Waters, Andy Razaf, Annette Hanshaw, Benny Goodman, Jack Teagarden, Mildred Bailey, Joe Haymes, Fats Waller, Boswell Sisters, Phil Harris, Judy Garland, Ray Noble, Lena Horne, Frankie Laine, Vaughn Monroe, Sarah Vaughan, Maxine Sullivan, Louis Armstrong, Dinah Washington, Lee Wiley, Sammy Davis Jr., Helen Merrill].

4863 Warren, Harry, 1893–1981

Harry Warren. [Series: American songbook, vol. 14]. Smithsonian: RD 048-14. 1932–87. [Ginger Rogers, Dick Powell, Glenn Miller, Harry James, Helen Forrest, Ray Eberle, Dick Haymes, Maxine Sullivan, Judy Garland, Fred Astaire, Nat King Cole, Jo Stafford, Tony Bennett, Rosemary Clooney, Teddi King, Vic Damone, Jackie and Roy, David Allyn, Hi-Los, Mel Tormé, Maureen McGovern, and others].

4864 Weill, Kurt, 1900–1950

Kurt Weill. [Series: American songbook, vol. 17]. Smithsonian: RD 048-17. 1941–87. [Louis Armstrong, Helen Forrest, Mary Martin, Bing Crosby, Lee Wiley, Buddy Clark, Kaye Ballard, Greta Keller, Hi-Los, Sarah Vaughan, Lotte Lenya, June Christy, Tony Bennett, Judy Garland, Georgia Brown, Dorothy Loudon, Lena Horne, and others].

4865 Whiting, Richard, 1891–1938

Richard Whiting. [Series: American songbook, vol. 22]. Smithsonian: RD 048-22. 1929–88. [Margaret Whiting, Maurice Chevalier, Jeanette MacDonald, Rudy Vallee, Ethel Merman, Boswell Sisters, Alice Faye, Shirley Temple, Lee Wiley, Tony Martin, Billie Holiday, Dick Powell, Kate Smith, Mel Tormé, Bing Crosby, Carmen McRae, Nat King Cole, Tony Bennett, Doris Day, Jeri Southern, Susannah McCorkle, and others].

4866 Youmans, Vincent, 1898–1946

Vincent Youmans. [Series: American songbook, vol. 20]. Smithsonian: RD 048-20. 1926–74. [Frank Sinatra, Beatrice Lillie, Fred Astaire, Rudy Vallee, Al Bowlly, Mildred Bailey, Andrews Sisters, Dinah Shore, Mary Martin, John Raitt, Lee Wiley, Doris Day, Elaine Strich, Roy Hamilton, Judy Garland, Liza Minnelli, and others].

Pre–World War II

This section covers popular music from early recordings just after 1900 (*see* 4879, 4883, and 4887) through 1945. Artists who established themselves during this period but whose careers extended further are listed here.

Anthologies

4867 * *Brother, can you spare a dime?: American song during the Great Depression.* New World: NW 270. LP. 1931–41. [Woody Guthrie, Shirley Temple, Rudy Vallee, Bing Crosby, Glen Gray, Dick Powell, Glenn Miller, Bill Broonzy, Uncle Dave Macon, Delmore Brothers, Gene Autry, Almanac Singers, and others]. OP

4868 *Brother, can you spare a dime?: great American songs of the Depression.* Pro Arte/Fanfare: CDD-486. 1930–37. [Ben Selvin, Harry Richman, Ruth Etting, Casa Loma Orchestra, Bing Crosby, Ben Bernie, Connie Boswell, Dick Powell, Fred Waring, Paul Robeson, Cliff Edwards, Paul Whiteman, Rudy Vallee, and others].

4869 *Can't help lovin' that man.* [Series: Art deco]. Columbia/Legacy: CK 52855. 1925–34. [Sam Lanin, Fred Rich, Joe Haymes, Bing Crosby, Travelers, Guy Lombardo, Cliff Edwards, Paul Whiteman, Will Osborne, and others].

4870 ** *Come, Josephine, in my flying machine.* New World: NW 233. LP. 1910–29. [Harry MacDonough, American Quartet, Blanche Ring, Billy Murray, Bert Williams, Nora Bayes, Al Jolson, Blossom Seeley, Vernon Dalhart, and others]. OP

4871 * *The crooners.* [Series: Art deco]. Columbia/Legacy: C2K 52942. 2CD set. 1926–41. [Willard Robison, Gene Austin, Seger Ellis, Smith Ballew, Bing Crosby, Harlan Lattimore, Russ Columbo, Red McKenzie, Cliff Edwards, Pinky Tomlin, Chick Bullock, Jack Teagarden, Harold Arlen, Buddy Clark, Eddy Howard, Frank Sinatra, Dick Haymes, and others].

4872 * *An experiment in modern music: Paul Whiteman at Aeolian Hall.* Smithsonian: 2028. 2LP set. 1917–27. [Paul Whiteman, George Gershwin, Zez Confrey, Jean Goldkette, Original Dixieland Jazz Band, Art Hickman, and others]. OP

4873 *Flappers, vamps and sweet young things.* ASV Living Era: CD AJA 5015. 1924–31. [Libby

Holman, Kate Smith, Sophie Tucker, Marion Harris, Blossom Seeley, Annette Hanshaw, Ruth Etting, Greta Keller, Helen Morgan, Helen Kane, Gertrude Lawrence, and others].

4874 *The Great Depression: American music in the '30s.* Columbia: CK 57589. 1927–41. [Rudy Vallee, Louis Armstrong, Duke Ellington, Victoria Spivey, Barbecue Bob, Blind Willie Johnson, Casa Loma Orchestra, Ted Lewis, Red Norvo, Billie Holiday, Bill Cox, Chick Bullock, Memphis Minnie, Hal Kemp, Artie Shaw, Horace Heidt, and others].

4875 *The human orchestra: rhythm quartets in the thirties.* Clanka Lanka: 144.003. LP. 1932–40. [Five Breezes, Golden Gate Quartet, Norfolk Jazz Quartet, Mills Brothers, Ink Spots, Five Jones Boys, and others].

4876 * *It had to be you: popular keyboard from the days of the speakeasy to the television era.* New World: NW 298. LP. [1977]. [Zez Confrey, Eddy Duchin, Roger Williams, Frankie Carle, Liberace, and others]. OP

4877 *Legendary bands of the 20s.* Pro Arte/Fanfare: CDD 484. 1925–30. [Paul Whiteman, Ted Weems, Guy Lombardo, Coon-Sanders, Ipana Troubadours, Ben Pollack, Fred Waring, George Olsen, Nat Shilkret, Harry Reser, Vincent Lopez, Ted Lewis, Isham Jones, Jean Goldkette, Ben Bernie, Rudy Vallee, Ben Selvin, and others].

4878 *Legendary entertainers.* Pro Arte/Fanfare: CDD 483. 1921–29. [Guy Lombardo, Paul Whiteman, Ted Lewis, Helen Kane, Cliff Edwards, Helen Morgan, Gene Austin, Ruth Etting, Wendell Hall, Fanny Brice, Annette Hanshaw, Eddie Cantor, Kate Smith, Jack Smith, Gertrude Lawrence, Harry Richman, Sophie Tucker, Frank Crumit, and others].

4879 * *Minstrels and tunesmiths: the commercial roots of early country music.* John Edwards Memorial Foundation: JEMF-109. LP. 1902–23. [Len Spencer, Arthur Collins, Fred Van Eps, May Irwin, Wendell Hall, Dan Quinn, Henry Burr, Kitty Cheatam, Peerless Quartet, and others].

4880 ** *The music goes round and around: the golden years of Tin Pan Alley.* New World: NW 248. LP. 1930–39. [Russ Columbo, Bing Crosby, Louis Armstrong, Mildred Bailey, Connie Boswell, Pha Terrell, Martha Raye, Ella Fitzgerald, Bea Wain, Jimmie Lunceford, and others]. OP

4881 * *Nipper's all-time greatest hits: the 40's, vol. 1.* RCA: 9855-2-R. 1938–44. [Artie Shaw, Duke Ellington, David Rose, Sammy Kaye, Glenn Miller, Tommy Dorsey, Frank Sinatra, King Sisters, Freddy Martin, Dinah Shore, Charlie Barnet, Spike Jones, Vaughn Monroe, Lena Horne, and others].

4882 *Nipper's all-time greatest hits: the 40's, vol. 2.* RCA: 9864-2-R. 1945–49. [Erskine Hawkins, Spike Jones, Perry Como, Betty Hutton, Count Basie, Louis Prima, Eddy Arnold, and others].

4883 ** *Nipper's greatest hits: 1901–1920.* RCA: 3031-2-R. 1905–19. [Billy Murray, Nora Bayes, Al Jolson, Len Spencer, Sousa's Band, George M. Cohan, Ada Jones, John McCormick, Enrico Caruso, Marion Harris, Ben Selvin, and others]. OP

4884 * *Nipper's greatest hits: the 20's, vol. 1.* RCA: 2258-2-R. 1920–29. [Gene Austin, Fred Waring, Nat Shilkret, Paul Whiteman, Eddie Cantor, Vernon Dalhart, Jean Goldkette, Fanny Brice, Duke Ellington, Johnny Hamp, George Gershwin, and others].

4885 * *Nipper's greatest hits: the 30's, vol. 1.* RCA: 9971-2-R. 1929–39. [Leo Reisman, Fanny Brice, Bing Crosby, Maurice Chevalier, Fred Astaire, Cab Calloway, Mae West, Tommy Dorsey, Wayne King, Fats Waller, Benny Goodman, Guy Lombardo, Larry Clinton, Glenn Miller, Kate Smith, and others].

4886 *Nipper's greatest hits: the 30's, vol. 2.* RCA: 9972-2-R. 1930–39. [Rudy Vallee, Mildred Bailey, Fred Waring, Leo Reisman, Russ Columbo, Helen Morgan, Louis Armstrong, Eddy Duchin, Paul Whiteman, Jeanette MacDonald and Nelson Eddy, Hal Kemp, Artie Shaw, Tommy Dorsey, Glenn Miller, Benny Goodman, and others].

4887 *Phono-cylinders, vols. 1–2.* Folkways: 3886/3887. 2AC set. 1904–16. [Len Spencer, Edison Military Band, Kerry Mills, Arthur Collins, Ada Jones, Billy Murray, George W. Johnson, and others].

4888 * *Praise the Lord and pass the ammunition: songs of World Wars I and II.* New World: NW 222. LP. 1915–46. [Spike Jones, Kay Kyser, Al Jolson, Helen Forrest, American Quartet, Nora Bayes, Peerless Quartet, Dick Robertson, Kenny Baker, and others]. OP

4889 ** *Sentimental journey: pop vocal classics, vol. 1.* Rhino: 71249. 1942–46. [Les Brown, Doris Day, Bing Crosby, Dick Haymes, Dinah Shore, Mills Brothers, Betty Hutton, Woody Herman, Billy Eckstine, Judy Garland, Harry James, Helen Forrest, Vaughn Monroe, Margaret Whiting, Martha Tilton, Johnny Mercer, Jo Stafford, Paul Weston, Andy Russell, Lena Horne, Frank Sinatra, Nat King Cole].

4890 *16 most requested songs of the 1940s, vol. 1.* Columbia: CK 45108. 1941–49. [Les Brown, Doris Day, Xavier Cugat, Harry James, Benny Goodman, Kay Kyser, Dinah Shore, and others].

4891 *16 most requested songs of the 1940s, vol. 2.* Columbia: CK 45109. 1939–49. [Harry James, Benny Goodman, Xavier Cugat, Frankie Carle, Les Brown, Kay Kyser, Dinah Shore, Buddy Clark, and others].

4892 *Songs that got us through World War II.* Rhino: 70960. 1941–45. [Andrews Sisters, Tommy Dorsey, Frank Sinatra, Mills Brothers, Harry James, Jo Stafford, Ink Spots, Jimmy Dorsey, Les Brown, Vaughn Monroe, Louis Armstrong, and others].

4893 * *Sophisticated ladies.* [Series: Art deco]. Columbia: C2K 52943. 2CD set. 1929–40. [Ruth Etting, Helen Morgan, Greta Keller, Annette Hanshaw, Ethel Waters, Connie Boswell, Boswell Sisters, Frances Langford, Alice Faye, Lee Wiley, Helen Ward, Ella Logan, Maxine Sullivan, Mildred Bailey, Nan Wynn, Ginny Simms, and others].

4894 * *Swing time! The fabulous big band era.* Columbia: C3K 52862. 3CD set. 1925–55. [Harry James, Claude Thornhill, Bunny Berigan, Benny Goodman, Woody Herman, Will Bradley, Ray Noble, Louis Prima, Don Albert, Cab Calloway, Duke Ellington, Charlie Barnet, Jimmy Dorsey, Paul Whiteman, Glenn Miller, Ben Pollack, Les Brown, Gene Krupa, Tommy Dorsey, Count Basie, Ted Lewis, Casa Loma Orchestra, Jan Savitt, Bob Crosby, Fletcher Henderson, Chick Webb, Jimmie Lunceford, and others].

4895 * *This is art deco.* Columbia/Legacy: CK 57111. 1913–82. [Bert Williams, Al Jolson, Cliff Edwards, Gertrude Lawrence, Sophie Tucker, Bing Crosby, Eddie Cantor, Guy Lombardo, Boswell Sisters, Mills Brothers, Mae West, Ethel Merman, Fred Astaire, Marlene Dietrich, Dean Martin, Judy Garland, Helen Humes, Alberta Hunter, and others].

4896 *We'll meet again: love songs of World War II.* Smithsonian: 2706 (RD 100). 2CD set. 1939–45. [Benny Goodman, Peggy Lee, Tony Martin, Artie Shaw, Dinah Shore, Adelaide Hall, Glenn Miller, Ink Spots, Connie Boswell, Marlene Dietrich, Bob Eberly, Jimmy Dorsey, Mary Martin, Lew Stone, Vera Lynn, Dick Haymes, Ambrose, Woody Herman, Tommy Dorsey, Xavier Cugat, Frank Sinatra, Mills Brothers, Frankie Carle, Les Brown, Bing Crosby, Duke Ellington, and others].

4897 ** *Yes sir, that's my baby: the golden years of Tin Pan Alley.* New World: NW 279. LP. 1920–29. [Paul Whiteman, Al Jolson, Fred Waring, Ted Lewis, Jack Smith, Ruth Etting, Sophie Tucker, Cliff Edwards, Gene Austin, Rudy Vallee, Louis Armstrong, and others]. OP

4898 *Your hit parade: 1943.* Time-Life: R912-20 (HPD-20). 1943. [From the series, Your hit parade, covering the years 1940–59. Glenn Miller, Harry James, Ink Spots, Bing Crosby, Dinah Shore, Vaughn Monroe, Tommy Dorsey, Lena Horne, Dick Haymes, Benny Goodman, Mills Brothers, Xavier Cugat, Al Dexter, and others].

Individual Artists or Groups

4899 * Andrews Sisters
50th anniversary, vol. 1. MCA: MCAD-42044. 1937–50.

4900 Armstrong, Louis, 1901–1971. *See* 4343 and 4345

4901 Astaire, Fred, 1899–1987
  4901.1 *Fred Astaire sings.* MCA: MCAD-1552 (Kapp). 1958.
  4901.2 ** *Starring Fred Astaire.* Columbia: C2K 44233. 2CD set. 1932–38.
  4901.3 *Top hat: hits from Hollywood.* Columbia: CK 64172. 1935–37.

4902 Boswell Sisters
That's how rhythm was born. Columbia/Legacy: CK 66977. 1931–35.

4903 * Boswell Sisters and Connie Boswell, 1907–1976
It's the girls! ASV Living Era: CD AJA 5014. 1925–31.

4904 Bradley, Will, 1912–1989, and Ray McKinley, 1910–1995
Best of the big bands. Columbia: CK 46151. 1939–41.

4905 Cantor, Eddie, 1892–1964
  4905.1 *The best of Eddie Cantor: a centennial celebration.* RCA: 07863-66033-2. 1917–57.
  4905.2 *The Columbia years.* Columbia: C2K 57148. 2CD set. 1922–40.

4906 Crosby, Bing, 1903–1977
  4906.1 * *Bing: his legendary years.* MCA: MCAD4-10887. 4CD set. 1931–57.
  4906.2 *The crooner.* Columbia: C3K 44229. 3CD set. 1928–34. OP
  4906.3 *Greatest hits.* MCA: MCAD-1620. 1939–47.

4906.4 *Pennies from heaven.* Pro Arte/Fanfare: CCD 432. 1931–36.

4906.5 ** *16 most requested songs.* Columbia: CK 48974. 1931–34. [Item 4906.2 covers material comparable to item 4906.5 but in greater depth and with better packaging and notes].

4907   Crumit, Frank, 1889–1943

Gay caballero. Pro Arte: CDD 3407 (Victor). 1925–35.

4908   Cugat, Xavier, 1900–1990

Bim bam bum. Harlequin: HQ CD 14. 1935–40.

4909 * Dorsey, Jimmy, 1904–1957

Greatest hits. MCA: MCAC-252. AC. 1938–44. *See also* 4364

4910 ** Dorsey, Tommy, 1905–1956

The seventeen number ones. RCA: 9973-2-R. 1935–42.

4911 * Dorsey, Tommy, 1905–1956, and Frank Sinatra, 1915–

All time greatest hits, vol. 1. RCA Bluebird: 8324-2-R. 1940–42.

4912   Duchin, Eddy, 1910–1951

Best of the big bands. Columbia: CK 46150. 1932–40.

4913   Etting, Ruth, 1907–1978

Ten cents a dance. ASV Living Era: CD AJA 5008. 1926–30.

4914   Fitzgerald, Ella, 1918–1996. *See* 4812

4915 ** Garland, Judy, 1922–1969

The best of the Decca years, vol. 1. MCA: MCAD-31345. 1937–45.

4916   Goodman, Benny, 1909–1986. *See* 4374

4917   Gray, Glen, 1906–1963. *See* 4377

4918   Haymes, Dick, 1916–1980

The best of Dick Haymes. MCA: MCAC2-4097 (Decca). AC. 1943–49.

4919 * Horne, Lena, 1917–

Stormy weather: the legendary Lena. RCA Bluebird: 9985-2-RB. 1941–58.

4920   Ink Spots

4920.1 ** *Greatest hits.* MCA: MCAD-31347. 1939–46.

4920.2 *Swing high, swing low.* ASV Living Era: CD AJA 5082. 1936–40.

4921 * James, Harry, 1916–1983

Best of the big bands. Columbia: CK 45341. 1939–45.

4922   Jolson, Al, 1886–1950

4922.1 *The best of the Decca years.* MCA: MCAD-10505. 1945–47.

4922.2 *Brunswick rarities.* MCA: MCAC-1560. AC. 1926–30.

4922.3 ** *You ain't heard nothin' yet: Jolie's finest Columbia recordings.* Columbia: CK 53419. 1913–32.

4922.4 *You made me love you: his first recordings, vol. 1.* Stash: ST-CD-564. 1911–16.

4923 * Jones, Spike, 1911–1965

The best of Spike Jones and his City Slickers. RCA: 53748-2. 1942–49.

4924   Kemp, Hal, 1905–1940

Best of the big bands. Columbia: CK 45346. 1933–37. OP

4925   Kyser, Kay, 1906–1985

Best of the big bands. Columbia: CK 45343. 1938–48.

4926   Lombardo, Guy, 1902–1977

4926.1 *Auld lang syne.* Pro Arte/Fanfare: CCD 592. 1928–39.

4926.2 * *16 most requested songs.* Columbia: CK 44407. 1932–34.

4927 * Mercer, Johnny, 1909–1976

Johnny Mercer. [Series: Capitol collectors]. Capitol: 92125. 1942–52.

4928 * Merman, Ethel, 1909–1984

You're the top. Pro Arte/Fanfare: CDD 473. 1931–40.

4929   Miller, Glenn, 1904–1944

4929.1 ** *Chattanooga choo choo: the #1 hits.* RCA Bluebird: 3102-2-RB. 1939–42. [Item 4929.2 covers material comparable to item 4929.1 but in greater depth and with better packaging and notes].

4929.2 *The popular recordings.* RCA Bluebird: 9785-2-RB. 3CD set. 1938–42.

4930   Mills Brothers

4930.1 ** *The best of the Decca years.* MCA: MCAD-31348. 1941–55.

4930.2 *Four boys and a guitar: the essential Mills Brothers.* Columbia/Legacy: CK 57713. 1932–34.

4931 Ossman, Vess, 1868–1923, and Fred Van Eps, 1878–1960

Kings of ragtime banjo. Yazoo: 1044. [1894–1920].

4932 Reser, Harry, 1896–1965

Banjo crackerjax. Yazoo: 1048. 1922–30.

4933 Scott, Raymond, 1910–1994

Reckless nights and Turkish twilights: the music of Raymond Scott. Columbia: CK 53028. 1937–40.

4934 Shaw, Artie, 1910– . *See* 4415

4935 Smith, Kate, 1907–1986

God bless America. Pro Arte: CDD 518. 1929–39.

4936 Vallee, Rudy, 1901–1986

4936.1 *Heigh-ho everybody, this is Rudy Vallee.* ASV Living Era: CD AJA 5009. 1928–30.

4936.2 *Vagabond lover.* Pro Arte/Fanfare: CDD 459. 1928–39.

4937 ** Waters, Ethel, 1896–1977

On stage and screen. Sony Music Special Products: A-2792. 1925–40.

4938 Whiteman, Paul, 1890–1967

4938.1 * *Paul Whiteman: the king of jazz.* ASV Living Era: CD AJA 5170. 1920–36.

4938.2 *The Victor masters featuring Bing Crosby.* RCA: 9678-2-R. 1927–35.

Post–World War II

The styles of these postwar and contemporary artists (sometimes marketed today as "easy listening" or "lite" music) derive fundamentally from the prerock period, but they may show influences of rock (as in "soft rock"), rhythm and blues, and other more recent idioms.

Anthologies

4939 *Ahmet Ertegun's New York cabaret music.* Atlantic: 82308-2. 4CD set. 1951–85. [Sylvia Syms, Chris Connor, Mabel Mercer, Bobby Short, Carmen McRae, Hugh Shannon, Mel Tormé, and others].

4940 * *Birth of a dream: Capitol's early hits.* Capitol: 98664. 1942–49. [Freddie Slack, Billie Holiday, Tex Ritter, Johnny Mercer, Jo Stafford, Stan Kenton, June Christy, Betty Hutton, Andy Russell, Merle Travis, Peggy Lee, Mel Tormé, Margaret Whiting, Les Paul, Nat King Cole, Tennessee Ernie Ford, and others]. OP

4941 * *Nipper's greatest hits: the 50's, vol. 1.* RCA: 8466-2-R. 1950–59. [Dinah Shore, Mario Lanza, Pee Wee King, Eartha Kitt, Eddie Fisher, Kay Starr, Elvis Presley, Harry Belafonte, Ames Brothers, Perry Como, Browns, Neil Sedaka, Jim Reeves, and others].

4942 *Nipper's greatest hits: the 50's, vol. 2.* RCA: 8467-2-R. 1950–59. [Phil Harris, Mario Lanza, Eddie Fisher, Ames Brothers, Perry Como, Elvis Presley, Harry Belafonte, Jim Reeves, Perez Prado, Neil Sedaka, Della Reese, Isley Brothers, and others].

4943 *Nipper's greatest hits: the 60's, vol. 1.* RCA: 8474-2-R. 1960–69. [Elvis Presley, Sam Cooke, Floyd Cramer, Tokens, Paul Anka, Neil Sedaka, Al Hirt, Eddy Arnold, Jefferson Airplane, Jose Feliciano, Guess Who, Henry Mancini, Friends of Distinction, and others].

4944 *Nipper's greatest hits: the 60's, vol. 2.* RCA: 8475-2-R. 1960–69. [Browns, Hank Locklin, Sam Cooke, Duane Eddy, Bobby Bare, Gale Garnett, Barry Sadler, Ed Ames, Hugo Montenegro, Youngbloods, Harry Nilsson, Elvis Presley, and others].

4945 * *Radio classics of the fifties.* Columbia: CK 45017. 1951–59. [Tony Bennett, Rosemary Clooney, Johnny Mathis, Doris Day, Frankie Laine, Four Lads, Johnny Ray, and others].

4946 *Sentimental journey: Capitol's great ladies of song.* Capitol: 98014. 1942–63. [Ella Mae Morse, Billie Holiday, Peggy Lee, Keely Smith, Dinah Shore, Margaret Whiting, and others]. OP

4947 ** *Sentimental journey: pop vocal classics, vol. 2.* Rhino: 71250. 1947–50. [Bing Crosby, Peggy Lee, Doris Day, Buddy Clark, Dinah Shore, Vaughn Monroe, Patti Page, Billy Eckstine, Frankie Laine, Evelyn Knight, Mel Tormé, Eileen Barton, Dick Haymes, Margaret Whiting, Teresa Brewer, Art Lund].

4948 ** *Sentimental journey: pop vocal classics, vol. 3.* Rhino: 71251. 1950–54. [Tony Bennett, Johnny Ray, Peggy Lee, Rosemary Clooney, Georgia Gibbs, Billy Eckstine, Percy Faith, Jo Stafford, Kay Starr, Tony Martin, Kitty Kallen, Dean Martin, Al Martino, Les Paul and Mary Ford, Don Cornell, Doris Day, Guy Mitchell, Eddie Fisher].

4949 * *Sentimental journey: pop vocal classics, vol. 4.* Rhino: 71252. 1954–59. [Bobby Darin, Peggy Lee, Debbie Reynolds, Joan Weber, Dinah Washington, Vic Damone, Guy Mitchell, Johnny Mathis, Doris Day, Gogi Grant, Dean Martin, Patti Page, Judy Garland, Jane Morgan, Sylvia Syms, Tony Bennett, Sammy Davis Jr.].

4950 *16 most requested songs: the 1950s, vol. 1.* Columbia: CK 45110. 1950–57. [Guy Mitchell, Tony Bennett, Frankie Laine, Johnny Ray, Percy Faith, Four Lads, Doris Day, Rosemary Clooney, Mitch Miller, Ray Conniff, Johnny Mathis, and others].

4951 *16 most requested songs: the 1950s, vol. 2.* Columbia: CK 45111. 1950–57. [Sammy Kaye, Guy Mitchell, Johnny Ray, Frankie Laine, Percy Faith, Tony Bennett, Rosemary Clooney, Four Lads, Doris Day, Louis Armstrong, Johnny Mathis, Vic Damone, Marty Robbins, and others].

4952 *Sweet and lovely: Capitol's great ladies of song.* Capitol: 97802. 1944–65. [Judy Garland, Dakota Staton, Lena Horne, Kay Starr, Peggy Lee, Keely Smith, Margaret Whiting, Nancy Wilson, and others].

4953 *Your hit parade: 1958.* Time-Life: R912-11 (HDP-11). 1958. [From the series, Your hit parade, covering the years 1940–59. Chordettes, Jimmie Rodgers, Nat King Cole, Perez Prado, Pat Boone, Doris Day, Platters, Perry Como, Mitch Miller, and others].

Individual Artists or Groups

4954 * Abba
Gold: greatest hits. Polydor: 314-517007-2. 1974–83.

4955 * Alpert, Herb, 1937–
Herb Alpert and the Tijuana Brass. [Series: Classics, no. 1]. A&M: 75021-2501-2. 1962–68.

4956 Anderson, Leroy, 1908–1975
The Leroy Anderson collection. MCA: MCAD2-99815. 2CD set. 1950–62.

4957 Anka, Paul, 1941–
30th anniversary collection: his all time greatest hits. Rhino: 71489. 2CD set. 1957–78.

4958 Anthony, Ray, 1922–
Ray Anthony. [Series: Capitol collectors]. Capitol: 94079. 1949–62.

4959 Belafonte, Harry, 1927–
4959.1 * *All-time greatest hits, vol. 1.* RCA: 6877-2-R. 1952–69.
4959.2 *Calypso.* RCA: 53801-2 (LPM 1248). 1956.

4960 Bennett, Tony, 1926–
4960.1 *Forty years: the artistry of Tony Bennett.* Columbia: C4K 46843. 4CD set. 1950–89.
4960.2 ** *16 most requested songs.* Columbia: CK 40215. 1950–64.

4961 Boone, Pat, 1934–
Pat Boone's greatest hits. MCA: MCAD-10885 (Dot). 1955–62.

4962 Brewer, Teresa, 1931–
The best of Teresa Brewer. MCA: MCAD-1545 (Coral). 1950–57.

4963 Callen, Michael, 1955–1993
Purple heart. Significant Other: SO 881. 1985, 1987.

4964 * Carpenters
The singles. A&M: 75021-3601-2. 1969–73.

4965 Clark, Buddy, 1912–1949
16 most requested songs. Columbia: CK 48976. 1946–49.

4966 Clooney, Rosemary, 1928–
4966.1 *Girl singer.* Concord Jazz: CCD-4496. 1991.
4966.2 * *Rosemary Clooney sings the lyrics of Johnny Mercer.* Concord Jazz: CCD-4333. 1987.
4966.3 *16 most requested songs.* Columbia: CK 44403. 1951–54.

4967 Cole, Nat King, 1917–1965
4967.1 * *The best of the Nat King Cole Trio: the vocal classics.* Capitol Jazz: 33571. 1942–46.
4967.2 ** *The greatest hits.* Capitol: 29687. 1943–64. [Item 4967.5 covers material comparable to item 4967.2 but in greater depth and with better packaging and notes].
4967.3 ** *Jumpin' at Capitol: the best of the Nat King Cole Trio.* Rhino: 71009. 1942–50. OP
4967.4 *Love is the thing.* Capitol: 46648 (824). 1957.
4967.5 *Nat King Cole.* Capitol: 99777. 4CD set. 1943–64.

4968 * Como, Perry, 1912–
All-time greatest hits, vol. 1. RCA: 8323-2-R. 1945–70.

4969 Connick, Harry, 1967–
25. Columbia: CK 53172. 1992.

4970 Conniff, Ray, 1916–
'S marvelous. Columbia: CK 8037. 1957.

4971 Darin, Bobby, 1936–1973. *See* 5516

4972 Day, Doris, 1922–
Greatest hits. Columbia: CK 8635. 1948–58.

4973 Day, Doris, 1922– , and Les Brown, 1912–
Best of the big bands. Columbia: CK 46224. 1945–47.

4974 Denver, John, 1943–
Greatest hits. RCA: PCD1-0374. 1971–77.

4975 Diamond, Neil, 1941–
His 12 greatest hits. MCA: MCAD–37252. 1968–72.

4976 Easton, Sheena, 1959–
The best of Sheena Easton. EMI: 91754. 1980–84.

4977 * Eckstine, Billy, 1914–1993
Everything I have is yours: the best of the MGM years. Verve: 819442-2 (MGM). 2CD set. 1947–57.

4978 Faith, Percy, 1908–1976
Greatest hits. Columbia: CK 8637. 1950–60.

4979 Farrell, Eileen, 1920–
My very best. Reference: RR60-CD. 1988, 1991.

4980 Fifth Dimension
Greatest hits on earth. Arista: ARCD-8335. 1967–72.

4981 Fisher, Eddie, 1928–
All-time greatest hits, vol. 1. RCA: 9592-2-R. 1951–56.

4982 Flirtations
4982.1 *The Flirtations.* Significant Other: SO 902. 1989–90.

4982.2 * *The Flirtations: live, out on the road.* Significant Other: FL 1002. 1991.

4983 Fogelberg, Dan, 1951–
Greatest hits. Epic: EK 38308. 1975–81.

4984 Four Aces
The Four Aces' greatest hits. MCA: MCAD-10886. 1951–55.

4985 * Four Freshmen
The Four Freshmen. [Series: Capitol collectors]. Capitol: 93197. 1951–63.

4986 Four Lads
16 most requested songs. Columbia: CK 46158. 1952–58.

4987 G, Kenny, 1959–
Silhouette. Arista: ARCD-8457. 1988.

4988 Garland, Judy, 1922–1969
Judy at Carnegie Hall. Capitol: 90013. 2CD set. 1961.

4989 Gleason, Jackie, 1916–1987
Music to make you misty/Night winds. Capitol: 92088. 1954, 1956.

4990 Hibbler, Al, 1915–
After the lights go down low. Atlantic: 1251-2. 1950–51.

4991 Houston, Whitney, 1963–
Whitney Houston. Arista: ARCD-8212. 1985.

4992 * Joel, Billy, 1949–
Greatest hits, vols. 1–2. Columbia: G2K 40121. 2CD set. 1973–85.

4993 Laine, Cleo, 1928–
Cleo at Carnegie: the 10th anniversary concert. RCA: 09026-61665-2 (DRG 2101). 1983.

4994 Laine, Frankie, 1913–
4994.1 *The Frankie Laine collection: the Mercury years.* Mercury: 314-510435-2. 1946–50.

4994.2 *16 most requested songs.* Columbia: CK 45029. 1951–57.

4995 Lanin, Lester, 1911–
Best of the big bands. Columbia: CK 46149. [1990].

4996 Lanza, Mario, 1921–1959
The great Caruso/Caruso favorites. RCA: 60049-2-RG. 1950, 1959.

4997 Lavner, Lynn
Butch fatale. Bent: 32499. 1992.

4998 Lee, Peggy, 1920–

4998.1 *Fever and other hits.* Capitol: 36258. 1946–67.

4998.2 ** *Peggy Lee.* [Series: Capitol collectors]. Capitol: 93195. 1945–50.

4999 Light, Enoch, 1905–1978

Provocative percussion. Project 3: PRD-5118 (Command 806). 1960.

5000 * Mancini, Henry, 1924–1994

All-time greatest hits, vol. 1. RCA: 8321-2-R. 1988.

5001 Manhattan Transfer

5001.1 * *The very best of the Manhattan Transfer.* Rhino/Atlantic: 71560 (19319). 1975–87.

5001.2 *Vocalese.* Atlantic: 81266-2. 1985.

5002 Manilow, Barry, 1946–

Greatest hits, vol. 1. Arista: ARCD-8598. 1973–78.

5003 Mantovani, 1905–1980

Golden hits. London: 800085-2. [1967].

5004 * Martin, Dean, 1917–1995

Dean Martin. [Series: Capitol collectors]. Capitol: 91633. 1948–60.

5005 Mathis, Johnny, 1935–

5005.1 *The best of Johnny Mathis 1975–1980.* Columbia: CK 36871. 1975–80.

5005.2 *Heavenly.* Columbia: CK 8152. 1959.

5005.3 * *Johnny's greatest hits.* Columbia: CK 34667 (1133). 1957–58.

5006 McGuire Sisters

Greatest hits. MCA: MCAD-31341 (Coral). 1954–61.

5007 Midler, Bette, 1945–

Experience the divine: greatest hits. Atlantic: 82497-2. 1972–91.

5008 Miller, Mitch, 1911–

Sing along with Mitch. Columbia: CK 8004 (1160). 1958.

5009 Minnelli, Liza, 1946–

Liza Minnelli at Carnegie Hall (highlights). Telarc: CD-85505. 1987.

5010 Morse, Ella Mae, 1924–

Ella Mae Morse. [Series: Capitol collectors]. Capitol: 95288. 1942–53.

5011 New York City Gay Men's Chorus

5011.1 *Love lives on.* Virgin Classics: 91647. 1991.

5011.2 * *New York, New York: a Broadway extravaganza.* Pro Arte: CCD 594 (CGD 198). 1984.

5012 Newton-John, Olivia, 1948–

Back to basics: the essential collection. Geffen: GEFD-24470. 1971–92.

5013 Nilsson, Harry, 1941–1994

Personal best: the Harry Nilsson anthology. RCA: 07863-66354-2. 2CD set. 1967–77.

5014 Page, Patti, 1927–

5014.1 *The Patti Page collection, vol. 1.* Mercury: 314-510433-2. 1947–52.

5014.2 *The Patti Page collection, vol. 2.* Mercury: 314-510434-2. 1952–62.

5015 Paul, Les, 1916–

5015.1 ** *The best of the Capitol masters.* Capitol: 99617. 1947–55. [Item 5015.2 covers material comparable to item 5015.1 but in greater depth and with better packaging and notes].

5015.2 *The legend and the legacy.* Capitol: 97654. 4CD set. 1940–59.

5016 Prima, Louis, 1911–1978

Louis Prima. [Series: Capitol collectors]. Capitol: 94072. 1957–59.

5017 Reddy, Helen, 1942–

Greatest hits. Capitol: 46490. 1971–75.

5018 Rodgers, Jimmie, 1933–

The best of Jimmie Rodgers. Rhino: 70942 (Roulette/Dot/A&M). 1957–67.

5019 Romanovsky and Phillips

5019.1 * *Be political, not polite.* Fresh Fruit: FF 104. 1991.

5019.2 *Brave boys: the best and more of Romanovsky and Phillips.* Fresh Fruit: FF 107. 1984–94.

5020 Schuur, Diane

Diane Schuur collection. GRP: GRD-9591. [1989].

5021 San Francisco Gay Men's Chorus

5021.1 *How fair this place.* American Helix/Golden Gate Performing Arts: SFGMC-92-1A (SFG 10-91). 1991.

5021.2 *San Francisco Gay Men's Chorus tours America '81.* Golden Gate Records: SFG 81. 1981.

5022 Seattle Men's Chorus

Over the rainbow! Emerald City Arts, 1990.

5023 * Shore, Dinah, 1917–1994

16 most requested songs. Columbia: CK 45315. 1946–49.

5024 Short, Bobby, 1926–

50 by Bobby Short. Atlantic: 81715-2. 2CD set. 1955–75.

5025 Simone, Nina, 1933–

The best of Nina Simone. Philips: 822846-2. 1964–66.

5026 Sinatra, Frank, 1915–

5026.1 * *The Capitol years.* Capitol: 94317. 3CD set. 1953–60.

5026.2 *Come fly with me.* Capitol: 48469 (920). 1958.

5026.3 ** *The essence of Frank Sinatra.* Columbia: CK 57152. 1943–52. [Item 5026.9 covers material comparable to item 5026.3 but in greater depth and with better packaging and notes].

5026.4 ** *Frank Sinatra.* [Series: Capitol collectors]. Capitol: 92160. 1953–60. [Item 5026.1 covers material comparable to item 5026.4 but in greater depth and with better packaging and notes].

5026.5 * *In the wee small hours.* Capitol: 96826 (581). 1955.

5026.6 *Nice 'n' easy.* Capitol: 96827 (1417). 1960.

5026.7 * *Songs for swinging lovers.* Capitol: 46570 (653). 1956.

5026.8 * *The very good years.* Reprise: 26501-2. 1960–80.

5026.9 *The voice.* Columbia: C4K 40343. 4CD set. 1943–52.

5027 Stafford, Jo, 1920–

Jo Stafford. [Series: Capitol collectors]. Capitol: 91638. 1943–50.

5028 Starr, Kay, 1922–

Kay Starr. [Series: Capitol collectors]. Capitol: 94080. 1947–63.

5029 Streisand, Barbra, 1942–

5029.1 ** *Greatest hits.* Columbia: CK 9968. 1963–69.

5029.2 * *Greatest hits, vol. 2.* Columbia: CK 35679. 1970–78.

5029.3 *Just for the record.* Columbia: C4K 44111. 4CD set. 1955–88.

5030 Tormé, Mel, 1925– . *See* 4838

5031 Turtle Creek Chorale

5031.1 *From the heart.* Turtle Creek Chorale: 113023-D5-0169-1 (TCC 1). 1990.

5031.2 * *Testament.* Reference Recordings: RR-49CD. 1992.

5032 Vaughan, Sarah, 1924–1990. *See* 4839

5033 Vaughn, Billy, 1931–1991

The best of Billy Vaughn. MCA: MCAC2-4164. 2AC set. 1954–71.

5034 Vinton, Bobby, 1935–

Greatest hits. Epic: EK 26098. 1962–64.

5035 * Warwick, Dionne, 1940–

The Dionne Warwick collection. Rhino: 71100. 1962–69.

5036 Washington, Dinah, 1924–1963

5036.1 *The complete Dinah Washington, vol. 6.* Mercury: 838956-2. 3CD set. 1958–60.

5036.2 * *Dinah Washington.* [Series: Compact jazz]. Mercury: 830 700-2. 1954–61.

See also 5343

5037 Weinberg, Tom Wilson

Get used to it! Aboveground: AR106CD. 1992–93.

5038 Welk, Lawrence, 1903–1992

Best of Lawrence Welk. Ranwood: R-8226-CD. [1987].

5039 Whiting, Margaret, 1924–

Margaret Whiting. [Series: Capitol collectors]. Capitol: 93194. 1942–56.

5040 Williams, Andy, 1928–

16 most requested songs. Columbia: CK 40213. [1956–67].

5041 Williams, Roger, 1925–

Roger Williams greatest hits. MCA: MCAD-63 (Kapp). [1971].

5042 Wilson, Nancy, 1937–

Yesterday's love songs, today's blues. Capitol: 96265 (2012). 1963–64.

5043 Windy City Gay Chorus

Mostly love. Windy City Performing Arts: WCGC 2. 1987–90.

New Age

This section covers the plurality of styles marketed since the late 1970s as "new age." Consult the index for specific listings under the new age–related *ambient, meditation,* and *worldbeat fusion.*

Anthologies

5044 * *Anthems: ten years of Living Music.* Living Music: LD-0023. [1992]. [Paul Winter, Eugene Friesen, Oscar Castro-Neves, Paul Halley, Glen Velez, and others].

5045 *Fruits of our labor.* Global Pacific: GP-79320. [1986]. [Steven Kindler, Bob Kindler, Paul Greaver, Aeolus, Ben Tavera King, Richard Garneau, and others].

5046 *Magnum mysterium: a special collection of sacred music classics.* Celestial Harmonies: 14060-2. [1987].

5047 *The Narada collection.* Narada: ND-39100. [1988]. [Michael Jones, Peter Buffett, Spencer Brewer, David Lanz, Eric Tingstad, Nancy Rumbel, David Arkenstone, and others].

5048 ** *Narada decade: the anniversary collection.* Narada: ND2-63911. 2CD set. [1993]. [Michael Jones, Peter Buffett, Spencer Brewer, Ancient Future, David Arkenstone, David Lanz, Michael Gettel, and others].

5049 *Narada wilderness collection.* Narada: ND-63905. [1990]. [David Arkenstone, Spencer Brewer, Eric Tingstad, Nancy Rumbel, Peter Buffett, David Lanz, and others].

5050 *New age music, vol. 1.* Innovative Communications: IC-710051. [1987]. [Jean-Michel Jarre, Klaus Schulze, Tangerine Dream, and others].

5051 *Pioneers of the new age.* Columbia: CK 44314. 1972–80. [Wendy Carlos, Weather Report, Paul Winter, Paul Horn, Terry Riley, and others].

5052 *Starflight 1.* [Series: Hearts of Space radio program]. Hearts of Space: HS100-2. 1986. [Kevin Braheny, Steve Roach, Tim Clark, Michael Amerian, and others].

5053 *Sunday morning coffee.* American Gramophone: AGCD 100. [1991]. [Chip Davis, Richard Burmer, Jackson Berkey, Doug Smith, and others].

5054 * *This is Higher Octave music, vol. 2.* Higher Octave: HOMCD-7042. [1991]. [Ottmar Liebert, William Aura, Eko, Bruce Becvar, Osamu Kitajima, Cusco, and others].

5055 ** *Windham Hill: the first ten years.* Windham Hill: WD-1095. 2CD set. 1977–87. [William Ackerman, Alex De Grassi, George Winston, Shadowfax, Liz Story, Michael Hedges, Scott Cossu, Montreux, Mark Isham, Philip Aaberg, Nightnoise, and others].

5056 *Windham Hill sampler '82.* Windham Hill: WD-1024. [1982]. [William Ackerman, George Winston, Michael Hedges, Stein and Walder, Shadowfax, Liz Story, Anger and Higbie, Scott Cossu, Alex De Grassi, and others].

5057 *Windham Hill sampler '84.* Windham Hill: WD-1035. [1984]. [Michael Hedges, Mark Isham, William Ackerman, George Winston, Shadowfax, Alex De Grassi, Scott Cossu, Oskay and O'Domhaill, and others].

5058 *Windham Hill sampler '86.* Windham Hill: WD-1048. [1986]. [Michael Manring, Liz Story, Stein and Walder, George Winston, Marshall and Anger, Philip Aaberg, Mark Isham, Shadowfax, Malcolm Dalglish, and others].

5059 *Windham Hill sampler '89.* Windham Hill: WD-1082. [1989]. [Paul McCandless, William Ackerman, Philip Aaberg, Therese Schroeder-Sheker, Michael Manring, Scott Cossu, Nightnoise, Metamora, and others].

5060 * *The world of Private Music.* Private Music: 2009-2-P. [1986]. [Yanni, Patrick O'Hearn, Lucia Hwong, Ancient Dreams, and others].

Individual Artists or Groups

5061 Aaberg, Philip

High plains. Windham Hill: CD-1037. [1985].

5062 Ackerman, William, 1949–

5062.1 *Conferring with the moon: pieces for guitar.* Windham Hill: CD-1050. [1986].

5062.2 *In search of the turtle's navel.* Windham Hill: WD-1001. [1976].

5063 Arkenstone, David
Valley of the clouds. Narada: ND-62001. 1987.

5064 * Budd, Harold, 1936–
Pavillion of dreams. Caroline: EEG-30-2 (Editions EG). 1976.

5065 Budd, Harold, 1936– , and Brian Eno, 1948–
The plateau of mirror. Caroline: EEG-18-2 (Editions EG). [1980].

5066 Ciani, Suzanne
The Private Music of Suzanne Ciani. Private Music: 1005-82103-2. [1992].

5067 Cossu, Scott
A Windham Hill retrospective. Windham Hill: 01934-11112-2. 1980–89.

5068 Dalglish, Malcolm
Jogging the memory. Windham Hill: CD-1046. 1985.

5069 De Grassi, Alex, 1952–
Southern exposure. Windham Hill: WD-1030. 1983.

5070 * Demby, Constance
Novus magnificat. Hearts of Space: HS-11003-2. [1986].

5071 Deuter, C. H., 1945–
Nirvana road. Kuckuck: 11068-2. [1984].

5072 * Eno, Brian, 1948–
Music for airports. Editions EG: CAROL-1516-2. 1978.

5073 * Enya (Eithne Ni Bhraonain), 1961–
Watermark. Warner Bros.: 26774-2 [1988].

5074 * Gardner, Kay
Ocean moon (Mooncircles/Emerging). Wise/Women Enterprises: WWE85CD. 1975, 1978.

5075 Halpern, Steven
Spectrum suite. Sound RX: SRX-7770. 1975.

5076 * Hedges, Michael, 1953–
Aerial boundaries. Windham Hill: CD-1032. [1984].

5077 ** Horn, Paul, 1930–
Inside the Taj Mahal. Kuckuck: 11062-2. 1968.

5078 * Isham, Mark
Vapor drawings. Windham Hill: CD-1027. 1983.

5079 * Jarre, Jean-Michel, 1948–
Oxygene. Dreyfus: DRY-CD-36140 (Polydor 6112). 1976.

5080 Jones, Michael
5080.1 * *Michael's music: a Michael Jones retrospective.* Narada: ND-64002. 1984–89.
5080.2 *Pianoscapes.* Narada: ND-61001. 1985.

5081 Kelly, Georgia
Seapeace. Global Pacific: 79307. 1978.

5082 Lanz, David
Cristofori's dream. Narada Lotus: ND-61021. 1987–88.

5083 Liebert, Ottmar, 1963–
Nouveau flamenco. Higher Octave: HOMCD-7026. [1990].

5084 * Lynch, Ray, 1943–
Deep breakfast. Windham Hill: 01934-11118-2. [1986].

5085 * Mannheim Steamroller
Fresh aire. American Gramophone: AGCD-355. [1974–75].

5086 Marshall, Mike, and Darol Anger
Chiaroscuro. Windham Hill: WD-1043. [1985].

5087 McKennitt, Loreena, 1957–
The visit. Warner Bros.: 26880-2. 1992.

5088 Montreux
Let them say. Windham Hill: WD-1084. [1989].

5089 Newton, James, 1953–
Echo canyon. Celestial Harmonies: 13012-2. 1984.

5090 ** Oldfield, Mike, 1953–
Tubular bells. Virgin: 86007. 1973.

5091 ** Oregon
The essential Oregon. Vanguard: VCD-109/110. [1972–76]. *See also* 4702

5092 * Penguin Cafe Orchestra
Penguin Cafe Orchestra. Editions EG: CAROL-1543-2. 1981.

5093 Popol Vuh
5093.1 *In the gardens of Pharao/Aguirre.* Celestial Harmonies: 13008-2 (CEL 008/9). 1972–82.

5093.2 *Tantric songs/Hosianna mantra.* Celestial Harmonies: 13006-2. [1981].

5094 Riley, Terry, 1935– . *See* 3889

5095 Roach, Steve

Dreamtime return. Fortuna: 18055-2. 2CD set. [1988].

5096 Rypdal, Terje, 1947–

5096.1 * *ECM works.* ECM: 78118-20428-2 (825428). 1971–81.

5096.2 *Odyssey.* ECM: 78118-21067-2 (1067/68). 1975.

5097 * Scott, Tony, 1921–

Music for Zen meditation. Verve: 817209-2 (V6 8634). 1964.

5098 Shadowfax

What goes around: the best of Shadowfax. Windham Hill: CD-1104. 1982–86.

5099 Stearns, Michael

Chronos. Sonic Atmospheres: CD-312. 1985.

5100 ** Tangerine Dream

Stratosfear. Virgin: 86092. 1976.

5101 Tibbetts, Steve

YR. ECM: 78118-21355-2 (Frammis). 1980.

5102 Tingstad, Eric, and Nancy Rumbel

Homeland. Narada/Sona Gaia: ND-61026. [1990].

5103 Turtle Island String Quartet

Turtle Island String Quartet. Windham Hill: WD-0110. [1988].

5104 Vangelis, 1943–

5104.1 *Antarctica: music from the soundtrack.* Polydor: 815732-2. 1983.

5104.2 * *China.* Polydor: 813653-2. 1978.

5104.3 *Opera sauvage.* Polydor: 829663-2. 1978–79.

5105 Vollenweider, Andreas

5105.1 * *Behind the gardens, behind the wall, under the tree.* CBS: MK 37793. [1981].

5105.2 *Caverna magica.* CBS: MK 37827. 1982.

5106 Winston, George, 1949–

5106.1 * *Autumn.* Windham Hill: CD-1012. 1980.

5106.2 ** *December.* Windham Hill: CD-1025. 1982.

5107 Winter, Paul, 1939–

5107.1 *Canyon.* Living Music: LD-0006. 1980–85.

5107.2 * *Icarus.* Epic: EK 31643 or Living Music: LD-0004. 1972.

5107.3 * *Wolf eyes: a retrospective.* Living Music: LD0018. 1980–88.

5108 Wolff, Henry, and Nancy Hennings

Tibetan bells II. Celestial Harmonies: 13005-2. 1978.

Rhythm and Blues, Soul, and Rap

Compiled by
**William E. Anderson
and Kent Underwood**

T he term *rhythm and blues* (r&b) was first applied by the music industry to Black popular music in the late 1940s. The first section of this chapter covers the various styles of African American popular vocal and dance music since World War II, including rhythm and blues itself, soul music, Motown, funk, and disco. (Consult the index for listings under these and other genre terms.) A section on rap music concludes the chapter.

Rhythm and Blues, Soul, and Related Genres

Anthologies

5109 *Atlantic honkers: a rhythm and blues saxophone anthology.* Atlantic: 81666. 2LP set. 1947–70. [Joe Morris, Tiny Grimes, Red Prysock, Frank Culley, Willis Jackson, Jesse Stone, Hal Singer, Sam "The Man" Taylor, Arnett Cobb, King Curtis]. OP

5110 ** *Atlantic rhythm and blues, 1947–1974.* Atlantic: 82305-2. 8CD set. 1947–74. [This material was previously released on seven single CDs (Atlantic: 81293-2/81299-2), now out-of-print].

5111 *Atlantic sisters of soul.* Rhino: 71037. 1965–73. [Sweet Inspirations, Barbara Lynn, Betty LaVette, Tammi Lynn, and others].

5112 *The best of Ace Records: the r&b hits.* Scotti Bros.: 75406-2. 1955–60. [Huey Smith, Bobby Marchan, Earl King, Red Tyler, Al Collins, and others].

5113 *Best of Chess r&b, vol. 1.* Chess: CHD-31317. 1956–65. [Moonglows, Miracles, Jimmy McCracklin, Vibrations, Etta James, Clarence Henry, Bobby Moore, Jan Bradley, Billy Stewart, Little Milton, and others].

5114 *Best of Chess r&b, vol. 2.* Chess: CHD-31318. 1964–69. [Billy Stewart, Tony Clarke, Mitty Collier, Radiants, Little Milton, Dells, Laura Lee, Fontella Bass, Ramsey Lewis, Jackie Ross, Etta James, and others].

5115 *The best of Holland-Dozier-Holland.* HDH: 3907 (Invictus/Hot Wax). 1970–73. [Flaming Ember, 8th Day, Chairmen of the Board, Honey Cone, and others].

5116 ** *Best of the girl groups, vol. 1.* Rhino: 70988. 1961–66. [Shangri Las, Chiffons, Dixie Cups, Shirelles, Betty Everett, and others].

5117 *Best of the girl groups, vol. 2.* Rhino: 70989. 1958–65. [Angels, Chiffons, Little Eva, Cookies, Shirelles, Essex, Exciters, and others].

5118 ** *Blues masters, vol. 5: jump blues classics.* Rhino: 71125. 1947–57. [Joe Turner, Wynonie Harris, Roy Brown, Tiny Bradshaw, Jackie Brenston, Roy Milton, Big Mama Thornton, Bull Moose Jackson, Ruth Brown, and others].

5119 * *Blues masters, vol. 13: New York City blues.* Rhino: 71131. 1944–56. [Lionel Hampton, Duke Ellington, Buddy Johnson, Hot Lips Page, Joe Morris, Eddie "Cleanhead" Vinson, Arnett Cobb, Lucky Millinder, Erskine Hawkins, Joe Turner, Cootie Williams, Johnny Hodges, Al Hibbler, Jesse Stone, Big Maybelle, Sam "The Man" Taylor, Count Basie, Joe Williams, Al Sears].

5120 *Blues masters, vol. 14: more jump blues.* Rhino: 71133. 1946–59. [Louis Jordan, Professor Longhair, Ruth Brown, Joe Turner, Louis Prima, Floyd Dixon, Joe Liggins, LaVern Baker, Sam Price, Big Maybelle, Faye Adams, Joe Morris, Piano Red, Wynonie Harris, and others].

5121 *Chicago soul: the legendary Brunswick/ Dakar hits.* Epic: PG2 39895. 2LP set. 1965–75. [Barbara Acklin, Tyrone Davis, Chi-Lites, Gene Chandler, and others]. OP

5122 *Collector's choice.* Rounder: CD 2082 (Ric/ Ron). 1959–64. [Professor Longhair, Irma Thomas, Tommy Ridgley, Eddie Bo, Al Johnson, Joe Jones, and others].

5123 *The complete Stax-Volt singles.* Atlantic: 82218-2. 9CD set. 1959–68. [Otis Redding, Sam and Dave, Booker T and the MGs, Eddie Floyd, Rufus Thomas, Carla Thomas, Albert King, William Bell, Johnnie Taylor, and others].

5124 ** *Crescent City soul highlights.* EMI: 37355. [1966]. [Fats Domino, Spiders, Smiley Lewis, Shirley and Lee, Dave Bartholomew, Showmen, Barbara George, Jewel King, Archibald, Clarence Garlow, Bobby Mitchell, Earl King, Benny Spellman, Ernie K-Doe, Chris Kenner, Jessie Hill, Irma Thomas, Roy Brown]. [Item 5125 covers material comparable to item 5124 but in greater depth and with better packaging and notes].

5125 * *Crescent City soul: the sound of New Orleans.* EMI: 37350. 4CD set. 1947–74. [Professor Longhair, Lloyd Price, Fats Domino, Spiders, Smiley Lewis, Shirley and Lee, Guitar Slim, Sugar Boy Crawford, Little Richard, Clarence "Frogman" Henry, Dave Bartholomew, Huey Smith, Prince La La, Showmen, Barbara George, Lee Dorsey, Tommy Ridgley, Jewel King, Archibald, Clarence Garlow, Bobby Mitchell, Lee Allen, Earl King, Benny Spellman, Ernie K-Doe, Chris Kenner, Aaron Neville, Jessie Hill, Irma Thomas, Roy Brown, Dr. John, Allen Toussaint, Meters, and others.]

5126 *Didn't it blow your mind!: soul hits of the '70s, vol. 1.* Rhino: 70781. 1969–70. [Friends of Distinction, Winstons, Eddie Holman, Chairmen of the Board, Brook Benton, Edwin Hawkins, Delfonics, and others].

5127 *Didn't it blow your mind!: soul hits of the '70s, vol. 2.* Rhino: 70782. 1969–70. [Tyrone Davis, Moments, Five Stairsteps, Freda Payne, Three Degrees, and others].

5128 *Didn't it blow your mind!: soul hits of the '70s, vol. 3.* Rhino: 70783. 1970. [Edwin Starr, Watts 103rd Street Rhythm Band, Gene Chandler, and others].

5129 *Didn't it blow your mind!: soul hits of the '70s, vol. 4.* Rhino: 70784. 1970–71. [King Floyd, Chairmen of the Board, Chi-Lites, Brenda and the Tabulations, and others].

5130 *Didn't it blow your mind!: soul hits of the '70s, vol. 5.* Rhino: 70785. 1971. [Honey Cone, Freda Payne, Jean Knight, Undisputed Truth, and others].

5131 *Didn't it blow your mind!: soul hits of the '70s, vol. 6.* Rhino: 70786. 1971. [Dramatics, Bill Withers, Isaac Hayes, Chi-Lites, Persuaders, Staple Singers, and others].

5132 *Didn't it blow your mind!: soul hits of the '70s, vol. 7.* Rhino: 70787. 1971–72. [Dennis Coffey, Joe Simon, Betty Wright, Dramatics, Chi-Lites, and others].

5133 * *Didn't it blow your mind!: soul hits of the '70s, vol. 8.* Rhino: 70788. 1972. [Joe Tex, Staple Singers, Bill Withers, Luther Ingram, O'Jays, Joe Simon, and others].

5134 *Didn't it blow your mind!: soul hits of the '70s, vol. 9.* Rhino: 70789. 1972–73. [Mel and Tim, Curtis Mayfield, Harold Melvin, Four Tops, Billy Paul, and others].

5135 *Didn't it blow your mind!: soul hits of the '70s, vol. 10.* Rhino: 70790. 1972–73. [Curtis Mayfield, War, Four Tops, Independents, Sylvia, and others].

5136 *Didn't it blow your mind!: soul hits of the '70s, vol. 11.* Rhino: 70551. 1972–73. [Barry White, Pointer Sisters, Eddie Kendricks, Ann Peebles, Staple Singers, Gladys Knight, JB's, Dells, and others].

5137 *Didn't it blow your mind!: soul hits of the '70s, vol. 12.* Rhino: 70552. 1973–74. [O'Jays, Manu Dibango, Eddie Kendricks, Bobby Womack, MFSB, Harold Melvin, Kool and the Gang, and others].

5138 *Didn't it blow your mind!: soul hits of the '70s, vol. 13.* Rhino: 70553. 1973–74. [Blue Magic, Rufus, Johnny Bristol, BT Express, Kool and the Gang, and others].

5139 *Didn't it blow your mind!: soul hits of the '70s, vol. 14.* Rhino: 70554. 1974–75. [Ohio Players, Labelle, O'Jays, Latimore, AWB, BT Express, Miracles, Shirley and Company, and others].

5140 *Didn't it blow your mind!: soul hits of the '70s, vol. 15.* Rhino: 70555. 1974–75. [Rufus, Ben E. King, Blackbyrds, Minnie Riperton, Tavares, Joe Simon, Staple Singers, Gwen McCrae, Major Harris, Shirley Brown, and others].

5141 ** *The disco years, vol. 1: turn the beat around.* Rhino: 70984. 1974–78. [Van McCoy, Shirley and Company, Rose Royce, Trammps, KC and the Sunshine Band, Diana Ross, Thelma Houston, Vicki Sue Robinson, Taste of Honey, Sylvester, Peter Brown, and others].

5142 * *The disco years, vol. 2: on the beat.* Rhino: 70985. 1978–82. [Chic, Anita Ward, Gloria Gaynor, Lipps Inc., Kool and the Gang, Village People, Blondie, Cheryl Lynn, and others].

5143 * *The disco years, vol. 3: boogie fever.* Rhino: 70274. 1973–80. [Sylvers, Carol Douglas, Village People, Jackson 5, Chic, Sister Sledge, Donna Summer, Amii Stewart, and others].

5144 *The disco years, vol. 4: lost in music.* Rhino: 70275. 1977–85. [Chic, Sister Sledge, Diana Ross, Kool and the Gang, Donna Summer, and others].

5145 *The disco years, vol. 5: must be the music.* Rhino: 70276. 1974–86. [Evelyn King, Cheryl Lynn, Donna Summer, Heatwave, Diana Ross, S.O.S. Band, and others].

5146 *Duke-Peacock's greatest hits.* MCA: MCAD-10666. 1952–73. [Big Mama Thornton, Junior Parker, Bobby Bland, Marie Adams, James Booker, Joe Hinton, Johnny Ace, O. V. Wright, Carl Carlton, and others].

5147 *The Fire/Fury Records story.* Capricorn: 42009-2. 2CD set. 1957–62. [Produced by Bobby Robinson. Wilbert Harrison, Buster Brown, Lee Dorsey, Bobby Marchan, Gladys Knight, Elmore James, Tarheel Slim and Little Ann, King Curtis, Les Cooper, and others].

5148 * *Get down tonight: the best of T. K. Records.* Rhino: 71003. 1972–80. [Gwen McCrae, George McCrae, KC and the Sunshine Band, Betty Wright, Timmy Thomas, Peter Brown, Foxy, and others].

5149 *Hi times: the Hi Records r&b years.* Right Stuff: 30584. 3CD set. 1958–78. [Bill Black, Willie Mitchell, Al Green, Ann Peebles, Syl Johnson, Otis Clay, O. V. Wright, and others].

5150 * *The history of Hi Records rhythm and blues, vol. 1: the beginnings.* Hi/MCA: MCAD-25226. 1959–72. [Bill Black, Willie Mitchell, Ann Peebles, Al Green, Otis Clay, and others. Item 5146 covers material comparable to item 5147 but in greater depth and with better packaging and notes.] OP

5151 ** *Hitsville USA: the Motown singles collection.* Motown: 37463-6312-2. 4CD set. 1959–71. [Contours, Four Tops, Marvin Gaye, Isley Brothers, Jackson 5, Gladys Knight, Martha and The Vandellas, Marvelettes, Miracles, Edwin Starr, Supremes, Temptations, Jr. Walker and the All Stars, Mary Wells, Stevie Wonder, Kim Weston, Brenda Holloway, and others].

5152 *Hitsville USA: the Motown singles collection, vol. 2.* Motown: 37463-6358-2. 4CD set. 1972–92. [Lionel Richie, Michael Jackson, Jackson 5, Supremes, Four Tops, Temptations, Stevie Wonder, Gladys Knight, Diana Ross, Marvin Gaye, Eddie Kendricks, Smokey Robinson, Thelma Houston, Commodores, Switch, Rick James, Teena Marie, Dazz Band, DeBarge, and others].

5153 * *In yo' face: the history of funk, vol. 1.* Rhino: 71431. 1970–74. [James Brown, Sly and the Family Stone, Funkadelic, Charles Wright, King Floyd, Curtis Mayfield, Eddie Kendricks, War; Earth, Wind and Fire; Parliament, and others].

5154 *In yo' face: the history of funk, vol. 2.* Rhino: 71432. 1971–75. [James Brown, Sly and the Family

Stone, Curtis Mayfield, Kool and the Gang, O'Jays, AWB, Rufus; Earth, Wind and Fire; and others].

5155 * *In yo' face: the history of funk, vol. 3.* Rhino: 71433. 1973–77. [Kool and the Gang, James Brown, O'Jays, Isley Brothers, Parliament, Rufus, Cameo, Brothers Johnson, Graham Central Station, and others].

5156 * *In yo' face: the history of funk, vol. 4.* Rhino: 71434. 1973–78. [Sly and the Family Stone, James Brown, Kool and the Gang, Parliament, Bootsy Collins, Marvin Gaye; Earth, Wind and Fire; Isley Brothers, and others].

5157 * *In yo' face: the history of funk, vol. 5.* Rhino: 71435. 1974–80. [Sly and the Family Stone, Con-FunkShun, Parliament, Fatback, Bar-Kays, Chuck Brown, Gap Band, Rick James, Zapp, Cameo, and others].

5158 * *The King r&b box set.* King: KBSCD-7002. 4CD set. 1945–68. [Bull Moose Jackson, Five Royales, Roy Brown, Swallows, Dominoes, Hank Ballard, Wynonie Harris, Lucky Millinder, Julia Lee, Todd Rhodes, James Brown, Tiny Bradshaw, Bill Doggett, and others].

5159 * *Mercury r&b 1946–1962.* Mercury: 838243-2. 2CD set. 1946–62. [Dinah Washington, Eddie "Cleanhead" Vinson, Roy Byrd (Professor Longhair), Buddy and Ella Johnson, Louis Jordan, Clyde McPhatter, and others].

5160 *The Minit Records story.* EMI: E2 30879. 2CD set. 1959–70. [Ernie K-Doe, Benny Spellman, Jessie Hill, Chris Kenner, Irma Thomas, Eskew Reeder, Bobby Womack, O'Jays, Ike and Tina Turner, and others].

5161 ** *Muscle Shoals sound.* Rhino: 71517. 1961–72. [Arthur Alexander, Jimmy Hughes, Percy Sledge, James and Bobby Purify, Wilson Pickett, Aretha Franklin, Arthur Conley, Etta James, Clarence Carter, R. B. Greaves, Staple Singers, and others].

5162 *New Orleans Jazz and Heritage Festival 1976.* Rhino: 71111. 1976. [Allen Toussaint, Lee Dorsey, Ernie K-Doe, Irma Thomas, and others].

5163 *The OKeh rhythm and blues story.* Epic/Legacy: E3K 48912. 3CD set. 1949–57. [Chris Powell, Red Saunders, Big Maybelle, Chuck Willis, Ravens, Larry Darnell, Treniers, Annie Laurie, Paul Gayten, Hadda Brooks, Titus Turner, Screamin' Jay Hawkins, Andre Williams, and others].

5164 * *OKeh soul.* Sony Music Special Products: A 37321 (OKeh). 1962–67. [Major Lance, Billy Butler, Walter Jackson, Artistics, Vibrations, and others].

5165 * *Phil Spector: back to mono.* Phil Spector/Abkco: 7118-2 (Philles). 4CD set. 1958–69. [Crystals, Ronettes, Righteous Brothers, Darlene Love, and others].

5166 *Pimps, players and private eyes.* Sire: 26624-2. 1971–74. [Bobby Womack, Impressions, Four Tops, Marvin Gaye, Isaac Hayes, Willie Hutch, Curtis Mayfield, and others].

5167 ** *The r&b box: 30 years of rhythm and blues.* Rhino: R2 71806. 6CD set. 1943–72. [Louis Jordan, Buddy Johnson, Illinois Jacquet, Joe Liggins, Lionel Hampton, Jimmy Liggins, Johnny Moore, Charles Brown, Ravens, Roy Milton, Julia Lee, Nellie Lutcher, Mabel Scott, Amos Milburn, Paul Williams, Big Jay McNeely, Dinah Washington, Johnny Otis, Percy Mayfield, Jackie Brenston, Five Keys, Lloyd Price, Ruth Brown, Orioles, Joe Turner, Professor Longhair, Clovers, Spaniels, Penguins, LaVern Baker, Moonglows, Ray Charles, Johnny Ace, Clyde McPhatter, Drifters, Shirley & Lee, Cadillacs, James Brown, Fats Domino, Big Maybelle, Chuck Willis, Dells, Jesse Belvin, Coasters, Jackie Wilson, Chantels, Huey Smith, Impressions, Wilbert Harrison, Flamingos, Dee Clark, Etta James, Bobby Bland, Solomon Burke, Mary Wells, Chuck Jackson, Booker T and the MGs, Marvin Gaye, Miracles, Joe Tex, Little Milton, Four Tops, Isley Brothers, Wilson Pickett, Percy Sledge, Temptations, Eddie Floyd, Aaron Neville, Otis Redding, James Carr, Aretha Franklin, Sam and Dave, B. B. King, Brook Benton, Ike and Tina Turner, Spinners, and others].

5168 *Rock instrumental classics, vol. 4: soul.* Rhino: 71604. 1961–73. [Booker T and the MGs, King Curtis, Mar-Keys, Hugh Masekela, Bar-Kays, Ray Barretto, Cannonball Adderley, Young-Holt Unlimited, Ramsey Lewis, Manu Dibango, Mongo Santamaria, El Chicano, and others].

5169 ** *The roots of rock and roll.* Savoy: ZDS-4415. 1947–56. [Paul Williams, Hal Singer, Johnny Otis, Little Esther, Varetta Dillard, Big Maybelle, Ravens, and others]. OP

5170 *The Scepter Records story.* Capricorn: 2-42003. 3CD set. 1959–72. [Shirelles, Maxine Brown, Isley Brothers, Chuck Jackson, Dionne Warwick, Kingsmen, Esquires, B. J. Thomas, and others].

5171 *Soul shots: a collection of sixties soul classics, vol. 1.* Rhino: 75774. 1962–69. [J. J. Jackson, James Brown, Dyke and the Blazers, Fontella Bass, Intruders, King Curtis, Lorraine Ellison, James and Bobby Purify, and others].

5172 *Soul shots: a collection of sixties soul classics, vol. 2.* Rhino: 75770. 1961–69. [Johnnie Taylor, Bobby Moore, Eddie Holman, Deon Jackson, Dells, Booker T and the MGs, Chuck Jackson, Major Lance, Linda Jones, and others].

5173 *Soul shots: a collection of sixties soul classics, vol. 3.* Rhino: 75757. 1959–68. [Capitols, Edwin Starr, Impressions, Sweet Inspirations, James Carr, Dells, O. V. Wright, James and Bobby Purify, and others].

5174 *Southern rhythm 'n' rock: the best of Excello Records, vol. 2.* Rhino: 70897. 1954–65. [Gladiolas, Jerry McCain, Arthur Gunter, Earl Gaines, Lillian Offit, Louis Brooks, King Crooners, and others].

5175 *Stars of the Apollo Theatre.* Columbia: C2K 53407. 2CD set. 1927–65. [Bessie Smith, Buck and Bubbles, Butterbeans and Susie, Mills Brothers, Cab Calloway, Cootie Williams, Eddie "Cleanhead" Vinson, Slim Gaillard, Ida Cox, Jimmy Rushing, Count Basie, Big Maybelle, Screamin' Jay Hawkins, Aretha Franklin, and others].

5176 ** *Straighten up and fly right: rhythm and blues from the close of the swing era to the dawn of rock 'n' roll.* New World: NW 261. LP. 1938–56. [Lionel Hampton, Joe Turner, Golden Gate Quartet, Nat King Cole, Cecil Gant, Louis Jordan, T-Bone Walker, Wynonie Harris, Ravens, Tiny Bradshaw, Lightnin' Hopkins, Clovers, Big Mama Thornton, Ruth Brown, Orioles, Muddy Waters]. OP

5177 * *Ten years of #1 hits.* Philadelphia International/CBS: ZK 39307. 1972–79. [Billy Paul, MFSB, O'Jays, Archie Bell, Lou Rawls, Teddy Pendergrass, McFadden and Whitehead].

5178 * *This is how it all began, vol. 1.* Specialty: 2117. LP/AC. 1945–55. [John Lee Hooker, Mercy Dee, Roy Milton, Joe Liggins, Percy Mayfield, Camille Howard, Jimmy Liggins, Soul Stirrers, Alex Bradford, Swan Silvertones, and others].

5179 * *Top of the Stax: 20 greatest hits.* Stax: SCD-88005-2. 1962, 1966–74. [Sam and Dave, Eddie Floyd, Staple Singers, Carla Thomas, Soul Children, Shirley Brown, Johnnie Taylor, Little Milton, Jean Knight, Rufus Thomas, Booker T and the MGs, Mel

and Tim, Dramatics, Emotions, Otis Redding, Frederick Knight, Isaac Hayes].

5180 *A tribute to Black entertainers.* Columbia: C2K 52454. 2CD set. 1919–82. [Bert Williams, Ethel Waters, Louis Armstrong, Slim and Slam, Jimmie Lunceford, Count Basie, Pete Johnson, Billie Holiday, Lena Horne, Cab Calloway, Mills Brothers, Duke Ellington, Sarah Vaughan, Ella Fitzgerald, O'Jays, Isley Brothers, Sly and the Family Stone, and others].

5181 *The Vee-Jay story: celebrating 40 years of classic hits.* Vee-Jay: NVS2-3-400. 3CD set. 1953–65. [Spaniels, Jerry Butler, El Dorados, Gene Chandler, Dells, Dee Clark, Roscoe Gordon, Betty Everett, Little Richard, Jimmy Reed, Elmore James, Eddie Taylor, John Lee Hooker, and others].

Individual Artists or Groups

5182 Adams, Faye, ca. 1925–

Golden classics. Collectables: COL-CD-5122 (Herald). [1953–57].

5183 Alexander, Arthur, 1940–1993

The ultimate Arthur Alexander. Razor & Tie: 2014 (Dot). 1961–64, 1975.

5184 Atlantic Starr

Atlantic Starr. [Series: Classics, vol. 10]. A&M: 75021-2508-2. 1978–85.

5185 Baker, Anita, 1957–

Rapture. Elektra: 60444-2. 1986.

5186 * Baker, LaVern, 1929–

Soul on fire: the best of LaVern Baker. Atlantic: 82311-2. 1953–62.

5187 * Ballard, Hank, 1936– , and the Midnighters

Sexy ways: the best of Hank Ballard and the Midnighters. Rhino: 71512 (Federal/King). 1953–61.

5188 Bar-Kays

The best of the Bar-Kays. Mercury: 314 514 823-2. 1976–89.

5189 Bell, William, 1939–

The best of William Bell. Stax: SCD-8541-2. 1968–74.

5190 Benton, Brook, 1931–1988

The best of Brook Benton. Mercury: 830772-2. 1959–64.

5191 Big Maybelle, 1924–1972

The complete OKeh sessions. Epic: EK 53417 (OKeh). 1952–55.

5192 Bland, Bobby, 1932– . *See 4225*

5193 Bonds, Gary U. S., 1939–

School of rock 'n' roll. Rhino: 70971 (Legrand). 1960–62.

5194 Booker T and the MGs

The very best of Booker T and the MG's. Rhino: 71738 (Stax). 1962–71.

5195 Bostic, Earl, 1913–1965

Earl Bostic blows a fuse. Charly: CDCHARLY 241 (King). 1946–58.

5196 Bradshaw, Tiny, 1905–1958

Breakin' up the house. Charly: CD 43 (King). 1950–52. OP

5197 Brown, Bobby, 1969–

Don't be cruel. MCA: MCAD-42185. 1988.

5198 ** Brown, Charles, 1922–

Driftin' blues: the best of Charles Brown. EMI: 97989 (Aladdin). 1945–56.

5199 Brown, Chuck, 1936– , and the Soul Searchers

Bustin' loose. Valley Vue: 53903 (Source). 1978.

5200 Brown, James, 1928–

5200.1 *Live at the Apollo.* Polydor: 823001-2. 1967.

5200.2 * *Live at the Apollo: October 24, 1962.* Polydor: 843479-2. 1962.

5200.3 * *Roots of a revolution.* Polydor: 817304-2 (Federal/King). 2CD set. 1956–64.

5200.4 * *Star time.* Polydor: 849108-2 (King). 4CD set. 1956–84.

5200.5 ** *20 all-time greatest hits.* Polydor: 314-511326-2. 1956–72. [Item 5200.4 covers material comparable to item 5200.5 but in greater depth and with better packaging and notes].

5201 Brown, Roy, 1925–1981

5201.1 * *Good rocking tonight: the best of Roy Brown.* Rhino: 71545 (DeLuxe/King). 1947–57.

5201.2 *Laughing but crying.* Route 66: RBD-2 (DeLuxe). 1947–59.

5202 Brown, Ruth, 1928–

Miss Rhythm. Atlantic: 82061-2. 2CD set. 1949–60.

5203 Bryson, Peabo, 1951–

The Peabo Bryson collection. Capitol: 46071. 1978–83.

5204 Burke, Solomon, 1936–

5204.1 * *The best of Solomon Burke.* Atlantic: 8109-2. 1960–67. [Item 5204.2 covers material comparable to item 5204.1 but in greater depth and with better packaging and notes].

5204.2 *Home in your heart: the best of Solomon Burke.* Rhino/Atlantic: 70284. 2CD set. 1960–68.

5204.3 *Soul alive!* Rounder: CD 11521. 1981.

5205 Butler, Jerry, 1939–

5205.1 * *The best of Jerry Butler.* Rhino: 75881 (Vee-Jay/Mercury). 1958–69.

5205.2 *The very best of Jerry Butler.* Mercury: 314-510967-2. 1967–72.

5206 * Cameo

The best of Cameo. Polydor: 314 514824-2 (Chocolate City/Atlanta Artists). 1977–87.

5207 Carr, James, 1942–

The essential James Carr. Razor & Tie: CD 2060. (Goldwax). 1966–69.

5208 Carter, Clarence, 1936–

Snatching it back: the best of Clarence Carter. Rhino/Atlantic: 70286. 1963, 1966–71.

5209 Charles, Ray, 1930–

5209.1 * *Anthology.* Rhino: 75759 (ABC). 1960–68.

5209.2 ** *The best of Ray Charles: the Atlantic years.* Rhino: 71722. 1953–59. [Item 5209.4 covers material comparable to item 5209.2 but in greater depth and with better packaging and notes].

5209.3 *The birth of a legend.* Ebony: EY2CD-8001/02 (Downbeat/Swingtime). 2CD set. 1949–52.

5209.4 * *The birth of soul.* Atlantic: 82310-2. 3CD set. 1952–59.

5209.5 *Modern sounds in country and western music.* Rhino: 70099 (ABC). 1962.

5209.6 *Ray Charles live.* Atlantic: 81732-2. 1958–59.

5210 Chi-Lites

Greatest hits. Rhino: 70532 (Brunswick). 1969–74.

5211 Chic

Dance, dance, dance: the best of Chic. Atlantic: 82333-2. 1977–83.

5212   Clark, Dee, 1938–1990

Raindrops. Vee-Jay: NVD2-703. 1958–62.

5213   Clovers

Down in the alley: the best of the Clovers. Atlantic: 82312-2. 1951–55.

5214   Coasters

5214.1 * *50 coastin' hits.* Rhino: 71090 (Spark/Atco). 2CD set. 1954–68.

5214.2 ** *The very best of the Coasters.* Rhino: 71597 (Atco). 1954–61. [Item 5214.1 covers material comparable to item 5214.2 but in greater depth and with better packaging and notes].

5215   Cole, Natalie, 1950–

Natalie Cole collection. Capitol: 46619. 1975–81.

5216   Collins, Bootsy, 1951–

Back in the day: the best of Bootsy Collins. Warner Bros.: 26581-2. 1972, 1976–82.

5217   Commodores

All the great hits. Motown: 37463-6028-2. 1974–81.

5218   Cooke, Sam, 1935–1964

5218.1 *Feel it!: live at the Harlem Square Club.* RCA: PCD1-5181. 1963.

5218.2 ** *The man and his music.* RCA: PCD1-7127 (Keen). 1956–64.

5219   Crystals

The best of the Crystals. Phil Spector/Abkco: 7214-2 (Philles). 1961–64.

5220   Darnell, Larry, 1929–1983

I'll get along somehow. Route 66: KIX-19 (Regal). LP. 1949–57. OP

5221   Davis, Tyrone, 1938–

Greatest hits. Rhino: 70533 (Dakar). 1968–75.

5222   Dazz Band

Greatest hits. Motown: 37463-5387-2. 1981–84.

5223   Delfonics

The best of the Delfonics. Arista: ARCD-8333 (Philly Groove). 1968–72.

5224   Dells

On their corner: the best of the Dells. Chess: CHD-9333 (Cadet). 1966–74.

5225 *   Doggett, Bill, 1916–1996

Leaps and bounds. Charly: CDCHARLY 281 (King). 1952–59.

5226   Domino, Fats, 1928–

5226.1 ** *The fat man: 25 classic performances.* EMI: 52326. 1949–61. [Item 5226.2 covers material comparable to item 5226.1 but in greater depth and with better packaging and notes].

5226.2 *"They call me the fat man . . .": the legendary Imperial recordings.* EMI: 96784. 4CD set. 1949–62.

5227   Dominoes

Sixty minute men: the best of Billy Ward and his Dominoes. Rhino: 71509 (Federal). 1950–57.

5228   Dorsey, Lee, 1924–1986

5228.1 * *Great googa mooga.* Charly: CD NEV 3 (Fury/Amy/Polydor/ABC). 2CD set. 1960–78.

5228.2 *Yes we can . . . and then some.* Polydor: 314 517865-2 (24-4042). 1963, 1970.

5229   Dr. John (Mac Rebennack), 1941–

Mos' scocious: the Dr. John anthology. Rhino: 71450. 2CD set. 1959–89.

5230   Dramatics

The best of the Dramatics. Stax: FCD-60-003. 1971–74.

5231   Drifters

5231.1 * *All time greatest hits and more.* Atlantic: 81931-2. 2CD set. 1959–65.

5231.2 * *Let the boogie woogie roll.* Atlantic: 81927-2. 2CD set. 1953–58.

5231.3 ** *The very best of the Drifters.* Rhino: 71211 (Atlantic). 1959–65. [Item 5231.1 covers material comparable to item 5231.3 but in greater depth and with better packaging and notes].

5232   Earth, Wind and Fire

5232.1 ** *The best of Earth, Wind and Fire, vol. 1.* Columbia: CK 35647. 1975–78.

5232.2 *The best of Earth, Wind and Fire, vol. 2.* Columbia: CK 45013. 1974–88.

5233   Falcons

I found a love. Relic: 7012. 1960–64.

5234   Five Keys

The Aladdin years. Collectables: 5632 (EMI 96056). 1951–53.

5235 * Five Royales

Monkey hips and rice: the "5" Royales anthology. Rhino: 71546 (Apollo/King). 2CD set. 1951–62.

5236 Flack, Roberta, 1939–

The best of Roberta Flack. Atlantic: 19317-2. 1971–81.

5237 Flamingos

The best of the Flamingos. Rhino: 70967. 1953–61.

5238 Four Tops

5238.1 * *Anthology.* Motown: 37463-0809-2. 2CD set. 1964–72.

5238.2 *The best of the Four Tops.* MCA: MCAD-27019 (Dunhill/ABC). 1972–76.

5239 Franklin, Aretha, 1942–

5239.1 *Aretha: jazz to soul.* Columbia: C2K 48515. 2CD set. 1961–67.

5239.2 *Greatest hits.* Arista: 07822-18722-2. 1980–94.

5239.3 *I never loved a man the way I love you.* Rhino: 71934 (Atlantic 8139). 1967.

5239.4 *Lady soul.* Rhino: 71933 (Atlantic 8176). 1968.

5239.5 * *Queen of soul: the Atlantic recordings.* Rhino/Atlantic: 71063. 4CD set. 1967–76.

5239.6 ** *The very best of Aretha Franklin, vol. 1.* Rhino: 71598 (Atlantic). 1967–70.

5239.7 * *The very best of Aretha Franklin, vol. 2.* Rhino: 71599 (Atlantic). 1970–76.

5240 * Funkadelic

One nation under a groove. Priority: 53872 (Warner Bros. 3209). 1978.

5241 Gant, Cecil, 1913–1951

Cecil Gant. Krazy Kat: KKCD03 (Gilt-Edge). 1944–46.

5242 Gap Band

The best of the Gap Band. Mercury: 314 522457-2. 1979–83.

5243 Gaye, Marvin, 1939–1984

5243.1 ** *Anthology.* Motown: 37463-0791-2 (Tamla). 2CD set. 1962–77.

5243.2 * *Let's get it on.* Motown: 37463-5192-2 (Tamla). 1973.

5243.3 ** *What's goin' on.* Motown: 37463-5339-2 (Tamla). 1971.

5244 Gayten, Paul, 1920– , and Annie Laurie

Regal Records in New Orleans. Specialty: SPCD-2169-2. 1949–51.

5245 Green, Al, 1946–

5245.1 * *Al Green explores your mind.* The Right Stuff: 30581 (Hi: 32087). 1972.

5245.2 ** *Greatest hits.* The Right Stuff: 30800 (Hi). 1970–77.

5245.3 *I'm still in love with you.* The Right Stuff: 27627 (Hi 32074). 1972.

5246 Griffin Brothers

Riffin' with the Griffin Brothers Orchestra. Ace: CHD 136 (Dot). LP. 1950–52. OP

5247 Grimes, Tiny, 1916–1989

Tiny Grimes and his Rockin' Highlanders. Krazy Kat: KKCD01 (Gotham). 1949–53.

5248 Guy

Guy. MCA: MCAD-42176. 1988.

5249 Hamilton, Roy, 1929–1969

16 most requested songs. Columbia: CK 57902 (Epic). 1954–61.

5250 * Harris, Wynonie, 1915–1969

Bloodshot eyes: the best of Wynonie Harris. Rhino: 71544 (King). 1947–54.

5251 Hathaway, Donny, 1945–1979

A Donny Hathaway collection. Atlantic: 82092-2. 1969–78.

5252 Hayes, Isaac, 1942–

Greatest hit singles. Stax: SCD-8515-2 (Enterprise). 1969–73.

5253 Humes, Helen, 1913–1981

Be-baba-leba. Whiskey, Women, and . . . : 701. 1944–52.

5254 Hunter, Ivory Joe, 1914–1974

5254.1 *7th Street boogie.* Route 66: KIX CD 4. 1946–50.

5254.2 * *Since I met you baby: the best of Ivory Joe Hunter.* Razor & Tie: RE 2052 (MGM/Atlantic). 1949–58.

5255 Intruders

Super hits. Philadelphia International/CBS: ZK 32131. 1966–70.

5256 Isley Brothers

5256.1 * *Greatest hits, vol. 1.* Columbia: ZK 39240 (T-Neck). 1969–83.

5256.2 *Isley Brothers story, vol. 1: rockin' soul.* Rhino: 70908 (RCA/Wand/Tamla). 1959–68.

5257 * Jackson, Bull Moose, 1919–1989

Badman Jackson, that's me. Charly: CDCHARLY 274 (King). 1945–55.

5258 Jackson, Janet, 1966–

Janet Jackson's Rhythm Nation 1814. A&M: 75021-3920-2. 1989.

5259 Jackson, Michael, 1958–

5259.1 ** *Off the wall.* Epic: EK 35745. 1979.

5259.2 * *Thriller.* Epic: EK 38112. 1982.

5260 Jackson, Millie, 1944–

Caught up. South Bound: SEW-003 (Spring 6703). 1974.

5261 * Jackson 5

Anthology. Motown: 37463-0868-2. 2CD set. 1969–75.

5262 James, Etta, 1938–

5262.1 * *The essential Etta James.* Chess: CHD2-9341 (Argo/Cadet). 2CD set. 1960–75.

5262.2 *R&B dynamite.* Flair/Virgin: 86232 (Modern). 1954–58.

5262.3 *The right time.* Elektra: 61347-2. 1992.

5263 James, Rick, 1952–

Bustin' out: the very best of Rick James. Motown: 314 530305-2 (Gordy). 1978–86.

5264 * Johnson, Buddy, 1915–1977

Walk 'em: the Decca sessions. Ace: CDCHD 623 (Decca). 1941–52.

5265 Johnson, Marv, 1938–

The best of Marv Johnson, you've got what it takes. EMI: 98895 (United Artists). 1958–63.

5266 Jordan, Louis, 1908–1975

5266.1 ** *The best of Louis Jordan.* Decca Jazz: GRD-664 (MCA 4079). 1941–54.

5266.2 * *Five guys named Moe: original Decca recordings, vol. 2.* MCA: MCAD-10503. 1942–52.

5266.3 *Just say Moe! mo' of the best of Louis Jordan.* Rhino: 71144. 1942–73.

5267 Kenner, Chris, 1929–1977

I like it like that. Collectables: COLCD-5166 (Instant). 1960–67.

5268 King, Ben E., 1938–

Stand by me: the best of Ben E. King. Atlantic: 80213-2. 1959–64, 1975.

5269 Knight, Gladys, 1944– , and the Pips

5269.1 *Anthology.* Motown: 31453-0483-2 (Soul). 2CD set. 1967–73.

5269.2 * *Soul survivors: the best of Gladys Knight and the Pips.* Rhino: 70756 (Buddah/Columbia/MCA). 1973–88.

5270 Kool and the Gang

5270.1 * *The best of Kool and the Gang 1969–1976.* Mercury: 314 514822-2 (De-Lite). 1969–76.

5270.2 *The best of Kool and the Gang 1979–1987.* Mercury: 314 522458-2 (De-Lite). 1979–87.

5271 LaBelle, Patti, 1944–

The best of Patti LaBelle. Epic: EK 36997. 1974–80.

5272 Lee, Julia, 1902–1958

Ugly papa. Juke Box Lil: 603 (Capitol). 1945–57.

5273 Liggins, Jimmy, 1922–

Jimmy Liggins and his Drops of Joy. Specialty: SPCD-7005-2. 1947–51.

5274 Liggins, Joe, 1915–1987

Joe Liggins and the Honeydrippers. Specialty: SPCD-7006-2. 1950–54.

5275 Little Willie John, 1937–1968

Fever: the best of Little Willie John. Rhino: 71511 (King). 1955–62.

5276 Lutcher, Nellie, 1915–

The best of Nellie Lutcher. Capitol Jazz: 35039. 1947–51.

5277 Manhattans

Greatest hits. Columbia: CK 36861. 1973–80.

5278 Marvelettes

5278.1 *Deliver: the singles.* Motown: 37463-6259-2 (Tamla). 2CD set. 1961–71.

5278.2 * *Greatest hits.* Motown: 37463-5180-2 (Tamla). 1961–66. [Item 5278.1 covers material comparable to item 5278.2 but in greater depth and with better packaging and notes].

5279 Mayfield, Curtis, 1942– , and the Impressions

5279.1 * *Curtis Mayfield and the Impressions: the anthology.* MCA: MCAD2-10664 (ABC, Curtom). 2CD set. 1961–77.

5279.2 ** *Greatest hits.* MCA: MCAD-31338 (ABC). 1961–68. [Item 5279.1 covers material comparable to item 5279.2 but in greater depth and with better packaging and notes].

5280 ** Mayfield, Percy, 1920–1984

Poet of the blues. Specialty: SPCD-7001-2. 1950–54.

5281 Maze

The greatest hits of Maze featuring Frankie Beverly: lifelines, vol. 1. Capitol: 92810. 1977–85.

5282 McPhatter, Clyde, 1932–1972

Deep sea ball: the best of Clyde McPhatter. Atlantic: 82314-2. 1955–59.

5283 * Melvin, Harold, 1939– , and the Blue Notes

If you don't know me by now: the best of Harold Melvin and the Blue Notes. Philadelphia International/CBS: ZK 66338 (34232). 1972–76.

5284 * Meters

Funkify your life: the Meters anthology. Rhino: 71869 (Josie/Reprise/Warner Bros.). 2CD set. 1969–77.

5285 * Milburn, Amos, 1927–1980

The best of Amos Milburn: down the road apiece. EMI: 27229 (Aladdin). 1946–57.

5286 * Millinder, Lucky, 1900–1966

Lucky days. MCA: 1319 (Decca). LP. 1941–45. OP

5287 Mills, Stephanie, 1957–

In my life: greatest hits. Casablanca: 832519-2. 1979–84.

5288 * Milton, Roy, 1907–1983

Roy Milton and his Solid Senders. Specialty: SPCD-7004-2. 1945–52.

5289 Mimms, Garnet, 1933–

Cry baby: the best of Garnet Mimms. EMI: 80183 (United Artists). 1963–67.

5290 * Moonglows

Blue velvet: the ultimate collection. Chess: CHD2-9345. 2CD set. 1953–59.

5291 Neville Brothers

Treacherous: a history of the Neville Brothers. Rhino: 71494. 2CD set. 1955–85.

5292 New Edition

Greatest hits, vol. 1. MCA: MCAD-10434. 1983–88.

5293 Ohio Players

Gold. Mercury: 824461-2. 1974–77.

5294 ** O'Jays

Love train: the best of the O'Jays. Columbia: ZK 66114 (Philadelphia International). 1972–76.

5295 * Orioles

The Orioles sing their greatest hits. Collectables: 5408 (Jubilee). 1948–54.

5296 Otis, Johnny, 1921–

5296.1 *The Johnny Otis Show: live at Monterey.* Epic: EK 53628 (30471). 1970. [Johnny Otis, Esther Phillips, Eddie "Cleanhead" Vinson, Joe Turner, Ivory Joe Hunter, Roy Brown, Pee Wee Crayton, Roy Milton, and others].

5296.2 * *The original Johnny Otis Show.* Savoy: SV-0266 (SJL-2230). 1945–51.

5297 Parker, Ray, Jr., 1954–

Greatest hits. Arista: ARCD-8294. 1977–83.

5298 Parliament

5298.1 ** *Parliament's greatest hits.* Casablanca: 822637-2. 1974–80. [Item 5298.2 covers material comparable to item 5298.1 but in greater depth and with better packaging and notes].

5298.2 * *Tear the roof off.* Casablanca: 314 514417-2. 2CD set. 1974–80.

5299 Pendergrass, Teddy, 1950–

TP. The Right Stuff: 66691 (Philadelphia International). 1980.

5300 Phillips, Little Esther, 1935–1984

Better beware. Charly: CDCHARLY 248 (Federal). 1951–53.

5301 Pickett, Wilson, 1941–

5301.1 * *A man and a half: the best of Wilson Pickett.* Rhino/Atlantic: 70287. 2CD set. 1961–71.

5301.2 ** *The very best of Wilson Pickett.* Rhino/Atlantic: 71212. 1962–71. [Item 5301.1 covers material comparable to item 5301.2 but in greater depth and with better packaging and notes].

5302 Price, Lloyd, 1933–

5302.1 *Lawdy!* Specialty: SPCD-7010-2. 1952–54.

5302.2 *Lloyd Price's greatest hits: the original ABC-Paramount recordings.* MCA: MCAD-11184 (ABC). 1957–60.

5303 Prince, 1958–

5303.1 ** *The hits 1.* Paisley Park: 45431-2. 1979–92.

5303.2 * *1999.* Warner Bros.: 23720-2. 1982.

5303.3 *Purple rain.* Warner Bros.: 25110-2. 1984.

5303.4 *Sign 'o' the times.* Paisley Park: 25577-2. 2CD set. 1987.

5304 Professor Longhair (Roy Byrd), 1918–1980

5304.1 *Crawfish fiesta.* Alligator: ALCD 4718. 1979.

5304.2 ** *'Fess: the Professor Longhair anthology.* Rhino: 71502. 2CD set. 1949–80.

5304.3 * *New Orleans piano.* Atlantic: 7225-2. 1949, 1953.

5305 Ravens

The greatest group of them all: "Old man river." Savoy: SV-260 (National). 1947–51.

5306 Redding, Otis, 1941–1967

5306.1 *Otis! the definitive Otis Redding.* Rhino: 71439 (Volt). 4CD set. 1960–67.

5306.2 ** *The very best of Otis Redding.* Rhino: 71147 (Volt). 1963–67. [Item 5306.1 covers material comparable to item 5306.2 but in greater depth and with better packaging and notes].

5307 Reeves, Martha, 1941– , and the Vandellas

5307.1 * *Greatest hits.* Motown: 37463-5204-2 (Gordy). 1962–66. [Item 5307.2 covers material comparable to item 5307.1 but in greater depth and with better packaging and notes].

5307.2 *Live wire! the singles.* Motown: 37463-6313-2 (Gordy). 2CD set. 1962–72.

5308 Rhodes, Todd, 1900–1965

Dance music that hits the spot. Swingtime: ST 1020 (King). LP. 1949–54. OP

5309 Richie, Lionel, 1949–

Can't slow down. Motown: 37463-6059-2. 1983.

5310 Robinson, Smokey, 1940–

Blame it on love, and all the great hits. Motown: 37463-5401-2 (Tamla). 1973–83.

5311 ** Robinson, Smokey, 1940– , and the Miracles

Anthology. Motown: 31453-0472-2 (793). 2CD set. 1958–75.

5312 Ronettes

The best of the Ronettes. Phil Spector/Abkco: 7212-2 (Philles). 1963–69.

5313 Ross, Diana, 1944–

Anthology. Motown: 37463-6049-2. 2CD set. 1970–81.

5314 ** Ross, Diana, 1944– , and the Supremes

Anthology. Motown: 37463-0794-2. 2CD set. 1962–69.

5315 Rufus (featuring Chaka Khan)

Rags to Rufus. MCA: MCAD-31365 (ABC 809). 1974.

5316 * Sam and Dave

The very best of Sam and Dave. Rhino: 71871 (Stax). 1965–69.

5317 Shalamar

Greatest hits. Solar/Epic: ZK 75308. 1978–87. OP

5318 * Shirelles

The very best of the Shirelles. Rhino: 71807 (Scepter). 1959–64.

5319 Simon, Joe, 1943–

Lookin' back: the best of Joe Simon. Charly: CD 144 (Sound Stage). 1966–70. OP

5320 Sledge, Percy, 1941–

It tears me up: the best of Percy Sledge. Rhino/Atlantic: 70285. 1966–71.

5321 Sly, 1944– , and the Family Stone

5321.1 ** *Anthology.* Epic: EGK 37071. 1968–73.

5321.2 *There's a riot goin' on.* Epic: EK 30986. 1971.

5322 Smith, Huey, 1934–

Serious clownin': the history of Huey "Piano" Smith and the Clowns. Rhino: 70222 (Ace). LP. 1957–60. OP

5323 Spaniels

Goodnight sweetheart, goodnight. Vee-Jay: NVD2-704. 1953–60.

5324 * Spinners

The very best of the Spinners. Rhino: 71213 (VIP/Atlantic). 1970–80.

5325   Staple Singers

The best of the Staple Singers. Stax: FCD-60-007. 1970–74.

5326   Stewart, Billy, 1937–1970

One more time: the Chess years. Chess: CHD-6027. 1962–68.

5327   Stylistics

The best of the Stylistics. Amherst: AMH-9743 (Avco). 1971–74.

5328   Summer, Donna, 1948–

On the radio: greatest hits, vols. 1–2. Casablanca: 822558-2. 1975–80.

5329   Sylvester, 1946–1988

The original hits. Fantasy: FCD-7710-2. 1977–81.

5330   Tate, Howard, 1943–

Get it while you can: the legendary sessions. Mercury: 526868-2 (Verve V6-5022). 1966–68.

5331   Tavares

The best of Tavares. [Series: Capitol gold]. Capitol: 89380. 1973–81.

5332   Taylor, Johnnie, 1938–

Chronicle. Stax: FCD-60-006. 1968–75.

5333 **   Temptations

Anthology. Motown: 37463-0782-2 (Gordy). 2CD set. 1964–84.

5334   Tex, Joe, 1933–1982

The very best of Joe Tex. Rhino: 72565 (Dial). 1964–72.

5335   Thomas, Irma, 1941–

Sweet soul queen of New Orleans: the Irma Thomas collection. Razor & Tie: RE 2097-2 (Minit/Imperial). 1961–65.

5336   Toussaint, Allen, 1938–

The Allen Toussaint collection. Reprise: 26549-2. 1970–78.

5337   Turner, Ike, 1931–

5337.1   *I like Ike! the best of Ike Turner.* Rhino: 71819. 1951–72.

5337.2   *Trail blazer.* Charly: CDCHARLY 263 (Federal). 1954–58.

5338 *   Turner, Ike, 1931– , and Tina Turner, 1938–

Proud Mary: the best of Ike and Tina Turner. EMI: 95846 (Sue/Minit/Liberty/United Artists). 1960–62, 1970–75.

5339   Turner, Joe, 1911–1985

5339.1   *Big, bad and blue: the Big Joe Turner anthology.* Rhino: 71550. 3CD set. 1938–83.

5339.2 **   *Big Joe Turner's greatest hits.* Atlantic: 81752-2. 1951–58.

5339.3   *The rhythm and blues years.* Atlantic: 81663-2. 1951–59.

5340 *   Vandross, Luther, 1951–

The best of Luther Vandross: the best of love. Epic: E2K 45320. 2CD set. 1980–89.

5341   Walker, Jr., 1942–1995, and the All Stars

Greatest hits. Motown: 37463-5208-2 (Soul). 1965–69.

5342   War

The best of War . . . and more. Avenue/Rhino: 70072 (UA/MCA). 1971–77.

5343   Washington, Dinah, 1924–1963

5343.1 *   *The complete Dinah Washington on Mercury, vol. 1.* Mercury: 832444-2. 3CD set. 1946–49.

5343.2 **   *First issue: the Dinah Washington story (the original recordings).* Mercury: 314 514841-2. 2CD set. 1943–61.

5343.3   *Mellow mama.* Delmark: DD 451 (Apollo). 1945.

5344 *   Wells, Mary, 1943–1992

Greatest hits. Motown: 37463-5233-2. 1960–64.

5345   White, Barry, 1944–

All-time greatest hits. Mercury: 314 522459-2 (20th Century). 1973–78.

5346   Wild Tchoupitoulas

The Wild Tchoupitoulas. Antilles: ANCD 7052. 1976.

5347   Williams, Larry, 1935–1980

Bad boy. Specialty: SPCD-7002-2. 1957–59.

5348 *   Willis, Chuck, 1928–1959

Let's jump tonight. Epic: EK 53619 (OKeh). 1951–56.

5349 Wilson, Jackie, 1934–1984

5349.1 *Mr. Excitement!* Rhino: 70775 (Brunswick). 3CD set. 1956–75.

5349.2 ** *The very best of Jackie Wilson.* Rhino: 71559 (Brunswick). 1957–67. [Item 5349.1 covers material comparable to item 5349.2 but in greater depth and with better packaging and notes].

5350 Withers, Bill, 1938–

Lean on me: the best of Bill Withers. Columbia: CK 52924 (Sussex). 1971–81.

5351 Witherspoon, Jimmy, 1923–

Blowin' in from Kansas City. Flair/Virgin: 86299 (Modern). 1948–52.

5352 Womack, Bobby, 1944–

Midnight mover: the Bobby Womack collection. MI: 27673 (Minit/United Artists). 2CD set. 1967–76.

5353 Wonder, Stevie, 1950–

5353.1 * *Greatest hits.* Motown: 37463-0282-2 (Tamla). 1963–67.

5353.2 *Greatest hits, vol. 2.* Motown: 37463-0313-2 (Tamla). 1968–71.

5353.3 ** *Innervisions.* Motown: 37463-0326-2 (Tamla). 1973.

5353.4 ** *Original musiquarium.* Motown: 37463-6002-2 (Tamla). 2CD set. 1972–82.

5353.5 *Songs in the key of life.* Motown: 37463-0340-2 (Tamla). 1976.

5353.6 *Talking book.* Motown: 37463-0319-2 (Tamla). 1972.

5354 Wright, O. V., 1939–1980

The soul of O. V. Wright. Duke-Peacock/MCA: MCAD-10670 (Backbeat). 1965–74.

Rap (Hip-Hop)

This section surveys the development of rap from its emergence in the late 1970s to the present.

Anthologies

5355 ** *Hip-hop greats: classic raps.* Rhino: 70957. 1979–85. [Sugarhill Gang, Fat Boys, Grandmaster Flash, Run-D.M.C., Kurtis Blow, and others].

5356 *Street jams: electric funk, part 1.* Rhino: 70575. 1982–84. [Afrika Bambaataa, Planet Patrol, Herbie Hancock, Newcleus, and others].

5357 *Street jams: electric funk, part 2.* Rhino: 70576. 1982–85. [Newcleus, Jonzun Crew, Ice-T, Shannon, and others].

5358 *Street jams: hip hop from the top, part 1.* Rhino: 70577. 1979–85. [Sugarhill Gang, Kurtis Blow, Grandmaster Flash, Whodini, and others].

5359 *Street jams: hip hop from the top, part 2.* Rhino: 70578. 1981–85. [Grandmaster Flash, Run-D.M.C., Whodini, Kurtis Blow, Roxanne, and others].

5360 * *Tommy Boy's greatest beats.* Tommy Boy: TBCD-1005. 1981–84. [Afrika Bambaataa, Jonzun Crew, Force MD's, and others].

5361 *West Coast rap: the first dynasty, vol. 1.* Rhino: 70590. 1981–86. [Ice-T, Egyptian Lover, 2 Live Crew, Timex Social Club, and others].

5362 *West Coast rap: the first dynasty, vol. 2.* Rhino: 70591. 1982–88. [Ice-T, Bobby Jimmy and the Critters, Kid Frost, Egyptian Lover, and others].

Individual Artists or Groups

5363 * Arrested Development

3 years, 5 months, and 2 days in the life of—. Chrysalis: 21929. 1992.

5364 Bambaataa, Afrika, 1960–

Planet rock, the album. Tommy Boy: TBCD 823 (1007). 1982.

5365 Beastie Boys

5365.1 *Ill communication.* Grand Royal/Capitol: 28599. 1994.

5365.2 ** *Licenced to ill.* Def Jam/Polygram: 314 527 351-2 (CK 40238). 1986.

5366 * Boogie Down Productions (KRS-One)

Criminal minded. B-Boy: BB CD 4787. 1987.

5367 Cypress Hill

Cypress Hill. Ruff House/Columbia: CK 47889. 1991.

5368 * De La Soul

3 feet high and rising. Tommy Boy: TBCD 1019. 1989.

5369 Digable Planets

Reachin' (a new refutation of time and space). Pendulum: 61414-2. 1993.

5370 Digital Underground

Sex packets. Tommy Boy: TBCD 1026. 1990.

5371 Dr. Dre

The chronic. Interscope: P2 57128. 1992.

5372 EPMD

Strictly business. Priority: CDL 57135 (Fresh 82006). 1988.

5373 Eric B. and Rakim

Paid in full. 4th and Broadway: 16244-4005-2. 1986.

5374 Gang Starr

Step in the arena. Chrysalis: 21798. 1990.

5375 * Grandmaster Flash, Melle Mel, and the Furious Five

The message from Beat Street: the best of Grandmaster Flash, Melle Mel, and the Furious Five. Rhino: 71606 (Sugar Hill). 1980–84.

5376 * Guru

Jazzmatazz, vol. 1: an experimental fusion of hip-hop and jazz. Chrysalis: 21998. 1993.

5377 Hammer, M. C., 1962–

Please Hammer don't hurt 'em. Capitol: 92857. 1990.

5378 Ice Cube, 1969–

AmeriKKKa's most wanted. Priority: CDL57120. 1990.

5379 * Ice-T, 1958–

O. G.: original gangster. Sire: 26492-2. 1991.

5380 Jungle Brothers

Done by the forces of nature. Warner Bros.: 26072-2. 1989.

5381 Kool Moe Dee

How ya like me now. Jive: 1079-2-J. 1987.

5382 KRS-One, 1965– . *See* 5366

5383 L. L. Kool J, 1969–

   5383.1 * *Mama said knock you out.* Def Jam/Polygram: 314 523 477-2 (CK 46888). 1990.

   5383.2 *Radio.* Def Jam/Polygram: 314 527 352-2 (CK 40239). 1985.

5384 MC Lyte, 1970–

Lyte as a rock. First Priority: 90905-2. 1988.

5385 * N.W.A.

Straight outta Compton. Ruthless/Priority: SL57102. 1988.

5386 * P.M. Dawn

Of the heart, of the soul, and of the cross. Gee Street/Island: 314 510 276-2. 1991.

5387 Poor Righteous Teachers

Holy intellect. Profile: PCD-1289. 1990.

5388 Public Enemy

   5388.1 ** *Fear of a black planet.* Def Jam/Polygram: 314 523 446-2 (CK 45413). 1990.

   5388.2 *Greatest misses.* Def Jam/Polygram: 314 523 487-2 (CK 53014). 1987–92.

5389 * Queen Latifah, 1970–

All hail the queen. Tommy Boy: TBCD 1022. 1989.

5390 * Run-D.M.C.

Together forever: greatest hits. Profile: PCD-1419. 1983–91.

5391 Salt-n-Pepa

Blacks' magic. Next Plateau/London: 828 362-2. 1990.

5392 Shinehead

Unity. African Love/Elektra: 60802-2. 1988.

5393 * Snoop Doggy Dogg, 1971–

Doggystyle. Death Row/Interscope: 50605 (92279). 1993.

5394 Tribe Called Quest

People's instinctive travels and the paths of rhythm. Zomba/Jive: 1331-2-J. 1990.

5395 Yo-Yo, 1971–

Make way for the motherlode. East West/Atlantic: 91605-2. 1991.

25

Rock

Compiled by
William E. Anderson
and Kent Underwood

This chapter covers rock music from its beginnings in the 1950s to the present. Consult the index under "rock" for decade-by-decade chronological listings and for various genre terms for rock (*rockabilly, British-invasion, folk-rock, heavy metal, punk,* etc.).

Anthologies

5396 ** *Beatle originals.* Rhino: 70071. LP. 1957–62. [Larry Williams, Carl Perkins, Shirelles, Little Richard, Buddy Holly, Arthur Alexander, and others. Original versions of songs subsequently recorded by the Beatles]. OP

5397 ** *Best of doo wop ballads.* Rhino: 75763. 1954–61. [Dion and the Belmonts, Five Satins, Dells, Moonglows, Penguins, Flamingos, Spaniels, and others].

5398 ** *Best of doo wop uptempo.* Rhino: 75764. 1954–63. [Dell-Vikings, El Dorados, Silhouettes, Crows, Cadillacs, Dion and the Belmonts, Frankie Lymon and the Teenagers, and others].

5399 *Best of the bubblegum years.* Special Music Co.: SCD-4914 (Buddah). 1967–70. [Ohio Express, Lemon Pipers, 1910 Fruitgum Co., Music Explosion, and others].

5400 ** *The British invasion: the history of British rock, vol. 1.* Rhino: 70319. 1963–65. [Kinks, Gerry and the Pacemakers, Searchers, Zombies, Yardbirds, and others].

5401 * *The British invasion: the history of British rock, vol. 2.* Rhino: 70320. 1964–65. [Kinks, Manfred Mann, Gerry and the Pacemakers, Searchers, Yardbirds, Hollies, Zombies, and others].

5402 * *The British invasion: the history of British rock, vol. 3.* Rhino: 70321. 1964–66. [Searchers, Gerry and the Pacemakers, Manfred Mann, Kinks, Hollies, Zombies, Yardbirds, and others].

5403 * *The British invasion: the history of British rock, vol. 4.* Rhino: 70322. 1965–67. [Yardbirds, Kinks, Hollies, Zombies, Spencer Davis Group, Gerry and the Pacemakers, Manfred Mann, and others].

5404 * *The British invasion: the history of British rock, vol. 5.* Rhino: 70323. 1962–66. [Tornadoes, Them, Beatles, Wayne Fontana and the Mindbenders, Pretty Things, Moody Blues, and others].

5405 *The British invasion: the history of British rock, vol. 6.* Rhino: 70324. 1964–67. [Hollies, Them, Manfred Mann, and others].

5406 *The British invasion: the history of British rock, vol. 7.* Rhino: 70325. 1965–67. [Easybeats, Gerry and the Pacemakers, Hollies, Bee Gees, and others].

5407 * *The British invasion: the history of British rock, vol. 8.* Rhino: 70326. 1966–72. [Spencer Davis Group, Cream, Hollies, Troggs, Procul Harum, Move, Moody Blues, Eric Burdon, Bee Gees, Status Quo, and others].

5408 *The British invasion: the history of British rock, vol. 9.* Rhino: 70327. 1967–72. [Cream, Bee Gees, Hollies, Joe Cocker, and others].

5409 *Bubblegum classics: the ultimate collection of pure pop music, vol. 1.* Varese Sarabande: VSD-5535. 1966–73. [Ohio Express, Boyce and Hart, Tommy Roe, Fifth Estate, 1910 Fruitgum Co., Dawn, Partridge Family, and others].

5410 ** *D.I.Y. anarchy in the UK: UK punk I.* Rhino: 71171. 1976–77. [Sex Pistols, Damned, Stranglers, Jam, Adverts, Buzzcocks, Wire, and others].

5411 ** *D.I.Y. blank generation: the New York scene.* Rhino: 71175. 1975–78. [Ramones, Patti Smith, Blondie, Richard Hell, Television, and others].

5412 *D.I.Y. the modern world: UK punk II.* Rhino: 71172. 1977–78. [Jam, Generation X, Buzzcocks, Wire, Siouxsie and the Banshees, Magazine, The Fall, and others]. OP

5413 * *D.I.Y. teenage kicks: UK pop I.* Rhino: 71173. 1976–79. [Nick Lowe, Motors, Tom Robinson, Squeeze, XTC, and others]. OP

5414 *The doo wop box: 101 vocal group gems from the golden age of rock 'n' roll.* Rhino: 71463. 4CD set. 1948–87. [Orioles, Ravens, Five Keys, Crows, Drifters, Spaniels, Chords, Penguins, Moonglows, Turbans, Platters, Cadillacs, Teenagers, Flamingos, Clovers, Five Satins, Dells, Dell-Vikings, Silhouettes, Chantels, Impressions, Elegants, Imperials, Dion and the Belmonts, Skyliners, Impalas, Zodiacs, Jive Five, Randy and the Rainbows, and others].

5415 *Even more nuggets, vol. 3.* Rhino: 75754. 1965–67. [Electric Prunes, Shadows of Knight, Strawberry Alarm Clock, Barbarians, Cyrkle, and others].

5416 *Faster and louder: hardcore punk, vol. 1.* Rhino: 71224. 1977–89. [Dead Kennedys, Bad Brains, Circle Jerks, Angry Samoans, Mission of Burma, Hüsker Dü, Suicidal Tendencies, and others].

5417 * *Groove 'n' grind: '50s and '60s dance hits.* Rhino: 70992. 1957–67. [Capitols, Little Eva, Miracles, Dyke and the Blazers, Bobby Freeman, and others].

5418 *Have a nice day: super hits of the seventies, vol. 5.* Rhino: 70925. 1971. [Lobo, Richie Havens, Jerry Reed; Hamilton, Joe Frank and Reynolds; Raiders, Fortunes, Tommy James, and others. Volumes 1–4 and 6–22 in this series are also available].

5419 *Heavy metal memories.* Rhino: 70986. 1970–83. [Kiss, Alice Cooper, Grand Funk Railroad, Humble Pie, Blue Öyster Cult, Ted Nugent, and others]. OP

5420 *The history of Latino rock, vol. 1: the Eastside sound.* Zyanya/Rhino: 061. LP/AC. 1956–65. [Ritchie Valens, Chan Romero, Thee Midnighters, Premiers, Cannibal and the Headhunters, and others]. OP

5421 * *Legends of guitar: rock—the '50s, vol. 1.* Rhino: 70719. 1951–59. [Chuck Berry, Bo Diddley, Bill Haley, Duane Eddy, Les Paul, Eddie Cochran, Link Wray, Gene Vincent, Buddy Holly, Carl Perkins, and others]. OP

5422 * *Legends of guitar: rock—the '50s, vol. 2.* Rhino: 70561. 1955–59. [Rick Nelson, Billy Riley, Ike Turner, Mickey Baker, Buddy Holly, Scotty Moore, Johnny Burnette, Gene Vincent, Santo and Johnny, Bill Haley, Eddie Cochran, Chuck Berry, Duane Eddy, Ritchie Valens, and others].

5423 *Legends of guitar: rock—the '60s, vol. 1.* Rhino: 70720. 1959–69. [Ventures, Yardbirds, Lonnie Mack, Jimi Hendrix, Chet Atkins, Frank Zappa, Steve Cropper, Dick Dale, Shadows, Byrds, Kinks, and others]. OP

5424 *Legends of guitar: rock—the '60s, vol. 2.* Rhino: 70562. 1960–70. [Jeff Beck, Jerry Garcia, Cream, John Mayall, Allman Brothers, and others].

5425 *Legends of guitar: rock—the '70s.* Rhino: 70721. 1969–79. [James Gang, Lynyrd Skynyrd,

Bonnie Raitt, Rick Derringer, Ted Nugent, Grand Funk Railroad, Tom Petty, Frank Zappa, and others].

5426 *Memphis rocks: rockabilly in Memphis.* Smithsonian: 2705 (CD-051). 1954–68. [Warren Smith, Billy Lee Riley, Sonny Burgess, Charlie Feathers, Carl Mann, Carl Perkins, Johnny Cash, Jerry Lee Lewis, Roy Orbison, and others].

5427 *Metal age: the roots of metal.* Rhino: 70272. 1970–81. [Beck, Bogart and Appice; Ten Years After, Bachman-Turner Overdrive, Robin Trower, Blue Öyster Cult, Motörhead, and others].

5428 *More nuggets, vol. 2.* Rhino: 75777. 1965–68. [Blues Magoos, Castaways, Music Machine, Five Americans, Nightcrawlers, Standells, and others].

5429 * *Never mind the mainstream . . . the best of MTV's 120 Minutes, vol. 1.* Rhino: 70545. 1986–90. [Red Hot Chili Peppers, Soul Asylum, Mission UK, The Church, Cocteau Twins, Julian Cope, Sinead O'Connor, Sonic Youth, Robyn Hitchcock, World Party, XTC, They Might Be Giants, Camper Van Beethoven, and others].

5430 * *Never mind the mainstream . . . the best of MTV's 120 Minutes, vol. 2.* Rhino: 70546. 1980–89. [R.E.M., Public Image, Ramones, X, Ministry, Morrissey, Jesus and Mary Chain, Echo and the Bunnymen, Joy Division, New Order, Depeche Mode, Sugarcubes, Hüsker Dü, Violent Femmes, Wire, and others].

5431 ** *Nuggets: classics from the psychedelic sixties, vol. 1.* Rhino: 75892. 1964–69. [Standells, Seeds, Count Five, Easybeats, Syndicate of Sound, Monkees, Troggs, Amboy Dukes, and others].

5432 *Outpunk dance party: a queer punk compilation.* Outpunk: OUT 12CD. 1994. [Pansy Division, Tribe, and others].

5433 * *Rebel rousers: Southern rock classics.* Rhino: 70586. 1969–82. [Allman Brothers, Black Oak Arkansas, Wet Willie, Elvin Bishop, Marshall Tucker Band, Lynyrd Skynyrd, and others].

5434 *Red hot + dance.* Columbia: CK 52826. [1992]. [Madonna, Seal, George Michael, P. M. Dawn, Sly and the Family Stone, Lisa Stansfield, EMF, and others].

5435 ** *Rock and roll—the early days.* RCA: PCD1-5463. 1948–57. [Chords, Wynonie Harris, Big Mama Thornton, Muddy Waters, Joe Turner, Bill Haley, Elvis Presley, Carl Perkins, Chuck Berry, Bo Diddley, Little Richard, Jerry Lee Lewis].

5436 * *Rock instrumental classics, vol. 1: the '50s.* Rhino: 71601. 1957–59. [Duane Eddy, Champs, Santo and Johnny, Link Wray, Cozy Cole, Dave "Baby" Cortez, Johnny and the Hurricanes, Sandy Nelson, Lee Allen, and others].

5437 * *Rock instrumental classics, vol. 2: the '60s.* Rhino: 71602. 1959–68. [Ventures, Lonnie Mack, Tornadoes, Duane Eddy, Mason Williams, and others].

5438 * *Rock o rama.* Abkco: 4222 (Cameo/Parkway). 2LP set. 1957–66. [Chubby Checker, Orlons, DeeDee Sharp, Rays, Tymes, Dovells, Bobby Rydell, ? and the Mysterians, and others]. OP

5439 * *Rock this town: rockabilly hits, vol. 1.* Rhino: 70741. 1952–58. [Johnny Burnette, Carl Perkins, Roy Orbison, Gene Vincent, Jerry Lee Lewis, Ritchie Valens, Bill Haley, Buddy Holly, Rick Nelson, and others].

5440 *Rock this town: rockabilly hits, vol. 2.* Rhino: 70742. 1957–83. [Eddie Cochran, Wanda Jackson, Jack Scott, Ronnie Hawkins, and others].

5441 *Rockabilly classics.* MCA: MCAD-5935. 1956–61. [Dale Hawkins, Sanford Clark, Buddy Holly, Roy Hall, Moon Mullican, Brenda Lee, Johnny Burnette, and others]. OP

5442 * *Roots of British rock.* Sire: SASH-3711-2. 2LP set. 1956–63. [Tommy Steele, Lonnie Donegan, Chris Barber, Adam Faith, Cliff Richards, Shadows, Billy Fury, Johnny Kidd, Marty Wilde, Springfields, Tornadoes, and others]. OP

5443 *San Francisco nights.* Rhino: 70536. 1965–68. [Beau Brummels, Youngbloods, Sly and the Family Stone, Quicksilver Messenger Service, Country Joe and the Fish, Blue Cheer, and others]. OP

5444 ** *Shake rattle and roll: rock 'n' roll in the 1950s.* New World: NW 249. LP. 1951–62. [Joe Turner, Jerry Lee Lewis, Ray Charles, Coasters, Fats Domino, Jackie Wilson, Bill Haley, Buddy Holly, Chuck Berry, and others]. OP

5445 *Songs of protest.* Rhino: 70734. 1962–71. [Barry McGuire, Sonny Bono, Turtles, Country Joe and the Fish, Rascals, Eric Burdon, Janis Ian, Temptations, Edwin Starr, Phil Ochs, Donovan, and others].

5446 *Space daze: a 2 hour mind journey of electronic ambient space rock.* Cleopatra: CLEO-7616-2. 2CD set. [197?–199?]. [Kraftwerk, Psychic TV, Hawkwind, The Orb, Legendary Pink Dots, Gong, Alien Sex Fiend, Brian Eno, Syd Barrett, Amon Duul 2, Nik Turner, Tangerine Dream, and others].

5447 *The Stiff Records box set.* Rhino: 71062. 4CD set. 1975–87. [Nick Lowe, Damned, Richard Hell, Elvis Costello, Adverts, Dave Edmunds, Wreckless Eric, Ian Dury, Graham Parker, Lene Lovich, Devo, Rachel Sweet, Madness, Pogues, and others].

5448 *Stone rock blues: the original songs covered by the Rolling Stones.* Chess: CHD-9347. 1948–61. [Chuck Berry, Muddy Waters, Bo Diddley, Howlin' Wolf, Arthur Alexander, Buddy Holly, Dale Hawkins. Original versions of songs subsequently recorded by the Rolling Stones].

5449 ** *The Sun story.* Rhino: 75884. 1953–59. [Elvis Presley, Carl Perkins, Jerry Lee Lewis, Billy Riley, Johnny Cash, Roy Orbison, Bill Justis, Carl Mann, Charlie Rich, Warren Smith, and others].

5450 * *Surfin' hits.* Rhino: 70089. 1962–65. [Beach Boys, Jan and Dean, Surfaris, Chantays, Dick Dale, Marketts, and others].

5451 * *Teen idols.* Rhino: 70180. LP/AC. 1957–62. [Paul Anka, Frankie Avalon, Dion, Bobby Vee, Fabian, Johnny Tillotson, Del Shannon, and others]. OP

5452 * *Texas music, vol. 3: garage bands and psychedelia.* Rhino: 71783. [196?]. [Roy Head, Bobby Fuller, Sam the Sham, Sir Douglas, Steve Miller, 13th Floor Elevators, Johnny Winter, and others].

5453 *This are Two Tone.* Chrysalis: 21745. 1979–82. [Specials, Madness, English Beat, Selector, and others].

5454 * *This is how it all began, vol. 2: the golden age of rock 'n' roll on Specialty Records.* Specialty: 2118. LP/AC. 1952–58. [Lloyd Price, Little Richard, Larry Williams, Jesse Belvin, Sam Cooke, Art Neville, Don and Dewey, and others].

Individual Artists or Groups

5455 AC/DC

Back in black. Atlantic: 92418-2 (16018). 1980.

5456 * Adam, Margie

The best of Margie Adam. Olivia: CD 961. 1990.

5457 * Aerosmith

Greatest hits. Columbia: CK 57367 (36865). 1974–82.

5458 Alice Cooper, 1948–

Greatest hits. Warner Bros.: 3107-2. 1970–73.

5459 Allman Brothers

    5459.1 *Dreams.* Polydor: 839417-2. 4CD set. 1968–85.

    5459.2 ** *Live at the Fillmore East.* Polydor: 823273-2. 2CD set. 1971.

5460 Amos, Tori, 1963–

Little earthquakes. Atlantic: 82358-2. 1991.

5461 * Animals

The best of the Animals. Abkco: 4324-2 (MGM). 1964–65.

5462 Anthrax

Among the living. Island: 422 842 447-2 (90584). 1987.

5463 Armatrading, Joan, 1950–

Track record. A&M: 75021-3319-2. 1976–83.

5464 B-52s

The B-52s. Warner Bros.: 3355-2. 1979.

5465 Bad Brains

Rock for light. Caroline: CAROL 1613-2. 1983.

5466 The Band

    5466.1 *Across the great divide.* Capitol: 89565. 3CD set. 1961–86.

    5466.2 ** *The Band.* Capitol: 46493. 1969.

    5466.3 ** *Music from Big Pink.* Capitol: 46069. 1968.

See also 5534

5467 Band of Susans

Love agenda. Blast First/Restless: 71425-2. 1989.

5468 Bangles

Greatest hits. Columbia: CK 46125. 1984–88.

5469 Beach Boys

    5469.1 ** *Endless summer.* Capitol: 46467. 1963–66.

    5469.2 *Pet sounds.* Capitol: 37667 (2458). 1966.

5470 Beastie Boys. *See 5365*

5471 Beatles

5471.1 *Abbey Road.* Capitol: 46446. 1969.

5471.2 ** *The Beatles: past masters, vol. 1.* Capitol: 90043. 1962–65.

5471.3 ** *The Beatles: past masters, vol. 2.* Capitol: 90044. 1966–70.

5471.4 * *Beatles for sale.* Capitol: 46438. 1964.

5471.5 * *The Beatles* ["White album"]. Capitol: 46443. 2CD set. 1968.

5471.6 * *A hard day's night.* Capitol: 46437. 1964.

5471.7 *Help!* Capitol: 46439. 1965.

5471.8 *Let it be.* Capitol: 46447. 1970.

5471.9 *Live at the Star Club, vol. 1.* Sony Music Special Products: AK 48544. 1962.

5471.10 ** *Please please me.* Capitol: 46435. 1963.

5471.11 ** *Revolver.* Capitol: 46441. 1966.

5471.12 ** *Rubber soul.* Capitol: 46440. 1966.

5471.13 ** *Sgt. Pepper's Lonely Hearts Club Band.* Capitol: 46442. 1967.

5471.14 * *With the Beatles.* Capitol: 46436. 1963.

5472 Beck, Jeff, 1944–

5472.1 *Blow by blow.* Epic: EK 33409. 1975.

5472.2 *Truth.* Epic: EK 47412. 1968.

5473 Bee Gees

Best of the Bee Gees, vol. 1. Polydor: 831594-2 (Atco). 1967–69.

5474 Benatar, Pat, 1953–

Best shots. Chrysalis: 21715. 1979–88.

5475 Berry, Chuck, 1926–

5475.1 * *Chuck Berry: the Chess box.* Chess: CHD3-80001. 3CD set. 1955–73.

5475.2 ** *The great 28.* Chess: CHD-92500. 1955–65. [Item 5475.1 covers material comparable to item 5475.2 but in greater depth and with better packaging and notes].

5476 * Big Brother and the Holding Co.

Cheap thrills. Columbia: CK 9700. 1968. [With Janis Joplin].

5477 Big Star

#1 record; Radio City. Stax: FCD-60-025-2 (Ardent). 1972–73.

5478 Black Flag

Damaged. SST: SSTCD-007. 1980–81.

5479 Black Sabbath

Paranoid. Warner Bros.: 3104-2. 1971.

5480 Blasters

Collection. Slash: 26451-2. 1980–85.

5481 Blondie

The best of Blondie. Chrysalis: 21337. 1977–80.

5482 Blood, Sweat and Tears

5482.1 *Blood, Sweat and Tears.* Columbia: CK 9720. 1969.

5482.2 *Child is father to the man.* Columbia: CK 9619. 1968.

5483 Blue Öyster Cult

Agents of fortune. Columbia: CK 34164. 1976.

5484 * Bo Diddley, 1928–

The Chess box. Chess: CHD2-19502. 2CD set. 1955–68.

5485 Bon Jovi

Slippery when wet. Mercury: 830264-2. 1986.

5486 Boston

Boston. Epic: EK 34188. 1976.

5487 Bowie, David, 1947–

5487.1 *Bowie: the singles.* Rykodisc: RCD-10218 (RCA/EMI). 2CD set. 1969–93.

5487.2 * *ChangesBowie.* Rykodisc: RCD-20171 (RCA). 1969–84. [Item 5487.1 covers material comparable to item 5487.2 but in greater depth and with better packaging and notes].

5487.3 *The rise and fall of Ziggy Stardust.* Rykodisc: RCD-10134 (RCA 4702). 1972.

5488 Bragg, Billy, 1958–

Back to basics. Elektra: 60726-2. 1985.

5489 Bronski Beat

The age of consent. MCA: MCAD-5538. 1984. OP

5490 Browne, Jackson, 1948–

The pretender. Elektra: 107-2. 1976.

5491 * Buffalo Springfield

Retrospective. Atco: 38-105-2. 1966–68.

5492 Bush, Kate, 1958–

The whole story. EMI America: 46414. 1978–85.

5493 Buzzcocks

Singles going steady. I.R.S./CEMA: 13153. 1977–79.

5494   Byrds

5494.1   *The Byrds.* Columbia: C4K 46773. 4CD set. 1965–90.

5494.2 ** *Greatest hits.* Columbia: CK 9516. 1965–67. [Item 5494.1 covers material comparable to item 5494.2 but in greater depth and with better packaging and notes].

5495   Cabaret Voltaire

Living legends. Mute: 71476-2. 1975–81.

5496   Cale, John, 1940–

Seducing down the door: the John Cale collection. Rhino: 71685. 2CD set. 1970–90.

5497   Captain Beefheart, 1941–

5497.1   *Shiny beast (bat chain puller).* Bizarre/ Straight: 70365. 1978.

5497.2   *Trout mask replica.* Reprise: 2027-2. 1969.

5498   Cars

Greatest hits. Elektra: 60464-2. 1978–84.

5499   Cash, Johnny, 1932– . *See* 5810.3

5500   Chicago

Greatest hits, vol. 1. Columbia: CK 33900. 1970–74.

5501 * Christian, Meg

The best of Meg Christian. Olivia: ORCD 957. 1973–84.

5502   Christian, Meg, and Cris Williamson

Meg/Cris at Carnegie Hall. Second Wave/Olivia: CD 933. 1982.

5503   Clapton, Eric, 1945–

5503.1 * *Crossroads.* Polydor: 835261-2. 4CD set. 1963–87.

5503.2   *461 Ocean Boulevard.* Polydor: 811697-2. 1974.

5504   Clash

5504.1 * *The Clash.* Epic: EK 36060. 1977.

5504.2 ** *London calling.* Epic: EGK 36328. 1979.

5505 * Cochran, Eddie, 1938–1960

Eddie Cochran, vol. 1. EMI: 92809 (Liberty). 1957–60.

5506   Cocker, Joe, 1944–

Greatest hits. A&M: 75021-3257-2. 1969–74.

5507   Collins, Phil, 1951–

No jacket required. Atlantic: 81240-2. 1985.

5508   Cooder, Ry, 1947–

5508.1   *Into the purple valley.* Reprise: 2052-2. 1972.

5508.2   *Paradise and lunch.* Reprise: 2179-2. 1974.

5509   Costello, Elvis, 1955–

5509.1 ** *My aim is true.* Rykodisc: RCD-20271 (Columbia 35037). 1977.

5509.2   *This year's model.* Rykodisc: RCD-20272 (Columbia 35331). 1978.

5509.3 * *Very best of Elvis Costello and the Attractions.* Rykodisc: RCD-40283 (Columbia). 1977–86.

5510   Country Joe and the Fish

The collected Country Joe and the Fish. Vanguard: VCD-111. 1965–70.

5511   Cream

5511.1 ** *The very best of Cream.* Polydor: 314 523752-2 (Atco). 1966–68.

5511.2   *Wheels of fire.* Polydor: 827578-2. 2CD set. 1968.

5512 ** Creedence Clearwater Revival

Chronicle. Fantasy: FCD-CCR2-2. 1968–72.

5513   Crenshaw, Marshall, 1954–

Field day. Warner Bros.: 23873-2. 1983.

5514   Crosby, Stills and Nash

Crosby, Stills and Nash. Atlantic: 82651-2 (8229). 1969.

5515   Cure

Standing on a beach: the singles. Elektra: 60477-2. 1979–85.

5516   Darin, Bobby, 1936–1973

Splish splash: the best of Bobby Darin, vol. 1. Atco: 91794-2. 1958–66.

5517   Dave Clark Five

The history of the Dave Clark Five. Hollywood: 2061 61482-2 (Epic). 2CD set. 1964–67.

5518   Dead Kennedys

Fresh fruit for rotting vegetables. Alternative Tentacles: Virus 1 CD. 1980.

5519 Deep Purple
Machine head. Warner Bros.: 3100-2. 1972.

5520 Def Leppard
Hysteria. Mercury: 830675-2. 1987.

5521 * Derek and the Dominos
Layla and other assorted love songs. RSO/Polydor: 847090-2. 1970.

5522 Devo
Q: are we not men? A: we are Devo. Warner Bros.: 3239-2. 1978.

5523 * Difranco, Ani, 1970–
Puddle dive. Righteous Babe: RBR CD-4. 1993.

5524 Dinosaur Jr.
You're living all over me. SST: SSTCD-130. 1987.

5525 * Dion, 1939– , and the Belmonts
The wanderer. Laurie: 3CD 105. 1958–63.

5526 Dire Straits
Money for nothing. Warner Bros.: 25794-2. 1978–85.

5527 Domino, Fats, 1928– . *See* 5226

5528 Donovan, 1946–
5528.1 * *Greatest hits.* Epic: EK 26439. 1966–68. [Item 5528.2 covers material comparable to item 5528.1 but in greater depth and with better packaging and notes].

5528.2 *Troubadour: the definitive collection.* Epic: E2K 46986. 2CD set. 1964–76.

5529 Doobie Brothers
Best of the Doobies. Warner Bros.: 3112-2. 1971–76.

5530 Doors
5530.1 *The best of the Doors.* Elektra: 60345-2. 2CD set. 1967–71.

5530.2 * *The Doors.* Elektra: 74007-2. 1967.

5531 Drake, Nick, 1948–1974
Way to blue: an introduction to Nick Drake. Hannibal: HNCD 1386. 1969–72.

5532 Duran Duran
Decade. Capitol: 93178. 1983–89.

5533 Dylan, Bob, 1941–
5533.1 * *Blonde on blonde.* Columbia: CGK 841. 1966.

5533.2 *Blood on the tracks.* Columbia: CK 33235. 1975.

5533.3 ** *Bringing it all back home.* Columbia: CK 9128. 1965.

5533.4 ** *Highway 61 revisited.* Columbia: CK 9189. 1965.

5533.5 *John Wesley Harding.* Columbia: CK 9604. 1968.
See also 5817 and 6526

5534 Dylan, Bob, 1941– , and the Band
The basement tapes. Columbia: C2K 33682. 2CD set. 1967.

5535 * Eagles
Greatest hits, 1971–1975. Asylum: 105-2. 1971–75.

5536 Eddy, Duane, 1938–
Twang thang: the Duane Eddy anthology. Rhino: 71223 (Jamie/RCA/Capitol). 2CD set. 1957–86.

5537 Einsturzende Neubauten
80–83 strategien gegen architekturen = 80–83 strategies against architecture. Homestead: HMS063-2 (Positive). 1983.

5538 Electric Light Orchestra
ELO's greatest hits. Jet/CBS: ZK 36310. 1973–78.

5539 English Beat
What is beat? I.R.S./A&M: 44797-0040-2. 1980–83.

5540 Eno, Brian, 1948–
5540.1 *Another green world.* Editions EG: CAROL-1512-2. 1975.

5540.2 *Before and after science.* Editions EG: CAROL-1513-2. 1977.

5541 Erasure
Pop! the first 20 hits. Sire: 45153-2. 1985–92.

5542 Etheridge, Melissa, 1961–
Yes I am. Island: 422 848660-2. 1993.

5543 Eurythmics
Greatest hits. Arista: ARCD-8680 (RCA). 1983–89.

5544 Everly Brothers
5544.1 ** *Cadence classics: their 20 greatest hits.* Rhino: 5258. 1957–60.

5544.2 *Golden hits.* Warner Bros.: 1471-2. 1960–62.

5545   Fairport Convention

    5545.1   *Liege and lief.* A&M: 75021-4257-2. 1969.

    5545.2   * *Unhalfbricking.* Hannibal: HNCD 4418 (A&M 4206). 1969.

    5545.3   *What we did on our holidays.* Hannibal: HNCD 4430 (A&M 4185). 1968.

5546   Faithfull, Marianne, 1946–

Broken English. Island: 422-842355-2. 1979.

5547   Fanny

Fanny. Reprise: 6417. LP. 1970. OP

5548   Feelies

Crazy rhythms. A&M: 75021-5319-2 (Stiff). 1980.

5549   * Ferry, Bryan, 1945– , and Roxy Music

Street life: 20 great hits. Reprise: 25857-2. 1972–85.

5550   * Fleetwood Mac

Rumours. Warner Bros.: 3010-2. 1977.

5551   Flipper

The generic album. Def American: 26915-2 (Subterranean). 1982.

5552   Flying Burrito Brothers

Farther along: the best of the Flying Burrito Brothers. A&M: 75021-5216-2. 1968–72.

5553   Foreigner

The very best . . . and beyond. Atlantic: 89999-2. 1977–91.

5554   Four Seasons

Anthology. Rhino: 71490 (Vee-Jay/Philips). 2CD set. 1962–74.

5555   Francis, Connie, 1938–

The very best of Connie Francis. Polydor: 827569-2 (MGM). 1957–64.

5556   * Gabriel, Peter, 1950–

Shaking the tree: 16 golden greats. Geffen: 24326-2. 1977–90.

5557   Gang of Four

Entertainment. Warner Bros.: 43047-2. 1979.

5558   Genesis

    5558.1   *Invisible touch.* Atlantic: 81641-2. 1986.

    5558.2   *The lamb lies down on Broadway.* Atco: 82677-2 (401-2). 2CD set. 1974.

5559   Go-Betweens

1978–1990. Capitol: 94681. 1978–90. OP

5560   Go-Go's

Greatest. I.R.S./A&M: 44797-0059-2. 1981–86.

5561   Golden Palominos

History (1982–1985). Metronome: 72651-2 (Celluloid). 1982–86.

5562   Gore, Lesley, 1946–

Golden hits of Lesley Gore. Mercury: 810370-2. 1963–67.

5563   Grand Funk Railroad

Grand Funk Railroad. [Series: Capitol collectors]. Capitol: 90608. 1969–75.

5564   Grateful Dead

    5564.1   * *Live Dead.* Warner Bros.: 1830-2. 1970.

    5564.2   *Workingman's Dead.* Warner Bros.: 1869-2. 1970.

5565   Guns 'n' Roses

Appetite for destruction. Geffen: 24148-2. 1987.

5566   Haley, Bill, 1925–1981

    5566.1   *From the original master tapes.* MCA: MCAD-5539 (Decca). 1954–56.

    5566.2   * *Rock the joint.* Schoolkids: SKR-1529/Rollercoaster: RCCD 3001 (Essex). 1951–53.

5567   * Hall, Daryl, 1948– , and John Oates, 1949–

Rock 'n' soul, part 1. RCA: PCD1-4858. 1976–83.

5568   * Harvey, P. J., 1970–

Dry. Indigo: 162 555001-2. 1992.

5569   Hawkins, Ronnie, 1935–

The best of Ronnie Hawkins and the Hawks. Rhino: 70966 (Roulette). 1959–63, 1970.

5570   Heart

Greatest hits/live. Epic: EGK 36888. 1976–81.

5571   Hendrix, Jimi, 1942–1970

    5571.1   *Are you experienced?* MCA: MCAD-10893 (Reprise 6261). 1967.

    5571.2   *Axis: bold as love.* MCA: MCAD-10894 (Reprise 6281). 1967.

    5571.3   ** *Electric ladyland.* MCA: MCAD-10895 (Reprise 6307). 1968.

5571.4 * *Jimi Hendrix: Woodstock.* MCA: MCAD-11063. 1969.

5571.5 *Jimi plays Monterey* (soundtrack). Reprise: 25358-2. 1967. OP

5571.6 *Live at Winterland.* Rykodisc: RCD-20038. 1968.

5571.7 *Radio One.* Rykodisc: RCD-20078. 1967.

5571.8 ** *Smash hits.* Reprise: 2276-2. 1966–68. OP

5571.9 ** *The ultimate experience.* MCA: MCAD-10829. 1966–70. [Items 5571.8 and 5571.9 cover similar material].

5572 Henley, Don, 1947–
Building the perfect beast. Geffen: 24026-2. 1984.

5573 Henry Cow
Unrest. T.E.C. Tones: 16026 or ESD: 80492 (Red). 1979.

5574 Hole
Live through this. DGC: DGCD 24631. 1994.

5575 * Hollies
Best of the Hollies. EMI: 35985 (Imperial). 1963–68.

5576 Holly, Buddy, 1936–1959

5576.1 *The Buddy Holly collection.* MCA: MCAD2-10883 (Decca, Coral). 2CD set. 1957–58.

5576.2 ** *Legend: from the original master tapes.* MCA: MCAD-5540 (Decca, Coral). 1957–58. [Item 5576.1 covers material comparable to item 5576.2 but in greater depth and with better packaging and notes].

5577 Hüsker Dü
New day rising. SST: SSTCD-031. 1985.

5578 Ian, Janis, 1951–
Breaking silence. Morgan Creek: 2959-20023-2. 1992.

5579 Iggy, 1947– , and the Stooges
Raw power. Columbia: CK 32111. 1973.

5580 Incredible String Band
The hangman's beautiful daughter. Hannibal: HNCD 4421 (Elektra 74021). 1967.

5581 Iron Maiden
Number of the beast. Capitol: 46364. 1982.

5582 Jam
Snap! Polydor: 821712-2. 1977–80.

5583 James, Tommy, 1947– , and the Shondells
The very best of Tommy James and the Shondells. Rhino: 71214 (Roulette). 1966–71.

5584 Jan and Dean
Surf city: the best of Jan and Dean. EMI: 92772. 1961–66.

5585 Jane's Addiction
Nothing's shocking. Warner Bros.: 25727-2. 1988.

5586 Jefferson Airplane

5586.1 *Jefferson Airplane loves you.* RCA: 07863-61110-2. 3CD set. 1962–74.

5586.2 ** *Surrealistic pillow.* RCA: 07863-66598-2 (LSP-3766). 1967.

5587 Jesus and Mary Chain
Psychocandy. Def American: 25383-2. 1985.

5588 Jethro Tull
M.U.: the best of Jethro Tull. Chrysalis: 21078. 1968–75.

5589 Jett, Joan, 1960–
I love rock 'n' roll. Blackheart: 747 (Boardwalk 33243). 1981.

5590 John, Elton, 1947–

5590.1 ** *Greatest hits, vol. 1.* Polydor: 314-512532-2 (Uni/MCA). 1970–74.

5590.2 *Greatest hits, vol. 2.* Polydor: 314-512533-2. 1972–76.

5591 Jones, Rickie Lee, 1954–
Rickie Lee Jones. Warner Bros.: 3296-2. 1979.

5592 Joplin, Janis, 1943–1970
Pearl. Columbia: CK 30322. 1971. *See also* 5476

5593 Journey
Escape. Columbia: CK 37408. 1981.

5594 Joy Division
Unknown pleasures. Quest/Warner Bros.: 25840-2. 1979.

5595 Judas Priest
Metal works. Columbia: C2K 53932. 2CD set. 1973–93.

5596 Kaiser, Henry, 1952– , and Fred Frith, 1949–
With enemies like these, who needs friends? SST: SSTCD 147 (Metalanguage). 1980.

5597 * King, Carole, 1942–
Tapestry. Ode/CBS: EK 34946. 1971.

5598 * King Crimson
The abbreviated King Crimson: heartbeat. Editions EG: CAROL-1467-2. 1969–84.

5599 Kinks
5599.1 * *Greatest hits, vol. 1.* Rhino: 70086 (Reprise). 1964–66.
5599.2 *The Kink kronikles.* Reprise: 6454-2. 2CD set. 1966–70.

5600 Kiss
Kiss alive II. Casablanca: 822781-2. 2CD set. 1978.

5601 Kraftwerk
Autobahn. Elektra: 25326-2 (Vertigo). 1975.

5602 Lauper, Cyndi, 1953–
She's so unusual. Portrait/CBS: RK 38930. 1983.

5603 Led Zeppelin
5603.1 ** *Led Zeppelin II.* Atlantic: 82633-2 (8236). 1969.
5603.2 * *Led Zeppelin* [IV: "Zo-so"]. Atlantic: 19129-2 (7208). 1971.

5604 Lennon, John, 1940–1980
Shaved fish. Capitol: 46642. 1969–75.

5605 Lewis, Huey, 1950–
Sports. Chrysalis: 21412. 1983.

5606 ** Lewis, Jerry Lee, 1935–
18 original greatest hits. Rhino: 70255 (Sun). 1956–63.

5607 Little Feat
Waiting for Columbus. Warner Bros.: 3140-2. 1977.

5608 Little Richard, 1935–
5608.1 ** *The Georgia peach.* Specialty: SPCD-7012-2. 1955–57.
5608.2 *Shut up! a collection of rare tracks.* Rhino: 70236. LP. 1951–64. OP

5609 Living Colour
Vivid. Epic: EK 44099. 1988.

5610 Los Lobos
5610.1 * *How will the wolf survive?* Slash: 25177-2. 1984.

5610.2 *Just another band from East L.A.: a collection.* Slash/Warner Bros.: 45367-2. 2CD set. 1978–93.

5611 Lovin' Spoonful
Anthology. Rhino: 70944 (Kama Sutra). 1965–68.

5612 Lowe, Nick, 1949–
Basher: the best of Nick Lowe. Columbia: CK 45313. 1978–88.

5613 Lymon, Frankie, 1942–1968
The best of Frankie Lymon and the Teenagers. Rhino: 70918 (Gee). 1956–60.

5614 Lynyrd Skynyrd
Gold and platinum. MCA: MCAD2-6898. 2CD set. 1973–78.

5615 * Madonna, 1958–
The immaculate collection. Sire: 26440-2. 1984–90.

5616 Mamas and the Papas
16 of their greatest hits. MCA: MCAD-5701 (Dunhill). 1965–68.

5617 Marshall Tucker Band
Greatest hits. AJK Music: 799-2 (Capricorn). 1973–77.

5618 McCartney, Paul, 1942–
All the best. Capitol: 48287. 1970–86.

5619 MC5
Back in the U.S.A. Rhino: 71033 (Atlantic). 1970.

5620 Meat Puppets
Meat Puppets II. SST: SSTCD-019. 1983.

5621 Megadeth
Peace sells . . . but who's buying? Capitol: 46370. 1986.

5622 Mekons
Original sin. Twin/Tone: 89164-2. 1989.

5623 Mellencamp, John Cougar, 1951–
Scarecrow. Riva/Mercury: 824865-2. 1985.

5624 Metallica
Metallica. Elektra: 61113-2. 1991.

5625 Midnight Oil
Diesel and dust. Columbia: CK 40967. 1988.

5626 Miller, Steve, 1943–

5626.1 *The best of Steve Miller, 1968–1973.* Capitol: 95271. 1968–73.

5626.2 *Greatest hits 1974–78.* Capitol: 46101. 1974–78.

5627 Mitchell, Joni, 1943–

5627.1 *Blue.* Reprise: 2038-2. 1971.

5627.2 * *Court and spark.* Asylum: 1001-2. 1974.

5628 Moby Grape

Vintage: the very best of Moby Grape. Columbia: C2K 53041. 2CD set. 1967–70.

5629 Monkees

Greatest hits. Rhino: 72190 (Colgems). 1966–68, 1987.

5630 Moody Blues

Greatest hits. Threshold: 840659-2. 1967–88.

5631 Morrison, Van, 1945–

5631.1 * *Astral weeks.* Warner Bros.: 1768-2. 1968.

5631.2 ** *Moondance.* Warner Bros.: 3103-2. 1970.

5631.3 *Saint Dominic's preview.* Warner Bros.: 2633-2. 1972.

5632 Motörhead

No remorse. Roadrunner: 9354. 1978–84.

5633 Mott the Hoople

Greatest hits. Columbia: CK 34368. 1972–76.

5634 Muldaur, Maria, 1943–

Maria Muldaur. Reprise: 2148-2. 1974.

5635 Napalm Death

Fear, emptiness, despair. Earache/Columbia: CK 64361. 1993.

5636 Nelson, Rick, 1940–1985

5636.1 *Rick Nelson, vol. 2.* EMI: 95219 (Imperial). 1957–62.

5636.2 *Ricky Nelson, vol. 1.* EMI: 92771 (Imperial). 1957–60.

5637 New Order

Substance. Quest/Warner Bros.: 25621-2. 2CD set. 1981–87.

5638 New York Dolls

New York Dolls. Mercury: 832752-2. 1973.

5639 Newman, Randy, 1944–

5639.1 *Sail away.* Reprise: 2064-2. 1972.

5639.2 * *12 songs.* Reprise: 6373-2. 1970.

5640 * Nine Inch Nails

The downward spiral. TVT/Interscope: 92346-2. 1994.

5641 Nirvana

5641.1 *In utero.* DCG: DGCD-24607. 1993.

5641.2 ** *Nevermind.* DGC: DGCD-24425. 1991.

5642 NRBQ

Peek-a-boo: the best of NRBQ. Rhino: 70770. 2CD set. 1969–89.

5643 Nugent, Ted, 1948–

Great gonzos: the best of Ted Nugent. Epic: EK 37667. 1975–81.

5644 Nyro, Laura, 1947–

Eli and the 13th confession. Columbia: CK 9626. 1968.

5645 O'Connor, Sinead, 1966–

I do not want what I haven't got. Chrysalis: 21759. 1990.

5646 * Orbison, Roy, 1936–1988

For the lonely: 18 greatest hits. Rhino: 71493 (Sun/Monument). 1956–64.

5647 Parker, Graham, 1950–

Squeezing out sparks. Arista: ARCD-8075. 1979.

5648 Parsons, Gram, 1946–1973

GP/Grievous angel. Reprise: 26108-2. 1973–74.

5649 Pavement

Slanted and enchanted. Matador: OLE 038-2. 1992.

5650 * Pearl Jam

Ten. Epic Associated: ZK-47857. 1991.

5651 Pentangle

Early classics. Shanachie: 79078. 1968–70.

5652 Pere Ubu

5652.1 * *Datapanik in the year zero.* Geffen: DGCD5-24969. 5CD set. 1975–82.

5652.2 *The tenement years.* Enigma: 73343. 1987.

5653 * Perkins, Carl, 1932–

Original Sun greatest hits. Rhino: 75890. 1955–57.

5654 Pet Shop Boys

Discography: the complete singles collection. EMI: 97097. 1985–91.

5655 Petty, Tom, 1953– , and the Heartbreakers

Greatest hits. MCA: MCAD-10813. 1976–93.

5656 Phair, Liz, 1967–

Exile in Guyville. Matador: OLE 051-2. 1993.

5657 Pink Floyd

5657.1 * *Dark side of the moon.* Capitol: 46001. 1973.

5657.2 *Saucerful of secrets.* Capitol: 46383 (Tower). 1968.

5657.3 *The wall.* Columbia: C2K 36183. 2CD set. 1979.

5657.4 *Works.* Capitol: 46478 (12276). 1967–73.

5658 Pitney, Gene, 1941–

Anthology. Rhino: 75896 (Musicor). 1961–68.

5659 Pixies

Doolittle. Elektra: 60856-2. 1989.

5660 * Platters

The magic touch: an anthology. Mercury: 314-510314-2. 2CD set. 1955–61.

5661 Pogues

If I should fall from grace with God. Island: 422 842878-2. 1988.

5662 * Police

Every breath you take: the singles. A&M: 75021-3902-2. 1978–83.

5663 Presley, Elvis, 1935–1977

5663.1 *The king of rock 'n' roll: the complete 50's masters.* RCA: 07863-66050-2. 5CD set. 1953–58.

5663.2 ** *The number one hits.* RCA: 6382-2-R. 1956–69. [Item 5663.4 covers material comparable to item 5663.2 but in greater depth.]

5663.3 ** *The Sun sessions CD.* RCA: 6414–2–R. 1954–55.

5663.4 * *Top ten hits.* RCA: 6383-2-R. 2CD set. 1956–72.

5664 * Pretenders

The singles. Sire: 25664-2. 1979–86.

5665 Procol Harum

Procol Harum. [Series: A&M classics, vol. 17]. A&M: 75021-2515-2. 1967–72.

5666 Psychedelic Furs

All of this and nothing. Columbia: CK 44377. 1980–88.

5667 Public Image Ltd.

Second edition (Metal box). Warner Bros.: 3288-2. 1980.

5668 Queen

Greatest hits. Hollywood: 2061 61265-2 (Elektra). 1974–81.

5669 Quicksilver Messenger Service

5669.1 *Quicksilver Messenger Service.* Capitol: 91146 (2904). 1968.

5669.2 *Sons of Mercury.* Rhino: 70747 (Capitol). 2CD set. 1968–75.

5670 Raitt, Bonnie, 1949–

5670.1 *Give it up.* Warner Bros.: 2643-2. 1972.

5670.2 * *Nick of time.* Capitol: 91268. 1989.

5671 Ramones

5671.1 * *All the stuff (and more), vol. 1.* Sire: 26220-2. 1976–77.

5671.2 *All the stuff (and more), vol. 2.* Sire: 26618-2. 1977–78.

5672 * Rascals

The very best of the Rascals. Rhino/Atlantic: 71277. 1965–71.

5673 Raspberries

The Raspberries. [Series: Capitol collectors]. Capitol: 92126. 1972–74.

5674 Reed, Lou, 1944–

Walk on the wild side: the best of Lou Reed. RCA: 3753-2-R. 1972–76.

5675 R.E.M.

5675.1 * *Automatic for the people.* Warner Bros.: 45055-2. 1992.

5675.2 ** *Eponymous.* I.R.S./MCA: IRSD-6262. 1981–87.

5676 REO Speedwagon

The hits. Epic: EK 44202. 1977–88.

5677 * Replacements

Let it be. Twin/Tone: 8441-2. 1984.

5678 Residents

5678.1 *Eskimo.* T.E.C. Tones: 7096-2 (Ralph). 1979.

5678.2 *The Residents' commercial album: 50 songs.* East Side Digital: ESD 80202 (Ralph 8052). 1980.

5679 Revere, Paul, 1942– , and the Raiders

The essential ride: '63–'67. Columbia: CK 48949. 1963–67.

5680 Richman, Jonathan, 1951–

The modern lovers. Rhino: 70091 (Beserkly). 1976.

5681 Righteous Brothers

The very best of the Righteous Brothers: unchained melody. Verve: 847248-2. 1964–68.

5682 Rolling Stones

5682.1 *Aftermath.* Abkco: 7476-2. 1966.

5682.2 * *Beggars banquet.* Abkco: 7539-2. 1968.

5682.3 * *Exile on Main Street.* Virgin: 39524 (Rolling Stones 2900). 1972.

5682.4 ** *Hot rocks 1964–1971.* Abkco: 6667-2 (London). 2CD set. 1964–69. [Item 5682.8 covers material comparable to item 5682.4 but in greater depth and with better packaging and notes].

5682.5 *Let it bleed.* Abkco: 8004-2. 1969.

5682.6 *Rewind.* Rolling Stones Records: CK 40505. 1971–84. OP

5682.7 *The Rolling Stones, now!* Abkco: 7420-2. 1965.

5682.8 * *Singles collection: the London years.* Abkco: 1231-2. 3CD set. 1963–69.

5683 Rollins Band

End of silence. Imago: 21006-2. 1992.

5684 * Ronstadt, Linda, 1946–

Greatest hits. Elektra: 106-2. 1967–75.

5685 Runaways

The best of the Runaways. Mercury: 826279-2. 1976–77.

5686 Rundgren, Todd, 1948–

Anthology. Rhino: 71491. 2CD set. 1968–85.

5687 Rush

Chronicles. Mercury: 838936-2. 2CD set. 1974–89.

5688 Ryder, Mitch, 1945–

Rev up: the best of Mitch Ryder and the Detroit Wheels. Rhino: 70941 (New Voice). 1966–71.

5689 Sahm, Doug, 1942–

The best of Doug Sahm and the Sir Douglas Quintet. Mercury: 846586-2. 1968–75.

5690 Santana

5690.1 *Abraxas.* Columbia: CK 30130. 1970.

5690.2 * *Santana.* Columbia: CK 9781. 1968.

5690.3 *Viva Santana!* Columbia: C2K 44344. 2CD set. 1967–86.

5691 Scaggs, Boz, 1944–

Silk degrees. Columbia: CK 33920. 1976.

5692 Searchers

Greatest hits. Rhino: 75773 (Kapp). 1963–67.

5693 Sedaka, Neil, 1939–

All time greatest hits. RCA: 6876-2-R. 1958–63.

5694 Seger, Bob, 1945–

5694.1 *Greatest hits.* Capitol: 30334. 1975–94.

5694.2 *Live bullet.* Capitol: 46085 (11523). 2CD set. 1975.

5695 * Sex Pistols

Never mind the bollocks here's the Sex Pistols. Warner Bros.: 3147-2. 1977.

5696 Shannon, Del, 1939–1990

Greatest hits. Rhino: 70977 (Big Top/Amy). 1961–65.

5697 ** Simon and Garfunkel

Greatest hits. Columbia: CK 31350. 1965–70.

5698 Simon, Carly, 1945–

The best of Carly Simon. Elektra: 109-2. 1971–75.

5699 Simon, Paul, 1941–

5699.1 ** *Graceland.* Warner Bros.: 25477-2. 1986.

5699.2 * *Negotiations and love songs.* Warner Bros.: 25789-2. 1971–86.

5700 Slayer

Reign in blood. Def American: 24131-2. 1986.

5701 Sly, 1944– , and the Family Stone. *See* 5321

5702 Smashing Pumpkins

Siamese dream. Virgin: 88267. 1993.

5703 * Smith, Patti, 1946–

Horses. Arista: 07822-18827-2 (8362). 1975.

5704 Smiths

The queen is dead. Sire: 25426-2. 1985.

5705 Snow, Phoebe, 1952–

The best of Phoebe Snow. Columbia: CK 37091. 1974–78.

5706 Soft Machine

Third. Columbia: CGK 30339. 1970.

5707 Somerville, Jimmy, 1961–

The singles collection. London: 828226-2. 1984–90.

5708 Sonic Youth

5708.1 ** *Daydream nation.* DGC: DGCD-24515 (Blast First 75403). 1988.

5708.2 *Sister.* DGC: DGCD-24514 (SST-134). 1987.

5709 Sonny and Cher

The beat goes on: the best of Sonny and Cher. Atco: 91796-2. 1965–67.

5710 Soundgarden

Superunknown. A&M: 314 540 198-2. 1994.

5711 Specials

The singles collection. Chrysalis: 21823. 1979–84.

5712 Spencer Davis Group

The best of the Spencer Davis Group. EMI: 46598 (United Artists). 1964–67.

5713 Spirit

Time circle. Epic: E2K 47363. 2CD set. 1968–72.

5714 Springsteen, Bruce, 1949–

5714.1 * *Born in the USA.* Columbia: CK 38653. 1984.

5714.2 ** *Born to run.* Columbia: CK 33795. 1975.

5715 Squeeze

Singles: 45's and under. A&M: 75021-3338-2. 1978–82.

5716 Steeleye Span

Spanning the years. Chrysalis/EMI: 32236. 2CD set. 1970–91.

5717 Steely Dan

A decade of Steely Dan. MCA: MCAD-5570. 1972–82.

5718 Steppenwolf

16 greatest hits. MCA: MCAD-37049 (Dunhill). 1968–70.

5719 Stevens, Cat, 1947–

Greatest hits. A&M: 75021-4519-2. 1971–75.

5720 Stewart, Rod, 1945–

5720.1 *Downtown train: selections from the storyteller anthology.* Warner Bros.: 26158-2. 1976–89.

5720.2 *Every picture tells a story.* Mercury: 822385-2. 1971.

5721 Stooges

The Stooges. Elektra: 74051-2. 1969.

5722 T. Rex (Marc Bolan, 1947–1977)

Electric warrior. Reprise: 6466-2. 1971.

5723 Talking Heads

5723.1 * *Remain in light.* Sire: 6095-2. 1980.

5723.2 ** *Talking Heads favorites/Sand in the Vaseline.* Sire: 26760-2. 2CD set. 1976–91.

5724 * Taylor, James, 1948–

Sweet baby James. Warner Bros.: 1843-2. 1970.

5725 ** Television

Marquee moon. Elektra: 1098-2. 1977.

5726 Ten Years After

The essential Ten Years After. Chrysalis: 21857. [1968–70].

5727 Thompson, Richard, 1949–

Watching the dark: the essential retrospective. Hannibal: HNCD 5303. 3CD set. 1969–92.

5728 ** Thompson, Richard, 1949– , and Linda Thompson, 1948–

Shoot out the lights. Hannibal: HNCD 1303. 1982.

5729 Three Dog Night

Joy to the world (greatest hits). MCA: MCAD-1466 (Dunhill). 1969–74.

5730 Traffic

5730.1 * *Mr. Fantasy.* Island: 422-842783-2. 1967.

5730.2 *Smiling phases.* Island: 314-510553-2. 2CD set. 1967–74.

5730.3 *Traffic.* Island: 422-842590-2. 1968.

5731 Trull, Teresa

A step away. Redwood: RRCD 412. 1986.

5732 * Turner, Tina, 1938–

Private dancer. Capitol: 46041 (12330). 1984. *See also 5338*

5733 Turtles

20 greatest hits. Rhino: 5160 (White Whale). 1965–69.

5734 U2

5734.1 * *The Joshua tree.* Island: 422-842298-2. 1987.

5734.2 *War.* Island: 422-811148-2. 1983.

5735 Valens, Ritchie, 1941–1959

The best of Ritchie Valens. Rhino: 70178 (Del-Fi). 1958–59.

5736 Van Halen

5736.1 *1984.* Warner Bros.: 23985-2. 1983.

5736.2 ** *Van Halen.* Warner Bros.: 3075-2. 1978.

5737 Vee, Bobby, 1943–

Bobby Vee. [Series: Legendary masters]. EMI: 92774 (Liberty). 1959–68.

5738 Velvet Underground

5738.1 *Loaded.* Warner Special Products: 27613-2 (Cotillion). 1970.

5738.2 *The Velvet Underground.* Verve: 815454-2. 1969.

5738.3 ** *The Velvet Underground and Nico.* Verve: 823290-2. 1967.

5739 Ventures

Walk don't run: the best of the Ventures. EMI: 93451 (Dolton). 1960–68.

5740 Vincent, Gene, 1935–1971

Gene Vincent. [Series: Capitol collectors]. Capitol: 94074. 1956–58.

5741 Violent Femmes

Violent Femmes. Slash: 23845-2. 1982–83.

5742 Waits, Tom, 1947–

Rain dogs. Island: 422-826382-2. 1985.

5743 Wham

Make it big. Columbia: CK 39595. 1984.

5744 Who

5744.1 * *Live at Leeds.* MCA: MCAD-11215 (Decca 79175). 1970.

5744.2 ** *Meaty beaty big and bouncy.* MCA: MCAD-37001 (Decca). 1965–70.

5744.3 *30 years of maximum r&b.* MCA: MCAD4-11020. 4CD set. 1964–89.

5744.4 *Tommy.* MCA: MCAD-10801 (Decca 7205). 1969.

5744.5 * *Who's next.* MCA: MCAD-37217 (Decca 79182). 1971.

5745 Williams, Lucinda, 1953–

Lucinda Williams. Chameleon: 61387-2 (Rough Trade 47). 1988.

5746 Williamson, Cris

5746.1 * *The best of Cris Williamson.* Olivia: CD 959. 1971–84.

5746.2 *The changer and the changed.* Olivia: ORCD 904. 1975.

5747 Winwood, Stevie, 1948–

Chronicles. Island: 422-842364-2. 1977–86.

5748 Wray, Link, 1935–

Rumble!: the best of Link Wray. Rhino: 71222 (Cadence/Epic/Swan). 1958–76.

5749 X

Los Angeles/Wild gift. Slash: 25771-2. 1980–81.

5750 XTC

Waxworks: some singles. Geffen: GEFD-4037. 1977–82.

5751 Yardbirds

5751.1 *Five live Yardbirds.* Rhino: 70189. 1964.

5751.2 * *Greatest hits, vol. 1* Rhino: 75895 (Epic). 1964–66.

5752 Yes

Fragile. Atlantic: 82667-2 (7211). 1972.

5753 Young, Neil, 1945–

5753.1 ** *Decade.* Reprise: 2257-2. 2CD set. 1966–76.

5753.2 *Ragged glory.* Reprise: 26315-2. 1990.

5753.3 *Rust never sleeps.* Reprise: 2295-2. 1979.

5754   Zappa, Frank, 1940–1993

   5754.1   *Hot rats.* Rykodisc: RCD-10508 (Bizarre 6356). 1969.

   5754.2 ** *Strictly commercial: the best of Frank Zappa.* Rykodisc: RCD-40500. 1966–88.

5755   Zappa, Frank, 1940–1993, and the Mothers of Invention

   5755.1   *Absolutely free.* Rykodisc: RCD-10502. (Verve 5013). 1967.

5755.2 * *We're only in it for the money.* Rykodisc: RCD-10503 (Verve 5045). 1967.

5756   Zevon, Warren, 1947–

A quiet normal life: the best of Warren Zevon. Asylum: 60503-2. 1976–82.

5757   Z. Z. Top

Greatest hits. Warner Bros.: 26846-2. 1970–90.

26

Country and Western

Compiled by
**Linda Gross and the staff of the Country Music Foundation
and William E. Anderson**

T his chapter comprises historical and contemporary country and western music, including western swing, honky-tonk, and bluegrass. (Consult the index for listings under these and other genre terms.) In addition to "General Anthologies," the chapter is divided chronologically into two main sections, "Pre–World War II" and "Post–World War II."

General Anthologies

5758 * *Back in the saddle again.* New World: NW 314-2/315-2. 2CD set. 1925–80. [Harry McClintock, Carl T. Sprague, Wilf Carter, Patsy Montana, Sons of the Pioneers, Tex Ritter, and others].

5759 ** *Classic country music: a Smithsonian collection.* Smithsonian: 2050 (RD 042). 4CD set. 1924–86. [Gid Tanner, Uncle Dave Macon, Vernon Dalhart, Carter Family, Jimmie Rodgers, Gene Autry, Milton Brown, Roy Acuff, Patsy Montana, Sons of the Pioneers, Bob Wills, Ernest Tubb, Eddy Arnold, Hank Williams, Loretta Lynn, Lefty Frizzell, George Jones, Gram Parsons, Willie Nelson,

Emmylou Harris, Alabama, Dolly Parton, Judds, and others].

5760 * *Columbia country classics, vol. 1: the golden age.* Columbia: CK 46029. 1935–53. [Carter Family, Roy Acuff, Chuck Wagon Gang, Gene Autry, Bob Wills, Patsy Montana, Bill Monroe, and others].

5761 * *Country music: in the modern era.* New World: NW 207. LP. 1942–75. [Eddy Arnold, Lefty Frizzell, Ray Price, Hank Snow, Kitty Wells, Ernest Tubb, Patsy Cline, Chet Atkins, Elvis Presley, Jim Reeves, Marty Robbins, Loretta Lynn, Johnny Cash, Buck Owens, Roger Miller, Merle Haggard, Dolly Parton, Kris Kristofferson]. OP

5762 * *Country music: South and West.* New World: NW 287. LP. 1929–75. [Jimmie Rodgers, Carter Family, Gene Autry, Monroe Brothers, Milton Brown, Blue Sky Boys, Patsy Montana, Roy Acuff, Sons of the Pioneers, Merle Travis, Bob Wills, and others]. OP

5763 *From the vaults: Decca country classics.* MCA: MCAD3-11069. 3CD set. 1934–73. [Stuart Hamblen, Milton Brown, Carter Family, Leo Soileau,

Tex Ritter, Bill Carlisle, Cliff Bruner, Jimmie Davis, Sons of the Pioneers, Ernest Tubb, Floyd Tillman, Delmore Brothers, Red Foley, Bill Monroe, Kitty Wells, Red Sovine, Webb Pierce, Jimmy Martin, Patsy Cline, Osborne Brothers, Loretta Lynn, Conway Twitty, and others].

5764 ** *Heroes of country music, vol. 1: legends of western swing.* Rhino: 72440 (71900). 1932–57. [Milton Brown, Light Crust Doughboys, Bob Wills, Tex Williams, Leon McAuliffe, Hank Thompson, Cliff Bruner, Hank Penny, Johnnie Lee Wills, Spade Cooley, and others].

5765 ** *Heroes of country music, vol. 2: legends of honky tonk.* Rhino: 72441 (71901). 1936–67. [Al Dexter, Ernest Tubb, Floyd Tillman, Hank Williams, Red Foley, Johnny Bond, Hank Thompson, Carl Smith, Red Sovine, Lefty Frizzell, George Jones, Cliff Bruner, Ted Daffan, Leon Payne, Hawkshaw Hawkins, Charlie Walker, and others].

5766 * *Heroes of country music, vol. 4: legends of the West Coast.* Rhino: 72443 (71903). 1941–63. [Jack Guthrie, Jimmy Wakely, Tennessee Ernie Ford, Tex Ritter, Skeets McDonald, Joe Maphis, Jean Shepard, Ferlin Husky, Buck Owens, Merle Haggard, Gene Autry, Sons of the Pioneers, Al Dexter, Spade Cooley, Maddox Brothers and Rose, Wynn Stewart, and others].

5767 * *Legends of guitar: country, vol. 1.* Rhino: 70718. 1935–80. [Larry Collins, Joe Maphis, Marty Robbins, Grady Martin, Merle Travis, Milton Brown, Bob Dunn, Spade Cooley, Chet Atkins, Bob Wills, Leon McAuliffe, Eldon Shamblin, Arthur Smith, Carl Perkins, Doc Watson, Byrds, and others].

5768 * *Legends of guitar: country, vol. 2.* Rhino: 70723. 1928–86. [Carter Family, Chet Atkins, Jerry Byrd, James Burton, Clarence White, Merle Travis, Little Jimmy Dickens, Roy Clark, Jerry Reed, Tony Rice, Hank Garland, Grady Martin, Albert Lee, and others].

5769 * *Sixty years of the Grand Ole Opry.* RCA: CPK2-9507: 2AC set. 1928–85. [Uncle Dave Macon, Crook Brothers, DeFord Bailey, Gully Jumpers, Asher Sizemore, Bradley Kincaid, Delmore Brothers, Bill Monroe, Ernest Tubb, Eddy Arnold, Pee Wee King, Willis Brothers, Johnny and Jack, Minnie Pearl, Grandpa Jones, Chet Atkins, Hank Snow, Jordanaires, Don Gibson, Jim Reeves, Porter Wagoner, Bobby Bare, Skeeter Davis, Lester Flatt, Willie Nelson, Dolly Parton, Ronnie Milsap, Osborne Brothers, and others].

5770 *Songs of the West.* [vol. 1: *Cowboy classics;* vol. 2: *Silver screen cowboys;* vol. 3: *Gene Autry and Roy Rogers;* vol. 4: *Movie and television themes*]. Rhino: 71263. 4CD set. 1934–90. [Available individually as Rhino: 71681/71684. Gene Autry, Sons of the Pioneers, Tex Ritter, Walter Brennan, Marty Robbins, Patsy Montana, Riders in the Sky, Rex Allen, Roy Rogers, Dale Evans, Bob Wills, Jimmy Wakely, Al Caiola, Hugo Montenegro, Frankie Laine, Johnny Cash, and others].

5771 * *Texas music, vol. 2: western swing & honky tonk.* Rhino: 71782. 1935–75. [Bob Wills, Light Crust Doughboys, Milton Brown, Cliff Bruner, Ernest Tubb, Floyd Tillman, Harry Choates, Lefty Frizzell, Hank Thompson, Johnny Gimble, Asleep at the Wheel, Ted Daffan, Al Dexter, and others].

Pre–World War II

This section covers the earliest country music recordings in the 1920s through 1945. Artists who established themselves during these years but whose careers extended further are listed here.

Anthologies

5772 ** *Are you from Dixie?: great country brother teams of the 1930's.* RCA: 8417-2-R. 1930–39. [Allen Brothers, Delmore Brothers, Dixon Brothers, Monroe Brothers, Blue Sky Boys, and others]. OP

5773 ** *The Bristol sessions.* Country Music Foundation: CMF-011-D (Victor). 2CD set. 1927. [Jimmie Rodgers, Carter Family, Ernest V. Stoneman, Blind Alfred Reed, West Virginia Coon Hunters, and others].

5774 *OKeh western swing.* Sony Music Special Products: A 37324. 1927–50. [Bob Wills, Spade Cooley, Leon McAuliffe, and others].

5775 *Old-time mountain ballads.* County: COCD 3504. 1926–29. [G. B. Grayson, B. F. Shelton, Buell Kazee, Clarence Ashley, Uncle Dave Macon, Ernest Stoneman, Blind Alfred Reed, and others].

5776 * *Ragged but right: great country string bands of the 1930's.* RCA: 8416-2-R. 1933–38. [Riley Puckett, Gid Tanner and His Skillet Lickers, Prairie Ramblers, J. E. Mainer, Wade Mainer, and others]. OP

5777 *Under the double eagle: great western swing bands of the 1930's, vol. 1.* RCA: 2101-2-R. 1934–35. [Bill Boyd and his Cowboy Ramblers, Milton Brown and his Musical Brownies]. OP

5778 * *White country blues: a lighter shade of blue.* Columbia: C2K 47466. 2CD set. 1926–38. [Frank Hutchison, Charlie Poole, Darby and Tarlton, Riley Puckett, Roy Acuff, Cliff Carlisle, Callahan Brothers, Allen Brothers, and others].

Individual Artists or Groups

5779 * Acuff, Roy, 1903–1992

The essential Roy Acuff. Columbia: CK 48956. 1936–49.

5780 Autry, Gene, 1907–

The essential Gene Autry. Columbia: CK 48957. 1933–46.

5781 Blue Sky Boys

5781.1 *The Blue Sky Boys (Bill and Earl Bolick).* RCA Bluebird: AXM2-5525. 2LP set. 1936–50. OP

5781.2 *In concert, 1964.* Rounder: CD 11536. 1964.

5782 Carter Family

5782.1 ** *Anchored in love.* Rounder: CD 1064 (Victor). 1927–28.

5782.2 * *The Carter Family.* [Series: Country Music Hall of Fame]. MCA: MCAD-10088 (Decca). 1936–38.

5782.3 ** *My Clinch Mountain home.* Rounder: CD 1065 (Victor). 1928–29. [Additional volumes from Rounder (1066/1072) complete this series].

5783 Davis, Jimmie, 1902–

Jimmie Davis. [Series: Country Music Hall of Fame]. MCA: MCAD-10087 (Decca). 1934–53. OP

5784 Hofner, Adolph, 1916–

South Texas swing. Arhoolie: CD-7029. 1936–5?.

5785 Macon, Uncle Dave, 1870–1952

Uncle Dave Macon. [Series: Country Music Hall of Fame]. MCA: MCAD-10546. 1926–34.

5786 Rodgers, Jimmie, 1897–1933

5786.1 * *America's blue yodeler.* Rounder: CD 1060 (Victor). 1930–31.

5786.2 *Down the old road.* Rounder: CD 1061 (Victor). 1931–32.

5786.3 * *The early years.* Rounder: CD 1057 (Victor). 1928–29.

5786.4 ** *First sessions.* Rounder: CD 1056 (Victor). 1927–28.

5786.5 *Last sessions.* Rounder: CD 1063 (Victor). 1933.

5786.6 * *No hard time.* Rounder: CD 1062 (Victor). 1932.

5786.7 *On the way up.* Rounder: CD 1058 (Victor). 1929.

5786.8 *Riding high.* Rounder: CD 1059 (Victor). 1929–30.

5787 * Sons of the Pioneers

Sons of the Pioneers. [Series: Country Music Hall of Fame]. MCA: MCAD-10090 (Decca). 1934–54.

5788 Wills, Bob, 1905–1975

5788.1 * *Anthology.* Rhino: 70744. 2CD set. 1935–73.

5788.2 ** *Anthology: 24 greatest hits.* Sony Music Special Products: A 32416. 1935–46.

5788.3 *The essential Bob Wills.* Columbia: CK 48958. 1935–47. [Items 5788.2 and 5788.3 cover similar material].

Post–World War II

Anthologies

5789 *All-time country and western hits.* King/Highland: KCD-537. 1946–53. [Cowboy Copas, Moon Mullican, Bonnie Lou, Grandpa Jones, Delmore Brothers, Reno and Smiley, Wayne Raney, and others].

5790 * *American banjo: three finger and Scruggs style.* Smithsonian/Folkways: SF 40037 (Folkways 2314). 1956.

5791 * *The best of bluegrass, vol. 1: standards.* Mercury: 848979-2. 1948–63. [Stanley Brothers, Carl Story, Lester Flatt and Earl Scruggs, Country Gentlemen, Red Allen, Osborne Brothers, and others].

5792 *Blue ribbon bluegrass.* Rounder: CD AN 11. [1993]. [Cox Family, Nashville Bluegrass Band, Alison Krauss, Ricky Skaggs, Johnson Mountain Boys, Laurie Lewis, Tony Rice, J. D. Crowe, and others].

5793 *The bluegrass album.* Rounder: CD 0140. 1980. [J. D. Crowe, Bobby Hicks, Doyle Lawson, Todd Phillips, Tony Rice].

5794 * *Columbia country classics, vol. 2: honky tonk heroes.* Columbia: CK 46030. 1946–62. [Floyd Tillman, George Morgan, Carl Smith, Ray Price, and others].

5795 *Hank Williams songbook.* Columbia: CK 47995. 1946–60. [Molly O'Day, Jimmy Dickens, Ray Price, Anita Carter, Marty Robbins, Carl Smith, Johnny Cash, and others].

5796 ** *Hills and home: thirty years of bluegrass.* New World: NW 225. LP. 1946–76. [Bill Monroe, Lester Flatt and Earl Scruggs, Stanley Brothers, Reno and Smiley, Mac Wiseman, Bill Clifton, Jimmy Martin, Jim and Jesse, Osborne Brothers, Country Gentlemen, New Grass Revival, and others]. OP

5797 *Mountain music, bluegrass style.* Smithsonian/Folkways: SF 40038 (Folkways FA 2318). 1960. [Don Stover, Tex Logan, Chubby Anthony, Earl Taylor].

5798 *The outlaws.* RCA: 5976-2-R (1321). [1976]. [Waylon Jennings, Willie Nelson, Jessi Colter, Tompall Glaser].

5799 *Traditions in country music.* Capitol: 98669. 1945–58. [Tex Ritter, Merle Travis, Cliffie Stone, Jimmy Wakely, Leon Payne, Tennessee Ernie Ford, Hank Thompson, Ferlin Husky, Louvin Brothers, Sonny James, Faron Young, and others].

5800 *Will the circle be unbroken?* EMI: 46589 (UA 9801). 2CD set. 1972. [Nitty Gritty Dirt Band, Doc Watson, Roy Acuff, Maybelle Carter, Merle Travis, Earl Scruggs, and others].

Individual Artists or Groups

5801 Alabama
Greatest hits. RCA: PCD1-7170. 1980–86.

5802 * Anderson, John, 1954–
Greatest hits. Warner Bros.: 25169-2. 1979–83.

5803 Arnold, Eddy, 1918–
Best of Eddy Arnold. RCA: 3675-2-R. 1946–66.

5804 Bandy, Moe, 1944–
Greatest hits. Columbia: CK 38315. 1975–81.

5805 Black, Clint, 1962–
Killin' time. RCA: 9668-2-R. 1989.

5806 Brooks, Garth, 1962–
Garth Brooks. Liberty: 90897. 1989.

5807 Byrds
Sweetheart of the rodeo. Columbia: CK 9670. 1968.

5808 Campbell, Glen, 1936–
Very best of Glen Campbell. Liberty: 46483. 1967–77.

5809 Carpenter, Mary-Chapin, 1958–
Come on come on. Columbia: CK 48881. 1992.

5810 Cash, Johnny, 1932–
5810.1 * *Columbia records 1958–1986.* Columbia: CGK 40637. 1958–86. [Item 5810.2 covers material comparable to item 5810.1 but in greater depth and with better packaging and notes].
5810.2 *The essential Johnny Cash.* Columbia: C3K 47991. 3CD set. 1955–83.
5810.3 ** *Sun years.* Rhino: 70950. 1955–58.

5811 Cash, Rosanne, 1955–
Hits 1979–1989. Columbia: CK 45054. 1979–89.

5812 Cline, Patsy, 1932–1963
5812.1 ** *Greatest hits.* MCA: MCAD-12 (Decca). 1957–63. [Item 5812.2 covers material comparable to item 5812.1 but in greater depth and with better packaging and notes].
5812.2 * *The Patsy Cline collection.* MCA: MCAD4-10421 (Decca). 4CD set. 1954–63.

5813 Country Gentlemen
Country songs, old and new. Smithsonian/Folkways: SF 40004. 1959.

5814 Crowe, J. D., 1937–
J. D. Crowe and the New South. Rounder: CD 0044. 1975.

5815 * Delmore Brothers
Freight train boogie. Ace: CDCH 455 (King). 1946–52.

5816 Dillards
There is a time. Vanguard: VCD 131/132. 1963–70.

5817 Dylan, Bob, 1941–
Nashville skyline. Columbia: CK 9825. 1969.

5818 Ely, Joe, 1947–
Honky tonk masquerade. MCA: MCAD-10220 (2333). 1978.

5819 Everly Brothers. *See* 5544

5820 Flatt, Lester, 1914–1979, Earl Scruggs, 1924– , and the Foggy Mountain Boys
5820.1 * *The complete Mercury sessions.* Mercury: 314 512644-2. 1948–50.

5820.2 *Foggy Mountain banjo.* Sony Music Special Products: A 23392 (CS 8364). 1961.

5820.3 ** *The golden era.* Rounder: CD SS 05 (Columbia). 1950–55.

5821 * Foley, Red, 1910–1968
Red Foley. [Series: Country Music Hall of Fame]. MCA: MCAD-10084 (Decca). 1944–53.

5822 Ford, Tennessee Ernie, 1919–1991
5822.1 *16 tons of boogie: the best of Tennessee Ernie Ford.* Rhino: 70975 (Capitol). 1949–55. [Items 5822.1 and 5822.2 cover similar material].

5822.2 *Tennessee Ernie Ford.* [Series: Capitol collectors]. Capitol: 95291. 1949–65. OP

5823 ** Frizzell, Lefty, 1928–1975
The best of Lefty Frizzell. Rhino: 71005 (Columbia). 1950–65.

5824 Gibson, Don, 1928–
All-time greatest hits. RCA: 2295-2-R. 1957–66.

5825 Gill, Vince, 1957–
When I call your name. MCA: MCAD-42321. 1989.

5826 * Gosdin, Vern, 1934–
Chiseled in stone. Columbia: CK 40982. 1987.

5827 Haggard, Merle, 1937–
5827.1 ** *Merle Haggard.* [Series: Capitol collectors.] Capitol: 93191. 1965–76.

5827.2 *More of the best.* Rhino: 70917 (Capitol/MCA). 1963–81.

5828 Harris, Emmylou, 1949–
5828.1 *At the Ryman.* Reprise: 26664-2. 1992.

5828.2 ** *Profile: the best of Emmylou Harris.* Warner Bros.: 3258-2. 1974–77.

5829 Horton, Johnny, 1929–1960
American originals. Columbia: CK 45071. 1956–61.

5830 Jackson, Alan, 1958–
Here in the real world. Arista: ARCD-8623. 1989.

5831 Jackson, Stonewall, 1932–
Dynamic Stonewall Jackson. Sony Music Special Products: A-8186 (CL1391). 1959.

5832 Jackson, Wanda, 1937–
Rockin' in the country: the best of Wanda Jackson. Rhino: 70990 (Capitol). 1957–70.

5833 * Jennings, Waylon, 1937–
Waylon Jennings: collector's series. RCA: 07863-58400-2. 1972–82.

5834 * Johnson Mountain Boys
At the old schoolhouse. Rounder: CD 0260/0261. 2CD set. 1988.

5835 Jones, George, 1931–
5835.1 * *Anniversary: ten years of hits.* Epic: EGK 38323. 1972–82.

5835.2 ** *The best of George Jones.* Rhino: 70531. 1955–67.

5836 * Jones, George, 1931– , and Tammy Wynette, 1942–
Greatest hits. Epic: EK 34716. 1971–77.

5837 Judds
Greatest hits. RCA: 8318-2-R. 1984–88.

5838 * Kentucky Colonels
Appalachian swing! Rounder: CD SS 31 (World Pacific). 1964.

5839 Krauss, Alison, 1971–
Every time you say goodbye. Rounder: CD 0285. 1992.

5840 lang, k.d. (Kathy Dawn), 1961–
Shadowland. Sire: 25724-2. 1988.

5841 Lawson, Doyle, 1944– , and Quicksilver
Rock my soul. Sugar Hill: SH-CD-3717. 1981.

5842 Lee, Brenda, 1944–
Anthology, vols. 1–2. MCA: MCAD2-10384. 2CD set. 1956–80.

5843 Lewis, Jerry Lee, 1935–
Killer: the Mercury years, vol. 1. Mercury: 836935-2. 1963–68.

5844 * Louvin Brothers
When I stop dreaming: the best of the Louvin Brothers. Razor & Tie: RAZCD-2068 (Capitol). 1952–62.

5845 Loveless, Patty, 1957–
Up against my heart. MCA: MCAD-10336. 1991.

5846 ** Lynn, Loretta, 1935–
Loretta Lynn. [Series: Country Music Hall of Fame]. MCA: MCAD-10083 (Decca). 1961–76.

5847 * Lynn, Loretta, 1935– , and Conway Twitty, 1933–1993

Very best of Loretta Lynn and Conway Twitty. MCA: MCAD-31236 (937). 1971–78.

5848   Maddox Brothers and Rose

America's most colorful hillbilly band: their original recordings, vol. 1. Arhoolie: CD 391 (Four Star). 1946–51.

5849 * Martin, Jimmy, 1927–

You don't know my mind. Rounder: CD SS 21 (Decca). 1956–66.

5850   McEntire, Reba, 1955–

5850.1 *The best of Reba McEntire.* Mercury: 824342-2. 1980–83.

5850.2 *Greatest hits.* MCA: MCAD-5979. 1984–87.

5851   Miller, Roger, 1936–1992

Golden hits. Mercury: 826261-2. 1964–66.

5852   Monroe, Bill, 1911–1996

5852.1 *Bill Monroe.* [Series: Country Music Hall of Fame]. MCA: MCAD-10082 (Decca). 1950–88. OP

5852.2 ** *The essential Bill Monroe and his Blue Grass Boys.* Columbia: C2K 52478. 2CD set. 1945–49.

5852.3 *In the pines.* County: 114 (Decca). 1950–53.

5852.4 *Mule skinner blues.* RCA: 2494-2-R. 1940–41. OP

5852.5 * *The music of Bill Monroe 1936–1994.* MCA: MCAD4-11048. 4CD set. 1936–94.

5853   Nashville Bluegrass Band

The boys are back in town. Sugar Hill: SH-CD-3778. 1990.

5854   Nelson, Willie, 1933–

5854.1 *Nite life: greatest hits and rare tracks.* Rhino: 70987. 1959–71.

5854.2 * *Red headed stranger.* Columbia: CK 33482. 1975.

5855   New Grass Revival

Live. Sugar Hill: SH-CD-3771. 1989.

5856   Owens, Buck, 1929–

5856.1 * *The Buck Owens collection.* Rhino: 71016 (Capitol/Warner). 3CD set. 1959–90.

5856.2 ** *Very best of Buck Owens, vol. 1.* Rhino: 71816. 1959–72. [Item 5856.1 covers material comparable to item 5856.2 but in greater depth and with better packaging and notes].

5857 * Parton, Dolly, 1946–

The RCA years. RCA: 07863-66127-2. 2CD set. 1967–86.

5858 ** Parton, Dolly, 1946– , Linda Ronstadt, 1946– , and Emmylou Harris, 1949–

Trio. Warner Bros.: 25491-2. 1987.

5859   Pierce, Webb, 1926–1991

King of the honky-tonk. Country Music Foundation: CMF019-D (Decca). 1952–59.

5860   Price, Ray, 1926–

The essential Ray Price. Columbia: CK 48532. 1951–62.

5861   Pride, Charlie, 1938–

The best of Charlie Pride. RCA: 5968-2-R (LSP 4223). 1966–69.

5862 * Reeves, Jim, 1924–1964

Welcome to my world: the essential Jim Reeves collection. RCA: 07863-66125-2. 2CD set. 1949–64.

5863 * Reno, Don, 1927–1984, and Red Smiley, 1925–1972

Don Reno and Red Smiley and the Tennessee Cut-ups: the early years. King/Highland Music: KBSCD-7001. 4CD set. 1951–59.

5864   Riders in the Sky

Best of the West. Rounder: CD 11517. 1980–83.

5865   Ritter, Tex, 1905–1974

Tex Ritter. [Series: Capitol collectors]. Capitol: 95036. 1942–73. OP

5866 * Robbins, Marty, 1925–1982

The essential Marty Robbins. Columbia: C2K 48537. 2CD set. 1951–82.

5867   Seldom Scene

The Seldom Scene live at the Cellar Door. Rebel: CD-1103. 1974.

5868 * Skaggs, Ricky, 1954–

Waitin' for the sun to shine. Epic: EK 37193. 1981.

5869   Smith, Carl, 1927–

The essential Carl Smith. Columbia: CK 47996. 1950–56.

5870 ** Snow, Hank, 1914–

I'm movin' on and other great country hits. RCA: 9968-2-R. 1949–56.

5871 Stanley Brothers

5871.1 ** *Angel band: the classic Mercury recordings.* Mercury: 314 528191-2. 1953–57.

5871.2 * *The early Starday King years 1958–1961.* Starday/King/Highland Music: KBSCD-7000. 4CD set. 1958–61.

5871.3 *The Stanley Brothers: Stanley series, vol. 3, no. 4.* Copper Creek: CCCD-5512. 1958.

5872 Statler Brothers

Best of the Statler Brothers, vol. 1. Mercury: 822524-2. 1970–75.

5873 Stewart, Gary, 1945–

Out of hand. Hightone: HCD 8026 (RCA). 1975.

5874 Strait, George, 1952–

Greatest hits. MCA: MCAD-5567. 1981–84.

5875 Texas Tornados

Texas Tornados. Reprise: 26251-2. 1990. [Freddie Fender, Flaco Jiménez, Augie Meyer, Doug Sahm].

5876 Thompson, Hank, 1925–

Hank Thompson. [Series: Vintage collections]. Capitol Nashville: 36901. 1947–61.

5877 Travis, Merle, 1917–1983

Best of Merle Travis. Rhino: 70993 (Capitol). 1946–53.

5878 * Travis, Randy, 1959–

Storms of life. Warner Bros.: 25435-2. 1986.

5879 * Tubb, Ernest, 1914–1984

Ernest Tubb. [Series: Country Music Hall of Fame]. MCA: MCAD-10086 (Decca). 1941–65.

5880 Tucker, Tanya, 1958–

Greatest hits. Columbia: CK 33355. 1972–75.

5881 * Twitty, Conway, 1933–1993

Silver anniversary collection. MCA: MCAD-8035. 1965–89.

5882 Wagoner, Porter, 1930– , and Dolly Parton, 1946–

5882.1 *Porter Wagoner and Dolly Parton.* Lassoes and Spurs: BMG 17269-2 (RCA). [1967–73]. [Items 5882.1 and 5882.2 cover similar material].

5882.2 *Sweet harmony.* Pair: PCD2-1013 (RCA). [1967–72].

5883 Watson, Gene, 1943–

Greatest hits. Curb: 77393 (Capitol). 1975–80, 1984.

5884 * Wells, Kitty, 1918–

Kitty Wells. [Series: Country Music Hall of Fame]. MCA: MCAD-10081 (Decca). 1952–65.

5885 Williams, Don, 1939–

20 greatest hits. MCA: MCAD-5944. 1973–84.

5886 Williams, Hank, 1923–1953

5886.1 ** *40 greatest hits.* Polydor: 821233-2 (MGM). 2CD set. 1947–53. [Item 5886.2 covers material comparable to item 5886.1 but in greater depth and with better packaging and notes].

5886.2 * *The original singles collection—plus.* Polydor: 847194-2 (MGM). 3CD set. 1947–53.

5887 Williams, Hank, Jr., 1949–

Hank Williams, Jr.'s greatest hits. Warner Bros./Curb: 60193-2. 1979–81.

5888 Wiseman, Mac, 1925–

Early Dot recordings, vol. 3. MCA/County: CCS-CD-113. 1952–54.

5889 Wynette, Tammy, 1942–

5889.1 ** *Anniversary: twenty years of hits.* Epic: EGK 40625. 1966–80. [Item 5889.2 covers material comparable to item 5889.1 but in greater depth and with better packaging and notes].

5889.2 * *Tears of fire: the 25th anniversary collection.* Epic: E3K 52741. 3CD set. 1964–91.

5890 Yoakam, Dwight, 1954–

Guitars, Cadillacs, etc., etc. Reprise: 25372-2. 1986.

5891 Young, Faron, 1932–

Live fast, love hard: original Capitol recordings. Country Music Foundation: CMF-020D. 1952–62.

Gospel and Other Popular Christian Music

Compiled by
William E. Anderson

T his chapter covers gospel and other popular Christian music of twentieth-century America in four sections: "General Anthologies," "African American Traditions," "Southern White Traditions," and "Contemporary Christian and Inspirational Music." Throughout its history, popular religious music typically has been recorded by small labels and distributed through Bible stores, by mail order, and at performances, and much of it remains unavailable through the usual commercial sources. Although additional labels have broadened distribution, it may still be difficult to provide balanced coverage of all traditions and styles.

General Anthologies

5892 ** *Brighten the corner where you are: Black and white urban hymnody.* New World: NW 224. LP/AC. 1909–75. [Rosetta Tharpe, Kings of Harmony, Soul Stirrers, Famous Blue Jay Singers, Fairfield Four, Roberta Martin, Willie Mae Ford Smith, Marion Williams, Homer Rodeheaver, George Beverly Shea, and others]. OP

5893 * *The gospel tradition: the roots and the branches, vol. 1.* Columbia: CK 47333. 1927–56. [Blind Willie Johnson, Washington Phillips, Carter Family, Mitchell's Christian Singers, Humbard Family, Charioteers, Chuck Wagon Gang, and others].

African American Traditions (Gospel and Related Styles, 1920s–1990s)

Anthologies

5894 * *All of my appointed time: forty years of a cappella gospel singing.* Mojo: 308 (Jass 640/Stash 114). 1936–76. [Golden Gate Quartet, Kings of Harmony, Blue Jay Singers, Soul Stirrers, Georgia Peach, Bessie Griffin, Golden Harps, Marion Williams].

5895 *Amazing grace.* Collectables: COL CD-5336 (Gotham). 1949–55. [Harmonizing Four, Edna Gallmon Cooke, Davis Sisters, Dixie Hummingbirds, Echo Gospel Singers, and others].

5896 *Atlanta gospel.* Gospel Heritage: HT 312. LP. 1946–52. [Georgia Peach, Five Trumpets, Reliable Jubilee Singers, and others].

5897 * *The best of Nashboro gospel.* Nashboro: 4001. 1951–68. [Angelic Gospel Singers, Consolers, Edna Gallmon Cooke, Swanee Quintet, Fairfield Four, Supreme Angels, and others].

5898 * *Birmingham quartet anthology.* Clanka Lanka: 144.001/002. 2LP set. 1926–53. [Birmingham Jubilee Singers, Famous Blue Jay Singers, CIO Singers, Heavenly Gospel Singers, Ravizee Singers, and others].

5899 * *Black gospel singing (A capella gospel singing/ The golden age of gospel singing).* Folklyric/Arhoolie: C 223 (9045/9046). AC. 1936–54. [Georgia Peach, Alphabetical Four, Dixie Hummingbirds, Heavenly Gospel Singers, Spirit of Memphis Quartet, Bessie Griffin, Davis Sisters, Five Blind Boys of Mississippi, and others].

5900 * *Black nativity: gospel on Broadway.* Vee-Jay: NVG2-501 (5022). 1961. [Alex Bradford, Marion Williams, Stars of Faith, and others].

5901 * *Bless my bones—Memphis gospel radio, the fifties.* Rounder: 2063. AC. 1948–72. [Songbirds of the South, Spirit of Memphis Quartet, Brewster-aires, Queen C. Anderson, Southern Wonders, and others].

5902 *Cleveland gospel.* Gospel Heritage: HT 316. LP. [194?]–1958. [Elite Jewels, Friendly Brothers, Shield Brothers, National Kings of Harmony, and others].

5903 *The earliest Negro vocal quartets.* Document: DOCD-5061. 1894–1928. [Dinwiddie Colored Quartet, Old South Quartet, Apollo Male Quartet, and others].

5904 ** *Father and sons.* Spirit Feel: SFD-1001. 1939–55. [R. H. Harris, Soul Stirrers, Five Blind Boys of Mississippi, Sensational Nightingales].

5905 *Get right with God: hot gospel.* Gospel Heritage: HT CD 01. 1947–53. [Radio Four, National Independent Gospel Singers, Five Blind Boys of Mississippi, Southern Harmonaires, and others].

5906 *Glad I found the Lord: Chicago gospel.* Gospel Heritage: HT CD 08. 1937–47. [Famous Blue Jay Singers, Golden Eagle Gospel Singers, Gospel Songbirds, Norfleet Brothers, Heavenly Kings, and others].

5907 * *Good news.* Charly: CDCHARLY 98 (Vee-Jay). 1954–64. [Caravans, Five Blind Boys of Mississippi, Harmonizing Four, Highway QCs, Staple Singers, Swan Silvertones, and others].

5908 ** *The gospel sound.* Columbia: C2K 57160 (31086). 2CD set. 1926–68. [Blind Willie Johnson, Golden Gate Quartet, Arizona Dranes, Mitchell's Christian Singers, Rev. J. M. Gates, Dorothy Love Coates, Mahalia Jackson, Marion Williams, Staple Singers, Abyssinian Baptist Choir, Dixie Hummingbirds, Angelic Gospel Singers].

5909 * *The gospel sound, vol. 2.* Columbia: 31595. 2LP set. 1928–66. [Blind Willie Johnson, Golden Gate Quartet, Arizona Dranes, Mitchell's Christian Singers, Rev. J. M. Gates, Dorothy Love Coates, Mahalia Jackson, Pilgrim Travelers, Marion Williams, Staple Singers, Bessie Griffin, R. H. Harris, and others]. OP

5910 ** *The gospel sound of Spirit Feel.* Spirit Feel: 1012. 1947–86. [Rosetta Tharpe, Mahalia Jackson, Soul Stirrers, Robert Anderson, Ernestine Washington, Roberta Martin, Spirit of Memphis, Jessie Mae Renfro, Dixie Hummingbirds, Clara Ward, Sensational Nightingales, Fairfield Four, Consolers, Marion Williams, and others].

5911 * *Gospel warriors: over 50 years of great solo performances.* Spirit Feel: SFD-1003. 1931–82. [Rosetta Tharpe, Georgia Peach, Clara Ward, Marion Williams, Bessie Griffin, Frances Steadman, and others].

5912 * *The great gospel men.* Spirit Feel/Shanachie: 6005. 1947–86. [Brother Joe May, Norsalus McKissick, Robert Anderson, J. Robert Bradley, Alex Bradford, J. Earle Hines, Eugene Smith, James Cleveland, R. L. Knowles].

5913 * *The great gospel women.* Spirit Feel/ Shanachie: 6004. 1939–91. [Mahalia Jackson, Willie Mae Ford Smith, Rosetta Tharpe, Marion Williams, Clara Ward, Cora Martin, Dorothy Love Coates, Roberta Martin, Marie Knight, Frances Steadman, and others].

5914 * *The great 1955 Shrine concert.* Specialty: SPCD-7045-2. 1955. [Pilgrim Travelers, Caravans, Joe May, Soul Stirrers, Dorothy Love Coates and the Original Gospel Harmonettes, and others].

5915 ** *Greatest gospel gems.* Specialty: SPCD-7206-2. 1948–58. [Soul Stirrers, Alex Bradford, Swan Silvertones, Chosen Gospel Singers, Gospel

Harmonettes, Five Blind Boys of Alabama, Joe May, Pilgrim Travelers, Robert Anderson, Wynona Carr, and others].

5916 ** *I hear music in the air: a treasury of gospel music.* RCA: 2099-2-R. 1926–42. [Rev. J. M. Gates, Golden Gate Quartet, Heavenly Gospel Singers, Southern Sons, and others].

5917 *Jesus put a song in my soul.* Gospel Heritage: HT CD 10. 1948–58. [Clara Ward, Selah Jubilee Singers, Friendly Brothers, and others].

5918 ** *Jubilation!: great gospel performances, vol. 1: Black gospel.* Rhino: 70288. 1937–75. [Mahalia Jackson, Roberta Martin, Angelic Gospel Singers, Golden Gate Quartet, Georgia Peach, Soul Stirrers, Clara Ward, Swan Silvertones, James Cleveland, Dixie Hummingbirds, Shirley Caesar, Pilgrim Travelers, Edwin Hawkins, and others].

5919 ** *Jubilation!: great gospel performances, vol. 2: more Black gospel.* Rhino: 70289. 1938–64. [Soul Stirrers, Mahalia Jackson, Davis Sisters, Caravans, Alex Bradford, Staple Singers, Five Blind Boys of Mississippi, Swan Silvertones, Gospel Harmonettes, and others].

5920 * *Jubilee to gospel: a selection of commercially recorded Black religious music.* JEMF: 108. LP. 1921–53. [Wings over Jordan, Utica Institute Jubilee Singers, Birmingham Jubilee Singers, Golden Gate Quartet, Norfolk Jazz Quartet, Famous Blue Jay Singers, Heavenly Gospel Singers, Georgia Peach, Alphabetical Four, Selah Jubilee Singers, Fairfield Four, and others].

5921 * *Malaco's greatest gospel hits, vol. 1.* Malaco: MAL 6004 CD. [1989]. [Florida Mass Choir, Vanessa Bell Armstrong, Williams Brothers, Willie Banks, Keith Pringle, Jackson Southernaires, and others].

5922 * *Mother Smith and her children.* Spirit Feel: SFD-1010. 1950–87. [Willie Mae Ford Smith, Martha Bass, Joe May, Edna Gallmon Cooke].

5923 *Negro religious songs and services.* Library of Congress: L 10. AC. 1936–42.

5924 *New Orleans gospel quartets.* Gospel Heritage: HT CD 12. 1947–56. [Jackson Gospel Singers, New Orleans Humming Four, Zion Harmonizers, Southern Harps, and others].

5925 *None but the righteous: Chess gospel greats.* Chess: CHD-9336. 1951–72. [Aretha Franklin, Soul Stirrers, Violinaires, Martha Bass, and others].

5926 *On one accord: singing and praying bands of Tidewater, Maryland and Delaware.* Global Village Music: CD 225. 1986–91.

5927 *One in the spirit: the ladies of gospel.* Starsong: SSD 8202. [1991]. [Clark Sisters, Barrett Sisters, Tramaine Hawkins, Albertina Walker, Shirley Caesar, and others].

5928 * *Preachin' the gospel: holy blues.* Columbia: CK 46779. 1927–53. [Blind Willie Johnson, Arizona Dranes, Washington Phillips, and others].

5929 * *Precious Lord: new recordings of the great gospel songs of Thomas A. Dorsey.* Columbia: CK 57164 (CG 32151). [1973]. [Bessie Griffin, Marion Williams, Alex Bradford, Delois Barrett Campbell, R. H. Harris, Sallie Martin, Thomas A. Dorsey].

5930 * *Say amen, somebody: music from the original soundtrack and more.* DRG: CDXP-12584. [1983]. [Thomas A. Dorsey, Sallie Martin, Willie Mae Ford Smith, Barrett Sisters, O'Neal Twins, and others].

5931 ** *Stars of the gospel highway.* Spirit Feel: 1008. AC. 1947–56. [Roberta Martin Singers, Original Gospel Harmonettes, Davis Sisters].

5932 *The storm is passing over: reverends and their congregations post-war gospel.* Global Village Music: C 203. AC. 1947–51. [Rev. Samuel Kelsey, Rev. R. A. Daniels, Rev. W. M. Rimson, Rev. Benjamin H. Brodie].

5933 *Wade in the water, vol. 1: African American spirituals: the concert tradition.* Smithsonian/Folkways: SFW CD 40072. 1993.

5934 *Wade in the water, vol. 2: African American congregational singing: 19th century roots.* Smithsonian/Folkways: SFW CD 40073. 1989, 1992.

5935 *Wade in the water, vol. 3: African American gospel: the pioneering composers.* Smithsonian/Folkways: SFW CD 40074. 1992–93. [Thomas A. Dorsey, Roberta Martin, Charles A. Tindley, and others].

5936 *Wade in the water, vol. 4: African American community gospel.* Smithsonian/Folkways: SFW CD 40075. 1992–93.

Individual Artists or Groups

5937 * Abyssinian Baptist Gospel Choir
Shakin' the rafters. Columbia: CK 47335 (CS 8348). 1960.

5938 Allen, Rance

The best of the Rance Allen Group. Stax: SCD-8540-2 (Gospel Truth). 1971–79.

5939 Andrews, Inez, 1929–

5939.1 *Lord don't move the mountain.* MCA Special Products: MCAC-20651 (ABC/Songbird). AC. 1972.

5939.2 *The two sides of Inez Andrews.* Spirit Feel/Shanachie: 6019 (1006). [1989].

5940 Angelic Gospel Singers

5940.1 *The best of the Angelic Gospel Singers.* Nashboro: 4509. 1955–64.

5940.2 * *Touch me Lord Jesus.* Gospel Heritage: HT CD 11 (Gotham). 1949–55.

5941 * Armstrong, Vanessa Bell, 1953–

Greatest hits. Muscle Shoals Sound: MSCD 8012. [1991].

5942 Bailey, Philip, 1951–

The best of Philip Bailey: a gospel collection. Word/Epic: EK 77004. 1984–89.

5943 Baylor, Helen

Highly recommended. Word/Epic: EK 47763. 1990.

5944 * Bradford, Alex, 1927–1978

Too close. Specialty: SPCD-7042-2. 1953–58.

5945 Broadnax, Wilbur, 1916–

Little axe: so many years. Gospel Jubilee: 1403. LP. [194?–195?].

5946 Brownlee, Archie, and the Five Blind Boys of Mississippi

You done what the doctor couldn't do. Gospel Jubilee: RBD 1402. 1948–59.

5947 Brunson, Milton, and the Thompson Community Singers

If I be lifted. Word/Epic: EK 48791 (Rejoice). 1987.

5948 ** Caesar, Shirley, 1938–

Her very best. Word/Epic: EK 47806. 1979–87.

5949 Caravans

5949.1 ** *The best of the Caravans.* Savoy: 7012. AC. 1952–58. [Albertina Walker, Cassietta George, Dorothy Norwood, Inez Andrews, Shirley Caesar, and others].

5949.2 *Seek ye the Lord/The soul of the Caravans.* Vee-Jay: NGV2-608 (5026/5038). 1962–63. [Albertina Walker, Cassietta George, Shirley Caesar, and others].

5950 Chosen Gospel Singers

The lifeboat. Specialty: SPCD-7014-2. 1952–55.

5951 * Clark, Mattie Moss

The best of the Southwest Michigan State Choir of the Church of God in Christ. Savoy: 7032. AC. [1979].

5952 * Clark Sisters

Is my living in vain: the dynamic Clark Sisters with Mattie Moss Clark. Sony Music Special Products: A 22145 (New Birth 7056). [198?].

5953 Cleveland, James, 1932–1991

5953.1 *Amazing grace.* Savoy: 14260. AC. 1970. [With the Southern California Choir].

5953.2 ** *The best of Rev. James Cleveland and the Gospel Music Workshop of America Mass Choir.* Savoy: SCD 7111. [1993].

5953.3 *I don't feel noways tired.* Savoy: 7024. AC. 1979. [With the Salem Inspirational Choir].

5953.4 ** *Out on a hill.* Savoy: 14045. LP. 1961.

5953.5 * *Peace be still.* Savoy: 14076. LP/AC. 1963.

5954 Coates, Dorothy Love, 1928–

The best of Dorothy Love Coates and the Original Gospel Harmonettes. Specialty: SPCD-7205-2. 1951–56.

5955 Commissioned

Complete: Go tell somebody/I'm going on. Light: 51416-1068-2. 1985–86.

5956 Consolers

The best of the Consolers. Nashboro: CD 4502. 1955–73.

5957 * Davis Sisters

The best of the Davis Sisters. Savoy: 7017. AC. 1955–68.

5958 Dixie Hummingbirds

5958.1 ** *The best of the Dixie Hummingbirds.* MCA Special Products: MCAD-22043 (Peacock 138). 1953–66.

5958.2 *Complete recorded works 1939–1947 in chronological order.* Document: 5491 (Decca/Apollo). 1939–47.

5959 Dixon, Jessy, 1938–

I know what prayer can do. Word/Epic: EK 47789. [1989].

5960   Fairfield Four

Standing on the rock. Ace: CDCHD 449 (Dot). 1949–54.

5961   Five Blind Boys of Alabama

Oh Lord stand by me/Marching up to Zion. Specialty: SPCD-7203-2. 1953–58.

5962 *   Five Blind Boys of Mississippi

The best of the Five Blind Boys of Mississippi. MCA Special Products: MCAD-22047 (Peacock 139). 1951–61.

5963   Florida Mass Choir

Lord you keep on proving yourself to me. Savoy: 7078. AC. 1982.

5964 **   Franklin, Aretha, 1942– , and James Cleveland, 1932–1991

Amazing grace. Atlantic: 906-2. 2CD set. 1972.

5965   Georgia Mass Choir

Hold on, help is on the way. Savoy: 7098. 1989.

5966   Golden Gate Quartet

5966.1 *Swing down chariot.* Columbia: CK 47131. 1941–50.

5966.2 * *Travelin' shoes.* RCA Bluebird: 66063-2. 1937–39.

5967   Gospel Music Workshop of America Mass Choir

Recorded 'live' in Cleveland, Ohio. Savoy: 7004. AC. 1975.

5968   Gospelaires of Dayton, Ohio

Can I get a witness/Bones in the valley. Mobile Fidelity: MFCD-763 (Peacock). 1961–68.

5969   Green, Al, 1946–

5969.1 * *One in a million.* Word/Epic: EK 77000. 1980–84.

5969.2 *Soul survivor.* A&M: 75021-5150-2. 1987.

5970   Griffin, Bessie, 1923–1990

Even me. Spirit Feel: 1009. AC. 1948–87.

5971   Harmonizing Four

The Harmonizing Four/God will take care of you. Vee-Jay: NVG2-604 (5002/5009). 1957–59.

5972   Hawkins, Edwin, 1943–

5972.1 * *Music and Arts Seminar Chicago Choir.* Fixit: CDF-9205. 1991.

5972.2 *Oh happy day.* Buddah: 75517-49512-2 (Pavillion). 1969.

5973 **   Hawkins, Walter, 1949–

Love alive. CGI: 51416-1012-2 (Light 5686). 1975.

5974   Highway QCs

Jesus is waiting. Vee-Jay: NVG2-603 (5005/5007). 1955–60.

5975   Jackson, Mahalia, 1911–1972

5975.1 ** *The Apollo sessions, 1946–1951.* Pair: PCD-2-1332 (Apollo). 1946–51.

5975.2 *Bless this house.* Columbia: PCT 8761 (CL 899). AC. 1956.

5975.3 * *Gospels, spirituals, and hymns.* Columbia: C2K 47083. 2CD set. 1954–67.

5975.4 *Mahalia Jackson, vol. 2* Columbia: C2K 48924. 2CD set. 1954–69.

5976   Jackson Southernaires

Greatest hits. Malaco: 4402. [1976–85].

5977 *   Johnson, Blind Willie, 1902–1949

The complete Blind Willie Johnson. Columbia: C2K 52835. 2CD set. 1927–30.

5978   Kee, John P., and the New Life Community Choir

Wait on him. Verity: 01241-43003-2 (Tyscot 89415). 1989.

5979   Los Angeles Mass Choir

Can't hold back. CGI: 51416-1013-2. 1990.

5980   Martin, Roberta, 1907–1969

5980.1 * *The best of the Roberta Martin Singers.* Savoy: 7018. AC. 1957–66.

5980.2 ** *The old ship of Zion.* Kenwood: 507 (Apollo). LP. 1949–55. OP

5981   Martin, Sallie, 1896–1988, and Cora Martin, 1927–

Throw out the lifeline. Specialty: SPCD-7043-2. 1950–52.

5982   May, Brother Joe, 1912–1972

Thunderbolt of the Middle West. Specialty: SPCD-7033-2. 1952–55.

5983   Meditation Singers

Good news. Specialty: SPCD-7032-2. 1953–59.

5984 * Mighty Clouds of Joy

The best of the Mighty Clouds of Joy, vol. 1. MCA Special Products: MCAD-22045 (Peacock 136). 1960–66.

5985 Mississippi Mass Choir

Mississippi Mass Choir: live in Jackson, Mississippi. Malaco: 6008. 1990.

5986 New Jersey Mass Choir

At their best. CGI: 51416-1016-2 (Light 7-115-74040-2). 1991.

5987 New Jerusalem Baptist Church Choir

Show me the way. Sound of Gospel: SOG-2D160C. AC. 1987.

5988 Norfolk Jubilee Quartet

Norfolk Jubilee Quartet. Gospel Heritage: HT 310. LP. 1927–38.

5989 Norwood, Dorothy, 1930–

The denied mother. Savoy: 14140. LP/AC. 1965.

5990 Phillips, Washington, 1891–1938

I am born to preach the gospel. Yazoo: 2003. 1927–29.

5991 Pilgrim Travelers

The best of the Pilgrim Travelers. Specialty: SPCD-7204-2. 1948–56.

5992 * Sensational Nightingales

The best of the Sensational Nightingales. MCA Special Products: MCAD-22044 (Peacock 137). 1956–66.

5993 Silver Leaf Quartet

Complete recorded works in chronological order. Document: DOCD 5352. 1928–31.

5994 Smallwood, Richard, 1948–

Richard Smallwood Singers: portrait. Word/Epic: EK 48559. [1991].

5995 Smith, Harold, and the Majestics

James Cleveland presents Harold Smith and the Majestics: Lord, help me to hold out. Savoy: 14319. AC. 1973.

5996 Soul Stirrers

5996.1 *Gospel music.* Vivid: VSCD 506 (Aladdin). 1947–48.

5996.2 *Jesus gave me water.* Specialty: SPCD-7031-2. 1951–55.

5996.3 ** *Sam Cooke with the Soul Stirrers.* Specialty: SPCD-7009-2. 1951–57.

5996.4 * *Shine on me.* Specialty: SPCD-7013-2. 1950.

5997 Spirit of Memphis

When Mother's gone. Gospel Jubilee: 1404. LP. 1948–58.

5998 Staple Singers

5998.1 *Freedom highway.* Columbia: CK 47334. 1964–66.

5998.2 * *Uncloudy day/Will the circle be unbroken.* Vee-Jay: NVG2-600 (5000/5008). 1955–60.

See also 5325

5999 Stars of Faith

Gospel songs. Savoy: 14024. LP. 1958. OP

6000 Swan Silvertones

6000.1 *Gospel soul.* King: KBGCD 468. 1946–51.

6000.2 * *Love lifted me/My rock.* Specialty: SPCD-7202-2. 1952–53.

6000.3 ** *Swan Silvertones/Singin' in my soul.* Vee-Jay: NVG2-609 (5003/5006). 1956–60.

6001 Swanee Quintet

The best of the Swanee Quintet. Nashboro: CD 4503. 1953–66.

6002 * Tharpe, Sister Rosetta, 1915–1973

Complete recorded works, 1938–1944, vols. 1–2. Document: DOCD 5334; DOCD 5335 (Decca). 2 CDs. 1938–44.

6003 Trumpeteers

Milky white way. Gospel Jubilee: 1401-2. 1949–52.

6004 Vails, Donald, 1947– , and the Donald Vails Choraleers

What a wonderful savior I've found. Savoy: 7025. 1979.

6005 * Walker, Albertina, 1930– , with James Cleveland, 1943–

Please be patient with me. Savoy: 14527. AC. 1980.

6006 ** Ward Singers

The best of the famous Ward Singers. Savoy: 7015. AC. 1948–64.

6007 West Angeles C.O.G.I.C. Mass Choir

Saints in praise: their very best. Sparrow: SPD 1572. [1996].

6008 Williams, Marion, 1927–1994

6008.1 *If we ever needed the Lord before.* Columbia: CK 48951. 1965, 1973.

6008.2 * *My soul looks back: the genius of Marion Williams.* Spirit Feel/Shanachie: 6011. 1962–92.

6009 * Williams, Marion, 1927–1994, and the Stars of Faith

God and me. Vee-Jay: NVG2-610 (5024/5031). 1962–63.

6010 Williams Brothers

Greatest hits, vol. 1. Malaco: 4451. [1991].

6011 Winans

Return. Quest/Warner Bros.: 26161-2. 1990.

6012 Winans, Bebe, and Cece Winans

Heaven. Capitol: 90959. 1988.

6013 Wiregrass Sacred Harp Singers

The colored Sacred Harp. New World: 80433-2. 1993.

Southern White Traditions (1920s–1990s)

Anthologies

6014 *Children of the heavenly king: religious expression in the Central Blue Ridge.* Library of Congress: L69/L70. 2AC set. 1978–79.

6015 ** *The gospel ship: Baptist hymns and white spirituals from the Southern mountains.* New World: 80294-2. 1977. [Field recordings made by Alan Lomax in Kentucky, Virginia, and Arkansas].

6016 *Jubilation!: great gospel performances, vol. 3: country gospel.* Rhino: 70290. 1929–81. [Hank Williams, Lester Flatt and Earl Scruggs, Kitty Wells, Louvin Brothers, Carter Family, Roy Acuff, Martha Carson, Bill Monroe, Ernest Tubb, Doyle Lawson, Ricky Scaggs, and others].

6017 *Primitive Baptist hymns of the Blue Ridge.* University of North Carolina Press: 0-8078-4083-1. LP. 1976.

6018 *Sacred Harp singing.* Library of Congress Recording Laboratory: AFS L11. AC. 1942. [Recorded by George Pullen Jackson and Alan Lomax in 1942 in Birmingham, Alabama].

6019 * *Something got a hold of me: a treasury of sacred music.* RCA: 2100-2-R. 1927–41. [Carter Family, Monroe Brothers, Blue Sky Boys, Dixon Brothers, Blind Alfred Reed, Wade Mainer, Uncle Dave Macon, and others].

Individual Artists or Groups

6020 * Alabama Sacred Harp Convention

White spirituals from the Sacred Harp. New World: 80205-2. 1959.

6021 * Blackwood Brothers Quartet

The best of the Blackwood Brothers Quartet. RCA: 07863-61090-4. [1992].

6022 * Cathedrals

Masters of gospel. Heartwarming/Benson: 84418-2876-2. [1992].

6023 Chuck Wagon Gang

Columbia historic edition. Columbia: PCT 40152. AC. 1936–60.

6024 Florida Boys

Together. Canaan/Word: 701 9955 533. 1986.

6025 Ford, Tennessee Ernie, 1919–1991

Country gospel classics, vol. 1. Capitol: 95849. [1991].

6026 Kingsmen

Masters of gospel. Riversong/Benson: 84418-2880-2. 1977–87.

6027 Old Harp Singers of Eastern Tennessee

Old Harp singing. Smithsonian/Folkways: 2356. AC. 1951.

6028 Presley, Elvis, 1935–1977

Elvis gospel: known only to him. RCA: 9586-2-R. 1957–71.

6029 Speers

Masters of gospel. Riversong/Benson: 84418-2929-2. 1970–86.

6030 Statesmen Quartet

The best of the Statesmen Quartet. RCA: 07863-61094-4. AC. [1992].

6031 West, Harry, 1926– , and Jeanie West, 1933–
Favorite gospel songs. Smithsonian/Folkways:
2357. AC. [1957].

Contemporary Christian and Inspirational Music (1960s–1990s)

6032 Ashton, Susan, 1967–
Angels of mercy. Sparrow: SPD-1327. 1992.

6033 Becker, Margaret, 1959–
Steps of faith. Sparrow: SPD-1354. 1987–91.

6034 Carman, 1956–
The absolute best. Sparrow: SPD-1339. [1993].

6035 * Chapman, Steven Curtis, 1962–
For the sake of the call. Sparrow: SPD-1258. 1990.

6036 Crouch, Andrae, 1942–
6036.1 * *Andrae Crouch, vol. 1: the classics.*
CGI: 51416-1009-2 (711 5750 629). [1991].

6036.2 *This is another day.* CGI: 51416-1053-2
(Light 5683). 1976.

6037 Gaithers
The early works. Benson: 84418-2893-2. 1974–83.

6038 * Grant, Amy, 1960–
The collection. Reunion/BMG: 07863-66258-2
(24340). 1979–86.

6039 Green, Keith, 1953–1982
Ministry years, vol. 1. Sparrow: SPD-1146. 2CD set.
1977–79.

6040 Happy Goodman Family
Goodman greats. Canaan/Word: 701 9889 530. AC.
1982.

6041 * Harris, Larnelle
The best of 10 years, vol. 1. Benson: 84418-2840-2.
[1980–90].

6042 * Imperials
The very best of the Imperials. Dayspring/Word:
701 4025 570. [1981].

6043 Keaggy, Phil
Phil Keaggy and Sunday's child. Myrrh/Word: 701
6876 616. 1988.

6044 Omartian, Michael
White horse/Adam again. Myrrh/Word: 701 6894
614. 1974–75.

6045 * Patti, Sandi, 1956–
Finest moments. Word/Epic: EK 47739. [1978–86].

6046 Peacock, Charlie
Love life. Sparrow: SPD-1303. 1991.

6047 Petra
Petra. Word/Epic: EK 48802. 1974.

6048 2nd Chapter of Acts
20. Sparrow: SPD-1332. 2CD set. 1972–92.

6049 Shea, George Beverly, 1909–
May the good Lord bless and keep you. RCA/
Camden: CAK-2515. AC. [196?].

6050 Smith, Michael W.
The first decade. Reunion/BMG: 07863-66314-2.
1983–93.

6051 Taff, Russ, 1953–
Under their influence. Word/Epic: EK 47733. 1991.
OP

6052 Take 6
Take 6. Reprise: 25670-2. 1988.

28

Musicals and Operettas, Motion Pictures and Television Shows

Compiled by
Kent Underwood

Musicals (Broadway, London, Hollywood) and Operettas

Anthologies

6053 ** *American musical theater: shows, songs, and stars.* Smithsonian: RD 036 (A4 20483). 4CD set. 1906–64. [Chronological survey of classic shows from *The fortune teller* (1898) to *Fiddler on the roof* (1964)].

6054 *Movie musicals, 1927–1936.* ABC: 836 044-2. 1927–36. [Al Jolson, Ginger Rogers, Fred Astaire, Maurice Chevalier, Gloria Swanson, Mae West, and others].

6055 *Music from the New York stage, vols. 1–4.* Pearl: GEMM CDS 9050-9052. 3CD set; GEMM CDS 9053-9055. 3CD set; GEMM CDS 9056-9058. 3CD set; GEMM CDS 9059-9061. 3CD set. 1890–1920.

Individual Shows (by Composer)

Consult the index under *Musicals* for an alphabetical list of shows by title.

6056 ** Arlen, Harold, 1905–1986

The wizard of Oz. (Motion picture soundtrack). Sony: AK 45356. 1939.

6057 Bart, Lionel, 1930–

Oliver! (Original Broadway cast). RCA: 4113-2-RG. 1962.

6058 * Berlin, Irving, 1888–1989

Annie get your gun. (Original Broadway cast). MCA: MCAD-10047. 1946.

6059 Bernstein, Leonard, 1918–1990

6059.1 *Candide.*
- (Original Broadway cast). Sony: SK 48017. 1956.
- (Final revised version; studio cast conducted by the composer). Deutsche Grammophon: 429734-2. 2CD set. 1989.

6059.2 *On the town.*
- (Original Broadway cast). Columbia: CK 2038. 1960.

- (Studio cast conducted by Michael Tilson Thomas). Deutsche Grammophon: 437 516-2. 1992.

6059.3 *A quiet place* [incorporating his *Trouble in Tahiti*]. (Studio cast conducted by the composer). Deutsche Grammophon: 419 761-2. 2CD set. 1986.

**6059.4 ** West side story.*

- (Motion picture soundtrack). Sony: SK 48211. 1960.

- (Original Broadway cast). Sony: CK 32603. 1957.

- (Studio cast conducted by the composer). Deutsche Grammophon: 415 253-2. 2CD set. 1985. [With his *On the waterfront*].

- (Highlights from the studio cast conducted by the composer). Deutsche Grammophon: 415 963-2. 1985.

6060 * Bock, Jerry, 1928–

Fiddler on the roof. (Original Broadway cast). RCA: RCD1-7060. 1964.

6061 * Casey, Warren

Grease. (Original Broadway cast). Polydor: 827 548-2. 1972.

6062 Charlap, Moose, 1928–

Peter Pan. (Original Broadway cast). RCA: 3762-2-RG. 1954.

6063 Coleman, Cy, 1929–

6063.1 *City of angels.* (Original Broadway cast). Columbia: CK 46067. 1990.

6063.2 *Sweet Charity.* (Original Broadway cast). Columbia: CK 2900. 1966.

6063.3 *Wildcat.* (Original Broadway cast). RCA: 60353-2-RG. 1960.

6064 Coward, Noel, 1899–1973

6064.1 *The girl who came to supper.* (Original Broadway cast). Sony: SK 48210. 1963.

6064.2 *The master's voice: his HMV recordings, 1928–1953.* Angel: 0777 7 54919 2. 4CD set. 1928–53.

6064.3 *Sail away.* (Original Broadway cast). Broadway Angel: ZDM 7 64759 2 9. 1961.

6065 * Ellington, Duke, 1899–1974

Sophisticated ladies. (Broadway revival cast). RCA: 07863-56208-2. 1981.

6066 Finn, William

March of the falsettos. (Original cast). DRG: CDSBL 12581. 1981.

6067 Geld, Gary

Shenandoah. (Original Broadway cast). RCA: 3763-2-RG. 1975.

6068 Gershwin, George, 1898–1937

6068.1 *Funny face.* (Motion picture soundtrack). DRG: CDS 15001. 1955.

6068.2 * *Girl crazy.* (Studio cast conducted by John Mauceri). Elektra Nonesuch: 79250-2. 1990.

6068.3 * *Lady be good.* (Studio cast conducted by Eric Stern). Elektra Nonesuch: 79308-2. 1992.

6068.4 *Of thee I sing.* (Broadway revival cast). Broadway Angel: ZDM 7 65025 2 9. 1952.

6068.5 *Oh, Kay!* (Studio cast conducted by Eric Stern). Nonesuch: 79361-2. 1995.

6068.6 *Pardon my English.* (Studio cast conducted by Eric Stern). Elektra Nonesuch: 79338-2. 1994.

**6068.7 ** Porgy and Bess*

- (Original Broadway cast). MCA: MCAD-10520. 1940–42.

- (Houston Grand Opera/John DeMain). RCA: RCD3-2109. 3CD set. 1977.

- (Studio cast conducted by Lorin Maazel). London: 414 559-2. 4CD set. 1976.

- (Studio cast conducted by Simon Rattle). EMI: CDS 7 49568 2. 3CD set. 1989.

6068.8 * *Strike up the band.* (Studio cast conducted by John Mauceri). Elektra Nonesuch: 79273-2. 2CD set. 1991.

6069 Gesner, Clark

You're a good man, Charlie Brown. (Original cast). Polydor: 820 267-2. 1986.

6070 Gilbert and Sullivan. *See* 6100

**6071 ** Hamlisch, Marvin, 1944–

Chorus line. (Original New York Shakespeare Festival cast). Columbia: CK 33581. 1975.

6072 Herbert, Victor, 1856–1924

Music of Victor Herbert. (Various performers). Smithsonian: R 017. 3LP set. 1898–1923. OP

6073 Herman, Jerry, 1933–

6073.1 * *La cage aux folles.* (Original Broadway cast). RCA: RCD1-4824. 1983.

6073.2 ** *Hello, Dolly.*

- (Original Broadway cast with Carol Channing). RCA: 3814-2-RG. 1964.
- (Original Broadway cast with Pearl Bailey). RCA: 1147-2-RG. 1967.

6073.3 *Mame.* (Original Broadway cast). Columbia: CK 3000. 1966.

6074 Joplin, Scott, 1868–1917

Treemonisha. (Houston Grand Opera/Gunther Schuller). Deutsche Grammophon: 435 709-2. 2CD set. 1976.

6075 Kander, John, 1927–

6075.1 * *Cabaret.* (Original Broadway cast). Columbia: CK 3040. 1966.

6075.2 *Kiss of the spider woman.* (Original Broadway cast). RCA: 09026-61579-2. 1992.

6076 ** Kern, Jerome, 1885–1945

Showboat.

- (Studio cast conducted by John McGlinn). EMI: CDS 7 49108 2. 3CD set. 1988.
- (Highlights from the above). EMI: CDC 7 49847 2. 1988.

6077 Lane, Burton, 1912–

Finian's rainbow. (Original Broadway cast). Columbia: CK 4062. 1947.

6078 Lehár, Franz, 1870–1948

The merry widow. See 3485

6079 Leigh, Mitch, 1928–

Man of La Mancha. (Original Broadway cast). MCA: MCAD-31065. 1973.

6080 Lloyd Webber, Andrew, 1948–

6080.1 *Cats.* (Original London cast). Geffen: 2017-2. 2CD set. 1981.

6080.2 *Jesus Christ superstar.* (Original London cast). MCA: MCA2-10000. 2CD set. 1970.

6080.3 * *Joseph and the amazing technicolor dreamcoat.* (Original London cast). MCA: MCAD-399. 1974.

6080.4 ** *Phantom of the opera.* (Original London cast). Polydor: 831 273-2. 2CD set. 1987.

6081 Loesser, Frank, 1910–1969

6081.1 * *Guys and dolls.*

- (Original Broadway cast). MCA: MCAD-10301. 1950.
- (Broadway revival cast). RCA: 09026-61317-2. 1992.

6081.2 * *How to succeed in business without really trying.* (Original Broadway cast). RCA: 60352-2-RG. 1961.

6081.3 *Most happy fella.* (Original Broadway cast). Sony: S2K 48010. 2CD set. 1956.

6082 Loewe, Frederick, 1901–1988

6082.1 *Brigadoon.* (Studio cast conducted by John McGlinn). EMI: 7 54481 2. 2CD set. 1991.

6082.2 * *Camelot.* (Original Broadway cast). Columbia: CK 32602. 1960.

6082.3 *Gigi.* (Motion picture soundtrack). CBS Special Products: AK 45395. 1958.

6082.4 ** *My fair lady.* (Original Broadway cast). Columbia: CK 5090. 1956.

6082.5 *Paint your wagon.* (Original Broadway cast). RCA: 60243-2-RG. 1951.

6083 ** MacDermot, Galt, 1928–

Hair. (Original off-Broadway cast). RCA: 1150-2-RC. 1968.

6084 Menken, Alan, 1949–

6084.1 *Beauty and the beast.* (Original Broadway cast). Walt Disney: 60861-2. 1991.

6084.2 * *Little shop of horrors.* (Original Broadway cast). Geffen: GEFD 2020. 1982.

6085 * Newley, Anthony, 1931–

The roar of the greasepaint, the smell of the crowd. (Original Broadway cast). RCA: 60351-2-RG. 1965.

6086 Ngema, Mbongeni

Sarafina! (Original Broadway cast). RCA: 9307-2-RC. 1988.

6087 Offenbach, Jacques, 1819–1880

Orpheus in the underworld. See 3495.3

6088 Porter, Cole, 1891–1964

6088.1 *Anything goes.* (Broadway revival cast). Epic: EK 15100. 1962.

6088.2 *Can-can.* (Original Broadway cast). Angel: ZDM 7 64664 2. 1953.

6088.3 * *Kiss me, Kate.* (Original Broadway cast). Columbia: CK 4140. 1949.

6089 Rodgers, Richard, 1902–1979

6089.1 *Allegro.* (Original Broadway cast). RCA: 07863-52758-2. 1947.

6089.2 *Babes in arms.* (Studio cast conducted by Evans Haile). New World: NW 386-2. 1989.

6089.3 * *Carousel.*

- (Original Broadway cast). MCA: MCAD-10048. 1945.

- (Studio cast conducted by Paul Gamignani). MCA: MCAD-6209. 1987.

6089.4 *Do I hear a waltz?* (Original Broadway cast). Sony: SK 48206. 1965.

6089.5 *Flower drum song.* (Original Broadway cast). Columbia: CK 2009. 1958.

6089.6 * *The king and I.* (Original Broadway cast). MCA: MCAD-10049. 1951.

6089.7 * *Oklahoma!* (Original Broadway cast). MCA: MCAD-10046. 1943.

6089.8 *On your toes.* (Original Broadway cast). Polydor: 813 667-2. 1983.

6089.9 *Pal Joey.* (Original Broadway cast). Broadway Angel: ZDM 7 64696 2. 1952.

6089.10 ** *The sound of music.*

- (Original Broadway cast). Columbia: CK 32601. 1959.

- (Motion picture soundtrack). RCA: PCD1-2005. 1965.

6089.11 * *South Pacific.* (Original Broadway cast). Columbia: CK 32604. 1949.

6090 Romberg, Sigmund, 1887–1951

The student prince. (Studio cast conducted by John Owen Edwards). TER: CDTER2 1172. 1989.

6091 Ross, Jerry, 1926–1955, and Richard Adler, 1921–

6091.1 * *Damn Yankees.* (Original Broadway cast). RCA: 3948-2-RG. 1955.

6091.2 *Pajama game.* (Original Broadway cast). Columbia: CK 32606. 1954.

6092 Schmidt, Harvey, 1929–

6092.1 * *The fantasticks.* (Original cast). Polydor: 821 943-2. 1979.

6092.2 *I do! I do!* (Original Broadway cast). RCA: 1128-2-RC. 1966.

6093 Schönberg, Claude-Michel, 1944–

6093.1 * *Les misérables.* (Original Broadway cast). Geffen: 9 24151-2. 2CD set. 1987.

6093.2 *Miss Saigon.* (Original London cast). Geffen: 24271-2. 2CD set. 1990.

6094 Schwartz, Stephen, 1949–

6094.1 *Godspell.* (Original off-Broadway cast). Arista: ARCD 8304. 1971.

6094.2 *Pippin.* (Original cast). Motown: MOTD-5243D. 1972.

6095 Sondheim, Stephen, 1930–

6095.1 *Anyone can whistle.* (Original Broadway cast). Columbia: CK 2480. 1964.

6095.2 ** *Company.* (Original Broadway cast). Columbia: CK 3550. 1970.

6095.3 * *Follies.* (Concert cast conducted by Carlo Svina). RCA: RCD2-7128. 2CD set. 1985. [With his *Stavisky: music from the original soundtrack*].

6095.4 * *A funny thing happened on the way to the forum.* (Original Broadway cast). Broadway Angel: ZDM 7 64770 2. 1962.

6095.5 *Into the woods.* (Original Broadway cast). RCA: 6796-2-RC. 2CD set. 1987.

6095.6 ** *A little night music.* (Original Broadway cast). Columbia: CK 32265. 1973.

6095.7 *Merrily we roll along.* (Original Broadway cast). RCA: RCD1-5840. 1982–86.

6095.8 *Pacific overtures.* (Original Broadway cast). RCA: RCD1-4407. 1976.

6095.9 *Passion.* (Original Broadway cast). Broadway Angel: CDQ 5 55251 2 3. 1994.

6095.10 *Sunday in the park with George.* (Original Broadway cast). RCA: RCD1-5042. 1984.

6095.11 ** *Sweeny Todd.* (Original Broadway cast). RCA: 3379-2-RC. 1979.

6096 Strauss, Johann, 1825–1899

Die Fledermaus. See 3515.1

6097 Strouse, Charles, 1928–

6097.1 * *Annie.* (Original Broadway cast). Columbia: CK 34712. 1977.

6097.2 *Bye bye Birdie.* (Original Broadway cast). Columbia: CK 2025. 1960.

6098 Stuart, Leslie, 1866–1928

Florodora. (Original London cast). Opal: CD 9835. 1899–1915.

6099 Styne, Jule, 1905–1994

6099.1 *Bells are ringing.* (Original Broadway cast). Columbia: CK 2006. 1956.

6099.2 * *Funny girl.*

- (Original Broadway cast). Broadway Angel: ZDM 7 65070 2. 1964.
- (Motion picture soundtrack). Columbia: CK 3220. 1968.

6099.3 * *Gypsy.* (Original Broadway cast). Columbia: CK 32607. 1959.

6100 Sullivan, Arthur, Sir, 1842–1900

6100.1 *The gondoliers.* (D'Oyly Carte Opera/John Pryce-Jones). Sony: S2K 58895. 2CD set. 1991.

6100.2 * *H.M.S. Pinafore.* (Welsh National Opera/ Charles Mackerras). Telarc: 80374. 1994.

6100.3 *Iolanthe.* (D'Oyly Carte Opera/Malcolm Sargent). Arabesque: Z 8066-2. 2CD set. 1900–12.

6100.4 ** *The Mikado.* (Welsh National Opera/ Charles Mackerras). Telarc: 80284. 1991.

6100.5 *Patience.* (D'Oyly Carte Opera/Isidore Godfrey). London: 425 193-2. 2CD set. 1961.

6100.6 ** *The pirates of Penzance.* (Welsh National Opera/Charles Mackerras). Telarc: 80353. 1993.

6100.7 *The yeomen of the guard.* (D'Oyly Carte Opera/John Owen Edwards). Sony: S2K 58901. 2CD set. 1992.

6101 Waller, Fats, 1904–1943

Ain't misbehavin'. (Broadway revival cast). RCA: 2965-2-RC. 2CD set. 1978.

6102 * Warren, Harry, 1893–1981

42nd Street. (Broadway revival cast). RCA: RCD1-3891. 1980.

6103 Weill, Kurt, 1900–1950

6103.1 ** *Aufstieg und Fall der Stadt Mahagonny (Rise and fall of the city of Mahagonny).* See 3656.1

6103.2 * *Lost in the stars*

- (Original Broadway cast). MCA: MCAD-10302. 1949.
- (Studio cast conducted by Julius Rudel). MusicMasters: 01612-67100-2. 1992.

6103.3 *Street scene.* (Scottish Opera/John Mauceri). London: 433 371-2. 2CD set. 1989–90.

6103.4 *Threepenny opera.* See 3656.3

6104 Willson, Meredith, 1902–1984

6104.1 ** *The music man.*

- (Original Broadway cast). Broadway Angel: ZDM 7 64663 2. 1957.
- (Motion picture soundtrack). Warner Bros.: 1459-2. 1962.

6104.2 *The unsinkable Molly Brown.* (Original Broadway cast). Broadway Angel: ZDM 7 64761 2. 1960.

6105 Wright, Robert Craig, 1914–

6105.1 *Kismet.*

- (Original Broadway cast). Columbia: CK 32605. 1953.
- (Studio cast conducted by Paul Gemignani). Sony: SK 46438. 1991.

6105.2 *Song of Norway.* (Studio cast conducted by John Owen Edwards). TER: CDTER2 1173. 2CD set. 1990.

6106 Youmans, Vincent, 1898–1946

No, no, Nanette. (Broadway revival cast). Columbia: CK 30563. 1971.

Motion Pictures and Television Shows

Anthologies

6107 * *The envelope please: Academy Award winning songs.* Rhino: 71868. 5CD set. 1934–93.

6108 *Hitchcock, master of mayhem.* (San Diego Symphony/Lalo Schifrin). Pro Arte: CDS 524. 1990. [Music by Bernard Herrmann, Franz Waxman, and Lalo Schifrin].

6109 *'Round midnight.* Columbia: CK 40464. 1986. [With Dexter Gordon, Herbie Hancock, Chet Baker, Wayne Shorter, Freddie Hubbard, and others].

6110 *Stormy weather.* [Series: Classics, vol. 2]. Fox/ Arista: 07822-11007-2. 1943. [With Fats Waller, Lena Horne, Bill Robinson, and Cab Calloway].

6111 * *Television's greatest hits.* TeeVee Toons: TVT 1100/1200/1300. 3CD set. 195?–198?.

Individual Composers

6112 Barron, Louis, 1920– , and Bebe Barron, 1927–

Forbidden planet. GNP Crescendo: PRD-001. 1954.

6113 Barry, John, 1933–

The Cotton Club. Geffen: GEFD-24062. 1984.

6114 Bradley, Scott

Tex Avery cartoons: music for the Tex Avery original soundtracks. Milan: 73138 35635-2. 1943.

6115 Burns, Ralph, 1922– , and Georgie Auld, 1919–1990

New York, New York. EMI-Manhattan: 46090. 1977.

6116 Coleman, Ornette, 1930– , and Howard Shore

Naked lunch. Milan: 73138-35614-2. 1992.

6117 Davis, Miles, 1926–1991

Ascenseur pour l'echafaud = Lift to the scaffold: complete recordings. Fontana/Philips: 836 305-2. 1957.

6118 Elfman, Danny

Music for a darkened theatre. MCA: MCAD-10065. 1990.

6119 * Ellington, Duke, 1899–1974

Anatomy of a murder. Rykodisc: RCD-10039 (Columbia CL 1360). 1959.

6120 Goodman, Benny, 1909–1986

The Benny Goodman story. MCA: MCAD-4055. 1955.

6121 Hancock, Herbie, 1940–

Blow up. Sony Music Special Products: AK-52418. 1966.

6122 Herrmann, Bernard, 1911–1975

Citizen Kane: the classic film scores of Bernard Herrmann. (National Philharmonic/Charles Gerhart). RCA: 0707-2-RG. 1974. *See also 6108*

6123 James, Harry, 1916–1983

Young man with a horn. Sony Music Special Products: BT-852. AC. 1949.

6124 Korngold, Erich Wolfgang, 1897–1957

Elizabeth & Essex: classic film scores of Erich Wolfgang Korngold. (National Philharmonic/Charles Gerhart). RCA: 0185-2-RG. 1973.

6125 Lewis, John, 1920–

Odds against tomorrow. Signature/CBS: AK 47487 (UA 5063). 1959. OP

6126 Mancini, Henry, 1924–1994

6126.1 *Mancini in surround: mostly monsters, murders & mysteries.* (Mancini Pops Orchestra/ Henry Mancini). RCA: 60471-2-RC. 1990.

6126.2 *Music from the films of Blake Edwards.* [Series: Film composers, vol. 4]. RCA: 2414-2-R. 1991.

6127 Marsalis, Branford, 1960–

Mo' better blues. Columbia: CK 46792. 1990.

6128 Morricone, Ennio, 1928–

The legendary Italian westerns. [Series: Film composers, vol. 2]. RCA: 9974-2-R. 1990.

6129 * O'Brien, Richard

The rocky horror picture show. Rhino: 70712. 1976.

6130 Rollins, Sonny, 1929– , and Oliver Nelson, 1932–1975

Alfie. MCA: MCAD-39107 (Impulse 9111). 1966.

6131 Rózsa, Miklós, 1907–1995

Spellbound: the classic film scores of Miklós Rózsa. RCA: 0911-2-RG. 1975.

6132 Schifrin, Lalo, 1932– . *See 6108*

6133 Scott, Raymond, 1910–1994. *See 4933*

6134 * Stalling, Carl W., 1888–1974

The Carl Stalling project: music from Warner Bros. cartoons, 1936–1958. Warner Bros.: 26027-2. 1936–58.

6135 Steiner, Max, 1888–1971

Now, voyager: the classic film scores of Max Steiner. (National Philharmonic/Charles Gerhart). RCA: 0136-2-RG. 1973.

6136 Tiomkin, Dimitri, 1894–1979

Lost horizon: classic film scores of Dimitri Tiomkin. (National Philharmonic/Charles Gerhart). RCA: 1669-2-RG. 1976.

6137 Waxman, Franz, 1906–1967

Sunset Boulevard: the classic film scores of Franz Waxman. (National Philharmonic/Charles Gerhart). RCA: 0708-2-RG. 1974. *See also 6108*

6138 Williams, John, 1932–

6138.1 * *The classic Spielberg scores.* Sony: SK 68419. [199?].

6138.2 * *Space-taculars.* Philips: 446 728-2. [199?].

Children's Music

Compiled by
**members of the Children's Services Division
of the Columbus Metropolitan Library, Columbus, Ohio**

This chapter consists of seven sections. The first three are suggested age-group categories, but any of these recordings might have a wider age appeal. Some albums are specifically geared to sing-alongs and activities (*see* 6136, 6138, 6144, 6146, 6148, 6149, 6153, 6159, 6160, 6161, 6164, 6172, 6174, 6178.3, and 6195) but many others are well suited to participation by both children and adults. Listings for "Multicultural Music," "Religious and Holiday Music," "Classical Music for Children," and "Lullabies" conclude the chapter.

Babies and Toddlers

6139   Bartels, Joanie

6139.1   *Dancin' magic.* Discovery Music/BMG Music: 02184-94408-2 (DM-8). 1991.

6139.2 * *Sillytime magic.* Discovery Music/BMG Music: 02184-94404-2 (DM-5). 1989.

6140   Beall, Pamela Conn, and Susan Hagen Nipp
Wee sing nursery rhymes and lullabies. PSS!/Price Stearn Sloan, Inc.: 0843 114223. AC. 1985. [Includes booklet].

6141   Hammett, Carol

6141.1 ** *It's toddler time.* Kimbo: KIM 0815C. AC. 1982.

6141.2 * *Toddlers on parade.* Kimbo: KIM 9002C. AC. 1985.

6142   McGrath, Bob, 1932– , and Katharine Smithrim

6142.1 * *The baby record.* Golden: 41007. AC. 1983.

6142.2   *Songs and games for toddlers.* Golden: 41016. AC. 1985.

6143   Palmer, Hap, 1942–

6143.1 * *Baby song.* Educational Activities: CD 713. 1991.

6143.2   *Hap Palmer sings classic nursery rhymes.* Activity: CD 646. 1991.

Preschool

Anthologies

6144 * *The best of Sesame Street.* Children's Television Workshop/Sight of Sound: GNL-220 (4105). 1987.

Individual Artists or Groups

6145 ** Chenille Sisters

1–2–3 for kids. Red House: RHR CD-33. 1989.

6146 * Fink, Cathy

Grandma slid down the mountain. Rounder: CD 8010. 1987.

6147 * Grammer, Red, and Kathy Grammer

Can you sound just like me? (Rolling along singing a song). Children's Group: 4203-4-Y. AC. 1983.

6148 McGrath, Bob, 1932–

6148.1 ** *Bob's favorite street songs.* A&M: 75021-0414-2. 1991.

6148.2 ** *If you're happy and you know it. Sing along with Bob #1.* Golden: 41009. AC. 1984.

6148.3 * *Sing along with Bob #2.* Golden: 41014. AC. 1990.

6149 Monet, Lisa

Circle time. Music for Little People: 42559-4 (MLP 215). AC. 1986.

6150 Palmer, Hap, 1942–

6150.1 *Sally the swinging snake.* Educational Activities: CD 617. 1986.

6150.2 * *Walter the waltzing worm.* Educational Activities: CD 555. 1982.

6151 Parachute Express

Shakin' it! Walt Disney: 60826-2. 1992.

6152 Raffi, 1948–

6152.1 * *More singable songs.* Shoreline/Rounder: CD 8052 (Troubadour). 1977.

6152.2 ** *Raffi in concert with the Rise and Shine Band.* Shoreline/Rounder: CD 8059 (Troubadour). 1989.

6152.3 *Rise and shine.* Shoreline/Rounder: CD 8055 (Troubadour). 1982.

6152.4 * *Singable songs for the very young.* Shoreline/Rounder: CD 8051 (Troubadour). 1976.

6153 Rogers, Fred (Mister Rogers)

A place of our own. Mister Rogers' Neighborhood: MRN 8104C. AC. 1970.

6154 Roth, Kevin

6154.1 *Dinosaurs and dragons.* Sony Kids' Music: LK 52811 (Marlboro: JAK07). 1990.

6154.2 * *Unbearable bears and other children's songs.* Marlboro: JAK01. 1986.

6155 Scelsa, Greg, and Steve Millang

6155.1 *Playing favorites.* Youngheart: YR 012-CD. 1991.

6155.2 * *We all live together, vols. 1–4.* Youngheart: YM 001CD/YM 004CD. 4 CDs. 1975–80.

6156 Seeger, Pete, 1919–

Stories and songs for little children. High Windy Audio: HW 1207. [198?].

6157 Sharon, Lois and Bram

6157.1 * *Mainly Mother Goose.* Elephant/Drive: DE2-43206 (0301). 1984.

6157.2 ** *One elephant went out to play = One elephant deux elephants.* Elephant/Drive: DE 2-43212 (0305). 1978.

6157.3 * *Smorgasbord.* Elephant/A&M: 25651-0304-4 (7902). AC. 1979.

School Age or All Ages

Anthologies

6158 ** *The Disney collection: best-loved songs from Disney movies, television shows and theme parks, vol. 1.* Walt Disney: 60816-2. 1991.

6159 *For our children.* Walt Disney: 60616-2. 1991. [Ziggy Marley, Bob Dylan, Sting, Paul McCartney, Little Richard, Bruce Springsteen, Brian Wilson, Bette Midler, Elton John, James Taylor, Carole King, Harry Nilsson, and others].

6160 *The music of Disney: a legacy of song.* Walt Disney: 60957-2. 3CD set. 1933–91.

Individual Artists or Groups

6161 Alsop, Peter, and Bill Harley, 1954–

In the hospital. Moose School Music: MS 503. AC. 1989.

6162   Arnold, Linda

Happiness cake. A&M: 75021-0405-4 (Ariel). AC. 1988.

6163   Beall, Pamela Conn, and Susan Hagen Nipp

6163.1   *Wee sing.* PSS!/Price Stearn Sloan, Inc.: 0843 105224. AC. 1979. [Includes booklet].

6163.2   *Wee sing America.* PSS!/Price Stearn Sloan, Inc.: 0843 137991. AC. 1987. [Includes booklet].

6164   Buck, Dennis

Car songs: vocal and music. Kimbo: KIM 9119C. AC. 1990.

6165   * Cassidy, Nancy

Kids' songs. Klutz: AC. 1986.

6166   Chapin, Tom

6166.1   ** *Family tree.* Sony Kids' Music: LK 48990 (Sundance Music 0402). 1988.

6166.2   * *Moonboat.* Sony Kids' Music: LK 53599 (Sundance Music 0403). 1989.

6167   Foote, Norman

If the shoe fits—. Walt Disney: 60835-2. 1992.

6168   Glazer, Tom

Children's greatest hits, vol. 1. Songs Music: 689 (CMS) AC. [197?].

6169   Guthrie, Woody, 1912–1967

Songs to grow on for mother and child. Smithsonian/Folkways: SF 45035. 1956.

6170   Harley, Bill, 1954–

50 ways to fool your mother. Round River: RRR 102. AC. 1986.

6171   Jenkins, Ella

6171.1   *Early early childhood songs.* Smithsonian/Folkways: SF 45015 (FC 7630). AC. 1982, 1990.

6171.2   * *You'll sing a song and I'll sing a song.* Smithsonian/Folkways: SF 45010 (FC 7664). 1989.

6172   Little Richard, 1935–

Shake it all about. Walt Disney: 60849-2. 1992.

6173   Loggins, Kenny, 1948–

Return to Pooh Corner. Sony Wonder: LK 57674. 1994.

6174   McCutcheon, John, 1952–

6174.1   * *Howjadoo.* Rounder: CD 8009. 1983.

6174.2   * *Mail myself to you.* Rounder: CD 8016. 1988.

6175   Muldaur, Maria, 1943–

One the sunny side of the street. Music for Little People: 42503-2. 1990.

6176   Pease, Tom

Boogie! boogie! boogie! Tomorrow River Music: SES-112C. AC. [1985].

6177   Penner, Fred

6177.1   ** *Collections.* Oak Street Music/BMG Kidz: 06847-84218-2 (A&M 0410). 1989.

6177.2   * *Special delivery.* Troubadour: CL-0027 (Shoreline). AC. 1983.

6178   ** Peter, Paul, and Mary

Peter, Paul and Mommy. Warner Bros.: 1785-2. 1969.

6179   Polisar, Barry Louis

Captured live and in the act. Rainbow Morning: 4879. AC. 1978.

6180   Rosenshontz

It's the truth. Lightyear Entertainment: 72259-75184-2. 1984.

6181   Rosenthal, Phil

The paw paw patch. American Melody: AM-C-104. AC. 1986–87.

6182   Scruggs, Joe

6182.1   * *Deep in the jungle.* Shadow Play/Educational Graphics Press: SPD 104 (913). 1987.

6182.2   ** *Late last night.* Shadow Play/Educational Graphics Press: SPD 101 (421). 1984.

6182.3   * *Traffic jams: songs for the car.* Educational Graphics Press: LLS 604. AC. 1985.

6183   * Seeger, Mike, 1933– , and Peggy Seeger, 1935–

American folksongs for children. Rounder: 8001/2 (11543/44). 2CD set. [1977].

6184   Seeger, Mike, 1933– , Peggy Seeger, 1935– , Barbara Seeger, and Penny Seeger

Animal folksongs for children—and other people! Rounder: CD 8023/24. [1992].

6185 * Seeger, Pete, 1919–

Abiyoyo and other story songs for children. Smithsonian/Folkways: SF 45001. 1958.

6186 * Thomas, Marlo, and Friends

Free to be . . . you and me. Arista: ARCD-8325. 1972.

6187 Tickle Tune Typhoon

Hug the earth. Music for Little People: MLP 236 (TTTCA 002). AC. 1985.

Multicultural Music

Anthologies

6188 * *Family folk festival: a multi-cultural sing-along.* Music for Little People: 42506-2 (D-2105). 1990. [John McCutcheon, Maria Muldaur, Sweet Honey in the Rock, Smothers Brothers, Doc Watson, Pete Seeger, Lillian Allen, Claudia Gomez, Taj Mahal, Amber McInnis].

6189 *Shake it to the one that you love the best: play songs and lullabies from Black musical traditions.* Music for Little People: MLP 2211 (JM 20581). AC. 1989.

Individual Artists or Groups

6190 Doucet, Michael, 1951–

Le hoogie boogie: Louisiana French music for children. Rounder: CD 8022. 1992.

6191 * Grammer, Red, and Kathy Grammer

Teaching peace. Smilin' Atcha/Children's Group: CGD 4202. 1986.

6192 Jenkins, Ella

Multicultural children's songs. Smithsonian/Folkways: SF 45045. 1995.

6193 Ladysmith Black Mambazo

Gift of the tortoise: a musical journey through Southern Africa. Music for Little People: 42553-2. 1994.

6194 ** Sweet Honey in the Rock

All for freedom. Music for Little People: 42505-2 (D-2230). 1989.

6195 Taj Mahal, 1940–

Shake sugaree. Music for Little People: 42502-2 (D-272). 1988.

Religious and Holiday Music

Anthologies

6196 *Chanukah at home.* Rounder: CD 8017. 1988. [Dan Crow, Marcia Berman, Uncle Ruthie Buell, J. P. Nightingale, Fred Sokolow].

Individual Artists or Groups

6197 Avni, Fran

6197.1 *Mostly matzah.* Music for Little People: MLP 488 (Lemonstone 1001). AC. 1983. [Passover].

6197.2 *The seventh day.* Music for Little People: MLP 268 (Lemonstone 1003). AC. 1984.

6198 Beall, Pamela Conn, and Susan Hagen Nipp

Wee sing Bible songs. PSS!/Price Stearn Sloan, Inc.: 0843 11780X. 1986.

6199 Palmer, Hap, 1942–

Hap Palmer's holiday magic. Hap-Pal: HP 108-2 (KUSA-006). 1990.

6200 Penner, Fred

The season: a family Christmas celebration. Oak Street Music: 06847-84228-2 (A&M 0412). 1990.

6201 Raffi, 1948–

Raffi's Christmas album. Shoreline/Rounder: CD 8056 (Troubadour). 1983.

6202 Scelsa, Greg, and Steve Millang

Holidays and special times. Youngheart: D2-74815. 1989.

6203 Scruggs, Joe

Merry Christmas. Shadow Play/Educational Graphics Press: SPR 150. 1989.

Classical Music for Children

Anthologies

6204 ** *Bernstein favorites: children's classics.* (New York Philharmonic/Leonard Bernstein). Sony Classical: SFK 46712. 1960, [1991]. [Prokofiev, Sergey: *Peter and the wolf;* Saint-Saëns, Camille: *Carnival of the animals;* and Britten, Benjamin: *The young person's guide to the orchestra*].

6205 *Daydreams and lullabies: a celebration of poetry, songs and classical music.* Classical Kids/BMG Music: 06847-84208-2. 1992.

Individual Artists or Groups

6206 * Bach, Johann Sebastian, 1685–1750

Mr. Bach comes to call. Classical Kids/BMG Music: 06847-84235-2 (CGD 4201). 1988.

6207 ** Beethoven, Ludwig van, 1770–1827

Beethoven lives upstairs. Classical Kids/BMG Music: 06847-84236-2 (CGD 4200). 1989.

6208 * Kleinsinger, George, 1914–

Tubby the tuba.

- (Carol Channing/Cincinnati Pops Orchestra/ Erich Kunzel). Caedmon: CPN-1623. AC. [1979]. [With Prokofiev, Sergey: *Peter and the Wolf*].
- (Manhattan Transfer/Naples Philharmonic/Timothy Russell). Summit: DCD 152. 1993.

6209 Louchard, Ric

6209.1 *G'morning Johann: classical piano solos for morning time.* Music for Little People: 42501-2 (D 2266). 1991.

6209.2 *G'night Wolfgang: classical piano solos for bedtime.* Music for Little People: 42500-2 (D 2108). 1989.

6210 Mozart, Wolfgang Amadeus, 1756–1791

Mozart's magic fantasy: a journey through the Magic Flute. Classical Kids/BMG Music: 06847-84237-2 (4204). 1990.

6211 Poulenc, Francis, 1899–1963

The story of Babar, the little elephant. (Pro Musica Chamber Players/Timothy Russell). D'Note Kids: DCD 175. 1994.

6212 Prokofiev, Sergey, 1891–1953

Peter and the wolf. See 6204 and 6208

6213 Vivaldi, Antonio, 1678–1741

Vivaldi's ring of mystery. Classical Kids/BMG Music: 06847-84206-2. 1991.

Lullabies

6214 * Ballingham, Pamala

A treasury of Earth Mother lullabies. Earth Mother: EMP 05B. 1987.

6215 * Bartels, Joanie

Lullaby magic. Discovery Music: 02184-94400-2 (DM-1). 1985.

6216 Bergman, Steve

Sweet baby dreams: calming music for expectant mothers, crying babies and children. Steve Bergman. AC. 1981.

6217 Carfra, Pat

Songs for sleepyheads and out-of-beds! LL Records/A&M Canada: JOY 5. AC. 1984.

6218 * Crosse, Jon

Lullabies go jazz. Jazz Cat: JCC 101. 1985.

6219 Herdman, Priscilla

Star dreamer: nightsongs & lullabies. Alacazam: ALA 1001. 1988.

6220 Roth, Kevin

Lullabies for little dreamers. Sony Kids' Music: LK 48887 (Marlboro 696). [1985].

30

Holidays, Special Occasions, Patriotic Music, and Miscellaneous

Compiled by
William E. Anderson

General Anthologies

6221 * *Music for all occasions: birthdays, graduation, Christmas, Fourth of July, St. Patrick's Day.* RCA: 09026-61488-2. 1993. [Also includes music for Valentine's Day, Memorial Day, weddings, Halloween, Thanksgiving, and New Year's Day].

Holidays

Christmas Carols (Traditional Choral Styles)

6222 *The carol album: seven centuries of Christmas music.* (Taverner Consort/Andrew Parrott). EMI: 49809. 1989.

6223 *Carols around the world.* (Quink). Telarc: CD-80202. 1989.

6224 *Carols for Christmas, vols. 1–2.* (Royal College of Music Chamber Choir/David Willcocks). Rykodisc: RCD 10004/10005. 2CD set. 1984.

6225 *Christmas Day in the morning: a Revels celebration of the winter solstice.* (Revels Company/John Langstaff). Revels: CD 1087. 1987.

6226 *Christmas with the Vienna Boys Choir.* (Vienna Boys Choir/Hermann Prey/Placido Domingo). RCA: 7930-2-RG. 1988.

6227 ** *A festival of carols.* (Robert Shaw Chorale). RCA: 6429-2-RG. 1987.

6228 *A festival of carols in brass.* (Philadelphia Brass Ensemble). CBS: MK 7033. 1967.

6229 *The joy of Christmas.* (Mormon Tabernacle Choir/Leonard Bernstein). CBS: XMT 6499. AC. [196?].

6230 *A little Christmas music.* (King's Singers). EMI: 49909. 1989.

6231 *Noel, noel! French Christmas music, 1200–1600.* (Boston Camerata/Joel Cohen). Erato: 45420-2. [1990].

6232 *O come all ye faithful.* (King's College Choir). Argo: 414042-2. 1984.

6233 *O holy night.* (Luciano Pavarotti). London: 414044-2 (26473). 1976.

6234 * *An old-fashioned Christmas: caroling with the Western Wind.* (Western Wind). Nonesuch: 79053-2. 1983.

6235 * *An old world Christmas: holiday favorites from Europe.* Deutsche Grammophon: 413 657-2. [1980].

6236 * *Sing we noel: Christmas music from England and early America.* (Boston Camerata/Joel Cohen). Nonesuch: 71354-2. 1978.

6237 *Sweet was the song.* (Smithsonian Chamber Players). Smithsonian: ND 040. 1990.

6238 *Thys Yool: a medieval Christmas.* (Martin Best). Nimbus: NI 5137. 1988.

6239 * *A Victorian christmas.* (Robert DeCormier Singers). Arabesque: Z6525. 1984.

6240 *Weihnachtskonzert = A Christmas concert.* (Regensburger Domspatzen). Deutsche Grammophon: 413 724-2. 1980.

Christmas Carols (Jazz, Blues, R&B, Folk, and Popular Styles)

Anthologies

6241 *The best of cool Yule.* Rhino: 75767. 1954–76. [Brenda Lee, Drifters, James Brown, Ventures, and others].

6242 *A big band Christmas.* Columbia: CK 40948. 1988. [Les Brown, Harry James, Benny Goodman, Lester Lanin, and others].

6243 ** *Billboard greatest Christmas hits, 1935–1954.* Rhino: 70637. 1935–54. [Bing Crosby, Gene Autry, Nat King Cole, Spike Jones, Jimmy Boyd, Eartha Kitt, and others].

6244 ** *Billboard greatest Christmas hits, 1955–present.* Rhino: 70636. 1955–83. [Bobby Helms, Brenda Lee, Chipmunks, Harry Simeone Chorale, Elvis Presley, Charles Brown, Drifters, Harry Belafonte, and others].

6245 * *Blue Yule: Christmas blues and r&b classics.* Rhino: 70568. 1950–90. [Charles Brown, Lightnin' Hopkins, Roy Milton, Canned Heat, Sonny Boy Williamson, John Lee Hooker, Louis Jordan, Jimmy Liggins, and others].

6246 *Bummed out Christmas.* Rhino: 70912. 1956–87. [Everly Brothers, George Jones, Sonics, Staple Singers, and others].

6247 *A Christmas gift for you from Phil Spector.* Abkco: 4005-2 (Philles). 1963. [Crystals, Ronettes, Darlene Love, Bob B. Soxx and the Blue Jeans].

6248 *Doo wop Christmas.* Rhino: 71057. 1948–89. [Orioles, Penguins, Drifters, Five Keys, Cadillacs, Moonglows, and others].

6249 *Dr. Demento presents: the greatest Christmas novelty CD of all time.* Rhino: 75755. 1947–[198?]. [Chipmunks, Spike Jones, Singing Dogs, Stan Freberg, Elmo and Patsy, Yogi Yorgesson, Allan Sherman, and others].

6250 *Enchanted carols: a feast of Christmas music with Victorian music boxes, handbells, church bells, barrel organs, street pianos, handbell choirs and brass bands.* Saydisc: CD-SDL-327. 1981.

6251 *Hillbilly holiday.* Rhino: 70195. 1945–72. [Bill Monroe, Tex Ritter, Brenda Lee, Willie Nelson, Hank Snow, and others].

6252 *Hipsters' holiday: vocal jazz and r&b classics.* Rhino: 70910. 1946–89. [Louis Armstrong, Eartha Kitt, Lambert, Hendricks and Ross, Miles Davis, Mabel Scott, Babs Gonzales, Lena Horne, and others].

6253 * *Jingle bell jazz.* Columbia: CK 40166 (36803+). 1961–69, 1985. [Duke Ellington, Lionel Hampton, Carmen McRae, Dave Brubeck, Herbie Hancock, Miles Davis, Dexter Gordon, McCoy Tyner, Heath Brothers, Wynton Marsalis, Paquito D'Rivera, and others].

6254 * *The original soul Christmas.* Rhino: 71788 (Atco 269+). 1968. [King Curtis, William Bell, Otis Redding, Clarence Carter, Carla Thomas, Booker T, Joe Tex, and others].

6255 *Our Christmas.* Word/Epic: EK 48580. [1991]. [Amy Grant, Sandi Patti, Al Green, Michael Smith, and others].

6256 *A winter's solstice.* Windham Hill: WD-1045. 1985. [William Ackerman, Philip Aaberg, Liz Story, Mark Isham, and others].

6257 *Yule struttin': a Blue Note Christmas.* Blue Note: 94857. 1990. [Bobby Watson, Lou Rawls, Chet Baker, Dexter Gordon, and others].

Individual Artists or Groups

6258 * Brown, James, 1928–
Santa's got a brand new bag. Rhino: 70194. 1966–70.

6259 * Cole, Nat King, 1917–1965

The Christmas song. Capitol: 46318 (1967). 1963.

6260 * Crosby, Bing, 1903–1977

Merry Christmas. MCA: MCAD-31143 (Decca 8128). 1945.

6261 * Fitzgerald, Ella, 1918–1996

Ella wishes you a swinging Christmas. Verve: 827150-2. 1960.

6262 Ford, Tennessee Ernie, 1919–1991

The star carol. Capitol: 91010. 1988.

6263 * Guaraldi, Vince, 1928–1976

A Charlie Brown Christmas. Fantasy: FCD-8431-2. 1970.

6264 Harris, Emmylou, 1949–

Light of the stable: the Christmas album. Warner Bros.: 3484-2. 1975–79.

6265 Jackson 5

Jackson 5 Christmas album. Motown: 37463-5250-2 (713). 1970.

6266 * Jackson, Mahalia, 1911–1972

Silent night. Columbia: CK 38304 (CL 702). 1955.

6267 Jones, Spike, 1911–1965

It's a Spike Jones Christmas. Rhino: 70196 (Verve). 1956.

6268 Mannheim Steamroller

Mannheim Steamroller Christmas. American Gramophone: AGCD-1984. 1984.

6269 Nelson, Willie, 1933–

Pretty paper. Columbia: CK 36189. 1979.

6270 * Presley, Elvis, 1935–1977

Elvis Christmas classics. RCA: 9801-2-R. 1957, 1971.

6271 Roches

We three kings. MCA/Paradox: MCAD-10020. 1990.

6272 Seeger, Mike, 1933– , Peggy Seeger, 1935– , and Penny Seeger

American folk songs for Christmas. Rounder: CD 0268/0269. 2CD set. 1989.

6273 Seeger, Pete, 1919–

Traditional Christmas carols. Smithsonian/Folkways: SF 40024. [1989].

6274 * Sinatra, Frank, 1915–

The Sinatra Christmas album. Capitol: 48329 (894). 1957.

6275 Streisand, Barbra, 1942–

A Christmas album. Columbia: CK 9557. 1967.

6276 * Temptations

The Temptations' Christmas card. Motown: 37463-5251-2 (Gordy 951). 1970.

6277 Winter, Paul, 1939–

Wintersong. Living Music: LD0012. 1986.

Halloween

6278 *Chiller.* (Cincinnati Pops/Erich Kunzel). Telarc: CD-80189. [1989].

6279 *Fright night: music that goes bump in the night.* CBS: MDK 45530. [1989].

6280 ** *Halloween hits.* Rhino: 70535. 1991. [Bobby "Boris" Picket, Jumpin' Gene Simmons, Ray Parker Jr., Sheb Wooley, Ran-Dells, Screamin' Jay Hawkins, and others].

6281 *Halloween horrors.* A&M: 75021-3152-2. 1977. ["The Story of Halloween" and sound effects].

6282 *Halloween stomp: jazz and big band dance music for a haunted house party.* Jass: J-CD-623. 1929–50. [Ray Noble, Cab Calloway, Louis Prima, Don Redman, Charlie Barnet, and others].

Jewish Holidays

See "Israel and Jewish Diaspora" in chapter 36

Kwanzaa

6283 *Kwanzaa.* Rounder: CD 2133. 1994. [James Brown, Aretha Franklin, Thomas Mapfumo, Clifton Chenier, Mahlathini and the Mahotella Queens, Oumou Sangare, Tabu Ley, and others].

Weddings

6284 *Everybody's favorite wedding music.* (Marni Nixon/John Cullum/Bert Lucarelli). Essex Entertainment: ESD-7050. 1991.

6285 *Music for weddings.* EMI: 62524. 1988.

6286 *Rockin' and rollin' wedding songs, vol. 1.* Rhino: 70588. [1992]. [Paul Anka, Beach Boys, Dixie

Cups, Captain and Tennille, 5th Dimension, Little Esther, Willows, Paul and Paula, and others].

6287 *Rockin' and rollin' wedding songs, vol. 2.* Rhino: 70589. [1992]. [Platters, Al Green, Jimmy Soul, Big Bopper, Lloyd Price, and others].

6288 *There is love (the wedding songs).* Scotti Bros.: 75262-2. 1992.

6289 *The wedding album.* RCA: 6207-2-RC. 1984. [Virgil Fox, Robert Shaw Chorale, Canadian Brass, and others].

6290 *The wedding album.* (Anthony Newman). Sony Masterworks: MDK 47273. 1991. [Organ].

6291 *Wedding favourites.* (Stephen Cleobury). London: 421 638-2. 1979. [Organ].

Sports and College Songs

6292 *Greatest college football marches.* (University of Michigan Band). Vanguard: VCD 29/30. 1971, 1987.

6293 *Touchdown! world's greatest college fight songs.* (Florida State University Seminole Band). Pro Arte/Intersound: CDD 511. 1990.

National Anthems and Patriotic Music

6294 *Battle cry of freedom.* (Robert Shaw Chorale). RCA: 60814-2-RG. 1962, 1991.

6295 * *Collections of national anthems, vol. 1* [Europe/U.S.S.R./Asia]. (Regimental Band of the Coldstream Guards). Denon: 4500-2. 1990.

6296 * *Collections of national anthems, vol. 2* [Americas/Africa/Middle East/Oceania]. (Regimental Band of the Coldstream Guards). Denon: 4501-2. 1990.

6297 *God bless America.* (Mormon Tabernacle Choir). Sony: MDK 48295. 1973–76, 1992.

6298 *National anthems of the world.* (Vienna State Opera Orchestra). Legacy: CD 301. [196?].

6299 *USA.* (Concert Arts Symphonic Band). EMI/Angel: 47422. 1986.

6300 *World anthems.* (English Chamber Orchestra). RCA: 09026-61344-2. 1992.

Sound Effects

6301 * *Authentic sound effects, vols. 1–3.* Elektra: 60731-2/60733-2. 3 CDs. [1987].

6302 *BBC sound effects library.* BBC/Films for the Humanities and Sciences: CD SFX 001-040. 40CD set. [1984–90]. [Includes printed guide-index].

Folk and Traditional Musics
of the United States and Canada

Compiled by
**William E. Anderson
and Laurel Sercombe**

his chapter is organized into seven sections: "Native American," "Hawaii," "African American," "Anglo-American," "Other European Immigrants," "Middle Eastern and Asian Immigrants," and "Canada." Hispanic music in the United States is covered in chapter 32, "Traditional and Popular Musics of the Caribbean and Latin America."

Native American (American Indian)

General Anthologies

6303 ** *An anthology of North American Indian and Eskimo music.* Ed. by Michael I. Asch. Smithsonian/Folkways: 4541. 2AC set. [1973].

6304 *Creation's journey: Native American music.* Smithsonian/Folkways: SF 40410. 1992–93.

6305 ** *A cry from the earth: music of the North American Indians.* Ed. by John Bierhorst. Smithsonian/Folkways: 37777. AC. 1894–1963. [Tlingit, Kwakiutl, Eskimo, Navajo, Arapaho, Comanche, Hopi, Yuman, Chippewa, Iroquois, Choctaw, Penob-

scot, Zuni, Cherokee, Nez Perce, Teton Sioux, Pima, Delaware, Kiowa, and others].

6306 *Native flute collection.* Talking Taco Records: TT111. [1991].

6307 *The song of the Indian.* Canyon: 6050. AC. [1960–81].

6308 ** *Songs of earth, water, fire and sky: music of the American Indian.* New World: 80246-2. 1975. [Cherokee, Seneca, Navajo, Arapaho, Creek, Pueblo, Yurok, Plains].

6309 *Washo-Peyote songs: songs of American Indian Church.* Smithsonian/Folkways: 4384. AC. 1954.

Northeast and Southeast Cultures

6310 * *Delaware, Cherokee, Choctaw, Creek.* [Series: Music of the American Indian]. Library of Congress: L 37. AC. 1940–52.

6311 * *Honor the earth powwow: songs of the Great Lakes Indians.* Rykodisc: RCD 10199. 1990.

6312 *Ojibway music from Minnesota: a century of song for voice and drum.* [Series: Minnesota musical traditions]. Minnesota Historical Society: C-003. AC. 1899–1988.

6313 *Plains Chippewa/Metis music from Turtle Mountain.* Smithsonian/Folkways: SF 40411 (4140). 1984.

6314 *Seneca songs from Coldspring Longhouse.* Library of Congress: L 17. AC. 1941–45.

6315 *Songs and dances of Great Lakes Indians.* Ed. by Gertrude Prokosch Kurath. Smithsonian/Folkways: 4003. AC. 1952–54.

6316 * *Songs and dances of the Eastern Indians from Medicine Spring and Allegany.* New World: 80337-2. 1985. [Cherokee, Creek, Seneca, Iroquois].

6317 *Songs from the Iroquois Longhouse.* Library of Congress: L 6. AC. 1941.

6318 *Songs of the Chippewa.* Library of Congress: L 22. AC. 1910–30.

6319 *Songs of the Menomonee, Mandan, and Hidatsa.* Library of Congress: L 33. AC. 1910–30.

6320 *Songs of the Muskogee Creek, parts 1–2.* Indian House: IH 3001-3002. 2 ACs. 1969. [Recorded at Seminole, Oklahoma].

6321 *Songs of the Seminole Indians of Florida.* Smithsonian/Folkways: 4383. AC. 1931–33.

6322 *Stomp dance: Muskogee, Seminole, Yuchi, vol. 1.* Indian House: IH 3003-C. AC. 1978.

6323 *Where the ravens roost: Cherokee traditional songs of Walker Calhoun.* Mountain Heritage Center: MHC-1. AC. 1988.

Plains Cultures

Anthologies

6324 *An historical album of Blackfoot Indian music.* Smithsonian/Folkways: 34001. AC. 1979.

6325 *Indian music of the Canadian plains.* Smithsonian/Folkways: 4464. AC. 1955.

6326 *Music of the American Indian: Kiowa.* Library of Congress: L 35. AC. 1940–52.

6327 ** *Plains: Comanche, Cheyenne, Kiowa, Caddo, Wichita, Pawnee.* [Series: Music of the

American Indian]. Library of Congress: AFS L 39. AC. 1940–52.

6328 * *Powwow songs: music of the Plains Indians.* New World: 80343-2. 1975.

6329 *Social songs of the Arapaho sun dance.* Canyon: CR-6080. AC. [1971]. [Recorded in Fort Washakie, Wyoming].

6330 * *Songs of Indian Territory: Native American music traditions of Oklahoma.* State Arts Council of Oklahoma/Center of the American Indian: [n.n.]. AC. [1989].

6331 *Songs of the Sioux.* Library of Congress: L 23. AC. 1910–30.

6332 *Sounds of Indian America: Plains and Southwest.* Indian House: IH 9501. 1969. [Recorded at the 48th Inter-Tribal Indian Ceremonial, Gallup, New Mexico].

6333 * *Takini: music and songs of the Lakota Sioux.* Le Chant du Monde: CMT 274 1000. 1994.

Individual Group

6334 Ashland Singers
Northern Cheyenne war dance. Indian House: 4201. 1974.

Southwest Cultures

Anthologies

6335 * *Apache.* [Series: Music of the American Indian]. Library of Congress: L 42. AC. 1940–52.

6336 * *Chicken scratch fiesta.* Canyon: 8055-2. AC. 1981. [Elvin Kelly y Los Reyes, Molinas, and others].

6337 * *Handgame of the Kiowa, Kiowa Apache, and Comanche, vol. 1.* Indian House: IH 2501-C. 1968.

6338 * *Hopi Katcina songs and six other songs by Hopi chanters.* Smithsonian/Folkways: 4394. AC. 1924.

6339 *Indian music of the Southwest.* Smithsonian/Folkways: 8850. AC. 1957.

6340 * *Music of New Mexico: Native American traditions.* Smithsonian/Folkways: SF 40408. 1990–92.

6341 * *Music of the American Indians of the Southwest.* Smithsonian/Folkways: 4420. AC. 1951.

6342 *Music of the Plains Apache.* Smithsonian/Folkways: 4252. AC. 1968.

6343 *Navajo songs: recorded by Laura Bolton in 1933 and 1940.* Smithsonian/Folkways: SF 40403. 1933, 1940.

6344 * *Navajo songs from Canyon de Chelly.* New World: 80406-2. 1975.

6345 * *Oku shareh: turtle dance songs of San Juan Pueblo.* New World: 80301-2. 1974.

6346 *Songs of the Papago.* Library of Congress: L 31. AC. 1910–30.

6347 *Songs of the Yuma, Cocapa, and Yaqui.* Library of Congress: L 24. AC. 1910–30.

6348 * *Talking spirits: Native American music from the Hopi, Zuni and San Juan Pueblos.* Music of the World: CDT-126. [1992].

6349 *Taos Pueblo round dance songs, vol. 1.* Indian House: 1006. AC. 1987. *See also 6329*

See also 6332 and 7062

Individual Artists or Groups

6350 Garcia, Peter, and the Garcia Brothers
Songs of my people. Music of the World: CDT-133. 1988–93.

6351 * Kinlechene, Kee, and Yátzá
Songs of the Navaho. JVC: VICG-5334. 1993.

6352 Southern Maiden Singers
Navajo skip dance and two-step songs. Indian House: 1535. AC. 1984.

6353 Turtle Mountain Singers
Navajo social dance songs. Indian House: 1523. AC. 1987.

Great Basin, Plateau, California, and Northwest Coast Cultures

6354 ** *Great Basin: Paiute, Washo, Ute, Bannock, Shoshone.* [Series: Music of the American Indian]. Library of Congress: L 38. AC. 1940–52.

6355 * *Indian music of the Pacific Northwest Coast.* Smithsonian/Folkways: 4523. AC. 1947–53.

6356 *Ishi: the last Yahi.* [Series: Music and word]. Wild Sanctuary: WSC 1604. AC. 1911–14.

6357 *Nez Perce stories.* [Series: Music and word]. Wild Sanctuary: [n.n.]. AC. 1972. [Songs and stories by Elizabeth Wilson].

6358 ** *Northwest (Puget Sound).* [Series: Music of the American Indian]. Library of Congress: L 34. AC. 1940–52.

6359 *Songs and dances of the Flathead Indians.* Smithsonian/Folkways: 4445. AC. 1953.

6360 *Songs and stories from Neah Bay by Helen Peterson of the Makah tribe.* Canyon: C-6125. LP/AC. [1976].

6361 * *Songs of love, luck, animals and magic: music of the Yurok and Tolowa Indians.* New World: 80297-2. 1976.

6362 *Songs of the Nootka and Quileute.* Library of Congress: L 32. AC. 1910–30.

6363 *Songs of the Pawnee and Northern Ute.* Library of Congress: L 25. AC. 1910–30.

6364 *Songs of the Warm Springs Indian Reservation.* Canyon: 6123. LP/AC. 1975. [Recorded in Warm Springs, Oregon].

6365 *Stick game songs by Joe Washington.* Canyon: C-6124. LP/AC. [1975]. [Recorded in Lummi, Washington].

6366 *Umatilla tribal songs.* Canyon: 6131. LP/AC. [1975]. [Umatilla Tribal Singers].

6367 *Utes.* Canyon: 6113. AC. 1974. [Performed by singers from Ignacio, Colorado, and White Mesa, Utah].

6368 *Yakima Nation singers of Satus Longhouse.* Canyon: 6126. LP/AC. 1974. [Recorded in Satus, Washington].

Arctic and Subarctic Cultures

6369 *Alaskan Eskimo songs and stories.* University of Washington Press: UWP-902. LP/AC. 1972.

6370 * *Canada: Inuit games and songs.* [Series: UNESCO collection]. Auvidis: D 8032. 1974–76.

6371 * *Canada: jeux vocaux des Inuit (Inuit du Caribou, Netsilik et Igloolik).* Ocora: C 559071. 1989.

6372   *Chants et tambours Inuit de Thulé au Detroit de Bering.* Ocora: C 559021. 1988.

6373   *Music of the Inuit: the Copper Eskimo tradition.* [Series: UNESCO collection]. Auvidis: D 8053. 1982.

Contemporary and Intertribal

Anthologies

6374   *Heartbeat: voices of First Nations women.* Smithsonian/Folkways: SF 40415. 1995.

6375   *Indian songs of today.* Library of Congress: L 36. AC. 1940–52.

6376   *Moving within the circle: contemporary Native American music and dance.* World Music Press: WMP 012. AC. [1993]. [Companion tape for the book by Bryan Burton].

6377   *Solo flights, vol. 1.* Sound of America Records (SOAR): 124. [1991]. [XIT, Douglas Spotted Eagle, Cathedral Lake Singers, Billie Nez, and others].

Individual Artists or Groups

6378   Badland Singers
Live at United Tribes, vol. 1. Indian House: 4106. AC. 1979.

6379   Bala-Sinem Choir
American Indian songs and chants. Canyon: 6110. AC. [1973].

6380   Black Lodge Singers
Pow-wow highway songs. Sound of America Records (SOAR): SOA-CD-RD-125. 1991.

6381   Coyote Oldman
In Medicine River. Coyote Oldman: 5. 1993.

6382   Gu-Achi Fiddlers
Old time O'odham fiddle music. Canyon: 8082. AC. [1988].

6383   Ironwood Singers
Traditional songs of the Sioux: live at the Rosebud Fair. Indian House: IH 4321. 1978.

6384   Nakai, R. Carlos, 1946–

    6384.1 * *Changes: Native American flute music, vol. 1.* Canyon: CR-615. 1982.

    6384.2   *Sundance season.* Celestial Harmonies: 13024-2. 1987.

6385   Nevaquaya, Doc Tate, 1932–
Comanche flute music. Smithsonian/Folkways: 4328. AC. 1978.

6386   Red Earth Singers
Red Earth Singers of Tama, Iowa: "live." Indian House: 4503. AC. 1990.

6387   White Eagle Singers
Intertribal pow-wow songs. Canyon: 6197. AC. 1987.

Hawaii

Anthologies

6388   *Hawaiian drum dance chants: sounds of power in time.* Smithsonian/Folkways: SF 40015. 1923–89.

6389 * *Hawaiian rainbow.* Rounder: 6018. LP/AC. 1988. [Raymond Kane, Andy Cummings, Michael Kahkina, and others].

6390 ** *Hawaiian steel guitar classics.* Folklyric/Arhoolie: CD 7027. 1927–38. [Sol Hoopii, Kalama's Quartet, King Namahi, Kane's Hawaiians, and others].

6391   *Hawaii's great contemporary classics.* Hawaiian Collection Series: HCS-1. 1987. [Olomana, Kapono Beamer, Gabby Pahinui, Makaha Sons of Niihau, and others].

6392 * *The history of slack key guitar.* [Series: Vintage Hawaiian treasures, vol. 7]. Hana Ola/Cord International: HOCD 24000. 1946–50. [Gabby Pahinui and others].

6393   *Hula blues: vintage steel guitar instrumentals of the 30's and 40's.* Rounder: C 1012. AC. [193?–194?]. [Sol Hoopii, Frank Ferara, Jim and Bob, Roy Smeck, and others].

6394   *Music of Hawaii.* Harlequin: HQCD 28. 1929–52. [Benny Nawahi, Tau Moe, Sol Hoopii, Lani McIntire, and others].

6395   *Puerto Rican music in Hawaii: kachi-kachi.* Smithsonian/Folkways: SF 40014. 1985.

6396 * *Vintage Hawaiian music: steel guitar masters.* Rounder: CD 1052. 1928–34. [King Benny Nawahi, Sol Hoopii, Tau Moe, Sam Ku West, Jim and Bob, and others].

6397 ** *Vintage Hawaiian music: the great singers.* Rounder: CD 1053. 1928–34. [Rose Moe, Kalama's Quartet, Sol Hoopii, George Ku, and others].

Individual Artists or Groups

6398 * Hoopii, Sol, 1902–1953

Master of the Hawaiian guitar, vols. 1–2. Rounder: CD 1024/CD 1025. 1926–51.

6399 Kalama's Quartet

Early Hawaiian classics. Folklyric/Arhoolie: CD 7028. 1927–32.

6400 Kane, Raymond, 1925–

Master of the slack key guitar. Rounder: 6020. AC. 1987.

6401 * Pahinui, Gabby, 1921–1980

The best of Gabby Pahinui, vols. 1–2. Hula Records: CDHS-578/CDHS-585. 2 CDs. [1981], [1989].

6402 Tau Moe Family, with Bob Brozman

Ho'omana'o I na mele o ka wa u'i (remembering the songs of our youth). Rounder: CD 6028. 1929, 1988.

African American

Recordings in this section document various premodern folk idioms by African American performers. *See also* chapter 21, "Blues" and chapter 27, "Gospel and Other Popular Christian Music."

Anthologies

6403 * *Been in the storm so long: spirituals, folk tales and children's games from John's Island, South Carolina.* Smithsonian/Folkways: SF 40031. 1963–65.

6404 *Country Negro jam session.* Arhoolie: CD 372 (Folklyric). 1959–62. [Butch Cage, Willie Thomas, Smokey Babe, Robert Pete Williams, and others].

6405 * *Georgia sea island songs.* New World: 80278-2. 1960–61. [Bessie Jones, Hobart Smith, Joe Armstrong, and others].

6406 *Traveling through the jungle: fife and drum band music from the Deep South.* Testament: TCD 5017 (2223). 1942, 1970.

Individual Artists or Groups

6407 Baker, Etta, 1915–

One-dime blues. Rounder: CD 2112. 1988–90.

6408 * Cotten, Elizabeth, 1893–1987

Freight train and other North Carolina folk songs. Smithsonian/Folkways: SF 40009. 1957–58.

6409 Davis, Reverend Gary, 1896–1972

Reverend Gary Davis at Newport. Vanguard: VMD-73008. 1965.

6410 Menhaden Chanteymen

Won't you help me to raise 'em. Global Village: CD 220. 1989. [Authentic net hauling songs from an African American fishery].

Anglo-American

The term *Anglo-American* refers here not just to England but to the dominant North American strain of folk music whose musical and linguistic roots are in the English-speaking British Isles. The general anthologies listed below consist primarily of Anglo-American music, but some collections do contain selections from African American or other ethnicities.

General Anthologies

6411 ** *Anthology of American folk music, vol. 1: ballads.* Smithsonian/Folkways: 2951. 2AC set. 1927–32. [Clarence Ashley, Coley Jones, Buell Kazee, Carolina Tar Heels, G. B. Grayson, Kelly Harrell, Carter Family, Frank Hutchison, Charlie Poole, Mississippi John Hurt, Furry Lewis, and others].

6412 ** *Anthology of American folk music, vol. 2: social music.* Smithsonian/Folkways: 2952. 2AC set. 1927–32. [Prince Albert Hunt's Texas Ramblers, Eck Robertson, Jim Baxter, Henry Thomas, Jim Jackson, Joseph Falcon, Breaux Freres, Rev. J. M. Gates, Alabama Sacred Harp Singers, Bascom Lamar Lunsford, Blind Willie Johnson, Carter Family, Ernest Phipps, Rev. F. W. McGee, and others].

6413 ** *Anthology of American folk music, vol. 3: songs.* Smithsonian/Folkways: 2953. 2AC set. 1927–32. [Clarence Ashley, Buell Kazee, Gus Cannon, Dock Boggs, Bascom Lamar Lunsford, Ernest Stoneman, Memphis Jug Band, Carter Family, Clemo Breaux, Joseph Falcon, Blind Lemon Jefferson, Sleepy John Estes, Ramblin' Thomas, Uncle Dave Macon, Mississippi John Hurt, Ken Maynard, Henry Thomas, and others].

6414 * *Brave boys: New England traditions in folk music.* New World: 80239-2. 1959–77.

6415 *Cowboy songs on Folkways.* Smithsonian/ Folkways: SF 40043. 1944–65. [Woody Guthrie, John Lomax, Leadbelly, Cisco Houston, Peter La-Farge, Rosalie Sorrels, Harry Jackson, Ray Reed, and others].

6416 * *Early mandolin classics, vol. 1.* Rounder: CD 1050. 1927–34. [Yank Rachell, Gid Tanner's Skillet Lickers, Dallas String Band, Canario y su Grupo, Giovanni Gioviale, Ctphyhha Opkectpa, and others].

6417 ** *Folk music in America, vol. 1: religious music: congregational and ceremonial.* Library of Congress: LBC 1. AC. 1902–71. [Ernest Stoneman, Yaqui Indians, Dinwiddie Colored Quartet, Rev. F. W. McGee, Cantor Isaiah Meisels, Arizona Dranes, and others].

6418 ** *Folk music in America, vol. 2: songs of love, courtship, and marriage.* Library of Congress: LBC 2. LP/AC. 1925–64. [Lonnie Johnson, Yank Rachell, Bill Monroe, Lydia Mendoza, Carter Family, Carolina Tar Heels, Blue Sky Boys, Wade Mainer, and others].

6419 ** *Folk music in America, vol. 3: dance music: breakdowns and waltzes.* Library of Congress: LBC 3. AC. 1927–75. [Little Buddy Doyle, Adolph Hofner, Bog Trotters, East Texas Serenaders, Uncle Dave Macon, and others].

6420 ** *Folk music in America, vol. 4: dance music: reels, polkas, and more.* Library of Congress: LBC 4. AC. 1926–75. [Pawlo Humeniuk, Sady Courville, Dennis McGee, Gid Tanner, and others].

6421 ** *Folk music in America, vol. 5: dance music: ragtime, jazz, and more.* Library of Congress: LBC 5. AC. 1917–75. [Bog Trotters, Kanui and Lula, East Texas Serenaders, Clifford Hayes, Bob Wills, State Street Stompers, and others].

6422 ** *Folk music in America, vol. 6: songs of migration and immigration.* Library of Congress: LBC 6. AC. 1927–75. [Roy Acuff, Frank Hovington, Cow Cow Davenport, Gabriel Brown, and others].

6423 ** *Folk music in America, vol. 7: songs of complaint and protest.* Library of Congress: LBC 7. AC. 1928–65. [Wilmoth Houdini, Bumble Bee Slim, Ernest V. Stoneman, J. B. Lenoir, Lester Flatt and Earl Scruggs, Bessie Tucker, Walter Roland, and others].

6424 ** *Folk music in America, vol. 8: songs of labor and livelihood.* Library of Congress: LBC 8. AC. 1927–76. [Clara Smith, Merle Travis, Blue Sky Boys, Big Chief Ellis, and others].

6425 ** *Folk music in America, vol. 9: songs of death and tragedy.* Library of Congress: LBC 9. LP. 1927–76. [Blue Sky Boys, Ernest Tubb, Fields Ward, Grandpa Jones, John Cephas, Ernest V. Stoneman, Dixon Brothers, and others].

6426 ** *Folk music in America, vol. 10: songs of war and history.* Library of Congress: LBC 10. LP/AC. 1927–62. [Blue Sky Boys, Wilmoth Houdini, Roy Acuff, Springback James, David "Honeyboy" Edwards, Lulu Belle and Scotty, Louisiana Red, and others].

6427 ** *Folk music in America, vol. 11: songs of humor and hilarity.* Library of Congress: LBC 11. AC. 1927–75. [Sylvester Weaver, Bumble Bee Slim, Fiddlin' John Carson, and others].

6428 ** *Folk music in America, vol. 12: songs of local history and events.* Library of Congress: LBC 12. AC. 1928–75. [Lone Star Cowboys, Carter Family, Papa Charlie Jackson, Lonnie Johnson, Jimmie Davis, Uncle Dave Macon, Amadé Ardoin, Blue Sky Boys, and others].

6429 ** *Folk music in America, vol. 13: songs of childhood.* Library of Congress: LBC 13. AC. 1927–75. [Carolina Tar Heels, Gid Tanner, Speckled Red, Byrd Moore, Molly O'Day, Ernest Stoneman, Frank Hovington, and others].

6430 ** *Folk music in America, vol. 14: solo and display music.* Library of Congress: LBC 14. AC. 1896–1975. [Lonnie Johnson, Uncle Dave Macon, Sylvester Weaver, Vess Ossman, Tommy Jarrell, Amadé Ardoin, James P. Johnson, Montana Taylor, J. E. Mainer, and others].

6431 ** *Folk music in America, vol. 15: religious music: solo and performance.* Library of Congress: LBC 15. AC. 1890–1975. [Elder Charlie Beck, Elder R. Wilson, Bunk Johnson, Fiddlin' John Carson, Kitty Wells, and others].

6432 *Folk music U.S.A.* Smithsonian/Folkways: 4530. 2AC set. [1958].

6433 ** *Folk song America: a 20th century revival.* Smithsonian: 2702 (RD-046). 4CD set. 1919–87. [Buell Kazee, John Jacob Niles, Almanac Singers, Leadbelly, Woody Guthrie, Richard Dyer-Bennet, Josh White, Burl Ives, Weavers, Oscar Brand, Harry Belafonte, Bill Broonzy, Odetta, Jean Ritchie, Kingston Trio, Joan Baez, New Lost City Ramblers, Cisco Houston, Limelighters, Dave Van Ronk, Jack Elliott, Lester Flatt and Earl Scruggs, Clancy Brothers, Peggy Seeger, Pete Seeger, Bob Dylan, Tom

Rush, Tom Paxton, Doc Watson, Ian and Sylvia, Byrds, Buffy Sainte-Marie, Jim Kweskin, Simon and Garfunkel, Phil Ochs, Judy Collins, Steve Goodman, Taj Mahal, Sweet Honey in the Rock, and others].

6434 ** *Going down the valley: vocal and instrumental styles in folk music from the South.* New World: NW 236. LP. 1926–38. [Carter Brothers, Ernest Stoneman, Uncle Dave Macon, Gid Tanner, Charlie Poole, Callahan Brothers, Allen Brothers, Coon Creek Girls, Wade Mainer, and others]. OP

6435 * *I'm on my journey home: vocal styles and resources in folk music.* New World: NW 223. LP. 1929–75. [Darby and Tarlton, Delmore Brothers, Denson Quartet, and others]. OP

6436 * *New Britain: the roots of American folksong.* (Boston Camerata/Joel Cohen). Erato: 2292-45474-2. [1990].

6437 * *Oh my little darling: folk song types.* New World: NW 245. LP. 1923–59. [Almeda Riddle, Fields Ward, Fiddlin' John Carson, Sarah Ogan, Clarence Ashley, Wade Mainer, Ernest Phipps, and others]. OP

6438 ** *Old-country music in a new land: folk music of immigrants from Europe and the Near East.* New World: NW 264. LP. 1916–55. [Krestyanskyj Orkestr, Mike Laphacak, Braca Kapugi, Patrick Killoran, Morrison and McKenna, Lydia Mendoza, Santiago Jiménez Sr., Dennis McGee, Elise Deshotel, Vart Sarkisian, Nahem Simon, Harilaos Piperakis, and others]. OP

6439 * *Roots 'n' blues: the retrospective.* Columbia: C4K 47911. 4CD set. 1925–50. [Charlie Poole, Frank Hutchison, Hersal Thomas, Rev. J. M. Gates, Fiddlin' John Carson, Washington Phillips, Barbecue Bob, Allen Brothers, Coley Jones, Mississippi John Hurt, Mamie Smith, Pink Anderson, Roosevelt Sykes, Hokum Boys, Atlanta Sacred Harp Singers, Joe Falcon, Gid Tanner, Mississippi Sheiks, Lonnie Johnson, Darby and Tarlton, Bo Carter, Peetie Wheatstraw, Light Crust Doughboys, Blind Willie McTell, Charlie Patton, Walter Roland, Lucille Bogan, Leroy Carr, Josh White, Bumble Bee Slim, Bill Broonzy, Albert Ammons, Cliff Carlisle, Callahan Brothers, Humbard Family, Homer Harris, Adolf Hofner, Big Maceo, Bill Monroe, Gene Autry, Big Joe Williams, Molly O'Day, and others].

6440 * *That's my rabbit, my dog caught it: traditional Southern instrumental styles.* [Series: Recorded anthology of American music]. New World: NW 226. LP. 1925–77. [Hobart Smith, Joseph Falcon, Dennis McGee, Arthur Smith, Bill Boyd, and others]. OP

Premodern Folk Music (Field Recordings and Traditional Performers)

The recordings listed here, made mostly before 1960, preserve rural folk traditions as performed typically by nonprofessional musicians.

Anthologies

6441 * *American fiddle tunes from the Archives of Folksong.* Library of Congress: L 62. AC. 1934–46.

6442 * *American sea songs and shanties.* Library of Congress: L 26/L 27. 2AC set. 1939–51.

6443 * *Anglo-American ballads.* Library of Congress: L 1. AC. 1934–41.

6444 *Anglo-American ballads.* Library of Congress: L 7. LP/AC. 1937–42.

6445 *Anglo-American shanties, lyric songs, dance tunes and spirituals.* Library of Congress: L 2. AC. 1937–41.

6446 * *Anglo-American songs and ballads.* Library of Congress: L 12. LP/AC. 1941–46.

6447 *Anglo-American songs and ballads.* Library of Congress: L 14. LP/AC. 1941–46.

6448 *Anglo-American songs and ballads.* Library of Congress: L 20. LP/AC. 1938–46.

6449 *Anglo-American songs and ballads.* Library of Congress: L 21. AC. 1938–47.

6450 *Ballads and songs of the Blue Ridge Mountains: persistence and change.* Smithsonian/Folkways: 3831. AC. 1968.

6451 * *Child ballads traditional in the United States, vols. 1–2.* Library of Congress: L 57/L 58. 2 ACs. 1935–50.

6452 * *Cowboy songs, ballads, and cattle calls from Texas.* Library of Congress: L 28. LP/AC. 1941–48.

6453 * *Fine times at our house: traditional music of Indiana.* Smithsonian/Folkways: 3809. AC. 1962–64.

6454 *Five miles out of town.* [Series: Traditional music of the Cumberland plateau, vol. 2: *music of the Big South Fork area*]. County: 787. LP/AC. [1987].

6455 *Folk music from Wisconsin.* Library of Congress: L 55. AC. 1940–46.

6456 *Folksongs and ballads, vol. 3.* Augusta Heritage: 009. AC. 1987–90. [Holley Hundley, Wavie Chappell, Homer Sampson, Hazel Stover].

6457 *Georgia folk: a sampler of traditional sounds.* Global Village Music: SC 03. AC. 1928–89.

6458 *Gettin' up the stairs.* [Series: Traditional music of the Cumberland plateau, vol. 1: *music of the Big South Fork area*]. County: 786. LP/AC. [1987].

6459 *The Hammons Family: a study of a West Virginia family's traditions.* Library of Congress: AFS L65-L66. 2 LPs/2 ACs. 1970–72.

6460 * *Instrumental music and songs of the Southern Appalachians.* Legacy International: CD 329 (Tradition 1007). 1956. [Etta Baker, Hobart Smith, Eric Darling, and others].

6461 *It's just the same today: the Barnicle-Cadle field recordings from eastern Tennessee and Kentucky.* Tennessee Folklore Society: TFS-108. LP. 1938–49.

6462 *The Library of Congress banjo collection.* Rounder: 0237. LP/AC. 1937–46.

6463 *Mississippi folk voices.* Southern Culture: SC 1700. LP/AC. 1968–72. [Napoleon Strickland, Bill Mitchell, Son Thomas, Chapman Family, and others].

6464 * *Mountain music of Kentucky.* Smithsonian/Folkways: SF 40077 (2317). 2CD set. 1959. [Roscoe Holcomb, George Davis, Marion Sumner, Lee Sexton, Bill Cornett, Willie Chapman, Granville Bowlin, and others].

6465 *Mountain valley music: grassroots music from western North Carolina and north Georgia.* John C. Campbell Folk School: C-4417. AC. 1990.

6466 * *New England traditional fiddling: an anthology of recordings, 1926–1975.* JEMF Records: JEMF 105. LP. 1926–75.

6467 *Now that's a good tune: masters of traditional Missouri fiddling.* Grey Eagle: 101. 2LP/2AC set. 1984–89.

6468 * *Old love songs and ballads from the Big Laurel, North Carolina.* Smithsonian/Folkways: 2309. AC. 1963. [Dillard Chandler, Cas Wallin, and others].

6469 * *Old Mother Hippletoe: rural and urban children's songs.* New World: NW 291. LP. 1933–78. OP

6470 *Play and dance songs and tunes.* Library of Congress: L 9. AC. 1936–42.

6471 *Railroad songs and ballads.* Library of Congress: L 61. AC. 1936–59.

6472 *Shaking down the acorns: traditional music and stories from Pocahontas and Greenbrier Counties, West Virginia.* Rounder: 0018. LP. 1970–72. [Members of the Hammons Family and others].

6473 *Songs and ballads of the anthracite miners.* Library of Congress: L 16. AC. 1946.

6474 *Songs and ballads of the bituminous miners.* Library of Congress: L 60. AC. 1940.

6475 *Songs of the Michigan lumberjacks.* Library of Congress: L 56. LP/AC. 1938–48.

6476 *Songs of the Mormons and songs of the West.* Library of Congress: L 30. AC. 1938–49.

6477 * *Sounds of the South: a musical journey from the Georgia Sea Islands to the Mississippi Delta recorded in the field by Alan Lomax.* Atlantic: 82496-2. 4CD set. 1959. [Fred McDowell, Hobart Smith, Almeda Riddle, Texas Gladden, John Dudley, and others].

6478 *Traditional music from Grayson and Carroll Counties.* Smithsonian/Folkways: 3811. AC. 1958–61. [Vester Jones, Glen Smith, Wade Ward, Glen Neaves, Ed Spencer].

6479 *Virginia traditions: southwest Virginia blues.* [Series: Blue Ridge Institute]. Global Village: C 1008 (BRI 008). AC. 1928–40, 1962–84. [Carl Martin, Carter Family, Dock Boggs, Byrd Moore, and others].

6480 *The Watson Family.* Smithsonian/Folkways: SF 40012 (2366). 1960–65, 1976. [Doc Watson, Gaither Carlton, Annie Watson, Rosa Lee Watson, Merle Watson, and others].

Individual Artists or Groups

6481 Gunning, Sarah Ogan, 1910–

Girl of constant sorrow. Folk Legacy: C-26. AC. 1964.

6482 Jackson, Aunt Molly, 1880–1960

The Library of Congress recordings. Rounder: 1002. LP. 1939. OP

6483 * Jarrell, Tommy, 1901–1985, and Fred Cockerham, 1901–198?

Tommy and Fred: best fiddle-banjo duets. County: CD-2702. 1968–73.

6484 McClintock, Harry, 1882–1957

6484.1 *Hallelujah! I'm a bum.* Rounder: 1009 (Victor). LP. 1928–29. OP

6484.2 *Haywire Mac.* Smithsonian/Folkways: 5272. AC. 1953.

6485 Proffitt, Frank, 1913–1969

Frank Proffitt sings folk songs. Smithsonian/Folkways: 2360. AC. 1961.

6486 * Riddle, Almeda, 1898–1986

Ballads and hymns of the Ozarks. Rounder: 0017. LP. 1972.

6487 Sexton, Morgan, 1911–1992

Shady Grove: traditional Appalachian banjo player. June Appal: JA 0066. 1989–90.

6488 * Watson, Doc, 1923– , and Clarence Ashley, 1895–1967

The original Folkways recordings (old time music at Clarence Ashley's). Smithsonian/Folkways: SF 40029/30 (2355/2359). 2CD set. 1960–62.

6489 Workman, Nimrod, 1895–1994

Passing thru the garden. June Appal: 001. LP/AC. 1972–73.

Modern and Contemporary Folk Music

The folk music in this section is of the modern, urban type, dating mostly from 1950 onward and representing the work of professional musicians who either re-create traditional songs or compose new music in traditional idioms.

Anthologies

6490 * *Don't mourn—organize! songs of labor songwriter Joe Hill.* Smithsonian/Folkways: SF 40026. 1940–90. [Utah Phillips, Harry McClintock, Paul Robeson, Pete Seeger, Joe Glazer, Cisco Houston, Earl Robinson, Hazel Dickens, Billy Bragg, Si Kahn, and others].

6491 *The evening concerts: the Newport Folk Festival 1963.* Vanguard: VCD 77002. 1963. [Mississippi John Hurt, Ramblin' Jack Elliott, Ian and Sylvia, Joan Baez, Bob Dylan, Freedom Singers, and others].

6492 * *A family of friends: women's music sampler.* Tsunami: 1003. 1993. [Jamie Anderson, Pam Hall, Alix Dobkin, Sue Fink, Venus Envy, Yer Girlfriend, and others].

6493 *Fast folk musical magazine.* Box 938, Village Station, New York, NY 10014. (212) 274-1636. [A magazine of contemporary folk performers with an accompanying compact disc].

6494 *Feeding the flame: songs by men to end AIDS.* Flying Fish: FF 70541. 1990. [Fred Small, Michael Callen, Romanovsky and Phillips, Flirtations, Pete Seeger, and others].

6495 *Folk classics: roots of American folk music.* Columbia: CK 45026. 1935–66. [Leadbelly, Pete Seeger, Burl Ives, Ramblin' Jack Elliott, Brothers Four, and others].

6496 * *Greatest folksingers of the '60s.* Vanguard: VCD-17/18. 2CD set. [196?]. [Weavers, Pete Seeger, Joan Baez, Phil Ochs, Ian and Sylvia, Eric Andersen, Buffy Sainte-Marie, Odetta, Doc Watson, Jim Kweskin, Bob Gibson, Tom Paxton, Bob Dylan, New Lost City Ramblers, Oscar Brand, Jean Ritchie, and others].

6497 *In country: folk songs of Americans in the Vietnam War.* Flying Fish: FF 70552. 1991.

6498 ** *New acoustic music.* Rykodisc: RCD 20002 (Rounder). [1985]. [Bela Fleck, David Grisman, Jerry Douglas, Tony Rice, Rob Wasserman, Russ Barenberg, Alan Stivell, Tony Trischka, Mike Marshall, Norman Blake, Pierre Bensusan, Sam Bush, Mark O'Connor, and others].

6499 *Newport broadside: topical songs at the Newport Folk Festival.* Vanguard: VCD 77003. 1963. [Bob Dylan, Pete Seeger, Tom Paxton, Phil Ochs, Joan Baez, and others].

6500 *Rounder banjo.* Rounder: CD 11542. [1987]. [J. D. Crowe, Alan Munde, Bill Keith, John Hartford, Tony Trischka, Snuffy Jenkins, Bela Fleck, Don Stover, and others].

6501 *Rounder fiddle.* Rounder: CD 11565. [1990]. [Vassar Clements, Alison Krauss, Richard Greene, Clark Kessinger, Mark O'Connor, Blaine Sprouse, Bobby Hicks, Byron Berline, Matt Glaser, Kenny Kosek, and others].

6502 * *Rounder folk.* Rykodisc: RCD 20018 (Rounder). [1985]. [Norman Blake, Patty Larkin, John Fahey, Bela Fleck, Tony Rice, Nanci Griffith,

Bill Morrissey, Christine Lavin, Guy Van Duser, Cathy Fink, John McCutcheon, and others].

6503 * *Rounder guitar: a collection of acoustic guitar.* Rounder: CD 11541. 1965–86. [Tony Rice, Russ Barenberg, Artie Traum, Guy Van Duser, Norman Blake, and others].

6504 *Rounder old-time music.* Rounder: CD 11510. 1952–86. [Norman Blake, Hazel Dickens, Ricky Scaggs, Whitstein Brothers, Blue Sky Boys, Louvin Brothers, Doc Watson, Mark O'Connor, and others].

6505 ** *Troubadours of the folk era, vol. 1.* Rhino: 70262. 1945–66. [Woody Guthrie, Joan Baez, Ian and Sylvia, Odetta, Buffy Sainte-Marie, Dave Van Ronk, Ramblin' Jack Elliott, Donovan, and others].

6506 ** *Troubadours of the folk era, vol. 2.* Rhino: 70263. 1962–69. [Pete Seeger, Tom Rush, Joni Mitchell, Judy Collins, Tom Paxton, Tim Hardin, Phil Ochs, Jim Kweskin, and others].

6507 ** *Troubadours of the folk era, vol. 3: the groups.* Rhino: 70264. 1957–64. [Weavers, Kingston Trio, Limelighters, New Lost City Ramblers, Brothers Four, New Christy Minstrels, Jim Kweskin, and others].

6508 ** *Troubadours of the folk era, vol. 4: singer-songwriters of the 70s.* Rhino: 71843. 1970–77. [James Taylor, Steve Goodman, Joan Baez, Jesse Winchester, Kate and Anna McGarrigle, Nitty Gritty Dirt Band, Loudon Wainwright III, Judee Sill, Don McLean, Janis Ian, Harry Chapin, John Prine, Rosalie Sorrels, Arlo Guthrie, Phoebe Snow, John Sebastian, Kate Wolf, Townes Van Zandt].

6509 * *Troubadours of the folk era, vol. 5: singer-songwriters of the 80s.* Rhino: 71844. 1978–91. [Steve Forbert, Phranc, Washington Squares, Suzanne Vega, Peter Case, Roches, Billy Bragg, Victoria Williams, John Gorka, Shawn Colvin, Nanci Griffith, Bruce Cockburn, Lucinda Williams, and others].

6510 ** *Voices of the civil rights movement: Black American freedom songs.* Smithsonian/Folkways: SF 40084 (2024). 2CD set. 1960–66.

6511 *Walls to roses: songs of changing men.* Smithsonian/Folkways: 37587. AC. 1978. [Charlie Murphy, Chris Tanner, Jeff Langley, George Fulgenini-Shakor, Blackberri, and others].

6512 *Winter moon: a celebration of gay and lesbian singers and songwriters . . . and friends.* Streeter: STCD-1003. 1995. [Cris Williamson, Michael Callen, Lucie Blue Tremblay, Holly Near, Fred Small, Flirtations, and others].

Individual Artists or Groups

6513   Almanac Singers
Talking union. Smithsonian/Folkways: 5285. AC. 1940–42.

6514   Baez, Joan, 1941–
> **6514.1** *Diamonds and rust.* A&M: 75021-3233-2. 1975.
> **6514.2** * *The first ten years.* Vanguard: VCD-6560/61. 1960–70.
> **6514.3** *Joan Baez in concert.* Vanguard: VCD-113/14. 1962–63.

6515   Blake, Norman, 1938– , and Nancy Blake
The Norman and Nancy Blake compact disc. Rounder: CD 11505. 1979–82.

6516   Block, Rory, 1949–
Best blues and originals. Rounder: CD 11525. 1981–86.

6517   Bok, Gordon, 1939–
North wind's clearing: songs of the Maine coast. Folk-Legacy: CD-1005. 1970–83.

6518   Casselberry-DuPree
City down. Ladyslipper: LS 203 (Iceberg 215). 1986.

6519   Chapman, Tracy, 1964–
Tracy Chapman. Elektra: 60774-2. 1988.

6520   Cohen, Leonard, 1934–
Songs of Leonard Cohen. Columbia: CK 9533. 1968.

6521   Collins, Judy, 1939–
> **6521.1** * *Colors of the day: the best of Judy Collins.* Elektra: 75030-2. 1966–70.
> **6521.2** *In my life.* Elektra: 74027-2. 1966.
> **6521.3** *Recollections.* Elektra: 61350-2. 1963–65.

6522   Cooney, Michael. *The cheese stands alone.* Folk-Legacy: C-35. AC. [1968].

6523   Dement, Iris, 1961–
Infamous angel. Warner Bros.: 45238-2 (Philo 1138). 1992.

6524   Dickens, Hazel
A few old memories. Rounder: CD 11529. [1987].

6525 * Dobkin, Alix

Love and politics, a 30 year saga. Women's Wax Works: A007cd. 1992.

6526 Dylan, Bob, 1941–

6526.1 *Another side of Bob Dylan.* Columbia: CK 8993. 1964.

6526.2 *Biograph.* Columbia: C3K 38830. 3CD set. 1961–81.

6526.3 * *The freewheelin' Bob Dylan.* Columbia: CK 8786. 1963.

6526.4 * *Greatest hits.* Columbia: CK 9463. 1962–67.

6526.5 ** *The times they are a-changin'.* Columbia: CK 8905. 1964.

See also 5533 and 5817

6527 Elliott, Ramblin' Jack, 1931–

Hard travelin'. Fantasy: FCD-24720-2. 1960–61.

6528 Fahey, John, 1939–

Return of the repressed: the John Fahey anthology. Rhino: 71737. 2CD set. 1963–90.

6529 Ferrel, Frank

Yankee dreams: wicked good fiddling from New England. Flying Fish: FF 70572. 1990.

6530 Fjell, Judy

Livin' on dreams. Honey Pie Music: HMP106CD. 1989.

6531 Flower, Robin

First dibs. Flying Fish: FF 90326. AC. 1984.

6532 Goodman, Steve, 1948–1984

City of New Orleans. Pair: PCD2-1233 (Buddah). 1971–72.

6533 Gorka, John

I know. Red House: 18. 1987.

6534 Griffith, Nanci, 1953–

One fair summer evening. MCA: MCAD-42255. 1988.

6535 * Grisman, David, 1945–

The David Grisman Quintet. Rhino: 71468 (Kaleidoscope 5). 1976.

6536 Grossman, Stefan, 1945–

Shining shadows. Shanachie: 97020. 1985.

6537 Guthrie, Arlo, 1947–

The best of Arlo Guthrie. Warner Bros.: 3117-2. 1967–76.

6538 Guthrie, Woody, 1912–1967

6538.1 *Columbia River collection.* Rounder: CD 1036. 1941.

6538.2 ** *Dust Bowl ballads.* Rounder: CD 1040. 1940.

6538.3 * *The greatest songs of Woody Guthrie.* Vanguard: VCD-35/36. [1972]. [Joan Baez, Ramblin' Jack Elliott, Woody Guthrie, Cisco Houston, Odetta, Weavers, and others].

6538.4 * *The Library of Congress recordings.* Rounder: CD 1041/1042/1043. 3CD set. 1940.

6539 ** Guthrie, Woody, 1912–1967, and Leadbelly, 1885–1949

Folkways: the original vision. Smithsonian/Folkways: SF 40001. 1940–47.

6540 Hardin, Tim, 1941–1980

Reason to believe: the best of Tim Hardin. Polydor: 833954-2. 1966–69.

6541 Havens, Richie, 1941–

Resume: the best of Richie Havens. Rhino: 71187. 1965–72.

6542 Houston, Cisco, 1918–1961

The Folkways years. Smithsonian/Folkways: SF 40059. 1944–61.

6543 Hurley, Michael, 1941– , the Unholy Modal Rounders, and Jeffrey Frederick

Have moicy! Rounder: CD 3010. 1976.

6544 Ian and Sylvia

Greatest hits. Vanguard: VCD-5/6. 1962–68.

6545 Indigo Girls

Indigo Girls. Epic: 45044. 1989.

6546 Ives, Burl, 1909–1995

Greatest hits. MCA: MCAD-11439 (Decca). 1945–63.

6547 Kahn, Si, 1941–

I'll be there: songs for jobs with justice. Flying Fish: FF 70509. 1989.

6548 * Kingston Trio

The Kingston Trio. Capitol: 92710. 1958–64.

6549 Kottke, Leo, 1945–

6549.1 * *6- and 12-string guitar.* Rhino: 71612 (Takoma 1024). 1969.

6549.2 *A shout toward noon.* Private Music: 2007-2-P. [1986].

6550 Kweskin, Jim, 1940–

Greatest hits. Vanguard: VCD-13/14. 1963–67.

6551 Lavin, Christine

Attainable love. Philo: CD PH 1132. [1990].

6552 * Leadbelly, 1885–1949

Leadbelly sings folk songs. Smithsonian/Folkways: SF 40010. 1946–48. *See also* 4172

6553 Lightfoot, Gordon, 1938–

Best of Gordon Lightfoot. EMI: 48396. 1965–69.

6554 Limelighters

Tonight in person. RCA: 2272-2-R. 1961.

6555 * McCutcheon, John, 1952–

Water from another time: a retrospective. Rounder: CD 11555. 1974–89.

6556 * McGarrigle, Kate, 1946– , and Anna McGarrigle, 1944–

Kate and Anna McGarrigle. Hannibal: HNCD 4401 (Warner Bros. 2862). 1975.

6557 Morrissey, Bill, 1951–

North. Philo: CD PH 1106. 1986.

6558 Murphy, Charlie

Catch the fire. Iceberg: ICE 5103. AC. 1986. OP

6559 * Near, Holly, 1949–

Imagine my surprise. Redwood: RRD-401. 1978.

6560 New Lost City Ramblers

The early years. Smithsonian/Folkways: SF 40036. 1958–62.

6561 Ochs, Phil, 1940–1976

6561.1 * *There but for fortune.* Elektra: 60832-2. 1964–66.

6561.2 *The war is over: the best of Phil Ochs.* A&M: 75021-5215-2. 1967–70.

6562 Odetta, 1930–

Odetta at Town Hall. Vanguard: VMD-2109. 1963.

6563 Ostroushko, Peter

Sluz duz music. Rounder: CD 0204. 1985.

6564 Paxton, Tom, 1937–

6564.1 *Ramblin' boy.* Elektra: 7277. LP. 1964. OP

6564.2 *The very best of Tom Paxton.* Flying Fish: FF 70519. 1986.

6565 Peter, Paul and Mary

6565.1 *In concert.* Warner Bros.: 1555-2. 1965.

6565.2 *Peter, Paul and Mary.* Warner Bros.: 1449-2. 1962.

6565.3 ** *10 years together: the best of Peter, Paul and Mary.* Warner Bros.: 3105-2. 1962–69.

6566 Phillips, U. Utah (Bruce), 1939–

Good though! Philo: 1004. 1973.

6567 Phranc, 1957–

6567.1 * *Folksinger.* Island: 422 846358-2. 1985. OP

6567.2 *I enjoy being a girl.* Island: 422 842579-2 (91259-2). 1989. OP

6568 Prine, John, 1946–

6568.1 *Great days: the John Prine anthology.* Rhino: 71400. 2CD set. 1971–91.

6568.2 * *Prime Prine.* Atlantic: 18202-2. 1971–75. [Item 6568.1 covers material comparable to item 6568.2 but in greater depth and with better packaging and notes].

6569 Red Clay Ramblers

Twisted laurel/Merchant's lunch. Flying Fish: FF 70055. 1976–77.

6570 Ritchie, Jean, 1922–

6570.1 * *British traditional ballads in the Southern Mountains: Child ballads, vols. 1–2.* Smithsonian/Folkways: 2301/02. AC. 1961.

6570.2 *The most dulcimer.* Greenhays: GR 70714. 1984.

6571 Ritchie, Jean, 1922– , and Doc Watson, 1923–

Live at Folk City. Smithsonian/Folkways: SF 40005 (FA 2426). 1963.

6572 * Roches

The Roches. Warner Bros.: 3298-2. 1979.

6573 * Rush, Tom, 1941–

The circle game. Elektra: 74018-2. 1968.

6574 Sainte-Marie, Buffy, 1941–

The best of Buffy Sainte-Marie. Vanguard: VCD-3/4. 1964–72.

6575 Seeger, Mike, 1933–

Solo: old time country music. Rounder: CD 0278. 1991.

6576 Seeger, Peggy, 1935–

The Folkways years: songs of love and politics. Smithsonian/Folkways: SF 40048. 1955–92.

6577 Seeger, Pete, 1919–

6577.1 *American industrial ballads.* Smithsonian/Folkways: SF 40058. 1956.

6577.2 ** *The essential Pete Seeger.* Vanguard: VCD-97/98 (Folkways). 1950–74.

6577.3 * *We shall overcome: the complete Carnegie Hall concert.* Columbia: C2K 45312. 2CD set. 1963.

6578 Sorrels, Rosalie, 1933–

Report from Grimes Creek. Green Linnet: 2105. 1991.

6579 Spence, Bill

The hammered dulcimer. Front Hall: FHR-302CD (01/05). 1972–75.

6580 Staines, Bill, 1947–

The first million miles. Rounder: CD 11560. 1975–88.

6581 Sweet Honey in the Rock

6581.1 ** *Breaths.* Flying Fish: FF 70105. 1981–83.

6581.2 *Live at Carnegie Hall.* Flying Fish: FF 70106. 1987.

6582 Terry, Sonny, 1911–1986, and Brownie McGhee, 1915–1996. *See 4279*

6583 Tremblay, Lucie Blue

Tendresse. Olivia: ORCD 955. 1989.

6584 Van Duser, Guy

American finger style guitar. Rounder: CD 11533. 1977–85.

6585 Van Ronk, Dave, 1936–

The Folkways years. Smithsonian/Folkways: SF 40041. 1959–61.

6586 Van Zandt, Townes, 1940–1997

Live at the Old Quarter. Tomato/Rhino: 71245 (TOM-2-7001). 1977.

6587 Wainwright, Loudon, III, 1946–

A live one. Rounder: CD 3050. 1976–78.

6588 Watson, Doc, 1923–

6588.1 ** *The essential Doc Watson.* Vanguard: VCD-45/46. 1963–64.

6588.2 *The Vanguard years.* Vanguard: VCD-155/58-2. 4CD set. 1963–71.

6589 Weavers

6589.1 *The best of the Decca years.* MCA: MCAD-11465. [1949–54].

6589.2 ** *The Weavers at Carnegie Hall.* Vanguard: VMD-73101. 1955.

6590 White, Josh, 1908–1969

The best of Josh White. Elektra: EKS-75008. 2LP set. 1954–60. OP

6591 Winchester, Jesse, 1944–

The best of Jesse Winchester. Rhino: 70085 (Bearsville). 1971–81.

6592 Wolf, Kate, 1942–1986

Gold in California: a retrospective of recordings. Rhino: 71485 (Kaleidoscope 3001). 2CD set. 1975–85.

Other European Immigrants

French (Cajun and Zydeco)

This section covers music of French-speaking whites (Cajun) and French-speaking African Americans (zydeco) centered in the state of Louisiana.

General Anthologies

6593 * *Alligator stomp, vol. 1: Cajun and zydeco classics.* Rhino: 70946. [1990]. [Rockin' Sidney, Rockin' Dopsie, D. L. Menard, Clifton Chenier, Johnnie Allan, Jo-el Sonnier, Rusty and Doug Kershaw, Boozoo Chavis, Beausoleil, Queen Ida, and others].

6594 *Alligator stomp, vol. 2: Cajun and zydeco classics.* Rhino: 70740. [1990]. [Terrance Simien, Balfa Brothers, Queen Ida, Clifton Chenier, Jo-el Sonnier, Rusty and Doug Kershaw, Boozoo Chavis, Beausoleil, Buckwheat Zydeco, Rockin' Dopsie, John Delafose, Nathan Abshire, Iry LeJeune, D. L. Menard, and others].

6595 *Alligator stomp, vol. 3: Cajun and zydeco classics.* Rhino: 70312. [1992]. [Beausoleil, C. J. Chenier, Savoy-Doucet Band, Rockin' Dopsie, Eddie LeJeune, John Delafose, Clifton Chenier, Buckwheat Zydeco, Balfa Brothers, Filè, and others].

6596 * *Alligator stomp, vol. 5: Cajun and zydeco, the next generation.* Rhino: 71846. [1995]. [Terrance Simien, Steve Riley, Beau Jocque, C. J. Chenier, Beausoleil, John Delafose, Nathan and the Zydeco Cha Chas, Wayne Toups, Chubby Carrier, David Doucet, Basin Brothers, Bruce Daigrepont, and others].

6597 *Another Saturday night: classic recordings from the Louisiana bayous.* Ace: CDCH 288. 1961–87. [Tommy McLain, Belton Richard, Cookie and His Cupcakes, Carol Fran, Johnnie Allan, Austin Pitre, Rufus Jagneaux, and others].

6598 * *Cajun music and zydeco.* Rounder: CD 11572. [1992]. [Clifton Chenier, Boozoo Chavis, Dewey Balfa, Buckwheat Zydeco, Beausoleil, Dennis McGee, Zachary Richard, Steve Riley, and others].

6599 ** *J'ai été au bal (I went to the dance): the Cajun and zydeco music of Louisiana, vols. 1–2.* Arhoolie: CD 331/CD 332. 2 CDs. 1928–88. [Queen Ida, Michael Doucet, Canray Fontenot, Dennis McGee, Amadé Ardoin, Nathan Abshire, Marc Savoy, Joe and Cleoma Breaux, Hackberry Ramblers, Leo Soileau, Harry Choates, Iry LeJeune, Clifton Chenier, D. L. Menard, Johnnie Allan, Dewey Balfa, John Delafose, Boozoo Chavis, Wayne Toups, and others].

6600 *Louisiana Cajun and Creole music: the Lomax recordings.* Swallow: 8003-2. 2LP set. 1934.

CAJUN ANTHOLOGIES

6601 *Cajun, vol. 1: Abbeville breakdown.* Columbia: CK 46220. 1929–39. [Breaux Family, Joe Falcon, Alley Boys of Abbeville].

6602 *Cajun honky tonk: the Khoury recordings: the early 1950s.* Arhoolie: CD 427. [195?]. [Nathan Abshire, Harry Choates, Floyd LeBlanc, Lawrence Walker, and others].

6603 * *Cajun social music.* Smithsonian/Folkways: SF 40006 (FA2621). 1975. [Nathan Abshire, Marc Savoy, Hector Duhon, and others].

6604 * *Folksongs of the Louisiana Acadians.* Folklyric/Arhoolie: CD 359 (5009+). 1956–59.

6605 * *Le gran mamou: a Cajun music anthology, the historic Victor/Bluebird sessions.* Country Music Foundation: CMF-013-D. 1928–41. [Leo Soileau, Amadé Ardoin, Dennis McGee, Nathan Abshire, Hackberry Ramblers, and others].

6606 * *Louisiana Cajun French music from the Southwest Prairies, vols. 1–2.* Rounder: CD 6001/6002. 2 CDs. 1964–67. [Balfa Brothers, Austin Pitre, Boisec Ardoin, and others].

6607 ** *Louisiana Cajun music special.* Swallow: CD-103. [1963–81]. [Nathan Abshire, Balfa Brothers, Mamou Playboys, D. L. Menard, Lionel Courmier, and others].

INDIVIDUAL ARTISTS OR GROUPS—CAJUN

6608   Abshire, Nathan, 1913–1981
French blues. Arhoolie: CD 373 (Khoury). 1949–56.

6609 *   Balfa Brothers
The Balfa Brothers play traditional Cajun music, vols. 1–2. Swallow: CD-6011. 1965, 1974.

6610   Balfa, Dewey, 1927–1992, Marc Savoy, 1940–, and D. L. Menard, 1932–
Under a green oak tree. Arhoolie: CD 312. 1976.

6611   Beausoleil
   6611.1 * *Allons à Lafayette and more with Canray Fontenot.* Arhoolie: CD 308. 1981, 1985.
   6611.2 ** *Bayou deluxe: the best of Michael Doucet and Beausoleil.* Rhino: 71169. 1980–92.

6612 *   Choates, Harry, 1922–1951
The fiddle king of Cajun swing. Arhoolie: CD 380 (Gold Star). 1946–50.

6613   Doucet, Michael, 1951–
Beau solo. Arhoolie: CD 321. 1989.

6614   Hackberry Ramblers
Early recordings. Old Timey: OT127. AC. 1935–48.

6615   Kershaw, Doug, 1936–
The best of Doug Kershaw. Warner Bros.: 25964-2. 1972–78.

6616 *   LeJeune, Iry, 1928–1955
Cajun's greatest: the definitive collection. Ace: CDCHD 428 (Goldband). 1948–55.

6617   Menard, D. L., 1932–
No matter where you at, there you are. Rounder: CD 6021. 1988.

6618   Menard, D. L., 1932– , and Austin Pitre, 1918–1981
The Swallow recordings. Ace: CDCHD 327. 1959–63, 1971.

6619 Richard, Zachary, 1950–

Zack's bon ton. Rounder: CD 6027. 1988.

6620 * Riley, Steve

Steve Riley and the Mamou Playboys. Rounder: CD 6038. [1990].

6621 Soileau, Leo, 1904–1980

Pioneer Cajun fiddler. Folklyric/Arhoolie: 9057. AC. 1929–37.

6622 Sonnier, Jo-el, 1946–

Cajun life. Rounder: CD 3049. [1988].

ZYDECO ANTHOLOGIES

6623 ** *Zydeco champs.* Arhoolie: CD 328. 1928–88. [Clifton Chenier, Amadé Ardoin, Conray Fontenot, Boisec Ardoin, Clarence Garlow, John Delafose, Sam Brothers, C. J. Chenier, and others].

6624 *Zydeco, vol. 1: the early years.* Arhoolie: CD 307. 1949, 1954, 1961–62. [Sidney Babineaux, Herbert Sam, Willie Green, Clifton Chenier, Clarence Garlow, and others].

INDIVIDUAL ARTISTS OR GROUPS—ZYDECO

6625 Ardoin, Amadé, ca. 1896–1941

I'm never comin' back. Folklyric/Arhoolie: CD-7007. 1930–34.

6626 Buckwheat Zydeco, 1947–

6626.1 * *Buckwheat's zydeco party.* Rounder: CD 11528. 1983–87.

6626.2 *Menagerie: the essential zydeco collection.* Mango: 162-539929-2. 1987–90.

6627 Chavis, Boozoo, 1930–

The Lake Charles atomic bomb (original Goldband recordings). Rounder: CD 2097. 1955–[196?].

6628 Chenier, Clifton, 1925–1987

6628.1 ** *Louisiana blues and zydeco.* Arhoolie: CD 329. 1964–67.

6628.2 * *Zydeco dynamite: the Clifton Chenier anthology.* Rhino: 71194. 2CD set. 1954–84.

6629 Delafose, John, 1939–1994

Joe Pete got two women. Arhoolie: CD 335. 1980–82.

6630 Queen Ida, 1930–

On tour. GNP Crescendo: GNPD-2147. 1982.

German and Swiss

Anthologies

6631 * *Ach ya! traditional German-American music from Wisconsin.* Folklore Village Farm: FVF 301. 2LP set. 1939–85.

6632 * *Swissconsin, my homeland: Swiss folk music in Wisconsin.* Wisconsin Folklife Center: 8801-C. AC. 1926–88.

Individual Artist

6633 Britton, George

Pennsylvania Dutch folk songs. Smithsonian/Folkways: 2215. AC. 1961.

Irish

Anthologies

6634 *Cherish the ladies: Irish women musicians in America.* Shanachie: 79053. 1985. [Liz Carroll, Eileen Ivers, and others].

6635 * *Dear old Erin's isle: Irish traditional music from America.* Nimbus: NI 5350. 1992. [Seamus Egan, Liz Carroll, Kevin Burke, Jimmy Keane, Joe Shannon, and others].

6636 ** *From Galway to Dublin: traditional Irish music.* Rounder: CD 1087. 1921–59. [Recorded in Ireland, England, and the United States; Frank Quinn, Paddy Killoran, Michael Coleman, Tom Morrison, James Mullan, and others].

6637 *The green fields of America: live in concert.* Green Linnet: GLCD 1096. 1988. [Mick Moloney, Eileen Ivers, Seamus Egan, Jimmy Keane, and others].

6638 ** *I'm leaving Tipperary: classic Irish traditional music recorded in America in the '20s and '30s.* GlobeStyle: CDORBD 082. [192?–193?]. [Hugh Gillespie, James Morrison, Michael Hanafin, Tom Ennis, Dan Sullivan, Flanagan Brothers, John McGettigan, and others].

6639 * *Irish-American dance music and songs.* Folklyric: 9010. LP. [192?–193?]. [Frank Quinn, Patrick Killoran, John Griffin, Flanagan Brothers, and others]. OP

6640 *Irish dance music.* Smithsonian/Folkways: 8821. AC. 1928–63.

6641 *Irish music from Cleveland, vols. 1–2.* Smithsonian/Folkways: 3517/3521. AC. 1977–78.

6642 *My love is in America: the Boston College Irish Fiddle Festival.* Green Linnet: GLCD 1110. 1990.

Individual Artists

6643 Carroll, Liz

Liz Carroll. Green Linnet: GLCD 1092. 1988.

6644 * Coleman, Michael, 1891–1945

Michael Coleman: 1891–1945. Viva Voce: 004. 2CD set. 1921–36.

Italian

6645 *Calabria bella, dove t'hai lasciate.* [Series: Italian folk music in New York and New Jersey, vol. 2]. Smithsonian/Folkways: 34042. AC. 1975–78.

6646 *Chesta e la voci ca canuscite = This is the voice you know: southern Italian mountain music from Calabria, Campania, Basilicata and Abruzzi.* Global Village: C 675. AC. [1985].

6647 * *In mezz'una strada trovai una pianta di rosa.* [Series: Italian folk music in New York and New Jersey, vol. 1]. Smithsonian/Folkways: 34041. AC. 1975–78.

6648 *Italian folk songs collected in Italian-speaking communities in New York City and Chicago.* Smithsonian/Folkways: 4010. AC. 1963–64.

6649 *Italian string virtuosi.* Rounder: CD 1095. 1908–32.

6650 ** *Rimpianto: Italian music in America.* Global Village: C 601. AC. 1915–29.

Scandinavian, Finnish, and Baltic

Anthologies

6651 *Accordions in the cutover: field recordings of ethnic music from Lake Superior's south shore.* Northland College: AITC. 2LP set. 1979–81. [Also includes Eastern European–American music].

6652 * *Across the fields.* [Series: Traditional Norwegian-American music from Wisconsin, vol. 1]. Folklore Village Farm/Wisconsin Folklife Center: FVF 201-C. AC. 1981–82.

6653 *American Swedish Spelmans Trio: old country folk fiddling.* Rounder: 6004. LP. 1977.

6654 *Children of the Finnish immigrant: Finnish-American music from upper Michigan.* Thimbleberry: THC 1008. AC. [1990].

6655 *From Sweden to America: emigrant and immigrant songs.* Caprice: CAP-2011. 2LP set. 1914–80.

6656 *Lithuanian folk songs in the United States.* Smithsonian/Folkways: 4009. AC. 1949–50.

6657 * *Nikolina: early Scandinavian bands and entertainers.* Banjar: BR-1840. AC. 1904–49. [Olle i Stratthult, Lager and Olzen, Eddie Jahrl, Arvid Franzen, and others].

6658 * *Norwegian-American music from Minnesota: old-time and traditional favorites.* [Series: Minnesota musical traditions]. Minnesota Historical Society: C-002. AC. 1987–88.

6659 *Scandinavian-American folk dance music, vol. 1: the Norwegians in Minnesota.* Banjar: BR-1825. LP. 1974.

6660 *Siirtolaisen muistoja: the immigrants' memories.* Ohelma: PK 40115 (RCA). AC. [1978]. [Compilation of remastered 78 rpm recordings].

6661 *Tunes and songs of Finland.* Smithsonian/Folkways: 6856. AC. 1957. [Adolf Stark, Aino Karelia].

6662 * *Tunes from the Amerika trunk.* [Series: Traditional Norwegian-American music from Wisconsin, vol. 2]. Folklore Village Farm/Wisconsin Folklife Center: FVF 202-C. AC. 1983–84.

Individual Artists or Groups

6663 Ameriikan Poijat

Finnish brass in America. Global Village: CD 810. 1993.

6664 * Turpeinen, Viola, 1909–1958

The early days: Finnish-American dance music. Thimbleberry: THC 1006. AC. 1928–38.

Slavic and Balkan

Anthologies

6665 *Ethnic dance music in Northern Indiana: Greek, Macedonian, Serbian and Croatian.* Archives of Traditional Music: [n.n.]. AC. 1950–87.

6666 * *Music of Eastern Europe: Albanian, Greek, and South Slavic traditions in the United States.* [Series: Sounds of the world]. Music Educators National Conference: 3038. 3AC set. [1989].

6667 *Nova domovina/A new homeland: Balkan Slavic music from the industrial Midwest.* Ohio Arts Council: OAC 601. LP. 1978–79.

6668 *Polish highlanders/na zywo gesle: music from the southern Tatra Mountains.* Modal Music: 911. AC. [1990].

6669 * *Polish village music: historic Polish American recordings.* Folklyric/Arhoolie: CD 7031 (9026). 1928–32.

6670 * *'Spiew juchasa/Song of the shepherd: songs of the Slavic Americans.* New World: NW 283. LP. 1926–50. OP

6671 * *Texas-Czech, Bohemian and Moravian bands: historic recordings.* Folklyric/Arhoolie: CD 7026. 1929–59. [Baca's Orchestra, Adolph Pavlas, Joe Patek, Adolph Hofner, and others].

6672 * *Ukrainian village music: historic recordings.* Folklyric/Arhoolie: CD 7030. 1928–33.

Individual Artists or Groups

6673 * Data, Marisha
Polish song favorites. Sajewski: 8882. AC. [194?–195?].

6674 * Humeniuk, Pawlo, 1884–1965
King of the Ukrainian fiddlers. Arhoolie: CD 7025. 1925–27.

6675 Moskowitz, Joseph, 1879–1954
The art of the cymbalom: the music of Joseph Moskowitz. Rounder: CD 1126. 1916–53.

6676 Papagika, Marika, 1890–1943
Greek popular and rebetica music in New York. Alma Criolla: CD 802. 1918–29.

6677 * Plehal Brothers
The Plehal Brothers: Tom and Eddie: rare recordings from the 1930s. Banjar: BR-1850. AC. 1938–41.

See also Greece in chapter 33

Polka

Anthologies

6678 * *Best of Cleveland.* JB: LP. [196?]. [Lenny Zadel, Polka Sharps, Ray Krakowski].

6679 ** *Chicagoland polkas.* Dana: LP 1246. LP. [195?]. [Eddie Zima, Johnny Bomba, Steve Adamczyk].

6680 * *Minnesota polka: dance music from four traditions.* [Series: Minnesota musical traditions]. Minnesota Historical Society: C-004. AC. 1965–90.

6681 *Two guys from Cleveland.* Kerebo: 2005. AC. [1990]. [Ray Budzilek, Joe Oberaitis].

Individual Artists or Groups

6682 Adamczyk, Steve
Polka music hall of fame album. Chicago Polkas: 4303. AC. [1970].

6683 Ampol-Aires
Polish nite life in Chicago. Ampol: 25001 (5004). [196?].

6684 Bay State IV
Salutes the polka stars. Polka Train: 8401. AC. [198?].

6685 Blazonczyk, Eddie, and the Versatones
6685.1 * *Another polka celebration.* Bel-Aire: CD-3039. 1986.
6685.2 *Polka concert.* Bel-Aire: 3023. AC. 1975.
6685.3 ** *Polkatime: 20 of the best from Eddie Blazonczyk and the Versatones.* Cleveland International: CIR 1003-2. 1968–94.

6686 Brave Combo
Musical varieties. Rounder: CD 11546. 1981, 1984.

6687 Canadian Fiddlestix
Blazing fiddles. WAM: 20068. AC. 1983.

6688 Check, John, and the Wisconsin Dutchmen
The Wisconsin Dutchmen present all originals: original polka, waltz and schottische selections. North Star Appli: NSA 178 CD. 1994.

6689 * Connecticut Twins
Holiday in Poland. Stella: SLP 926. LP. [196?].

6690 * Dyna-Tones
Live wire. WRS/World Renowned Sounds: 20067. AC. 1982.

6691 G-Notes
At last. WAM: 4029. AC. [198?].

6692 Golonka, Stas
Hooked on honkey. WRS/World Renowned Sounds: 20082. AC. 1985.

6693   Gomulka, Lenny, and Chicago Push

6693.1 ** *From the polka capital.* Bel-Aire: 4064. AC. 1983.

6693.2 *Join the polka generation.* WRS/World Renowned Sounds: 20092. AC. 1988.

6693.3 *Most requested hits.* WRS/World Renowned Sounds: WRD 2803. 1992.

6694 * Gosz, Romy, 1911–1966

Roman Gosz and his orchestra, vols. 1–2. Polkaland: LP-30/LP-33. 2 LPs. 1931–36.

6695 * Groller, Walt, 1931–

I wish I were a little boy. Chalet: 316. AC. [197?].

6696 * Haller, Hank

Thank you dear and give her roses. Haller: 5022. AC. 1986.

6697 * Happy Louie and Julcia

Polkarisma. Halo: 5032. AC. 1986.

6698   Henry, Ray

Unforgettable hits. Deb: DEB-105. 194?–7?.

6699 * Li'l Wally (Jagiello)

Polka time. Jay Jay: 5155. AC. 1987.

6700   Lush, Marion

6700.1 ** *The golden voice of polkas.* Dyno: 1650. [1985].

6700.2 *Na zdrowie!* Dyno: 1606 (Starr 544-545). AC. [1970].

6701   Meixner, Al

Small world of polkas. EC: 1891. AC. [198?].

6702   Moostash Joe Polka Band

Our favorite music, vol. 4: polkas and waltzes. Czech Records: 80. AC. 1987.

6703   Mrozinski Brothers Aleatoric Ensemble

In session. Aleatoric: 1003. AC. 1982.

6704   New Brass

Roll out the barrel. WAM: 20035. AC. 1977.

6705   Oberaitis, Joe

Pan Jozef: past-present-future. Kerebo: 2004. AC. [1991?].

6706   Ostanek, Walter

6706.1 * *Polka stalgia, vols. 1–2.* WRS/World Renowned Sounds: 100007/8. AC. 1988.

6706.2 *35th anniversary.* WRS/World Renowned Sounds: WRD 1800 (10015). 1993.

6707 ** Pecon, Johnny, 1915–1975

Polkas by Pecon with Lou Trebar. Delta International: DI-7019-LPS. LP. [197?].

6708   Rotondi

Play on. ROM: 26001. 1986, 1988.

6709 ** Six Fat Dutchmen

Greatest hits, vol. 1. Polka City: 1006. AC. [198?].

6710 * Solek, Walt

Clown prince of polkas. KSD: 7222 (Dana 598-12). [195?].

6711   Sturr, Jimmy

A polka just for me. Starr: 563. 1986.

6712   Tercek, Al

Polka power. Delta International: DI-7015-LPS. LP. [197?].

6713 * Vadnal, Johnny

Slovenian style polka specials. Jay Jay: JJ-5071. AC. [195?].

6714   Weber, Jimmy, and The Sounds

Soundsational polkas. WAM: 20087. AC. 1987.

6715 * Wilfahrt, Whoopee John, 1893–1961

Whoopee John story, vol. 1. Polka City: 1004. AC. [197?].

6716 * Witkowski, Bernie, 1916–

World's greatest polka band. Stella: SLP 900. LP. [195?–196?].

6717 * Wojnarowski, Frank

The best of Frank Wojnarowski. Dyno: 1655. [19??].

6718   Yankovic, Frankie, 1915–

6718.1 *48 polka and waltz medleys.* Ross: 6626-2. [198?].

6718.2 ** *Greatest hits.* Columbia: CK 9287. [198?].

6718.3 *70 years of hits.* Polydor: 422 830024-4. AC. 1985.

6719 * Zima, Eddie, 1923–1966

Polka music hall of fame. Chicago: LP-4701. [19-?]. OP

Middle Eastern and Asian Immigrants

Anthologies

6720 *Armenians on 8th Avenue.* Traditional Crossroads: 4279. [194?]. [Kanuni Garbis, Marko Melkon, "Sugar Mary" Vartanian, and others].

6721 * *Eternal voices: traditional Vietnamese music in the United States.* New Alliance: NAR CD 053. 2CD set. 1987.

6722 ** *Music of East Asia: Chinese, Korean, and Japanese traditions in the United States.* [Series: Sounds of the world]. Music Educators National Conference: MENC 3036. 3AC set. [1989].

6723 ** *Music of the Middle East: Arab, Persian/ Iranian, and Turkish traditions in the United States.* [Series: Sounds of the world]. Music Educators National Conference: MENC 3040. 3AC set. [1990].

6724 *Songs of departure: Vietnamese traditional music in Dallas and Fort Worth.* Documentary Arts: 110. AC. [1990].

Individual Artists

6725 Hagopian, Richard, 1937– , and Buddy Sarkissian

Kef time: exciting sounds of the Middle East. Traditional Crossroads: TCRO 4269. [196?].

Canada (French and British)

See also 6325, 6369, 6370, 6371, 6372, 6373, 6520, 6544, 6553, 6687

Anthologies

6726 *La belle province, Québec: French-Canadian folk songs.* Monitor: MFS-51714. AC. [197?]. [Alexander Zelkin and Denise Berard].

6727 *The Doukhobors of British Columbia.* Smithsonian/Folkways: 8972. AC. 1962.

6728 * *Folklore: anthology of Canadian music.* Radio Canada International: ACM 39 CD 1–5. 5CD set. 1990.

6729 *Folksongs of Saskatchewan.* Smithsonian/Folkways: 4312. AC. 1963. [Includes Welsh-, German-, Ukrainian-, Icelandic-, French-, and Anglo-Canadian, as well as Indian, songs].

6730 *Masters of French Canadian music, vols. 1–4.* Smithsonian/Folkways: RF 110/111/114/115. 4 ACs. 1926–45. [Joseph Allard, Phillipe Bruneau, Gabriel Labbe, Alfred Montmarquette, Henry Lacroix].

6731 *Québec: groupes folkloriques provinciaux.* Planett: 242015. 1991.

6732 *Songs from Cape Breton Island.* Smithsonian/ Folkways: 4450. AC. 1953.

6733 *Songs of French Canada.* Smithsonian/ Folkways: 4482. AC. 1957.

6734 *A taste of Atlantic Canada.* Ground Swell: GRS-59. 1993.

6735 * *Traditional music from Cape Breton Island.* Nimbus: NI-5383. 1993.

Individual Artists or Groups

6736 Ad Vielle Que Pourra

Ad Vielle Que Pourra. Green Linnet: GLCD 1099. 1989.

6737 Amyot, Robert

Sur la Vignolon: chansons de Québec. Auvidis Ethnic: B 6740. [199?].

6738 La Bottine Souriante

La traversée de l'Atlantique. Green Linnet: GLCD 3043. 1988.

6739 Cormier, Joseph, 1927–

Joseph Cormier and friends: old time wedding reels, and other favorite Scottish fiddle tunes. Rounder: CD 7013. 1992.

6740 Girardon, Evelyne

Amour de fusain. Ocora: C 559043. 1988.

6741 Lampron, Jean-Luc

Canada: danses du Québec. PlayaSound/Auvidis: PS 65080. 1991.

6742 McGarrigle, Kate, 1946– , and Anna McGarrigle, 1944–

French record. Hannibal: HNCD 1302. 1981. *See also* 6556

6743 Pancerzewski, Joe, 1905–

Brand new old fiddle tunes. Voyager: VRCS 335. AC. 1988.

6744 Tyson, Ian, 1933–

And stood there amazed. Vanguard: VCD 79471. 1990–91.

32

Traditional and Popular Musics of the Caribbean and Latin America

Compiled by
**Mark McKnight and
William E. Anderson**

T his chapter comprises traditional and popular musics from the Caribbean, Central America, and South America by their Spanish-speaking, Portuguese-speaking, French-speaking, English-speaking, and indigenous Indian peoples. Latino traditions of the United States (Texas and Southwest border regions, New York City, and Miami) are also included, but composers associated primarily with the Western Classical tradition are covered in that section of the book. The chapter is divided into six sections: "General Anthologies"; "Salsa, Latin Jazz, and Related Styles"; "Caribbean"; "Mexico and Southwestern United States"; "Central America"; and "South America."

General Anthologies

6745 *Africa in America: music from 19 countries.* Corason: MTCD 115/7. 3CD set. [194?]–1992. [Selections from Cuba, Haiti, Belize, Honduras, Brazil, United States, Surinam, Dominican Republic, Venezuela, Panama, Guatemala, Puerto Rico, Mexico, Peru, Jamaica, Antigua, Guadeloupe, Martinique, Nicaragua, and Colombia].

6746 *Amérique du sud: musiques hispaniques.* Auvidis Ethnic: B 6782. 1992. [Traditional and popular music from Colombia, Argentina, El Salvador, Bolivia, and Venezuela].

6747 *Amérique du sud: musiques indiennes.* Auvidis Ethnic: B 6783. 1992. [Traditional songs and instrumental music of Indian peoples of Bolivia, Venezuela, Argentina, Peru, Mexico, and Colombia].

6748 *Grands carnavals d'Amérique de Rio à Quebec.* PlayaSound: PS 65008. 1987. [Carnival music of the northern and southern Americas].

6749 *Musica de la tierra, vols. 1–2.* Music of the World: CDC-206–CDC-207. 2 CDs. 1992. [Music from various Latin American countries].

6750 *Percussions d'Amérique latine.* Arion: ARN 64023. 1986. [Latin American percussion].

6751 *The spirit cries: music from the rainforests of South America and the Caribbean.* Rykodisc: RCD 10250. 1949–87. [Field recordings from the Archive of Folk Culture, Library of Congress; music from Belize, Panama, Colombia, Peru, French Guiana, Surinam, and Jamaica].

Salsa, Latin Jazz, and Related Styles (Including New York City, Miami, and Pan-Caribbean Artists)

Anthologies

6752 * *The best of the mambo, vol. 1.* RCA Tropical: 3310-2-RL. 1949–57. [Machito, Tito Puente, Perez Prado, Beny Moré, Tito Rodriguez, Noro Morales, and others].

6753 * *Caliente = Hot: Puerto Rican and Cuban musical expression in New York.* New World: 80244-2. 1976. [Hector Rivera, Julito Collazo, Victor Montanez, Armando Sanchez, and others].

6754 ** *The Latin vogue.* Charly: CDCHARLY 229. [196?–197?]. [Tito Puente, Celia Cruz, Ray Barretto, Machito, Candido, Johnny Colon, Fania All Stars, Larry Harlow, Ismael Rivera, Eddie Palmieri, Charlie Palmieri, and others].

6755 * *Mambo mania: the kings and queens of mambo.* Rhino: 71881. 1949–80. [Celia Cruz, La Sonora Matancera, Perez Prado, Mongo Santamaria, Hector Rivera, Beny Moré, Ray Barretto, Tito Puente, Tito Rodriguez, Machito, Xavier Cugat, Cachao, Cal Tjader, Septeto Nacional de Ignacio Pineiro, and others].

6756 * *Salsa fresca! dance hits of the '90s.* Rhino: 72195. [1996]. [Frankie Ruiz, Grupo Niche, Willie Colon, Pete "El Conde" Rodriguez, Luis Enrique, Gilberto Santa Rosa, Willie Rosario, Eddie Santiago, and others].

6757 * *Salsa greats: ritmo caliente.* Charly: CD CHARLY 131. [1976]. [Tito Puente, Ruben Blades, Ray Barretto, Willie Colon, Larry Harlow, Johnny Pacheco, Eddie Palmieri, Ricardo Ray, Bobby Valentín, and others].

6758 ** *Salsa greats, vol. 2.* Fania: JMCD 524. [1978]. [Eddie Palmieri, Tito Puente, Ray Barretto, Larry Harlow, Willie Colon, Johnny Pacheco, Bobby Valentín, Ricardo Ray, and others].

6759 *Sixties gold.* Musica Latina: SPCD 53. [196?]. [Ray Barretto, Joe Cuba, Mongo Santamaria, and others].

6760 *Las Tres flautas.* Fania: 561. 1980. [Jose Fajardo, Johnny Pacheco, Pupi Legarreta].

6761 *Tres grandes orquestas e interpretes de la musica Afro Cubana, vol. 1.* RCA Tropical: 74321-15702-2. 1950–60. [Tito Puente, Beny Moré, Tito Rodriguez].

6762 * *We got Latin soul.* Charly: CDCHARLY 91. 1963–67. [Joe Cuba, Ray Barretto, Tito Puente, Joe Bataan, Fania All Stars, and others].

Individual Artists or Groups

6763 Armenteros, Alfredo "Chocolate," ca. 1926– *Prefiero el son.* SAR: SLPCD 1009. 1980.

6764 Barretto, Ray, 1929–
6764.1 *Acid.* Fania: SLP 346. 1967.
6764.2 *Rican/struction.* Fania: JMCD 552. 1979.

6765 Batachanga
Mañana para los niños. Earth Beat: 2557. 1989.

6766 Bauza, Mario, 1911–1993
6766.1 *My time is now.* Messidor: CD 15824-2. 1992.
6766.2 *Tanga.* Messidor: CD 15819-2. 1991.

6767 Blades, Ruben, 1948–
6767.1 *Bohemio y poeta.* Fania: JMCD 541. 1979.
6767.2 *Maestra vida.* Fania: JMCD 576/JMCD 577. 2 CDs. 1980.
6767.3 * *Ruben Blades y Sol del Solar live!* Elektra: 60868-2. 1989.

6768 Blades, Ruben, 1948– , and Willie Colon, 1950–
Siembra. Fania: JMCD-537. 1978.

6769 Chirino, Willy
Amandote. CBS: 80249 (10542). [1988].

6770 Colon, Willie, 1950–
6770.1 *The best.* Globo/Sony: 80747. [1992].
6770.2 *The best II.* Globo/Sony: 81463. [1994].
6770.3 * *The good, the bad, the ugly.* Fania: SLP 484. 1975.
6770.4 *Willie.* Fania: SLP 464. 1974.

6771 Cortijo, Rafael, d. 1983
Time machine. Musical Productions: MP 3108. 1974.

6772 Cruz, Celia
6772.1 *Azucar negra.* RMM: CDZ-80985. 1993.
6772.2 * *La incomparable.* Seeco: SCCD 9136. 1951–60. [With La Sonora Matancera].

6772.3 ** *Introducing the queen of salsa.* Charly: CDCHARLY 130. 1966–[197?].

6773   Cruz, Celia, and Johnny Pacheco, 1935–

Celia and Johnny. Vaya: VS 31. 1974.

6774   Cruz, Celia, and Ray Barretto, 1929–

Ritmo en el corazon. Fania: JMCD 651. [1981].

6775   Cruz, Celia, and Willie Colon, 1950–

Cruz & Colon: only they could have made this album. Vaya: JMVS66. 1977.

6776   D'Rivera, Paquito, 1946–

La Habana-Rio conexion. Messidor: CD 15820-2. 1992.

6777   D'Rivera, Paquito, 1946– , and Arturo Sandoval, 1949–

Reunion. Messidor: 15805-2. 1990.

6778   Estefan, Gloria, 1957–

Mi tierra. Epic: EK 53807. 1993.

6779   Fania All Stars

6779.1   *Fania All Stars: live at Yankee Stadium, vol. 1.* Fania: 476. 1975.

6779.2   *Los hits gordos de Fania = Fania All Stars' greatest hits.* Fania: JMCD 511. 1977.

6780   Fé, Alfredo de la

Salsa and charanga. Discos Fuentes: 10127 (6019). 1991.

6781   Feliciano, Cheo

The best of Cheo Feliciano with the Joe Cuba Sextette. Polydor: 314 521 076-2. [1993].

6782   Fiol, Henry, 1947–

Sonero. Earthworks: STEW 19 (CAROL 2418). 1983–86.

6783   Gonzalez, Jerry, 1949– , and the Fort Apache Band

Rumba para Monk. Sunnyside: 1036. 1988–89.

6784   Irakere

6784.1   *The best of Irakere.* Columbia: CK 57719 (35655/36107). 1978–80.

6784.2   *Live at Ronnie Scott's.* World Pacific: CDP80598. 1993.

6785   Lavoe, Hector, 1946–

Lavoe. Fania: JM 700. 2CD set. [1993?].

6786   Machito, 1912–1984

6786.1   *Latin soul plus jazz (Kenya).* Charly: CDCHARLY 149 (Tico 1314). 1957–58.

6786.2 ** *Mucho macho.* Pablo: PACD-2625-712-2. 1948–49.

See also 4456

6787   Marin, Orlando, 1934–

6787.1   *Saxophobia.* Mucho Music: MMICD1024. [1993?]. [Featuring Charlie Palmieri and Louie Ramirez].

6787.2   *Se te quemo la casa.* Alegre: JMAS6015. 1978.

6788   Morales, Noro, 1911–1964

His piano and rhythm. Ansonia: 1272. 1961.

6789   Orquesta Conexion Latina

Calorcito. ENJA: 4072. 1984.

6790   Orquestra Rytmo Africa-Cubana

La charanga 1980. TKIOS Musique: 7779. [1992?].

6791 * Pacheco, Johnny, 1935–

Introducing Johnny Pacheco. Charly: CD 165. [1989?].

6792   Pacheco, Johnny, 1935– , and Pete "El Conde" Rodriguez

Los compadres. Fania: SLP-CD-400. 1972.

6793   Palmieri, Charlie, 1927–1988

Charanga Duboney: echoes of an era. West Side Latino: 240. [196?].

6794   Palmieri, Eddie, 1936–

6794.1   *Champagne.* Tico: 1165. 1968.

6794.2 * *Sun of Latin music.* Musical Productions: MP-3109 CD. 1973.

6794.3   *Unfinished masterpiece.* Coco: MP3120. [1975].

6795   Pozo, Chano, 1915–1948, and Arsenio Rodriguez, 1911–1970

Legendary sessions. Tumbao: TCD-017. 1947–53.

6796   Prado, Perez, 1916–1989

6796.1   *Kuba-mambo.* Tumbao: TCD-006. 1947–49.

6796.2 ** *Mondo mambo! the best of Perez Prado & his orchestra.* Rhino: 71889. 1950–62.

6797   Puente, Tito, 1923–

6797.1 ** *Dance mania.* RCA: 2467-2-RL (LSP 1692). 1958.

6797.2 *The mambo king: 100th LP.* RMM Records: CDT 80680. 1991.

6797.3 *Mambo macoco.* Tumbao: TCD-018. 1949–51.

6797.4 *Night beat/Mucho Puente, plus!* Bear Family: 15686 (RCA LPM-1447/LSP-1479). 1955–58.

6797.5 *Un poco loco.* Concord Picante: CCD-4329. 1987.

6797.6 *Top percussion.* RCA: 3264-2-RL. 1957.

6798 Rodríguez, Arsenio, 1911–1970

6798.1 ** *A todos los barrios.* RCA Latino: 3336-2-RL. 1946–50.

6798.2 *Como se goza en el barrio.* Tumbao: TCD-022. 1953.

6799 Rodríguez, Tito, 1923–1973

6799.1 *The best of Tito Rodríguez, vol. 1.* RCA Tropical: 3419-2-RL. 1955–56.

6799.2 *Mambo mona.* Tumbao: TCD-014. 1949–51.

6799.3 * *Tito Rodríguez at the Palladium.* Palladium: PCD-5108. 1958.

6800 Rogers, Shorty, 1924–1994

Afro-Cuban influence. [Series: Tropical]. RCA: 3449-2-RL (LPM 1763). 1958.

6801 Rosario, Willie, 1930–

Gracias mundo. Inca: SLP 1056. 1977.

6802 Ruiz, Hilton, 1952–

Manhattan mambo. Telarc: CD-83322. 1992.

6803 Ruiz, Rey, 1966–

Mi media mitad. Sony Tropical: 81185. 1994.

6804 Sanabria, Bobby, and Ascensión

New York City ache. Flying Fish: FF 70630. [1993].

6805 Sanchez, Poncho, 1951–

Bien sabroso! Concord Picante: CCD-4239. 1983.

6806 Sandoval, Arturo, 1949–

Tumbaito. Messidor: CD 15974-2. 1986.

6807 Santa Rosa, Gilberto, 1950–

A dos tiempos de un tiempo. Sony: 80895. 1992.

6808 Santamaria, Mongo, 1922–

6808.1 *Afro roots.* Prestige/Fantasy: PCD-24018-2. 1958–59.

6808.2 *Mongo at the Village Gate.* Fantasy: OJCCD-490-2 (Riverside 93529). 1963.

6808.3 *Our man in Havana.* Fantasy: FCD-24729-2. 1960.

6808.4 *Skins.* Milestone/Fantasy: MCD-47038-2. 1962.

6809 Tjader, Cal, 1925–1982

Los ritmos calientes. Fantasy: FCD-24712-2 (3216/3262). 1954–57.

6810 Totico (Eugene Arango)

Totico y sus Rumberos. Montuno: 515. 1981.

6811 Valdez, Carlos "Patato," 1926–

Patato y Totico. Mediterraneo: MDC-10065. (Verve V6-5037). [196?].

See also "Cuba," below, and "Puerto Rico" (page 483)

Caribbean

General Anthologies

6812 *Caribbean beat: soca, kaseko, merengue, cadence, zouk, ska, compas.* Intuition: INT 3112 2. [1993]. [Gazoline, Wilfrido Vargas, Laurel Aitken, and others].

6813 *Caribbean beat, vol. 2.* Intuition: INT 3126 2. [1995]. [Imagination Brass, Toumpak, Dixie Band, Skatalites, Dede Saint-Prix, Arrow, and others].

6814 ** *Caribbean currents: a panorama of Caribbean music.* Rounder: CD 1120-21. 2CD set. [1997].

6815 *Dancehall reggaespañol.* Columbia: 48526. [1991]. [El General, Cutty Ranks, Sugar Minott, Cocoa Tea, Lisa M, Rude Girl (La Atrevida), and others].

6816 *Mento/merengue/méringue: country dance music from Jamaica, Grand Cayman, Haiti & the Dominican Republic.* Original Music: OMCD 028. [1995]. [Recorded by John Storm Roberts].

6817 *Under the coconut tree: music from Grand Cayman and Tortola.* Original Music: OMCD 025 (OMC 201). 1982.

Cuba

Anthologies

6818 * *Afro-Cuba: a musical anthology.* Rounder: CD 1088. 1994.

6819 *Antologia de la música Cubana, vols. 1–4.* Artex: CD 045-CD 048. 4 CDs. 193?–91.

6820 ** *A carnival of Cuban music.* [Series: Routes of rhythm, vol. 1]. Rounder: CD 5049. [1990]. [Xavier Cugat, Don Azpiazu, Chano Pozo, Dizzy Gillespie, Perez Prado, Arsenio Rodriguez, Celia Cruz, Tito Puente, Ruben Blades, and others].

6821 *Casa de la Trova: Santiago de Cuba.* Corason: COCD 120. [1994].

6822 *Cuba: fully charged.* Earthworks: STEW 30 (CAROL-2429). [1993]. [N.G. La Banda, Sierra Maestra, and others].

6823 *Cuba: musica campesina = musique populaire.* Auvidis: B 6758. 1985–88. [Afro-Cuban music].

6824 ** *Cuban counterpoint: history of the son montuno.* Rounder: CD 1078. 1946–60. [Arsenio Rodriguez, Celia Cruz, Septeto Nacional de Ignacio Pineiro, Sextéto Habanero, and others].

6825 * *Cuban dance party.* [Series: Routes of rhythm, vol. 2]. Rounder: CD 5050. 1990. [Irakere, Los Van Van, Estrellas Cubanas, Septeto Nacional de Ignacio Pineiro, Orquesta Orestes Lopez, Isaac Oviedo, Son de la Loma].

6826 * *Cuban gold: que se sepa!: yo soy de la Habana.* Qbadisc: QB-9006. [1993]. [Los Van Van, Irakere, Grupo Manguare, Orquesta Original de Manzanillo, and others].

6827 ** *Dancing with the enemy: incredible dance hits of the 60's and 70's.* [Series: Cuba classics, vol. 2]. Luaka Bop/Warner Bros.: 26580-2. [1991]. [Orquesta Revé, Los Van Van, and others].

6828 ** *Diablo al infierno.* [Series: Cuba classics, vol. 3]. Luaka Bop/Warner Bros.: 45107-2. [1992]. [Irakere, N. G. La Banda, Los Van Van, Síntesis, Dan Den, and others].

6829 *La gloria eres tu: boleros clasicos, vol. 1.* RCA Tropical: 3404-2-RL. 1953–58. [Orquesta Aragon, Beny Moré, Tito Rodriguez, Tito Puente, and others].

6830 *Hot music from Cuba.* Harlequin: HQ CD 23. 1907–37. [Trio Matamoros, Sextéto Habanero, Sextéto Nacional, and others].

6831 *Joyas de la música cubana, vols. 1–3.* Artex: CD-022/023/024. 3 CDs. [19-?].

6832 *Real rumba from Cuba.* Corason: COCD 110. 1985, 1988. [Los Muñequitos de Matanzas, Cutumba, and others].

6833 * *Sabroso!: Havana hits.* Earthworks: STEW 11 (CAROL-2411/V 91312). [1989]. [Celina Gonzalez, Irakere, Los Van Van, Orquesta Revé, and others].

6834 *Septetos cubanos: sones de Cuba.* Corason: MTCD 113/4. 2CD set. 1990. [Septeto Nacional de Ignacio Pineiro, Cuarteto Patria, and others].

6835 ** *Sextétos cubanos, vol. 1.* Folklyric/Arhoolie: CD 7003. 1929–30. [Sextéto Munamar, Sextéto Machin, Sextéto Nacional, Sextéto Matancero].

6836 * *Sextétos cubanos, vol. 2.* Folklyric/Arhoolie: CD 7006. 1926–28. [Sextéto Boloña, Sextéto Occidente, Sextéto Matancero, Sextéto Nacional].

Individual Artists or Groups

6837 Alvarez, Adalberto
Adalberto Alavarez y su son. Egrem/Artex: CD-011. 1990.

6838 Azpiazu, Don, 1893–1943
Don Azpiazu and his Havana Casino Orchestra. Harlequin: HQ CD 10. [193?].

6839 Cardona, Milton
Bembe. American Clavé: AMC 1004. 1985. [Ritual percussion music for Santeria liturgy].

6840 Conjunto Matamoros
Conjunto Matamoros with Beny Moré. Tumbao: TCD-020. 1945–47.

6841 Cuarteto Patria
A una coqueta. Corason: COCD 106. 1986–93.

6842 Gonzalez, Celina, 1928–
   6842.1 *Fiesta guajira.* World Circuit: WCD 034. [198?].
   6842.2 *Que viva chango!* Qbadisc: QB 9004. [197?–198?].

6843 Grupo Afrocuba de Matanzas
Rituales afrocubanos. Egrem: EGCD0058. [19-?].

6844 Grupo Folklorico de Cuba
Toques y cantos de santos, vols. 1–2. Cubilandio: 511; 513. 2 CDs. 1993.

6845 López, Israel "Cachao," 1918–
Descargas cubanas. Maype: CD 122. [199?].

6846 La Lupe
Mongo introduces La Lupe. Milestone: MCD-9210-2 (Fantasy). 1962–63.

6847 Mendoza, Celeste
Cuba. A.S.P.I.C.: X55516. 1993.

6848 Milanes, Pablo
Cancionero. World Pacific: 80596. [1993].

6849 Moré, Beny, 1919–1963
 6849.1 ** *The most from Beny Moré.* RCA Tropical: 2445-2-RL. 1955–57.
 6849.2 *Y hoy como ayer.* RCA Tropical: 3204-2-RL. 1956–58.

6850 Muñequitos de Matanzas
 6850.1 *Congo yambumba.* Qbadisc: QB 9014. 1983.
 6850.2 *Rumba caliente 88/77.* Qbadisc: QB 9005. 1977, 1988.

6851 N. G. La Banda
En la calle. Qbadisc: QB 9002. 1989–90.

6852 Orquesta Aragon
The heart of Havana, vol. 1. RCA: 3204-2-RL. 1956–57.

6853 Orquesta Casino de la Playa
Memories of Cuba. Tumbao: TCD-003. 1937–44.

6854 * Orquesta Revé
La explosion del momento! Realworld: CAROL-2303-2 (91301). [1989].

6855 Orquesta Ritmo Oriental
Historia de la ritmo, vols. 1–2. Qbadisc: 9007-9008. 2 CDs. 1974–88.

6856 Oviedo, Isaac
Isaac Oviedo. [Series: Routes of rhythm, vol. 3]. Rounder: CD 5055. 1981, 1984.

6857 Los Papines
Tambores cubanos. EGREM: EGCD0037. [19-?].

6858 Puebla, Carlos
Carlos Puebla y sus Tradicionales. EGREM-ARTEX: CD-013. 1992.

6859 Rodriguez, Silvio, 1946–
 6859.1 * *Greatest hits.* [Series: Cuba classics, vol. 1]. Luaka Bop/Warner Bros.: 26480-2. 1975–88.
 6859.2 *Dias y flores: songs of the Nueva Trova Cubana.* Hannibal: HNCD-1322. 1975.

6860 Santamaria, Mongo. *See 6808*

6861 Saquito, Nico, 1901–1982
Goodbye Mr. Cat. World Circuit: WCD 035. 1982.

6862 * Sextéto Habanero
Las raices del son. Tumbao: TCD-009. 1925–31.

6863 Síntesis
Ancestros. Qbadisc: QB 9001. 1987.

6864 Sonora Matancera
Celebrando con la Sonora Matancera: 65 aniversario. TH-Rodven: TH-2630. [1989]. [Featuring Celia Cruz, Bobby Capo, and Ismael Rivera].

6865 * Trio Matamoros
The legendary Trio Matamoros. Tumbao: TCD-016. 1928–37.

6866 Valdes, Vicentico
Algo de ti. Seeco/Tropical: 90521. 1991.

6867 * Los Van Van
Dancing wet = Bailando mojado: seven years of Cuba's #1 dance band. World Pacific: 80600. 1984–90.

6868 * Varela, Carlos
Monedas al aire. Qbadisc: QB 9010. 1993.

6869 Viejo Lázaro
Dan den. Qbadisc: 9009. [199?].

Dominican Republic

Anthologies

6870 * *Aqui esta el merengue* Karen/BMG: 3440-2-RL (KLP-112). [1992]. [Juan Luis Guerra, Wilfrido Vargas, Sergio Vargas, Las Chicas del Can, and others].

6871 *Bachatazo, vol. 1.* Discos Jose Luis: JLR 116. [1991].

6872 * *Essential merengue: stripping the parrots.* Corason: CO-122. [1995].

6873 *Singers of the cibao.* Original: OML403c. AC. 1986.
See also 6881

Individual Artists or Groups

6874 Guerra, Juan Luis, 1957–
 6874.1 *Areito.* Karen: 3456-2-RL (CDK 146). 1992.
 6874.2 * *Bachata rosa.* Karen/BMG: 3230-2-RL (KCD 136). 1990.

6875   Pochi y su Cocoband. *La faldita.* Kubaney: KCD 224. 1990.

6876   Ulloa, Francisco

6876.1 *¡Merengue!* GlobeStyle: CDORB 020 (Kubaney). 1985.

6876.2 *Ultramerengue!* Xenophile/Green Linnet: GLCD 4004. 1992.

6877 * Vargas, Wilfrido, 1949–

El rey del merengue: 15 grandes exitos. Sonotone: SO-1441. 1990.

6878 ** Ventura, Johnny

Johnny Ventura. Kubaney: CD 117. 1987.

6879   Viloria, Angel

Merengues: los exitos de Angel Viloria, vol. 1. Ansonia: HGCD 1206. [195?].

Haiti

Anthologies

6880   *The beat of Haiti.* Mini: MRSD 1012. 1969–83. [Tabou Combo, Coupe Cloué, Bossa Combo, Les Shleu Shleu, and others].

6881 * *Caribbean revels: Haitian rara and Dominican gaga.* Smithsonian/Folkways: SF 40402. 1976–78.

6882 * *Couleur compas, vol. 1: Haiti cheri.* Declic: 302217. 1978–94. [Coupe Cloué, Shah Shah, Tabou Combo, Les Freres deJean, and others].

6883   *Divine horsemen: the voodoo gods of Haiti.* Lyrichord: LLCT 7341. AC. 1947–51.

6884 * *The drums of Vodou.* White Cliffs Media: WCM 9338. [1994]. [Featuring master drummer Frisner Augustin. Accompanies book of same title by Lois Wilcken].

6885   *Folk music from Haiti.* Lyrichord LLCT: 7340. AC. 1947–51.

6886 ** *Konbit: burning rhythms of Haiti.* A&M: 75021-5281-2. 1957–89. [Ensemble Nemours Jean-Baptiste, Tabou Combo, Mini All Stars, and others]. OP

6887   *Meringue: "Haiti cherie."* Corason: COCD 107. 1983.

6888 ** *Rhythms of rapture: sacred musics of Haitian Vodou.* Smithsonian/Folkways: SF 40464. 1947–95.

6889   *Voodoo trance music: ritual drums of Haiti.* Lyrichord: LLCT 7279. AC. 1974.

Individual Artists or Groups

6890   Boukan Ginen

Jou a rive. Xenophile/Green Linnet: XCD 4024. [1995].

6891 ** Boukman Eksperyans

Vodou adjae. Mango: 162 539899-2. 1989.

6892   Coupe Cloué

Maximum compas from Haiti. Earthworks: STEW 27 (CAROL-2426). [197?–198?].

6893 * Ensemble Nemours Jean-Baptiste

Musical tour of Haiti. Ansonia: HGCD 1280. [196?].

6894   Michel, Emeline

The best of Emeline Michel. Cobalt: 09262-2. [1993].

6895   Mini All Stars

Happy anniversary Mr. Mini. Mini: MRSD 2020. [1991].

6896   Tabou Combo

1979–1986, vol. 5. Mini: MRSD 1020. 1979–86.

Jamaica

Traditional Music

ANTHOLOGIES

6897 * *Drums of defiance: Maroon music from the earliest free Black communities of Jamaica.* Smithsonian/Folkways: SF 40412. 1977–91.

6898   *From Kongo to Zion: Black music traditions of Jamaica.* Heartbeat: C-HB-17. AC. 1974–79. OP

INDIVIDUAL ARTIST

6899   Jolly Boys

6899.1 *Pop 'n' mento.* First Warning/Rykodisc: RCD 10185. 1989.

6899.2 *Roots of reggae.* Lyrichord: LLCT 7314. AC. 1986.

Reggae, Ska, and Related Genres

ANTHOLOGIES

6900 * *The best of Studio One, vol. 1.* Heartbeat: CDHB 07. [1987]. [Marcia Griffiths, Alton Ellis, Johnnie Osbourne, Dennis Brown, Heptones, Gladiators, Sugar Minott, Wailing Souls, and others].

6901 *Dancehall stylee: the best of reggae dancehall music, vol. 2.* Profile: PCD 1291. 1990. [Barrington Levy, Freddie McGregor, Shabba Ranks, and others].

6902 * *Duke Reid's treasure chest: Treasure Isle rock steady.* Heartbeat: CDHB 95/96. 2CD set. [1992]. [Melodians, Alton Ellis, U Roy, Paragons, and others].

6903 * *Explosive rock steady: Joe Gibbs' Amalgamated label.* Heartbeat: CDHB 72. 1967–73. [Lee Perry, Pioneers, Cool Sticky, Sir Lord Comic, and others].

6904 *First family of reggae.* Shanachie: SH 9100. [1991]. [Joe Higgs, Lucky Dube, Bunny Wailer, Rita Marley, Judy Mowatt, Yellowman, Alpha Blondy, Mutabaruka, Augustus Pablo, Dennis Brown, Linton Kwesi Johnson, Culture, Eeek-a-Mouse, Gregory Isaacs, Ras Michael].

6905 ** *The harder they come* [soundtrack]. Mango: 162 539202-2. [1972]. [Jimmy Cliff, Toots and the Maytals, Melodians, Desmond Dekker, and others].

6906 * *Intensified!: original ska.* Mango: 162 539524-2. 1962–66. [Baba Brooks, Don Drummond, Skatalites, Maytals, Tommy McCook, and others].

6907 * *Jammin'.* Mango: 162 539924-2. 1968–89. [Bob Marley and the Wailers, Third World, Toots and the Maytals, Aswad, Jimmy Cliff, Marcia Griffiths, Slickers, Desmond Dekker, Black Uhuru, Lorna Bennett, Heptones, Dennis Brown, Mighty Diamonds, Junior Murvin, and others].

6908 *Keep on coming through the door: Jamaican deejay music.* Trojan: CDTRL 255. 1969–73. [U Roy, Dillinger, Dennis Alcapone, Prince Far I, and others].

6909 *Me gone buck wild: reggae dance hall killers.* Shanachie: 43091. [1991]. [Shabba Ranks, Gregory Isaacs, Cocoa Tea, Yellowman, Frankie Paul, Papa San, Judy Mowatt, and others].

6910 *Reggae dance party.* RAS: 3018. 1987. [Barrington Levy, Michigan and Smiley, Don Carlos, Black Uhuru, Sugar Minott, Gregory Isaacs, and others].

6911 * *Roots of reggae, vol. 1: ska.* Rhino: 72438. 1959–67. [Laurel Aitken, Derrick Morgan, Prince Buster, Blues Busters, Justin Hinds, Maytals, and others].

6912 * *Roots of reggae, vol. 2: rock steady.* Rhino: 72439. 1966–70. [Alton Ellis, Justin Hinds, Prince Buster, Techniques, Ken Boothe, Delroy Wilson, Melodians, Uniques, Bob Andy, Tommy McCook, and others].

6913 *Solid gold, Coxsone style.* Heartbeat: CD HB 80. [197?]. [John Holt, Alton Ellis, Abyssinians, Jackie Mittoo, Delroy Wilson, Ernest Ranglin, Dennis Brown, and others].

6914 *Strictly for rockers.* [Series: Reggae greats]. Mango: 162 539796-2. 1975–84. [Augustus Pablo, Wailing Souls, Bunny Wailer, Culture, Judy Mowatt, Freddy McGregor, Ina Kamoze, Sugar Minott, and others].

6915 ** *This is reggae music.* Mango: 162 539251-2. [1974]. [Wailers, Joe Higgs, Jimmy Cliff, Toots and the Maytals, Heptones, and others].

6916 * *This is reggae music, vol. 2.* Mango: 162 539327-2. [1975]. [Third World, Heptones, Augustus Pablo, Burning Spear, and others].

6917 ** *This is reggae music, vol. 3.* Mango: 162 539391-2. [1976]. [Junior Murvin, Lee Perry, Max Romeo, Justin Hines, Burning Spear, Bunny Wailer, Peter Tosh, Aswad, and others].

6918 ** *Tougher than tough: the story of Jamaican music.* Mango: 162 539935-2. 4CD set. 1959–92. [Laurel Aitken, Derrick Morgan, Skatalites, Prince Buster, Toots and the Maytals, Alton Ellis, Delroy Wilson, Ken Boothe, Jimmy Cliff, Millie Small, Desmond Dekker, Marcia Griffiths, Bob Marley, Wailers, Dennis Brown, Heptones, U Roy, Black Uhuru, Burning Spear, Mighty Diamonds, Culture, Gregory Isaacs, Barrington Levy, Super Cat, Tiger, Shabba Ranks, Buju Banton, Shaggy, and others].

6919 * *Towering dub inferno: the Roir tapes.* Rykodisc: RCD 20152. [1990]. [Lee Perry, Scientist, Ras Michael, Prince Far I, Black Uhuru, Roots Radics, and others].

6920 * *The Trojan story.* Trojan: CDTRD 402. 2CD set. 1961–71. [Skatalites, Techniques, Alton Ellis, Jimmy Cliff, Big Youth, Dennis Alcapone, U Roy, Dennis Brown, Desmond Dekker, Heptones, Toots and the Maytals, Pioneers, Peter Tosh, Byron Lee, Ken Boothe, Upsetters, John Holt, and others].

INDIVIDUAL ARTISTS OR GROUPS

6921 Aswad

Crucial tracks. Mango: 162 539833-2. [1989].

6922   Big Youth
Some great Big Youth. Heartbeat: CD HB 03. 1981.

6923   Black Uhuru
6923.1 * *Liberation: the Island anthology.* Island: 314 518 282-2. 2CD set. 1980–83.
6923.2   *Red.* Mango: 162 539625-2. 1981.

6924   Bolo, Yami, 1970–
Up life street. Heartbeat: CD HB 114. 1992.

6925 * Brown, Dennis, 1957–
Some like it hot. Heartbeat: CD HB 107 (Observer). [197?].

6926 * Burning Spear
Marcus Garvey. Mango: 162 539377-2. 1975.

6927   Cliff, Jimmy, 1948–
Reggae greats. Mango: 162 539794-2. 1967–73.

6928 * Culture
Two sevens clash. Shanachie: 44001. 1987.

6929   Dekker, Desmond, 1942–
Rockin' steady: the best of Desmond Dekker. Rhino: 70271. 1963–73.

6930   Ellis, Alton, 1944–
Cry tough. Heartbeat: CD HB 106. 1966–67.

6931   Griffiths, Marcia, 1954–
Naturally. Shanachie: 44014. [197?].

6932   Heptones
6932.1 * *Night food.* Mango: 162 539381-2. 1976.
6932.2   *Party time.* Mango: 162 539456-2. 1977.

6933   Hibbert, Toots, 194?– , and the Maytals
6933.1 ** *Funky Kingston.* Mango: 162 539330-2. 1973.
6933.2   *Reggae greats.* Mango: 162 539781-2. 1968–84.

6934   Higgs, Joe, 1940–
Blackman know yourself. Shanachie: 43077. 1990.

6935   Inner Circle
The best of Inner Circle featuring Jacob Miller. Mango: 162 539931-2. 1977–80.

6936 * Isaacs, Gregory, 1951–
Night nurse. Mango: 162 539721-2. 1982.

6937   Itals
Early recordings. Nighthawk: 310. 1971–79.

6938   Johnson, Linton Kwesi, 1952–
Forces of victory. Mango: 162 539566-2. 1979.

6939   King Tubby (Osbourne Ruddock), 1941–
King Tubby's special. Trojan: CDTRD 409. 2CD set. 1973–76.

6940   Levy, Barrington, 1964–
Broader than Broadway. Profile: PCD 1294. [198?].

6941   Marley, Bob, 1945–1981, and the Wailers
6941.1 * *Burnin'.* Tuff Gong/Island: 422 846200-2. 1973.
6941.2 * *Catch a fire.* Tuff Gong/Island: 422 846201-2. 1972.
6941.3 ** *Legend: the best of Bob Marley and the Wailers.* Tuff Gong/Island: 422 846210-2 (90169). 1972–80.
6941.4 ** *Natty dread.* Tuff Gong/Island: 422 846204-2. 1974.
6941.5 * *Songs of freedom.* Tuff Gong/Island: 314 512280-2. 4CD set. 1962–80.
6941.6   *Survival.* Tuff Gong/Island: 422 846202-2. 1979.

6942   Marley, Rita
Who feels it knows it. Shanachie: 43003. 1981.

6943   Marley, Ziggy, 1968–
Conscious party. Virgin: 86038 (90878). 1988.

6944   McGregor, Freddie
Bobby Babylon. Heartbeat: CD HB 3502. [1991].

6945   Meditations
Deeper roots: the best of the Meditations. Heartbeat: CD HB 158. [197?–198?].

6946 * Mighty Diamonds
Go seek your rights. Front Line: CAROL-1678-2 (Virgin). 1976–79.

6947   Moses, Pablo, 1952–
A song. Mango: 162 539541-2. 1980.

6948   Mowatt, Judy
Black woman. Shanachie: 43011. 1991.

6949   Mutabaruka, 1952–
Check it! Alligator: ALCD 8306. 1983.

6950 Pablo, Augustus

6950.1 * *East of the River Nile.* Message/Shanachie: 1003. [1983]. OP

6950.2 *King Tubby meets rockers uptown.* Shanachie: 44019 (Message 1007). 1976.

6951 * Perry, Lee "Scratch," 1940–
Reggae greats. Mango: 162 539792-2. 1976–77.

6952 Ras Michael
Rally round. Shanachie: 43027. 1985.

6953 Reid, Junior, 1965–
One blood. Big Life/Mercury: 843557-2. 1990.

6954 * Shabba Ranks, 1965–
As raw as ever. Epic: EK 47310. 1991.

6955 * Skatalites
Ska voovee. Shanachie: SH 45009. 1993.

6956 Sly (Dunbar, 1952–) and Robbie (Shakespeare, 1953–)
Rhythm killers. Island: 422 842785-2 (90585). 1987.

6957 * Steel Pulse
Reggae greats. Mango: 162 539783-2. 1978–80.

6958 Super Cat
Don dada. Columbia: CK 52435. 1992.

6959 Third World

6959.1 *96 degrees in the shade.* Mango: 162 539830-2. 1977.

6959.2 * *Reggae ambassadors: 20th anniversary collection.* Mercury: 314 518294-2 (Island/ Columbia). 2CD set. 1975–92.

6960 Tiger, 1960–
A me named Tiger. RAS: RASCD: 3021. 1986.

6961 Toots and the Maytals. *See 6933*

6962 * Tosh, Peter, 1944–1987
Equal rights. Columbia: CK 34670. 1977.

6963 * UB40
Labour of love. A&M: 75021-4980-2 (Virgin). 1983.

6964 Wailer, Bunny, 1947–
Blackheart man. Mango: 162 539415-2. 1976.

6965 Yabby You
One love, one heart. Shanachie: 43016. 1992.

6966 Yellowman
Zungguzungguzungguzeng. Shanachie: 48012 (Greensleeves). 1983.

Puerto Rico

Anthologies

6967 *Bien jibaro: country music.* Rounder: CD 5056. [1994?].

6968 *Folk music of Puerto Rico.* [Series: Folk music of the Americas]. Library of Congress: AFS L 18. LP/AC. 1946.

6969 ** *The music of Puerto Rico.* Harlequin: HQ CD 22. 1929–46. [Canario, Cuarteto Marcano, Sextéto Okeh, and others].

Individual Artists or Groups

6970 Batacumbele
Con un poco de songó. Disco Hit: DHTLP-008-CD. 1981.

6971 * Canario (Manuel Jiménez), 1895–1975
Plenas. Ansonia: HGCD-1232. [1990].

6972 Cortijo, Rafael, d. 1983
El alma de un pueblo. Polygram Latino: 314-521604-2. [1994?]. *See also 6771*

6973 Cortijo, Rafael, d. 1983, and Kako, 1937–
Ritmos y cantos callejeros. Ansonia: HGCD 1477. 1970.

6974 * Cortijo, Rafael, d. 1983, Ismael Rivera, and Nelson Pinedo
16 exitos. Discos Fuentes: 16114. [195?].

6975 El Gran Combo

6975.1 *Tribute to the Messiah.* Combo: 1906. [199?].

6975.2 * *25th anniversary.* Combo: RCSCD 2050. 1962–87.

6976 Padilla, Pedro
Vuelva en alas del placer. Rounder: 5003. LP. 1975. OP

6977 Los Pleneros de la 21 and Conjunto Melodia Tropical
Puerto Rico, Puerto Rico mi tierra natal. Shanachie: 65001. [1990].

6978 Santa Rosa, Gilberto. *See 6807*

6979   Sextéto Borinquen

El auténtico. Ansonia: ANSCD 1312. [199?].

6980   Sonora Ponceña

6980.1   *New heights.* Inca: 11064 (1074). 1980.

6980.2 *   *Soul of Puerto Rico.* Charly: CDCHARLY 307. 1975–90.

Trinidad and Tobago

Steel Bands

ANTHOLOGIES

6981   *Carnival jump-up: steelbands of Trinidad and Tobago.* Delos: DE 4014. 1987–89.

6982   *The heart of steel: featuring steelbands of Trinidad and Tobago.* Flying Fish: FF 70522. 1990.

6983 *   *Pan champs, vol. 1.* Blue Rhythm: BRD 1111. 1990. [Solo Harmonites, Phase II Pan Groove, Amoco Renegades, and others].

6984   *Pan classics: competition performances from the world's finest steel bands.* Blue Rhythm: BRCD 1114. 1992.

6985 *   *Panorama: steelbands of Trinidad and Tobago.* Delos: 13491-4015-2. 1991.

6986 *   *Steel band des Caraibes.* Arion: ARN 64082. 1981.

INDIVIDUAL GROUP

6987   Our Boys Steel Orchestra

Pan night and day. Mango: CCD 9822. [1988].

Calypso and Soca

ANTHOLOGIES

6988 *   *Ah feel to party: best of Straker's.* Rounder: CD 5066/67. 2CD set. 1973–93. [Chalkdust, Calypso Rose, Shadow, Singing Francine, Black Stalin, Duke, Winston Soso, Lord Melody, and others].

6989 *   *Calypso breakaway.* Rounder: CD 1054. 1927–41. [Attila the Hun, The Tiger, The Executor, The Caresser, Lord Beginner, and others].

6990   *Calypso calaloo: early carnival music in Trinidad.* Rounder: CD 1105. 1914–[195?]. [Lionel Belasco, Roaring Lion, Lovey's Band, The Tiger, Houdini, Lord Executor, Lord Invader, and others].

**6991 ** **   *Calypso carnival.* Rounder: CD 1077. 1936–41. [The Lion, The Tiger, The Growler, Lionel Belasco, Atilla the Hun, The Caresser, Wilmoth Houdini, Lord Invader, Lord Executor, and others].

6992 *   *Calypso pioneers.* Rounder: CD 1039. 1912–37. [Wilmoth Houdini, Attila the Hun, Lovey's Band, Merrick's Orchestra, and others].

**6993 ** **   *Calypso season.* Mango: 162 539861-2. 1989. [Bally, Tambu, Sparrow, David Rudder, and others].

6994 *   *Calypsos from Trinidad: politics, intrigue and violence in the 1930s.* Folklyric/Arhoolie: CD 7004. 1935–39. [Attila the Hun, The Tiger, The Lion, The Executor, The Caresser, Lord Beginner, and others].

6995 *   *Heat in de place: soca music from Trinidad.* Rounder: CD 5041. [1990]. [Bally, Shadow, Johnny King, Singing Francine, and others].

6996   *Say what? double entendre soca music from Trinidad.* Rounder: CD 5042. [1990]. [Shadow, Bally, Rio, Plainclothes, Poser, Monarch].

6997 *   *Wind your waist: the ultimate soca dance party.* Shanachie: 64034. [1991]. [Arrow, Shadow, Tambu, and others].

INDIVIDUAL ARTISTS OR GROUPS

6998   Arrow (Alphonsus Cassell)

Knock dem dead. Mango: 162 539809-2. 1988.

6999   Black Stalin, 1941–

Roots rock soca. Rounder: CD 5038. [1991].

7000   Calypso Rose

Soca diva. Ice: 931202. 1993.

7001   Crazy

Crazymania. JW: JWCR 043. 1991–92.

7002   Growling Tiger (The Tiger)

Knockdown calypsos. Rounder: CD 5006. 1979.

7003   Houdini, Wilmoth, 1895–1973

Poor but ambitious: calypso classics from Trinidad. Folklyric/Arhoolie: CD 7010. 1928–40.

7004 *   Kitchener, Lord, 1921–

Klassik Kitchener, vol. 1. Ice: 931102. [1993].

7005   Roaring Lion, 1910?–

Standing proud. Ice: 930202. [193?].

7006 Rudder, David, 1953– , and Charlie's Roots
Haiti. Sire: 25723-2. 1987.

7007 Shadow
Columbus lied. Shanachie: 64033. 1988–90.

7008 * Sparrow, 1935–
Mighty Sparrow, vol. 1. Ice: 921002. [1992].

Other Caribbean Islands
(Including the Bahamas, Barbados, Guadeloupe, Martinique, St. Lucia, and U.S. Virgin Islands)

Anthologies

7009 * *Au bal antillais: Creole beguines from Martinique.* Folklyric/Arhoolie: CD 7013. 1929–51. [Alexandre Stellio, Don Barreto, and others].

7010 ** *Dance! cadence!* GlobeStyle: CDORB 002. 1985. [Michel Godzum, George Decimus, Eugene Mona, and others].

7011 * *Fire in de wave.* Ice: 941502. [1994]. [Gabby, Grynner, Bert "Panta" Brown].

7012 * *Hurricane zouk.* Earthworks: STEW 02 (CAROL-2402/V 90882). [1988]. [Jacob Desvarieux, Pierre Edouard Decimus, Francky Vincent, Vikings, and others].

7013 *Musical traditions of St. Lucia, West Indies.* Smithsonian/Folkways: SF 40916. 1975–87.

7014 *Tumba, cuarta and ka'i: music from Aruba, Bonaire and Curaçao.* Original Music: OMCD 202. 1982. [Music of Aruba, Bonaire, and Curaçao].

7015 *West Indies: an island carnival.* Nonesuch: 72091-2. 1969–71.

7016 *Zoop zoop zoop! music of the U.S. Virgin Islands.* New World: 80427-2. 1957–85.

7017 * *Zouk attack.* Rounder: CD 5037. [1992].

Individual Artists or Groups

7018 Blinky and the Roadmasters
Crucian scratch band music. Rounder: CD 5047. 1990.

7019 Gazoline
Zouk obsession. Shanachie 64021. [1990].

7020 Kassav'
  7020.1 *Majestik zouk.* Columbia: CK 45353. 1989.
  7020.2 ** *Zouk is the only medicine we have.* Greensleeves: GRE2 2001. [1989].

7021 Malavoi
L'autre style. Hibiscus: 88052-2. 1975–82.

7022 Marce et Tumpak
Zouk chouv. GlobeStyle: CDORB 035. 1987.

7023 * Mona, Eugene
Collection prestige de la musique caribéenne, vol. 1. Hibiscus/Polygram: 191213-2. 1975–78.

7024 Negrit, Eric
Kompa ka, vol. 1. Sonodisc: CDS 74041. [19-?].

7025 Ransay, Max
Atuomo. Hibiscus: 191157-2. [198?].

7026 Red Plastic Bag
Movements! Pond Side/J & M: PS 006. LP. 1985.

7027 Spence, Joseph, 1910–1984
  7027.1 * *The complete Folkways recordings.* Smithsonian/Folkways: SF 40066. 1958.
  7027.2 ** *Happy all the time.* Hannibal: HNCD 4419. 1964.

7028 Vikings
Guadeloupe: les precurseurs du zouk. Coco Sound/Hibiscus: 88054-2. 1974–78.

Mexico and Southwestern United States
Mexico
Anthologies

7029 * *Antologia del son de Mexico = Anthology of Mexican sones.* Corason: COCD 101/2/3. 3CD set. [1985].

7030 *Folk music of Mexico.* [Series: Music of the Americas]. Library of Congress: AFS L 19. LP/AC. 1944–46.

7031 *Folkstyles of Mexico and Colombia.* Music of the World: CDT-113. [1986]. [Los Pregoneros Del Puerto, Aires Colombianos, Lydia Mendoza].

7032 *Mexican Indian traditions.* [Series: UNESCO collection]. Auvidis: D 8304. 1992.

7033   *Mexico: fiestas of Chiapas and Oaxaca.* Nonesuch Explorer: 72070-2. 1976.

7034   *Mexico, voz y sentimiento, vols. 1–2.* CBS Discos: CD-80437/Sony Discos: CDZ-80649. 2 CDs. [1990, 1991].

7035   *Pure Purepechan: pirekuas y abajeños.* Corason: COCD119. [1994].

7036   *Voces de Mexico.* Globo/Sony: CDZ-81225. [1994]. [Ana Gabriel, Vicente Fernandez, Jose Alfredo Jiménez, Vikki Carr, Los Panchos, Angeles Ochoa, Yuri, Javier Solis, and others].

Individual Artists or Groups

7037   Bernal, Rozenda

Rozenda Bernal con mariachi. Capitol/EMI Latin: 42376. 1990.

7038   * Los Bukis

Me volvi a acordar de ti. Melody: CDML 001. 1989.

7039   Los Camperos de Valles

El triunfo: sones de la Huasteca. Corason: COCD104. 1986.

7040   Campesinos de Michoacán

Canciones de mi tierra. [Series: Music of Mexico, vol. 4]. Arhoolie: 3024. AC. 1985–87.

7041   Cardenas, Guty, 1905–1932

El ruiseñor yucateco. Alma Criolla: ACCD 801. 1928–32.

7042   Conjunto Alma de Apatzingán

Arriba! tierra caliente. [Series: Music of Mexico, vol. 2: *Michoacán*]. Arhoolie: CD 426 (Alborada). 1993.

7043   Conjunto Alma Jarocha

Sones jarochos. [Series: Music of Mexico, vol. 1: *Veracruz*]. Arhoolie: CD 354. 1978.

7044   Hernandez Chabez, Carlos, with Los Trovadores

Songs of Mexico. JVC: VICG 5335. 1994.

7045   ** Jiménez, José Alfredo, d. 1974

Homenaje a José Alfredo Jiménez. CBS Discos International: CDA-10432. [19-?].

7046   Lara, Agustín, 1900–1970

7046.1   *Agustín Lara.* [Series: 20 exitos]. RCA: 3307-2-RL. [19-?].

7046.2   *Agustín Lara y sus interpretes.* Orfeon: 25CDN-501. [19-?].

7047   * Mariachi Coculense de Cirilo Marmolejo

Mariachi Coculense "Rodriguez" de Cirilo Marmolejo. [Series: Mexico's pioneer mariachis, vol. 1]. Folklyric/Arhoolie: CD 7011. 1926–36.

7048   Mariachi Reyes del Aserradero

Sones de Jalisco. Corason: CORA 108. [1993].

7049   Mariachi Tapatío de José Marmolejo

El autentico. [Series: Mexico's pioneer mariachis, vol. 2]. Folklyric/Arhoolie: CD 7012. 1937–44.

7050   ** Mariachi Vargas de Tecalitlan

Their first recordings. [Series: Mexico's pioneer mariachis, vol. 3]. Folklyric/Arhoolie: CD 7015. 1937–47.

7051   Negrete, Jorge, 1911–1953

Los grandes exitos de Jorge Negrete, vol. 2. RCA International: 7374-2-RL. [194?].

7052   Ochoa, Angeles

Juntito a ti. Sony: CD-80663. 1991.

7053   Los Pregoneros del Puerto

Music of Veracruz: the sones jarochos of Los Pregoneros del Puerto. Rounder: CD 5048. 1990.

7054   Reyes, Lucha, 1906–1944

15 exitos de Lucha Reyes. BMG/Mexico: 77192. [19-?].

7055   Reynoso, Juan

El Paganini de la tierra caliente. Corason: COCD 105. 1972–93.

7056   Solis, Javier

15 autenticos exitos. CBS Discos International: CD-80282. 1990.

7057   Tapia, Oscar Moreno, and Los Mecateros

Songs of Mexico, vol. 2. JVC: VICG 5336. 1994.

7058   Los Tigres del Norte

7058.1   *Corridos prohibidos.* FonoVisa: FPCD 8815. 1989.

7058.2   * *Mi buena suerte.* FonoVisa: FPCD 8831. 1989.

7059   Los Tres Ases

Siluetas en trio. RCA/BMG: 3402-2-RL. 1958.

7060 * Trio Los Panchos

20 de colección. Sony: CD-81129. [1993].

7061 * Valentín, Juan

El rey del mariachi y la banda: 14 super exitos. Capitol/EMI Latin: 42789. [1993].

Tex-Mex and Other Hispanic American Music of the Southwestern United States

Anthologies

7062 * *Borderlands: from conjunto to chicken scratch—music from the Rio Grande Valley of Texas and Southern Arizona.* Smithsonian/Folkways: SF 40418. 1946–92. [Narciso Martínez, Lydia Mendoza, Los Dos Gilbertos, Ramon Ayala, Roberto Pulido, Molinas, Southern Scratch, and others].

7063 * *Conjunto! Texas-Mexican border music, vol. 1.* Rounder: CD 6023. [1988]. [Tony de la Rosa, Steve Jordan, Flaco Jiménez, Ramon Ayala, and others].

7064 * *Conjunto! Texas-Mexican border music, vol. 2.* Rounder: CD 6024. [1988]. [El Conjunto Bernal, Tony de la Rosa, Valerio Longoria, Ramon Ayala, and others].

7065 *Conjunto! Texas-Mexican border music, vol. 3.* Rounder: CD 6030. [1990]. [Flaco Jiménez, Steve Jordan, Valerio Longoria, Roberto Pulido, and others].

7066 *Conjunto! Texas-Mexican border music, vol. 4.* Rounder: CD 6034. [1990]. [Steve Jordan, Flaco Jimenéz, Los Cachorros, Valerio Longoria, and others].

7067 *Conjunto! Texas-Mexican border music, vol. 5: polkas de oro.* Rounder: CD 6051. [1994]. [Ruben Naranjo, Tony de la Rosa, Valerio Longoria, Los Dos Gilbertos, Ruben Vela, and others].

7068 *Conjunto! Texas-Mexican border music, vol. 6: contrabando.* Rounder: CD 6052. [1994]. [Angel Flores, Los Dos Gilbertos, Ruben Naranjo, Tony de la Rosa, and others].

7069 *Corridos and tragedias de la frontera: first recordings of historic Mexican-American ballads.* [Series: Mexican-American border music, vols. 6–7]. Folklyric/Arhoolie: CD 7019/20. 2CD set. 1928–37.

7070 * *Dark and light in Spanish New Mexico.* New World: 80292-2. 1940, 1970. [Luis Montoya, Ricardo Archuleta, Vincente Padilla, Melitaclon Roybal].

7071 ** *Mexican-American border music, vol. 1: an introduction: Pioneer recording artists.* Folklyric/Arhoolie: CD 7001. 1928–58. [Bruno Villareal, Narciso Martínez, Lydia Mendoza, Santiago Jiménez Sr., Valerio Longoria, and others].

7072 *Music of New Mexico: Hispanic traditions.* Smithsonian/Folkways: SF 40409. 1973–92.

7073 *Orquestas tejanas.* [Series: Tejano roots]. Arhoolie: CD 368 (Ideal). 1947–60. [Beto Villa, Isidro López, Pedro Bugarin, Balde Gonzalez, and others].

7074 * *San Antonio's conjuntos in the 1950s.* [Series: Tejano roots]. Arhoolie: CD 376 (Rio). 1948–57. [Ada Garcia, Conjunto San Antonio Alegre, Juanita y Maria Mendoza, Flaco Jiménez, Trio San Antonio, Valerio Longoria, Los Pavos Reales, and others].

7075 *Spanish and Mexican folk music of New Mexico.* Smithsonian/Folkways: 4426. AC. 1946–51.

7076 ** *Tejano roots = Raices tejanas: the roots of Tejano and conjunto music.* [Series: Tejano roots]. Arhoolie: CD 341 (Ideal). 1946–69. [Narciso Martínez, Lydia Mendoza, Tony de la Rosa, Carmen y Laura, Beto Villa, Juan López, Isidro López, Valerio Longoria, Freddie Fender, and others].

7077 *Tex-Mex conjuntos.* Arhoolie: CD 311. 1970, 1974. [Los Pingüinos del Norte, Fred Zimmerle's Trio San Antonio].

7078 ** *The Texas-Mexican conjunto: history of a working-class music.* Arhoolie: C 9049. AC. 1936–66. [Bruno Villareal, Narciso Martínez, Santiago Jiménez Sr., Pedro Ayala, Los Alegres de Teran, Valerio Longoria, Tony de la Rosa, Ruben Vela, Conjunto Bernal, Los Relampagos].

7079 * *The women.* [Series: Tejano roots]. Arhoolie: CD 343 (Ideal). 1946–70. [Carmen y Laura, Las Abajenos, Las Rancheritas, Lydia Mendoza, and others].

Individual Artists or Groups

7080 Ayala, Ramon

Corridos del '91. Freddie: FMCD-1572. 1991.

7081 Conjunto Bernal

Mi unico camino. Arhoolie: CD 344. 1954–60.

7082 De la Rosa, Tony, 1931–

  7082.1 *Asi se baila en Tejas.* Rounder: CD 6046. 1991.

7082.2 * *Atotonilco.* [Series: Tejano roots]. Arhoolie: CD 362 (Ideal). 1953–64.

7083   Fender, Freddie, 1937–

Canciones de mi barrio. [Series: Tejano roots]. Arhoolie: CD 366. 1959–64.

7084   Jiménez, Flaco, 1931–

7084.1 ** *Ay te dejo en San Antonio y mas.* Arhoolie: CD 318. 1979, 1985.

7084.2   *Un mojado sin licensia.* Arhoolie: CD 396. 1955–67.

7085   Jiménez, Santiago, Sr., 1913–1984

Don Santiago Jiménez: his first and last recordings. [Series: Tejano roots]. Arhoolie: CD 414. 1937, 1979.

7086   Jiménez, Santiago, Jr., 1944–

7086.1   *Familia y tradición.* Rounder: CD 6033. 1989.

7086.2   *El mero, mero de San Antonio.* Arhoolie: CD 317. 1981–88.

7087   Jordan, Steve, 1938–

7087.1 * *The many sounds of Steve Jordan.* Arhoolie: CD 319. 1963, 1970.

7087.2   *The return of El Parche.* Rounder: CD 6019 (Freddie). 1976–84.

7088   Longoria, Valerio, 1924–

7088.1   *Caballo viejo.* Arhoolie: CD 336. 1989.

7088.2 * *Texas conjunto pioneer.* [Series: Tejano roots]. Arhoolie: CD 358 (Ideal). 1951–63.

7089   López, Isidro, 1933–

El Indio. [Series: Tejano roots]. Arhoolie: CD 363 (Ideal). 1954–63.

7090   López, Juan, 1922–

El rey de la redova. [Series: Tejano roots]. Arhoolie: CD 407 (Ideal). [195?].

7091 * Martínez, Narciso, 1911–1992

Father of the Texas-Mexican conjunto. [Series: Tejano roots]. Arhoolie: CD 361 (Ideal). 1946–61.

7092   Mazz

Que esperabas. EMI Latin: 27738. 1993.

7093   Mendoza, Lydia, 1916–

7093.1   *La gloria de Texas.* Arhoolie: CD 3012. 1979.

7093.2 ** *Mal hombre.* [Series: Mexican-American border music, vol. 2]. Arhoolie: CD 7002. 1928–38.

7094   Navaira, Emilio

Southern exposure. EMI Latin: 42838. 1993.

7095   Los Pavos Reales

"Early hits" y las primeras grabaciones de Los Hermanos Torres-Garcia. Arhoolie: CD 410 (DRC/Ideal). [1949], 1962–64.

7096   Sanchez, Joe, Delio Villareal, and Ray Casias

Matachines: social and religious music of northern New Mexico. Ubik Sound: 13. AC. 1990.

7097   Selena, 1971–1995

12 super exitos. [Series: Tejano classics]. EMI Latin: 30907. [1994].

7098   Valdez, Chayito

15 exitos. Fonovisa: 4011. [1991].

7099   Villa, Beto, 1915–1986

Father of orquesta Tejano. [Series: Tejano roots]. Arhoolie: CD 364 (Ideal). 1948–54.

7100   Ybarra, Eva

A mi San Antonio. Rounder: CD 6056. 1993.

Central America

Belize

Anthologies

7101   *Brukdon: shine eye gal: Belizean calypso.* Corason: COCD-118. 1978, 1985. [Mini-Musical Female Duet, Brad Pattico & Co., Ethnic Boom 'n Chime Band, Belizean Boom 'n Chime Band, The Tigers, Mahogany Chips].

Individual Group

7102   Chatuye

Heartbeat in the music. Arhoolie: CD 383. 1992.

Costa Rica

7103   *Calypsos: African-Limonese music from Costa Rica.* Lyrichord: LYRCD 7412. [1988].

El Salvador

7104   Yolocamba I-Ta

Cara o cruz. Flying Fish: FF 70503. 1988.

Guatemala

7105 *Guatemala: les célèbres marimbas.* Arion: ARN 64261. 1993.

Honduras

7106 Lita Ariran

Honduras: songs of the Garifuna. JVC: VICG-5337. 1993.

Nicaragua

7107 *Concierto por la paz: April in Managua.* Ocarina: NCLP-5001. 2LP set. 1984. [Reissued on CD by Varagram. Peace concert featuring popular performers from Uruguay, Mexico, Cuba, Brazil, Argentina, and Nicaragua].

7108 *Nicaragua presente! music from Nicaragua libre.* Rounder: CD 11564. 1989.

7109 *Soul vibrations: Black history/Black culture: Afro-Nicaraguan music.* Redwood: RR 9104. [1991].

Panama

Anthology

7110 *Street music of Panama.* Original Music: OMCD 008. [196?].

Individual Artists or Groups

7111 Danzas Panama

Instrumental folk music of Panama. JVC: VICG-5338. 1991.

7112 El General

El poder de El General. RCA: 3433-2-RL. 1992.

South America

General Anthologies and Transnational Performers

7113 * *Music of the Andes.* Hemisphere/EMI: 28190. [1994]. [Inti-Illimani, Quilapayun, Victor Jara, Conjunto Kollahuara, Illapu].

7114 Sukay

Huayrasan. Flying Fish: FF 70501. 1988.

Argentina

Anthologies

7115 *Argentina: tritonic musics of the north-west.* [Series: UNESCO collection]. Auvidis: D 8208. 1988.

7116 *Argentina canta asi: the best of Argentine tango and folk music.* Philips: 832 020-2. [1987]. [Mercedes Sosa, Osvaldo Pugliese, Astor Piazzolla, Los Tucu-Tucu, Ernesto Baffa, Raul Lavie, and others].

7117 *Argentine: chamamé: musique du Paraná.* (Rudy Flores/Nini Flores). Ocora: C 560052. 1993.

7118 *Argentine: musical patrimony of the north-west provinces.* PlayaSound: PS 65073. [1991].

7119 * *Buenos Aires by night: 20 historic tango originals by Argentina's musical legends.* EMI: 0777 7 89180 8 (CDEMS 1487). 1934–93. [Carlos Gardel, Hector Varela, Anibal Troilo, Osvaldo Pugliese, Francisco Canaro, Sextéto Mayór, and others].

7120 ** *Historia del tango.* Music Hall: MHCD 10.001-2/10.002-2. 2CD set. 1934–77. [Carlos di Sarli, Anibal Troilo, Roberto Firpo, Julio de Caro, Astor Piazzolla, and others].

7121 *Indians of the Gran Chaco.* Lyrichord: LLCT 7295. AC. 1975.

7122 *Instrumental tangos of the golden age.* Harlequin: HQ CD 45. [1994]. [Francisco Canaro, Anibal Troilo, Roberto Firpo, Julio de Caro, Carlos di Sarli, and others].

7123 *Tango Argentina: original cast.* Atlantic: 81636-2. 1986. [Broadway show featuring Sextéto Mayór and Sextéto Berlingieri].

7124 *Tango in Paris.* Fremeaux: FA 012. 2CD set. 1907–41. [Carlos Gardel, Rafael Canaro, Bachicha, Alina de Silva, and others].

7125 *The tango project.* Nonesuch: 79030-2. 1982. [Performed by William Schimmel and others. Compositions by G. H. Matos Rodriguez, Carlos Gardel, Enrique Santos Discépolo, José Padilla, Juan de Diós Filiberto, Eduardo Arolas, and others].

7126 * *Tangos para aficionados, vol. 1.* Phontastic: CD 7578. 1930–45. [Carlos Gardel, Roberto Firpo, Francisco Canaro, Anibal Troilo, and others].

Individual Artists or Groups

7127   Alba, Haydée

Tango argentin. Ocora: C 559091. 1989–90.

7128   Deluigi, Silvana

Tanguera: woman in tango. Wergo Spectrum: SM 1503-2. 1989.

7129   Firpo, Roberto, 1884–1969

Alma de Bohemio. El Bandoneon: EBCD 8. 1936–37, 1947.

7130   Francini, Enrique Mario, with Armando Pontier

Tango, vol. 1. JVC: VICG-5342. 1980.

7131   García, Carlos, 1914–

Argentina. JVC: VICG-5343. 1980.

7132   Gardel, Carlos, 1890–1935

7132.1 * *Carlos Gardel, le créateur du tango argentin.* Forlane: UCD-19032. [1992].

7132.2 *16 exitos, vols. 1–2.* Capitol/EMI Latin: 42196/42197. 1930–35.

7133   Lara, Roberto

Argentina: the guitar of the Pampas. Lyrichord: LLCT7253. AC. [1973].

7134   Piazzolla, Astor, 1921–1992

7134.1 *La historia del tango, vol. 1.* Polydor: 314 511638-2. [1991].

7134.2 *The late masterpieces: the complete work on American Clavé.* American Clavé: AMCL 1022 (1013, 1019, 1021). 3CD set. 1986–88. [Includes all material on item 7134.3].

7134.3 ** *Tango: zero hour = Tango: hora zero.* American Clavé: AMCL 1013. 1986.

7135   Pugliese, Osvaldo, 1905–

Osvaldo Pugliese y su Orquesta Tipica. El Bandoneon: EBCD 5. 1949.

7136   Sextéto Mayór

A passion for tango: authentic tangos from Argentina. Angel: 54857. 1993.

7137 * Sosa, Mercedes, 1935–

Gracias a la vida. Polygram Latino: 832314-2. 1987.

7138   Sosa, Mercedes, 1935– , León Gieco, and Milton Nascimento, 1942–

Corazón americano. Tropical Music: 68.913. 1984. [Live recording from 1984 celebrating the end of the Argentine dictatorship].

7139   Torres, Jaime

Charango. Messidor: CD 15949-2. [1985].

7140   Troilo, Anibal, 1914–1975

El inmortal "Pichuco." El Bandoneon: EBCD 1. 1941.

7141   Yupanqui, Atahualpa

30 ans de chansons. Le Chant du Monde: LDX 274 750. 1983–87.

Bolivia

Anthologies

7142   *Bolivia: calendar music in the central valleys.* Le Chant du Monde: LDX 274 938. 1992.

7143   *Bolivia: panpipes.* [Series: UNESCO collection]. Auvidis: D 8009. 1965–73.

7144   *Pukajwayra.* Lyrichord: LYRCD-7361. [198?].

Individual Artists or Groups

7145 * Awatinas

Bolivia: de coleccion. Inbofon: CDB-538. 1993.

7146   Bolivia Manta

7146.1   *Music of the Andes: Pak'cha.* Auvidis: A 6127. 1987.

7146.2   *Quechua music.* A.S.P.I.C.: X 55502. 1989. [Also featuring Nanda Manachi].

7147   Cavour Aramayo, Ernesto

La partida. Tudor: TUD-885. 1990.

7148   Junaro, Emma

Canta a Matilde Casazola "Mi corazon en la ciudad." Riverboat Stern's: TUGCD 1003. 1992.

7149   Los Kjarkas

El arbol de mi destino. Discolandia: CD 27. 1992.

7150   Rumillajta

7150.1   *Atahuallpa: Andean music from Bolivia.* Rumillajta Recordings: RUMI 931CD. 1993.

7150.2 * *Urupampa: Andean music from Bolivia.* Rumillajta Recordings: RUMI 911CD. 1990.

Brazil

Anthologies

7151   *Afro-Bahian religious songs from Brazil: songs of the African cult groups.* [Series: Folk music of the Americas]. Library of Congress: AFS L 13. LP/AC. 1941–42.

7152 * *Afro Brasil.* Verve: 845326-2. 1977–90. [Caetano Veloso, Maria Bethania, Margareth Menezes, Beth Carvalho, Alcione, Nana Vasconcelos, Alceu Valenca, and others].

7153 * *Afros e afoxés da Bahia.* Mango: 162 539893-2. [1988]. [Oludum, Ara Ketu, and others].

7154 *Amazônia: festival and cult music from northern Brazil.* Lyrichord: LYRCD 7300. 1975.

7155 *Asa branca: accordion forró from Brazil.* Rykodisc: RCD 20154. 1978–87. [Luiz Gonzaga, Dominguinhos, and others].

7156 *Axé Brazil: the Afro-Brazilian music of Brazil.* World Pacific: 95057. 1972–90. [Clara Nunes, Geronimo, Djavan, Simone, Gonzaguinha, Marisa Monte, and others].

7157 ** *Beleza tropical.* [Series: Brazil classics, vol. 1]. Sire: 25805-2. [1989]. [Jorge Ben, Maria Bethania, Gal Costa, Gilberto Gil, Caetano Veloso, Chico Buarque, Milton Nascimento, Nazare Pereira].

7158 ** *Bossa nova Brasil.* Verve: 314 515762-2 (845325-2). [1990]. [João Gilberto, Antonio Carlos Jobim, Gal Costa, Elis Regina, Astrud Gilberto, and others].

7159 * *Brazil: a century of song.* Blue Jackel Entertainment: 5000-2. 4CD set. 1939–95. [Carmen Miranda, Ary Barroso, Martinho da Vila, João Gilberto, Oscar Castro-Neves, Beth Carvalho, Toquinho, Chico Buarque, Baden Powell, Gal Costa, Clara Nunes, Alcione, Simone, Jorge Ben, Ivan Lins, Marisa Monte, Daniela Mercury, Olodum, Milton Nascimento, and others].

7160 * *Brazil: the Bororo world of sound.* [Series: UNESCO collection]. Auvidis: D 8201. 1987.

7161 ** *Brazil forró: music for maids and taxi drivers.* Rounder: CD 5044. [1989].

7162 * *Brazil—roots—samba.* Rounder: CD 5045. [1989].

7163 *Brazilliance: the music of rhythm.* Rykodisc: RCD 20153. 1977–89.

7164 *Bresil musiques du haut Xingu.* Ocora: C 580022. 1969–75.

7165 *Capoeira: senzala de santos: Brésil, capoeira, samba de roca, maculelê.* Buda: 92575-2. [1994].

7166 * *Capoeira Angola from Salvador, Brazil.* Smithsonian/Folkways: SF 40465. 1994.

7167 *Forró etc.: music of the Brazilian northeast.* [Series: Brazil classics, vol. 3]. Luaka Bop/Warner Bros.: 26323-2. [1991].

7168 *Historia del carnival de Brasil.* Ubatuqui: UBCD 20003/4/5. 3CD set. 1902–52.

7169 * *Nordeste Brasil.* Verve: 845327-2. [1990]. [Milton Nascimento, Gal Costa, Gilberto Gil, Elba Ramahlo, and others].

7170 ** *O samba.* [Series: Brazil classics, vol. 2]. Sire: 26019-2. [1989]. [Clara Nunes, Alcione, Beth Carvalho, Martinho da Vila, and others].

7171 *Ritual music of the Kayapó-Xikrin, Brazil.* Smithsonian/Folkways: SF 40433. 1988.

7172 * *Samba Brasil.* Verve: 314 515761-2 (845324-2). [1990]. [Caetano Veloso, João Bosco, Alcione, Beth Carvalho, and others].

7173 *Tempo de Bahia.* Melodie: 48105-2. [1989]. [Moraes Moreira, Ara Ketu, Olodum, and others].

Individual Artists or Groups

7174 Agepê
Agepê. [Series: Minha historia]. Philips: 314 518 215-2. [1993].

7175 Alcione, 1947–
Alcione. Philips: 836 440-2. 1975–80.

7176 Amaro de Souza Ensemble
Suadades do Brasil: rythmes, chants, danses, instruments percussion du Bresil. Arion: ARN 64165. [1991].

7177 Ara Ketu
Ara Ketu. Seven Gates: SGDL 0001. 1992.

7178 Bahia Black
Ritual beating system. Axiom: 314-510 856-2. 1992. [Featuring Carlinhos Brown, with Olodum percussion ensemble, Wayne Shorter, Herbie Hancock, Bernie Worrell, and Henry Threadgill].

7179 Bandolim, Jacob do, 1918–1969
Mandolin master of Brazil: original classic recordings, vol. 1. Acoustic Disc: ACD-3 (RCA Brazil). 1955–66.

7180 Ben, Jorge, 1940–
7180.1 *Benjor.* Tropical Storm/WEA: 56619. 1989.

7180.2 * *Jorge Ben.* [Series: Personalidade]. Philips: 832 806-2. [1987].

7181 * Bethania, Maria, 1946–
Alibi. Verve: 836011-2. 1988.

7182 Bonfá, Luiz, 1922–
The Bonfá magic. Caju Music/Fantasy: MCD-9202-2. 1991.

7183 Bosco, João, 1946–
Odile odila. Verve: 314 512024-2. 1982–86.

7184 Buarque, Chico, 1944–
A arte de Chico Buarque. Fontana/Polygram: 836241-2. [1988].

7185 Costa, Gal, 1945–
Aquarela do Brasil. Philips: 836017-2. 1988.

7186 Costa, Paulinho da, 1948–
Agora. Fantasy: OJCCD-630-2 (Pablo 2310 785). 1976.

7187 Gil, Gilberto, 1942–
7187.1 *Gilberto Gil.* [Series: Personalidade]. Philips: 832 216-2. [1987].
7187.2 * *Parabolic.* Tropical Storm/WEA Latina: 76292-2. 1992.

7188 Gilberto, Astrud, 1940–
The Astrud Gilberto album. [Series: The silver collection]. Verve: 823 451-2. 1965–70.

7189 Gilberto, João, 1931–
7189.1 *João Gilberto.* Polygram: 848 507-2. [1991].
7189.2 *The legendary João Gilberto.* World Pacific: 93891. 1958–61.

7190 Gismonti, Egberto, 1947– , and Nana Vasconcelos, 1945–
Danca das cabecas. ECM: 78118-21089-2 (1089). 1976.

7191 Gonzaguinha, 1945–
Gonzaguinha. Tropical Music: 68.951. 1984.

7192 Os Ingênuos
Os Ingenuos play choros from Brazil. Nimbus: NI 5338. 1992.

7193 Jobim, Antonio Carlos, 1927–1994
A arte de Tom Jobim. Verve: 836 253-2. [1988].

7194 ** Jobim, Antonio Carlos, 1927–1994, and Elis Regina, 1945–1982
Elis and Tom. Verve: 824418-2. 1974.

7195 Menezes, Margareth, 1962–
7195.1 *Eligibo.* Mango: 162 539855-2. 1990.
7195.2 *Kindala.* Mango: 162 539917-2. 1991.

7196 Mercury, Daniela
O canto da cidade. Globo: CDZ 80998 2464348. 1992.

7197 Miranda, Carmen, 1909–1955
The Brazilian recordings. Harlequin: HQ CD 33. 1935–40.

7198 Nascimento, Milton, 1942–
7198.1 *A arte de Milton Nascimento.* Philips: 829 302-2. [1988]. [With Caetano Veloso, Gal Costa, Chico Buarque].
7198.2 ** *Clube da esquina.* World Pacific: 30429 (6005-6). 1972.
7198.3 *Minha historia.* Philips: 314 514440-2. 1970–89.

7199 Nunes, Clara, 1943–1983
The best of Clara Nunes. World Pacific: 96866. [1992].

7200 Oficina de Cordas
Pernambuco's music, Brazil. Nimbus: NI-5398. 1993.

7201 Olodum
Revolution in motion. World Circuit: WCD 031 (Continental). 1992.

7202 Pé de Serra Forró Band
Dance music from the countryside. Wergo/Spectrum: SM-1509 2. 1992.

7203 Pereira, Nazare
Ritmos da Amazonia. PlayaSound: PS 65030. 1988.

7204 Purim, Flora, 1942–
Stories to tell. Fantasy: OJCCD-619-2 (Milestone 9058). 1974. [With Airto].

7205 Quarteto Negro
Quarteto Negro. Auvidis Ethnic: B 6146. 1987.

7206 Reflexú
Reflexú's Da mãe África. Mango: 162-539 901-2. 1987.

7207 Regina, Elis, 1945–1982

Essa mulher. WEA Latina: WH 55900-2. 1979.

7208 Sivuca

Norte forte. Tropical Music: 68.959. 1994.

7209 Timbalada

Timbalada. Philips: 314 518 068-2. [1993].

7210 Veloso, Caetano, 1942–

7210.1 *Circuladô.* Elektra Musician: 79277-2. 1991.

7210.2 * *Estrangeiro.* Elektra Musician: 60898-2. 1989.

7211 Veloso, Caetano, 1942– , and Gilberto Gil, 1942–

Tropicalia 2. Elektra Nonesuch: 79339-2. 1993.

7212 Vila, Martinho da, 1938–

7212.1 *Batuqueiro.* Braziloid: BRD 4004. 1988.

7212.2 *Meu samba feliz.* Tropical Music: 68.911. 1969–82.

7213 Viola, Paulinho da

Eu canto samba. RCA: CD 10.015. 1989.

7214 Xangai

North-east Brasilian popular songs. Auvidis Ethnic: B 6135. 1984–86.

7215 Zé, Tom

7215.1 *The best of Tom Zé.* [Series: Brazil classics, vol. 4]. Luaka Bop/Warner Bros.: 26396-2. 1973–79.

7215.2 *Return of Tom Zé.* [Series: Brazil classics, vol. 5]. Luaka Bop/Warner Bros.: 45118-2. 1992.

Chile

Anthology

7216 *Chile: Hispano-Chilean Metisse traditional music.* [Series: UNESCO collection]. Auvidis: D-8001. 1975.

Individual Artists or Groups

7217 Cárcamo, Pablo

Mi Chiloé. ARC Music: EUCD 1095. 1990.

7218 Ensemble Musica Criolla

Musique traditionelle du Chile. Buda: 82474-2. [1983].

7219 Inti-Illimani

Inti-Illimani 2: la nueva cancion chilena. Monitor: MCD 71794. [197?].

7220 * Jara, Victor, 1938–1973

Vientos del pueblo. Monitor: MCD 61778. [1974].

7221 Parra, Violeta, 1917–1967

7221.1 *Cantos campesinos.* Alerce: CDA 0151. [1992].

7221.2 *Que canto Violeta Parra.* [Series: El folklore de Chile, vol. 4]. EMI: 99019. [1957].

7222 Quilapayun

Latitudes. Alerce: CDA-0149. 1992.

Colombia

Anthologies

7223 *Afro-Hispanic music from western Colombia and Ecuador.* Smithsonian/Folkways: 4376. AC. [1965].

7224 ** *Cumbia cumbia.* World Circuit: WCD 016 (Fuentes). [195?–198?]. [Pedro Laza, Sonora Dinamita, and others].

7225 * *Cumbia cumbia, vol. 2.* World Circuit: WCD 033. 1954–72.

7226 * *Fiesta vallenata.* Shanachie: 64014. [1986].

7227 *Musique tropicale de Colombie, vol. 2.* Fuentes/Sonodisc: CD 70002. 1987, 1989.

7228 * *Sueño Colombiano.* Mango: 842391-2 (Discos Fuentes). [1990]. [Joe Arroyo, La Sonora Cienaguera, Corraleros de Majagual, Afredo de la Fé, Fruko y sus Tesos, Latin Brothers, Los Titanes, and others].

Individual Artists or Groups

7229 Aires Colombianos. *See 7031*

7230 Arroyo, Joe, 1955–

7230.1 *En acción.* Discos Fuentes: 10083. 1989.

7230.2 * *Rebellión.* World Circuit: WCD 012 (Fuentes). 1981–89.

7230.3 *20 aniversario Joe Arroyo: 12 grandes exitos con Fruko y Sus Tesos and the Latin Brothers.* Discos Fuentes: SOF-1643. 1991.

7231   Cabrera, Jorge

Charanga vallenata. GlobeStyle: ORB 019. LP. [1982].

7232   Corraleros de Majagual

14 grandes exitos. Discos Fuentes: SOF-5659. LP. [1988].

7233   Cuesta, Ivan, 1946– , and his Baltimore Vallenatos

A ti, Colombia. Arhoolie: CD-388. 1992.

7234   Díaz, Diomedes, and Nicolas "Colacho" Mendoza

¡Cantando! [Series: Accordions that shook the world]. GlobeStyle: CDORB 055. 1989.

7235   Duran, Alejandro, 1919–

16 grandes exitos. Discos Fuentes: 16031. [199?].

7236   Grupo Niche

Grandes exitos. Globo/BMG: 9878-2RL. 1989.

7237   Gutiérrez, Alfredo

El palito. BMG/INT: 8544-4-RL. AC. [19-?].

7238   Meliyara, La India

La sonora Meliyara. Riverboat: TUGCD 1005. 1992.

7239   Meriño Brothers

Vallenato dynamos! [Series: Accordions that shook the world]. GlobeStyle: CDORB 049. 1988.

7240   Meza, Lisandro

Lisandro's cumbia. World Circuit: WCD 026 (Sonolux). 1983–91.

7241   Orquesta Guayacan

7241.1   *A puro golpe.* RMM: CD-81252. 1994.

7241.2   *Con el corazon abierto.* RMM: CD2-80983. 1993.

7242   Peregoyo y su Combo Vacana

Tropicalisimo. World Circuit: WCD 015 (Discos Fuentes). 1972.

7243   Sonora Dinamita

7243.1   *De nuevo 16 exitos.* Discos Fuentes: SOF-1632. [1989].

7243.2   *Es un escandalo.* New World Presents: 9434. 1993.

7243.3   *Super exitos!* Vedisco/Discos Fuentes: 1065-2. [1994].

7244   Torres, Roberto, 1940–

Al fin . . . ! lo mejor de Roberto. Globo/Sony Discos: CDZ-80683. 1991.

7245   Vives, Carlos

Clasicos de la provincia. Sonolux/Philips: 314 518 884-2. 1993.

Ecuador

7246   Jatun Cayambe

Ecuador. A.S.P.I.C.: X 55505. 1989.

7247   Karu Nan

Chimbaloma: Ecuadorian folk music. Tumi: CD 027. 1993.

See also 7223

Guyana

7248   Emigre, Viviane

Jambe dlo. T.D.M. Production: Dan's A 041. [198?].

Paraguay

7249   Basaldua, Papi, and Grupo Cantares

Songs of Paraguay. JVC: VICG-5341. 1989.

7250   Tzaud, Jean-Pierre

Paraguayan harp. PlayaSound: PS 65128. [1994].

Peru

Anthologies

7251   *Afro-Peruvian classics: the soul of Black Peru.* Luaka Bop/Warner Bros.: 45878-2. 1971–92.

7252   *Festivals of Cusco.* [Series: Traditional music of Peru, vol. 1]. Smithsonian/Folkways: SF 40466. 1989.

7253   * *Flutes and strings of the Andes: native musicians from the Altiplano.* Music of the World: CDT-106. 1943–84.

7254   ** *Huayno music of Peru, vols. 1–2.* Arhoolie: CD 320/338. 2 CDs. 1949–91.

7255   * *Huaynos and Huaylas: the real music of Peru.* GlobeStyle: CDORBD 064. 1991.

7256   *Kingdom of the sun: Peru's Inca heritage; Fiestas of Peru: music of the high Andes.* [Series: Explorer]. Nonesuch: 79197-2. 1968.

TRADITIONAL AND POPULAR MUSICS OF THE CARIBBEAN AND LATIN AMERICA **495**

7257 *The Mantaro Valley.* [Series: Traditional music of Peru, vol. 2]. Smithsonian/Folkways: SF 40467. 1985.

7258 *Mountain music of Peru, vols. 1–2.* Smithsonian/Folkways: SF 40020; SF 40406 (FE 4539). 2 CDs. 1964–89.

7259 *Peru: music from the land of Macchu Picchu.* Lyrichord: LYRCD 7294. 1975.

7260 *Peru, musica negra: traditional and modern music of Afro-Peruvians.* A.S.P.I.C.: X 55515. [1992?].

7261 *Your struggle is your glory: music of Peru.* Arhoolie: 3025. AC. 1964–83.

Individual Artists or Groups

7262 Aragon, Gabriel, and Antonio Sulca
The Inca harp: laments and dances. Lyrichord: LLCT 7359. AC. [1980].

7263 Ayllu Sulca
Music of the Incas: Andean harp and violin music from Ayacucho, Peru. Lyrichord: LYRCD 7348. [197?].

7264 Chocolate
Chocolate: Peru's master percussionist. Lyrichord: LYRCD 7417. 1990.

7265 Grupo Belen de Tarma
Chicha. Tumi: TUMICD 045. 1994.

Surinam

7266 *Switi: hot, Kaseko music.* Dutch Music Foundation: SPN 010. [1993].

Uruguay

Individual Artists or Groups

7267 Marino-Rivero, René, and Maria Dunkel
Bandoneon pure. [Series: Traditional music of the world, vol. 5]. Smithsonian/Folkways: SF 40431. 1991.

7268 Roos, Jaime, 1953–
Repertorio. DG Discos Argentina: ECD 65008. [199?].

Venezuela

Anthologies

7269 *Folk music of Venezuela.* [Series: Folk music of the Americas]. Library of Congress: AFS L 15. LP/AC. 1939–43.

7270 *Los grandes del llano.* Sonografica: 10270. [19-?].

Individual Artists or Groups

7271 * D'Leon, Oscar, 1943–
El rey de los soneros. Sonero: CDZ-80823. 1992.

7272 Frometa, Billo, and Simon Díaz
Lo mejor de Billo y Simon. Leon: CD-1121-2. [198?].

7273 Guaco
Lo mejor de Guaco. Sonotone: SO-1439. [199?].

7274 Grupo Vera
Venezuela: salsa and tradition. PlayaSound: PS 65097. [1992].

7275 Maracaibo Ensemble
Flûtes, harpe, et guitars du Venezuela. Arion: ARN 64160. [1975].

7276 Los Melodicos
Distintos! Velvet/Rodven: 200289. [19-?].

7277 Orquesta de la Luz
La aventura. Ariola/BMG: 74321-17399-2. 1993.

33

Traditional and Popular Musics of Europe

Compiled by
William E. Anderson
and Kent Underwood

This chapter encompasses the indigenous national musics of Europe other than Western classical. Arrangement is by country, with the continent organized into three main sections: "United Kingdom and Ireland"; "Western Europe and Scandinavia"; and "Eastern Europe" (including the Baltics, the Balkans, and the western, historically Christian republics of the former Soviet Union). See also chapter 31, "Folk and Traditional Musics of the United States and Canada," for music of European immigrants in North America.

United Kingdom and Ireland

General Anthologies

7278 * *The big squeeze: masters of the Celtic accordion.* Green Linnet: GLCD 1093. [1988]. [Joe Burke, Phil Cunningham, Bill McComiskey, John Whelan, and others].

7279 *Celtic odyssey: a contemporary Celtic journey.* Narada: ND-63912. [1993]. [Altan, Capercaille,

Moving Hearts, Relativity, Alasdair Fraser, Sileas, and others].

7280 ** *The Celts rise again.* Green Linnet: GLCD 104. 1986–90. [Patrick Street, Tannahill Weavers, Capercaille, Liz Carroll, Andy M. Stewart, Joe Burke, Matt Molloy, Phil Cunningham, and others].

7281 ** *Flight of the Green Linnet—Celtic music: the next generation.* Rykodisc: RCD 20075 (Green Linnet 103). [1979–87].

7282 * *The heart of the Gaels: a collection of Celtic music.* Green Linnet: GLCD 105. [1992]. [Altan, John Cunningham, Gerald Trimble, Patrick Street, Tannahill Weavers, Dick Gaughan, Matt Molloy, Andy Irvine, Sean Keane, and others].

7283 *Playing with fire: the Celtic fiddle collection.* Green Linnet: GLCD 1101. [1989]. [Kevin Burke, Liz Carroll, John Cunningham, Eileen Ivers, Brendan Mulvihill, and others].

7284 *25 years of world pipe champions.* Lismor: LEOM 9034. [1990].

Individual Artists or Groups

7285 ** Boys of the Lough

Live at Carnegie Hall. Sage Arts: 0301-2. 1988.

7286 Relativity

Relativity. Green Linnet: GLCD 1059. 1984. [John and Phil Cunningham, Tríona Ní Dhomhnaill, Mícheál Ó Dhomhnaill].

England

Anthologies

7287 * *The cutting edge: a selection of contemporary British roots music.* Cooking Vinyl: 001. [1989]. [Oyster Band, Rory McLeod, Edward II and the Red Hot Polkas, Deighton Family, and others].

7288 *An evening with Henry Russell.* Nonesuch: H-71338. LP. 1976. [Songs by Henry Russell, 1812–1900, performed by Clifford Jackson and William Bolcom]. OP

7289 *Hidden English: a celebration of English traditional music.* Topic: TSCD 600. [1983].

7290 * *The iron muse: a panorama of industrial folk music.* Topic: TSCD 465. 1963. [A. L. Lloyd, Ewan MacColl, Dick Gaughan, Ray Fisher, Louis Killen, Anne Briggs, and others].

7291 *Morris on.* Hannibal: HNCD 4406. 1972. [John Kirkpatrick, Ashley Hutchings, Richard Thompson, and others].

7292 *There'll always be an England.* ASV Living Era: CD AJA 5069. 1939. [Billy Cotton, Joe Loss, Vera Lynn, Flanagan and Allen, Nat Gonella, Ambrose, Lew Stone, Geraldo, Harry Roy, Jack Hylton, Gracie Fields, and others].

7293 ** *Troubadours of British folk, vol. 1.* Rhino: 72160. 1955–72. [Lonnie Donegan, Ewan MacColl, Ray and Archie Fisher, Davy Graham, Donovan, Jean Redpath, Watersons, A. L. Lloyd, Martin Carthy, Bert Jansch, Anne Briggs, Incredible String Band, Shirley and Dolly Collins, Pentangle, Fairport Convention, Steeleye Span, and others].

7294 * *Troubadours of British folk, vol. 2.* Rhino: 72161. 1969–75. [Fairport Convention, Albion Country Band, Traffic, Nick Drake, Fotheringay, Roy Harper, Ralph McTell, Amazing Blondel, Lindisfarne, Steeleye Span, Richard and Linda Thompson, and others].

7295 * *Troubadours of British folk, vol. 3.* Rhino: 72162. 1976–95. [Maddy Pryor, June Tabor, Dougie MacLean, Silly Wizard, Tannahill Weavers, Dick Gaughan, Billy Bragg, Oyster Band, Richard Thompson, Mouth Music, and others].

7296 *Up with the curtain: songs of the Variety Theater.* ASV Living Era: CD AJA 5076. 1935–42. [Lupino Laine, Max Miller, Arthur Tracy, Max and Harry Nesbitt, Geraldo, Jack Hylton, Flanagan and Allen, and others].

7297 * *Your own . . . your very own: stars of the music hall.* ASV Living Era: CD AJA 5004. 1901–29. [Harry Champion, Marie Lloyd, Charles Coborn, Dan Leno, George Formby, G. H. Chirgwin, Billy Merson, Jack Pleasants, Harry Lauder, Wilkie Bard, G. H. Elliott, Albert Whelan, and others].

Individual Artists or Groups

7298 Ambrose, Bert, 1897–1971

Ambrose and his Orchestra. ASV Living Era: ASL 5066. 1937–38.

7299 Bailey, Roy, 1935–

What you do with what you've got. Fuse: 399. 1975–91.

7300 * Bowlly, Al, 1899–1941

Al Bowlly with Ray Noble. ABC: 836170-2. 1931–34.

7301 * Carthy, Martin, 1941–

The collection. Green Linnet: GLCD 1136. 1974–89.

7302 Copper Family

Coppersongs. English Folk Dance and Song Society: VWML004C. AC. 1952, 1987.

7303 House Band

Stonetown. Green Linnet: GLCD 3060. 1991.

7304 Jansch, Bert, 1943– , and John Renbourn

Stepping stones. Vanguard: VMD 6506 (Transatlantic). 1968.

7305 MacColl, Ewan, 1915–1989

7305.1 * *Black and white: the definitive Ewan MacColl.* Green Linnet: GLCD 3058. 1972–86.

7305.2 ** *The real MacColl.* Topic: TSCD 463. 1959–66.

7306 * Oyster Band

From Little Rock to Leipzig. Rykodisc: RCD 50098. 1989–90.

7307 * Pryor, Maddy, and June Tabor, 1947–

Silly sisters. Shanachie: 79040 (CHR 1101). 1976.

7308 Tabor, June, 1947–

Airs and graces. Shanachie: 79055. 1976.

7309 Tester, Scan, 1887–1972

I never played to many posh dances. Topic: 2-12T455/6. 2LP set. [1990].

7310 Tickell, Kathryn, 1967–

Signs. Black Crow: CRO CD 230. 1993.

7311 * Watersons

For pence and spicy ale. Topic: CD 462/Shanachie: 79088. 1975–77.

Ireland

Anthologies

7312 *The gentlemen pipers: classic recordings of Irish traditional piping.* GlobeStyle: GSTY 84 (Topic). [1995]. [Liam Walsh, William Andrews, Leo Rowsome, Willie Clancy, Seamus Ennis, and others].

7313 * *An Ireland of treasures: the voices and the melodies of Ireland.* Capitol: 96577. 1913–48.

7314 * *Moore's Irish melodies.* (Lucy Shelton and others). Elektra Nonesuch: 79059-4. AC. 1982. [From the collection of Thomas Moore, 1779–1852].

7315 *The rushy mountain: classic music from Sliabh Luachra.* GlobeStyle: GSTY 85 (Topic). 1952–77.

7316 ** *Treasure of my heart: classic recordings from the Topic catalogue of Irish traditional music.* GlobeStyle: CDORBD 081. [193?]–1993. [William Andrews, Willie Clancy, Leo Rowsome, James Morrison, Hugh Gillespie, Joe Heaney, Dan Sullivan, Flanagan Brothers, McPeake Family, Boys of the Lough, Paddy Tunney, Seamus Ennis, and others].

Individual Artists or Groups

7317 * Altan

The first ten years. Green Linnet: GLCD 1153. 1986–95.

7318 Black, Mary, 1955–

Mary Black collected. Gifthorse: 10006 (Dara). 1982–88.

7319 ** Bothy Band

The best of the Bothy Band. Green Linnet: GLCD 3001. [1981].

7320 ** Chieftains

Chieftains 5. Shanachie: 79025. 1975.

7321 * Clancy Brothers and Tommy Makem

The best of the Clancy Brothers and Tommy Makem. Legacy International: CD 320 (Tradition). 1956–57.

7322 * Clannad

Clannad in concert. Shanachie: 79030. 1978.

7323 Davey, Shaun

Brendan voyage. Tara: 3006. 1980.

7324 * DeDannan

The best of DeDannan. Shanachie: 79047. 1986.

7325 Derrane, Joe

Irish accordion masters. Copley: COP 5009. 1948–53.

7326 Ennis, Seamus, 1912–1982

The wandering minstrel. Green Linnet: GLCD 3078 (Topic). 1974.

7327 Keane, Dolores

Sail og rua. Green Linnet: GLCD 3033. 1983.

7328 Patrick Street

All in good time. Green Linnet: GLCD 1125. 1993.

7329 * Planxty

The Planxty collection. Shanachie: 79012. [1972–74].

Scotland

Anthology

7330 ** *A celebration of Scottish music.* Temple: COMD 2003. [1988]. [Battlefield Band, Alison Kinnaird, Christine Primrose, Shotts and Dykehead Caledonia Pipe Band, Hamish Moore, and others].

Individual Artists or Groups

7331 * Battlefield Band

Home ground. Temple: CMD 2034. 1989.

7332 Capercaille
Sidewaulk. Green Linnet: GLCD 1094. 1989.

7333 Cormack, Arthur
Nuair bha mi og. Temple: COMD 2016. 1984.

7334 Cunningham, Phil
Airs and graces. Green Linnet: GLCD 3032. 1984.

7335 Fisher, Archie
Will ye gang love. Green Linnet: GLCD 3076 (Topic 277). 1976.

7336 * Gaughan, Dick
Handful of earth. Green Linnet: GLCD 3062. 1981.

7337 MacLean, Dougie, 1954–
Craigie dhu. Dunkeld: DUNCD 001. 1982–83.

7338 Redpath, Jean, 1937–
7338.1 *First flight.* Rounder: CD 11556 (Elektra). 1962–64.
7338.2 *The songs of Robert Burns, vols. 1–2.* Philo: 1187 (1037/1048). 1976, 1980.

7339 Sileas
Delighted with harps. Green Linnet: GLCD 3039. 1986.

7340 ** Silly Wizard
Live wizardry: the best of Silly Wizard in concert. Green Linnet: GLCD 3036/37. 1988.

7341 * Tannahill Weavers
The best of the Tannahill Weavers. Green Linnet: GLCD 1100. 1979–89.

Wales

7342 Ar Log
Ar Log o IV i V. Sain: SCD 9068. 1984, 1988.

7343 Evans, Meredydd
Welsh folk-songs. Smithsonian/Folkways: 6835. AC. [1954].

7344 Fulton, Cheryl Ann
The airs of Wales. Koch: 3-7071-2 H1. 1990.

7345 George, Siwsann
Traditional songs of Wales = Caneuon traddodiadol Cymru. Saydisc: CD-SDL 406. 1993.

7346 * Gorky's Zygotic Mynci
Introducing Gorky's Zygotic Mynci. Mercury: 314 532816-2 (Ankst). 1994–95.

Western Europe and Scandinavia

Austria

Anthologies

7347 *Austrian folk music, vol. 1: the eastern provinces.* Arhoolie: 3001. LP. 1967.

7348 *Austrian folk music, vol. 2: the western and southern provinces.* Arhoolie: 3003. LP. 1971.

7349 ** *Cithare autrichienne = Austrian zither.* PlayaSound: PS 65067. [1990].

7350 * *Die schönsten Jödler der Bergen = The best of Alpine yodeling, vols. 1–3.* Koch: 321122/330023/330039. 3 CDs. [1984–88].

7351 *So hab'n ma's in Breitensee gern: 1910–1926.* (Fritz Matauschek and ensemble). Basilisk: DOCD 3011. [1910–26].

7352 *Sound of the Tyrol.* Koch: 321680. 1986.

7353 *Spielt's ma an Tanz auf: die Nachfolger der Brüder Schrammel um die Jahrhundertwende (1899–1914) = The successors of the Schrammel Brothers around the turn of the century.* Basilisk: DOCD 310. 1899–1914.

7354 *Wien bleibt Wien: Viennese songs and Schrammel music.* Koch: 322554. [1990].

7355 *Zither-Perlen.* Koch: 321 660. [198?].

Individual Artists or Groups

7356 * Biedermeier Ensemble Wien
Musik des Biedermeier. Denon: CO-72587. 1988.

7357 Kollo, René, 1937–
Im Land der Lieder. Koch: H 321 656. [1983].

7358 Wiener Sängerknaben
Volks- & Kinderlieder = Folk songs & songs for children. Philips: 400 014-2 (6514 188). 1981.

Belgium

7359 *Belgique: ballades, danses et chansons de Flandre et Wallonie.* Ocora: C 580061 (558 594). 1952–80.

7360 *Flemish folk music.* (Brabants Volksorkest). René Gailly: CD87 043. [1988].

Denmark

7361   Haugaard, Dan

Danish folk songs. Smithsonian/Folkways: 6857. AC. [1957].

7362   Livstykke

Traditionals arranged by Dronningens Livstykke. Pan: CD 136. 1976–84.

Finland

Anthologies

7363   *Finnish folk music.* (Kaustisen Purppuripelimannit/Konsta Jylhä). Finlandia: 566072/566082. 2CD set. 1970–72.

7364   *Setusongs.* [Series: Music from Finno-Ugric peoples, vol. 1]. Mipu Music: MIPUCD 104. 1990.

Individual Artists or Groups

7365   * JPP (Jarvelan Pikkupelimannit)

Devil's polska: new Finnish folk fiddling. Xenophile/Green Linnet: GLCD 4012. 1991.

7366   Kalaniemi, Maria, 1964–

Maria Kalaniemi. Xenophile/Green Linnet: GLCD 4013. 1992.

7367   Mattlar, Marja

Pariisi & Vuorenkylä. Buda: 82885-2. [1993].

7368   Ottopasuuna

Ottopasuuna. Xenophile/Green Linnet: GLCD 4005. 1991.

7369   Pokela, Martti, 1944–

The old and new: kantele. ARC Music: EUCD 1040. 1969, 1977.

7370   * Värttinä

Seleniko. Xenophile/Green Linnet: GLCD 4006. 1992.

France

Anthologies

7371   *Accordeon, 1913–1941.* Discotheque des Halles: DH 002. 2CD set. 1913–41. [Adolph Deprince, Marceau, Emile Prudhomme, Emile Vacher, Gus Viseur, Frehel, Jean Gabin, Edith Piaf, and others].

7372   *Chansons de métiers de Provence et du Comtat Venaissin.* (Jean-Marie Carlotti and others). Ocora: C 559079. [1989].

7373   *Chants de Basse-Bretagne: eur zon hervez ma zantimant.* (Arnaud Maisonneuve). Ocora: C 558082. 1989.

7374   *Chants du Centre-Bretagne: an heñchou treuz.* (Erik Marchand and others). Ocora: C 559084. [1990].

7375   * *Corsica: chants polyphoniques.* (E Voce di u Cumune/Marcel Pérès). Harmonia Mundi: HMC 901256. 1986.

7376   * *Corsica: religious music of oral tradition from Rusio.* [Series: UNESCO collection]. Auvidis: D 8012. 1976.

7377   *50 chansons de France.* Double Gold: DBG 2-53009. 2CD set. [19-?]. [Charles Trenet, Juliette Greco, Edith Piaf, Guy Beart, Georges Brassens, Catherine Sauvage, Gilbert Bicaud, Yves Montand, Jacques Brel, Serge Gainsbourg, and others].

7378   * *France: bagpipes of central France.* (Jean Blanchard and others). [Series: UNESCO collection]. Auvidis: D 8202. 1987–89.

7379   * *Musique de Bretagne.* Buda: 92524-2. [199?].

7380   * *Musiques, chants et danses de Bretagne.* Keltia Musique: KMCD 01. [1986]. [Dan Ar Bras, Patrick Molard, Sonerien Du, Kemper Pipe Band, and others].

7381   *Musiques de Basse-Auvergne: Eau forte.* (Les Brayauds). Ocora: C 559083. 1989.

7382   ** *Musique pour cornemuses et accordéons: Matins gris.* (Christian Vesvre and others). Ocora: C 559081. 1988.

7383   *Musiques pour vielle à roue: "Bleu nuit."* (Gilles Chabenat and others). Ocora: C 559046. [1988].

7384   *Musiques pour vielle à roue en Auvergne et Bourbonnais.* (Patrick Bouffard and others). Ocora: C 560007. 1989.

7385   *Musiques sacrées: Settimana Santa in Bunifazziu.* [Series: Corse, vol. 1]. Ocora: C 559086. 1989.

7386   *Le paradis des Celtes = The paradise of the Celts.* (Gwenva). Auvidis Ethnic: B 6763. [1992].

7387   ** *Paris after dark: a collection of the finest French cabaret artists and songs from the 1920's to the 1950's.* EMI (England): CDP 7 90667-2. 1928–55. [Edith Piaf, Tino Rossi, Josephine Baker,

Maurice Chevalier, Mistinguett, Lucienne Boyer, Frehel, Jean Sablon, Charles Trenet, and others].

7388 * *Paris blues: the French realist singers.* EMI (England): CDP 7 96446-2. 1926–58. [Edith Piaf, Juliette Greco, Frehel, and others].

7389 *A table in Montmartre: 20 vintage titles with the heartbeat of Paris.* EMI: 7 99103 2. 1912–64. [Edith Piaf, Jean Sablon, Charles Trenet, Lucienne Boyer, Tino Rossi, Mistinguett, Maurice Chevalier, Stephane Grapelli, and others].

Individual Artists or Groups

7390 Achiary, Beñat
Pays basque: Arranca. [Series: En France]. Ocora: C 559045. 1988.

7391 Aznavour, Charles, 1924–
20 chansons d'or. Musarm: MU 700014 (Trema 710267). [1993].

7392 * Brel, Jacques, 1929–1978
Jacques Brel. [Series: Master série]. Polydor: 816458-2. 1983.

7393 Chevalier, Maurice, 1888–1972
Ma cherie. Pro Arte/Fanfare: CDD 438. [192?–193?].

7394 Clastrier, Valentin, 1947–
Valentin Clastrier. [Series: Grandes maîtres de la vielle à roue = Great masters of the hurdy-gurdy]. Auvidis Ethnic: B 6130. 1984, 1987.

7395 Corou de Berra
"Asa nisi masa": Nice, Piémont, Ligurie: chants des Alpes méridionales. Buda: 92607-2. 1993.

7396 Frehel, 1891–1951
L'inoubliable et inoubliée. Chansophone: CHCD 100. 1908, 1928–30.

7397 Kaas, Patricia, 1966–
Scène de vie. Columbia: CK 47845. 1991.

7398 * Kornog
Première: music from Brittany. Green Linnet: GLCD 1055. 1983.

7399 Le Tron, Bruno
Valhermeil. Auvidis Ethnic: B 6742. [199?].

7400 ** Malicorne
Légende. Hannibal: HNCD 1360. 1978–86.

7401 Montand, Yves, 1921–1991
Yves Montand. Philips: 824784-2. 1961–81.

7402 Négresses Vertes, Les
Mlah. Sire: 26029-2. 1989.

7403 ** Piaf, Edith, 1915–1963
The voice of the sparrow: the very best of Edith Piaf. Capitol: 96632. [19-?].

7404 Rossi, Tino, 1907–1983
J'attendrai: the best of Tino Rossi. EMI: CDP 7 99102 2. 1934–78.

7405 Stivell, Alan, 1943–
Journée à la maison. Rounder: CD 3062. 1987.

7406 Trio Erik Marchand
An tri breur. Silex: Y225008. 1991.

Germany

Anthologies

7407 * *Berlin by night: songs of stage, screen and radio in the Weimar Republic and the Third Reich.* EMI: CDP 7 96331 2. 1930–43. [Will Glahe, Helmut Zacharias, Late Anderson, and others].

7408 *Best-loved German folk songs.* Monitor: MCD 61398. [1963].

7409 *Folk songs from Bavaria.* Laserlight: 15182. [1989].

7410 *German drinking songs.* Legacy International: CD 304. [1988].

7411 *German drinking songs.* (Die Bleibtreu Sanger). Monitor: MCD 61419. [1964].

7412 *Das gibt's nur einmal.* Bear Family: BCD 15628 (Amiga 8001). 3CD set. 1930–44. [Marlene Dietrich, Willy Fritsch, Goomabay Dance Band, and others].

7413 *Mit Zither und Hackbrett.* Koch: 322442. [1990].

7414 *Oktoberfest in Germany.* Laserlight: 15181. [1989].

Individual Artists or Groups

7415 * Dietrich, Marlene, 1901–1992
The cosmopolitan Marlene Dietrich. Columbia: CK 53209. 1951–54.

7416 * Prey, Hermann, 1929–

Deutsche Volkslieder = German folk-songs. Capriccio: 10 115. [1986].

7417 Salon-Orchester Cölln

Berliner Salon. Deutsche Harmonia Mundi: 16 9529 2. 1985.

Italy

Anthologies

7418 *Atlante di musica tradizionale = Roots music atlas.* Newtone: NT 6736. 2CD set. [199?].

7419 ** *Bella ciao: chansons du peuple en Italie.* Harmonia Mundi: HMA 190734. [1975].

7420 *In dialetto sardo.* Heritage: HTCD 20. 1930–32. [Antioco Marras, Pietro Testoni, Gavino de Lunas].

7421 *Italy after dark = Italia nostalgica.* EMI: 0777 7 80023 2. [1992]. [Renato Carosone, Carlo Buti, Beniamino Gigli, and others].

7422 *Musiques de fêtes de Calabre = Calabria: feste e musica tradizionale.* [Series: Inédit]. Maison des Cultures du Monde: W 260051. 1983–93.

7423 ** *Polyphonies de Sardaigne = Polyphonies of Sardinia.* Le Chant du Monde: LDX 274 760. 1979–80.

7424 * *San Remo Festival: the golden years, vols. 1–4.* Replay: 14201/14202/14205/14206. 4 CDs. [195?–196?].

7425 *Sardaigne: musique de bergers et chants.* Arion: ARN 64283. 1979.

7426 *Sardaigne: polyphonies de la semaine sainte = Sardinia: polyphony for Holy Week.* Le Chant du Monde: LDX 274 936. 1985–91.

7427 *Sicily: music of the Holy Week.* [Series: UNESCO collection]. Auvidis: D 8210. 1982–90.

7428 *Zampogne en Italie = Zampogne: Italian bagpipes: Latium, Molise, Companie, Basilicate, Calabre et Sicilie.* Silex: Y225111. 1969–90.

Individual Artists or Groups

7429 Arbore, Renzo, and L'Orchestra Italiana

Napoli: due punti e a capo. Elektra/Musician: 61676-2. 1993.

7430 * Buscaglione, Fred

The greatest hits. Replay: RMCD 4003. [19-?].

7431 * Carosone, Renato

I successi di Renato Carosone. Replay: RMCD 4001. [195?].

7432 Ciapa Rusa

Antologia = Anthology. Robi Droli/Newtone: RDC 5015. 2CD set. [1989–19?].

7433 Ferri, Gabriella

L'eco del core. Replay: 4031. [196?].

7434 I Giullardi di Piazza

Dea fortuna. Shanachie: 21010. AC. 1989. OP

7435 Pavarotti, Luciano, 1935–

    7435.1 *Mamma.* London: 411 959-2. 1984.

    7435.2 ** *Volare: popular Italian songs.* London: 421 052-2. 1987.

7436 Ritmia

Maybe the sea. Shanachie: 64007. AC. 1989. OP

7437 Squadra

La Squadra: chansons génoises. Buda: 92571-2. [1990].

Malta

7438 *Folk songs and music from Malta.* (George Bonavia). Smithsonian/Folkways: 4047. AC. 1964.

7439 *Malte: ballades et joutes chantées.* (Frans Baldachino/Karmeu Bonnici). [Series: Inédit]. Maison des Cultures du Monde: W 260040. [1992].

Netherlands

Anthology

7440 *Folksongs and dances of the Netherlands.* Smithsonian/Folkways: 4036. AC. [1963].

Individual Artist

7441 Kunst, Jaap, 1891–1960

Living folksongs and dance-tunes from the Netherlands. Smithsonian/Folkways: 3576. AC. [1956].

Norway

Anthologies

7442 *Chants et danses de Norvège = Norwegian songs and dances.* PlayaSound: PS 65065. 1990.

7443 ** *Nordisk sang: music of Norway: selections from the Helio catalogue.* New Albion: NA031CD. 1957–88.

Individual Artists or Groups

7444 Bjorgum, Hallvard T., 1956– , and Torleiv H. Bjorgum, 1921–

Dolkaren: the best of Hallvard T. & Torleiv H. Bjorgum. Sylvartun: SYLVCD 3. [1989].

7445 Buen, Knut

As quick as fire: the art of the Norwegian hardanger fiddle. Henry Street/Rounder: HSR 0002. 1979–92.

7446 Lande, Vidar

Fiddle and hardanger fiddle music from Agder. [Series: UNESCO collection]. Auvidis: D 8063. [1996].

7447 * Nyhus, Sven, 1932–

Traditional Norwegian fiddle music. Shanachie: 21003. [1981].

7448 * Persen, Mari Boine

Gula gula. Real World/Virgin: 86222 (91631). 1989.

7449 Sorbye, Lief

Springdans: songs & dances from Norway. ARC: EUCD 1056. [1987].

Portugal

Anthologies

7450 * *Fado de Coimbra.* Heritage: HT CD 15. 1926–30.

7451 * *Fado de Lisboa, vol. 1: fados from Portugal.* Heritage: HT CD 14. 1928–36.

7452 *Fado de Lisboa, vol. 3: Lisbon women.* Heritage: HT CD 24. 1928–31.

7453 ** *Musical traditions of Portugal.* [Series: Traditional music of the world, vol. 9]. Smithsonian/Folkways: SF 40435. [1994].

7454 *Un parfum de fado = A spirit of fado, vols. 1–6.* PlayaSound: PS 65701-65706. 6 CDs. [199?]. [Carlos do Carmo, Armenio de Melo, Jose Maria Nobrega, and others].

7455 * *Portugal: Portuguese traditional music.* [Series: UNESCO collection]. Auvidis: D 8008. 1971.

7456 *Portuguese string music.* Heritage: HT CD 05. 1908–31. [Grupo Bahianinho, Orchestra da Notias, and others. Also includes Brazilian and Cape Verdean groups.]

7457 *Trás-os-Montes: chants du blé et cornemuses de berger.* Ocora: C 580035. 1978.

Individual Artists or Groups

7458 Menano, Antonio, 1895–1969

Antonio Menano. [Series: Fado's archives, vol. 5]. Heritage: HT CD 31. 1927–28.

7459 Paredes, Carlos

Guitarra portuguesa. Nonesuch: 79203-2. 1969–70.

7460 Rodrigues, Amalia, 1920–

> **7460.1** *Fados e guitarradas.* Accord: 401132 (Festival 113). [1989].

> **7460.2** * *Portugal's great Amalia Rodrigues.* Monitor: MCD 61442. 1956.

7461 Soares, Fernando Machado

Portugal: fado de Coimbra. Ocora: C 559041. 1987.

Spain

Anthologies

7462 *The best of sevillanas, vol. 1.* Oro: CD 701-2. [197?]. [Los Hermanos Reyes, El Pali, Los Marismenos, Amigos de Gines, and others].

7463 * *Cante flamenco: recorded live in Andalucia.* Nimbus: NI 5251. 1989.

7464 * *Cante gitano: gypsy flamenco.* Nimbus: NI 5168. 1988.

7465 *Cobles catalanes.* Silex: Y225102. [1992].

7466 ** *Duende: from traditional masters to Gypsy rock.* Ellipsis Arts: CD 3350. 3CD set. [1994]. [Luis de Cordoba, Enrique Morente, Camaron de la Isla, Lole y Manuel, Susi, Niña de los Peines, Tomatito, Paco de Lucia, Manolo Sanlucar, Sabicas, Pepe Habichuela, Ramón Montoya, Ketama, Amalgama, Strunz and Farah, Pata Negra, and others].

7467 ** *Early cante flamenco: classic recordings from the 1930s.* Arhoolie: CD 326. 1934–39. [Antonio Mairena, Manolo Caracol, Pepe Pinto, Niña de los Peines, and others].

7468 ** *Flamenco: grandes figuras.* Le Chant du Monde: 274944. [19-?]. [Niña de los Peines, Manolo Caracol, Antonio Mairena, Terremoto de Jerez, Ramón Montoya, Sabicas, and others].

7469 *Musiques catalanes d'aujourd'hui.* Silex: Y225013. [1992].

7470 * *The young Flamencos = Los jovenes flamencos.* Hannibal: HNCD 1370. 1983–90. [Pata Negra, Ketama, Rafael Riquini, Pepe Habichuela, and others].

Individual Artists or Groups

7471   Amaya, Carmen, 1913–1963

Carmen Amaya. [Series: Grands cantaores [figures] du flamenco, vol. 6]. Le Chant du Monde: LDX 274 880. [198?].

7472   Cadiz, Beni de, 1929–1990

Beni de Cadiz. [Series: Grands cantaores du flamenco, vol. 17]. Le Chant du Monde: LDX 274 992. [1994].

7473   Camaron de la Isla (Jose Monge Cruz), 1951–1992

   7473.1   *Camaron de la Isla.* [Series: Grands cantaores du flamenco, vol. 15]. Le Chant du Monde: LDX 274 957. [19-?].

   7473.2   * *Una leyenda flamenco, vols. 1 & 2.* Polygram Latino: 314 512822-2/314 512823-2. 2 CDs. 1970–92.

7474   Caracol, Manolo, 1909–1973

Manolo Caracol. [Series: Grands cantaores du flamenco, vol. 7]. Le Chant du Monde: LDX 274 899. 1958.

7475   Gallego, Jacinto, ca. 1901–1971

El Nino de Almaden. [Series: Grands cantaores du flamenco, vol. 2]. Le Chant du Monde: LDX 274 830. 1957–63.

7476   Gregorio el Borrico, Tio

Tio Gregorio el Borrico. [Series: Grandes figures du flamenco, vol. 12]. Le Chant du Monde: LDX 274 928. [19-?].

7477   Iglesias, Julio, 1943–

Julio. Columbia: CK 38640. 1983.

7478   Ketama

Y es ke me han kambiao los tiempos. Mango: 162 539879-2. 1990.

7479   Lagun Arteak

Chants du pays basque. Arion: ARN 64223. 1993.

7480   Linares, Carmen

La luna en el río. Auvidis Ethnic: B6753. 1991.

7481   Lucía, Paco de, 1947–

   7481.1   ** *Entre dos aguas.* Verve: 814106-2. 1973.

   7481.2   * *Siroco.* Verve: 830913-2. 1987.

7482   Mairena, Antonio, 1909–1983

Antonio Mairena. [Series: Grands cantaores du flamenco, vol. 9]. Le Chant du Monde: LDX 274 911. [198?].

7483   Manuel de Agujeta

Manuel de Agujeta. [Series: Grands cantaores du flamenco, vol. 8]. Le Chant du Monde: LDX 274 900. [198?].

7484   Marchena, Pepe

Pepe Marchena. [Series: Grands cantaores du flamenco, vol. 10]. Le Chant du Monde: LDX 274 912. [19-?].

7485   Martirio

Estoy mala. Nuevos Medios: 13211. [198?].

7486   Milladoiro

Castellum honesti: Celtic music from Spain. Green Linnet: GLCD 3055. [1991].

7487   Montoya, Ramón, 1880–1949

Ramón Montoya. [Series: Grandes figures du flamenco, vol. 5]. Le Chant du Monde: LDX 274 879. 1936.

7488   Nunez Melendez, Jose, 1887–198?

Pepe de la Matrona. [Series: Grands cantaores du flamenco, vol. 1]. Le Chant du Monde: LDX 274 829. 1957–63.

7489   Orfeó Catalá

Chansons traditionnelles de Catalogne. Harmonia Mundi: HMI 1907006. 1992.

7490   * Pastora, Pavon, 1890–1969

La Nina de los Peines. [Series: Grands cantaores du flamenco, vol. 3]. Le Chant du Monde: LDX 274 859. [193?–194?].

7491   Pata Negra

Blues de la frontera. Hannibal: HNCD 1309. 1987.

7492   Péña, Paco

   7492.1   *Flamenco.* Philips: 826904-2. 1971.

   7492.2   *Misa flamenca.* Nimbus: NI 5288. 1990.

7493   Ricardo, Nino de, 1909–1972

Nino de Ricardo. [Series: Grandes figures du flamenco, vol. 11]. Le Chant du Monde: LDX 274 927. 1955, [1991].

7494   Sabicas, 1912–1990

Sabicas. [Series: Grandes figures du flamenco, vol. 14]. Le Chant du Monde: LDX 274 935. [1992].

7495   Soto el Sordera, Manuel

Manuel Soto el Sordera. [Series: Grands cantaores du flamenco, vol. 13]. Le Chant du Monde: LDX 274 958. [19-?].

7496 Terremoto, Fernando, 1934–1981

Terremoto de Jerez. [Series: Grands cantaores du flamenco, vol. 4]. Le Chant du Monde: LDX 274 860. [198?].

7497 Utrera, Fernanda de, 1923–

Fernanda et Bernarda de Utrera. Ocora: C 558642/ 43. 2CD set. 1984.

7498 Vargas, Antonia Gilibert, 1925–1975

La Perla de Cadiz. [Series: Grands cantaores du flamenco, vol. 13]. Le Chant du Monde: LDX 274 934. [1992].

Sweden

Anthologies

7499 ** *Arsringar: Swedish folk music.* Manifest: MNW 194-95. 2CD set. 1970–90. [Groupa, Filarfolket, Norrlatar, J. P. Nystroms, Rojas Jonas, Lena Willemark, Ale Moller, and others].

7500 *Suède-Norvège: musiques des vallées scandinaves.* Ocora: C 560008. 1992.

Individual Artists or Groups

7501 Absolut Folk

Musiques traditionnelles de Suède. Silex: 225215. 1993.

7502 * Filarfolket

Vintervals. resource: RESCD 504 (Amalthea 76). 1980–90.

7503 Hedningarna

Kaksi! Xource/Sweden: Xoucd 101. 1991–92.

7504 Norrlatar

Sign of the raven. resource: RESCD 506 (Manifest). 1973–91.

7505 Svart Kaffe

Musique traditionnelle de Suède. Planett: 242054. 1992.

7506 Vásen

Essence: Swedish music. Auvidis Ethnic: B 6787. 1993.

Switzerland

7507 *Jüüzli: jodel du Muotatal (Suisse).* Le Chant du Monde: LDX 274 716. 1979.

7508 ** *Switzerland: Zäuerli: Yodels of Appenzell.* [Series: UNESCO collection]. Auvidis: D 8026. 1979.

7509 *Zur Ehre des Alphorns = In praise of the Alphorn.* Claves: CD 50-500. [1970].

Eastern Europe
(Including the Baltics, the Balkans, and Westerly Republics of the Former Soviet Union)

General Anthologies

7510 *Musique traditionnelle des Balkans.* (Nikola and others). Harmonia Mundi: HMA 1903007. 1990. [Greek, Bulgarian, Macedonian, Romanian, Turkish, and Arabic traditions].

7511 * *Voix des pays baltes: Lettonie, Lituanie, Estonie.* [Series: Inédit]. Maison des Cultures du Monde: W 260055. 1994. [Latvia, Lithuania, Estonia].

Albania

Anthologies

7512 *L'Albanie mystèrieuse = Mysterious Albania.* Disques Pierre Verany: PV 750010. [1995].

7513 * *Albanie: polyphonies vocales et instrumentales = Albania: vocal and instrumental polyphony.* Le Chant du Monde: LDX 274 897. [1988].

7514 *Famille Lela de Permet: polyphonies vocales et instrumentales d'Albanie.* Indigo/Harmonia Mundi: LBLC 2503. [1992].

7515 *Folk music of Albania.* Topic: TSCD 904. 1965.

7516 *There where the avalanche stops.* Touch/UK: CD 3311. 1988.

Individual Artist

7517 Licursi, Silvana

Far from the land of eagles: Albanian folk songs from southern Italy. Lyrichord: LYRCD 7413. 1989.

Armenia

Anthologies

7518 *Armenia: liturgical chants for Lent and Easter.* (Choir of the Makhitarist Community of San Lazzaro, Venice). [Series: UNESCO collection]. Auvidis: D 8015. 1974.

7519 *Arménie: chants liturgiques du moyen-age et musique instrumentale.* Ocora: C559001 (OCR 66). [1973].

7520 *Chants liturgiques armeniens = Armenian liturgical chants.* (Armenian Choir of Sofia/Bedros Papazian). Jade: JADC 056. 1992.

7521 *Haut-Karabagh; musiques de front = Upper Karabagh: musics from the front.* [Series: Mosaique]. Silex: Y225218. 1993.

Individual Artists or Groups

7522 Darbinian, Hovannes
The art of the Armenian târ. MEG: 003. 1988–89.

7523 Gasparian, Djivan
Moon shines at night. All Saints: CAROL 6604-2. [1993].

7524 ** Hagopian, Richard, 1937–
Armenian music through the ages. Smithsonian/Folkways: SF 40414. 1993.

7525 Kalaschjan
Rural and urban traditional music from Armenia. Wergo: SM 1505-2 (281505-2). 1991.

7526 Komitas, Vardapet, 1869–1935
Yerketsoghutuink srbo pataraki = Divine liturgy. (Choir of St. Gayané Cathedral). New Albion: NA033CD. 1988.

7527 Pehlivanian, Elia
Elia Pahlivanian, kanonne: musique traditionnelle d'Arménie. Buda: 82442-2. [198?].

Belarus

7528 *Byelorussia: musical folklore of the Polessye.* [Series: UNESCO collection]. Auvidis: D 8005. [197?].

7529 *USSR choral music festival.* Art & Electronics/MCA: AED 10609. 1991. [Music of Belarus and Lithuania].

Bosnia

See under Yugoslavia

Bulgaria
Anthologies

7530 *Bulgaria: gaida orchestra: bagpipe music from the Rhodope Mountains.* JVC: VICG-5224-2. 1991.

7531 *Bulgaria = Bulgarie.* [Series: UNESCO collection]. Auvidis: D 8019. 1980–82. [Traditional vocal and instrumental music].

7532 *Bulgarian brass: military and civil brass bands.* Pan: 153. [1995].

7533 *Bulgarian village singing: two women started to sing.* Rounder: CD 1055. 1978–88.

7534 *Du Danube au Balkan.* [Series: Anthologie de la musique bulgare, vol. 5]. Le Chant du Monde: CMT 274 981. 1976–81.

7535 ** *A harvest, a shepherd, a bride: village music of Bulgaria; In the shadow of the mountain: Bulgarian folk music.* [Series: Explorer]. Elektra Nonesuch: 79195-2. 1970–71.

7536 ** *Music of Bulgaria: the original 1955 recording.* [Series: Explorer]. (Ensemble of the Bulgarian Republic/Philippe Koutev). Elektra Nonesuch: 72011-2. 1955.

7537 * *Musique du pays Chope.* [Series: Anthologie de la musique bulgare, vol. 1]. Le Chant du Monde: CMT 274 970. 1977–82.

7538 ** *Le mystère des voix bulgares.* (Bulgarian State Radio and Television Female Vocal Choir). Nonesuch: 79165-2. 1987.

7539 *Le mystère des voix bulgares, vol. 2.* (Bulgarian State Radio and Television Female Vocal Choir and others). Nonesuch: 79201-2. 1957–87.

7540 * *Pirin.* [Series: Anthologie de la musique bulgare, vol. 4]. Le Chant du Monde: CMT 274 979. 1976–81.

7541 * *Rhodope—Dobroudja.* [Series: Anthologie de la musique bulgare, vol. 2]. Le Chant du Monde: CMT 274 975. 1976–81.

7542 *Song of the Bulgarian women.* (Sofia Women's Choir/Zdravko Mihaylov). Auvidis Ethnic: B 6138. 1988.

7543 * *Thrace.* [Series: Anthologie de la musique bulgare, vol. 3]. Le Chant du Monde: CMT 274 977. 1976–81.

7544 *Vocal traditions of Bulgaria: Bulgarian village traditional song from the archives of Radio Sofia.* Saydisc: CD-SDL 396. [1992].

Individual Artists or Groups

7545 * Papasov, Ivo, 1952–
Balkanology. Hannibal: HNCD 1363. 1991.

7546 Sestri Biserovi (Bisserov Sisters)
Bulgarian polyphony, vol. 2. JVC: VICG-5223. 1991.

7547 Trio Bulgarka

The forest is crying. Hannibal: HNCD 1342. 1988.

Croatia

See under Yugoslavia

Czech Republic and Slovak Republic (former Czechoslovakia)

Anthologies

7548 *Bohemian folk songs from Chodsko.* Supraphon: 11 2143. 1970–85.

7549 *Czech folk songs and dances.* Apon: 2472. LP. [196?].

7550 *Czeching in.* Škoda: SK0005-2. [1996].

7551 *Famous Slovak folk songs and dances.* Apon: 2474. LP. [196?].

7552 ** *Hody, hody, doprovody: Bohemian folk songs.* Supraphon: 11 1592-2 711. [1967–89].

7553 *K. u. K. Festkonzert: die schönsten böhmischen Märsche, Polkas und Walzer = the most famous Bohemian marches, polkas and waltzes.* (Czech Philharmonic/Václav Neumann). Orfeo: C 107 101 A/170 201 A. 2 CDs. 1983.

7554 *Moravian folk songs and dances.* Supraphon: 11 094. [19-?].

7555 *Songs of Moravia.* Apon: 2437. [196?].

Individual Group

7556 Musica Bohemica

Hajej, nynej: lullabies from Bohemia and Moravia. Supraphon: 11 1516-2 731. 1990.

Estonia

See 7511 and 7658

Georgia

Anthologies

7557 *Folk music from Georgia today.* Welt Musik/Wergo: 281510-2 (SM 1510-2). 1991. [Soinari, Mzetamze, Mtiebi].

7558 * *Georgian polyphony, vol. 1: choral music from Caucasia.* JVC: VICG-5003-2. 1987.

7559 *Georgian polyphony, vol. 2.* (Martve Boys' Chorus/Angzor Erkomainishvili). JVC: VICG-5004-2. 1988.

7560 *Georgian polyphony, vol. 3.* (Tinandari Male Chorus Group). JVC: VICG-5225-2. 1989.

7561 ** *Georgie: polyphonies de Svanétie = Georgia: polyphony of Svaneti.* Le Chant du Monde: LDX 274 990. 1991.

See also 7658

Individual Group

7562 Rustavi Choir

Georgian voices. Nonesuch: 79224-2 (Melodiya). 1981, 1988.

Greece

Anthologies

7563 * *Anthologia demotikou tragoudiou = Anthology of Greek folk songs, vol. 1: 1929–1940.* Greek Archives/F.M.: 666. 1929–40.

7564 ** *The best of bouzouki.* Koch: 321 889. [1988]. [Music by Stavros Xarhakos, Manos Hadjidakis, Mikis Theodorakis].

7565 * *Byzantine Mass: Akathistos hymn.* (Greek Byzantine Choir/Lycourgos Angelopoulos). Playa-Sound: PS 65118/PS 65119. 2CD set. [1989].

7566 * *Chant byzantin: passion et resurrection.* (Chorale of Saint-Julien-le-Pauvre/Marie Keyrouz). Harmonia Mundi: HMC 901315. 1989.

7567 * *Dimotiki anthologia "Kalamatiana-Sirta."* EMI/Regal: 14C 045 707532. [1987]. [Iota Lidia, Rita Abatsi, Yoryos Nakos, Papasideres, and others].

7568 * *Grèce: chansons et danses populaires = Greece: folk songs and dances.* VDE-Gallo: CD-552. 1930–59.

7569 *Grèce: les grands époques du chant sacré byzantin (XIVe–XVIIIe siècles).* (Ensemble Theodore Vassilikos). Ocora: C 559075. 1988.

7570 ** *Greece: traditional music.* [Series: UNESCO collection]. Auvidis: D 8018. 1973.

7571 *Greece: vocal monodies.* [Series: UNESCO collection]. Auvidis: D 8056. 1979.

7572 * *Greek folk instruments, vol. 1: lyra: Konstantinoupoles, Kretes, Pontou = Constantinople, Cretan, Pontic.* F.M.: 678. [1994].

7573 * *Greek folk instruments, vol. 2: santouri = sandouri.* F.M.: 679. [1994]. [Nikos Kalaintzes-Bintagialas, 1925– , santur].

7574 * *Greek folk instruments, vol. 3: phlogera = floghera.* F.M.: 680. [1994]. [Aristeides Vasilares, 1932–].

7575 *Greek traditional village music and dance.* [Series: World music library, vol. 76]. King: KICC 5176. [1994].

7576 ** *Greek-Oriental rebetica: songs and dances in the Asia Minor style, the golden years.* Folklyric/Arhoolie: CD 7005. 1911–37. [Rita Abadzi, Rosa Ezkenazi, Marika Papagika, Dhimitrios Semsis, and others].

7577 * *Hellenikos phonographos, vol. 1: to rebetiko tragoudi stem [oten] Amerike, 1920–1940 = the rebetiko song in America, 1920–1940.* Greek Archives/F.M.: 627. 1927–35.

7578 * *Hellenikos phonographos, vol. 2: to rebetiko tragoudi stem Amerike, 1945–1960 = the rebetiko song in America, 1945–1960.* Greek Archives/F.M.: 628. 1950–59.

7579 * *Hellenikos phonographos, vol. 3: to rebetiko tragoudi stem Amerike, 1945–1960 = the rebetiko song in America, 1945–1960.* Greek Archives/F.M.: 629. 1945–60.

7580 *Hellenikos phonographos, vol. 4: anamnese Smyrnes = memory of Smyrna.* Greek Archives/F.M.: 630. [19-?].

7581 *Hellenikos phonographos, vol. 5: tragoudia tou upokosmou = songs of the underground.* Greek Archives/F.M.: 631. [19-?].

7582 *Hellenikos phonographos, vol. 6: gunaikes tou rebetikou tragoudiou = women of the rebetiko song.* Greek Archives/F.M.: 632. [19-?].

7583 *Hellenikos phonographos, vol. 7: 'agnostes echographeseis Smyrneikon tragoudion = unknown recordings of songs from Smyrna, 1922–1940.* Greek Archives/F.M.: 633. 1922–40.

7584 *Hellenikos phonographos, vol. 8: Armenioi, Evraioi, Tourkoi, Tsigganoi stis pallies echographeseis = Armenians, Jews, Turks & Gypsies in old recordings.* Greek Archives/F.M.: 634. [19-?].

7585 *Hellenikos phonographos, vol. 9: he Konstantinoupole stis pales echographeseis = Constantinople in old recordings.* Greek Archives/F.M.: 635. [19-?].

7586 *Hellenikos phonographos, vol. 10: phones tou rebetiko se demotika tragoudia = traditional songs by rebetiko singers.* Greek Archives/F.M.: 636. 1920–36.

7587 *Hellenikos phonographos, vol. 11: tragoudia tou perithoriou = songs of outlaws.* Greek Archives/F.M.: 637. [19-?].

7588 *Hellenikos phonographos, vol. 12: 'agnostes echographeseis rebetikon tragoudion = unknown recordings of the rebetico songs, 1922–1940.* Greek Archives/F.M.: 638. 1922–40.

7589 ** *Liturgie byzantine.* (Greek Byzantine Choir/Lycourgos Angelopoulos). Le Chant du Monde: LDX 274 971. 1990.

7590 * *Music of ancient Greece.* (Christodoulos Halaris and ensemble). Orata: ORANGM 2013. [1992].

7591 *Music of the Greek bouzouki.* ARC Music: EUCD 1206 (Dorchester 9006). [1992]. [Athenians, Romiosini, Michalis Terzis].

7592 * *Musique de la Grèce antique.* (Atrium Musicae/Gregorio Paniagua). Harmonia Mundi: HMA 1901015. 1978.

7593 *Musique sacrée Byzantine: grand chant octo-tonal à la Vierge [de] Pétros Béréketis.* (Ensemble Theodore Vassilikos). Ocora: C 558682. 1982.

7594 ** *Rembetica: historic urban folksongs from Greece.* Rounder: CD 1079. 1906–46. [Rosa Eskenazi, Vassilis Tsitsanis, Markos Vamvakaris, Stratos, Rita Abatzi, Marika Papagika, and others].

7595 * *Rempetiko* [soundtrack]. CBS: 4506372. [1983]. [Stavros Xarhakos, Nikos Gkatsos, Giannes Tsarouches].

7596 *Zorba the Greek and others hits.* (Popular Orchestra). Mythos/F.M.: 605. [19-?].

Individual Artists or Groups

7597 Angéla
Rebetika: songs of the Greek soul. Auvidis Ethnic: B 6744. [1990].

7598 Annabouboula
In the baths of Constantinople. Shanachie: 64022. 1990.

7599 Constandinou, Christos
Grèce: bouzouki et touberleki. Arion: ARN 64089. [1988].

7600 Dalaras, George

The Greek voice. Tropical Music: 68.954. 1991.

7601 Hiotis, Manolis

30 chronia. EMI: 14C 234 71130-71131. 2AC set. 1980.

7602 Mangas, Yiorgos

Yiorgos Mangas. GlobeStyle: CDORB 021. 1985.

7603 * Mouskouri, Nana, 1936–

Only love: the very best of Nana Mouskouri. Philips: 314 510229-2. [19-?].

7604 Takoutsia

Grèce Epire. [Series: Inédit]. Maison des Cultures du Monde: W 260020. 1984–85.

7605 Theodorakis, Mikis, 1925–

7605.1 * *The best of Mikis Theodorakis.* Koch: 321888. [19-?].

7605.2 *Grand final du concert.* Le Chant du Monde: LDX 274 889. 1977–78.

7606 * Tsitsanes, Vassiles, 1915–1984

Hommage a Tsitsanis. Ocora: C559010. 1980.

7607 * Vamvakaris, Markos, 1905–

40 years. EMI: 711262. 1932–72.

Hungary

Anthologies

7608 *Hongrie: chants tziganes = Hungary: Gypsy folksongs.* Quintana: QUI 903028. 1991.

7609 ** *Hongrie: le dernier passage.* Ocora: C 580031. 1982.

7610 *Hongrie: musique tzigane = Hungarian Gypsy music.* (Sándor Lakatos and ensemble). Harmonia Mundi: HMP 3903009. 1990.

7611 *Hungarian folk music from Szatmar region.* Hungaroton: HCD 18192. [1991].

7612 *Hungary: the Gypsy violin.* (László Berki and ensemble). JVC: VICG-5270-2. 1992.

7613 *Musiques traditionnelles de Hongrie = Hungarian traditional music.* PlayaSound: PS 65117. [1990].

7614 *Tziganes: Paris/Berlin/Budapest.* Fremeaux F&A: CD 006. 2CD set. 1910–35.

Individual Artists or Groups

7615 Balogh, Kálmán, 1959–

The Gypsy-cimbalom. ARC Music: EUCD 1102. [1988].

7616 Fodor, Sandor, 1922–

Hungarian folk music from Transylvania. Hungaroton: HCD 18122. 1989.

7617 Kalyi Jag Group

Chants tziganes de Hongrie. PlayaSound: PS 65112 (Hungaroton HCD 18199). 1990.

7618 Muzsikás

7618.1 ** *Marta Sebestyen and Muzsikás.* Hannibal: HNCD 1330. [1987].

7618.2 *The prisoner's song.* Hannibal: HNCD 1341. 1986.

7619 * Ökrös Ensemble

Transylvanian portraits: Hungarian village music from Transylvania. Koch World: 3-4004-2. 1993.

7620 Salonisti

Hej Cigány: i Salonisti spielen Musik aus dem Zigeunersalon. EMI: 49137. 1987.

7621 Sánta, Ferenc

Csárdás: Hungarian Gypsy music. Naxos: 8.550954. 1994.

7622 Sebö

Hungarian folk music. Rounder: CD 5005. 1980.

7623 Vujicsics

Vujicsics: Serbian music from southern Hungary. Hannibal: HNCD 1310. 1988.

Latvia

Anthologies

7624 * *Lettonie: musiques des rite solaires = Latvia: music of solar rites.* [Series: Inédit]. Maison des Cultures du Monde: W 260062. 1993.

Individual Group

7625 Dzintars

Songs of amber. Rykodisc: RCD 10130. 1989.

Lithuania

7626 *Lithuanian songs and dances.* Monitor: 51305. AC. [1961].

See also 7511, 7529, and 7658

Macedonia

See under Yugoslavia

Poland

Anthologies

7627   *Polish folk music.* (State Folk Song and Dance Company "Slásk"/Stanislaw Hadyna). Polskie Nagrania: PNCD054. [1990?].

7628   *Polish folk songs and dances.* Smithsonian/Folkways: 6848. AC. 1952.

7629   *Polkas from Poland.* Polskie Nagrania: PNCD23. 1967–81.

7630 ** *Pologne: chansons et danses populaires = Poland: folk songs and dances.* VDE-Gallo: CD 757. 1972–92.

7631   *Pologne: danses = Poland: dances.* Arion: ARN 64188. [1992].

Individual Artists or Groups

7632   Polish State Folk Ballet

Slask. Monitor: 51-325. AC. [1959].

7633   Trebunia Family Band

Music of the Tatra Mountains, Poland. Nimbus: NI-5437. [1995].

7634   Zawadzki, Bolek

Bolek singing Polish favorites; Memories of Poland. Monitor: MCD 61409. 1964–66.

Romania

Anthologies

7635   *Cantari la nunta: musiques de noces en Valachie = Wedding music from Wallachia.* Auvidis Ethnic: B 6799. [1994].

7636 * *La doina Roumaine = Romanian doina.* Pierre Verany: PV 750006. [1994].

7637   *La Moldavie: l'art du bratsch.* Buda: 92596-2. 1993.

7638 ** *Panpipe music and folksongs of Romania.* [Series: World music library, vol. 47]. King: KICC 5147. 1987.

7639 ** *Reflections of Romania: village and urban folk traditions.* [Series: Explorer]. Elektra Nonesuch: 72092-4. AC. 1977.

7640   *Roumanie: musique de villages = Village music from Romania.* VDE-Gallo: CD 537/539. 3CD set. 1933–43.

7641   *Roumanie: musiques de mariage du Maramurés.* Ocora: C 580052. 1973.

7642   *Roumanie: polyphonie vocale des Aroumains = Rumania: vocal polyphony of the Arumanians.* Le Chant du Monde: LDX 274 803. 1980–81.

7643   *Roumanie: le vraie tradition de Transylvanie.* Ocora: C 559 070. 1974–79.

Individual Artists or Groups

7644   Syrinx

Musique tzigane en Roumanie = Romanian Gipsy music. Arion: ARN 64236. 1971–72.

7645   Szaszcsavas Band

Musique instrumentale de Transylvania = Instrumental folk music from Transylvania. Quintana: QUI 903072. 1992.

7646   Taraf de Carancebes

Taraf de Carancebes: musiciens du Banat. Silex: Y225208. 1992.

7647   Taraf de Clejani

Musique des Tsiganes de Valachie. Ocora: C 559036. [1988].

7648   Taraf de Haidouks

7648.1   *Honourable brigands, magic horses and evil eye.* Crammed Discs: CRAW 13. 1994.

7648.2 * *Musique des Tziganes de Roumanie.* Crammed Discs: CRAW 2 CD. 1991.

7649   Trio Pandelescu

Trio Pandelescu. [Series: Mosaïque]. Silex: Y225206. 1991.

7650 * Zamfir, Georghe, 1941–

Les flûtes roumaines. Arion: ARN 64004. 1968.

Russian Federation and Soviet Union

See also individual republics of the former Soviet Union in this chapter and in chapter 36, "Classical, Traditional, and Popular Musics of Northern Africa, the Middle East, and Central Asia."

Anthologies

7651   *Anthologie historique du chant religieux russe = Historical anthology of Russian sacred chant.* Le Chant du Monde: LDC 288 071. 1989–91.

7652 *Chants des femmes de la vielle Russie =
Women's songs from old Russia: traditions de
Kiéba, Bransk et des Simielski de Sibérie.* [Series:
Inédit]. Maison des Cultures du Monde: W 260018.
1990.

7653 * *Chants des peuples de Russie = Songs of the
peoples of Russia: regions of Briansk, Tula,
Arkhangelsk, Sverdlovsk, Tartary, Krasnodar,
Kharkov.* Le Chant du Monde: CDM 274 978. 1994.

7654 *Chants orthodoxes anciens et monastiques =
Ancient and monastic orthodox chants.* (Male
Choir Drevneruski Rospev/Anatoly Grindenko). Le
Chant du Monde/Saison Russe: LCD 288003. 1989.

7655 * *Chants traditionnelles russes = Russian traditional songs.* Auvidis Ethnic: B 6792. [1994].

7656 *Les fêtes de l'année liturgique orthodoxe =
The feasts of the orthodox liturgical year.* (Ural
Choir/Valadislav Novik). Le Chant du Monde: LCD
288 076/077. 2CD set. 1994.

7657 *Mother Volga = Volga matj: music of the Volga
Ugrians.* Pan: 2008. 1968–71, 1991.

7658 ** *Musics of the Soviet Union.* Smithsonian/
Folkways: SF 40002. [1989]. [Folk instrumental
music and songs of Lithuania, Estonia, Russia,
Tuva, Azerbaijan, and Georgia].

7659 *Musiques de la toundra et de taïga: Bouriates,
Yakoutes et Toungouses d'URSS.* [Series: Inédit,
vol. 7]. Maison des Cultures du Monde: W 260019.
1987, 1990.

7660 *Old believers: music of the Nekrasov Cos-
sacks.* Smithsonian/Folkways: SF 40462. 1989–90.

7661 ** *Russian Orthodox chants.* [Series: UNESCO
collection]. (Choir of the Dormition Church of the
Novodevichy Convent/Petr Polyakov). Auvidis: D
8301. 1987.

7662 *Voix de l'orient soviètique.* [Series: Inédit].
Maison des Cultures du Monde: W 260008. 1985.

7663 * *Voyage en U.R.S.S.: musique des peuples de
l'U.R.S.S. = Music of the peoples of the U.S.S.R.* Le
Chant du Monde: LDX 274920/274925. 6CD set.
[1990].

Individual Artists or Groups

7664 Andreyev Balalaika Ensemble
Balalaika! Monitor: MCD 61713. [1990].

7665 Baba Yaga
Back in the U.S.S.R. Flametree: FLTRCD 514. [199?].

7666 Gorby, Sarah
Chansons russes et tziganes. Arion: ARN 64249.
[1993].

7667 ** Odessa Balalaikas
The art of the balalaika. Elektra Nonesuch:
79034-2. 1981.

7668 Patriarchal Choir Moscow
Russian folk songs. Naxos: 8.550781. 1993.

7669 * Pokrovsky, Dmitri, ca. 1944–1996
The wild field. Realworld: CAROL-2316-2 (91736).
1991. *See also* 3643.45

7670 Svetlana
Chansons russes. Ocora: C 559098. 1990.

7671 Terem Quartet
Terem. RealWorld: CAROL-2321-2. 1993.

7672 Vysotsky, Vladimir, 1938–1980
    7672.1 *Le monument.* Le Chant du Monde: LDX
    274 997. 1973–76.
    7672.2 * *Selected songs.* Melodiya: SUCD 60-
    00293. [1974–75].

Tuva (Autonomous Republic of the Russian Federation)

ANTHOLOGY

7673 *Tuva: voices from the center of Asia.* Smith-
sonian/Folkways: SF 40017. 1987–88.

INDIVIDUAL ARTISTS OR GROUPS

7674 * Huun-Huur-Tu
60 horses in my herd: old songs and tunes of Tuva.
Shanachie: 64050. 1993.

7675 Sainkho
Out of Tuva. CramWorld/Sony: CRAW 6 (2866-2).
1986–88.

7676 Shu-De
Voices from the distant steppe. RealWorld: CAROL-
2339-2. 1992. *See also* 7658

Serbia

See under Yugoslavia

Slovak Republic

See under Czech Republic

Slovenia

See under Yugoslavia

Tuva

See under Russian Federation

Ukraine

Anthologies

7677 *Chants traditionnels de l'Ukraine.* (Ukranian Children's Choir of Odessa). Auvidis Ethnic: B 6780. 1992.

7678 * *Musiques traditionnelles d'Ukraine = Traditional music from Ukraine.* [Series: Mosaïque]. Silex: Y225211. [1993].

7679 * *Musiques traditionnelles d'Ukraine = Traditional music from Ukraine, vol. 2: Polésie, Poltava, Kiev, etc.* [Series: Mosaïque]. Silex: Y225216. 1992–93.

7680 *Ukraine: traditional music.* [Series: UNESCO collection]. Auvidis: D 8206. [1991].

7681 *Ukrainian dances.* Monitor: MCD 71790. 1978.

7682 *Voix ukrainiennes = Ukranian voices.* PlayaSound: PS 65114. 1993.

Individual Group

7683 Baron Samedi Percussions
Diakouyou. Silex: Y225020. 1992.

Yugoslavia (Including the Republics of Bosnia, Croatia, Macedonia, Serbia, and Slovenia)

Anthologies

7684 ** *Bosnia: echoes from an endangered world.* Smithsonian/Folkways: SF 40407. 1984–85.

7685 *Chant religieux serbes et bulgares = Serbian and Bulgarian religious chants.* (Rybine Male Choir/Valery Rybine). Le Chant du Monde/Saison Russe: RUS 289 087. 1993.

7686 *Chants & danses croates = Croatian folksongs and dances.* Quintana/Harmonia Mundi: QUI 903071. 1953–85.

7687 *Danses de Macédoine, Yugoslavia = Macedonia dances, Yugoslavia.* PlayaSound: PS 65076. [1991].

7688 * *Islamic ritual from the province of Kosovo.* [Series: UNESCO collection]. Auvidis: D 8055. 1973.

7689 *Musics from Yugoslavia.* Buda: 92490-2. [1992].

7690 *Serbia: pastoral dances and melodies.* Auvidis Ethnic: B 6759. [197?].

7691 *Songs of a Macedonian Gypsy.* (Esma Redžepova/Usnija Jašarova). Monitor: MCD 71496. [195?].

7692 ** *Village music of Yugoslavia: songs and dances from Bosnia-Herzegovina, Croatia & Macedonia.* [Series: Explorer]. Elektra Nonesuch: 72042-2. 1970.

7693 *Yougoslavie: Serbie orientale: les bougies du paradis.* Ocora: C 580041. 1970–78.

7694 *Yugoslav folk music.* Lyrichord: LLCT 7189. AC. [1968].

Individual Artists or Groups

7695 Ensemble Ulvi Erguner
Oslobodenje: quotidien indépendant de Bosnie-Herzégovine. Al Sur: ALCD 109. 1964, 1991.

7696 Estacada, B.
Chants & danses de Yougoslavie. PlayaSound: PS 65044. [1989].

7697 * Kalesijski Zvuci
Bosnian breakdown: the unpronounceable beat of Sarajevo. GlobeStyle: CDORBD 074. 1991.

7698 Stojiljkovic, Jova
Blow, Besir blow!!! GlobeStyle: CDORBD 038. 1989.

7699 Tamburaski sastav "Veritas"
Mi smo Šokci: Croatian folklore from Yugoslavia. ARC Music: EUCD 1078. [1989].

International Anthologies and Worldbeat Fusion

Compiled by
William E. Anderson

International Anthologies

This section contains transnational, cross-cultural compilations of traditional and popular music. Some focus on a particular musical characteristic, while others celebrate globalism itself.

7700 * *The ace and deuce of pipering.* Heritage: HT CD 21. 1906–47.

7701 * *Africando, vol. 1: trovador.* Stern's Africa: STCD 1045. 1993. [West African and Latin American musicians].

7702 * *Africando, vol. 2: tierra tradicional.* Stern's Africa: STCD 1055. 1994. [West African and Latin American musicians].

7703 * *The big bang: in the beginning was the drum.* Ellipsis Arts: CD 3400. 3CD set. 1974–94.

7704 * *Boiling point: music from hot countries.* World Circuit: WCD 022. [1991]. [Joe Arroyo, Ali Farka Toure, Oumou Sangare, Orchestra Baobab, Dimi Mint Abba, Abdel Gadir Salim, and others].

7705 ** *Dances of the world: music from the Nonesuch Explorer series.* Elektra Nonesuch: 79167-2. 1966–80.

7706 *Frozen brass: Africa and Latin America.* [Series: Anthology of brass band music no. 2: ethnic series]. Pan: PAN 2026. 1991–92.

7707 *Frozen brass: Asia.* [Series: Anthology of brass band music no. 1: ethnic series]. Pan: PAN 2020. 1949–92.

7708 * *Global celebration.* Ellipsis Arts: CD 3230. 4CD set. [1993?]. [vol. 1: *Dancing with the gods;* vol. 2: *Earth spirit;* vol. 3: *Passages;* vol. 4: *Gatherings*]. [Bachir Attar, Mongo Santamaria, I Giullardi di Piazza, James Cleveland, Matt Molloy, Nahawa Doumbia, Sebö, Alfredo Gutiérrez, Ali Hassan Khan, Klezmatics, Virunga, Abana Ba Nassery, Varttina, Tarika Sammy, Nass El Ghiwane, M'Mah Sylla, Saba Saba!, Orchestra Marrabenta, Mahlathini and the Mahotella Queens, Bo Dollis, Monk Boudreaux, Marce and Tumpak, and others].

7709 ** *Global divas: voices from women of the world.* Rounder: CD 5062/3/4. 3CD set. [1995]. [Celina Gonzalez, Varttina, Nasida Ria, Oumou Sangare, Marlene Dietrich, Djur Djura, Gal Costa, Maria Bethania, Lydia Mendoza, Dimi Mint Abba, Rosa Eskenazi, Fairuz, Marian Anderson, Amalia Rodrigues, Carmen Linares, Celia Cruz, Houria Aichi, Calypso Rose, Patsy Cline, Miriam Makeba, Edith Piaf, Hibari Misora, Lucha Reyes, Tarika Sammy, Bulgarian State Radio and Television Female Vocal Choir, Maria Olga Pineros, Aretha Franklin, Elis Regina, Cedella Marley-Booker, Mercedes Sosa, Les Amazones de Guinee, Marta Sebestyen, Oum Kalsoum, Lata Mangeshkar, Mahotella Queens, Cheikha Remitti, Idjah Hadidjah, and others].

7710 ** *Instruments de musique du monde = Musical instruments of the world.* Le Chant du Monde: LDX 274 675. [197?].

7711 * *Mbuki mvuki: terrestrial hits selected from the catalog of Original Music.* Original Music: OMCD 017. [195?]–84.

7712 ** *Planet squeezebox: accordion music from around the world.* Ellipsis Arts: CD 3470. 3CD set. [1995]. [Gus Viseur, Attwenger, Maria Kalaniemi, Phil Cunningham, Joe Derrane, Steve Riley, Lynn August, Pauline Oliveros, Guy Klucevsek, Brave Combo, Steve Jordan, Eva Ybarra, Lisandro Meza, Astor Piazzolla, Zagazougou, Raul Barboza, I. K. Dairo, Tshwatla Makala, Abdel Aziz El Mubarak, Hussan Ramzy, Ivan Kirev, Klezmer Conservatory Band, and others].

7713 * *Roots Piranhas: sound tracks into world music.* Piranha: PIR 48-2 (EFA CD 01898). [19-?]. [Eduardo Durao, Stella Chiweshe, Noise Khanyile, Orchestra Marrabenta Star, Ali Hassan Kuban, Klezmatics, Tukul Band, and others].

7714 ** *The secret museum of mankind, vols. 1–3: ethnic music classics.* Yazoo: 7004/7006. 3 CDs. 1925–48. [Compilation of remastered 78 rpm recordings from the four hemispheres].

7715 ** *Tambours de terre = Drums of the earth, vol. 1: Africa, America.* Auvidis Ethnic: B 6773. 1990. [Ivory Coast, Ghana, Senegal, Morocco, Surinam, Guyane, Cuba].

7716 ** *Tambours de terre = Drums of the earth, vol. 2: Asia.* Auvidis Ethnic: B 6774. 1990. [Iraq, Iran, Nepal, India].

7717 * *Voices: a compilation of the world's greatest choirs.* Mesa: 79026. 3CD set. [1991].

Worldbeat Fusion

Musicians in this section draw on a variety of traditional and modern idioms in the creation of a contemporary, cross-cultural synthesis.

Anthologies

7718 *Planet soup: a stirring collection of cross-cultural collaborations and musical hybrids.* Ellipsis Arts: CD3450. 3CD set. 1985–95. [Ray Lema, Astor Piazzolla, Peter Kater, R. Carlos Nakai, Varttina, Africando, Henry Kaiser, Dissidenten, Ali Hassan Kuban, Jon Hassell, Farafina, Wolfstone, Pierre Dorge, Ketama, and others].

7719 *Sona Gaia collection one.* Sona Gaia/Narada: ND-62764. 1986–90. [Ira Stein and Russell Walder, Ancient Future, Michael Gettel, Michael Pluznick, Max Lasser, and others].

7720 * *Songhai.* Hannibal: HNCD 1323. 1989. [Ketama, Toumani Diabaté, Danny Thompson].

Individual Artists or Groups

7721 Ancient Future
Natural rhythms. Philo: CD PH 9006. 1981.

7722 Chandra, Sheila, 1965–
7722.1 * *Silk.* Shanachie: 64035. 1983–90.
7722.2 *Weaving my ancestors' voices.* Realworld: CAROL-2322-2. 1993.

7723 * Cooder, Ry, 1947– , and Vishwa Mohan Bhatt
A meeting by the river. Water Lily Acoustics: WLA-CS-29-CD. 1992.

7724 Dissidenten
Sahara electrik. Shanachie: 64005. 1988.

7725 Do'a
Ancient beauty. Philo: CD PH 9004. 1981.

7726 Garbarek, Jan, 1947– , and Ustad Fateh Ali Khan
Ragas and sagas. ECM: 78118-21442 (511263-2). 1990.

7727 Gipsy Kings
7727.1 *Allegria.* Elektra: 61019-2. 1982–83.
7727.2 * *Gipsy Kings.* Elektra: 60845-2. 1988.

7728 Hart, Mickey, 1950–

7728.1 * *At the edge.* Rykodisc: RCD 10124. 1975–90.

7728.2 *Planet drum.* Rykodisc: RCD 10206. 1991.

7729 ** Hassell, Jon, 1937–

Fourth world, vol. 1: possible musics. Editions EG: CAROL-1537-2. 1980.

7730 Hwong, Lucia

House of sleeping beauties. Private Music: 2006-2-P. [1985].

7731 * Kitajima, Osamu

Osamu. Island: ILPS 9426. LP. 1977. OP

7732 * Kitaro, 1953–

Silk road. Kuckuck: 12051-2. 2CD set. 1980.

7733 Libana

Sojourns. Shanachie: 67001. 1989.

7734 * Mariano, Charlie, 1923– , and the Karnataka College of Percussion featuring R. A. Ramamani

Jyothi. ECM: 811 548-2 (1256). 1983.

7735 Mgrdichian, George

One man's passion. Shanachie: 65004. [1990].

7736 Micus, Stephan, 1953–

Wings over water. ECM: 78118-23338-2 (JAPO 60038). 1982.

7737 Les Miserables Brass Band

Manic traditions. Northeastern: NR 5004-CD. 1989.

7738 * Mouth Music

Mouth music. Triple Earth/Rykodisc: RCD 10196. 1991.

7739 Olatunji, Babatunde, 1939–

Drums of passion: the beat. Rykodisc: RCD 10107. 1986.

7740 Outback

Baka. Hannibal: HNCD 1357. 1990.

7741 * Stivell, Alan, 1943–

Renaissance of the Celtic harp. Rounder: CD 3067. 1987.

7742 * 3 Mustaphas 3

Soup of the century. Rykodisc: RCD 10195. [1990].

7743 * Zap Mama

Adventures in Afropea 1. Luaka Bop/Warner Bros.: 45183-2. 1993.

Traditional and Popular Musics
of Sub-Saharan Africa

Compiled by
**Suzanne Flandreau, William E. Anderson,
and Kent Underwood**

T his chapter comprises music of the African countries south of the Sahara Desert plus the islands of Mauritius, La Réunion, and the Seychelles in the Indian Ocean. Countries are arranged alphabetically within four regional groups: western, central, eastern, and southern. The Arab countries of northern Africa are covered in chapter 36, "Classical, Traditional, and Popular Musics of Northern Africa, the Middle East, and Central Asia."

General Anthologies

7744 ** *Africa dances.* Original Music: OMCD 002. [195?–197?].

7745 * *Africa: drum, chant & instrumental music.* [Series: Explorer]. Elektra Nonesuch: 72073-2. 1976. [Recorded in Niger, Mali, and Upper Volta (Burkina Faso)].

7746 ** *Africa: never stand still.* Ellipsis Arts: CD 3300. 3CD set. [1994]. [Youssou N'Dour, Ladysmith Black Mambazo, Salif Keita, Baaba Maal, Tarika

Sammy, Aurlus Mabele and Loketo, Thomas Mapfumo, Ali Farka Toure, Les Têtes Brulées, Remmy Ongala, Oliver Mutukudzi, Abdul T-Jay, Pierre Akendengue, Robson Banda, Lulu Masilela, Gabriel Omolo, Dulce and Orchestra Marrabenta, Martin K. Obeng, Kapere Jazz Band, Bellemou Messaoud, Barrister, Pepe Kalle, Oumou Sangare, Papa Wemba, Dimi Mint Abba, Kanda Bongo Man, Stella Chiweshe, Sir Shina Peters, Soul Brothers, Bonga, and others].

7747 *Africa: south of the Sahara.* Smithsonian/Folkways: 4503. 2AC set. 1957.

7748 * *African acoustic: sounds eastern and southern.* Original Music: OMCD 001. [1988].

7749 * *African drum/chant/instrumentals.* [Series: Explorer]. Elektra Nonesuch: 72073-2. 1976. [Recorded in Niger, Mali, and Upper Volta].

7750 *African journey: a search for the roots of the blues.* Sonet: SNTF 667 (Vanguard 73014/15). 1974. [Recorded by Samuel Charters in Gambia, Senegal, Mali, Ghana, and Togo].

7751 * *African moves: soukous, highlife and juju music.* Rounder: CD 11513. 1983–87. [Somo Somo, Tabu Ley, M'bilia Bel, Ebenezer Obey, Segun Adewale, African Brothers, Hi-Life International, and others].

7752 * *African moves, vol. 2.* Stern's Africa: STCD 1029. [1989]. [Kasse Mady, Papa Wemba, Thione Seck, Kante Manfila, Aster Aweke, Cheb Khaled, Ismael Lo, Salif Keita].

7753 ** *African rhythms and instruments.* Lyrichord: LYRCD 7328; 7338; 7339. 3 CDs. 1969.

7754 * *African tribal music and dances.* Legacy International: CD 328 (Vogue 193). 1952. [Recorded in Guinea and Ivory Coast].

7755 * *An anthology of African music, vols. 1–14.* [Series: UNESCO collection]. Bärenreiter/Musicaphon: BM 30 L 2301/2314. 14LP set. [195?–197?]. OP

7756 *Music of Africa series, vols. 1–10.* Kaleidophone: KMA 1–10. 10LP/10AC set. 1972. OP

7757 *Out of Africa.* Rykodisc: RCD 20059. [1988]. [Mahotella Queens, Youssou N'Dour, Ebenezer Obey, and others].

7758 *Sound d'Afrique, vols. 1–2.* Mango: 162 539697-2; 162 539754-2. 2 CDs. [1981–82].

7759 *Spirit of African Sanctus: the original recordings of David Fanshawe.* Saydisc: SDL 389. 1969–73. [Recorded in Egypt, Sudan, Uganda, and Kenya].

7760 * *Telling stories of the sea.* [Series: Adventures in Afropea, vol. 3]. Luaka Bop/Warner Bros.: 45669-2. [1995]. [Bonga, Cesaria Evora, Andre Mingas, Waldemar Bastos, Pedro Ramos, Dany Silva, and others].

7761 ** *30 ans de musique africaine.* Africa No. 1/Sonodisc: CD 52910. 1960–89. [Joseph Kabaselle, Hilarion Nguema, Rochereau, Docteur Nico, Bantous Jazz, Manu Dibango, Miriam Makeba, Pierre Akendengue, Koffi Olomide, Mory Kante, Franco, Alpha Blondy, Pepe Kalle, and others].

African Reggae

Anthology

7762 * *Black star liner: reggae from Africa.* Heartbeat: CD HB 16. 1976–81. [Sonny Okosun, Victor Uwaifo, Bongos Ikwue, Sabanoh 75, and others].

Individual Artists or Groups

7763 * Alpha Blondy, 1953–
The best of Alpha Blondy. Shanachie: 43075. 1983–89.

7764 Dube, Lucky, 1967–
Prisoner. Shanachie: 43073. 1991.

7765 Fashek, Majek
Prisoner of conscience. Mango: 162 539870-2. 1990.

7766 Okosun, Sonny, 1947–
Liberation. Shanachie: 43019. 1978–84.

Western Africa

Benin

Anthologies

7767 *Benin: Bariba and Somba music.* [Series: UNESCO collection]. Auvidis: D 8057. 1974.

7768 * *Benin: rhythms and songs for the vodun.* VDE-Gallo: CD-612. 1973–74.

7769 ** *Yoruba drums from Benin, West Africa.* Smithsonian/Folkways: SF 40440. 1987.

Individual Artists or Groups

7770 * Kidjo, Angelique, 1960–
Logozo. Mango: 162 539918-2. 1991.

7771 Orchestre T. P. Poly-rythmo de cotonou
0 + 0 = 0. Tangent: TAN 7007. LP. [198?]. OP

7772 Pedro, Gnonnas
La compilation. [Series: Musique afro-cubaine. vol. 1]. Ledoux/Melodie: 79556-2. [1994].

Burkina Faso (Upper Volta)

Anthologies

7773 *Rhythms of the grasslands.* [Series: Music of Upper Volta, vol. 2]. Nonesuch: 72090. LP. 1973–75. OP

7774 *Savannah rhythms.* [Series: Music of Upper Volta, vol. 1]. Nonesuch: 72087. LP. 1973–75. OP

Individual Artists or Groups

7775 Farafina
Faso denou. Realworld: CAROL-2328-2. 1992.

7776   Frères Coulibaly

Anka dia: musique et chants du Burkina Faso. Auvidis Ethnic: B 6775. 1991.

Cape Verde

Anthologies

7777 * *Cape Verde: anthology 1959–1992.* Buda: 92614-2. 2CD set. 1959–92.

7778   *Music from Cape Verde.* Caprice: CAP 21451. 1993.

Individual Artists or Groups

7779   Bana

Chante la magie du Cap Vert. Lusafrica/Melodie: 08630-2. 1994.

7780 * Evora, Cesaria

Miss Perfumado. Lusafrica/Melodie: 79540-2. 1992.

7781   Finacon

Simplicidade. Melodie: 79558-2. 1994.

Chad

7782   *Chad: music from Tibesti.* Le Chant du Monde: LDX 274 722. 1969–79.

7783   *Music of Chad.* Smithsonian/Folkways: 4337. AC. 1966.

Gambia

Anthologies

7784   *Gambia's music, vol. 1.* Smithsonian/Folkways: 4521. 2AC set. 1978.

7785   *Sounds of West Africa: the kora & the xylophone.* Lyrichord: LYRCD 7308. [1977]. [Foday Musa Suso and other unnamed musicians, recorded in Ghana, Gambia, and Senegal].

7786   *Wolof music of Senegal and the Gambia.* Smithsonian/Folkways: 4462. AC. 1955.

Individual Artists or Groups

7787 * Ancient Heart

Mandinka and Fulani music of the Gambia. Axiom: 539880-2. 1990.

7788   Jobareth, Amadu Bansang

Tabara. Music of the World: CDT-129. 1987.

7789   Konte, Alhaji Bai, 1920–1983

Kora melodies from the Republic of the Gambia, West Africa. Rounder: CD 5001. 1973.

7790   Ly, Mamadou, 1937–

Mandinka drum master. Village Pulse/Stern's Africa: VP-1001. 1992.

7791   Suso, Foday Musa, 1953–

7791.1   *Kora music from the Gambia.* Smithsonian/Folkways: 8510. AC. 1976.

7791.2   *Mansa bendung = Welcome to the king.* Flying Fish: FF 70380. 1986.

7792   Suso, Salieu

Griot. Lyrichord: LYRCD 7418. [1993].

Ghana

Anthologies

7793 * *Drum gahu: good-time drumming from the Ewe people of Ghana and Togo.* White Cliffs Media: WCM 9494. [1987].

7794   *Drums of West Africa: ritual music of Ghana.* Lyrichord: LYRCD 7307. 1974–76.

7795 * *Ghana: ancient ceremonies, songs & dance music.* [Series: Explorer]. Elektra Nonesuch: 72082-2. [1979].

7796   *Ghana: music of the northern tribes.* Lyrichord: LYRCD 7321. 1976.

7797 * *Giants of danceband highlife.* Original Music: OMCD 011. [195?–197?]. [E. T. Mensah, Ramblers, Professional Uhuru].

7798 * *The guitar and the gun: a collection of Ghanian highlife dance music, vols. 1–2.* Africagram: A DRY 1/A DRY 6. 2 LPs. 1983, 1985.

7799   *I've found my love: 1960's guitar band highlife of Ghana.* Original Music: OMCD 019. [1993].

7800   *Master drummers of Dagbon* [vol. 1]. Rounder: CD 5016. 1981.

7801   *Master drummers of Dagbon, vol. 2: drumming from northern Ghana.* Rounder: CD 5046. 1981.

7802   *Money no be sand: Afro-lypso/Pidgin highlife/ Afro-rock/Afro-soul.* Original Music: OMCD 031. 1958–71. [E. T. Mensah, Charlotte Dada, Ramblers, Eddie Okonta, Eric Akaeze, Charles Iwegbue, and others].

7803 *Music of the Dogoma (Dagomba) from Ghana.* Smithsonian/Folkways: 4324. AC. 1976.

7804 * *Rhythms of life, songs of wisdom: Akan music from Ghana, West Africa.* Smithsonian/Folkways: SF 40463. 1992–93.

Individual Artists or Groups

7805 Addy, Mustapha Tettey, 1942–

   7805.1 ** *Mustapha Tettey Addy: master drummer from Ghana.* Lyrichord: LYRCD 7250. 1974.

   7805.2 *Les percussions du Ghana.* Arion: 64055. 1979.

7806 Addy, Obo, 1936–

Okropong: traditional music of Ghana. EarthBeat: 42508-2. 1989.

7807 African Brothers

Me poma. Rounder: 5018 (Stern's Africa 1004). AC. 1984.

7808 * Agyeman, Eric

Highlife safari. Stern's Africa: STCD 3002 (Apogee 013). 1978.

7809 Amponsah, Daniel (Koo Nimo), 1934–

Osabarima. Adasa/Stern's Africa: ADCD 102. 1976.

7810 * Crentsil, A. B., 1950– , and Sweet Talks

Hollywood highlife party/Moses. Popular African Music: ADC 301 (Philips 635 4034). 1978, 1982.

7811 De Souza, Ignace, 1937–

The great unknowns. Original Music: OMCD 026. [195?–196?].

7812 Kobom, Joseph

Xylophone music from Ghana. White Cliffs Media: WCM 9516. [1992].

7813 Konadu, Alex

One man thousand: live in London. World Circuit: WCD 009. 1988.

7814 Lobi, Kakraba

The world of Kakraba Lobi. JVC: VICG-5014 (VID 25014). 1985.

7815 * Mensah, E. T., 1919– , and Tempos Dance Band

Day by day. RetroAfric: RETRO 3CD. [195?–196?].

7816 Osibisa

Osibisa. Lineca/Line: 9.01266 (MCA 32). 1971.

7817 Pan African Orchestra

Opus 1. Realworld: CAROL 2350-2. 1994.

Guinea

Anthologies

7818 *Guinée: anthologie du balafon mandingue.* Buda: 92520-2. 2CD set. 1991.

7819 *Guinée: les Peuls du Wassolon: la danse des chasseurs.* Ocora: C 558679. 1986.

7820 *Guinée: récits et épopées.* Ocora: C 560009. 1986.

7821 *Guinée, Sénégal.* [Series: Le chant des enfants du monde, vol. 1]. Arion: ARN 64259. 1990.

Individual Artists or Groups

7822 * Amazones de Guinée

Au coeur de Paris and M'mah Sylla. Bolibana/ Melodie: 42076-2. 1983.

7823 Ballets Africains

Les Ballets Africains: ensemble national de la République de Guinée. Buda: 925792. 1993.

7824 * Bembeya Jazz National

Regard sur le passé. Syliphone: 42064-2. 1982.

7825 Camara, Ladji, 1923–

Les ballets africains de Papa Ladji Camara. Lyrichord: LYRCD 7419. [198?].

7826 Diabaté, Prince, and Amara Sanoh

Prince Diabaté et Amara Sanoh: Guinea: chant et kora. Buda: 92578-2. 1993.

7827 Diabaté, Sona, 1958–

Girls of Guinea. Shanachie: 65007. 1988.

7828 * Jawara, Jali Musa, 1961–

Yasimika. Hannibal: HNCD 1355. 1983.

7829 Kante, Mory, 1951–

Akwaba beach. Polydor: 833119-2 (Barclay: 281833). 1987.

7830 Kouyate, Ousmane, 1952–

Domba. Mango: 162 539886-2. 1990.

7831 Kouyate, Sory Kandia

Doua. Sonodisc: CDS 6815. 1970.

7832 ** Percussions de Guinée

Les Percussions de Guinée, vol. 2. Buda: 92586-2. 1993.

7833 Wassa

Guinée: chants & percussions de la Basse-Côte. Buda: 92518-2. 1991.

Guinea-Bissau

7834 Naka, Ramiro, 1955–

Salvador. Mango: 162 539921-2. 1990.

Ivory Coast (Côte-d'Ivoire)
Anthologies

7835 *The Baoulé of the Ivory Coast.* Smithsonian/Folkways: 4476. AC. 1954–55.

7836 *Côte-d'Ivoire: a Senufo-Fodonon funerary vigil.* [Series: UNESCO collection]. Auvidis: D 8203. 1989.

7837 *Côte-d'Ivoire: Baule vocal music.* [Series: UNESCO collection]. Auvidis: D 8048. 1965–66.

7838 * *Côte-d'Ivoire: masques Dan.* Ocora: C 580048 (OCR 52). 1965–67.

7839 *Côte-d'Ivoire: tom-tom fantasy: live performances from the mask festival.* JVC: VICG-5010. 1987.

7840 *Ivory Coast, Senufo: music for Fodonon funerals.* Le Chant du Monde: CNR 274 838. 1976–82.

Individual Artists or Groups

7841 Alpha Blondy. *See* 7763

7842 Dje Dje, Ernesto, d. 1983

Tizere. Star: SHA 032. [197?].

7843 Dramé, Adama, 1954–

Adama Dramé, tambour djembé. Auvidis Ethnic: B 6126. 1987.

7844 Foliba

Percussions mandingues = Mandingo drums, vol. 2. PlayaSound: PS 65122. 1993.

7845 Kone, Aicha

Poro dance. Sonodisc: CD 92008. 1992.

7846 Le Zagazougou

Zagazougou coup. Piranha: PIR 49-2 (CD 01899). 1993.

Liberia

7847 *Folk music of Liberia.* Smithsonian/Folkways: 4465. AC. 1954.

7848 *Music of the Kpelle of Liberia.* Smithsonian/Folkways: 4385. AC. 1970.

7849 *Music of the Vai of Liberia.* Smithsonian/Folkways: 4388. AC. 1977–81.

Mali
Anthologies

7850 * *Musiques du Mali: Banzoumana; Sira Moury.* Syllart/Melodie: 38901-2/38902-2. Two 2CD sets. 1965–80. [Sidiki Diabaté, Rail Band, Salif Keita, Les Ambassadeurs, Maravillas, Super Biton, Nahawa Doumbia, Fanta Demba, and others].

7851 * *Première anthologie de la musique malienne, vols. 1–6.* Bärenreiter-Musicaphon: BM 30 L 2501/2506. 6LP set. [197?]. OP

7852 ** *The Wassoulou sound: women of Mali* [vol. 1]. Stern's Africa: STCD 1035. [1991]. [Sali Sidibe, Coumba Sidibe, Oumou Sangare, Dienaba Diakite, and others].

7853 * *The Wassoulou sound, vol. 2: women of Mali.* Stern's Africa: STCD 1048. [1994]. [Coumba Sidibe, Sali Sidibe, Djeneba Seck, Nahawa Doumbia, and others].

Individual Artists or Groups

7854 * Les Ambassadeurs

Les Ambassadeurs International, featuring Salif Keita. Rounder: CD 5053. [197?].

7855 Diabaté, Zani, 1947–

Zani Diabaté and the Super Djata Band. Mango: 162 539814-2. 1985.

7856 Doumbia, Nahawa

Nyama toutou/Didadi. Stern's Africa: STCD 1033. 1988–90.

7857 Kanté, Mamadou

Les tambours du Mali. PlayaSound: PS 65132. [1992].

7858 ** Keita, Salif, 1949–

Soro. Mango: 162 539808-2. 1987.

7859 * Mady, Kasse, 1955–

Kela tradition. Stern's Africa: STCD 1034. 1990.

7860 Sacko, Ousmane, 1940– , and Yakaré Diabaté
Mali: la nuit des griots. Ocora: C 559009. 1983.

7861 Samaké, Sibiri
Les chasseurs de Sebenikoro et leur griot Sibiri Samaké. Buda: 92523-2. 1990.

7862 Sangare, Oumou, 1968–
    7862.1 *Ko sira.* World Circuit: WCD 036. 1992.
    7862.2 ** *Moussoulou.* World Circuit: WCD 021. 1988.

7863 Super Rail Band
New dimensions in rail culture. GlobeStyle: CDORB 001. 1982.

7864 Toure, Ali Farka, 1939–
    7864.1 ** *Ali Farka Toure.* Mango: 162 539826-2. 1987.
    7864.2 *Talking Timbuktu.* Hannibal: HNCD 1381. 1993.

Mauritania

Anthology

7865 *Mauritanie, vols. 1–2: anthololgie de la musique maure: Hodh oriental.* Ocora: 558 532/33. 2LP set. 1975–76. OP

Individual Artists or Groups

7866 ** Abba, Dimi Mint
Music and songs of Mauritania. Auvidis Ethnic: B 6768. 1991.

7867 * Eide, Khalifa Ould, and Dimi Mint Abba
Moorish music in Mauritania. World Circuit: WCD 019. [1990].

Niger

Anthologies

7868 *Anthologie de la musique du Niger.* Ocora: C 559056. 1963.

7869 ** *The Fulani.* [Series: UNESCO collection]. Auvidis: D 8006. 1972–74.

7870 *Nomades du désert.* PlayaSound: PS 65009. 1983.

7871 *Percussions d'Afrique.* PlayaSound: PS 65004. 1983.

Individual Artists

7872 Poussy, Moussa, and Saadou Bori
Niamey twice. Stern's Africa: STCD 1057. [1994].

Nigeria

Anthologies

7873 * *African music.* Vertigo: 814480-1. LP. 1971–82. [Victor Uwaifo, Victor Olaiya, Rex Lawson, Celestine Ukwu, Prince Nico Mbarga, Stephen Osadebe, Mike Ejeagha, and others]. OP

7874 *Azagas and archibogs: the sixties sound of Lagos highlife.* Original Music: OMCD 014. [1991].

7875 *Drums of the Yoruba of Nigeria.* Smithsonian/Folkways: 4441. AC. 1951.

7876 *The Igede of Nigeria: drumming, chanting and exotic percussion.* Music of the World: CDT-117. 1978–79.

7877 *Juju roots: 1930s–1950s.* Rounder: CD 5017. 1936–[196?].

7878 *Lucky Stars & Rosy Mornings: the 60s Ibadan juju scene.* Original Music: OMCD 037. 1967–71.

7879 *Music from the villages of Northeastern Nigeria.* Smithsonian/Folkways: 4532. AC. 1969.

7880 *Music of the Jos Plateau and other regions of Nigeria.* Smithsonian/Folkways: 4321. AC. 1958–59.

7881 *Nigeria: music of the Yoruba people.* Lyrichord: LLCT 7389. AC. 1983.

7882 *Yoruba street percussion: agidigbo, apala, sakara, fuji, juju, waka.* Original Music: OMCD 016. [196?].

Individual Artists or Groups

7883 ** Ade, King Sunny, 1946–
Juju music. Mango: 162 539712-2. 1982.

7884 * Barrister, Sikiru Ayinde, 1948–
New fuji garbage. GlobeStyle: CDORBD 067. 1990.

7885 * Dairo, I. K., 1930–
Juju master. Original Music: OMCD 009 (Decca DWAPS 2253/2269). 1961–[196?].

7886 Kollington, Ayinla, 1953–
Ijo yoyo. Kollington: KRLP 35. LP/AC. 1991.

7887   Kuti, Fela Anikulapo, 1938–

7887.1   *Beasts of no nation.* Shanachie: 43070. 1988.

7887.2 ** *Music is the weapon of the future, vols. 1–2.* Just'in/Baya/Wotre Music Distribution: 760443; 760444. 2 CDs. 1975–84.

7888 * Mbarga, Prince Nico, 1950–

Aki special. Rounder: CD 11545. 1976.

7889 * Obey, Ebenezer, 1942–

Juju jubilee. Shanachie: 43031. 1985.

7890 * Oriental Brothers

Heavy on the highlife. Original Music: OMCD 012. 1973–88.

7891   Osadebe, Chief Stephen Osita, 1934–

Kedu America. Xenophile/Green Linnet: XENO 4044. 1994.

7892   Peters, Sir Shina, 1958–

Shinamania. Flametree: TIMBCD 501. 1990.

7893   Twins Seven Seven, 1944–

Nigerian beat. [Series: World music library, vol. 49]. King: KICC 5149. 1989.

Senegal

Anthologies

7894   *Dakar '92.* Revue Noire/Insitut Francais de Dakar: RN 7. 1992.

7895   *Messe et chants au Monastère de Keur Moussa.* Arion: ARN 64095. [1980]. [Benedictine chants and hymns].

7896   *Percussions-Sénégal.* PlayaSound: PS 33508. [198?].

7897   *Sénégal: kora, balafon, guitare, percussions, chants.* Arion: ARN 64163. [1991].

7898   *Sénégal: musique des Peul et des Tenda.* Ocora: C 560043. 1961–83.

7899   *Tom-tom arabesque: the session of cross beat drums in Shell Island, Senegal.* JVC: VID-25009. 1987.

See also Gambia

Individual Artists or Groups

7900 * Baobab Orchestre

Pirate's choice. World Circuit: WCD 014. 1982.

7901   Cissoko, Sunjui

Songs of the griots II. JVC: VICG-5227. 1990.

7902   Diatta, Pascal, and Sona Mane

Simnade + 4. Rogue: FMSD 5017. 1988.

7903   Etoile de Dakar

Thiapathioly. [Series: Etoile de Dakar, vol. 2]. Stern's Africa: STCD 3006. 1979.

7904   Konté, Lamine

7904.1   *La kora du Sénégal: les rythmes, les percussion, la voix de Lamine Konté.* Arion: 64036. [1976].

7904.2   *Senegal: songs of the griots.* JVC: VICG-5008. 1986.

7905   Lo, Ismael

Diawar. Stern's Africa: STCD 1027. 1989.

7906 * Maal, Baaba, 1953– , and Mansour Seck

Djam leeli. Mango: 162 539840-2 (Rogue). 1984.

7907   N'Dour, Youssou, 1959–

7907.1 ** *Immigrés.* Earthworks: STEW 10 (CAROL-2410/V 91020). 1984.

7907.2 * *Set.* Virgin: 86195 (91426). 1990.

7908   Orchestra Africa Djembé

The drums of Gorée: Senegal. PlayaSound: PS 65104. [1993].

7909   Seck, Thione, 1955–

Daaly (Le pouvoir d'un coeur pur). Stern's Africa: STCD 1070 (1023). 1988, [1997].

7910 * Toure Kunda

Dance of the leaves: the Celluloid recordings. Metrotone: 72664-2. 1983–87.

Sierra Leone

Anthologies

7911   *African elegant: Sierra Leone's Kru/Krio calypso connection.* Original Music: OMCD 015. [195?–19-?]. [Ebenezer Calender, Famous Scrubbs, and others].

7912   *Music of Sierra Leone: Kono Mende farmers' songs.* Smithsonian/Folkways: 4330. AC. 1978.

7913   *Music of the Mende of Sierra Leone.* Smithsonian/Folkways: 4322. AC. 1965.

7914   *Sierra Leone: musiques traditionnelles.* Ocora: C 580036. 1976–77.

Individual Artists

7915 * Rogie, Sooliman E., 1927–1994
The '60s sounds of S. E. Rogie. Cooking Vinyl: COOK 010 (Rogiphone 2). AC. 1960–69.

7916 T-Jay, Adbul, and Rokoto
Kanka kuru. Rogue: FMSD 5018. 1989.

Togo

7917 *Togo: music from West Africa.* Rounder: CD 5004. 1978.

See also 7793

Central Africa

General Anthology

7918 * *Bantu: musique traditionelle, musique moderne.* CICIBA (Centre International des Civilisations Bantu): CIC 8401/8402. 2LP set. 1968–84.

Cameroon

Anthologies

7919 * *The African typic collection.* Earthworks: STEW 12 (CAROL-2412/V 91313). 1984–88. [Sam Fan Thomas, Charlotte Mbango, Koko Ateba, Tam Tam 2000].

7920 *Cameroon: Baka Pygmy music.* [Series: UNESCO collection]. Auvidis: D 8029. 1975.

7921 * *Fleurs musicales du Cameroon.* Afro-Vision: FMC 001/2/3. 3LP/3AC set. [1983]. [Eboa Lottin, Bebe Manga, Manu Dibango, Francis Bebey, Anne-Marie Nzie, and others].

7922 *Flûtes et rythmes du Cameroun.* Buda: 82460-2. [1983].

7923 *Makossa connection, vols. 1–4.* TJR/Sonodisc: CD AT 107-CD AT 110. 4 CDs. [1993]. [Alhadji Toure, Charlotte Mbango, Moni Bile, Prince Eyango, Ben Decca, Lapiro de Mbanga, Guy Lobe, Epee and Koum, Petit Pays, and others].

7924 *Messes au Cameroun = African Masses.* PlayaSound: PS 65054. [1990].

7925 *Music of the Cameroons.* Smithsonian/Folkways: 4372. AC. 1959.

7926 *Music of the Cameroons: the Fulani of the north.* Lyrichord: LLCT 7334. AC. 1975–76.

Individual Artists or Groups

7927 Bebey, Francis, 1929–
Nandolo/With love. Original Music: OMCD 027. 1963–94.

7928 Bilé, Moni, 1957–
10e anniversaire: best of Moni Bilé. Sonodisc: CD 52711. 1991.

7929 Dibango, Manu, 1933–
7929.1 *Negropolitaines.* Soul Paris/Melodie: 85905-2. 1992.
7929.2 * *Seventie's.* Soul Paris/Sonodisc: SPCD 8701. 1987.

7930 Epee and Koum
Makossa collection non-stop. Sonodisc: ATO 83. LP/AC. 1991. OP

7931 Génies Noirs de Douala
Les Génies Noirs de Douala: percussions & danses du Cameroun. Arion: ARN 64112. 1990.

7932 Lobe, Guy
Ambiances. Sonodisc: CD 72828. 1994.

7933 Mbango, Charlotte
Konkai makossa. TJR/Sonodisc: CDAT 502 (Toure Jim's). 1989.

7934 Nzie, Anne-Marie, 1932–
Liberté. Tangent: TC 0003. LP/AC. 1984. OP

7935 * Les Têtes Brulées
Hotheads. Shanachie: 64030. 1990.

7936 * Thomas, Sam Fan, 1952–
Sam Fan Thomas: si tcha. Kanibal/Sonodisc: CD 59801. 1986.

7937 Les Veterans
Au village. Tangent: TC 0007. LP/AC. 1985–87. OP

Central African Republic

7938 *Aka Pygmy music.* [Series: UNESCO collection]. Auvidis: D 8054. 1971.

7939 *Anthologie de la musique des Pygmées Aka.* Ocora: C 559012/559013. 2CD set. 1972–77.

7940 *Centrafrique: musique Gbáyá: chants à penser.* Ocora: C 580008 (558 524). 1977.

7941   *Central Africa: sanza music in the land of the Gbaya.* VDE: CD-755. 1977.

7942   *Central African Republic: Banda polyphony.* [Series: UNESCO collection]. Auvidis: D 8043. 1975.

7943   *Central African Republic: music for xylophones.* Le Chant du Monde: LDX 274932. 1977–90.

7944   *Central African Republic: music of the Dendi, Nzakara, Banda, Linda, Gbaya, Banda-dakpa, Nobaka, Aka Pygmies.* [Series: UNESCO collection]. Auvidis: D 8020. 1982.

7945   *Polyphonies vocales des Pygmées Mbenzele: Republique Centrafricaine.* [Series: Inédit]. Maison des Cultures du Monde: W 260 042. 1986.

Congo

Anthology

7946   *Congo: cérémonie du Bobé.* Ocora: C 560010. 1990.

Individual Group

7947   * Les Bantous de la Capitale

Les Bantous de la Capitale (1963–1969). Sonodisc: CD 36527. 1963–69.

Gabon

Anthologies

7948   *Gabon: musique des Pygmées Bibayak: chantres de l'épopée.* Ocora: C 559053. 1966–73.

7949   *Music from an equatorial microcosm: Fang Bwiti music from Gabon Republic.* Smithsonian/Folkways: 4214. AC. 1959–60.

Individual Artists

7950   Akendengue, Pierre, 1944–

Passé composé. Encore/Melodie: 493402. 1973–86.

7951   Nguema, Hilarion

Crise économique. Haissam: MH 107. LP/AC. 1988.

Zaire

Anthologies

7952   *L'African Fiesta, vol. 1.* African/Sonodisc: CD 36509. 1962–63. [Dr. Nico, Rochereau, Roger Izeyidi].

7953   *Afrique centrale: tambours Kongo.* Buda: 92525-2. [199?].

7954   * *Compact d'Afrique.* GlobeStyle: CDORB 907. [1986]. [Aurlus Mabele, Choc Stars, Kanda Bongo Man, Papa Wemba, Quatre Etoiles, and others].

7955   * *Compilation jeunes orchestres zairoises.* African/Sonodisc: CD 36517. 1971–75. [Orchestre Bella Bella and others].

7956   * *Compilation musique congolo-zairoise.* African/Sonodisc: CD 36531. 1972–73. [Mpongo Love, Orchestre Thu-Zahina, Zaiko Langa Langa].

7957   * *Heartbeat soukous.* Earthworks: STEW 03 (CAROL-2403/V 90883). [1987]. [Kanda Bongo Man, Nyboma, Pepe Kalle, Bopol, and others].

7958   *Mangbetu: Haut-Uele.* Fonti Musicali: FMD 193. 1984–88.

7959   ** *Mbuti pygmies of the Ituri rainforest.* Smithsonian/Folkways: SF 40401. 1957–58.

7960   ** *Les merveilles du passé 1957–1975.* African/Sonodisc: CD 36501. 1957–75. [Joseph Kabassele, Franco, Orchestre Veve, Orchestre Negro Succes, Rochereau, Zaiko Langa Langa, and others].

7961   * *Music of the rainforest pygmies.* Lyrichord: LYRCD 7157. [1961].

7962   *Musique congolo-zairoise.* [Series: Merveilles du passé, vol. 1]. African/Sonodisc: CD 36504. 1962–73. [Orchestre Bantous, Orchestre Conga Succes, Orchestre Veve, and others].

7963   *Musique congolo-zairoise.* [Series: Merveilles du passé, vol. 2]. African/Sonodisc: CD 36507. 1962–71. [Orchestre Bantous, Orchestre Cobantou, Orchestre Negro Succes, Orchestre Conga Succes, Orchestre Veve, and others].

7964   *Musique congolo-zairoise.* [Series: Merveilles du passé, vol. 3]. African/Sonodisc: CD 36510. 1966–71. [Orchestre Veve, Orchestre Conga Succes, Orchestre Cobantou, and others].

7965   *Musiques urbaines à Kinshasa.* Ocora: C 559007. 1978.

7966   * *Nico, Kwamy, Rochereau et l'African Fiesta.* African/Sonodisc: CD 36512. [196?]. [Dr. Nico, Rochereau, Kwamy, and others].

7967   *Roots of OK jazz.* [Series: Zaire classics, vol. 3]. Crammed Discs: CRAW 7. 1955–56. [Franco,

Vicky, Rossignol, Jean-Serge Essous, De La Lune, and others].

7968 ** *Sound of Kinshasa: guitar classics from Zaire.* Original Music: OMCD 010. [195?–197?]. [Franco, Kalle, Rochereau, Dr. Nico, and others].

7969 *Zaire: African Mass.* (Children's Choir of Lwiro Catholic Church). JVC: VICG-5299. 1983.

7970 *Zaire: entre les lacs et la forêt: la musique des Nande.* VDE-Gallo: CD-652. 1986–88.

7971 *Zaire: music of the Shi people.* JVC: VICG-5228. 1983.

7972 *Zaire: polyphonies Mongo.* Ocora: C 580050. 1970–72.

7973 *Zaire: polyphony of the deep rain forest: music of the Ituri pygmies.* JVC: VICG-5015. 1983.

Individual Artists or Groups

7974 Bel, M'bilia, 1959–
Bameli soy. Shanachie: 43025. 1985.

7975 Boziana, Bozi, et L'Anti Choc
Doukoure, vol. 2. Flash Diffusion: FDB 300003. [198?].

7976 Choc Stars
Engombe. Flash Diffusion: FDB 300007. [198?].

7977 Franco, 1938–1989
   7977.1 *Franco et le tout puissant O.K. Jazz: Mario.* Sonodisc: CD 8461. 1985, 1989.
   7977.2 ** *Franco et l'OK Jazz: 1970/1971/1972.* African/Sonodisc: CD 36514. 1970–72.
   7977.3 *Franco et l'OK Jazz, vols. 1–3.* [Series: Merveilles du passé]. African/Sonodisc: CD 36502/CD 36505/CD 36508. 3 CDs. 1957–62.
   7977.4 * *20ème anniversaire, vol. 1.* African/Sonodisc: CD 50382. 1976.

7978 Franco, 1938–1989, and Tabu Ley (Rochereau), 1940–
Omona wapi. Shanachie: 43024. 1983.

7979 Jocker, Evoloko, and Langa Langa Stars
Mingelina B 52. Flash Diffusion: FDB 300058. 1991.

7980 * Kabassele, Joseph, 1930–1983
Grand kalle et l'African Jazz, vols. 1–2. [Series: Merveilles du passé]. African/Sonodisc: CD 36503/CD 36506. 1958–62.

7981 Kalle, Pepe, 1951–
Gigantafrique. GlobeStyle: CDORB 062. 1990.

7982 * Kanda Bongo Man, 1955–
Amour fou = Crazy love. Hannibal: HNCD 1337. 1984.

7983 Lema, Ray, 1946–
Gaia. Mango: 162 539895-2. 1990.

7984 Ley, Tabu (Rochereau), 1940–
   7984.1 *Le Seigneur Rochereau.* African/Sonodisc: CD 36515. 1966–68.
   7984.2 ** *Tabu Ley.* Shanachie: 43017. 1984.

7985 Loketo
Extra ball. Shanachie: 64028. 1990.

7986 Mangwana, Sam, 1945–
Aladji. Shanachie: 64017. 1988.

7987 M'Benza, Syran
Symbiose. Stern's Africa: HYSA 1185 CD. 1991.

7988 Mounka, Pamelo, 1945–
Des plus grands succes de Pamelo Mounka, vol. 1. Karac/Sonodisc: 44430. 1981.

7989 Muana, Tshala, 1955–
Soukous siren. Shanachie: 64031. 1991.

7990 Mwenda, Jean Bosco, 1925–
Mwenda wa bayeke. Rounder: CD 5061. 1988.

7991 Nico, Dr., 1939–1985, et l'African Fiesta Sukisa
   7991.1 ** *Eternel Docteur Nico.* African/Sonodisc: CD 36516. 1966–68.
   7991.2 * *1967/1968/1969.* African/Sonodisc: CD 36524. 1967–69.

7992 Olomide, Koffi
Tcha tcho. Stern's Africa: STCD 1031. 1988–90.

7993 Quatre Etoiles
Sangonini. Stern's Africa: STCD 1049. 1986. [Bopol, Nyboma, Syran M'Benza, Wuta-Mayi].

7994 Swede Swede
Toleki bango (Miles ahead). Crammed Discs: CRAW 1CD. 1991.

7995 Wemba, Papa, 1953–
Papa Wemba. Stern's Africa: STCD 1026. 1988.

7996   Wenge Musica

Bouger bouger (Mulolo). Natari/Africassette: NACD 9401. 1988.

7997   Zaiko Langa Langa

7997.1 * *L'authentique Zaiko Langa Langa.* Sonodisc: CD 8487. 1987.

7997.2 *Zaire-Ghana.* RetroAfric: RETRO 5CD. 1976.

Eastern Africa (Including Horn of Africa and East African Islands)

General Anthology

7998 *Africa: ceremonial & folk music.* [Series: Explorer]. Nonesuch: 72063. LP. 1975. [Recorded in Uganda, Kenya, and Tanzania]. OP

Burundi

Anthology

7999 * *Burundi: musiques traditionnelles.* Ocora: C 559003. 1967.

Individual Groups

8000 * Batimbo

Tambours du Burundi = Burundi drums. Playa-Sound: PS 65089. 1991.

8001   Les Maîtres-Tambours du Burundi

8001.1 *The Drummers of Burundi = Les Tambourinaires du Burundi.* Realworld: CAROL-2338-2. 1987.

8001.2 ** *Les Maîtres-Tambours du Burundi.* Arion: ARN 64016. 1981.

8002   Rukinzo Legacy

Sacred drums. [Series: World music library, vol. 100]. King: KICC 5200. 1994.

Comoros

8003 *Comores: musiques traditionnelles de l'île d'Anrouan.* [Series: Inédit]. Maison des Cultures du Monde: W 260058. 1983–92.

Ethiopia

Anthologies

8004 *Amharic hits and experimental traditions from Ethiopia.* Piranha: PIR 44-2 (CD 01894). [199?]. [Ethio Stars, Tukul Band].

8005 *L'Assomption à Dábrá Gánnát: l'eglise orthodoxe éthiopienne de Jerusalem.* Ocora: C 560027/28. 2CD set. 1989.

8006 *Ethiopia: musiques traditionnelles.* Playa-Sound: PS 65074. 1990–91.

8007 ** *Ethiopie: musiques vocales et instrumentales.* Ocora: C 580055/56 (OCR 44/OCR 75). 2CD set. 1962–71.

8008 *Ethiopia: polyphony of the Dorze.* Le Chant du Monde: CNR 274646. 1974–75.

8009 *Ethiopia: the harp of Apollo: songs accompanied by the kirar.* JVC: VICG-5013. 1989.

8010 * *Ethiopian groove: the golden seventies.* Blue Silver: 002-2 (Kaifa). 1976–77. [Aster Aweke, Wallias Band, Alemayehu Eshete, Bzunesh Bekele, Ayalew Mesfin, and others].

8011 *Folk music and ceremonies of Ethiopia.* Smithsonian/Folkways: 4354. AC. 1972.

8012 *Music from Ethiopia.* Caprice: CAP 21432. 1992.

Individual Artists

8013 * Ahmed, Mahmoud

Ere mela mela. Hannibal: HNCD 1354. 1975–78.

8014 * Aweke, Aster, 1961–

Aster. Columbia: CK 46848. 1989.

8015   Damessae, Seleshe

Songs from Ethiopia today. Wergo: CD SM 1516-2. 1993.

8016   Eshete, Alemayehu

Addis Ababa: new beat music from Ethiopia. Shanachie: 64045. 1993.

Kenya

Anthologies

8017 *Before benga 1: Kenya dry.* Original Music: OMCD 021. [1993].

8018 * *Before benga 2: the Nairobi sound.* Original Music: OMCD 022. [195?–196?].

8019 * *Guitar paradise of east Africa.* Earthworks: STEW 21 (CAROL-2420). [1990]. [Daniel Kamau, Simba Wanyika, Orchestre Super Mazembe, Kilimambogo Brothers, and others].

8020 * *Kenya & Tanzania: witchcraft & ritual music.* [Series: Explorer]. Elektra Nonesuch: 72066-2. [1975].

8021 * *Kenya dance mania.* Earthworks: STEW 24 (CAROL-2423). 1976–[198?]. [Gabriel Omolo, Maroon Commandos, Les Wanyika, Daniel Kamau, and others].

8022 *Kenya: musiques du Nyanza.* Ocora: C 560022/23. 2CD set. [1993].

8023 *Luo roots: musical currents from western Kenya.* GlobeStyle: CDORBD 061. 1989. [Kapere Jazz Band, Orchestra Nyanza Success, and others].

8024 ** *Missa Luba: an African mass.* (Muungano National Choir/Boniface Mganga). Philips: 426 836-2. 1990. [With Kenyan folk melodies].

8025 * *The Nairobi beat: Kenyan pop music today.* Rounder: CD 5030. [1989]. [Shirati Mbiri Young Stars, Kilimambogo Brothers, Maroon Commandos, Kalambaya Sisters, and others].

8026 * *Songs the Swahili sing: classics from the Kenya coast.* Original Music: OMCD 024. [1984].

Individual Artists or Groups

8027 Abana ba Nasery

Nursery boys go ahead. Xenophile/Green Linnet: GLCD 4002. 1992.

8028 Konde, Fundi

Retrospective, vol. 1. RetroAfric: RETRO 8CD. 1947–56.

8029 Mapangala, Samba, 195?– , and Orchestre Virunga

Feet on fire. Stern's Africa: STCD 1036. 1991.

8030 * Misiani, Daniel O., 1940– , and Shirati Jazz

Benga blast. Earthworks: STEW 13 (CAROL-2413/V91314). 1989.

8031 National Percussion Group of Kenya

Roots: African drums. Denon: DC-8559 (38C39-7276). 1984.

8032 Simba Wanyika

Pepea. Kameleon/Stern's Africa: KMLN CD 01. [1992].

8033 * Zein Musical Party

Mtindo wa Mombasa = The style of Mombasa. GlobeStyle: CDORBD 066. 1989.

Madagascar

Anthologies

8034 *Madagascar: Antandroy country, south-west coast.* Ocora: C 560077. 1994.

8035 * *Madagascar: possession et poésie.* Ocora: C 580046. 1967–69.

8036 * *Madagasikara 1: current traditional music of Madagascar.* GlobeStyle: CDORBD 012. 1986.

8037 * *Madagasikara 2: current popular music of Madagascar.* GlobeStyle: CDORBD 013. 1986. [Mahaleo, Rossy, Tarika Sammy, and others].

8038 *Madagaskar 1: Musik aus Antananarivo.* Feuer & Eis: fuec 704. 1989. [Rossy, Tarika Sammy, Jean Emilien, and others].

8039 * *Music of Madagascar: classic recordings of the 1930s.* Yazoo: 7003. [193?].

8040 *A world out of time: Henry Kaiser and David Lindley in Madagascar.* Shanachie: 64041. 1991.

Individual Artists or Groups

8041 D'Gary

Malagasy guitar. Shanachie: 65009. 1993.

8042 Jaojoby

Salegy! hot dance music from Madagascar. Xenophile/Green Linnet: 4040 (Rogue). 1992.

8043 Rakotofra, 1925–

Flute master of Madagascar. [Series: Madagasikara, vol. 3]. GlobeStyle: ORBD 027. LP. 1985.

8044 Randafison, Sylvestre, 1928–

The art of Randafison Sylvestre. JVC: VICG-5012 (VID 25012). 1989. [With Rakotofra and Patrice Ratsimbazafy].

8045 * Rokotozafy, 1933–197?

Valiha malaza = Famous valiha: historical recordings from the 1960s. [Series: Madagasikara, vol. 4]. GlobeStyle: CDORBD 028. [196?].

8046 Rossy

Island of ghosts. Realworld: CAROL-2318-2 (91782). 1991.

8047 * Tarika Sammy

Fanafody. Xenophile/Green Linnet: GLCD 4003 (Rogue). 1992.

Mauritius

Anthologies

8048 *Île Maurice: séga ravanne mauricien; Séga tambour de l'île Rodrigues.* Ocora: C 580060. 1981.

8049 *Sega dance.* Tambour: CD TAMB 1. [199?].

Individual Artist

8050 Ti Frère, 1900–

Île Maurice: hommage à Ti Frère. Ocora: C 560019. 1989.

Réunion

Anthology

8051 *La Réunion: danses et chansons.* (Groupe folklorique de la Réunion). Auvidis: A 6122. 1979–81.

Individual Artists or Groups

8052 Farreyrol, Jacqueline

Mon île: folklore de la Réunion: romances créoles, ségas, maloyas. Auvidis Ethnic: B 6155. [199?].

8053 * Ziskakan

Ziskakan. Mango: 162-539 938-2. 1993.

Rwanda

Anthology

8054 *Songs of the Watutsi.* Smithsonian/Folkways: 4428. AC. 1952.

Individual Artist

8055 Kayirebwa, Cecile, 1946–

Rwanda. GlobeStyle: CDORBD 083. 1986, 1990.

Seychelles

8056 *Creole islands of the Indian Ocean: Seychelles, Maurice, Réunion.* PlayaSound: PS 65010. 1987.

8057 *Seychelles: musiques oubliées "des îles": danses et romances de l'ancienne France.* Ocora: C 559055. 1976–77.

Somalia

8058 *Baujun ballads.* Smithsonian/Folkways: 8504. AC. 1962.

8059 *Jamiila: songs from a Somali city.* Original Music: OMCD 007. 1984.

Sudan

Anthologies

8060 *Rain in the hills: Beja ballads of Port Sudan.* Original Music: OMCD 029. [1995].

8061 * *Sounds of Sudan.* World Circuit: WCD 018. 1986. [Abdel Gadir Salim, Abdel Aziz El Mubarak, Mohamed Gubara].

Individual Artists or Groups

8062 Hamza el Din
    8062.1 *Eclipse.* Rykodisc: RCD 10103. 1978.
    8062.2 *Music of Nubia.* Vanguard: VMD 79164. 1964.
    8062.3 *A song of the Nile.* JVC: VICG-5007 (VID-25007). 1982.

8063 Mubarak, Abdel Aziz El, 1951–

Straight from the heart. World Circuit: WCD 010. 1989.

8064 Salim, Abdel Gadir

The Merdoum Kings play songs of love. Shanachie: 64039. 1991.

8065 Wardi, Mohamed

Live in Addis Ababa. Rags Music: RPM 001-2. 1994.

Tanzania

Anthologies

8066 *Dada Kidawa/Sister Kidawa: classic dance hits from Tanzania.* Original Music: OMCD 032. 1964–69. [Cuban Marimba Band, Kiko Kids, Western Jazz Band, Nuta Jazz Band, and others].

8067 *Mateso: master musicians of Tanzania.* Triple Earth: TERRACD 104. 1985. [Hukwe Zawose, Dickson Mkwama, and others].

8068 *Music of Tanzania.* [Series: World music library, vol. 50]. King: KICC 5150. [1987].

8069 *Taarab 3: the music of Zanzibar.* GlobeStyle: CDORBD 040. 1988.

8070 *Tanzania dance bands, vol. 2.* Monsun/Line: MSCD 9.01117. [1991]. [Orchestra Maquis, Tshimanga Assosa, Juwata Jazz, IOSS, and others].

8071 *The Tanzania sound.* Original Music: OMCD 018. 1950–[196?]. [Salim Abdulla, Nuta Jazz Band, and others].

8072 *Tanzanie: chants des Wagogo et des Kuria.* [Series: Inédit]. Maison des Cultures du Monde: W 260041. [1992].

Individual Artists or Groups

8073 * Black Star Musical Club and Lucky Star Musical Club
Nyota: classic taarab from Tanga. GlobeStyle: CDORB 044 (MZURI). 1969–76.

8074 Ikhwani Safaa Music Club
Taarab 2: the music of Zanzibar. GlobeStyle: CDORB 033. 1988.

8075 Ongala, Remmy, 1947–
Songs for the poor man. Realworld: CAROL-2305-2 (91315). 1990.

8076 * Orchestre DDC Mlimani Park
Sikinde. [Series: Tanzania dance bands, vol. 1]. Africassette: AC9402 CD (Monsun/Line 9.00902). 1980–87.

8077 Zawose, Hukwe Ubi, 1940–
Tanzania: the art of Hukwe Zawose. JVC: VICG-5011. [1989].

Uganda
Anthologies

8078 *The Kampala sound.* Original Music: OMCD 013. 1964–68.

8079 ** *Ouganda: aux sources du Nil.* Ocora: C 560032. 1991.

Individual Artists or Groups

8080 Muyinda, Evalisto
Traditional music of the Baganda. Pan: 2003. 1991.

8081 Oryema, Geoffrey
Exile. Realworld: CAROL-2313-2 (91629). 1990.

8082 Samite
Dance my children, dance. Shanachie: 65003. 1989.

Southern Africa
Angola
Anthologies

8083 *Music and musicians from the Angolan border.* Lyrichord: LLCT 7311. AC. 1973–76.

8084 *Sanza and guitar: music of the Bena Luluwa of Angola and Zaire.* Lyrichord: LLCT 7313. AC. 1973–76.

Individual Artists or Groups

8085 Bonga, Kuenda, 1942–
Paz em Angola. Rounder: CD 5052. 1988–89.

8086 Orquestra Os Jovens do Prenda
Berlin festa! Piranha: PIR 40-2 (CD 01890). 1990.

Botswana

8087 * *Healing dance music of the Kalahari San.* Smithsonian/Folkways: 4316. AC. 1968–72.

8088 * *Instrumental music of the Kalahari San.* Smithsonian/Folkways: 4315. AC. 1951–72.

Lesotho

8089 * *Music of Lesotho.* Smithsonian/Folkways: 4224. AC. 1972–75.

Malawi
Anthology

8090 * *Chants et rythmes du Malawi.* PlayaSound PS 65140. [1994]. [Kasambwe Brothers, Makazi Band, and others].

8091 *Music tradition of Malawi = Tradition musicale du Malawi.* [Series: UNESCO collection]. Auvidis: D 8265. 1991.

Individual Artist

8092 Namoko, Alan, and Chimvu Jazz
Ana osiidwa: the orphans. Pamtondo: PAM 004. 1992.

Mozambique
Anthologies

8093 *Music from Mozambique* [vol. 1]. Smithsonian/Folkways: 4310. AC. 1978–79.

8094 ** *Music from Mozambique, vol. 2: Chopi timbila.* Smithsonian/Folkways: 4318. AC. 1981.

8095 * *Music from Mozambique, vol. 3.* Smithsonian/Folkways: 4319. AC. [1983].

8096 *Saba saba!* GlobeStyle: CDORBD 077. 1989. [Mil-Quinhento, Conjunto Nimala de Lalauah].

Individual Artists or Groups

8097 Durao, Eduardo

Timbila: new Chopi music. GlobeStyle: CDORB 065. 1991.

8098 Eyuphuro

Mama Mosambiki. Realworld: CAROL-2309-2 (91347). 1989.

8099 * Marrabenta Star de Mozambique

Independance. Piranha: PIR 15-2 (CD 01862). 1989.

8100 Mbande, Venancio

Timbila ta Venancio Mbande, Mozambique: xylophone music from the Chopi people. [Series: Welt Musik]. Haus der Kulturen der Welt/Wergo: SM 1513-2. 1992.

South Africa

Anthologies

8101 * *Drum: South African jazz and jive.* Monsun/ Line: MSCD 9.01092. 1954–60. [Lemmy "Special" Mabaso, Manhattan Brothers, Skylarks, Spokes Mashiyane, Miriam Makeba, Kippie Moeketsi, Hugh Masekela, and others].

8102 * *Freedom fire.* [Series: The indestructible beat of Soweto, vol. 3]. Earthworks: STEW 17 (CAROL-2416/V 91409). [198?]. [Mahlathini, Mahotella Queens, Malombo, and others].

8103 * *From marabi to disco: 42 years of township music.* Gallo: CDZA 61. 1939–81. [Dorothy Masuka, Miriam Makeba, Soul Brothers, and others].

8104 * *The heartbeat of Soweto: Zulu, Shangaan, Tsonga jive.* Shanachie: 43051. [1988].

8105 * *Homeland: a collection of Black South African music.* Rounder: CD 11549. [1987].

8106 ** *The indestructible beat of Soweto* [vol. 1]. Shanachie: 43033/Earthworks: STEW 14. 1981–84. [Mahlathini, Ladysmith Black Mambazo, and others].

8107 *Jive Soweto.* [Series: The indestructible beat of Soweto, vol. 4]. Earthworks: STEW 26 (CAROL-2425). [1992]. [Soul Brothers, Ihashi Elimhlophe, Mahlathini, Mahotella Queens, Sipho Mabuse, and others].

8108 ** *The kings and queens of township jive: modern roots of the incredible beat of Soweto.* Earthworks: STEW 20 (CAROL-2419). [196?–

197?]. [Mahlathini, Mahotella Queens, Soul Brothers, West Nkosi, Lulu Masilela, and others].

8109 * *Mbube roots: Zulu choral music from South Africa.* Rounder: CD 5025. 1932–69.

8110 * *Singing in an open space: Zulu rhythm and harmony.* Rounder: CD 5027. 1962–82.

8111 *Siya hamba! 1950s South African country and small town sounds.* Original Music: OMCD 003. [1989].

8112 *South African music.* (National Symphony Orchestra of the S.A.B.C.). Marco Polo: 8.223709. 1994. [Works by Theo Wendt, Henry Lissant-Collins, Michael Mosoeu Moerane, Gideon Fagan].

8113 * *Thunder before dawn.* [Series: The indestructible beat of Soweto, vol. 2]. Earthworks: STEW 01 (CAROL-2401/V 90866). 1983–85. [Mahlathini, Mahotella Queens, Malombo, and others].

8114 * *Township swing jazz, vol. 1.* Harlequin: HQ CD 08. [194?–195?]. [Skylarks, Dolly Rathebe, Jazz Dazzlers, Father Huddleston Band, Eastern City Seven, and others].

8115 * *Urban Africa: jive hits of the townships.* Polydor: 841470-2. [1990]. [Yvonne Chaka Chaka, Lucky Dube, Mahlathini, Mahotella Queens, Stimela, Chicco, Miriam Makeba, and others].

8116 * *Zulu songs from South Africa.* Lyrichord: LLCT 7401. AC. 1982.

Individual Artists or Groups

8117 Clegg, Johnny, 1953– , and Savuka
Third world child. Capitol: 46778. 1987.

8118 Clegg, Johnny, 1953– , and Sipho Mchunu
The best of Juluka. Rhythm Safari: CDL 57138. 1979–84.

8119 * Dark City Sisters
Dark City Sisters and Flying Jazz Queens. Earthworks: STEW 31. [196?].

8120 Khanyile, Noise, 1943–
The art of Noise. GlobeStyle: CDORB 045. 1988–89.

8121 Ladysmith Black Mambazo
8121.1 ** *Classic tracks.* Shanachie: 43074. 1990.
8121.2 *Shaka Zulu.* Warner Bros.: 25582-2. 1987.

8122 Mahlathini

The lion of Soweto. Earthworks: STEW 04 (CAROL-2404/V 90867). [197?].

8123 Mahlathini and the Mahotella Queens

8123.1 ** *The lion roars.* Shanachie: 43081. [196?–197?].

8123.2 *Paris-Soweto.* Urban Africa/Polydor: 839676-2 (66829-2). 1990.

8123.3 * *Thokozile.* Earthworks: STEW 06 (CAROL-2406/V 90920). 1988.

8124 Mahotella Queens

Izibani zomgqashiyo. Shanachie: 43036. 1977.

8125 Makeba, Miriam, 1932–

8125.1 *Africa.* Novus/RCA: 3155-2. 1960–65.

8125.2 * *The best of Miriam Makeba and the Skylarks.* Kaz: KAZ CD 26. 1956–59.

8125.3 *Sangoma.* Warner Bros.: 25673-2. 1988.

8126 Mashiyane, Spokes

King kwela. [Series: African classics]. Celluloid: 66891-2. 1958.

8127 Mbuli, Mzwakhe

Resistance is defense. Earthworks: STEW 25 (CAROL-2424). 1992.

8128 Ngobeni, Obed

My wife bought a taxi. Shanachie: 64003. 1989.

8129 Seema, Puseletso, and Tau Ea Linare

He o oe oe! GlobeStyle: ORB 003. LP. 1981.

8130 * Soul Brothers

Jive explosion. Earthworks: STEW 08 (CAROL-2408/V 90999). 1983–86.

8131 Tabane, Philip, and Malombo

Unh! Nonesuch: 79225-2. 1989.

Zambia

Anthologies

8132 *From the copperbelt: Zambian miners' songs.* Original Music: OMCD 004. 1957.

8133 *Zambia!! an introduction.* Mondeca/Demon: 0015. [1989]. [Amayenge, Shalawambe, Kazembe, Fire Family, P. K. Chisala, and others].

8134 * *Zambiance!* GlobeStyle: CDORB O37. 1985–87. [Shalawambe, Kalambo Hit Parade, Amayenge, Fire Family, and others].

Individual Artist

8135 Nkhata, Alick, 1922–

Shalapo. RetroAfric: RETRO 4CD. 1949–59.

Zimbabwe

Anthologies

8136 * *Africa: Shona mbira music.* [Series: Explorer]. Nonesuch: 72077. LP. 1977. OP

8137 *Jit: the movie plus other big hits.* Earthworks: STEW 23 (CAROL-2422). [1991]. [Oliver Mutukudzi, John Chibadura, Robson Banda, Jonah Sithole, and others].

8138 *Music from the Petauke of Northern Rhodesia, vols. 1–2.* Smithsonian/Folkways: 4201/4202. 2ACs. 1961.

8139 ** *Spirit of the eagle.* [Series: Zimbabwe frontline, vol. 2]. Earthworks: STEW 18 (CAROL-2417/V 91410). [1990]. [Thomas Mapfumo, Four Brothers, Jonah Moyo, Nyami Nyami Sounds, and others].

8140 * *Zimbabwe frontline* [vol. 1]. Earthworks: STEW 09 (CAROL-2409/V 91001). 1980–86. [Thomas Mapfumo, Jonah Moyo, Four Brothers, Robson Banda, and others].

8141 *Zimbabwe: the Ndebele people.* Jecklin: JD 654-2. 1989.

8142 ** *Zimbabwe: the soul of mbira.* [Series: Explorer]. Nonesuch: 72054-2. 1972.

Individual Artists or Groups

8143 Bhundu Boys

Shabini. DiscAfrique: AFRI CD 002 (8802). 1986.

8144 Chiweshe, Stella

Kumusha. Piranha: PIR 42-2 (CD 01892). 1990.

8145 Four Brothers

Makorokoto: the best of the Four Brothers. Atomic Theory: ATD 1106 (Cooking Vinyl 014). 1988.

8146 Manyeruke, Machanic, 195?–

Machanic Manyeruke and the Puritans. Flying Fish: FF 70553. 1989.

8147 Mapfumo, Thomas, 1945–

8147.1 * *The chimurenga singles.* Shanachie: 43066. 1976–80.

8147.2 *Corruption.* Mango: 162 539848-2. 1989.

8147.3 *Shumba: vital hits of Zimbabwe.* Earthworks: STEW 22 (CAROL-2421). 1975–84.

8148 * Maraire, Dumisani
Chaminuka. Music of the World: CDC 208. 1989.

8149 Masuka, Dorothy
Pata pata. Mango: 162 539911-2. 1991.

8150 Moyo, Jonah and Devera Ngwena
Taxi driver. K-KO/Stern's Africa: KKO-1. LP. 1988. OP

8151 Mtukudzi, Oliver, 1952–
Shoko: Tuku music from the townships of Zimbabwe. Piranha: PIR 30-2 (CD 01880). 1990.

8152 Mujuru, Ephat
Rhythms of life. Lyrichord: LYRCD 7407. [1988].

36

Classical, Traditional, and Popular Musics of Northern Africa, the Middle East, and Central Asia

Compiled by
**Kent Underwood and
William E. Anderson**

C itations in this chapter are listed by country and organized into four regional-cultural groupings: "Northern Africa"; "Israel and Jewish Diaspora" (including Jewish music of the United States and Europe); "Arab Middle East, Iran, and Turkey"; and "Central Asia" (including the eastern Muslim republics of the former Soviet Union).

Transnational

Anthologies

8153 * *Archives de la musique arabe.* Ocora: C 558678. 1908–20.

8154 ** *Couleur Orient-Maghreb.* Declic: 302134. 1990–94. [Cheb Khaled, Cheb Mami, Chaba Fadela, Idir, Reinette l'Oranaise, Warda, Najat Aatabou, Lili Boniche, Nass el Ghiwane, and others].

8155 * *Music in the world of Islam.* Topic: TSCD 901/903. 3CD set. 1960–75.

8156 *A recital from the Holy Quran: Surat Yusuf.* (Mahmoud Khalil El Houssary). Orient: CDO 101. [199?].

8157 * *Le saint Coran, vols. 1–6.* (Sheikh Abdelbasset Abdessamad). Artistes Arabes Associés: AAA 050; 070; 080; 090; 095; 100. 6 CDs. [1993].

Individual Artists

8158 * Fish, Robert Arthur, 1948–
Rhythmic essence: the art of the dumbek. Lyrichord: LYRCD-7411. [1991].

8159 * Racy, Ali Jihad, 1943–
Taqasim: improvisation in Arab music. Lyrichord: LYRCD 7374. [198?].

8160 ** Shaheen, Simon, 1955–
Turath = Heritage: Simon Shaheen performs masterworks of the Middle East. CMP: CD 3006. 1991.

Northern Africa

Algeria

Anthologies

8161 *Algeria: Sahara: music of Gourara.* [Series: UNESCO collection]. Auvidis: D 8037. 1974.

8162 * *Hoggar: musique des Touareg.* Le Chant du Monde: LDXZ 274974. 1980.

8163 * *Nûba çika; Nûba zidane; Nûba des înklabat, mode mouel.* (Ensemble Essoundoussïa/Ensemble Ahbab Cheikh Larbi Bensari). Ocora: C 560044/560045. 2CD set. 1993–94.

8164 * *Pop-rai and rachid style.* [Series: Rai rebels, vol. 2]. Earthworks: STEW 15 (CAROL-2414/V 91407). 1981–88. [Cheb Zahouani, Cheb Khaled, Cheb Sahraoui, Chaba Zahouania, Cheb Anouar, and others].

8165 ** *Rai rebels.* Earthworks: STEW 07 (CAROL-2407/V 91000). [1988]. [Chaba Fadela, Cheb Khaled, Chaba Zahouania, Cheb Hamid, and others].

Individual Artists or Groups

8166 Aichi, Houria
Songs of the Aures: Arabico-berber song. Auvidis Ethnic: B 6749. 1990.

8167 Alla, 1946–
Foundou de Bechar = Foundou from Bechar. Al Sur: ALCD 110. 1992.

8168 * Djur Djura
Voice of silence: the best of Djur Djura. [Series: Adventures in Afropea, vol. 2]. Luaka Bop/Warner Bros.: 45211-2. 1978–86.

8169 Fadela, Chaba
You are mine. Mango: 162 539827-2. 1988.

8170 Farqani, Muhammed al-Tahir, 1928–
Maluf de Constantine. Ocora: C 560002. 1991.

8171 Khaled, Cheb
Cheb Khaled: la voix du Maghreb = Young Khaled: the voice of Maghreb. Buda: 82873-2. 1993.

8172 * Khaled, Cheb, and Safy Boutella
Kutché. Stern's Africa: STCD 1024 (Intuition 90934). 1987–88.

8173 Leyris, Raymond, 1912–1961
Concert public de malouf a l'Université Populaire de Constantine, 1954. Al Sur: ALCD 133/134. 2CD set. 1954.

8174 Mami, Cheb, 1966–
Prince of rai. Shanachie: 64013. 1989.

8175 Messaoud, Bellemou
Le père du rai. World Circuit: WCD 011. 1988.

8176 Remitti, Cheikha
Ghir el baroud. Michel Levy Productions/Sonodisc: MLPCD 306. 1989.

8177 Tetma, Cheikha
Musique arabo-andalouse: école de Tlemcen Cheikha Tetma. Artistes Arabes Associés: AAA 067. [193?].

Egypt

Anthologies

8178 * *L'age d'or de la musique égyptienne = The golden age of Egyptian music.* Artistes Arabes Associés: AAA 043. 1905–30.

8179 ** *Classical music of Egypt.* [Series: World music library, vol. 70]. King: KICC 5170. 1991.

8180 * *Egypt: taqâsîm & layâlî: Cairo tradition.* [Series: UNESCO collection]. (Takht Ensemble of Cairo). Auvidis: D 8038. 1971.

8181 *Music of the Nile Valley.* Lyrichord: LYRCD 7355. [198?].

8182 * *The music of upper and lower Egypt.* Ryko-disc: RCD 10106. 1978.

8183 * *Vocal music of Egypt.* [Series: World music library, vol. 69]. King: KICC 5169. 1991.

8184 ** *Y'alla: hitlist Egypt.* Mango: 162 539873-2. [1990]. [Mohamed Mounir, Ehab Tawfik, Shaaban el-Rahim, Magdy Talaat, Hanan, and others].

Individual Artists or Groups

8185 Abdul Wahab, Mohammed, 1910–1990
8185.1 * *Mohamed Abdelwahab, vols. 1–10.* [Series: Archives de la musique arabe]. Club du Disque Arabe: AAA 011; AAA 013–AAA 021. 10 CDs. 1920–39.
8185.2 *The music of Mohamed Abdel Wahab.* (Simon Shaheen). Axiom: 422 846 754-2 (539 865-2). [1990].

8186 * Atrash, Farid, 1915–1974

Les années 30. Club du Disque Arabe: AAA 053. [193?–196?].

8187 Hafiz, Abd al-Halim, 1927–1977

Risalah min taht al-ma. Soutelphan/EMI: GSTP 503. 1988.

8188 * Kuban, Ali Hassan

From Nubia to Cairo. Shanachie: 64036. 1980.

8189 Misri, Husayn

Zagal. Auvidis Ethnic: B 6781. 1993.

8190 Musiciens du Nil (Musicians of the Nile)

8190.1 ** *Egypte.* Ocora: C 559006. 1976–79.

8190.2 *Luxor to Isna.* Realworld: CAROL-2307-2 (91316). 1986–89.

8191 Racy, Ali Jihad, 1943–

Ancient Egypt. Lyrichord: LYRCD 7347. 1978.

8192 * Redouane, Aicha, 1962–

Egypte. Ocora: C 560020. 1993.

8193 Umm Kulthum, 1898–1975

8193.1 ** *El atlaal.* Sono Cairo: SONO 101. [194?].

8193.2 * *Fat el mead.* Sono Cairo: SONO 105. [19-?].

8193.3 *Oum Kaltsoum, vols. 1–8.* Club du Disque Arabe: AAA 005; AAA 024–AAA 030. 8 CDs. 1926–37.

Morocco

Anthologies

8194 ** *Apocalypse across the sky: the master musicians of Jajouka featuring Bachir Attar.* Axiom: 314 510857-2. 1991.

8195 *Gnawa music of Marakesh: night spirit masters.* Axiom: 314 510147-2. 1991.

8196 * *Maroc: anthologie d'al-melhûn: traditions des Fes, Meknes, Sale, Marrakech.* [Series: Inédit]. Maison des Cultures du Monde: W 260016. 3CD set. 1990.

8197 *Maroc: anthologie des Rwâyes: chants de musiques Berberes du sous.* [Series: Inédit]. Maison des Cultures du Monde: W 260023. 4CD set. 1990.

8198 * *Maroc: musique gharnati: nuba ramal (selection).* (Ahmad Pirou and ensemble). [Series:

Inédit]. Maison des Cultures du Monde: W 260017. 1990.

8199 *Maroc: musiques de la haute montagne.* Buda: 92580-2. 1993.

8200 *Nawbat al-istihlal = Nûbâ al-îstihlâl.* (Haj Abdelkrim al-Rais and ensemble). [Series: Inédit; Musique andaluci-marocaine]. Maison des Cultures du Monde: W 260028. 7CD set. 1990.

8201 * *Nubat al-Isbihan = Nûbâ al-Îsbihân.* (Mohammed Larbi Temsamani and ensemble). [Series: Inédit; Anthologie "al-âla"]. Maison des Cultures du Monde: W 260024. 6CD set. 1992.

8202 *Nubat al-Ushshaq = Nûbâ al-Ushshâq.* (Muhammad Tawd and ensemble). [Series: Inédit; Anthologie "al-âla"]. Maison des Cultures du Monde: W 260014. 6CD set. 1989.

8203 *Nubat gharibat al-Husayn = Nûbâ ghâribât al-Husâyn.* (Abd al-Karim al-Rais and ensemble). [Series: Inédit; Anthologie "al-âla"]. Maison des Cultures du Monde: W 260010. 6CD set. 1989.

Individual Artists or Groups

8204 * Aatabou, Najat

The voice of the Atlas. GlobeStyle: CDORBD 069. 1984–87.

8205 * Aisha Kandisha's Jarring Effects

El buya. Barraka el Farnatshi/Stern's Africa: BARBARITY 002. 1988–89.

8206 Belkhyat, Abdelhadi

El kamar el ahmar. Tichkaphone/Sonodisc: TCK CD 05. [199?].

8207 Cherkaoui, Abdeslam

Morocco: the Arabic tradition of Moroccan music. [Series: UNESCO collection]. Auvidis: D 8002. 1976–77.

8208 * Hakmoun, Hassan

Trance. RealWorld: CAROL-2334-2. [1993].

8209 Nass el Ghiwane

8209.1 * *Chants gnawa du Maroc.* Buda: 82468-2. 1985.

8209.2 *Les meilleur de Nass el Ghiwane.* Blue Silver: 071-2. [1993].

Tunisia

Anthologies

8210 * *Nawbat al-asbahan = Nûbâ al-asbahân.* (Abdelhamid Bel Eljia and others). [Series: Inédit; Tunisie: anthologie du malouf]. Maison des Cultures du Monde: W 260046. 1962.

8211 *Nawbat al-dhil = Nûbâ al-dhîl.* (Abdelhamıd Bel Eljia and others). [Series: Inédit; Tunisie: anthologie du malouf]. Maison des Cultures du Monde: W 260044. 1959.

8212 *Nawbat al-Iraq = Nûbâ al-Irâq.* (Abdelhamid Bel Eljia and others). [Series: Inédit; Tunisie: anthologie du malouf]. Maison des Cultures du Monde: W 260047. 1960.

8213 *Nawbat al-ramal = Nûbâ al-ramal.* (Abdelhamid Bel Eljia and others). [Series: Inédit; Tunisie: anthologie du malouf]. Maison des Cultures du Monde: W 260045. 1960.

8214 *Nawbat al-sikah = Nûbâ al-sîka.* (al-Nasir Zaghandah and others). [Series: Inédit; Tunisie: anthologie du malouf]. Maison des Cultures du Monde: W 260059. 1994.

Individual Artist

8215 Bushnak, Lutfi

Maluf Tunisi = Malouf tunisien. [Series: Inédit]. Maison des Cultures du Monde: W 260053. 1993.

Israel and Jewish Diaspora (Including U.S. and European Jewish Music)

Anthologies

8216 *The Chanukkah story.* (Western Wind/Theodore Bikel). Western Wind: WW 1818CD. 1991.

8217 * *Chazanim and chazanut = Cantors and cantorials.* Pearl: GEMM CD 9313. 1904–36. [Gershon Sirota, Mordecai Hershman, Israel Leib Tkatsch, Zevulun Kwartin, Ben Zion Kapov-Kagan, Moses Mirsky, David Moshe Steinberg, Joseph Rosenblatt].

8218 *Echoes of the temple: cantors in prayer and folksong.* Pearl: GEMM CD 9126. 1922–36. [Gershon Sirota, Leib Glantz, Moses Mirsky, Joseph Rosenblatt, Salomo Pinkasovitch, and others].

8219 *Folklore yiddish d'Europe centrale = Yiddish folklore from central Europe.* (Budapester Klezmer Band). Quintana/Harmonia Mundi: QUI 903070. 1991.

8220 *Hazanout: chants liturgiques juifs.* [Series: Inédit]. Maison des Cultures du Monde: W 260005. 1986.

8221 ** *Jakie, jazz 'em up: old-time klezmer music.* Global Village: CD 101. 1912–26. [Abe Schwartz, Mishka Tsiganoff, Art Shryer, Harry Kandel, and others].

8222 *Jewish life, the old country.* Smithsonian/Folkways: 3801. AC. 1963.

8223 *Jewish songs from Bulgaria.* Gega New: GD 157. [1994].

8224 * *Klezmer music: early Yiddish instrumental music, the first recordings.* Folklyric/Arhoolie: C 9034. AC. 1910–27.

8225 *Klezmer music 1910–1942: recordings from the YIVO archives.* Global Village: C 104. AC. 1910–42.

8226 ** *Klezmer pioneers: European and American recordings.* Rounder: CD 1089. 1905–52. [Art Shryer, Abe Schwartz, Kandel's Orchestra, Dave Tarras, Sam Musiker, and others].

8227 *Klezmer plus! old time Yiddish dance music featuring Sid Beckerman and Howie Leess.* Flying Fish: FF 70488. 1991.

8228 *Liturgie juive: sept grands cantors = Jewish liturgy: seven great cantors.* [Series: Musique du monde]. Buda: 92581-2. 2CD set. [193?]. [Pierre Pinchik, Berele Chagy, Zavel Kwartin, David Roitman, Yossele Rosenblatt, Mordecai Hershman, Gershon Sirota].

8229 *Liturgies juives d'Ethiopie.* [Series: Inédit]. Maison des Cultures du Monde: W 260013. 1986. [Liturgical chant of the Ethiopian Jews (Falashas)].

8230 *Liturgy of Dohány Street Synagogue, Budapest.* (Sándor Kovács). Hungaroton: HCD 18134-2. [1986].

8231 *Mi-metav shire Yisrael = The very best of Israel.* NMC Music/CBS: 460815-2. [1988].

8232 *Music of the Bukharan Jewish ensemble Shashmaqam: Central Asia in Forest Hills, New York.* Smithsonian/Folkways: SF 40054. 1990.

8233 *Musique liturgique juive = Jewish liturgical music.* (Adolphe Attia and others). Le Chant du Monde: CMT 274 993. 1994.

8234 * *Mysteries of the Sabbath: classic cantorial recordings, 1907–47.* Yazoo: 7002. 1907–47. [Leib Glantz, Pierre Pinchik, David Roitman, Yossele Rosenblatt, Mordecai Hershman, Zavel Kwartin, Sophie Kurtzer, Gershon Sirota, Zindel Sapoznik, Yeshaya Meisels, and others].

8235 *Partisans of Vilna: the songs of World War II Jewish resistance.* Flying Fish: FF 70450. [1989].

8236 *The Passover story.* (Western Wind/Theodore Bikel). Western Wind: WW 1800CD. 1991.

8237 *Romances sefardies = Sephardic songs.* (Françoise Altan). Buda: 92529-2. 1992.

8238 *Shalom: Folklore und neue Songs aus Israel.* Calig: CAL 50594. [1979].

8239 *Shalom Israel.* Atoll: ATO 8605. [1987].

8240 * *The Yemenite Jews: Jewish-Yemenite diwan.* [Series: UNESCO collection]. Auvidis: D 8024. 1976–77.

Individual Artists or Groups

8241 Aguado, Bienvenida
Chants judéo-espagnols de la Méditerranée orientale. [Series: Inédit]. Maison des Cultures du Monde: W 260054. 1993.

8242 Alhambra
The art of Judeo-Spanish song. Global Village: CD 127. [1988].

8243 Argov, Zohar
Be-metav lehite ha-zahav = Greatest hits. Reuveni Brothers: C.D.R. 009-011. 3CD set. [197?–198?].

8244 Bikel, Theodore, 1924–
8244.1 *Theodore Bikel sings Jewish folk songs.* Bainbridge: BCD-2507 (Elektra). 1959.

8244.2 * *Theodore Bikel sings Yiddish theatre & folk songs.* Bainbridge: BCD-2504 (Elektra). [1964].

8245 * Bloemendal, Hans
The Amsterdam Synagogue: chants throughout the Jewish year. Philips: 422 030-2. 1960–66.

8246 * Brave Old World
Klezmer music. Flying Fish: FF 70560. 1991.

8247 Carlebach, Shlomo, 1926–1994
8247.1 *Mikdash melekh: in the palace of the king.* Vanguard: VMD 79192. 1965.

8247.2 * *Shlomo Carlebach at the Village Gate.* Vanguard: 2133-2. 1963.

8248 ** Damari, Shoshana
Israeli, Yiddish, Yemenite, and other folk songs. Vanguard: OVC 6025. 1961–63.

8249 Esim, Janet
Sefardim: songs of Spanish Jews from Turkey. Feuer & Eis: FUEC 710. 1992.

8250 Estah
Esta. Buda: 82851-2. 1990.

8251 Frankel, Judy
Sephardic songs of love and hope = Canticas sephardis de amor y esperansa. Global Village: CD 157. [1992].

8252 Fuchs, Leo
Leo Fuchs sings Yiddish theatre favorites. Greater Recording Co.: GRC 174. LP. [192?–193?].

8253 Gebirtig, Mordecai, 1877–1942
Kracow ghetto notebook. Koch: 3-7295-2H1. 1993.

8254 * Haza, Ofra, 1959–
Fifty gates of wisdom. Shanachie: 64002. 1984.

8255 Jontef
Klezmer music & Yiddish songs. ARC Music: EUCD 1303. 1995.

8256 Kandel, Harry
Russian sher: master of klezmer music. Global Village: CD 128. 1917–21.

8257 Kapelye
8257.1 *Chicken.* Shanachie: 21007. 1986.

8257.2 * *Kapelye on the air: old-time Jewish-American radio.* Shanachie: 67005. 1994.

8258 Katz, Mickey, 1909–1985
8258.1 *Don Byron plays the music of Mickey Katz.* Elektra Nonesuch: 79313-2. 1993.

8258.2 ** *Simcha time! Mickey Katz plays for weddings, bar mitzvahs and brisses (the klezmer sessions).* World Pacific: 30453. 1950–66.

8259 * Klezmatics
Rhythm + Jews. Flying Fish: FF 70591. 1992.

8260   Klezmer Conservatory Band

Old world beat. Rounder: CD 3115. 1991.

8261   Klezmorim

Metropolis. Flying Fish: FF 70258. 1993.

8262 * Kol Aviv

Chants et danses d'Israël. Arion: ARN 64033. [1975].

8263 * Lamandier, Esther

Romances. Aliénor: AL 1012. 1984.

8264 * Lebedeff, Aaron, 1873–1960

The best of Aaron Lebedeff. Greater Recording Co.: GRC 182. LP. [192?–193?].

8265   Leiser, Moshe, 1956–

Chansons yiddish: tendresses et rage. Ocora: C 558652. 1985.

8266   Levy, Gloria

Sephardic folk songs. Smithsonian/Folkways: 8737. AC. 1959.

8267   Massel Klezmorim

Is gewejn a folk. ARC Music: EUCD 1059. 1986.

8268   Mazeltones

Latkes & lattes. Global Village: CD 159. [1993].

8269   Miller, Sima

Heritage: the art of the Yiddish folk song, vols. 1–5. Global Village: C 123/124/130/131/132. 5 ACs. [198?].

8270 * Muzsikás

Máramaros: the lost Jewish music of Transylvania. Hannibal: HNCD 1373. [1993].

8271 * Mystic Fugu Orchestra

Zohar. Tzadik: TZ 7106. 1995.

8272   Nirenberg, Mariam

Folksongs in the East European Jewish tradition. Global Village: C 117. AC. 1946–83.

8273   Peerce, Jan, 1904–

8273.1 ** *The art of the cantor: Chanukah—the Sabbath—High Holy Days.* Vanguard: VCD 72017. 1966.

8273.2 *Jan Peerce today: cantorial masterpieces.* Vanguard: 71277-2. 1980.

8274   Picon, Molly, 1898–1992

Molly Picon at the Yiddish Theatre. Greater Recording Co.: GRC 220. LP. [192?–193?].

8275   Pinkasovicz, Salomo, 1886–1951

Cantor Salomo Pinkasovitch: his great recordings, 1920–1930. Pearl: GEMM CD 9015. 1920–30.

8276   Rubin, Joel

Zeydes un eyniklekh = Grandfathers and grandsons: Jewish-American wedding music from the repertoire of Dave Tarras. Wergo Spectrum: SM 1610-2. 1993.

8277   Satz, Ludwig, 1891–1944

Ludwig Satz at the Yiddish Theatre. Greater Recording Co.: GRC 172. LP. [192?–193?].

8278   Schaechter-Widman, Lifshe, 1893–1974

Az di furst avek: a Yiddish folksinger from the Bukovina. Global Village: C 111. AC. 1954.

8279   Secunda, Sholom, 1894–1974

8279.1 *Kol nidre service.* (Richard Tucker). Sony Masterworks: MDK 35207. 1959.

8279.2 *Passover seder festival: a Passover service.* (Richard Tucker). Sony Masterworks: MDK 48304. 1947, 1962.

8280   Seewald, Zahava

Ashkenaz songs. Sub Rosa/Le Coeur du Monde: SR 89. 1994.

8281 * Sittner, Ora

Chants hébreux d'Israël et d'Orient = Hebrew songs from Israel and the Orient. Al Sur: ALCD 139. 1994.

8282   Statman, Andy

The Andy Statman Klezmer Orchestra. Shanachie: 21004. 1992.

8283   Sulam

Klezmer music from Tel Aviv. Haus der Kulturen der Welt/Wergo: SM 1506-2 (281506-2). 1990.

8284   Tarras, Dave, 1897–1987

8284.1 * *Master of klezmer music, vol. 1.* Global Village: CD 105. 1929–49.

8284.2 *Yiddish-American klezmer music.* Yazoo: 7001. 1925–56.

8285   Voice of the Turtle

8285.1 *Balkan vistas, Spanish dreams: music of the Spanish Jews of Bulgaria and Yugoslavia.* [Series: Paths of exile, quincentenary series, vol. 3]. Titanic: Ti-203. [1991].

8285.2 *Bridges of song: music of the Spanish Jews of Morocco.* [Series: Paths of exile, quincentenary series, vol. 2]. Titanic: Ti-189. [1990].

8285.3 *Circle of fire: a Hanukah concert.* [Series: Songs of the Sephardim, vol. 5]. Titanic: Ti-159. 1986.

8285.4 *From the shores of the Golden Horn: music of the Spanish Jews of Turkey.* [Series: Paths of exile, quincentenary series, vol. 1]. Titanic: Ti-173. [1989].

8286 West End Klezmorim

Freylekhs 21. Global Village: CD 153. [1991].

8287 Zimet, Ben

Chants yiddish = Yidishe folks-lider. Buda: 82440-2. [198?].

8288 Zmiros

Eclectic klezz. Global Village: CD 110. 1985.

Arab Middle East, Iran, and Turkey

Transnational

8289 ** *Les chants des femmes = Women's songs.* [Series: Anthologie musicale de la peninsule arabique, vol. 4]. VDE-Gallo: VDE CD-783. 1968–90.

8290 ** *Middle East: sung poetry.* [Series: UNESCO collection]. Auvidis: D 8025. [1975]. [Feyzullah Tchinar, Hossein Ghavami, Mohammed-Ali Tedjo, Ibrahim Alouane Jerad].

8291 *Musique classique arabe.* (Al Kindi). Auvidis Ethnic: B 6735. [1989].

8292 *Poesie chantee des bedouins = Sung poetry of the Beduins* [sic]. [Series: Anthologie musicale de la peninsule arabique, vol. 1]. VDE-Gallo: VDE CD-780. 1970–72.

8293 *Sif safaa: new music from the Middle East.* Hemisphere/EMI: 32255. [1995]. [Mohamed Mounir, Hanan, Hamdi Ahmed, Saleh Khairy, Hohamed Fouad, Abu Hilal, Kazim al Sahir].

8294 *Le sowt, musique des villes = Sowt, music from the city.* [Series: Anthologie musicale de la peninsule arabique, vol. 3]. VDE-Gallo: VDE CD-782. 1971–76.

Bahrain

8295 * *Bahrain: fidjeri, songs of the pearl divers.* [Series: UNESCO collection]. Auvidis: D 8046. 1976.

8296 *La musique de Bahrein = The music of Bahrain.* Artistes Arabes Associés: AAA 104. [193?].

8297 *Musique des pêcheurs de perles = Music of the pearl divers.* [Series: Anthologie musicale de la peninsule arabique, vol. 2]. VDE-Gallo: VDE CD-781. 1970–75.

Iran

Anthologies

8298 *Baloutchistan: musiques d'extase et de guerison.* Ocora: C 580017/580018. 2CD set. 1978–90.

8299 *Classical music of Iran: the Dastgah systems.* Smithsonian/Folkways: SF 40039. 1966.

8300 *Folk music of Iran: the Luristan & Fars provinces.* Lyrichord: LLCT 7261. AC. 1972.

8301 * *Iran: les maîtres de la musique traditionnelle.* Ocora: C 560024/560026. 3CD set. 1979–88.

8302 ** *Iran: Persian classical music.* (Faramarz Payvar and ensemble). [Series: Explorer]. Elektra Nonesuch: 72060-2. 1973.

8303 * *Kurdish music.* [Series: UNESCO collection]. Auvidis: D 8023. 1972.

8304 *Kurdistan: zikr et chants soufis.* Ocora: C 560071/560072. 2CD set. 1993.

8305 * *Music of Iran, vol. 1.* [Series: World music library, vol. 5]. King: KICC 5105. 1989.

8306 * *Music of Iran, vol. 2.* [Series: World music library, vol. 6]. King: KICC 5106. 1989.

8307 *The music of Lorestan, Iran.* (Shahmirza Moradi/Reza Moradi). Nimbus: NI 5397. [1994].

8308 ** *Musique iranienne.* (Djamchid Chemirani/Madjid Kiani/Daryoush Tala'i). Harmonia Mundi: HMC 90391. 1976–79.

Individual Artists or Groups

8309 Bina, Sina

Iran: musique du sud du Khorassan. Buda: 92583-2. [199?].

8310 * Chemirani, Djamchid

Djamchid Chemirani, zarb. Auvidis Ethnic: B 6752. 1991.

8311   Ensemble Moshtaq

Music savante persane = Persian art music. Buda: 92532-2. 1992.

8312 * Googoosh

Jadeh. [Series: The best of Googoosh, vol. 1]. Caltex: 2040. [198?].

8313   Haydeh

Ashnai. Caltex: 2061. [197?].

8314   Khaladj, Madjid, 1962–

Iran: l'art du tombak (zarb) = The art of tombak (zarb). Buda: 92594-2. 1993.

8315 * Kiâni, Majid

Majid Kiâni, santur. Auvidis: B 6756. 1991.

8316   Manahedji, Behnam

Behnam Manahedji: master of the Persian santoor. Wergo/Haus der Kulturen der Welt: SM 1508-2. 1993.

8317 * Omoumi, Hossein

Persian classical music. Nimbus: NI 5359. 1992.

8318   Parisa, Fatemer Vaezi, and Seyyed Noureddin Razavi

Classical vocal art of Persia. JVC: VICG-5269. 1978.

8319   Perwer, Sivan, 1955–

Songs from Kurdistan. Auvidis Ethnic: B 6145. 1988.

8320   Shadjariân, Mohammad Rezâ

Musique classique persane. Ocora: C 559097. 1989.

8321   Shusha

Persian love songs & mystic chants. Lyrichord: LYRCD 7235. [1972].

8322   Tabrizizadeh, Mahmoud

Musique persane = Persian music. Al Sur: ALCD 112. [199?].

Iraq
Anthologies

8323 * *Iraq: iqa'at: traditional rhythmic structures.* [Series: UNESCO collection]. Auvidis: D 8044. 1976.

8324 ** *Music of Iraq.* [Series: World music library, vol. 4]. King: KICC 5104. 1975–77.

Individual Artists or Groups

8325   Ali, Safwat Mohammed

Iraqi music: ud taqsim and pasta. [Series: World music library, vol. 3]. King: KICC 5103. 1981.

8326   Bachir, Munir, 1930–

8326.1 ** *Maqamat.* [Series: Inédit]. Maison des Cultures du Monde: W 260050. 1993.

8326.2   *Munir Bachir en concert live à Paris.* [Series: Inédit]. Maison des Cultures du Monde: W 260006. 1987.

Kuwait
Anthology

8327   *Sahra maa nujum al-Kuwaiti = Stars of Kuwait, vol. 1.* Bou Zaid Phone: BUZ CD 503. [198?]. [Rabab, Nawaal, Adul Karim Kader, and others].

Individual Artist

8328   Rabab

Rabab: al-juz al-thani = The best of Rabab, vol. 2. Bou Zaid Phone: BUZ CD 508. [198?].

Lebanon
Anthologies

8329   *Arabic songs of Lebanon and Egypt.* Smithsonian/Folkways: 6925. AC. [1956].

8330   *Chant traditionnel Maronite: noël, passion, résurrection.* (Marie Keyrouz and ensemble). Harmonia Mundi: HMC 901350. 1990.

8331 * *Folk songs & dances from Lebanon.* Sawt al-Sharq/Digital Press Hellas: VDLCD 533. [1991?].

8332   *Laments of Lebanon.* Smithsonian/Folkways: 4046. AC. 1965–70.

Individual Artists or Groups

8333   El Roumi, Majida

Words. Music Master: MMCD 002. 1991.

8334 * Fayruz

The very best of Fairuz. [Series: Voix de l'Oriente]. Sawt al-Sharq: VDLCD 501. [1987].

Oman

8335   *Oman: traditional arts of the Sultanate of Oman.* [Series: UNESCO collection]. Auvidis: D 8211. 1990–91.

Palestine

8336 *Arabic and Druse music.* Smithsonian/Folkways: 4480. [1956].

8337 *Folk music of Palestine.* Smithsonian/Folkways: 4408. AC. [1951].

8338 * *Palestine: music of the intifada.* Venture/Virgin: VE 29. [199?].

Saudi Arabia

Anthology

8339 * *At-Tawhid: épopée musicale = a musical epic.* [Series: Inédit]. Maison des Cultures du Monde: W 260001. 1994.

Individual Artists or Groups

8340   Abduh, Muhammad

 8340.1 * *Mohammed Abdu: Abaa'd.* Sawt al-Jazirah/Music Master: MACD 501. [198?].

 8340.2 *Sabiyat = Folk songs.* Sawt al-Jazirah/Music Master: MACD 516/517. 2CD set. [1991].

8341   Ettab

The very best of Ettab. Relax-In/EMI Greece: REL CD 513. [1989].

Syria

Anthologies

8342 * *Syria: Islamic ritual zikr in Aleppo.* [Series: UNESCO collection]. Auvidis: D 8013. 1973.

8343 *Syrian Orthodox Church: Antioch liturgy.* [Series: UNESCO collection]. Auvidis: D 8039. 1982.

8344 ** *Syrie: muezzins d'Alep: chants religeux de l'Islam = Syria: muezzins of Alep: religious songs of Islam.* Ocora: C 580038. 1975.

8345 *Syrie: musique des Derviches tourneurs de Damas.* (Shaykh Hamza Shakkûr and ensemble). Auvidis Ethnic: B 6813. 1994.

8346 * *Wasla d'alep: chants traditionnels de Syrie.* (Sabri Moudallal and ensemble). [Series: Inédit]. Maison des Cultures du Monde: W 260007. 1988.

Individual Artists or Groups

8347   Arafeh, Souheil

Magic touch. Byblos/EMI Greece: TC-PL 908. AC. 1977.

8348 *   Azrié, Abed

Aromates. [Series: Explorer]. Elektra Nonesuch: 79241-2. [1990].

8349   Lamandier, Esther

Chants chrétiens araméens. Aliénor: AL 1034. 1989.

8350   Sabbagh, Farhan

Recital de oud à Berlin. Artistes Arabes Associés: AAA 047. [1992].

Turkey

Anthologies

8351 *The best of Turkey.* Atoll/Sonodisc: ATO 8649-2. [1990]. [Baris Manco, Cem Karaca, Zeki Muren, Ibrahim Tatlises, and others].

8352 *Celebrations: Turkish classical music: tribute to Yunus Emre.* (National Choir of Turkish Classical Music/Nevzad Atlig). [Series: UNESCO collection]. Auvidis: D 8303. 1991.

8353 *Chants du harem.* [Series: Musique ottomane = Ottoman music]. (Women's Ensemble of Istanbul). Al Sur: ALCD 127. 1993.

8354 *Istanbul 1925.* Traditional Crossroads: 4266. 1925–50.

8355 * *The Janissaries: martial music of the Ottoman Empire.* (Ensemble of the Turkish Republican Army/Kudsi Erguner). Auvidis Ethnic: B 6738. 1990.

8356 *Masters of Turkish music.* Rounder: CD 1051. [190?–192?].

8357 * *Musique traditionnelle turque: pièces instrumentales.* Ocora: C 558584. LP. 1971. OP

8358 *Song creators in Eastern Turkey.* [Series: Traditional music of the world, vol. 6]. Smithsonian/Folkways: SF 40432. 1990–92.

8359 * *Turkey: the sacred Koran: Islamic chants of the Ottoman Empire.* (Ibrahim Canakkeleli and others). JVC: VICG-5006. [1990].

8360 *Turkish military band music of the Ottoman Empire.* [Series: World music library, vol. 1]. King: KICC 5101. 1969–77.

8361 *Turquie: archives de la musique turque, vols. 1–2.* Ocora: C 560081/560082. 2 CDs. 1903–35.

8362 *Turquie: Aşik: chants d'amour et de sagesse d'Anatolie.* (Nuray Hafiftaş and others). [Series: Inédit]. Maison des Cultures du Monde: W 260025. 1991.

8363 *Turquie: musique soufi: ilahi et nefes.* (Nezih Uzel/Kudsi Ergüner). [Series: Inédit]. Maison des Cultures du Monde: W 260021. 1990.

Individual Artists or Groups

8364 Cicek, Ali Ekber

Turkish Sufi music: folk lute of Anatolia. Lyrichord: LYRCD 7392. [198?].

8365 Ergüner, Kudsi, 1952–

8365.1 * *Fasl: music of the Ottoman Empire.* Auvidis Ethnic: B 6737. 1990.

8365.2 *Sufi music of Turkey.* CMP: CD 3005. 1990.

8365.3 * *Turkey: the Turkish ney.* [Series: UNESCO collection]. Auvidis: D 8204. 1990.

8366 * Erköse Ensemble

Tzigane: the Gypsy music of Turkey. CMP: CD 3010. 1992.

8367 Firat, Ozan

Turquie: musique des troubadours. Auvidis: B 6771. 1992.

8368 Kenkulian, Hrant, 1901–1978

Udi Hrant: the early recordings, vols. 1–2. Traditional Crossroads: CD 4270/4271. 2 CDs. 1935–50.

8369 * Necdet Yaşar Ensemble

Music of Turkey. Music of the World: CDT-128. 1989.

8370 Özkan, Talip, 1939–

8370.1 * *L'art vivant de Talip Özkan.* Ocora: C 580047. 1980.

8370.2 *Turquie: l'art du tanbûr.* Ocora: C 560042. 1993.

8371 Sipahi, Nesrin

Sharki: love songs of Istanbul. CMP: CMPD 3009. 1992.

8372 Tanrikorur, Cinuçen, 1938–
Turquie. Ocora: C 580045 (558754). 1983.

Yemen

8373 *Yemen: traditional music of the north.* [Series: UNESCO collection]. Auvidis: D 8004. 1977–78.

Central Asia

General Anthologies

8374 * *Asie centrale: traditions classiques.* Ocora: C 560035/560036. 2CD set. 1990–93.

8375 *Music on the silk roads.* Auvidis Ethnic: B 6776. 1991.

8376 *The secret museum of mankind, vol. 4: Central Asia: ethnic music classics.* Yazoo: 7007. 1925–48.

Afghanistan

Anthologies

8377 *Afghanistan.* (Mohammad Naim and others). PlayaSound: PS 65058. [1980].

8378 *Afghanistan: chants des Pashai.* Le Chant du Monde: LDX 274752. 1970–71.

Individual Artist

8379 ** Herawi, Aziz
Master of Afghani lutes. Arhoolie: CD-387. 1992.

Azerbaijan

Anthology

8380 * *Azerbayjan: musique traditionnelle = Azerbaijan: traditional music.* Le Chant du Monde: LDX 274901. 1984–85.

Individual Artists or Groups

8381 Abdullaev, Aqakhân

Mugam d'Azerbaijan. [Series: Inédit; Anthologie du muğam d'Azerbaijan, vol. 6]. Maison des Cultures du Monde: W 260052. 1992.

8382 Aliev, Hâbil

Viele kementche. [Series: Great masters of the kamânche fiddle]. Auvidis Ethnic: B 6767. [1992].

8383 Huseynov, Hâji Bâbâ

Mugam d'Azerbaijan. [Series: Inédit; Anthologie du mugam d'Azerbaijan, vol. 3]. Maison des Cultures du Monde: W 260026. 1991.

8384 Ismailova, Sakine

Sakine Ismailova. [Series: Inédit; Anthologie du mugam d'Azerbaijan, vol. 5]. Maison des Cultures du Monde: W 260049. 1993.

8385 Kassimov, Alem

Alem Kassimov, vols. 1–2: mugam d'Azerbaijan. [Series: Inédit: anthologie du mugam d'Azerbaijan, vols. 1–2]. Maison des Cultures du Monde: W 260012; 260015. 2 CDs. 1989.

8386 Mansurov, Bahrâm, 1911–1984

Azerbaijan: Azerbaijani mugam. [Series: UNESCO collection]. Auvidis: D 8045. 1974.

8387 Trio Jabbar Garyaghdu Oghlu

Trio Jabbâr Garyaghdu Oghlu: mugam d'Azerbaijan. [Series: Inédit]. Maison des Cultures du Monde: W 260037. 1991.

Kazakhstan

8388 *Dombra music of Kazakhstan.* [Series: World music library, vol. 99]. King: KICC 5199. 1991.

8389 * *Music of Kazakhstan.* [Series: World music library, vol. 66]. King: KICC 5166. 1991.

Kurdistan

See Iran

Tajikistan

Anthologies

8390 * *Musiques savantes et populaires du Tadjikistan = Art and rural music of Tadzhikistan.* (Dav-

latmand) [Series: Inédit]. Maison des Cultures du Monde: W 260038. 1992.

8391 *Tadjikistan: musiques populaires du Sud.* Fonti Musicali: fmd 189. 1989–90.

8392 *Tajik music of Badakhshan.* [Series: UNESCO collection]. Auvidis: D 8212. 1988–91.

Individual Artist

8393 ** Sadikova, Goltchereh

Tadjikistan: falak. Fonti Musicali: FMD 192. 1991.

Turkmenistan

Anthologies

8394 *Instrumental music of Turkmenistan.* [Series: World music library, vol. 75]. King: KICC 5175. 1993.

8395 *Turkmen epic singing: Köroglu.* [Series: UNESCO collection]. Auvidis: D 8213. 1988–91.

Individual Group

8396 Ashkhabad

City of love. Realworld: CAROL-2329-2. 1992.

Uzbekistan

Anthologies

8397 ** *Bukhara: musical crossroads of Asia.* Smithsonian/Folkways: SF 40050. 1990.

8398 *Music of Central Asia: Uzbekistan.* [Series: World music library, vol. 8]. King: KICC 5108. 1985.

Individual Artist

8399 Yultchieva, Monâjât

Ouzbékistan: Monâjât Yultchieva. Ocora: C 560060. 1994.

37

Classical, Traditional, and Popular Musics of Asia and Oceania

Compiled by
Kent Underwood and
William E. Anderson

T his chapter encompasses the indigenous musics of Asia and Oceania. Citations are listed by country, and countries are grouped into four regions: "North and Northeast Asia," "South Asia," "Southeast Asia," and "Oceania."

General Anthologies

8400 * *Musiques de l'Islam d'Asie = Islamic music of Asia: Pakistan, Inde, Malasie, Indonésie.* [Series: Inédit]. Maison des Cultures du Monde: W 260022. [1991].

North and Northeast Asia

China

Anthologies

8401 *Buddhist music of Tianjin.* (Tianjin Buddhist Music Ensemble). Nimbus: NI 5416. 1993.

8402 * *China: Buddhist music of the Ming dynasty.* (Zhihuasi Temple monks). JVC: VICG 5259. 1992.

8403 *China: Chuida wind and percussive ensembles.* [Series: UNESCO collection]. Auvidis: D 8209. 1987.

8404 *China's instrumental heritage.* (Liang Tsai-Ping and others). Lyrichord: LYRCD 792. [1960].

8405 * *Chine: fanbai: chant liturgique bouddhique.* (Quanzhou Temple monks). Ocora: C 559080. 1987.

8406 *Chine: fanbai: chant liturgique bouddhique: leçon du matin à Shanghai = Morning service in Shanghai.* (Longhua Temple monks). Ocora: C 560075. 1992.

8407 *Chine: hautbois du nord-est = Shawms from north-east China, vols. 1–2.* Buda: 92612-2; 92613-2. 2 CDs. 1994.

8408 * *Chine: musique ancienne de Chang'an.* (Ensemble of the Xian Conservatory). [Series: Inédit]. Maison des Cultures du Monde: W 260036. 1991.

8409 ** *Chine: musique classique.* Ocora: C 559039. 1957–71.

8410 *Chinese music of the Han people.* [Series: World music library, vol. 40]. (Yao-Xing Chen and others). King: KICC 5140. 1985.

8411 *Dongjing music in Yunnan China.* (Ancient Music Band of Nanjian). [Series: World music library, vols. 89–90]. King: KICC 5189/5190. 2 CDs. 1994.

8412 * *Floating petals—wild geese—the moon on high: music of the Chinese pipa.* (Lui Pui-Yuen). [Series: Explorer]. Elektra Nonesuch: 72085-2. 1979.

8413 *Hong Kong: instrumental music.* [Series: UNESCO collection]. Auvidis: D 8031. 1974.

8414 * *The Hugo masters: an anthology of Chinese classical music, vols. 1–4.* Celestial Harmonies: 13042-2/13045-2. 4 CDs. [1992].

8415 *Instrumental music of the Uighurs.* [Series: World music library, vol. 38]. King: KICC 5138. 1989.

8416 * *An introduction to Chinese opera.* Marco Polo: 8.223930-8.223933 (Hong Kong 6.340371). 4CD set. [1985].

8417 ** *The monkey king: the world of Peking opera.* (Chinese Academy of Peking Opera). JVC: VICG-5016. 1979.

8418 *Music from the People's Republic of China.* Rounder: CD 4008. 1976.

8419 *Music of Chinese minorities.* [Series: World music library, vol. 42]. King: KICC 5142. 1981–85.

8420 *Music of the dynasties of China.* Inside Sound: ISC-2895. [1995].

8421 * *Music of the Song Dynasty (960–1279 A.D.)* (Liu De-Hai and others). Hong Kong Records: 8.242110. 1986.

8422 *Music of Yi people in Yunnan, China.* [Series: World music library, vol. 88]. King: KICC 5188. 1994.

8423 * *Opera de Pekin: La forêt en feu: La Princesse Cent-Fleurs = Peking opera: The forest on fire: The Princess Hundred Flowers.* (Dalian Troupe). Buda: 92618-2. 1994.

8424 *Opéra du Sichuan: La légende de Serpent Blanc = Sichuan opera: The legend of White Snake.* (Sichuan Opera Troupe no. 3 of Chengdu). Buda: 92555-2. 2CD set. 1992.

8425 *Le pavillon aux pivoines = The peony pavillion: Chinese classical opera kunqu.* (Lan Ting Chinese Opera Troupe). Auvidis/Inedit: W 260060. 2CD set. 1994.

8426 *Popular Jiangnan music.* (Ma Sheng-Long and others). Hong Kong Records: 8.880015. 1982.

8427 * *Rain dropping on the banana tree: an anthology of Chinese classical music.* Rounder: CD 1125. 1902–30.

8428 *Sizhu = Silk bamboo: chamber music of South China.* [Series: Anthology of music in China, vol. 3]. Pan: 2030. 1986–94.

8429 * *Turkestan chinois: Xinjiang: musiques ouigoures.* Ocora: C 559092/559093. 2CD set. 1988–89.

8430 *Vocal music of the Uighurs.* (Sinkiang Uigur Autonomous Region Khotan District Art Troupe). [Series: World music library, vol. 39]. King: KICC 5139. 1989.

8431 *Yazhou xiongfeng: di shiyi ju Yayun hui gegu = The valiant spirit of Asia: songs of the 11th Asia games.* Zhongguo Guangbo Yinxiang Chubanshe: BM-025. 1990.

Individual Artists or Groups

8432 ** Cercle d'Art Populaire
Chine: musique classique vivante. Ocora: 559049. 1988.

8433 Chen, Qilian
Qilian Chen sings Chinese songs. Pavane: ADW 7299. [1993].

8434 Chen, Xiaoyong, and Huihong Ou
Orchidee: traditional zheng and qin music. Wergo: SM 1603-2 (281 603-2). 1990.

8435 Chiang, Chien-hua, 1961–
Jiang Jian-hua plays compositions for er-hu and symphony orchestra. Hong Kong Records: 8.880037. 1983. [Music by Hua Yan-Jun, Dai Hong-Wei, Zhang Xie-Cheng, Liu Tian-Hua, and others].

8436   Chinese Music Ensemble of New York

Beloved Chinese songs. Chesky: WO 121. 1994.

8437 * Cui Jian

Yiwu suoyou (I have nothing). EMI: CDFH-50037. 1989.

8438   Dai, Xiaolian

China: the art of the qin zither. Auvidis Ethnic: B 6765. 1992.

8439 * Fleuve Jaune

Fleuve jaune = Yellow river: instrumental music of China. Auvidis Ethnic: B 6757. 1991.

8440   Guo Brothers

Yuan. Realworld: CAROL-2310-2 (91345). 1990.

8441   He, Shu-feng, 1955–

Chinese pipa. [Series: World music library, vol. 43]. King: KICC 5143. 1981.

8442 * Hsu, Hung

Song of the pipa. Hong Kong Records: 8.880033. 1983.

8443   Hu, Zhihou

Music of the guanzi. JVC: VICG 5260. 1992.

8444   Jing Ying Soloists

> **8444.1** *Evening song: traditional Chinese instrumental music.* Saydisc: SDL 368. 1987.
>
> **8444.2** * *Like waves against the sand: Chinese music for er-hu, pi-pa, di-zi, yang-qin, and Chinese percussion.* Saydisc: SDL 325. 1981.

8445 * Li, Xiangting

Chine: l'art du qin. Ocora: C 560001. 1990.

8446 * Lin, Shih-cheng, 1922–

Chine: l'art du pipa. Ocora: C 560046. 1988.

8447 * Liu, Hung-chun, 1946–

Fantastic pipes of China. JVC: VID-25017. 1986.

8448   Thundering Dragon

Thundering Dragon: percussion music from China. Wergo/Welt Musik: SM 1519-2. 1993.

8449   Tsai, Hsiao-yüeh

> **8449.1** ** *Chine: Nan-kouan, vol. 1: musique et chant courtois de la Chine du Sud.* Ocora: C 559004. 1982.
>
> **8449.2** * *Chine: Nan-kouan, vols. 4–6: chants courtois de la Chine du Sud.* Ocora: C 560039/ 560041. 3CD set. 1991.

8450 ** Wu, Man, 1963–

Pipa: Chinese traditional and contemporary music. Nimbus: NI 5368. 1993.

8451 * Wu, Suhua

China: the art of the erhu fiddle. Auvidis Ethnic: B 6764. 1992.

8452   Wu, Wenguang

Music of the qin. JVC: VICG-5213. 1991.

8453   Yu, Cheng

Classical Chinese pipa. ARC: EUCD 1176. 1991.

8454   Yuan, Lily

The ancient art music of China. Lyrichord: LYRCD 7409. [1990].

Japan

Anthologies

8455   *Japan: gagaku: court music of Japan.* (Tokyo Gakuso). JVC: VICG-5354. 1981.

8456   *Japan: music of the Bunraku theatre.* (Tsudayo Takemoto/Danshichi Takezawa). JVC: VICG-5356. 1986.

8457 ** *Japan: music of the koto.* (Kinichi Nakanoshima and others). JVC: VICG-5358. [1994].

8458   *Japan: music of the Noh theatre.* (Noh Hayashi Ensemble). JVC: VICG-5355. 1973–76.

8459 ** *Japan: music of the shakuhachi.* (Gorō Yamaguchi and others). JVC: VICG-5357. [1994].

8460   *Japan: O-Suwa-Daiko drums.* [Series: UNESCO collection]. Auvidis: D 8030. 1978.

8461   *Japan: semiclassical and folk music.* [Series: UNESCO collection]. Auvidis: D 8016. 1974.

8462 * *Japan: Shomyo Buddhist ritual.* [Series: UNESCO collection]. Auvidis: D 8036. 1974.

8463   *Japan: Shomyo: Japanese Buddhist ritual of the Shin-gon sect.* JVC: VICG-5353. 1993.

8464   *Japanese koto consort: koto, shamisen, shakuhachi and voice.* (Kofu Kikusui and others). Lyrichord: LYRCD 7205. [1960].

8465 * *Japanese masterpieces for the shakuhachi: played by the masters of Meian-ryu, Kimpu-ryu, Tozan-ryu, Ikuta-ryu and Kikusue-ryu at Daruaden of Ninzenji and Meianji, Koyto, Japan.* Lyrichord: LYRCD 7176. [196?].

8466 * *Japanese traditional music, vol. 1: gagaku.* King/Seven Seas: KICH 2001. 1989.

8467 * *Japanese traditional music, vol. 2: nōgaku.* King/Seven Seas: KICH 2002. [1990].

8468 * *Japanese traditional music, vol. 3: kabuki.* King/Seven Seas: KICH 2003. 1985.

8469 * *Japanese traditional music, vol. 4: biwa.* King/Seven Seas: KICH 2004. [1990].

8470 * *Japanese traditional music, vol. 5: shakuhachi.* King/Seven Seas: KICH 2005. [1990].

8471 * *Japanese traditional music, vol. 6: sō.* King/ Seven Seas: KICH 2006. [1990].

8472 * *Japanese traditional music, vol. 7: sankyoku.* King/Seven Seas: KICH 2007. [1990].

8473 * *Japanese traditional music, vol. 8: shamisen I.* King/Seven Seas: KICH 2008. [1990].

8474 * *Japanese traditional music, vol. 9: shamisen II.* King/Seven Seas: KICH 2009. [1990].

8475 * *Japanese traditional music, vol. 10: percussion.* King/Seven Seas: KICH 2010. [1990].

8476 *Music of Japanese people, vol. 1: harmony of Japanese music.* King/Seven Seas: KICH 2021. [1991].

8477 *Music of Japanese people, vol. 2: Japanese dance music.* King/Seven Seas: KICH 2022. [1991].

8478 *Music of Japanese people, vol. 3: Japanese work songs.* King/Seven Seas: KICH 2023. [1991].

8479 *Music of Japanese people, vol. 4: jam session of tsugaru-shamisen.* King/Seven Seas: KICH 2024. [1991].

8480 * *Music of Japanese people, vol. 5: music of Okinawa.* King/Seven Seas: KICH 2025. [1991].

8481 * *Music of Japanese people, vol. 6: music of Yaeyama and Miyako.* King/Seven Seas: KICH 2026. 1963–73.

8482 * *Music of Japanese people, vol. 7: music of Amami.* King/Seven Seas: KICH 2027. [1991].

8483 * *Music of Japanese people, vol. 8: music of Japanese festivals.* King/Seven Seas: KICH 2028. [1991].

Individual Artists or Groups

8484 Boredoms
Wow2/Life is OK! Avant: AVAN 026. 1992.

8485 Ensemble Nipponia
8485.1 ** *Japan: Kabuki and other traditional music.* [Series: Explorer]. Nonesuch: 72084-2. 1978.
8485.2 ** *Japan: traditional vocal & instrumental music.* [Series: Explorer]. Elektra Nonesuch: 72072-2. 1976.

8486 Japanese Koto Orchestra
Otone no Nagare ni Sote. Lyrichord: LYRCD 7167. 1967.

8487 Kadekaru, Rinsho
Folk songs of Okinawa. JVC: VICG-5360-2. 1994.

8488 * Kina, Shoukichi, 1948–
The best of Shoukichi Kina: peppermint tea house. [Series: Asia classics, vol. 2]. Luaka Bop/Warner Bros.: 45159-2. 1966–91.

8489 Kitajima, Osamu, 1949–
Benzaiten. Antilles: AN-7016. LP. 1974. OP

8490 Kitaro. *See* 7732

8491 Kodo
Heartbeat drummers of Japan. Sheffield Lab: CD KODO. 1985.

8492 * Mihashi, Michiya
Tokusen minyo best 20. King: K30H-5288. AC. 1986.

8493 Misora, Hibari, 1937–1989
8493.1 *Misora Hibari zenkyokushu.* Nippon Columbia: CSR-1246. AC. 1985.
8493.2 * *Tabi hitotose: geino seikatsu 40-shunen kinen.* Nippon Columbia: CAR 1432. AC. 1986.

8494 * Miyata, Kōhachiro
Shakuhachi: the Japanese flute. [Series: Explorer]. Elektra Nonesuch: 72076-2. 1976.

8495 Sakamoto, Ryuchi, 1952–
Beauty. Virgin: 86132. 1990.

8496 Shang Shang Typhoon
Shang Shang Typhoon 2. Tristar/Sony: WK 57781. 1991.

8497   Shonen Knife

Let's knife. Virgin: 86638. 1993.

8498   Taira, Yoshihisa

Celebrations: tribute to Noguchi. [Series: UNESCO collection]. Auvidis: D 8302. 1989.

8499   Takio Band (Takio Ito)

Takio. CBS-Sony: CD32 DH 5123. 1984.

8500 *   Ueda, Junko

Japon: h'epopée des Heike = Japan: the epic of the Heike. VDE-Gallo: CD 650. 1990.

8501   Yamaguchi, Gorō, 1933–

Great masters of the shakuhachi flute. Auvidis: A 6139. 1988.

8502   Yano, Akiko

Akiko Yano. Elektra Nonesuch: 72044-2. 1971.

8503 *   Yonin no Kai Ensemble

Japon: sankyoku. Ocora: C 560070. 1994.

Korea

Anthologies

8504   *Korea.* [Series: UNESCO collection]. Auvidis: D 8010. 1972.

8505 *   *Korea: folkloric instrumental traditions, vol. 1: sinawi and sanjo.* JVC: VICG-5020. 1988.

8506   *Korea: ritual songs from the island of Chindo.* VDE-Gallo: 756. 1990–92.

8507   *Korea: shamanistic ceremonies of the eastern seaboard.* (Kim Suk Chul Ensemble). JVC: VICG-5261. 1991.

8508   *Korean court music.* (Orchestra of the National Music Institute, Seoul/Kim Ki-su). Lyrichord: LYRCD 7206. [1969].

8509 *   *P'ansori: Korea's epic vocal art & instrumental music.* [Series: Explorer]. Elektra Nonesuch: 72049-2. 1972.

8510   *Sinawi music of Korea.* [Series: World music library, vol. 63]. King: KICC 5163. 1984.

8511 **   *Traditional Korean music: sanjo and vocal music.* [Series: World music library, vol. 91]. King: KICC 5191. 1984.

Individual Artists or Groups

8512 *   Chukp'a, 1911–1989

Korean kayagum music: sanjo. [Series: World music library, vol. 44]. King: KICC 5144. 1985.

8513   Hwang, Pyong-gi, 1936–

8513.1   *Kayagum masterpieces, vol. 1.* SEM: DS 0034. 1993.

8513.2   *Mountain rhyme.* Arcadia: 1994-2. [1992].

8514 *   Jong Nong Ak Ho Ensemble

Corée: musique instrumentale de la tradition classique. Ocora: C 558701. 1982.

8515   Jung, Jung Min

Korea: Simchongga: the epic vocal art of pansori. JVC: VICG-5019. 1988.

8516 *   Samul Nori

Record of changes. CMP: CMPCD 3002. 1990.

8517   Song, Kum-nyong

Music of the kayagum. JVC: VICG-5108. 1986.

8518   Yi, Kum-mi

Folk songs, vol. 1: songs of the Khonggi District. JVC: VICG-5022. 1988.

8519   Yi, Mi-ja

Yi Mi-ja taepyogok moum. Chigu: JCDS-0015. [19??].

8520   Yi, Son-hui

Sejong Munhwa Hoegwan kongyon sirhwang. Seoul: SPCD-243. AC. 1990.

Mongolia

Anthologies

8521   *The art of morin khuur.* (Guo Min and others). [Series: World music library, vol. 65]. King: KICC 5165. 1992.

8522 *   *Mongolia: traditional music.* [Series: UNESCO collection]. Auvidis: D 8207. 1990.

8523   *Mongolian epic song: zhangar.* [Series: World music library, vol. 36]. King: KICC 5136. 1985.

8524   *Mongolian instrumental music.* [Series: World music library, vol. 34]. King: KICC 5134. [1988].

8525 *Mongolian songs of Ottoman Empire.* (Namjil Norovbanzad and others). [Series: World music library, vol. 33]. King: KICC 5133. [1988].

Individual Artist

8526 Či Bulag

Mongolian morin khuur. [Series: World music library, vol. 35]. King: KICC 5135. 1985.

Taiwan

8527 *Polyphonies vocales des Aborigenes de Taïwan.* [Series: Inédit]. Maison des Cultures du Monde: W 260011. 1966, 1988.

8528 *Taiwan: music of the aboriginal tribes.* Jecklin Disco: JD 653-2. 1987.

8529 *Taiwan: musique des peuple minoritaires = Music from the ethnic minorities of Taiwan.* Arion: ARN 64109. 1989.

8530 *Taiwan: the Confucious temple ceremony.* Jecklin Disco: JD 652-2. 1987.

See also China

South Asia

Bangladesh

8531 *Bangladesh: les Garos de la forêt de Madhupur.* Ocora: C 580054. [1982].

8532 *Chants mystiques baûls du Bangladesh: dans la tradition de l'ordre Lâlan Shâhîl.* (Muhmmad Shâhjahân Miah and others). [Series: Inédit]. Maison des Cultures du Monde: W 260039. 1991.

Bhutan

See Tibet and Bhutan

India

Anthologies

8533 *Bengale: chants des "fous" = Bengal: songs of the "madmen."* Le Chant du Monde: LDX 274 715. 1978–79.

8534 *Bhangra power.* Multitone: BHANGRA 1. [1988]. [Amarjit Sidhu, Gurdev Dev, Johal, Surjit Sahota, and others].

8535 *Chants in praise of Krishna.* JVC: VICG-5034. 1988.

8536 * *CompilASIAN # 1.* Indipop/MNW: INDCD 1. 1983–90. [Asha Bhosle, Lata Mangeshkar, Najma, Bapphi Lahiri, Sheila Chandra, and others].

8537 * *Dance raja dance: the South Indian film music of Vijaya Anand.* [Series: Asia classics, vol. 1]. Luaka Bop/Warner Bros.: 26847-2. 1983–92.

8538 *Disco bhangra: wedding bands from Rajasthan.* Avant: 031. 1987–89.

8539 *Festive drums of Kerala.* [Series: World music library, vol. 20]. King: KICC 5120. 1988.

8540 * *Golden voices from the silver screen: classic Indian film soundtrack songs from the television series "Movie mahal," vols. 1–3.* GlobeStyle: CDORBD 054/056/059. 3 CDs. 1955–81. [Asha Bhosle, Mukesh, Lata Mangeshkar, Mohammed Rafi, and others].

8541 *Great artistes, great ghazals, vols. 1–2.* Sirocco/CBS Gramophone: SIR CD 006/007. 2 CDs. [1988]. [Asha Bhosle, Ghulam Ali, Salma Agha, Mehdi Hassan, Chitra and Jagjit Singh, Hariharan, Nirmal and Manhar Udhas, and others].

8542 * *Inde du nord: Mithila: chants d'amour de Vidyapati = North India: Mithila: love songs of Vidyapati.* Ocora: C 580063. 1974.

8543 *Inde du sud: musiques rituelles et théâtre du Kerala = South India: ritual music and theatre of Kerala.* Le Chant du Monde: LDX 274 910. 1981–83.

8544 *India: North Indian folk music.* [Series: UNESCO collection]. Auvidis: D 8033. 1972.

8545 *Khazana: a treasury of ghazals, vol. 1.* Music India: ASM 1318. [1982]. [Jagjit and Chitra Singh, Anup Jalota, Ahmed and Mohamed Hussain, and others].

8546 *Le Mahabharata: musiques, chants et rythmes du Kathakali.* Auvidis Ethnic: B 6778. 1978.

8547 *Music of the bansuri: a flute of Rajasthan.* JVC: VICG-5220. 1989. [Rajendra and Ajay Prasanna and others].

8548 *North India: instrumental music of mediaeval India.* [Series: UNESCO collection]. Auvidis: D 8205. 1991. [Asad Ali Khan, Gopal Das].

8549 ** *North India: instrumental music: rudra vena, vichitra veena, sarod, shahnai.* [Series: UNESCO collection]. Auvidis: D 8021. 1974. [Asad Ali Khan, Gopal Krishna, Ashok Roy, Hira Lal].

8550 ** *North India: instrumental music: sitar, flute, sarangi.* [Series: UNESCO collection]. Auvidis: D 8017. 1972. [Ghulam Hussain Khan, Bhola Nath, Nazir Ahmad].

8551 *Orissi dance music: an ancient performance from Orissa.* JVC: VICG-5268. 1986.

8552 *Le Râmâyana: musiques, chants et rythmes du Kathakali.* Auvidis Ethnic: B 6779. 1978.

8553 * *Swara bushani: a compilation of the great masters of Carnatic music.* Oriental: AAMS CD 166/167. 2CD set. [1992].

8554 *Vintage music from India: early twentieth-century classical & light classical music.* Rounder: CD 1083. 1906–[192?].

8555 *Yaadgaar thumriyan.* Gramophone Company of India/EMI: PMLP 5209. 1990. [Bhimsen Joshi, Bade Ghulam Ali Khan, Kishori Amonkar, Prabha Atre, Shobha Gurtu, Lakshmi Shankar, Begum Akhtar, and others].

Individual Artists or Groups

8556 Akhtar, Begum, d. 1974
Ghazals. Music India: CDNF 154. [1991].

8557 * Akhtar, Najma
Qareeb. Shanachie: 64009. 1987–88.

8558 * Alaap
Best of Alaap. Multitone: DMUT 001. [1988].

8559 * Balachander, S., 1927–
Veena virtuoso. [Series: World music library, vol. 19]. King: KICC 5119. 1982.

8560 Banerjee, Nikhil, 1931–1986
8560.1 *The hundred-minute raga: Purabi Kalyan.* Raga: 207. 2CD set. 1982.
8560.2 *Immortal sitar of Pandit Nikhil Banerjee.* Chhanda Dhara: SNCD 8886. [1986].
8560.3 * *Rag Hemant.* Raga: 214. 1970.

8561 Bawa, Gurmeet, 1944–
Love and life in the Punjab. [Series: World music library, vol. 16]. King: KICC 5116. 1988.

8562 Bhatt, Vishwa Mohan
Saradamani. Water Lily Acoustics: WLA-ES-23-CD. 1991.

8563 Bhattacharya, Tarun
Sargam: santur, shenai & tabla. Music of the World: CDT-132. 1993.

8564 Chaurasia, Hariprasad
8564.1 * *Rag Ahir bhairav; Marriage song.* Nimbus: NI 5111. 1987.
8564.2 *Raga Darbari kanada; Dhun in raga Mishra pilu.* Nimbus: NI 5365. 1990.

8565 Dagar, Zia Mohiuddin, 1929–
Raga Pancham kosh; Raga Malkauns. [Series: Great masters of the rudra-veena]. Auvidis Ethnic: B 6131. 1988.

8566 Dagar Brothers
8566.1 * *Dhrupad: vocal art of Hindustan.* JVC: VICG-5032. 1988.
8566.2 *Rag Kambhoji.* Music of the World: CDT-114. [1989].

8567 Das Gupta, Buddhadev, 1933–
8567.1 * *Morning concert: Ahir bhairav.* Raga: 206. 1989.
8567.2 *Rag Nayak ki kanra.* Raga: 210. 1989.

8568 Devi, Girija
Girija Devi, Zakir Hussain. Moment: MR 1004. 1989.

8569 * Ganguly, Rita
Thumri and dadra: vocal art of Hindustan. JVC: VICG 5347. 1989.

8570 * Gopalakrishnan, K. S.
Carnatic flute. Haus der Kulturen der Welt/Wergo: SM-1502-2. 1991.

8571 * Hussain, Zakir, 1951–
Super percussion of India. [Series: World music library, vol. 13]. King: KICC 5113. 1988.

8572 Jasraj, Pandit, 1930–
8572.1 *Hussaini kanra; Bhajan.* Moment: MR 1009. 1992.
8572.2 *Invocation.* Water Lily Acoustic: WLA-ES-31-CD. 1992.
8572.3 ** *The meditative music of Pandit Jasraj.* Oriental: CD 187. [198?].

8572.4 * *Ornamental voice.* Chhanda Dhara: SNCD 74289. [1989].

8573 Jayadeva, 12th cent.
Gita govinda: Jayadeva's lyrical poem. (Ragunath Panigrahi and others). Auvidis Ethnic: B 6152. 3CD set. [1982].

8574 Joshi, Bhimsen, 1922–
Hindustani vocal music. [Series: World music library, vol. 14]. King: KICC 5114. [1989].

8575 Katkar, Shruti, 1951–
Shruti Sadolikar. [Series: Hindustani classical vocal]. Nimbus: NI 5346. 1991.

8576 Khan, Ali Akbar, 1922–
8576.1 *The emperor of the sarod: live, vols. 1–2.* Chhanda Dhara: SNCD 70293/71090. 2 CDs. 1990–[1993?].
8576.2 *Raga Basant mukhari with jogia.* Chhanda Dhara: SNCD 3386. [1985].
8576.3 * *Signature series, vols. 1–4.* AAMP: CD 9001; CD 9002; CD 9404; CD 9405. 4 CDs. [196?]–1973.
8576.4 ** *Then and now.* AMMP: CD9507. 1955, 1994.

8577 * Khan, Ali Akbar, 1922– , and L. Subramaniam
Duet. Ravi Shankar Music Circle: RSMC-D-103. [1981].

8578 Khan, Amjad Ali, 1945–
Inde du nord. Ocora: C 560011. 1992.

8579 * Khan, Bismillah, 1916–
Shenai nawaz: vibrant sounds of shenai. Oriental: CD 126. [198?].

8580 Khan, Ghulam Mustafa, 1933–
Ghulam Mustafa Khan. [Series: Hindustani classical vocal]. Nimbus: NI 5409. 1992.

8581 Khan, Imrat
8581.1 * *Rag Madhur ranjani.* Music of the World: CDT-123. [1992].
8581.2 *Raga Marwa.* Nimbus: NI 5356. [1992].

8582 Khan, Jaffar Hussain
Qawwali de l'Inde du Norde. [Series: Inédit]. Maison des Cultures du Monde: W 260048. 1992.

8583 Khan, Sabri
Raga Darbari; Raga Multani. Auvidis Ethnic: B 6754. 1991.

8584 Khan, Sultan
Singing sarangi of Sultan Khan. Chhanda Dhara: SP 83988. [1988].

8585 * Khan, Vilayat, 1924–
Raga Jaijaivanti. India Archive: CD 1010. 1991.

8586 * Krishnan, Ramnad, d. 1973
Ramnad Krishnan: Vidwan: music of south India, songs of the Carnatic tradition. [Series: Explorer]. Elektra Nonesuch: 72023-2. 1967.

8587 * Mangeshkar, Lata, 1929–
The legend. EMI India: CDPM 1180. [1987].

8588 Mukesh, d. 1976
Hits all the way. EMI India: CD PMLP 5017. [1988].

8589 * Mukherjee, Budhaditya, 1955–
Budhaditya Mukherjee. Nimbus: NI 5221. 1989.

8590 Narayan, Brij, 1952–
Raga Lalit; Raga Bairagi bhairav. Nimbus: NI 5263. 1990.

8591 Narayan, Ram, 1927–
8591.1 ** *Pandit Ram Narayan.* Ocora: C 559060. 1978.
8591.2 *Sonorous strings of sarangi.* Oriental: CD-118. [1989].

8592 * Pran Nath, 1918–1996
Ragas of morning and night. Gramavision: GNA 61008-2. 1968.

8593 Ram Chandra
Musique classique de l'Inde: style Dhrupad. Buda: 82459-2. [198?].

8594 Ramani, N., 1934–
Classical Karnatic flute. Nimbus: NI 5257. 1990.

8595 Ravikiran, N.
South Indian ragas: young star of gottuvadyam. Chhanda Dhara: SNCD 15987. [1987].

8596 Sachdev, Gurubachan Singh
Bansuri: the bamboo flute of India. Lyrichord: LYRCD 7405. [1980].

8597 Sangeet, Apna
Greatest hits. Sirocco: SIR 005. [198?].

8598   Santhanam, Maharajapuram

Musique karnatique = Karnatic music. Auvidis Ethnic: B 6746. 1991.

8599 * Sayeeram, Aruna

Chant karnatique = Karnatic song. Auvidis Ethnic: B 6747. 1990.

8600 * Shankar, Daya

Daya Shankar's shahnai-ensemble with Pandit Anant Lal. Chhanda Dhara: SNCD 74589. [1989].

8601   Shankar, Lakshmi

8601.1 *Evening concert.* Ravi Shankar Music Circle: RSMC-D-102. 1986.

8601.2 * *Les heures et les saisons.* Ocora: C 558615. 1983.

8601.3 ** *Songs of devotion.* Auvidis Ethnic: B 6745. 1990.

8602   Shankar, Lakshminaravana, 1950–

Raga Aberi. Music of the World: CDT-131. [1995].

8603   Shankar, Ravi, 1920–

8603.1 *Golden jubilee concert.* Chhanda Dhara: SNCD 70390. 1990.

8603.2 ** *Live at the Monterey International Pop Festival.* One Way: S21 56848. 1967.

8603.3 * *Pandit Ravi Shankar.* Ocora: C 558674. 1986.

8604 * Shankar, Ravi, 1920– , and Ali Akbar Khan, 1922–

Ragas. Fantasy: FCD-24714-2. 1964–65.

8605   Sharma, Shiv Kumar, 1938–

8605.1 *Rag Madhuvanti; Rag Misra tilang.* Nimbus: NI 5110. 1987.

8605.2 *Raga Jog.* Auvidis Ethnic: B 6766. 1991.

8606   Sridhar, Krishnamurti, 1948–

8606.1 *Nadanjali: Raga Malkauns.* Auvidis Ethnic: B 6736. 1990.

8606.2 *Raga Kaushik kanada.* Auvidis: B 6507. 1984.

8607 * Srinivasier, Semmangudi R., 1908–

The doyen of Carnatic music. Oriental: CD 163/CD 164. 2CD set. [1979].

8608   Subramaniam, L., 1947–

8608.1 * *L. Subramaniam en concert.* Ocora: C 558656. 1983.

8608.2 *Three ragas for solo violin.* Nimbus: NI 5323. 1991.

8608.3 *Le violon de l'Inde du sud.* Ocora: C 559029. 1980.

8609   Sultana, Parween, 1950– , and Dilshad Khan

8609.1 * *From dawn until night: Hindustani song.* Auvidis Ethnic: B 6748. 1991.

8609.2 *The impeccable soprano and the innovative tenor.* Oriental: CD 185. [199?].

8610   Udhas, Pankaj

Chitti aai hai. Music India: CDF 026. [19-?].

Nepal

Anthologies

8611   *Folk music of Nepal.* [Series: World music library, vol. 74]. King: KICC 5174. 1993.

8612   *Nepal: musique de fête chez les Newar = Festival music of the Newar.* VDE-Gallo: CD-553. 1952, 1973.

Individual Artist

8613   Singh, Tara Bir

Nepal sitar. Wergo Spectrum: SM 1045-50. 1985.

Pakistan

Anthology

8614   *Qawwali, expression de l'essential désir = Qawwali, the essence of desire.* (Mehr Ali/Sheher Ali). Buda: 92611-2. [199?].

Individual Artists or Groups

8615   Ali, Ghulam

Greatest hits of Gulam [Ghulam] *Ali.* Sirocco: SIR CD 006. [1988].

8616   Hassan, Mehdi

Greatest ghazals. Sirocco: SIR 001. [196?].

8617   Khan, Nusrat Fateh Ali, 1948–

8617.1 *Devotional and love songs.* Realworld: CAROL-2300-2. 1988.

8617.2 * *Nusrat Fateh Ali Khan en concert à Paris, vols. 1–5.* Ocora: C 558658/558659/ 559072/559073/559074. 5 CDs in 3 containers. 1985–88.

8617.3 ** *Shahbaaz.* Realworld: CAROL-2315-2. [1991].

8617.4 * *Shahen-Shah.* Realworld: CAROL-2302-2. 1989.

8618 Parveen, Abida

Chants soufis du Pakistan = Pakistani Sufi songs: qâl, ġhazal et kâfî. [Series: Inédit]. Maison des Cultures du Monde: W 260003. 1994.

8619 Rathore, Mohamed Subhan

Pakistani music: the rubab of Kashmir. [Series: World music library, vol. 9]. King: KICC 5109. 1981.

8620 Sabri Brothers

8620.1 *Pakistan: the music of the Qawal.* [Series: UNESCO collection]. Auvidis: D 8028. 1975.

8620.2 * *Ya habib.* Realworld: CAROL-2311-2 (91346). 1990.

Sri Lanka

Anthologies

8621 *Gamelans et tambours des îles: Bali; Sri Lanka.* Arion: ARN 64203. [197?].

8622 *Sri Lanka: comédies et opéras populaires = Popular comedies and operas.* Le Chant du Monde: CMT 274 1006. 1979.

8623 *Sri Lanka: musiques rituelles et religieuses.* Ocora: C 580037. 1979.

Individual Artist

8624 Jayasingha, Anura, 1950–

Welcome to Sri Lanka. Arion: ARN 64087. [1990].

Tibet and Bhutan
(Including Tibetan Exiles in India)

8625 *Ladakh: musique de monastère et de village = Ladakh: monastic and village music.* Le Chant du Monde: LDX 274 662. 1976.

8626 *Tibet: traditions rituelles des Bonpos.* Ocora: C 580016. 1981–83.

8627 *Tibetan Buddhism.* (Shartse College of Ganden Monastery/Lobsang Tenzin). Bridge: BCD 9015. 1987.

8628 *Tibetan Buddhism: tantras of Gyütö.* [Series: Explorer]. Nonesuch: 79198-2. 1972.

8629 ** *Tibetan Buddhism: the ritual orchestra and chants.* [Series: Explorer]. Nonesuch: 72071-2. 1973.

8630 * *Tibetan Buddhist rites from the monasteries of Bhutan, vols. 1–4.* Lyrichord: LYRCD 7255/7258. 4 CDs. 1971.

8631 *Tibetan ritual.* [Series: UNESCO collection]. Auvidis: D 8034. 1970.

Southeast Asia

Burma

See Myanmar

Cambodia

8632 * *Cambodge.* (Cambodian Royal Ballet Orchestra and Chorus). [Series: Les musiques du Ramayana, vol. 2]. Ocora: C 560015. 1964.

8633 *Cambodge: musique classique khmère, théâtre d'ombres et chants de mariage.* [Series: Inédit]. Maison des Cultures du Monde: W 260002. 1991–94.

8634 * *Cambodge: musique de l'exil = Cambodia: music of the exil[e].* VDE/Gallo: CD-698. 1980–84.

8635 ** *Cambodge: musiques du Palais Royal (années soixante—).* Ocora: C 560034. 1966–70.

8636 *Cambodia: royal music.* [Series: UNESCO collection]. Auvidis: D 8011. 1970.

8637 *Homrong.* (National Dance Company of Cambodia). Realworld: CAROL-2317-2 (91734). 1990.

8638 *9 gong gamelan.* [Series: Music of Cambodia, vol. 1]. Celestial Harmonies: 13074-2. [1993].

8639 *Royal court music.* [Series: Music of Cambodia, vol. 2]. Celestial Harmonies: 13075-2. [1993].

8640 *Solo instrumental music.* [Series: Music of Cambodia, vol. 3]. Celestial Harmonies: 13076-2. [1994].

Indonesia

Anthologies

8641 *Asmat dream.* [Series: New music Indonesia, vol. 1]. Lyrichord: LYRCD 7415. 1989. [Compositions by Harry Roesli, Afryanto Suhendi, Nano S., and Ekagustdiman Dody Satya].

8642 * *Bali: gamelan and kecak.* [Series: Explorer]. Nonesuch: 79204-2. 1987.

8643 *Bali: les grands gong kebyar des années soixante.* Ocora: C 560057/58. 2CD set. 1969–71.

8644 *Bali: musique pour le gong gede.* Ocora: C 559002. 1972.

8645 *Bali-Sunda.* [Series: Les musiques du Ramayana, vol. 3]. Ocora: C 560016. 1971–73.

8646 * *Batak of Northern Sumatra.* New Albion: NA046CD. [1992].

8647 *Betawi and Sundanese music of the north coast of Java: topeng Betawi, tanjidor, ajeng.* [Series: Music of Indonesia, vol. 5]. Smithsonian/Folkways: SF 40421. 1990–92.

8648 *Court music of Kraton Surakarta.* [Series: World music library, vol. 51]. King: KICC 5151. 1992.

8649 ** *The gamelan music of Bali.* [Series: World music library, vol. 26]. King: KICC 5126. 1990.

8650 *The gamelan of Cirebon.* [Series: World music library, vol. 30]. King: KICC 5130. 1989.

8651 *Gender wayang pemarwan: music for the Balinese shadow play "The Mahabharata."* (Sekehe Gender Bharata Muni). CMP: CD 3014. 1989.

8652 *The heavenly orchestra of Bali.* (Gamelan Semar Pegulingan Saih Pitu). CMP: CD 3008. 1991.

8653 * *Indonesian popular music: kroncong, dangdut, and laggam jawa.* [Series: Music of Indonesia, vol. 2]. Smithsonian/Folkways: SF CD 40056. [197?]–90.

8654 * *Java: Langen Mandra Wanara: opéra de Danuredjo VII.* Ocora: C 559014/15. 2CD set. 1975.

8655 * *Java: palais royal de Yogyakarta, vol. 1: les danses de cour.* Ocora: C 560067. 1970–73.

8656 * *Java: palais royal de Yogyakarta, vol. 2: la musique instrumentale.* Ocora: C 560068. 1970–73.

8657 *Java: Sundanese folk music.* [Series: UNESCO collection]. Auvidis: D 8051. 1972.

8658 ** *Javanese court gamelan.* [Series: Explorer]. Elektra Nonesuch: 72044-2. 1971.

8659 * *Jegog: the bamboo gamelan of Bali.* (Werdi Sentana). CMP: CD 3011. 1991.

8660 * *Kecak: a Balinese music drama.* (Kecak Ganda Sari/I Gusti Putu Putra). Bridge: BCD 9019. 1987.

8661 *Mana 689.* [Series: New music Indonesia, vol. 2]. Lyrichord: LYRCD 7420. 1989. [Compositions by Otok Bima Sidarta, Blacius Subono, I Wayan Sadra, Pande Made Sukerta].

8662 * *Music for the gods: the Fahnestock South Sea expedition: Indonesia.* [Series: Library of Congress: endangered music project]. Rykodisc: RCD 10315. 1941.

8663 *Music from the forests of Riau and Mentawai.* [Series: Music of Indonesia, vol. 7]. Smithsonian/Folkways: SF 40423. 1990–93.

8664 ** *Music from the morning of the world: the Balinese gamelan & Ketjak, the Ramayana monkey chant.* [Series: Explorer]. Elektra Nonesuch: 79196-2. 1966.

8665 *Music from the outskirts of Jakarta.* [Series: Music of Indonesia, vol. 3]. Smithsonian/Folkways: SF CD 40057. 1991.

8666 *Music of Nias & North Sumatra: Hoho, Gendang Karo, Gondang Toba.* [Series: Music of Indonesia, vol. 4]. Smithsonian/Folkways: SF 40420. 1990–91.

8667 *Music of sasandu.* (Yakob Mberu). [Series: World music library, vol. 79]. King: KICC 5179. 1992.

8668 *Night music of West Sumatra: saluang, rabab Pariaman, dendang Pauah.* [Series: Music of Indonesia, vol. 6]. Smithsonian/Folkways: SF 40422. 1992.

8669 *Songs before dawn: gandrung banyuwangi.* [Series: Music of Indonesia, vol. 1]. Smithsonian/Folkways: SF CD 40055. 1991.

8670 *Street music of Java.* Original Music: OMCD 006. 1976, 1978.

8671 * *Sundanese classical music.* [Series: World music library, vol. 31]. King: KICC 5131. 1986.

8672 *Vocal and instrumental music from east and central Flores.* [Series: Music of Indonesia, vol. 8]. Smithsonian/Folkways: SF 40424. 1993–94.

8673 *Vocal music of central and west Flores.* [Series: Music of Indonesia, vol. 9]. Smithsonian/Folkways: SF 40425. 1993–94.

Individual Artists or Groups

8674 * Hadidjah, Idjah
Tonggeret. Icon/Nonesuch: 79173-2. 1979–86.

8675 * Komariah, Euis

Jaipongan Java. GlobeStyle: CDORB 057. 1990.

8676 Kurnia, Detty

Coyor panon. Flame Tree: FLTRCD 519. 1992.

8677 Nasida Ria

Keadilan: qasidah music from Java. Piranha: PIR 26-2 (CD 01876). [19-?].

8678 * Sadra, I Wayan, 1953–

Karya. [Series: New music Indonesia, vol. 3]. Lyrichord: LYRCD 7421. 1987–90.

8679 * Wasitodiningrat, K. R. T., 1909–

The music of K. R. T. Wasitodiningrat. (Gamelan Sekar Tunjung). CMP: CD 3007. 1990.

Laos

8680 ** *Laos: Lam Saravane: musique pour le khene.* (Soubane Vongath and others). Ocora: C 559058. 1977.

8681 *Laos: traditional music of the south.* [Series: UNESCO collection]. Auvidis: D 8042. 1972–73.

8682 *Music from southern Laos.* (Molam Lao). Nimbus: NI 5401. 1993.

Malaysia

Anthologies

8683 *Dangdut Melayu = Malay dangdut.* [Series: Koleksi lagu-lagu terbaik]. EMI: 07243 (8280552 6). [1993]. [Zaleha Hamid, Sharifah Aini, Herman Tino, and others].

8684 *Dream songs and healing sounds in the rainforests of Malaysia.* Smithsonian/Folkways: SF 40417. 1981–91.

Individual Artist

8685 Ramlee, P., 1929–1973

Kenangan abadi, vols. 1–2. EMI (Singapore): TC 7011/7012. 2AC set. 1955–73.

Myanmar (Burma)

Anthologies

8686 * *Birmanie: musique d'art.* Ocora: C 559019/ 559020. 2CD set. 1975–79.

8687 *Hsaing waing of Myanmar.* (U Sein Win and ensemble). [Series: World music library, vol. 62]. King: KICC 5162. 1992.

8688 ** *Music of Myanmar.* [Series: World music library, vol. 32]. King: KICC 5132. 1981–87.

Individual Artist

8689 Yee, Moe Moe, 1957–

Burmese harp: Myanmar music. PlayaSound: PS 65135. 1994.

Philippines

Anthologies

8690 *Music of the Magindanao in the Philippines, vols. 1–2.* Smithsonian/Folkways: 4536. 2 AC set. [1961].

8691 * *Philippine gong music from Lanao: Muranao kakolintang, vols. 1–2.* Lyrichord: LLCT 7322; 7326. 2 ACs. [1978].

8692 *Philippines: musique de hautes-terres Palawan = Palawan highlands music.* Le Chant du Monde: LDX 274 865. 1970–83.

Individual Artists or Groups

8693 * Aguilar, Freddie

Katarungan. Ghani Enterprise: KM558. AC. [198?].

8694 Apo Hiking Society

The best of Apo Hiking Society. WEA/Universal: CDP-94,601. [1991].

8695 ** Bayanihan Philippine Dance Company

Bayanihan Philippine Dance Company, vols. 1–2. Monitor: MFS-71322/MFS-409. 2 CDs. 1959.

8696 Inang Laya

Atsay ng mundo. Dypro: DYP 86/15. 1989.

Thailand

Anthologies

8697 ** *Classical music of Thailand.* [Series: World music library, vol. 25]. King: KICC 5125. 1991.

8698 *Instrumental music of northeast Thailand.* [Series: World music library, vol. 24]. King: KICC 5124. 1991.

8699 * *Mo lam singing of northeast Thailand.* [Series: World music library, vol. 23]. King: KICC 5123. 1991.

8700 *Music of northeast Thailand.* [Series: World music library, vol. 59]. King: KICC 5159. 1991.

8701 *Royal court music of Thailand.* Smithsonian/Folkways: SF 40413. 1994.

8702 *Thailand: classical instrumental traditions.* JVC: VICG-5262. 1976.

8703 *Thailand: the music of Chieng Mai.* [Series: UNESCO collection]. Auvidis: D 8007. 1971.

8704 * *Virtuosi of Thai classical music.* [Series: World music library, vol. 58]. King: KICC 5158. 1991.

Individual Groups

8705 * Fong Naam Ensemble
Thai classical music. Marco Polo: 8.223197/8.223198. 2CD set. 1990.

8706 Isan Slete
The flower of Isan: songs and music from northeast Thailand. GlobeStyle: CDORBD 051. 1989.

8707 Prasit Thawon Ensemble
Thai classical music. Nimbus: NI 5412. 1993.

Vietnam

Anthologies

8708 * *Instrumental music of Vietnam.* [Series: World music library, vol. 60]. King: KICC 5160. 1991.

8709 *Music from Viet Nam.* Caprice: CAP 21406. 1991. [Phong Lun Group, Quy Bon, Kim Sinh, and others].

8710 *Music of North and South Vietnam: theater music of the South—sung poetry of the North.* Ed. by Stephen Addiss. Smithsonian/Folkways: 4219. AC. 1971.

8711 ** *The music of Vietnam, vols. 1.1–1.2.* Celestial Harmonies: 13082-2/13083-2. 2 CDs. [1994].

8712 *Stilling time: traditional musics of Vietnam.* Innova: 112. 1993–94.

8713 * *String instruments of Vietnam.* [Series: World music library, vol. 21]. King: KICC 5121. 1991.

8714 *Vietnam: ca tru & quan ho: traditional music.* [Series: UNESCO collection]. Auvidis: D 8035. 1976.

8715 *Vietnam: court theatre music: hat-bôi.* [Series: UNESCO collection]. Auvidis: D 8058. 1985.

8716 *Vietnam: hát chèo: traditional folk theatre.* [Series: UNESCO collection]. Auvidis: D 8022. 1976.

8717 *Viêt-Nam: instruments et ensemble de musique traditionnelle = traditional music instruments and ensembles.* Arion: ARN 64303. 1984.

8718 *Viêt-nam: poésies et chants.* (Trân Van Khê/Trân Thi Thuy Ngoc). Ocora: C 560054. 1994.

8719 *Vietnam: tradition of the South.* [Series: UNESCO collection]. Auvidis: D 8049. 1975.

8720 *Vietnamese folk theatre: Hat cheo.* (Quy Bon Family). [Series: World music library, vol. 22]. King: KICC 5122. 1991.

Individual Artists or Groups

8721 Jimmii, J. C.
Ngu'ó'i con gái = The girl. Jimmii: CDR2003. [1993].

8722 Kim, Sinh, 1930–
The art of Kim Sinh. [Series: World music library, vol. 61]. King: KICC 5161. 1991.

8723 Trân, Quang Hai, 1944–
Vietnamese zither: the water and the wind. Playa-Sound: PS 65103. [1993].

Oceania
Australia

Anthologies

8724 *Les Aborigènes: chants & danses de l'Australie du Nord.* Arion: ARN 64056. 1979.

8725 * *Australia: aboriginal music.* [Series: UNESCO collection]. Auvidis: D 8040. 1959–69.

8726 *Australia: songs of the aborigines and traditional music of Papua, New Guinea.* Lyrichord: LYRCD 7331. 1963–64.

8727 *Dawn until dusk: tribal song and didgeridoo.* (Adam Plack and others). Australian Music International: AMI 3003-2. [1992].

Individual Artists or Groups

8728 Bogle, Eric, 1944–
Scraps of paper. Flying Fish: FF 70311. 1983.

8729 Hudson, David
Rainbow serpent. Celestial Harmonies: 13096-2. 1995.

8730 * Maralung, Alan
Bunggridj-bunggridj: Wangga songs. [Series: Traditional music of the world, vol. 4]. Smithsonian/ Folkways: SF 40430. 1988.

8731 Roach, Archie
Charcoal lane. Hightone: HCD 8037. 1992.

8732 * Yothu Yindi
Tribal voice. Hollywood: 61288-2. 1992.

Hawaii

See chapter 31, "Folk and Traditional Musics of the United States and Canada"

New Caledonia

8733 *Chants Kanaks = Kanak songs: feasts and lullabies.* Le Chant du Monde: LDX 274 909. 1984–87.

New Hebrides

See Vanuatu

New Zealand

8734 *He toa takatini: a selection of authentic Maori songs & chants.* Ode: CD ODE 1007. [1987].

8735 *Maori songs of New Zealand.* Smithsonian/ Folkways: 4433. AC. [1952].

Papua New Guinea

8736 *Aborigines of Papua New Guinea: music from the Sepik Province.* PlayaSound: PS 65107. 1992.

8737 * *Musiques de Papouasie Nouvelle Guinée = Music of Papua New Guinea.* Buda: 92570-2. 1992–93.

8738 *Papua New Guinea: the coast of the Western Province.* Jecklin: JD 655-2. 1963–64.

8739 *Voices of the rainforest.* Rykodisc: RCD 10173. [1991].

See also 8726

Polynesia

8740 *Percussions polynesiennes = South Pacific drums.* PlayaSound: PS 65066. [1990].

8741 *South Pacific aparima.* Manuiti/PlayaSound: PS 65092. 1965–75.

8742 ** *South Pacific songs and rhythms.* Playa-Sound: PS 65108. 1985.

8743 *Spirit of Polynesia.* Saydisc: CD-SDL403. 1978–88.

Solomon Islands

8744 *Îles Salomon: ensemble de flûtes de Pan 'aré 'aré = 'Are'are panpipe ensembles.* Le Chant du Monde: LDX274 961/62. 2CD set. 1974–75.

8745 *Îles Salomon: musique de Guadalcanal.* Ocora: C 580049. 1970.

8746 *Polyphonies des Îles Salomon = Polyphonies of the Solomon Islands.* Le Chant du Monde: LDX 274 663. 1974.

8747 *Solomon Islands: Fataleka and Baegu music from Malaita.* [Series: UNESCO collection]. Auvidis: D 8027. 1969–70.

Tahiti

Anthologies

8748 *Tahiti: belle epoque* [vol. 1]: *all time Tahitian favorites.* Manuiti/PlayaSound: S 65807. 1940–67.

8749 *Tahiti: belle epoque, vol. 2: Mila et Loma.* Manuiti/PlayaSound: S 65809. [196?].

8750 *Tahiti: belle epoque, vol. 3: Original Barefoot Boys from the 60s.* Manuiti/PlayaSound: S 65811. 1967–68.

8751 *Tahiti: belle epoque, vol. 4: songs of the atolls and the islands.* Manuiti/PlayaSound: S 65816. 1955–66.

8752 *Vahine: chanteuses de Tahiti.* PlayaSound: PS 65038. [1989].

Individual Groups

8753 Royal Tahitian Dance Company
The Royal Tahitian Dance Company. Monitor: MCD 71758. [1974].

8754 * Tahitian Choir
Rapa iti. Triloka: 7192-2. 1993.

8755 * Temaeva

Coco's Temaeva: royal folkloric group of Tahiti. Manuiti/PlayaSound: S 65185. 1966–87.

Tuvalu

8756   *Tuvalu: a Polynesian atoll society.* [Series: Anthology of Pacific music, vol. 5]. Pan: 2055. 1990.

Vanuatu (New Hebrides)

8757   *Vanuatu (Nouvelles-Hébriden = New Hebrides): singsing-danis kastom = musiques coutumières = custom music.* VDE-Gallo: CD-796. 1972–77.

APPENDIXES

SUPPLIERS OF SCORES

Music Suppliers and Ordering

Ordering printed music may require new procedures in a library's general acquisitions department, especially because most book distributors do not handle printed music. Most music is published by firms outside the general book trade, and nearly all musical works may be published in more than one format. The distributors below specialize in music and have staff who can offer advice and assistance.

When ordering, specify composer, title, instrumentation for the version of the work desired, publisher and publisher's number, price, and, most essentially, the format (i.e., score, score and parts, parts alone, piano-vocal score, orchestral score, or chamber score).

General Music Distributors in the United States

Broude Brothers, Ltd.
   141 White Oaks Road
   Williamstown, MA 01267
   (413) 458-8131 phone and fax

Educational Music Service
   13 Elkay Drive
   Chester, NY 10918
   (914) 469-5790 phone
   (914) 469-5817 fax

Theodore Front Musical Literature, Inc.
   16122 Cohasset Street
   Van Nuys, CA 91406
   (818) 994-1902 phone
   (818) 994-0419 fax
   71431.1732@compuserve.com

J. W. Pepper & Son, Inc.
   P.O. Box 850
   Valley Forge, PA 19482-9985
   (800) 345-6296 phone
   (610) 993-0563 fax
   cslater@jwpepper.com

General Music Distributors in Europe

Blackwell's Music Library Services
  Hythe Bridge Street
  Oxford OX1 2ET
  United Kingdom
  011-44-1865-792792, ext. 294, phone
  011-44-1865-249483 fax

Otto Harrassowitz
  P.O. Box 2929
  Taunusstrasse 5
  65019 Wiesbaden
  Germany
  49-611-5300 phone
  49-611-530-56-0 fax
  service@harrassowitz.de

  North American office
    P.O. Box 10
    Columbia, MD 21045-0010
    (800) 348-6886 phone
    (410) 964-3013 fax
    service@ottosvc.com

Specialized Music Distributors

The following suppliers specialize in music for a particular instrument or group of instruments:

Music for Brass

Robert King Music Sales, Inc.
  140 Main Street
  North Easton, MA 02356-1499
  no telephone number
  (508) 238-2571 fax

Music for Double Bass

Lemur Music Company
  P.O. Box 1137
  San Juan Capistrano, CA 92693
  (800) 246-2277 phone
  (714) 493-8565 fax

Music for Guitar

Editions Orphée
  1240 Clubview Boulevard N
  Columbus, OH 43235-1226
  (614) 846-9517 phone
  (614) 846-9794 fax
  mophee@iwaynet.net

Guitar Solo
  1411 Clement Street
  San Francisco, CA 94118
  (415) 896-1144 phone
  (415) 896-1155 fax

Music for Harp

International Music Service
  133 West 69th Street
  New York, NY 10023
  (212) 874-3360 phone
  (212) 580-9829 fax

Lyon & Healy
  168 North Ogden
  Chicago, IL 60607
  attn: Accessory Dept.
  (800) 621-3881 phone
  (312) 786-1881 phone
  (312) 226-1502 fax
  lyonhealy@earthlink.net

Vanderbilt Music Company
  P.O. Box 456
  Bloomington, IN 47402
  (800) 533-7200 phone
  (812) 333-5255 phone
  (812) 333-5257 fax

Music for Percussion

Steve Weiss Music
  P.O. Box 20885
  Philadelphia, PA 19141
  (215) 329-1637 phone
  (215) 324-3999 phone
  (215) 329-3519 fax

Music for Recorder

Courtly Music Unlimited, Inc.
  84 Main Street
  Warrensburg, NY 12885
  (800) 274-2443 phone
  (518) 623-2869 fax
  courtlym@aol.com

SUPPLIERS OF SOUND RECORDINGS

Mail-Order Distributors

These companies distribute a variety of labels, and many offer discounts to libraries. For domestic recordings, the distributors who handle the greatest range of labels and types of music are Audio Buff, CD One Stop, Professional Media Service, and Valley Record Distributors. Annotations indicate a particular area of specialty. "Catalog" means that the buyer is advised to obtain the distributor's catalog before ordering anything.

Artex Publication Exchange, Inc.
   8306 Mills Drive, Suite 241
   Miami, FL 33183
   (305) 256-0162 phone
   (305) 252-1813 fax

      Cuban music. Catalog

Audio Buff Company, Inc.
   P.O. Box 2628
   Athens, OH 45701-5428
   (614) 593-3014 phone
   (614) 592-6693 fax
   mraudbuffco@delphi.com

      Domestic and imported labels. Will special
      order

Brazil CDs
   P.O. Box 382282
   Cambridge, MA 02238
   (617) 524-5030 phone

      Brazilian music. Imports. Catalog

Canyon Records and Indian Arts
   4143 North Sixteenth Street
   Phoenix, AZ 85016
   (602) 266-4823 phone
   (602) 265-2402 fax

      North American Indians. Catalog

CD One Stop
   13 Francis J. Clarke Circle
   Bethel, CT 06801
   (800) 388-8889 phone
   (203) 798-8852 fax

      U.S.–produced or U.S.–distributed labels.
      Catalog

County Sales
   P.O. Box 191
   Floyd, VA 24091
   (540) 745-2001 phone
   (540) 745-2008 fax

      North American traditional music. Catalog

Descarga Latin Music Mail-Order Company
328 Flatbush Avenue, Suite 180
Brooklyn, NY 11238
(800) 377-2647, ext. 25, phone
(718) 693-1316 fax
descarga@aol.com

    Latin American music. Catalog

Elderly Instruments
1100 North Washington
P.O. Box 14210
Lansing, MI 48901
(517) 372-7890 phone
(517) 372-4161 phone
(517) 372-5155 fax
web@elderly.com

    North American and international traditional
    music. Catalog

Interstate Music
20 Endwell Road
Bexhill-on-Sea
East Sussex TN4 01EA
United Kingdom
011-44-1424-219847 phone

    Blues and international music. British labels.
    Catalog

Irish Books
580 Broadway, Room 1103
New York, NY 10012
(212) 274-1923 phone
(212) 431-5413 fax
acpmpf@inch.com

    Irish music. Catalog

Ladyslipper
P.O. Box 3124
Durham, NC 27715
(800) 634-6044 phone
(919) 683-1570 phone
(800) 577-7892 fax
info@ladyslipper.org

    Women's, gay, and lesbian music. Catalog

Marginal Distribution
277 George Street North
Unit 102
Peterborough, Ontario K9J 3G9
Canada
(705) 745-2326 phone and fax
marginal@ptbo.igs.net

    Contemporary avant-garde; alternative jazz and
    rock. Small labels. Catalog

Nonsequitur, Inc.
P.O. Box 344
Albuquerque, NM 87103-0344
(505) 224-9483 phone and fax

    Contemporary avant-garde. Small labels.
    Catalog

North Country Distributors
Cadence Building
Redwood, NY 13679
(315) 287-2852 phone
(315) 287-2860 fax
northcountry@cadencebuilding.com

    Contemporary avant-garde; alternative jazz and
    rock. Small labels. Catalog

Professional Media Service Corp.
19122 S. Vermont Ave.
Gardena, CA 90248
(800) 223-7672 phone
(310) 532-9024 phone
(800) 253-8853 fax
(310) 532-0131 fax

    U.S.-produced or U.S.-distributed labels.

Roots & Rhythm
P.O. Box 2216
El Cerrito, CA 94577
(510) 614-5353 phone
(510) 614-8833 fax
roots@hooked.net
http://www.bluesworld.com/roots.html

    North American and international traditional
    music. Classic blues and rhythm and blues.
    Catalog

Rounder Mail Order
One Camp Street
Cambridge, MA 02140
(800) 443-4727 phone
(617) 661-6308 phone
(617) 868-8769 fax
info@rounder.com
order@rounder.com
http://www.rounder.com

    North American and international traditional
    music. Catalog

Silo Music
P.O. Box 429
South Main Street
Waterbury, VT 05676-0429
(800) 342-0295 phone
(802) 244-5178 phone
(802) 244-6128 fax
order@silo=alcazar.com

> Folk and new age. Catalog

Stern's Music U.S., Inc.
598 Broadway, 7th Floor
New York, NY 10012
(212) 925-1648 phone
(212) 925-1689 fax

> African, Middle Eastern, and other international music. Catalog

Valley Record Distributors
P.O. Box 2057
Woodland, CA 95776
(800) 845-8444 phone
(800) 999-1794 fax
valley@vrd.com

> U.S.–produced and U.S.–distributed labels. Catalog

Wayside Music
P.O. Box 8427
Silver Spring, MD 20907
(301) 589-1819 fax

> Contemporary avant-garde; alternative jazz and rock. Catalog

World Music Institute
49 W. 27th Street, Suite 930
New York, NY 10001
(212) 545-7536 phone
(212) 889-2771 fax
worldmus@aol.com

> African, Asian, Middle Eastern, European, North and South American traditional music. Imports. Catalog

Individual Labels

Specialty labels not included in *Schwann Opus* or *Schwann Spectrum* (see p. 573, "Sound Recordings," "General,") are listed here.

Ansonia Records
380 Kamena Street
Fairview, NJ 07022
(201) 945-7600 phone
(201) 945-9042 fax

Archives of Traditional Music
Morrison Hall
Indiana University
Bloomington, IN 47405

Augusta Heritage Recordings
100 Campus Drive
Davis & Elkins College
Elkins, WV 26241
(304) 637-1209 phone
(304) 637-1317 fax
augusta@DnE.wvnet.edu

Banjar Records
P.O. Box 32164
7440 University Avenue NE
Minneapolis, MN 55432
(612) 755-9829 phone

Bel-Aire Records
7208 South Harlem Avenue
Bridgeview, IL 60455
(708) 594-5182 phone
(708) 448-5494 fax

Benson Music Group
365 Great Circle Road
Nashville, TN 37228
(800) 688-2505 phone
(615) 742-6848 phone

John C. Campbell Folk School
Route 1, Box 14A
Brasstown, NC 28902
(704) 837-2775 phone
(704) 837-8637 fax

Charly Records Limited
156–166 Ilderton Road
London SE15 1NT
United Kingdom
011-44-071-639-8603 phone
011-44-071-639-2532 fax

Documentary Arts
P.O. Box 140244
Dallas, TX 75214
(214) 824-3377 phone

Folklore Village Farm Records
See Wisconsin Folklife Center

Folkways
See Smithsonian/Folkways Recordings

Grey Eagle Records
Extension Publications
115 South Fifth Street
Columbia, MO 65211

Malaco/Savoy Records
P.O. Box 9287
Jackson, MS 39287-9287
(800) 962-5226 phone
(601) 977-4164 fax

Minnesota Historical Society Press
Order Dept. 105
345 Kellogg Boulevard West
St. Paul, MN 55102-1906
(800) 647-7827 phone
(612) 297-3243 phone
(612) 297-1345 fax

Modal Music
P.O. Box 4614
Oak Brook, IL 60521

Mountain Heritage Center
Western Carolina University
Cullowhee, NC 28723
(704) 227-7129 phone

Multicultural Media
RR 3, P.O. Box 6655
Granger Road
Barre, VT 05641
(800) 550-9675 phone
(802) 229-1834 fax
mcm@multiculturalmedia.com

Music Educators National Conference
Publication Sales
1902 Association Drive
Reston, VA 22091

North Star Appli
1451 W. Mason Street
Green Bay, WI 54303

Organization of American States/Inter-American
Musical Editions
1889 F Street NW, 2nd Floor
Washington, DC 20006

Qbadisc
P.O. Box 1256, Old Chelsea Station
New York, NY 10011

Savoy
See Malaco

Smithsonian/Folkways Recordings (for cassette
copies of original Folkways LPs)
414 Hungerford Drive, Suite 444
Rockville, MD 20850
(800) 410-9815 phone
(301) 443-2314 phone
(301) 443-1819 fax
folkways@aol.com

Smithsonian Recordings (for CDs on the
Smithsonian or Smithsonian/Folkways labels)
P.O. Box 700
Holmes, PA 19043
(800) 669-1559 phone
(800) 927-7377 phone
(610) 586-3232 fax

Southern Culture Records
c/o Center for the Study of Southern Culture
The University of Mississippi
University, MS 38677

Sparrow Distribution
101 Winners Circle
Brentwood, TN 37027
(800) 877-4443 phone
(615) 371-6980 fax

Tennessee Folklore Society
Middle Tennessee State University
P.O. Box 201
Murfreesboro, TN 37132

Thimbleberry Recordings
c/o Postman North
Route 1, Box 195
Calumet, MI 49913

Time-Life
1450 E. Pasham Road
Richmond, VA 23280
(800) 621-7026 phone
(804) 261-1397 fax
http:\\www.timelifecs.com

Ubik Sound
P.O. Box 4771
Albuquerque, NM 87196
(505) 843-9396 phone

Vee-Jay Limited Partnership
8857 W. Olympic Boulevard, Suite 200
Beverly Hills, CA 90211
(310) 657-9814 phone
(310) 657-2331 fax
allnations@earthlink.net

Viva Voce
See Irish Books

Wisconsin Folklife Center
100 South 2nd Street
Mount Horeb, WI 53572

Word Distribution International
Distribution Center
7300 Imperial Drive
P.O. Box 2518
Waco, TX 76702
(800) 933-9673 phone
(817) 772-4200 phone
(817) 772-5474 fax

World Music Press
P.O. Box 2565
Danbury, CT 06813
(800) 810-2040 phone
(203) 748-1131 phone
(203) 748-3432 fax
wmpress@aol.com

World Renowned Sounds (WRS)
Box 91906
Cleveland, OH 44101

BIBLIOGRAPHIC RESOURCES

Scores

Bassoon Music

Beebe, Jon P. *Music for unaccompanied solo bassoon: an annotated bibliography.* Jefferson, N.C.: McFarland, 1990. 0-8995-0463-9.

Bulling, Burchard. *Fagott Bibliographie.* Wilhelmshaven, Germany: F. Noetzel, 1989. 3-7959-0315-7.

Jansen, Will. *The bassoon: its history, construction, makers, players, and music.* 5 vols. Buren, The Netherlands: Uitgeverij F. Knuf, 1978. 9-060-27446-6 (set).

Koenigsbeck, Bodo. *Bassoon bibliography.* Monteux, France: Musica Rara, 1994. 2-95006-462-0.

Wilkins, Wayne. *The index of bassoon music.* Magnolia, Ark.: Music Register, 1976; supplements: 1976–77, 1978.

Brass Music

Anderson, Paul G. *Brass ensemble music guide.* Evanston, Ill.: Instrumentalist, 1978.

———. *Brass solo and study material music guide.* Evanston, Ill.: Instrumentalist, 1976.

Decker, Richard G. *A bibliography of music for three heterogeneous brass instruments alone and in chamber ensembles.* Oneonta, N.Y.: Swift-Dorr, 1976.

Fasman, Mark J. *Brass bibliography: sources on the history, literature, pedagogy, performance, and acoustics of brass instruments.* Bloomington: Indiana University Press, 1990. 0-253-32130-1.

Horne, Aaron. *Brass music of Black composers: a bibliography.* Westport, Conn.: Greenwood Publications Group, 1996. 0-313-29826-2.

Thompson, J. Mark. *French music for low brass instruments: an annotated bibliography.* Bloomington: Indiana University Press, 1994. 0-253-35993-7.

Chamber Music

Baron, John H. *Chamber music: a research and information guide.* New York: Garland, 1987. 0-8240-8346-6.

Berger, Melvin. *Guide to chamber music: a listener's companion.* New York: Anchor/Doubleday, 1990. 0-385-41149-9.

Cobbett, Walter Willson. *Cyclopedic survey of chamber music.* 2nd ed. New York: Oxford University Press, 1963.

Hinson, Maurice. *The piano in chamber ensemble: an annotated guide.* Bloomington: Indiana University Press, 1978. 0-253-34493-X.

Rangel-Ribeiro, Victor, and Robert Markel. *Chamber music: an international guide to works and their instrumentation.* New York: Facts on File, 1992. 0-8160-2296-8.

Chamber Music for Winds

Gillespie, James E. *The reed trio: an annotated bibliography of original published works.* Warren, Mich.: Information Coordinators, 1971.

Helm, Sanford M. *Catalog of chamber music for wind instruments.* Rev. and corrected printing. New York: Da Capo Press, 1969.

Houser, Roy. *Catalogue of chamber music for woodwind instruments.* New York: Da Capo Press, 1973.

Peters, Harry B. *The literature of the woodwind quintet.* Metuchen, N.J.: Scarecrow Press, 1971.

Secrist-Schmedes, Barbara. *Wind chamber music: winds with piano and woodwind quintets, an annotated guide.* Metuchen, N.J.: Scarecrow Press, 1996. 0-8108-3111-2.

Choral Music

Choral music in print. Philadelphia: Musicdata, 1985– . vol. 1: *Sacred choral music,* 2nd ed., 1985, with 1988 and 1992 supplements. vol. 2: *Secular choral music,* 2nd ed., 1987, with 1991 and 1993 supplements.

DeVenney, David P. *Nineteenth-century American choral music: an annotated guide.* Berkeley, Calif.: Fallen Leaf Press, 1987. 0-914913-08-5.

——— and Craig R. Johnson. *The chorus in opera: a guide to the repertory.* Metuchen, N.J.: Scarecrow Press, 1992. 0-8108-2620-8.

Green, Jonathan D. *A conductor's guide to choral-orchestral works.* Metuchen, N.J.: Scarecrow Press, 1993. 0-8108-2712-3.

Laster, James. *Catalogue of choral music arranged in Biblical order.* Metuchen, N.J.: Scarecrow Press, 1983. 0-8108-1592-3.

White, Evelyn Davidson. *Choral music by African-American composers: a selected, annotated bibliography.* 2nd ed. Lanham, Md.: Scarecrow Press, 1995. 0-8108-3037-X.

White, J. Perry. *Twentieth-century choral music: an annotated bibliography of music suitable for use by high school choirs.* 2nd ed. Metuchen, N.J.: Scarecrow Press, 1990. 0-8108-2394-2.

Clarinet Music

Brymer, Jack. *Clarinet.* 1st American ed. New York: Schirmer Books, 1977. 0-02-871430-X.

Gee, Harry R. *Clarinet Solos de concours, 1897–1980: an annotated bibliography.* Bloomington: Indiana University Press, 1981. 0-253-13577-X.

Pino, David. *The clarinet and clarinet playing.* New York: Scribner's, 1980. 0-684-16624-0.

Rehfeldt, Phillip. *New directions for clarinet.* Rev. ed. Berkeley: University of California Press, 1994. 0-520-03379-5.

Thurston, Frederick. *Clarinet technique.* 4th ed. New York: Oxford University Press, 1985. 0-19-322364-3.

Wilkins, Wayne. *The index of clarinet music.* Magnolia, Ark.: Music Register, 1975.

Double Bass Music

Grodner, Murray. *Comprehensive catalog of available literature for the double bass.* 3rd ed. Albuquerque: Lemur Musical Research, 1974.

Flute Music

Howell, Thomas. *The avant-garde flute: a handbook for composers and flutists.* Berkeley: University of California Press, 1974. 0-520-02305-6.

Pellerite, James J. *A handbook of literature for the flute: a compilation of graded method materials, solos, and ensemble music for flutes.* Rev. 3rd ed. Bloomington, Ind.: Zālo Publications, 1978. 0-931200-69-5.

Pierreuse, Bernard. *Flûte littérature.* Paris: Société des Éditions Jobert, 1982. Distributed in U.S. by Édition musicales transatlantiques. 2-8589-4000-2.

Toff, Nancy. *The flute book.* 2nd ed. New York: Oxford University Press, 1996. 0-19-510502-8.

Vester, Frans. *Flute music of the 18th century: an annotated bibliography.* Monteux, France: Musica Rara, 1985. 2-9500-6461-2.

———. *Flute repertoire catalog: 10,000 titles.* London: Musica Rara, 1967.

Wilkins, Wayne. *The index of flute music, including The index of baroque trio sonatas.* Magnolia, Ark.: Music Register, 1974; supplements: 1974, 1975, 1976–77, 1978.

Guitar Music

Mijndert, Jape. *Classical guitar music in print.* Music-in-print series, vol. 7. Philadelphia: Musicdata, 1989. 0-88478-025-2.

Stimpson, Michael. *The guitar: a guide for students and teachers.* New York: Oxford University Press, 1988. 0-19-317419-7 (hardcover), 0-19-317421-9 (pbk.).

Harp Music

Michel, Catherine, and François Lesure. *Répertoire de la musique pour harpe publiée du XVIIe au début du XIXe siècle: bibliographie.* Paris: Aux Amateurs de Livres International, 1990.

Palkovic, Mark. *Harp music bibliography: compositions for solo harp and harp ensemble.* Bloomington: Indiana University Press, 1995. 0-253-32887-X.

Torgerson, Helena Stone. *Harp music: a digest, classified alphabetically and in grades according to degrees of difficulty.* Chicago: Lyon and Healy, 1916.

Zingel, Hans Joachim. *Verzeichnis der Harfenmusik.* Hofheim am Taunus: Hofmeister, 1965.

Horn Music

Brüchle, Bernhard. *Horn-Bibliographie, I–III.* Wilhelmshaven, Germany: Heinrichshofen, 1970.

Oboe or English Horn Music

Gifford, Virginia Snodgrass. *Music for oboe, oboe d'amore, and English horn: a bibliography of materials at the Library of Congress.* Westport, Conn.: Greenwood Press, 1983. 0-3132-3762-X.

Haynes, Bruce. *Music for oboe, 1650–1800: a bibliography.* 2nd ed. Berkeley, Calif.: Fallen Leaf Press, 1992. 0-914013-15-8.

McMullen, William Wallace. *Soloistic English horn literature from 1736–1984.* Stuyvesant, N.Y.: Pendragon Press, 1994. 0-918728-78-9.

Wilkins, Wayne. *The index of oboe music, including The index of baroque trio sonatas.* Magnolia, Ark.: Music Register, 1976; supplements: 1977, 1978.

Orchestral Music

Daniels, David. *Orchestral music: a handbook.* 3rd ed. Metuchen, N.J.: Scarecrow Press, 1996. 0-8108-3228-3.

The Edward A. Fleischer Collection of Orchestral Music in the Free Library of Philadelphia: a cumulative catalog, 1929–1977. Boston: G. K. Hall, 1979. 0-8161-7942-5.

Farish, Margaret K. *Orchestral music in print.* Philadelphia: Musicdata, 1979. 0-88478-010-4. 1983 supplement, 0-88478-014-7. Master index, 1994, 0-88478-034-1.

Green, Jonathan D. *A conductor's guide to choral-orchestral works.* Metuchen, N.J.: Scarecrow Press, 1994. 0-8108-2712-3.

Hinson, Maurice. *Music for piano and orchestra: an annotated guide.* Enl. ed. Bloomington: Indiana University Press, 1993. 0-253-33953-7.

Koshgarian, Richard. *American orchestral music: a performance catalog.* Metuchen, N.J.: Scarecrow Press, 1992. 0-8108-2632-1.

Saltonstall, Cecilia Drinker, and Henry Saltonstall. *A new catalog of music for small orchestra.* Clifton, N.J.: European American Music, 1978. 0-913574-14-7.

Organ Music

Arnold, Corliss Richard. *Organ literature: a comprehensive survey.* 3rd ed. 2 vols. Metuchen, N.J.: Scarecrow, 1995. 0-8108-2964-9 (v.1), 0-8108-2965-7 (v.2), 0-8108-2970-3 (set).

Kratzenstein, Marilou. *Survey of organ literature and editions.* Ames: Iowa State University Press, 1980. 0-8138-1050-7.

Lukas, Viktor. *A guide to organ music.* Portland, Ore.: Amadeus, 1989. 0-93134-010-1.

Organ music in print. 2nd ed. Philadelphia: Music-data, 1984. 0-88478-015-5. 1990 supplement, 0-88478-026-0.

Percussion Music

Bajzek, Dieter. *Percussion: an annotated bibliography, with special emphasis on contemporary notation and performance.* Metuchen, N.J.: Scarecrow Press, 1988. 0-8108-2107-9.

Percussive Arts Society. *Solo and ensemble literature for percussion.* Terre Haute, Ind.: Percussive Arts Society, 1978.

Siwe, Thomas. *Percussion ensemble and solo literature.* Champaign, Ill.: Media Press, 1993. 0-9645891-0-5. This is succeeded by the following two books:

————. *Percussion ensemble literature.* Champaign, Ill.: Media Press, 1996. 0-9635891-2-1.

————. *Percussion solo literature.* Champaign, Ill.: Media Press, 1995. 0-9635891-1-3.

Vincent, David W. *A percussionist's guide to orchestral excerpts.* Columbia, S.C.: Broad River, 1980. 0-932614-01-9.

Piano or Harpsichord Music

Arneson, Arne Jon. *The harpsichord booke: being a plaine & simple index to printed collections of musick by different masters of the harpsichord, spinnet, clavichord, & virginall.* Madison, Wisc.: Index House, 1986. 0-936697-00-8.

Chang, Frederic Ming, and Albert Faurot. *Concert piano repertoire: a manual of solo literature for artists and performers.* Metuchen, N.J.: Scarecrow, 1976. 0-8108-0937-0.

————. *Team piano repertoire: a manual of music for multiple players at one or more pianos.* Metuchen, N.J.: Scarecrow, 1976. 0-8108-0937-0.

Friskin, James. *Music for the piano: a handbook of concert and teaching material from 1580 to 1952.* New York: Dover, 1973. 0-486-22918-1.

Fuszek, Rita M. *Piano music in collections: an index.* Warren, Mich.: Information Coordinators, 1982. 0-89990-012-7.

Hinson, Maurice. *Guide to the pianist's repertoire.* 2nd rev. enl. ed. Bloomington: Indiana University Press, 1987. 0-253-32656-7.

————. *Music for more than one piano: an annotated guide.* Bloomington: Indiana University Press, 1983. 0-253-33952-9.

————. *Music for piano and orchestra: an annotated guide.* Enl. ed. Bloomington: Indiana University Press, 1993. 0-253-33953-7.

————. *The pianist's guide to transcriptions, arrangements, and paraphrases.* Bloomington: Indiana University Press, 1990. 0-253-32745-8.

Horne, Aaron. *Keyboard music of Black composers: a bibliography.* Westport, Conn.: Greenwood Press, 1992. 0-313-27939-X.

Lubin, Ernest. *The piano duet: a guide for pianists.* New York: Da Capo Press, 1976. 0-306-80045-4.

McGraw, Cameron. *Piano duet repertoire: music originally written for one piano four hands.* Bloomington: Indiana University Press, 1981. 0-253-14766-2.

Meggett, Joan M. *Keyboard music by women composers: a catalog and bibliography.* Westport, Conn.: Greenwood Press, 1981. 0-313-22833-7.

Recorder Music

Letteron, Claude. *Catalogue général: musique pour flûte à bec = General Katalog: Musik für Blockflöte = General catalogue: music for recorder = Catálogo general: música para flauta dulce.* Paris: Éditions Aug. Zurfluh, 1989. 2-87750-056-X.

Saxophone Music

Gee, Harry R. *Saxophone soloists and their music, 1844–1985: an annotated bibliography.* Bloomington: Indiana University Press, 1986. 0-253-35091-3.

Londeix, Jean-Marie. *150 years of music for saxophone: bibliographical index of music and educational literature for the saxophone, 1844–1994.* Cherry Hill, N.J.: Roncorp, 1994. 0-939103-04-4.

Wilkins, Wayne. *The index of saxophone music.* Magnolia, Ark.: Music Register, 1979.

Score Anthologies

Heyer, Anna Harriett. *Historical sets, collected editions, and monuments of music: a guide to their contents.* 3rd ed. 2 vols. Chicago: American Library Association, 1980. 0-8389-0288-X (set).

Hilton, Ruth B. *An index to early music in selected anthologies.* Clifton, N.J.: European American Music Corp., 1978.

Murray, Sterling E. *Anthologies of music: an annotated index.* 2nd ed. Warren, Mich.: Harmonie Park Press, 1992. 0-89990-061-5.

Perone, James E. *Musical anthologies for analytical study: a bibliography.* Westport, Conn.: Greenwood Press, 1995. 0-313-29595-6.

String Music

Farish, Margaret K. *String music in print.* 2nd ed. Philadelphia: Musicdata, 1980. Supplement: 1984. 0-88478-016-3.

Trombone Music

Arling, Harry J. *Trombone chamber music: an annotated bibliography.* Enl. 2nd ed. Clearwater, Fla.: Brass Press, 1983.

Bäumer, Hermann, Reinke Eisenberg, and Franz Schulte-Huermann. *Annotated bibliography of trombone literature = Kommentierte Bibliographie der Literatur für Posaune.* Detmold, Germany: Edition Piccolo, 1995– . Multiple vols.

Everett, Thomas G. *Annotated guide to bass trombone literature.* 3rd ed., rev. and enl. Clearwater, Fla.: Brass Press, 1985.

Gregory, Robin. *The trombone: the instrument and its music.* New York: Praeger, 1973.

Kagarice, Vern. *Annotated guide to trombone solos with band and orchestra.* Lebanon, Ind.: Studio Publications Recordings, 1974.

———. *Solos for the student trombonist: an annotated bibliography.* Clearwater, Fla.: Brass Press, 1979.

Werden, David R., and Dennis W. Winter. *Euphonium music guide.* New London, Conn.: Whaling Music, 1983.

Trumpet or Cornet Music

Carnovale, Norbert, and Paul F. Doerksen. *Twentieth-century music for trumpet and orchestra: an annotated bibliography.* Special supplement to the February 1994 *ITG Journal.* 2nd rev. ed. Clearwater, Fla.: Brass Press, 1994. 0-914282-81-2.

Collver, Michael, and Bruce Dickey. *A catalog of music for the cornet.* Bloomington: Indiana University Press, 1995. 0-253-20974-9.

Tuba Music

Bevan, Clifford. *The tuba family.* New York: Scribners, 1978. 0-684-15477-3.

Mason, J. Kent. *The tuba handbook.* Toronto: Sonante Pub., 1977. 0-969-06560-4.

Morris, R. Winston, and Edward Goldstein. *The tuba source book.* Bloomington: Indiana University Press, 1995. 0-253-32889-6.

Werden, David R., and Dennis W. Winter. *Euphonium music guide.* New London, Conn.: Whaling Music, 1983.

Viola Music

Barrett, Henry. *The viola: complete guide for teachers and students.* 2nd ed., rev. and enl. Tuscaloosa: University of Alabama Press, 1978.

Johnson, Christine Ann. *Viola source materials: an annotated bibliography.* D.M. thesis, Florida State University, 1988.

Letz, Hans. *Music for the violin and viola.* New York: Rinehart & Company, 1948. Lists works featuring solo violin and solo viola, not violin and viola duets.

Wilkins, Wayne. *The index of viola music.* Magnolia, Ark.: Music Register, 1976. Supplements: 1976–77, 1978.

Williams, Michael D. *Music for viola.* Detroit studies in music bibliography, no. 42. Detroit: Information Coordinators, 1979.

Zeyringer, Franz. *Literatur für Viola: Verzeichnis der Werke für Viola-Solo, Duos mit Viola, Trios mit Viola, Viola-Solo mit Begleitung, Blockflöte mit Viola, Gesang mit Viola und der Schul- und Studienwerke für Viola = Literature for viola: catalogue of works for viola solo, duos with viola, trios with viola, solo viola with accompaniment, recorder with viola, voice with viola, and methods, etudes and exercises for viola.* Neue, erw. Ausg. Hartberg, Austria: Schonwetter, 1985.

Violin Music

Edlund, Harry. *Music for solo violin, unaccompanied.* High Wycombe, Bucks, England: P. Marcan Publications, 1989.

Johnson, Rose-Marie. *Violin music by women composers: a bio-bibliographical guide.* Westport, Conn.: Greenwood Press, 1989. 0-313-26652-2.

Letz, Hans. *Music for the violin and viola.* New York: Rinehart & Company, 1948. Lists works featuring solo violin or solo viola, not violin and viola duets.

Wilkins, Wayne. *The index of violin music.* Magnolia, Ark.: Music Register, n.d. Supplements: 1973, 1974, 1975, 1976–77, 1978.

Violoncello Music

Cowling, Elizabeth. *The cello.* New York: Scribner's, 1975. Nearly half the book is an essay on cello literature that includes several useful lists.

Homuth, Donald. *Cello music since 1960: a bibliography of solo, chamber, and orchestral works for the solo cellist.* Fallen Leaf reference books in music, 26. Berkeley, Calif.: Fallen Leaf Press, 1994. 0-914913-27-1.

Kenneson, Claude. *Bibliography of cello ensemble music.* Detroit: Harmonie Park Press, 1974.

Markevitch, Dmitry. *The solo cello: a bibliography of the unaccompanied violoncello literature.* Berkeley, Calif.: Fallen Leaf Press, 1989. 0-914913-12-3.

Pleeth, William. *Cello.* Compiled and ed. by Nona Pyron. New York: Schirmer Books, 1982. 0-02-872060-1. Lists "neglected but recommended cello works."

Wilkins, Wayne. *The index of cello music, including The index of baroque trio sonatas.* Magnolia, Ark.: Music Register, 1979.

Vocal Music

Bloom, Ken. *American song: the complete musical theatre companion, 1900–1994.* 2nd ed. 2 vols. New York: Schirmer Books, 1995. 0-02-870484-3 (set).

———. *Hollywood song: the complete film and musical companion.* New York: Facts on File, 1995. 0-8160-2002-7.

Borroff, Edith. *American operas: a checklist.* Warren, Mich.: Harmonie Park Press, 1992. 0-89990-063-1.

Coffin, Berton. *The singer's repertoire.* 2nd ed. 5 vols. New York: Scarecrow Press, 1960–62.

DeCharms, Desiree, and Paul F. Breed. *Songs in collections: an index.* Detroit: Information Service, 1966.

Dunlap, Kay, and Barbara Winchester. *Vocal chamber music: a performer's guide.* New York: Garland, 1985. 0-8240-9003-0.

Espina, Noni. *Repertoire for the solo voice: a fully annotated guide to works for the solo voice published in modern editions and covering material from the 13th century to the present.* 2 vols. Metuchen, N.J.: Scarecrow Press, 1977. 0-8108-0943-5 (set).

Goleeke, Tom. *Literature for voice: an index of songs in collections and a source book for teachers of singing.* Metuchen, N.J.: Scarecrow Press, 1984. 0-8108-1702-0.

Goodfellow, William D. *SongCite: an index to popular songs.* New York: Garland, 1995. 0-8153-2059-0.

Havlice, Patricia Pate. *Popular song index.* Metuchen, N.J.: Scarecrow Press, 1975. 0-8108-0820-X. First supplement: 1978, 0-8108-1099-9; second supplement: 1984, 0-8108-1642-3; third supplement: 1989, 0-8108-2202-4.

Johnson, Harold Earle. *Operas on American subjects.* New York: Coleman-Ross, 1964.

Kagen, Sergius. *Music for the voice: a descriptive list of concert and teaching materials.* Rev. ed. Bloomington: Indiana University Press, 1968.

Laster, James. *Catalogue of vocal solos and duets arranged in Biblical order.* Metuchen, N.J.: Scarecrow Press, 1984. 0-8108-1748-9.

Lax, Roger. *The great song thesaurus.* 2nd ed., updated and expanded. New York: Oxford University Press, 1989. 0-19-505408-3.

Lissauer, Robert. *Lissauer's encyclopedia of popular music in America: 1888 to the present.* 2nd ed. New York: Facts on File, 1996. 0-8160-3238-6.

Lust, Patricia. *American vocal chamber music, 1945–1980: an annotated bibliography.* Westport, Conn.: Greenwood Press, 1985. 0-313-24599-1.

Lynch, Richard Chigley. *Musicals!: a directory of musical properties available for production.* 2nd ed. Chicago: American Library Association, 1994. 0-8389-0627-3.

Manning, Jane. *New vocal repertory: an introduction.* New York: Taplinger, 1987. 0-8008-5557-4 (pbk.).

Marco, Guy A. *Opera: a research and information guide.* New York: Garland, 1984. 0-8240-8999-5.

Nardone, Thomas R. *Classical vocal music in print.* Philadelphia: Musicdata, 1976. 1985 supplement by Gary S. Eslinger and F. Mark Daugherty. Musicdata, 1986. 0-88478-018-X. 1995 supplement by F. Mark Daugherty. Musicdata, 1995. 0-88478-035-X.

Northouse, Cameron. *Twentieth-century opera in England and the United States.* Boston: G. K. Hall, 1976. 0-8161-7896-8.

Ord, Alan J. *Songs for bass voice: an annotated guide to works for bass voice.* Metuchen, N.J.: Scarecrow Press, 1994. 0-8108-2897-9.

Parsons, Charles H. *An opera bibliography.* 2 vols. Lewiston, N.Y.: Edwin Mellen Press, 1995. 0-88946-416-2 (v.1), 0-88946-417-0 (v.2).

Sears, Minnie Earl. *Song index: an index to more than 12,000 songs in 177 song collections, comprising 262 volumes.* New York: H. W. Wilson, 1926. *Supplement: an index to more than 7000 songs in 104 song collections, comprising 124 volumes.* New York: H. W. Wilson, 1934.

Stubblebine, Donald J. *Broadway sheet music: a comprehensive listing of published music from Broadway and other stage shows, 1918–1993.* Jefferson, N.C.: McFarland, 1996. 0-7864-0047-1.

United States. Library of Congress. Music Division. *Dramatic music: catalogue of full scores in the collection of the Library of Congress.* New York: Da Capo Press, 1969.

Villamil, Victoria Etnier. *A singer's guide to the American art song, 1870–1980.* Metuchen, N.J.: Scarecrow Press, 1993. 0-8108-2774-3.

Woodwind Music

Voxman, Himie. *Woodwind solo and study material music guide.* Evanston, Ill.: Instrumentalist, 1975.

Sound Recordings

Listed here are further sources of information for collection development of sound recordings. Titles marked with an asterisk would be especially useful in collecting that goes beyond the limits of BML3.

General

Davis, Elizabeth A. *Index to the New World Recorded Anthology of American Music: a user's guide to the initial one hundred recordings.* New York: Norton, 1981.

Erlewine, Michael, and Scott Bultman, eds. *All music guide: the best CDs, albums and tapes.* 3rd ed. San Francisco: Miller Freeman, 1997.

Gray, Michael H. *Bibliography of discographies, vol. 3: popular music.* New York: Bowker, 1983.

O'Neil, Thomas. *The Grammys: for the record.* New York: Penguin, 1993.

*Schaefer, John. *New sounds: a listener's guide to new music.* New York: Harper & Row, 1987.

Schwann opus. Santa Fe: Stereophile Quarterly periodical, available by subscription or singly in many record stores. Current in-print listings for most domestically produced or distributed labels in classical music.

Schwann spectrum. Santa Fe: Stereophile Quarterly periodical, available by subscription or singly in many record stores. Current in-print listings for most domestically produced or distributed labels in jazz, rock, and other genres of popular music.

Shapiro, Nat, and Bruce Pollock, eds. *Popular music, 1920–1979: a revised cumulation.* Detroit: Gale, 1985.

Tudor, Dean. *Popular music, an annotated guide to recordings.* Littleton, Colo.: Libraries Unlimited, 1983.

Whitburn, Joel. *Top pop albums, 1955–1992.* Menomonee Falls, Wisc.: Record Research, 1993.

———. *Top pop singles, 1955–1996.* Menomonee Falls, Wisc.: Record Research, 1996.

African Music

See World Music

Asian Music

See World Music

Blues/Rhythm and Blues

Cohn, Lawrence. *Nothing but the blues: the music and the musicians,* pp. 410–13. New York: Abbeville Press, 1993.

Godrich, John, and Robert M. W. Dixon. *Blues and gospel records, 1890–1943.* 4th ed. New York: Oxford University Press, 1997.

Guralnick, Peter. *The listener's guide to the blues.* New York: Facts on File, 1982.

———. *Sweet soul music: rhythm and blues and the southern dream of freedom,* pp. 415–30. New York: Harper & Row, 1986.

Leadbitter, Mike and Neil Slaven. *Blues records, 1943–1970: a selective discography.* 2 vols. London: Record Information Services, 1987–94.

*Oliver, Paul, ed. *The new Blackwell guide to recorded blues.* Oxford: Blackwell, 1996.

Palmer, Robert. *Deep blues,* pp. 279–93. New York: Viking, 1981.

*Pruter, Robert, ed. *The Blackwell guide to soul recordings.* Oxford: Blackwell, 1993.

Whitburn, Joel. *Top r&b singles 1942–1995.* Menomonee Falls, Wisc.: Record Research, 1996.

Children's Music

*Jarnow, Jill. *All ears: how to choose and use recorded music for children.* New York: Penguin, 1991.

*Sale, Laurie. *Growing up with music: a guide to the best recorded music for children.* New York: Avon, 1992.

Country Music

*Allen, Bob, ed. *The Blackwell guide to recorded country music.* Oxford: Blackwell, 1994.

*Kingsbury, Paul, ed. *Country on compact disc: the essential guide to the music by the Country Music Foundation.* New York: Grove Press, 1993.

Morthland, John. *The best of country music.* Garden City, N.Y.: Doubleday, 1984.

Oermann, Robert K., and Douglas B. Green. *The listener's guide to country music.* New York: Facts on File, 1983.

Whitburn, Joel. *Top country singles 1944–1993.* Menomonee Falls, Wisc.: Record Research, 1994.

Folk and Ethnic Music (U.S.)

American folk music and folklore recordings: a selected list. Washington, D.C.: Library of Congress American Folklife Center, 1984– .

Broven, John. *South to Louisiana,* pp. 338–44. Gretna, La.: Pelican, 1983.

*Cohen, Norm. *Traditional Anglo-American folk music: an annotated discography of published sound recordings.* New York: Garland, 1994.

Ethnic recordings in America: a neglected heritage, pp.175–229. Studies in American folklife, vol. 1. Washington, D.C.: Library of Congress American Folklife Center, 1982.

Greene, Victor. *A passion for polka: old-time ethnic music in America,* pp. 329–32. Berkeley: University of California Press, 1992.

Keil, Charles, and Angeliki V. Keil. *Polka happiness,* pp. 213–15. Philadelphia: Temple University Press, 1992.

Lifton, Sarah. *The listener's guide to folk music.* New York: Facts on File, 1983.

Loza, Steven. *Barrio rhythm: Mexican American music in Los Angeles,* pp. 299–301. Urbana: University of Illinois Press, 1993.

Pena, Manuel. *The Texas-Mexican conjunto: history of a working-class music,* p. 213. Austin: University of Texas Press, 1985.

Roberts, John Storm. *The Latin tinge: the impact of Latin American music on the United States,* pp. 234–38. New York: Oxford University Press, 1979; Tivoli, N.Y.: Original Music, 1985.

Sandberg, Larry, and Dick Weissman. *The folk music sourcebook.* Rev. ed. New York: Da Capo Press, 1989.

Spottswood, Richard K. *Ethnic music on records: a discography of ethnic recordings produced in the United States, 1893 to 1942.* Urbana: University of Illinois Press, 1990.

Tudor, Dean, and Nancy Tudor. *Grass roots music.* Littleton, Colo.: Libraries Unlimited, 1979.

Gay and Lesbian Music/Women's Music

Gough, Cal, and Ellen Greenblatt. *Gay and lesbian library service,* pp. 253–74. Jefferson, N.C.: McFarland, 1990.

*Grega, Will. *Outsounds: the gay and lesbian music alternative.* New York: Pop Front, 1996.

Gospel Music

Hayes, Cedric J. *A discography of gospel records 1937–1971.* København: Knudsen, 1973.

———— and Robert Laughton. *Gospel records 1943–1969: a Black music discography.* London: Record Information Services, 1992–93.

Heilbut, Tony. *The gospel sound: good news and bad times,* pp. 327–37. 2nd rev. ed. New York: Limelight, 1987.

Reagon, Bernice Johnson, ed. *We'll understand it by and by: pioneering African American gospel composers,* pp. 351–54. Washington, D.C.: Smithsonian Institution Press, 1992.

Holiday Music

Marsh, Dave, and Steve Propes. *Merry Christmas, baby: holiday music from Bing to Sting.* Boston: Little, Brown, 1993.

Jazz

Allen, Daniel. *Bibliography of discographies, vol. 2: jazz.* New York: Bowker, 1981.

Bruyninckx, Walter. *Sixty years of recorded jazz.* Mechelen, Belgium: [Bruyninckx], [1978–81]. Specialized multivolume discography for larger collections.

Carr, Ian, Digby Fairweather, and Brian Priestley. *Jazz: the rough guide.* London: Rough Guides, 1995.

*Cook, Richard, and Brian Morton. *The Penguin guide to jazz on compact disc.* 3rd ed. London: Penguin, 1996.

Friedwald, Will. *Jazz singing: America's great voices from Bessie Smith to bebop and beyond,* pp. 433–73. New York: Collier, 1992.

*Harrison, Max, Charles Fox, and Eric Thacker. *The essential jazz records, vol. 1: ragtime to swing.* Westport, Conn.: Greenwood, 1984.

*Harrison, Max, Alun Morgan, Ronald Atkins, et al. *Modern jazz: the essential records.* London: Aquarius, 1978.

Kernfeld, Barry. *The Blackwell guide to recorded jazz,* 2nd ed. Oxford: Blackwell, 1995.

Lord, Tom. *The jazz discography.* West Vancouver, B.C.: Lord Music Reference, 1992– . Specialized multivolume discography for larger collections.

Piazza, Tom. *The guide to classic recorded jazz.* Iowa City: University of Iowa Press, 1995.

Placksin, Sally. *American women in jazz,* pp. 303–22. New York: Seaview Books, 1982.

Raben, Erik. *Jazz records, 1942–1980: a discography.* Copenhagen: JazzMedia Aps, 1987– . Specialized historical discography for larger collections.

Rust, Brian. *Jazz records, 1897–1942.* 5th ed. Chigwell, Essex, England: Storyville Publications, [1982]. Specialized historical discography for larger collections.

Stroff, Stephen M. *Discovering great jazz: a new listener's guide to the sounds and styles of the top musicians and their recordings on CDs, LPs, and cassettes.* New York: Newmarket Press, 1991.

Latin American Music

See World Music

Middle Eastern Music

See World Music

New Age

*Bedard, Gilles. *Au coeur de la musique nouvel age.* Montreal: Louise Courteau, 1991.

*Birosik, Patti Jean. *The new age music guide: profiles and recordings of 500 top new age musicians.* New York: Collier, 1989.

Melton, J. Gordon. *New age encyclopedia,* pp. 295–300. Detroit: Gale, 1990.

Popular Music, Pre–World War II

American music before 1865 in print and on records: a biblio-discography. ISAM monographs, no. 6. Brooklyn, N.Y.: Brooklyn College Institute for Studies in American Music, 1976. Updated in *Notes: the quarterly journal of the Music Library Association* 34 (1978): 571–80; and 37 (1980): 31–36.

Hemming, Roy, and David Hajdu. *Discovering great singers of classic pop,* pp. 235–77. New York: Newmarket Press, 1991.

Kinkle, Roger D. *The complete encyclopedia of popular music and jazz, 1900–1950.* New Rochelle, N.Y.: Arlington House, 1974.

Rust, Brian. *The American dance band discography 1917–1942.* New Rochelle, N.Y.: Arlington House, 1975.

———— and Allen G. Debus. *The complete entertainment discography: from 1897 to 1942.* 2nd ed. New York: Da Capo Press, 1989.

Whitburn, Joel. *Pop memories 1890–1954.* Menomenee Falls, Wisc.: Record Research, 1986.

Rock

*Christgau, Robert. *Christgau's record guide: the '80s.* New York: Pantheon, 1990; New York: Da Capo Press, 1994.

*————. *Rock albums of the seventies: a critical guide.* New Haven: Ticknor & Fields, 1981; New York: Da Capo Press, 1990.

*DeCurtis, Anthony, James Henke, and Holly George-Warren, eds. *The Rolling Stone album guide.* New York: Random House, 1992.

DeCurtis, Anthony, James Henke, Holly George-Warren, et al. *The Rolling Stone illustrated history of rock & roll: the definitive history of the most important artists and their music.* New York: Random House, 1992.

Felder, Rachel. *Manic pop thrill,* pp. 161–70. Hopewell, N.Y.: Ecco Press, 1993.

*Robbins, Ira, ed. *The Trouser Press guide to '90s rock.* 5th ed. New York: Simon & Shuster, 1997.

*Shapiro, Bill. *Rock & roll review: a guide to good rock on CD.* Kansas City: Andrews and McMeel, 1991.

Western Classical Music

Greenfield, Edward, Robert Layton, Ivan March, et al. *The Penguin guide to opera on compact disc.* London: Penguin, 1993.

Gruber, Paul, ed. *The Metropolitan Opera guide to recorded opera.* New York: Norton, 1993.

*March, Ivan, ed. *The Penguin guide to compact discs and cassettes.* New ed., rev. and expanded. London and New York: Penguin, 1996.

Myers, Kurtz. *Index to record reviews, 1978–1983: based on material originally published in Notes,* the quarterly journal of the Music Library Association between 1978 and 1983. Boston: G. K. Hall, 1985.

————. *Index to record reviews, 1984–1987: based on material originally published in Notes, the quarterly journal of the Music Library Association between 1984 and 1987.* Boston: G. K. Hall, 1989.

————, Richard LeSeur, Paul Cauthen, et al. "Index to record reviews." *Notes: the quarterly journal of the Music Library Association.* Quarterly index, since 1987.

Rosenberg, Kenyon C. *A basic classical and operatic recordings collection on compact discs for libraries: a buying guide.* Metuchen, N.J.: Scarecrow, 1990.

World Music

*Barlow, Sean, and Banning Eyre, eds. *Afropop: an illustrated guide to contemporary African music.* Edison, N.J.: Chartwell Books, 1995.

*Broughton, Simon, Mark Ellingham, David Muddyman, et al. *World music: the rough guide.* London: Rough Guides, 1994.

Ewens, Graeme. *Africa o-ye! A celebration of African music,* pp. 216–17. New York: Da Capo Press, 1992.

*Graham, Ronnie. *The Da Capo guide to contemporary African music.* New York: Da Capo Press, 1988.

*————. *The world of African music.* Stern's guide to contemporary African music, vol. 2. London: Pluto Press; Chicago: Research Associates, 1992.

Jessup, Lynne. *World music: a source book for teaching.* Danbury, Conn.: World Music Press, 1988.

Manuel, Peter. *Popular musics of the non-western world: an introductory survey.* New York: Oxford University Press, 1988.

McGowan, Chris, and Ricardo Pessanha. *The Brazilian sound: samba, bossa nova, and the popular music of Brazil,* pp. 205–10. New York: Billboard Books, 1991.

Stapleton, Chris, and Chris May. *African rock: the pop music of a continent.* New York: Dutton, 1990.

*Sweeney, Philip. *The Virgin directory of world music.* New York: Holt, 1991.

INDEXES TO SCORES

All Scores

This index lists all items in part 1, "Scores," each indexed to its entry number. Works by a single composer are indexed under the composer's name; anthologies (collections of music by more than one composer) are indexed under title.

INDEX TO SOUND RECORDINGS

The personal and corporate names in the index are almost without exception limited to the primary creators of the music (i.e., the composers for classical works and the principal recording artists for vernacular genres). For reasons of space, interpreters, editors, producers, and others who might also be included within a citation are not generally indexed. Subject terms in the index are given as a complement to the table of contents and provide an additional layer of access.

Bryson, Peabo *5203*
BT Express *5138, 5139*
Buarque, Chico *7157, 7159, 7184, 7198.1*
Bubblegum music
  Anthologies *5399, 5409*
  James, Tommy *5583*
  Monkees *5629*
Bubbles, John W. *4850.2*
Buck and Bubbles *5175*
Buck, Dennis *6164*
Buckwheat Zydeco *6594, 6595, 6598, 6626*
Budd, Harold *5064, 5065*
Budzilek, Ray *6681*
Buen, Knut *7445*
Buffalo Springfield *5491*
Buffett, Peter *5048*
Buju Banton *6918*
Bukis, Los *7038*
Bulgarian State Radio and Television
  Female Vocal Choir *7538, 7539, 7709*
Bull, John *3142, 3229, 3235*
Bullock, Chick *4871, 4874*
Bumble Bee Slim *4099, 4121, 4122, 4128, 4135, 6423, 6427, 6439*
Bumcke, Gustav *3662*
Bunn, Teddy *4294*
Buonamente, Giovanni Battista *3389, 3391*
Burdon, Eric *5407, 5445*
Burgess, Sonny *5426*
Burke, Joe *7278, 7280*
Burke, Kevin *6635, 7283*
Burke, Solomon *5167, 5204*
Burmer, Richard *5053*
Burnette, Johnny *5422, 5439, 5441*
Burning Spear *6916, 6917, 6918, 6926*
Burns, Ralph *6115*
Burns, Robert *7338.2*
Burnside, R. L. *4203*
Burr, Henry *4879*
Burrell, Kenny *4294, 4298, 4445, 4511, 4512*
Burse, Charlie *4123*
Burton, Gary *4513, 4514, 4515*
Burton, James *5768*
Burton, Richard *4854*
Buscaglione, Fred *7430*
Bush, Kate *5492*
Bush, Sam *6498*
Bushnak, Lufti *8215*
Busnois, Antoine *3143, 3186.2, 3210, 3213*
Busoni, Ferruccio *3554*
Bussotti, Sylvano *3718, 3993, 3997*
Buster, Prince *6911, 6912, 6918*

Buti, Carlo *7421*
Butler, Billy *5164*
Butler, Jerry *5181, 5205*
Butler, Martin *3960*
Butterbeans and Susie *5175*
Butterfield, Paul *4198, 4199, 4228*
Butterworth, George *3651.9*
Buxtehude, Dietrich *3275, 3367, 3368, 3369*
Buzzcocks *5410, 5412, 5493*
Byard, Jaki *4436, 4447, 4516*
Byas, Don *4293, 4299, 4353*
Byrd, Charlie *4294, 4445*
Byrd, Donald *4517*
Byrd, Jerry *5768*
Byrd, Roy *see* Professor Longhair
Byrd, William *3144, 3152.1, 3207, 3209, 3211, 3229, 3235, 3237, 3248*
Byrds *5423, 5494, 5767, 5807, 6433*
Byrne, David *4857.3, 5723*
Byron, Carl *3955*
Byron, Don *4518, 8258.1*

Cabanilles, Juan *3276, 3362, 3372, 3384*
Cabaret music: Anthologies *4939*
Cabaret Voltaire *5495*
Cabezón, Antonio de *3209, 3247, 3265, 3384*
Cabezón, Hernando de *3209*
Cabrera, Jorge *7231*
Caccini, Francesca *3277*
Caccini, Giulio *3278, 3379, 3388, 3390*
Cachao *6755, 6845*
Cachorros, Los *7066*
Cadéac, Pierre *3218*
Cadenet *3097*
Cadillacs *5167, 5398, 5414, 6248*
Cadiz, Beni de *7472*
Caesar, Shirley *5918, 5927, 5948, 5949*
Cage, Butch *6404*
Cage, John *3628.5, 3661, 3669, 3719, 3982, 3983, 3985, 3990, 3994, 3996, 3997, 4007, 4008, 4014, 4021, 4027, 4030*
Cain, Jackie *see* Jackie and Roy
Caiola, Al *5770*
Caldara, Antonio *3251, 3270.46, 3279, 3388*
Cale, John *5496*
Calender, Ebenezer *7911*
Callahan Brothers *5778, 6434, 6439*
Callen, Michael *4963, 6494, 6512*
Calloway, Cab *4315, 4321, 4327, 4328, 4338, 4354, 4801, 4803,*

4850.1, 4861, 4885, 4894, 5175, 6110, 6282
Calvi, Carlo *3376*
Calypso
  Anthologies *6989, 6990, 6991, 6992, 6993, 6994, 7101, 7103*
  Growling Tiger *7002*
  Houdini, Wilmoth *7003*
  Kitchener, Lord *7004*
  Roaring Lion *7005*
  Shadow *7007*
  Sparrow *7008*
Calypso Rose *6988, 7000, 7709*
Camara, Ladji *7825*
Camaron de la Isla *7466, 7473*
Cambrai, Jacques de *3104*
Cameo *5155, 5157, 5206*
Cameron, Allison *3956*
Campbell, Dolois Barrett *5929*
Campbell, Glen *5808*
Camper Van Beethoven *5429*
Camperos de Valles, Los *7039*
Campesinos de Michoacán *7040*
Campion, Thomas *3145, 3224, 3227, 3228, 3234, 3236*
Canadian Fiddlestix *6687*
Canario *6969, 6971*
Canario y su Grupo *6416*
Canaro, Francisco *7119, 7122, 7126*
Canaro, Rafael *7124*
Candido *6754*
Canned Heat *4199, 4229, 6245*
Cannibal and the Headhunters *5420*
Cannon, Gus *4099, 4106, 4142, 4147, 4150, 6413*
Cannon's Jug Stompers *4151, 4155*
Canteloube, Joseph *3555*
Cantor, Eddie *4845.2, 4878, 4884, 4895, 4905*
Capercaille *7279, 7280, 7332*
Capirola, Vincenzo *3231, 3252*
Capitol Records: Anthologies *4940, 4946, 4952*
Capitols *5173, 5417*
Capo, Bobby *6864*
Capoeira: Anthologies *7165, 7166*
Captain Beefheart *5497*
Cara, Marchetto *3240, 3247, 3249*
Caracol, Manolo *7467, 7468, 7474*
Caravans *5907, 5914, 5919, 5949*
Cárcamo, Pablo *7217*
Cardenal, Peire *3102*
Cardenas, Guty *7041*
Cardew, Cornelius *3685*
Cardona, Milton *4446, 6839*
Cardoso, Manuel *3146*
Cardot *3256*
Caresser, The *6989, 6994*

Guy, Buddy *4239*
Howlin' Wolf *4246*
James, Elmore *4248*
Lenoir, J. B. *4254*
Little Walter *4258*
Magic Sam *4260*
Muddy Waters *4264*
Nighthawk, Robert *4266*
Reed, Jimmy *4268*
Rogers, Jimmy *4269*
Rush, Otis *4270*
Shines, Johnny *4273*
Wells, Junior *4288*
Williamson, Sonny Boy (Rice Miller) *4290*
Chicago jazz: Anthologies *4303, 4304, 4305, 4320*
Chicago Push *6693*
Chicago soul music *see* Soul music, Chicago
Chicas del Can, Las *6870*
Chicco *8115*
Chicken scratch music: Anthologies *6336, 7062*
Chieftains *7320*
Chiffons *5116, 5117*
Chihara, Paul *3636.14*
Child ballads *6450, 6570*
Childes, Mary Ellen *3975*
Chimvu Jazz *8092*
Chinese Music Ensemble of New York *8436*
Chipmunks *6244, 6249*
Chirgwin, G. H. *7297*
Chirino, Willy *6769*
Chisala, P. K. *8133*
Chiweshe, Stella *7713, 7746, 8144*
Choates, Harry *5771, 6599, 6602, 6612*
Choc Stars *7954, 7976*
Chocolate *7264*
Chopin, Frédéric *3458, 3508.23*
Chordettes *4953*
Chords *5414, 5435*
Chosen Gospel Singers *5915, 5950*
Chou, Lung *3724*
Chou, Wen-chung *3725*
Chowning, John M. *3726*
Christian, Charlie *4294, 4297, 4299, 4357, 4374.4*
Christian, Meg *5501, 5502*
Christmas music *4035, 6222–6277*
Christy, June *4810, 4860, 4861, 4864, 4940*
Chuck Wagon Gang *5760, 5893, 6023*
Chukp'a *8512*
Church, The *5429*
Či Bulag *8526*
Ciani, Suzanne *5066*

Ciapa Rusa *7432*
Ciconia, Johannes *3041, 3134*
Cilèa, Francesco *3459*
Cima, Andrea *3379*
Cima, Giovanni Paolo *3395*
CIO Singers *5898*
Circle *4527*
Circle Jerks *5416*
Circus music: Anthologies *4086*
Cissoko, Sunjui *7901*
Civil War music (U.S.): Anthologies *4052, 4053, 4054, 4055, 4056, 4057, 4058*
Civitate, Antonio de *3134*
Clérambault, Louis Nicolas *3288, 3328*
Clancy Brothers *6433, 7321*
Clancy, Willie *7312, 7316*
Clannad *7322*
Clapton, Eric *4217, 5503*
Clarinet Summit *4528*
Clark, Buddy *4859, 4864, 4871, 4891, 4947, 4965*
Clark, Dave *see* Dave Clark Five
Clark, Dee *5167, 5181, 5212*
Clark, Mattie Moss *5951, 5952*
Clark, Roy *5768*
Clark, Sanford *5441*
Clark Sisters *5927, 5952*
Clark, Sonny *4529*
Clark, Tim *5052*
Clarke, Herbert L. *4078, 4080, 4084*
Clarke, Jeremiah *3287, 3371*
Clarke, Kenny *4437, 4440, 4441, 4677*
Clarke, Rebecca *3558*
Clarke, Tony *5114*
Clash *5504*
Classic blues *see* Vaudeville blues
Clay, Otis *4230, 5149, 5150*
Clayton, Buck *4358, 4469*
Clayton, Doctor *4213*
Clegg, Johnny *8117, 8118*
Clemens non Papa, Jacobus *3148, 3248*
Clementi, Muzio *3405*
Clements, Vassar *6501*
Cleveland, James *5912, 5918, 5953, 5964, 6005, 7708*
Cliff, Jimmy *6905, 6907, 6915, 6918, 6920, 6927*
Clifton, Bill *5796*
Cline, Patsy *5761, 5763, 5812, 7709*
Clinton, Larry *4885*
Clooney, Rosemary *4843, 4845.2, 4846.2, 4847, 4848, 4852, 4863, 4945, 4948, 4950, 4951, 4966*
Clovers *5167, 5176, 5213, 5414*

Club blues
Brown, Charles *5198*
Charles, Ray *5209.3*
Hunter, Ivory Joe *5254*
Mayfield, Percy *5280*
Milburn, Amos *5285*
Coasters *5110, 5167, 5214, 5444*
Coates, Dorothy Love *5908, 5909, 5913, 5914, 5915, 5931, 5954*
Cobb, Arnett *5109, 5119*
Cobham, Billy *4530*
Coborn, Charles *7297*
Cobra Records: Anthologies *4202*
Cochran, Eddie *5421, 5422, 5440, 5505*
Cochrane, Chris *3968*
Cockburn, Bruce *6509*
Cocker, Joe *5408, 5506*
Cockerham, Fred *6483*
Cocoa Tea *6815, 6909*
Cocoband *6875*
Cocteau Twins *5429*
Codax, Martin *3042, 3108, 3123*
Coffey, Dennis *5132*
Cogan, Robert *3980*
Cohan, George M. *4883*
Cohen, Leonard *6520*
Cohn, Al *4531*
Cole, Ann *4102*
Cole, Bob *4067*
Cole, Cozy *5436*
Cole, Nat King *4296, 4359, 4843, 4844, 4848, 4849, 4850.1, 4853, 4854, 4858, 4863, 4865, 4889, 4940, 4953, 4967, 5176, 6243, 6259*
Cole, Natalie *5215*
Coleman, Anthony *3968*
Coleman, Cy *4847, 6063*
Coleman, Jaybird *4112, 4126*
Coleman, Michael *6636, 6644*
Coleman, Ornette *4008, 4299, 4449, 4532, 4672, 6116*
Coleman, Steve *4533*
Coleridge-Taylor, Samuel *3460*
Collarde, Edward *3211*
Collazo, Julito *6753*
Collier, Mitty *5114*
Collins, Al *5112*
Collins, Albert *4101, 4200, 4208, 4213, 4215, 4221, 4231, 4232*
Collins, Arthur *4091, 4879, 4887*
Collins, Bootsy *5156, 5216*
Collins, Dolly *7293*
Collins, Judy *6433, 6506, 6521*
Collins, Larry *5767*
Collins, Nicholas *3727, 3974*
Collins, Phil *5507*
Collins, Sam *4130*
Collins, Shirley *7293*

Garfunkel, Art *5697, 6433*
Garland, Hank *4294, 5768*
Garland, Judy *4843, 4844, 4845.1,*
   4849, 4850.1, 4850.2, 4852,
   4853, 4856, 4857.1, 4857.2,
   4858, 4859, 4860, 4862, 4863,
   4864, 4866, 4889, 4895, 4915,
   4949, 4952, 4988
Garland, Peter *3766*
Garlow, Clarence *5124, 5125,*
   6623, 6624
Garneau, Richard *5045*
Garner, Erroll *4292, 4296, 4299,*
   4373, 4850.2
Garnett, Gale *4944*
Garrett, Kenny *4578*
Garsi da Parma, Santino *3208*
Garton, Brad *3960*
Gasparyan, Djivan *7523*
Gastoldi, Giovanni Giacomo *3212,*
   3237, 3244, 3246
Gates, J. M., Rev. *4147, 5908,*
   5909, 5916, 6412, 6439
Gaughan, Dick *7282, 7290, 7295,*
   7336
Gaultier, Denis *3299, 3386*
Gaultier, Ennemond *3300, 3386*
Gay, John *3301*
Gay/lesbian interest
   Anthologies *4144, 4857.3, 4869,*
     5432, 5434, 6492, 6494, 6511
   Adam, Margie *5456*
   All the rage (Ostertag) *3865*
   Bronski Beat *5489*
   Cage aux folles, La (Herman)
     6073.1
   Callen, Michael *4963*
   Casselberry-DuPree *6518*
   Christian, Meg *5501, 5502*
   Dobkin, Alix *6525*
   Erasure *5541*
   Etheridge, Melissa *5542*
   Fjell, Judy *6530*
   Flirtations *4982*
   Flower, Robin *6531*
   Gardner, Kay *5074*
   I T S O F O M O (Neill) *3856*
   Ian, Janis *5578*
   Kiss of the spider woman (Kander)
     6075.2
   Lavner, Lynn *4997*
   March of the falsettos (Finn)
     6066
   Murphy, Charlie *6558*
   Near, Holly *6559*
   New York City Gay Men's Chorus
     5011
   Phranc *6567*
   Resurrection (Davies) *3734.5*
   Romanovsky and Phillips *5019*

   San Francisco Gay Men's Chorus
     5021
   Seattle Men's Chorus *5022*
   Somerville, Jimmy *5707*
   Symphony no. 1 (Corigliano)
     3728.2
   Tremblay, Lucie Blue *6583*
   Trull, Teresa *5731*
   Turtle Creek Chorale *5031*
   Weinberg, Tom Wilson *5037*
   Williamson, Chris *5502, 5746*
   Windy City Gay Chorus *5043*
Gay men's choruses
   New York City Gay Men's Chorus
     5011
   San Francisco Gay Men's Chorus
     5021
   Seattle Men's Chorus *5022*
   Turtle Creek Chorale *5031*
   Windy City Gay Chorus *5043*
Gaye, Marvin *5151, 5152, 5156,*
   5166, 5167, 5243
Gaynor, Gloria *5142*
Gayten, Paul *5163, 5244*
Gazoline *6812, 7019*
Gebirtig, Mordecai *8253*
Geld, Gary *6067*
Geminiani, Francesco *3302*
General, El *6815, 7112*
Generation X *5412*
Genesis *5558*
Génies Noirs de Douala *7931*
George, Barbara *5124, 5125*
George, Cassietta *5949*
George, Siwsann *7345*
Georgia blues (pre-war)
   Anthologies *4122*
   Barbecue Bob *4152*
   McTell, Blind Willie *4173*
Georgia Mass Choir *5965*
Georgia Peach *5894, 5896, 5899,*
   5911, 5918, 5920
Georgia Tom (Thomas A. Dorsey)
   4160
Geraldo *7292, 7296*
Gerhard, Roberto *3573, 4000*
Geronimo *7156*
Gerry and the Pacemakers *5400,*
   5401, 5402, 5403, 5406
Gershwin, George *3574, 3997,*
   4850, 4872, 4884, 6068
Gervaise, Claude *3218*
Gesner, Clark *6069*
Gesualdo, Carlo *3162, 3238*
Gettel, Michael *5048, 7719*
Getz, Stan *4299, 4444, 4455, 4579,*
   4580, 4581
Ghent, Emmanuel *3962*
Gherardello, da Firenze *3110,*
   3112, 3114

Ghiselin, Johannes *3210*
Ghizeghem, Hayne van see Hayne,
   van Ghizeghem
Gianoncelli, Bernardo *3208*
Gibbons, Orlando *3163, 3229,*
   3237
Gibbs, Georgia *4948*
Gibbs, Mike *4582*
Gibbs, Terry *4441, 4583*
Gibson, Bob *6496*
Gibson, Don *5769, 5824*
Gibson, Jon *4028*
Gideon, Miriam *3767, 3991*
Gieco, León *7138*
Gigli, Beniamino *7421*
Gil, Gilberto *7157, 7169, 7187,*
   7211
Gilbert and Sullivan see Sullivan,
   Arthur, Sir
Gilbert, Henry *3556*
Gilberto, Astrud *7158, 7188*
Gilberto, João *4580, 7158, 7159,*
   7189
Gill, Vince *5825*
Gillebert, de Berneville *3104*
Gillespie, Dizzy *4299, 4302, 4338,*
   4404.3, 4417, 4437, 4438, 4439,
   4440, 4441, 4451, 4456, 4584,
   4703.14, 4704, 6820
Gillespie, Hugh *6638, 7316*
Gillum, Jazz *4119, 4126*
Gilmore, John *4491*
Gimble, Johnny *5771*
Ginastera, Alberto *3575, 3620.6,*
   3664
Giordani, Tommaso *3388*
Giordano, Umberto *3470*
Giovanelli, Ruggiero *3246*
Giovanni, da Cascia *3111, 3112*
Gioviale, Giovanni *6416*
Gipsy Kings *7727*
Giramo, Pietro Antonio *3221*
Girardon, Evelyne *6740*
Giraut, de Borneil *3097, 3099,*
   3100, 3101, 3104
Girl groups
   Anthologies *5116, 5117*
   Crystals *5219*
   Martha and the Vandellas *5307*
   Marvelettes *5278*
   Ronettes *5312*
   Shirelles *5318*
   Supremes *5314*
Gismonti, Egberto *4595, 7190*
Giteck, Janice *3768*
Giuffre, Jimmy *4443, 4585*
Giuliani, Mauro *3471, 3496.3*
Giullardi di Piazza, I *7434, 7708*
Gkatsos, Nikos *7595*
Gladden, Texas *6477*

Heptones   *6900, 6907, 6915, 6916, 6918, 6920, 6932*
Herawi, Aziz   *8379*
Herbert, Victor   *6072*
Herbst, Johannes   *4034*
Herdman, Priscilla   *6219*
Herman, Jerry   *6073*
Herman, Woody   *4300, 4302, 4338, 4384, 4439, 4441, 4453, 4856, 4889, 4894, 4896*
Hermanos Reyes   *7462*
Hermanos Torres-Garcia, Los   *7095*
Hernandez, Alonso   *3240*
Hernandez Chabez, Carlos   *7044*
Herrmann, Bernard   *6108, 6122*
Hersch, Fred   *3955*
Hershman, Mordecai   *8217, 8228, 8234*
Hewitt, James   *4059*
Hi-Life International   *7751*
Hi-Los   *4854, 4861, 4863, 4864*
Hi Records: Anthologies   *5149, 5150*
Hibbert, Toots *see* Toots and the Maytals
Hibbler, Al   *4990, 5119*
Hickman, Art   *4872*
Hicks, Bobby   *5793, 6501*
Hicks, Robert *see* Barbecue Bob
Hidalgo, Juan   *3309, 3360, 3362, 3380*
Hideki, Kato   *3977*
Higbie, Barbara   *5056*
Higgs, Joe   *6904, 6915, 6934*
Highlife
    Anthologies   *7751, 7797, 7798, 7799, 7873, 7874*
    African Brothers   *7807*
    Agyeman, Eric   *7808*
    Crentsil, A. B.   *7810*
    Konadu, Alex   *7813*
    Mbarga, Prince Nico   *7888*
    Mensah, E. T.   *7815*
    Oriental Brothers   *7890*
    Osadebe, Chief Stephen Osita   *7891*
    Osibisa   *7816*
Highway QCs   *5907, 5974*
Hildegard, Saint   *3044*
Hill, Andrew   *4608*
Hill, Bertha "Chippie"   *4148*
Hill, Jessie   *5124, 5125, 5160*
Hill, Joe   *6490*
Hill, Z. Z.   *4196, 4213, 4215, 4218, 4242*
Hiller, Lejaren Arthur   *3784*
Hindemith, Paul   *3543.13, 3545.11, 3586, 3672*
Hinds, Justin   *6911, 6912*

Hines, Earl   *4292, 4296, 4299, 4300, 4302, 4303, 4308, 4315, 4320, 4322, 4328, 4332, 4338, 4343.10, 4343.11, 4385*
Hines, J. Earle   *5912*
Hines, Justin   *6917*
Hinton, Joe   *5146*
Hiotis, Manolis   *7601*
Hirsch, Shelley   *3957, 3968, 3974*
Hirt, Al   *4943*
Hitchcock, Robyn   *5429*
Ho, Fred *see* Houn, Fred
Hoddinott, Alun   *3785*
Hodes, Art   *4293, 4386*
Hodges, Johnny   *4307, 4312, 4322, 4371, 4448, 5119*
Hofer, Maria   *3534*
Hofhaimer, Paul   *3210, 3237*
Hofner, Adolph   *5784, 6419, 6439, 6671*
Hogan, Silas   *4216*
Hoiby, Lee   *3955*
Hokum Boys   *6439*
Holborne, Anthony   *3211, 3234, 3250, 3263*
Holcomb, Roscoe   *6464*
Hole   *5574*
Holiday, Billie   *4293, 4299, 4321, 4338, 4803, 4804, 4816, 4843, 4845.2, 4846.1, 4848, 4849, 4850.2, 4851, 4852, 4853, 4855, 4856, 4857.1, 4857.2, 4858, 4865, 4874, 4940, 4946, 5180*
Holland, Dave   *4527, 4609, 4723*
Holland-Dozier-Holland (song writers-producers): Anthologies   *5115, 5151*
Holliday, Judy   *4845.2, 4851, 4859, 4860*
Hollies   *5401, 5402, 5403, 5405, 5406, 5407, 5575*
Holliger, Heinz   *3786*
Holloway, Brenda   *5151*
Holly, Buddy   *5396, 5421, 5439, 5441, 5444, 5448, 5576*
Holman, Bill   *4631.1*
Holman, Eddie   *5126, 5172*
Holman, Libby   *4873*
Holmboe, Vagn   *3787*
Holst, Gustav   *3587*
Holt, John   *6913, 6920*
Holyoke, Samuel   *4063*
Homler, Anna   *3954*
Honegger, Arthur   *3588, 3617.20, 3674*
Honey Cone   *5115, 5130*
Honky-tonk music
    Anthologies   *5765, 5771, 5794*
    Frizzell, Lefty   *5823*
    Haggard, Merle   *5827*

    Horton, Johnny   *5829*
    Jones, George   *5835*
    Owens, Buck   *5856*
    Pierce, Webb   *5859*
    Price, Ray   *5860*
    Thompson, Hank   *5876*
    Tubb, Ernest   *5879*
    Williams, Hank   *5886*
Hooker, Earl   *4200, 4205, 4207, 4243*
Hooker, John Lee   *4099, 4199, 4205, 4208, 4213, 4244, 5178, 5181, 6245*
Hoopii, Sol   *6390, 6393, 6394, 6396, 6397, 6398*
Hope, Elmo   *4610*
Hopkins, Claude   *4300, 4321*
Hopkins, Lightnin'   *4099, 4101, 4104, 4205, 4206, 4213, 4245, 5176, 6245*
Hopkinson, Francis   *4034*
Horn, Paul   *5051, 5077*
Horn, Shirley   *4817*
Hornburg, Lupold   *3107*
Horne, Lena   *4843, 4844, 4848, 4850.1, 4850.2, 4852, 4853, 4857.1, 4857.2, 4858, 4860, 4861, 4862, 4864, 4881, 4889, 4898, 4919, 4952, 5180, 6110, 6252*
Horton, Johnny   *5829*
Horton, Walter   *4194, 4198, 4202*
Hostia, Pietro da   *3225*
Houdini, Wilmoth   *6423, 6426, 6990, 6991, 6992, 7003*
Houn, Fred   *4025, 4611*
House Band   *7303*
House, Son   *4099, 4103, 4127, 4131, 4141, 4165, 4199, 4205*
Houston, Cisco   *6415, 6433, 6490, 6538.3, 6542*
Houston, Thelma   *5141, 5152*
Houston, Whitney   *4991*
Hovda, Eleanor   *4001, 4025*
Hovhaness, Alan   *3788, 3990*
Hovington, Frank   *6422, 6429*
Howard, Camille   *5178*
Howard, Eddy   *4871*
Howard, Joseph E.   *4067, 4074*
Howell, Peg Leg   *4108, 4122, 4144, 4146*
Howlin' Wolf   *4099, 4102, 4103, 4106, 4195, 4197, 4201, 4207, 4213, 4218, 4222, 4246, 5448*
Hrant, Udi *see* Kenkulian, Hrant
Hsu, Hung   *8442, 8445*
Hu, Zhihou   *8443*
Hubbard, Freddie   *4612, 4775, 6109*
Hudson, David   *8729*
Hudson, Hattie   *4129*